Research Methodology
Concepts and Cases

Research Methodology
Concepts and Cases

Second Edition

Dr Deepak Chawla
Distinguished Professor, Dean (Research & Fellow Programme)
International Management Institute (IMI)
New Delhi

Dr Neena Sondhi
Professor
International Management Institute (IMI)
New Delhi

VIKAS® PUBLISHING HOUSE PVT LTD

VIKAS® PUBLISHING HOUSE PRIVATE LIMITED
E-28, Sector-8, Noida-201301 (UP), India
Phone: +91-120-4078900 • Fax: +91-120-4078999
Registered Office: A-27, 2nd Floor, Mohan Co-operative Industrial Estate, New Delhi-110044
E-mail: helpline@vikaspublishing.com • Website: www.vikaspublishing.com

SALES AND MARKETING OFFICES OF VIKAS® AND S CHAND AND COMPANY LIMITED

Chennai : Ph: 044-2363 2120, chennai@schandpublishing.com
Guwahati : Ph: 0361-2738 811, 2735 640, guwahati@schandpublishing.com
Hyderabad : Ph: 040-4018 6018, hyderabad@schandpublishing.com
Jalandhar : Ph: 0181-4645 630, jalandhar@schandpublishing.com
Kolkata : Ph: 033-2335 7458, 2335 3914, kolkata@schandpublishing.com
Lucknow : Ph: 0522-4003 633, lucknow@schandpublishing.com
Mumbai : Ph: 022-2500 0297, mumbai@schandpublishing.com
Patna : Ph: 0612-2260 011, patna@schandpublishing.com

Research Methodology—Concepts and Cases
ISBN: 978-93259-8239-0

Product Code: V8REM60BMGT10ENAB16

First Published 2011
Second Edition 2016
Reprinted in 2020, 2021, 2022 (Twice), 2023 (Thrice)
Reprint 2024 (Twice)
Reprint 2025

PRINTED IN INDIA
By Vikas Publishing House Private Limited, Plot 20/4, Site-IV, Industrial Area Sahibabad, Ghaziabad-201010 and Published by Vikas Publishing House Private Limited, E-28, Sector-8, Noida-201301

To the memory of my

Parents

(Late) Shrimati Sushila Devi Chawla and (Late) Shri Lila Dhar Chawla

Brothers

(Late) Prof. R C Chawla
Retd Principal, Govt Bikram College of Commerce, Patiala
(Late) Dr Dinkar Chawla, MBBS, MS
Senior Surgeon
and

Sister and Brother-in-law
(Late) Mrs Kiran Makhija and (Late) Mr Vinay Makhija

Deepak Chawla

To my parents

Sudershan & Shashi Ghai

for their unselfish love and nurturance

To my husband

Anil,

my inspiration and strength

To my children

Kanika & Kartik

for their everlasting belief in me

To all my Gurus and teachers

who taught me all that I know....

Neena Sondhi

Instruction to Download Free SPSS 14-day Trial Version

1. Type the link in your browser. http://www14.software.ibm.com/download/data/web/en_US/trialprograms/W110742E06714B29.html
2. Select your operating system by choosing the radio button. For e.g., if your operating system is Windows XP Professional, select the appropriate radio button and click Continue.
3. Register by filling in your personal details.
4. Once registered, you can login to download the trial software.

Foreword

An important pillar of the bridge that connects 'Management as Art' to 'Management as Science' is a foundation course in Research Methodology, which MBA students are required to take. It is a basis for inculcating 'research as a value' for effective decision-making, a value which is difficult to imbibe when the course is seen merely as an academic one, where theoretical foundations and concepts have to be learnt more as necessary obstacles to be overcome in the journey to acquire an MBA, but with little prospect of utilizing the knowledge in practical situations they would encounter later in their professional lives. This is precisely the challenge that the authors have sought to address in this book.

Professor Deepak Chawla is a reputed teacher of Statistics, Research Methodology, Marketing Research and Business Forecasting, having long years of experience in teaching these subjects to MBA students. He is a seasoned researcher and scholar, with contributions in various functional areas of management like Marketing, Finance, Economics and, most recently, in Knowledge Management. Professor Neena Sondhi is a distinguished academic in the area of Marketing, Research Methodology and Marketing Research. She brings extensive experience of teaching and applying research methodology to management problems. The two have produced a book that can be read at two levels simultaneously—at one level for the exposition of the discipline of statistics and for its intrinsic beauty and concepts, and at another, for the techniques and methodology of research for their power and sweep of applications. The authors, through a carefully chartered path into Research Methodologies, systematically ease the student's journey into researching a whole spectrum of management problems, analysing them, and then drawing meaningful and utilizable conclusions.

A noteworthy and invaluable feature of this book is the large number of cases drawn from a variety of situations that help the students understand the concepts and applications of different techniques. Two cases run throughout the book and provide a constant backdrop for learning the concepts and methodologies that are discussed as one progresses through the book. Thirty-five end-of-chapter cases help show how in different real contexts the statistical concepts and research methodologies are indeed applied. Another noteworthy feature is the extensive SPSS applications on problems and cases. Indeed, many problems have been worked out and discussed using both conventional methods and SPSS software. Furthermore, in order to anchor the treatment to reality, real-life data have been used for the cases.

'This is a book by teachers who understand what difficulties the students face, what conceptual cul-de-sac they can get into, the difference between knowing a technique and applying it successfully. Therefore, they have kept the students' needs directly in view while deciding on the style and treatment of the subject and its scope. This is a book that students will enjoy learning from. It is also a book that other teachers of Research Methodology to management students will find useful.

I commend the authors for bringing out a truly valuable textbook.

Professor Ashoka Chandra
Former Special Secretary, Education, Ministry of Human Resource Development, Government of India
Currently, Principal Adviser to International Management Institute (IMI),
Chairman, Centre for Management of Innovation and Technology, IMI, and
Chairman, Centre for Social Sector Governance, IMI.

Preface to the Second Edition

We have received an overwhelming response for *Research Methodology: Concepts and Cases* from faculty members, research scholars and students of educational institutions across the country. Alongside, appreciation and praise for our efforts to bring out such a useful book, we have received valuable feedback and suggestions to further improve the contents of the book. We thank them for the same and accordingly have made the following additions in the second edition of the book.

Addition and updating: There were chapters and section where we have clarified the process or construct in some cases; we have added new sections and additional analysis to enhance the learning and interpretation of the research topic/technique. Some of these are as follows:

1. In the second chapter on *Formulations of the business research problem & development of research hypotheses*, the concept of moderator and mediator variable is described in detail - both as text and diagrammatically.
2. The chapter on *Analysis of variance techniques* has been revised and post-hoc analysis has been discussed under one way analysis of variance.
3. In chapter 5 that is *Secondary data collection methods*, the section on syndicate research has been further expanded with the help of examples.
4. The chapter 18 on *Cluster analysis* has been rearranged so as to make the reading smooth for the readers. The cases of continuous and discrete data have been explained separately.
5. The chapter 19 on *Multidimensional scaling and perceptual mapping* has been explained at length by giving all possible measurement questions and conditions under which multi-dimensional scaling can be carried out. Further it also discusses attribute based perceptual mapping using Factor analysis.
6. The *Conjoint analysis* appeared as an addendum in the previous edition of the book. It appears as a separate chapter 20 as per the suggestions of our readers.
7. A number of new examples have been added in various chapters to illustrate the concepts that are discussed.
8. The data set for *Cases and problems* that have been added in this edition are also available in the form of EXCEL and SPSS format on a CD that is provided with the book.

New to the addition: The greatest benefit of the book, for which scholars and academicians and practitioners have appreciated our book has been its hands on and application based approach. Hence we have strengthened the application aspect considerably in this edition in the following way.

1. There are new conceptual and application questions in majority of the chapters. This offers the learner ample opportunity to apply the chapter learning on decision problems.
2. The chapters' questions have also been complemented by adding 15 new cases in the second edition of the book. This edition thus has a total of 52 cases.The new cases that have been added in this edition are as follows:
   - Case 2.4 Fortune at the last frontier (A)
   - Case 3.3 Fortune at the last frontier (B)
   - Case 4.1 Keshav furniture pvt. Ltd.
   - Case 6.4 Fortune at the last frontier (C)
   - Case 6.5 Career in service sector vs manufacturing sector - The case of MBA aspirants

- Case 9.3 Yaseer restaurent
- Case 11.2 Second hand classified websites in India: Usage and trust amongst customers
- Case 12.3 Change in the lifestyle of youth after the gangrape incident of December 16, 2012
- Case 12.4 Perceived organizational support, role overload and work family conflict in IT industry
- Case 13.4 Perception of Delhiites about Delhi metro
- Case 15.2 Shyam foods pvt. Ltd.
- Case 18.3 Danish International (D)
- Case 19.3 A shirt on my back
- Case 20.1 Burman tea company
- Case 3 Daag Acchhe hain! (Comprehensive case)

3. In the digital age, researchers across the world have made active use of the internet to carry out research. Thus a new addendum on online research has been added in the book. This deals with the unique aspects and indices that are of exclusive use when conducting and measuring on the virtual platform.

The revised instructor manual is available with the publisher and Faculty members adopting the book may contact them for a copy of the same. We would be delighted to receive the comments and suggestions on the second edition of the boo.

Dr Deepak Chawla
Distinguished Professor

Dr Neena Sondhi
Professor

Preface

Every truth has four corners: as a teacher I give you one corner, and it is for you to find the other three.

...Confucius

Research Methodology: Concepts and Cases is like Confucius' corner, a tool, an ever-evolving and changing process that will always take on different nuances based on the unique philosophy of every reader and researcher who uses it. But it is our staunch belief that once you have reached the last page of this volume, the other three corners—which might vary, based on a researcher's area of interest—will not seem to be such a daunting task. Research would then become a simplified, practical and necessary path that you would confidently undertake.

The significance of business research in the Indian context gained increasing impetus in the early 1990s, with the major economic reforms implemented post liberalization by the Indian government. India was a growing and lucrative market, with a huge exodus towards urban living. Thus, a number of multinationals decided to set up their business here. However, they needed to understand the Indian consumer, the marketplace, the operating systems and most significantly, the competition; and one of the ways which could make this possible was through research. On the other hand, since the market was spoiled for choice and the buyer rather than the seller was dictating the terms, Indian companies had to revisit the way they would need to conduct their business. Hence, the value of business research to seek specific answers became important. Research in marketing was an existing reality but the scope had widened and from simple consumer studies, organizations had started looking at advertising research and new product research in a big way. Simple percentages and pie charts were no longer sufficient; more accurate and focused findings that could be effectively built into business strategies were required.

This increasing significance and usage of research tools were not isolated just to the marketing domain. Other areas of business like finance and human resources were also relying on and greatly benefitting from research undertaken for specific purposes. With a number of BPOs and KPOs being set up by organizations from developed countries, job opportunities for the Indian working population were increasing by leaps and bounds. The flip side of this was that companies started facing increasing attrition, organizational stress and dissatisfied employees. As a measure to retain and nurture human capital, a number of studies were carried out on employee satisfaction, career planning, work-life balance, organizational climate surveys, training need analysis and other related areas.

Behavioural finance was an area that even financial analysts who were earlier skeptical about structured research study, now recognized as an important emerging area of research. Investment decisions were an area of concern not only for the Indian investor but also for companies offering the financial instrument. Thus, financial research took on a new meaning in this panorama. Competition from domestic and international players forced even the existing market leaders into improving business efficiency through operations research and real-time analysis.

Research, which was once an academic exercise carried out mostly by research scholars and doctoral students, was fast becoming an important technique that was a critical part of any business school curriculum. It was no longer regarded as a theoretical, insignificant course; both the learner and the recruiter had understood that this was going to be an extremely important modus operandi, which could add tremendous value to any job role. At the workplace too, managers who outsource research must also be able to understand and evaluate the merit of research findings.

However, despite the present need and significance of business research, we, as teachers of this course on Business Research, have, for some time now, been aware that though business managers require to equip themselves to handle the unique needs of the fiercely competitive Indian industrial realm, the material and books available on the subject are not adequate enough to handle the complexity and technological advancements that have taken place in the area. Either the text is too mathematical for those who do not have a mathematical background, or if the statistical techniques have been addressed in detail, the business interpretation is missing, leaving the readers clueless on how to make any sense of the obtained numbers by converting them into business decisions. There are good books on qualitative research but they lean more towards the abstract; readers then find it difficult to understand and apply to them for their specific needs.

Of the books that are being used actively for the university system, most are too theoretical and just provide definitions with practically no illustrations. Numerous methods and techniques explained have become obsolete and redundant in the current scenario. The resulting outcome is that either the field of research is a one-eyed monster to be avoided at all costs; or a bitter pill that one swallows by rote and forgets later.

Looking at the above scenario, both of us realized that it was time to pick up our pens and turn scribes. Our effort would be to instill a comprehensive and step-wise understanding of the research process with a balanced blend of theory, techniques and Indian illustrations—from all business areas that might be of relevance to the reader. We were also aware that the text had to be simple, interesting and succinct.

Reader and Learner

This book makes no presumptions and can be used with confidence and conviction by both students and experienced managers who need to make business sense of the data and information that is culled out through research groups. The conceptual base has been provided in comprehensive, yet simplistic detail, addressing even the minutest explanations required by the reader. The language maintains a careful balance between technical know-how and business jargon. Every chapter is profusely illustrated with business problems related to all domains—marketing, finance, human resource and operations. Thus, no matter what the interest area may be, the universal and adaptable nature of the research process is concisely demonstrated.

At all stages in the compilation we have been careful in ensuring that the usefulness and comprehension is broad based. Every chapter includes simple and direct end-of-the-chapter questions which serve to recapitulate the learning at the first level, while the application questions and cases take the learner to the next level—beyond concepts to be able to crystallize and apply the learning in real time. The volume also has the potential to be an excellent learning guide both for the business manager and research scholars as it provides both rigorous, yet simplified understanding of the step-wise progression of the research process.

Organization of Content

The book has been essentially divided into six sections and covers the entire research process. There are also two topics which have been added as an addendum to cover the entire syllabi of all national and international universities and business schools in the country.

Section I consists of four chapters. Chapter 1 covers the research process in its totality. Chapter 2 is devoted to conceptualizing and designing of the problem to be investigated. Depending on the need of the researcher this may then be converted into a working hypothesis, to be tested in the later stages. Chapters 3 and 4 cover all the three basic research designs—exploratory, descriptive and experimental. The sub-divisions of each one are dealt with in detail in the two chapters.

Section II also consists of four chapters. This section is devoted to the data collection techniques available to the researcher. It covers in complete depth the secondary and primary data collection methods. Chapter 6 provides details on all the qualitative techniques available to the researcher. Chapters 7 and 8 deal with the quantitative scales and questionnaire.

Section III focuses on the fieldwork once the measuring scale/questionnaire is ready. The respondent's selection or sampling plan for collecting the primary data is discussed in Chapter 9. Chapter 10 is an extremely critical chapter as the information collected now needs to be processed for analysis. Thus this chapter talks about coding, tabulating and editing of the data collected from the primary methods.

Section IV consists of the analysis done for testing the research hypotheses. This covers a wide range of methods beginning with univariate and bivariate analysis in Chapters 11 and 12. An entire chapter is devoted to the analysis of variance methods and the last chapter in this section discusses the non-parametric methods actively used by the business researcher.

Section V comprises five important advanced data analysis methods used for research. Individual chapters are devoted to correlation and regression analysis; factor analysis; discriminant analysis; cluster analysis and multidimensional scaling.

Section VI comprises only one chapter devoted to the writing and presentation of research results. This is very important and often handled superficially by most researchers as part of the research study. Thus, illustrations and stepwise guidelines of compiling and disseminating the study results are presented here.

Addendum to the book: Two topics that we felt would make this a complete volume were conjoint analysis and research ethics. We have formulated short, comprehensive guides on the two.

Key Features of the Book

Some specific advantages and highlights of the book you are about to be read and learn from are:

- No mathematical aptitude or knowledge required to understand the simple logic and steps of conducting data analysis.
- Coverage of all topics and areas that are taught at all universities and business schools in the country.
- Real-time researched examples from all domains of business management and a fine blend of theory and application in every chapter.
- Complete and comprehensive chapters devoted to important multivariate techniques, rather than only a single chapter that gives a brief introduction to every technique.
- Detailed explanations of complex analytical terms in simple reader-friendly language, with appropriate illustrations in every data analysis chapter.
- Explicit instructions on the preconditions and assumptions for using every data collection method and data analysis technique.
- SPSS instructions provided to take the reader through stepwise data analysis commands for every data analysis technique.
- Evaluation exercises and learning applications in the form of objective and subjective questions at the end of every chapter.
- Thirty-five end-of-chapter Indian cases for the reader to apply his/her learning on.
- Two comprehensive cases to practise the learning garnered from every topic in the book.
- SPSS data sets for all examples and problems as well as cases given across the book.
- Useful for postgraduate students of business management as well as disciplines in social sciences such as psychology and sociology. It can also serve as a research project guide for M Phil. and PhD scholars.
- Emphasis on clear interpretation of study results into theoretical and applied implications lends it enhanced value in terms of its utility for business managers, regardless of the sector.

Final Word ....

As we near the completion of the Herculean task of compiling this book on *Research Methodology: Concepts and Cases*, we are exhilarated at the magnitude of the task accomplished and yet humbled at the journey of learning this book took us on. There were times we formalized what we knew and others when we learnt anew and transcended new boundaries. It seems like only yesterday that Research Methodology was a subject that was so tedious and difficult to comprehend. All the problems, gaps in understanding and the monotony of the subject that we had experienced at the learner stage ourselves stood us in good stead as we were able to put ourselves in the shoes of learners as they who would unravel the intricate and complex research process.

Research for both of us is a passion and an endless journey that takes us in diverse directions to traverse new grounds and validate old theories. The quest for knowledge and learning never ends and we are but humble learners in this ever-evolving field of research. And you, our readers, can facilitate our new voyage of research through your valuable feedback in the form of comments and advice as you set forth on your research path by using this book as a learning tool.

Deepak Chawla
dchawla@imi.edu
Neena Sondhi
neenasondhi@imi.edu

Acknowledgements

The conceptualization and publication of this book was a rigorous and voluminous task and it would not have been accomplished without the encouragement and support of many of our associates and well-wishers. We would like to take this opportunity to express our gratitude to all of them in their various capacities.

We would like to thank Dr Pritam Singh, the Director General of International Management Institute (IMI), New Delhi, for his inspirational support in the publishing of this book. This work was initiated when late Dr C. S. Venkataratnam was the Director of the institute. We are grateful to the management of IMI for the infrastructural facilities and support provided to us in developing this comprehensive volume. Prof. Ashoka Chandra had been a constant source of inspiration and encouragement from the very beginning of the project. We gratefully thank him for sparing his valuable time from his busy schedule to write the foreword for the book. We appreciate the encouragement and support of our faculty and colleagues, with a special word of gratitude for Prof. Himanshu Joshi for his invaluable help and advice in the SPSS section of Chapter 10. Appreciation is also due to the experts, friends and professional colleagues from other reputed business schools, who were our sternest critics and staunchest supporters in believing the significance and magnitude of contribution in the compilation of this book. At every stage, we are grateful for the critical and valuable reviewing of the text in order to improve the readability and coverage of the book.

The success of a publication is not possible without the unstinting faith of a publisher and a team that staunchly believes that the document under preparation is a winning product. This faith was also one of the constant driving forces that provided us the encouragement to move forward. We would like to thank you enitre editorial team of Vikas Publishing House.

No effort made by either one of us would have been possible without the patient and consistent support of each of our individual families, whose faith and love for us was a constant source of inspiration and reassurance for us. A special word of thanks to the corporates, where some of the illustrative cases reported in the book were carried out. All students and research investigators who contributed in various ways in providing valuable data and inputs are also acknowledged here.

We would also like to record our gratitude and appreciation to Ms Vandana Sehgal and Ms Jaspreet Kaur for their tireless and patient typing and in carrying out various computer runs on SPSS and EXCEL in the preparation of the manuscript. And last, but not the least, we would like to express our gratitude to the Almighty without whose benevolence nothing in this world would see the light of the day.

Deepak Chawla
Neena Sondhi

Contents

Section 2
Data Collection, Measurement and Scaling

SECTION 3
RESPONDENTS SELECTION AND DATA PREPARATION

SECTION 4
PRELIMINARY DATA ANALYSIS AND INTERPRETATION

SECTION 5
ADVANCED DATA ANALYSIS TECHNIQUES

List of Cases

Section 1

RESEARCH PROCESS: PROBLEM DEFINITION, HYPOTHESIS FORMULATION AND RESEARCH DESIGNS

This section introduces the reader to the scientific and structured process of research, which distinguishes it from a simplistic method of business enquiry.

Chapter 1 Introduction to Business Research

Chapter 1 provides a broad overview of the essential process of research. It starts with problem formulation and statement of hypotheses and covers research designs, data collection and respondent sampling, followed by data refining, analysis and interpretation in brief. The chapter goes on to discuss different types of research—an orientation ranging from basic to applied studies is discussed at length with their sub-classifications into exploratory and conclusive studies as well. Insight is also provided into research applications in the field of marketing, finance, human resources and operations. Clear elucidation of criteria of a robust research study is also provided. The chapter also has a detailed appendix, devoted to preparation and compilation of a research proposal.

Chapter 2 Formulation of the Research Problem and Development of the Research Hypotheses

Chapter 2 traces the path of converting a management dilemma into a research question that lends itself to scientific enquiry. The process of problem formulation requires a comprehensive collation of facts. This is done through inputs from industry and topic experts, organizational analysis, review of existing and problem-specific literature and sometimes loosely structured group discussions with respondents. Every problem must be broken down into specific components, i.e., the units of analysis and the study variables—independent and dependent. The chapter concludes by discussing in detail the process of hypotheses generation and elucidating the types of hypotheses available to a researcher.

Chapter 3 Research Designs: Exploratory and Descriptive

Chapter 3 provides the classification of different types of research designs available to the researcher. Once the researcher has crystallized the research problem and objectives, the next step is to design the study execution plan. This stage is known as the research design stage. The first step, which is generally a precursor to most research studies, is an exploratory design based on a mix of secondary and loosely structured qualitative methods. The more structured descriptive designs, with the sub-classification into cross-sectional and longitudinal designs, are discussed at length with appropriate illustrations from different business domains.

Chapter 4 Experimental Research Designs

Chapter 4 starts by defining an experiment and explains the concept of causality and the necessary conditions required for making causal inferences. The concepts of internal and external validity of the experiments are explained and the factors affecting them are detailed. The experimental designs could be classified into (1) pre-experimental design (2) quasi-experimental designs (3) true experimental designs and (4) statistical designs. Under each of the four heads, various designs are covered. The true experimental designs enable the researchers to eliminate the effect of extraneous variables from both control and experimental group. The statistical designs help to study the effect of more than one independent variable on the dependent variable and also help to control the effect of extraneous variables.

1

CHAPTER

Introduction to Business Research

Learning Objectives

By the end of the chapter, you should be able to:

1. Understand the relevance and role of research in management and the significance of the research tool in all functional areas of management.
2. Cognize and distinguish between the different kinds of research available, based on the purpose and nature of the management decision.
3. Apprehend the steps that need to be accomplished in order to complete the research study.
4. Formulate a research proposal for a research endeavour.
5. Interpret the basics of quality checks needed to classify research as a meaningful and 'good' research.

16 September 2008: Ravi Mathaiyya, CEO of EEE—a KPO set up as an ancillary of a US-based credit card company, operating from Noida—read the story of the Lehmann Brothers, Merrill Lynch and the other financial disasters in the US. He reeled under the shocking story of the 158-year-old conglomerate which had just collapsed like a pack of cards. Of late, when the business was not doing well, it seemed that this sub-prime crisis would eventually hit the banking, credit and related sectors in a big way. What would be the impact on the KPOs catering to the US market? On the human front, the company was not doing as well as it should have considering the fact that it was voted amongst 'the top ten companies to work for in India' by a popular business magazine. The attrition figures were as high as 67 per cent in the last six months. Why didn't his employees want to stay? What was the magic ingredient that would provide a conducive work environment for employees to work in and enjoy themselves? Could the answer be compensation, flexible work policies, job enrichment or rotation exercises?

Ravi was an optimistic and futuristic kind of person. He was always looking at exploring and expanding his business. Had the time come for him to look for and evaluate new pastures? Food retailing seemed to be an interesting business proposition that Ramesh Kumar, his batchmate, was expanding into. How big was this market? Was it an organized or an unorganized sector? How did the consumer carry out his or her grocery shopping? What was the nature of operations in terms of supply chain and distribution? How could he develop an effective marketing strategy?

Alternatively, he could venture into syndicate market research. He could train and absorb his existing employees into a new venture. Would the employees be willing to take this opportunity? How would the organizational goals match his/her personal career goals? There were so many questions in his mind but no single magic formula that could help him arrive at the answers that he wanted. It seemed to Ravi that the answer might lie in the annals of the subject in his B-School, that he often kept as last on his study list—research. He was certain that research would help and provide him with the information required to arrive at a viable answer/solution to his dilemma. He had big plans and a revolutionary vision of what the future might hold. But how did one carry out a research for realizing them? How did one communicate and convert and then measure and evaluate whether the path that he wanted to traverse would really lead to success? Was there a risk? Could he measure it and what really was the answer?

LEARNING OBJECTIVE 1
Understand the relevance and role of research in management and the significance of the research tool in all functional areas of management.

Ravi is atypical of most managers and perhaps you, who might, at your individual or organizational level, face a similar decision dilemma. Effective decisions pave the way to managerial success and this requires reducing the element of risk and uncertainty. There are different schools of thought on what could be the magic mantra for this—some say it is on-the-job experience; others call it 'a strong gut feel'; and some say it is the gambler's luck.

The authors believe that all this is possible but not before you have availed the scientific method of enquiry, followed a structured approach to collect and analyse information and then eventually subjected it to the manager's judgement. This is no magic mantra but a scientific and structured tool available to every manager, namely—Research.

WHAT IS RESEARCH?

Research is a tool that is a building block and a sustaining pillar of every discipline—scientific or otherwise—that one knows of. Before comprehending the true meaning of the term, we would like to make it clear that this book primarily focuses on the process of business research. The premise of this decision-oriented enquiry is vast and may range from the simplistic view, which involves compilation and validation of information, to an exhaustive theory and model construction. To distinguish between non-scientific and scientific method, we would like to consider a few definitions of research.

One of the earliest distinctions was made by Lundberg (1942) who stated 'Scientific methods consist of systematic observation, classification, and interpretation of data. Now obviously, this process is one in which nearly all people engage in their daily life. The main difference between our day-to-day generalizations and the conclusions usually recognized as the scientific method lies in the degree of formality, rigorousness, verifiability, and general validity of the latter.'

Fred Kerlinger (1986) also validated the thought and stated that 'Scientific research is a systematic, controlled and critical investigation of propositions about various phenomena.' Grinnell (1993) has simplified the debate and stated 'The word *research* is composed of two syllables, *re* and *search*. The dictionary defines the former as a prefix meaning again, anew or over again and the latter as a verb meaning to examine closely and carefully, to test and try, or to probe. Together they form a noun describing a careful, systematic, patient study and investigation in some field of knowledge, undertaken to establish facts or principles.'

Management research is an unbiased, structured and sequential method of enquiry, directed towards a clear implicit or explicit business objective. This enquiry might lead to validating the existing postulates or arriving at new theories and models.

Thus, drawing from the common threads of the above definitions, we derive that management research is *an unbiased, structured, and sequential method of enquiry, directed towards a clear implicit or explicit business objective. This enquiry might lead to validating existing postulates or arriving at new theories and models.*

The most important and difficult task of a researcher is to be as objective and neutral as possible. The temptation to skew the results in the hypothesized direction has to be avoided at all costs. Magazine articles and newspaper surveys which want to prove a point might want to skew the opinion polls in favour of the Capitalists or the Republicans, or on the need for reservation versus no reservation in educational institutes but a researcher has to collect and display the findings of the research as objectively as possible.

Let us look at another example, a domestic hearing-aid company is not able to keep above the red line and has identified inventory management in the company as probably one of the areas that needs to be refurbished. You take stock of the existing shipping, storing and delivery operations and find that you are losing out to a local competitor who is selling hearing aids at a much higher premium, because of out-of-stock conditions at your end. You track this down to a faulty inventory reporting system, where the data about stocks is provided for a cycle of 40 days. A small impromptu survey with retailers stocking your products and the pathology labs recommending your products confirms your observations. You study the latest inventory management techniques available. You isolate three different practices and work out the feasibility of implementing each one of them in the company. The one that seems to be the most cost- and time-effective is the one you choose and develop an inventory model which you implement for the base hearing aids (incidentally, these are your largest selling models). At regular intervals you monitor the sales data and compare it with past sales data. You realize you have a probable winner on hand. So you extrapolate the result to the other two more expensive and technologically superior models and prepare a report on the proposed inventory management model with cost implications to the management. What do we observe here? A structured and sequential method of enquiry was conducted. The method systematically developed a new model, validated it and at the same time addressed the immediate management problem faced by the company. In your opinion do you perceive that some research has been carried out?

A **researcher** should work towards a goal, whether immediate or futuristic, else the research loses its significance in the field of management.

The last most important aspect of our definition that needs to be carefully considered is the decision-assisting nature of business research. Thus, as Easterby-Smith *et al.* (2002) state, business research must have some practical consequences, either immediately, when it is conducted for solving an immediate business problem or when the theory or model developed can be implemented and tested in a business setting. The world of business demands that managers and researchers work towards a goal—whether immediate or futuristic, else the research loses its significance in the field of management.

TYPES OF RESEARCH

The above discussion seems to be leading to a truly Gestaltian perspective of business research, which should be theoretically and technically sound and yet have immediate and topological significance in the world of business. Hodgkinson *et al.* (2001) have also supported this argument, which states that business research must be able to withstand the requirement of both theory and practice.

LEARNING OBJECTIVE 2
Cognize and distinguish between different kinds of research available, based on the purpose and nature of the management decision.

Within this domain of creating and propagating theories and models and resolving immediate managerial problems, the purpose and context of your research project might be conceptualized differently. Sometimes this may be done for a purely academic reason of a need to know or to investigate some best practices—inventory management, or a new cause and effect relationship, work-family conflict and its impact on turnover intentions. The purpose behind the study is wider and all-encompassing, where the benefits generated would be applicable to the entire business community. The context is vast and time period flexible. This research is termed to be *fundamental* or *basic* research. On the other end of the continuum, you have more contextual and restricted studies. For example, your product which was declared a winner in the test marketing that you conducted is not able to take off after the product launch and you need to identify the reasons for this, in order to take corrective action. Thus the study you undertake would have limited relevance and be able to generate knowledge specific to the problem situation. This would be of practical value to the specific organization. Secondly, it has implications for immediate action. This action-oriented research is termed as *applied research.*

Fundamental/basic research is vast and the time period involved in it is flexible. Whereas in applied research, the goal is action-oriented and focuses on immediate results.

However, at this juncture we would like to advise the reader not to look at the two as opposites of each other. They, in fact, just lie at two ends of a continuum and in certain situations, merge or lead to the other. For example, you might need to study the impact of a merger between two large business corporations on employee morale and subsequent turnover intention. The findings of the study might reveal an intricate impact of other individual and organizational correlates which could be modifying the relationship. The recommendations would thus look at a vast spectrum of amendments required in HR policies. This is direct and applied research. In case the relationship between the two variables is further investigated in similar and different organizations, the researchers might be able to develop a broader model and framework to explain turnover intentions. Thus the research which started as contextual might lead to some fundamental and basic research which expands the body of knowledge. The process followed in both basic and applied research is systematic and scientific; the difference between them could simply be a matter of context and purpose.

Research studies can also be classified on the basis of the nature of enquiry or the objective behind the conduction. The orientation of this book—in terms of research design, methodology and analysis—is based on this distinction, thus at this stage we would like to clearly distinguish between these.

Exploratory Research

Exploratory research allows the researcher to gain a better understanding of the concept and provides direction in order to initiate a more structured research.

As the name suggests, **exploratory researches** are conducted to resolve ambiguity. Differing mainly in design from descriptive research, exploratory research is used principally to gain a deeper understanding of something. Its role is to provide direction to subsequent and more structured and rigorous research. A review of market opportunities available to a prospective entrepreneur; an informal survey conducted to identify the problem in the supply chain of a product; different ways that women professionals adapt to manage work-family conflict are examples of this kind of research. As can be seen, studies of this nature are less structured, more flexible in approach and are not conducted to test or validate any preconceived propositions; in fact exploratory research could lead to some testable hypotheses. Some schools have also called them pilot or feasibility studies. It is the first step the researcher takes into the unknown, to explore new frontiers which determine whether a full-scale investigation is worthwhile. Exploratory studies are also conducted to develop, refine or test the designed measuring instruments. For example, in designing a questionnaire to measure the parameters an individual looks at while taking an investment decision, one needs to first explore the benefits of a financial instrument, which could be the advantages sought by a consumer while saving. Another case could be that we identify the selection parameters a person considers while enrolling for a pilot training institute. After an assessment is made about the importance of the parameters considered, one can then work out the financial feasibility of setting up a private pilot training institute.

The nature of the study being loosely structured means the researcher's skill in observing and recording all possible information and impressions determines the accuracy of the findings. Along with the researcher's versatility, there are other ways in which findings of the exploratory research can be greatly enhanced. These will be discussed in detail in the data collection chapters.

Conclusive Research

Conclusive research tests and authenticates the propositions revealed by exploratory research. It is usually quantitative in nature.

The findings and propositions developed as a consequence of exploratory research might be tested and authenticated by conclusive research. This kind of research study is especially carried out to test and validate formulated hypotheses and specified relationships. In contrast to exploratory research, these studies are more structured and definite. The variables and constructs in the research are clearly defined with explicit quantifiable indications or simply, the variables can be denoted in the form of numbers that can be quantified and summarized. The timeframe of the study and respondent selection is more formal and representative. The emphasis on reliability and validity of the research findings assume critical significance as the concluded results might need to be implemented, in case it is an applied research study. For example, if a research study has to be conducted to test the impact of a new data monitoring programme on the inventory management system of a hearing aids' manufacturer, then the impact needs to be clearly discernible for the management to install the monitoring system.

It is to be noted, however, that it is not always the exploratory that leads to the conclusive. Sometimes the hypothesized relationship to be tested might be spelled out by the manager as the problem to be investigated. An example is testing the level of consumer satisfaction with different insurance policies that an organization has offered to consumers at large. A simple differentiation between the two broad areas of research is presented in Table 1.1.

As shown in Figure 1.1, conclusive research can further be divided into descriptive and causal research. This categorization is basically made based on the nature of investigation required.

Descriptive research

Descriptive research aims at elucidating the data and primary characteristics about the object/situation/concept under study.

As the name suggests, descriptive research is undertaken to describe the situation, community, phenomenon, outcome or programme. The main goal of this type of research is to describe the data and characteristics about what is being studied. The annual census carried out by the Government of India is an example of descriptive research. It is contemporary, topical and time-bound. It addresses the establishment or exploration of a formulated proposition. For example, the study might want to distinguish between the characteristics of the customers who buy normal petrol and those who buy premium petrol. Is the consumption of organic food more in affluent South Delhi as compared to the other areas in Delhi? What is the level of involvement

TABLE 1.1 Differences between exploratory and conclusive research

EXPLORATORY RESEARCH	CONCLUSIVE RESEARCH
Is loosely structured in design	Is well structured and systematic in design
Is flexible and investigative in methodology	Has a formal and definitive methodology that needs to be followed and tested
Does not involve testing of hypotheses	Most conclusive researches are carried out to test the fomulated hypotheses
Findings might be topic-specific and might not have much relevance outside the researcher's domain	Findings are significant as they have a theoretical or applied implication

FIGURE 1.1
Types of research

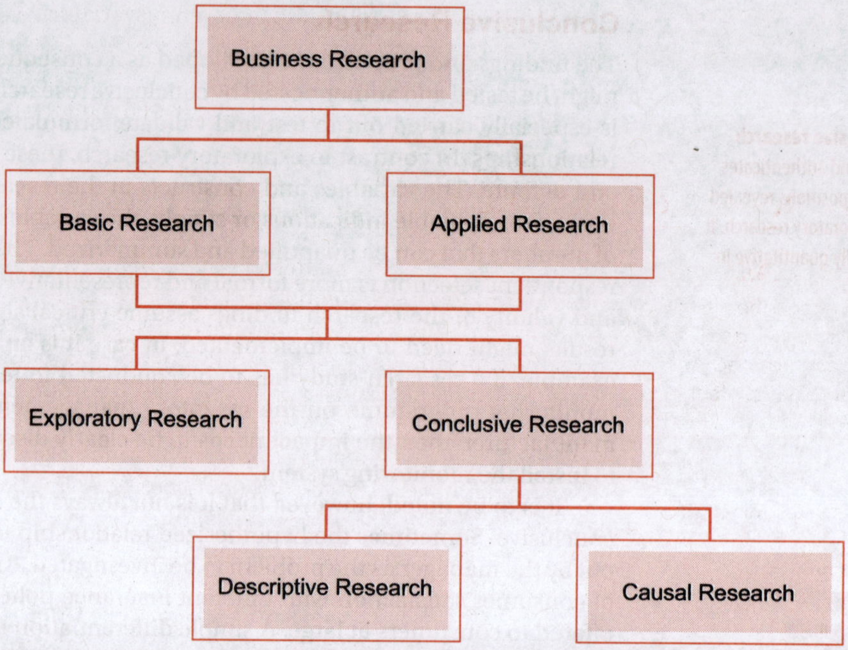

of middle-level versus senior-level managers in a company's stock-related decisions? Organizational climate studies are conducted in different organizations. A study of inventory management practices in the best-managed companies is another example. The commonality between all these research studies is the fact that unlike the exploratory, these are being conducted to test specific hypotheses and trends. They are relatively more structured and require a formal, specific and systematic approach to sampling, collecting information, collating and testing the data to verify the research assumptions.

The findings of descriptive studies are largely of a diagnostic nature, i.e., the studies indicate the existing symptoms of a particular situation without establishing the causality of the relationship.

Causal research

Causal research is concerned with exploring the effect of one variable on another. It requires a rigid sequential approach to sampling, data collection and data analysis.

To address the need for establishing causality, there is another kind of conclusive research study called causal research. These studies establish the why and the how of a phenomenon. Causal research explores the effect of one thing on another and more specifically, the effect of one variable on another. They are highly structured and require a rigid sequential approach to sampling, data collection and data analysis. The design of the study takes on a critical significance here. To establish a reliable and testable relationship between two or more constructs or variables, the other influencing variables must be controlled so that their impact on the effect can be eliminated or minimized. For example, to study the impact of flexible work policies on turnover intentions, the other intervening variables, of age, marital status, organizational commitment and job autonomy would need to be controlled.

CONCEPT CHECK

1. What do you understand by the term 'research'?
2. Define exploratory research and conclusive research.
3. What is the difference between exploratory research and conclusive research?

This method of controlling the intervening variables will be discussed in detail in the subsequent chapter. This kind of research, like research in pure sciences, requires experimentation to establish causality. In majority of the situations, it is quantitative in nature and requires statistical testing of the information collected.

THE PROCESS OF RESEARCH

LEARNING OBJECTIVE 3

Apprehend the steps that need to be accomplished in order to complete the research study.

Business research, no matter what the objective and thrust behind it, essentially needs to follow a sequential and structured path. The stages might overlap and sometimes be bypassed or eliminated in some research studies. While conducting research, information is gathered through a sound and scientific research process. Each year organizations spend enormous amounts of money for research and development in order to maintain their competitive edge. Some authors might call the interlinked and systematic progression as an oversimplification of the process, as every research has a unique orientation and methodology. While we do not disagree with the notion, we would nevertheless like to propose a broad framework that is often used as a blueprint or map and is usually followed in most researches. The process of research according to us is cyclic in nature and is interlinked at every stage (Figure 1.2). In the following paragraphs we will briefly discuss the steps that, in general, any research study might follow:

The **process of research** is cyclic in nature and is interlinked at every stage.

The Management Dilemma

Any research needs to be triggered by the need and desire to know more. This need might be merely because we want to discover and reinstate some relationships, the orientation might be purely academic with the purpose of uncovering some new perspectives to existing phenomena (basic or fundamental research) or there might be an immediate business decision that requires additional information acquisitions and analysis in order to arrive at any effective and workable solution (applied research). For example, an HR consultant or professor might wish to study some aspect of the work-life balance phenomenon or a soft drinks manufacturer might want to test the acceptability of fruit-based juices to his product portfolio.

Defining the Research Problem

Defining a research problem is a kind of prelude to the end result one hopes to achieve and therefore it requires considerable thought and analysis.

This is the first and the most critical step of the research journey. Some authors might object to the word *problem* as it indicates a negative nuance to the process. We would like to clarify the reason for this usage. It is because the entire sequence of the discovery is oriented towards looking for a solution(s) to the researcher's dilemma. It is a prelude to the end result that we hope to achieve, which is why this step itself may require considerable thought and analysis; as unless there is a clear definition of *what* one is seeking and for what *purpose*, it is not possible to begin. For example, in the area of work-life balance, the researcher might be looking at the impact of work-family conflict on turnover intentions. It might be felt that when it comes to women professionals, we might perceive that rather than role (job role) conflict, it could be her work-family conflict that might impact her job commitment, which, in turn, could impact her intention to quit (turnover intention). A clear definition of what is meant by work-family conflict, job commitment, and turnover intentions needs to be made so that there is complete clarity in the mind of the researcher regarding the elements of the constructs that he/she would need to collect information on.

Formulating the Research Hypotheses

In this given model, we have made broken lines to link the research problem definition stage and the hypotheses formulation stage. The reason behind a research study might not always begin with a hypothesis; in fact, the task of the study might be to collect rich, in-depth and detailed data that might lead to, at the end of the study, some indicative propositions that can be construed as hypotheses to be tested in subsequent research. This is most often the case with descriptive research. For example, in a research that is studying the economic indicators of human development in a country, the study is directed towards indicating the standing of the country on the defined variables and is not an authentication of the relationship between the concepts. The outcome may give an indication of the probable relationship between longevity, literacy and purchasing power parity (PPP), and the outcome of which might be constructed into a hypothesized formulation of the Human Development Index.

Hypothesis is the presupposition of the expected direction of the results of a research.

Hypothesis is, in fact, the presupposition of the expected direction of the results of the research. For example, it might be hypothesized that the research might be oriented towards testing a direct relationship between work-family conflict and turnover intentions. Higher the conflict, higher is the intention to leave. Conversion of the defined problem into a working hypotheses will be discussed in Chapter 2.

Developing the Research Proposal

Once the management dilemma has been converted into a defined problem and a working hypothesis, the next step is to develop a framework of the plan of investigation. Sometimes this step is carried out simultaneously with the research design formulation and sometimes after the data collection and sampling plan have been crystallized. The reason for its placement before the other stages is that a proposal is most often a time- and objective-bound commitment that a researcher needs to make to himself or the manager for whom the study is being carried out. It needs to spell out the research problem, the scope and the objectives of the study and the operational plan for achieving the same. The proposal is a flexible contract about the proposed methodology and once it is formalized and accepted, the research is ready for initiation.

Research Design Formulation

Based on the orientation of the research, i.e., exploratory, descriptive or causal, the researcher has a number of techniques for testing the stated objectives. These methods have a clear indication of the process of systematically controlling the variables under study in order to be able to establish the association or causality of the relationship under the study. Since critical managerial decisions are dependent on research outputs, the strength and accuracy of the findings can be ensured only through rigorous experimentation. Since the main task of the design is to explain how the research problem will be investigated, the logic or justification for the selected design needs to be explicit, accurate and measurable. For example, an exploratory study investigating the kind of hearing disorders prevalent in India might require a loosely designed framework of secondary information through historical hospital data, or discussions with some experts—like doctors and pathologists—to arrive at conclusions. However, the acceptability of some price points of a digital hearing aid might require a controlled and empirical study in the field (depending on time and cost resources) or under simulated conditions to measure the price and acceptability relationship.

Sampling Design

A researcher should avoid probability of error by selecting a **sample** that is free from every bias and ensuring that the degree of precision/error is measurable.

This section refers to how one goes about making an investigation of the respondent population to be studied. It is not always possible to study the entire population. Thus, one goes about studying a small and representative sub-group of the same. This sub-group is referred to as the sample of the study. There are different techniques available for selecting the group based on certain assumptions. For example, would you conduct your price sensitivity study on ENT doctors or consumers using hearing aids? Is the acceptability of the fruit-based beverage by the consumer to be measured based on retailers of beverage products, consumers of juices, consumers of water or consumer of the manufacturer's brand? These are questions which, once selected, will indicate the direction of the results and the group and determine the accuracy of the decision based on the findings. The most important criteria for this selection would be the *representativeness* of the sample selected from the population under study. The second rule to avoid a probability of error in prediction is that the selected sample should be free from researcher's bias and the degree of precision/error should be measurable and small enough to be deducted from the results.

Two categories of sampling designs available to the researcher are probability and non-probability. The selection of one or the other depends on the nature of the research, degree of accuracy required (the probability sampling techniques reveal more accurate results) and the time and financial resources available for the research.

Another critical decision the researcher needs to take is to determine the optimal sample size to be selected in order to obtain results that can be considered as representative of the population under study. This is a structured and scientific procedure and the researcher can take informed decisions based on certain mathematical computations. This would be studied in subsequent chapters.

Planning and Collecting the Data for Research

Primary data is original and is collected first hand for a study. **Secondary data**, on the other hand, is the information that has been collected and compiled earlier.

In the model (Figure 1.2), we have placed planning and collecting data for research as simultaneous to the sampling plan. This is because these two—based on the research design—need to be developed concurrently. The reason for this is that the sampling plan helps in identifying the population under study and the data collection plan helps in working out ways of obtaining information from the specified population. There are a huge variety and number of data collection instruments available to the researcher. Broadly, these may be classified into secondary and primary data methods. Each has multiple sub-divisions available. Primary, as the name suggests, is original and collected first hand for the problem under study. There are a variety of primary data methods available to the researcher ranging from subjective, non-quantifiable interviews, focus group discussions, personal/telephonic interviews/mail survey to the well-structured and quantifiable questionnaires. Secondary data is information that has been collected and compiled earlier. For example, company records, magazine articles, expert opinion surveys, sales records, customer feedback, government data and previous researches done on the topic of interest. For example, a study that measures the acceptability of orange-flavoured drink versus natural orange juice by consumers requires empirical and primary information. On the other hand, a descriptive financial investment behaviour study of consumers might be able to make use of secondary data. There are sub-steps involved at this stage—primary data instrument design and pilot testing. For example, if we want to measure the work-family conflict experienced by women in the health care sector and the steps that women professionals take to balance this, the study requires empirical data collection and instrument design. Once the instrument has been designed, it has to be tested and refined (pilot testing) before actual data collection can take place. In case a pre-constructed instrument is available and has been developed to measure the specific construct, the two steps of instrument design and testing can be done away with (indicated by the broken lines for these steps in the model in Figure 1.2).

This step in the research process requires careful and rigorous quality checks to ensure the reliability and validity of the data collected. There are measurement options available to establish these criteria for the data collection instrument, which have been discussed in the subsequent chapter. Once the instrument is ready, the field work begins and the data is collected from the respondent population based on the devised sampling plan.

Data Refining and Preparation for Analysis

The collected data should be **edited** and **refined** for any omissions and irregularities. It should be then **coded** and **tabulated** for statistical analysis.

Once the data is collected, it must be refined and processed in the format required for evaluating the information in order to answer the research question(s) and test the formulated hypotheses (if any). This stage requires editing of the data for any omissions and irregularities. Then it is coded and tabulated in a manner in which it can be subjected to statistical testing.

In case of data which is subjective and qualitative, the information collected has to be post coded into broad categories to be able to arrive at any inference and conclusion. For example, in-depth exit interviews will have to be carefully filtered and categorized *after* the conduction rather than before the conduction.

Data Analysis and Interpretation of Findings

Univariate, bivariate and **multivariate** analysis can be done to examine a single variable, two variables or more than two variables given under a specific study.

This is actually the crux of the researcher's contribution to the study. This stage requires, firstly, the selection of analytical tools for assessing the information collected to realize the research objectives. There are a number of statistical techniques available to the researcher—parametric and non-parametric techniques—these are selected based on the type of study, degree of accuracy required, the sampling plan used and the nature of the questions asked. In case the analysis requires testing a single variable under study, *univariate data analysis* method is used. In case one is testing or measuring the relationship between two variables, then one makes use of *bivariate analysis* methods; and if the variables being investigated are more than two, then one uses *multivariate analysis* of data. For analysing subjective and qualitative data, there are various other methods available which will be discussed in Chapter 6.

The technique chosen must be carefully decided upon and justified, as a wrong test or criterion selection can have hazardous effects on the study results. The selection criteria for the tests, the assumptions and the preconditions for each, are discussed in detail in later chapters.

Once the data has been analysed and summarized, the skill of the researcher in linking the results with the research objectives, stating clearly the implications of the findings and doing all this with an objective and rational approach, is the ultimate test.

The Research Report and Implications for the Manager's Dilemma

The report compilation that starts from the problem formulation to the interpretation is the final part of the process. As we stated earlier, business research is ultimately always directed towards answering the question 'so what are the implications for

FIGURE 1.2
The process of research

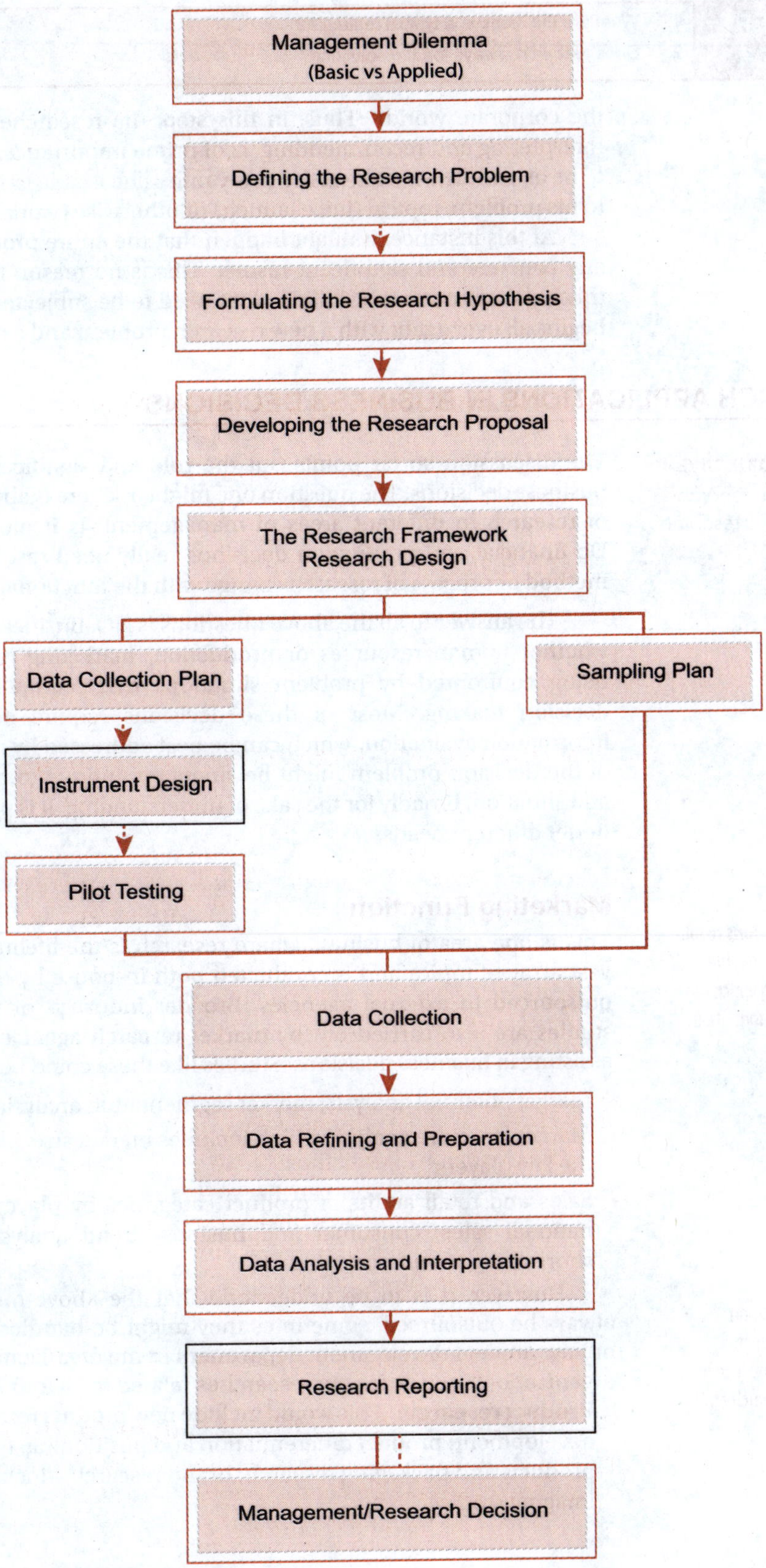

CONCEPT CHECK	1. What are the steps in a typical research? 2. Does research always lead to solutions?

the corporate world?' Thus, in this step, the researcher's expertise in analysing, interpreting and recommending, is of prime importance. The manager is not going to be as enthusiastic about the study unless he is able to clearly foresee the solution to his problem, topical (juice launch) or otherwise (work-life balance).

At this instance, it might happen that the entire process is carried out without any concrete and significant results. This is no reason for being disheartened, as this indicates other possibilities that need to be subjected to research and the loop begins all over again with a new research problem and a different perspective.

RESEARCH APPLICATIONS IN BUSINESS DECISIONS

LEARNING OBJECTIVE 4
Formulate a research proposal for a research endeavour.

The discussion so far points out the role and significance of research in aiding business decisions. The question one might ask here is about the critical importance of research in different areas of management. Is it most relevant in marketing? Do financial and production decisions really need research assistance? Does the method or process of research change with the functional area?

The answer to all the above questions is NO. Business managers in each field—whether human resources or production, marketing or finance—are constantly being confronted by problem situations that require effective and actionable decision making. Most of these decisions require additional information or information evaluation, which can be best addressed by research. While the nature of the decision problem might be singularly unique to the manager, organization and situation, broadly for the sake of understanding, it is possible to categorize them under different heads.

Marketing Function

Problem situations require effective and actionable decision-making which can be assisted by information evaluation.

This is one area of business where research is the lifeline and is carried out on a vast array of topics and is conducted both in-house by the organization itself and outsourced to external agencies. Broader industry- or product-category-specific studies are also carried out by market research agencies and sold as reports for assisting in business decisions. Studies like these could be:

- Market potential analysis; market segmentation analysis and demand estimation
- Market structure analysis which includes market size, players and market share of the key players
- Sales and retail audits of product categories by players and regions as well as national sales; consumer and business trend analysis—sometimes including short-/long-term forecasting

Four Ps of marketing research are product research, pricing research, promotional research and place research.

However, it is to be understood that the above-mentioned areas need not always be outsourced; sometimes they might be handled by a dedicated research or new product development department in the organizations. Other than these, an organization also carries out researches related to all four Ps of marketing such as:

1. **Product research:** This would include new product research; product testing and development; product differentiation and positioning; testing and evaluating new products and packaging research; brand research—including equity to tracks and imaging studies.

2. **Pricing research:** Price determination research; evaluating customer value; competitor pricing strategies; alternative pricing models and implications.
3. **Promotional Research:** Includes everything from designing of the communication mix to design of advertisements, copy testing, measuring the impact of alternative media vehicles, impact of competitors' strategy.
4. **Place research:** Includes locational analysis, design and planning of distribution channels and measuring the effectiveness of the distribution network.

These days, with the onset of increased competition and the need to convert customers into committed customers, customer relationship management (CRM), customer satisfaction, loyalty studies and lead user analysis are also areas in which significant research is being carried out.

Personnel and Human Resource Management

Critical success factor analysis is done both at individual and organizational level.

Human resources (HR) and organizational behaviour is an area which involves basic or fundamental research as a lot of academic, macro-level research may be adapted and implemented by organizations into their policies and programmes. Applied HR research by contrast is more predictive and solution-oriented. Though there are a number of academic and organizational areas in which research is conducted, yet some key contemporary areas which seem to attract more research are as follows:

- **Performance management:** Leadership analysis development and evaluation; organizational climate and work environment studies; talent and aptitude analysis and management; organizational change implementation, management and effectiveness analysis.
- **Employee selection and staffing:** This includes pre- and on-the-job employee assessment and analysis; staffing studies.
- **Organizational planning and development:** Culture assessment—either organization-specific or the study of individual and merged culture analysis for mergers and acquisitions; manpower planning and development.
- **Incentive and benefit studies:** These include job analysis and performance appraisal studies; recognition and reward studies, hierarchical compensation analysis; employee benefits and reward analysis, both within the organization and industry best practices.
- **Training and development:** These include training need gap analysis; training development modules; monitoring and assessing impact and effectiveness of training.
- **Other areas:** These include employee relationship analysis; labour studies; negotiation and wage settlement studies; absenteeism and accident analysis; turnover and attrition studies and work-life balance analysis.

Critical success factor analysis and employer branding are some emerging areas in which HR research is being carried out. The first is a participative form of management technique, developed by Rockart (1981) in which the employees of an organization identify their critical success factors and help in customizing and incorporating them in developing the mission and vision of their organization. The idea is that a synchronized objective will benefit both the individual and the organization, and which will lead to a commitment and ownership on the part of the employees. Employer branding is another area which is being actively investigated as the customer perception (in this case it is the internal customer, i.e., the employee) about the employer or the employing organization has a strong and direct impact on his intentions to stay or leave. Thus, this is a subjective qualitative construct which can have hazardous effect on organizational effectiveness and efficiency.

Financial and Accounting Research

Financial and accounting research is a mix of historical and empirical research.

The area of financial and accounting research is so vast that it is difficult to provide a pen sketch of the research areas. In this section, we are providing just a brief overview of some research topics:

- **Asset pricing, corporate finance and capital markets:** The focus here is on stock market response to corporate actions (IPOs, takeovers and mergers), financial reporting (earnings and firm-specific announcements) and the impact of factors on returns, e.g., liquidity and volume.
- **Financial derivatives and interest rate and credit risk modeling:** This includes analysing interest rate derivatives, development and validation of corporate credit rating models and associated derivatives; analysing corporate decision making and investment risk appraisal.
- **Market-based accounting research:** Analysis of corporate financial reporting behaviour; accounting-based valuations; evaluation and usage of accounting information by investors and evaluation of management compensation schemes.
- **Auditing and accountability:** This includes both private and public sector accounting studies, analysis of audit regulations; analysis of different audit methodologies; governance and accountability of audit committees.
- **Financial econometrics:** This includes modelling and forecasting in volatility, risk estimation and analysis.
- **Other related areas of investigation:** These are in merchant banking and insurance sector and business policy and economics areas.

Considering the nature of the decision required in this area, the research is a mix of historical and empirical research. Behavioural finance is a new and contemporary area in which, probably, for the first time subjective and perceptual variables are being studied for their predictive value in determining consumer sentiments.

Production and Operation Management

This area of management is one in which quantifiable implementation of the research results takes on huge cost and process implications. Research in this area is highly focused and problem-specific. The decision areas in which research studies are carried out are as follows:

- **Operation planning:** These include product/service design and development, and resource allocation and capacity planning.
- **Demand forecasting and decision analysis**
- **Process planning:** Production scheduling and material requirement management; work design planning and monitoring.
- **Project management and maintenance management studies**
- **Logistics and supply chain and inventory management analysis**
- **Quality estimation and assurance studies:** These include total quality management (TQM) and quality certification analysis.

This area of management also invites academic research which might be macro and general but helps in developing technologies such as JIT (just-in-time technology) and EOQ (economy order quantity—an inventory management model) which are then adapted by organizations for optimizing operations.

Cross-Functional Research

Cross-functional research requires an open orientation where experts from across the discipline contribute to and gain from the study.

Business management being an integrated amalgamation of all these and other areas sometimes requires a unified thought and approach to research. These studies require an open orientation where experts from across the disciplines contribute to and gain from the study. For example, an area such as new product development requires the commitment of the marketing, production and consumer insights team to exploit new opportunities. Other areas requiring cross functional efforts are as follows:

- Corporate governance and the role of social values and ethics and their integration into a company's working is an area that is of critical significance to any organization.

THE SIX GOLDEN RULES TO BRINGING VALUE BACK TO RESEARCH

The business world across the globe is extremely enthusiastic when it comes to cost cutting at the expense of research. So is there a way out? Can researchers survive the axe and build faith in conventional research and rebuild the value of their profession?

Focus on targeting and positioning: Philip Kotler says, 'If you nail targeting and positioning, everything else will follow.' Do not fall into the trap of picking a target in nanoseconds (as with 93 per cent of American brands) with no discernible positioning at all. 'Rigorous analysis of unimpeachable data' should be your mantra as you work hard to find the financially optimal target and a uniquely compelling positioning.

Open the windows and get out of the box: Make sure that it covers 'out-of-the-box' concepts, product/service attributes and benefits, and eventually analysis-stuff that is different than anything currently being used in its category. As my mom used to say, 'If all you do is what you have done, all you will get is what you got.' And that is not good enough!

Take the time to get it right: Rarely is speed the most important concern for marketers, even though they may think and act as if it is. Yes, there are some technology businesses that change at high speed, so speed of marketing research is of essence. But in most industries and for most decision areas, things change very slowly. It is more important to do it right the first time than to keep doing it over and over again.

Drop the jargon: While it may impress our friends and colleagues, research jargon confuses those not 'in the know' and leads to questions about what exactly the research is providing. Define terms for both the technically and non-technically inclined, not only in terms of the process, (i.e., data collection techniques, formulae, modeling), but also in terms of the type of information the analysis will provide.

Quantify the ROI of different research approaches: Take a typical US$ 20 million TV campaign, for instance. The average cost to produce one finished 30-second commercial is US$ 320,000, but it takes only about US$ 25,000 apiece to produce an animatic or photomatic—a rough version of a commercial—and US$ 20,000 for a research firm to test it. Two commercials cost US$ 90,000 in creative and research; four commercials, US$ 1,80,000. Rather than risking US$ 3,20,000 on one execution that will most likely yield return of 1 per cent to 4 per cent (the ROI of most advertising campaigns), why not spend US$ 5,00,000 (US$ 3,20,000 + US$ 1,80,000) to improve the probability of choosing the execution that will give 20 per cent ROI, or US$ 4 million? Presenting research choices in terms of greater profit potential gives marketers quantified information they can use to justify a decision to senior management.

Focus on research innovations that truly save time rather than cut corners: Many researchers have focused R&D efforts on developing faster data collection techniques, often through the Internet. On the surface, some new techniques appear faster, but a deeper look reveals the increase in speed is the result of cutting a few corners. The result is less representativeness and lower response rates. While the Internet and other technologies certainly offer opportunities for overcoming many of the impediments to quick data collection, such as distance, incidence and cost constraints, true innovations should preserve the integrity of data rather than sacrifice it for speed.

Source: Adapted from Clancy and Krieg (2000).

- Technical support systems, enterprise resource planning systems, knowledge management, and data mining and warehousing are integrated areas requiring research on managing coordinated efforts across divisions.
- Ecological and environmental analysis; legal analysis of managerial actions; human rights and discrimination studies.

FEATURES OF A GOOD RESEARCH STUDY

LEARNING OBJECTIVE 5
Interpret the basics of quality checks needed to classify research as meaningful and 'good' research.

In the above sections, we learnt that one method of arriving at solutions to our professional dilemmas is through research. This method of enquiry, we will subsequently learn can vary from the loosely structured method based on observations and impressions to the strictly scientific and quantifiable methods. However, whatever be the method of enquiry, it must adhere to certain historically established criteria to be termed as business research. For a research to be of value and to authenticate or contribute to the body of knowledge, we feel that it must possess the following characteristics:

(a) It must have a clearly stated purpose that implicit as when the *purpose* is to develop a new system of inventory management or explicit to establish quality standards for the service delivery model in our mobile eye care unit. This not only refers to the objective of the study, but also precise definition of the scope and domain of the study. The variables and constructs that are being investigated—service delivery model, quality standards, inventory management—need to be defined in clear and precise terms.

Research can assist one in arriving at some possible solutions to the existing **professional dilemmas.**

(b) It must follow a *systematic and detailed plan* for investigating the research problem. The source from which information is to be collected about quality standards inventory models has to be listed. In case the data is to be collected from a sample of suppliers, retailers and pathologists for investigating the gaps in the current inventory model, the detailing of how representativeness of the sample to the total population is to be ensured along with estimated error has to be specified. The systematic conduction also requires that all the steps in the research process are interlinked and sequential in nature.

(c) The selection of techniques of collecting information, sampling plans and data analysis techniques must be supported by a logical *justification.* In case you are selecting a secondary data source only or going for an online survey, or rather than going to pathologists going to the ENT specialists for your hearing aid study, the reason for doing so, along with a clear demonstrable link to the research purpose is an absolute must.

A researcher should not disclose his/her **biases** at any cost as it may limit the approach and horizon of a study.

(d) The results of the study must be presented in an *unbiased, objective* and *neutral manner*. The significant findings can, at best, be supported by past researches, research approach and limitation, or by expert opinion. The researchers' own judgements and biases should not be revealed at any cost, even when the scope of the study demands providing recommendations.

(e) The research that you undertake can never be fruitful if it cuts corners or if it exploits the rights of the respondents. Thus, the research at every stage and at any cost must maintain the *highest ethical standards.* For example, for the

CONCEPT CHECK	
	1. Enunciate the research application areas in various fields of management.
	2. What are the six golden rules of research?
	3. What are the features of a good research study?

hearing aids study, if through the survey we identify the pivotal influence of the pathologist in the hearing aid purchase decision; the pathologists could be given a commission for bad mouthing the competitor's products to steer the customers towards our product even when there is a delay in delivery, thus improving our profits without any major changes implemented in the faulty inventory reporting. But this would be unethical.

(f) And lastly, the reason for a structured, ethical, justifiable and objective approach is the fact that the research carried out by us must be *replicable*. This means that the process followed by us must be 'reliable', i.e., in case the study is carried out under similar constraints and conditions, it should be able to reveal similar results. We are not talking about identical results as there is a contribution of extraneous and chance factors which will be discussed in subsequent chapters.

SUMMARY

- Research is a quintessential tool, no matter what the field of learning is. It takes on special significance in the area of management as it would aid in more informed decision-making by business managers. The researcher might carry out a basic or an applied research based on his orientation. Basic research is carried out for the purpose of adding to the body of management science and usually does not have immediate utility. On the other hand, applied research is more problem-centric and is focused towards a specific business problem to which the manager-researcher is seeking an answer.
- There are other categorizations for classifying business research. Exploratory research is usually preliminary, loosely-designed study carried out to get the actual study perspective. On the other end of the continuum are conclusive research studies, which are clearly designed and follow a sequential progression to arrive at concrete findings. Conclusive research can be of two types—descriptive or causal studies. Descriptive, as the name conveys, are formulated to describe the environment/population under study in comprehensive detail and by following a predefined structure. Causal research studies are the most scientific in nature as they are designed to study a cause and effect relationship in a controlled environment. These studies are basically predictive in nature.
- Any research study usually follows a structured sequence of steps. These are:
    1. Developing and defining the research problem
    2. Formulating the study hypothesis
    3. Developing the study plan or proposal
    4. Identifying the research design
    5. Designing the sampling approach
    6. Conceptualizing and developing the data collection plan
    7. Executing data analysis
    8. Working out data inference and conclusions
    9. Compiling and preparing the research report
- Each of these steps requires a formal and well-defined approach.
- In the area of business management, each of the disciplines such as marketing, finance, human resources and operations have adapted and modified the research process to develop models and approaches which are unique and customized to the applications. This could be as simple as customer feedback or as complex as a highly structured and quantitative demand forecasting and analysis.
- Lastly, for any research to be recognized as significant and contributing to the field of management, it must follow some basic tenets, i.e., it must be unbiased and systematic in conduction. It must have a clearly defined agenda or purpose and if the study conditions are explicitly followed, the findings obtained should be replicable.

KEY TERMS

- Applied research
- Basic research
- Bivariate data analysis
- Business domain research
- Causal research
- Conclusive research
- Criteria for research
- Cross-functional research
- Descriptive research
- Experimentation
- Exploratory research
- Multivariate data analysis
- Non-probability sampling designs
- Primary data collection methods
- Probability sampling designs
- Research designs
- Research hypotheses
- Research proposal
- Sampling designs
- Scientific method
- Secondary data collection methods
- Sequential plan
- Univariate data analysis

CHAPTER REVIEW QUESTIONS

Objective Type Questions

State whether the following statements are true (T) or false (F).

1. Research is a tool that is specific to certain disciplines.
2. Applied research is the kind of research where one needs to apply specific statistical procedures.
3. In basic research, the context is vast and the time period is flexible.
4. Exploratory research always leads to a conclusive research study.
5. Both exploratory and conclusive research studies are carried out to test the research hypothesis.
6. Descriptive studies require experimentation to establish relationships between variables.
7. If one wants to state the current specializations that business management students are opting for, one conducts a causal research study.
8. The HR manager who wishes to undertake a study to find out the reasons for attrition in the organization so that she can make necessary changes in the existing employee policies; is carrying out an applied research study.
9. The research process is a precise and essentially a sequential process.
10. Research design is the flexible contract between the researcher and the client about the methodology of the study.
11. The group of individuals from whom one needs to collect data for the study is called the sample.
12. The most important decision to be taken in sampling the population is regarding the size of the sample.
13. Changes in the research orientation will cause changes in the research design selection as well.
14. In case one wants to know the various promotion schemes that have been used by all the competitors in the market, one must conduct a primary data collection exercise as the first step.
15. In case there are multiple variables under study, one will need to conduct bivariate analysis of data.
16. Critical factor analysis and employer branding are some emerging areas in marketing research.
17. In case one finds that the formulated research hypothesis has been negated, it can be safely said that the process of research was not carried out.
18. The researcher must clearly state his/her opinion about the findings of the study while reporting in the end.
19. Research method is a broad term, while research methodology is specific to a particular research problem.
20. One of the most important features of a good research study is replicability of findings.

Conceptual Questions

1. How would you define business research? What are the major components of a good research study? Illustrate with an example.
2. What is of more value to the corporate world—basic, fundamental, or applied research? Justify your reasoning.

3. Does exploratory research always lead to conclusive research? Give adequate examples to explain your perspective.
4. 'The research process involves a series of interrelated and intricate steps.' Does every research study necessarily need to satisfy all the conditions and be carried out in this sequence? Explain.
5. Besides functional research being carried out in an organization, the new era has seen a series of cross-functional studies being conducted. Can you identify some study areas like this, besides those listed in the chapter?

Application Questions

1. Does the opening vignette in the begining of this chapter require research? Why/why not? In case your answer is yes, what type of research would you advocate to EEE?
2. You are a business manager with the ITC group of hotels. You receive a customer satisfaction report on your international hotels from the research agency to which you had outsourced the work. What or how will you evaluate the quality of work done in the study?
3. A lot of business magazines conduct surveys, for example the best management schools in the country; the top ten banks in the country; the best schools to study in, etc. What do you think of these studies, would you call them research? Why/why not?
4. Faced with increasing absenteeism and low productivity, your HR manager proposes that a job satisfaction study across levels is required in the company. What do you think of this research question? Do you think such a study would help the manager in resolving his dilemma? Explain.
5. Select any research paper from a management journal in any area of your choice. Work backwards for it, i.e., if you were to submit a research proposal for this study, how would you design it?

Appendix – 1.1: HOW TO FORMULATE THE BUSINESS RESEARCH PROPOSAL

We have learnt in this chapter that research always begins with a purpose. Research is either the researcher's own pursuit, or it is carried out to address and answer a specific managerial question and arrive at an applicable solution. This clear statement of purpose guides the research process; however, for a study to qualify as research, it must be planned and systematic. Thus, the researcher needs to formalize this plan of pursuing the study. This framework or plan is termed as the research proposal. *A research proposal is a formal document that presents the research objectives, design of achieving these objectives and the expected outcomes/deliverables of the study.*

This step is essential both for academic and corporate research, as it clearly establishes the researcher's conceptualization of the research process that is intended to address the research questions. Through this written document the reader (academic expert or manager) is able to assess the rigour and validity of the study and whether or not it will result in an objective and accurate answer to the research problem. In a business or corporate setting, this step is often preceded by a PR (Proposal Request). Here the manager or the corporate spells out his decision problem and objectives and requests the potential suppliers of research to work out a research plan/proposal to address the stated issues. Thus, the research proposal submitted in such cases allows the manager to assess the credentials of the research agency or researcher as well as the proposed plan and to compare them with other proposals submitted. Then the manager selects the one that he feels would be able to most effectively (in terms of cost, time and accuracy) achieve the stated research goals.

Another advantage of a formal proposal is that sometimes the manager may not be able to clearly identify or enunciate his problem or the researcher might not be able to comprehend and convert the decision into a viable and workable research problem. The researcher lists out the objectives of the study and then together with the manager, is able to review whether or not the listed objectives and direction of the study will be able to deliver the necessary inputs required for arriving at a workable solution.

For the researcher, the document provides an opportunity to identify any shortfalls in the logic or the assumption of the study. When the researcher defines the flow and order of the steps required in the research process, he is also creating a mechanism for identifying probabilities of possible interrelated or simultaneous activities that can be carried out. It also helps to monitor the methodical work being carried out to accomplish the project.

Basically the proposals formulated could be of three types. The first is the academic research proposal that might be generated by students or academicians pursuing the study for fundamental academic research. An example is an academician wanting to explore the viability of different eco-friendly packaging options available to a manufacturer.

The second type of proposals are internal to an organization and are submitted to the management for approval and funding. They are of a highly focused nature and are oriented towards solving immediate problems. For example, a pharmaceutical company, which has developed a new hair growing formulation; wants to test whether to package the liquid in a spray type or capped dispenser. The solutions are time-driven and applicability is only for this product. These studies do not require extensive literature review but do require clearly stated research objectives, for the management to assess the nature of work required.

The third type of proposals have the base or origin within the company, but the scope and nature of the study requires a more structured and objective research. For example, if the above stated pharmaceutical company wishes to explore the herbal cosmetic market and wants market analysis and feasibility study conducted; the PR might be spelt out to solicit proposals to address the research question, and execute an outsourced research.

Contents of a research proposal

As stated above, the requirements and the origin of the research would direct the sequential formulation of the research proposal. However, there is a broad framework that most proposals adhere to. In this section, we will briefly discuss these steps.

Executive summary

This is a broad overview or abstract that spells out the purpose and objective of the study. In a short paragraph the author gives a summary about the management problem/academic concern, which is the backdrop of the study. The probable research questions which might need to be answered in order to arrive at any conclusive results are further listed.

Background of the problem

This is the detailed background of the management problem. It requires a sequential and systematic build-up to the research questions and also a compelling reason for pursuing the study. The researcher has to be able to demonstrate that there could be a number of ways in which the management dilemma could be addressed. For example, in the pharmaceutical company, the product testing could be done internally in the company, or the two sample bottles could be formulated and tested for their acceptability amongst probable consumers or retailers stocking the product; or the two prototypes would be developed and test launched and tested for their sales potential. The researcher thus has to spell out all probabilities and then systematically and logically argue for the intended research study. This section has to be explicit, objective and written in simple language, avoiding any metaphors or idioms to dramatize the plan. The logical arguments should speak for themselves and be able to convince the reader of the need for the study in order to find probable solutions to the management dilemma.

Problem statement and research objectives

The clear definition of the problem broken down into specific objectives is the next step. This section is crisp and to the point. It begins by stating the main thrust area of the study. For example, in the above case, the problem statement could be:

To test the acceptability of a spray or capped bottle dispenser for a new hair growing formulation. The basic objectives of this research would be to:

- Determine the comparative preference of the two prototypes amongst customers of hair growing solutions
- To conduct a sample usage test of both the bottles with the identified population
- To assess the ease of use for the bottles amongst the respondents
- To prepare a comparative analysis of the advantages and problems associated with each bottle, on the basis of the sample usage test
- To prepare a detailed feasibility report on the basis of the findings

If the study is addressed towards testing some assumptions in the form of hypotheses, they have to be clearly stated in this section.

Research design

This is the working section of the proposal as it needs to indicate the logical and systematic approach intended to be followed in order to achieve the listed objectives. This would include specifying the population to be studied, the sampling process and plan, sample size and selection. It also details the information areas of the study and the probable sources of data, i.e., the data collection methods. In case the process has to include an instrument design, then the intended approach needs to be detailed here. A note of caution has to be given here, this is not a simple statement of the sampling and data collection plan, it requires a clear and logical justification of using the techniques over a wide gamut of methods available for research. For example, in the pharmaceutical study—a before and after design, a respondent population of customers who use like products and the use of a structured questionnaire over other methods, have to be justified.

Scheduling the research

The time-bound dissemination of the study with the major phases of the research has to be presented. This can be done using the CPM/GANTT/PERT charts. This gives a clear mechanism for monitoring and managing the research task. It also has the additional benefit of providing the researcher with a means of spelling out the payment points linked to the delivered phase outputs.

Results and outcomes of the research

Here the clear terms of contract or expected outcomes of the study have to be spelt out. This is essential even if it is an academic research. The expected deliverables need to clearly demonstrate how the researcher intends to link the findings of the proposed study design to the stated research objectives. For example, in the pharmaceutical study, the expected deliverables are:

- To identify the usage problems with each bottle type.
- To recommend on the basis of the sample study which bottle to use for packaging the liquid.

Costing and budgeting of the research

In all instances of business research, both internal and external, an estimated cost of the study is required. A typical sample budget format with payment schedules is presented in the following sample proposal.

In addition to these sections, academic research requires a review of related literature section; this generally follows the 'problem background' section. If the proposal is meant to establish the credentials of the research supplier, then detailed qualifications of the research team, including the research experience in the required or related area, help to aid in the selection of the research proposal.

Sometimes, the research study requires an understanding of some technical terms or explanations of the constructs under study; in such cases the researcher needs to attach a glossary of terms in the appendix of the research proposal.

The last section of the proposal is to state the complete details of the references used in the formulation of the research proposal. Thus the data source and address has to be attached with the formulated document.

Appendix – 1.2: SAMPLE RESEARCH PROPOSAL

Executive summary

The 1980s was an era that saw the emergence of environmental issues. They were no longer the preserve of the social activist or the rigid revolutionist, environmentalism 'has become a competitive issue in the market place'.

Consumers who are environmentally aware place additional requirements on manufacturers, distributors and marketers. Food has cultural and social implications and food choice has become more broadly influenced by symbolic values; thus one of the offshoots of this new lifestyle shift is the increasing demand for organically grown products. However, the nature of the product demands a marketing strategy very different from normally grown food products. The question is also if there is really a market in the country for organic products. If yes then what is the size of the market and how we cater to the needs of the consumers. The imperative for any manufacturer of organic food products is to gauge the demand and then analyse how to address this. A highly lucrative market driven by premium pricing is extremely enticing if there is scope for capturing it.

Background

In recent years, all over the world, people are showing more concern for health and environment than ever before. There are enough evidences of deterioration of soil quality and water pollution due to chemical inputs in agriculture. Research studies have also indicated presence of harmful chemicals in food and milk at dangerous levels.

Thus, there is a growing concern over health risks associated with consumption of food with residues of agro-chemicals used in production. Heightened awareness of health and environmental issues in India and other countries has generated interest in organic farming. Demand for organic food is increasing and is expected to grow. Government of India has recognized this new developing market and estimated more than USD 13 billion export market with growth rate of 5–10 per cent in the next five years. Indian government has launched a national programme to boost organic food production. Under this scheme, producers will be linked to export markets and poor farmers would receive assistance. (*Asia Times*, 25 January 2001).

While Government of India is encouraging organic farming for improving export business, the domestic market also cannot be ignored. In most of the cities in India, demand for organic food is increasing rapidly. Number of retail stores and number of brands of various food products is increasing every year. However, organic food is considered to be premium quality and that much more expensive compared to conventionally grown food. Thus organic food is beyond the reach of middle class and poor people.

Though many NGOs in India are encouraging farmers towards organic farming and there are many stores in cities selling organic products, supply of these items is very limited. There are frequent instances when consumers do not get what they want and are forced to buy non-organic food.

Apart from the lack of awareness about organic produce, the organic food market has multifold problems:

- Consumers have problem of purchasing what they want in a required quantity at the time of their need.
- Distributors and retailers have problem of irregular supply and very low demand.
- Farmers have problem of producing, storing and marketing.

Unless all the three components are managed well, organic farming and marketing in the domestic market will not take off to the desired extent.

Practical/scientific utility

Health and fitness conscious society of today will be more and more conscious about their food intake also. Thus, demand for food free from harmful chemicals will increase with time. Organic food will be in demand across all the sections of society. It will be necessary to meet these demands.

Considering the farmers' or producers' point of view, for sustainable farming it would be necessary for them to switch over to organic farming to maintain the fertility of soil. Organic farming is cheaper compared to chemical farming and requires less amount of water because of specific ways of farming.

There are enough evidences of fertile land converted into wasteland because of chemical farming. There are also enough incidents of polluted water (ground and surface) due to chemical farming. Thus organic farming needs to be encouraged for both reasons, growing demand as well as to maintain the environment and water quality.

With this brief background of need of organic farming, we think that it is necessary to examine the issues of demand and supply management of organic farming, which is not done.

If farmers are assured about the demand of organic products and provided distribution channels, they will switch over to organic farming. This will benefit the farmers to manage soil and fertility of land. Society will be benefited in general and will have less polluted water.

Problem statement

The present study proposes to understand the growing demand pattern for organic fruits, vegetables and processed food products in the domestic Indian market and analyse the gap between demand and supply.

Research objectives

1. Estimate the production of selected organic farm products in various states and study the present distribution system:
   (a) The categories would include all fruits and vegetables.
   (b) Preserved food products like jams, juices, pulp and concentrates would also be studied.
   (c) All condiments, pulses, flour, rice and cereals would be studied.
   (d) Snack food products like biscuits and namkeens are also to be studied.
   (e) Study the supply chain—in terms of the farmer producer, the certification of the produce, the wholesaler/agent, the organic distributor and the retailer(s).
2. Estimate the domestic demand for the mentioned products at the national level.
   (a) This would be done for all the items, both for the existing and potential buyers of organic products.
   (b) The analysis would be done at the macro level, i.e., for the country as well as at the micro level, i.e., a regionwise analysis.
3. Understand the current pricing methodology adopted by organic players.
4. Identify the current strategies utilized for marketing organic food products.
5. SWOT of all the leading players would be attempted region wise.
6. Forecast the potential for organic products in the domestic market.

Assumption and hypothesis

These are as follows:

- **Assumption:** We assume that majority of people and farmers are aware of benefits of organic food and if it were easily available at affordable price; consumers would be willing to buy organic food produce. Presently, consumption of organic produce is very little compared to non-organic food because of high price and unavailability when required.
- **Hypothesis:** There is wide gap between demand and supply of organic produce. Gap can be reduced if farmers are encouraged to pracise organic farming and will reduce the pollution of water and soil.

Review of literature

Research work done and in progress in India

Some pioneering work has been conducted on organic farming in India, but it is still not of the proportions required for estimating and gauging the emerging market for organic food. Some recent work done on the subject is as follows:

Garibay and Jyoti (2003) conducted a large scale survey to assess the potential for organic products in India and in the international market and specified the steps required to achieve world class quality standards. They estimate the domestic sales of organic products at 1050 tonnes, which accounts for barely 7.5 per cent of the total organic production. This study undertaken by FIBL and ORG-MARG estimates the area under organic agriculture to be 2775 hectares (0.0015 per cent of gross cultivated area in India). But another estimation undertaken by SOEL-Survey shows that the land area under organic cropping is 41,000 hectare. The total numbers of organic farms in the country as per SOEL-Survey are 5661 but FIBL and

ORG-MARG survey puts it as 1426. Some of the major organically produced agricultural crops in India include spices, pulses, fruits, vegetables and oil seeds.

Singh (2003) in his paper on organic farming locates the rationale for organic farming and trade in the problems of conventional farming and trade practices, both international and domestic, and documents the Indian experience in organic production and trade. It explores the main issues in this sector and discusses strategies for its better performance from a marketing and competitiveness perspective.

The GOI (2003) working group report on organic farming led to the 10th Five-Year Plan, which emphasizes the promotion of organic farming with the use of organic waste, integrated pest management (IPM) and integrated nutrient management (INM). Even the 9th Five-Year Plan had emphasized the promotion of organic produce in plantation crops, spices and condiments with the use of organic and bio inputs for protection of environment and promotion of sustainable agriculture.

Research work done and in progress abroad

Wier, Hansen and Smed (2001) have analysed the consumption of organic food in Denmark in the 1990s. Their estimation of the demand elasticity demonstrated that the price sensitivity for organic products is higher than conventional products which clearly indicates the relevance of levies and subsidies on price conditions and the resulting demand.

Dryer (2004) focused on the natural *foods* industry in the US. Natural and organic food sales keep chalking up double-digit sales gains and milk and dairy products are among the growth leaders. *Organic foods* sales grew to $4.5 billion during 2002, an increase of 17 per cent. In the organic foods category, milk and dairy products accounted for about 14 per cent of total sales.

Tregear, Dent and McGregor (1994) conducted a research to investigate demand for organic foods by focusing on consumer attitude and motivations, product availability and retail options. A nationwide survey in UK revealed a nascent and evolving consumer most willing to purchase if the price differential was low.

Zygmont (2000) in his paper on export potential for US organic food has also found evidence of important consumer factors like awareness, motivation and willingness to pay as influencing organic consumption.

Some investigations have focused only on the production and demand of the produce.

Yussefi and Miller (2003) have found that worldwide sales of organic products reached 26 billion US $ in 2001, with fast moving products being milk products and vegetables. The annual growth rate of the market is 20 per cent. The biggest Asian market according to them is Japan with popular products imported being frozen vegetables, meat, tea and bananas.

SOL survey (2001) found that 15.8 million hectares are organically managed worldwide. Presently majority of this area is in Australia (7.6 million hectares), Argentina (5.5 million), Italy (1 million). Asia's produce is only 0.33 per cent, i.e., 50,000 hectares.

A comprehensive report on the world market for organic food and beverages was compiled by ITC (2000). This states that worldwide 130 countries are producing organic food and beverages. The market for organic food and beverages is growing rapidly in Western Europe, North America, Japan and Australia, with retail sales of organic food and beverages reaching an estimated $20 billion in 2001.

Research design

Demand–supply management is a critical process for agricultural produce.

Demand forecast drives supply chain and in this case, supply depends upon farmers' choice of organic farming, which is not conventional, farmers' choice of the crop and finally the weather (monsoon). We propose to develop a demand-supply matrix considering these factors.

At exploratory phase of the study, for identification of the products to be included in study, organizations involved in marketing of organic products will be visited and based on semi-structured interviews and sales data, items sold in those outlets will be classified into three classes according to sale and need. Fast moving items will be considered for study. Demand pattern of these items will be studied.

1. **Stage I:** This would involve data collection from secondary sources such as journals, articles, government publications and company literature. This would assist in estimating the production of organic products, traditional products and supply systems in practice.
2. **Stage II:** At this stage, primary research will be conducted in three phases.
   - **Expert opinion sample survey:** Agriculture researchers, policy-makers and farmers will be interviewed to collect information regarding organic farming and its necessity.

     Sample size: Ten agricultural researchers and five policy makers from central and state governments.
   - **Farmer's study:** Farmers doing organic as well as conventional farming will be included for studying problems related to organic farming and marketing organic produce. Study areas for the purpose will be Uttarakhand, Uttar Pradesh, Haryana, Gujarat, Rajasthan, Kerala, Karnataka and Tamil Nadu where organic farming is becoming popular.

     Sample size: Twenty farmers (conventional) + 20 farmers (organic) from each state.

- **Supplier's analysis:** In depth study will be carried out with some major manufacturers/suppliers of organic products. Their current trading, pricing and distribution practices will be studied. Supplier's study will be done in select cities like Delhi, Mumbai, Chennai, Ahmedabad and Bengaluru where demand for organic products is growing.

  Sample size: Ten leading manufacturers/suppliers in the country would be studied in depth; also five retailers and five distributors from each city under study.

3. **Stage III: Pricing of organic produce:** Current practices for pricing of the products will be examined and sensitivity analysis can be done for fixing prices by considering variables such as demand, volume of product and importance of the product and farmers' margin.

   Data processing will be done by us with the help of research associates and by using appropriate software for analysis.

Results and practical utility of the research

Findings of the report will be useful to all the policy-making agencies for defining or redefining policies regarding farming in India.

Findings will also be useful to all those involved and related to organic farming to decide their crop pattern and production.

Organizations involved in marketing and supplying organic products to society can use these findings to develop or modify their distribution systems and marketing strategies.

Duration of Project/Study and Phasing of the Work Plan

Duration of the project/study will be as follows:

- Total duration in days/weeks/months: 24 months
- Equivalent number of quarters: Four

Quarterwise phasing of activities will be as follows:

Work Plan S. No.	Tasks to be Accomplished	Week(s)
Quarter I	Exploratory study	8 weeks
	Secondary data collection	12 weeks
	Preparation of questionnaires	4 weeks
Quarter II	Pilot survey	8 weeks
	Expert opinion survey	10 weeks
	Manufacturers/supplier analysis	10 weeks
Quarter III	Retailer and distributor analysis	10 weeks
	Farmer survey	16 weeks
Quarter IV	Price sensitivity analysis	4 weeks
	Data processing	5 weeks
	Data analysis	5 weeks
	First draft report	8 weeks
	Final project report	4 weeks

Costing and Budget

Yearwise/itemwise recurring and non-recurring expenditure may be furnished (as shown in the tables below):

(A) Recurring Expenditure

Items	Year I (INR)	Year II (INR)	Total
1. Salary/Honorarium	360000.00	380000.00	740000.00
2. Travel	200000.00	100000.00	300000.00
3. Stationery, typing and printing	50000.00	40000.00	90000.00
4. Contingencies	50000.00	50000.00	100000.00
5. Others (Specify) boarding	200000.00	100000.00	300000.00
Total	860000.00	670000.00	1530000.00

(B) Non-Recurring Expenditure

Items	Year I	Year II	Total
1. Books and journals related to work	20000.00	10000.0	30000.00
2. Laptop computer	80000.00	–	80000.00
3. Digital camera	10000.00	–	10000.00
Total	110000.00	10000.00	120000.00
Grand Total (A+B)	1530000.00	120000.00	1650000.00

Answers to Objective Type Questions

1. False	2. False	3. True	4. False	5. False
6. False	7. False	8. True	9. True	10. False
11. True	12. False	13. True	14. False	15. False
16. False	17. False	18. False	19. True	20. True

REFERENCES

Clancy K J and P C Krieg. "Suriving Death Wish Research". *Marketing Research* 13 (4) 2000: 8–12.

Department of Agriculture and Rural Development. "Organic Production, a Viable Alternative for Northern Ireland," 2000. http://www.organic-research.com/news/2000/2000112.htm.

Dryer, J. *The Organic Option*, 105 (9) 2004: 24

Easterby-Smith, M, R Thorpe and A Lowe. *Management Research: An Introduction*, 2nd edn. London: Sage, 2002.

Garibay S V and K Jyoti. *Market Opportunities and Challenges for Indian Organic Products*, Study funded by Swiss State Secretariat of Economic Affairs, February 2003.

GoI (Government of India). *Report of the Working Group on Organic and Biodynamic Farming for the10th Five-Year Plan*. Planning Commission, GoI, New Delhi: September, 2001.

Grinnell, Richard Jr (ed.). *Social Work, Research and Evaluation* 4th edn. Itasca, Illinois: F E Peacock Publishers, 1993.

Hodgkinson, G P, P Herrior and N Anderson. "Re-aligning the Stakeholders in Management Research: Lessons from Industrial, Work and Organizational Psychology", *British Journal of Management*, 12, Special Edition, 2001: 41–8.

Kerlinger, Fred N. *Foundations of Behavioural Research* 3rd edn. New York: Holt, Rinehart and Winston, 1986.

Lundberg, George A., *Social Research—A Study in Methods of Gathering Data*. 2nd edn. New York: Longmans, Green & Co.,1942.

Miller, H and M Yussefi. "Organic Agriculture Worldwide, Statistics and Future Prospects', SOL (74): 2001.

Rockart, John F. "A Primer on Critical Success Factors". *In The Rise of Managerial Computing: The Best of the Center for Information Systems Research*, edited by Christine V Bullen. Homewood, IL: Dow Jones-Irwin, 1981.

Singh, S. "Marketing of Organic Produce and Minor Forest Produce," Chairman's Report on Theme 1 of the 17th Annual Conference of the Indian Society of Agricultural Marketing (ISAM), *Indian Journal of Agricultural Marketing* 17(3) 2003.

SOEL Survey (2003). Downloaded in April 2003 from www.soel.de/oekolandbau/welweit_reports.html

Tregear, A, J B Dent and M J McGregor. "The Demand for Organically Grown Produce," *British Food Journal* 96 (4)1994: 21–25.

Wier, M, L G Hansen and S Smed. "Explaining Demand for Organic Foods," Paper for the 11th Annual EAERE Conference, Southhampton, 2001.

Yussefi, M and H Miller (eds.). *The World of Organic Agriculture 2003–Statistics and Future Prospects*. IFOAM. Germany: Tholey-Theley, 2003.

Zygmont, J. "US Organic Fruit: Export Opportunities and Competition in the International Market". Paper presented at the Washington Horticultural Association's 96th Annual Meeting and Trade Show, Yokima, Washington DC, 6 December 2000.

BIBLIOGRAPHY

Boyd, Harper W, Jr Ralph Westfall and Stanley F Stasch. *Marketing Research: Text and Cases*. 7th edn. Richard D Irwin, Inc., 2002.

Green, Paul E and Donald S Tull. Research for Marketing Decisions. 4th edn. New Delhi: Prentice Hall of India Private Ltd, 1986.

Kothari, C R. *Research Methodology Methods and Techniques*. 2nd edn. New Delhi: Wiley Eastern Limited, 1990.

Malhotra, Naresh K. Marketing Research – An Applied Orientation. 3rd edn. New Delhi: Pearson Education, 2002.

Organic Food Co., UK. *Organic Food Market Triples over Three Years*. 2000.

Pannerselvam, R. *Research Methodology*. New Delhi: Prentice Hall of India Pvt. Ltd, 2004.

Tull, Donald S and Del I Hawkins. *Marketing Research: Measurement & Method*. 6th edn. New Delhi: Prentice Hall of India Pvt. Ltd, 1993.

Wright, S. "Europe Goes Organic," *Food Ingredients Europe* 3 (1997): 39–43.

2

CHAPTER

Formulation of the Research Problem and Development of the Research Hypotheses

Learning Objectives

By the end of the chapter, you should be able to:

1. Apply both deductive and inductive reasoning strategies to formulate a research problem.
2. Have a clear and precise understanding of what are the components of a scientific and objective research model.
3. Reduce the decision needs into distinct and clearly spelt research questions.
4. Identify propositions and convert them into testable research hypotheses depending on the nature of research.

'These research agency people have amazing sixth sense, before you can even spell out the information you need to arrive at a viable and workable decision, they come up with all the details about the kind of research you are most likely to need. Clairvoyant, that's what they are', commented awestruck Nachiketa Dubey. 'How do you say that?' asked her old batchmate Ravikesh. 'Well, only the other day I was in a meeting with the project director of Jagriti Research and told her about our extremely creative and dedicated team of project managers, some of whom were from the best universities across the world and yet the status of our project deadlines was extremely dismal. Therefore, we were not in a position to meet the deadline of even the smallest operation despite a lag time of 45 days. I said that I was at my wits end'.

And this lady tells me, 'Sir, the first thing we need to do is to identify the project areas which are manageable and require support; second; identify the jobs for which you may need to outsource; third, you need to do an internal homework of the talent and maybe a reorganization of the team based on an assessment of their capabilities, would be required. Fourth you need a standardized manual of procedures which can be modified by the project team and management information system (MIS) in place so that the progress on the project is updated at all times with all members of the team.' Before I could catch my breath, she said 'I think most of the data is available internally, the background of the team with work experience can be provided to us, and we will work on some benchmarked teams' data and prepare probable structural formats for the team. There we would take your inputs as well as that of the team members and fine tune. For the MIS if need be, our people can work on this with your employees and have it ready simultaneously.' 'Now, how did she know the root and probable solutions to my problems, so she has to be clairvoyant, right!'.

Ravikesh said 'Well let me tell you, what she followed was a simple stepwise logical analysis of the basic problems which were responsible for your dilemma. Next, she split it into smaller information needs which could serve as inputs into probable solutions. There is no eureka about it, it is a simple stepwise approach to problem solving that you need to adopt and pursue. Believe me, it is no rocket science, you apply this to any decision that you need to take, and believe me, it works. I used this when I had to plan my son's higher studies. I named it Project Rohan, where I had identified that

I needed to collect information on the universities available, the selection process, the finances required, the educational loans available; the preparation my son needed to do and career prospects following different degrees. Let me tell you that Project Rohan was successful and Rohan is at MIT doing his masters in Information Management Systems. And now I have Project Ritika'.

'Your daughter? Another university candidate?' quizzed Nachiketa.

'No project—marriage this time.'

The crux of the scientific approach to identifying and pursuing a research path is to identify the 'what', i.e., what is the exact research question to which you are seeking an answer. The second important thing is that the process of arriving at the question should be logical and follow a line of reasoning that can lend itself to scientific enquiry. However, we would like to sound a note of caution here. The challenge for a business manager is not only to identify and define the decision problem; the bigger challenge is to convert the decision into a research problem that can lend itself to scientific enquiry. As Powers *et al.* (1985) have put it 'Potential research questions may occur to us on a regular basis, but the process of formulating them in a meaningful way is not at all an easy task'. One needs to narrow down the decision problem and rephrase it into researchable terms. Yegidis and Weinback (1991) have also referred to the complexity of phrasing the decision in research terms.

The second concern in formulating business research problems is the fact that more often than not, managers become aware of problems, seek information and arrive at decisions under conditions of bonded rationality. A concept formalized by March and Simon (1958) which implies that managers do not always work and take decisions in a perfectly rational sequence. The model says that information search or problem recognition phase like any other behaviour has to be motivated. Unless the manager is driven by present levels of dissatisfaction or by high expected value of outcomes, the process does not start. The next implication of the model is that in most instances, a manager does not have access to complete and perfect information. And further, the manager might try to seek reasonably convenient and quick information that meets minimal rather than optimal standards.

THE SCIENTIFIC THOUGHT

LEARNING OBJECTIVE 1

Apply both deductive and inductive reasoning strategies to formulate a research problem.

The real requirement, as pointed out by our protagonist Ravikesh in the opening vignette, is not the identification of the decision situation but applying a thought process that can take a panoramic view of the business decision. One needs to reason logically and effectively to cover all the probable alternatives that need to be addressed in order to arrive at any concrete basis for decision making. This reasoning approach could be deductive or inductive or a combination of both.

1. **Deductive thought:** This kind of logic is a culmination, a conclusion or an inference drawn as a consequence of certain reasoned facts. The reasons cited have to be real and not a figment of the researcher's judgement and second, the deductions or conclusions must essentially be an outcome of the same reasons. For example, if we summarize for Ms Dubey's problem that:

   All well-executed projects have well-integrated teams. (Reason 1)
   The ABC project has many shortfalls. (Reason 2)
   The ABC project team is not a very cohesive and integrated team. (Inference)

Deductive thought can be defined as a logic which includes drawing culmination/conclusion/inference from a given list of certain facts.

A note of caution here is that the above could be only two probable reasons; this inference is justified if we look at only these facts. Thus, unless all probable reasons have been isolated and identified, the nature of the inference is incomplete.

2. **Inductive thought:** On the other end of the continuum is inductive thought. Here there is no strong and absolute cause and effect between the reasons stated and the inference drawn. Inductive reasoning calls for generating a conclusion that is beyond the facts or information stated. In the same example of the ABC project, we might begin by asking a question, 'What is the reason for the ABC project not being executed on time?' And a probable answer could be that the project team is not making a coordinated effort. Again, this is only one explanation and there could be other inductive hypotheses as well, for example:

   The vendors and suppliers are ineffective in maintaining and managing the raw material and supplies.

   or

   The local authorities are extremely corrupt. At each stage, they deliberately put an official spoke in the wheel and do not let the next phase of the project be achieved till their 'rightful' share is negotiated and delivered.

   or

   The workers union in the area is very strong and is on a go-slow call which prevents the execution of work on time.

   Thus, the fact of the matter is that inductive thought draws assumptions and hypothesis which could explain the phenomena observed and yet there could be other propositions which might explain the event as well as the one generated by the manager/researcher. Each one of them has a potential truth in it. However, we have more confidence in some over the others, so we select them and seek further information in order to get confirmation.

Inductive thought does not involve any absolute cause and effect relationship between a set of reasons and inferences.

CONCEPT CHECK

1. Define deductive thought by citing an example.
2. What is inductive thought?
3. Elaborate the term 'research problem' in your own words.

In practice, scientific thought actually makes use of both inductive and deductive reasoning in a chronological order. We might question the phenomena by an inductive hypothes and then collect more facts and reasons to deduct that the hypothesized conclusion is correct.

DEFINING THE RESEARCH PROBLEM

LEARNING OBJECTIVE 2
Have a clear and precise understanding of what are the components of a scientific and objective research model.

The first and the most important step of the research process is to identify the path of enquiry in the form of a research problem. It is like the onset of a journey, in this instance the research journey, and the identification of the problem gives an indication of the expected result being sought. A research problem can be defined as a gap or uncertainty in the decision makers' existing body of knowledge which inhibits efficient decision making. Sometimes it may so happen that there might be multiple reasons for these gaps and identifying one of these and pursuing its solution, might be the problem. As Kerlinger (1986) states, 'If one wants to solve a problem, one must generally know what the problem is. It can be said that a large part of the problem lies in knowing what one is trying to do.' The defined research problem might be classified as simple or complex (Hicks, 1991). Simple problems are those that are easy to comprehend and their components and identified relationships are linear and easy to understand, e.g., the relation between cigarette smoking and lung cancer. Complex problems on the other hand, talks about interrelationship between antecedents and subsequently with

A gap or uncertainty which hampers the process of efficient decision making in a given body of knowledge is called a **research problem.**

the consequential component. Sometimes the relation might be further impacted by the moderating effect of external variables as well, e.g., the effect of job autonomy and organizational commitment on work exhaustion, at the same time considering the interacting (combined) effect of autonomy and commitment. This might be further different for males and females. These kinds of problems require a model or framework to be developed to define the research approach.

Thus, the significance of a clear and well-defined research problem cannot be overemphasized, as an ambiguous and general issue does not lend itself to scientific enquiry. Even though different researchers have their own methodology and perspective in formulating the research topic, a general framework which might assist in problem formulation is given below.

Problem Identification Process

Problem identification process is action oriented and requires a narrowing down of a broad decision problem to the level of information oriented problem in order to arrive at a meaningful conclusion.

The problem recognition process invariably starts with the decision maker and some difficulty or decision dilemma that he/she might be facing. This is an action oriented problem that addresses the question of what the decision maker should do. Sometimes, this might be related to actual and immediate difficulties faced by the manager (applied research) or gaps experienced in the existing body of knowledge (basic research). The broad decision problem has to be narrowed down to information oriented problem which focuses on the data or information required to arrive at any meaningful conclusion. Given in Figure 2.1 is a set of decision problems and the subsequent research problems that might address them.

Management decision problem

The entire process explained above begins with the acknowledgement and identification of the difficulty encountered by the business manager/researcher. If the manager is skilled enough and the nature of the problem requires to be resolved by him or her alone, the problem identification process is handled by him or her, else he or she outsources it to a researcher or a research agency. This step requires the author to carry out a problem appraisal, which would involve a comprehensive audit of the origin and symptoms of the diagnosed business problem. For illustration, let us take the first problem listed in the Figure 2.1. An organic farmer and trader in Uttarakhand, Nirmal farms, wants to sell his organic food products in the domestic Indian market. However, he is not aware if this is a viable business opportunity and since he does not have the expertise or time to undertake any research to aid in the formulation of the marketing strategy, he decides to outsource the study.

The management can also outsource the **problem identification process** to a research agency in case of lack of time, means or knowledge regarding the market pulse.

Discussion with subject experts

The next step involves getting the problem in the right perspective through discussions with industry and subject experts. These individuals are knowledgeable about the industry as well as the organization. They could be found both within and outside the company. The information on the current and probable scenario required is obtained with the assistance of a semi-structured interview. Thus, the researcher must have a predetermined set of questions related to the doubts experienced in problem formulation. It should be remembered that the purpose of the interview is simply to gain clarity on the problem area and not to arrive at any kind of conclusions or solutions to the problem. For example, for the organic food study, the researcher might decide to go to food experts in the Ministry for Food and Agriculture or agricultural economists or retailers stocking health food as well as doctors and dieticians. This data however is not sufficient in most cases while in

FIGURE 2.1 Converting management decision problem into research problem*

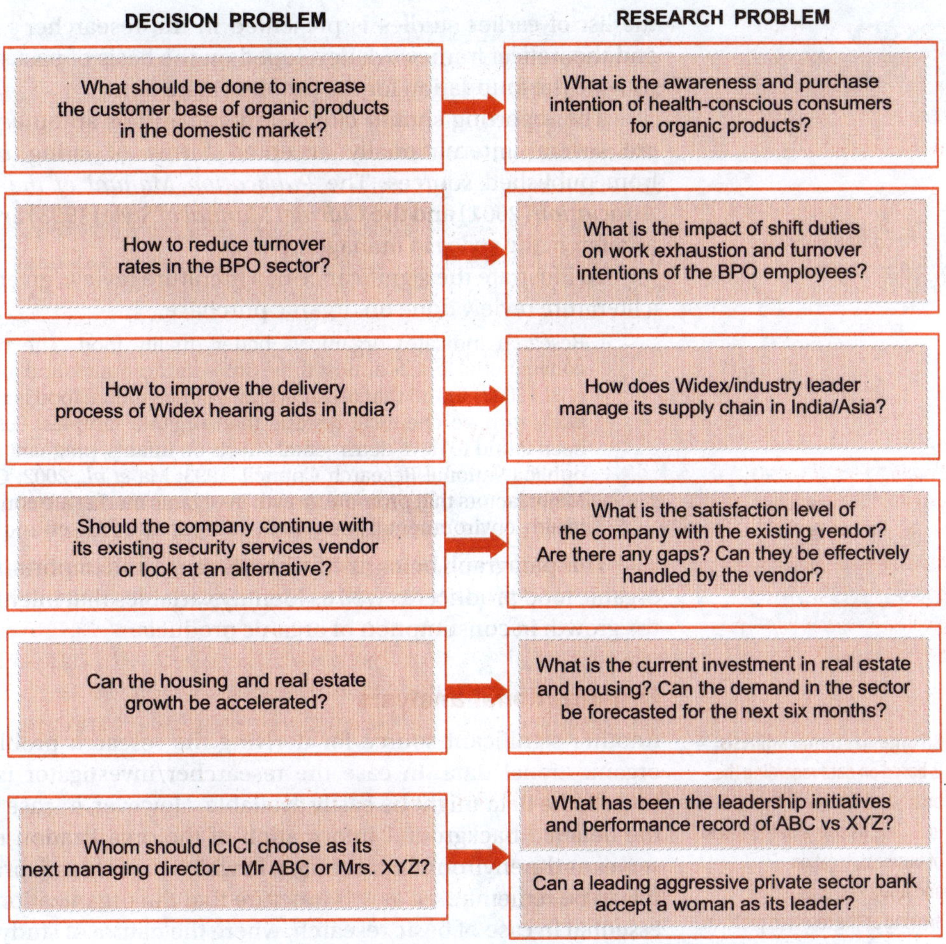

*The transgression from the first to the second column is not an easy task and requires a sequential stepwise approach (presented in Figure 2.3)

other cases, accessibility to subject experts might be an extremely difficult task as they might not be available. The information should, in practice, be supplemented with secondary data in the form of theoretical as well as organizational facts.

Review of existing literature

A literature review is a comprehensive compilation of the information obtained from published and unpublished sources of data in the specific area of interest to the researcher. This may include journals, newspapers, magazines, reports, government publications, and also computerized databases. The advantage of the survey is that it provides different perspectives and methodologies to be used to investigate the problem, as well as identify possible variables that may need to be investigated. Second, the survey might also uncover the fact that the research problem being considered has already been investigated and this might be useful in solving the decision dilemma. It also helps in narrowing the scope of the study into a manageable research problem that is relevant, significant and testable.

A literature review involves a comprehensive compilation of the information obtained from both published and unpublished sources of data which belong to the specific interest area of the researcher.

Once the data has been collected from different sources, the researcher must collate all information together in a cogent and logical manner instead of just listing the previous findings. This documentation must avoid plagiarism and ensure that the list of earlier studies is presented in the researcher's own words. The logical and theoretical framework developed on the basis of past studies should be able to provide the foundation for the problem statement.

The reporting should cite clearly the author and the year of the study. There are several internationally accepted forms of citing references and quoting from published sources. The *Publication Manual of the American Psychological Association* (2001) and the *Chicago Manual of Style* (1993) are academically accepted as referencing styles in management.

To illustrate the significance of a literature review, given below is a small part of a literature review done on organic purchase.

> Research indicates organic is better quality food. The pesticide residue in conventional food is almost three times the amount found in organic food. Baker *et al.* (2002) found that on an average, conventional food is more than five times likely to have chemical residue than organic samples. Pesticides toxicity has been found to have detrimental effects on infants, pregnant women and general public (National Research Council, 1993; Ma *et al.*, 2002; Guillete et al., 1998) Major factors that promote growth in organic market are consumer awareness of health, environmental issues and food scandals (Yossefi and Willer, 2002).

This paragraph helps justify the relevance and importance of organic versus non organic food products as well as identify variables that might contribute positively to the growth in consumption of organic products.

Organizational analysis

An **organizational analysis** is based on data regarding the origin and history of the firm including its size, assets, nature of business, location and resources. It assists in arriving at the research problem.

Another significant source for deriving the research problem is the industry and organizational data. In case the researcher/investigator is the manager himself/herself, the data might be easily available. However, in case the study is outsourced, the detailed background information of the organization must be compiled, as it serves as the environmental context in which the research problem has to be defined. It is to be remembered at this juncture that the organizational context might not be essential in case of basic research, where the nature of study is more generic.

This data needs to include the organizational demographics—origin and history of the firm; size, assets, nature of business, location and resources; management philosophy and policies as well as the detailed organizational structure, with the job descriptions.

Qualitative survey

Sometimes the expert interview, secondary data and organizational information might not be enough to define the problem. In such a case, an exploratory qualitative survey might be required to get an insight into the behavioural or perceptual aspects of the problem. These might be based on small samples and might make use of focus group discussions or pilot surveys with the respondent population to help uncover relevant and topical issues which might have a significant bearing on the problem definition.

In the organic food research, focus group discussions with young and old consumers revealed the level of awareness about organic food and consumer sentiments related to purchase of more expensive but a healthy alternative food product.

Management research problem

A **variable**, in general, is a symbol to which we can assign numerals or values. It can be dichotomous, discrete or indefinite.

Once the audit process of secondary review and interviews and survey is over, the researcher is ready to focus and define the issues of concern, that need to be investigated further, in the form of an unambiguous and clearly-defined research problem. Once again it is essential to remember that simply using the word 'problem' does not mean there is something wrong that has to be corrected, it simply indicates the gaps in information or knowledge base available to the researcher. These might be the reason for his inability to take the correct decision. Second, identifying all possible dimensions of the problem might be a monumental and impossible task for the researcher. For example, the lack of sales of a new product launch could be due to consumer perceptions about the product, ineffective supply chain, gaps in the distribution network, competitor offerings or advertising ineffectiveness. It is the researcher who has to identify and then refine the most probable cause of the problem and formalize it as the research problem. This would be achieved through the four preliminary investigative steps indicated above.

Last, the researcher must be able to isolate the underlying issues from the symptoms of the problem. For example, in the organic food study, the manufacturer has an outlet in an up market area in Delhi, and is constantly doing some attractive sales promotion but there is no substantial increase in sales. Here the real problem is lack of awareness and motivation on the part of the consumer about the benefits of organic food. Thus the low sales are primarily a consequence of lack of awareness and purchase intention.

To address the problems of clarity and focus, we need to understand the components of a well defined problem. These are:

The **unit of analysis** is that particular source from which the required information is obtained. It can be individual(s), department, organization or an industry.

1. **The unit of analysis:** The researcher must specify in the problem statement the individual(s) from whom the research information is to be collected and on whom the research results are applicable. This could be the entire organization, departments, groups or individuals. In the organic food study, for example, the retailer who has to be targeted for stocking the product as well as the end consumer could be the unit of analysis. Thus, the information required for decision might sometimes require investigation at multiple levels.
2. **Research variables:** The research problem also requires identification of the key variables under the particular study. To carry out an investigation, it becomes imperative to convert the concepts and constructs to be studied into empirically testable and observable variables. A variable is generally a symbol to which we assign numerals or values. A variable may be dichotomous in nature, that is, it can possess only two values such as male-female or customer-non-customer. Values that can only fit into prescribed number of categories are discrete variables, for example, occupations can be: Teacher (1), Civil Servant (2), Private Sector Professional (3) and Self-employed (4). There are still others that possess an indefinite set, e.g., age, income and production data.

   Variables can be further classified into five categories, depending on the role they play in the problem under consideration.

A **dependent variable (DV)** is measurable and quantifiable variable in nature. It is the most crucial variable to be analysed in a given research study.

- **Dependent variable:** The most important variable to be studied and analysed in research study is the dependent variable (DV). The entire research process is involved in either describing this variable or investigating the probable causes of the observed effect. Thus, this in essence has to be reduced to a measurable and quantifiable variable. For example, in the organic food study, the consumer's purchase intentions and the retailers stocking intentions as well as sales of organic food products in the domestic market, could all serve as the dependent variable.

  A financial researcher might be interested in investigating the Indian consumers' investment behaviour, post the recent financial slow down. In another study, the HR head at Cognizant Technologies would like to study the organizational commitment and turnover intentions of short and long tenure employees in the company.

  Hence, as can be seen from the above examples, it might be possible that in the same study there might be more than one dependent variable.

- **Independent variable:** Any variable that can be stated as influencing or impacting the dependent variable is referred to as an independent variable (IV). More often than not, the task of the research study is to establish the causality of the relationship between the independent and the dependent variable(s). The proposed relations are then tested through various research designs.

  In the organic food study, the consumers' attitude towards healthy lifestyle could impact their organic purchase intention. Thus, attitude becomes the independent and intention the dependent variable. Another researcher might want to assess the impact of job autonomy and role stress on the organizational commitment of the employees; here job autonomy and role stress are independent variables.

Moderating variables (MVs) are the ones that have a strong contingent effect on the relationship between the independent and dependent variables. They have the potential to modify the direction and magnitude of the above stated association.

- **Moderating variables:** Moderating variables are the ones that have a strong contingent effect on the relationship between the independent and dependent variables. These variables have to be considered in the expected pattern of relationship as they modify the direction as well as the magnitude of the independent–dependent association. In the organic food study, the strength of the relation between attitude and intention might be modified by the education and the income level of the buyer. Here, education and income are the moderating variables (MVs).

In a consulting firm, the management is looking at the option of introducing flexi-time work schedule. Thus, a study might need to be taken to see whether there will be an increase in productivity of each individual worker (DV) subsequent to the introduction of a flexi-time (IV) work schedule.

In real time situations and actual work settings, this proposition might need to be revised to take into account other impacting variables. This second independent variable might need to be introduced because it has a significant contribution on the stated relationship. Thus, we might like to modify the above statement as follows:

There will be an increase in productivity of each individual worker (DV) subsequent to the introduction of a flexi-time (IV) work schedule, especially amongst women employees (MV).

There might be instances when confusion might arise between a moderating variable and an independent variable.

Consider the following situation:

- ***Proposition 1:*** Turnover intention (DV) is an inverse function of organizational commitment (IV), especially for workers who have a higher job satisfaction level (MV).

While another study might have the following proposition to test.

- ***Proposition 2:*** Turnover intention (DV) is an inverse function of job satisfaction (IV), especially for workers who have a higher organizational commitment (MV).

Thus, the two propositions are studying the relation between the same three variables. However the decision to classify one as independent and the other as moderating depends on the research interest of the decision maker.

To understand the impact and role of the moderator variable let us represent the relationships graphically (Figure 2.2). Here *a* represents the effect of the independent variable (job satisfaction); *b* represents the effect of the second variable moderator variable (organizational commitment) and *c* represents the moderating effect, which is the combined effect of the moderating variable and the independent variable on the dependent variable. Thus, the effect of *c* has to be large enough and significant enough (statistically) to prove the moderation hypotheses.

An intervening variable (IVV) is a temporal occurrence which follows the independent variable and precedes the dependent variable.

- **Intervening variables:** An intervening variable (IVV) has a temporal connotation to it. It generally follows the occurrence of the independent variable and precedes the dependent variable. Tuckman (1972) defines it as 'that factor which

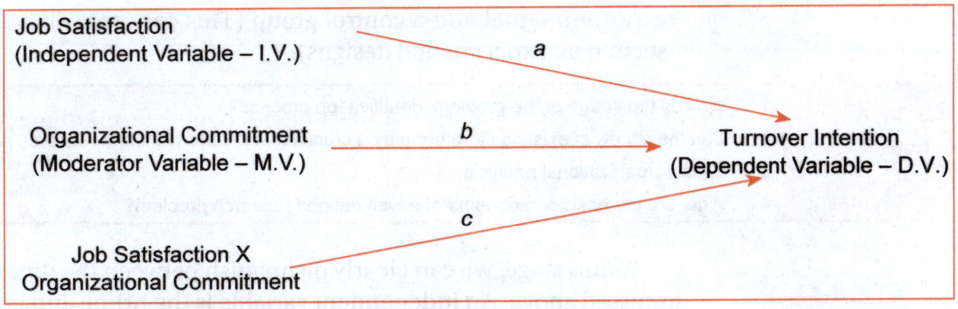

FIGURE 2.2 Graphical representation of moderating variable: Proposition 2

Note: a, b and *c* are hypothesized to be negative according to theory.

theoretically affects the observed phenomena but cannot be seen, measured, or manipulated; its effects must be inferred from the effects of the independent variable and moderator variables on the observed phenomenon.'

For example, in the previous case, There is an increase in job satisfaction (IVV) of each individual worker, subsequent to the introduction of a flexi-time (IV) work schedule, which eventually affects the Individual's productivity (DV), especially amongst women employees (MV). Another example would be, the introduction of an electronic advertisement for the new diet drink (IV) will result in increased brand awareness (IVV), which in turn will impact the first quarter sales (DV).This would be significantly higher amongst the younger female population (MV).

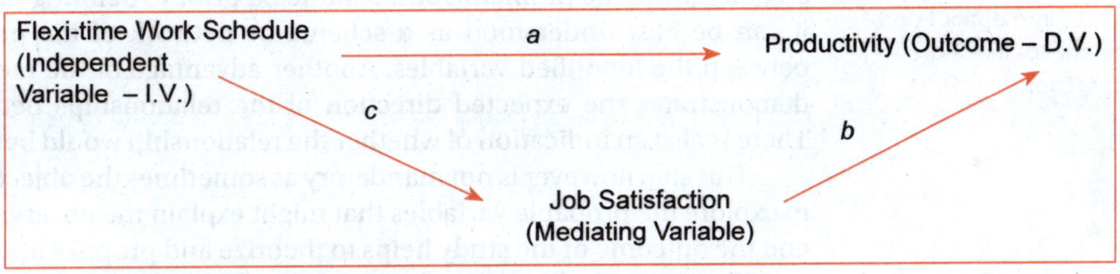

FIGURE 2.3 Graphical representation of mediating variable

Note: b, c = indirect effect, *a* = direct effect

In current research terminology, the intervening variable is also called a mediating variable, as it mediates the strength and direction of the relationship between the independent and dependent variable (Figure 2.3). For example in the above case, the direct effect of the predictor or the independent variable is measured by *a*; and the mediating impact of the mediating variable is represented by *b*. However, the point to be noted is that the independent variable acts on the mediating variable as represented by *c*. Thus, to prove a mediating relationship, one would expect that the effect of *b* would be more than the effect of *a* and that this could be proven to be significantly significant. The best case of mediation would be if *a* was zero or the predictor had no direct effect on the outcome variable. The impact of the mediating variable is assessed by the method of structural equation modeling. However, the discussion on the method is beyond the scope of this book.

Extraneous variables (EV) are responsible for the chance variations that are often observed in a research investigation. In most cases, they are limited to a peculiar group.

- **Extraneous variables:** Besides the moderating and intervening variables, there might still exist a number of extraneous variables (EVs) which could affect the defined relationship but might have been excluded from the study. These would most often account for the chance variations observed in the research investigation. For example, a tyrannical boss; family pressures or nature of the industry could impact the flexi-time impact, but since these would be applicable to individual cases, they might not heavily impact the direction of the findings. However, in case the effect is substantial, the researcher might try to block their effect by using an experimental and a control group (This concept will be discussed later in the section on experimental designs).

CONCEPT CHECK	
	1. What is the nature of the problem identification process?
	2. Can the review of existing literature play a crucial role in approaching a research problem?
	3. Define organizational analysis.
	4. What are the basic components of a well-defined research problem?

At this stage, we can clearly distinguish between the different kinds of variables discussed above. An independent variable is the prime antecedent condition which is qualified as explaining the variance in the dependent variable; the intervening variable follows the occurrence of the independent variable and may in turn impact the dependent variable; the moderating variable is a contributing variable which might impact the defined relationship; the extraneous variables are outside the domain of the study and responsible for chance variations, but in some instances, their effect might need to be controlled.

THEORETICAL FOUNDATION AND MODEL BUILDING

LEARNING OBJECTIVE 3
Reduce the decision needs into distinct and clearly spelt research questions.

Having identified and defined the variables under study, the next step requires operationalizing the stated relationship in the form of a theoretical framework. This is an outcome of the problem audit conducted prior to defining the research problem; it can be best understood as a schema or network of the probable relationship between the identified variables. Another advantage of the model is that it clearly demonstrates the expected direction of the relationships between the concepts. There is also an indication of whether the relationship would be positive or negative.

This step however is not mandatory as sometimes the objective of the research is to explore the probable variables that might explain the observed phenomena (DV) and the outcome of the study helps to theorize and propose a conceptual model.

A **theoretical framework** is a schema or network of the probable relationship between the identified variables. It is a powerful driving force behind the research process.

The theoretical framework, once formulated, is a powerful driving force behind the research process and ought to be comprehensively developed. It requires a thorough understanding of both theory and opinion.

Given below is a predictive model for turnover intentions developed to explain the high rate of attrition amongst BPO professionals. Once validated, it is of course possible to test it in different contexts and differing respondent population.

The Turnover Intention Model

The proposed model to predict turnover intention is specified as mentioned below:

$$TI = f(WE, OC, A, MS, TWE) \qquad ...(1)$$

Where, TI = Turnover intention

WE = Work exhaustion

OC = Organizational commitment

A = Age

MS = Marital status

TWE = Total work experience

A theoretical framework can be explained verbally as a **verbal model**, in a graphical form as a **graphical model** and can be reduced to mathematical equations and represented as a **mathematical model**.

The theoretical construct of work exhaustion is influenced by Perceived Workload (PWL), Fairness of Reward (FOR), Job Autonomy (JA) and Work Family Conflict (WFC) [Adapted from Ahuja, Chudoba and Kacman, 2007]. This can be mathematically written as:

$$WE = f(PWL, FOR, JA, WFC) \qquad ...(2)$$

FIGURE 2.4 Proposed model for turnover intention

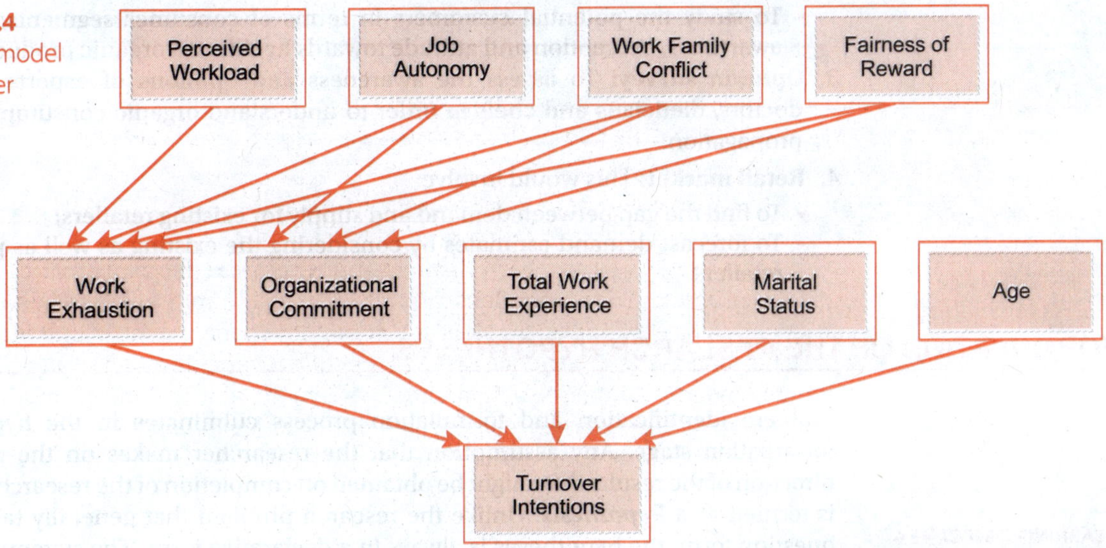

Similarly, Organizational Commitment depends upon Job Autonomy, Work-Family Conflict, Fairness of Reward and Work Exhaustion (WE) [Adapted from—Ahuja, Chudoba and Kacmar, 2007]. Therefore, this can be stated mathematically as

$$OC = f(JA, WFC, FOR, WE) \quad ...(3)$$

The model is diagrammatically represented in Figure 2.4.

The formulated framework has been explained verbally as a ***verbal model***. The flowchart of the relationship between independent and intervening variables has been demonstrated in graphical form as a ***graphical model*** and the same have been also reduced to three mathematical equations specifying the relationship between the same in the form of a ***mathematical model***. What needs to be understood is that all three compliment each other and are basically representatives of the same framework.

Statement of Research Objectives

Research objectives are to be formulated according to the basic, thrust areas of the research which are crucial to the study being conducted.

Next, the research question(s) that were formulated need to be broken down and spelt out as tasks or objectives that need to be met in order to answer the research question.

Based on the framework of the study, the researcher has to numerically list the thrust areas of research. This section makes active use of verbs such as 'to find out', 'to determine', 'to establish', and 'to measure' so as to spell out the objectives of the study. In certain cases, the main objectives of the study might need to be broken down into sub-objectives which clearly state the tasks to be accomplished.

In the organic food research, the objectives and sub-objectives of the study were as follows:

1. **To study the existing organic market:** This would involve:
   - To categorize the organic products available in Delhi into grain, snacks, herbs, pickles, squashes, fruits and vegetables;
   - To estimate the demand pattern of various products for each of the above categories;
   - To understand the marketing strategies adopted by different players for promoting and propagating organic products.
2. **Consumer diagnostic research:** This would entail:
   - To study the existing consumer profile, i.e., perception and attitudes towards organic products and purchase and consumption patterns;

- To study the potential customers in terms of consumer segments, level of awareness, perception and attitude towards health and organic products.

3. **Opinion survey:** To assess the awareness and opinions of experts such as doctors, dieticians and chefs in order to understand organic consumption and propagation.
4. **Retail market:** This would involve:
   - To find the gap between demand and supply for existing retailers;
   - To forecast demand estimates by considering the existing as well as potential retailers.

FORMULATION OF THE RESEARCH HYPOTHESES

LEARNING OBJECTIVE 4
Identify propositions and convert them into testable research hypotheses depending on the nature of research.

Problem identification and formulation process culminates in the hypotheses formulation stage. Any assumption that the researcher makes on the probable direction of the results that might be obtained on completion of the research process is termed as a ***hypothesis***. Unlike the research problem that generally takes on a question form, the hypotheses is always in a declarative form. The statements thus formulated can lend themselves to empirical enquiry. Kerlinger (1986) defines a hypothesis as '...a conjectual statement of the relationship between two or more variables.' According to Grinnell (1993), 'A hypotheses is written in such a way that it can be proven or disproven by valid and reliable data—it is in order to obtain these data that we perform our study.'

While designing any hypotheses, there are a few criteria that the researcher must fulfil. These are:

- A hypothesis must be formulated in simple, clear, and declarative form. A broad hypothesis might not be empirically testable. Thus, it might be advisable to make the hypothesis unidimensional, and to be testing only one relationship between only two variables at a time.
  - Consumer liking for the electronic advertisement for the new diet drink will have positive impact on brand awareness of the drink.
  - High organizational commitment will lead to lower turnover intention.
- A hypothesis must be measurable and quantifiable so that the statistical authenticity of the relationship can be established.
- A hypothesis is a conjectual statement based on the existing literature and theories about the topic and not based on the gut feel or subjective judgement of the researcher.
- The validation of the hypothesis would necessarily involve testing the statistical significance of the hypothesized relation. For example, the above two hypotheses would need to use correlation and regression analysis respectively to test the stated relationship.

A hypothesis can be **descriptive** or **relational**, while the former is a statement about the magnitude, trend or behaviour of a population under study, the latter typically states the expected relationship between two variables.

The formulated hypothesis could be of two types:

1. **Descriptive hypothesis:** This is simply a statement about the magnitude, trend or behaviour of a population under study. Based on past records, the researcher makes some presumptions about the variable under study. For example:
   - Students from the pure science background score 90–95 per cent on a course on Quantitative Methods.
   - The current advertisement for the diet drink will have a 20–25 per cent recall rate.
   - The attrition rate in the BPO sector is almost 33 per cent.
   - The literacy rate in the city of Indore is 100 per cent.

FIGURE 2.5
Problem identification process

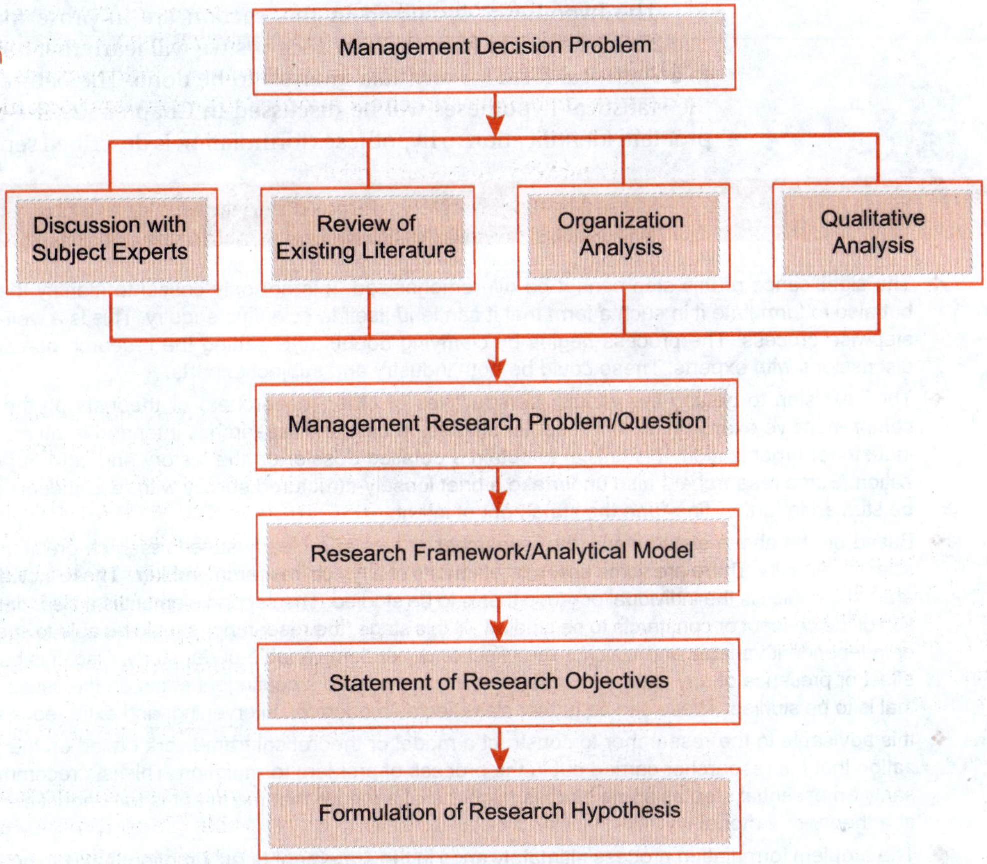

2. **Relational hypothesis:** These are the typical kind of hypotheses which state the expected relationship between two variables. While stating the relation if the researcher makes use of words such as increase, decrease, less than or more than, the hypothesis is stated to be directional or one-tailed hypothesis.

CONCEPT CHECK

1. State two advantages of model building.
2. Define the term 'hypothesis.'
3. What criteria should be fulfilled by a researcher while developing a hypothesis?
4. How would you differentiate between various types of hypotheses?

For example,

- Higher the likeability of the advertisement, the higher is the recall rate.
- Higher the work exhaustion experienced by the BPO professional, higher is the turnover intention of the person.

A directional or **one-tailed hypothesis** involves the usage of words such as increase, decrease, less than or more than. Whereas, in a **two-tailed hypothesis,** there is not enough reasonable supportive data to hypothesize the expected direction of the relationship.

However, sometimes the researcher might not have reasonable supportive data to hypothesize the expected direction of the relationship. In this case, he or she would leave the hypothesis as non-directional or two-tailed.

For example,

- There is a relation between quality of working life and job satisfaction experienced by employees.
- Ban on smoking has an impact on the cigarette sales.
- Anxiety is related to performance.

The hypotheses discussed in this section are in prose form and in a verbal declarative sentence form. In later sections we will learn that it needs to be reduced to a statistical form for any data analysis to be done. The nature and formulation of the statistical hypotheses will be discussed in Chapter 12. The complete process of problem identification to hypotheses formulation is described separately in Figure 2.5.

SUMMARY

- The significance of this step cannot be overemphasized. It is not only critical to identify the decision to be made but also to formulate it in such a form that it can lend itself to scientific enquiry. This is a well-integrated, linked and stepwise process. The process begins by clarifying doubts and getting the research perspective on the basis of discussions with experts. These could be both industry and subject experts.
- The next step to getting the various perspectives of other researchers or theorists on the topic is to conduct a comprehensive examination of the earlier studies. In case the research is intended to be carried out in a particular industry or organization, it is critical to obtain a detailed dossier on the history and current practices of the organization. Some researchers also undertake a brief loosely-structured survey with respondents from the population to be studied to further fine-tune the statement of intent.
- Based on the above stated steps, the researcher arrives at a clearly stated research problem that can lend itself to scientific enquiry. There are some essential elements of a typical research problem. These include specifying the unit of analysis—which is the individual or group that is to be studied. The second element is a clear definition and categorization of the concept or constructs to be studied. At this stage, the researcher should be able to specify what is the causal or independent variable and which is the effect or dependent variable under study. Also, it is best to acknowledge the effect or presence of any external variables which might have a contingent effect on the cause and effect relationship that is to be studied. These can be further classified as moderator, intervening, and extraneous variables.
- It is advisable to the researcher to construct a model or theoretical framework based on the stepwise conceptualization that the researcher carried out in the process of problem formulation. This is a recommended but not necessarily an essential step as some studies might be of a nature that the intent is to conduct the study and then arrive at a theory or a model.
- The problem formulation process ultimately ends in the statement or assumption that is to be authenticated through the research process. This proposition is termed as the research hypothesis. The formulated hypothesis could be descriptive in nature in that it only makes an assumption about the probability of occurrence or it might be relational in nature which indicates the probability of relationship between two or more variables. The hypotheses formulated at the beginning of the study are in statement or verbal form; however later in the course of research, they need to be reduced to statistical form, so that they can be adequately tested.

KEY TERMS

- Decision problem
- Deductive thought
- Dependent variable
- Descriptive hypothesis
- Extraneous variable
- Graphical model
- Hypothesis
- Independent variable
- Inductive thought
- Intervening variable
- Literature review
- Mathematical model
- Model building
- Moderating variable
- Organizational analysis
- Relational hypothesis
- Research problem
- Unit of analysis
- Variable

CHAPTER REVIEW QUESTIONS

Objective Type Questions

State whether the following statements are true (T) or false (F).

1. Deductive thought demands generating a conclusion beyond the available facts and information.

2. A business research problem leads to defining the business decision problem.
3. A valuable source of problem formulation is based on informal interviews conducted with industry experts.
4. *The Chicago Manual of Style* provides information on the method of collecting secondary data.
5. Organizational analysis involves collecting literature related to the organization under study.
6. Formulation of the research problem does not require primary data collection.
7. The persons from whom research related information is to be collected are called unit of analysis.
8. Discrete variables can have only two discrete values.
9. The causal variable is also called an independent variable.
10. The dependent variable is also called the effect.
11. The variables that have a significant contingent effect on the cause and effect relationship are called intervening variables.
12. The effect of a moderating variable can be possibly reduced by using a control group.
13. If one evaluates the impact of the pedagogy of Prof. N S on the research methods course grades of students, then Prof. N S, here, is the unit of analysis.
14. In the above example, the course grades of the students are the dependent variable in the study.
15. In problem number xiii, the prior knowledge of statistics that some students might have is the moderating variable.
16. All hypotheses are always formulated in question form.
17. If one is formulating a proposition about the magnitude or behaviour of a particular population, we call it a descriptive hypothesis.
18. Role ambiguity is related to role conflict—this is an example of a directional hypothesis.
19. All research problems must be stated in a question form.
20. A hypothesis that has two sub-hypotheses is called two-directional hypothesis.

Conceptual Questions

1. How would you distinguish between a management decision problem and a management research problem? Do all decision problems require research? Explain and illustrate with examples.
2. What are the components of a sound research problem? Illustrate with examples.
3. 'The manager/researcher is not equipped to arrive at a focused and precise research question, till he carries out a thorough inventory check of the problem area.' Examine the above statement and justify with examples why you agree/disagree with it.
4. Select a research problem, enlist the variables in the problem and formulate a theoretical framework to demonstrate the link between the variables under study.
5. What is a research hypothesis? Do all researches require hypotheses formulation? Explain.
6. 'Hypotheses are the guiding force in any research study.' Justify and explain.

Application Questions

1. The Indian Army wants to ascertain why young students do not select the armed forces as a career option in their graduation.
   (a) How would you formulate a research problem to resolve the dilemma?
   (b) What would be the variables under study?
   (c) How would you generate descriptive and relational hypotheses for your study?
2. The diet drink manufacturer in the study finds that young women are more health conscious and are looking at low calorie options. Thus, any communication or advertisement for the product has to emphasize the health aspect. The purchase probability is also influenced by their education level and the nature of their profession. Other factors such as available brands, celebrity endorsement and dieticians' recommendations also have an impact on them.
   (a) Identify your research problem and hypotheses.
   (b) Identify and classify the variables under study.
   (c) Is it possible to generate a theoretical framework for the study?

3. The training manager at ABC corporation has asked you to identify the kind of training programmes that should be offered to the young recruits who have joined as management trainees and are to be imparted five additional general management programmes along with their specific job training modules. The trainees are a mixed bunch of engineering and management graduates.
   (a) Formulate your research problem.
   (b) Identify the sources you would use to carry out a problem audit.
   (c) State your research objectives and the research hypotheses.

4. The highly successful "God's Own Country" campaign by Kerala Tourism and Mr Amitabh Bachan's series of ads on Gujarat titled "Come, breathe in a bit of Gujarat" have created tremendous visibility for the states. The state governments, however, feel that besides tourism, these campaigns have had an indirect impact on other aspects of development in the respective states. For example, in terms of real estate prices and other avenues as well. The central government would like to assess the direct and indirect impact of these campaigns on various developmental metrics. If you were to conduct a research for the government:
   (a) How would you formulate your management research questions?
   (b) How would you carry out a problem audit? Explain in detail the steps you would carry out for this.
   (c) State your research objectives and research hypotheses.

5. The relation between Indian sentiments and investment in gold has been well established since time immemorial. However, recent investment surveys have shown that the yellow metal has lost some lustre and the younger investor is looking at other financial instruments. A large banking and investment conglomerate would like to assess whether financial sentiments are different in old and young investors. What is the pattern of investment in the last decade and whether there are any shifts related to the global sub-prime crisis? The Bank CMD is of the firm opinion that investment is not always a rational and well deliberated decision, and there could be multiple factors impacting this. As an investment counselor and consultant, the organization should be aware of this and suitably build this into its financial products and services to service the investment better and also lead to increased profits for the company. In the light of this scenario:
   (a) How would you formulate your management research questions?
   (b) How would you carry out a problem audit? Explain in detail the steps you would take for this.
   (c) What could be the mix of variables that could impact the investor decisions? Is it possible to represent the same through a theoretical framework?
   (d) State your study objectives and research hypotheses.

CASE 2.1

ONLINE BOOKING—HAS THE TIME COME?

The day is not very far when the Indian travellers can criss-cross the globe with just a few clicks. Taking e-commerce and information technology services a step further, the Indian travel industry is composing itself to usher in the era of e-ticketing.

On-line booking involves pursuing of available information on travel websites and then making a reservation. However, if you are not the kind who prefers a particular airline, then you can check out travel sites, which collate flights details of all airlines, and are the apt place to book or bid for air tickets. Travel portals, such as, travelguru.com, arzoo.com, yatra.com, indiatimes.com, rediff.com, makemytrip.com, and cleartrip.com, would provide you all details of flights along with their fares in an ascending order, i.e., the lowest priced, ticket is featured first, on its web page.

The number of consumers who book travel tickets online is growing. But a switch from offline environment to online environment creates certain doubts in the minds of consumers. Such doubts have been termed as perceived risks in literature.

Also, the Internet revolution has brought about significant changes in market transparency, defined as the availability and accessibility of information to market participants. For example, air travellers can use online travel agencies to browse through hundreds of travel offers to their destination, compared to typically few offers from a traditional travel agent or airline prior to the Internet era.

Generally, market transparency seems to benefit consumers because they are able to better discern the product that best fits their needs at a better price. However, there still is a large percentage of population who get their tickets booked through the traditional queuing system.

The advent of e-ticket booking over the past couple of years has led to the mushrooming of online travel agencies. These online service providers have in fact come up with a wide variety of services for faster and more convenient mode of ticket booking. They offer a host of services starting from booking something as mundane as a train or flight ticket to something as exotic as a holiday. They offer various packages which have the entire itinerary for the proposed holiday. They even offer a convenient pick-up and drop service. With such a range of services being offered at your fingertips, expectations are that more and more number of travellers would start using such easy, fast and convenient services as compared to the conventional booking process across a reservation counter. Yet, we still observe long queues at the various reservation counters. And, we also know that there are a number of people who use the online services available to book their travel than through traditional travel booking counters.

Srininandan Rao, CEO of Ghoom.com, a travel portal that has been in existence for the past three years wondered whether he can look at a bigger customer base for his travel booking business or look at an alternative e-business.

QUESTIONS

1. What is the kind of research study that you can undertake for Mr Rao?
2. Formulate the research problem and the objectives of your study. Can you suggest an alternative research approach that you can take?
3. Develop a working hypothesis for your study.

CASE 2.2

DANISH INTERNATIONAL (A)

Shameem had been with the organization for a fortnight now and was due to meet Raghu. He opened the door and walked in.

Raghu asked him to be seated and said, 'So doctor, what is the diagnosis?'

Shameem Naqib had been recently hired as the company counsellor at Danish International, as Raghu Narang, the CEO, felt that he was fed up with his team of non-performers. He had hand-picked the Band II decision makers from the most prestigious and growing enterprises. Each one came with a proven track record of strategic turnarounds they had managed in their respective roles. So why this inertia at DI? The salaries and perks were competitive, reasonable autonomy was permitted in decision-making and yet nothing was moving.

There had been two major mergers and the responsibilities had increased somewhat. When Shameem went to meet Sid Malhotra, the bright star who had joined six months back, he was reported absent and seemed to be suffering from hypertension and angina pain. His colleague in the next cabin was not aware that Sid had not come for the past four days. As he was talking to Raghu's secretary, he could hear Kamini Bansal, the HR head, yelling at the top of her voice at a new recruit, who after six weeks of joining had come to ask her about her job role.

The Band III executives had been with the company for a tenure of 5–15 years and yet had not been able to make it to the Band II position (except two lady employees). They were laidback, extremely critical and yet surprisingly were not moving.

Raghu also seemed a peculiar guy, he had hired him as the counsellor and was also making some structural changes as suggested by a Vastu expert, to nullify the effect of 'evil spirits'. He had a history of hiring the best brains, and then trying to fit them into some role in the organization. And in case someone did not fit in, firing him without any remorse. He had changed his nature of business thrice and on the personal front, he was on the verge of his second divorce.

The company had a great infrastructure, attractive compensation packages and yet the place reeked of apathy. It was like a stagnant pool of the best talent. Was it possible to undertake-operation clean up?

QUESTIONS

1. What is the management decision problem that Shameem is likely to narrate to Raghu Narang?
2. Convert and formulate it into a research problem and state the objectives of your study. Can you suggest a theoretical framework about what you propose to study?
3. Develop the working hypothesis for your study.

CASE 2.3

BHARAT SPORTS DAILY (A)

Mr Anil Mehra, a senior executive with a leading newspaper published from Delhi, was frustrated with his job. His idea of launching an exclusive sports daily was not warmly received by the top management. Anil Mehra had written a few notes explaining the need for launching such a daily. However, he was not able to convince his superior, Mr Ashok Kapoor. Mr Kapoor had specifically asked him the estimates of demand for such a paper in the first year of the launch and for which Mehra had no answers based on any scientific research. Kapoor had told him clearly that unless he convinced him about the need for such a paper with the help of an empirical study, he would not be able to help him out.

Anil Mehra was a graduate in English (Hons) from Delhi University and had obtained a diploma in journalism in 1982. For the last 12–13 years he had worked with many newspapers and business magazines and it was his knowledge which was inducing him to go for this type of a venture. He was regretting not having a business background, which would have helped him to carry out an MR study for which his boss had assured him sponsorship from the newspaper. However, the amount for the research study was too small for him to contact any MR agency for help. The total budget for the study was ₹50,000. Just as Anil thought of putting in his papers and starting a sports daily on his own, he received a phone call from his friend Prof. Ravi Sharma, who was working with one of the leading management institutions of India. Prof. Sharma was on a visit to Delhi for a consulting assignment and thought of calling Anil. Anil was thrilled to receive the phone call and fixed up a meeting with him for the next evening. Prof. Sharma was accompanied by one of his colleagues, Prof. Singh. The conversation which went between Anil, Prof. Sharma, and Prof. Singh is as follows:

Prof. Sharma: Anil, Why do you look so upset? What is wrong with you? Any problem with the job?

Anil: I feel I shouldn't have gone for journalism and should have opted for management as career, like you.

Prof. Singh: Mr Mehra, I do not think yours is a bad line. However, please tell us if we could be of any help to you.

Anil: Prof. Singh, I want that we should come up with an exclusive sports daily (in English). I gave this idea to my boss. However, I am not able to convince him as he feels that it is only my hunch that there exists a demand for such a daily. He wants me to give specific estimates through a scientifically conducted research and I find myself totally at a loss.

Prof. Sharma: Anil, suppose you bring out such a daily, who will be the buyers?

Anil: What do you mean by this?

Prof. Sharma: I mean who are the people you think would be interested in reading such a sports daily, what are their age groups, education, profession, income, etc.?

Prof. Singh: Further, how much do you think people would be ready to pay for such a sports daily?

Anil: Well, Prof. Singh, let me tell you one thing that in this business, the price of a newspaper is immaterial for us. In fact, things like the cost of printing is much higher than the price charged from the customer.

Prof. Singh: How will it be a viable proposition?

Anil: It becomes viable just because the money is recovered through advertisements and if the circulation is high, more and more companies advertise their products in the newspapers.

Prof. Sharma: Anil, there is a sports section in all the newspapers. Why would people go for another one?

Anil: Ravi, you are right that all the newspapers have a sports section but I do not think that sports lovers are satisfied with the material covered there.

Prof. Singh: I think there would be variations in the amount of satisfaction the readers derive depending upon which newspapers they read. Further, I feel that they can satisfy there love for sports by going through general magazines, sports coverage on TV, sports videos, sports coverage on radio, and sports magazines and if that be the case, I have my doubts that there would be enough readership for such a sports daily.

Anil: Well, Prof. Singh, you are right. The programmes on TV and coverage on radio is on a specific time and the sports lovers may not have time to spare during those hours. Further, general magazines and sports magazines are usually quarterly or monthly and as such would be providing only stale material on sports.

Prof. Sharma: Prof. Singh, I think Anil has a point. However, it would be interesting to know the interests of the sports lovers for specific games so that one could know which games the sports daily should emphasize. Further, what is the profile of the people who like some specific games.

Prof. Singh: I have another question. At what time should the sports daily be brought out. That is to say should we bring it out in the morning or in the afternoon or in the late evening hours.

Anil: Look, Prof. Singh, these are all my problems and I have to convince my boss on all these issues. Please help me get a study conducted with the help of your students. I am sorry we have limited funds. We would be able to reimburse their travelling expenses plus give them a token honorarium for their efforts.

Prof. Singh: Mr Mehra, you do not have to worry about it. We would send two of our intelligent, hardworking and dedicated students to your organization for their summer job when they would conduct the study for you. Meanwhile, please tell me where would you like to launch this exclusive sports daily? Further, if you have any information you think would be relevant to this study, kindly hand it over to us.

Anil: Naturally, the sports daily has to be launched in Delhi on a trial basis. We have no idea what other information you are looking for. If you could spell out the same, I will try to supply it.

QUESTIONS

1. What is the management decision problem in this case?
2. How would you translate the management decision problem into research problem?
3. Explain the various steps that would be involved in the conduct of the study.

(*Note:* **Please note that when this case was written, cable TV was not launched in the Indian market. Therefore analyse the case in the light of this information.)**

CASE 2.4

FORTUNE AT THE LAST FRONTIER (A)

Nikhil Thareja belonged to the third generation of builders Thareja & Sons. The company had been started by Nikhil's grandfather, Lala Harbans Lal Thareja, after partition in 1947. From a small construction set up in a two-BHK house in Malviya Nagar, the company scaled new heights under Nikhil's father, Sampat Lal Thareja. The company worked in the areas of commercial space, residential complexes, and also undertook some industrial projects. Now, the ball was in Nikhil's court and the expectations from the 35-year-old London School of Economics finance major were huge. Today was the D-Day when he was to take over a new expansion unit that his grandfather and father had envisioned for their bright young heir.

Nikhil strode purposefully into his grandfather's cabin and asked "So Lalaji, what is this exciting plan that you have for me?" Lalaji (Lala Harbans Lal was affectionately called Lalaji by all) smiled exultantly and handed him a blue dossier marked 'Confidential'. Nikhil could hardly wait to open it. He quickly tore open the envelope and read the title and looked up aghast, wondering if his 85-year-old grandfather had gone senile. Lalaji watched his puzzled grandson from his wise old eyes and said "What I am giving you is challenging, futuristic and an exciting opportunity which I know has a great potential. I have been watching the world pass by and I know that the real fortune in a fully saturated market place lies not with an impudent and aggressive Young India, but a 'young' 60-year-old Indian who has the capital and the desire to enjoy the spoils of his labor. Your Lalaji has not lost his marbles , I challenge you to get the best of-what-do you call them—research agencies—to do a market feasibility study for you and then get back to me." Nikhil looked from his grandfather, whom he considered one of the most iconic entrepreneurs of his time, to the report in front of him. The embossed golden letters of the report glittered in the morning light as they spelt out: "Twilight Luxury- Retirement solutions: for those who reinvent life". Had his grandfather read the market signals correctly? Could there really be an attractive business opportunity with the senior population? And that too in India?

Housing Solution for Senior Citizens

There has been a definite change in the way the senior citizen lives his life today. The multinationals that came to India in the 1990s provided lucrative job opportunities—as a result, the senior of today has better financial cushion and investments today. There was also exposure to Western colleagues and their lifestyle. Due to these factors, the senior citizen's approach to life is different today. He may retire from his job, but not from life, and he has started looking beyond simple and frugal living after retirement, where you only think of *sanyas*. With better medical facilities and improved life expectancy, the elder wants to live his life amongst all the material comforts that he can buy. They have the financial means but not the physical energy, so they are open to buying any facility that can help them live their silver years in both comfort and style, with no physical and mental stress.

Worldwide, there are generally three different options available for the senior in terms of retirement solutions. The first is independent living homes—these are meant for those who are of reasonably good health and are able to manage life on their own. The second housing solution is for those who require physical or medical help and need assistance to manage daily chores. The third is for those who require medical care and treatment.

Thareja Builders were looking at the first category, where the senior was in considerably good health to look for a comfortable and desirable housing, which also had appreciation potential. Some successful retirement housing projects in India were:

1. Ashianna Utsav Retirement resorts (Bhivadi, Lavasa, Jaipur, Rajasthan)
2. Athashri (Pune , Maharashtra)
3. Brindavan Hill View (Coimbatore, Tamil Nadu)
4. Dignity Lifestyle (Mumbai, Maharashtra)
5. Shriram Senior Living (Bangalore, Karnataka)
6. AVI Vintage home (Gurgaon, Bangalore, Kolkata, Vishakhapatnam)
7. Serene Covai Properties (Coimbatore, Puducherry, Chennai, Mysore, Hyderabad)

Here again, the trend so far was of three kinds

- **Complete sales model:** This entails complete ownership for the buyer and requires considerable capital investment. These solutions also have some special provisions in terms of medical support, food and utility payment support; entertainment and recreation facilities to match the needs of old age. The additional facilities, of course, come at a separate and market-driven cost.
- **Lease deposit model:** Here, the senior citizen pays a one-time deposit and the rest is payable as monthly fees. Some part of the deposit is non-refundable. For example, there is a housing solution for cottage living near Mumbai, where the initial deposit is 13 lakh, of which 4 lakh is non-refundable. Besides, there is a monthly charge of 10,000; of this six months' charges are taken as advance security deposit. Besides this, there are charges for transport, telephone, television, Internet and medical facilities, and food is charged on actuals.
- **Pure rental model:** This is the easiest and most hassle-free option for the senior. Here again, there is a deposit and security fee but the initial capital investment required is not huge. The other charges are on actuals or in the form of monthly charges. However, the downside of these solutions is that these places lack permanency, as the rentals are for a period of 1-6 months and moving in and out might be a big hassle in old age.

The Decision

Higher life expectancy, better financial reserves and a positive and ego-expressive mindset have made the senior population an attractive market. However, Nikhil Thareja still felt that to evaluate the merit of this business opportunity, he needed to do a comprehensive research on the existing consumers, as well as the market.

QUESTIONS

1. Identify the management decision problem. Can you generate the kind of research this would require? Here, you need to look at multiple research problems that could address Mr Tharejas' dilemma and help in his decision making.
2. For identifying a research problem what kind of problem audit would you recommend? Elaborate on the steps you would undertake to conduct this study.
3. Of these select one business research problem that you believe will best address the decision needs. Give reasons for your selection.

Answers to Objective Type Questions

1. False	2. False	3. True	4. False	5. True
6. False	7. True	8. False	11. True	10. True
11. False	12. True	13. False	14. True	15. True
16. False	17. True	18. False	19. True	20. False

REFERENCES

Ahuja, M K, K A Chudoba and C J Kacmar, "IT Road Warriors: Balancing Work –family Conflict, Job Autonomy and Work Overload to Mitigate Turnover Intentions," *MIS Quarterly* 31(1) 2007: 1–17.

Baker, B, *et al.* "Pesticide Residues in Conventional, Integrated Pest Management (IPM)-Grown and Organic Foods: Insights from Three US Data Sets," *Food Additives and Contaminants* 19 (5)2002: 427–46.

Grinnell, R Jr (ed.). *Social Work, Research and Evaluation.* 4th edn. Itasca, Illinois: F E Peacock Publishers, 1993.

Guillette, E A *et al.* "An Anthropological Approach to the Evaluation of Preschool Children Exposed to Pesticides in Mexico," *Environmental Health Perspectives* 106 (6)1998: 347–53.

Kerlinger, F N. *Foundations of Behavioural Research.* 3rd edn. New York: Holt, Rinehart and Winston, 1986.

Mae X *et al.* '*Critical Windows of Exposure to Household Pesticides and Risk of Childhood Leukemia*,' *Environment Health Perspectives* 110 (9) 2002: 955–60.

March, J G and H A Simon. *Organisations.* New York: John Wiley & Sons, 1958.

National Research Council. *Pesticides in the Diets of Infants and Children.* Washington D C: National Academy Press, 1993.

Powers, G T, M M Thomas and G T Beverly. *Practice Focused Research: Integrating Human Practice and Research*. Englewoods Cliffs, NJ: Prentice Hall, 1985.

Yegidis, B and R Weinback. *Research Methods for Social Workers*. New York: Longman, 1991.

Yussefi, M and H Miller. *Organic Agriculture World Wide 2002, Statistics and Future Prospects.* International Federation of Organic Agriculture Movements. Germany: 2002.

Zikmund, William G. *Business Research Methods.* 5th edn. Bengaluru: Thompson South-Western, 1997.

BIBLIOGRAPHY

Burns, Robert B. *Introduction to Research Methods.* London: Sage Publications, 2000.

Dwivedi, R S. *Research Methods in Behavioural Sciences. New* Delhi: Macmillan India Ltd, 1997.

Green, Paul E and Donald S Tull. *Research for Marketing Decisions*. 4th edn. New Delhi: Prentice Hall of India Pvt. Ltd, 1986.

Malhotra, Naresh K. *Marketing Research–An Applied Orientation*. 3rd edn. New Delhi: Pearson Education, 2002.

Moore, J E. "One Road to Turnover: An Examination of Work Exhaustion in Technology Professionals," *MIS Quarterly.* Vol. 24, March (2000): 141-68.

Pannerselvam, R. *Research Methodology*. New Delhi: Prentice Hall of India Pvt. Ltd, 2004.

Tull, Donald S and Del I Hawkins. *Marketing Research: Measurement & Method.* 6th edn. New Delhi: Prentice Hall of India Pvt. Ltd, 1993.

3

CHAPTER

Research Designs: Exploratory and Descriptive

Learning Objectives

By the end of the chapter, you should be able to:

1. Identify the framework or design you intend to use to arrive at answers to the research questions framed by you.
2. Appreciate the numerous options available to you in formulating the research design.
3. Understand the nature of exploratory and two-tiered research designs.
4. Understand the techniques and stages in descriptive studies.
5. Understand and interpret cross-sectional and longitudinal designs.

As Anamika Rathore looked out from the 15th floor window of her Buzy Bee (BB) home solution office at the dismal January fog which was masking the bustling and cheerful view of Connaught Circus, it seemed that a similar fog had enveloped her normally decisive mind.

The company had been set up two years back in this prime location. They imported cabinets of all shapes and sizes, made from superior quality buffed steel and aluminium. The product category showed great promise and the pundits had predicted an unparalleled growth of 28 per cent in the coming year and expected it to rise further by 11 per cent in the subsequent year. But somehow BB was not in the radar of the potential buyer. Kaffe, Godrej and even regional and unbranded manufacturers enjoyed better sales than BB.

Anamika had suggested that they study the buying behaviour of the residents of builder apartments and society flats as they could be potential customers. The next step would be to identify the reasons for the lost opportunity. Anant Chacko, the CEO, took her suggestion seriously and agreed to sponsor the survey. However, he asked her to present a blueprint of the proposed investigation.

A blueprint for a short survey? Is that not making a simple thing so complicated? After all, it is not a building that she intends to construct that he was asking for the architectural design. That's what happens with these aggressive young people who have a fancy, glitzy MBA from abroad. Then she suddenly remembered Nilesh, who was with a local market research firm, and immediately called him up. 'Hi Nilesh, Anamika here, I need your help. Can you help me design a survey?' 'Hi Ani, sure. What kind of a design would you be looking at?' and he rattled off a set of names and assumptions. Anamika was flummoxed, what had she let herself in for?

The CEO was right in the stipulation that he had made. In fact, most researches lose out because either the research design was not conceptualized properly, or the design formulated was weak. Daft (1995), while reviewing the academic articles for the *Academy of Management Journal* and the *Administrative Science Quarterly*, states that 20 per cent of the reasons for rejection was inadequate study design. Grunow (1995), further corroborates and states that this weak area was discovered in both the published as well as the unpublished articles that he analysed. For a single research problem, different design options might exist, however, they have to be carefully selected based upon the deciding criteria and requirement of the study. This point will be further elaborated when the criteria of a well-structured research design are discussed in the chapter.

Thus, given certain preconditions, the researcher has multiple approaches to study the same problem (Hitt *et al.*, 1998). In fact, for the same research question, both qualitative and quantitative approach could be taken (Bartunek *et al.*, 1993) for example, to establish the human development status of a country, we can look at the quality of life (qualitative) that people enjoy or look at certain quantifiable parameters like longevity, literacy and purchasing power parity (quantitative).

This is an approach that became acceptable only in the later half of the 20th century, as the earlier school of thought was more based upon the objective nature of theory building—the positivist paradigm. This only accepted designs which called for an empirical observation and were followed by a certain level of statistical analysis (Ackroyd, 1996). The constructivists, on the other hand, argue for more divergent and behaviour specific techniques that are not a spillover from the natural sciences, and thus, follow a more qualitative approach (Jorgensen, 1989; Atkinson and Hammersley,1994). However, what needs to be considered by the researcher is what best suits and matches the research objectives; and only after that, he should take a position and proceed with the choice of the study.

THE NATURE OF RESEARCH DESIGNS

LEARNING OBJECTIVE 1
Identify the framework or design you intend to use to arrive at answers to the research questions framed by you.

Once you have established the *what* of the study, i.e., the research problem, the next step is the *how* of the study, which specifies the method of achieving the stated research objectives in the best possible manner.

As stated earlier, different paradigms will guide the selection of the gamut of techniques available. These differences in approach have led to varying definitions of what constitutes a research design.

Green *et al.* (2008) defines research designs as 'the specification of methods and procedures for acquiring the information needed. It is the overall operational pattern or framework of the project that stipulates what information is to be collected from which sources by what procedures. If it is a good design, it will insure that the information obtained is relevant to the research questions and that it was collected by objective and economical procedures.'

A **research design** is based on a framework and provides a direction to the investigation being conducted in the most efficient manner.

Thyer (1993) states that, 'A traditional research design is a blueprint or detailed plan for how a research study is to be completed—operationalizing variables so they can be measured, selecting a sample of interest to study, collecting data to be used as a basis for testing hypotheses, and analysing the results.' The essential requirement of the design is thus to provide a framework and direction to the investigation in the most efficient manner. Sellitz *et al.* (1962) states that 'A research design is the arrangement of conditions for collection and analysis of data in a manner that aims to combine relevance to the research purpose with economy in procedure.'

One of the most comprehensive and holistic definition has been given by Kerlinger (1995). He refers to a research design as, '..... a plan, structure and strategy of investigation so conceived as to obtain answers to research questions or problems. The plan is the complete scheme or programme of the research. It includes an outline of what the investigator will do from writing the hypotheses and their operational implications to the final analysis of data.'

Research design is the framework that has been created to seek answers to research questions. On the other hand, **research method** is the technique to collect the information required.

Thus, the formulated design must ensure three basic tenets:

(a) Convert the research question and the stated assumptions/hypotheses into operational variables that can be measured.
(b) Specify the process that would be followed to complete the above task, as efficiently and economically as possible.
(c) Specify the 'control mechanism(s)' that would be used to ensure that the effect of other variables that could impact the outcome of the study have been controlled.

The important consideration is that none of these assumptions can be foregone; all of them must be addressed succinctly and adequately in the design for it to be able to lead on to the methods to be used for collecting the problem-specific information. Thus, it follows the problem definition stage and precedes the data collection stage. However, this is not an irreversible step. Sometimes when the researcher is operationally defining the variables for study, it might emerge that the research question needs to be restructured and consecutively the approach for data collection also might oscillate from the quantitative to the qualitative or vice versa.

At this juncture, one needs to understand the distinction between research design and research method. While the design is the specific framework that has been created to seek answers to the research question, the research method is the technique to collect the information required to answer the research problem, given the created framework.

Thus, research designs have a critical and directive role to play in the research process. The execution details of the research question to be investigated are referred to as the research design.

FORMULATION OF THE RESEARCH DESIGN: PROCESS

LEARNING OBJECTIVE 2
Appreciate the numerous options available to you in formulating the research design.

Once the researcher has identified the research scope and objectives, he has also established his/her epistemological position. This could be positivistic—in which case the method of enquiry would necessarily be scientific and empirical. Subsequently, this would require a statistical method of analysis (Ackroyd, 1996). The constructivists on the other hand argue for methods that are richer and more applicable to the social sciences, unlike the more pedantic experimental approach. Qualitative is a more definitive choice here than the quantitative (Atkinson and Hammersley, 1994). Yet another approach is the principle of triangulation (Jick, 1979), which advocates the simultaneous or a sequential use of the qualitative and quantitative methods of investigation. The proponents state that when the findings from diverse methods are collated, then the results are richer, more wholistic and this, in turn, improves the sanctity of the analysis.

The principle of triangulation advocates the simultaneous or a sequential use of qualitative and quantitative methods of investigation.

The formulated research questions are then, through a comprehensive theoretical review, put into a practical perspective. The conceptual design thus developed requires and entails specifications of the variables under study as well as approach to the analysis. This might in turn lead to a refining or rephrasing of the defined research questions. Thus, the formulation of the research design is not a stagnant stage in the research process; rather it is an ongoing backward and forward integrated process by itself.

- **An illustration:** Let us take the example of the organic food study. The formulated research problem was:

To investigate the consumer decision-making process for organic food products and to segment the market according to the basket size.

On conducting an extensive review of the literature, it was found that organic consumption is not always a self-driven choice; rather it could be the seller who might influence the product choice. Thus, a research design was formulated to study the organic consumer's decision stages. However, once the design is selected and a proposed sampling plan is developed, the next step required is that the constructs and the variables to be studied must be operationalized. On defining the organic consumer, we realized the significance of the psychographics of the individual—the attitude, interest and opinion—which were extremely critical. Thus, to get a wholistic view, one needs to look at the psychographic profile of the existing consumer, as well as of the potential consumer with a similar mindset. This led to a revision of the research problem:

To investigate the consumer decision-making process for organic food products and to segment the market—existing and potential—according to their psychographic profile.

CLASSIFICATION OF RESEARCH DESIGNS

LEARNING OBJECTIVE 3
Understand the nature of exploratory and two-tiered research designs.

The researcher has a number of designs available to him for investigating the research objectives. There are various typologies that can be adopted for classifying them. The classification that is universally followed and is simple to comprehend is the one based upon the objective or the purpose of the study. A simple classification that is based upon the research needs ranging from simple and loosely structured to the specific and more formally structured is given in Figure 3.1. This depiction shows the two types of researches—exploratory and conclusive as separate design options, with subcategories in each.

The demarcation between the designs in practice is not this compartmentalized. Thus, a more appropriate approach would be to view the designs on a continuum as in Figure 3.2. Hence, in case the research objective is diffused and requires a fine-tuning and refinement, one uses the exploratory design, this might lead to the slightly more concrete descriptive design—here one describes all the aspects of the constructs and concepts under study. This leads to a more structured and controlled causal research design.

The research design classification that is universally followed and simple to comprehend is the one based upon the objective or purpose of the study.

In this chapter, exploratory and descriptive research designs are discussed in detail. The causal design requires to be understood for its mathematical presumptions and that would be dealt with in the next chapter.

Exploratory Research Design

Exploratory designs, as stated earlier, are the simplest and most loosely structured designs. As the name suggests, the basic objective of the study is to explore and obtain clarity about the problem situation. It is flexible in its approach and it mostly involves a qualitative investigation. The sample size is not strictly representative and at times it might only involve unstructured interviews with a couple of subject experts. The essential purpose of the study is to:

- Define and conceptualize the research problem to be investigated
- Explore and evaluate the diverse and multiple research opportunities
- Assist in the development and formulation of the research hypotheses
- Operationalize and define the variables and constructs under study
- Identify the possible nature of relationships that might exist between the variables under study
- Explore the external factors and variables that might impact the research

FIGURE 3.1
Classification of research designs

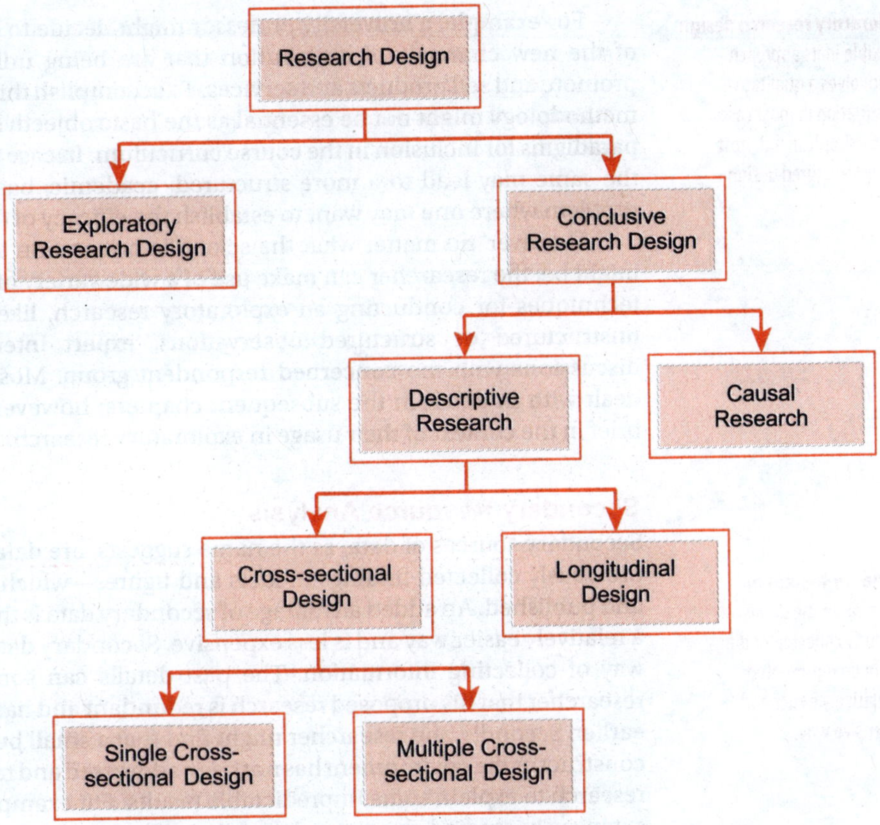

FIGURE 3.2
Research designs—a continuous process

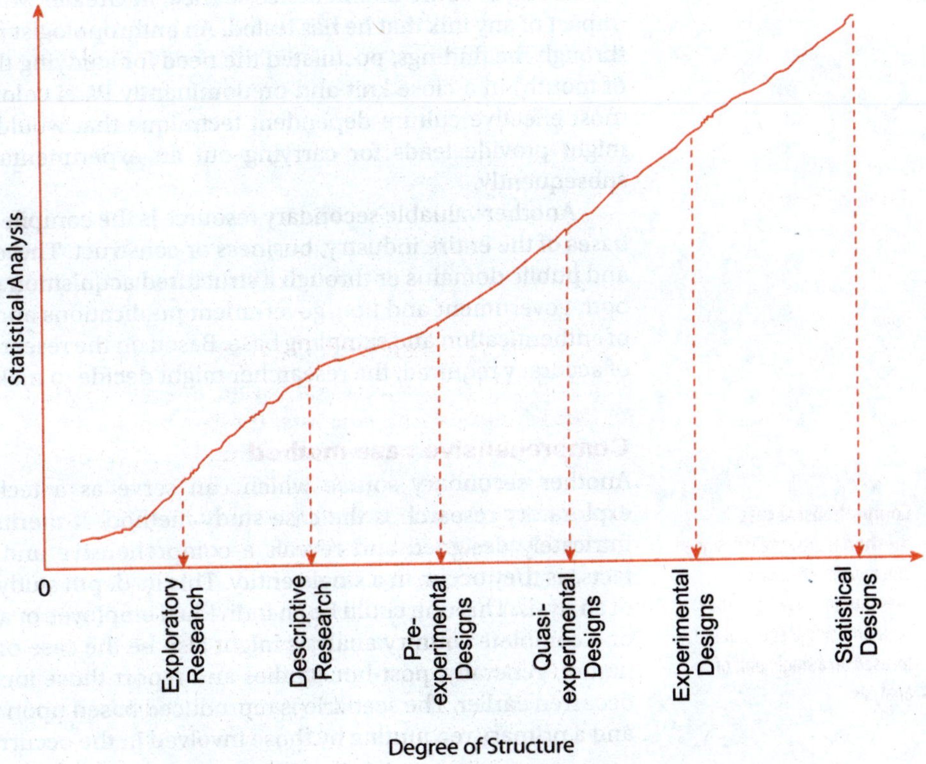

Exploratory research design is flexible in its approach and involves a qualitative investigation in most cases. It is the simplest and most loosely structured design.

For example, a university professor might decide to do an exploratory analysis of the new channels of distribution that are being utilized by the marketers to promote and sell products and services. To accomplish this, a structured and defined methodology might not be essential as the basic objective is to understand the new paradigms for inclusion in the course curriculum. In case the findings are of interest, the same may lead to a more structured, academic, basic research or an applied problem where one may want to establish the efficacy of different methods.

However, no matter what the scientific orientation and the research objective might be, the researcher can make use of a wide variety of established methods and techniques for conducting an exploratory research, like secondary data sources, unstructured or structured observations, expert interviews and focus group discussions with the concerned respondent group. Most of these techniques are dealt with in detail in the subsequent chapters; however, we will discuss them in brief in the context of their usage in exploratory research.

Secondary Resource Analysis

Secondary sources of data contain the details of previously collected findings and can be represented in a relatively easier and inexpensive way.

Secondary sources of data, as the name suggests, are data in terms of the details of previously collected findings in facts and figures—which have been authenticated and published. An added advantage of secondary data is that it can be represented in a relatively easier way and is less expensive. Secondary data is a fast and inexpensive way of collecting information. The past details can sometimes point out to the researcher that his proposed research is redundant and has already been established earlier. Secondly, the researcher might find that a small but significant aspect of the construct or the environment has not been addressed and might require a full-fledged research to explain some unpredictable results. For example, a marketer might have extensively studied the potential of the different channels of communication for promoting a 'home maintenance service' in Greater Mumbai. However, there is no impact of any mix that he has tested. An anthropologist research associate, on going through the findings, postulated the need for studying the potential of WOM (word of mouth) in a close knit and predominantly Parsi colony where this might be the most effective culture-dependent technique that would work. Thus, such insights might provide leads for carrying out an experimental and conclusive research subsequently.

Another valuable secondary resource is the compiled and readily available data bases of the entire industry, business or construct. These might be available on free and public domains or through a structured acquisition process and cost. These are both government and non-government publications and would have varying levels of authentication and sampling base. Based on the research constraints and the level of accuracy required, the researcher might decide to make use of them.

Comprehensive case method

Comprehensive case method is intricately designed and reveals a complete presentation of facts as they occur in a single entity. It is focused on a single unit of analysis.

Another secondary source which can serve as a technique for conducting an exploratory research is the case study method. It merits separate mention as it is intricately designed and reveals a comprehensive and complete presentation of facts, as they occur, in a single entity. This in-depth study is focused on a single unit of analysis. This unit could be an individual employee or a customer; an organization or a complete country analysis might also be the case of interest. They are by their nature, generally, post-hoc studies and report those incidences which might have occurred earlier. The scenario is reproduced based upon the secondary information and a primary recounting by those involved in the occurrence. Thus, there might be an element of bias as the data, in most cases, become a judgemental analysis rather than a simple recounting of events.

For example, BCA Corporation wants to implement a performance appraisal system in the organization and is debating between the merits of a traditional appraisal system and a 360° appraisal system. For a historical understanding of the two techniques, the HR director makes use of the theoretical works done on the constructs. However, the roll-out plans and repercussions and the management issue were not very clear. This could be better understood when they studied in-depth case studies on Allied Association which had implemented traditional appraisal formats, and Surakhsha International-360° systems. Thus, the two exploratory researches carried out were sufficient to arrive at a decision in terms of what would work best for the organization.

Expert opinion survey

Expert opinion survey is conducted when no previous information or data is available on a topic of research. It is formal and structured in general.

There might be a situation at times when the topic of a research is such that there is no previous information available on it. Thus, in these cases, it is advisable to seek help from the experts who might be able to provide some valuable insights based upon their experience in the field or with the concept. This approach of collecting particulars from significant and erudite people is referred to as the expert opinion survey. This methodology might be formal and structured and might be useful when being authenticated or supported by a secondary/primary research or it might be fluid and unstructured and might require an in-depth interviewing of the expert. For example, the evaluation of the merit of marketing organic food products in the domestic Indian market cannot be done with the help of secondary data as no such structured data sources exist. In this case the following can be contacted:

- Doctors and dieticians as experts would be able to provide information about the products and the level to which they would advocate organic food products as a healthier alternative.
- Chefs who are experimental and innovative and might look at providing a better value to the clients. However, this would require evaluating their level of awareness and perspective on the viability of providing organically prepared dishes.
- Pragmatic retailers who are looking at new ways of generating footfalls and conversions by offering contemporary and futuristic products. Again, awareness about the product, past experience with selling healthier lifestyle products would need to be probed to gauge their positive or negative reactions to the new marketing initiatives.

It is advisable to quiz different expert sources as no expert, no matter how learned or erudite, can be solely relied upon to arrive at any conclusions.

These could be useful in measuring the viability of the proposed plan. Discussions with knowledgeable people may reveal some information regarding who might be considered as potential consumers. Secondly, the question whether a healthy proposition or a lifestyle proposition would work better to capture the targeted consumers needs to be examined.

Thus, this method can play a directional role in shaping the research study. However, a note of caution is also necessary as by its very nature, it is a loosely structured and skewed method, thus supporting it with some secondary data or subsequently validating the presumptions through a primary research is recommended. Another aspect to be kept in mind is that no expert, no matter how vast and significant his experience is, can be solely relied upon to arrive at any conclusions, as in the example stated above. It is also advisable to quiz different expert sources. Notwithstanding these constraints, this technique is of great value to any researcher, no matter what his/her area of interest is. The more varied the perspective, more Gestaltian is the research approach, which will result in a meaningful contribution to the field of study.

Focus group discussions

Focus group discussions technique is originally rooted in sociology and is most staunchly advocated and used for consumer and motivational research studies.

Another alternative approach to interviewing is to carry out discussions with significant individuals associated with the problem under study. This technique, though originally rooted in sociology, is actively used in all branches of behavioural sciences. However, it has a special significance in management and here also it is most staunchly advocated and used for consumer and motivational research studies. In a typical focus group, there is a carefully selected small set of individuals representative of the larger respondent population under study. It is called a focus group as the selected members discuss the concerned topic for the duration of 90 minutes to, sometimes, two hours. Usually the group comprises six to ten individuals. The number thus stated is because less than six would not be able to throw enough perspectives for the discussion and there might emerge a one-sided or a skewed discussion on the topic. On the other hand, more than ten might lead to more confusion rather than any fruitful discussion and that would be unwieldy to manage. Generally, these discussions are carried out in neutral settings by a trained observer, also referred to as the moderator. The moderator, in most cases, does not participate in the discussion. His prime objective is to manage a relatively non-structured and informal discussion. He initiates the process and then maneuvers it to steer it only to the desired information needs. Sometimes, there is more than one observer to record the verbal and non-verbal content of the discussion. The conduction and recording of the dialogue requires considerable skill and behavioural understanding and the management of group dynamics. In the organic food product study, the focus group discussions were carried out with the typical consumers/buyers of grocery products. The objective was to establish the level of awareness about health hazards, environmental concerns and awareness of organic food products. A series of such focus group discussions carried out across four metros—Delhi, Mumbai, Bengaluru and Hyderabad—revealed that even though the new age consumer was concerned about health, the awareness about organic products was extremely low to non-existent.

Two-tiered Research Design

The **two-tiered research design** involves the formulation of the research question and the design framework.

Once an exploratory study using a loosely structured exploratory design is over, the researcher would have a greater clarity and direction, leading subsequently to a more structured research that he might undertake. Thus, he would manage to achieve the following:

- A comprehensive and focused research question, which will clearly indicate the orientation the study intends to take
- Finding out through various sources as listed above that the need for a conclusive research study is not there and the decision-maker can make use of the exploratory results to assist in the decision making
- Developing both the general and the specific hypotheses or presumptions of the likelihood of certain trends or outcomes
- Developing clarity on the framework and methodology best suited to achieve the formulated research objectives

This is/might be the first rung of a two-tiered research design where the first step is to formulate the research question and the second-tier is more formal and

CONCEPT CHECK

1. What is the basic nature of research designs?
2. Define exploratory research design.
3. Illustrate the importance of comprehensive case method.
4. What is meant by two-tiered research design?

structured and refers to the design framework defined earlier in the chapter. In most instances, the researchers avoid the first rung and move on to the second, due to the additional cost and time involved. However, it is advocated strongly that the exploratory stage can be extremely significant in reducing the risks of ambiguous and redundant research objectives.

Descriptive Research Designs

LEARNING OBJECTIVE 4
Understand the techniques and stages in descriptive studies.

The second set of research designs, discussed in the chapter, is more structured and formal in nature. These are termed as the descriptive designs. As the name implies, the objective of these studies is to provide a comprehensive and detailed explanation of the phenomena under study. The intended objective might be to:

- Give a detailed sketch or profile of the respondent population being studied. This might require a structured primary collation of the information to understand the concerned population. For example, a marketer to design his advertising and sales promotion campaign for high-end watches, would require a holistic profile of the population which buys high-end luxury products. Thus a descriptive study, which generates data on the *who, what, when, where, why* and *how* of luxury accessory brand purchase would be the design necessary to fulfil the research objectives.

Descriptive designs provide a comprehensive and detailed explanation of the phenomena under study. However, it lacks the precision and accuracy of experimental designs.

- There might be a temporal component to this design, that is, the description might be in a stagnant time period or be stretched across collecting the relevant information in different stages in a stipulated time period.
- The studies are also carried out to measure the simultaneous occurrence of certain phenomena or variables. For example, a researcher who wants to establish the relationship between market flux and investment behaviour might carry out a descriptive research to establish the correlation between the two variables under study.

Conducting descriptive research

Descriptive research, as we stated earlier, is a framework used for a conclusive research. It, however, lacks the precision and accuracy of experimental designs, yet it lends itself to a wide spectrum of situations and is more frequently used in business research. Based on the temporal collection of the research information, descriptive research is further subdivided into two categories: cross-sectional studies and longitudinal studies.

LEARNING OBJECTIVE 5
Understand and interpret cross-sectional and longitudinal designs.

Cross-sectional studies

Cross-sectional study investigates a specific chunk of the population under study. It is scientific in its approach.

As the name suggests, the study involves a slice of the population just as in scientific experiments one takes a cross-section of the leaf or the cheek cells to study the cell structure under the microscope, similarly one takes a current subdivision of the population and studies the nature of the relevant variables being investigated.

There are two essential characteristics of cross-sectional studies:

- The cross-sectional study is carried out at a single moment in time and thus the applicability is most relevant for a specific period. For example, a cross-sectional study on the attitude of Americans towards Asian-Americans, pre- and post-9/11, was vastly different and a study done in 2011 would reveal a different attitude and behaviour towards the population which might not be absolutely in line with that found earlier.

- Secondly, these studies are carried out on a section of respondents from the population units under study (e.g., organizational employees, voters, consumers, industry sectors). This sample is under consideration and under investigation only for the time coordinate of the study.

- **Illustrative case:** A Danish ice cream company wanted to find out how to target the Indian consumer to indulge in high-end ice creams. Thus, they outsourced to a local market research firm to find out the dessert consumption habits of an upper class, metro Indian consumer. The study was conducted during March–May 2008 on 1,000 Indian metro consumers in the upper income bracket.

The consumer survey conducted revealed that most Indians have a sweet tooth and prefer to eat their specific regional concoctions at home. However, when they are out, they love experimenting and generally look at exotic, foreign desserts or if lost for choice, opt for an ice cream, especially in summer. The highlights of the findings were as follows:

- 92.6 per cent of the sample stated ice cream as the first plus the second choice.
- 81 per cent stated ice cream as their first choice.
- Regional brands were the popular choice of most consumers.
- The recall of foreign brands was, however, only 15 per cent in the total population.
- The recall of foreign brands amongst globetrotters (who had made at least five trips to a foreign country in the last two years) was 39 per cent.
- 92 per cent agreed with the statement that a person's social status is an important determinant of who he/she is.
- 76 per cent believed, that what you eat and 85 per cent believed that where you eat, are influenced by the social class you belong to.
- 83 per cent usually eat out once every fortnight, 72 per cent eat out once every weekend.
- 64 per cent eat an ice cream outside at least once a week.
- 61.5 per cent were willing to experiment with exotic desserts, even if they were exorbitantly priced.

The ice cream company concluded from the findings that the market, at least in the metros, was ready. However, it was a niche segment and a better audience base could be found amongst the savvy urban Indian traveller. Another conclusion was that even though the ice cream was healthy and natural, it would have to take a lifestyle positioning in order to melt the Indian heart.

Cross-sectional survey, which is conducted on different sample groups at different time intervals, is called cohort analysis.

There are also situations in which the population being studied is not of a homogeneous nature and there is a divergence in the characteristics under study. Thus it becomes essential to study the sub-segments independently. This variation of the design is termed as *multiple cross-sectional studies*. Usually this multi-sample analysis is carried out at the same moment in time. However, there might be instances when the data is obtained from different samples at different time intervals and then they are compared. *Cohort analysis* is the name given to such cross-sectional surveys conducted on different sample groups at different time intervals. Cohorts are essentially groups of people who share a time zone or have experienced an event that took place at a particular time period. For example, in the 9/11 case, if we study and compare the attitudes of middle-aged Americans versus teenaged Americans towards Asian-Americans, post the event, it would be a cohort analysis.

The technique is especially useful in predicting election results, cohorts of males-females, different religious sects, urban-rural or region-wise cohorts are studied by leading opinion poll experts like Nielsen, Gallup and others.

Cross-sectionals studies are extremely useful to study current patterns of behaviour or opinion. However, respondent's likelihood of future decisions or delving too far in the past to determine the difference between the present and the past behaviour is not a wise choice. In such cases, a study that is anchored for information collection at different moments in time is a better technique. The results would be more reliable and valid. The advantage would be that rather than relying on the respondent's memory or prediction, an actual monitoring of behaviour patterns would take place over time.

Longitudinal studies

A single sample of the identified population that is studied over a stretched period of time is termed as a **longitudinal study design.**

A single sample of the identified population that is studied over a stretched period of time is termed as a longitudinal study design. A panel of consumers specifically chosen to study their grocery purchase pattern is an example of a longitudinal design. There are certain distinguishing features of the longitudinal studies:

- The study involves the selection of a representative panel, or a group of individuals that typically represent the population under study.
- The second feature involves the repeated measurement of the group over fixed intervals of time. This measurement is specifically made for the variables under study.
- A distinguishing and mandatory feature of the design is that once the sample is selected, it needs to stay constant over the period of the study. That means the number of panel members has to be the same. Thus, in case a panel member due to some reason leaves the panel, it is critical to replace him/her with a representative member from the population under study.

Thus, the two descriptive designs basically differ in their temporal components and secondly, in the stability of the sample unit selection over time. However, which one is selected depends upon the research objectives. Also, though they are visualized conceptually as two ends of a continuum, in practice, the two might merge or complement each other in usage.

Longitudinal studies are often referred to as **time series design** due to the repeated measurements taken over time.

For example, a management school that has just started a PGDM in human resource management wants to ascertain the stakeholders' (students, recruiters, programme faculty) attitude toward the programme structure and student quality and to monitor and alter the programme, relative to the changes in those attitudes over time. Specifically, suppose the B-school wants to measure this six-monthly, at the time of placements and six months after the trainee has worked on the job. For this objective, the ideal design would be the longitudinal design. However, this might work for the recruiter population but cannot be used for student effectiveness as a cross-section of that year's pass outs would need to be studied. Thus, it might not require the formulation of a fixed panel of respondents for this purpose and instead a cross-sectional sample might be used for the post-training analysis. However, the faculty sample could be a fixed panel selected for monitoring the change over time.

For determining a change or consistency on the measured variable over time, the ideal design is the longitudinal studies. These are sometimes referred to as the *time-series design* due to the repeated measurement overtime.

CONCEPT CHECK

1. What is desciptive research? How is it conducted?
2. Differentiate between cross-sectional and longitudinal studies.

Repeated measurements, as stated above, can be derived from the same sample, kept constant over time or on a representative but different group selected for every study stage. Even though the two collections would be under the domain of a longitudinal design, the obtained results and conclusions might be vastly different. This would be clear from the illustrative case given below.

- **Illustrative case:** The customer portfolio management division of a large private bank wanted to study the investment behaviour of bank customers in government instruments, mutual funds and securities, bullion and fixed deposits. This analysis was done for every quarter in a year for a period of five years. The survey was done on a different but stock sample of 1,000 bank customers for each quarter and the results obtained are shown in Table 3.1. Two conclusions pertaining to the researcher's attitude emerged. First, government instruments were the most popular option, with approximately 45 per cent customers. Second, the overall percentage of the division amongst the other three options is more or less stable over time.

TABLE 3.1
Results of longitudinal bank investment study

Use of	Quarter 1	Quarter 2	Quarter 3	Quarter 4
Govt institutions	45	43	43	45
MF and others	21	17	18	15
Bullion	15	22	21	19
FD	19	18	18	21
Total	100	100	100	100

Another option that the bank had was to form a panel of the regular customers and assess their periodic investments in these instruments; here the same group of people would be interviewed in the five-year period. The findings and conclusions obtained here would be slightly different, in case the sample remained the same. Such a panel study, in addition to indicating an overall investment behaviour, would have made it possible to monitor the options balanced between each other by the same group over time, and also how overall the quarter still showed a uniform pattern. This data will be available only if the customers studied remain constant at each data collection phase.

To illustrate the advantage of longitudinal data, let us consider two cases. The results from the two are presented in Tables 3.2 and 3.3. In both the tables, the figures, the values under 'Row Total' represent the total investment made in the instrument quarter 1 and the numbers under 'Column Total' represent the behaviour at the end of quarter 2. The overall investment spread is the same at the end of each time period. Thus, the results of the study as indicated earlier still hold true. However, the two tables contain additional information about the movement of the decision taken. The first row of the numbers in Table 3.2 reveals that of the 45 consumers who invested in goverment securities in period 1, 25 invested in the same in quarter 2, 5 moved to mutual funds, 10 to bullion and 5 got FDs made. Now consider the first row of numbers in Table 3.3. These numbers reveal that of the 45 consumers who invested in government securities, 43 still invested in the same in period 2, 1 put his money in mutual funds and one switched to bullion. The other investment options in the two cases can be similarly interpreted.

A true panel involves a committed sample group that is more likely to tolerate an extended or long data collecting sessions.

Thus, in case one, the investors who play safe and invest only in the fixed deposits more or less demonstrate the same behaviour. However, the other investors fluctuate between options. In case two, however, the investors are more rigid and conservative and remain with the same options.

Such longitudinal study using the same section of respondents thus provides more accurate data than one using a series of different samples. These kinds of panels are defined as true panels and the ones using a different group every time are called omnibus panels.

Advantages of a true panel are that it has a more committed sample group that is likely to tolerate extended or long data collecting sessions. Secondly, the profile information is a one time task and need not be collected every time. Thus, a useful respondent time can be spent on collecting some research-specific information.

After a certain period of time the panel members are **changed** so that new perspectives can be obtained.

However, the problem is getting a committed group of people for the entire study period. Secondly, there is an element of mortality and attrition where the members of the panel might leave midway and the replaced new recruits might be vastly different and could skew the results in an absolutely different direction. A third disadvantage is the highly structured study situation which might be responsible for a consistent and structured behaviour, which might not be the case in the real or field conditions.

To deal with this, the research agencies making use of such panels try to make certain that people behave normally and do not demonstrate exaggerated or artificial behaviour. Also steps are taken to get new members who match the behaviour of the leaving members. Thirdly, after a certain period of time, the panel members are changed so that new perspectives can be obtained.

Thus, there are advantages and drawbacks in both the descriptive designs, the level of accuracy required, the nature of the monitored behaviour and the degree of influence of demographic and psychographic variables determines the design decision; or the researcher might decide to use a combination of the two for more accurate results.

TABLE 3.2 Investment behaviour of regular consumers: Case 1

Customer Investments Quarter 1	Customer investments Quarter 2			FD	Row Total
	Government instruments	MF & others	Bullion		
Govt institutions	25	5	10	5	45
MF & others	8	4	9	0	21
Bullion	4	8	3	0	15
FD	6	0	0	13	19
Column Total	43	17	22	18	100

TABLE 3.3 Investment behaviour of regular customers: Case 2

Customer Investments Quarter 1	Customer investments: Quarter 2			FD	Row Total
	Government instruments	MF & others	Bullion		
Govt institutions	43	0	1	1	45
MF & others	0	16	3	2	21
Bullion	0	1	13	1	15
FD	0	0	5	14	19
Column Total	43	17	22	18	100

SUMMARY

- The research design is the blueprint or the framework for carrying out the research study. It indicates the plan constituted in order to give the necessary direction to the research study. At this juncture, the orientation of the researcher, whether scientific or positivist or constructivist and qualitative, would influence the design that is created to test the research hypotheses formulated in the earlier stage.
- Even though every design would be unique to the investigated question, it is possible to group them on the basis of the basic tenets of the guiding approach.
- The design can be loosely structured and investigative in nature. These are the exploratory designs. The design involves a comprehensive study of the earlier work done on the topic and an expert or/and a respondent survey. These designs are usually a prelude to and might lead to the more structured conclusive design which is more directional and involves creating a structured approach in order to test the study hypotheses. In case the hypothesis formulated is descriptive in nature, the study design would also be descriptive. Here, there is a time constraint to the study and, more often than not, the studies are topical in nature. The study involves collecting the *who, what, why, where, when* and *how* about the population under study.
- Descriptive studies can further be divided into cross-sectional, i.e., studying a section of the population at a single time period and reporting on the occurrence/non-occurrence of the variable under study. In case the study is conducted on a single population, it is termed as single cross-sectional and in case, it is done on more than one segment viewed as separate groups it is called multiple cross-sectional designs.
- Another type of descriptive desgn is the longitudinal design. Here, a selected sample is studied at different intervals (fixed) of time to measure the variable(s) under study. The design involves tracking the change in the studied variable over time. Since staggered data is available, it is also possible to compare the findings of different time periods.
- The conclusive research designs could also be causal in nature; these are called experimental designs. Since there are a number of further subdivisions possible in this category, they will be discussed in detail in the next chapter.

KEY TERMS

- Case study method
- Classification of designs
- Cohort analysis
- Conclusive research designs
- Cross-sectional studies
- Descriptive research design
- Expert opinion survey
- Exploratory research designs
- Focus group discussions
- Longitudinal studies
- Multiple cross-sectional designs
- Research blueprint
- Secondary resource analysis
- Single cross-sectional designs
- Two-tiered research design

CHAPTER REVIEW QUESTIONS

Objective Type Questions

State whether the following statements are true (T) or false (F).

1. Research designs are the blueprint of the research study to be conducted.
2. Research design formulation follows the problem definition and the data collection stage.
3. Research design is a dynamic process and permits modification and realignment during the course of the study.
4. Triangulation approach advocates the complimentary use of both qualitative and quantitative methods of investigation.
5. The most loosely structured research designs are called pre-experimental designs.
6. Exploratory research designs can help define variables and constructs under study.
7. The case study method is generally focused on a single unit of analysis.
8. The moderator in a focus group discussion is always a participant.
9. Expert opinion survey and respondent group discussions together form a two-tiered research design.

10. A research study that tracks the profile of a typical social networking user is an example of an exploratory research design.
11. TRPs (television rating performance) of soap operas on TV are generally based on cross-sectional designs.
12. The unit of analysis in the above design would be the advertiser who advertises during the serial time.
13. If one wants to assess changes in investment behaviour of general public over time, the best design available to the researcher is a longitudinal design.
14. A study to analyse the profile of the supporters of Anna Hazare would need a cross-sectional research design.
15. Married couples are the unit of analysis in a cohort analysis.
16. Different groups of people tested over a single stretch of time is a special characteristic of a longitudinal design.
17. The research variable in a longitudinal research design is studied over fixed intervals in time.
18. Descriptive designs do not require any quantitative statistical analysis.
19. In case the cross-section of the population that needs to be studied is not homogenous, then the researcher will have to make use of mixed cross-sectional designs.
20. Time series analyses are a form of longitudinal designs.

Conceptual Questions

1. How would you define a research design? What are the significant elements of a research design? Illustrate with examples.
2. How are research designs classified? What are the distinguishing features of each classification? Differentiate by giving appropriate examples.
3. 'Even though exploratory research designs are lowest in terms of accuracy of findings, it is recommended that no research must be carried out without them'. Examine the above statement and justify with examples why you agree/disagree with it.
4. 'Majority of the research designs are exploratory cum descriptive in nature in business research.' How?
5. Distinguish between cross-sectional and longitudinal designs. In what situations would you recommend the usage of one over the other?
6. Distinguish between:
   (a) Exploratory and descriptive research designs
   (b) Cross-sectional versus multi-cross-sectional designs
   (c) Omnibus versus true panels

Application Questions

1. You are a research executive with a university offering a number of postgraduate courses like M Com, MCA and MBA. Though any kind of educational qualification enhances one's personality, still you believe that the two-year MBA programme offered by the university has a slow and steady impact on the personality development (especially in terms of introversion/extroversion) of the students.
   What is the recommended research design? Justify your selection. What would be the variables, hypotheses and the population under study?
2. You are the HRD manager with ABB (India). ABB has recently taken over a major unit in Kolkata. You are sent on a posting there and are given the task of introducing a new operation scheme which your parent organization feels will improve efficiency. But you perceive during your stay that there is an underlying dissatisfaction amongst the employees and it is essential to gauge their view and opinion about the takeover and their expectations before introducing the scheme.
   What is the recommended research design? Justify your selection. What would be the variables, hypotheses and the population under study?
3. Butamal Kirorimal is a small jeweller from Jodhpur with limited resources. He is into the business of designing and selling traditional Rajasthani jewellery. He believes that having an exquisite and a mystically arranged display on the Palace on Wheels will suitably boost his sales. He also feels that foreigners rather than Indians would be influenced more. It is the month of September 2009 and by the end of the year, he wants to decide whether to go in for the display or not.
   What is the recommended research design? Justify your selection. What would be the variables, hypotheses and the population under study?

CASE 3.1

KEEP YOUR CITY CLEAN: ENVIRONMENTAL CONCERNS

Over the last decade, recycling of household waste has become an extremely important behaviour across the nations. However, in Asian countries this fluctuates from one country to the other. China is the leader amongst waste management while India, an equally large country, still has a long way to go. Though these are essentially policy driven or community driven initiatives, there are a number of attitudinal and motivational barriers to recycling, acting at an individual level.

Punita Nagarajan, a business studies graduate with a keen interest in environmental issues, read about this in a special report in the newspaper. She recognized a potential business opportunity. It seemed obvious to her that there was scope for a potentially lucrative business related to some aspect of household recycling. All she had to do was work out some way of alleviating the inconvenience people associated with recycling.

Punita decided that a door-to-door recycling service may be a profitable way to get people to recycle. She believed that households would be willing to pay a small fee to have their waste collected on a weekly basis, from outside their home. Punita discussed this idea with a few friends, who were very receptive, reinforcing Punita's views that this was indeed a good business opportunity. However, before she developed a detailed business plan, she decided it was necessary to confirm her thoughts and suspicions regarding the consumer's views about recycling. In particular, she needed to check that her ideas, about convenience and recycling, were on the right track. To do this, she decided to conduct some research into attitudes towards household recycling.

QUESTIONS

1. What is the kind of research design you would advocate here?
2. Identify your variables and the population under study.
3. Can you suggest any alternative design? Why/why not?

CASE 3.2

DANISH INTERNATIONAL (B)

Shameem answered that the team was apathetic and there could be multiple reasons for this apathy. Thus, it was essential that the team be studied to identify what was the group reaction to the working conditions at Danish. Also it was important to identify what was perceived as the major problem area. Shameem was also of the opinion that there might be a difference between the old and new employees. Thus this angle also was to be given due recognition when conducting a survey. Raghu said, 'this seems to be a logical approach to the problem, but don't you think that before you go to the team members you must at least identify what could be the reasons for the lacklustre performance at Danish by looking at the other organizations or by talking to the human resource consultants who have some experience of the same'?

Shameem listened attentively and said, 'I think there is a lot of merit in what you say. So this is what I will do __________.'

QUESTIONS

1. What is the research design(s) Shameem is likely to recommend? Why?
2. Identify the variables, hypotheses and the units under study.
3. How could you possibly improve the accuracy of the results obtained?

CASE 3.3

FORTUNE AT THE LAST FRONTIER (B)

Nikhil Thareja belonged to the third generation of Thareja & Sons Builders, a company started by Nikhil's grandfather Lala Harbans Lal Thareja in 1947. Nikhil Thareja, the heir apparent of Thareja & Sons, had been called by his grandfather and given his first independent Strategic Business Unit (SBU). The plan was to set up a new project, "Twilight Luxury: Retirement Solutions for Those Who Reinvent Life". The idea was to set up retirement solutions or housing for senior citizens who had the resources and who could manage an independent lifestyle.

Though Nikhil was apprehensive about the business idea, he respected his grandfather's wishes. He also decided to make a success of the challenging opportunity and to have a strategy that was focused and thus watertight enough to minimize the risk of failure. For this purpose, he felt that a need gap analysis was needed. He knew that in the information world that he lived in, the market data on the segment as well as the industry of old-age housing solutions would not be a problem.

Thareja Builders had the brand image of delivering to those who *felt with the heart* rather than those who *thought with the mind.* Thus, he felt that to *feel with the heart*, he needed to conduct a comprehensive study on the Indian senior. The study would assess his physical, emotional and aesthetic needs; what a home or housing solution meant for him/her; if the need was of comfort or stylish luxury—companionship or hassle-free living; the kind of utility and medical support the person was looking for. What was the long-term purpose of the investment? Was it an asset that he wanted to leave for his loved ones? or if he was philanthropic enough to leave it to others like him who may need a home but did not have the means to do so or simply leave it to charity.

Nikhil also felt that the retirement housing would find more takers amongst the urban SEC A consumers. However, he felt that there might be a difference in how an old couple looked at the offering as compared to a widowed senior. Nikhil Thareja picked up the phone to call Shantanu Roy, his classmate at London School of Business, who ran a highly successful research agency in Mumbai. "Hi Shantanu, this is Nikhil here. I have a highly confidential business assignment for you that is of critical importance for me and I have full faith that you will be able to give me the correct directions. This is what I want you to do ..."

QUESTIONS

1. Based on Nikhil Thareja's decision dilemma problem, identify the research questions. Is there a need to define any constructs or variables at this stage?
2. What research design do you think is Shantanu Roy likely to suggest?
3. Is an alternative research design possible on this study? Why/why not?

Answers to Objective Type Questions

1. True	2. False	3. True	4. True	5. False
6. True	7. True	8. False	9. False	10. False
11. False	12. False	13. True	14. True	15. False
16. False	17. True	18. False	19. False	20. True

REFERENCES

Ackroyd, S. "The Quality of Qualitative Methods: Qualitative or Quality Methodology for Organization Studies," *Organization* 3 (3) 1996: 439–51.

Atkinson, P and M Hammersley. "Ethnography and Participant Observation," *Handbook of Qualitative Research,* edited by N K Denzin and Y S Lincoln (Thousand Oaks, CA: Sage, 1994) 248–61.

Bartunek, J M, P Bobko and N Venkataraman. Guest co-editors' introduction to "Towards Innovation and Diversity in Management Research Methods" *Academy of Management Journal* 36 (6) 1993: 1362–73.

Daft, R L. "Why I Recommended That Your Manuscript Be Rejected and What You Can Do About It," in *Publishing in the Organizational Sciences,* edited by L L Cummings and P L Frost, 2nd edn. (Thousand Oaks, CA: Sage, 1995)164–82.

Green, P G, D S Tull and G A Albaum. *Research for Marketing decisions.* 5th edn. New Delhi: Prentice Hall of India, 2008.

Grunow, D. "The Research Design in Organization Studies," *Organization Science*, 6 (1) 1995: 93–103.

HItt, M A, J Gimeno and R E Hoskisson. "Current and Future Research Methods in Strategic Management", *Organizational Research Methods* 1 (1) 1998: 6–44.

Jick, T D. "Mixing Qualitative and Quantitative Methods: Triangulation in Action," *Administrative Science Quarterly* 24 (1979): 602–11.

Jorgensen, D L. *Participant Observation: A Methodology for Human Studies*. Newbury Park, CA: Sage, 1989.

Hair, Joseph F Jr, Robert, P Bush and David J Ortinau, *Marketing Research–A Practical Approach for the New Millennium. New* Delhi: McGraw-Hill Higher Education, 1999.

Kerlinger, F N. *The Foundation of Behavioural Science*. New York: Holt, Rinehart and Winston, 1995.

Selltiz, C, L S Wrightman and S W Cook, in collaboration with G I Balch *et al. Research Methods in Social Relations*, New York: Holt, Rinehart and Winston, 1976.

Thyer, B A. *Successful Publishing in Scholarly Journals, Survival Skills for Scholars Series 11.* Thousand Oaks, CA: Sage, 1994.

BIBLIOGRAPHY

Gilbert, A Churchill, Jr and Dawn Iacobucci. *Marketing Research Methodological Foundations.* 8th edn. New Delhi: Thompson South-Western, 2002.

Harper, W Boyd, Jr Ralph Westfall and Stanley F Stasch, *Marketing Research: Text and Cases.* 7th edn. New Delhi: Richard D Irwin, Inc., 2002.

Malhotra, Naresh K. *Marketing Researc – An Applied Orientation.* 3rd edn. New Delhi: Pearson Education, 2002.

Easwaran, Sunanda and Sharmila J Singh. *Marketing Research–Concepts, Practices and Cases.* New Delhi: Oxford University Press, 2006.

Kinnear, Thomas C and James R Taylor. *Marketing Research: An Applied Approach,* 5th edn. New York: McGraw Hill, Inc., 1996.

Tull, Donald S and Del I Hawkins. *Marketing Research: Measurement and Method*. 6th edn. New Delhi: Prentice Hall of India Pvt. Ltd., 1993

Zikmund, William G. *Business Research Methods,* 5th edn. Dryden Press, Harcourt Brace College Publishers, 1997.

4

CHAPTER

Experimental Research Designs

Learning Objectives

By the end of the chapter, you should be able to:

1. Define an experiment and explain the concept of causality.
2. Discuss the necessary conditions for drawing causal inferences.
3. Explain the basic concepts that are used in experiments.
4. Explain the difference between internal and external validity of the experiment.
5. Explain the factors affecting internal validity of the experiment.
6. Describe the factors affecting external validity of the experiment.
7. Discuss the methods to control extraneous variables.
8. Distinguish between laboratory and field experiments.
9. Explain the classification of experimental designs into four categories—pre-experimental, quasi-experimental, true experimental design and statistical designs.

In 1991 Bajaj Enterprises set up a chain of supermarkets in all the Indian metros. These supermarkets sell a broad line of household and kitchen appliances. While the supermarkets in other metros were doing well, the one in Delhi NCR was showing a stagnant growth of 2–2.5 per cent per annum. The General Manager (Sales) was concerned and was thinking of ways to boost the sales. A meeting of the senior marketing officials was called to discuss the issue. Many suggestions came up including increasing the advertising budget, reducing the prices of slow-moving items, and giving a discount to loyal customers. One of the suggestions was to offer a discount of 5 per cent in the form of coupons to customers who opt for a bulk purchase of ₹2,500/- and above. It was decided that these customers would be given 5 per cent discount coupons that they could redeem within a three-month period. It was argued that this would gradually result in increasing sales and profits of the supermarkets. However, a market researcher who was part of the discussion team argued that the sale increase depended upon a host of factors such as the size of the supermarket, location, the layout, point-of-purchase (POP) displays, competitor's prices and competitor's advertising expenses besides other variables. The regulation of many of these was beyond their control. The GM (Sales) also gave a thought to designing a study in order to examine the impact of the entire idea of discount on the bulk purchase scheme and gradually on the net sales and profits of the supermarkets. The members also realized that the extraneous factors would have to be controlled so as to infer a causality.

This chapter discusses the issues involved in inferring a cause and effect relationship. A number of concepts would be discussed which would help in setting up experiments to establish causality. The limitations of various designs in removing the influence of extraneous variables will also be covered under this chapter.

WHAT IS AN EXPERIMENT?

LEARNING OBJECTIVE 1
Define an experiment and explain the concept of causality.

An experiment is generally used to infer a causality. In an experiment, a researcher actively manipulates one or more causal variables and measures their effects on the dependent variables of interest. Since any changes in the dependent variable may be caused by a number of other variables, the relationship between cause and effect often tends to be probabilistic in nature. It is virtually impossible to prove a causality. One can only infer a cause-and-effect relationship. It is, therefore, essential to understand the whole concept of causality. To illustrate this concept, an example follows in the paragraph below.

Causality

The sales manager of a soft drink bottling company sends some of his sales personnel for a new sales training programme. Three months after they return from the training programme, the sales in the territory where this sales force was working increases by 20 per cent. The sales manager concludes that the training programme is very effective and, therefore, the sales force from the other territories should also be sent for the same. What the sales manager is trying to infer is that the sales training is a causal variable and increased sales is an effect variable. Do we agree to this statement? This statement may not be true as the increase in sales may not be due to the sales training programme alone. It could occur because of a host of factors e.g., reduction in the price of the soft drink, a strike at the competitor's plant, increase in the price of the competitor's product, reduction in the quality of competing products, weather conditions and so on. Therefore, it is very important that the sales manager understands the conditions under which such causal statements can be made. There are three necessary conditions for making causal inferences.

NECESSARY CONDITIONS FOR MAKING CAUSAL INFERENCES

LEARNING OBJECTIVE 2
Discuss the necessary conditions for drawing causal inferences.

The following are the necessary conditions for making causal inferences:

1. **Concomitant variation:** Concomitant variation is the extent to which a cause X and effect Y occur together or vary together. This means that there has to be a strong association between the training programme and increased sales. Moreover, both of them need to occur together. However, a strong association between the two does not imply causality. The high association between these two variables could be due to the influence of other extraneous factors which may be influencing both the variables or it may be the of result of random variations.

2. **Time order of occurrence of variables:** This condition means that the causal variable must occur prior to or simultaneously with the effect variable. This means that sales training must have taken place either before or simultaneously with the increased sales. However, just because sales training took place prior to an increase in sales will not help in inferring causality. It might have been due to a mere coincidence and thus, cannot help in inferring causality.

Concomitant variation is the extent to which a cause X and effect Y occur together or vary together.

Furthermore, it is quite possible for each of the two events to be both cause and effect of each other. In the illustrated example, the sales training programme may cause an increase in sales, and increased sales may result in keeping company some spare funds for training etc. Therefore, the relationship between the two variables could be that they alternatively 'feed' each other.

Even if it can be shown that there is a concomitant variation between the sales training programme and the increased sales and the time occurrence of all variables, there is still a question left unanswered whether other variables which could 'cause' increased sales have remained in a constant position. This is explained in the next point.

The **objective of an experiment** is to measure the influence of the independent variables on a dependent variable while keeping the effect of other extraneous variables constant.

3. **Absence of other possible causal factors:** As mentioned earlier, the increase in sales of soft drink could have been due to many other factors besides the sales training. There could be a strike at the competitor's plant, resulting in an overall reduction in supply, weather conditions, the increased price of the competitor's product or a problem at the distribution channel at the competitor's end. The sales training programme may be a causal variable if all the other factors mentioned above were kept constant or otherwise controlled.

As a matter of fact, the researcher cannot rule out the influence of other causal factors such as the weather condition. However, it will be seen later that it may be possible to control some or more of the extraneous variables by the use of experimental design. It may be possible to balance the effect of some uncontrolled factors. This may help in measuring random variations resulting from uncontrolled measures.

Experiments are used to seek help in identifying a cause-and-effect relationship. The objective of an experiment is to measure the influence of the independent variables on a dependent variable while keeping the effect of other extraneous variables constant. Experiments may be used to arrive at conclusive answers in the following situations:

- Can a change in the package design of a product enhance its sales?
- Should a supermarket introduce a discount scheme on bulk purchase to increase its sales?
- Will an increase in the shelf space allocated to a brand of a particular product increase its sales?
- Will a reduction in the price of the menu items of a restaurant increase sales?
- What will be the impact of POP display of 'Arrow' shirts on their sales?
- Which of several promotional techniques is most effective in increasing the sales of a product?
- What is the impact of increasing the proportion of female counter clerks from 30 to 60 per cent on the sales of the store?
- Does mentoring help in acclimatizing a person to the organizational culture?
- Does organizational climate impact the quality of working life of a company?
- What is the impact of change in home loan rates on the investor investment in real estate?

In order to have a good understanding of experimentation, it would be useful to learn some basic concepts and definition used in experiments.

CONCEPT CHECK

1. Define the term 'experiment'.
2. What is a concomitant variation?
3. What is the significance of the time order of occurrence of variables in establishing causality?

CONCEPTS USED IN EXPERIMENTS

LEARNING OBJECTIVE 3
Explain the basic concepts used in experiments.

The following are some concepts used in experiments:

- **Independent variables:** Independent variables are also known as explanatory variables or treatments. The levels of these variables are manipulated (changed) by researchers to measure their effects on the dependent variable. In the case of our example, independent variable (treatment) consisted of the sales training programme.
- **Test units:** Test units are those entities on which treatments are applied. The researcher is often interested in measuring the effect of treatment on test units. The examples of test units include individuals, organizations and geographic areas. In the case of our example, test units were the sales personnel who were sent for the training programme.
- **Dependent variables:** These variables measure the effect of treatments (independent variable) on the test units. The examples of dependent variables can include sales, profits, market share and brand awareness. In the case of our example, dependent variable consisted of sales.
- **Experiment:** An experiment is executed when the researcher manipulates one or more independent variables and measures their effect on the dependent variables while controlling the effect of the extraneous variables. Our example of sending some sales personnel for the training and thereby measuring the effect on the sales qualifies for an experiment.

Extraneous variables can weaken the results of the experiment performed to establish a cause and effect relationship.

- **Extraneous variables:** These are the variables other than the independent variables which influence the response of test units to treatments. Examples of extraneous variables could be store size, advertising efforts of competitors, government policies, temperature, food intake, and geographical location. In our example, some of the extraneous variables could be weather condition, a strike at competitor's plant, a problem at the distribution channel at the competitor's end. These variables can weaken the results of the experiment performed to establish a cause-and-effect relationship.

VALIDITY IN EXPERIMENTATION

LEARNING OBJECTIVE 4
Explain the difference between internal and external validity of the experiment.

For conducting an experiment, it is essential to specify:

- Treatments (independent variables) to be manipulated
- Test units to be used
- Dependent variables to be measured
- Procedure for dealing with the extraneous variables.

The researcher has two goals while conducting an experiment:

1. To draw valid conclusions about the effect of treatments (independent variables) on the dependent variables.
2. To make generalizations about the results to a wider population. Here, the concern of the first goal lies with internal validity, whereas the second one is concerned with the external validity.

Internal validity tries to examine whether the observed effect on a dependent variable is actually caused by the treatment in question. On the other hand, external validity refers to the generalisation of the results of an experiment.

- **Internal validity:** Internal validity tries to examine whether the observed effect on a dependent variable is actually caused by the treatments (independent variables) in question. For an experiment to be possessing internal validity, all the other causal factors except the one whose influence is being examined should be absent. Internal validity is the basic minimum that must be present. It is impossible to draw inferences about the causal relationship between the independent and dependent variables if the observed effects on test units are influenced by extraneous variables. Control of extraneous variables is a necessary condition for inferring causality. Without internal validity, the experiment gets confounded.

- **External validity:** External validity refers to the generalization of the results of an experiment. The concern is whether the result of an experiment can be generalized beyond the experimental situations. If it is possible to generalize the results, then to what population, settings, times, independent variables and the dependent variables can the results be projected.

It is desired to have an experiment that is valid both internally and externally. However, in reality, a researcher might have to make a trade-off between one type of validity for another. To remove the influence of an extraneous variable, a researcher may set up an experiment with artificial setting, thereby increasing its internal validity. However, in the process the external validity will be reduced.

Definition of Symbols

To facilitate the discussion of exogenous variables present in a specific experimental design, a set of symbols most commonly used in such experimental research are defined below:

X = The exposure of a test group to an experimental treatment whose effect is to be measured.
O = The measurement or observation of the dependent variable.
R = The random assignment of test units or groups to separate treatments.

In addition to above, the following conventions are generally used:

- Movement from left to right indicates the time sequence of events.
- All symbols in one row indicate that the subject belongs to that specific treatment group.
- Vertical arrangement of the symbols means that these symbols refer to the events or activities that occur simultaneously.

Example 1: Consider the following symbolic arrangement:

$$O_1 \quad X \quad O_2 \quad O_3$$

There is one group whose members were not selected randomly. The group of test unit was exposed to treatment X. The measurement (O_1) on the group was taken prior to applying treatment X. Two measurements (O_2, O_3) on the group were taken after the application of the treatment at different points of time.

Example 2: Consider the symbolic arrangement:

$$\begin{array}{llll} R & O_1 & X & O_2 \\ R & & X & O_3 \end{array}$$

The above scheme indicates that the two groups of individuals were assigned at random (R) to two treatment groups at the same times. Both groups received the same treatment X at the same time. The first group received both a pretest (O_1) and post-test measurement (O_2). The second group received the post-test measurement (O_3) at the same time as the first group received the post-test measurement (O_2).

FACTORS AFFECTING INTERNAL VALIDITY OF THE EXPERIMENT

LEARNING OBJECTIVE 5
Explain the factors affecting internal validity of the experiment.

As discussed earlier, there is a need to control the influence of extraneous variables so as to ensure that the experiment has not been confounded. The following extraneous variables may threaten the internal validity of an experiment.

1. **History:** History in the present context does not refer to the occurrence of events before the experiment. History here refers to those specific events that are external to the experiment but occur at the same time as the experiment. Consider the following experiment:

$$O_1 \quad X \quad O_2$$

History, in this context, refers to those specific events that are external to the experiment but occur at the same time as the experiment.

where X denotes treatment (sales training programme) and the symbols O_1 and O_2 may represent the sale before and after the training programme. The difference (O_2 - O_1) may indicate the treatment effect. Even if this difference is positive, this may not be attributed to the training programme as this may be due to an improvement in the general economic condition between O_1 and O_2. This is because the training programme is not the only variable causing a positive difference between O_2 and O_1. As a matter of fact, the higher the time difference between the two observations, higher are the chances of history confounding an experiment.

2. **Maturation:** Maturation is similar to history except that it is concerned with the changes in a test unit occurring with the passage of time. These changes are not due to the impact of treatments. Examples of maturation include people becoming older, more experienced, tired, or uninterested. Referring to our example, sales people might have gained maturity as with passage of time they become experienced and understand their job better. It is not only people who change over time, so do stores, geographic regions and organizations. Stores change over time in terms of physical layout, décor, traffic and composition. Again, longer the time difference between O_1 and O_2, the greater are the chances of maturation effect to occur.

The main **testing** effect occurs when the first observation influences the second observation.

3. **Testing:** It is concerned with the possible effect on the experiment of taking a measurement on the dependent variable before presentation of the treatment. Testing effects are of two kinds: (i) main testing effect and (ii) reactive or interactive testing effect. The main testing effect occurs when the first observation influences the second observation. This is responsible for compromising with the internal validity of the experiment. Consider, as an example, a questionnaire filled up by the respondents before being exposed to the treatment. Now, after being subjected to the treatment, they are likely to respond differently. This is because they are now 'experts' with the questionnaire.

   Consider the example of the sales training programme mentioned earlier. If the respondents become aware during the experimentation that their behaviour is being measured, this can sensitize and bias the responses. For example, if sales people know that they are being sent for the training to know its effectiveness, they would become 'sensitized' and behave differently.

4. **Instrumentation:** It refers to the effect caused by the changes in measuring instrument used for taking an observation. At times, a measurement instrument may be modified during the course of an experiment resulting in confounding of that particular experiment.

Suppose the difference in 'rupee' sales 'before' and 'after' the training programme is used to measure the effectiveness of the training programme, a price difference during the time interval could make a substantial difference in the inference. A 'change in price' would be the change of instrumentation.

Presenting the pre and post-test questionnaire in a different fashion, experience of the invigilator, and a change in the mood of the investigators are some of the examples of changing instrumentation.

Statistical regression occurs when the test units with extreme scores are chosen for exposure to the treatment.

5. **Statistical regression:** The effect of statistical regression occurs when the test units with extreme scores (either extremely favourable or extremely unfavourable) are chosen for exposure to the treatment. The effect is that test units with extreme scores tend to move towards an average score with the passage of time. Suppose in the example of the sales training programme, the sales people with extremely poor performance are sent for the training programme. An increase in sales after the training programme may be attributed to the regression effect. This is because test units with extreme score have more room for a change, so a variation is more likely to be there. Random occurrences (weather, luck, festive seasons), might have helped good and poor performance of sales people in the pre-test measurement. These random occurrences will turn some of the poor performers' into better performers thereby confounding the experiment.
6. **Selection bias:** This refers to the improper assignments of test units to treatments. Test units may be assigned to the treatment groups in such a way that the groups differ on the dependent variable prior to the presentation of the treatment. Selection bias can occur if test units self-select their groups or are assigned to the groups on the basis of the researcher's judgment. The selection of test units to the treatment group should be random.
7. **Test unit mortality:** Some of the test units might drop out from the experiment while it is in progress or some may refuse to continue with the experiment. In the case of sales training example, some sales people may quit the organization before completing the training successfully. There is no way of finding out whether those who were not improving quit the organization. It is also not possible to measure whether those who left would have produced the same results as those who completed the training programme.

The types of extraneous variables discussed above are not mutually exclusive. They can occur together and interact with each other. These extraneous variables can provide alternative explanations regarding what is being observed in an experiment and our objective should be to eliminate the possibility of these effects confounding the results.

FACTORS AFFECTING EXTERNAL VALIDITY

LEARNING OBJECTIVE 6
Describe the factors affecting external validity of the experiment.

While the internal validity of an experiment is concerned with the absence of all possible causal factors except the one whose influence is being examined, external validity raises the issues of generalizability of the findings. The factors affecting external validity of the experiment are listed below:

- The environment at the time of test may be different from the environment of the real world where these results are to be generalized. For example, a commercial advertisement may be shown to a set of prospective customers and their reaction to the advertisement may be very favourable. However, if the same advertisement appears while the respondents are watching TV at home with their family members, they may not like to see it and switch to another channel. In this example, the environment in the two situations is completely different and has come in the way to generalize the results.

- Population used for experimentation of the test may not be similar to the population where the results of the experiments are to be applied. Suppose the students of a college are asked to perform a task that could be manipulated to study the effects on their performance. However, the findings of this study cannot be generalized to the real world when the same task is assigned to the employees of an organization. This is because the employees and the nature of job in this particular organization may be quite different.
- Results obtained in a 5–6 week test may not hold in an application of 12 months. Suppose a company wants to launch ice cream in Delhi NCR. The results of the survey conducted during the months of May and June may be extremely favourable. These results would certainly not be applicable during the winter months in December and January, thereby raising questions on the generalizability of the results.
- Treatment at the time of the test may be different from the treatment of the real world. This can happen when while testing the effect of a treatment, it is administered in the form of a pill and in reality it is given as a part of a cereal.

CONCEPT CHECK

1. What are the concepts used in experiments?
2. What is meant by the terms 'internal validity' and 'external validity'?
3. Define the set of symbols commonly used in experimental research.
4. Name the prime factors that affect the internal and external validity of a particular experiment.

METHODS TO CONTROL EXTRANEOUS VARIABLES

LEARNING OBJECTIVE 7
Discuss the methods to control extraneous variables.

As discussed in the previous sections, extraneous variables pose a threat to the internal and external validity of the experiment. They affect the dependent variable and confound the results of the experiment. Therefore, there is a need to control the extraneous variables as they represent alternative explanations of crucial experimental results.

The researcher has four methods to control the effect of extraneous variables. These are randomization, matching, use of specific experimental design and statistical control. These methods are discussed below:

1. **Randomization:** It refers to the random assignments of test units to experimental groups. Treatments are also randomly assigned to the experimental groups. Because of random assignment, extraneous factors will be operating in experimental groups. However, for randomization to be effective, a large sample size is required.
2. **Matching:** Another way of controlling extraneous variables is to match the various groups by confounding variables. Suppose there are 120 people to be distributed in three groups. If there are 45 females among the 120 members, then each of the three groups is assigned 15 females. This way, the effect of gender can be distributed among all three groups. Likewise, other confounding variables like age, income, years of work experience could be distributed among the three groups. The other examples of matching variables can be price, sales, size or location of store. However, there are two drawbacks of matching. It may

be not possible to match all the confounding variables to various groups. Further, matched characteristics may not be relevant to the dependent variable.

3. **Use of experimental designs:** Some of the experimental designs may be very useful in eliminating the influence of extraneous variables. In the subsequent sections, these experimental designs and their role in eliminating the extraneous factors will be discussed.
4. **Statistical control:** If all the above discussed methods fail to eliminate the effect of extraneous variables among the treatment group, then the experiment in question gets confounded and it is not possible to make any causal inferences. However, there is still one way of handling the confounding variable. It may be possible to statistically control the effects of this variable on the dependent variable by the use of a technique called analysis of covariance (ANCOVA). This topic is beyond the scope of this text.

ENVIRONMENTS OF CONDUCTING EXPERIMENTS

LEARNING OBJECTIVE 8
Distinguish between laboratory and field experiments.

There are two types of environments in which the experiment can be conducted. These are called laboratory environment and field environment. In a laboratory experiment, the researcher conducts the experiment in an artificial environment constructed exclusively for the experiment. Suppose the interest is in studying the effectiveness of a TV commercial. If the test units are made to see a test commercial in a theatre or in a room, the environment would of a laboratory experiment. Field experiment is conducted in actual market conditions. There is no attempt to change the real-life nature of the environment. Showing of test commercial in an actual TV telecast is an example of a field experiment.

In a **laboratory experiment** the researcher works in an artificial environment to conduct a study whereas in a **field experiement** an actual market condition is used for the same.

There are certain advantages of laboratory experiments over field experiments. Laboratory experiments have higher internal validity as they provide the researcher with maximum control over the maximum number of confounding variables. Since the laboratory experiment is conducted in a carefully monitored environment, the effect of history can be minimized. The results of a laboratory experiment could be repeated with almost similar subjects and environments. Laboratory experiments are generally shorter in duration, make use of smaller number of test units, easier to conduct and relatively less expensive than field experiments.

However, laboratory experiments lack in external validity i.e., it is not possible to generalize the results of the experiment. Experiments conducted in the field have lower internal validity. The ability to generalize the results of the experiment is possible in case of a field experiment, thereby leading to higher external validity. In the light of the above-mentioned facts, researchers need to take a decision whether to use a laboratory experiment or a field experiment. These two types of experiments play complementary roles in real life situations.

A CLASSIFICATION OF EXPERIMENTAL DESIGNS

Experimental design can be classified as pre-experimental, quasi-experimental, true experimental and statistical. Pre-experimental designs include the one-shot case study, the one-group pre-test-post-test design and the static group comparison. Tests included under quasi-experimental designs are time series and multiple time series. True-experimental designs include pre-test-post-test control group, post-test-only control group, and Solomon four-group design. The

LEARNING OBJECTIVE 9
Explain the classification of experimental designs into four categories—pre-experimental design, quasi-experimental design, true experimental design and statistical design.

statistical designs include completely randomized design, randomized blocks, factorial and Latin square designs. To have a glimpse of the classification, these are presented in Figure 4.1.

Pre-experimental Designs

Pre-experimental designs do not make use of any randomization procedures to control the extraneous variables. Therefore, the internal validity of such designs is questionable. Three designs included in this category are elaborated below:

One-shot case study is also called the after–only design and may be symbolically presented as:
X O

1. **One-shot case study:** This design is also known as the after-only design and may be presented symbolically as:

$$X \quad O$$

This means that only one test group is subjected to the treatment *X* and then a measurement on the dependent variable is taken *O*. It may be noted that the symbol *R* does not appear in this design. This means there was no random assignment of test units to the treatment group. This means that the test units were either self-selected or arbitrarily selected by the researcher. In the sales training programme example, the sales manager might have chosen those sales people whom he likes or may ask the sales people to volunteer for the training programme.

FIGURE 4.1
Classification of experimental design

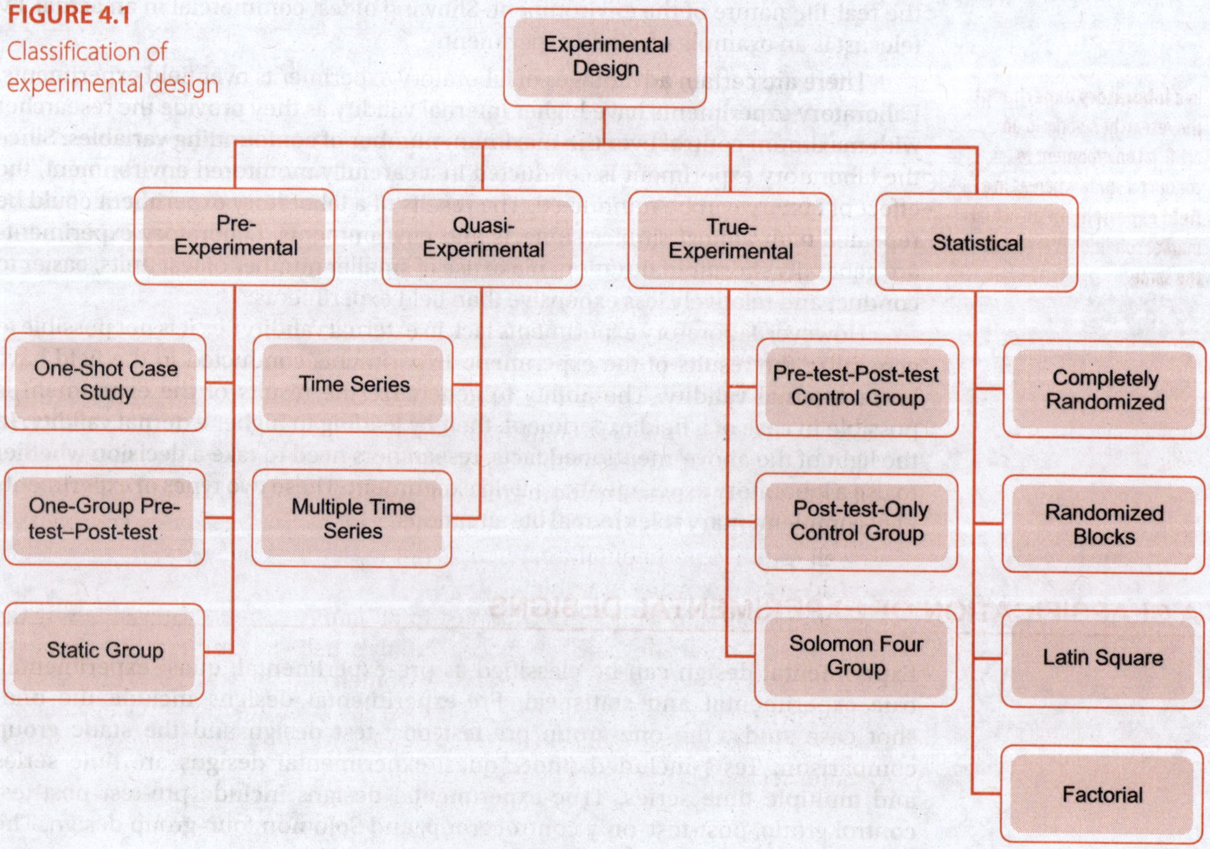

Let us examine another example here. The objective is to study the impact of an extra ten days' credit period (X) on a credit card payment time (O) and one decides to study the relationship/impact by offering this to the customers who make an average usage of ₹25,000/- per month. The problem in this case would be that no measure was taken to establish their payment behaviour prior to the extended period. Hence, no valid conclusion can be made from this design. There is no pre-treatment observation on performance. The level of 'O' might be affected by several uncontrolled extraneous factors like history, maturation, selection bias and test unit mortality. These uncontrolled extraneous variables will confound the experiment and render the design internally invalid.

One-group pre-test–post-test design is also known as before–after without control group design and may be symbolically written as: $O_1 \ X \ O_2$

2. **One-group pre-test-post-test design:** This design is also called before-after without control group design. This design may be written symbolically as:

$$O_1 \quad X \quad O_2$$

In this design also, test units are not selected at random as the symbol 'R' is not appearing here. The test units are subjected to the treatment X and both pre-treatment (O_1) and post-treatment measurement (O_2) are taken. For instance, in the credit card example, one might take the payment time before and after the extended ten-days' period. One may be tempted to compute treatment effect as $O_2 - O_1$, which may not be really so, as this difference could be the result of many uncontrolled extraneous factors like history, maturation, testing, instrumentation, regression, selection and mortality. This would make the design invalid for making any causal inferences on account of the following reasons:

- The economic condition might have changed during the two periods (history).
- The test units may mature over time (maturation).
- The pre-test measurement on the test units may influence the performance (testing).
- The prices of goods might have changed over time (instrumentation).
- Test units might not have been selected at random (selection bias).
- Some test units might have left before the experiment was complete (mortality).
- Test units might be self-selected on the basis of the current poor performance and may have a better period ahead because of sheer luck (regression).

Static group comparison uses two treatment groups in which test units are not selected at random. This design is presented as:
Group 1–$X \ O_1$
Group 2– O_2

3. **Static group comparison:** This design is symbolically written as:

Group 1	–	X	O_1
Group 2	–		O_2

This design uses two treatment groups. Test units in both the groups are not selected at random. The first group, called the experimental group, is subjected to the treatment X, whereas the second group, namely, the control group, is not subjected to any treatment. Both groups are measured only after the treatment has been presented. Thus, it is critical to understand that in this design the exposure as well as the experimental treatment is not under the control of the researcher. Consider the following example:

A study wants to assess the relationship of 'family support' (measured by the presence of domestic help or spouse/family's help in carrying out domestic chores) with the work-life balance of BPO women employees. Here, the presence or absence of help is ascertained and then we can measure the work-life balance. Thus the design is essentially *ex-post facto* and any segregation into experimental or control group is not made by the researcher.

The treatment effect could be measured by $O_1 - O_2$. However, this difference could be attributed to at least selection bias and mortality. Moreover, since the test units are not selected at random, the two groups could differ prior to the application of treatment. All these are sufficient to make the design invalid for drawing any causal inferences.

Quasi-experimental Designs

Quasi-experimental design lacks complete control of scheduling of treatment and also lacks the ability to randomize test units' exposure to treatments.

In quasi-experimental design the researcher can control when measurements are taken and on whom they are taken. However, this design lacks complete control of scheduling of treatment and also lacks the ability to randomize test units' exposure to treatments. As the experimental control is lacking, the possibility of getting confounded results is very high. Therefore, the researchers should be aware of what variables are not controlled and the effects of such variables should be incorporated into the findings. There are two forms of quasi-experimental designs.

1. **Time series design:** This design involves a series of periodic measurements on the dependent variable for a group of test unit. The treatment X is then administered and a series of periodic measurements are again taken to measure the effect of treatment. This design may be written symbolically as:

$$O_1 \quad O_2 \quad O_3 \quad O_4 \quad X \quad O_5 \quad O_6 \quad O_7 \quad O_8$$

The above is a quasi-experimental design since there is no randomization of treatment to test units. Further, the timing of treatment presentation as well as which of the test units are exposed to the treatment may not be within the researcher's control. Because of the multiple observations in time series design, the effect of maturation, main testing effect, instrumentation and statistical regression can be ruled out. If test units are selected at random, selection bias can be reduced. Further, if a strong measure like giving certain incentives to the respondents is introduced, mortality effect can more or less be controlled.

The results of a **time series design** may be affected by an interactive testing effect because multiple measurements are made on these test units.

The major drawback of this experiment is the inability of a researcher to control the effect of history. The results of the experiment may be affected by an interactive testing effect because multiple measurements are made on these test units. If a researcher could keep a record of key changes in various unusual economic activities and if no changes are found, one can reasonably conclude that the treatment has exerted an effect on test unit.

This design may look similar to the one group pre-test-post-test design given by $O_4 \; X \; O_5$. However, there are differences as in case of time series design, a number of periodic measurements are taken both before and after the application of the treatment. But in the case of one group pre-test–post-test design, one measurement is taken prior to the treatment and one after that.

The results of taking multiple measurements can be compared with one group pre-test–post-test design. This is shown in Figure 4.2, where X (treatment) is the new advertising campaign and the measurement on dependent variable represents the market share at certain periodic intervals. Six different scenarios (A to F) are presented.

The case of one group pre-test–post-test design would be shown as $O_4 \; X \; O_5$ and the analysis of the results would indicate some positive effects of the new advertising campaign in situations A, B, D and E, whereas in situations C and F, advertising would not be having any effect. The conclusion in the case of time series design would be as follows:

- In situation A, the campaign had a short-run positive effect, after which market share was sustained.

FIGURE 4.2
Possible results of a time series experiment

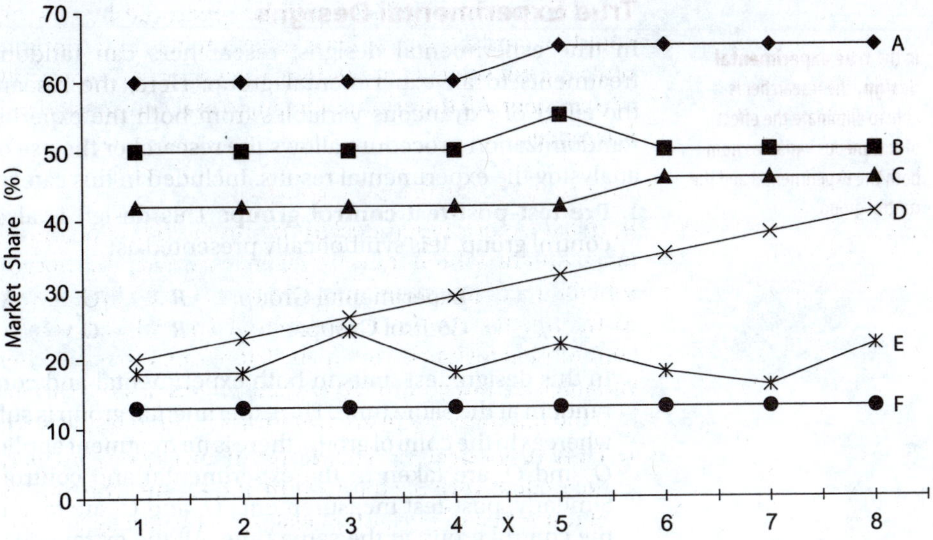

Source: Adopted with modification from Thomas C. Kinnear & James R. Taylor, "Marketing Research: An Applied Approach", McGraw-Hill, Inc., Fifth Edition

- In situation B, the new advertising campaign had a short-run positive effect. The rise in market share was temporary. The market share reverts to the level which was there before the application of the treatment.
- In situation C, the treatment had a delayed positive effect and, accordingly, it took longer time to appear.
- In situation D, E, and F the changes that occur after the application of treatment are in line with what occurred prior to the application of treatment. Therefore, the new advertising campaign had no effect on the market share.

Therefore it is seen that by taking multiple observations, the results have altogether different interpretations and inferences.

Multiple time series design involves the addition of the 'control group' which is not subjected to any treatment.

2. **Multiple time series design:** In this design, one more group called the 'control group' is added to the time series design. The design may be diagrammed symbolically as:

Experimental Group:	O_1	O_2	O_3	O_4	X	O_5	O_6	O_7	O_8
Control Group:	O'_1	O'_2	O'_3	O'_4		O'_5	O'_6	O'_7	O'_8

The experimental group is subjected to the treatment X, whereas the control group is without any treatment. Taking the example of the sales training programme, the sales training would represent treatment, and observations O_1, O_2, O_3 ... would represent sales volume of this group. The test unit of the control group would compromise sales people who are not sent for the training programme. The measurement on the sales volume is denoted by O'_1, O'_2, O'_3, ... etc. The measurement on the sales for both the groups is taken after the training programme. The treatment effect (sales training) is found by comparing the average sales of the two groups before and after the training programme. The major drawback of this design is the possibility of the interactive effect in the experimental group.

True Experimental Designs

In the **true experimental design,** the researcher is able to eliminate the effect of extraneous variables from both the experimental and the control group.

In true experimental designs, researchers can randomly assign test units and treatments to an experimental group. Here, the researcher is able to eliminate the effect of extraneous variables from both the experimental and control group. Randomization procedure allows the researcher the use of statistical techniques for analysing the experimental results. Included in this category are the following:

1. **Pre-test–post-test control group:** This design is also called before-after with control group. It is symbolically presented as:

Experimental Group:	R	O_1	X	O_2
Control Group:	R	O_3		O_4

   In this design, test units in both experimental and control group are selected at random at the same time. The experimental group is subjected to the treatment X, whereas in the control group, there is no treatment applied. Pre-test measurements O_1 and O_3 are taken in the experimental and control group at the same time. Similarly, post-test measurements O_2 and O_4 are taken for the experimental and the control group at the same time. All the extraneous variables operate equally on both the experimental and control group because of randomization. Therefore, the only difference in the two groups is the effect of treatment in the experimental group.

   If the difference in the post-test and pre-test measurements of experimental and control group is denoted by A and B respectively, then

$$A = O_2 - O_1 = \text{Treatment + extraneous variables}$$
$$B = O_4 - O_3 = \text{Extraneous variables}$$

   The extraneous variables would include history, maturation, testing, instrumentation, statistical regression, selection bias and test unit mortality. However, it may be worth noting that the interactive testing effect would be present only in the experimental group and would be missing in the control group. This is because only the experimental group is subjected to the treatment. Therefore $A - B = (O_2 - O_1) - (O_4 - O_3)$ = treatment effect which would include interactive testing effect. Therefore, it is doubtful to generalize the results of the experiment.

2. **Post-test-only control group design:** This design is also named as after-only with one control group and is presented symbolically as:

Experimental Group:	R	X	O_1
Control Group:	R		O_2

   Here, the test units in both the experimental and the control group are selected at random. The experimental group is subjected to the treatment X, and post-test measurements are taken on both experimental (O_1) and control group (O_2) at the same time. The post-test measurement (O_1) on experimental group comprises treatment effect and all other extraneous variables, whereas O_2 comprises only extraneous variables. Therefore, the difference in the post-test measurement of experimental and control group is taken as a measure of treatment effect. Hence,

$$\begin{aligned} O_1 - O_2 &= \text{(Treatment effect + extraneous factors) - (extraneous factors)} \\ &= \text{Treatment effect} \end{aligned}$$

   As pre-test measurement is absent, the effect of instrumentation and interactive testing effect is ruled out. As there is a random assignment of test units to both the groups, it can be approximately assumed that both the groups were equal prior to the application of treatment to the experimental group. Further, one can always assume that the test units' mortality affects each group equally. One can always justify these assumptions by taking a large randomized sample. This design is widely used in marketing research.

The Solomon four-group design is referred to as "ideal controlled experiment" as it helps the researcher to remove the influence of extraneous variables and that of the interactive testing effect.

3. **Solomon four-group design:** This design is also called four-group six-study design. This is also referred to as 'ideal controlled experiment'. As will be seen, this design helps the researcher to remove the influence of extraneous variables and also that of the interactive testing effect. This design is symbolically presented as:

Experiment Group 1	R	O_1	X	O_2
Control Group 1	R	O_3		O_4
Experiment Group 2	R		X	O_5
Control Group 2	R			O_6

In the above design test units are selected at random in all the four groups. It is seen that the experimental group 2 and control group 2 are not given any pre-test measurement, whereas experimental group 1 and control group 1 are subjected to pre-test measurement O_1 and O_3 respectively. Both experimental groups 1 and 2 are subjected to the same treatment X at the same time.

As the experimental group 2 and control group 2 are not subjected to pre-test measurement, we would need their estimates to remove the influence of extraneous variables and interactive testing effect. As test units from all the four groups are chosen at random, it can be assumed that all the four groups are equal before experiment. Therefore, the pre-test measurements O_1 and O_3 on experimental and control group 1 can be used as an estimate of the pre-test measurement of experimental and control group 2. The results of difference of various post-test and pre-test measurement would give the following results:

Experimental Group 1:

$O_2 - O_1$ = Treatment effect + extraneous factors without interactive testing effect + interactive testing effect ...(i)

Control Group 1:

$O_4 - O_3$ = Extraneous factors without interactive testing effect ...(ii)

As this group was not subjected to any treatment, there would not be any interactive testing effect.

Experimental Group 2:

$O_5 - O_1$ = Treatment effect + extraneous factors without interactive testing effect ...(iii)

$O_5 - O_3$ = Treatment effect + extraneous factors without testing effect ...(iv)

As there was actually no pre-test measurement, the interactive testing effect cannot occur here.

Control Group 2:

$O_6 - O_1$ = (Extraneous factors without testing effect) ...(v)

$O_6 - O_3$ = (Extraneous factors without testing effect) ...(vi)

As the group was not subjected to any treatment, the difference in measurement would only indicate the effect of extraneous factors without interactive testing effect.

By taking the average of (v) and (vi), one gets:

$$O_6 - \frac{O_1 + O_3}{2} = \text{(Extraneous factors without testing effect)} \quad \text{...(vii)}$$

By taking the average of (iii) and (iv), one obtains:

$$O_5 - \frac{O_1 + O_3}{2} = \text{Treatment effect + extraneous factors without testing effect} \quad \text{...(viii)}$$

By subtracting (vii) from (viii), one obtains:

$$\left(O_5 - \frac{O_1 + O_3}{2}\right) - \left(O_6 - \frac{O_1 + O_3}{2}\right) = O_5 - O_6 = \text{Treatment effect}$$

By subtracting (viii) from (i), one obtains:

$$O_2 - O_1 - \left(O_5 - \frac{O_1 + O_3}{2}\right) = \text{Interacting testing effect}$$

Therefore, this design has helped not only in measuring the effect of treatment, but also in obtaining magnitude of the interactive testing effect and extraneous factors.

The Solomon four-group design is useful for businesses where establishing cause-and-effect relationship is crucial for survival.

To conduct this experimental design, the time and cost required are enormous and therefore, this design is not commonly used in research. However, as seen, this experimental design guarantees the maximum internal validity. In businesses where establishing cause-and-effect relationship is very crucial for survival, this design is useful.

Statistical Designs

Statistical designs allow for statistical control and analysis of external variables. The main advantages of statistical design are the following:

- The effect of more than one level of independent variable on the dependent variable can be manipulated.
- The effect of more than one independent variable can be examined.
- The effect of specific extraneous variable can be controlled.

Included in this category are the following designs:

Completely randomized design allows a researcher to investigate the effect of one independent variable on the dependent variable.

1. **Completely randomized design:** This design is used when a researcher is investigating the effect of one independent variable on the dependent variable. The independent variable is required to be measured in nominal scale i.e. it should have a number of categories. Each of the categories of the independent variable is considered as the treatment. The basic assumption of this design is that there are no differences in the test units. All the test units are treated alike and randomly assigned to the test groups. This means that there are no extraneous variables that could influence the outcome.

   Suppose we know that the sales of a product is influenced by the price level. In this case, sales are a dependent variable and the price is the independent variable. Let there be three levels of price, namely, low, medium and high. We wish to determine the most effective price level, i.e., at which price level the sale is highest. Here the test units are the stores which are randomly assigned to the three treatment levels. The average sales for each price level is computed and examined to see whether there is any significant difference in the sale at various price levels. The statistical technique to test for such a difference is called analysis of variance (ANOVA).

The main limitation of the **completely randomized design** is that it does not take into account the effect of extraneous variables on the dependent variable.

This design suffers from the main limitation that it does not take into account the effect of extraneous variables on the dependent variable. The possible extraneous variables in the present example could be the size of the store, the competitor's price and price of the substitute product in question. This design assumes that all the extraneous factors have the same influence on all the test units which may not be true in reality. This design is very simple and inexpensive to conduct.

2. **Randomized block design:** As discussed, the main limitation of the completely randomized design is that all extraneous variables were assumed to be constant over all the treatment groups. This may not be true. There may be extraneous variables influencing the dependent variable. In the randomized block design it is possible to separate the influence of one extraneous variable on a particular dependent variable, thereby providing a clear picture of the impact of treatment on test units.

   In the example considered in the completely randomized design, the price level (low, medium and high) was considered as an independent variable and all the test units (stores) were assumed to be more or less equal. However, all stores may not be of the same size and, therefore, can be classified as small, medium and large size stores. In this design, the extraneous variable, like the size of the store could be treated as different blocks. Now the treatments are randomly assigned to the blocks in such a way that each treatment appears in each block at least once. The purpose of forming these blocks is that it is hoped that the scores of the test units within each block would be more or less homogeneous when the treatment is absent. What is assumed here is that block (size of the store) is correlated with the dependent variable (sales). It may be noted that blocking is done prior to the application of the treatment.

   In a **randomized block Design,** it is assumed that block is correlated with the dependent variable. Blocking is done prior to the application of the treatment.

   In this experiment one might randomly assign 12 small-sized stores to three price levels in such a way that there are four stores for each of the three price levels. Similarly, 12 medium-sized stores and 12 large-sized stores may be randomly assigned to three price levels. Now the technique of analysis of variance could be employed to analyse the effect of treatment on the dependent variable and to separate out the influence of extraneous variable (size of store) from the experiment.

3. **Latin square design:** This design is employed when the researcher is interested in separating out the influence of two extraneous variables. Suppose the interest is to study the influence of price (treatment) on sales. Let there be three levels of price categories, namely, low (X_1), medium (X_2) and high (X_3). The sales could be influenced by two extraneous variables, namely, store size and type of packaging. For the application of the Latin square design, the number of categories of two extraneous variables should be equal to the number of levels of treatments. This is a necessary condition for the use of Latin square design. The store could be of size – small (1), medium (2) and large (3) and type of packaging could be I, II and III. The Table 4.1 below presents the layout of the Latin square design.

   Latin square design has a very complex setup and is quite expensive to execute but it helps to measure statistically the effect of a treatment on the dependent variable.

TABLE 4.1
Latin square design for various levels of price

Store Size	Packaging		
	I	II	III
1 (Small)	X_1	X_2	X_3
2 (Medium)	X_2	X_3	X_1
3 (Large)	X_3	X_1	X_2

It may be noted that the rows and columns represent those extraneous variables whose effect is to be controlled and measured. There are three categories of row variable (size of store) and three categories of column variable (type of packaging). This would result in 3 × 3 Latin square.

One point that has to be kept in mind is that the treatment should be assigned randomly to cells in such a way that each treatment occurs once and only once in each row and in each column. The treatments exhibited in Table 4.1 satisfy this condition.

Use of this design helps to measure statistically the effect of a treatment on the dependent variable and also the measurement of an error resulting from two extraneous variables. This design, indeed has a very complex setup and is quite expensive to execute.

A factorial design is employed to measure the effect of two or more independent variables at various levels.

4. **Factorial design:** A factorial design may be employed to measure the effect of two or more independent variables at various levels. The factorial designs allow interaction between the variables. An interaction is said to take place when the simultaneous effect of two or more variables is different from the sum of their individual effects. An individual may have a high preference for mangoes and may also like ice-cream, which does not mean that he would like mango ice cream, leading to an interaction.

The sales of a product may be influenced by two factors, namely, price level and store size. There may be three levels of price—low (A_1), medium (A_2) and high (A_3). The store size could be categorized into small (B_1) and big (B_2). This could be conceptualized as a two-factor design with information reported in the form of a table. In the table, each level of one factor may be presented as a row and each level of another variable would be presented as a column. This example could be summarized in the form of a table having three rows and two columns. This would require 3 × 2 = 6 cells. Therefore, six different levels of treatment combinations would be produced, each with a specific level of price and store size. The respondents would be randomly selected and randomly assigned to the six cells. The tabular presentation of 3 × 2 factorial design is given in Table 4.2.

TABLE 4.2
3 × 2 factorial design for price level and store size

Price	Store	
	Small (B_1)	Big (B_2)
Low Level (A_1)	A_1B_1	A_1B_2
Medium Level (A_2)	A_2B_1	A_2B_2
High Level (A_3)	A_3B_1	A_3B_2

Respondents in each cell receive a specified treatment combination. For example, respondents in the upper left hand corner cell would face small level of price and small store. Similarly, the respondents in the lower right hand corner cell will be subjected to both high price level and big store.

The main advantages of factorial design are:

- It is possible to measure the main effects and interaction effect of two or more independent variables at various levels.
- It allows a saving of time and effort because all observations are employed to study the effects of each factor.
- The conclusion reached using factorial design has broader applications as each factor is studied with different combinations of other factors.

The limitation of this design is that the number of combinations (number of cells) increases with increased number of factors and levels. However, a fractional factorial design could be used if interest is in studying only a few of the interactions or main effects.

CONCEPT CHECK

1. How would you control the appearance of extraneous variables in an experiment?
2. What is the influence exerted by an environment upon the conducting of an experiment?
3. Classify and segregate the various types of experimental designs. Which, according to you, is the most effective and why?

SUMMARY

- Experiments are used to infer causality where the researcher actively manipulates one or more causal variables and measure their effects on the dependent variable. There are three necessary conditions for inferring causality: (i) concomitant variation (ii) time order of occurrence of variables, and (iii) the absence of other possible causal factors. Various concepts like independent variables (treatments), test units, dependent variables, exogenous variables are used in conducting an experiment. An experiment can be conducted under different environmental conditions, namely, laboratory and field. The researcher has two goals while conducting an experiment: (i) to keep the internal validity of the experiment very high and (ii) to make generalization of the results of the experiments to a wider population. Internal validity is concerned with examining the absence of all the causal factors except the one whose influence is being examined on the dependent variable. External validity, on the other hand, refers to the generalization of the results of the experiment. There are various factors affecting the internal validity of the experiment. These are history, maturation, testing, instrumentation, statistical regression, selection bias and test units' mortality. Similarly, there are factors influencing the external validity of an experiment. Some of the factors may be common to both the internal and the external validity of the experiment. The methods of controlling the effects of extraneous variables are also discussed.
- Experimental designs are classified into pre-experimental, quasi-experimental, true-experimental, and statistical design. Under pre-experimental design are included (i) one-shot case study, (ii) one-group pre-test–post-test design and (iii) static group comparison. The pre-experimental designs do not make use of randomization procedure in order to control the extraneous variables. Therefore, the internal validity of such experiments remains doubtful. Under quasi-experimental design are discussed (i) time series design and (ii) multiple time series design. In these designs the researcher has control over when the measurements are to be taken and on whom they are taken. However, the design lacks complete control of scheduling of treatment and also lacks ability to randomize test units exposure to treatments. Included in the category of true-experimental design are (i) pre-test–post-test control group, (ii) post-test–only control group and (iii) Solomon four-group design. In these designs, the researcher can randomly assign test units and treatments to experimental groups. The researcher is able to eliminate the effect of extraneous variables from both control and experimental groups. The statistical designs covered here are (i) completely randomized design, (ii) randomized block design, (iii) Latin square design, and (iv) factorial design. The statistical designs help to (i) study the effect of more than one level of independent variables on the dependent variable; (ii) study the effect of more than one independent variable and (iii) the effect of specific extraneous variables.

KEY TERMS

- Causality
- Completely randomized design
- Concomitant variation
- Control group
- Dependent variables
- Experiment
- Experimental group
- External validity
- Extraneous variables
- Factorial design
- History
- Independent variables
- Instrumentation
- Internal validity
- Latin square design
- Levels of independent variables
- Maturation
- Multiple time series design
- One-group pre-test–post-test design
- One-shot case study
- Physical control
- Post-test–only control group
- Pre-experimental design
- Pre-test–post-test control group
- Quasi-experimental design
- Randomization
- Randomized block design
- Selection bias
- Solomon four-group design
- Static group comparison
- Statistical designs
- Statistical regression
- Test unit mortality
- Test units
- Testing
- Time series design
- True experimental designs

CHAPTER REVIEW QUESTIONS

Objective Type Questions

State whether the following statements are true (T) or false (F).

1. The main advantage of the time series design is that it is possible to control the effect of history.
2. Test marketing is a form of laboratory experiment.
3. Mortality effect is more serious in field experiments than laboratory experiments.
4. Selection bias is not a problem in experiments involving just one group.
5. The one group after–only design is a quasi-experimental design.
6. Two group before–after design is a quasi-experimental design.
7. In the time series design the influence of history to confound the results is very high.
8. In the completely randomized design, it is assumed that there are no extraneous variables which could influence the outcome.
9. In the randomized block design, it is assumed that the scores on the dependent variable in each of the block would be more or less same.
10. The Latin square design can handle the influence of more than two extraneous variables.
11. The interactive testing effect would not occur for a group not subjected to any treatment.
12. In the quasi-experimental design the timing of the treatment presentation as well as which test units are exposed to the treatment may not be under the control of the researcher.
13. Changes in the economic environment can lead to history effect.
14. In a factorial design with three price levels and four promotional display alternatives, the number of interactions to be tested would be 12.
15. In a Latin-square design each treatment occurs only once in each row and in each column.
16. Laboratory experiments are low on internal validity but high on external validity.
17. To reduce selection bias, it is suggested to include a control group in the experiment.

18. In an experiment, the researcher manipulates one or more variables to measure its effect on the dependent variable.
19. When the events occur before the conduct of the experiment, the history effect comes to confound the experiment.
20. Independent variables are also called treatments.

Conceptual Questions

1. Differentiate between a laboratory experiment and a field experiment.
2. Explain the various extraneous variables which can influence the internal validity of an experiment.
3. What is causality? Discuss the necessary condition for inferring causality between two variables.
4. Define an experiment. What are the extraneous variables affecting the external validity of an experiment?
5. Discuss a completely randomized design. What are its limitations? How can a randomized block design take care of the limitation of such a design?
6. How does quasi-experimental design differ from true experiment design?
7. Define research design. Describe some of the important research designs used in the researches of social sciences.
8. Explain the meaning of causal relationship and discuss the conditions required for establishing it.
9. How is experimental design different from a descriptive research design? Explain with the help of an example.
10. What is the advantage of a random assignment of test units to an experimental design?
11. What are the extraneous variables which influence the internal and the external validity of experiments?
12. What are the different ways of controlling extraneous variables?
13. How do lab experiments differ from field experiments? What are the advantages of lab experiments over field experiments and vice versa?
14. Explain with the help of an example an interactive testing effect.
15. How does a time series experiment allow for the control of some extraneous variables?
16. What are the strengths and weaknesses of a factorial design?
17. Describe each of the following design:
    (a) Completely randomized design
    (b) Randomized block design
    (c) Factorial design
    (d) Latin square design
18. Design an experiment to determine which of the two fast foods—pizza and burger—are preferred by consumers in the age group of 18 to 21.

Application Questions

1. A set of MBA students from various business schools are administered a questionnaire to seek their perception about the image of a company. They are then shown a TV commercial about the same company. After viewing the programme, the same set of students are again administered the same questionnaire.
    (i) Diagram the experiment.
    (ii) Identify dependent variable, treatment, extraneous variables and test unit.
    (iii) What do you think could be the purpose of the experiment?
    (iv) Comment on the validity of the experiment.
2. To examine the effectiveness of a diet drink on weight reduction, a sample of respondents is selected at random. These respondents are divided randomly into two groups, each having the same numbers. Members of both groups are weighed weekly for a period of three months. For the next two months, members of one group are given the diet drink. The weights of members of both the groups are taken weekly for the next one month.
    (i) Discuss the purpose of this experiment.
    (ii) Diagram the experiment.
    (iii) Identify test units, dependent variable, independent variable, and extraneous variables.
    (iv) What purpose does each group serve?
    (v) Comment on the internal and external validity of the experiment.

3. Consider a telephone instrument manufacturing company wanting to measure the influence of different colors by keeping all the remaining features of the instrument same. Discuss various methods to control the effect of extraneous variables while measuring the influence of colours on the sales. Your answer should be specific and not general.
4. You are employed by the product manager of Tarai Foods Ltd. who wants to know the ideal price differential between the company's frozen vegetables and those marketed by Mother Diary. The customers of the frozen vegetables are mostly working women. Identify your variables, test units, hypotheses, and the research design to be used. Represent it diagrammatically and state the method of analysis.
5. The manager of Archies online wants to measure the effect of length of time between order of placement and the delivery of the merchandise on the amount of goods returned by the customers. The delay between order and delivery they want to test are one week, two weeks and three weeks. Identify your variables, hypotheses and test units. What is your research design. Represent it diagrammatically and state your method of analysis.
6. Butamal Kirorimal is a small jeweller from Jodhpur with limited resources. He is into the business of designing and selling traditional Rajasthani jewellery. He believes that having an exquisite and mystically arranged display on the Palace on Wheels will suitably boost the sale. He also feels that foreigners rather than Indians would be influenced more. It is the month of September 2010 and by the end of the year he wants to decide whether to go in for the display or not. Identify your variables, hypotheses and test units. What is your research design? Represent it diagrammatically and state your method of analysis.
7. You are asked to develop an experiment for studying the effect that monetary compensation has on the response rates secured from personal interview of certain people. This study will involve 300 people who will be assigned to one of the following conditions: (1) no compensation, (2) compensation of ₹250. A number of sensitive issues will be explored concerning various social problems and 300 people will be drawn from the adult population. Identify your variables, hypotheses and test units. What is your research design? Represent it diagrammatically and state your method of analysis.

Answers to Objective Type Questions

1. False	2. False	3. True	4. True	5. False
6. False	7. True	8. True	9. True	10. False
11. True	12. True	13. True	14. True	15. True
16. False	17. False	18. True	19. False	20. True

CASE 4.1

KESHAV FURNITURE PVT. LTD.

Keshav Furniture Pvt. Ltd. was established in 1950, and since its inception, has shown an average growth rate of 12 per cent per annum. Specializing in home and office furniture, it has also been exporting its products for the last seven years. Over the years, the company has gained reputation for its durable and comfortable designer products, which offer lots of convenience to the users.

Mr Keshav Prasad, the owner of the company, was happy with the growth of the company. According to him, 'Our products are far superior to that of our competitors in terms of quality, durability, range of designs and value for money.'

The real estate prices in Delhi and its neighboring areas of Gurgaon and Noida have gone up at an exponential rate. Therefore, the demand for studio apartments and small two-bedroom flats is increasing. Mr Prasad is considering launching three styles of sofas ideally suited for two-bedroom flats. These sofas are compact, occupy very little space and are affordable.

The price range for the three styles varies from ₹70,000 to 75,000. There is a difference of about 10 per cent in their cost of production.

Mr Prasad was wondering which style of sofa would sell the most, and the reasons thereof. A meeting of the top management was called to discuss the same. During the discussion a point that came up was that the sale need not only depend on the style of the sofa but also on the size of store where the sofas are sold. It was therefore decided to conduct an experiment which would help to answer whether the sales would vary across styles and store size.

QUESTION

1. How would you design an experiment to achieve the objectives stated above?

BIBLIOGRAPHY

Adams, John, Hafiz T A Khan, Robert Raeside and David White. *Research Methods for Graduate Business and Social Studies*. New Delhi: Response, 2007.

Aggarwal, L N and Diwan, Parag. *Research Methodology and Management Decisions*. New Delhi: Global Business Press, 1997.

Beherug, N, Sethna. *Research Methods in Marketing Management*. New Delhi: Tata McGraw-Hill Publishing Company Ltd, 1984.

Bhattacharyya, Dipak Kumar. *Research Methodology*. New Delhi: Excel Books, 2006.

Boyd, Harper, W. Jr. Ralph Westfall and Stanley F Stasch. *Marketing Research: Text and Cases*, 7th edn. Richard D. Irwin, Inc., 2002.

Burns, Robert B. *Introduction to Research Methods*. London: Sage Publications, 2000.

Churchill, Gilbert A Jr and Dawn Iacobucci. *Marketing Research Methodological Foundations*. 8th edn. New Delhi: Thompson South Western, 2002.

Cooper R, Donald. *Business Research Methods*. New Delhi: Tata McGraw-Hill Publishing Company Ltd, 2006.

Dwivedi, R S. *Research Methods in Behavioural Sciences*. Delhi: MacMillan India Ltd, 1997.

Easwaran, Sunanda and Sharmila J Singh. *Marketing Research – Concepts, Practices, and Cases*. New Delhi: Oxford University Press, 2006.

Emory, William C. *Business Research Methods*, Illinois: Richard D. Irwin, 1976.

Gay, L R. *Research Methods for Business and Management*. New York: MacMillan Publishing Company, 1992.

Gill, John. *Research Methods for Managers*. London: Sage Publications, 2002.

Graziano, Anthony, M. *Research Methods: A Process of Inquiry*. Boston: Allyn and Bacon, 2000.

Green, Paul E and Donald S Tull. *Research for Marketing Decisions,* 4th edn. Prentice Hall of India Private Ltd, 1986.

Hair Joseph, F. Jr., Robert, P. Bush, David, J. Ortinau. *Marketing Research – A Practical Approach for the New Millennium*. Delhi: McGraw Hill Higher Education, 1999.

Kinnear, Thomas C and James R Taylor. *Marketing Research: An Applied Approach*, 5th edn. New York: McGraw Hill, Inc., 1996.

Kothari, C R. *Research Methodology Methods & Techniques*, 2nd edn. New Delhi: Wiley Eastern Limited, 1990.

Malhotra, Naresh K. *Marketing Research – An Applied Orientation*, 3rd edn. Pearson Education, 2002.

Michael, V P. *Research Methodology in Management*. Mumbai: Himalaya Publishing House, 2000.

Nargundkar, Rajendra. *Marketing Research (Text and Cases)*. New Delhi: Tata McGraw Hill Publishing Company Ltd, 2002.

Nation, Jack, R. *Research Methods*. New Jersey: Prentice Hall, 1997.

Pannerselvam, R. *Research Methodology*. New Delhi: Prentice Hall of India Pvt Ltd, 2004.

Sekaram, Uma. *Research Methods for Business: A Skill Building Approach*. Singapore: John Wiley & Sons (Asia) Pte Ltd, 2003.

Shajahan, S. *Marketing Research – Concepts & Practices in India*. New Delhi: McMillan India Ltd, 2005.

Sharma B A V, Ravindra D Prasad and P Satyanarayana (eds). *Research Methods in Social Sciences*. New Delhi: Sterling Publishers Private Ltd, 1983.

Tripathi, P C. *A Textbook of Research Methodology in Social Sciences*. New Delhi: Sultan Chand & Sons, 2007.

Trochim, William M. *Research Methods*. New Delhi: Biztantra, 2003.

Tull, Donald, S and Del, I Hawkins. *Marketing Research: Measurement & Method*, 6th edn. Prentice Hall of India Pvt. Ltd, 1993.

Zikmund, William G. *Business Research Methods*, 5th edn. Dryden Press, Harcourt Brace College Publishers, 1997.

[illegible]

QUESTION [illegible]

[illegible]

[illegible]

Ahuja, [illegible] Dawson, Catherine [illegible] Researcher's Handbook: [illegible] Methods for Graduate Business and Social Studies, New Delhi: [illegible], 2007. [illegible]

[illegible] Phillip, [illegible] Business Press, 1987. [illegible]

[illegible] Research Methodology, New Delhi: [illegible] Books, 2000.

[illegible] Richard D. Irwin, 1976.

[illegible] London: [illegible], 2002.

[illegible] Prentice-Hall, 1975.

[illegible] New Delhi: [illegible], 2005.

[illegible] New Delhi: [illegible], 2003.

Section 2

DATA COLLECTION, MEASUREMENT AND SCALING

Once the research problem has been formalized and the execution plan or design has been formulated, the researcher needs to collect information and data oriented towards seeking answers to the research enquiry. This section is devoted to the data collection options available to the researcher.

Chapter 5 Secondary Data Collection Methods

Chapter 5 begins by discussing at length the various kinds of secondary data methods available to the researcher. The internal sources of data include sales, employee and financial records, as well as company records. External sources of data include published, syndicate and electronic sources. All these are detailed and discussed at length here. Each of the external sources is further divided into sub groups like government and non-government; individual and industrial syndicate sources. Comprehensive information is provided on various kinds of electronic independent sources, as well as databases.

Chapter 6 Qualitative Methods of Data Collection

Chapter 6 provides a complete coverage of the qualitative sources of data. It begins with the simple observation method and moves on to the popular interview and focus group discussions. The methodology and assumptions with step-wise instructions and illustrations are provided. Complex and skilled techniques like projective techniques, content analysis and sociometry are also discussed. The chapter ends by providing insights on emerging qualitative methods in business research.

Chapter 7 Attitude Measurement and Scaling

Chapter 7 deals with measurement and scaling. It discusses the basic characteristics of four types of measurements—nominal, ordinal, interval and ratio—and the permissible statistics associated with these measurements. Then it goes on to discuss various types of scaling techniques. One way of classifying the scales is to divide them into two groups, namely, single item and multiple item scale. Another way the scales can be classified is in terms of comparative and non-comparative scales. Under comparative scales, paired comparison, constant sum, rank order and Q-sort scales are discussed. The non-comparative scales are further classified into graphic rating scales and itemized rating scales. The itemized rating scales are further divided into Likert, Semantic Differential, and Stapel Scale. The chapter also discusses criteria for evaluating the measuring instrument through reliability, validity and sensitivity. The reliability is tested with the help of (1) test-retest reliability, (2) split-half reliability and (3) Cronbach alpha. The methods of measuring validity are content validity, concurrent validity and predictive validity.

Chapter 8 Questionnaire Desining

Chapter 8 is a detailed description with multiple illustrations about the most commonly used method of data collection—the questionnaire method. The chapter begins by stating the well structured and developed questionnaire design process. Different types of questionnaire formats and type of questions that can be used are discussed with ample illustrations. Guidelines for every aspect of selecting the questions based on the information needs; including the procedure for preparing the physical form, as well as how to conduct a pilot test are enunciated at length here.

CHAPTER 5

Secondary Data Collection Methods

Learning Objectives

By the end of the chapter, you should be able to:

1. Differentiate between primary and secondary sources of data.
2. Understand both the benefits and limitations of secondary data.
3. Identify the criteria or quality checks to be used when evaluating secondary information and gain familiarity with reporting and concluding from past records and data.
4. Distinguish between the various types and sources of secondary data.

'Twenty per cent more, buy one get one free or scratch cards—which one of our schemes worked best? The Gujarat Milk Product company is also launching new schemes every month, like combo deals, 50 per cent extra and storing jar. So, what really works? What is the magic formula?' quizzed Ranjit Shah, VP (Sales), northern region, Mom Dairy. He was in a monthly review meeting with his sales executives across the region.

Mom Dairy had established a stronghold in the NCR and the north in the past decade and was able to cater to the vociferous milk and milk product demand of the northern consumer. However, 2010 appeared to be a challenging year as another giant, GMP, was making its presence felt, through aggressive and head-on sales collision. The category in point was ice-creams and ice-lollies. Sales promotion targeted at the retailer and the consumer was being made with fervour.

Shah also showed concern about erratic sales in areas near schools and colleges where Mom Dairy vendors demonstrated varying results. Nivedita, the sales officer of western region (Delhi) stated, 'Sir, we can track the response for our schemes by observing the sales tracks corresponding to the areas and time periods of the relevant promotion through our MIS.'

'What about GMP's track? Secondly, I also need some inputs on making my reach more lucrative, especially in schools.'

Charu, a new incumbent from Jigyasa market research agency, confidently advised, 'Sir, to improve and manage the current situation in a better manner, we need to backtrack and use a structured and broad-based panel data and audits'. 'Panels and audits? How authentic and reliable would these sources be? And when a plethora of such data products exist, how do I know what and how to select?'

Charu is right when she suggests backtracking and looking at the past performance to forecast some strategies for the next period. Panel data and retail audits are but a few examples of what could be the nature of such sources.

CLASSIFICATION OF DATA

LEARNING OBJECTIVE 1
Differentiate between primary and secondary sources of data.

To understand the multitude of choices available to a researcher for collecting the project/study-specific information, one needs to be fully cognizant of the resources available for the study and the level of accuracy required. To appreciate the truth of this statement, one needs to examine the gamut of methods available to the researcher. The data sources could be either contextual and primary or historical and secondary in nature (Figure 5.1).

Primary data is original, problem- or project-specific and collected for serving a particular purpose. Its authenticity or relevance is reasonably high.

Primary data as the name suggests is original, problem- or project-specific and collected for the specific objectives and needs spelt out by the researcher. The authenticity and relevance is reasonably high. The monetary and resource implications of this are quite high and sometimes a researcher might not have the resources or the time or both to go ahead with this method. In this case, the researcher can look at alternative sources of data which are economical and authentic enough to take the study forward. These include the second category of data sources—namely the secondary data.

Secondary data is not topical or research-specific. It can be economically and quickly collected by the decision-maker in a short span of time.

Secondary data as the name implies is that information which is not topical or research- specific and has been collected and compiled by some other researcher or investigative body. The said information is recorded and published in a structured format, and thus, is quicker to access and manage. Secondly, in most instances, unless it is a data product, it is not too expensive to collect. As suggested in the opening vignette, the data to track consumer preferences is readily available and the information required is readily available as a data product or as the audit information which the researcher or the organization can procure and use it for arriving at quick decisions. In comparison to the original research-centric data, secondary data can be economically and quickly collected by the decision maker in a short span of time. Also the information collected is contextual; what is primary and original for one researcher would essentially become secondary and historical for someone else.

FIGURE 5.1
Sources of research information

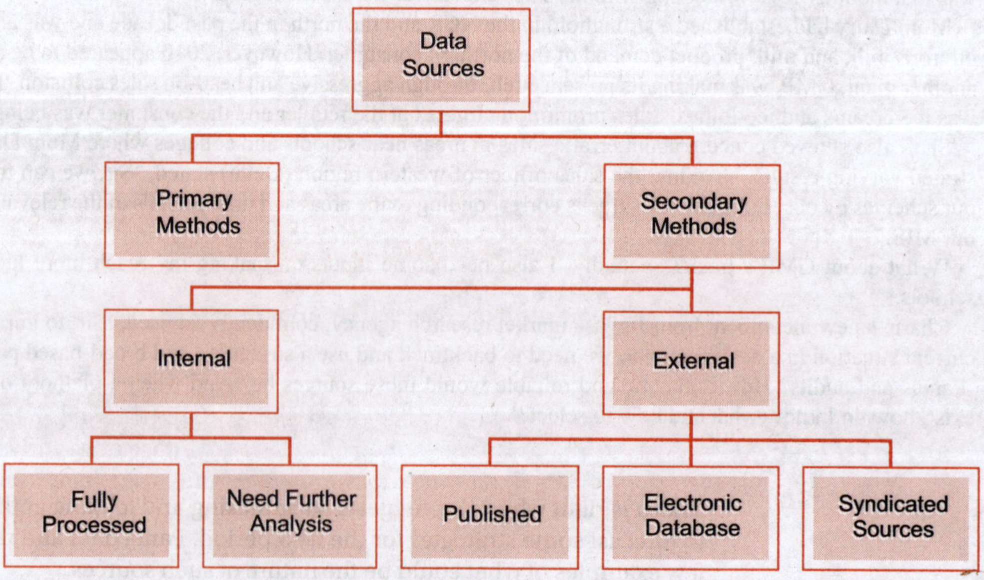

RESEARCH APPLICATIONS OF SECONDARY DATA

Secondary data can be used in multiple stages during the course of a business research study:

- **Problem identification and formulation stage:** Existing information on the topic under study is useful in giving a conceptual framework for the investigation. For example, if a researcher is interested in investigating the investor's perception of market risk, and he tracks investment behaviour of different quarters, alongside political, economic and social occurrences, he would be in a position to isolate the predictive variables he might wish to study.
- **Hypotheses designing:** Previous research studies done in the area as well as the industry trends and market facts could help in speculating on the expected directions of the study results. For example, the researcher in the above example might predict a positive, linear relationship between economic parameters like GDP and GNP and the choice of investment instruments and a linear negative relation between inflation rate and investment behaviour.

In most cases, **past studies** on the subject make the current study simpler as the researcher can make use of the findings of the earlier studies.

- **Sampling considerations:** There might be respondent related databases available to seek respondent statistics and relevant contact details. These would assist as the sampling frame for collection of primary information. For example, in the investment study, let us say the researcher wants to conduct study amongst upper income class individuals. He can then collect information on the size and spread through suitable census data.
- **Primary base:** The secondary information collected can be adequately used to design the primary data collection instruments, in order to phrase and design appropriate queries. Sometimes, the past studies done on the subject make the current study simpler, as the researcher can make use of the previously designed questionnaires. These have been standardized and validated earlier, thus the level of confidence and accuracy would be higher as compared to a new instrument.
- **Validation and authentication board:** Earlier records and studies as well as data pools can also be used to support or validate the information collected through primary sources.

Before we examine the wide range of the secondary sources available to the business researcher, it is essential that one is aware of the merits and demerits of using secondary sources.

BENEFITS AND DRAWBACKS OF SECONDARY DATA

LEARNING OBJECTIVE 2
Understand both the benefits and limitations of secondary data.

Both benefits and drawbacks of secondary data have been discussed below:

Benefits

As we can observe, the usage of secondary data offers numerous advantages over primary data. This makes their inclusion in a research study almost mandatory. There are multiple reasons why we staunchly advocate their usage.

Resource advantage involves making use of secondary information which, in turn, saves immensely in terms of both cost and time.

1. **Resource advantage:** The predominant and most important argument in support is the resource advantage. Any research or survey that is making use of secondary information will be able to save immensely in terms of both cost and time (Ghouri and Gronhaugh, 2002). VCare is a house maintenance company, located at Jaya Nagar, Bengaluru, and wants to assess the customer acceptance in the neighbouring areas. For this it wants to know: How many people reside in own

houses/apartments? How many have double income households? And how many are in the income bracket of 1 lakh+ per month?

Thus, the latest city census data available can be accessed to arrive at these figures. Therefore, it is advocated that the investigator must first find out about the availability of probable, previously collected data, before venturing into primary data collection. The time saved in collecting information can be gainfully used for analysing and interpreting the data.

2. **Accessibility of data:** The other major advantage of secondary sources is that, once the information has been collected and compiled in a structured manner as a publication, accessing it for one's individual research purpose becomes much easier than collecting it for a singular study. Census data as the one mentioned above is generally available through a government source and is usually free of charge. However, in case VCare wants market data, in terms of size, players and volume—one might need to go to the commercial data sources which might be available for a cost, depending on the sample size and research agency repute. However, even when the data is purchased, the cost of the information would be much less as compared to collecting it on one's own.
3. **Accuracy and stability of data:** As stated in the above case, data that is collected by recognized bodies and on a large scale has the additional advantage of accuracy and reliability (Stewart and Kamins, 1993). Thus, any interpretation of primary findings or supportive logic for an implementation decision would be more precise. Moreover, since the data is collected and compiled by an outside body, it can be readily and easily accessed by other researchers as well (Denscombe, 1998).

Secondary data can be used to compare and support the primary research findings of the investigators.

4. **Assessment of data:** Another plus point of collecting secondary data is that the information can be used to compare and support the primary research findings of the investigators. In case the study was conducted on a representative sample of the population, the findings could be used to estimate the applicability on a larger population. Even if the findings of the earlier collected information are in contrast with the current findings, it is still useful as it might reveal the presence of certain moderator variables which might be operating in the two research conditions.

However, there is need for caution as well because in using secondary data, there might be some constraints and disadvantages as well.

Drawbacks

The drawbacks of secondary data are due to the following reasons:

1. **Applicability of data:** What one needs to remember in case of secondary data is the purpose for which the information was collected. It was unique to that study and thus cannot be an absolute fit for the current research. As a result of this, the information might not be applicable or relevant for the current objective. (Denscombe, 1998). The typical differences that emerge in such cases are with relation to the variables and the units being used to measure it. For example, market optimism or buoyancy by one researcher might be reflected by the consumer's spending in that quarter; while one might be interested in measuring buoyancy in terms of the investment in equity and growth funds.

Another significant difference is in terms of the time period. The information that one might be using for the current research might have been collected in a different time coordinate or in a different environment. The implication of this divergence in the research base is that there might be multiple modifying variables, which might not be apparent like the socio-cultural environment, climatic effects and political factors. However, these might be responsible for skewing the direction of the findings.

Multiple modifying variables might not be apparent such as socio-cultural factors, climatic effects and political factors and yet can skew the direction of the findings.

2. **Accuracy of data:** While application of the data might be an issue, there is a sincere concern before one relies on the information gathered by another source—that is the level of trust one can have on the same. The concerns are three: Who, Why and How?

The first level of accuracy depends upon who was the investigator or the investigative agency. The reputation of the organization/person becomes extremely critical in establishing the truth of the findings as well as believing the inferences drawn in the quoted research. The second is the reason for collecting the data. For example, if a certain political party collects information on the potential voters and an independent market research agency collects information on the spread of the opinions—positive and negative—towards various political parties, one is more likely to rely on the second source. The reliability would be higher due to the reasons given below:

- Since the agency specializes in conducting opinion polls and has a vast experience as well as a respondent base, the chances of error would be minimized.
- The political party might have a hidden agenda of securing the campaign sponsorship through the survey conducted, while the independent body would be free from this bias.

Last but not the least is the data collection process of the study in terms of sample selection and sampling characteristics used to identify the respondent population. This is very important as this would be a clear indicator of the applicability of the results when extrapolating to the larger population.

CONCEPT CHECK

1. How will you classify data?
2. Discuss the main sources of secondary data.
3. What are the benefits and drawbacks of secondary data?

EVALUATION OF SECONDARY DATA—RESEARCH AUTHENTICATION

LEARNING OBJECTIVE 3

Identify the criteria or the quality checks to be used when evaluating secondary information and gain familiarity with reporting and concluding from past research and data.

Even though the data collected through other sources is valuable and critical to the research that one is undertaking, there must be certain quality checks that a researcher sometimes must undertake. On first reviewing the information, it may seem applicable and useful but on a closer examination, one might find either a mismatch with the framed research objectives or a doubt regarding the methodology or the analysis of the study. Thus, a set of evaluative measures can be employed before one decides to use it for the present study.

Methodology Check

Methodology check involves the evaluation of the process or design used to collect the data or respondent sampling or data analysis.

The first evaluative criterion is the process or design used to collect the data so that in case there has been an element of skewed respondent selection or bias, one can detect it here. The verification one needs to attempt is for the following:

- **Sampling considerations:** This has to be done in terms of the defining criteria; the sampling frame; the respondent selection; response rate and the quality of data recording.
- **Methodology of data:** In terms of quality of instrument design and nature of fieldwork. This is critical as one might find that the variables measured are not as required by the current study (Jacob, 1994).
- **Analytical tools used and subsequent reporting and interpretation of results:** The problem that might occur here is that, while interpreting the

findings the author might do so using his own personal judgement, which might not be based on any particular school of thought. Thus, taking the study report prima facie might be risky (Denscombe, 1998).

Further these checks also help the researcher establish whether the earlier assumptions and findings can be extrapolated on the present study.

Accuracy Check

Accuracy check determines the significance of the source of information from where the data was collected for a specific study.

Dochartaigh et al. (2002) emphasize upon the significance of the source of information. The researcher must determine whether the data is accurate enough for the purpose of the present study. If the study has been conducted and the findings compiled by a reputed source, the reliability of using it as a base for further research is higher, viz., one conducted by a relative newcomer or on a small scale. In case information is from such a source, it would be advisable to collect similar data from multiple sources and then collate the findings. A related problem that might occur is when different studies/sources report contrary findings. In such a case, a short pilot study, supported by an expert opinion survey would help achieve the right perspective. This is termed as cross-check verification (Partzer, 1996).

Another problem of accuracy is when the data is deliberately manipulated for the purpose of the study. This might happen in reporting of accidents and mishaps by supervisors and managers, in order to improve the safety records of the organization. Customer satisfaction surveys might decide to include only the consumer feedback data which was average to very good rather than very poor to very good thus presenting the findings demonstrating a high customer satisfaction.

The inaccuracy could also be in the presentation of the findings, i.e., the scale used might artificially enhance or play down the results. This is illustrated in the example below.

Example 5.1

Misrepresentation of data—Bhagyshree evaluated the use of tabulated presentations in the company reports as part of her research study. Based on a sample of data collected from 53 companies' reports, she found that 29 per cent organizations made use of graphical data presentations, while 100 per cent made use of tables.

What was alarming was that 59 per cent of the figures made use of distorted graphical presentations. Either the size of the bar or the scale used was manipulated to do this. Thus, the interpretation might be misleading about the rate of change or growth. A frequently used mechanism was not to start the value axis at zero as is demonstrated in the following graph.

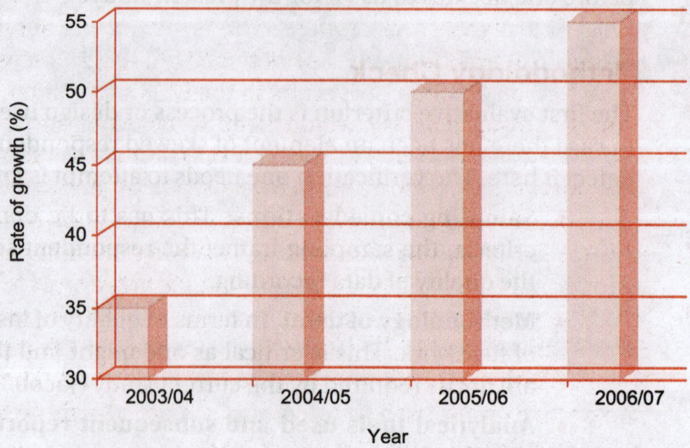

Topical Check

Topical check aims at investigating the information that is being used or cited in the research study for periodical upgradations.

Any information that is being used or cited in the research study needs also to be subjected to a topical check. It might happen that there is a considerable time lag between the earlier reported findings on the subject and the research being conducted now. A case in point is the census data, which is collected once in five years. However, if one is looking at the impact of variables such as age distribution and gender composition on the purchase patterns of personal care products, five years is a period where trends and fashions might have changed and presumptions or hypotheses made on the basis of such a data might be erroneous. To address these problems, a number of market research firms have started publishing syndicated sources (will be discussed later in the chapter) which are periodically updated.

Cost-benefit Analysis

Last but not the least is the financial check. Kervin (1999) states that before making use of secondary data, one needs to measure the cost of procuring the data, viz., the advantage of the information. This is applicable in the case of industry reports, market research data or readership surveys which might cost a considerable sum and the research funds might not be adequate for the purpose.

CONCEPT CHECK

1. What is meant by methodology check?
2. Define accuracy check and topical check.
3. How would you define cost-benefit analysis?

Example 5.2

Secondary data—*Active Parenting* is a national magazine launched from Delhi. It published the results of a study conducted to find out the features parents consider most important when selecting a pre-nursery school for their child. In the order of importance, these characteristics are safety, cost, infrastructure, location, child care, teaching pedagogy, teacher attitude, and the number of admissions to reputed secondary schools. *Active Parenting* then ranked 20 schools in the NCR according to these characteristics.

This article would be a useful source of secondary data for the pre-nursery school M Pride (MP) in conducting a market research study to identify aspects of school amenities that should be improved. However, before using the data, MP should evaluate according to several criteria.

First, the methodology used to collect the data for this survey needs to be evaluated in detail. As is the practice, *Active Parenting* has at the end of the survey indicated the methodology used in the study. A poll of 2,500 parents with children in the age group of 2–3 years was studied. The results of the survey had a 5 per cent error margin. The first thing MP needs to do is to determine whether 5 per cent is good enough to extrapolate the results to the NCR population.

Another issue that MP would need to consider is the time period of the study and the survey purpose in taking a decision on the utility of the survey findings. This survey was conducted before the Delhi government's directive on nursery admissions, which were more based on the school-residence distance. Thus, the features a parent might be looking at while evaluating a pre-nursery school might have changed. Secondly, the purpose of the survey was to acquaint the NCR parents with the options available and to build awareness on how to decide about the school for their child. Thus, the idea is to address the topical need of the hour and it is not really scientifically designed or conducted. The survey simply presents a perspective on parent opinion and is not necessarily aimed at addressing the need of the supplier—in this case the school.

The survey was conducted by CRB MR Agency for *Active Parenting* magazine. Thus, the reputation of the agency in conducting such surveys might need to be examined first. To validate the selection of the evaluative criteria, the school might look at some similar studies conducted by other MR agencies within the country or outside. Another related aspect about the methodology is the definition of the evaluation variables. For example, 'cost' in the survey was the cost inclusive of the school fees plus the transportation cost as well as the school uniform, while MP would like to evaluate 'cost' only in terms of the school fees.

However, despite all these drawbacks, the *Active Parenting* article is a cost-effective way of starting a customer expectation or a satisfaction study. For instance, it might be useful in formulating the problem's scope and objective, but, because of the article's limitations in regard to the time period, sampling, research design, and reliability, the researcher must look at some alternative studies as well as primary data collection methods.

CLASSIFICATION OF SECONDARY DATA

LEARNING OBJECTIVE 4
Distinguish between various types and sources of secondary data.

As we saw earlier in Figure 5.1, the information sources could be research-specific and primary or ex-post facto and secondary in nature. Secondary data can further be divided into either internal or external sources. Internal, as the name implies, is organization- or environment-specific source and includes the historical output and records available with the organization which might be the backdrop of the study. This would be directly accessible to the researcher in case he is part of the organization. However it might not be easily available to an investigator who is an outsider. The data that is independent of the organization and covers the larger industry-scape would be available through outside sources. This might be available to the researcher in the form of published material, computerized databases or data compiled by syndicated services. Discussed below are the major internal sources of data.

Internal Sources of Data

Secondary data can be internal or external. Internal is the organization- or environment-specific source, whereas external is based upon the sources available outside an institution.

Compilation of various kinds of information and data is mandatory for any organization that exists. Some sources of internal information are presented in Figure 5.2.

The facts and information may be available (like the employee data) in a format where it can be directly used for data interpretation or analysis, however there might be certain studies for which the data from different heads would need to be processed before it can be further used. For example, in case one wants to calculate the capacity of the utilization and profitability of an organization then for this one needs the employee numbers, shift attendance, units made and sold as well as inventory figures. These have to be, then, evaluated against the financial statements.

FIGURE 5.2
Internal sources of data

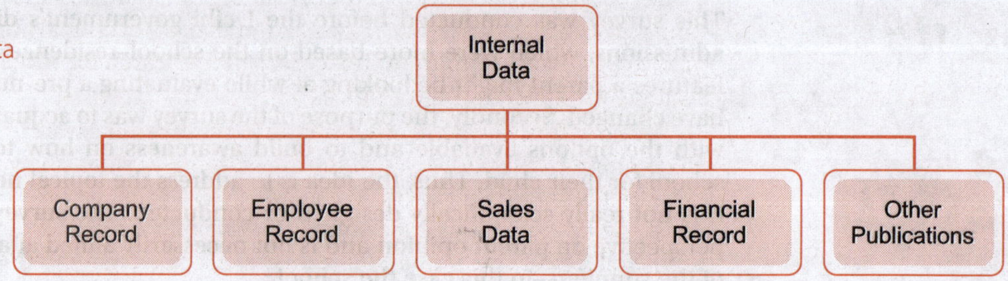

1. **Company records:** This would entail all the data about the inception, the owners, and the mission and vision statements, infrastructure and other details including both the process and manufacturing (if any) and sales, as well as a historical timeline of the events. Policy documents, minutes of meetings and legal papers would come under this head. The access to some part of this data might be available on the public domains. However, there might be certain documents like corporate plans for the next year(s) which might not be available.

Company and employee records play a crucial role in determining the capacity, utilization and profitability of the organization.

2. **Employee records:** All details regarding the employees (regular and part-time) would be part of employee records. This would include all the demographic information, as well as all the performance and discipline data available with reference to the individual. Performance appraisal records, satisfaction/dissatisfaction data as well as the exit interview data would also be available in the organization's annals. Sometimes, the decision maker can review the impact of certain policy changes, through performance data. Also, attrition and absenteeism data could serve as indicators for primary research required. For a service firm, employee records are more significant as people here are a part of the delivery process.
3. **Sales data:** This is an extremely valuable source and can be the most important part of the data collection process for a market research study. The data can take on different forms:
4. **Cash register receipt:** This is the simplest, most frequently recorded and available data. It would be used to reveal data under different conditions. For example, sales by product line, by major departments, by specific stores, geographical regions, by cash versus credit purchases, at specific time periods/days and the size of purchase bills.
5. **Salespersons' call records:** This is a document to be prepared and updated every day by each individual salesperson. This can reveal a wealth of information about the potential customer, classification of the customer in terms of product requirement/company product purchase, as well as the popular products, the products that are hard to sell, information sought by the customer, customer's usage pattern and the demand analysis. The reports can also provide vital leads for a product's redesign or new product development. The data is also critical for creating job descriptions and building incentives into the system for motivating the sales force. The information needed and the presentation and negotiation required also help in designing more customized training and development initiatives.
6. **Sales invoices:** Customer who has placed an order with the company, his complete details including the size of the order, location, price by unit, terms of sale and shipment details (if any). This information set helps to forecast the annual demand for the product as well as evaluate the adequacy of sales and delivery.
7. **Financial records and sales reports:** These reveal total sales made against projected sales data, total sales by rupees and units, comparative sales performance across quarters, across regions, product categories, as well as subsequent to different sales promotion activities. Financial records in terms of sales expenses, sales revenue, sales overhead costs and profits are some of the most important output data recorded by an organization that are of critical importance as these are the dependent variables in most cases in a research for which the decision maker tries to establish the causation.

Besides this, there are other published sources like warranty records, CRM data and customer grievance data which are extremely critical in evaluating the health of a product or an organization. There are also internal records of the published data about the organization; for example, newspaper or magazine coverage or articles published about the manufactured or a marketed product, e.g., business school ratings, harmful trans fats found in burgers and French fries as related to fast food burger chains.

There are some significant advantages of using internal data sources. First, they are readily accessible and economical to use. Secondly, they are topical and updated to the latest time period with a great amount of precision and details. However, despite these obvious advantages, most researchers do not explore the organizational archives in the first stage. A prime reason why this source is not actively sought is because it is a cumbersome task to collect information from multiple sources and then putting it together for the research study.

The organization of large volumes of information into clusters of data based upon user requirements is called **data mining.**

However, with the advent of technology, this task has been made simple and extremely fast with various data base techniques. Most organizations today maintain a data warehouse, which is essentially a computerized storehouse for the data bases that can organize large volumes of information into clusters of data based upon the user requirement. This process of organizing the data is termed as data mining. The researcher/investigator has the provision through this technique to create multi-dimensional analysis and reports based upon a unidimensional original data set. Various software programmes and languages are used to detect patterns and trends from the data like the neural networks, tree models, estimation, market basket analysis, genetic algorithms, clustering, classification, etc. In fact these techniques make the prediction of the outcome so effective and involving a minimal error that a lot of firms are actively relying on data mining of the internal data sources, viz., the external data or primary data for implementing planned strategies.

External Data Sources

As stated earlier, information that is collected and compiled by an outside source that is external to the organization is referred to as external source of data. Included under this head (Figure 5.1) are published sources, computer-based information sources and syndicated sources. Each of these would be discussed separately in this section.

Published data

Published data can be procured both from official and government sources or from reports compiled by individuals, private research agencies or organizations.

The most frequently used and most easily available data information that is compiled by using public or private sources. There could be a plethora of information available on the same topic from varied sources. For the sake of the avid researcher who would like to explore these options, listed below are some potential information sources.

There could be two kinds of published data—one that is from the official and government sources—this could include census data, policy documents and historical archives; the other kind of data is that which has been prepared by individuals or private agencies or organizations. This could be in the form of books, periodicals, industry data such as directories and guides.

1. **Government sources:** The Indian government publishes a lot of documents that are readily available and are extremely useful for the purpose of providing background data. This could be available on public domains or might be retrieved by special permission. The publications are usually available, for example the population or census data and other publications.
    - **Census data:** Considering the size of the Indian subcontinent, one needs to understand the magnitude of the data available and the intensity of effort required to record information from all parts of the country. Recently, the Census 2010 has been carried out and the quality of census data promises to be very high and the data has been collected in a much more detailed format.

Statistical data collected by the government is highly detailed, varied and accurate. In this category, census data often provides a reliable base.

- **Other government publications:** In addition to the census, the Indian government collects and publishes a great deal of statistical data. The Planning Commission of India has in its archives all the details on economic planning and outcomes of the country. Other sources are budget and legislative documents and other economic surveys done related to the trade and culture of the country. The data could be further available at the micro level, that is the state level as well. Today, with the advent of technology, most of this is available in computerized form. Listed in Table 5.1 is an illustration of some of the sources. One may find that the list is neither complete nor exhaustive. The objective is to give the researcher a flavour of the kind of recorded information available to him for his study. Another point to be noted is that while we have listed the Indian sources, similar data is available for most countries.

TABLE 5.1
Secondary data—government publications

	Sub-type	Sources	Data	Uses
1.	Census data conducted every ten years throughout the country	Registrar General of India conducting census survey http://censusindia.gov.in/	Size of the population and its distribution by age, sex, occupation and income levels. 2011 census took many more variables to get a better picture of the population	Population information is significant as the forecasts of purchase, estimates of growth and development, as well as policy decisions can be made on this basis
2.	Statistical Abstract India – annually	CSO (Central Statistical Organization) for the past 5 years http://www.mospi.gov.in/cso_test1.htm	Education, health, residential information at the state level is part of this document	Making demand, estimations and a state-level assessment of government support and policy changes can be made
3.	White paper on national income	CSO http://www.mospi.gov.in/cso_test1.htm	Estimates of national income, savings and consumption	Significant indication of the financial trends; investment forecasts and monetary policy formulation
4.	Annual Survey of Industries – all industries	CSO – no. of units, persons employed, capital output ratio, turnover, etc. http://www.mospi.gov.in/cso_test1.htm		Information on existing units gives perspective on the Industrial development and helps in creating the employee profile
5.	Monthly survey of selected industries	CSO http://www.mospi.gov.in/cso_test1.htm	Production statistics in detail	Demand–supply estimations
6.	Foreign Trade of India Monthly Statistics	Director General of Commercial Intelligence http://www.dgciskol.nic.in/	Exports and imports countrywise and productwise	Forecast, manufacturing and trade estimations

Contd...

	Sub-type	Sources	Data	Uses
7.	Wholesale price index – weekly all-India Consumer Price Index	Ministry of Commerce and Industry http://india.gov.in/sectors/commerce/ministry_commerce.php	Reporting of prices of products like food articles, foodgrains, minerals, fuel, power, lights, lubricants, textiles, chemicals, metal, machinery and transport	Establishing price bands of product categories; pricing estimations for new products; determining consumer spend
8.	Economic Survey – annual publication	Dept. of Economic Affairs, Ministry of Finance, patterns, currency and finance http://finmin.nic.in/the_ministry/dept_eco_affairs/	Descriptive reporting of the current economic status	Estimations of the future and evaluation of policy decisions and extraneous factors in that period
9.	National Sample Survey (NSS)	Ministry of Planning http://www.planningcommission.gov.in/	Social, economic, demographic, industrial and agricultural statistics	Significant for making policy decisions as well as studying sociological patterns

2. **Other data sources:** This source is the most voluminous and most frequently used, in every research study. The information could be in the form of books, periodicals, journals, newspapers, magazines, reports, and trade literature. The data could also be available as compilations in the form of guides, directories and indices.

- **Books and periodicals:** Books and periodicals are the simplest, easily accessible and user friendly form of documented material. The volumes could carry information ranging from constructs, technical details and cultural data to just a collection of views on the topic of interest to the researcher.
- **Guides:** These are an instructive source of standard or recurring information. A guide may subsequently lead into identifying other important sources of directories, trade associations and trade publications. In fact it is advisable to begin a study by exploring such guides.
- **Directories and indices:** Directories are useful as they may again lead to a source or a pool of specific information. Indices, on the other hand, serve as a collection of the location of information on a particular topic in several different publications.

Directories, books and periodicals are thoroughly compiled sources which are easily accessible and most frequently used in many research studies.

- **Standard non-governmental statistical data:** Published statistical data are of great interest to researchers. Graphic and statistical analyses can be performed on these data to draw important insights. There are renowned private agencies which periodically compile and publish this kind of data and they are considered extremely significant in their contribution to understanding the market. Important sources of non-governmental statistical data include Standard and Poor's Statistical Service, Moody's Industrial manual and data from agencies such as NASSCOM & MAIT (IT Industry); SIAM (automobile industry); CETMA, IEEMA (electronics) and IPPAI (power). Reports and documents available from renowned bodies like the World Bank, United Nations and World Trade Organization are also valuable sources of secondary information. Some non-government data sources are presented in Table 5.2.

TABLE 5.2
Secondary data—Non-government publications

	Sub-type	Sources	Data	Uses
1.	Company Working Results – Stock Exchange Directory	Bombay Stock Exchange http://www.bseindia.com/	A complete database of the companies registered with the stock exchange and comprehensive details about stock policies and current share prices	Significant in determining the financial health of various sectors as well as assessment of corporate funding and predictions of outcomes
2.	Status reports by various commodity boards	The commodity board or the industry associations like Jute Board, Cotton Industry, Sugar Association, Pulses Board, Metal Board, Chemicals, Spices, Fertilizers, Coir, Pesticides, Rubber, Handicrafts, Plantation Boards, etc.	Detailed information on current assets – in terms of units, current production figures and market condition	These are useful for individual sectors in working out their plans as well as evaluating causes of success or failure
3.	Industry associations on problems faced by private sector, etc.	FICCI, ASSOCHAM, AIMA, Association of Chartered Accountants and Financial Analysts, Indo-American Chamber of Commerce, etc. http://www.ficci.com/ http://www.assocham.org/ http://www.aima-ind.org/ www.iaccindia.com/	Cases/ comprehensive reports by the supplier or user or any other section associated with the sector	Cognizance of the gaps and problems in the effective functioning of the organization; trouble shooting
4.	Export-related data – commodity-wise	Leather Exports Promotion Council, Apparel Export Promotion Council, Handicrafts, Spices, Tea, Exim Bank, http://www.leatherindia.org/ http://www.aepcindia.com/	Product- and country-wise data on the export figures as well as information on existing policies related to the sector	To estimate the demand; gauge opportunities for trade and impetus required in terms of manufacturing and policy changes
5.	Retail Store Audit on pharmaceutical, veterinary, consumer products	ORG (Operations Research Group); Monthly reports on urban sector; Quarterly reports on rural sector	The touch point for this data is retailer, who provides the figures related to product sales; the data is very comprehensive and covers most brands. The data is region-specific and covers both inventory and goods sold	Market analysis and market structure mapping with estimations of market share of leading brands. The audit can also be used to study consumption trends at different time periods or subsequent to sales promotion or other activities
6.	National Readership Survey (NRS)	IMRB survey of reading behaviour for different segments as well as different products http://www.imrbint.com/	Today these surveys are done by various bodies with different sample bases. Today the survey base has become younger, with the age of the reader lowered to 12+	Media planning and measuring exposure as well as reach for product categories

Contd...

	Sub-type	Sources	Data	Uses
7.	Thompson Indices: Urban market index, rural market index	Hindustan Thompson Associates	All towns with population of more than one lakh are covered and information of demographic and socio-economic variables are given for each city with Mumbai as base. The rural index similarly covers about 400 districts with socio-economic indicators like value of agriculture output, etc.	The inclinations to purchase consumer products are directly related to socio-economic development of communities in general. The indices provide barometers to measure such potentials for each city and has implications for the researcher in terms of data collection sources

However, no matter how vast and differentiated is the published data source available to the researcher, hunting from huge volumes is truly a herculean task and can be extremely tedious. With the advent of computer technology, today, most published information is also available in the form of computerized databases.

Computer-stored data

Information that was earlier stored as a printed document is now available in an electronic form. The growth in computerized databases has been impressive and it is estimated that 4750 online databases (Aaker et al., 2000) are available to the business researcher. Infor-mation retrieval from such sources is extremely fast and can be accomplished in a most user-friendly fashion. The databases available to the researcher can be classified on the basis of the type of information or by the method of storage and recovery (Figure 5.3).

Reference databases are also called bibliographic databases as they provide online indices and abstracts.

1. **Based on content of information:** These could be of two kinds:
   - **Reference databases:** These refer users to the articles, research papers, abstracts and other printed news contained in other sources. They provide online indices and abstracts and are thus also called bibliographic databases. Using reference databases has the following advantages:
     (a) They are up-to-date summaries or references to a wide assortment of articles appearing in thousands of business magazines, trade journals, government reports, and newspapers throughout the world.
     (b) The information is accessed by using commonly used keywords, rather than author or title. For example, The word 'coke' will initiate a search that will collate all documents that contain that word.
     (c) One can also use a combination of terms to arrive at the information that could be indirectly supportive of the topic under study. For example, One may look at 'coke+ alternative fuels' to arrive at the combustion alternatives available for a consumer.
   - **Source databases:** These provide numerical data, complete text, or a combination of both. Unlike, abstracts and addresses in the reference database, source databases usually provide complete textual or numerical information. They can be classified into: (1) Full-text information sources, (2) Economic and

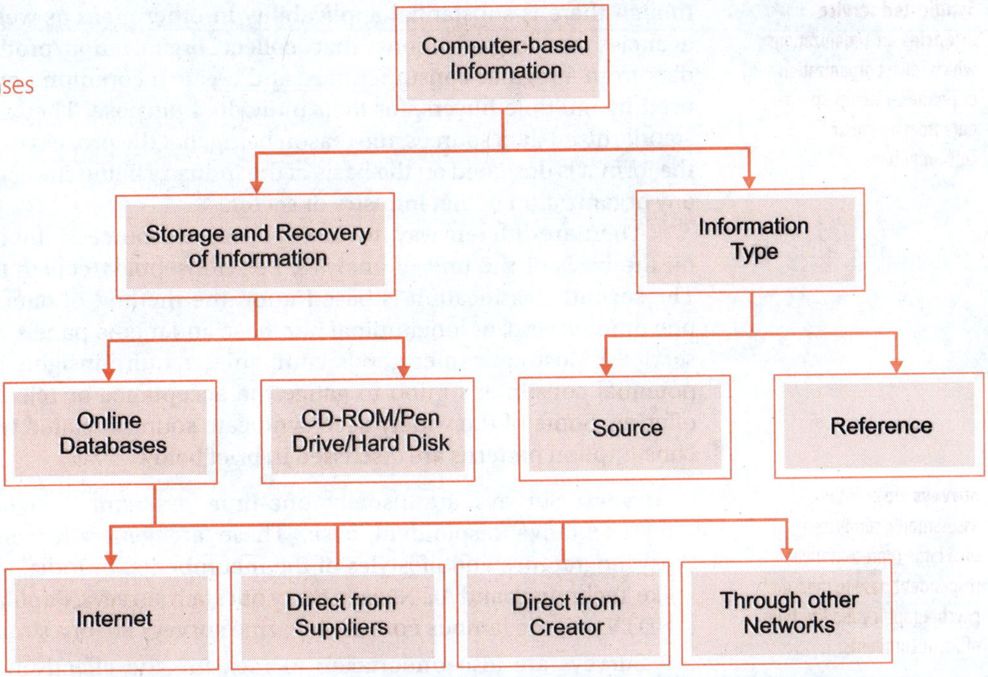

FIGURE 5.3 Classifications of computerized databases

financial statistical databases such as Standard and Poor's Compstat Services and Value Line Database, and (3) Online data and descriptive bases such as: American Business Directory, which lists over 10 million companies, mainly private. It also lists government officials and professionals, such as physicians and attorneys. There are also indicative estimates of the sales and market share; Standard and Poor's Corporate Description Plus News includes business description of 12,000 public companies, incorporation history, earnings and finances, capitalization summary, stocks and bond data; Data-Star full-text market research reports. Focus Market Research is also available here, which includes Euromonitor, ICC Keynote Report, Investext, Frost and Sullivan, European Pharmaceutical Market Research and Freedonia Industry and Business Report.

2. **Based on storage and recovery mechanisms:** Another useful way of classifying databases is based on their method of storage and retrieval.

- **Online databases:** These can be accessed in real time directly from the producers of the database or through a vendor. Examples include ABI/Inform, EBSCO and Emerald.
- **CD-ROM databases:** The technology of the portable devices for storing and retrieving information, has made the job of the researcher much simpler. The main advantage of CD-ROM over online access is that there are no time or physical access issues involved. Secondly, the financial implications are also one-time, during purchase, the most powerful CD-ROM applications usually are sold by an annual subscription or a one-time fee for an unlimited data access. Typically, the user receives a disk with updated information each week, month or quarter. Almost all the reference and source databases that are available online are also available on CD-ROM.

Syndicated data sources

Among the largest and most frequently used external information sources are syndicated sources. They are most actively used in marketing research studies,

Syndicated service agencies are organizations which collect organization or product-cateogy specific data from a regular consumer base.

though there is substantial applicability in other areas as well. Syndicated service agencies are organizations that collect organization/product-category-specific data from a regular consumer base and create a common pool of data that can be used by multiple buyers, for their individual purpose. They are also referred to as standardized data sources, the reason being that the process remains structured and the format is designed on the basis of the industry being studies and is not specific to any organization in that industry or sector.

There are different ways to classify syndicate sources. Either they can be classified on the basis of the unit of analysis, i.e., households/consumers or organizations. The second classification is based upon the method of data collection, i.e., from one time surveys, or longitudinal purchase and media panels, or electronic scanner services. Most consumer goods companies require insights into their existing or potential consumer's mind to gauge the acceptance or rejection of their product offering. Some of the widely used syndicate sources related with the behavior and consumption patterns are discussed in brief below.

Surveys are one-time assessments conducted on a large representative respondent base to measure psychographics and lifestyles of the incumbents.

1. **Surveys:** Surveys are usually one-time assessments conducted on a large representative respondent base. These are generally conducted to measure psychographics and lifestyles of the incumbents. In India, a number of agencies like Technopak and AC Nielsen carry out such surveys. Popular news channels like NDTV and the famous Forbes magazine surveys are of a similar nature.

   Surveys are also undertaken to measure the effectiveness of advertising in print and electronic media. This measure of effectiveness becomes extremely critical in the case of TV advertising. The evaluations can be done at home or in a simulated environment. The viewers are shown the commercials and then asked to provide insights about preferences related to the product being advertised and the commercial itself.

   However, the data is not free from certain limitations, the most important being stagnancy in terms of both time and the respondent group that is studied. Thus, taking it as population-wide phenomena is not possible and secondly, the applicability of the results is also mostly topical. Another limitation is that the researcher has to rely primarily upon the respondents' self-reports. There is a gap between what people say and what they actually do. Fallacies might occur because of a poor recall or because the respondent gave socially desirable responses.

   Some interesting surveys that can have bearing on the formulating or modification in existing business strategies are the voter and public opinion polls that are published in Times magazine by Yankelovich's surveys. The company also comes out with a **Yankelovich MONITOR** that is an annual survey on changing social values. Similar polls are conducted by ORG, IMRB, C-FORE, etc. in India and are published in national dailies and magazines. Popular surveys are those related to management institutes that rate the business-school based on the perceptions of the various stakeholders.

2. **Consumer purchase panels:** Sometimes, to authenticate the primary or study-specific data collected on a small scale, it is wise to support the findings by information obtained from the structured panel data. As discussed in chapter 3, panels are actually conducted to collect information for a longitudinal design. These are relatively stable group of respondents; these could be individuals, household groups, or companies who are studied over specific time periods with a stipulated measuring time and parameter to be analyzed. The essential feature of a panel is that the respondent unit needs to maintain a record of its purchase activities.

3. **Household purchase panels:** These selected respondent groups specifically record certain identified purchases, generally related to household products and groceries. Either this is done through an auditor, who regularly and periodically visits the panel member to record the purchases or the person can self-record. One of the most trusted and widely-used panels are IMRB household panels. These are carefully constructed with the unit of analysis being the decision maker for grocery products. This is done across segments and follows a disproportionate stratified sampling plan. The person maintains a log of the purchase in terms of product category, brand, pack size, number of units and special offers. This serves as a useful base for targeting and predicting consumer preferences.
   - **Diary panels:** Earlier, this was done manually in a diary provided by the recording agency. This followed a particular prescribed format and was extremely easy to maintain. These panels provide critical information used by manufacturers and marketers to forecast the probable sales, manage demand and supply, estimate market position, evaluate brand loyalty and brand switching behaviour and to profile the heavy users as well as non-users. Since the data is periodic in nature, it can also be used to measure the impact of various alterations made in the product or promotion mix. This was used as the input for a specified quarter for the products being recorded. However, the problem with this method was that it was dependent on the respondent's effort; in case there was a fallacy in recording or lapse, the inferences might change drastically.
   - **Home scan panels:** With the advent of technology, now the diary has been replaced by an electronic recorder and the records can be submitted online. The household panel member uses a hand held scanner to scan all bar coded products purchased and bought home from market outlets. Generally, these service providers compensate the panelists for their effort with cash or gifts in kind.

Media panels make use of different kinds of electronic equipment to automatically record the consumer viewing behaviour.

4. **Media-based standardized services:** A very popular and important syndicated, standardized sources are those related to the information related to media exposure and measurement. This helps organizations measure the effectiveness of their existing communication plans and also for planning ahead.
5. **Readership surveys:** To effectively work out a media mix and decide about the media vehicles to be used for the advertising campaign one needs to be fully conversant with the media habits of the different segments of the population.
6. **National readership survey:** It is one such syndicate source (refer to Table 5.2 for a snapshot). This was an independent survey conducted by ORG and IMRB; however, it was merged with the **Indian Readership Survey** and is today published as Indian Readership Survey under the auspices of Media Research users Council.
   - **Source and respondent base:** It is conducted by HANSA research and is the largest and most comprehensive readership survey across the world with a respondent based of 256,000 respondents. It is conducted over 1178 towns and 2894 villages. The report is compiled for readership and viewing related to newspapers, radio, cinema and TV programs, at city, state, zonal and all India level. It also provides extensive information related to consumption of various consumer goods, mostly in the FMCG (fast moving consumer goods) section.
   - **Methodology and analysis:** Once the fieldwork is accomplished the data is weighed against the census data collected for the entire population of India. Thus the readership and consumption habits are extrapolated to the population.

- **Usage:** The media habits are extremely useful for any company, whether FMCG or otherwise in designing their promotional plan for the targeted population. And since there is a standardized procedure available one can design plans for a longer duration as well. The readership data can also be used for identifying test marketing and targeted promotional plans.

  IMRB also comes out with a specific survey about the reading habits of executives and professionals in India (**BRS-Businessmen's Readership Survey**). It has the data base of approximately 9000 readers across 12 major metros and mini-metros across the country. MARG also does study about the media habits of young readers in its **Children Readership Survey (CMS).** This covers not only publications but also TV viewing and cinema habits of young children.

  NOP World's **Starch Readership Survey** does not only indicate the readership but are based on interview data and indicates what exactly the reader saw and read the advertisement.

  There are different categories of readership from:

  1. Saw and noted
  2. Saw and associated with the advertised brand
  3. Saw and read partly (remember portions of the ad.)
  4. Saw and recall most (remember 75% of the ad.)

  The Starch report gives ad ranks and also analyzes and presents the impact of advertisement size, placement, color, visual vs verbal content, etc. Starch also has another metrics called **Adnorms**; this is interesting as it provides the readership by the type and size of advertisement appearing in the *Business Week*. Thus the advertiser can also see the impact of advertising and creativity on the viewer and plan better.

7. **Television rating indices:** These are special kind of syndicate research services related to television viewership behaviour.

   - **The information provided:** Panels are created for collecting information related to promotion and advertising. The task of the media panel is to make use of different kinds of electronic equipment to automatically record consumer viewing behaviour. This, then, serves various needs of the marketer. The **Nielsen Television Index (NTI)**, a product source from AC Nielsen, is one of the most reliable and user-friendly data sources.
   - **The method of data computation:** The recording in these cases is not done manually but with a device called 'people meter.' First, the agency selects the respondents representing the different sections of society according to the established criteria, next to each television in the household this device is attached. The recording is done on two parameters—first which channel and which programme is being watched, for how long and secondly, it also records who is viewing the programme. The information at the end of each day is daily uploaded via telephone lines on a central processing unit and is analyzed through a predesigned programme on multiple parameters and this information is made available to all the prescribing channels in the television industry.

     From the information collected, Nielsen is able to assess the number and other segment details of the household/individuals viewing a particular television show. Thus, macro-level and micro-level details of the consumer audience can be derived.
   - **Data usage**: These indices are then used to calculate the television rating points (TRP). The TRPs are calculated by other agencies such as IMRB as well. These indices are used by the channels to compute advertising rates for

the advertisements to be aired during specific shows. It can also be used by various companies like Unilever, Pepsico, Cadburys and others for their media planning.

8. **Radio listeners' indices:** The reach of one of the cheapest and most effective passive media vehicle is the radio. One of the oldest and most respected and comprehensive radio listeners' index is the **Arbitron ratings.** It involves selecting members from randomly generated phone numbers, to ensure that unlisted numbers are also part of the panel. These members were provided a dairy to record the radio channel they had listened to. However these are now replaced by a PPM (Portable People meter) that automatically records the station listened to. Arbitron data helps the companies identify the time of listening and in case there is a station which has more in car listening or commuter listening a company can identify where it wants to slot its radio jingles secondly the station itself might benefit in terms of the kind of program, traffic or sports or news information that it wants to deliver to its listeners.

9. **Internet and multimedia services:** A related product category that Nielsen has gone into is the usage of Internet services. Nielsen/NetRatings Inc. (www.netratings.com) collects usage data from Internet using households and work users. The service was launched in 1999. The sites frequented are recorded and the report gives comprehensive details on ranking by sites, traffic details on the sites, time of visit and frequency of the sites visited and now with so much e-commerce happening, it also tracks the trading and purchase patterns with consumer details, transaction time and payment mode. The effectiveness of banner advertising and interactive content is also reported. This service is also available with IMRB.

    However, the reports are not without errors, the foremost being misrepresentation and sample group response bias. The panels might cover the diversity of the consumer. This problem is further aggravated by false recording, refusal to respond and mortality of the panel members (some members might leave the panel and be replaced by some other members, thus the buying patterns might change significantly). Another problem is that a product like toothpaste or a beverage might be purchased by different people in the household, but the recording is done by only one. Thus, what might be interpreted as brand switching, might simply be different recording made by some one else who bought a different drink.

    There also contemporary media usage which is highly effective in reaching a younger and more experimental audience which is also being actively recorded as standardized syndicate sources. **Soundscan** records the respondents' behavior regarding the downloading of music from various online platforms. **Bookscan** and **videoscan** track the downloading of pre recorded videos and books form online platforms.

10. **Scanner devices and individual source systems:** To overcome the problems of panel data, a new service is provided by research agencies through electronic scanner devices. This recording innovation has considerably revolutionized the standardized sources of data recording. Today, almost all manufacturers identify their produced lots by bar codes, and therefore, every merchandise that reaches a retail outlet necessarily has a bar code. This, when passed over a laser scanner, optically reads and records the bar-coded description (the Universal Product Code or UPC) printed on each package. This sensing links the product to the current price of the same stored in the attached computer and this linkage then delivers the sales receipt. The slip records the time of the transaction as well as the total value of all the products purchased by the consumer. Information

printed on the sales slip includes descriptions as well as prices of all the items purchased. Any coupon redemptions and transaction mode can also be tested to measure the consumer response.

There are different kinds of scanner data available, namely sales volume tracking data, scanner panels—and scanner panels with cable television. Sales volume tracking data simply provides information on the product/category movement on the brand purchased, size, price and variant—like flavour. These are simply based on sales receipts. If the information on shelf placement, cooperative advertising or point of sales display is also recorded in the computer memory, it is possible to measure the impact on the product sales as well. AC Nielsen tracks over 2,00,000 stores across more than 65 countries through their scan tracking services.

Data collected from a scanner record helps to draw a consumer profile specific for a product category and brand.

The scanner panels involve giving some selected households and their members an ID card that can be read by the electronic scanner of the stores where they go to buy their provisions. The individual just needs to give his/her scanner card on the billing counter, so that the entire basket gets recorded each time he/she purchases. Thus, this is easier as there is no need to record purchases as the shopping record for that individual can be built more accurately and can be subjected to record and analysis almost immediately. There are also home scan panels where, selected panelists are provided with hand devices which can scan and record once the members run it over their purchases. This information, like the electronic diaries, is then transmitted onto the central unit at Nielsen through telephone lines. Thus, the data helps to draw a consumer profile specific for a product category and brand. The response to promotions as well as buying patterns is critical data for manufacturers and traders in devising their marketing strategies as well as measuring the effectiveness of the current one.

An alternative to household scanner panel is one that provides the panel members with specific cable connections. Then to test the response and impact of different commercials they deliberately manipulate the airing by 'splitting' the members into two or multiple groups and target different advertisements at different time slots and across programmes to measure the variation in impact. Thus, it serves as a controlled environment which can be made available to companies to conduct controlled experiments in a representative setting.

During an **audit**, a designated company representative/auditor visits the retail and wholesale outlets registered with the research agency and physically makes a note of the existing product records.

Retail and home scanners can be used for tracking product sales, impact of various price points, monitoring the supply chain and managing stocks. Scanner panels with cable TV may be used for concept and new product testing, advertising decisions and evaluating the effectiveness of the promotional strategy, as they provide a readily-available experimental and yet a natural testing environment . The disadvantage is, as with the diary panels, there could be a skewed representation. Secondly, it provides bare product movement without the extremely valuable qualitative inputs. The third issue is the geographic representation of the findings, especially in rural and interior belts where scanning and electronic recording of purchase patterns are slightly difficult.

Institutional syndicated data

These are of the following types:

- **Retail store audits:** These are typical cyclic data and usually require human auditing and recording. The sales cycle or recording usually matches the purchase patterns in that industry and the sales are tracked with reference to brands, sizes, package types, flavors or variants, etc. The formula used for this recording is as follows:

Sales = (Beginning inventory + purchase made/deliveries) – ending inventory.

The researcher also records, alongside the following data any general or brand or retailer specific promotion or activity that might be happening at the recording time. This would help to explain any variations in the buying pattern due to these extraneous factors. This data can be used to then calculate market and brand share as well as for forecasting future demand.

The ORG (Operation Research Group) publishes two monthly reports—one on consumer products (50 consumer products) and another on pharmaceutical products (9000 brands). These are collected on a pan-India fixed retailer sample base (refer to Table 5.2 for snapshot). Similarly, AC Nielsen publishes Nielsen Retail index for four major reporting groups—grocery products, drugs, alcoholic beverages and other merchandise. IMRB (Indian Market Research Bureau) publishes *Market PULSE*, which is the retail audit report for 22 consumer products.

- **Wholesalers' audits:** Another audit service provided for a few segments are whole sale audits, these measure warehouse movement. Participating operators, include, wholesalers, super and hyper markets and frozen-food warehouses. These account for a huge volume of the product availability in the area.

This data can be used to compose the market structure, along with market share; competitive activity; channel effectiveness and inventory control; managing and developing sales promotion plans and last but not the least, forecasting product movement.

Audits, however, are extremely superficial in terms of predicting consumer sentiments and satisfaction. Another disadvantage is that all markets are not covered by the retail boundary. Also, the data is available at fixed time period and the minor movements, which might serve as significant predictors of market dynamics, are sometimes lost.

In this chapter, the intention was to only provide a flavour of the huge mass of information that is available in a well documented and standardized form. Sometimes, the economies of scale can advocate the use of these data sources to provide reasonably accurate inferences for the researcher investigator. And as we have seen with the advent of technological advancement the accuracy and collection is extremely quick and exhaustive at the same time.

CONCEPT CHECK

1. What are the primary internal sources of data?
2. Classiffy external data sources.
3. Write a short note om computer-stored data.
4. What is meant by institutional syndicated data?

SUMMARY

- To analyse a typical management research problem, the only base available to a researcher is information. This information in the language of research is called data. The researcher has access to two major sources of this data. The data collected might be original and project specific as in primary sources or it might have been collected, compiled and published by some one else and the relevant information is used by the researcher for his study. This source is termed as secondary data. This is the source discussed in detail in this chapter.
- The secondary information that is collected by the researcher can be put to multiple uses. This could be for formulating the research question or for honing the research hypothesis. Respondent population's address or statistics could have been compiled as a database and this can be used for defining the selected sample. The prior studies or information sources could also be used in designing the primary instrument to be used for the study. Lastly, the data could be used to validate the findings from the primary sources. Thus, the secondary sources are useful, fast and cost-effective way of testing and achieving the study objectives.
- However, there might be certain drawbacks of using them. The accuracy and applicability of the sources might be questionable. Thus, it is advised that a methodology, accuracy and recency-temporal authentication be conducted before using the information compiled through a secondary source.

- ❖ Secondary data could be collected and compiled within the organization/industry. These are termed as internal sources of data. These might include the company history, employee data and records, company policies, sales and financial records as well as other publications like newspaper and articles.
- ❖ When data collected by an outside source, these are termed as external data sources. These are further divided into published sources—both government and non-government sources. These carry complete details of the methodology and respondent base. Thus, it is possible to authenticate and use the information collected with confidence.
- ❖ User-friendly, fast and cost-effective secondary sources are computer-based sources available today. Ease of use and easy availability are making this source the most useful information base for researchers across the globe and across management areas.
- ❖ The third kind of secondary sources are volumes/databases available from multiple research agencies as their respective products. They are common data pools that can be used with ease by multiple buyers based on their individual requirement. The syndicate sources are available on the basis of individual units or organisational units. The information is updated over fixed time intervals and is usually high in accuracy as it is compiled over large and representative samples.

KEY TERMS

- Company records
- Data collection methods
- Data mining
- Data warehousing
- Electronic data sources
- Employee records
- External data sources
- Government data sources
- Household panels
- Internal data sources
- Non-government data sources
- Primary methods
- Published data
- Research authentication
- Retail audits
- Sales data
- Secondary methods
- Syndicated data sources
- Television rating performance (TRP)
- Wholesale audits

CHAPTER REVIEW QUESTIONS

Objective Type Questions

State whether the following statements are true (T) or false (F).

1. The data that is always collected first in a research study is called primary data.
2. Secondary data is not always specific to the research problem under study.
3. Census data is an example of primary data source.
4. Sampling frame of the respondent population is an example of secondary data.
5. Primary data methods have a significant time and cost advantage over secondary data.
6. Cross-check verification by conducting a short pilot study at times is carried out to authenticate the secondary data collected.
7. Cash register receipt is an example of external secondary data sources.
8. Annual demand forecast can be made by using sales invoices of company salesmen.
9. Customer grievance data available with the company is an important source of primary data.
10. Computerized records of company information are called data warehouses.
11. The process of organizing this stored data, as mentioned in Question (X) is called CRM.
12. Statistical abstracts of India are prepared by the Central Statistical Organization.
13. Director General of Commercial Intelligence prepares the White Paper on National Income.
14. Consumer price index is prepared by the Ministry of Commerce and Industry.
15. Ministry of Social Welfare prepares the National Sample Survey (NSS).
16. Poor's Statistical Services are a government publication on the people below the poverty line.

17. SIAM is an agency that provides data about all service industries in India.
18. NRS refers to National Readership Survey.
19. Emerald and EBSCO are important online databases available to the researcher.
20. Net Ratings Inc. is a syndicate data source prepared by IMRB.

Conceptual Questions

1. Distinguish between secondary and primary methods of data collection. Is it possible to use secondary data methods as substitutes of primary methods? Justify your answer with suitable illustrations.
2. How can secondary data be classified? Elaborate on each type with suitable examples.
3. How can one establish the authenticity of the information collected by secondary sources? Are there clear quality checks that a researcher must be aware about?
4. 'Majority of the researches make use of primary sources of data and secondary data sources do not really contribute to a scientific enquiry.' Do you agree/disagree with this statement? Explain.
5. 'Technology and computer applications have been a major boost to syndicated data sources'. Explain the assumption made in the statement with suitable examples.
6. What are syndicated data sources? Elaborate on the various types of sources available, giving a suitable example for each type.
7. Distinguish between internal and external sources of data collection. In what situations would you recommend the usage of one over the other?
8. Distinguish between:
   (a) Purchase panels and media panels
   (b) Government and non-government data sources
   (c) Individual and industrial data sources

Application Questions

1. You plan to export semi-precious stones from Jaipur to countries like:
   (a) USA
   (b) Canada
   (c) European Union
   What would be the nature of information required by you? How would secondary data sources help you here?
2. You have your own Sonpari Productions and have recently come up with a children's programme called 'Hindustan', it is all about knowing your country. You need to take a decision on:
   (a) Which channel to approach?
   (b) What should be the time slot?
   (c) What should be the advertisement rates?
   (d) Who would be the target audience?
   (e) How should you communicate to them about your programme?
   What would be the nature of the information required by you? How would secondary data sources help you here?
3. You have been approached by Rohit Bal, who wants to start an economy line and would like to know:
   (a) How is the fashion market composed?
   (b) What is the profile of the avid fashion followers?
   (c) What are the potential segments you can convert into fashion followers?
   (d) What is their buying behaviour like?
   (e) How can you approach and market to this segment?
   (f) Would it be lucrative to move there?
   What would be the nature of information required by you? How would secondary data sources help you here?
4. Rajeev Mulchandani has decided to become a freelance financial advisor and advise his clients on:
   (a) Share options
   (b) Insurance schemes

What would be the nature of information that would assist him in the task? How would secondary data sources help him here?

5. Meera Sanyal has decided to open a placement agency. Kindly advice her on:
   (a) What would be the ideal location for her setup?
   (b) Who should she target—in terms of both individual and corporate clients?
   (c) What databases would come in useful here?

   What would be the nature of information that would assist her in the task? How would secondary data sources help her here?
6. Visit the website of IMRB (**www.imrb.com**) and AC Nielsen (**www.acnielsen.com**) and write a descriptive account of the syndicate data sources available with them.
7. The Census 2010 used a methodology that is far superior to the earlier census. Evaluate the new versus the old by visiting the website and comment on the improvements made. Do you think this could have been further improved? How?

CASE 5.1

THE PINK DILEMMA

The Indian television industry has seen an exponential growth since the satellite television first came to India. Today, though cable penetration is only about 70 per cent (according to various industry estimates), this class of people watching cable tv is defined as the 'consuming class' in India. By 2002, the share of cable and satellite television was 86.9 per cent of the total television advertising as against a meagre 31.3 per cent in 1994. Hindi general entertainment television is the fuel for growth in the television industry with a 46.8 per cent share of the total viewership and an even higher 57.4 per cent share of the total advertising revenue. Sony Entertainment Television is a key player in this space and has been a consistent and strong number two behind Star Plus, which has been the undisputed leader since July 2000. In India, most homes are single-TV homes. Hindi is the preferred language for consuming entertainment across India (except the four southern states) and that makes the Hindi general entertainment television an intensely competitive space. It consists of five players. Star Plus has been the undisputed leader since July 2000 and has significantly consolidated its position thereafter. In September 2003, Star Plus had nearly five times as much viewership as its nearest rival Sony Entertainment Television. The other contenders are Zee TV, Sahara TV and SAB TV. The key factor is that during primetime (specifically in the 9–10 pm slot) which is the focus of this case, the females influence the choice of channel to view.

Sony Entertainment Television dominated the 9–10 pm band, with two of its leading shows, Kkusum and Kutumb until mid 2002 after which the 4 daily shows of Star Plus took over.

Despite several high profile attempts to regain lost audiences, Sony Entertainment Television's share in this band continued to erode. Star Plus had established a clear dominance over Sony Entertainment Television. (Star Plus average range of Television Ratings (TVRs) is approximately 13.2 TVRs, as compared to Sony Entertainment Television's 1.3 TVRs). Besides, Sony Entertainment Television was now perceived as a 'me-too' to Star Plus.

Sony Entertainment Television realized that women were the primary target audience who could get eyeballs for the channel. The challenge, therefore, was to create and sell a distinct viewing alternative, going beyond the clichéd family dramas with storylines revolving around family conflicts and kitchen politics which is the predominant fare on general entertainment channels today.

QUESTIONS

1. What could be the probable sources of establishing the market share of the channel that are used in the case? Can one rely on the authenticity of Sony's dominance? Why/why not?
2. To help Sony achieve its target of understanding what Indian women want, what secondary data sources would you suggest?

Answers to Objective Type Questions

1. False	2. True	3. False	4. True	5. False
6. True	7. False	8. True	9. False	10. True
11. False	12. True	13. False	14. True	15. False
16. False	17. False	18. True	19. True	20. False

REFERENCES

Aaker, D A, V Kumar and G S Day. *Marketing Research*, 7th edn. Singapore: John Wiley & Sons, 2000.

Denscombe, M. *The Good Research Guide*. Buckingham: Open University Press, 1998.

Dochartaigh, N O. *The Internet Research Handbook: A Practical Guide for Students and Researchers in the Social Sciences*. London: Sage, 2002.

Ghauri, P and K Gronhaugh. *Research Methods in Business Studies: A Practical Guide*. 2nd edn. Harlow: Prentice Hall, 2002.

Jacob, H. "Using Published Data: Errors and Remedies," in *Research Practice,* edited by M S Lewis-Beck, (London, Sage and Toppan Publishing, 1994) 339–89.

Kervin, J B. *Methods for Business Research*. 2nd edn. New York: HarperCollins, 1999.

Patzer, G L. *Using Secondary Data in Market Research. United States and World-wide*. Westport, CT: Quorum Books, 1996.

Stewart, D W and M A Kamins. *Secondary Research: Information Sources and Methods*. 2nd edn. Newbury Park, CA: Sage, 1993.

BIBLIOGRAPHY

Bhattacharyya, D K. *Research Methodology*. New Delhi: Excel Books, 2006.

Boyd, Harper W Jr, Ralph Westfall and Stanley F Stasch, *Marketing Research: Text and Cases*. 7th edn. Richard D Irwin, Inc., 2002.

Green P E and T S Donald. *Research for Marketing Decisions*. 4th edn. New Delhi: Prentice Hall of India Private Ltd, 1986.

Malhotra, N K. *Marketing Research–An Applied Orientation*. New Delhi: Pearson Education, 3rd edn., 2002.

Pannerselvam, R. *Research Methodology*. New Delhi: Prentice Hall of India Pvt. Ltd, 2004.

Easwaran, Sunanda and Sharmila J Singh. *Marketing Research–Concepts, Practices and Cases*. New Delhi: Oxford University Press, 2006.

6 CHAPTER

Qualitative Methods of Data Collection

Learning Objectives

By the end of the chapter, you should be able to:

1. Identify the situations which would benefit from qualitative information.
2. Distinguish between qualitative and quantitative methods of data collection.
3. Understand the various types of qualitative research methods and the significance of observation as a qualitative method with a clear understanding on how to ensure objectivity in reporting.
4. Understand the conduct and analysis of a focus group discussion.
5. Design and conduct in-depth interviews and ensure objectivity in reporting.
6. Understand qualitative methods, originating in other disciplines, now used actively in business research.

Ritu Kalmadi, editor of Young Indian, was driving down to her office at Bhikaji Cama Place, New Delhi, and was trying to beat the office rush at 10 a.m. She had a meeting with her creative team listed as her first appointment for the day at 11.30 a.m. They had to sit down and freeze the layout of the articles and columns for the new fortnightly magazine of Satrangi publications. The English magazine was targeted towards the 14 to 18-year-olds, typically residing in a metro. The traffic light had just turned red, so Ritu stopped and started thinking about how she would design a winner of a magazine. She had been the editor of a popular women's magazine, so this assignment should not be tough. Her meanderings were broken by the loud blaring of a cacophonic horn. She looked back and saw a young girl of probably 15 or 16 yelling at her from a huge monstrous Scorpio. When Ritu opened her window and pointed towards the signal, the young, purple-streaked girl driver shouted 'So move your jalopy you old cow! I wonder why senile buddhis like you get behind a wheel.' Ritu was aghast. The young girl was probably as old as Manjari, her daughter, so she reprimanded her and said, 'Young lady, mind your language,' to which the reply was 'Shut up and get lost'. Just then the light turned green and the Scorpio brushed dangerously close to her Accent, hooting and whizzing away.

Ritu took her car to the side and sat shaken for a moment. Was this the audience for which Young Indian was meant? Good Heavens! The team did not have a clue. The new-age teenager was beyond comprehension. What were her/his likes and dislikes? Whom did he/she look up to? Why were Roadies and LoveNet such favourite programmes for them? Did they have any kind of value system? What were their fears and insecurities? Was life only Facebook and friends or did these teenagers have any goals in life?

Questions galore and despite having the company of her daughter at home, Ritu was not sure whether she and her team even remotely understood the people for whom they were creating an offering. They required some serious in-depth understanding of the potential reader. Suddenly, she remembered her niece, who was pursuing a masters in psychology, telling her about inkblot tests and something called a TAT, which unravelled the personality of individuals. Maybe a sensitive analysis that attempted to create a typical persona of this new Indian teenager would help design a periodical specially meant for them.

Ritu started her car and realized that she still had a lot to learn. There would be more work required but it was also going to be exciting and challenging to unravel the subjective mysteries of the young mind. She had always swept aside the subconscious and latent explanations of why people act unpredictably, but maybe there was merit in what Sigmund Freud had prophesized. She reached office and sprinted across to the discussion room and opened the door. 'Hi guys! Let's leave the copy and become creative for a while. We need to do a little more subjective and qualitative homework before we surge ahead. This is what I propose we do'.

Ritu is absolutely correct and wise in her approach. Numbers and chemical equations might be fine for predicting rainfalls and genetic constitutions. However, when one needed to strategize and deliver to the human mind, one had to go deeper and understand what makes him/her tick; and the best way to do this is through a qualitative analysis.

As discussed in the last chapter, Primary data source available to the researcher is original, first-hand data. This might be qualitative or quantitative in nature (as shown in Figure 6.1). Qualitative research as an approach contributing to management thought took a very long time to be accepted as such. There was considerable interest generated when in 1825, JB Savarin published *The Physiology of Taste*, where he stated 'Tell me what you eat and I will tell you what you are.' Personality and human emotions and needs were being analysed in the area of organizational behaviour. However, the analysis was usually done by structured, quantitative, measurable techniques. William Henry (1956) with his Thematic Apperception Tests (TAT) provided subjective methods which could be used to analyse and interpret certain reasons behind why

FIGURE 6.1 Classification of qualitative data sources

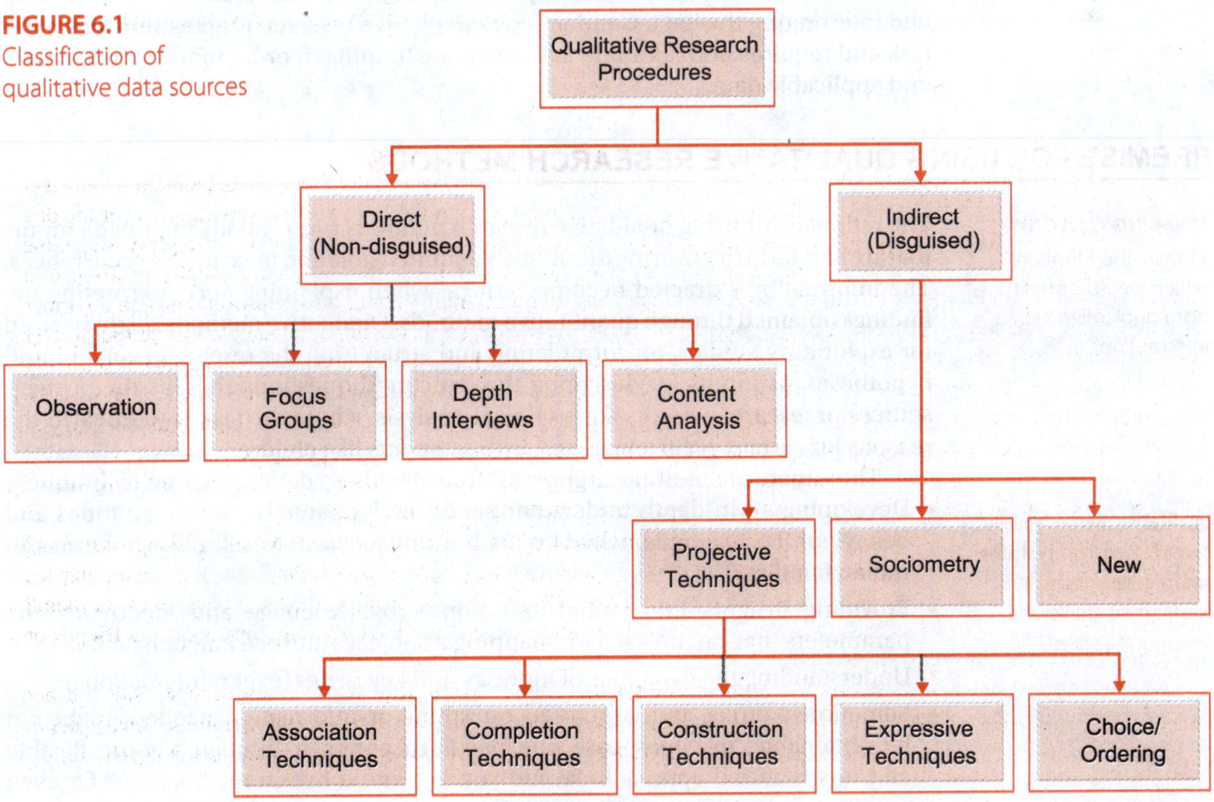

people think and behave in a certain way. This was perceived to have a lot of merit in understanding the employees in an organization and secondly, it could explain how brands were symbolic of their lives. No matter what is the management area one is using a qualitative approach, one has to begin with the most significant proponents of the movement—Glaser and Strauss (1967). In the *Discovery of Grounded Theory*, they challenged the positivists and used an inductive approach (based on simple real life observations) to understand various human and business processes and used these to formulate a formal theory. There have been a number of proponents of the movement who have taken this thought forward, developed and modified the method of capturing this fluid reality and attempted to make sense from the symbolic behaviour and words used by the individuals, organizations, and policy-makers. Locke (2001) an active supporter of the theory, vouches for the use of this theory in the field of management as it is able to make sense of the complexity of the phenomena observed, has realistic usefulness and is especially useful in the new areas where change is constant and the variables are multiple. Thus, the presumption is that there are multiple realities as experienced and interpreted by different people in their own unique fashion.

Qualitative research goes beyond the observable of constructs and variables. The information collected is more in-depth and intensive.

Qualitative research, thus, is presumed to go beyond the observable constructs and variables that are not visible or measurable; rather they have to be deduced by various methods. There are a variety of such methods which will be discussed in detail in this chapter. However, common premise of all these are that they are relatively loosely structured and require a closer dialogue or interaction between the investigator and the respondent. The information collected is more in-depth and intensive and results in rich insights and perspectives than those delivered through a more formal and structured method. However, since the element of subjectivity is high, they require a lot of objectivity on the part of the investigator while collecting and interpreting the data. Conducting a qualitative research is an extremely skillful task and requires both aptitude and adequate training in order to result in valuable and applicable data.

PREMISE FOR USING QUALITATIVE RESEARCH METHODS

LEARNING OBJECTIVE 1
Identify the situations which would benefit from qualitative information.

The rationale for using qualitative research methods is essentially to provide inputs that are helpful in uncovering the motives behind visible and measurable occurrences. The information extracted becomes critical when explaining and interpreting the findings obtained through quantitative methods. Qualitative methods might be used for exploratory studies, for formulating and structuring the research problem and hypotheses, as inputs for designing the structured questionnaires, as the primary sources of research enquiry for a clinical analysis, where the task is to unearth the reasons for certain occurrences and with segments like children.

Qualitative methods might be used for exploratory studies and for gaining an insight into the mind, attitude and behaviour of a subject.

Thus, there are multiple arguments for using these data-collection techniques:

- Developing an in-depth understanding of the individuals, beliefs, attitudes and behaviour. For example, why is it such a difficult task to sell old age homes to Indian families?
- Providing insights into verbal and non-verbal language and identifying the parameters that can be used for mapping a subject's attitude and behaviour.
- Understanding the dynamics of industry and key issues (expert interactions).
- Sometimes, direct and structured questions or information needed might not be obtainable, in which case one needs to obtain it through a more flexible and unstructured approach. Would you get into a live-in relationship? Or even

a relatively simple question like what aspects of your boss do you think need correction?

- Checking how individuals interpret the work-related policies or occurrences or product attributes/message/pricing.
- Getting reactions to ideas and identifying likes/dislikes of human beings.
- Sparking off new ideas and brainstorming. What does a consumer look for in probiotic curd, digestive enzymes or low fat food? Tata's Nano might mean something for a two-wheeler owner and something entirely different for a four-wheeler owner. Based upon the reaction to the car, the company can decide its positioning.
- Certain behaviour seems to be non-comprehensible by the respondent also, in which case the latent motives need to be unearthed through other methods. For example, why do you want to get a tattoo on your arm? Or why do you not take any initiative in a team discussion even when your senior asks you to? The classic example in this case is the half-filled glass, interpreted differently by optimists and pessimists.
- Each individual's organization of reality is unique and his reaction would be uniquely dependent on that. Thus, it becomes critical to make sense of this through an unstructured and ambiguous stimulus (Kerlinger, 1986).

DISTINGUISHING QUALITATIVE FROM QUANTITATIVE DATA METHODS

LEARNING OBJECTIVE 2
Distinguish between qualitative and quantitative methods of data collection.

To comprehend the distinction between the two approaches, one needs to appreciate the contribution of each to the research process one intends to undertake in order to address the research questions (Refer Chapter 1).

Research Objective

Qualitative research is used to explore, describe or understand a certain phenomenon. It is loosely structured and open to interpretations.

Qualitative research: It can be used to explore, describe or understand the reasons for a certain phenomenon. For example, to understand what a low-cost car means to an Indian consumer, this kind of investigation would be required.

Quantitative research: When the data to be studied needs to be quantified and subjected to a suitable analysis in order to generalize the findings to the population at large or to be able to quantify and explain and predict the occurrence of a certain phenomenon. For example, to measure the purchase intentions for Nano as a function of the demographic variables of income, family size and distance travelled, one would need to use quantitative methods.

Research Design

Qualitative research: The design is exploratory or descriptive, loosely structured and open to interpretation and presumptions.

Quantitative research: The design is structured and has a measurable set of variables with a presumption about testing them.

Sampling Plan

Qualitative research: Only a small sample is manageable as the information required needs to be extracted by a flexible and sometimes lengthy procedure.

Quantitative research: Large representative samples can be measured and the data collected can be based upon a shorter time span with a larger number. Chances of error in extrapolating it to a larger population are less and measurable.

Data Collection

Qualitative research: The data collection is in-depth and collected through a more interactive and unstructured approach. Data collected includes both the verbal and non-verbal responses. Methodology requires a well-trained investigator.

Quantitative research: The data collected is formatted and structured. The nature of interrogation is more of stimulus-response type. The data collected is usually verbal and well-articulated. Interrogation does not need extensive training on the part of the investigator.

Data Analysis

Qualitative research: Interpretation of data is textual and usually non-statistical.

Quantitative research: Interpretation of data entails various levels of statistical testing.

Research Deliverables

Qualitative research: The initial and ultimate objective is to explain the findings from more structured sources.

Quantitative research: The findings must be conclusive and demonstrate clear indications of the decisive action and generalizations.

Quantitative research predicts the occurrence of a certain phenomenon. It is formatted and structured and usually conclusive.

Before we discuss the various methods of qualitative nature, it is essential to remember that even though the information obtained is rich and extensive, it is diagnostic and not evaluative in nature, thus, should not be used for generalizations on to larger respondent groups. Secondly, because of the nature of the conduction, they always cover smaller sample groups or individuals. Thus, they are indicative rather than predictive in nature. And lastly, they indicate the direction of respondent sentiments and should not be mistaken for the strength of the reactions. Thus, what is advocated is that the two approaches—qualitative and quantitative—are not to be treated as the extreme ends of a theoretical continuum. A business researcher should take them as complementary and supportive in order to get measurable as well as humanistic inputs for taking informed decisions.

CONCEPT CHECK	1. Elaborate on the basic premise for using qualitative research methods. 2. Differentiate between qualitative and quantitative data collection methods.

METHODS OF QUALITATIVE RESEARCH

LEARNING OBJECTIVE 3
Understand the various types of qualitative research methods and the significance of observation as a qualitative method with a clear understanding on how to ensure objectivity in the reporting.

The researcher has a whole range of methods available to him for conducting qualitative research. Most of these have been derived from other branches of social sciences and have been adapted to suit the needs of the business researcher. They can be either directed towards the manifest or the apparent, like the observation method, group discussions and structured interviews. These can be conducted with relative ease and the analysis is also not very difficult. On the other hand, they could be directed towards the latent, and the conduction and interpretation requires considerable skill and training. Projective techniques and semiotics are some examples of this approach.

Observation Method

This direct method of data collection is one of the most appropriate methods to use in case of descriptive research. Yet, it most often gets ignored as it appears too simplistic a procedure. Observation is a skill that most of us use consciously and unconsciously in our everyday life as well. It might be carried out in a naturalistic environment where there are no control elements or it might be carried out in a simulated environment under certain controlled conditions. There are arguments in support of both the approaches. The task of the observer-investigator is not to question or discuss with the individuals whose behaviour is being studied. The event being observed might involve a live observation and reporting or it might involve observing and inferring from a recording of the event. Thus, the method of observation involves viewing and recording individuals, groups, organizations or events in a scientific manner in order to collect valuable data related to the topic under study.

In a **structured format**, the nature of content to be recorded and the format and broad areas of recording are predetermined.

The mode of observation could be in a standardized and structured format. Here, the nature of content to be recorded and the format and the broad areas of recording are predetermined. Thus, the observer's bias is reduced and the authenticity and reliability of the information collected is higher. For example, Fisher Price toys carry out an observational study whenever they come out with a new toy. The observer is supposed to record the appeal of the toy for a child, i.e., how often does he/she pick it up from a collection of the toys available. What is the attention span in terms of how long is it able to engage the child? Is there any safety issue with the toy? What was the reaction of the child while/after playing with the toy? Thus, for a clearly defined information need, in terms of parameters to be noted, it is an extremely useful and a non-intrusive method. This method is useful for cross-sectional descriptive studies.

In an **unstructured observation**, there is a lack of clearly defined objectives and the chances of an observer's biases remain high.

The antithesis of this is called the *unstructured observation*. Here, the observer is supposed to make a note of whatever he understands as relevant for the research study. This kind of approach is more useful in exploratory studies where there is a lack of clearly-defined objectives and one is still trying to identify what parameters need to be investigated and the nature of relationship between these and the causal variable. Since it lacks structure, the chances of observer's bias are high as the observer has his/her own presumptions about the situation being observed. To overcome the shortcomings of this, one generally has multiple observers for the same situation in order to get different perspectives about the same instance. An example of this is the observation of consumer experiences at a service location—this could be a bank, a restaurant or a doctor's clinic to get an insight into the intangible needs and individual behaviour of service personnel. It could give clear indications of the elements that might create an unhappy experience or might lead to customer delight. In this case, giving clear mandates about what to observe might miss out on important elements of the service experience which might be critical in delivering a superior value. However, one needs to remember that the observation is always of behavioural variables, assumptions about the affective or cognitive element impacting the behaviour have to be assumed and hypothesized and later validated through consumer response through other methods.

However, it is critical here to understand that the researcher must have a preconceived plan to capture the observations made. It is not to be treated as a blank sheet where the observer reports what he sees. The aspects to be observed might be clearly listed as in an audit form, or they could be indicative areas on which the observation is to be made. Presented here is an observation sheet that was used in the organic food products study. This sheet includes both an audit form and broad indicative areas.

OBSERVATION SHEET: ORGANIC RETAILER

Name of Store: Location: Size of Store:

Store personnel (number):

Store personnel (attitude):

Store atmosphere:

Approximate footfalls
Weekdays: weekends

Percentage of conversions
Weekdays: weekends

Please mark (✓) the items that you stock in your store

Product	Stock	Product	Stock
TEA		CEREALS	
Organic Tea		Amaranth	
Flavoured		Amaranth Popped	
SNACKS		Amaranth Breakfast Cereal	
Cookies (Ragi/Ramdana)		Jhangara	
Bread		Ragi	
Namkins		Ragi Atta	
SPICES		Maize	
Chilli Powder		Maize Atta	
Chilli Red		Wheat Atta	
Dhania Powder		Wheat Dalia	
Dhania Seeds		Wheat Puffed	
Haldi Whole		PULSES	
Haldi Powder		Arhar Dal	
Mustard Powder		Bhatt Dal	
Sesame/Til		Kulath Dal	
Zeera		Masoor Dal	
PRESERVES		Moong Sabut	
Mango Pickle		Moong Dal	
Garlic Pickle		Kabuli Channa	
Mixed Pickle		Naurangi Dal	
Amla Chutney		Rajma (Brown/White)	
Ginger Ale		Rajma (Chitkabra)	
Burans Squash		Rajma (Mix)	
Lemon Squash		Rajma (Red Small)	

Product	Stock	Product	Stock
Malta Squash		Urad Dal	
Pudina Squash		Urad Whole	
		RICE	
ANY OTHER		Basmati Dehradun	
		Rice Khanda	
		Rice Rikhwa	
		Rice Unpolished	
		Rice Hansraj	
		Rice Red	
		Rice Kasturi	
		Rice Kelas	
		Rice Punjab Basmati	
		Rice Ramjavan	
		Rice Sela	

In a **disguised observation**, the respondent has no knowledge regarding him/her being under observation or study. It is quite the opposite in an undisguised observation.

Another way of distinguishing observations is the level of respondent consciousness about the scrutiny. This might be *disguised*; here the observation is done without the respondent's knowledge who has no idea that he/she is being observed. The advantage of this method is that since the respondent does not know, one is able to record the natural manner in which the person behaves and interacts with others in his environment. Sometimes this may be accomplished by having observers who are a part of the group or are employees of the organization. It is also possible to use other devices like a one way mirror or a hidden camera or a recorder. The only disadvantage is the privacy issue, as this is ethically an intrusion of an individual's right to privacy. On the other hand, the knowledge that the person is under observation can be conveyed to the respondent, and this is *undisguised observation*. There are different perspectives on the degree of artifice of the behaviour. The proponents state that the influence of the observer's presence is brief and does not really have any effect on the natural way a person behaves. While the other school of thought is that it distorts an individual's behaviour pattern drastically. The decision to choose one over the other depends upon the nature of the study. Whenever the objective is to study the latent, subconscious or an intangible aspect of human behaviour, it is recommended that one opts for disguised approach. However, when the observation is accepted as non-intrusive as it is a part of the process, for example in a group discussion or a formal meeting or moving around in a retail store under a close circuit TV surveillance, the undisguised approach can be used.

The observation method can also be distinguished on the basis of the setting in which the information is being collected. This could be natural observation, which as the name suggests, is carried out in real time locations, for example the observations of how employees interact with each other during breaks. On the other hand, it could be an *artificial* or *simulated* environment in which the respondent is to be observed. This is actively done in the armed forces where stress tests are carried out to measure an individual's tolerance level.

Thus, evaluating the reactions of respondents to the phenomena or strategies under study can be carried out at a smaller scale in a contrived situation, as these would help predict the behaviour likely to occur, in the actual situation. However, when the object is to study true reactions and not the supposed ones, natural observation is recommended.

There is a more recent differentiation that has come about and this has been effected through alternative technologically-advanced gadgets replacing human observations. Thus, the observation could be done by a human observer or a mechanical device.

In the **human observation technique**, the investigator is not supposed to contribute to the situation being observed. He must not send any verbal/non-verbal cues to the respondent and should remain neutral.

1. **Human observation:** As the name suggests, this technique involves observation and recording done by human observers. The investigator is considered to be like a 'fly on the wall', there has to be absolutely no contribution in any way to the situation being observed. This means he has to send no verbal or non-verbal cues to the respondent, which might impact the behaviour being observed.

   Human observation has both advantages and disadvantages of the human element. The analytical ability of the recorder makes this mode far superior to mechanical recording. As the observer observes, accordingly he infers and then records. Thus, if the observer views a supervisor giving a piece of his mind to his subordinate, the inference might be of non-supportive behaviour or autocratic and domineering attitude of the supervisor.

   However, this very advantage might prove to be a negative of the technique as well, for example based on the observer's own experience, he might report this as absolutely 'normal handling of a junior's mistake by the supervisor, or he might state this as 'an inhuman act to curtail an individual's basic human right to be.' Thus, maintaining objectivity while reporting and inferring is of critical importance. The exact definition of what are the parameters to be observed in the case of structured observation are extremely important. For example, if we need to observe them on the level of initiative that they take in delivering service, then it is essential to define the kind of behaviour that is part of the job role and that which might be construed as initiative. This is critical if observation is the major data-collection instrument for a descriptive study. This will ensure the reliability of the findings. The second concern is that of validity, for example a pleasant demeanour of a restaurant waiter might be stated as a positive predictor of consumer delight; however, the validity of such findings becomes questionable as for one observer this might be simply a pleasant smile, while the others might include an overall handling of the order right from the greeting to the final collection of payment. Thus, the construct validity (to be discussed in the chapter on Attitude and Measurement) of the method requires that the relation being studied of personnel attitude and customer satisfaction must have some theoretical base.

   This also has implications for the generalizability and applicability of the findings. Sometimes, the situation constructed like a packaging option or an advertisement might have indications only for the study situation, whereas others, like the supervisor–subordinate relations might have a wider application.

   The task of the observer is simple and predefined in case of a structured observation study as the format and the areas to be observed and recorded are clearly defined. In an unstructured observation, the observer records in a narrative form the entire event that he has observed. Subsequently, he assigns the behaviour to different categories. The reporting must ensure that these categories are exhaustive in covering the details noted and they are mutually exclusive. Another aspect to be noted is that the observer needs to be trained to report using 'natural' rather than 'judgemental' words. For example, if the narration involved reporting of the supervisor-suboridnate relationship, then, rather than reporting it as aggressive or normal, one needs to spell out what, according to the researcher, constitutes normal or aggressive behaviour, as what is normal according to one might be reported as aggressive by the other. Thus, it is advisable to record behaviour manifestations and then analyse the type of relationship.

In a **mechanical observation**, the recording is done through electronic medium; and is later subjected to an interpretation and analysis.

2. **Mechanical observation:** In these methods, man is replaced by machine. This might or might not involve directives by human hand. Generally, the recording is done continuously and later subjected to an interpretation and analysis.

Store cameras and cameras in banks and other service areas also provide vital information about consumer movement and behaviour patterns; as well as reaction to shelf placement or store displays. Another method was the one discussed for store panels in the previous chapter, the Universal Product Code (UPC). The UPC scanned by electric scanners in stores records information related to consumer purchases by product category, brand, store type, price and quantity. Another device is the turnstile located at the entrance of a store, mall, office or even traffic locations to collate data about individual or vehicular movement at different times of the day. AC Nielsen and others also record Internet usage through their Net scanners. The net surfing behaviour in terms of the time spent, sites visited and links used are extremely valuable insights into mapping consumer interests, as this helps in designing product and promotion offering, thus, catering to the needs and interests of the potential users.

Another device is the input used for media panel audits using people meter and audio meter. These are, as discussed in Chapter 5, devices which record the channel being watched, and in case of the people meter, also record who is watching it.

In contrast to the ones stated above, a number of mechanical observation devices need the respondent to be active in assisting the recording. To measures the impact on the skin, a popular technique is the psychogalvanometer, which measures galvanic skin response (GSR) or changes in the electrical resistance of the skin. Small electrodes are attached to the individual's skin and these electrodes are in turn attached to a monitor. The rationale behind this test is that any affective reaction of the individual results in a higher perspiration which, in turn, results in a change in the electrical resistance of the skin. This is recorded on the galvanometer. Thus, the respondent could be exposed to different kinds of packaging, advertisements and product composition, to note his reaction to them. The strength of the movement shown on the monitor indicates the respondent's reaction and impression about the stimuli.

There are a number of equipment to measure the impact of various stimuli on the sense of sight. Eye-tracking equipment such as oculometers, eye cameras or eye view minuters, record the movements of the eye. These devices can be used to determine how a respondent reacts to various aspects like advertisements, packaging options, shelf or store displays. The oculometer determines what the individual is looking at, while the pupilometer measures the interest of the person in the stimulus. The pupilometer measures changes in the diameter of the respondent's pupils. The technique involves exposing the individual to various images on a screen. A before- and after-test is conducted to measure any change in the pupil movement. The theoretical assumption is that any change in a cognitive activity is immediately reflected in the change in pupil size. The hypothesis being that more the increase in the size of the pupil, more positive is the attitude of the individual towards the stimulus.

Voice pitch meters measure emotional reactions of the individual by reporting on any change in the respondent's voice. The audio-compatible computer devices measure any change in the voice pitch of the person. The basic premise behind the usage of these devices is that certain affective and cognitive responses manifest themselves through the sensory outputs and thus can be subsequently measured. However, these are expensive to use and record and thus have not really found a widespread usage. Another problem is the impact of the simulated or artificial environment required to carry out these analysis, which might mask the true response or exaggerate it.

Other techniques used more in marketing research are, as reported in chapter 5, those of store or pantry audits. These require a physical recording and reporting by a human observer. The usual task is to count the number of units and convert it into counts. Pantry audits are done at the individual level and the observer makes a note of the products, brands and sizes bought by a consumer, However, this is an expensive field work and the consumer might not permit the audit. Secondly, the basket only reflects the current choice and not the rejected or the most preferred brands.

In trace analysis, the leftovers of the consumers' basket are evaluated to measure current trends and patterns of usage and disposal.

A related technique is that of Trace analysis; in this the remains or the leftovers of the consumers' basket—like his credit card spend, his recycle bin on his computer, his garbage (garbology) are evaluated to measure current trends and patterns of usage and disposal. The make and condition of cars in a parking lot near a locality can be used to ascertain the lifestyle and prosperity of the residents in the locality.

Observational techniques are an extremely useful method of primary data collection and are always a part of the inputs, whether accompanying other techniques, like interviews, discussions or questionnaire administration, or as the prime method of data collection. However, the disadvantage which they suffer from is that they are always behaviourally driven and cannot be used to investigate the reasons or causes of the observed behaviour. Another problem is that if one is observing the occurrence of a certain phenomenon, one has to wait for the event to occur.

One alternative to this is to study the recordings, whether verbal, written or audio-visual, in order to formulate the study-related inferences. This technique is called content analysis.

Content Analysis

Content analysis is original, first-hand and problem-specific. Due to these factors, it is categorized under primary methods.

This technique involves studying a previously recorded or reported communication and systematically and objectively breaking it up into more manageable units that are related to the topic under study. It is peculiar in its nature that it is classified as a primary data collection technique and yet makes use of previously produced or secondary data. However, since the analysis is original, first hand and problem specific, it is categorized under primary methods. Some researchers classify it under observation methods, the reason being that in this, one is also analysing the communication in order to measure or infer about variables. The only difference being that one analyses communication that is ex-post facto rather than live. One can content-analyse letters, diaries, minutes of meetings, articles, audio and video recordings, etc. The method is structured and systematic and thus of considerable credibility.

The first step involves defining U, or the *universe of content*. For example, in the case of Ritu, who wants to know what makes the young Indian tick, she could make use of the blogs written by youngsters, essays and reality shows featuring the age group. She decides that she wants to assess value systems, attitudes towards others/ elders, clarity of life goal and peer influences. This step is extremely critical as this indicates the assumptions or hypotheses the researcher might have formulated.

Universe of content can be reported in five different formats: word; theme; characters; space measure; time measure and item.

This universe can be reported in any of five different formats (Berelson, 1954). The smallest reported unit could be a *word*. This is especially useful as it can be easily subjected to a computer analysis. In Ritu's case, the values that she wants to evaluate are individualistic or collectivistic, aggressive or compliant. Thus, she can sift the communication and place words such as 'I' or 'we' under the respective heads. Words like 'hate' 'dislike' go under aggression and 'alright' 'fine' 'maybe not so good' for complacency. Then counts and frequencies are calculated to arrive at certain conclusions.

The next level is a *theme*. This is very useful but, a little difficult to quantify as this involves reporting the propositions and sentences or events as representing a theme. For example, disrespect towards elders is the theme and one picks out the following as a representative: a young teen's blog which says *my old man (father) has gone senile and needs to be sent to the looney bin for expecting me to become a space scientist, just because he could not become one...*

This categorization becomes more complex as the element of observer's bias comes into play. Thus, this kind of analysis could be extremely useful when carried out by an expert. However, in the case of an untrained analyst, the reliability and validity of the findings would be questionable.

The other units are *characters* and *space* and *time measures*. The character refers to the person producing the communication, for example the young teenager writing the blog. Space and time are more related to the physical format, i.e., the number of pages used, the length of the communication and the duration of the communication.

Percentage of agreement between the two analyses (Cohen, 1960)

$$K=\frac{Pr(a)-Pr(e)}{1-Pr(e)}$$

The last unit is the *item*, which is more Gestaltian in nature and refers to categorizing the entire communication as say 'responsible and respectful' or 'aggressive and amoral.' As in the case of theme, this categorization is equally complex as the observer's bias is likely to be high. Thus, to ensure the reliability of the findings, one may ask another coder to evaluate the same data. Cohen (1960) states the measuring of the percentage of agreement between the two analyses by the following formula:

$$K=\frac{Pr(a)-Pr(e)}{1-Pr(e)}$$

Here, Pr(a) is the relative observed agreement between the two raters. Pr(e) is the probability that this is due to chance. If the two raters are in complete agreement, then Kappa is 1. If there is no agreement, then Kappa = 0, 0.21–0.40 is fair, 0.41–0.80 is good and 0.81–1.00 is considered excellent.

Content analysis of large volumes becomes tedious and prone to error if handled by humans. Thus, there are various computer program available that can assist in the process. For computers running on Windows, one can use TEXTPACK, this is a dictionary word approach, where it can tag defined words for word frequency by sorting them alphabetically or by frequencies. Open-ended questions can be sorted by a program called Verbastat (generally used by corporate users) or Statpac, which has an automatic coding module and is of considerable use to individual researchers.

Content analysis is a very useful technique when one has a large quantity of text as data and it needs to be structured in order to arrive at some definite conclusions about the variables under study. Computer assistance has greatly aided in the active usage of the technique. However, it can appear too simplistic, when one reduces the whole data to counts or frequencies.

The next two methods that are being discussed now are the most frequently-used methods of qualitative research and are also strong in terms of reliability and validity of the findings.

CONCEPT CHECK	1. How would you define the observation method of qualitative research? 2. Distinguish between human and mechanical observation. 3. What is content analysis? 4. Define the units inolved in a content analysis.

FOCUS GROUP METHOD

LEARNING OBJECTIVE 4
Understand the conduct and analysis of a focus group discussion.

Focus group as a method developed in the 1940s in Columbia University by sociologist Robert Merton and his colleagues as part of a sociological technique. This was used as a method for measuring audience reaction to radio programmes (MacGregor and Morrison, 1995). In fact, the method was uniquely adapted and modified in different branches of social sciences namely anthropology (Wilson and Wilson 1945), sociology (Merton and Kendall, 1946), psychology (Bogardus, 1926), education (Edminton, 1944) and advertising (Smith, 1954). It essentially emerged as an alternative method which was more cost effective and less time consuming and could generate a large amount of information in a short time span. Another argument given in its favour was that group dynamics play a positive role in generating data that the individual would be hesitant about sharing when he was spoken to individually (Morgan and Krueger, 1997).

A focus group is a highly versatile and dynamic method of collecting information from a representative group of respondents. The process generally involves a moderator who maneuvers the discussion on the topic under study. There are a group of carefully-selected respondents who are specifically invited and gathered at a neutral setting. The moderator initiates the discussion and then the group carries it forward by holding a focused and an interactive discussion. The technique is extensively used and at the same time also criticized. While one school of thought places group dynamics at an important position, another negates its contribution as detrimental. We will examine these as we go along.

Key Elements of a Focus Group

A **focus group** is a highly versatile and dynamic method of collecting information from a representative group of respondents.

There are certain typical requirements for a conducive discussion. These need to be ensured in order to get meaningful and usable outputs from the technique.

- **Size:** The size of the group is extremely critical and should not be too large or too small. Fern (1983) stated that as every member is assumed to contribute meaningfully to the discussion, if the size of the group is too large then contribution by the members might not be premium. Ideal recommended size thus for a group discussion is 8 to 12 members. Less than eight would not generate all the possible perspectives on the topic and the group dynamics required for a meaningful session.
- **Nature:** Individuals who are from a similar background—in terms of demographic and psychographic traits—must be included, otherwise the disagreement might emerge as a result of other factors rather than the one under study. For example, a group of homemakers and working women discussing packaged food might not have a similar perspective towards the product because they have different roles to manage and balance; thus what is perceived as convenience by one is viewed as indifferent and careless attitude towards one's family by the other. The other requirement is that the respondents must be similar in terms of the subject/policy/product knowledge and experience with the product under study. Moreover, the participants should be carefully screened to meet a certain criteria.

- **Acquaintance:** It has been found that knowing each other in a group discussion is disruptive and hampers the free flow of the discussion and it is believed that people reveal their per-spectives more freely amongst strangers rather than friends (Feldwick and Winstanley,1986). Bristol (1999) found that men revealed more about themselves amongst strangers, while females were more comfortable amongst acquaintances. Thus, it is recommended that the group should consist of strangers rather than subjects who know each other. There are exceptions however in certain cases; this would be further discussed in a subsequent section.

The **setting** for a group discussion should be neutral, informal and comfortable. The external factors should be minimized.

- **Setting:** As far as possible, the external factors which might affect the nature of the discussion are to be minimized. One of these could be the space or setting in which the discussion takes place. Thus, it should be as neutral, informal and comfortable as possible. Even the ones that have one-way mirrors or cameras installed need to ensure that these gadgets are as unobtrusively placed as possible.
- **Time period:** The conduction of the discussion should be held in a single setting unless there is a before and after design which requires group perceptions, initially before the study variable is introduced; and later in order to gauge the group's reactions. The ideal duration of conduction should not exceed one and a half hour. This is usually preceded by a short rapport formation session between the moderator and the group members.
- **The recording:** Earlier there were human recorders, either sitting behind one-way mirrors or in the discussion room. Today, these have been replaced by cameras that video record the entire discussion. This can, then, be replayed for analysis and interpretation. The advantage over human recording is that one is able to observe the non-verbal cues and body language as well. This technology has been further enhanced and one can evaluate the discussion happening at one location, being observed and transmitted at another.

The **moderator** is the key conductor of the whole session and is supposed to supervise over the nature, content and the vallidity of the data collected.

- **The moderator:** He is the key conductor of the whole session. The nature, content and validity of the data collected are dependent to a large extent on the skills of the moderator. His role might be that of a participant where he might be a part of the group discussion or he might be a non-participant and has the task of rapport formation, initiating the discussion and steering the discussion forward. Morgan and Thomas (1996) have stated that any group task has two clear agendas. One is the conscious agenda to complete the overt task and the second, more important, plan is related to the unconscious. This is concerned with the emotional needs of the group and has been described differently as 'group mind', 'group as a whole' and 'group as a group'. The moderator is clearly responsible for this as he needs to work with the group as a group in order to maximize the group performance. Thus, he needs to possess some critical moderating skills like:
  - Ability to listen attentively and have a positive demeanour that encourages others to discuss. At the same time, he must be detached, and give no indication about his personal opinion in order to skew the discussion. He should be dressed in a manner that is informal and similar to the group.
  - He needs to make others feel comfortable, thus the language used should be in the subjects' lingo, with no use of technical words at all.
  - He needs to be flexible in approach, so that the discussion flows naturally rather than becoming compartmentalized into a question and answer session. At the same time, he also needs to act as a translator in case some one's point is not understood or interpreted correctly.

- He must also discreetly handle the overbearing and dominating participants and encourage all the members to contribute by drawing out the hesitant ones as well. Thus, sensitivity to the respondents' feelings must be present at all times.
- There is no external signal, so he needs to be sufficiently trained and acquainted with the topic to understand the specific interval when all the possible viewpoints get exhausted and the discussion needs to move on.

Summary and closure approach involves the elaboration of a point made by a participant to the other so as to forward the discussion.

In conducting the discussions, he might use the *summary and closure* approach where he might pick up a similar point made by a participant to another and summarize it and ask for his opinion. Another tactic that can be used is to bring in the *extreme opinions* on the topic, in case no counter points are coming through; this, then, is able to generate more arguments into the discussion. Sometimes, rather than the moderator introducing another viewpoint, he might ask 'is that all?' This might sometimes trigger a fresh stance.

Steps in Planning and Conducting Focus Groups

The focus group conduction has to be handled in a structured and stepwise manner as stated below:

(i) Clearly define and enlist the research objectives of the research study that require qualitative research.

(ii) Then these objectives have to be split into information needs to be answered by the group. These may be bulleted as topics of interest or as broad questions to be answered by the group.

(iii) Next, a list of characteristics needs to be prepared, which would be used to select the respondent group. Based on this screening, a questionnaire is prepared to measure the demographic, psychographics, topic-related familiarity and knowledge. In case of a product or policy, one also needs to find out the experience and attitude towards it. Next, a comprehensive moderator's outline for conducting the whole process needs to be charted out. Here, it is critical to involve the decision maker (if any), the business researcher as well as the moderator. This is done so that there is complete clarity for the moderator in terms of the intention and potential applicability of the discussion output. This involves extensive discussions among the researcher, client and the moderator. Another advantage of having a structured guideline is that in case of multiple moderators, who might need to conduct focus group discussions at different locales, collection of similar information and reliability of the method can be maintained.

(iv) After this, the actual focus group discussion is carried out. Different sociologists have enlisted various stages that take place in a focus group. The most famous and comprehensive is the linear model of group development formulated by Tuckman (1965). This has been adapted by Chrzanowska (2002) to explain stages in the Focus group discussions (Table 6.1).

(v) The focus group reveals rich and varied data, thus the analysis cannot be quantitative or even in frequencies. The summary of the findings are clubbed under different heads as indicated in the focus group objectives and reported in a narrative form. This may include expressions like 'majority of the participants were of the view' or 'there was a considerable disagreement on this issue'. A summary report on the focus group discussion held in the organic food study is presented below along with the moderator guide.

TABLE 6.1
Stages in a focus group discussion

Stage	Affective reactions	Behaviour patterns	Moderator's role
Forming	The group members are uncomfortable, insecure, and a little lost and apprehensive.	Silence or general talk, greetings and introductions. Mundane activity.	Tries to bring clarity by explaining the purpose of gathering together, and the expected behaviour during the discussion.
Storming	There is chaos, as emotions start flying with members questioning others and voicing their own opinion.	Arguments directed at each other or trying to seek support from the moderator. Generally there is rigidity in terms of sticking to ones position. The leaders and the followers emerge.	Does not take side. Play poker face and say that all opinions are welcome. Steers the direction to the topic rather than arguments which might go off the tangent. Tries to draw out the passive participants.
Norming	Cliques and sides start forming based on the stand that people have taken. More supportive and positive signals, especially non-verbal.	People have got the hang of the process and do not really need any steering by the moderator.	Takes it easy, and is more bothered about sequencing of information and managing time at this junction.
Performing	Individuals are subservient to the group, roles are flexible and task-oriented.	Sense of concentration and flow, everything seems easy, high energy, group works without being asked.	Introduces difficult issues, stimulus material, projective techniques.
Re-adjustment: There might be role reversals. People may have another perspective with which the loosely-defined cliques might not agree, so one of the earlier stages might emerge.			
Mourning	Group task nearing completion, so there might be a sense of loss as the energy generated with the discussion might be sapped.	If members do not feel that any clear stand is emerging, they might want to continue and not disband the group.	Signal conclusion. If you want to summarize, ask if any one has something to add. Thank everyone and disperse for refreshments or closure.

(Source: Chrzanowska, 2002)

MODERATOR GUIDE: ORGANIC FOOD PRODUCTS STUDY

Potential customers of organic food products

Rapport formation (5–8 minutes)

- Greetings
- Purpose of the focus group: (Brief from covering note)
- Ground rules – nature of a focus group
- Video recording and moderator's presence explained
- No right or wrong opinion
- Please speak as clearly as possible and listen to others' opinion as well
- Kindly speak in Hindi or English, whatever is more comfortable for you
- Brief 'get acquainted period'
- Participants' name, something about themselves that they would like to share with the group

Orientation towards health and environmental concerns (10–12 minutes)

- Everyday one hears of adulterated food and drinks, the alarming level of pesticides and fertilizers in food items. How much of this do you think is true? (Explore)
- Dose it bother you? PROBE
- What do you do at your personal end to safeguard yourself/your family from these effects? Please share your strategies/methods with all of us. PROBE

Organic food (30 minutes)

- Presentation of the concept with products (inform about both raw and the ready-to-use variety like preserves, biscuits, bread and snacks)
- How many of you have heard about this? EXPLORE
- Do you know that organic products have been available for almost a decade in the country but the level of awareness is very low?
- What should be done to improve the awareness about the products? EXPLORE

Marketing the product (30 minutes)

- Which products do you think would sell more? Why?
- What do you feel about the products (likes/dislikes)?
- How should these products be priced and packed?
- Where do you think these products should be sold?
- Do you think big brands or government or the farmers themselves should sell it?

Closing the discussion (10 minutes)

- Finally, I would like you to be creative and give me ideas about possible brand names that can be used by a company selling organic food.
- Is there anybody who feels that we left out something or would like a clarification from me or from another member? If necessary explore, else refine and summarize.
- Thank the respondent members for their contribution and close the session.

FOCUS GROUP SUMMARY: ORGANIC FOOD PRODUCTS STUDY

Potential customers of organic food products

Two separate focus group discussions were conducted—one in Noida (UP) and the other in Hi-Tech City, Hyderabad. The group at Noida was predominantly of housewives and the one in Hi-Tech had professionals from different walks of life. Their opinion on a variety of subjects was sought. A summary of the discussions is presented below:

Adulteration in food

All the participants were unanimously concerned about adulterated food that they and their families were consuming. The discussion went from pesticides to chemicals and spurious food products. The ladies felt that they experienced a lot of health problems, specifically acidity, because of adulteration in the food. Some stated that they tried to grind all masalas at home as they felt that most of the problem was with masalas. However, some felt that this was meaningless as the whole masala was adulterated and contaminated by chemical residues. Thus, even though it was a matter of concern for them, they felt helpless to verbalize the possible solution.

There was one lady (Noida group), however, who felt that some of the problems were exaggerated and were basically created by the media and were plain hype. Another lady (HT group) felt that the problem of pollution was too deep-rooted and just adulterated food or food grown with chemical fertilizers and pesticides was too elementary and small to comprehend the problem of health hazards of the general population.

Changes in lifestyle

The consumers observed major changes in the recent years. The groups were unanimously of the opinion that they were more health conscious and concerned than their mothers and grandmothers. The younger generation (post- teens especially) are extremely conscious about the nutritional content of their food. They actively avoid excess sugar and fats in their diet. As a regime, people said that they exercise in some form or the other. Some said they drink more water and include healthy supplements like sprouts and olive oil in their diets.

Awareness of organic food products

Almost all the consumers, with the exception of one, had read or heard of organic food. One respondent had tried the product and found it very tasty. Three of the group members, as stated earlier, were skeptical about the benefits of organic food.

Willingness to try

The product was formally introduced to the groups and their reactions were noted to the same. Most of them, with the exception of two, were extremely enthusiastic about the products and wanted to know more about them and had a number of queries about the availability, price, brands and benefits of the products.

Suggestions for marketing the product

- Divided opinion on who should sell the product. Some felt that a government-approved outlet like Mother Dairy/Trinetra should sell the products whereas others felt that there should be exclusive organic food outlets. There were two or three people who felt that there should be no distinction and the products should be available everywhere. Some were also of the opinion that the products could be sold at high-end grocery stores or departmental stores since this was an expensive product. One consumer suggested the vegetable *mandi* also as a possible outlet, however most of the others felt that the products would not be purchased by the masses.
- All the group members were unanimously of the opinion that they would buy a product only if it was certified as organic from an authentic and reputed body.
- The product should be vaccum packed, preferably in a brown paper packet with the label having the certification information and the source of the product clearly displayed.
- All felt that the price difference should not be too steep. At the same time, the Indian consumer who is buying a quality product accepts a price difference, so the product should be slightly expensive than the non-organic option.
- All the respondents felt that television was the best medium for promoting the product. All opined that there was a dire need for creating awareness. They felt that there was absolutely no visibility for the products and more availability and awareness would mean more sales and more organically converted consumers. Some suggested popular soap operas and others were in favour of educational programmes.
- Some respondents felt that product promotions should be effectively and widely-conducted by tying up with environment-related organizations that would be willing to promote a healthy cause.
- In terms of endorsement, they wanted sports personalities, film stars like Hema Malini, Simi Grewal, etc; and politicians like Menaka Gandhi and Sushma Swaraj endorsing the product, some even suggested common people who eat organic products and the farmer who produces.
- The groups were generally of the opinion that the campaigns should be targeted at housewives and school children who would be wonderful and effective change agents.
- Comparative advertising demonstrating the benefits of organic versus non-organic was another valuable suggestion discussed in the group. Some however argued for simply enlisting the benefits and resolving the myths about the products.
- Price and availability and the reputation of the organization or brand would be important issues in marketing the product effectively.
- Some punch lines suggested for the product were:
  - It is the future
  - The healthy alternative
  - *Shudh* and *swachh*
  - *Shuddhaahaar*
  - Healthorganic
  - Organic is healthy
  - Go organic

Types of Focus Groups

As stated earlier, there could be several variations to the standard procedure. Some such innovations and alternative approaches are presented below:

- **Two-way focus group:** Here one respondent group sits and listens to the other and after learning from them or understanding the needs of the group, carry out a discussion amongst themselves.

  For example, in a management school the faculty group could listen to the opinions and needs of the student group. Subsequently, a focus group of the faculty could be held to study the solutions or changes that they perceive need to be carried out in the dissemination of the programme.

A **dual-moderator group** involves two different moderators responsible for the management of group discussion and *'group mind'* respectively.

- **Dual-moderator group:** Here, there are two different moderators; one responsible for the overt task of managing the group discussion and the other for the second objective of managing the *'group mind'* in order to maximize the group performance.
- **Fencing-moderator group:** The two moderators take opposite sides on the topic being discussed and thus, in the short time available, ensure that all possible perspectives are thoroughly explored.
- **Friendship groups:** There are situations where the comfort level of the members needs to be high so that they elicit meaningful responses. This is especially the case when a supportive peer group encourages admission about the related organizations or people/issues. Stevens (2003) used the technique successfully when studying women groups for their experiential consumption of women magazines.
- **Mini-groups:** These groups might be of a smaller size (usually four to six) and are usually expert groups/committees that on account of their composition are able to decisively contribute to the topic under study.
- **Creativity groups:** These are usually of longer than one and a half hour duration and might take the workshop mode. Here, the entire group is instructed which then brainstorms into smaller sub-groups and then reassembles to present their sub-groups opinion. They might also stretch across a day or two. A variation of the technique uses projective methods to extract alternative thinking (Desai, 2002).

A **brand-obsessive group** consists of special respondent sub-strata who are passionately involved with a brand or product categroy.

- **Brand-obsessive groups:** These are special respondent sub-strata who are passionately involved with a brand or product category (say cars). They are selected as they can provide valuable insights that can be successfully incorporated into the brand's marketing strategy.

In an **online focus group discussion,** geographical locations are not a constraint and persons from varied locations can participate meaningfully in a discussion.

- **Online focus group:** This is a recent addition to the methodology and is extensively used today. Thus, it will be elaborated in detail. Like in the case of regular group process, the respondents are selected from an online list of people who have volunteered to participate in the discussion. They are then administered the screening questionnaire to measure their suitability. Once they qualify, they are given a time, a participating id and password and the venue where they need to be so that they can be connected with the others. The group size here varies from four to six, as otherwise there might be technical problems and lack of clarity in the voices received. To ensure a standardized way of responding, the respondents are mailed details of how to use specific symbols to express emotions, while typing the responses. For example, for denoting satisfaction or dissatisfaction the following symbols may be used: ☺ or ☹. These could also be coloured differently; also to show a higher degree of the emotion additional faces may be used. Besides, a brief about the purpose of the discussion and clarity on specific or technical terms is provided before the conduction. At the designated time, the group assembles in a web-based chat room and enters their id and password to log on. Here the chatting between the moderator and the participant is real time. Once the discussion is initiated, the group is on its own and chats amongst themselves, with the moderator playing the typical role. The session lasts for one to one and a half hour and the process is much faster than a normal focus group.

The *advantage* of the method is that geographic locations are not a constraint and persons from varied locations can participate meaningfully in the discussion. Also, since it does not require a commitment to be physically assembled at a particular place and time, people who are busy and otherwise are not able to participate, can also be tapped. Since the addresses of the members are available to the moderators, it is also possible subsequently to probe deeper at a later date or seek clarifications. The interaction is faceless so the person interacting is completely assured of his/her anonymity and is thus less inhibited. The method also has a cost advantage as compared to a traditional focus group. People are generally less inhibited in their responses and are more likely to fully express their thoughts. A lot of online focus groups go well past their allotted time since so many responses are expressed. Finally, as there is no travel, videotaping or facilities to arrange, the cost is much lower than for traditional focus groups. Firms are able to keep costs between one-fifth and one-half the cost of traditional focus groups.

However, the method can be actively and constructively used only with those who are computer savvy. Another disadvantage is that since anonymity is assured, actual authentication of the respondent being a part of the population under study might be a little difficult to establish. Thus, to verify the details, one may use the traditional telephone method and cross check the information. Since the person is typing his/her response, other sensory cues of tone, body language and facial expressions are not available. Thus, while the apparent emotions or attitudes can be tapped, however, the unconscious or subconscious cannot be judged.

These techniques have extensive use for companies that are into e-commerce. Most companies today have started using this technique to get employee reactions to various organizational issues, in what is termed as a 'virtual town hall meeting'. Thus, cyber dialogues can be carried out and meaningful feedback as well as population reaction can be measured with considerable ease and accuracy.

Evaluating Focus Group as a Method

Focus group discussions lead to idea generation as the dialogue between the members helps to define and rephrase the perspective into a usable solution.

Focus groups are extensively criticized and yet have widespread usage in all areas of business research, to the extent that the technique is considered by some as synonymous with qualitative research. Before concluding the discussion on focus groups, let us examine the benefits and drawbacks of using the method.

- **Idea generation:** As discussed earlier, the collective group mind creates an atmosphere where ideas and suggestions are churned out which are more holistic and significant than those that would be generated in an individual interview. The other advantage is that the group process works towards vetting each idea as it is presented. The dialogue between the members helps to refine and rephrase the perspective into a usable solution at the end of the discussion.
- **Group dynamics:** Once the moderator has initiated the debate and some members have expressed their opinion, the atmosphere becomes charged and the respondents' involvement with the topic increases with most members presenting reactions and counter reactions. The expressiveness becomes contagious and the contrived discussion slowly becomes a free-flowing discussion. As the comfort level of individuals with the other members increases, they start feeling at ease with the setting and expression becomes more open.
- **Process advantage:** The discussion situation permits considerable flexibility in extracting the relevant information as the flow of topics and the extent to which the topic can be debated is dependent upon the group members and the emerging dynamics. Also, the situation permits a simultaneous conduction and collection of information from a number of individuals at a single point of time.
- **Reliability and validity:** Since the objectives of the study have been listed out and the structure of the moderator outline is predetermined, the reliability of the information obtained is high. The mechanical recording of the data removes the element of human bias and error in the information collected.

However, the technique is not without shortcomings.

- **Group dynamics:** Group dynamics can also be a disadvantage of the process. On account of the group setting, the members might present a perspective not necessarily their own, but one that is along the lines of the group expression. This is the 'nodding dog syndrome,' which is often a result of group conformity.
- **Scientific process:** The group discussion must be treated as indicative and, thus, generalizing must be avoided. The answers obtained are varied and in a narrative form. Thus, coding and analysing this data is quite cumbersome.
- **Moderator/investigator bias:** As discussed in earlier sections, the success or failure of the process depends, to a large extent, on the skills of the moderator. An unbiased and sensitive moderator who is able to generate meaningful and unbiased discussions is quite a rarity.

CONCEPT CHECK

1. What is the technique that operates behind the focus group method?
2. Explain the steps in planning and conducting a focus group meeting.
3. What is the role of a moderator in a focus group?
4. Discuss the benefits and drawbacks of the focus group method.

PERSONAL INTERVIEW METHOD

LEARNING OBJECTIVE 5
Design and conduct in-depth interviews and ensure objectivity in reporting.

Another method of direct access to the respondents' school of thought is the personal interview method. Personal interview is a one-to-one interaction between the investigator/interviewer and the interviewee. The purpose of the dialogue is research specific and ranges from completely unstructured to highly structured. The definition of the structure depends upon the information needs of the research study. The interview has varied applications in business research and can be used effectively in various stages.

Personal interview is a one-to-one interaction between the investigator/ interviewer and the interviewee. The dialogue either can be both unstructured and structured.

- **Problem definition:** The interview method can be used right in the beginning of the study. Here, the researcher uses the method to get a better clarity about the topic under study. The interview can be carried out with the experts or with the members of the respondent population to get an indication about the variables to be studied in the actual research study. For example, in a study on devising a postgraduate management programme like what should be the research undertaken and what needs should it address; the investigator might carry out informal interviews with some academic experts as well as the student decision maker, to get a perspective on the information that needs to be collected. Thus, on the basis of the interviews, the following objectives would be formulated:
    - Identify the postgraduate options available to the students, both national and international.
    - Identify the selection process followed by benchmarked institutes.
    - Identify the process used by a typical undergraduate student in preparing a list of the institutes to apply in.
    - Based on the above objectives, identify the business model that a postgraduate institute needs to adapt to successfully reach out to the potential student group.
- **Exploratory research:** Once the steps or research objectives have been established, the researcher might need to do another round of semi-structured interviews to get a perspective on the variables to be studied, the definitions of these variables and any other information of relevance to the study topic. This helps in formulating the questions of the final measuring instrument of the study. For example, to achieve objective three in the above research study, it is imperative to find out the parameters considered by the students in selecting a professional management course. Thus, informal interviews would be held with

a few undergraduate students to find out what measures they use to arrive at a decision. At the same time, interviews would also be held with the deans of a few selected universities to find out the same.

Primary method of data collection is used when the area to be investigated is high on subjectivity and a structured method would not elicit any meaningful information.

- **Primary data collection:** There are situations when the method is used as a primary method of data collection, this is generally the case when the area to be investigated is high on subjectivity or individual sentiments and a structured method would not elicit any meaningful information. For example, if the study is about confidential, sensitive or embarrassing topics (impact of obesity on personal relations, the extent of unscrupulous dealings required for taking critical business decisions, etc.), and situations where conformity to social norms exists and the respondent is wary of deviant behaviour, may be easily swayed by group response (e.g., attitude towards cosmetic surgery), affective or compulsive consumption and situations where apparent explanations are not clear to the respondent also (superior-subordinate relations).
- **The interview process:** The steps undertaken for the conduction of a personal interview are somewhat similar in nature to a focus group discussion.
  - *Interview objective:* The information needs that are to be addressed by the instrument should be clearly spelt out as study objectives. This step includes a clear definition of the construct/variable(s) to be studied.
  - *Interview guidelines:* A typical interview may take from 20 minutes to close to an hour. A brief outline to be used by the investigator is formulated depending upon the contours of the interview.

The quality of the output and the depth of information collected depends upon the **probing and listening skills** of the interviewer.

- **Unstructured:** Absolutely no defined guidelines. Usually begins with a casually worded opening remark like 'so tell us/me something about yourself'. The cues are usually taken from what the subject says. The direction the interview will take is not known to the researcher also. The probability of subjectivity is very high and generalization from such an investigation is extremely difficult.
- **Semi-structured:** This has a more defined format and usually only the broad areas to be investigated are formulated. The questions, sequence and language are left to the investigator's choice. Probing is of critical importance in obtaining meaningful responses and uncovering hidden issues. After asking the initial question, the interviewer uses an unstructured format. The subsequent direction of the interview is determined by the respondent's initial reply, the interviewer's probes for elaboration and the respondent's answers.
- **Structured:** This format has highest reliability and validity. There is considerable structure to the questions and the questioning is also done on the basis of a prescribed sequence. They are sometimes used as the primary data collection instrument also.
  - *Interviewing skills:* The quality of the output and the depth of information collected depend upon the probing and listening skills of the interviewer. Thus, he needs to be a sympathetic listener and alert to cues from the respondent's answers, which might require further probing/clarification. He needs to be well-acquainted with the study objectives and aware about the deliverables of the study. His attitude needs to be as objective as possible and not in any way be directional or distorting the results or responses of the subject.
  - *Analysis and Interpretation:* The information collected is not subjected to any statistical analysis. Mostly the data is in narrative form, in the case of structured interviews it might be categorized after the conduction and be reported as 'most students seem to be using placements and infrastructure as the primary reason...' Sometimes the output of the interviews is subjected to a content analysis to achieve a better structure for the results obtained.

Given below is an interview guide created for a beverage purchase and consumption study.

INTERVIEW GUIDE: BEVERAGE PURCHASE AND CONSUMPTION

Introduction and Warm Up

Hi, I am conducting a short survey on soft drink consumption. Thus, I would just take some insights from you on your purchase. There are no right or wrong answers, however, since you consume soft drinks, your opinion is really important for understanding the purchase behaviour.

1. Tell me something about yourselves… what do you do—as in occupation… your hobbies…your interests? How would you describe yourself as a person? Do you generally plan and buy….
2. **PROBE FURTHER – PSYCHOGRAPHICS/LIFESTYLE**
3. **PURCHASE BEHAVIOUR :**
4. This soft drink that you have purchased….how do you generally consume it…. Chilled/cool, can/bottle, stand alone or mixed with something.
5. If I were to ask you to list occasions for soft drinks' purchase, they would be:

   ____

   ____

   ____

   ____
6. So when you are making this purchase, what triggers it:

- brand
- price
- deals
- taste
- packaging
- any other ____________

PROBE ALL ATTRIBUTES FOR REASONS. ***For example, what kind of deals? Packaging? brand image?***

7. Supposing your favourite brand is not available for purchase…..what do you do…….(PROBE)……do you move on to another store or pick up another brand……(PROBE) …….reason(s)
8. Supposing a company changes its packaging so that it is really eye catching, what is your reaction to it…… (PROBE)……reason(s)
9. **EXPOSE PICTURE**

   I am going to show you some display pictures. Please tell me which one do you think looks attractive….. (let the respondent select)…….(PROBE reasons for liking)……would this move customers to go and look around and purchase…….(reason)……..would it influence you to buy…..(reasons)
10. **EXPOSE PICTURE**

    I am going to show you a picture of a store. Where would you generally expect the soft drinks to be placed…..in your opinion, is this the right place or can it be put somewhere else…..REASON
11. Buy one get one free, a freebie, coupons, prizes. Do you get moved to try out and buy some of these?....... which ones did you try……REACTION
12. Soft drinks companies come up with a lot of ads…. can you tell me something about some ads? What do you recall…….. (**note**- degree of recall and if brand recalled was the right match)……..did it influence your purchase of the drink? PROBE

Thank you.

Categorization of Interviews

There are various kinds of interview methods available to the researcher. We have spoken earlier about a distinction based on the level of structure. The other classification is based on the mode of administering the interview. A classification table is presented in Figure 6.2.

FIGURE 6.2
Classification of personal interview methods

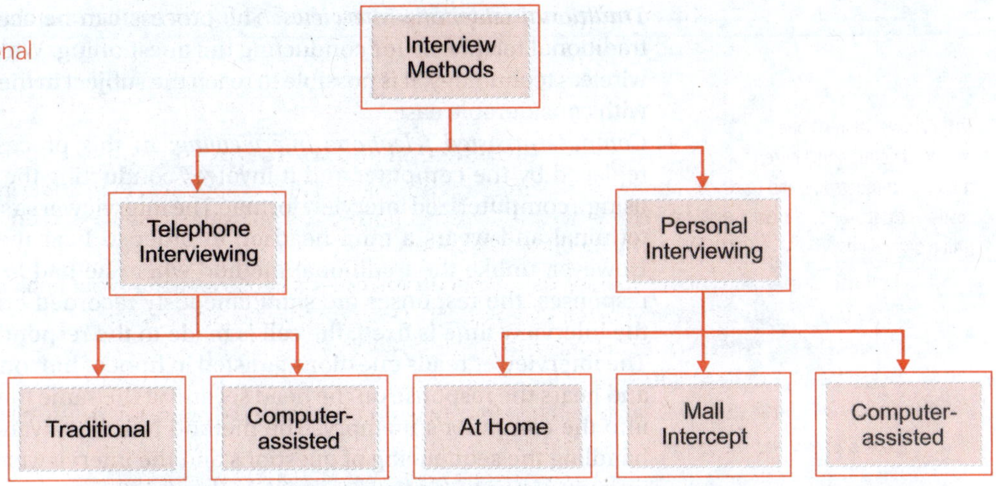

- **Personal methods:** These are the traditional one-to-one methods that have been used actively in all branches of social sciences. However, they are distinguished in terms of the place of conduction. These may be categorized as at-home, mall-intercept, or computer-assisted interviews.
  - *At-home interviews:* This face-to-face interaction takes place at the respondent's residence. Thus, the interviewer needs to initially contact the respondent to ascertain the interview time. The interviewer asks the respondent study-related questions and records the responses. The cost and time involved in conducting these interviews is considerable, which is the reason why they are avoided. However, they are used for syndicate research studies like pantry audits. The advantage of the technique is that it can be used in collaboration with observation to ascertain the lifestyle of the subject as well as get his/her responses.
  - *Mall-intercept interviews:* As the name suggests, this method involves conducting interviews with the respondents as they are shopping in malls. Sometimes, product testing or product reactions can be carried out through structured methods and followed by interviews to test the reactions. The advantage of the method is that a large number of subjects are accessible in a short time period, thus it is both cost and time effective. However, the time available is short, thus the questioning cannot be extensive and must get over in 20 to 30 minutes.
  - *Computer-assisted personal interviewing (CAPI):* These techniques are carried out with the help of the computer. In this form of interviewing, the respondent faces an assigned computer terminal and answers a questionnaire on the computer screen by using the keyboard or a mouse. A number of pre-designed packages are available to help the researcher design simple questions that are self-explanatory and instead of probing, the respondent is guided to a set of questions depending on the answer given. Thus, predetermined branches are formulated for probing a particular line of thought. There is usually an interviewer present at the time of respondent's computer-assisted interview and is available for help and guidance, if required. This is why they are called interviews and not questionnaires.

Computer-assisted personal interviewing (CAPI) is called so as there is usually an interviewer present at the time of the respondent's computer-assisted interview.

- **Telephone method:** The telephone method involves replacing the face-to-face interaction between the interviewer and interviewee, by questioning on telephones and calling up the subjects to asking them a set of questions. The advantage of the method is that geographic boundaries are not a constraint and the interview can be conducted at the individual respondent's location. The format and sequencing of the questions remains the same.

- *Traditional telephone interviews:* The process can be accomplished using the traditional telephone for conducting the questioning. With the improvement in wireless technology, it is possible to reach the subject in the remotest of locations with considerable ease.
- *Computer-assisted telephone interviewing:* In this process, the interviewer is replaced by the computer and it involves conducting the telephonic interview using a computerized interview format. The interviewer sits in front of a computer terminal and wears a mini-headset, in order to hear the respondent answer. However, unlike the traditional method where he had to manually record the responses, the responses are simultaneously recorded on the computer. Once the interview time is fixed, the call is made to the respondent by the computer. The interviewer reads questions as listed in front of him on the computer screen and hears the response on the head set and at the same time the answers are fed into the computer's memory. The method has the advantage of the computer handling the sequencing of questions and the interviewer is free to conduct the interview in reduced time and with higher accuracy.

Interview requires a one-to-one dialogue and, hence, it is more cumbersome and costly as compared to a focus group discussion.

The structured interview is one of the most powerful tools of qualitative data collection methods available to the researcher. It provides information that is richer in content as compared to the focus group. There is no pressure for conformity and reactions which might be lost in group conduction are explored in depth in this technique. Also for selected groups, (for example experts or retailers or representatives of the competing organizations), information can be better sought by the personal interview method. And as we have seen, with the advent of technological assistance, these interviews can be carried out at remote and far-off locations with the help of a telephone or a computer.

However, since the interview requires a one-to-one dialogue to be carried out, it is more cumbersome and costly as compared to a focus group discussion. Also conduction of interview requires considerable skills on the part of the interviewer and thus adequate training in interviewing skills is needed for capturing a comprehensive study-related data.

Thus far, the techniques that we have discussed are direct methods of data collection. These are actively used in almost all areas of business research. However, the discussion on qualitative methods would be incomplete if we did not discuss other methods of capturing rich, subjective data. These are not so frequently used as they require professionals for the conduction and thus might not be used by all. However, the quality of information and the nature of interpretations that can be made with these methods require a brief discussion and orientation to the techniques.

The first of these are the intriguing and ingenious projective techniques.

CONCEPT CHECK

1. What are the various stages involved in a personal interview method?
2. Classify the categories of interviews used for obtaining information.

PROJECTIVE TECHNIQUES

LEARNING OBJECTIVE 6

Understand qualitative methods, originating in other disciplines, now used actively in business research.

The idea of projecting one self or one's feelings on to ambiguous objects is the basic assumption in projective techniques. The 19th century saw the origin of these techniques in clinical and developmental psychology. However, it was after World War II that these techniques were adopted for use in advertising agencies and market research firms. Ernest Dichter (1960) was one of the pioneers who used these techniques in consumer and motivational research. Consumer Surveys and research were considered incomplete if they did not make use of projective techniques (Henry, 1956; Rogers and Beal, 1958; Newman, 1957). However, with the advent of technology and computer-aided analysis, these subjective methods were generally forgotten.

It was only in the 1990s that work done on semiotics, in-depth interviews and renewed interest in human emotions and needs, especially the latent needs and brand personalities led to resurgence of these methods (Belk et al., 1997 and Zaltman, 1997).

Unlike the other approaches discussed in the chapter, these methods involve indirect questioning. Instead of asking direct questions, the method involves a relatively ambiguous stimuli and indirect questions related to imaginary situations or people. The purpose of the research is to present a situation to the respondents to project their underlying needs, emotions, beliefs and attitudes on to this. The ambiguity of the situation is non-threatening and thus the person has no hesitation in revealing his true inner motivations and emotions. The more the degree of ambiguity, the more is the range of responses one gets from the respondents. In the theoretical sense, projective techniques unearth beliefs, attitudes and feelings that might underlie certain behaviour or interaction situations. Thus, the respondents' attitudes are uncovered by analysing their responses to the scenarios that are deliberately constructed to stimulate responses from the right side of the brain, which is stated to be the affective side. The second premise of projective techniques is to uncover the different levels of consciousness (Freud, 1911). Generally, the structured methods look at primary motivations; however, it is the underlying latent needs which might drive the individual to behave in a certain manner. The third is to reveal data that is inhibited by socially-desirable and correct responses. Sometimes individuals hesitate to express their prejudices or feelings towards other individuals, groups or objects. Indirect and ambiguous stimuli might reveal startling results in such cases. In psychology there are a wide variety of techniques available. These can be categorized on the basis of the conduction process. Some of these techniques are briefly discussed below.

The **projective techniques** uncover the different levels of consciousness of an individual's mind and reveal that data which is inhibited by socially-desirable and correct responses.

- **Association techniques:** These are the most frequently used methods in management research. They essentially involve presenting a stimulus to the respondent and he needs to respond with the first thing that comes to his mind. The method is essentially borrowed from clinical psychology, the most well known being the Rorschach Inkblot test. The set of inkblots are ambiguous in nature, however, these are standardized blots symmetrical in nature. The first few are in shades of black and white and the others are coloured. Each of these is presented in a sequence to the consumer. The responses, time taken, the direction in which the blot is turned, are noted. There are norms and scores available for evaluating the personality of the individual. They require a considerable amount of training in conduction and interpretation and, thus, are not commonly used. A technique based on the same principle is called the word association test. This found its earliest uses in 1936 by Houghton for advertising evaluations. The technique involves presenting a basket of words and the respondent needs to respond instantly with the first thing that comes to his mind. The critical words are disguised and come after a few neutral or mundane words. The idea is that the element of surprise will reveal associations that lie in the subconscious or the unconscious mind. The words which are selected to address the objectives of the study are called test words and the others are called fillers.

Rorschach Inkblot test and word association test are techniques that present a stimulus to the respondent and try to interpret his/her unconscious tendencies.

For example, to attest the extent of eco-friendly attitude of a community, one could have a number of words like 'environment,' 'plastic,' 'water,' 'earth,' 'tigers,' 'clean,' etc. These would be embedded in the fillers to see the extent to which the consumer is aware. The person's exact response is either noted or recorded; in case one is doing this manually, it is critical to note the reaction time of the person, as hesitating would mean that there was a latent response which the person was not comfortable about revealing. In this case, the response needs to be discarded or evaluated through other responses. Another variation of the test used in individual and brand personality is to ask the person to think of an animal/object that one associates with a brand or a person.

For example, the word 'wall' is associated with a famous Indian cricketer.

The obtained answers are measured in terms of:

(a) The similarity of responses given to a test word by a number of respondents
(b) Unique responses
(c) The time taken for a response
(d) Non-response

In case a person does not respond at all, it is assumed that the emotional block hampering the person is considerable. A person's attitudes and feelings related to the topic can be measured by this technique.

Illustration

Talking to elders: A popular pharmaceutical firm produces a range of expensive products meant for old-age consumers. The company plans to use television advertising to create awareness about the products. Word association was used to study old people's attitudes towards medication and supportive therapy. Six men and six women were selected to administer the test; they were matched on income, class, age, education and current status of living with their married sons/daughters. The test words used and the responses obtained are provided in Table 6.2.

The major responses are highlighted and reveal that the seniors are not afraid of dying, are realistic about failing health and supportive medicines or walking stick. However, they have clearly stated that they do not want to be embarrassed. Thus, talking about their health problems on a public medium and offering solutions would not be welcome. They are conscious and positive about medicines being essential, however, their dignity must be kept intact.

This research was taken as a reflection of the attitude of the elderly at large and the company does not use television advertising at all, rather it relies on doctors and chemists to push the product.

An extension of the association technique is the completion technique.

Sentence completion is the most popular technique used to map a respondent's attitude towards a product/situation/service.

- **Completion techniques:** These techniques involve presenting an incomplete object to the respondent, which can be completed by the respondent in any way that he/she deems appropriate. For example:

Old age is...

TABLE 6.2
Word association test

Test words	Responses		
Health	**Care (3)**	Bad (2)	Good (1)
Life	Difficult (2)	**Relaxed (3)**	Good (1)
Medicines	**Necessity (4)**	Prevention (2)	Avoid (1)
Walking stick	**Support (3)**	Avoid (2)	Carved ivory (1)
Adult diapers	**Embarrassment (4)**	Necessity (2)	
Treatment	In time (2)	**Expensive (4)**	
Bones	**Weak (3)**	**Brittle (3)**	
Death	**The end (1)**	**Inevitable (5)**	

Sentence completion is the most popular of all completion techniques and is inevitably used in almost all measuring instruments as an open-ended question. However, the incomplete sentence of a typical projective test needs to be more ambiguous than a typical open-ended question. Generally, they are given a single word or phrase and asked to fill it in, for example:

Working at IBM is.. Or

McDonald is...

Another extension of the technique is *story completion*. Here, the individual is given an incomplete story or idea. One provides a backdrop and a background for a possible topic. However, the possible end is left open-ended. The subject is supposed to complete the story and provide a conclusion. The theoretical assumption is that the completion of the story/sentence reflects the underlying attitude and personality traits of the person.

Thematic apperception tests (TAT) and **cartoon tests** belong to the branch of clinical psychology and the focus here is on the completion of a particular story, incident, picture or dialogue.

- **Construction techniques:** These techniques might appear similar to completion technique, however here, the focus is on the completed object, which could be a story, a picture, a dialogue or a description. Here, again, the level of ambiguity and scope for letting loose the respondents' imagination is vast.

  Clinical psychology has a whole range of construction techniques, but in this chapter we will refer only to the ones which are actively used in business research. These are:

  - *Story construction tests:* The most often used test is the thematic apperception test (TAT) developed by Henry (1956). There are a total of 20 pictures, most of them having the profile of a man, woman or child either clearly visible or diffused. The set of these pictures are given to the respondent and he/she is asked: What is happening here? What happened or led to this? What do you think is going to happen now? The assumption is, that in most instances the person puts himself/herself into the shoes of the protagonist and actually indicates how he/she would respond in the given situation. The story gives an indication of the person's personality and need structure. For example, an individual may be characterized as extroverted, or a pessimistic or high on creativity or high on dogmatism, and so on. The TAT is used extensively, in parts (a few selected pictures) or in totality in a number of organizations, including the armed forces. The usage is majorly done for selection and recruitment process.
  - *Cartoon tests:* The tests make use of animated characters in a particular situation (Masling, 1952). They are considered ambiguous as the figures bear no resemblance to a living being and thus are considered non-threatening. The cartoon usually has a picture that has two or more characters talking to each other; usually the statement/question by one character is denoted and one needs to fill in the response made by the other character. The picture has a direct relation with the topic under study and is assumed to reveal the respondent's attitude, feelings or intended behaviour. They are one of the easiest to administer, analyse and score.
- **Choice or ordering techniques:** These techniques involve presenting the respondents with an assortment of stimuli—in the form of pictures or statements—related to the study topic. The subject is supposed to sort them into categories, based on the study instructions given. For example, in a study on measuring desired supervisor–subordinate relations, a set of Tom and Jerry cartoon pictures were used, some in which Tom is overpowering Jerry, some neutral pictures where they are carrying out their respective tasks and others where Jerry, the mouse outwits Tom. The respondent needs to sort them into good, neutral and bad picture piles.

These sets are not similar to cartoon tests as they do not require completion or closure. These require sorting, in order to measure any stereotyped or typical behaviour of the respondent. The pictures that have been given to the person carry an expert score (that is they have been categorized on a rating scale to reveal different degrees of the attitude). The higher the selection of pictures with extreme scores, the more rigid is the respondent's attitude and in case modification or enhancement is required, the task would be more difficult. The test is used to measure attitudes and the strength of the existing attitude.

- **Expressive techniques:** The focus on the other five techniques was on the end result or the output. However, in expressive techniques, the method or means or expressions used in attempting the exercise are significant. The subject needs to express not his/her own feelings and opinions but those of the protagonist(s) in a given verbal or visual situation. Again the presumption is that people are uncomfortable giving personal opinion on a sensitive issue, but, do not mind or are less inhibitive when it is in the third person. There are many examples: Clay modelling—here the emphasis is on the manner in which the person uses or works with clay and not on the end result.

Psychodrama (Dichter, 1964)—here the person needs to take on the roles of living or inanimate object, like a brand(s) and carry out a dialogue.

Object personification (Vicary, 1951)—here the person personifies an inanimate object/brand/organization and assigns it human traits.

In the **role playing technique,** the respondents are asked to play the role or assume the behaviour of someone else. Similarly, the **third-person technique** reduces the social pressure about a sensitive issue.

Role playing is another technique that is used in business research. The respondents are asked to play the role or assume the behaviour of someone else. The details about the setting are given to the subject(s) and they are asked to take on different roles and enact the situation.

The third-person technique is again considered harmless as here, the respondent is presented with a verbal or visual situation and needs to express what might be the person's beliefs and attitudes. The person may be a friend, neighbour, colleague, or a 'typical' person. Asking the individual to respond in the third person reduces the social pressure, especially when the discussion or study is about a sensitive issue. For example, no respondent even when assured of anonymity, would own up to being open to an extra-marital affair; however, if asked whether a colleague/friend/person in his/her age group might show an inclination for the same, the answers might be starkly different.

Evaluating Projective Techniques

Thus, as can be seen from the description of the techniques available to the researcher, the projective techniques are unsurpassed in revealing latent yet significant responses. These would not surface through a more structured or standardized techniques like focus group discussions or interviews. The ambiguity and the third-person setting give the respondent a sufficient camouflage and confidence to feel comfortable about revealing attitudes, interests and beliefs about sensitive issues. There might also be instances where the respondent is unaware of his underlying motivations, beliefs and attitudes that are operating at a subconscious level. Projective techniques are helpful in unearthing these with considerable ease and expertise.

However, this richness of data also has its disadvantages. The conduction and analysis of the technique requires specialists and trained professionals. This is also the reason why the tests are expensive and time consuming in usage. Most of the techniques require varying degrees of ambiguity and the higher the ambiguity, the richer is the response. But, at the same time, it makes the analysis and interpretation difficult and subjective. Role playing and psychodrama require interaction and participation by the subject, thus the person who volunteers to participate in the study, might be unusual in some way. Therefore, generalizing the results of the analysis might be subject to error.

Sociometric Analysis

Sociometric analysis involves measuring the choice, communication and interpersonal relations of people in different groups.

This is a technique that has the group rather the individual as its unit of analysis and thus has its origin in sociology. Sociometry involves measuring the choice, communication and interpersonal relations of people in different groups. The computations made on the basis of these choices indicate the social attraction and avoidance in a group. The individual could be asked such sociometric questions like 'in the group (describe) with whom you would like to work/interact socially with,' 'out of the following (list of acquaintances) whom would you find as acceptable neighbours on either side of your home?' One may ask the individual to also carry out the reverse, that is, indicate whom from the group do they think would choose him/her?

In a **sociogram**, a one-way arrow indicates a one-way choice and a two-way arrow indicates a mutual choice.

- **Sociometric analysis of data:** The data obtained by these kinds of sociometric questions can be subjected to a quantitative analysis. For the behavioural researcher, the sociometric matrices and sociometric indices have research possibilities.
  - *Sociometric matrices:* The matrix in this case is an $n \times n$ matrix, where n is the number of people in the group. The choice matrix is based upon the answers given by the subjects to the sociometric question. For example, to a five-member group, we ask a sociometric question, 'from the group indicate two people you would like to take in your project team.' A selection is marked as one, otherwise the person gets a score of 0 (Table 6.3).

The interpretation of the matrix is first done at the macro level to add up the score for each person and assess the individual popularity of each person. For example, Ravdeep is the least popular and Shanti is the most popular person in the group. The micro analysis is to assess a one-way choice, a mutual choice and no choice. Based on these choices, one, two and non-directional graphs are made in the form of a *sociogram,* where a one-way arrow indicates a one-way choice and a two-way arrow indicates a mutual choice. However, this is simple when one has a

TABLE 6.3 Sociometric matrix of team choices: Team project question

	CHOICE SET					
	Nimit	**Shanti**	**Pooja**	**Ravdeep**	**Asmit**	**Rini**
Nimit	0	1	1	0	0	0
Shanti	1	0	0	0	1	0
Pooja	1	1	0	0	0	0
Ravdeep	0	1	0	0	1	0
Asmit	0	1	0	0	0	1
Rini	0	1	0	0	1	0
Σ	2	5	1	0	3	1

Note: The summation at the bottom indicates the number of times the person was chosen by his friends/colleagues. The choices are to be read row-wise, for example, Nimit chooses Shanti and Pooja, while Shanti chooses Nimit and Asmit.

small group but becomes complicated and difficult to decipher as the number of members increases.

- *Sociometric indices:* Based on the matrix drawn and the indicated choices, it is possible to obtain two quantitative measures. One is for the choice status of the person, i.e., how popular he/she is and the second is related to cohesion in a group.

The following is the formula for measuring the popularity or choice status of a person.

$$CS_j = \frac{\Sigma c_j}{n-1}$$

Group cohesiveness refers to the mutual bonding within the groups.

CS_j = the choice status of person j, Σc_j = the sum of choices in column j, and n = number of people in the group who were asked the sociometric question. For Shanti, CSs = 5/5 = 1.00 and for Ravdeep CSr = 0/5 = 0.

However, in an organizational set up, one is more interested in the group cohesiveness and how that would impact the functioning. Another popular index is the one to measure group cohesiveness. The person could be permitted to choose as many as he/she wants from the group for the task. The formula, then, is as follows:

$$Co = \frac{\Sigma (I \leftrightarrow j)}{\frac{n(n-1)}{2}}$$

Group cohesiveness is represented by Co and $\Sigma(I \leftrightarrow j)$ = sum of mutual choices (or mutual pairs). It divides the study pair by the ideal situation of all possible pairs. In the six-member group that we had, the number of possible pairs and the total number of possible pairs is 6 people taken 2 at a time.

$$\binom{6}{2} = \frac{6(6-1)}{2} = 15$$

If, in an unlimited choice situation, there were 2 mutual choices, then Co = 3/15 = 0.2, a rather low degree of cohesiveness. In case of limited choice, the formula is:

$$Co = \frac{\Sigma(I \leftrightarrow j)}{dn/2}.$$

Where d = the number of choices each individual is permitted (in the study case only 2). Thus the cohesiveness becomes Co = 3/(2 × 6/2) = 3/6 = .50, a reasonable degree of cohesiveness.

The above technique is useful in evaluating informal channels of communication in an organization. It can also be used effectively to measure the social and organizational prejudices that people might have. In a community or social group, one is also able to measure the star or potential leaders or opinion leaders, as they would have substantial influence in impacting the attitude of the group towards a product, brand or organizational change. The disadvantage of the method is that the findings do not have widespread applicability and can be used only for a limited group. The second limitation is that it is only indicative of the personal choice and not of the actual choice which might depend upon other factors. The person who is selected as the most popular might not be chosen because of his/her personal traits but on the basis of perceived benefits/power the person might have. Thus, it is advisable to use the method in conjunction with other, more structured techniques.

Afterthoughts on Qualitative Research

In this chapter we have attempted to expose the potential researcher to the rich and enigmatic world that is revealed through the use of qualitative techniques. As man becomes more sensitive to his environment and realizes that all the puzzles cannot be answered by simple mathematical functions, he appreciates the subjectivity of reasoning and the latent emotions behind it. To be able to stand out in a crowded marketplace, it is imperative to reach out and form a human connect. Whether with the external consumers in a marketing research or with the internal consumers in a behavioural research, the subconscious and the unconscious needs and emotions are extremely critical. An exercise such as this is just not possible if one does not make use of qualitative methods. There have been many new advancements done in the field with new techniques like netnography—study of internet communities and tweets and blogs available as representing virtual consumption groups and Monticello corrections—study of human consumption in history.

CONCEPT CHECK

1. How are projective techniques different from the others?
2. Elaborate on the construction techniques and choice or ordering techniques.
3. What is sociometric analysis?

SUMMARY

- One cannot overemphasize the significance of this class of methods. To comprehend the puzzle of acceptance and rejection of management offerings to the internal or external customer, the best approach available to the researcher is that of qualitative research. These are loosely-structured subjective methods designed to allow and instigate deep and insightful exploration of the respondents' mind. There are multiple arguments and examples of how qualitative approach has resulted in obtaining clarity about the quantitative phenomena. They are diametrically different from quantitative techniques and yet are not lacking in any way. Even though they are unstructured, they still have a well-defined methodology and plan of execution. They are not overtly diagnostic in nature; thus, a Gestaltian approach would be to use them in conjunction with quantitative methods.
- There are a number of rich and diverse qualitative methods available to the business researcher. Most of these have their origin in social sciences like psychology and sociology and have been adapted now to reveal more about human behaviour.
- The observation method is a technique which involves an apparent and a direct reporting of events as they occur. They are usually non-participative and the respondent does not offer any inputs into the data collected. The skill and objectivity in recording all the aspects of both non-verbal and verbal features of the event being observed is extremely critical. The method could involve a highly unstructured, ambiguous approach or the researcher might design a broad format of the areas on which the observations are to be made. The observation might be carried out either by human observers or by mechanical sources such as galvanometer for skin responses or pupilometer to measure eye movement. A derivation of the observation method is Trace analysis. Here the leftover things like credit card statements or the shopping basket is observed to measure current purchase and consumption.
- Content analysis is another qualitative method. This method involves analysing previously recorded communication and trying to break it down into inferences that will aid in achieving the study objectives. A typical content analysis might break down the information into words, theme, space, character, time and item according to a predefined rule. Today there are software programmes to assist the researcher in carrying out content analysis.
- Focus group techniques are one of the most widely and frequently used qualitative methods. They usually consist of 8–10 members who are led by a participant or a non-participant moderator into a structured and sequential discussion. The researcher prepares a discussion guide and maneuvers the discussion according to a definite pattern. The output is rich and precise and needs to be objectively interpreted for the study purpose. There are different types of focus group studies that can be carried out and the selection depends upon the research approach and design of the study.
- Another popular method is the personal interview method, which involves a one-to-one interaction between the interviewer and the interviewee to generate a dialogue that is carried out to achieve answers to the research

questions. The interview ranges from the unstructured to semi-structured to completely structured. The interview could be conducted over the telephone or as a traditional face-to-face personal method. In both the methods today, there has been considerable ease of conduction with the advent of computer-assisted interviews.

- Two other methods that are rich in terms of output but are difficult to conduct as they require considerable training on the part of the investigator are projective techniques and sociometry. Projective techniques are of five different kinds and essentially involve presenting the respondent a relatively ambiguous object on which he superimposes his own thoughts and feelings. The methods involve indirect questioning and analysis. Sociometry is a method of evaluating the group behaviour and intergroup relations. This technique is more of use in studies carried out in organizational behaviour and human resource areas.

KEY TERMS

- Association tests
- Completion techniques
- Computer-assisted interviews
- Construction techniques
- Content analysis
- Discussion guides
- Dual moderator groups
- Focus group discussions
- Group formation stages
- Human observation
- Mall intercept interviews
- Mechanical observation
- Moderator
- Netnography
- Observation method
- Oculometers
- Projective techniques
- Psycho galvanometer
- Qualitative research
- Semi-structured interviews
- Sociometric indices
- Sociometry
- Structured interviews
- Structured observation
- Telephonic interviews
- Trace analysis
- Two-way focus groups
- Unstructured interviews
- Unstructured observation

CHAPTER REVIEW QUESTIONS

Objective Type Questions

State whether the following statements are true (T) or false (F).

1. The richness of data collected by using qualitative methods is better than that collected through quantitative methods.
2. Qualitative methods are more costly and time consuming as compared to quantitative methods.
3. In case one wants to know why some people use plastic bags for carrying their grocery even after the imposition of a ban on plastic bags by the Delhi Government, one may use the observation method to collect the data.
4. Usually the observation method entails that the observation is disguised, i.e., carried out without the respondent's knowledge.
5. Usually when one wants to study latent or subconscious aspect of human behaviour, one makes use of disguised observation method.
6. Oculometers can be used to measure what attracts a consumer as he enters a retail store.
7. Pupilometers measure the blinking of eyelids over the pupil, when the respondent is exposed to stimuli.
8. Garbology is an observation technique where one evaluates a person's garbage.
9. The simplest level of analysis in content analysis is a theme.
10. Both focus group discussions and sociometry have their origin in sociology.
11. A discussion guide is the moderator guide who directs the discussion in a focus group discussion.
12. Eight to ten respondents are ideal for a focus group discussion.
13. Cliques and smaller sub-groups are made in the forming stage of group formation.
14. Mourning refers to the passing away of a popular member of the formed group.
15. CAPI refers to computer-assisted personal interviewing.

16. Projective techniques make use of multiple unambiguous objects to understand a person's underlying needs and emotions.
17. Rorschach Inkblot test is a kind of expressive technique.
18. Netnography involves understanding virtual communities.
19. The best method to study informal communication network in an organization is sociometry.
20. TAT is a technique borrowed from anthropology to understand group structure.

Conceptual Questions

1. Distinguish between the qualitative and the quantitative sources of data collection. Can qualitative methods be used for a conclusive research study? Justify your answer with suitable illustrations.
2. What are focus group discussions? Under what circumstances should they be used?
3. What is the observation method? What are the different types of observation methods available to the researcher? Elaborate with suitable examples.
4. Explain the interview method of data collection. What are the advancements that have been made in the technique? How has technology helped in the conduction of interviews?
5. 'Qualitative methods require special skills and techniques on the part of the investigator.' Examine the truth of the statement by using suitable examples.
6. What is content analysis? What is the process to be followed for conducting a content analysis study? Why is this called a primary data collection method even though it works on secondary data?
7. What are projective techniques? What are the different types of techniques available to a researcher? Explain with suitable examples.
8. Distinguish between:
   (a) Focus group discussions and personal interviews
   (b) Personal and mechanical observation methods
   (c) Completion and construction techniques
   (d) Actual and virtual focus groups
9. Write short notes on:
   (a) Sociometry
   (b) Content analysis
   (c) Computer-aided interviews

Application Questions

1. You have been assigned the task of carrying out an FGD for a new radio station—FM 42.0 Radio Chillz. The channel is meant for Generation Y (those born after 1980). You need to get information from the assigned group on:
   (a) What should be the punch line?
   (b) What kind of programmes should you air?
   (c) What would be the requirement if you hire RJ's (Radio Jockey)?

   Write down the discussion guide for the following study. What elements should the moderator be careful about? How will he screen the respondents?
2. Conduct a focus group for the following research study:

   LG is doing it, Colgate is doing it, Pepsodent is doing it, Add gel is doing it. i.e., targeting children

   The Information and Broadcasting Ministry want to set up a regulatory advertising body. As a part of the research team, you have been asked to conduct FGD'S to find out:
   (a) Should advertisements and sales promotions be targeted at children?
   (b) What are the moral issues that need to be taken care of?
   (c) If yes, for what age groups?
   (d) Which product categories?
   (e) What will be the screening questions?
   (f) Design the discussion guide and conduct FGD with 8–10 members.
   (g) Formulate a short two-page report on the study.

3. Conduct an interview (structured interview) to obtain information about:
   (a) Demographics
   (b) Psychographics
   (c) Lifestyle
   (d) Role models
   (e) Friends—the relevance of friendship in a person-specifically his/her life
      - What are the qualities he/she looks for in a friend?
      - Describe his/her friendship group.
      - Analyse himself/herself in terms of the kind of friend he/she is?
      - In this respect if she/he could improve on his/her one quality, what would it be?
      - A story or song he/she associates with true friendship.
4. Conduct a sociometric analysis amongst 10 relatives of yours to find out the popularity status and cohesiveness in your family. For this:
   (a) Design a sociometric question
   (b) Provide brief details about the ten selected members
   (c) Conduct the study and prepare the analysis
   (d) Prepare a short report, explaining the reasons you perceive are responsible for the finding
   (e) What could have been the limitations/biases of your study?

CASE 6.1

DANISH INTERNATIONAL (C)

Shameem was returning after an exhaustive session with P & Y consultants. The lady consultant had reviewed the information that he had provided about the working atmosphere at Danish.

She had also conducted a couple of visits to the office and had submitted her report. She had pointed out clearly that the indifference he had observed was a matter of serious concern. No benchmarked data would help as the problem was peculiar to the unit. She had advised that the attitude and emotions of the members would have to be analysed. She had told him that they had a couple of standardized tests that she could administer and prepare an action plan.

Shameem was not convinced as he knew that the issue needed to be handled at a different plane. Then he remembered the lady he had met from Transcend, the research beyond group, who had made a presentation yesterday about seeking the latent to work on the manifest. He recalled the book that he had read by Sigmund Freud and how it had made a lot of sense about why people reacted in a certain way. Yes, there was merit in the surreal. But this was business, should he go for the subjective?

He reached office, read the P & Y report, thought about what he believed, and picked up his phone and made the call ...

QUESTIONS

1. Who do you think he called? Why?
2. Are there any alternative technique(s) he could use? Explain by providing a template for collecting the information.

CASE 6.2

WHAT'S IN A CAR?

Shridhar from Bengaluru, had developed an electric car—VERVE (It is a fully automatic, no clutch, no gears), two-door hatchback, easily seating two adults and two children with a small turning radius of just 3.5 metres). It runs on batteries and as compared to other electric vehicles, has an onboard charger to facilitate easy charging which can be carried out by plugging into any 15 amp socket at home or work. A full battery charge takes less than seven hours and gives a range of 80 km. In a quick-charge mode (two-and-a-half hours) 80 per cent charge is attained which is good enough for 65 km. A full charge consumes just about 9 units of electricity. Somehow the product did not take off the way he expected. He is contemplating about repositioning the car. As he stood looking at the prototype, he knew that there were a couple of questions to which he must find answers before he undertook the repositioning exercise. Who should be the targeted segment—old people, young students just going to college, housewives, or ...? What should be the positioning stance? What kind of image would these customers relate to? Was a new name or punch-line required? How should the promotions be undertaken? Hyundai had done it with Shah Rukh Khan, should he also consider a celebrity? If yes who?

QUESTIONS

1. What kind of research study should Shridhar undertake? Define the objectives of his research.
2. Do the stated objectives have scope for a qualitative research?
3. Which method(s) would you recommend and why?
4. Can you construct a template for conducting the study? What element would you advice Shridhar to keep in mind, and why?

CASE 6.3

CANDY-HO! (A)

The evening sky was overcast. Looking out from the window of his office on the 12th floor, Sagar Ahuja could still see the etched out skyline of New Delhi. Sighing wearily, he turned his thoughts back to his comfortable job at Indore where he was marketing spicy Gujarati namkeen, and wondered what on earth he was doing in an alien city whose complexities and multiplicities seemed to defy any description to his simple mind. Having been a star performer at his regional office, and responsible for the launch of two revolutionary products for his company, he had been approached by head hunters to join Nefertiti—the famous global confectionary company in India. As his first assignment he had been given the job of swimming in deep waters and launch a new bubblegum that had been developed.

The Product

It was a sugar-coated, round-shaped, centre-filled liquid gel bubblegum in two flavours—strawberry and blueberry. The product was packed in mono pillow packs and was going to be priced at ₹1.00 per piece. The name of the product was to be *Moondrops*.

He had in front of him the results of a research conducted by Offspring research agency—a market research company specializing in child research studies.

Research Objectives

- To understand the meaning of a candy/bubblegum in a child's life.
- To analyse the response to two advertisements that had been created to market the bubblegum.
- To arrive at a decision on how to position and market the gum, and the advertisement that would be more suitable for the purpose.

Weighted base: Those whose favourite category is bubblegum and chewing gum	**771**
Like the taste/like to eat it	87
Soft to chew	26
Easily available everywhere	18
Helps in passing time/kills boredom/overcomes feeling of restlessness	18
Freshens breath	17
Taste you never get tired of/can keep eating repeatedly	11
Has variety of flavours	11
Not costly/Does not cost much	11
Improves taste of mouth/removes bad taste in mouth	10
Can be had any time of the day	10
Makes me feel happy/fun to have	9
Liked by my friends	7
Worth the price I pay for it/value for money	6

Data Source: Primary Research carried out by Nefertiti Company. Random Interviews with SEC A and B consumers equally split between male and female respondents, in the top eight cities, total sample size was 1,000 respondents.

FGD Analysis

The result of 24 focus groups across age groups and metros revealed the following data from a projective technique that involved personifying the bubblegum. The responses are across age groups and are in the decreasing order of most stated.

- *I want to play with my bubblegum*
- *The bubblegum has lots of friends—lot of names*
- *The bubblegum is very naughty—no one can catch him*
- *The bubblegum is my friend and helps me fight the older kids*
- *If all bubblegums were to fight, my bubblegum would win*
- *If I am feeling sad, my bubblegum would make me laugh*
- *My bubblegum is the bravest*

Post the FGC. Select respondents (children) were shown two advertisements. reaction to these are listed below:

(a) The race ad

The storyboard was that at a school annual function race, where the 'hero' of the story deliberately loses the race and comes third instead of first to get the third prize of two big jars of Moondrops. Followed by the punchline '*Moondrops ke liye kuch bhi ho sakta hai*'.

Reactions (with loud laughter)

All the kids were involved with the ad while viewing it and liked the storyboard with comments such as:

- '*It was interesting*'.

- '*Main soch raha tha ki yeh ladka ruk kyon gaya*'. (I was wondering why the boy stopped.)

The children enjoyed when the kid smiles with two big Moondrop jars in his hand.

- '*Jab who ladka race mein finish line ke pas aake ruk jata hai*'. (When the boy stops near the finish line.)
- '*Jab use third prize Moondrops milta hai aur use doorse do first and second prize wale ladke ghoor ke dekhte hain*'. (When he gets Moondrops as the third prize and the first and second prize winners stare at him.)
- *We feel proud to win a race even if we do not get any prize.*'
- '*If I win the race then Mummy and Daddy will anyway buy me Moondrops*'.
- '*Mein sirf Moondrops ke liye race nahin haroonga*'. (I'll never lose a race just for Moondrops.)
- '*Woh ladka buddhoo tha, kyonki usne jeeti hui race har di.*' (That boy was a fool, as he lost a race that he was winning.)

The kids were surprised when the child stops just near the finish line and when the other two children are surprised and shocked that he is getting the Moondrops as the third prize.

Empathy/Relatability

Not many of the kids could relate to the ad. They did not see themselves doing the same just for getting two jars of Moondrops, the underlying reason being that they had to lose (If they could finish first, then why finish third).

(b) Kitty party ad

The story starts with a child returning from school to see a kitty party in progress at home (lots of fat aunties chatting and eating samosas and pakoras). One fat aunty pulls his cheek affectionately and much to his disgust, kisses him. He then feels happy when his reward is a Moondrop from the fat aunty. Seeing that he gets a Moondrop when the aunty kisses him, he plays a prank on all the aunties by jumping on the table and the sofa and kissing all the aunties there. His reward is lots of Moondrops. Followed by the punchline, '*Moondrops ke liye kuch bhi ho sakta hai*'.

Reactions

The scene where the fat aunty kisses the boy and they show her fat lips. The boy kissing the aunties by jumping on the sofa, on the table and by kissing an aunty.

- '*Jab who moti aunty ke lips dikhate hain*'. (When they show the fat aunty's lips.)
- '*Jab who moti aunty use kiss karti hain*'. (When the fat aunty kisses him.)
- '*Jab who sari aunties ko kiss karta hai aur aunties hairan ho jati hain*'. (When he surprises all the aunties by kissing them.)

Likeability

- '*Dekhne mein maza aaya*' (It was fun to watch.)
- '*Jab usne aunties ko kiss kiya to bahut accha laga*' (It was really good to see him kissing the aunties.)
- '*Aunty ka face itna funny tha, unko dekh ke hasi aayi*' (Aunty's face was so funny that we felt like laughing.)

Empathy/Relatability

- '*Chhi, hum naughty nahin hain*' (Ugh, we are not naughty.)
- '*Aunty ko kiss nahin karenge, beizzati hoti hai.*' (Will not kiss the aunty, it is insulting.)
- '*Ganda lagta hai*'. (Don't like it.)
- '*Aunty ko kis karenge to manjan karna padega*'. (Will have to brush teeth if we kiss aunty.)

QUESTION

1. Can you help Mr Ahuja arrive at a decision?

CASE 6.4

FORTUNE AT THE LAST FRONTIER (C)

Nikhil Thareja belonged to the third generation of Thareja & Sons Builders. The company had been started by Nikhil's grandfather Lala Harbans Lal Thareja in 1947. Nikhil Thareja, the heir apparent for the Thareja & Sons Empire, had been called by his grandfather and given his first independent Strategic Business Unit (SBU). The plan was to set up "Twilight Luxury: Retirement Solutions for those Who Reinvent Life". The idea being to set up retirement solutions or housing for the senior citizens with resources and who could reasonably manage an independent life style.

Nikhil Thareja had done extensive research in terms of collecting market and consumer data on senior citizens in India. He had developed three housing concepts and studied the purchase intention for each of these solutions. His research had pointed out that the best option to be developed by Thareja Builders was Option A.

Option A

Luxury condominiums on the Delhi-Agra expressway. These would range from one-bedroom studio apartments to three-bedroom fully furnished apartments. The price would be 75 lakh to 1.25 crore. The apartments would be constructed as per environmental guidelines. The area would have only 100 such apartments. The facilities in the housing complex would include a library; a state-of-the-art movie theatre; fully functional kitchen; 24-hour transport, nursing care and tie-up with Apollo Hospital in Delhi for medical emergencies.

Nikhil's business development team was looking at developing the marketing strategy for the housing solution. Thus, the teams from Roy Research Agency (Nikhil Thareja's batchmate Shantanu Roy's research agency) decided to conduct the study at two levels.

Level 1

The objective of the first research was to:

- *Identify the typical consumer of "Twilight Luxury-Retirement solutions"*
- *Define effective and focused targeting principles for the segment*
- *Develop a clear and distinct positioning stance for the housing brand*

This was to be done at the company level. This would be done with the Board of directors of Thareja Builders; the Head of Corporate communications at Thareja builder; the Executive director marketing and 10 employees who had been working with the company for minimum five years with the company. The selection of the ten employees was done by selecting every 5th employee from the pool of 65 of this group.

For the purpose of an in-depth interview that was to last for 40–50 minutes, an in-depth discussion guide was prepared (Case exhibit-1).

Level 2

After level one result had been suitably conducted, level 2 of the study would be conducted with the identified population to be targeted. The objective of this stage was to:

- *Identify a viable concept for the "Twilight Luxury-Retirement solutions"*
- *Develop a clear and distinct brand positioning based on the concept note for the Housing brand*

This was to be done at the respondent level. Based on the identified characteristics of the targeted population 40 in-depth interviews were to be conducted. Each interview would take 40–60 minutes. The sample would be selected based on convenience sampling method. The in-depth interview guide for the respondent survey was also developed (Case exhibit-2).

QUESTIONS

1. In the light of the study objectives evaluate the two in-depth interview guides.
2. What are the chances of errors in using the guides? How would you advocate that these be reduced/ minimized? Make suitable recommendations.
3. Could any other qualitative research method have been used in this study? If yes which one? If not, why not?

Case Exhibit 1: Internal Discussion Guide

1. What kind of buyers do you think will look at buying the condominiums that would be made under the "Twilight luxury" name?
2. Describe the person/couple in complete graphical detail.
3. What are the demographic characteristics of this buyer? Age? Income? Education? Last profession? etc.
4. How would this consumer be similar or different to the kind of buyers who patronize Thareja Housing? Please go beyond the simple age of the two consumers.
5. Do you think that the decision to explore a Twilight Solution by the buyer would be on his/her own or under recommendation of an expert, e.g. a broker or property agent?
6. What kind of facilities would the Buyer be looking for from the supplier?
7. Do you think that we should set up our own infrastructure/ service to deliver these requirements (as stated in the last question) or outsource it?
8. How would the prospective buyer hear about/come to know about Twilight Luxury? Further what will the consumer/buyer want to know about the Housing project?
9. What should be the pricing of these apartments? Please remember we had discussed additional facilities as well. How should the costing of living + facilities be done?
10. Describe your visual image of "Twilight Luxury- Retirement Solutions". In the light of the discussion that we just had would you have any suggestion in terms of the tagline?

Case Exhibit 2: Consumer Discussion Guide

Introduction

Thank you for agreeing to talk to me today. My name is .... I am conducting this study for a respected infrastructural entrepreneur who is thinking of expanding into housing solutions. Please remember there are no right or wrong answers. It is your perception about the concept that I want to capture. Your ideas and insights are what will make this concept richer and better understood and developed. So shall we begin?

1. You see in front of you the gate of a housing complex. On the gate is written "Twilight Luxury: Retirement Solutions for those Who Reinvent Life". Please tell me what will you see once you enter the gate?
   - **Probe:** Landscape
   - **Probe:** Houses
   - **Probe:** Any other
2. If you knock on the door of an apartment/ house (take a cue from what he/she said in the earlier question for House) who will open the door?
   - **Probe:** Describe the person
   - **Probe:** Describe the interiors of the house/apartment
   - **Probe:** Anything else
3. If you further explore the surroundings of this complex, what else will you find? (PROBE: Ask the person to describe whatever he/she reports)
4. What will you see on this complex which is different from what you would see in any other complex?
5. If you were to describe this place to someone you know how would you describe it
   a. Your friend/acquaintance
   b. A person who is of 60 years of age

CASE 6.5

CAREER IN SERVICE SECTOR VS MANUFACTURING SECTOR – THE CASE OF MBA ASPIRANTS

Introduction

Service industries have traditionally ruled the economy across the world. The share of services in India's gross domestic product (GDP) at factor cost (at current prices) increased from 33.3 per cent (1950–51) to 56.5 per cent in 2012–13, as per advance estimates (AE).[1] The share of manufacturing in the GDP has hovered around 15–16 per cent. As per advance estimates made by the Central Statistics Office (CSO), the contribution of manufacturing to the GDP during 2012-13 is 15.2 per cent at factor cost, at 2004-05 prices.[2] The National Manufacturing Policy envisages that India's manufacturing sector should increase its share of GDP from 15 per cent at present to 25 per cent by 2022, in line with global peers.[3] RBI has also said that India needs to focus more on manufacturing in order to achieve a GDP growth more than 6.5 per cent.[4]

The output in manufacturing sectors has always shown positive growth, though the workforce lacks the required strength. Young people born during the 1980s and early 1990s, popularly referred to as Gen Y, particularly prefer a career in the service sector over manufacturing. The question, thus, arises, why a country like India with a high-growth-potential manufacturing industry is unable to attract and retain young talent in this sector. Though most manufacturing companies offer high compensation and incentive, the younger workforce still mostly prefer the service sector over the manufacturing sector. Manufacturing industry has a lot of potential to contribute significantly in the overall growth of the country. Therefore, attraction and retention of workforce, as well as analysis of shortfall of young talent in this sector is a subject matter of concern and should be addressed at the earliest. The productivity and output in manufacturing industries continue to grow even as manufacturing employment numbers drop in many countries.[5] No organization in manufacturing or any other sector can compete in the global economy without a highly skilled and motivated workforce.

Global manufacturing companies in most parts of the world faces a shortage of high-skilled workers and an aging workforce, resulting in a shortage of talent in these companies. Part of the answer to the growing problem may lie with Generation Y, which will constitute a significant proportion of the working-age population in the coming years. A failure to effectively attract and engage these new workers will significantly hamper manufacturers' competitiveness in the long run. Convincing this generation to pursue a career in the manufacturing sector, however, is a challenge in itself.

The problem is the negative image of the manufacturing sector, which is no longer seen as a leading source of high-reward career opportunities. Other industries afford attractive alternatives for talented young people. To attract these new workers, the manufacturing industry needs a model of talent management that will address the unique characteristics of this generation.

Purpose of the Study

The diminishing incoming talent can pose a serious threat to the long-term global competitiveness of manufacturing firms. Therefore, it is important to attract young talent into this sector. This talent gap varies a great deal across manufacturing industries and geographies in terms of magnitude, age, and skill type. The purpose of this study is to identify these elements which prevent the young talent, especially the management graduates, from joining this sector.

1 http://dipp.nic.in/English/questions/27022013/rs45.pdf

2 http://articles.economictimes.indiatimes.com/2013-03-17/news/37787192_1_bcg-report-people-productivity-competitiveness

3 http://articles.economictimes.indiatimes.com/2012-08-05/news/33049112_1_gdp-growth-pension-and-insurance-funds-governor-d-subbarao

4 http://www.deloitte.com/assets/Dcom-Global/Local%20Assets/Documents/dtt_dr_ talentcrisis070307.pdf

5 http://www.deloitte.com/assets/Dcom-Global/Local%20Assets/Documents/dtt_dr_ talentcrisis070307.pdf

Methodology

The research design employed in the present study is exploratory. A focus group discussion (FGD) is conducted, in which the participants are eight students pursuing MBA in Human Resource Management in a business school in Delhi. Responses during the FGD are recorded using audiotape and later transcribed in their entirety (transcription of FGD is presented in Appendix).

Appendix

Transcript of the Focus Group Discussion

Moderator: Hi, good afternoon people. First of all, thanks a lot for participating in the FGD process. The issue on which we are going to have a discussion is 'Preference of management graduates: manufacturing sector or the service sector?' To begin with, I would like all of you to introduce yourselves. The format of the introduction would be your name, your summer internship company, wherever applicable, and your dream company where you would like to work in future.

Preetesh: I am Preetesh and my summer internship company is Philips. I wish to work for a company like Mercer or EnY

Shishank: I am Shishank, my internship company is Pylon Consulting and my dream company is Best Buy.

Bhavna: I am Bhavna, my internship company is Deloitte and my dream company is Cadbury.

Simar: I am Simardeep Singh, my internship company is Capgemini, and I want to work in Walmart.

Isha: I am Isha, my internship company is Asian Paints, and I do not actually have a dream company, I would rather like to have the experience of everything, have not thought about it.

Bani: I am Bani Updhyay, I don't know about my internship company yet, my dream company would be in the banking sector.

Khushboo: I am Khushboo, I am not yet placed and about dream company, today the market is so bad, there is job crunch everywhere, so if I get a job either in manufacturing or service sector, I would take it.

Jalpan: Hi, I am Jalpan. Summer Internship Company is Hero MotoCorp and Dream Company is Google.

Moderator: Thanks a lot. To begin with the FGD, our first question to the group is, what do you think is the key fact that an MBA graduate looks for in a job? You can take a minute to think about it and please come up with two to three factors.

Simar: I think, compensation.

Bhavna: I think rather than compensation, Gen Y would be looking more towards work-life balance. It has become the focus of every individual now.

Khushboo: At any point of time, salary would definitely be a major deciding factor for your job but it would also depend on your interest like you all said. If you are heading towards your dream company, even if it offers a somewhat less compensation you would definitely go for it.

Jalpan: Major factor would be the application of what you have learnt. Many people coming for MBA feel that they have learnt something in engineering but are not being able to apply it. So it is the identity of a job, and the fact that you will be able to apply what you have learnt, is a critical factor. A young professional looks for these factors after postgraduation, primarily because after this, he may not study any further.

Isha: For a person like me, who is a fresher and does not have a dream company, the determining factor would be the job opportunities that I get, whether it is a compelling sector, how it suits my needs, at what point of career I am and how it will further enhance my career.

Moderator: So, suppose you are sitting for campus placement, what is the determining factor for you?

Isha: Initially, when you do not have prejudices against a company or a set mind or framework, the brand really matters. So, when Asian Paints had come, my aim was to crack it or RPG, which were the initial ones. Further down the line, other factors come in and then it is not the brand. Even if it is a small start-up, if it is giving me a good package and good opportunity to grow as a person and good job profile

Preetesh: Apart from the brand I look forward to a company which gives me recognition.

Moderator: You mean the job profile?

Preetesh: Not only that, but also the type of work I do. I should be in a company or department where I should feel important. Only when you join, you get to know of these things, like I have worked before, and there are situations where you work day and night for a particular project and you don't get recognition. Then your satisfaction level drops downs and you tend to stop giving your best for that job. Brand and compensation are important, but then at the same time, recognition is important.

Vedant: So you are talking about non-monetary rewards?

Preetesh: It can be tangible, intangible both.

Bani: As a fresher the determining factor would be the growth opportunities as I do not have experience. I would like to take up a job which offers me lot of opportunities and as I go down the line the work culture and the kind of environment that it offers to its employees would be the major determining factors.

Simar: In our college, companies like ICICI that offered a package of 9.5 lakh per annum, there is no question of manufacturing or service sector in that case, because each and every student had applied for the ICICI because of the package. I am just emphasizing that compensation is one of the major factors for people while selecting their companies in colleges like ours.

Simar: I think compensation is one of the major factors that play an important role in people selecting sectors in an MBA college like ours.

Moderator: Companies belonging to these two sectors—do they have a preference regarding which institutes they want to go to? Are you saying, service sector industries are more interested in 2nd level B-schools than the manufacturing industry?

Simar: As our economy is a service-oriented economy right now and around 80-90 per cent of the companies are service oriented, so manufacturing is like a subdued kind of sector. So few people are willing to go into manufacturing sectors, as there are not enough jobs.

Bhavna: Moreover, the jobs in manufacturing sectors are much more challenging than in the service sector. There is no work-life balance in the manufacturing sector, especially in Industrial Relations role. That is a challenge that I think Gen Y will not be willing to accept.

Jalpan: Rightly said, manufacturing sector is subdued and plays a small role in the economy, so companies that have vacancies prefer going to top colleges and then coming to tier 2 colleges.

Simar: I think that is the reason people prefer service-oriented industry, because they do not have exposure to the manufacturing sector.

Jalpan: There is no opportunity available in manufacturing sector.

Isha: Manufacturing companies are located out of metro areas. Metros are a big attraction for every other gen Y. They want to stay in metro areas, whereas manufacturing companies are in the areas like Surat and Ankleshwar, which are not attractive cities for Gen Y.

Preetesh: But I still believe that the people working in the manufacturing sector tend to save more because the cost of living is low in these locations as compared to metros.

Simar: It is changing fast. Now, people of Gen Y tend to spend more.

Preetesh: That is why they demand much better compensation.

Simar: That is why people are willing to spend their money and so they prefer metropolitan cities rather than any other the 2nd or 3rd tier city.

Isha: Then your work-life balance comes into picture. You like to spend your hard earned money when you like to spend as you have earned it. There are spending opportunities.

Khushboo: Whatever may be the sector, our generation is very brand-conscious. We want big names. In our summers also, nobody talks what kind of exiting projects you got but which company you got into. So if in manufacturing sector you are getting a big brand they may change their preferences; change their work life balance preference and anything.

Preetesh: Even if it's a manufacturing company and offers you better timing and work-life balance, say timings of 10-5, then you are staying less in the office rather than a service job, where you have to stay the entire day.

Simar: There is a perception that sitting in an office gives you a better reputation. A person's perception and psyche play a very important role.

Jalpan: While talking of MBA graduates, a lot of us are not aware of the nitty-gritties of the role we will play. Many things are decided on the basis of apparent values like brand, societal value, brand compensation and how the family will respond to it. These factors are not related to the job we will do.

Preetesh: We do not have any hands-on experience. Whatever we know, we know it through people who have been there and from market surveys. So maybe, joining a manufacturing firm may turn out to be a good experience.

Bani: I think it is all about consistency. You might take up a manufacturing job because of brand but how long will you be able to work there?

Simar: I think there are three external environmental pressures. Economic pressures, the social factors, and the kind of environment you were born and brought up in. Say, if you are brought up in Delhi, then you may join the service sector rather than manufacturing. If you have seen the manufacturing sector or have been in its vicinity, then it has a very big impact on the person.

Moderator: We have learnt in our course that if we have an Industrial Relations profile to begin with, it gives us a major leverage. Is that an important factor or we just move forward?

Simar: IR sector leverages our knowledge.

Moderator: We have studied in our course that if we have an IR profile to begin with, it leverages our career growth. So will an MBA graduate pursuing his course consider it as an important factor?

Bhavna: Yes, it is because starting with an IR role, it is easy to shift from an IR role to other roles of HR. But for one position of HR, which is not an IR role, but perhaps in service sector it is very difficult for that person to come back in manufacturing and handle the role of an IR. I believe that starting from an IR role, gaining experience there and progressing the career pattern is much better option.

Khushboo: I think it depends on your personality type. If you are not suitable for the manufacturing sector, then why go for it; you will rather pick up service industry. Ideally, it depends on our personality but if we don't have any option, then we judge our personality then we select a sector then a company. But today, since we do not have an option to judge our personality and then select a sector, then we select a company. So anyway, we have to get in any company where we are placed.

Moderator: Somebody said that jobs in manufacturing sectors are more challenging, whereas the service sector maintains more work-life balance in a person's life. Let us suppose a person is really career oriented and he wants to go up the career ladder. In that case, what do you think his decision would be?

Isha: For me, it would be manufacturing. If I am focused on my career I'll first go for manufacturing sector, probably later in life when I settle down, I have a family, so then I will see what kind of balance I will have. Then I may shift to service sector.

Moderator: So is it right to say that manufacturing sector is a stepping stone to a rise in career?

Isha: Yes

Moderator: Another question I would like to ask the group is, as Simar mentioned that India is now a service industry, so do you think the manufacturing sector in India has the potential to grow? There are many jobs in the manufacturing industry but MBA graduates are not willing to take these up for various reasons, which you guys have already cited.

Simar: Jobs are there because India will have the youngest population in the next 20 years, so the most important thing that we need to have is manpower. As being a power centre right now, we can have technology and all the other resources but manpower is the most important resource. I think we have the capability to become a very manufacturing-sector-oriented economy as well but that may take some time. It will have to be a gradual process. Shifting from service to manufacturing, people do not have the perception.

Moderator: What do you think will make an MBA graduate shift his or her perception from a service oriented industry to a manufacturing industry?

Shishank: I think, if we really want to move up the ladder, if we really want to become vice-president, HR, then we need to have exposure in all the fields of HR, from IR to recruitment to compensation. It is better to have an IR exposure at the beginning of your career rather than having at the very end. So if a person has high aspirations he should start in IR profile because after some time it becomes very difficult to move from service to manufacturing sector.

Moderator: Do you think women will not prefer a manufacturing sector job and would go for a service sector job?

All: Yes

Moderator: Why?

Bhavna: Because the role is much more challenging in the manufacturing sector.

Simar: Not that. Many employers do not want women at the factory site. There are many issues like labour issues related to them.

Shishank: Also, the glass ceiling is more significant in manufacturing than in service.

Khushboo: All the manufacturing plants are located in such remote locations so it will be difficult for women after marriage.

Isha: I think that is the driving factor in the differentiation. Similarly, when you start your career, being a girl, I would prefer the manufacturing sector because when I settle down in life later on, I cannot be in a manufacturing sector and I have to shift to the service sector.

Bhavna: I think the pressure of an IR person is much more demanding and challenging and I feel that women cannot give that much of time and dedication to the job.

Khushboo: I do not think dedication is a problem.

Bhavna: Because later on in life when you have a family to go back to, you would not prefer to stay in the office post 8 pm.

Simar: Even in the service sector you have to stay post 8 pm but nowadays these things are being taken care of.

Jalpan: It also depends on what kind of firm and what kind of facilities the manufacturing firm is providing. For example, the Reliance Jamnagar Refinery has the best township in the world and even women prefer to work in these kinds of sites.

Khushboo: Even in service industry, you are required to work 9 to 9 so even that kind of work is demanding and much more challenging than the work in the manufacturing sector. So, a lot depends on the firm.

Preetesh: So, for a manufacturing firm it is more important to provide basic amenities that one gets in a metro, because people prefer metros for their facilities. For a manufacturing firm located in a remote area they should have a township. Also, there is a bias among us that manufacturing firms have people who are more experienced. There are very few freshers who join manufacturing firms. So, for a manufacturing firm to flourish, they should have people from similar age group. They should have some criteria on the basis of which they should select a certain number of people from certain colleges who are fresher.

Moderator: Don't you think, if you join at a junior level and you know that there are people at the senior level in the manufacturing firms, you will have a better learning opportunity from them?

Preetesh: They should have the criteria that people from the younger generation are taken in for better salaries and opportunities so that we do not get scared that there are senior people in the company and we cannot adjust with them.

Moderator: Do you think the work culture plays a role in selecting a company?

Bani: Yes. In the service sector it is more flexible and adaptable. Relating to Gen Y, things can be changed more frequently, whereas in the manufacturing sector, the plants and refineries have a set pattern of work, so it is very difficult to bring about a change in their culture.

Moderator: What can the manufacturing sector do to attract Gen Y?

Simar: The most important role should be of the government. There should be certain minimum amenities for people coming into the manufacturing sector. There should be fixed policies that the manufacturing sector should maintain in order to sustain interest in this sector.

Jalpan: Additionally, if employee count goes beyond a certain number there should be provision for mandatory township and amenities near that manufacturing area. For example, the land near cities that are not used for agriculture should be given to industries to attract the young crowd. Gurgaon and Orissa are good examples of this.

Moderator: Thank you so much for your time and response.

QUESTIONS

1. Identify the underlying categories in the transcripts using content analysis. What do you recommend should be the unit for Content Analysis? (Refer chapter 6 for Unit of Content Analysis)
2. What are the major factors responsible for career inclination among MBA graduates?
3. What are the major reasons behind the non-preference and preference of students towards manufacturing sector?
4. Comment on the information sought through FGD in the light of objectives of study.

Answers to Objective Type Questions

1. True	2. True	3. False	4. False	5. True
6. True	7. False	8. True	5. False	10. True
11. False	12. True	13. False	14. False	15. True
16. False	17. False	18. True	19. True	20. False

REFERENCES

Belk, Russell W. *Handbook of Qualitative Research Methods in Marketing*. Edward Elgar Publishing Limited. Massachusetts, USA, 2006

Berelson, B. 'Content Analysis,' In *Handbook of Social Psychology,* edited by G Lindzey. (Reading: Mass Addison Wesley, 1954).

Bogardus, Emory S. 'The Group Interview.' *Journal of Applied Sociology*, 10 (1926) 372–82.

Bristol, Terry. 'Enhancing Focus Group Productivity: New Research and Insights,' in *Advances in Consumer Research*, edited by Eric J Arnould and Linda M Scott, vol. 26, Provo, UT: Association for Consumer Research, (1999) 479–82.

Chrzanowska, Joanna. *Interviewing Groups and Individuals in Qualitative Market Research*. London: Sage Publications, 2002.

Cohen J. 'A Coefficient of Agreement for Nominal Scales. *Educational and Psychological Measurement* 20 (37): 46 (1960).

Desai, Philly. *Methods Beyond Interviewing in Qualitative Market Research*. London: Sage, 2002.

Dichter, Ernest. *The Strategy of Desire*. Chicago: T V Broadman and Co. Ltd, 1960.

Dichter. Ernest. *Handbook of Consumer Motivation*. McGraw Hill Company, 1964. New York

Edminton, V. 'The Group Interview,' *Journal of Educational Research*, 37 (1944): 593–601.

Feldwick, Paul and Lorna Winstanley. 'Qualitative Recruitment: Policy and Practice' (Proceedings of the Market Research Society Conference, London, 1986) 57–72.

Fern, Edward F. 'Focus Groups: A Review of some Contradictory Evidence; Implications and Suggestions for Further Research,' in *Advances in Consumer Research,* edited by Richard R Bagozzi and Alice M Tybout, Vol.10, Provo UT: Association for Consumer Research (1983) 121–26.

Freud, Sigmund. 'Formulations on the Two Principles of Mental Functioning,' In *The Standard Edition of the Complete Psychological Works of Sigmund Freud,* edited by J Strachey and A Freud, Vol.12, London: Hogarth, 1911, 1956.

Glaser, B and A Strauss. *The Discovery of Grounded Theory*. New York: Aldine, 1967.

Henry, William E. *The Analysis of Fantasy*. New York: Wiley Sons, Inc., 1956.

Kerlinger, Fred N. *Foundations of Behavioural Research*, 3rd edn. A PRISM Indian Edition, 1986.

Locke, Karen. *Grounded Theory in Management Research*. London: Sage, 2001.

MacGregor, B and D E Morrison. 'From Focus Groups to Editing Groups: A New Method of Reception Analysis,' *Media, Culture and Society*, 17 (1), (1995): 141–50.

Masling, Joseph M. *The Preparation of a Projective Test for Assessing Attitudes Towards the International Motion Picture Service Film Program*. Philadelphia: Institute for Research in Human Relations, 1952.

Merton, Robert K and Patricia L Kendall. 'The Focused Interview,' *American Journal of Sociology*, 51 (1946): 541–57.

Morgan, David L and Richard A Krueger. *The Focus Group Kit*. Volumes 1–6, Thousand Oaks, CA: Sage, 1997.

Morgan, Helen and Kerry Thomas. 'A Psychodynamic Perspective on Group Processes,' in *Identities, Groups and Social Issues*, edited by Margaret Wetherell. (London: Open University/Sage, 1996) 63–117.

Newman, Joseph W. *Motivation Research and Marketing Management*. Cambridge, MA: Harvard University, 1957.

Rogers, Everett and G M Beal. 'Projective Techniques in Interviewing Farmers,' *Journal of Marketing*, 23 (1958): 177–83.

Smith, George R. *Motivation in Advertising and Marketing*. New York: McGraw Hill, 1954.

Stevens, Lorna, 'The Joys of Text: Women's Experiential Consumption of Magazines' (PhD thesis, University of Ulster, 2003).

Tuckman, B W. 'Developmental sequences in small groups,' *Psychological Bulletin*, 63, (1965): 384–99.

Tull, Donald S and Del I Hawkins. *Marketing Research: Measurement & Method*. 6th edn. New Delhi: Prentice Hall of India Pvt. Ltd, 1993.

Vicary, James M. 'How Psychiatric Methods Can be Applied to Market Research,' *Printers' Ink*, (1951): 39–40, 1951.

Wilson, Godfrey and Wilson, Morica. *The Analysis of Social Change Based on Observations in Central Africa,* Cambridge: The University Press, 1945.

Zaltman, Gerald. 'Rethinking Market Research: Putting People Back in,' *Journal of Marketing Research,* 34 (1997): 424–37.

BIBLIOGRAPHY

David, J Luck and Robin S Ronald. *Marketing Research*. 7th edn. New Delhi: Prentice Hall of India, 1998.

Gay, L R. *Research Methods for Business and Management*. New York: Macmillan Publishing Company, 1992.

Grbich, Carol. *Qualitative Data Analysis–An Introduction*. London: Sage Publications.

Green, Paul E and Donald S Tull. *Research for Marketing Decisions*. 4th edn. New Delhi: Prentice Hall of India Private Ltd, 1986.

Harper, W Boyd, Jr Ralph Westfall and Stanley F Stasch, *Marketing Research: Text and Cases*. 7th edn. New Delhi: Richard D Irwin, Inc., 2002.

Kinnear, Thomas C and James R Taylor. *Marketing Research: An Applied Approach*. 5th edn. New York: McGraw Hill, Inc., 1996.

Kothari, C R. *Research Methodology Methods and Techniques*. 2nd edn. New Delhi: Wiley Eastern Limited, 1990.

Kumar, Ranjit. *Research Methodology–A Step by Step Guide for Beginners*. 2nd edn. New Delhi: Pearson Publication, 2006.

McBurney, Donald H. *Research Methods*. 5th edn. Thomson Wadsworth Publication, 2006.

McDaniel, Carl and Roger Gates. *Marketing Research–The Impact of the Internet*. 5th edn. South-Western, 2002.

Pannerselvam, R. *Research Methodology*. New Delhi: Prentice Hall of India Pvt. Ltd, 2004.

Russell, Belk, Guliz Ger and Soren Askegaard. 'Consumer Desire in Three Cultures: Results of Projective Research,' in *Advances in Consumer Research,* edited by Merrie Brucks and Debbie MacInnis, vol. 24 (1997): 24–8.

Saunders, Mark, Philip Lewis and Adrian Thornhill. *Research Methods for Business Students,* 3rd edn. Pearson Publication.

Theitart, Raymond-Alian *et al*. *Doing Management Research–A Comprehensive Guide*. London: Sage Publications.

Trochim, William M K. *Research Methods*. 2nd edn. New Delhi: Biztantra, 2003.

William, Henry. *The Analysis of Fantasy*, New York: Wiley & Sons, Inc., 1956.

Zikmund, William G. *Business Research Methods*. 5th edn. Bengaluru: Thompson South-Western, 1997.

7

CHAPTER

Attitude Measurement and Scaling

Learning Objectives

By the end of the chapter, you should be able to:

1. Define measurement.
2. Distinguish between the four types of measurement scales.
3. Define attitude and its three components.
4. Discuss the various classifications of scales.
5. Define measurement error and explain the criteria for good measurement.

Three fresh MBAs joined a consulting company. The first assignment given to them was to design and conduct a study to compare the perception of the patrons of Domino's Pizza with Pizza Hut. As the first step, they conducted an exploratory research by informally talking to the management of both the pizza joints. They also conducted three focus groups so as to gain insight into what the consumers are actually looking at while buying pizza. The output of the unstructured interviews and focus groups resulted in identifying various information needs that could be used in designing the relevant questionnaire. Some of the relevant information was on gender, age, income, frequency and occasion of eating pizza, ranking of the attributes that are sought while choosing pizza joints, and comparative perceptions of Domino's and Pizza Hut. This information was to be employed in designing the questionnaire.

One question that came into the minds of the three MBAs was how to measure the attitude and analyse the information thus obtained from the survey. For this, it was necessary to assign numbers or symbols to the characteristics of the objects. Assignment of numbers permits a statistical analysis of the data. The numbers assigned and the subsequent analysis could be different, depending upon the type of question asked. On one hand, there can be questions used to measure different psychological aspects such as attitude, perception, image and preference of people with the help of a certain pre-defined set of stimuli. On the other hand, there can be questions on gender, marital status, ranking preference for different flavours, income and age.

The focus of this chapter is on different types of measurements and the statistical techniques that are applicable for the same. The various formats of a rating scale and the construction of the attitude measurement scale, along with the description of the distinct criteria involved in analysing a good measurement scale, are elaborated in this chapter.

INTRODUCTION

LEARNING OBJECTIVE 1
Define measurement.

The term **measurement** means assigning numbers or some other symbols to the characteristics of certain objects.

The term 'measurement' means assigning numbers or some other symbols to the characteristics of certain objects. When numbers are used, the researcher must have a rule for assigning a number to an observation in a way that provides an accurate description. We do not measure the object but some characteristics of it. Therefore, in research, people/consumers are not measured; what is measured only are their perceptions, attitude or any other relevant characteristics. There are two reasons for which numbers are usually assigned. First of all, numbers permit statistical analysis of the resulting data and secondly, they facilitate the communication of measurement results.

As mentioned earlier, the numbering is done based on certain rules. Therefore, the assignment of numbers to the characteristics must be isomorphic, i.e., there must be a one-to-one correspondence between the numbers and the characteristics being measured.

For example, same rupee figures should be assigned to a household with identical annual income. Only then numbers can be associated with specific characteristics of the measured object and vice versa. Further, they must not change over the objects or time. This means that the rules for a given assignment must be invariant over time or the object being measured.

Scaling is an extension of measurement. Scaling involves creating a continuum on which measurements on objects are located. Suppose you want to measure the satisfaction level towards Jet-Airways Airlines and a scale of 1 to 11 is used for the said purpose. This scale indicates the degree of dissatisfaction, with 1 = extremely dissatisfied and 11 = extremely satisfied. Measurement is the actual assignment of a number from 1 to 11 to each respondent whereas the scaling is the process of placing the respondent on a continuum with respect to their satisfaction towards Jet Airways.

TYPES OF MEASUREMENT SCALE

LEARNING OBJECTIVE 2
Distinguish between the four types of measurement scales.

There are four types of measurement scales—nominal, ordinal, interval and ratio scales. We will discuss each one of them in detail. The choice of the measurement scale has implications for the statistical technique to be used for data analysis.

Nominal scale: This is the lowest level of measurement. Here, numbers are assigned for the purpose of identification of the objects. Any object which is assigned a higher number is in no way superior to the one which is assigned a lower number. In the nominal scale there is a strict one-to-one correspondence between the numbers and the objects. Each number is assigned to only one object and each object has only one number assigned to it. It may be noted that the objects are divided into mutually exclusive and collectively exhaustive categories.

Examples of nominal scale:

- What is your religion?
  (a) Hinduism
  (b) Sikhism
  (c) Christianity
  (d) Islam
  (e) Any other, (please specify)

A Hindu may be assigned a number 1, a Sikh may be assigned a number 2, a Christian may be assigned a number 3 and so on. Any religion which is assigned a higher number is in no way superior to the one which is assigned a lower number. The assignment of numbers is only for the purpose of identification. We also note that all respondents have been divided into mutually exclusive and collectively exhaustive categories. For example:

- Are you married?
  - (a) Yes
  - (b) No

If a person is married, he or she may be assigned a number 101 and an unmarried person may be assigned a number 102.

- In which of the following departments do you work?
  - (a) Marketing
  - (b) HR
  - (c) Information Technology
  - (d) Operations
  - (e) Finance and Accounting
  - (f) Any other, (please specify)

Here also, a person working for the marketing department may be assigned a number 1, the one working for HR may be assigned a number 2 and so on.

Nominal scale measurements are used for identifying food habits (vegetarian or non-vegetarian), gender (male/female), caste, respondents, brands, attributes, stores, the players of a hockey team and so on.

The numbers assigned in a **nominal scale** cannot be added, subtracted, multiplied or divided.

The assigned numbers cannot be added, subtracted, multiplied or divided. The only arithmetic operations that can be carried out are the count of each category. Therefore, a frequency distribution table can be prepared for the nominal scale variables and mode of the distribution can be worked out. One can also use chi-square test and compute contingency coefficient using nominal scale variables.

An **ordinal scale measurement** tells whether an object has more or less of characteristics than some other objects.

Ordinal scale: This is the next higher level of measurement than the nominal scale measurement. One of the limitations of the nominal scale measurements is that we cannot say whether the assigned number to an object is higher or lower than the one assigned to another option. The ordinal scale measurement takes care of this limitation. An ordinal scale measurement tells whether an object has more or less of characteristics than some other objects. However, it cannot answer how much more or how much less. An ordinal scale tells us the relative positions of the objects and not the difference between the magnitudes of the objects. Suppose Shashi scores the highest marks in marketing and is ranked no. 1; Mohan scores the second highest marks and is ranked no. 2; and Krishna scores third highest marks and is ranked no. 3. However, from this statement we cannot say whether the difference in the marks scored by Shashi and Mohan is the same as between Mohan and Krishna. The only statement which can be made under ordinal scale is that Shashi has scored higher than Mohan and Mohan has scored higher than Krishna. The difference between the ranks does not have any meaningful interpretation in the sense that it cannot tell the difference in absolute marks between the three candidates. Another example of the ordinal scale could be the CAT score given in percentile form. Suppose a candidate's score is 95 percentile in the CAT exam. What it means is that 95 per cent of the candidates that appeared in the CAT examination have a score below this candidate, whereas only 5 per cent have scored more than him. The actual score is how much less or more cannot be known from this statement. Examples of the ordinal scale include quality ranking, rankings of the teams in a tournament, ranking of preference for colours, soft drinks, socio-economic class and occupational status, to mention a few. Some of the examples of ordinal scales are listed below:

- Rank the following attributes while choosing a restaurant for dinner. The most important attribute may be ranked one, the next important may be assigned a rank of 2 and so on.

Attribute	Rank
Food quality	
Prices	
Menu variety	
Ambience	
Service	

- Rank the following by placing a 1 beside the attribute you think is the most important, a 2 beside the attribute you think is the second most important and so on while purchasing a two-wheeler.

Attribute	Rank
After sale service	
Prices	
Re-sale value	
Fuel efficiency	
Aesthetic appeal	

The **ordinal scale** data can be converted into nominal scale data but not the other way round.

In the ordinal scale, the assigned ranks cannot be added, multiplied, subtracted or divided. One can compute median, percentiles and quartiles of the distribution. The other major statistical analysis which can be carried out is the rank order correlation coefficient, sign test. As the ordinal scale measurement is higher than the nominal scale measurement, all the statistical techniques which are applicable in the case of nominal scale measurement can also be used for the ordinal scale measurement. However, the reverse is not true. This is because ordinal scale data can be converted into nominal scale data but not the other way round.

In the **interval scale**, it is assumed that the respondent is able to answer the questions on a continuum scale.

Interval scale: The interval scale measurement is the next higher level of measurement. It takes care of the limitation of the ordinal scale measurement where the difference between the score on the ordinal scale does not have any meaningful interpretation. In the interval scale the difference of the score on the scale has meaningful interpretation. It is assumed that the respondent is able to answer the questions on a continuum scale. The mathematical form of the data on the interval scale may be written as

$$Y = a + bX \quad \text{where } a \neq 0$$

The interval scale data has an arbitrary origin (non-zero origin). The most common example of the interval scale data is the relationship between Celsius and Farenheit temperature. It is known that:

$$C° = \frac{5}{9}(F° - 32).$$

Therefore, $$C° = \frac{-160}{9} + \frac{5}{9}F°$$

This is of the form $Y = a + bX$, where $a = \frac{-160}{9}$ and $b = \frac{5}{9}$ and hence it represents the interval scale measurement. In the interval scale, the difference in score has a meaningful interpretation while the ratio of the score on this scale does not have a meaningful interpretation. This can be seen from the following interval scale question:

- How likely are you to buy a new designer carpet in the next six months?

	Very unlikely	Unlikely	Neutral	Likely	Very likely
Scale A	1	2	3	4	5
Scale B	0	1	2	3	4
Scale C	–2	–1	0	1	2

Suppose a respondent ticks the response category 'likely' and another respondent ticks the category 'unlikely'. If we use any of the scales A, B or C, we note that the difference between the scores in each case is 2. Whereas, when the ratio of the scores is taken, it is 2, 3 and –1 for the scales A, B and C respectively. Therefore, the ratio of the scores on the scale does not have a meaningful interpretation. The following are some examples of interval scale data.

- How important is price to you while buying a car?

Least important	Unimportant	Neutral	Important	Most important
1	2	3	4	5

- How do you rate the work environment of your organization?

Very good	Good	Neither good nor bad	Bad	Very bad
5	4	3	2	1

- The counter-clerks at ICICI Bank, (Vasant Kunj Branch) are very friendly.

Strongly disagree	Disagree	Neither agree nor disagree	Agree	Strongly agree
1	2	3	4	5

- Rate the life of the battery of your inverter.

Low 1 —— 2 —— 3 —— 4 —— 5 High

- Indicate the degree of satisfaction with the overall performance of Wagon R.

Very dissatisfied 1 —— 2 —— 3 —— 4 —— 5 Very satisfied

- How expensive is the restaurant 'Punjabi By Nature'?

Extremely expensive	Definitely expensive	Somewhat expensive	Somewhat inexpensive	Definitely inexpensive	Extremely inexpensive
1	2	3	4	5	6

- How likely are you to buy a new car within the next six months?

Definitely will buy	Probably will buy	Neutral	Probably will not buy	Definitely will not buy
1	2	3	4	5

The numbers on this scale can be added, subtracted, multiplied or divided. One can compute arithmetic mean, standard deviation, correlation coefficient and conduct a t-test, Z-test, regression analysis and factor analysis. As the interval scale data can be converted into the ordinal and the nominal scale data, therefore all the techniques applicable for the ordinal and the nominal scale data can also be used for interval scale data.

The mathematical form of the **ratio scale data** is given by $Y = bX$.

Ratio scale: This is the highest level of measurement and takes care of the limitations of the interval scale measurement, where the ratio of the measurements on the scale does not have a meaningful interpretation. The ratio scale measurement can be converted into interval, ordinal and nominal scale. But the other way round is not possible. The mathematical form of the ratio scale data is given by $Y = bX$. In this case, there is a natural zero (origin), whereas in the interval scale we had an arbitrary zero. Examples of the ratio scale data are weight, distance travelled, income and sales of a company, to mention a few. Consider the following examples for ratio scale measurements:

- How many chemist shops are there in your locality?
- How many students are there in the MBA programme at IIFT?
- How much distance do you need to travel from your residence to reach the railway station?

All the mathematical operations can be carried out using the ratio scale data. In addition to the statistical analysis mentioned in the interval, the ordinal and the nominal scale data, one can compute coefficient of variation, geometric mean and harmonic mean using the ratio scale measurement. The basic characteristics, examples and the statistical techniques applicable under each of the four scales are summarized in Table 7.1.

CONCEPT CHECK

1. What do you mean by the term 'measurement'?
2. Define a nominal scale.
3. How would you differentiate between an ordinal scale and an interval scale?

ATTITUDE

LEARNING OBJECTIVE 3
Define attitude and its three components.

An attitude is viewed as an enduring disposition to respond consistently in a given manner to various aspects of the world, including persons, events and objects. A company is able to sell its products or services when its customers have a favourable attitude towards its products/services. In the reverse scenario, the company will not be able to sustain itself for long. It, therefore, becomes very important to measure the attitude of the customers towards the company's products/services. Unfortunately, attitude cannot be measured directly. There are many variables which the researcher wishes to investigate as psychological variables and these cannot be directly observed. For example, we may have a favourable attitude towards a particular brand of toothpaste, but this attitude cannot be observed directly. In order to measure an

TABLE 7.1 Types of scale, characteristics, examples, permissible statistical techniques

Scale	Basic Characteristics	Examples	Permissible Statistics
Nominal	Numbers are used to label and classify objects	Players of Team India, Caste, Religion, Gender, Marital Status, Store Types, Brands, etc.	Percentages, Mode, Chi-square, Contingency coefficient, Binomial test
Ordinal	Numbers indicate the relative position of the objects, however the difference in the magnitude of the score cannot be known	Preference Ranking, Image Ranking, Social Class, etc.	Percentile, Quartiles, Median, Rank order correlation, Friedman ANOVA
Interval	Difference between the objects can be known, however the ratio of the scores has no meaning	Attitude, Opinion, Index Numbers	Product moment correlation coefficient, t-test, z-test, ANOVA, Regression Analysis, Factor Analysis
Ratio	Ratios of the score value have a meaningful interpretation	Age, Income, Market Share, Sales, Cost, etc.	Geometric means, Harmonic Means and Coefficient of variation

attitude, we make an inference based on the perceptions the customers have about the product/services. The attitude is derived from the perceptions. If the consumers have a favourable perception towards the products/services, the attitude will be favourable. Therefore, the attitudes are indirectly observed.

Basically, attitude has three components: cognitive, affective and intention (or action) components.

The **cognitive component** represents an individual's information and knowledge about an object.

Cognitive component: This component represents an individual's information and knowledge about an object. It includes awareness of the existence of the object, beliefs about the characteristics or attributes of the object and judgement about the relative importance of each of the attributes. In a survey, if the respondents are asked to name the companies manufacturing plastic products, some respondents may remember names like Tupperware, Modicare and Pearl Pet. This is called unaided recall awareness. More names are likely to be remembered when the investigator makes a mention of them. This is aided recall. It may be noted that the knowledge may not be limited only to the awareness. An individual can form beliefs or judgements about the characteristics or attributes of the plastic products manufacturing companies through advertisements, word of mouth, peer groups, etc. The examples of such beliefs could be that the products of Tupperware are of high quality, non-toxic and can be used in parties; a mutton dish can be cooked in a pressure cooker in less than 30 minutes; the Nano car gives a very high mileage as compared to the other small cars.

The **affective component** summarizes a person's overall feeling or emotions towards the objects.

Affective component: The affective component summarizes a person's overall feeling or emotions towards the objects. The examples for this component could be: the food cooked in a pressure cooker is tasty, taste of orange juice is good or the taste of bitter gourd is very bad. If there are a number of alternatives to choose from, liking is expressed in terms of preference for one alternative over the other. Among the various soft drinks like Pepsi, Coke, Limca and Sprite, the respondents might have to indicate the most preferred soft drinks, the second preferred one and so on. This is an example of the affective component. The other example could be that the plastic products produced by Pearl Pet are cheaper than Tupperware products; however, the quality of Tupperware products is better than that of Pearl Pet.

The **behavioural component** of an attitude reflects a predisposition to an action by reflecting the consumer's buying or purchase intention.

Intention or action component: This component of an attitude, also called the behavioural component, reflects a predisposition to an action by reflecting the consumer's buying or purchase intention. It also reflects a person's expectations of future behaviour towards an object. How likely a person is to buy a designer carpet may range from most likely to not at all likely, reflecting the purchase intentions. However, when one is talking about the purchase intentions, a time horizon has to be kept in mind as the intentions may undergo a change over time. The intentions incorporate information regarding the respondent's willingness to pay for the product.

There is a relationship between attitude and behaviour. If a consumer does not have a favourable attitude towards the product, he/she will certainly not buy the product. However, having a favourable attitude does not mean that it would be reflected in the purchase behaviour. This is because intention to buy a product has to be backed by the purchasing power of the consumer. Having a favourable attitude towards Mercedes Benz does not mean that a person is going to purchase it even if he does not have the ability to buy a product. Therefore, the relationship between the attitude and the purchase behaviour is a necessary condition for the purchase of the product but it is not a sufficient condition. This relationship could hold true at the aggregate level but not at the individual level.

CONCEPT CHECK

1. Define attitude.
2. What is meant by the term 'affective component'?

CLASSIFICATION OF SCALES

LEARNING OBJECTIVE 4
Discuss the various classifications of scales.

One of the ways of classifications of scales is in terms of the number of items in the scale. Based upon this, the following classification may be proposed:

Single Item vs Multiple Item Scale

Single item scale: In the single item scale, there is only one item to measure a given construct. For example:

Consider the following question:

- How satisfied are you with your current job?

  Very Dissatisfied
  Dissatisfied
  Neutral
  Satisfied
  Very satisfied

The problem with the above question is that there are many aspects to a job, like pay, work environment, rules and regulations, security of job and communication with the seniors. The respondent may be satisfied on some of the factors but may not on others. By asking a question as stated above, it will be difficult to analyse the problem areas. To overcome this problem, a multiple item scale is proposed.

In a **multiple item scale**, each item forms some part of the construct that the researcher is trying to measure.

Multiple item scale: In multiple item scale, there are many items that play a role in forming the underlying construct that the researcher is trying to measure. This is because each of the item forms some part of the construct (satisfaction) which the researcher is trying to measure. As an example, some of the following questions may be asked in a multiple item scale.

- How satisfied are you with the pay you are getting on your current job?
  Very dissatisfied
  Dissatisfied
  Neutral
  Satisfied
  Very satisfied
- How satisfied are you with the rules and regulations of your organization?
  Very dissatisfied
  Dissatisfied
  Neutral
  Satisfied
  Very satisfied
- How satisfied are you with the job security in your current job?
  Very dissatisfied
  Dissatisfied
  Neutral
  Satisfied
  Very satisfied

Comparative vs Non-comparative Scales

The scaling techniques used in research can also be classified into comparative and non-comparative scales (Figure 7.1).

FIGURE 7.1
Types of scaling techniques

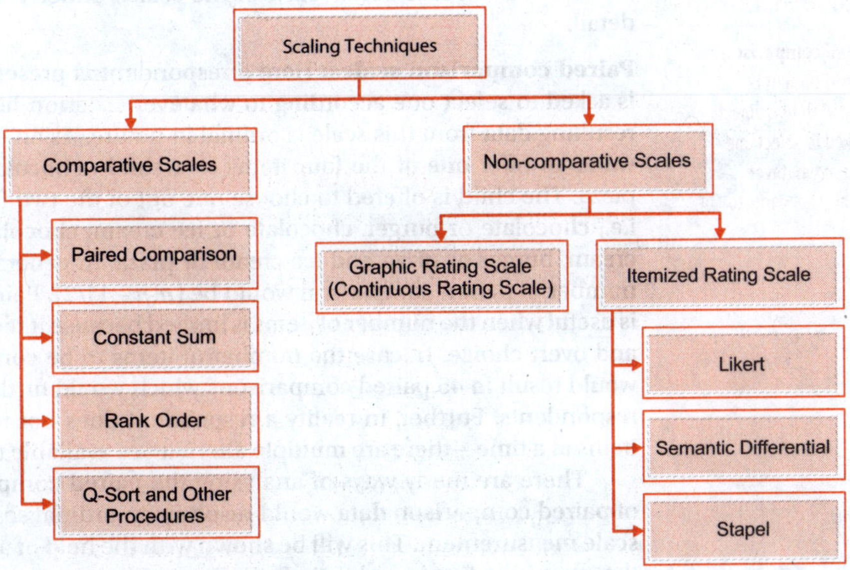

Comparative Scales

In comparative scales it is assumed that respondents make use of a standard frame of reference before answering the question. For example:

A question like 'How do you rate Barista in comparison to Cafe Coffee Day on quality of beverages?' is an example of the comparative rating scale. It involves the

In a **comparative scale**, it is assumed that a respondent makes use of a standard frame of reference before answering the question.

direct comparison of stimulus objects. For example, respondents may be asked whether they prefer Chinese in comparison to Indian food. Consider the following set of questions generally used to compare various attributes of Domino's Pizza and Pizza Hut.

- Please rate Domino's in comparison to Pizza Hut on the basis of your satisfaction level on an 11-point scale, based on the following parameters: (1 = Extremely poor, 6 = Average, 11 = Extremely good). Circle your response:

a.	Variety of menu options	1	2	3	4	5	6	7	8	9	10	11
b.	Value for money	1	2	3	4	5	6	7	8	9	10	11
c.	Speed of service (delivery time)	1	2	3	4	5	6	7	8	9	10	11
d.	Promotional offers	1	2	3	4	5	6	7	8	9	10	11
e.	Food quality	1	2	3	4	5	6	7	8	9	10	11
f.	Brand name	1	2	3	4	5	6	7	8	9	10	11
g.	Quality of service	1	2	3	4	5	6	7	8	9	10	11
h.	Convenience in terms of takeaway location	1	2	3	4	5	6	7	8	9	10	11
i.	Friendliness of the salesperson on the phone	1	2	3	4	5	6	7	8	9	10	11
j.	Quality of packaging	1	2	3	4	5	6	7	8	9	10	11
k.	Adaptation of Indian taste	1	2	3	4	5	6	7	8	9	10	11
l.	Side orders/appetizers	1	2	3	4	5	6	7	8	9	10	11

Comparative scale data is interpreted generally in a relative kind. The comparative scale includes paired comparison, rank order, constant sum scale and Q-sort technique to mention a few.

We will discuss below each of the scales under comparative rating scales in detail:

In a **paired comparison scale**, a respondent is presented with two objects and is asked to select one according to whatever criterion he/she wants to use.

Paired comparison scales: Here a respondent is presented with two objects and is asked to select one according to whatever criterion he or she wants to use. The resulting data from this scale is ordinal in nature. As an example, suppose a parent wants to offer one of the four items to a child—chocolate, burger, ice cream and pizza. The child is offered to choose one out of the two from the six possible pairs, i.e., chocolate or burger, chocolate or ice cream, chocolate or pizza, burger or ice cream, burger or pizza and ice cream or pizza. In general, if there are n items, the number of paired comparison would be $(n(n - 1)/2)$. Paired comparison technique is useful when the number of items is limited because it requires a direct comparison and overt choice. In case the number of items to be compared is large (say 10), it would result in 45 paired comparisons which would further result in fatigue for the respondents. Further, in reality a respondent does not make the choice from two items at a time—there are multiple alternatives available to him.

There are many ways of analysing the paired comparison data. The analysis of paired comparison data would result in an ordinal scale and also in an interval scale measurement. This will be shown with the help of an example. Let us assume that there are five brands—A, B, C, D and E—and a paired comparison with two brands at a time is presented to the respondent with the option to choose one of them. As there are five brands, it will result in 10 paired comparisons. Suppose this is administered to a sample of 250 respondents with the results as presented in Table 7.2.

TABLE 7.2
Paired comparison data

	A	B	C	D	E
A	–	0.60	0.30	0.60	0.35
B	0.40	–	0.28	0.70	0.40
C	0.70	0.72	–	0.65	0.10
D	0.40	0.30	0.35	–	0.42
E	0.65	0.60	0.90	0.58	–

The above table may be interpreted by assuming that the cell entry in the matrix represents the proportion of respondents who believe that 'the column brand is preferred over the row brand.' For example:

In brand A versus brand B comparison it can be said that 60 per cent of the respondents prefer brand B to brand A. Similarly, 30 per cent of the respondents prefer brand C to brand A and so on.

To develop the ordinal scale from the given paired comparison data in the above table, we can convert the entries in the table to 0 – 1 scores. This is to show whether the column brand dominates the row brand and vice versa. If the proportion is greater than 0.5 in the above table, a number of '1' is assigned to that cell, which means that the column brand is preferred over the row brand. Whenever the proportion is less than 0.5 in above table, a number of '0' is assigned to that cell, which means column brand does not dominate the row brand. The results are in Table 7.3.

TABLE 7.3
Conversion of paired comparison data into 0 to 1 form

	A	B	C	D	E
A	–	1	0	1	0
B	0	–	0	1	0
C	1	1	–	1	0
D	0	0	0	–	0
E	1	1	1	1	–
Total	2	3	1	4	0

To get the ordinal relationship among the brands, we total the columns. Here the ordinal scale of brands is D > B > A > C > E. This means brand D is the most preferred brand, followed by B, A, C and E.

In order to obtain the interval scale data from the paired comparison data as presented above, the entries in the table can be analysed by using a technique called Thurston's law of comparative judgement, which converts the ordinal judgements into the interval data. Here the proportions are assumed as probabilities and using the assumption of normality, Z-scores can be computed. Z-value has symmetric distribution with a mean of '0' and variance of '1.' If the proportion is less than 0.5, the corresponding Z-value has a negative sign and for the proportion that is greater than 0.5, the Z-score takes a positive value. The Z-scores for the paired comparison data is given in Table 7.4.

TABLE 7.4
Z-scores for paired comparison data

	A	B	C	D	E
A	0	0.255	–0.525	0.255	–0.38
B	–0.255	0	–0.58	0.525	–0.255
C	0.525	0.58	0	0.385	–1.28
D	–0.255	–0.525	–0.385	0	–0.2
E	0.38	0.255	1.28	0.2	0
Total Distance	0.395	0.565	–0.21	1.365	–2.115
Average Distance	0.079	0.113	–0.042	0.273	–0.423
Brand	D	B	A	C	E
Interval scale value with change of origin	0.696	0.536	0.502	0.381	0

The **average distance** is computed by dividing the total score by the number of brands. This way one obtains the absolute position of each brand.

The entries in Table 7.4 show the distance between two brands. Assuming that the scores can be added, the total distance is computed. The average distance is computed by dividing the total score by the number of brands. This way one obtains the absolute position of each brand. Now the highest negative values among all the column is added to each entry corresponding to the average value so that by change of origin, interval scale values can be obtained. This is shown in the last row and the values are of interval scale, indicating the difference between brands. Brand D is the most preferred brand and E is the least preferred brand and the distance between the two is 0.696. The distance between brand C and E equals 0.381.

In the **rank order scaling**, respondents are presented with several objects simultaneously and asked to order or rank them according to some criterion.

Rank order scaling: In the rank order scaling, respondents are presented with several objects simultaneously and asked to order or rank them according to some criterion. Consider, for example the following question:

- Rank the following soft drinks in order of your preference, the most preferred soft drink should be ranked one, the second most preferred should be ranked two and so on.

Soft Drinks	Rank
Coke	
Pepsi	
Limca	
Sprite	
Mirinda	
Seven Up	
Fanta	

Like paired comparison, this approach is also comparative in nature. The problem with this scale is that if a respondent does not like any of the above-mentioned soft drink and is forced to rank them in the order of his choice, then, the soft drink which is ranked one should be treated as the least disliked soft drink and similarly, the other rankings can be interpreted. This scale is very commonly used to measure preferences for brands as well as attributes. The rank order scaling results in the ordinal data.

In **constant sum rating scale**, the respondents are asked to allocate a total of 100 points between various objects and brands.

Constant sum rating scaling: In constant sum rating scale, the respondents are asked to allocate a total of 100 points between various objects and brands. The respondent distributes the points to the various objects in the order of his preference. Consider the following example:

- Allocate a total of 100 points among the various schools into which you would like to admit your child. The more the points you allocate to a school, more preferred it is to be considered. The points should be allocated in such a way that the sum total of the points allocated to various schools adds up to 100.

Schools	Points
DPS	
Modern School	
Mother's International	
APEEJAY	
DAV Public School	
Laxman Public School	
Tagore International	
TOTAL POINTS	100

Suppose Mother's International is awarded 30 points, whereas Laxman Public School is awarded 15 points, one can make a statement that the respondent rates Mother's International twice as high as Laxman Public School. This type of data is not only comparative in nature but could also result in ratio scale measurement. This type of scale is widely used in allocating weights which the consumer may assign to the various attributes of a product.

In a **Q-sort technique**, a rank order procedure is used in which objects are sorted into different piles based on their similarity with respect to certain criterion.

Q-sort technique: The Q-sort technique was developed to discriminate among a large number of objects quickly. This technique makes use of the rank order procedure in which objects are sorted into different piles based on their similarity with respect to certain criterion. Suppose there are 100 statements and an individual is asked to pile them into five groups, in such a way, that the strongly agreed statements could be put in one pile, agreed statements could be put in another pile, neutral statements form the third pile, disagreed statements come in the fourth pile and strongly disagreed statements form the fifth pile, and so on. The data generated in this way would be ordinal in nature. The distribution of the number of statement in each pile should be such that the resulting data may follow a normal distribution. The number of piles need not be restricted to 5. It could be as large as 10 or more as the large number increases the reliability or precision of the results.

Non-comparative Scales

In the **non-comparative scales**, the respondents do not make use of any frame of reference before answering the questions.

In the non-comparative scales, the respondents do not make use of any frame of reference before answering the questions. The resulting data is generally assumed to be interval or ratio scale. For example:

The respondent may be asked to evaluate the quality of food in a restaurant on a five point scale (1 = very poor, 2 = poor and 5 = very good). The non-comparative scales are divided into two categories, namely, the graphic rating scales and the itemized rating scales. The itemized rating scales are further divided into Likert scale, semantic differential scale and Stapel scale. All these come under the category of the multiple item scales.

Graphic rating scale

This is a continuous scale, also called graphic rating Scale. In the graphic rating scale the respondent is asked to tick his preference on a graph. Consider for example the following question:

- Please put a tick mark (✓) on the following line to indicate your preference for fast food.

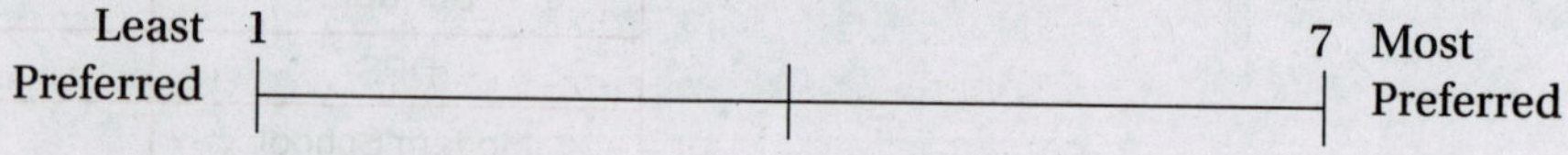

To measure the preference of an individual towards fast food one has to measure the distance from the extreme left to the position where a tick mark has been put. Higher the distance, higher would be the individual preference for fast food. This scale suffers from two limitations—one, if a respondent has put a tick mark at a particular position and after ten minutes, he or she is given another form to put a tick mark, it will virtually be impossible to put a tick at the same position as was done earlier. Does it mean that the respondent's preference for fast food has undergone a change in10 minutes? The basic assumption in this scale is that the respondents can distinguish the fine shade in differences between the preference/attitude which need not be the case. Further, the coding, editing and tabulation of data generated through such a procedure is a tedious task and researchers try to avoid using it. Another version of graphic scale could be the following:

- Please put a tick mark (✓) on the following line to indicate your preference for fast food.

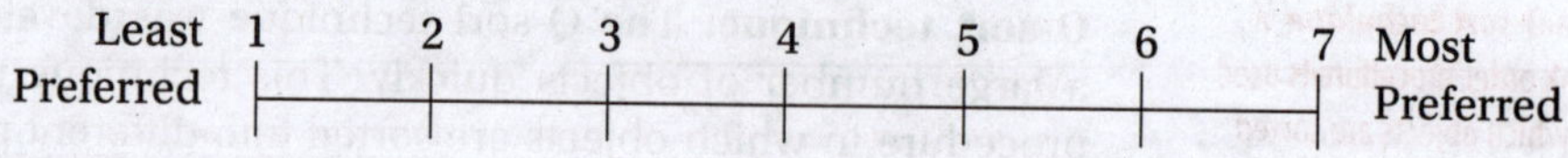

This is a slightly better version than the one discussed earlier. It will overcome the limitation of the scale to some extent. For example, if a respondent had earlier ticked between 5 and 6, it is likely that he would remember the same and the second time, he would tick very close to where he did earlier. This means that the difference in the two responses could be negligible.

Another way of presenting the graphic rating scale is through smiling face scale. The following example would illustrate the same.

- Please indicate how much do you like fast food by pointing to the face that best shows your attitude and taste. If you do not prefer it at all, you would point to face one. In case you prefer it the most, you would point to face seven.

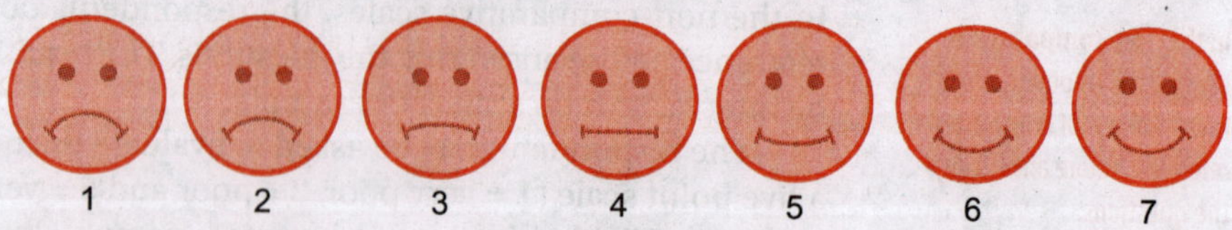

In the itemized rating scale, the respondents are provided with a scale that has a number of brief descriptions associated with each of the response categories.

Itemized rating scale

In the itemized rating scale, the respondents are provided with a scale that has a number of brief descriptions associated with each of the response categories. The response categories are ordered in terms of the scale position and the respondents are supposed to select the specified category that describes in the best possible way an object is rated. Itemized rating scales are widely used in survey research. There are certain issues that should be kept in mind while designing the itemized rating scale. These issues are:

Number of categories to be used: There is no hard and fast rule as to how many categories should be used in an itemized rating scale. However, it is a practice to use five or six categories. Some researches are of the opinion that more than five categories should be used in situations where small changes in attitudes are to be measured. There are others that argue that the respondents would find it difficult to distinguish between more than five categories. It is, however, a fact that the additional categories need not increase the precision with the attitude being measured. It is generally seen that researchers use five-category scales and in special cases, may increase or decrease the number of categories.

Odd or even number of categories: It has been a matter of debate among the researchers as to whether odd or even number of categories are to be used in survey research. By using even number of categories the scale would not have a neutral category and the respondent will be forced to choose either the positive or the negative side of the attitude. If odd numbers of categories are used, the respondent has the freedom to be neutral if he wants to be so. The Likert scale (to be discussed later) is a balanced rating scale with an odd number of categories and a neutral point. It is generally seen that if a respondent is not aware of the subject matter being measured by the scale, he would prefer to be neutral. However, if we have selected our unit of analysis to be one who is knowledgeable about the study being conducted and if he prefers to be neutral, we should not debar him from this opportunity.

A **balanced scale** has equal number of favouable and unfavourable categories.

Balanced versus unbalanced scales: A balanced scale is the one which has equal number of favourable and unfavourable categories. Examples of balanced and unbalanced scale are given below.

The following is the example of a balanced scale:

- How important is price to you in buying a new car?
  Very important
  Relatively important
  Neither important nor unimportant
  Relatively unimportant
  Very unimportant

In this question, there are five response categories, two of which emphasize the importance of price and two others that do not show its importance. The middle category is neutral.

The following is the example of the unbalanced scale.

- How important is price to you in buying a new car?
  More important than any other factor
  Extremely important
  Important
  Somewhat important
  Unimportant

In this question there are four response categories that are skewed towards the importance given to the price, whereas one category is for the unimportant side. Therefore, this question is an unbalanced question. In the unbalanced scale, the numbers of favourable and unfavourable categories are not the same. One could use an unbalanced scale depending upon the nature of attitude distribution to be measured. If the distribution is dominantly favourable, an unbalanced scale with more favourable categories than unfavourable categories should be appropriate. If an unbalanced scale is used, the nature and degree of the unbalance in the scale should be taken into account during the data analysis.

Verbal descriptions must be clearly and precisely worded so that the respondents are able to differentiate between them.

Nature and degree of verbal description: Many researchers believe that each category must have a verbal, numerical or pictorial description. Verbal description should be clearly and precisely worded so that the respondents are able to differentiate between them. Further, the researcher must decide whether to label every scale category, some scale categories, or only extreme scale categories. It is argued that a clearly defined response category increases the reliability of the measurement.

An important issue concerning the construction of an itemized rating scale is the use of a **forced scale versus non-forced scale.**

Forced versus non-forced scales: An important issue concerning the construction of an itemized rating scale is the use of a forced scale versus non-forced scale. In the forced scale, the respondent is forced to take a stand, whereas in the non-forced scale, the respondent can be neutral if he/she so desires. The argument for a forced scale is that those who are reluctant to reveal their attitude are encouraged to do so with the forced scale. Paired comparison scale, rank order scale and constant sum rating scales are examples of forced scales.

Physical form: There are many options that are available for the presentation of the scales. It could be presented vertically or horizontally. The categories could be expressed in boxes, discrete lines or as units on a continuum. They may or may not have numbers assigned to them. The numerical values, if used, may be positive, negative or both.

Suppose we want to measure the perception about Jet Airways using a multi-item scale. One of the questions is about the behaviour of the crew members. Given below is a set of scale configurations that may be used to measure their behaviour. The following are some of the examples where various forms of presenting the scales are shown:

The behaviour of the crew members of Jet Airways is:

1. Very bad ____ ____ ____ ____ ____ Very good
2. Very bad 1 2 3 4 5 Very good
3. ☐ Very bad
   ☐
   ☐ Neither bad nor good
   ☐
   ☐ Very good
4. Very bad Bad Neither bad nor good Good Very good
5. –2 Very bad –1 0 Neither bad nor good 1 2 Very good

Below we will describe some of the itemized rating scales which are very commonly used in survey research.

Likert scale is also called a summated scale because the scores on individual items can be added together to produce a total score for the respondent.

Likert scale: This is a multiple item agree–disagree five-point scale. The respondents are given a certain number of items (statements) on which they are asked to express their degree of agreement/disagreement. This is also called a summated scale because the scores on individual items can be added together to produce a total score for the respondent. An assumption of the Likert scale is that each of the items (statements) measures some aspect of a single common factor, otherwise the scores on the items cannot legitimately be summed up. In a typical research study, there are generally 25 to 30 items on a Likert scale.

To construct a Likert scale to measure a particular construct, a large number of statements pertaining to the construct are listed. These statements could range from 80 to 120. The identification of the statements is done through exploratory research which is carried out by conducting a focus group, unstructured interviews with knowledgeable people, literature survey, analysis of case studies and so on. Suppose we want to assess the image of a company. As a first step, an exploratory research may be conducted by having an informal interview with the customers, and employees of the company. The general public may also be contacted. A survey of the literature on the subject may also give a set of information that could be useful for constructing the statements. Suppose the number of statements to measure the constructs is 100 in number. Now samples of representative respondents are asked to state their degree of agreement/disagreement on those statements. Table 7.5 gives a few statements to assess the image of the company.

It may be noted that only anchor labels and no numerical values are assigned to the response categories. Once the scale is administered, numerical values are assigned to the response categories. The scale contains statements' some of which are favourable to the construct we are trying to measure and some are unfavourable to it.

For example, out of the ten statements given, statements numbering 1, 2, 4, 6 and 9 in Table 7.5 are favourable statements, whereas the remaining are unfavourable statements. The reason for having a mixture of favourable and unfavourable statements in a Likert scale is that the responses by the respondent should not become monotonous while answering the questions. Generally, in a Likert scale, there is an approximately equal number of favourable and unfavourable statements. Once the scale is administered, numerical values are assigned to the responses. The rule is that a 'strongly agree' response for a favourable statement should get the same numerical value as the 'strongly disagree' response of the unfavourable statement.

TABLE 7.5 Likert scale statements to measure the image of the company

No.	Statement	Strongly disagree	Disagree	Neither agree nor disagree	Agree	Strongly agree
1.	The company makes quality products			✓		
2.	It is a leader in technology					✓
3.	It doesn't care about the general public		✓			
4.	The company leads in R&D to improve products				✓	
5.	The company is not a good paymaster	✓				
6.	The products of the company go through stringent quality tests				✓	
7.	The company has not done anything to curb pollution		✓			
8.	It does not care about the community near its plant	✓				
9.	The company's stocks are good to buy or own				✓	
10.	The company does not have good labour relations		✓			

Suppose for a favourable statement the numbering is done as Strongly disagree = 1, Disagree = 2, Neither agree nor disagree = 3, Agree = 4 and Strongly agree = 5. Accordingly, an unfavourable statement would get the numerical values as Strongly disagree = 5, Disagree = 4, Neither agree nor disagree = 3, Agree = 2 and Strong agree = 1. In order to measure the image that the respondent has about the company, the scores are added.

For example, if a respondent has ticked (✓) statements numbering from one to ten as shown in Table 7.5, his total score would be 3 + 5 + 4 + 4 + 5 + 4 + 4 + 5 + 4 + 4 = 42 out of 50. Now if there are 100 respondents and 100 statements, the score on the image of the company can be worked out for each respondent by adding his/her scores on the 100 statements. The minimum score for each respondent will be 100, whereas the maximum score would be 500.

As mentioned earlier, a typical Likert scale comprises about 25–30 statements. In order to select 25 statements from the 100 statements, we need to discard some of them. The rule behind discarding the statements is that those items that are non-discriminating should be removed. The procedure for choosing 25 (say number of statements) is shown.

As mentioned earlier, the score for each of the respondents on each of the statements can be used to measure his/her total score about the image of the company. The data may look as given in Table 7.6.

Table 7.6 shows that the total score for respondent no. 1 is 410, whereas for respondent no. 2 it is 209. This means that respondent no. 1 has a more favourable image for the company as compared to respondent no. 2. Now, in order to select 25 statements, let us consider statements numbering i and j. We note that the statement no. j is more discriminating as compared to statement no. i. This is because the score on statement j is very highly correlated with the total score as compared to the scores on statement i. Therefore, if we have to choose between i and j, we will choose statement no. j. From this we can conclude that only those statements will be selected which have a very high correlation with the total score. Therefore, the 100 correlations are to be arranged in the ascending order of magnitudes corresponding to each statement and only top 25 statements having a high correlation with the total score need to be selected.

Another method of selecting the number of statements from a relatively large number of them is through the use of factor analysis. This aspect will be covered at the appropriate stage in the chapter on factor analysis.

TABLE 7.6 Total score and individual score of each respondent on various statements

	Scores of Statements									
Resp. No.	**1**	**2**	**3**	**..........**	**i**	**..........**	**j**	**..........**	**100**	**Total Score**
1	-	-	-	....	5	....	4	....	-	410
2	-	-	-	....	4	....	2	....	-	209
3	-	-	-	....	-	....	-	....	-	-
-	-	-	-	....	-	....	-	....	-	-
-	-	-	-	....	-	....	-	....	-	-
-	-	-	-	....	-	....	-	....	-	-
-	-	-	-	....	-	....	-	....	-	-
-	-	-	-	....	-	....	-	....	-	-
-	-	-	-	....	-	....	-	....	-	-
100	-	-	-	....	-	....	-	....	-	-

In a semantic differential scale, a respondent is required to rate each attitude or object on a number of five-or-seven point rating scales.

Semantic differential scale: This scale is widely used to compare the images of competing brands, companies or services. Here the respondent is required to rate each attitude or object on a number of five-or seven-point rating scales. This scale is bounded at each end by bipolar adjectives or phrases. The difference between Likert and Semantic differential scale is that in Likert scale, a number of statements (items) are presented to the respondents to express their degree of agreement/disagreement. However, in the semantic differential scale, bipolar adjectives or phrases are used. As in the case of Likert scale, the information on the phrases and adjectives is obtained through exploratory research. At times there may be a favourable or unfavourable descriptor (adjectives) on the right-hand side and on certain occasions these may be presented on the left-hand side. This rotation becomes necessary to avoid the halo effect. This is because the location of previous judgments on the scale may influence the subsequent judgements because of the carelessness of the respondents. The mid point of a bipolar scale is a neutral point. In the Likert scale, ten statements were used where respondents were asked to express their degree of agreement/disagreement regarding the image of the company. Taking the same example further, the semantic differential scale corresponding to those ten statements in Likert scale is shown below where the bipolar adjectives/phrases are separated by seven points. These points can be numbered as 1, 2, 3, ..., 7 or +3, +2, +1, 0, −1, −2, −3 for a favourable descriptor positioned on the left hand side. For an unfavourable descriptor the numberings would be reversed. A typical semantic differential scale where bipolar adjectives/phrases are positioned at the two extreme ends is given in Table 7.7.

TABLE 7.7
Select bipolar adjectives/phrases of semantic differential scale

1	Makes quality products	□ □ □ □ □ □ □ □	Does not make quality products
2	Leader in technology	□ □ □ □ □ □ □ □	Backward in technology
3	Does not care about general public	□ □ □ □ □ □ □ □	Cares about general public
4	Leads in R & D	□ □ □ □ □ □ □ □	Lagging behind in R&D
5	Not a good paymaster	□ □ □ □ □ □ □ □	A good paymaster
6	Products go through stringent quality test	□ □ □ □ □ □ □ □	Products don't go through quality test
7	Does nothing to curb pollution	□ □ □ □ □ □ □ □	Does a remarkable job in curbing pollution
8	Does not care about community near plants	□ □ □ □ □ □ □ □	Cares about community near plants
9	Company stocks good to buy	□ □ □ □ □ □ □ □	Not advisable to invest in company stock
10	Does not have good labour relations	□ □ □ □ □ □ □ □	Has good labour relations

Once the scale is constructed and administered to the representative respondents, the mean score for each of the descriptor is calculated. The scale is administered under the assumption that the numerical values assigned to the response categories are of interval scale in nature. This is generally the practice adopted by many researchers. However, if the response categories are treated as ordinal scale, instead of computing the arithmetic mean, median may be computed. In this example, we are treating the responses as the interval scale and hence the mean is computed. Once the mean for all the bipolar adjectives/phrases is computed we put the result in the form of a pictorial profile so as to make the comparison easy. At this time, all the favourable descriptors are kept on one side and all the unfavourable descriptors

TABLE 7.8
Pictorial profile based on semantic differential ratings

	Favourable descriptor	Unfavourable descriptor
1	Makes quality products	Does not make quality products
2	Leader in technology	Backward in technology
3	Cares about general public	Does not care about general public
4	Leads in R & D	Lagging behind in R&D
5	A good paymaster	Not a good paymaster
6	Products go through stringent quality test	Products do not go through quality test
7	Done remarkable job in curbing pollution	Done nothing to curb pollution
8	Cares about community near plants	Does not care about community near plants
9	Company stocks good to buy	Not advisable to invest in company stock
10	Has good labour relations	Does not have good labour relations

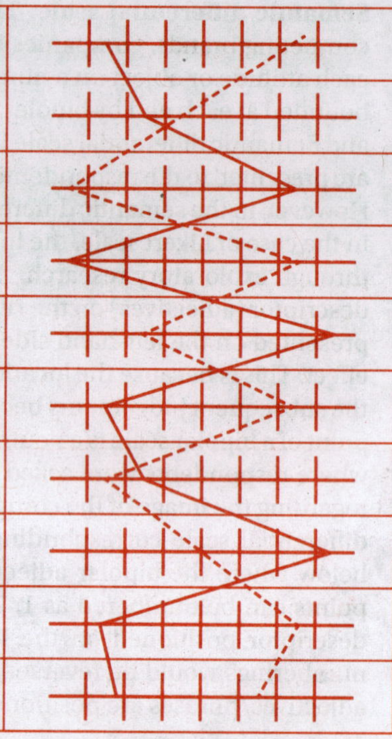

____________ Company A - - - - - - - - - Company B

are positioned at the other. In our example, we have positioned all the favourable descriptors for the two companies whose image we want to compare on the left hand side. This is shown in Table 7.8.

As per the results presented in the pictorial profile, Company A is better than Company B in the sense that it makes quality products, leads in R&D, its products go through stringent quality tests, its stocks are good to buy and it has good labour relations. Company B is ahead of Company A as it cares about general public and is a good paymaster. Company A is a better than Company B as it is leads in technology whereas Company B is better than Company A as it has done a remarkable job in curbing pollution. However, these differences are not statistically significant.

Stapel scale is used to measure the direction and intensity of an attitude.

Stapel scale: The Stapel scale is used to measure the direction and intensity of an attitude. At times, it may be difficult to use semantic differential scales because of the problem in creating bipolar adjectives.

RESTAURANT

+5	+5
+4	+4
+3	+3
+2*	+2
+1	+1
Quality of Food	***Quality of Service***
−1	−1
−2	−2
−3	−3
−4	−4
−5	−5*

The Stapel scale overcomes this problem by using only single adjectives. This scale generally has 10 categories involving numbering –5 to +5 without a neutral point and is usually presented in a vertical form. The job of the respondent is to indicate how accurately or inaccurately each term describes the object by selecting an appropriate numerical response category. If a positive higher number is selected by the respondent, it means the respondent is able to describe it more favourably. Suppose a restaurant is to be evaluated on quality of food and quality of service, then the Stapel scale would be presented as shown on the previous page:

In the above scale, the respondents are asked to evaluate how accurately each word or phrase describes the restaurant in question. They will choose a value of +5 if the restaurant very accurately describes the attribute and –5 if it does not describe at all correctly the word in question. Suppose a respondent has chosen his options as indicated by *. This shows that the respondent slightly prefers the quality of food and is of the opinion that the quality of service is totally useless.

CONCEPT CHECK

1. Distinguish between the Likert scale and semantic differential scale.
2. List the various forms of presenting the scales.
3. When is a Stapel scale used?

MEASUREMENT ERROR

LEARNING OBJECTIVE 5

Define measurement error and explain the criteria for good measurement.

Measurement error occurs when the observed measurement on a construct or concept deviates from its true values. The following is a list of the sources of measurement errors.

- There are factors like mood, fatigue and health of the respondent which may influence the observed response while the instrument is being administered.
- The variations in the environment in which measurements are taken may also result in a departure from the true value.
- There are situations when a respondent may not understand the question being asked and the interviewer may have to rephrase the same. While rephrasing the question the interviewer's bias may get into the responses. Also how the questionnaire is administered (telephone survey, personal interview with questionnaire or mail survey) will have its own impact on the responses.
- At times, some of the questions in the questionnaire may be ambiguous and some may be very difficult for the respondents to understand. Both of them can cause deviation from the correct response, thereby giving rise to measurement error.
- At times, the errors may be committed at the time of coding, entering of data from questionnaire to the spreadsheet on the computer and at the tabulation stage.

The observed measurement in any research need not be equal to the true measurement. The observed measurement can be written as

$$O = T + S + R$$

where, O = Observed measurement
T = True score
S = Systematic error
R = Random error

It may be noted that the total error consists of two components—systematic error and random error. Systematic error causes a constant bias in the measurement. Suppose there is a weighing scale that weighs 50 gm less for every one kg of product being weighed. The error would consistently remain the same irrespective of the kind of product and the time at which product is weighed. Random error on the other hand involves influences that bias the measurements but are not systematic. Suppose we use different weighing scales to weigh one kg of a product and if systematic error is assumed to be absent, we may find that recorded weights may fall within a range around the true value of the weight, thereby causing random error.

The **random error** on the other hand involves influences that bias the measurements but are not systematic.

Criteria for Good Measurement

There are three criteria for evaluating measurements: reliability, validity and sensitivity.

Reliability

Reliability is concerned with consistency, accuracy and predictability of the scale. It refers to the extent to which a measurement process is free from random errors. The reliability of a scale can be measured using the following methods:

In the **test–retest reliability,** repeated measurements of the same person or group using the same scale under the similar condition are taken.

Test–retest reliability: In this method, repeated measurements of the same person or group using the same scale under similar conditions are taken. A very high correlation between the two scores indicates that the scale is reliable. However, the following issues should be kept in mind before arriving at such a conclusion.

- What should be the appropriate time difference between the two observations is a question which requires attention. If the time difference between two consecutive observations is very small (say two or three weeks) it is very likely that the respondents would remember the previous answer and may give the same answer when the instrument is administered the second time. This will make the instrument reliable, which may not actually be the case. However, if the difference between the two observations is very large (say more than a year) it is quite likely that the respondent's answers to the various questions of the instrument might have actually undergone a change, resulting in poor reliability of the scale. Therefore, the researcher has to be very careful in deciding upon the time difference between the two observations. Generally, it is thought that a time difference of about five to six months is an ideal period.
- Another problem in this test is that the first measurement may change the response of the subject to the second measurement.
- The situational factors working on two different time periods may not be the same, which may result in different measurement in the two periods.
- The second reading on the same instrument from the same subject may produce boredom, anger or attempt to remember the answers given in an initial measurement.
- A favourable response with a brand during the period between the two tests might cause a shift in the individual rating by the subject.

A **high correlation** indicates that the internal consistency of the construct leads to greater reliability.

Split-half reliability method: This method is used in the case of multiple item scales. Here the number of items is randomly divided into two parts and a correlation coefficient between the two is obtained. A high correlation indicates that the internal consistency of the construct leads to greater reliability. Another measure which is used to test the internal consistency of a multiple item scale is the coefficient alpha (α) commonly known as cronbach alpha. The cronbach alpha computes the average of all possible split-half reliabilities for a multiple item scale. This coefficient demonstrates whether the average score of all split-half of reliabilities converge to a certain point or not.

The coefficient alpha does not address validity. However, many researchers use this as a sole indicator of validity. The alpha coefficient can take values between 0 and 1. The following values of alpha with their interpretations are suggested below:

$\alpha = 0$ means	There is no consistency between the various items of a multiple item scale
$\alpha = 1$ means	There is complete consistency between various items of a multiple item scale
$0.80 \leq \alpha \leq 0.95$ implies	There is very good reliability between the various items of a multiple item scale
$0.70 \leq \alpha \leq 0.80$ implies	There is good reliability between the various items of a multiple item scale
$0.60 \leq \alpha \leq 0.70$ implies	There is fair reliability between the various items of a multiple item scale
$\alpha < 0.60$ means	There is poor reliability between the various items of a multiple item scale

Validity

The **validity** of a scale refers to the question whether we are measuring what we want to measure.

The validity of a scale refers to the question whether we are measuring what we want to measure. Validity of the scale refers to the extent to which the measurement process is free from both systematic and random errors. The validity of a scale is a more serious issue than reliability. There are different ways to measure validity.

Content validity is also called face validity in which an expert provides subjective judgement to assess the appropriateness of the construct.

Content validity: This is also called face validity. It involves subjective judgement by an expert for assessing the appropriateness of the construct. For example, to measure the perception of a customer towards Jet Airways, a multiple item scale is developed. A set of 15 items is proposed. These items when combined in an index measure the perception of Jet Airways. In order to judge the content validity of these 15 items, a set of experts may be requested to examine the representativeness of the 15 items. The items covered may be lacking in the content validity if we have omitted behaviour of the crew, food quality, and food quantity, etc., from the list. In fact, conducting the exploratory research to exhaust the list of items measuring perception of the airline would be of immense help in such a case.

Concurrent validity: It is used to measure the validity of the new measuring techniques by correlating them with the established techniques. It involves computing the correlation coefficient of two measures of the same phenomena (for example, perception of an airline and image of a company) which are administered at the same time. We prepare a 15 item scale to measure the perception of Jet Airways, which is assumed to be a valid one. Suppose a researcher proposes an alternative and shorter technique. The concurrent validity of the new technique would be established if there is a high correlation between the two techniques when administered at the same time under similar or identical conditions.

Predictive validity: This involves the ability of a measured phenomena at one point of time to predict another phenomenon at a future point of time. If the correlation coefficient between the two is high, the initial measure is said to have a high predictive ability. As an example, consider the use of the common admission test (CAT) to shortlist candidates for admission to the MBA programme in a business school. The CAT scores are supposed to predict the candidate's aptitude for studies towards business education.

Sensitivity

The sensitivity of a scale is an important measurement concept, particularly when changes in attitudes are under investigation. Sensitivity refers to an instrument's ability to accurately measure the variability in a concept. A dichotomous response category such as agree or disagree does not allow the recording of any attitude changes. A more sensitive measure with numerous categories on the scale may be required. For example, adding strongly agree, agree, neither agree nor disagree, disagree and strongly disagree categories will increase the sensitivity of the scale. The sensitivity of scale based on a single question or a single item can be increased by adding questions or items. In other words, because composite measures allow for a greater range of possible scores, they are more sensitive than a single-item scale. Therefore, the sensitivity of the scale is generally increased by adding more response points or by adding scale items.

CONCEPT CHECK

1. List some of the factors that can cause a deviation in measurement.
2. What is a random error?
3. Explain content and concurrent validity.

SUMMARY

- 'Measurement' means the assignment of numbers or other symbols to the characteristics of certain objects. Scaling is an extension of measurement. Scaling involves creating a continuum on which measurements on the objects are located. There are four types of measurement scales: nominal, ordinal, interval and ratio scale.
- Attitude is a predisposition of the individual to evaluate some objects or symbol. Attitude cannot be observed directly. It may be inferred from the perceptions. Attitude has three components: cognitive, affective and intention or action component. Scales can be classified as single-item and multiple-item scales. Another classification could be whether the scales are comparative or non-comparative in nature. The comparative scales could be further classified into paired comparison scale, constant sum rating scale, rank order scale and Q-sort and other procedures. The non-comparative scales can be divided into graphic rating scales and itemized rating scales. The Itemized rating scales could be further classified into Likert scale, semantic differential scale and Stapel scale. There are various issues like (1) number of categories to be used, (2) odd or even number of categories, (3) balanced vs unbalanced scale, (4) nature and degree of verbal description, (5) forced vs non-forced scale, and (6) physical form that has to be kept in mind while constructing itemized scales.
- The observed measurement need not be equal to the true value of the measurement. Some systematic and random errors may be found in the observed measurement. There are three criteria for determining the accuracy of a measurement—reliability, validity and sensitivity. Reliability can be tested using test–retest reliability, split–half method and Cronbach alpha. The validity of a scale can be judged by content validity, concurrent validity and predictive validity of a measure. The sensitivity of an instrument examines the ability to measure the variability in a concept in an accurate manner.

KEY TERMS

- Attitude
- Balanced vs unbalanced scales
- Comparative scale
- Concurrent validity
- Constant sum rating scale
- Content validity
- Forced vs non-forced scales
- Graphic rating scale
- Interval scale
- Itemized rating scale
- Likert scale
- Measurement

- Measurement error
- Multiple-item scale
- Nominal scale
- Non-comparative scale
- Ordinal scale
- Paired comparison scale
- Predictive validity
- Q-sort technique
- Rank-order scaling
- Ratio scale
- Reliability
- Scaling
- Semantic differential scale
- Sensitivity
- Single-item scale
- Split–half reliability
- Stapel scale
- Test–retest reliability
- Validity

CHAPTER REVIEW QUESTIONS

Objective Type Questions

State whether the following statements are true (T) or false (F).

1. A nominal scale can only involve the assignment of numbers. Alphabets or symbols cannot be assigned.
2. When we measure the perceptions, attitudes, and preferences of consumers, we are measuring the objects or other relevant characteristics.
3. An ordinal scale indicates the relative position and the magnitude of the differences between the objects.
4. Ratios or differences between scale values are permissible in ratio scale.
5. Non-comparative scale data is generally assumed to be interval or ratio scaled.
6. In constant sum scaling, if an attribute is twice as important as some other attribute it receives twice as many points.
7. Systematic sources of error do have an adverse impact on reliability because they affect the measurement in a constant way and do not lead to inconsistency.
8. Reliability can be defined as the extent to which measures are free from random error, X_R.
9. Given its subjective nature, content validity alone is a sufficient measure of the validity of a scale.
10. A total (summated) score can be calculated for each respondent by summing across his score for all the items.
11. Profile analysis involves determining the average respondent ratings for each item.
12. The Likert scale is a balanced rating scale with an odd number of categories and a neutral point.
13. The Stapel scale is usually presented horizontally.
14. Reliability refers to the extent to which a scale produces valid results if repeated measurements are made.
15. A ratio-scaled variable is one that is constructed as the ratio of data on two other variables.
16. Coding and analysis of attitudinal data obtained through the use of 'pure' graphic rating scales can be done very quickly.
17. Numbers forming a nominal scale merely act as identification labels for different categories.
18. An itemized, forced-choice rating scale typically has an even number of response choices.
19. A comparative rating scale attempts to provide a common frame of reference to all respondents.
20. The reliability of an attitude scale is a necessary condition for its validity.

Conceptual Questions

1. Discuss with the help of examples the four key levels of measurement. What mathematical operations/statistical techniques are and are not permissible on data from each type of scale?
2. Discuss the major types of validity that concern a researcher in experimental designs.
3. Define attitude. Briefly explain the three components of attitude.
4. Explain an itemized rating scale. What are the various issues involved in constructing an itemized rating scale?
5. Suppose there are five banks located near your residence. Determine a constant sum rating scale to understand the preferences for these banks.
6. Distinguish between single-item and multiple-item scale. Should one prefer a multiple-item scale over the single-item scale? Explain with example.
7. What is measurement error? Discuss various types of measurement accuracy and the methods to measure them.
8. Briefly explain the concepts of reliability and validity.
9. What is the meaning of measurements in research? Give examples.
10. Discuss the applications of rating scales in various functional areas of management.
11. What is scaling? Describe the various scaling techniques used in business research.
12. Explain the various scaling techniques in measuring the variables.
13. What do you mean by measurement? Explain the most widely used classification of measurement scales with examples.

14. Describe each of the following:
    (a) Test–retest reliability
    (b) Split–half reliability
    (c) Cronbach alpha
    (d) Content validity
    (e) Predictive validity
    (f) Sensitivity
15. Explain with the help of examples the difference between Semantic differential scale and Stapel scale.
16. Discuss the methodology of developing ordinal and interval scale from paired comparison data.
17. What is test–retest reliability? What problems can be faced by the researchers by using the test–retest reliability measure?

Application Questions

1. Suppose Jet Airways wants to ascertain the image it has in the minds of its patrons. Construct a seven-item Likert and semantic differential scale to measure the perceived image of the airlines. Make sure that the seven items under each format correspond to the same seven dimensions.
2. Indicate the type of measurement scale you would use for each of the following characteristics. Why did you choose the scale you did? Develop the appropriate question for each characteristic and the scale chosen.
    (a) Colour of a dishwasher
    (b) Age of a TV
    (c) Occupation
    (d) Brand loyalty
    (e) Readership of a newspaper
    (f) Intention to purchase a TV
3. Suppose 100 consumers were asked to indicate their preference for five brands of car tyres, namely Dunlop, Modi, Ceat, Good year and MRF. Figures below indicate the proportion of times the brand mentioned in the column was preferred over the brand in the row.Compute the distance between the brands and comment on the results.

Brand	Brand				
	Dunlop	Modi	Ceat	Good Year	MRF
Dunlop	0.50	0.80	0.59	0.52	0.77
Modi	0.20	0.50	0.60	0.46	0.56
Ceat	0.41	0.40	0.50	0.61	0.60
Goodyear	0.48	0.54	0.39	0.50	0.67
MRF	0.23	0.44	0.40	0.33	0.50

4. Assume that a manufacturer of a line of packaged meat products wanted to evaluate consumer attitudes towards the brand. A panel of 500 regular consumers of the brand responded to a questionnaire that was sent to them and that included two attitude scales. The questionnaire produced the following results:
    - The average score for the sample on a 25-item Likert scale (five-point) was 105.
    - The average score for the sample on a 20-item semantic differential scale (seven-point) was 106.

   The vice president has asked you to indicate whether these customers have a favourable or unfavourable attitude towards the brand. What would you tell him? Please be specific.
5. Indicate the type of scale (nominal, ordinal, interval or ratio) that is being used in each of the following questions:
    (a) How large is the market size for shampoos?
    (b) In which of the following functional areas of management do you wish to specialize in the second year?
        (i) Marketing
        (ii) Finance
        (iii) HR
        (iv) IT
    (c) State the order of your preference for the following colours.
        (i) Grey
        (ii) White

(iii) Blue
(iv) Green
(v) Black

(d) Was the research methods course difficult to understand?
Yes__________ No___________

(e) In which month were you born?

(f) How do you rate the quality of food at the Golden Dragon restaurant?
1 = Very poor, 2 = Poor, 3 = Neither good nor poor, 4 = Good, 5 = Very good

6. For each of the following statements, identify the appropriate component of attitude.
   (a) I do not like carrot juice.
   (b) Ambala Cantonment is well connected by rail and road.
   (c) The compensation package for MBA graduates has gone down because of the recession.
   (d) I did not attend most of my classes in the second term because of my illness.
   (e) The Congress party won all but one Lok Sabha seat from Delhi.
   (f) I prefer plastic bottles to glass bottles.
   (g) I like the recent Vodafone advertisement on TV.
   (h) I understand that Santro gives a better mileage than Wagon R.
7. The table below presents a paired comparison data. It states the observed proportion by stating that brand *i* (column of the table) is preferred to brand *j* (row of the table). Use the data to prepare an ordinal and an interval scale.

PAIRED COMPARISON DATA

	BRAND *i*				
BRAND *j*	**A**	**B**	**C**	**D**	**E**
A	0.50	0.60	0.37	0.61	0.20
B	0.40	0.50	0.44	0.56	0.34
C	0.63	0.56	0.50	0.52	0.13
D	0.39	0.44	0.48	0.50	0.30
E	0.80	0.66	0.87	0.70	0.50

8. Develop a Likert scale to measure the perception of bank customers towards the concept of Internet banking.
9. Develop a semantic differential scale to measure the image of two coffee joints—Cafe Coffee Day and Barista.
10. Design a 5-item Likert scale to measure the opinion of the general public for what measures should be taken to ensure the safety of women in the Indian cities.
11. From a survey of the consumers of a product, the following inferences were drawn.
    (a) The image that users have of our company is 2.0 times as positive as that of non-users.
    (b) On an average the income of the users is twice that of non-users.
    (c) The preference of users of the product is 1.8 times that of non-users.
    (d) The product of the company was ranked no. 2 by the survey respondents.
    (e) The sale of the product has increased by 18% over the previous year.

    Critically evaluate the meaningfulness and legitimacy of these inferences.

CASE 7.1

TUPPERWARE INDIA PVT. LTD.

Tupperware is the world's largest plastic food container company. It markets its products in over 100 countries across the globe and is today a household name in every corner of the world.

Tupperware India Pvt. Ltd. is a wholly owned subsidiary of the US-based Tupperware Corporation, the world's leading manufacturer of high-quality plastic food storage and serving containers. The company started its operations in India in 1996 and the country has been recognized as the fastest growing market by Tupperware Worldwide. Its products were launched in Delhi (November 1996) followed by Mumbai in (April 1997) and in Bangalore and Chennai in (October 1997). Pune, Chandigarh and Hyderabad followed in 1998.

Starting off with just 12 products, Tupperware India today sells over 70 products that meet Tupperware's stringent international quality standards. At present, the company sells its products in over 35 cities through a sales network comprising over 35,000 consultants, 1500 managers and 75 distributors. Backed by a committed and dedicated staff, region offices in all metros, Tupperware India has the pride of being the fastest set-up operation in the history of Tupperware. The company has been growing so fast that today it is approximately three times larger than any other company in its products' category. The company's turnover as of now is over US $11.5 million.

A full-fledged manufacturing facility is today the nerve-centre of Tupperware's Indian operations. Located in Hyderabad, this plant employs state-of-the-art technology to manufacture over 65 products, each of them meeting stringent quality standards laid down by Tupperware's international norms. Set up in a record time of three months, this facility could soon go in for an expansion to meet the ever-increasing demand for Tupperware. The moulds used to make Tupperware are hand-tooled stainless steel and these moulds are common for all countries and move in different countries as per the requirements.

The company classified its products under various categories depending upon the purpose they serve. The main product line of the company is grouped as follows:

- Dry storage – Modular mates, canisters, etc.
- Tableware – Bread server, butter dish, curry server, etc.
- Food preparation – Masala keeper, magic flow, quick shakes
- Microwave – Soup mugs, crystalwave medium
- Refrigerator – Cool n fresh series, wondlier bowls, ice trays
- Lunch and outdoors – Tumblers, lunch boxes
- Canister – Store-all-canisters, oasis jug
- Classics – Classic slim launch, tropical cups.

Tupperware India has specially designed select tailormade products for the Indian homemaker to fulfill the unique needs of the Indian kitchen. 'Cinnamon microwave dish' in a dark blue colour keeps in mind *haldi* stains, 'Masala storage box' which can store up to seven dry spices, and a range of thalis, katoris, roti-keeper, pickle and oil containers have already been introduced in the market. These products combine aesthetics and functionality. They are ingeniously designed to offer versatility and convenience. Tupperware products have won several design awards worldwide. The products are manufactured with 100 per cent food grade virgin plastic and offer a lifetime guarantee against chipping, cracking or breaking under normal non-commercial use. They are light, unbreakable, non-toxic and odourless. They also have special airtight and liquid tight seals which lock in freshness and flavour. The products are not only designed elegantly and add functionality but also add vibrancy and colour to any kitchen and dining table. The products are available in soothing colours such as red, blue, pastels and green to match kitchen décor and consumer preference.

Tupperware India, at present, faces competition from stainless steel utensils and low-end plastic products both available at retail outlets across India. However, with increasing awareness of high-end food storage containers, the company will soon see itself up against more intense competition. Already companies like Modicare, Cutting Edge and Real Life have entered this segment, albeit with lower prices.

The company is growing rapidly and uses a direct selling method to reach its end customers. An empirical study was undertaken to understand the perception of consumers and dealers (consultant).

The study assumes significance since the outcome of this research would help Tupperware identify the areas in which the perception is poor and would, therefore, be able to identify the problem areas so as to take remedial action. This is necessary because Tupperware is facing competition from Modicare, Pearl Pet and Reallife and the results of the study will help it in consolidating its market position by identifying its strengths and weaknesses. Further, it would indicate why and on what parameters the perception of consumers versus non-consumers is different. This could enable the company to formulate appropriate strategy to attract the non-consumers use its product.

The objectives of the study were:

1. To understand the perception of Tupperware product users about the company. Specifically we want to answer the following questions:
   (a) What is the profile of the users of Tupperware product?
   (b) What is the awareness level (both aided and unaided recall) of the users of Tupperware products?
   (c) Is the perception different for a user belonging to a nuclear or a joint family?
   (d) Does the perception vary across marital status?
   (e) Does the perception vary across professions?
   (f) Does the perception vary across age groups?
   (g) Does the perception vary across education levels?
   (h) Does the perception vary across income groups?
   (i) What are the underlying significant factors of the perceptions of users?
2. What is the perception of the non-users of Tupperware products about the company? Specifically, we would attempt to answer the following questions:
   (a) What is the profile of the non-users of Tupperware product?
   (b) What is the awareness level (both aided and unaided recall) of the non-users of Tupperware products?
   (c) Is the perception different for a non-user belonging to a nuclear or joint family?
   (d) Does the perception vary across marital status?
   (e) Does the perception vary across professiones?
   (f) Does the perception vary across age group?
   (g) Does the perception vary across education levels?
   (h) Does the perception vary across income groups?
   (i) What are the underlying significant factors of the perceptions of non-users?
3. Is the overall perception different for user and non-user of the Tupperware product?

To carry out the objectives, a study was conducted. The following questionnaire was used for the purpose.

Questionnaire for User/Non-user Research

1. What type of storage food container do you use in your kitchen? (Please tick one or more)
   (a) Stainless Steel
   (b) Plastic Products
   (c) Glass containers
   (d) Any Other (Please specify)
2. (a) In case you use plastic containers for storage, are you aware of the company/companies manufacturing it?

   Yes ☐

   No ☐

   (b) If yes, name them ____________________

   ____

   ____

   ____

3. Which of the following plastic container manufacturing companies are you aware of? (Please tick the appropriate box, you may tick more than one.
   (a) Cutting Edge ☐
   (b) Modicare ☐
   (c) Real Life ☐
   (d) Tupperware ☐
   (e) Any other (please specify) ☐

4. In case you have ticked Tupperware, please tell us as to how did you come to know about the product 'Tupperware' (Please tick the appropriate box, you may tick more than one)
   (a) Advertisements ☐
   (b) Party plan ☐
   (c) Internet ☐
   (d) Women's magazines ☐
   (e) Word of mouth ☐
   (f) Any other (please specify) ☐

5. Do you use Tupperware products?
   Yes ☐
   No ☐
   (If the answer is No, you will still be having some perception about Tupperware's products, its quality and price. Therefore, please move to question 11 directly)

6. If answer to above question is yes, did you
   (a) Buy the product
   (b) Received as a gift
   (c) Both

7. If you bought the product as mentioned in the question 6 above, did you buy
   (a) Through party plan
   (b) Telephoning the dealer
   (c) Both

8. How often do you buy Tupperware products?
   (a) Once a month
   (b) Twice a month
   (c) More than two times in a month

9. How much money do you spend in a month on the purchase of Tupperware products? ______________

10. In your last purchase which of the following items were bought by you. (Please tick as many as you like)
    Dry storage ☐
    Tableware ☐
    Food preparation ☐
    Microwave containers ☐
    Refrigerator containers ☐
    Lunch and outdoor containers ☐
    Canister ☐
    Classics ☐

11. Given below are some statements, you are requested to state your degree of agreement/disagreement on each of the statements as mentioned below on a 5-point scale.

	Statement	***Completely Disagree***	***Disagree***	***No Opinion***	***Agree***	***Completely Agree***
A	Tupperware products are made with the state-of the-art technology					
B	Tupperware products are ideal for gifts					
C	Tupperware products are not available in different sizes					
D	The products are available in attractive colours					
E	The products do not provide good value for money					
F	I feel proud to serve food to my guests in Tupperware products					
G	My peer groups do not use Tupperware products					
H	The products are not easily available					
I	The designs of the products are such that they occupy a lot of shelf space					
J	The products provide a good look to the kitchen					
K	The spices kept in Tupperware containers retain their original flavour for long					
L	Tupperware products are very expensive					
M	Tupperware products offer a lifetime warranty without any requirement of proof of purchase					
N	The products go with my lifestyle					
O	Tupperware products are for daily use					
P	The products require special cleaning agent					
Q	Tupperware products retain stain marks (e.g., turmeric) after cleaning					
R	Parents feel very safe while their children handle the products					
S	The products usages are well demonstrated in the home party					
T	The company provides timely information on new products					
U	The products are not air/water-tight					
V	The products are inconvenient to use					
W	I have no inhibition in using products in a large gathering of guests					
X	Tupperware keeps adding new products to its range to suit the kitchen requirements					
Y	The shape of the products are very eye-catching					
Z	Tupperware products are quite sturdy					
aa	The products are non-toxic and odourless					
ab	The products are very heavy in weight to carry from one place to another					

12. You belong to a
    - Nuclear family ☐
    - Joint family ☐

13. Marital status
    - Single ☐
    - Married ☐
    - Widow/divorced ☐
14. If married, are both of you working or only one
    - Both ☐
    - One ☐
15. In case you are working, you are employed in
    - Private sector ☐
    - Public sector ☐
    - Self-employed ☐
    - Govt. service ☐
16. You belong to age group
    - 20 – 30 years ☐
    - 31 – 40 years ☐
    - 41 – 50 years ☐
    - 51 and above ☐
17. Your education
    - Less than graduation ☐
    - Graduate ☐
    - Postgraduate and above ☐
18. Your monthly household income
    - Up to ₹15,000 ☐
    - 15,001 – 30,000 ☐
    - 3,0001 – 45,000 ☐
    - 45,001 and above ☐
19. Do you or your spouse own the following:

(a) Credit card	Yes ☐	No ☐
(b) Four wheeler	Yes ☐	No ☐
(c) House	Yes ☐	No ☐
(d) Club membership	Yes ☐	No ☐
(e) Microwave oven	Yes ☐	No ☐

Please note that in the question no.11 statements numbers a, b, d, f, j, k, m, n, o, r, s, t, w, x, y, z, aa are favourable statements. The remaining are unfavourable statements.

QUESTIONS

1. Indicate the type of measurement (nominal, ordinal, interval or ratio) which is being used in each of the above questions.
2. Identify the questions which will be relevant for each of the objectives of the study.

Note: The case is based on a project report 'Perception Study of Tupperware India Pvt. Ltd,' by Gautam Sareen, Raman Chawla and Sandeep Bansal, participants of PGPM (2001–04), International Management Institute, New Delhi.

Answers to Objective Type Questions

1. False	2. False	3. False	4. True	5. True
6. True	7. True	8. True	9. False	10. True
11. True	12. True	13. False	14. False	15. False
16. False	17. True	18. False	19. True	20. True

BIBLIOGRAPHY

Aaker, David A, V Kumar and George S Day. *Marketing Research*. 7th edn. New Delhi: John Wiley & Sons, Inc., 2001.

Beri, G C. *Marketing Research*. 3rd edn. New Delhi: Tata McGraw-Hill Publishing Company Ltd, 2000.

Bhatnagar, O P. *Research Methods and Measurements in Behavioural and Social Sciences'*. New Delhi: Agricole Publishing Academy, 1981.

Bhattacharyya, Dipak Kumar. *Research Methodology*. New Delhi: Excel Books, 2006.

Churchill, Gilbert A Jr and Dawn Iacobucci. *Marketing Research Methodological Foundations*. 8th edn. New Delhi: Thomson South Western, 2002.

Cooper, Donald R and Schindler, Pamela S. *Business Research Method*. 6th edn. Tata McGraw Hill Publishing Company Ltd., 1998.

Cooper, Donald R. *Business Research Methods*. New Delhi: Tata Mcgraw Hill Publishing Company Ltd, 2006.

Emory, William C. *Business Research Methods*. Illinois: Richard D. Irwin, 1976.

Kinnear, Thomas C and James R Taylor. *Marketing Research – An Applied Approach*. 3rd edn. New York: McGraw-Hill Book Company, 1987.

Kothari, C R. *Research Methodology: Methods and Techniques*. New Delhi: Wiley Eastern, 1990.

Malhotra, Naresh K. *Marketing Research – An Applied Orientation*. 5th edn. Pearson Education, 2007.

Michael, V P. *Research Methodology in Management*. Mumbai: Himalaya Publishing House, 2000.

Nargundkar, Rajendra. *Research methods in Social Sciences*. New Delhi: Sterling Publishers Private Ltd, 1983.

Nargundkar, Rajendra. *Marketing Research – Text and Cases*. 3rd edn. New Delhi: Tata McGraw Hill Publishing Company Ltd, 2008.

Nation, Jack R. *Research Methods*. New Jersey: Prentice Hall, 1997.

Parasuraman, A, Dhruv Grewal, and Krishnan, R. *Marketing Research*. New Delhi: Biztantra, 2004.

Schwab, Donald P. *Research Methods for Organizational Studies*. Mahwah, Lawrence Erlaum Associates Publishers, 2005.

Sekaran, Uma. *Research Methods for Business: A Skill Building Approach*. Singapore: John Wiley & Sons (Asia) Pte Ltd, 2003.

Tripathi, P C. *A Textbook of Research Methodology in Social Sciences*. New Delhi: Sultan Chand & Sons, 2007.

Trochim, William M. *Research Methods*. New Delhi: Biztantra, 2003.

Zikmund, William G. *Business Research Methods*. Fort Worth: Dryden Press, 2000.

8

CHAPTER

Questionnaire Designing

Learning Objectives

By the end of the chapter, you should be able to:

1. Appreciate the situations that merit the usage of a well-designed questionnaire and approach various methods available for the same.
2. Understand the step-wise process involved in the design of a questionnaire.
3. Determine the content of the questions designed in order to encourage the person to respond meaningfully to them.
4. Determine the flow and sequence of the questioning method.
5. Pretest and administer the questionnaire with ease and accuracy.

'Madam, can you please fill in this feedback questionnaire about your experience of buying Toyota Corolla from Star Motors.' Chetan Singh, sales executive at Toyota Motors, made a request to Shalini Singh as her husband sat filling in the various forms and receiving the car papers. 'Oh, it was very satisfying and you were very prompt in helping us out with our doubts. You fill in whatever you want and I am ok with it.' 'No Ma'am, we need the feedback in your words. Please appreciate that this is not just an exercise. At Toyota, all the information that you give will be recorded and used for my appraisal and also, the score that I get on the basis of your feedback will be added to the score of the team to which I belong. All the incentives and bonuses that my team or I will get are dependent to a large extent on the customer experience we are able to deliver. So, I request you to please fill this. It will not take much time, as most of the questions are simple 'yes' and 'no' types.'

Shalini reluctantly took the form that Chetan handed out. It had questions listed on both sides; she looked at her husband, Ravi, and knew that he would take some time. She took a pen and started filling in the information required. At the outset, she saw that Chetan had been right. The questionnaire began by clearly mentioning the purpose of the form, to what use it would be put and why objectivity was important. Next, she saw that the whole process of the first interface with the executive, the follow-up, the information sought and the time taken to respond and the response itself was mentioned. Attitude of the personnel, amenities at the outlet, the refreshments offered were also included. Good heavens, there was not a thing that was missing. Each question had five response options and very smartly, there was no 'very bad' and the response options began with 'not satisfactory'. She did not think this was correct as the responses were very obviously skewed towards average or above average and the consumer did not have an option of communicating that their experience was not happy. She decided that she would definitely write this in the suggestion box at the end of the questionnaire. 'Shall we go', quizzed Ravi, to which she responded, 'just a couple of minutes more, let me finish this.' Ravi smiled and waited patiently.

A month after their purchase, Shalini got a parcel from Toyota Motors. She wonderingly opened it and found a beautiful keychain and a letter. The letter thanked her for her feedback on the form she had filled in at Toyota Motors. It went on to explain the reason why the questionnaire that she had filled in had only 'not satisfactory' and then 'average' as the response. The author informed her that even though the category went from 'not satisfactory' to 'excellent', if a customer gave 'not satisfactory' as a response, it was scored as –2 and 'average' had a score of 0. Thus, the executive would get the appropriate negative rating.

Shailini realized that Toyota took the feedback process really seriously and worked on it; probably that was the reason why they had been able to earn so much goodwill. She ran a beauty salon and thought that this questionnaire method was a good mechanism for conducting a quality check to see whether they were able to come up to the customer's expectations and, secondly, how they could deliver better value. Yes, there was a lot of merit in this, as she remembered, it hardly took any time and was easy to understand as well. When she discussed the idea with Ravi, he said, 'You do not need to make so much effort, just see whether your client is smiling or complaining and you can also judge her satisfaction by the tip she gives to the girls.' 'But that only tells me that she is happy or unhappy, not the WHY? No, I think I am going to get a questionnaire designed, the question is how do I do it?'

So is Ravi right or Shalini? Is it really essential to formulate a tedious questionnaire, when a simpler and easier mechanism of observation or verbal interview is available? The answer is explicit in Shalini's response about the 'Why'?

This is one of the most cost-effective methods which can be used with considerable ease by most individual and business researchers. It has the advantage of flexibility of approach and can be successfully adapted for most research studies. The instrument has been defined differently by various researchers. Some take the traditional view of a written document requiring the subject to record his/her own responses (Kervin, 1999), others have taken a broader perspective to include structured interview also as a questionnaire (Bell, 1999). It is essentially a data-collection instrument that has a pre-designed set of questions, following a particular structure (De Vaus, 2002). Since it includes a standard set of questions, it can be successfully used to collect information from a large sample in a reasonably short time period.

However, a note of caution is to be sounded here, as the usage of questionnaire as the best method in all research studies is not a foregone conclusion. For example, at the exploratory stage, when one is still trying to identify the information areas, variables and execution decision, it is advisable to use a more unstructured interview. Secondly, when the number of respondents is small and one needs to collect more subjective data and most of the questions to be asked are open-ended, then a standardized questionnaire is not advisable.

CRITERIA FOR QUESTIONNAIRE DESIGNING

When one is designing the questionnaire, there are certain criteria that must be kept in mind.

LEARNING OBJECTIVE 1

Appreciate the situations that merit the usage of a well-designed questionnaire and approach various methods available for the same.

The first and foremost requirement is that the spelt-out research objectives must be converted into clear questions which will extract answers from the respondent. This is not as easy as it sounds, for example, if one wants to know something like what is the margin that a company gives to the retailer? This cannot be converted into a direct question as no one will give the correct figure. Thus, one will have to ask a disguised question like may be a range of percentage estimates—2-5 per cent, 6-10 per cent, 11-15 per cent, 16-20 per cent, etc., or the retailer might not go beyond a yes, no or 'industry standard.'

The second requirement is, like the Toyota questionnaire, it should be designed to engage the respondent and encourage a meaningful response. For example, a questionnaire measuring stress cannot have a voluminous set of questions which fatigue the subject. The questions, thus, should be non-threatening, must encourage response and be clear to understand. One needs to remember that the essential usage of the instrument is to administer the same to a large base, thus there must be clarity and interest that should be part of the measure itself.

Lastly, the questions should be self-explanatory and not confusing as then the answers one gets might not be accurate or usable for analysis. This will be discussed in detail later, when we discuss the wording of the questions.

Types of Questionnaire

The basic requirement for a **questionnaire** is that spelt-out research objectives must be converted into clear questions.

There are many different types of questionnaire available to the researcher. The categorization can be done on the basis of a variety of parameters. The two which are most frequently used for designing purposes are the degree of construction or structure and the degree of concealment, of the research objectives. Construction or formalization refers to the degree to which the response category has been defined. Concealed refers to the degree to which the purpose of the study is explained or is clear to the respondent.

Instead of considering them as individual types, most research studies use a mixed format. Thus, they will be discussed here as a two-by-two matrix (Table 8.1).

TABLE 8.1 Types of questionnaire

	FORMALIZED	NON-FORMALIZED
UNCONCEALED	Most research studies use standardized questionnaires like these	The response categories have more flexibility
CONCEALED	Used for assessing psychographic and subjective constructs	Questionnaires using projective techniques or sociometric analysis

Formalized and unconcealed questionnaire: This is the one that is indiscriminately and most frequently used by all management researchers. For example, if a new brokerage firm wants to understand the investment behaviour of the population under study, they would structure the questions and answers as follows:

1. Do you carry out any investment(s)?
   Yes __________ No __________
   If yes, continue, else terminate.

2. Out of the following options, where do you invest (tick all that apply).
   Precious metals __________, real estate __________, stocks __________, government instruments __________, mutual funds __________, any other __________.

3. Who carries out your investments?
   Myself __________, agent __________, relative __________, friend __________, any other __________.
   In case the option ticked is self, please go to Q. 4, else skip.

4. What is your source of information for these decisions?
   Newspaper __________, investment magazines __________, company records, etc. __________, trading portals __________, agent __________.

This kind of structured questionnaire is easy to administer, as one can see that the questions are self-explanatory and, since the answer categories are defined as well, the respondent needs to read and tick the right answer. Another advantage with this form is that it can be administered effectively to a large number of people at the same time. Data tabulation and data analysis is also easier to compute than in other methods.

This format, as a consequence of its predefined composition, is able to produce relatively stable results and is reasonably high in its reliability. The validity, of course would be limited as the comprehensive meaning of the constructs and variables under study might not be holistic when it comes to structured and limited responses. In such cases, variables are made a part of the study and some open-ended questions as well as administration/additional instructions/probing by the field investigator could help in getting better results.

Concealed questionnaire tries to reveal the latent causes of behaviour which cannot be determined by direct questions. It maps basic values, opinions and beliefs.

Formalized and concealed questionnaire: The research studies which are trying to unravel the latent causes of behaviour cannot rely on direct questions. Thus, the respondent has to be given a set of questions that can give an indication of what are his basic values, opinions and beliefs, as these would influence how he would react to certain products or issues. For example, a publication house that wants to launch a newspaper wants to ascertain what are the general perceptions and current attitudes about newspapers. Asking a direct question would only reveal apparent information, thus, some disguised attitudinal questions would need to be asked in order to infer this.

Please indicate your level of agreement with the following statements:

SA – Strongly Agree; A – Agree; N – Neutral; D – Disagree; SD – Strongly Disagree

		SA	A	N	D	SD
1	The individual today is better informed about everything than before.					
2	I believe that one must live for the day and worry about tomorrow later.					
3	An individual must at all times keep abreast of what is happening in the world around him/her.					
4	Books are the best friends anyone can have.					
5	I generally read and then decide what to buy.					
6	My lifestyle is so hectic that I do not have time for reading the newspaper.					
7	The advent of radio, television and Internet have made the traditional information sources-like newspapers, redundant.					
8	A man/woman is known by what he/she reads.					

The logic behind these tests of attitude is that the questions do not seem to be in a particular direction and are apparently non-threatening, thus the respondent gives an answer which would be in the general direction of his/her attitudes.

The advantage of these questions is that since these are structured, one can ascertain their impact and quantify the same through statistical techniques. Secondly, it has been found that psychographic questions like these increase the subject coverage and improve the validity of the instrument as well. Most studies interested in quantifying the primary response data make use of questions that are designed both as formalized unconcealed and formalized concealed.

Unconstructed questions allow a respondent to express his/her attitude in a liberated and uninhibited manner.

Non-formalized unconcealed: Some researchers argue that the respondent is not really cognizant of his/her attitude towards certain things. Also, this method asks him to give structured responses to attitudinal statements that essentially express attitudes in a manner that the researcher or experts think is the correct way. This however might not be the way the person thinks. Thus, rather than giving them pre-designed response categories, it is better to give them unstructured questions where he has the freedom of expressing himself the way he wants to. Some examples of these kinds of questions are given below:

1. What has been the reason for the success of the 'lean management drive' that the organization has undertaken? Please specify FIVE most significant reasons according to YOU.
   (a) ________
   (b) ________
   (c) ________
   (d) ________
   (e) ________
2. Why do you think Maggi noodles are liked by young children? ________
3. How do you generally decide on where you are going to invest your money?
4. Give THREE reasons why you believe that the Commonwealth 2010 Games have helped the country?

The advantage of the method is that the respondent can respond in any way he/she believes is important. For example, for the last question, some people might respond by stating that it has boosted tourism in the country and contributed to the country's economy. Some might think it will encourage more international events to be held in the country. Some might also state that it is not a good idea and the government should instead be spending on improving the cause of the people who are below the poverty line.

Thus, one gets a comprehensive perspective on what the construct/product/policy means to the population at large; and at the micro level, what it means to people in different segments. The validity of these measures is higher than the previous two. However, quantification is a little tedious and one cannot go beyond frequency and percentages to represent the findings. The other problem is the researcher's bias which might lead to clubbing responses into categories which might not be homogenous in nature (this element of bias will be discussed in detail in Chapter 10).

Non-formalized, concealed: If the objective of the research study is to uncover socially unacceptable desires and latent or subconscious and unconscious motivations, the investigator makes use of questions of low structure and disguised purpose. The presumption behind this is that if the argument, the situation or question is ambiguous, it is most likely that the revelation it would result in would be more rich and meaningful. In Chapter 6, there was a discussion on projective techniques; these kinds of questionnaires are designed on the above-stated lines. The major weakness of these types of questionnaires is that being of a low structure, the interpretation required is highly skilled. Cost, time and effort are additional elements which might curtail the use of these techniques. A study conducted to measure to which segment should men's personal care toiletries (especially moisturizers and fairness creams) be targeted, the investigator designed two typical bachelors' shopping lists. One with a number of monthly grocery products as well as the normal male toiletries like shaving blades, gels, shampoos, etc., and the other list had the same grocery products and male toiletries but it had two additional items—Fair and Handsome fairness cream and sensitive skin moisturizer. The list was given to 20 young men to conceptualize/describe the person whose list this is. The answers obtained were as follows:

List with Cream and Moisturizer	List without Cream and Moisturizer
65 per cent said this person was good looking	10 per cent said this man was good looking
5 per cent said typical male	39 per cent said 30 plus in age
25 per cent said a 20-year-old	90 per cent said rugged and manly
48 per cent said has a girlfriend	38 per cent said has a girlfriend
46 per cent said has a boyfriend	No one spoke of boyfriend
26 per cent said spendthrift	21 per cent said thrifty
15 per cent said 'girly'	32 per cent said normal Indian male

Thus, as we can see, the normal Indian adult male is still going to take time to include beauty or cosmetic products into his normal personal care basket. Thus, it is wiser for the marketeers to target the younger metrosexual male who is a heavy spender.

In a **schedule**, the interviewer reads out each question and makes a note of the respondent's answers.

A **self-administered questionnaire** saves time, cost and manpower and, thus, it is advisable to use in case of a large sample.

Another useful way of categorizing questionnaires is on the method of administration. Thus, the questionnaire that has been prepared would necessitate a face-to-face interaction. In this case, the interviewer reads out each question and makes a note of the respondent's answers. This administration is called a *schedule*. It might have a mix of the questionnaire type as described in the section above and might have some structured and some unstructured questions. The investigator might also have a set of additional material like product prototypes or copy of advertisements. The investigator might also have a predetermined set of standardized questions or clarifications , which he can use to ask questions like 'why do you say that?' or 'can you explain this in detail' 'what I mean to ask is......' The other kind is the *self-administered questionnaire*, where the respondent reads all the instructions and questions on his own and records his own statements or responses. Thus, all the questions and instructions need to be explicit and self-explanatory.

The selection of one over the other depends on certain study prerequisites.

Population characteristics: In case the population is illiterate or unable to write the responses, then one must as a rule use the schedule, as the questionnaire cannot be effectively answered by the subject himself.

Population spread: In case the sample to be studied is large and dispersed, then one needs to use the questionnaire. Also when the resources available for the study, time, cost and manpower are limited, then schedules become expensive to use and it is advisable to use self-administered questionnaire.

Study area: In case one is studying a sensitive topic, like organizational climate or quality of working life, where the presence of an investigator might skew the answers in a more positive direction, then it is better that one uses the questionnaire. However, in case the motives and feelings are not well-developed and structured, one might need to do additional probing and in that case a schedule is better. If the objective is to explore concepts or trace the reaction of the sample population to new ideas and concepts, a schedule is advisable.

CONCEPT CHECK

1. What should be the criteria for questionnaire designing?
2. Elaborate on the various types of questionnaires available.
3. Distinguish between non-formalized, unconcealed and non-formalized concealed questionnaires.

There is another categorization that is based upon the mode of administration; this would be discussed in later sections of the chapter.

QUESTIONNAIRE DESIGN PROCEDURE

LEARNING OBJECTIVE 2
Understand the stepwise process involved in the design of a questionnaire.

In the earlier section, the researcher must have understood the great advantage he has in case he uses a questionnaire for his research purpose. However, one of the most difficult steps in the entire research process is designing a well-structured instrument. A number of scholars have attempted to create structured and sequential guidelines to be used by a researcher, no matter what his/her interest area. While not following any particular school of thought, presented below is a standardized process that a researcher can follow.

These, of course, might need to be modified depending upon the objectives of research. The steps are indicative of what one needs to accomplish, however, the final document that emerges and the effectiveness of the measure in extracting the study-related information, depends entirely upon the individual understanding of the researcher to be able to:

The steps involved in the **questionnaire design procedure** are not independent. In the actual conduction, there might be a simultaneous involvement of some.

- Effectively and comprehensively list out the research information areas.
- Convert these into meaningful research questions.
- Understand and use the language of the respondent.

The steps involved in designing a questionnaire are as follows (Figure 8.1): (1) Convert the research objectives into the information needed, (2) Method of administering the questionnaire, (3) Content of the questions, (4) Motivating the respondent to answer, (5) Determining the type of questions, (6) Question design criteria, (7) Determine the questionnaire structure, (8) Physical presentation of the questionnaire, (9) Pilot testing the questionnaire, (10) Standardizing the questionnaire.

Each of these would be discussed and illustrated in this section. The researcher needs to remember that these are not independent steps, where one needs to finish the first one to go on to the next one and so on. In the actual conduction, there might be a simultaneous conduction of some and one might not be able to draw clear cut boundaries between them. Also at times, the researcher might have to backtrack and modify an earlier task that he might have carried out.

Convert the research objectives into information areas: This is the first step of the design process. As stated in the flowchart, this is the most critical stage and the researcher/investigator is assumed to have done considerable exploratory work to have crystallized objectives of the study. As you recall from Chapter 3, this is also the stage that requires formation of the research design of the study. Thus, by this stage one assumes that one has achieved the following tasks:

- Spelt out clearly the specific research questions that the study will address.
- Converted these questions into statements of objectives.
- Operationalized the variables to be studied, i.e., the variables under study should have been clearly defined.
- Identified the direction of the relation or any other assumption one makes about the variables under study in the form of a hypothesis.
- Specified the information needed for the study, in this case one will look at the information needed from the primary data source.

Once these tasks are accomplished, one can prepare a tabled framework so that the questions which need to be developed become clear.

FIGURE 8.1
Questionnaire design process

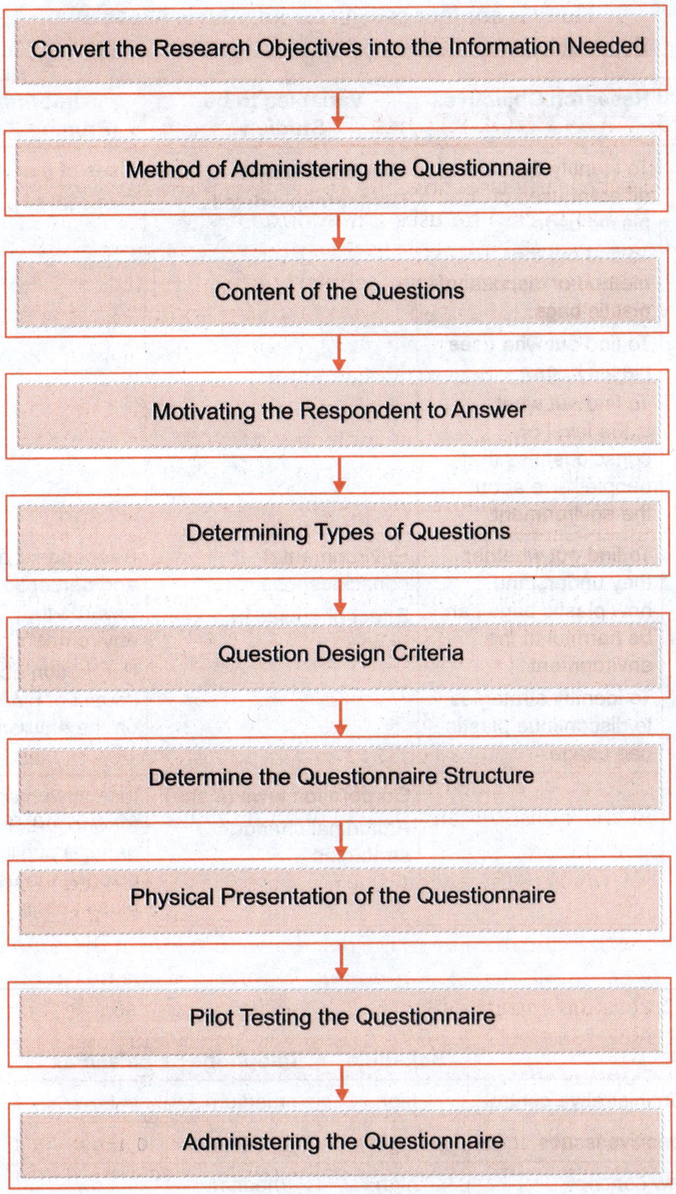

By this time, the respondent would have also developed a clear idea about the group that he would need to study. Thus, the characteristics of the population which might impact the constructs under study would also need to be studied in order to frame appropriate questions on these. At this stage, it might emerge that one needs to design separate questionnaires for the populations whose inputs are important, or have separate set of questions for those with different stands on the stated criteria. This stepwise process is explained in Table 8.2.

Method of administration: Once the researcher has identified his information area; he needs to specify how the information should be collected. The researcher usually has available to him a variety of methods for administering the study. The main methods are personal schedule (discussed earlier in the chapter) self-administered questionnaire through mail, fax, e-mail and web-based. There are different preconditions for using one method over the other. Also once the decision

TABLE 8.2
Framework for identifying information needs

Research Questions	Research Objectives	Variables to be Studied	Information (Primary Required)	Population to be Studied
What is the nature of plastic bag usage amongst people in the NCR (National Capital Region)?	To identify the different uses of plastic bags. To find out the method of disposal of plastic bags. To find out who uses plastic bags. To find out what is the level of consciousness that people have about the environment.	Usage behaviour Demographic details	Uses of plastic bags Disposal of plastic bags	Consumers Retailers
What is the level of environment consciousness amongst them?	To find out whether they understand how plastic bags can be harmful to the environment. To identify strategies to discontinue plastic bag usage.	Environmental consciousness. Effect of plastic bag usage	Respondent attitudes and perceptions towards the environment Perception about the impact of plastic bags on the environment	Consumer Retailer
What measures can be taken to encourage people not to use plastic bags?		Corporation laws (if any) Attitudinal change strategies	Indicative measures for encouraging the general public to discontinue use of plastic bags	Policy maker Consumer Retailer

TABLE 8.3
Mode of administration and design implications

	Schedule	Telephone	Mail/Fax	E-mail	Web-Based
Administrative control	high	medium	Low	low	low
Sensitive issues	high	medium	Low	low	low
New concept	high	medium	Low	low	low
Large sample	low	low	High	high	high
Cost/time taken	high	medium	Medium	low	low
Question structure	unstructured	either	structured	structured	structured
Sampling control	high	high	Medium	low	low
Response rate	high	high	Low	medium	low
Interviewer bias	high	high	low	low	low

has been taken about the method, one also needs to design different ways of asking the required information. Table 8.3 gives a template the researcher can use to take his administration decision and the kind of questions he must ask. As can be seen, a larger population can be covered by mail or fax. In case the population to be studied is computer literate, it is possible to use e-mail or web-designed surveys.

For a smaller population and more complex or sensitive issues, personal schedule is advisable. In computer-assisted dissemination (CAPI and CATI), complex skip and branching options are possible and randomization of questions to eliminate the order bias can be carried out with considerable ease. When the researcher wants to have a higher control over the way the questions are answered, i.e., the sequence and response time for answering, he should be using the schedule. By sampling control we mean who answers the questions. When one is interested in the decision maker's thought process and purchase process, one would not like to go to those users who might not always be the buyers, for example the housewife buying toothpaste for a toothpaste evaluation study is the respondent and not her son who might be using the toothpaste but who is, definitely, not the buyer. Sampling control, as we can see, is highest in schedule and lowest in a web-based survey.

As the researcher proceeds from one administration mode to another, the question structure and instructions change. The major reason for this is the presence or absence of the investigator. This has been illustrated in the example below.

Administration Mode and Question Structure

Schedule

Now I am going to give you a set of cards. Each card will have the name of one television serial (*Handover the cards to the respondent in a random order)*. I want you to examine them carefully (*give her some time to read all the names)*. I would request you to hand over the card which has the name of the serial you like to watch the most. (*Record the serial and keep this card with you*). Now, of the remaining nine serials, name your next most favourite serial (*continue the same process till the person is left with the last card)*

	TV serial	Rank Order
1.	1	________
2.	2	________
3.	3	________
4.	4	________
5.	5	________
6.	6	________
7.	7	________
8.	8	________
9.	9	________
10.	10	________

Telephone Questionnaire

Please listen very carefully; I am going to slowly read the names of ten popular TV serials. I want to know how much you prefer watching them. You need to use a 1 to 10 scale, where 1 means—I do not like watching it—and 10 means—I really like watching it. For those in between you may choose any number between 1 to 10. However, please remember that the higher the number, the more you like watching it. Now, I am going to name the serials one by one. In case the name is not clear, I will repeat the list again. So, the serial's name is ________. Please use a number between 1 to 10 as I had told you. Ok thank you, the next name is ________. And so on till all the 10 names have been read out and evaluated.

	Serial										
1.	*Balika Badhu*	1	2	3	4	5	6	7	8	9	10
2.	*Sathiya*	1	2	3	4	5	6	7	8	9	10

	Serial										
3.	*Sasural Genda Phool*	1	2	3	4	5	6	7	8	9	10
4.	*Bidai*	1	2	3	4	5	6	7	8	9	10
5.	*Pathshala*	1	2	3	4	5	6	7	8	9	10
6.	*Bandini*	1	2	3	4	5	6	7	8	9	10
7.	*Lapataganj*	1	2	3	4	5	6	7	8	9	10
8.	*Sajan Ghar Jaana Hai*	1	2	3	4	5	6	7	8	9	10
9.	*Tere Liye*	1	2	3	4	5	6	7	8	9	10
10.	*Uttaran*	1	2	3	4	5	6	7	8	9	10

Mail Questionnaire

In the next question you will find the names of ten popular Hindi serials that are being aired on television these days. You are requested to rank them in order of your preference. Start by identifying the serial which is your most favourite, to this you may give a rank of 1. Then from the rest of the nine, pick the second most preferred serial and give it a rank of 2. Please carry out this process till you have ranked all 10. The one you prefer the least should have a score of 10. You are also requested not to give two serials the same rank. The basis on which you decide to rank the serials is entirely dependent upon you. Once again, you are asked to rank all the 10 serials.

	Serial	Rank Order
1.	*Balika Badhu*	______
2.	*Sathiya*	______
3.	*Sasural Genda Phool*	______
4.	*Bidai*	______
5.	*Pathshala*	______
6.	*Bandini*	______
7.	*Lapataganj*	______
8.	*Sajan Ghar Jaana Hai*	______
9.	*Tere Liye*	______
10.	*Uttaran*	______

The pattern of instructions and the response structure for fax, e-mail and web surveys are similar. Thus, they have not been shown here separately.

Given the fact that the **time of a respondent** is precious, unless a question is adding to the data required for reaching an answer to the formulated problem it should not be included.

Content of the questionnaire: The next step, once the information needs and mode of administration has been decided, is to determine the matter to be included as questions in the measure. The decision to include or not include certain questions depends upon a certain criteria. Thus, the researcher needs to subject the questions designed by him to an objective quality check in order to ascertain what research objective/information need the question would be covering before using any of the framed questions.

How essential is it to ask the question? In the course of the research study, the researcher might formulate a number of questions which he thinks address the information needs of the study. Sometimes the researcher might find a particular question very intriguing or interesting and thus might decide to include it in the questionnaire. However, one needs to remember that the time of the respondent is precious and it should not be wasted. Unless a question is adding to the data required for reaching an answer to the formulated problem, it should not be included. For example, if one is studying the usage of plastic bags, then demographic questions on age group, occupation, education and gender might make sense but questions related to marital status, family size and the state to which the respondent belongs are not required as they have no direct relation with the usage or attitude towards plastic bags.

Sometimes, to gauge the information needs, the researcher might have to ask multiple questions, even though they might not seem to be related directly to the research objective. For example, instead of asking shopkeepers, who own a shop in a shopping centre, whether they would in the near future open an outlet in a mall, a set of questions were asked to understand the retailers' perception of shopping trends.

Please indicate your level of agreement with the following statements:

SA – Strongly Agree; A – Agree; N – Neutral; D – Disagree; SD – Strongly Disagree

	Compared to the Past (5-10 years)	SA	A	N	D	SD
1	The individual customer today shops more					
2	The consumer is well-informed about market offerings					
3	The consumer knows what he/she wants to buy before he enters the store					
4	The consumer today has more money to spend					
5	There are more shopping options available to the consumer today					

There are also times, especially in self-administered questionnaires, when one may ask some neutral questions at the beginning of the questionnaire to establish an involvement and rapport. For example, for a biofertilizer usage study, the following question was asked:

Farming for you is a:
- noble profession
- ancestral profession
- profession like any other
- profession that is not lucrative
- any other

Camouflaged or disguised questions are asked sometimes to keep the purpose or sponsorship of the project hidden. Here generally, the researcher might ask questions related to a set of brand names in the product category rather than asking questions only with reference to the company/brand one is interested in. For example, in a survey done on power drinks carried out by Gatorade, one might also have questions related to Powerade and Red Bull. Similar questions might be kept at different points in the study to assess the consistency of the respondent in answering. Questions like these add to the reliability of the scale.

Do we need to ask several questions instead of a single one? After deciding on the significance of the question, one needs to ascertain whether a single question will serve the purpose or should more than one question be asked. For example, in the TV serial study, assume that the second question after the ranking/rating question is:

'Why do you like the serial ______ (the one you ranked No. 1/prefer watching the most)?'

(Incorrect)

Here, one lady might say, 'Everyone in my family watches it.' While another might say, 'It deals with the problems of living in a typical Indian joint family system' and yet another might say, 'My friend recommended it to me.' The first relates to joint decision-making by the family, the second relates to an attribute of the programme, while the third tells us what the information source was for her.

Thus, we need to ask her:
'What do you like about______?'
'Who all in your household watch the serial?'
and
'How did you first hear about the serial?'
(Correct)

The **questionnaire** should be so designed as to stimulate the respondent to give comprehensive information regarding a particular topic under study.

Motivating the respondent to answer: The one thing the researcher must remember is that answering the questionnaire requires some effort on the part of the respondent. Thus, the questionnaire should be designed in a manner that it involves the respondent and motivates him/her to give comprehensive information. There might be two kinds of hindrances to active participation by the subject:

- The respondent might not be able to respond in the right manner.
- The respondent might be unwilling to part with the information.

We will discuss these situations and also understand how these need to be overcome, in order to be able to collect the data.

Assisting the respondent to provide the required information: There are three kinds of situations which might lead to inability to answer in a correct manner. Each of these is examined separately here:

Does the person have the required information? It has been found that once the respondents get into the rhythm of answering the questions, they answer questions even when they do not understand or have information about the construct being investigated. This is not because they are inherently dishonest; it is simply the result of confusion. For example, a young man whose personal care products are bought by his mother will not have any knowledge about the purchase process and decision. Yet, if asked, he will answer them based on his general understanding of the process.

Qualifying or **filter questions** measure the experience or knowledge of a respondent about the concerned research topic and thus, save time.

Another situation might be when the person has had no experience with the issue being investigated. Look at the following question:

How do you evaluate the negotiation skills module, viz., the communication and presentation skill module?
(Incorrect)

In this case it might be that the person has not undergone one or even both the modules, so how can he compare? Thus, in situations where not all the respondents are likely to be informed about the research topic, certain qualifying or *filter questions* that measure the experience or knowledge must be asked before the questions about the topics themselves. Filter questions enable the researcher to filter out the respondents who are not adequately informed. Thus, the correct question would have been:

Have you been through the following training modules?

- Negotiation skills module Yes/no
- Communication and presentation skills Yes/no

In case the answer to both is yes, please answer the following question, or else move to the next question.

How do you evaluate the negotiation skills module, viz., the communication and presentation skill module?
(Correct)

Does the person remember? Many a times, the question addressed might be putting too much stress on an individual's memory. All of us know that human memory might be short and yet sometimes while designing the questionnaire, one overlooks this. For example, consider the following questions:

How much did you spend on eating out last month? (Incorrect)
How many questions do you ask in a recruitment interview? (Incorrect)

As one can see, such questions far surpass any normal individual's memory bank. There have been a number of studies to demonstrate that people are generally not very good at remembering quantities. Usually, people forget significant events like birthdays or anniversaries. However, generally this is more related to pleasant days rather than bad days associated with accident or theft or even death anniversaries. Secondly, there is an element of the most recent events to remember. Thus, the employee will be able to better evaluate a training module that he attended last than those he attended in the whole year. A person remembers his recent big purchase details more than the last four major purchases.

Aided recall refers to the triggers which give a cue to the respondent so as to stimulate the memory and extract some forgotten material.

Forgotten material can be drawn out by giving cues to stimulate the memory. These triggers are termed as *aided recall.* For example, unaided recall of TV serials could be measured by questions such as follows, 'Which TV serials did you watch last week?' The aided recall approach on the other hand would assist in recall by giving a list of serials aired in the last week and then ask. 'Which of these serials did you watch last week?'

Thus, the questions listed above could have been rephrased as follows:

When you go out to eat, on an average your bill amount is:

Less than ₹100
₹101–250
₹251–500
More than ₹500

How often do you eat out in a week?

1–2 times.
3–4 times
5–6 times
Everyday
(correct)

From the following, tick the areas on which you ask questions in a typical recruitment interview:

Educational background
Subject knowledge
Previous experience
General awareness
Individual information

Once the respondent ticks the relevant areas, then a number of questions from the indicated areas are asked. It is also possible to use the constant sum scale (refer to Chapter 7) to indicate the percentage of questions asked from the area, so that the total adds up to 100 per cent.

Can the respondent articulate? The articulation does not refer to only enlisting the response. It also refers to not knowing what words to be used to articulate certain types of answers. For example, if you ask a respondent to:

- Describe a river rafting experience.
- The ambience of the new Levi's outlet. (Incorrect)

Most respondents would not know what phrases to use to give an answer. On the other hand, if the researcher uses a Semantic differential scale (Chapter 7), the respondent can be provided adjectives to choose from. It must be remembered that if the person does not know what words to use or finds the task of description too tedious, the person will not fill in the answers. Thus, in the above case, one can provide answer categories to the person as follows:

Describe the river rafting experience. (Correct)

1	Unexciting		Exciting
2	Bad		Good
3	Boring		Interesting
4	Cheap		Expensive
5	Safe		Dangerous

Assisting the respondent to answer: This is the second reason for not answering a question. It might happen that the person understands the question and also knows the answer, yet he is not willing to part with the information. We will discuss the situations which might result in this scenario.

At times, the respondent is not ready to part with the information as the perspective is not clear. Hence, the questions asked should possess **face validity.**

The perspective is not clear: The questions that are being asked must possess face validity (Chapter 7), i.e., they must not appear to be out of context with the other questions in the survey. Thus, a questionnaire which is measuring a person's quality of working life and poses questions as below will not be appreciated as the questions will seem to be suspicious and might be perceived as having a hidden agenda.

How many credit cards do you own?
When did you last go on a holiday?
How many movies do you watch in a fortnight?

People are not willing to answer questions they think do not make sense. Respondents are also hesitant about sharing personal demographic data such as age, income, and profession. Thus, the purpose of asking such questions has to be made explicit in the instructional note.

Thus, in the previous example, the researcher can justify that a spillover of a healthy quality of working life is also reflected in a person's way of living. Thus, we would like to know how you live.

In the second case of demographic data details, stating that 'We would like to determine which TV serials are preferred by people of different ages, incomes and professions, we need information on ...', will put the respondent at ease when sharing the data.

CONCEPT CHECK

1. How would you convert research objectives into information areas?
2. What should be the nature of the content of questionnaire?
3. How can one assist the respondent in order to extract maximum information?

Sensitive information: There might be instances when the question being asked might be embarrassing to the respondents and thus they would not be comfortable in disclosing the data required. Sometimes, this might diminish the respondent's willingness to respond to the other questions as well. These topics could be related to income, family life, political and religious beliefs, and socially undesirable habits and desires. A number of techniques are available to reduce the respondent's hesitation.

- Make a generic statement to soothe the anxieties and state that 'these days most women consume alcoholic drinks at social gatherings, followed by a question on alcohol consumption. This technique is called *counter biasing.*
- Place the sensitive question in between some seemingly neutral questions and then ask the questions at a rapid speed.
- The best way to get answers on sensitive issues is to use *the third-person technique* and ask the question as related to other people.

For example, questions such as the following will not get any answers.

Have you ever used fake receipts to claim your medical allowance? (Incorrect)

Have you ever spit tobacco on the road (to tobacco consumers)? (Incorrect)

However, in case the socially undesirable habit is in the context of a third person, the chances of getting indicative correct responses are possible. Thus the questions should be rephrased as follows:

Do you associate with people who use fake receipts to claim their medical allowance? (Correct)

Do you think tobacco consumers spit tobacco on the road? (Correct)

- For certain demographic questions like income and age, instead of using the ratio scale one must use class intervals:

'What is your household's annual income?' (Incorrect)

'What is your household's annual income?'
Under ₹25,000,
₹25,001–50,000,
₹50,001–75,000,
Over ₹75,000. (Correct)

- For sensitive issues as stated earlier, it is much better to use unstructured questions and probe only after the respondent is comfortable with the investigator.

DETERMINING THE TYPE OF QUESTIONS

LEARNING OBJECTIVE 3
Determine the content of the questions designed in order to encourage the person to respond meaningfully to the questions asked.

After deciding on the necessity of questions and the mode of administration, the researcher comes to taking a decision on the response categories. The essential difference is whether the response options would be given to the respondent or will they be left open to be completed in the respondent's own words. In this section we will begin by first discussing the open and then the closed-ended questions. The closed-ended, as can be seen in Figure 8.2, can be further divided into different types. These will be discussed in the later section.

Open-ended Questions

These are termed as open-ended, but the openness refers to the option of responding in one's own words. They are also referred to as unstructured questions

FIGURE 8.2
Types of question–response options

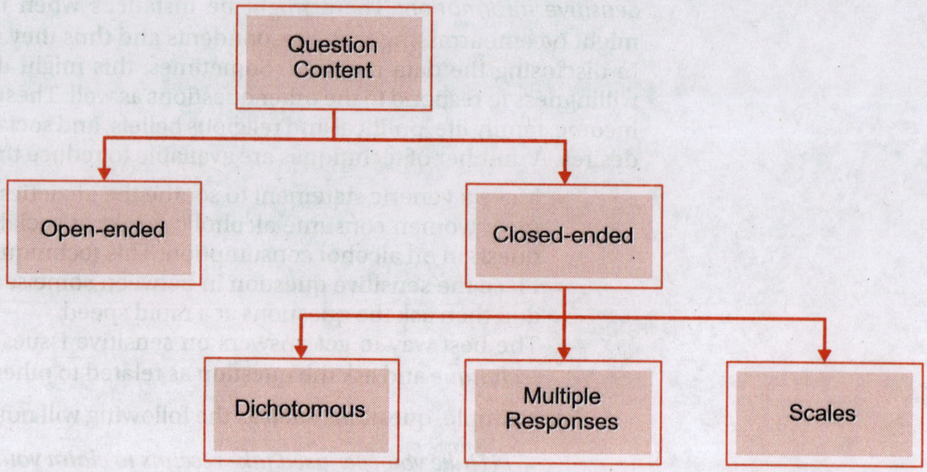

or free-response or free-answer questions. The researcher suggests no alternatives. Thus the words, logic and structure that a person would give while filling the answers is totally left to his discretion. Some illustrations of this type are listed below:

Open-ended questions are unstructured. Thus, the words, logic and structure are provided by a respondent and not the researcher.

- What is your age?
- How would you evaluate the work done by the present government?
- How much orange juice does this bottle contain?
- What is your reaction to this new custard powder?
- Why do you smoke Gold Flakes cigarettes?
- Which is your favourite TV serial?
- What training programme did you last attend?
- With whom in your work group do you interact with after office hours?
- How do you decide on the instrument in which you are going to invest?
- I like Nescafe because ______________
- My career goal is to ______________
- I think hybrid cars are ______________

The last three, as can be seen, are in a statement form (sentence completion, as discussed in Chapter 6) while the first few are in question form. For the second and sixth question, the person would need to spend more time and the answer might have multiple components, while the others would be one word or one liner (last three).

Open-ended questions can typically be used for three reasons. First, they can be used in the beginning to start the questioning process. For example, a questionnaire on investment behaviour could begin with:

How do you think people manage their savings?

This puts the respondent into the frame of answering investment-related questions. Yet, as can be seen, the question is in third person and, thus, is non-threatening.

Open-ended questions can also be used as probing or clarifying questions to understand the reason behind certain responses.

For example:
Why do you feel that way?

Thirdly, they can be used in the end as suggestions or final opinions.

For example:

'Any suggestion you would like to give in terms of improving the quality of the working life in your organization __________.'

These questions have the inherent advantage of improving the validity of the construct being studied. Also, they are not restrictive and the respondents are free to express any views. The observations and justifications can provide the researcher with valuable interpretative material. However, the interpretation and evaluation of the answers are open to the investigator's bias. This is especially the case with schedules, where the researcher might not record the exact words but what he interprets as what the person wants to convey.

Coding or categorizing the written responses for an open-ended question is expensive both in terms of time as well as finances. The coding problems will be discussed in detail in Chapter 10.

Open-ended questions are also dependent upon the respondent's skill to articulate well. Secondly, they are more suited to face-to-face interactions rather than the self-administered type, where there are chances of misinterpretation or a complete non-response as well.

However, despite the problems listed above, they are still recognized as rich and versatile sources of data collection. Proponents of the format have created a number of ways that subjectivity on the part of the researcher and effort on the part of the respondent can be greatly reduced. This will be discussed in detail in the precoding section in Chapter 10.

Closed-ended Questions

In these questions, both the question and response formats are structured and defined. The respondent only needs to select the option(s) that he feels are expressive of his opinion. There are three kinds of formats as we observed earlier—dichotomous questions, multiple-choice questions and those that have a scaled response.

Dichotomous questions have restrictive alternatives and provide the respondents only with two options.

1. **Dichotomous questions:** These are restrictive alternatives and provide the respondents only with two answers. These could be 'yes' or 'no,' like or dislike, similar or different, married or unmarried, etc.

Are you diabetic?	Yes/No
Have you read the new book by Dan Brown?	Yes/no
What kind of petrol do you use in your car?	Normal/Premium
What kind of cola do you drink?	Normal/diet
Your working hours in the organization are	fixed/flexible

The first two questions are monotonic in nature in the sense they study only the presence and absence; while the others present two distinctly different alternatives. The problem with these situations is that these are forced choices and one needs to select one of them. Sometimes they might be complemented by a neutral alternative, such as 'no opinion,' 'do not know,' 'both' or 'none.' Thus, the dilemma is whether to include a neutral response alternative. If there are only two choices, he is forced to take a stand even when he has no opinion on either or he is uncertain about the two options. However, the problem with the neutral category is that most respondents want to avoid taking a stand and use it as an escape, thus the researcher does not get any meaningful number for or against the issue under study. It is advisable not to force the issue in case a substantial number of people might have an in-between stand. For example, for the cola question, there might be a large number of people who drink both, thus the option of 'both' should be provided. If the ratio of neutral respondents is expected to be small, then it should be avoided as in the following case:

Who do you think will win the next Wimbledon men's single championship?
Roger Federer________
Rafael Nadal________
Neither

Dichotomous questions are the easiest type of questions to code and analyse. They are constructed on the nominal level of measurement and are categorical or binary in nature. A disadvantage of the method is that the wording of the question might result in different answers. For example, the two questions asked at different places in a questionnaire were as follows:

Do you think management schools should permit laptops in class? Yes/no
Do you think management schools should forbid laptops in class? Yes/No (Incorrect)

For the first question, there were 56 per cent respondents who said 'should not permit'. Essentially speaking, both the questions are identical and should give the same results. But it was found that 39 per cent of the same respondents said yes. To deal with this problem, it is suggested that the question should have both the options indicated in the question, for example:

Management schools should permit or forbid the use of laptops in class?
Permit/forbid

Another disadvantage of the method is that the simple binary response might be reflective of the current stand, but need not reflect what the person intends to do at a later date or when given some other factors. For example, two people might say that they are not going to buy the Nano in the next six months. But one might change his stand in case he has the resources to do so, let's say when he gets a bonus, while the other might be waiting for the car to get good performance ratings before taking a decision. Thus, a simple yes/no would not capture the reply; rather a question with multiple-choice responses would result in better answers.

2. Multiple-choice questions: Unlike dichotomous questions, the person is given a number of response alternatives here. He might be asked to choose the one that is most applicable. For example, this question was given to a retailer who is currently not selling organic food products:

Will you consider selling organic food products in your store?

☐ Definitely not in the next one year ☐ Probably not in the next one year
☐ Undecided ☐ Probably in the next one year
☐ Definitely in the next one year

Sometimes, multiple-choice questions do not have verbal but rather numerical options for the respondent to choose from, for example:

How much do you spend on grocery products (average in one month)?
Less than ₹2,500/-
Between ₹2,500–5,000/-
More than ₹5,000/-

Most multiple-choice questions are based upon ordinal or interval level of measurement. However, in instances like the one discussed below, the answers are on a nominal level. This is because each alternative selected is evaluated as a categorical variable having a yes or no answer.

In certain instances, when multiple options are given to a respondent, he can select all those that apply in that case. This is called **checklist**.

There could also be instances when multiple options are given to the respondent and he can select all those that apply in the case. These kinds of multiple-choice questions are called checklists. These are what have been earlier in the chapter termed as cues, as sometimes it is difficult to verbalize all the possible answers/reasons for the response given. For example, in the organic food study, the retailer who does not stock organic products was given multiple reasons as follows:

You do not currently sell organic food products because (Could be ≥ 1)

- ☐ You do not know about organic food products.
- ☐ You are not interested.
- ☐ You are interested but you do not know how to procure them.
- ☐ It is not profitable.
- ☐ The customer demand is too low.
- ☐ Organic products do not have attractive packaging.
- ☐ The product is too expensive for the typical customer who frequents your store.
- ☐ They have a poor shelf life.
- ☐ Organic food products are not supplied regularly.
- ☐ Any other ____________________

Most of the issues discussed with reference to itemized rating scales in Chapter 7 are applicable here as well. There are some additional concerns, with reference to multiple-choice questions, which deserve a special mention here.

The response options given to the respondents should be exhaustive. Secondly, the answers should be mutually exclusive and should be constructed in a manner that there is no scope for any overlap between the categories. The general practice in a good research study is to draw out these alternatives through the exploratory study done preceding the questionnaire. Here, depth interviews or focus group discussions might provide a set of all the possible choices. However, as a practice, the researcher must still have an open-ended 'any other' to cover contingencies (as can be seen from the example above).

As we have seen in the above two examples, the response(s) to be made differs in the two situations. In one there is only one choice that is to be indicated, while the other can have the person choosing multiple options. Thus, the instructions must be separately mentioned, in bold or should be highlighted so that the respondent knows what is required. This caution is especially necessary in self-administered questionnaires.

As mentioned earlier, the list of alternatives should be exhaustive and not tedious. This is because in case there are too many options, the task of evaluating them becomes difficult. In case the researcher is getting the responses through a schedule, it is advisable to use response cards with alternatives separately printed on each (as was the case with the name of the ten TV serials mentioned in an earlier example). In case this is a self-administered instrument, then the investigator could consider splitting the question into two and dividing the options to be processed for a single question.

Order of **position or location bias** can be managed in a schedule by shuffled response cards so that each respondent receives a differently numbered set.

A number of studies have been done on the impact of the position of alternatives on the selection process. This is termed as the *order of position or location bias*, i.e., a person's predisposition to select an option simply because it is placed in a particular place or order. The tendency is that when there are statements of intent or opinion, people usually pick up the first option (*primacy effect*) and sometimes the last (*recency effect*) as the one that applies. This can be managed in the schedule by shuffling and presenting the response cards so that for some respondents it comes first, for some in the end and for others, somewhere in between. This is not possible in mailed questionnaires unless multiple sets with shuffled response options are printed. This can be, however, managed in a web survey.

This order bias is somewhat different in case of numbers (quantities or prices) where there is a bias toward the central position on the list. This can also be managed in the same way as the statement options.

Multiple-choice questions can effectively cancel the researcher's bias that was inherent in the open-ended questions. Secondly, since they have pre-designed response options that require the person to pick one or all that apply, the administration is much faster. Data processing for these questions is much easier, as is quantification and analysis of the information collected.

Administering them might be easier, but designing exhaustive multiple-choice questions is a challenge. As stated earlier, the researcher will have to do an exploratory study to uncover possible alternatives or conduct an extensive secondary data analysis to identify the alternatives. The other problem is that though one includes an 'any other' option, most respondents play it safe and pick up one or few from the listed options only. Thus, the answers are restricted only to the predetermined set.

3. Scales: Scales refer to the attitudinal scales that were discussed in detail in Chapter 7. Since these questions have been discussed in detail in the earlier chapter, we will only illustrate this with an example. The following is a question which has five sub-questions designed on the Likert scale. These require simple agreement and disagreement on the part of the respondent. This scale is based on the interval level of measurement.

Given below are statements related to your organization. Please indicate your agreement/disagreement with each statement:

(1-Strongly Disagree →→→→ 5-Strongly Agree)	1	2	3	4	5
1. The people in my company know their roles very clearly.					
2. I want to complete my current task by hook or by crook.					
3. Existing systems are very effective.					
4. I feel the need for the organization to change.					
5. Top management is committed to long-term vision of creating value for organization.					

In the same questionnaire, depending upon the information need, one can use multiple questions that have been designed on different scales.

The advantage with these scaled questions is that they are easy to administer, no matter what be the mode. The other advantage is that coding and tabulating these questions are not difficult. Since the questions have been formulated by assigning numerical values to response categories, the quantification of subjective variables and attitudes becomes possible.

However, devising the questions so that they cover the construct under study, requires considerable effort, like the multiple-choice questions. In case the respondent has an additional perspective, it is not possible to extract it.

Criteria for Question Designing

Step six of the questionnaire involves translating the questions identified into meaningful questions. Utmost care is needed to word the questioning, in a manner that the question is clear and easy to understand by the respondent. A confusing question or a poorly-worded question might result in either no response or a wrong response. Both of these are detrimental to the purpose of the research study.

There are certain designing criteria that a researcher should adhere to when writing the research questions. We will illustrate and discuss these individually.

Quality check involves that the question formulated must clearly specify the issue concerned.

Clearly specify the issue: By reading the question, the person should be able to clearly understand the information need. To understand quality check, we can use the same template that the trainee newspaper journalists are advised to keep in mind while creating their first copy: namely, who, what, when, where, why, and how. The first four are applicable to all questions, the 'why' and 'how' might apply to some.

Which newspaper do you read? (Incorrect)

This might seem to be a well-defined and structured question. However, let us examine it carefully. The 'who' in this case could be the person filling in the questionnaire or it could be what he reads by virtue of the newspaper purchased by his family. The 'what' in this case is the newspaper being read. But what if the person reads more than one newspaper. Should he talk about the regular newspaper he reads, or the one he reads for business news, or the one he reads on weekends or the one he prefers to read most? The 'when' is not apparent as it could be stated as the one read on weekdays, weekends or the one he used to read earlier? The 'where' seems to be at home but is not apparent, as he could be reading the newspaper in the college library as well. A better way to word the question would be:

Which newspaper or newspapers did you personally read at home during the last month? In case of more than one newspaper, please list all that you read. (Correct)

Inclusion of **technical words** which are not used in everyday communication must be avoided. The language should be understandable.

Use simple terminology: The researcher must take care to ask questions in a language that is understood by the population under study. Technical words or difficult words that are not used in everyday communication must be avoided. Most people do not understand them, thus it is advisable to stay simple. For example, instead of asking '*Do you think the distribution of Mother Dairy ice cream is adequate?*' ask: '*Do you think Mother Dairy ice cream is readily available when you want to buy it?*'

Do you think thermal wear provides immunity? (Incorrect)
Do you think that thermal wear provides you protection from the cold? (Correct)

Sometimes words that are used might have a different meaning either in the local dialect or as a phrase. For example, a simple question like, '*When did you go to town?*' (incorrect) might get you the answer of the person's last visit to town or it may be taken as 'go to town' (go crazy or mad) and would be regarded as an insult. Thus the question can be rephrased as:

When did you last visit the town? (Correct)

Avoid ambiguity in questioning: The words used in the questionnaire should mean the same thing to all those answering the questionnaire. A lot of words are subjective and relative in meaning. Consider the following question:

How often do you visit Pizza Hut?

Never
Occasionally
Sometimes
Often
Regularly (Incorrect)

These are ambiguous measures, as *occasionally* in the above question, might be three to four times in a week for one person, while for another it could be three times in a month. Three youngsters who visit Pizza Hut once a month may check three different categories: occasionally, sometimes, and often. A much better wording for this question would be the following:

In a typical month, how often do you visit Pizza Hut?

Less than once
1 or 2 times
3 or 4 times
More than 4 times (Correct)

These responses are giving definite numbers and thus there is no chance of the person misunderstanding the words. Some questions use ambiguous words in the question itself. For example,

Do you download music regularly from LimeWire? Yes/no (Incorrect)

Here, the word 'regularly' can mean different numbers to different people. Thus, rather than a dichotomous question, it is advisable to rephrase it as follows:

How often do you down load from LimeWire?

Once a week
2–3 times in a week
4–5 times in a week
Every day (Correct)

Followed by the question:

On an average, for how many hours do you download in a single sitting?

Less than an hour
1 to 3 hours
3 ½ to 5 hours
More than 5 hours (Correct)

Leading questions provide a clue for the 'good' answer.

Avoid leading questions: Any question that provides a clue to the respondents in terms of the direction in which one wants them to answer is called a leading or biasing question. For example, '*Do you think that working mothers should buy ready-to-eat food when that might contain some chemical preservatives*?

Yes
No
Don't know (Incorrect)

The question would mostly generate a negative answer, as no working mother would like to buy something that is convenient but might be harmful. Thus, it is advisable to construct a neutral question as follows:

Do you think that working mothers should buy ready-to-eat food?

Yes
No
Don't know (Correct)

Even questions such as the following are suggestive in nature.

How long was the class session? Or how short was the class session? (Incorrect)

The individual, in this case, is reacting to short or long as the reference point. Thus, for the same class for the first question, the respondents said about 120 minutes and for the second, 90 minutes. Thus, we can use a measure in this kind of question and the question can be framed as follows:

For how many minutes did the class session run? (Correct)

A skewed response may also result if the name of the organization/brand is included in the question. Most respondents tend to be agreeable and would respond positively. For example, The question, '*Is Harvest Gold your favourite bread?*' is likely to bias the answers towards Harvest Gold. A better way to obtain the answers would be to ask, '*What is your favourite bread brand?*'

Similarly, quoting a reputed body or an expert like the Indian Medical Association certifies that...... can also bias the reply. In fact, even an ambiguous reference such as the one in the following example:

Industry experts think that flexible working hours positively affect work-life balance.' What is your opinion?
(Incorrect)

Here, there are two leads—'industry experts' and 'positively affect'. A better way of questioning the respondent would be:

What is the relation between flexi working hours and work-life balance?
No relation
Positively related
Negatively related

Loaded questions explore answers to sensitive issues.

Avoid loaded questions: Questions that address sensitive issues are termed as loaded questions and the response to these questions might not always be honest, as the person might not wish to admit the answer, even when assured about his anonymity. For example, questions such as follows will rarely get an affirmative answer:

Have you ever cheated on your spouse? (Incorrect)
Will you take dowry when you get married? (Incorrect)
Do you think your boss/supervisor is incompetent? (Incorrect)

Sensitive questions like this can be rephrased and camouflaged in a variety of ways as discussed earlier. For example, the first two questions could be constructed in the context of a third person as follows:

Do you think most people usually cheat on their spouses? (Correct)
Do you think most Indian men would take dowry when they get married? (Correct)

For the third question, it could be interspersed between a number of other questions and the questions can be read out rapidly as follows:

Do you think your friend is incompetent?
Do you think the government is incompetent?
Do you think your juniors are incompetent?
Do you think your driver is incompetent?
Do you think your boss/supervisor is incompetent? (Correct)
Do you think your neighbour is incompetent?
Do you think your mechanic is incompetent?

Avoid implicit choices and assumptions: In case the option being queried is done in isolation and the other alternatives the person might have are hidden, this is referred to as an implicit assumption. Thus, in case other choices are not specified in the response categories, the assumption made about the option being evaluated might not be correct. Consider the following two questions:

Would you prefer to work fixed hours, in a five-day week? (Incorrect)
Would you prefer to work fixed hours, in a five-day week or would you like to have a flexi-time 40 hours week? (Correct)

In the first question, the preference is being evaluated but the other alternatives against which he needs to do this are only implicit; while in the second question, it is explicit. Thus, the number of people who prefer a fixed schedule would be more realistic in the second case rather than in the first.

Thus, when there are multiple alternatives to the option being investigated, one must clearly spell them out. In case there are multiple alternatives and evaluation becomes difficult, as stated earlier, one may use response cards and ask the person to select from these.

The researcher might sometimes frame questions that require the respondent to make some implicit assumptions in order to give an answer. The answer is, thus, a consequence of the assumption made. However, different respondents might make different assumptions, thus, the moderator variable (Chapter 2) might be different for different individuals, and the assumptions that the researcher wants the respondent to keep in mind while answering the questions should be explicity stated in the question (itself). Examine the following questions:

Are you in favour of the Commonwealth Games 2010 that were held in India? (Incorrect)

Are you in favour of the Commonwealth Games 2010 that were held in India, if they resulted in increased revenue from tourism? (Correct)

In the first question, one will make certain assumptions about the impact of the Commonwealth Games and give a positive or a negative answer. This might be an increase in revenue from tourism, it could lead to an improvement in the existing infrastructure, and the surplus generated could be used for the development of the country. On the other hand, the second question is a better way to word this question as here the researcher has included only the moderator variable or the assumption that he believes is most significant.

A double-barrelled question includes two separate options separated usually by 'or' and 'an'. These should be avoided.

Avoid double-barrelled questions: As specified earlier, questions that have two separate options separated by an 'or' or an 'and' are like the following:

Do you think Nokia and Samsung have a wide variety of touch phones? Yes/no (Incorrect)

The problem is that the respondent might believe that Nokia has better phones or Samsung has better phones or both. These questions are referred to as *double-barrelled* and the researcher should always split them into two separate questions or the question should provide the two as response options. For example, a wide variety of touch phones is available for:

Nokia
Samsung
Both (Correct)

In the context of training needs analysis, consider the question:

Did the training you went through make you feel more motivated and effective in your job? (Incorrect)

Here, when the answer is 'no,' then we do not know whether he is not motivated or whether he is not effective at his job or both. Thus, to obtain the required information, we must split it into separate questions.

Did the training you went through make you feel motivated at your job? and

(Yes/No)

Did the training you went through make you more effective at your job?

(Yes/No)

(Correct)

CONCEPT CHECK	
	1. What are the various types of questions that can be included in a questionnaire?
	2. Discuss the basic criteria for question designing.

LEARNING OBJECTIVE 4
Determine the flow and sequence of the questioning method.

Questionnaire Structure

Once the researcher has formulated the questions and response options that he intends to use in the questionnaire, the next critical step is to put the questions together in a sequence that is reader/respondent-friendly and generates the required data in a short and effective manner. Thus, most questionnaires follow a standardized sequence of questions.

Instructions explain the purpose of questionnaire administration and introduce the respondent to the researcher's objective.

Instructions: The questionnaires always, even the schedules, begin with standardized instructions. These begin by greeting the respondent and then introducing the researcher or investigator and the affiliating body. The note then goes on to explain the purpose of questionnaire administration. Sometimes, as in disguised questionnaire format, the sponsoring organization/brand might not be revealed, rather the investigator would talk about the generic brand. For example, in the study on organic food products, the following instructions were given at the beginning of the questionnaire:

'Hi. We ________ are carrying out a market research on the purchase behaviour of grocery products/organic food. We are conducting a survey of consumers, retailers and experts in the NCR for the same.

As you are involved in the purchase and/or consumption of food products, we seek your cooperation for providing the following relevant information for our research. We value your contribution to our research and to the organic community who has been facing the problem in acquiring organic food products. We do appreciate your support and encouragement provided through this information. Thank you very much.'

Even though the study was conducted on behalf of a particular marketer of organic food products, in the instructions the name was not revealed, as this then would be termed as 'leading instructions' that might bias the consumer/respondent in favour of the brand.

In case it is a study done on the employees of an organization for any human resource issue, the researcher must give the correct introduction about himself and in the instructions should reassure by saying 'Please be assured that the study is for an academic purpose and the responses and results would not be shared with any other organization.'

Simple questions which do not require a lot of thinking or response time should be asked first as they build the tempo for answering the more difficult/sensitive questions later.

Opening questions: Then come the opening questions, these have to be non-threatening and yet lead the respondent to get into the right frame for answering the rest of the questions. For example, a questionnaire on understanding the consumer's buying behaviour in malls, can ask an opening question that is generic in nature, such as:

What is your opinion about shopping at a mall?

Most people like to share their perspective and this gets them into the responding mode and in the direction that the researcher wants. Thus, they serve the purpose of rapport formation even in a self-administered questionnaire.

Sometimes, the questionnaire might need to be filled in by people fulfilling a certain criteria. Thus, the first question is a qualifying question and would determine whether the person is eligible to answer the questions and in case the answer is yes, he continues with the responding; else the interview terminates.

Study questions: After the opening questions, the bulk of the instrument needs to be devoted to the main questions that are related to the specific information needs of the study. Here also, as a general rule, one goes from the general questions to the specific ones, following a sequential mode.

Another aspect of the questionnaire is that the simpler questions, which do not require a lot of thinking or response time should be asked first as they build the tempo for answering the more difficult/sensitive questions later on . This method of going in a sequential manner from the general to the specific is called the funnel approach. Like a funnel, the initial set of questions are broad and as one goes along the questions, the answers required become more specific as well as restrictive. There are instances when one might reverse the funnel and start the questioning with the specific questions and leave the general and open-ended questions for the end. Given below is a funnel-shaped questionnaire to assess pizza purchase behaviour.

Illustration: Screening Question

Please indicate whether you have purchased pizzas from (Could be ≥ 1)

- ☐ Pizza Corner ☐ Nirula's
- ☐ Pizza Hut ☐ Domino's
- ☐ Local bakery ☐ any other ________

(In case respondent has ticked BOTH Domino's and Pizza Hut, continue, else TERMINATE

1. How often do you order pizzas from outside? (Average)
   - ☐ Once in 2–3 months ☐ Once a month
   - ☐ Once a fortnight ☐ Once a week
   - ☐ 2–3 times in a week ☐ Every day
2. How is it purchased? (Could be ≥ 1)
   - ☐ Personal visit/take away ☐ Telephone (home delivery)
3. What are the preferred days for ordering the pizza?
   - ☐ Week days ☐ Weekends
   - ☐ Special occasions (Birthday party, guests, festivals)
4. What is generally the time for placing the order?
   - ☐ Lunch time ☐ Dinner time
   - ☐ Evening ☐ Any time
5. How much is your bill amount? (average)
   - ☐ < ₹200 ☐ ₹200–350
   - ☐ ₹351–500 ☐ > ₹500

Classification information: This is the information that is related to the basic socio-economic and demographic traits of the person. These might include name (kept optional in some cases), address, e-mail address and telephone number. Sometimes the socio-economic classification grid is presented to the respondent and he indicates by encircling the right choice. The SEC grid generally used is presented in Appendix 8.1.

There might be instances when the demographic questions might be asked right in the beginning as they could be the qualifying or screening questions. For

FIGURE 8.3
Sequence of branching questions for determining usage of travel portals

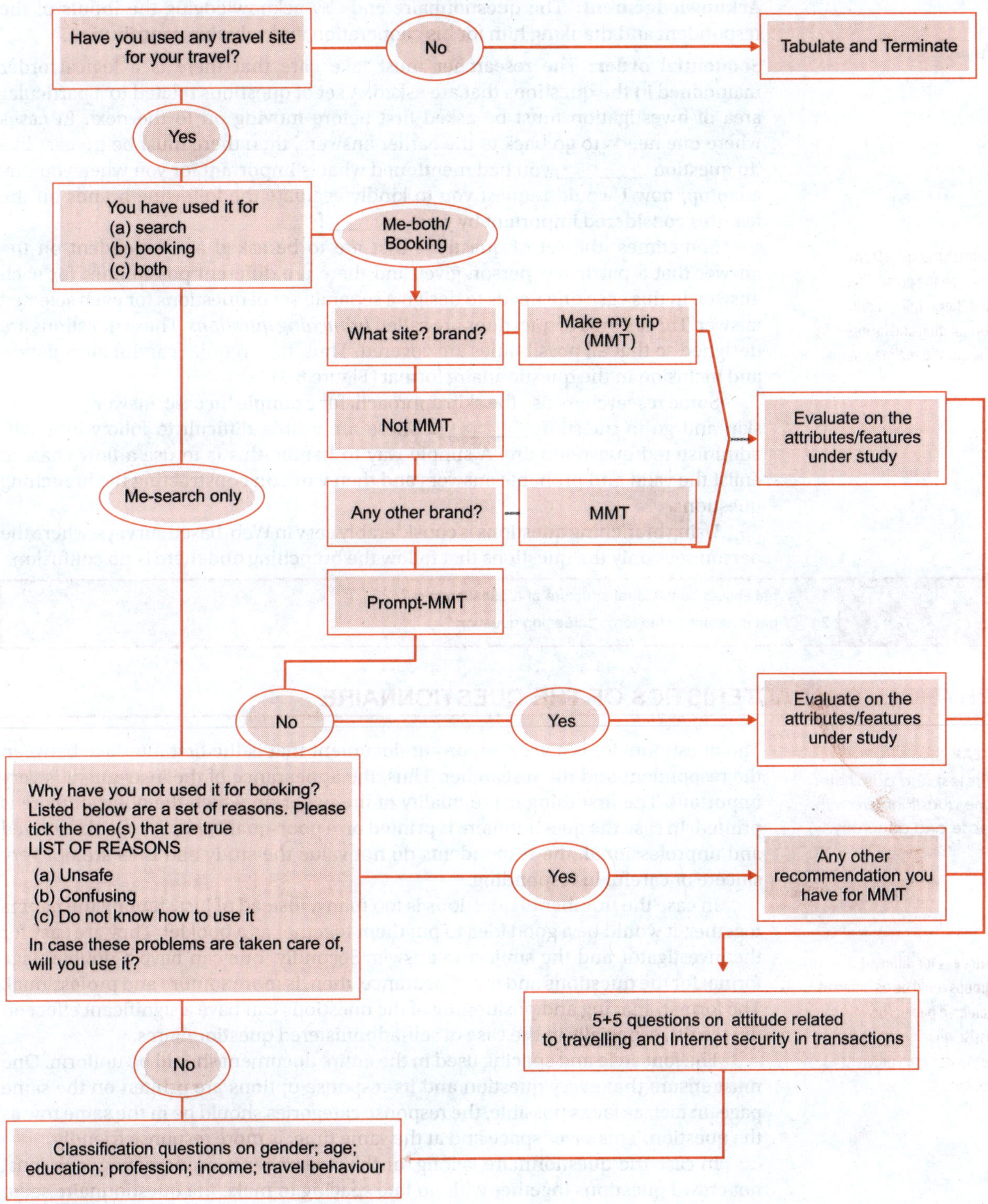

example, if the study is to be done on young working mothers living in Delhi, then all these details might need to be taken right in the beginning.

Acknowledgement: The questionnaire ends by acknowledging the inputs of the respondent and thanking him for his cooperation and valuable contribution.

Sequential order: The researcher must take care that there is a logical order maintained in the questions that are asked. A set of questions related to a particular area of investigation must be asked first before moving on to the next. In cases where one needs to go back to the earlier answers, then there must be triggers like 'In question ________ you had mentioned what is important for you when you buy a laptop; now I would request you to kindly evaluate the following brands on the features considered important by you ________.'

Branching questions cover all the possibilities and they require careful formulation and inclusion in the questionnaire format.

Sometimes, the set of questions that are to be asked are dependent on the answer that a particular person gives and there are different possibilities for each answer. In this case one needs to design a separate set of questions for each selected answer. These kinds of questions are called *branching questions*. These questions are designed so that all possibilities are covered. Thus, they require careful formulation and inclusion in the questionnaire format (Figure 8.3).

Some researchers use the skip approach, for example 'in case answer ________ skip and go to question ________.' These are a little difficult to follow in a self-administered questionnaire. A simple way to handle this is to use a flow chart to enlist the valid and probable answers and then work on constructing the branching questions.

Using branching questions is considerably easy in Web-based surveys, where the person sees only the questions that follow the branching and there is no confusion.

CONCEPT CHECK	
	1. What should be the ideal structure of a questionnaire?
	2. What is meant by the term 'screening question'?

PHYSICAL CHARACTERISTICS OF THE QUESTIONNAIRE

LEARNING OBJECTIVE 5
Pretest and administer the questionnaire with ease and accuracy.

The questionnaire is a very important document that is the first interface between the respondent and the researcher. Thus, the appearance of the instrument is very important. The first thing is the quality of the paper on which the questionnaire is printed. In case the questionnaire is printed on a poor-quality paper or looks tattered and unprofessional, the respondents do not value the study and thus are not very sincere or careful in responding.

In case the number of questions is too many, instead of just stapling the papers together, it would be a good idea to put them together as a booklet. They are easy for the investigator and the subject to answer. Secondly, one can have a double-page format for the questions and the appearance, then, is more sombre and professional. The format, spacing and positioning of the questions can have a significant effect on the results, especially in the case of self-administered questionnaires.

Surveys for different groups could be on different coloured paper. This may assist while grouping the responses from different segments.

The font style and spacing used in the entire document should be uniform. One must ensure that every question and its response options are printed on the same page. In fact, as far as possible, the response categories should be in the same row as the question. This saves space and at the same time, is more response friendly.

In case the questionnaire is long, or the researcher is economizing, one must not crowd questions together with no line spacing to make the questionnaire seem shorter. This format could result in error while recording as the person could fill the answer in the wrong row. Secondly, in case there are open-ended questions as well, the responses would be less revealing and shorter. The respondent might feel that this is going to be a really long and complex administration and may actually lose interest. Thus, though it is advisable to have short instruments that are not too taxing, but in case here is a research need for which the questions cannot be shortened, one must not clutter the appearance of the measuring instrument (questionnaire).

Although the use of colour does not really impact the quality of the response, sometimes it can be used to distinguish between the groups or for branching questions. Also, surveys for different groups could be on different coloured paper. This would be helpful when grouping the responses from different segments. For example, if Delhi is being studied as five zones, then the questionnaire used in each zone could be printed on a differently coloured paper.

As we saw in the last section, the questionnaire is segregated into different sections to address the various information needs. It is useful if the researcher divides the data needed into separate sections such as Sections A, B, C and so on.

Then the questions in each part should be numbered, especially, when one is using branching questions. The other advantage of numbering the questions is that after the conduction coding, entering the data obtained becomes much easier. Precoded questionnaires are easier to administer and record. We will be discussing coding of data in detail in Chapter 10.

In case there is any response instruction for an individual question, it must accompany the question. In case it is a schedule and there are instructions for asking the question as well as instructions for responding, the response instruction should be placed very close to the question. However, instructions about how to record the answer and any probing question that needs to be asked should be placed after the question. To distinguish the instructions from questions, one should use a different font style. For example, overall how satisfied (are/were) you with your [Domino's] experience? Would you say you are (READ LIST)?

Very satisfied...5
Satisfied...4
Neither satisfied nor dissatisfied...3
Dissatisfied...2
Or, Very dissatisfied...1
IN CASE OF 2 or 1
(PROBE) What was the reason(s) for your experience? Kindly explain ________

Pilot Testing of the Questionnaire

Pilot testing involves the testing and administration of the designed instrument on a small group of people from the population under study.

Pilot testing refers to testing and administering the designed instrument on a small group of people from the population under study. This is to essentially cover any errors that might have still remained even after the earlier eight steps. Every aspect of the questionnaire has to be tested and one must record all the experiences of the conduction, including the time taken to administer it. If the respondent had a problem understanding a question or response category, the investigator should verbatim record the instruction he/she gave to clarify the point as this then would need to be incorporated in the final version of the questionnaire. In case a question got no answers, then it might be essential to rephrase the entire question.

Even when the mode of administration is mail or Internet or self-administered tests, the pilot tests should always be done in a face-to-face interaction. Here, the researcher is able to observe and record responses, both verbal and non-verbal. Sometimes, the researcher might also get the questionnaire vetted by academic or industry experts for their inputs.

Once the essential changes have been made, the researcher might carry out one short trial and then go ahead with the actual administration. As far as possible, the pilot should be a small scale replica of the actual survey that would be subsequently conducted.

It is advisable to use multiple investigators for the pilot study. The group of investigators should be a mix of experienced and seasoned field investigators and inexperienced investigators as well. The inexperienced ones would be able to reveal the problems encountered in administering the measure, while the experienced field workers would be able to report respondent difficulties in answering the questions.

The respondent's experience of the pilot test can be recorded in two ways. One is protocol analysis where he is asked to speak out the reasoning in responding to the questions. This is recorded, as it helps to understand the underlying factors or mental processing involved in giving answers. The other method is called debriefing, where after the questionnaire has been completed, the person is asked to summarize his experience in terms of any problems experienced in answering or whether there was any confusion or fatigue while answering the questionnaire.

The researcher must then edit the questionnaire as required and carry out any further pilot tests. Once this is over, he enters the pilot data to explore and see whether the information that is being collected through the questionnaire would adequately furnish the information needs for which the instrument was designed.

Administering the Questionnaire

A questionnaire is a highly adaptable mechanism. It can be designed for every domain, branch and field of study.

Once all the nine steps have been completed, the final instrument is ready for conduction and the questionnaire needs to be administered according to the sampling plan. This will be discussed in detail in the next chapter on sampling.

Advantages and disadvantages of the questionnaire method: Thus, as we can see, designing a measuring instrument is an extremely structured, sequential and difficult task. However, once we have been able to give shape to the questionnaire, there are many advantages that it has over the other data collection methods discussed earlier.

Probably the greatest benefit of the method is its *adaptability*. There is, actually speaking, no domain and no branch for which a questionnaire cannot be designed. It can be shaped in a manner that can be easily understood by the population under study. The language, the content and the manner of questioning can be modified suitably. The instrument is particularly suitable for studies that are trying to establish the reasons for certain occurrences or behaviour. Here, methods like observations would not help as the motivations and intentions for the perspective have to be established. The second advantage is that it assures *anonymity* if it is self-administered by the respondent, as there is no pressure or embarrassment in revealing sensitive data. Secondly, a lot of questionnaires do not even require the person to fill in his/her name, which further offers a blanket of obscurity. Administering the questionnaire is much *faster* and *less expensive* as compared to other primary and a few secondary sources as well. The well-designed instrument can be *administered simultaneously* by a single researcher, thus it saves on both human and financial resources available for the study. There is considerable ease of quantitative coding and analysis of the obtained information as most response categories are closed-ended and based on the measurement levels as discussed in Chapter 7. Most individuals have a previous experience of filling in a questionnaire and thus are not uncomfortable with the elicitation of answers. The other qualitative techniques that we discussed in Chapter 6 could be influenced by the researcher's bias. However, the questionnaires minimize and almost eliminate this. There is no pressure of immediate response, thus the subject can fill in the questionnaire whenever he or she wants. However, the method does not come without any disadvantages.

The major disadvantage is that the inexpensive standardized instrument has a *limited applicability* for only those who can read and write. Even though it is possible to get the responses by reading out aloud, but then the time and cost advantage would be lost.

The **return ratio** is the number of people who return the duly filled in questionnaires.

The *return ratio*, i.e., the number of people who return the duly filled in questionnaires are sometimes not even 50 per cent of the number of forms distributed. This non-response could be because of various reasons. These reasons might range from lack of clarity of the purpose of the questionnaire to fact that the issue being questioned might be highly sensitive. However, one way to ensure that one gets the required sample for the study is to try and get a larger group of respondents, congregated at the same time to fill in the questionnaires.

Skewed sample response could be another problem. This can occur in two cases; one if the investigator distributes the same to his friends and acquaintances and second because of the self-selection of the subjects. This means that the ones who fill in the questionnaire and return it might not be the representatives of the population at large.

In case the person is not clear about a question, *clarification* with the researcher might not be possible. In case the person is filling in the questionnaire on his own, he might read the whole document first and the responses might be influenced by the way he is answering a previous or a subsequent question. Sometimes the person might genuinely be not able to respond, as either he does not remember ('how did you decide to buy your television ten years ago?') or he himself is not aware about how he took the decision ('why did you decide to buy this dress and not the other one?').

The **spontaneity of the response** gets faded if the respondent takes too much time in answering a particular question.

In most instances, the respondent is given sufficient time to respond, thus he thinks and gives his answers, in which case the *spontaneity* of response is lost and what the respondent reports is what he 'thinks is the right answer' and not 'what is the right answer.'

Questionnaire designing software/packages: With the advancement in computer programming, the task of the researcher is made much simpler and he/she is able to use different design packages available to compile the study questionnaire. Most of the sites and packages have developed area-specific methodologies, which help to customize the broadly-framed instrument to the research needs of the investigator. One can also help refine and modify a pre-designed questionnaire.

The package can also design questions based upon different levels of measurement, depending upon what is the nature of the data analysis required. The survey questionnaires can also be designed with branching questions and one has the provision of adding the company logo, different colours and graphics to make the instrument more user-friendly and attractive.

In some cases, the survey designing portals are also able to carry out the online survey and do preliminary data coding and entry as well. Some survey portals offering survey designing services are *www.sawtoothsoftware.com* and *www.surveymethods.com, www.zoomerang.com*. Most of these are user friendly and do not require special downloads and come with a free trial. The advantage of online surveys has been previously discussed; their advent has made questionnaire administration faster, cheaper and resulting in a higher response rate on the part of the respondent.

CONCEPT CHECK

1. Write a short note on the physical characteristics of a questionnaire.
2. What is pilot testing?
3. Discuss the benefits and drawbacks of the questionnaire method.

SUMMARY

- The most frequently used method of primary data collection is undoubtedly the questionnaire. It is simplest to design and execute. However, since most quantitative analysis is based upon the output from a questionnaire, it needs to be carefully designed to address the research objectives in the most accurate manner.
- On the basis of the questionnaire structure and intention, questionnaires can be categorized into unconcealed and formalized, concealed and formalized, unconcealed and non-formalized and concealed and non-formalized. Out of all these, the first one, that is the structured and undisguised is the most frequently-used type of questionnaire. Another categorization is based upon the mode of administration, that is, the investigator might ask the questions and record the answers, and is called a schedule. The other type is a self-administered questionnaire; here the responsibility of entering the responses lies with the respondents. The selection of any kind of instrument depends upon the study objectives and the study resources in terms of time and finance.
- The questionnaire design process is a step-wise and structured process which begins with converting the study objectives into information needs and specifying the population(s) from which the information needs to be tapped. Then, based upon the study constraints, the researcher could administer it through mail, email, web based, fax and telephone. Each mode has its own advantages and limitations and is selected accordingly.
- The question content has to be meticulously designed in order to extract the needed answers. The designed format should also be able to motivate the respondents to provide the necessary information. Available to the researcher are different question formats ranging from the open-ended, where the question is structured and the answer is unstructured, to the closed-ended where both the question and responses are structured. The closed-ended questions can be the simple dichotomous, multiple-choice questions or based on attitudinal scales. Once the content and the type of questions have been decided upon, the researcher has to design the questionnaire flow based on certain criteria. Once all this is done, the researcher also needs to take care of the physical features of the instrument, in terms of the font size, physical appearance, paper quality and others.
- Once the procedure is completed, then the first draft of the designed questionnaire needs to be pilot tested for any flaws and errors which are rectified and then the final instrument is appropriately administered for best results. The method has its merits and demerits, but is still one of the simplest and most cost-effective methods available to the business researcher, no matter what the area of study.

KEY TERMS

- Branching questions
- Closed-ended question
- Concealed questionnaire
- Dichotomous question
- Double-barrelled questions
- Formalized questionnaire
- Leading questions
- Loaded questions
- Location bias
- Mail questionnaire
- Multiple-choice question
- Non-formalized questionnaire
- Open-ended question
- Pilot testing
- Population spread
- Primacy effect
- Questionnaire
- Questionnaire frame work
- Rapport formation
- Recency effect
- Return ratio
- Scales
- Schedule
- Screening questions
- Self-administered questionnaire
- Socio-economic classification
- Study area
- Telephone questionnaire
- Unconcealed questionnaire

CHAPTER REVIEW QUESTIONS

Objective Type Questions

State whether the following statements are true (T) or false (F).

1. The non-formalized unconcealed questionnaire is the most frequently-used questionnaire.

2. The non-formalized concealed questionnaires require maximum skill in terms of interpretation.
3. The process of questionnaire administration is known as schedule.
4. Sampling control is highest in a web-based survey.
5. Interviewer bias is high in a telephonic survey.
6. The most cost-effective questionnaire administration method is through e-mail.
7. Response rate is highest in a mail interview.
8. Similar questions are asked at different points in the questionnaire to increase the validity of the questionnaire.
9. Qualifying questions are also termed as filter questions.
10. When the respondent gets a remuneration or aid to answer the questionnaire, it is called as aided recall.
11. 'These days you need to give a bribe to get your work done. Have you ever given a bribe?' this is an example of counter biasing.
12. 'Are you a vegetarian?—Yes/No' is an example of an open-ended question.
13. 'Do you sing and dance?' is an example of a double-barrelled question?
14. The tendency to select the last response option given to a person is called the recency effect.
15. 'It is alright to date two girls at the same time?' is an example of a leading question.
16. The questions that have multiple answers are called branching questions.
17. Testing the first draft of the questionnaire on a small sample of respondents is called pilot testing of the questionnaire.
18. 'Do you not think that all fairness creams make false claims? –Yes/No' is an example of a loaded question.
19. The number of people who return the filled-in questionnaire over the distributed questionnaire is called the return ratio.
20. The mailed questionnaire has limited applicability.

Conceptual Questions

1. What is a questionnaire? Can it be used in all situations? Why/why not? Support your answer with suitable examples.
2. What are the criteria of a sound questionnaire? How can one improve the quality of the instrument designed?
3. What are the advantages and disadvantages of the method? Illustrate with suitable examples.
4. What is the difference between a questionnaire and a schedule? What are the steps involved in the questionnaire design?
5. What principles should be followed for an ideal questionnaire design? Illustrate with suitable examples.
6. How can questionnaires assist in survey research? How will you design a questionnaire meant to measure the attitude towards banks and insurance services? Discuss by effectively using the steps in questionnaire design.
7. What are the different modes of administering a questionnaire? What are the conditions that merit the use of one over the other? Discuss by using suitable examples.
8. Write short notes on:
   (a) Software packages for designing questionnaires
   (b) Types of questions
   (c) Funnel approach to questionnaire designing
   (d) Pilot testing a questionnaire
9. Distinguish between:
   (a) Open-ended and closed-ended questions
   (b) Schedules and questionnaires
   (c) Structured vs unstructured questionnaires
   (d) Dichotomous questions vs multiple-choice questions

Application Questions

1. Prestige consulting services offer personalized investment advice to their customers. They are ocated at a prime location where corporate offices of major multinational companies are located. Thus, the organzation has a huge customer base of 2,450 platinum and 3,400 gold customers (based on the investment of over ₹10 lakh and between

₹5 to 10 lakh respectively). The management of Prestige is looking at expanding its operation in the other metros. Over the last several years, they have been offering advice in all financial instruments and other investment options. Management is concerned with how its customers rate the service and the personnel at the consultancy, and they would like to know the customers' impressions of Prestige. Design a mail questionnaire that can be sent to the bank's customers to obtain the desired information.

2. The administrators of Parents' Pride, one of the city's largest chain of pre-nursery schools, are concerned with the attitude parents have towards the various aspects of the school and whether they would recommend the school to their friends and colleagues. They have authorized the undertaking of a marketing research study to gather this information, and have directed that it cover the following areas—all the functions with which the parents and the child come into contact (such as admissions, school infrastructure, teachers, teachers' attitude, meals, fee structure, parent-teacher interaction, hygienic conditions and so on). Design a questionnaire that can be used for this study. Would your design change if this was a schedule? How?

3. Rainbow Seven is a regional brand of water whose share of the market has remained fairly stable for the past few years. The management wants to increase the brand's market share through the use of a more effective advertising theme. For the last two years, Rainbow's advertising has featured a well-known Bollywood actress who presents a 'safe and secure, always' message in all the commercials.

   The company knows that it needs to make the brand more progressive and needs to reposition it. Thus they wish to carry out a short study to know the perception about Rainbow as compared with the new brands available today. They feel that such information will help them structure the positioning exercise better. They are not sure whether a structured or an unstructured approach would be better. Thus, you are required to:

   (a) Design an unstructured and concealed questionnaire and

   (b) Design a formalized and unconcealed questionnaire.

   Justify your approach and specify what information needs you are covering in each.

   Which one, according to you, is a better approach for this exercise? Why?

4. Suppose you want to ascertain the amount of money students spend on eating outside. Assuming you want to ask just one question, how would you phrase it in each of the following forms: open-ended, dichotomous, and multiple-category? In what ways would the type of data obtained through each form differ?

CASE 8.1

MALLS FOR ALL

A research was undertaken to ascertain the attitude of the Delhi shopper towards the mall shopping experience. For the study, the researcher identified the following research objectives:

- To understand the typical Delhites' shopping behaviour
- To understand the parameters that influence his/her selection of a mall
- To understand the respondents' spending pattern in a mall
- To understand consumer awareness about specific malls in Delhi/NCR
- To understand the consumer's evaluation and satisfaction with respect to the malls that he/she has shopped in
- To adequately profile the typical Delhi mall shopper

Subsequently, a mailing questionnaire is to be designed for this purpose. The following questionnaire was designed for the study.

1. How would you evaluate the instrument as a whole? In terms of
   - questionnaire structure and sequencing
   - the clarity and content of the questions asked
2. Evaluate the questions in the light of the above stated objectives. That is, which question(s) was/were designed to match which objectives. Kindly list the same.
3. Has the questionnaire been effective in meeting the study objectives? Why/Why not?
4. How would you like to modify the questionnaire in the light of your answers to the above questions?

Instructions

1. The questionnaire deals with the analysis of consumers on their mall buying behaviour.
2. All the questions are quite general and simple but if there are any queries, then please feel free to clarify.
3. The questionnaire is solely an academic exercise, so please feel free to give us the information.

Name (Optional): Mr/Ms/Mrs

Mailing address (Area):

Age(in yrs):

- ☐ 10-20
- ☐ 21-30
- ☐ 31-40
- ☐ >40

Occupation:

- ☐ Student
- ☐ Housewife
- ☐ Professional/Service
- ☐ Self employed/Own Busines
- ☐ Others (Please specify________________)

1. Do you shop? Yes/No
   a) How often do you shop ?
      - ☐ Once a month
      - ☐ Twice a month
      - ☐ Thrice a month
      - ☐ More than thrice a month

   b) When do you prefer to shop ?
      - ☐ Weekdays morning
      - ☐ Weekend morning
      - ☐ Weekdays afternoon
      - ☐ Weekend afternoon
      - ☐ Weekdays evening
      - ☐ Weekend evening
2. Where do you shop normally?
   - ☐ A local area market (Could you please specify the market ______________)
   - ☐ A shopping mall
   - ☐ Both of the above
3. Please tell us about your awareness and number of visits to the following malls?

	Awareness (Tick)	***Number of visit (No. of times in a month)***
Ansal Plaza		
Sahara Mall		
Waves Noida		
Metropolitan Mall		
Ansals Faridabad		
DT's Gurgaon		

4. Please give your views on malls for the following aspects.

	Strongly agree	*Agree*	*Neutral*	*Disagree*	*Strongly disagree*
Malls are convenient					
Malls offer more variety					
Malls are hygienic					
Malls offer value for money					
Malls are more expensive					
The atmosphere in malls is very congenial					
Malls are fashionable					
Malls are good for outing with family/friends					

5. Please specify your spending for the following with respect to a mall.

Spending / *Reasons*	*0-10 per cent*	*10-20 per cent*	*>20 per cent*
For eating or drinking			
For entertainment (movies, etc.)			
For shopping			

6. How would you classify your spending behaviour (Can have multiple options)?
   - ☐ On the spot mood
   - ☐ Planned purchases
   - ☐ Linked spending (e.g., eating out if you have come for shopping)

7. Could you please give us your individual rating of the mall with respect to the following (Please rate from 1-5, good to bad)? (Please specify the name of the mall if you are taking a specific one______________)

V. Good __________ V. Bad

Availability of products	1	2	3	4	5
Eating joints	1	2	3	4	5
Multiplex/entertainment	1	2	3	4	5
Mall atmosphere	1	2	3	4	5
Facilities (AC, staff, parking)	1	2	3	4	5
Overall experience	1	2	3	4	5

Date: Place:

CASE 8.2

OUTLOOK OF *OUTLOOK*

The management of *Outlook* magazine finds that despite changes in the publication frequency, the magazine is still facing a stiff competition from the rival *India Today*. Thus, the management wanted to conduct a comparative survey for the two magazines and assess whether they had a distinct positioning. Who was the reader of *Outlook*? How did he/ she rate the magazine, and so on? The specific study objectives were to:

- Understand the consumer's magazine reading behavior
- Understand what the reader looks for in a general interest magazine
- Know how the reader evaluates *Outlook* and *India Today* in the light of these parameters, which he looks for in a magazine
- Evaluate the reader satisfaction with the individual magazines
- Establish the reasons for the satisfaction with each of the magazines
- Understand the positioning of the *India Today* and *Outlook* amongst the readers of the magazines
- Understand the consumer profile of the typical reader of the magazine

The team developed a questionnaire as presented below. Go through the questionnaire and answer the following questions:

1. How would you evaluate the instrument as a whole? In terms of
   - questionnaire structure and sequencing
   - the clarity and content of the questions asked
2. Evaluate the questions in the light of the above stated objectives. That is, which question(s) was/were designed to match which objectives. Kindly list the same.
3. Has the questionnaire been effective in meeting the study objectives? Why/Why not?
4. How would you like to modify the questionnaire in the light of your answers to the above questions?

Questionnaire

This is a survey on readership habits. We would be highly obliged if you could take out some time from your busy schedule and give us your valuable comments/inputs. Please note that this is an academic exercise and all the information will be kept confidential.

Name	***Monthly Household Income***
Age:	₹3,001 to ₹4,000
Sex:	₹4,001 to ₹5,000
Highest educational qualification:	₹5,001 to ₹6,000
Occupation:	₹6,001 to ₹8,000
Type of occupation:	₹8,001 to ₹10,000
Self-employed	₹10,001 to ₹12,000
Service	₹12,001 to ₹15,000
Phone:	₹15,001 to ₹20,000
Mobile:	₹20,001 to ₹30,000
	₹30,001 to ₹40,000
	₹40,001+

1. Which are the general interest magazines you are aware of?
2. Please tick the magazines that you are aware of from below:

The Week	
India Today	
Outlook	
Frontline	

3. Do you read *Outlook* or *India Today*?
   ☐ Yes (Both) ☐ Yes (*Outlook*)
   ☐ Yes (*India Today*) ☐ No
   If Yes (Both) then continue else, please terminate.
4. (a)Do you subscribe to the two magazines listed below?

	Outlook	*India Today*
Yes		
No		

   (b) If no, please mention 'source of acquiring the magazine'
   ☐ Borrow ☐ Buy from retail shops
   ☐ Library ☐ Office/Workplace
   ☐ Others (Please specify_______________)

5. I know that you read these magazines __________ Who else in your family reads these magazines?

Occupation	*Reads Outlook*	*Reads India Today*
College student		
School student		
Housewife		
Professional		
Self-employed/entrepreneur		
Grandparents		
Others (Pls specify) __________		

6. On a scale of 1 to 5, please rate each of the magazines on the following attributes:
   1: Completely disagree
   2: Somewhat disagree
   3: Neither agree nor disagree
   4: Somewhat agree
   5: Completely agree

Attribute	*Outlook*	*India Today*
This magazine gives me news first		
This magazine is very bold		
This magazines covers a variety of topics		
This magazine is truthful		
This magazine is read by elders		

Attribute	*Outlook*	*India Today*
This magazine is read by young people		
This magazine analyses information in-depth		
This magazine is for the highly inquisitive mind		
This magazine is very well researched		
This magazine gives attractive freebies		
This magazine gives me news which is spicy		
This magazine has very attractive issues		
This magazine is rich in content		
This magazine gives very predictable news		
This magazine gives relevant information only		
This magazine is intellectually stimulating		
This magazine provides me with an opinion		
This magazine is centered around politics		
This magazine gives me news as it is		
This magazine is for the practical people		
This magazine gives reliable news		

7. Can you recommend some changes in *Outlook* that you think it needs?
   (1) ______________________________
   (2) ______________________________
   (3) ______________________________

8. In the table below, please tick the articles/commodities that you own in each category:

Brand	*Range 1*	*Range 2*	*Range 3*
Watches	Above ₹6,000 Omega/Rolex/Cartier/Tissot/ Others ____________	₹1,500-6,000 Swatch/Tanishq/Tag Heur/ Others ____________	Below ₹1,500 Timex/HMT/Titan Others ____________
Mobiles	Above ₹15,000 Brand and Model ____________	₹7,000-15,000 Brand and Model ____________	Below ₹7,000 Brand and Model ____________
Car	Above ₹7 lakh Mercedes/Sonata/Skoda/Vectra Others ____________	₹4-7 Lacs Esteem/Accent/Bolero Others ____________	Below ₹4 Lacs Zen/Maruti 800/Alto/Santro/Palio Others____________

9. How satisfied are you (overall) with:
   A. *Outlook*
   B. *India Today*

Very satisfied/satisfied/neutral/dissatisfied/very dissatisfied

10. MARUTI Stands for Trust Stands for Taste
   (a) What do you think *Outlook* stands for?
   ____
   (b) What do you think *India Today* stands for?
   ____

CASE 8.3

WHAT DOES AN EMPLOYEE WANT?

An academic.....................................opportunities. The objectives of the study were as follows:

- To assess the growth and development opportunities available in IT companies.
- To form a comprehensive information sheet on the compensation packages for employees of various IT companies.
- To assess the trade-off that employees might make with respect to growth and development opportunities in case of an attractive compensation package
- To profile the typical employee in the IT sector
- The implication of the analysis for the IT industry

For this, they have developed a questionnaire as presented below. Go through the questionnaire and answer the following questions.

1. How would you evaluate the instrument as a whole? In terms of
   - questionnaire structure and sequencing
   - the clarity and content of the questions asked
2. Evaluate the questions in the light of the above stated objectives. That is, which question(s) was/were designed to match which objectives. Kindly list the same.
3. Has the questionnaire been effective in meeting the study objectives? Why/Why not?
4. How would you like to modify the questionnaire in the light of your answers to the above questions?

Research Questionnaire

Name: ______________________________

Working as: ______________________________

Name of the organization: ______________________

E-mail ID: ______________________________

Dated: ______________________________

Please fill the following questionnaire:

1. Are you currently employed in the IT sector?
   - Yes
   - No

   If yes, then continue.
2. Are you a permanent employee?
   - Yes
   - No
3. Marital Status
   - Single
   - Married
4. Work experience till date
   - Less than 3 months
   - 3 months–1 year
   - 1–3 years
   - 3–5 years
   - More than 5 years

5. Work experience in this organization
    - Less than 3 months
    - 3 months–1 year
    - 1– years
    - 3–5 years
    - More than 5 years
6. Mark your salary bracket (All figures are in INR)
    - Less than 20,000
    - 20,000–30,000
    - 30,001–40,000
    - 40,001–50,000
    - Above 50,000
7. Do you find sufficient growing opportunities in your current organization?
    - Yes
    - No
8. What is your priority?
    - Compensation hike
    - Current growth opportunity
9. Does your superior's view affect your decision of selecting pay hike or growth opportunities?
    - Yes
    - No
    - Can't say
10. Please rank the following growth opportunities as per your priority (Ranks: 1 to 7)
    - Promotion ____________________________
    - Onsite (working abroad at Onsite) ______
    - Training ______________________________
    - Higher Education (MBA, MS, etc.) _______
    - Switching to a better company _________
    - Better working environment ____________
    - Better assignments ____________________
11. What is the minimum hike in package at which you will be satisfied even when you are not getting any of the above mentioned growing opportunity?
    - 0–5 per cent
    - 6–10 per cent
    - 11–15 per cent
    - 16–20 per cent
    - 21–25 per cent
    - More than 25 per cent
12. Is money the only factor to continue your current job?
    - Yes
    - No
13. At what percentage hike in package are you willing to forego?
    (a) The promotion opportunity
        - 0–5 per cent
        - 6–10 per cent
        - 11–15 per cent

- 16–20 per cent
- 21–25 per cent
- 25–30 per cent
- More than 30 per cent
- Not willing to forego at any percentage hike

(b) The training opportunity?
- 0–5 per cent
- 6–10 per cent
- 11–15 per cent
- 16–20 per cent
- 21–25 per cent
- 25–30 per cent
- More than 30 per cent
- Not willing to forego at any percentage hike

(c) The onsite opportunity (working at the site)
- 0–5 per cent
- 6–10 per cent
- 11–15 per cent
- 16–20 per cent
- 21–25 per cent
- 25–30 per cent
- More than 30 per cent
- Not willing to forego at any percentage hike

(d) Higher education opportunity?
- 0–5 per cent
- 6–10 per cent
- 11–15 per cent
- 16–20 per cent
- 21–25 per cent
- 25–30 per cent
- More than 30 per cent
- Not willing to forego at any percentage hike

(e) Company-switching opportunity?
- 0–5 per cent
- 6–10 per cent
- 11–15 per cent
- 16–20 per cent
- 21–25 per cent
- 25–30 per cent
- More than 30 per cent
- Not willing to forego at any percentage hike

(f) Better working-climate opportunity?
- 0–5 per cent
- 6–10 per cent
- 11–15 per cent
- 16–20 per cent
- 21–25 per cent

- 25–30 per cent
- More than 30 per cent
- Not willing to forego at any percentage hike

(g) Better assignment opportunity?
- 0–5 per cent
- 6–10 per cent
- 11–15 per cent
- 16–20 per cent
- 21–25 per cent
- 25–30 per cent
- More than 30 per cent
- Not willing to forego at any percentage hike

(h) Working in the city of your choice?
- 0–5 per cent
- 6–10 per cent
- 11–15 per cent
- 16–20 per cent
- 21–25 per cent
- 25–30 per cent
- More than 30 per cent
- Not willing to forego at any percentage hike

14. What do you consider yourself, as per the following:
    - Underpaid
    - Overpaid
    - Paid as per the industry standards

15. Please mention any other growing opportunity which according to you is important but is not provided by your current organization.

    ____

    ____

16. Any other feedback you would like to share.

    ____

    ____

APPENDIX 8.1

Socio-economic Classification Table

Occupation	Education						
	Illiterate	School up to 4 years	School 5-9 years	SSC/HSC	Some College but not Graduate	Graduate/ Post-graduate – general	Graduate/ Post-graduate – Profes-sional
Unskilled worker	E2	E2	E1	D	D	D	D
Skilled worker	E2	E1	D	C	C	B2	B2
Petty Trader	E2	D	D	C	C	B2	B2
Shop owner	D	D	C	B2	B1	A2	A2
Businessman/ industrialist with no. of employees							
• None	D	C	B2	B1	A2	A2	A1
• 1-9	C	B2	B2	B1	A2	A1	A1
• 10 +	B1	B1	A2	A2	A1	A1	A1
Self-employed professional	D	D	D	B2	B1	A2	A1
Clerical/Salesman	D	D	D	C	B2	B1	B1
Supervisory level	D	D	C	C	B2	B1	A2
Officer/Executive • Junior	C	C	C	B2	B1	A2	A2
Officer/Executive • Middle/Senior	B1	B1	B1	B1	A2	A1	A1

Answers to Objective Type Questions

1. False
2. True
3. False
4. False
5. True
6. True
7. False
8. False
9. True
10. False
11. True
12. False
13. True
14. True
15. False
16. False
17. True
18. False
19. True
20. True

REFERENCES

Bell, J. *Doing Your Research Project.* 3rd edn. Buckingham: Open University Press, 1999.

De Vaus, D A. *Surveys in Social Research.* 5th edn. London: Routledge, 2002.

Kervin, J B. *Methods for Business Research,* 2nd edn. Reading, MA: Addison-Wesley, 1999.

BIBLIOGRAPHY

Boyd, Harper W, Jr, Ralph Westfall and Stanley F Stasch, *Marketing Research: Text and Cases.* 7th edn. Richard D Irwin, Inc., 2002.

Gay, L R. *Research Methods for Business and Management.* New York: Macmillan Publishing Company, 1992.

Grbich, Carol. *Qualitative Data Analysis–An Introduction*. London: Sage Publication, 2007.

Green, Paul E and Donald S Tull. *Research for Marketing Decisions*. 4th edn. New Delhi: Prentice Hall of India Private Ltd, 1986.

Kinnear, Thomas C and James R Taylor. *Marketing Research: An Applied Approach*, 5th edn. New York: McGraw Hill, Inc., 1996.

Kothari, C R. *Research Methodology Methods and Techniques*. 2nd edn. New Delhi: Wiley Eastern Limited, 1990.

Kumar, Ranjit. *Research Methodology–A Step by Step Guide for Beginners*. 2nd edn. New Delhi: Pearson Publication, 2005.

Luck, David J and Rubin, Ronald S. *Marketing Research*, 7th edn. New Delhi: Prentice Hall of India, 2008.

McBurney, Donald H. *Research Methods*. 5th edn. Singapore: Thomson Wadsworth Publication, 2002.

McDaniel, Carl and Roger Gates. *Marketing Research–The Impact of the Internet*. 5th edn. South-western, 2002.

Pannerselvam, R. *Research Methodology*. New Delhi: Prentice Hall of India Pvt. Ltd, 2004.

Saunders, Mark, Philip Lewis and Adrian Thornhill. *Research Methods for Business Students*. 3rd edn. New Delhi: Pearson Publication, 2008.

Theitart, Raymond-Alian, *et al*. *Doing Management Research–A Comprehensive Guide*. CA: Sage Publications, 2001.

Tull, Donald S and Del I Hawkins. *Marketing Research: Measurement & Method*. 6th edn. New Delhi: Prentice Hall of India Pvt. Ltd, 1993.

William, M K Trochim. *Research Methods*, 2nd edn. New Delhi: Biztantra, 2003.

Zikmund, William G. *Business Research Methods*, 5th edn. The Dryden Press, Harcourt Brace College Publishers, 1997.

Section 3

RESPONDENTS SELECTION AND DATA PREPARATION

This section discusses the method of sample selection and the process of refining and collating the collected data.

Chapter 9 begins with various sampling concepts. The distinction between sample and census is explained, and the advantages of sample over census are discussed. The chapter outlines two types of errors, namely, sampling and non-sampling error. The process of selecting the sample from the population is referred to as sampling design. This could be either one of two types, namely, probability and non-probability sampling design. Under probability sampling design, simple random sampling with replacement, simple random sampling without replacement, systematic sampling, stratified random sampling and cluster sampling are discussed. Under non-probability sampling design, convenience sampling, purposive sampling, snowball sampling and quota sampling are discussed. This chapter also explains the determination of sample size while estimating mean and proportion by using confidence interval approach.

Chapter 10 is a prelude to the data analysis section and introduces the researcher to the data preparation process. Starting with editing, both field and centralized in-house editing are discussed at length. Next, the process of codebook formulation and both pre-coding and post-coding of data are discussed with sample code books. The chapter moves on to classification of obtained primary data in the form of tables. The chapter also presents some exploratory methods of data analysis like bar and pie charts, histograms and stem and leaf displays. There is a detailed appendix on the SPSS package. This provides a step-by-step manual of introduction to basic features of the package, as well as data entry and variable transformation instructions.

9

CHAPTER

Sampling Considerations

Learning Objectives

By the end of the chapter, you should be able to:

1. Understand the basic concepts of sampling.
2. Distinguish between sample and census.
3. Differentiate between a sampling error and a non-sampling error.
4. Understand the meaning of sampling design.
5. Explain different types of probability sampling designs—simple random sampling with replacement, simple random sampling without replacement, systematic sampling, stratified sampling and cluster sampling.
6. Describe various types of non-probability sampling designs—convenience sampling, judgemental sampling, snowball sampling and quota sampling.
7. Estimate the sample size required while estimating the population mean and proportion.

The Delhi government introduced a ban on plastic bags in 2009. This decision was taken considering the fact that plastic bags are not biodegradable and it takes close to 60 years for them to decompose. Plastic bags are also the cause of other problems such as clogging of drainpipes and death of cattle that accidentally chew plastic bags.

According to the notification of the Delhi government, use, storage and sale of plastic bags of any kind or thickness in all those places where one gets the bags after shopping is banned. Anyone found violating the ban faces a maximum penalty of ₹1 lakh or five years' imprisonment or both, as per the Environment Protection Act. The Delhi Pollution Control Committee (DPCC) has formed a special inspection team for the purpose. The team is to visit the manufacturing and collecting units and initiate punishment for the violators.

Prakash Research Associates (PRA), a Delhi-based research organization specializing in environmental issues became interested in analysing the impact and effectiveness of the ban from the point of view of both the consumers and vendors. PRA assigned the project to three summer trainees from a business school with a total budget of ₹1.5 lakh, out of which a sum of ₹75,000/- was earmarked for a survey of consumers and vendors. The three summer trainees held discussions on various issues:

- How to define the population of consumers and vendors? How to prepare the sampling frame?
- How large should be the sample of consumers and vendors?
- What scheme should be used to select the sample of consumers and vendors?
- What would be the possible sources of error?

The above four issues and many more are addressed in this chapter.

Research objectives are generally translated into research questions that enable the researchers to identify the information needs. Once the information needs are specified, the sources of collecting the information are sought. Some of the information may be collected through secondary sources (published material), whereas the rest may be obtained through primary sources. The primary methods of collecting information could be the observation method, personal interview with questionnaire, telephone surveys and mail surveys. Surveys are, therefore, useful in information collection, and their analysis plays a vital role in finding answers to research questions. Survey respondents should be selected using the appropriate procedures, otherwise the researchers may not be able to get the right information to solve the problem under investigation. The process of selecting the right individuals, objects or events for the study is known as sampling. Sampling involves the study of a small number of individuals, objects chosen from a larger group.

SAMPLING CONCEPTS

LEARNING OBJECTIVE 1
Understand the basic concepts of sampling.

Before we get into the details of various issues pertaining to sampling, it would be appropriate to discuss some of the sampling concepts.

Population refers to any group of people or objects that form the subject of study in a particular survey.

Population: Population refers to any group of people or objects that form the subject of study in a particular survey and are similar in one or more ways. For example, the number of full-time MBA students in a business school could form one population. If there are 200 such students, the population size would be 200. We may be interested in understanding their perceptions about business education. If there are 200 class IV employees in an organization and we are interested in measuring their job satisfaction, all the 200 class IV employees would form the population of interest. If a TV manufacturing company produces 150 TVs per week and we are interested in estimating the proportion of defective TVs produced per week, all the 150 TVs would form our population. If, in an organization there are 1000 engineers, out of which 350 are mechanical engineers and we are interested in examining the proportion of mechanical engineers who intend to leave the organization within six months, all the 350 mechanical engineers would form the population of interest. If the interest is in studying how the patients in a hospital are looked after, then all the patients of the hospital would fall under the category of population.

Element: An element comprises a single member of the population. Out of the 350 mechanical engineers mentioned above, each mechanical engineer would form an element of the population. In the example of MBA students whose perception about the management education is of interest to us, each of the 200 MBA students will be an element of the population. This means that there will be 200 elements of the population.

The list of registered voters, number of students in a university and the telephone directory are some examples of **sampling frames**.

Sampling frame: Sampling frame comprises all the elements of a population with proper identification that is available to us for selection at any stage of sampling. For example, the list of registered voters in a constituency could form a sampling frame; the telephone directory; the number of students registered with a university; the attendance sheet of a particular class and the payroll of an organization are examples of sampling frames. When the population size is very large, it becomes virtually impossible to form a sampling frame. We know that there is a large number of consumers of soft drinks and, therefore, it becomes very difficult to form the sampling frame for the same.

Sample: It is a subset of the population. It comprises only some elements of the population. If out of the 350 mechanical engineers employed in an organization,

30 are surveyed regarding their intention to leave the organization in the next six months, these 30 members would constitute the sample.

A single member of a particular sample is called **sampling unit**.

Sampling unit: A sampling unit is a single member of the sample. If a sample of 50 students is taken from a population of 200 MBA students in a business school, then each of the 50 students is a sampling unit. Another example could be that if a sample of 50 patients is taken from a hospital to understand their perception about the services of the hospital, each of the 50 patients is a sampling unit.

Sampling: It is a process of selecting an adequate number of elements from the population so that the study of the sample will not only help in understanding the characteristics of the population but will also enable us to generalize the results. We will see later that there are two types of sampling designs—probability sampling design and non-probability sampling design.

Census is an examination of each and every element of the population.

Census (or complete enumeration): An examination of each and every element of the population is called census or complete enumeration. Census is an alternative to sampling. We will discuss the inherent advantages of sampling over a complete enumeration later.

Uses of Sampling in Real Life

In our day-to-day life we make use of the concept of sampling. There is hardly any person who has not made use of the concept in a real-life situation. Consider the following examples:

- Suppose you go to a grocery shop to purchase rice. You have been instructed by your mother to purchase good quality rice. On reaching the grocery shop you have the choice of buying the rice from any one of three bags. What is generally done is that you pick up a handful of rice from each bag, examine its quality and then decide about which bag's rice is to be bought. The concept of sampling is being used here as a handpick from each bag is a sample and examining the quality is a process by which you are trying to assess the quality of all the rice in the bag.
- Suppose you have a guest for dinner at your residence. Your mother prepares a number of dishes and before the guest arrives, she may give you a tablespoon of each of the dish to taste and tell her whether all the ingredients are in the right proportion or not. Again, a sample is being taken from each of the dish to know how each of them tastes.
- You go to a bookshop to buy a magazine. Before you decide to buy it, you may flip through its pages to know whether the contents of the magazines are of interest to you or not. Again, a sample of pages is taken from the magazine.

SAMPLE VS CENSUS

LEARNING OBJECTIVE 2
Distinguish between sample and census.

For a sample to be representative of the population, the **distribution of sampling units** in the sample has to be in the same proportion as the elements in the population.

In a research study, we are generally interested in studying the characteristics of a population. Suppose in a town there are 2 lakh households and we are interested in estimating the proportion of those households who spend their summer vacations in a hill station. This information can be obtained by asking every household in that town. If all the households in a population are asked to provide information, such a survey is called a census. There is an alternative way of obtaining the same information by choosing a subset of all the two lakh households and asking them for the same information. This subset is called a sample. Based upon the information obtained from the sample, a generalization about the population characteristic could be made. However, that sample has to be representative of the population. For a sample to be a representative of the population, the distribution of sampling units in the sample has to be in the same proportion as the elements in the population. For example, if in a town there are 50, 35 and 15 per cent households in lower, middle and upper income groups, then a sample taken from this population should have the same proportions in for it to be representative. There are several advantages of sample over census.

- Sample saves time and cost. Consider as an example that we are interested in estimating the monthly average household expenditure on food items by the people of Delhi. It is known that the population of Delhi is approximately 1.2 crore. Now, if we assume that there are five members per household, it would mean that the population comprises approximately 24 lakh households. Collecting data on the expenditure of each of the 24 lakh households on food items would be a very time-consuming and expensive exercise. This is because you will need to hire a number of investigators and train them before you conduct the survey on the 24 lakh households. Instead, if a sample of, say, 2000 households is chosen, the task would not only be finished faster but will be inexpensive, too.
- Many times a decision-maker may not have too much of time to wait till all the information is available. Therefore, a sample could come to his rescue.
- There are situations where a sample is the only option. When we want to estimate the average life of fluorescent bulbs, what is done is that they are burnt out completely. If we go for a complete enumeration there would not be anything left for use. Another example could be testing the quality of a photographic film. To test the quality, we need to expose it completely and the moment it is exposed it gets destroyed. Therefore, sample is the only choice.
- The study of a sample instead of complete enumeration may, at times, produce more reliable results. This is because by studying a sample, fatigue is reduced and fewer errors occur while collecting the data, especially when a large number of elements are involved.

A census is appropriate when the population size is small, e.g., the number of public sector banks in the country. Suppose the researcher is interested in collecting information from the top management of a bank regarding their views on the monetary policy announced by the Reserve Bank of India (RBI), in this case, a complete enumeration may be possible as the population size is not very large. As another example, consider a business school having a few students from Europe, East Africa, South East Asia and the Middle East. These students would have their own problems in settling down in the Indian environment because of the differences in social, cultural and environmental factors. To understand their concerns, a survey of population may be more appropriate. Therefore, a survey of population could be used when there is a lot of heterogeneity in the variables of interest and the population size is small.

A **census** is appropriate for a small population or when there is a lot of heterogeneity in the variables of interest.

CONCEPT CHECK

1. Define the basic concepts of sampling.
2. What is the use of sampling in real life?
3. How would you differentiate between a sample and a census?

SAMPLING VS NON-SAMPLING ERROR

LEARNING OBJECTIVE 3

Differentiate between a sampling and a non-sampling error.

There are two types of error that may occur while we are trying to estimate the population parameters from the sample. These are called sampling and non-sampling errors.

Sampling error: This error arises when a sample is not representative of the population. For example, if our population comprises 200 MBA students in a business school and we want to estimate the average height of these 200 students by taking a sample of 10 (say). Let us assume for the sake of simplicity that the true value of population mean (parameter) is known. When we estimate the average height of the sampled students, we may find that the sample mean is far away from the population mean. The difference between the sample mean and the population mean is called sampling error, and this could arise because the sample of 10 students may not be representative of the entire population. Suppose now we increase the sample size from 10 to 15, we may find that the sampling error reduces. This way, if we keep doing so, we may note that the sampling error reduces with the increase in sample size as an increased sample may result in increasing the representativeness of the sample.

Sampling error arises when a sample is not representative of the population.

Non-sampling error: This error arises not because a sample is not a representative of the population but because of other reasons. Some of these reasons are listed below:

A **non-sampling** error usually arises due to more varied reasons.

- The respondents when asked for information on a particular variable may not give the correct answers. If a person aged 48 is asked a question about his age, he may indicate the age to be 36, which may result in an error and in estimating the true value of the variable of interest.
- The error can arise while transferring the data from the questionnaire to the spreadsheet on the computer.
- There can be errors at the time of coding, tabulation and computation.
- If the population of the study is not properly defined, it could lead to errors.
- The chosen respondent may not be available to answer the questions or may refuse to be part of the study.
- There may be a sampling frame error. Suppose the population comprises households with low income, high income and middle class category. The researcher might decide to ignore the low-income category respondents and may take the sample only from the middle and the high-income category people.

SAMPLING DESIGN

LEARNING OBJECTIVE 4
Understand the meaning of sampling design.

Sampling design refers to the process of selecting samples from a population. There are two types of sampling designs—probability sampling design and non-probability sampling design. Probability sampling designs are used in conclusive research. In a probability sampling design, each and every element of the population has a known chance of being selected in the sample. The known chance does not mean equal chance. Simple random sampling is a special case of probability sampling design where every element of the population has both known and equal chance of being selected in the sample. In case of non-probability sampling design, the elements of the population do not have any known chance of being selected in the sample. These sampling designs are used in exploratory research.

PROBABILITY SAMPLING DESIGN

Under this, the following sampling designs would be covered—simple random sampling with replacement (SRSWR), simple random sampling without replacement (SRSWOR), systematic sampling, stratified random sampling and cluster sampling.

LEARNING OBJECTIVE 5
Explain different types of probability sampling designs—simple random sampling with replacement, simple random sampling without replacement, systematic sampling, stratified random sampling and cluster sampling.

Simple Random Sampling with Replacement

Under this scheme, a list of all the elements of the population from where the samples to be drawn is prepared. If there are 1000 elements in the population, we write the identification number or the name of all the 1000 elements on 1000 different slips. These are put in a box and shuffled properly. If there are 20 elements to be selected from the population, the simple random sampling procedure involves selecting a slip from the box and reading of the identification number. Once this is done, the chosen slip is put back to the box and again a slip is picked up and the identification number is read from that slip. This process continues till a sample of 20 is selected. Please note that the first element is chosen with a probability of 1/1000, the second one is also selected with the same probability and so are all the subsequent elements of the population.

An alternative way of selecting the samples from the population is by using random number tables. Table 9.1 gives an illustrative example of random numbers.

TABLE 9.1
Select four-digit random numbers

I	II	III	IV	V
2807	0495	6183	7871	9559
8016	5732	3448	0164	2367
1322	4678	8034	1139	1474
0843	4625	7407	9987	5734
2364	1187	4565	2343	9786
4885	8755	4355	5465	0575
3406	4678	5950	7222	8494
5927	6010	7545	8979	1041
4447	3476	9140	0736	2332
4968	7553	1073	2493	4251
7489	1630	2330	4250	6170
4010	2707	3925	6007	8089
6531	9784	5520	7764	0008
7052	3861	7115	9521	2192
6573	2793	8710	2127	3846
8094	3205	2030	3035	5765
8615	6092	1900	4792	7684
9136	4016	3495	6549	9603
9656	5246	5090	8306	1522
2017	8323	1685	3006	3441

Table 9.1 gives four-digit random numbers arranged in 20 rows and five columns. These random numbers can be generated by a computer programmed to scramble numbers. The logic for generating random number is that any number can be constructed from numbers 0 to 9. The probability that any one digit from 0 through 9 will appear is the same as that for any other digit and the appearance of the numbers is statistically independent. Further, the probability of one sequence of digits occurring is the same as that for any other sequence of the same length.

The use of random number table for selecting samples could be illustrated through an example. Suppose there are 75 students in a class and it is decided to select 15 out of the 75 students. These students can be numbered from 01 to 75. Now, to pick up 15 students using random numbers and following the scheme of simple random sampling with replacement, we proceed as follows:

- With eyes closed, we place our finger on a number on the random number table. Suppose it is on the first row and the first column of our table. Now, we go down the first two columns and choose two-digit random numbers running from 01 to 75. If any number greater than 75 appears, it gets rejected. This way, the first number to be selected would be 28. The second number is 80, which would be rejected as we are choosing numbers from 01 to 75. The next selected number would be 13, followed by 08, 23, 48, 34, 59, 44, 49, 74, 40, 65, 70 and 65. Note that 65 has appeared twice. Since we are using the scheme of simple random sampling with replacement, we would retain it. This way we have selected 14 samples. The 15th number selected would be 20. In brief, the scheme explained above states that any number greater than the population size (in this case 75) is rejected and only the numbers from 01 to 75 are selected. A number may get repeated because simple random sampling scheme is done with replacement.

Simple Random Sampling Without Replacement

In the case of simple random sample without replacement, the procedure is identical to what was explained in the case of simple random sampling with replacement. The only difference here is that the chosen slip is not placed back in the box. This way, the first unit would be selected with the probability of 1/1000, second unit with the probability of 1/999, the third will be selected with a probability of 1/998 and so on, till we select the required number of elements (in this case, 20) in our sample.

Simple random sampling is not used in consumer research as the population size is usually very large, which creates problems in the preparation of a sampling frame.

The simple random sampling (with or without replacement) is not used in a consumer research. This is because in a consumer research the population size is usually very large, which creates problems in the preparation of a sampling frame. For example, there is a large number of consumers of soft drinks, pizza, shampoo, soap, chocolate, etc. However, these (SRSWR and SRSWOR) designs could be useful when the population size is very small, for example, the number of steel/aluminum-producing companies in India and the number of banks in India. Since the population size is quite small, the preparation of a sampling frame does not create any problem.

Another problem with these (SRSWR and SRSWOR) designs is that we may not get a representative sample using such a scheme. Consider an example of a locality having 10,000 households, out of which 5,000 belong to low-income group, 3,500 belong to middle income group and the remaining 1,500 belong to high-income group. Suppose it is decided to take a sample of 100 households using the simple random sampling. The selected sample may not contain even a single household belonging to the high- and middle-income group and only the low-income households may get selected, thus, resulting in a non-representative sample.

Systematic Sampling

In **systematic sampling**, the entire population is arranged in a particular order according to a design.

Systematic sampling takes care of the limitation of the simple random sampling that the sample may not be a representative one. In this design, the entire population is arranged in a particular order. The order could be the calendar dates or the elements of a population arranged in an ascending or a descending order of the magnitude which may be assumed as random. List of subjects arranged in the alphabetical order could also be used and they are usually assumed to be random in order. Once this is done, the steps followed in the systematic sampling design are as follows:

- First of all, a sampling interval given by K = N/n is calculated, where N = the size of the population and n = the size of the sample. It is seen that the sampling interval K should be an integer. If it is not, it is rounded off to make it an integer.

- A random number is selected from 1 to K. Let us call it C.
- The first element to be selected from the ordered population would be C, the next element would be C + K and the subsequent one would be C + 2K and so on till a sample of size n is selected.

This way we can get representation from all the classes in the population and overcome the limitations of the simple random sampling. To take an example, assume that there are 1,000 grocery shops in a small town. These shops could be arranged in an ascending order of their sales, with the first shop having the smallest sales and the last shop having the highest sales. If it is decided to take a sample of 50 shops, then our sampling interval K will be equal to 1000 ÷ 50 = 20. Now we select a random number from 1 to 20. Suppose the chosen number is 10. This means that the shop number 10 will be selected first and then shop number 10 + 20 = 30 and the next one would be 10 + 2 × 20 = 50 and so on till all the 50 shops are selected. This way we can get a representative sample in the sense that it will contain small, medium and large shops.

In a **systematic sampling**, the first unit of sample is selected at random and having chosen this there is no control over the subsequent units of sample. Due to this reason, it is at times referred to as 'mixed sampling'.

It may be noted that in a systematic sampling the first unit of the sample is selected at random (probability sampling design) and having chosen this, we have no control over the subsequent units of sample (non-probability sampling). Because of this, this design at times is called mixed sampling.

The main advantage of systematic sampling design is its simplicity. When sampling from a list of population arranged in a particular order, one can easily choose a random start as described earlier. After having chosen a random start, every K^{th} item can be selected instead of going for a simple random selection. This design is statistically more efficient than a simple random sampling, provided the condition of ordering of the population is satisfied.

The use of systematic sampling is quite common as it is easy and cheap to select a systematic sample. In systematic sampling one does not have to jump back and forth all over the sampling frame wherever random number leads, and neither does one have to check for duplication of elements as compared to simple random sampling. Another advantage of a systematic sampling over simple random sampling is that one does not require a complete sampling frame to draw a systematic sample. The investigator may be instructed to interview every 10th customer entering a mall without a list of all customers.

There may be situations where it may not be possible to get a representative sample. The design can create problems if the sampling interval is a whole number multiple of some cycle related to the problem. On this design there may be a problem that there is a high probability of systematic bias creeping into the sample resulting in a non-representative sample. Consider, for example, the case of a certain PVR cinema hall where there may be a couple of snack bars. We may be interested in estimating the average daily sales of a particular snack bar in that PVR. Now, using the daily data with the population and sample size known, we compute a sampling interval which may be a multiple of seven. Using this, we may select our first element which would reflect one of the seven days of the week, say Friday. The next element would also be Friday, as our sampling interval is a multiple of seven and so the subsequent elements of the population. Therefore, our sample would comprise only Fridays and the sample would not reflect day of the week variation in the sales data, which could result in a non-representative sample. Therefore, while using daily data, care should be taken that our sampling interval is not a multiple of seven.

Stratified Random Sampling

Under this sampling design, the entire population (universe) is divided into strata (groups), which are mutually exclusive and collectively exhaustive. By mutually exclusive, it is meant that if an element belongs to one stratum, it cannot belong to any other stratum. Strata are collectively exhaustive if all the elements of various strata put together completely cover all the elements of the population. The elements are selected using a simple random sampling independently from each group.

Stratified random sampling is more efficient as compared to simple random sampling as dividing the population into various strata increases the representativeness of the sampling.

There are two reasons for using a stratified random sampling rather than simple random sampling. One is that the researchers are often interested in obtaining data about the component parts of a universe. For example, the researcher may be interested in knowing the average monthly sales of cell phones in 'large,' 'medium' and 'small' stores. In such a case, separate sampling from within each stratum would be called for. The second reason for using a stratified random sampling is that it is more efficient as compared to a simple random sampling. This is because dividing the population into various strata increases the representativness of the sampling as the elements of each stratum are homogeneous to each other.

There are certain issues that may be of interest while setting up a stratified random sample. These are:

The **criteria for stratification** should be related to the objectives of the study.

What criteria should be used for stratifying the universe (population)?

The criteria for stratification should be related to the objectives of the study. The entire population should be stratified in such a way that the elements are homogeneous within the strata, whereas there should be heterogeneity between strata. As an example, if the interest is to estimate the expenditure of households on entertainment, the appropriate criteria for stratification would be the household income. This is because the expenditure on entertainment and household income are highly correlated. As another example, if the objective of the study is to estimate the amount of money spent on cosmetics, then, gender could be used as an appropriate criteria for stratification. This is because it is known that though both men and women use cosmetics, the expenditure by women is much more than that of their male counterparts. Someone may argue out that gender may no longer remain the appropriate criteria if it is not backed by income. Therefore, the researcher might have to use two or more criteria for stratification depending upon the problem in hand. This would only increase the number of strata thereby making the sampling difficult.

Generally stratification is done on the basis of demographic variables like age, income, education and gender. Customers are usually stratified on the basis of life stages and income levels to study their buying patterns. Companies may be stratified according to size, industry, profits for analysing the stock market reactions.

How many strata should be constructed?

Going by common sense, as many strata as possible should be used so that the elements of each stratum will be as homogeneous as possible. However, it may not be practical to increase the number of strata and, therefore, the number may have to be limited. Too many strata may complicate the survey and make preparation and tabulation difficult. Costs of adding more strata may be more than the benefit obtained. Further the researcher may end up with the practical difficulty of preparing a separate sampli frame as the simple random samples are to be drawn from each stratum.

What should be appropriate number of samples size to be taken in each stratu

This question pertains to the number of observations to be taken out fro stratum. At the outset, one needs to determine the total sample size for the and then allocate it between each stratum. This may be explained as foll

Let there be a population of size N. Let this population be divid strata based on a certain criterion. Let N_1, N_2 and N_3 denote the si and 3 respectively, such that $N = N_1 + N_2 + N_3$. These strata are mutually exclusive and collectively exhaustive. Each of these three strata could be treated as three populations. Now, if a total sample of size n is to be taken from the population, the question arises that how much of the sample should be taken from strata 1, 2 and 3 respectively, so that the sum total of sample sizes from each strata adds up to n.

Let the size of the sample from first, second and third strata be n_1, n_2, and n_3 respectively such that $n = n_1 + n_2 + n_3$. Then, there are two schemes that may be used to determine the values of n_i, $(i = 1, 2, 3)$ from each strata. These are proportionate and disproportionate allocation schemes.

In the **proportionate allocation scheme**, the size of the sample in each stratum is proportional to the size of the population of the stratum.

Proportionate allocation scheme: In this scheme, the size of the sample in each stratum is proportional to the size of the population of the strata. As an example, if a bank wants to conduct a survey to understand the problems that its customers are facing, it may be appropriate to divide them into three strata based upon the size of their deposits with the bank. If we have 10,000 customers of a bank in such a way that 1,500 of them are big account holders (having deposits more than ₹10 lakh), 3,500 of them are medium sized account holders (having deposits of more than ₹2 lakh but less than ₹10 lakh), the remaining 5,000 are small account holders (having deposits of less than ₹2 lakh). Suppose the total budget for sampling is fixed at ₹20,000 and the cost of sampling a unit (customer) is ₹20. If a sample of 100 is to be chosen from all the three strata, the size of the sample from strata 1 would be:

$$n_1 = n \times \frac{N_1}{N} = 100 \times \frac{1500}{10000} = 15$$

The size of sample from strata 2 would be:

$$n_2 = n \times \frac{N_2}{N} = 100 \times \frac{3500}{10000} = 35$$

The size of sample from strata 3 would be:

$$n_3 = n \times \frac{N_3}{N} = 100 \times \frac{5000}{10000} = 50$$

This way the size of the sample chosen from each stratum is proportional to the size of the stratum. Once we have determined the sample size from each stratum, one may use the simple random sampling or the systematic sampling or any other sampling design to take out samples from each of the strata.

Disproportionate allocation: As per the proportionate allocation explained above, the sizes of the samples from strata 1, 2 and 3 are 15, 35 and 50 respectively. As it is known that the cost of sampling of a unit is ₹20 irrespective of the strata from where the sample is drawn, the bank would naturally be more interested in drawing a large sample from stratum 1, which has the big customers, as it gets most of its business fro strata 1. In other words, the bank may follow a disproportionate allocation of ... the importance of each stratum is not the same from the point of view of ... bank may like to take a sample of 45 from strata 1 and 40 and 15 from ... ively. Also, a large sample may be desired from the strata having

...pling

... sampling, the entire population is divided into various clusters in ... at the elements within the clusters are heterogeneous. However, there is homogeneity between the clusters. This design, therefore, is just the opposite of the stratified sampling design, where there was homogeneity within the strata and heterogeneity between the strata. To illustrate the example of a cluster sampling, one may assume that there is a company having its corporate office in a multi-storey building. In the first floor, we may assume that there is a marketing department where the offices of the president (marketing), vice president (marketing) and so on to the level of management trainee (marketing) are there. Naturally, there would be a lot of variation (heterogeneity) in the amount of salaries they draw and hence a high amount of variation in the amount of money spent on entertainment. Similarly, if the finance department is housed on the second floor, we may find almost a similar pattern. Same could be assumed for third, fourth and other floors. Now, if each of the floors could be treated as a cluster, we find that there is homogeneity between the clusters but there is a lot of heterogeneity within the clusters. Now, a sample of, say, 2 to 3 clusters is chosen at random and once having done so, each of the cluster is enumerated completely to be able to make an estimate of the amount of money the entire population spends on entertainment.

Examples of cluster sampling could include ad hoc organizational committees drawn from various departments to advise the CEO of a company on product development, new product ideas, evaluating alternative advertising programmes, budget allocations and marketing strategies. Each of the clusters comprises a heterogeneous collection of members with different interests, background, experience, value system and philosophy. The CEO of the company may be able to take strategic decisions based upon their combined advice.

A **cluster** may not contain heterogeneous elements. Therefore, the applicability of cluster sampling to an organizational context may be questioned.

Although the per unit costs of cluster sampling are much lower than those of other probability sampling, the applicability of cluster sampling to an organizational context may be questioned as a cluster may not contain heterogeneous elements. The condition of heterogeneity within the cluster and homogeneity between the clusters may not be met. As another example, the households in a block are to be similar rather than dissimilar and as a result, it may be difficult to form heterogeneous clusters.

Cluster sampling is useful when populations under a survey are widely dispersed and drawing a simple random sample may be impractical.

CONCEPT CHECK

1. Distinguish between sampling and non-sampling errors.
2. What is a sampling design?
3. Explain simple random sampling without replacement.
4. What is stratified random sampling?

NON-PROBABILITY SAMPLING DESIGNS

LEARNING OBJECTIVE 6

Describe various types of non-probability sampling designs—convenience sampling, judgemental sampling, snowball sampling and quota sampling.

Under the non-probability sampling, the following designs would be considered—convenience sampling, purposive (judgemental) sampling, snowball sampling and quota sampling.

Convenience Sampling

Convenience sampling is used to obtain information quickly and inexpensively. The only criterion for selecting sampling units in this scheme is the convenience of the researcher or the investigator. Mostly, the convenience samples used are neighbours, friends, family members, colleagues and 'passers-by.' This sampling

Convenience sampling is often used in the pre-test phase of a research study such as the pre-testing of a questionnaire.

design is often used in the pre-test phase of a research study such as the pre-testing of a questionnaire. Some of the examples of convenience sampling are:

- People interviewed in a shopping centre for their political opinion for a TV programme.
- Monitoring the price level in a grocery shop with the objective of inferring the trends in inflation in the economy.
- Requesting people to volunteer to test products.
- Using students or employees of an organization for conducting an experiment.
- Interviews conducted by a TV channel of people coming out of a cinema hall, to seek their opinion about the movie.
- A researcher visiting a few shops near his residence to observe which brand of a particular product people are buying, so as to draw a rough estimate of the market share of the brand.

In all the above situations, the sampling unit may either be self-selected or selected because of ease of availability. No effort is made to choose a representative sample. Therefore, in this design the difference between the population value (parameters) of interest and the sample value (statistic) is unknown both in terms of the magnitude and direction. Therefore, it is not possible to make an estimate of the sampling error and researchers won't be able to make a conclusive statement about the results from such a sample. It is because of this, convenience sampling should not be used in conclusive research (descriptive and causal research).

Convenience sampling is commonly used in exploratory research. This is because the purpose of an exploratory research is to gain an insight into the problem and generate a set of hypotheses which could be tested with the help of a conclusive research. When very little is known about a subject, a small-scale convenience sampling can be of use in the exploratory work to help understand the range of variability of responses in a subject area.

Judgemental Sampling

In **judgemental sampling,** the judgement of an expert is used to identify a representative sample. Empirically, this approach may not produce satisfactory results.

Under judgemental sampling, experts in a particular field choose what they believe to be the best sample for the study in question. The judgement sampling calls for special efforts to locate and gain access to the individuals who have the required information. Here, the judgement of an expert is used to identify a representative sample. For example, the shoppers at a shopping centre may serve to represent the residents of a city or some of the cities may be selected to represent a country. Judgemental sampling design is used when the required information is possessed by a limited number/category of people. This approach may not empirically produce satisfactory results and, may, therefore, curtail generalizability of the findings due to the fact that we are using a sample of experts (respondents) that are usually conveniently available to us. Further, there is no objective way to evaluate the precision of the results. A company wanting to launch a new product may use judgemental sampling for selecting 'experts' who have prior knowledge or experience of similar products. A focus group of such experts may be conducted to get valuable insights. Opinion leaders who are knowledgeable are included in the organizational context. Enlightened opinions (views and knowledge) constitute a rich data source. A very special effort is needed to locate and have access to individuals who possess the required information.

The most common application of judgemental sampling is in business-to-business (B to B) marketing. Here, a very small sample of lead users, key accounts or technologically sophisticated firms or individuals is regularly used to test new product concepts, producing programmes, etc.

Snowball Sampling

Snowball sampling is generally used when it is difficult to identify the members of the desired population, e.g., deep-sea divers, families with triplets, people using walking sticks, doctors specializing in a particular ailment, etc. Under this design each respondent, after being interviewed, is asked to identify one or more in the field. This could result in a very useful sample. The main problem is in making the initial contact. Once this is done, these cases identify more members of the population, who then identify further members and so on. It may be difficult to get a representative sample. One plausible reason for this could be that the initial respondents may identify other potential respondents who are similar to themselves. The next problem is to identify new cases.

Quota Sampling

In **quota sampling**, the sample is selected on the basis of certain demographic characteristics such as age, gender, occupation, education, etc.

In quota sampling, the sample includes a minimum number from each specified subgroup in the population. The sample is selected on the basis of certain demographic characteristics such as age, gender, occupation, education, income, etc. The investigator is asked to choose a sample that conforms to these parameters. Field workers are assigned quotas of the sample to be selected satisfying these characteristics.

A researcher wants to measure the job satisfaction level among the employees of a large organization and believes that the job satisfaction level varies across different types of employees. The organization is having 10 per cent, 15 per cent, 35 per cent and 40 per cent, class I, class II, class III and class IV, employees, respectively. If a sample of 200 employees is to be selected from the organization, then 20, 30, 70 and 80 employees from class I, class II, class III and class IV respectively should be selected from the population. Now, various investigators may be assigned quotas from each class in such a way that a sample of 200 employees is selected from various classes in the same proportion as mentioned in the population. For example, the first field worker may be assigned a quota of 10 employees from class I, 15 from class II, 20 from class III and 30 from class IV. Similarly, a second investigator may be assigned a different quota such that a total sample of 200 is selected in the same proportion as the population is distributed. Please note that the investigators may choose the employees from each class as conveniently available to them. Therefore, the sample may not be totally representative of the population, hence the findings of the research cannot be generalized. However, the reason for choosing this sampling design is the convenience it offers in terms of effort, cost and time.

In the example given above, it may be argued that job satisfaction is also influenced by education level, categorized as higher secondary or below, graduation, and postgraduation and above. By incorporating this variable, the distribution of population may look as given in Table 9.2. From the table, we may note that there are 8 per cent class I employees who are postgraduate and above, there are 35 per cent class IV employees with a higher secondary education and below and so on. Now, suppose a sample of size 200 is again proposed. In this case, the distribution of sample satisfying these two conditions in the same proportion in the population is given in Table 9.3.

TABLE 9.2
Distribution of population (percentage)

Education	Category of Employees				
	Class I	Class II	Class III	Class IV	Total
Postgraduation and above	8	5	5	0	18
Graduation	2	10	20	5	37
Higher Secondary and below	0	0	10	35	45
Total	10	15	35	40	100

TABLE 9.3
Distribution of sample (numbers)

Education	Category of Employees				
	Class I	Class II	Class III	Class IV	Total
Postgraduation and above	16	10	10	0	36
Graduation	4	20	40	10	74
Higher Secondary and below	0	0	20	70	90
Total	20	30	70	80	200

Table 9.3 indicates that a sample of 20 class II employees who are graduates should be selected. Likewise, a sample of 10 employees who possess postgraduate and above education should be selected. In the above table, the sample to be taken from each of the 12 cells has been specified. Having done so, each of the investigators is assigned a quota to collect information from the employees conforming to the above norms so that a sample of 200 is selected.

Quota sampling design may look similar to the stratified random sampling design. However, there are differences between the two. In the stratified sampling design, the selection of sample from each stratum is random but in the quota sampling, the respondents may be chosen at the convenience or judgement of the researchers. Further, as already stated, the results of stratified random sampling could be generalized, whereas it may not be possible in the case of quota sampling. Quota sampling has some advantages over the probabilistic techniques. This design is very economical and it does not take too much time to set it up. Also, the use of this design does not require a sampling frame.

Quota sampling does not require a sampling frame, is economical and does not take too much time to set up.

However, quota sampling also has certain weaknesses like:

- The total number of cells depends upon the number of control characteristics associated with the objectives of the study. If the control characteristics are large, the total number of cells increases, which may result in making the task of the investigator difficult.
- The chosen control characteristics should be related to the objectives of the study. The findings of the study could be misleading if any relevant parameter is omitted for one reason or the other.
- The investigator may visit those places where the chances of getting the respondents with the required control characteristics are high. The investigator could also avoid some responses that appear to be unfriendly. All this could result in making the findings of the study less reliable.

DETERMINATION OF SAMPLE SIZE

LEARNING OBJECTIVE 7
Estimate the sample size required while estimating the population mean and proportion.

The size of a sample depends upon the basic characteristics of the population, the type of information required from the survey and the cost involved. Therefore, a sample may vary in size for several reasons. The size of the population does not influence the size of the sample as will be shown later on.

There are various methods of determining the sample size in practice:

- Researchers may arbitrary decide the size of sample without giving any explicit consideration to the accuracy of the sample results or the cost of sampling. This arbitrary approach should be avoided.
- For some of the projects, the total budget for the field survey (usually mentioned) in a project proposal is allocated. If the cost of sampling per sample unit is known, one can easily obtain the sample size by dividing the total budget allocation by the cost of sampling per unit.
  This method concentrates only on the cost aspect of sampling, rather than the value of information obtained from such a sample.
- There are other researchers who decide on the sample size based on what was done by the other researchers in similar studies. Again, this approach cannot be a substitute for the formal scientific approach.
- The most commonly used approach for determining the size of sample is the confidence interval approach covered under inferential statistics. Below will be discussed this approach while determining the size of a sample for estimating population mean and population proportion. In a confidence interval approach, the following points are taken into account for determining the sample size in estimation of problems involving means:

The **size of a sample** depends upon the basic characteristics of the population, the type of information required from the survey and the cost involved.

(a) *The variability of the population:* It would be seen that the higher the variability as measured by the population standard deviation, larger will be the size of the sample. If the standard deviation of the population is unknown, a researcher may use the estimates of the standard deviation from previous studies. Alternatively, the estimates of the population standard deviation can be computed from the sample data.

If the researcher seeks **greater precision,** the resulting sample size would be large.

(b) *The confidence attached to the estimate:* It is a matter of judgement, how much confidence you want to attach to your estimate. Assuming a normal distribution, the higher the confidence the researcher wants for the estimate, larger will be sample size. This is because the value of the standard normal ordinate 'Z' will vary accordingly. For a 90 per cent confidence, the value of 'Z' would be 1.645 and for a 95 per cent confidence, the corresponding 'Z' value would be 1.96 and so on (see Annexure 1 at the end of the book). It would be seen later that a higher confidence would lead to a larger 'Z' value.

(c) *The allowable error or margin of error:* How accurate do we want our estimate to be is again a matter of judgement of the researcher. It will of course depend upon the objectives of the study and the consequence resulting from the higher inaccuracy. If the researcher seeks greater precision, the resulting sample size would be large.

Sample Size for Estimating Population Mean

We have learnt in the central limit theorem that the sampling distribution of the sample mean ($\bar{X}$) follows a normal distribution with a mean μ and a standard error $\sigma_{\bar{X}}$ irrespective of the shape of population distribution whenever the sample size is large. Symbolically, it may be written as:

$$\bar{X} \cap N(\mu, \sigma_{\bar{X}})$$
$$n \to 30$$

The above also holds true whenever samples are drawn from normal population. However, in that case, the requirement of a large sample is not there. The various notations are explained as under:

$\overline{X}$ = Sample mean

μ = Population mean

$\sigma_{\overline{X}}$ = Standard error of mean

n = Sample size

N = Population size

σ = Population standard deviation

The value of:

$\sigma_{\overline{X}} = \sigma/\sqrt{n}$ (when samples are drawn from an infinite population)

$= \frac{\sigma}{\sqrt{n}}\sqrt{\frac{N-n}{N-1}}$ (when samples are drawn from a finite population)

The expression: $\sqrt{\frac{N-n}{N-1}}$ **is called the finite population multiplier.**

The expression $\sqrt{\frac{N-n}{N-1}}$ is called the finite population multiplier and need not be used while sampling from a finite population provided $\frac{n}{N} < 0.05$.

The standard normal variate Z may be written as:

$$Z = \frac{\overline{X}-\mu}{\sigma_{\overline{X}}}$$

$$Z = \frac{\overline{X}-\mu}{\frac{\sigma}{\sqrt{n}}}$$

$$Z = \frac{\overline{X}-\mu}{\sigma}\sqrt{n}$$

$$Z = \frac{e\sqrt{n}}{\sigma}$$

where $\overline{X} - \mu = e$ = Margin of error

$$\therefore \quad n = \frac{Z^2\sigma^2}{e^2}$$

It may be noted from above that the size of the sample is directly proportional to the variability in the population and the value of Z for a confidence interval. It varies inversely with the size of the error. It may also be noted that the size of a sample does not depend upon the size of population. Below are given some worked out examples for the determination of a sample size.

Example 9.1

An economist is interested in estimating the average monthly household expenditure on food items by the households of a town. Based on past data, it is estimated that the standard deviation of the population on the monthly expenditure on food item is ₹30. With allowable error set at ₹7, estimate the sample size required at a 90 per cent confidence.

Solution:

90 per cent confidence ⇒ Z = 1.645

e = ₹7

σ = ₹30

$$n = \frac{Z^2 \sigma^2}{e^2}$$
$$= \frac{(1.645)^2 (30)^2}{(7)^2}$$
$$= 49.7025$$
$$= 50 \text{ (approx.)}$$

Example 9.2 You are given a population with a standard deviation of 8.6. Determine the sample size needed to estimate the mean of the population within ± 0.5 with a 99 per cent confidence.

Solution:

99 per cent confidence ⇒ Z = 2.575

$$e = \pm 0.5$$
$$\sigma = 8.6$$
$$n = \frac{Z^2 \sigma^2}{e^2}$$
$$= \frac{(2.575)^2 (8.6)^2}{(0.5)^2}$$
$$= 1961.60$$
$$= 1962 \text{ (approx.)}$$

Example 9.3 It is desired to estimate the mean life time of a certain kind of vacuum cleaner. Given that the population standard deviation σ = 320 days, how large a sample is needed to be able to assert with a confidence level of 96 per cent that the mean of the sample will differ from the population mean by less than 45 days?

Solution:

96 per cent confidence ⇒ Z = 2.055

$$e = 45$$
$$\sigma = 320$$
$$n = \frac{Z^2 \sigma^2}{e^2}$$
$$= \frac{(2.055)^2 (320)^2}{(45)^2}$$
$$= 213.55$$
$$= 214 \text{ (approx.)}$$

Determination of sample size for estimating the population proportion

If the sample proportion $\bar{p}$ is used to estimate the population proportion p, the standard error of $\bar{p}(\sigma_p)$ would be $\sqrt{\frac{pq}{n}}$, where q = 1 - p. Now assuming normal distribution, we have

$$\bar{p} \cap N\left(p, \sqrt{\frac{pq}{n}}\right)$$

Therefore, $$Z = \frac{\bar{p} - p}{\sqrt{\frac{pq}{n}}}$$

Therefore, margin of error $e = \bar{p} - p = Z\sqrt{\frac{pq}{n}}$

$$Z = \frac{e}{\sqrt{\frac{pq}{n}}}$$

$$Z = \frac{e\sqrt{n}}{\sqrt{pq}}$$

$$n = \frac{Z^2 pq}{e^2}$$

The above formula will be used if the value of population proportion p is known. If, however, p is unknown, we substitute the maximum value of pq in the above formula. It can be shown that the maximum value of pq is ¼ when p = ½ and q = ½. This is shown in Figure 9.1.

Therefore, $n = \frac{1}{4}\frac{Z^2}{e^2}$

FIGURE 9.1 Graph of pq corresponding to the values of p

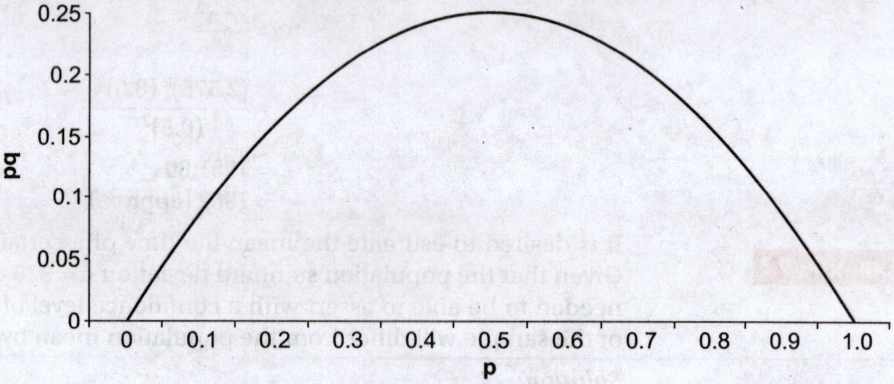

Let us consider a few examples for determining a sample size while estimating the population proportion.

Example 9.4

A market researcher for a consumer electronics company would like to study the television viewing habits of the residents of a particular, small city. What sample size is needed if he wishes to be 95 per cent confident of being within ± 0.035 of the true proportion who watch the evening news on at least three weeknights if no previous estimate is available?

Solution:

95 per cent confidence ⇒ Z = 1.96

$e = \pm .035$

$$n = \frac{1}{4}\frac{Z^2}{e^2}$$

$$= \frac{1}{4}\frac{(1.96)^2}{(.035)^2}$$

$$= 784$$

Example 9.5

A manager of a department store would like to study women's spending per year on cosmetics. He is interested in knowing the population proportion of women who purchase their cosmetics primarily from his store. If he wants to have a 90 per cent confidence of estimating the true proportion to be within ± 0.045, what sample size is needed?

Solution:

$$90 \text{ per cent confidence} \Rightarrow Z = 1.645$$
$$e = \pm .045$$
$$n = \frac{1}{4}\frac{Z^2}{e^2}$$
$$= \frac{1}{4}\frac{(1.645)^2}{(.045)^2}$$
$$= 334.0772$$
$$= 335 \text{ (approx.)}$$

Example 9.6 A consumer electronics company wants to determine the job satisfaction levels of its employees. For this, they ask a simple question, 'Are you satisfied with your job?' It was estimated that no more than 30 per cent of the employees would answer yes. What should be the sample size for this company to estimate the population proportion to ensure a 95 per cent confidence in result, and to be within 0.04 of the true population proportion?

Solution:

$$95 \text{ per cent confidence} \Rightarrow Z = 1.96$$
$$e = 0.04$$
$$p = 0.3$$
$$q = 0.7$$
$$n = \frac{Z^2 pq}{e^2}$$
$$= \frac{(1.96)^2 \times 0.3 \times 0.7}{(0.04)^2}$$
$$= 504.21$$
$$= 505 \text{ (approx.)}$$

Points to be noted for sample size determination

There are certain issues to be kept in mind before applying the formulas for the determination of sample size in this chapter. First of all, these formulas are applicable for simple random sampling only. Further, they relate to the sample size needed for the estimation of a particular characteristic of interest. In a survey, a researcher needs to estimate several characteristics of interests and each one of them may require a different sample size. In case the universe is divided into different strata, the accuracy required for determining the sample size for each strata may be different. However, the present method will not able to serve the requirement. Lastly, the formulas for sample size must be based upon adequate information about the universe.

CONCEPT CHECK

1. Discuss convenience sampling and purposive sampling.
2. What is quota sampling?
3. What are the various methods of determining the sample size in practice?

SUMMARY

- Surveys are useful in information collection. The analysis of the collected information is useful in finding answers to the research questions. The survey respondents should be selected using appropriate and right procedures. The process of selecting the right individuals, objects or events for the study is known as sampling. Before understanding the various issues pertaining to sampling, it is appropriate to understand the various related concepts like population, sampling frame, sample, sampling unit, sampling and census.
- The concept of sampling is used in our day-to-day life. An alternative to sample is census where each and every element of the population (universe) is examined. There are many advantages of sampling over complete enumeration. While estimating the population parameter using sample results, the researcher may incur two types of error—sampling and non-sampling error.
- The process of selecting samples from the population is referred to as sampling design. There are two types of sampling designs—probability sampling design and non-probability sampling design. Probability sampling designs are used in a conclusive research whereas non-probability sampling designs are appropriate for an exploratory research. In a probability sampling design, each and every element of the population has a known chance of being selected in the sample, whereas that is not the case with a non-probability sampling design.
- There are five probability sampling designs—the simple random sampling with replacement, simple random sampling without replacement, systematic sampling, stratified random sampling and cluster sampling. Each of them has its own merits and demerits. Under the non-probability sampling designs, the methods like *convenience sampling, judgemental sampling, snowball sampling* and *quota sampling* are discussed.
- The various methods of determining sample size are discussed and the actual determination of a sample size is shown using a confidence interval approach. The sample size for estimating the population mean and proportion is illustrated with the help of examples.

KEY TERMS

- Census
- Cluster sampling
- Convenience sampling
- Disproportionate allocation scheme
- Judgemental sampling
- Non-probability sampling design
- Non-sampling error
- Population
- Probability sampling design
- Proportionate allocation scheme
- Quota sampling
- Random number tables
- Representative sample
- Sample
- Sample size
- Sampling
- Sampling design
- Sampling error
- Sampling frame
- Sampling unit
- Simple random sampling with replacement
- Simple random sampling without replacement
- Snowball sampling
- Stratified sampling
- Systematic sampling

CHAPTER REVIEW QUESTIONS

Objective Type Questions

State whether the following statements are true (T) or false (F).

1. The effort required by a researcher in collecting a judgemental sample is more than that of a convenience sample.
2. If the number of control characteristics in a quota sampling is increased, it will result in decreasing the number of total cells.
3. In a cluster sampling, a few units are selected from every cluster of the population.
4. A convenience sample may contain more relevant units than a judgemental sample.
5. Simple random sampling does not play any role in proportionate stratified random sampling.

6. A judgemental sample provides a better representation of the population than a probability sample.
7. Non-probability methods are those in which the sample units are chosen purposefully.
8. A population which is being sampled is also called the universe.
9. Quota sampling is an example of a probability sampling design.
10. The difference between the sample result and the results obtained through a census using the identical procedure is known as sampling error.
11. Selection of every 15th subscriber to *Business India* is an example of random sampling.
12. When the confidence coefficient is increased from 95 to 99 per cent, the sample size increases roughly by half or more.
13. For using a random number table, the starting number is chosen arbitrarily.
14. There is no role of a simple random sampling in the proportionate stratified random sampling scheme.
15. Only the initial sample unit is chosen randomly in a systematic sampling.
16. A convenient sample is more likely to contain irrelevant units than a judgemental sample.
17. The sampling units are selected more flexibly in the probability sampling design than the non-probability sampling design.
18. Quota sampling is same as the stratified random sampling.
19. Judgement sampling is same as the purposive sampling.
20. Judgement samples can be used to make generalizations about a population of interest.

Conceptual Questions

1. What is the need of sampling? Discuss various probability sample techniques by giving their merits and demerits.
2. Explain the meanings of sample and sample design. Briefly discuss some most of the popular sample designs used in research.
3. What is the significance of sample selection in research? Explain the factors which should be considered while selecting a sample for research.
4. What is sampling? Discuss different sampling methods.
5. How do you distinguish between probability sampling and non-probability sampling?
6. What is a research design? Discuss the basis of stratification to be employed in sampling a public opinion on inflation.
7. Differentiate between the stratified random sampling and systematic sampling.
8. What is the significance of the concept of standard error in a sampling analysis?
9. Discuss any four sampling techniques with their relative merits and drawbacks.
10. Briefly describe the different types of sampling techniques with examples.
11. List the similarities and differences between the quota sampling and stratified sampling.
12. What is the main difference between a stratified sampling and cluster sampling?
13. What is a systematic sample? How is it selected? What are the advantages and disadvantages of systematic sample?

Application Questions

1. To determine the effectiveness of the advertising campaign for a new DVD player, the management would like to know what percentage of the households is aware of the new brand. The advertising agency thinks that this figure is as high as 70 per cent. The management would like a 95 per cent confidence interval and a margin of error not greater than plus or minus 2 per cent.
   (a) What sample size should be used for this study?
   (b) Suppose that the management wanted a 99 per cent confidence level with an error of plus or minus 3 per cent. How would the sample size change?
   (Given 95 per cent area is covered, within ± 1.96 standard deviations in a normal distribution. Also 99 per cent area is covered with ± 2.58 standard deviation in a normal distribution).
2. The management of a local restaurant wants to determine the average monthly amount spent by the households in restaurants. Some households in the target market do not spend anything at all, whereas other households spend as much as $ 300 per month. Management wants to be 95 per cent confident of the findings and does not want an error to exceed plus or minus $5.
   (a) What sample size should be used to determine the average monthly household expenditure?
   (b) After the survey was conducted, the average expenditure was found to be $ 90.30 and the standard deviation was $ 45. Construct a 95 per cent confidence interval. What can be said about the level of precision?
   (Given 95 per cent area is covered, within ± 1.96 standard deviations in a normal distribution).

3. A simple random sample has been drawn from a population of 2000 items. If we desire to estimate the percentage defective items with 1.5 per cent of the true value with 95 per cent probability, how large a sample needs to be drawn?
4. Determine the size of the sample for estimating the true weight of cereal containers for the universe with N = 5000 on the basis of the following information.
   (a) The variance of the weight equals 4 ounces on the basis of past records.
   (b) The error should be within 0.8 ounces of the true average weight with 99 per cent probability.

   Will there be any change in the size of the sample if we assume the population to be infinite?
5. An automobile insurance company wants to estimate from a sample about what proportion of its policy holders intend to buy a new car within the next six months. How large a sample is required to be able to assert with a 98 per cent confidence that the sample proportion and true proportion will differ by less than 0.025?
6. Explain the effect of the increasing degree of confidence from 90 to 95 per cent on the sample size when the standard error remains unchanged.
7. There is a residential locality where the residents comprise Hindus, Sikhs, Muslim, Jains and Christians. A survey is conducted to understand the food habits of the residents. Every 7th house is selected as the sample. Critically examine the sampling scheme.
8. Identify with a brief reasoning each of the following sampling methods.
   (a) The population of interest is in the alphabetical order. Starting with the 8th name, every 9th member thereafter was selected as a member of the sample. The sample, therefore, consisted of numbers 8, 17, 26, 35 and so on.
   (b) A large precinct was subdivided into 25 smaller areas. Then, five of these areas were selected at random, and residents in these five areas were interviewed.
   (c) Executives were subdivided into six groups—including banking executives, industrial executives, and insurance executives. Random samples were taken from each of these groups and the sample results were weighed according to the number in the group relative to the total.

CASE 9.1

MEHTA GARMENT COMPANY

Mr Mohan Mehta has a chain of restaurants in many cities of northern India and was interested in diversifying his business. His only son, Kamal, never wanted to be in the hospitality line. To settle Kamal into a line which would interest him, Mr Mehta decided to venture into garment manufacturing. He gave this idea to his son, who liked it very much. Kamal had already done a course in fashion designing and wanted to do something different for the consumers of this industry. An idea struck him that he should design garments for people who are very bulky but want a lean look after wearing readymade garments. The first thing that came to his mind was to have an estimate of people who wore large sized shirts (42 size and above) and large sized trousers (38 size and above).

A meeting was called of experts from the garment industry and a number of fashion designers to discuss on how they should proceed. A common concern for many of them was to know the size of such a market. Another issue that was bothering them was how to approach the respondents. It was believed that asking people about the size of their shirt or trouser may put them off and there may not be any worthwhile response. A suggestion that came up was that they should employ some observers at entrances of various malls and their job would be to look at people who walked into the malls and see whether the concerned person was wearing a big sized shirt or trouser. This would be a better way of approaching the respondents. This procedure would help them to estimate in a very simple way the proportion of people who wore big-sized garments.

QUESTIONS

1. Name the sampling design that is being used in the study.
2. What are the limitations of the design so chosen?
3. Can you suggest a better design?
4. What method of data collection is being employed?

CASE 9.2

HERBAL TOOTH POWDER

ABC Manufacturing Company had produced a herbal tooth powder five years back and was marketing the same in rural Punjab. The company is about 20 years old and is producing various toiletry products in Punjab. It had a name in the rural markets of Punjab. The herbal powder was launched only five years back and had shown a compound annual growth rate of 18 per cent. The CEO of the company, Mr Avtar Singh, was thinking of introducing the herbal tooth powder in the urban areas of Punjab.

Mr Singh got a preliminary research done with regard to the tooth powder market. The results of this research indicated that generally, people in urban areas preferred toothpaste instead of tooth powder. This was more so in case of young people below the age of 20 years. Mr Singh had a meeting with senior officials of the company and decided to get a research study conducted from a marketing research company with the following objectives:

- To estimate the proportion of population that used tooth powder.
- To understand the demographic and psychographic profile of people who used tooth powder.
- To understand the reasons for not using tooth powder.
- To get an understanding of the media habits of both the users and non-users of tooth powder.

The research team in the marketing research company defined the users of tooth powder as those who had bought tooth powder in the last six months. In order to select the users of tooth powder they conducted a preliminary study. A sample of 500 respondents was taken from Amritsar, Jalandhar, Ludhiana and Patiala. The results of the study indicated that out of the 500 respondents selected randomly, 20 per cent were below the age of 20. Out of the remaining 400 respondents, 30 per cent refused to participate in the study. Out of the remaining sample 60 per cent did not use tooth powder, 30 per cent bought it only once in a year or two and only 10 per cent of the respondents bought it at least once in six months. The cost of sampling 500 respondents was ₹40,000/-.

The company wanted to select 200 users from both Amritsar and Ludhiana, whereas 100 respondents were to be selected from Jalandhar and Patiala each. The remaining 300 users were to be selected from the remaining urban/semi-urban towns of Punjab. In brief, the marketing research company wanted a total sample of 900. It was argued that a large sample should be taken from larger cities.

A total budget of ₹4,00,000/- was allocated for the research, out of which ₹2,50,000/- was for the purpose of field work. One of the members of the research team indicated that the total budget for the field work would not be sufficient to get the desired number of users of tooth powder. He suggested that chemist shops and 'General *Kirana* Stores' could be contacted for identifying the users.

QUESTIONS

1. Will the money allocated for the fieldwork be sufficient to get the desired size of the sample from various towns of Punjab as mentioned in the case?
2. If the amount is not sufficient, how many users can be contacted with the given budget?
3. How would you define the population and the sampling frame in this case?
4. Do you agree with the statement that a large sample should be taken from towns with a large population?
5. Would it be advisable to contact general *kirana* stores and chemist shops for identifying the users?

CASE 9.3

YASEER RESTAURANT

Yaseer Ahmed retired as a chef from a 5-star hotel in Delhi and returned to his hometown Ramveerpur (population: 5 lakh) in Uttar Pradesh (UP). However, he found it difficult to settle back into the community. He realized that he needed a vocation to keep him occupied, otherwise, he might go into depression. He was still clueless about what to do, when his friend Samar Dewan visited him and asked him why he looked so morose. Yaseer explained his dilemma and asked his friend for advice, as Samar understood Ramveerpur and its residents better.

Samar pondered over the problem, and suggested that considering Yaseer's expertise in exotic cuisine, he should think about setting up a restaurant serving non-vegetarian food. The enterprise would be perfect, as Ramveerpur hardly had any restaurant serving good non-vegetarian cuisine. Yaseer liked the idea very much and thought the business would be lucrative and interesting. But before putting the idea into practice, he felt that it was important to have a rough estimate of the non-vegetarian population who went out for meals in a restaurant at least once in a typical week.

Samar recalled a hotel industry report, according to which Ramveerpur's population comprised 15 per cent Muslims, 20 per cent Sikhs, 10 per cent Jains, and 55 per cent Hindus. It was known that generally, Muslims were non-vegetarian, whereas 95 per cent of the Sikhs were non-vegetarian. The Jain population was totally vegetarian, whereas 20 per cent of the Hindu population was non-vegetarian. Further, the result of a report on hotel industry had indicated that more than 2 per cent of the population of the town ate out at least once a week.

The data definitely indicated a sound and profitable business opportunity. However, Yaseer felt that before setting up a restaurant serving non-vegetarian food, a quick survey should be conducted. He wanted to carry out a survey of the households to understand their preferences for various cuisines. All the households were assigned a serial number. He decided to survey 1000 households. His plan was to contact every 100th household in a particular locality and ask for their eating preferences.

QUESTIONS

1. What type of sampling design is being used in this case? Critically examine it and explain whether it could lead to any sampling frame error.
2. Suggest an alternative sampling design. Also indicate how the process must be carried out to execute your suggested design.
3. Suggest the possible sample size that should be taken out from each community and why?

Answers to Objective Type Questions

1. True	2. False	3. False	4. False	5. False
6. True	7. True	8. True	9. False	10. True
11. False	12. True	13. True	14. False	15. True
16. True	17. False	18. False	19 True	20. False

BIBLIOGRAPHY

Aaker, David A, V Kumar and George S Day. *Marketing Research,* 7th edn. Singapore: John Wiley & Sons, Inc., 2001.

Bhattacharyya, Dipak Kumar. *Research Methodology.* New Delhi: Excel Books, 2006.

Churchill, Gilbert A Jr and Dawn Lacobucci. *Marketing Research Methodological Foundations,* 8th edn. New Delhi: Thomson-South Western, 2002.

Cooper, Donald R. *Business Research Methods.* New Delhi: Tata McGraw-Hill Publishing Company Ltd., 2006.

Gay, L R. *Research Methods for Business and Management.* New York: Macmillan Publishing Company, 1992.

Kinnear, Thomas C and James R Taylor. *Marketing Research—An Applied Approach,* 3rd edn. New York: McGraw-Hill Book Company, 1987.

Kothari, C R. *Research Methodology: Methods and Techniques.* New Delhi: Wiley Eastern, 1990.

Malhotra, Naresh K. *Marketing Research—An Applied Orientation,* 5th edn. New Delhi: Pearson Education, 2007.

Nargundkar, Rajendra. *Marketing Research—Text and Cases,* 3rd edn. New Delhi: Tata McGraw Hill Publishing Company Ltd, 2008.

Nation, Jack R. *Research Methods.* New Jersey: Prentice Hall, 1997.

Parasuraman, A, Dhruv Grewal and R Krishnan. *Marketing Research (First Indian Adaptation).* New Delhi: Biztantra, 2004.

Sharma B A V, Ravindra D Prasad and P Satyanarayana (eds). *Research Methods in Social Sciences.* New Delhi: Sterling Publishers Private Ltd, 1983.

Saunders, Mark. *Research Methods for Business Students.* Singapore: Pearson Education (Pte.) Ltd., 2003.

Sekaram, Uma. *Research Methods for Business: A Skill Building Approach.* Singapore: John Wiley & Sons (Asia) Pte Ltd, 2003.

Tripathi, P C. *A Textbook of Research Methodology in Social Sciences.* New Delhi: Sultan Chand & Sons, 2007.

Trochim, William M. *Research Methods.* New Delhi: Biztantra, 2003.

Zikmund, William G. *Business Research Methods.* Fort Worth: Dryden Press, 2000.

10 CHAPTER

Data Processing

Learning Objectives

By the end of the chapter, you should be able to:

1. Understand the processing of the data collected before the data analysis.
2. Understand and carry out the checking and editing of the primary data as well as be able to carry out the necessary fieldwork required.
3. Code both the structured and unstructured questionnaires following certain guidelines.
4. Carry out the tabulation and entry of data in the required format.
5. Carry out preliminary statistical preparation of data.

'Whew, thank God we have the data under control now', said Sanjeev Chakrapani in a relaxed manner. 'Ok ladies and gentlemen, clear your tables and move out, I want everyone back on their seats at 8.30 tomorrow morning.' With collective grunts and groans, everyone trudged out of the Mind Site office at 1.30 a.m.

Sana waited for the BPO van of her friend Saraswati's office across the road, which she knew would be leaving soon. Around 2.00 a.m. Saraswati saw Sana outside her office and asked her what she was doing in the office at this late hour. Sana said, 'It's a long story, I'll tell you on the way back. By the way, I hope I can hitch a ride in your van.' 'No problem', said Saraswati and told the driver, 'Madam will also travel with us'.

'So, what happened?' asked Saraswati once the two had got into the van. 'Do you remember the educational research we had got for Sutlej Learning?' 'I think so…', said Saraswati.

'Well, we conducted tests in English, Maths, Science and Bangla for them in 28 schools in West Bengal. This was to assess the level of conceptual learning in these subjects. The tests were designed by school teachers who had taught from the Madhyamic Board syllabi. The questions were all translated into Bangla. Interestingly, even for the English questions the instructions were in Bangla'. 'Oh my God!' Saraswati exclaimed laughingly.

'Yes, well the assessment was done on 5,465 students and we had 5th, 6th, 8th and 9th grade scores. Once the tests were administered, we had to give it to some Bengali school teachers with the scoring key to evaluate and grade. The instructions for grading were given to them and they were told to correct and then give them a score based upon the answer. The scores were to be given as numbers.'

'Well, the corrected answer scripts arrived by courier the day before and we were all working on the double to enter all the marks so that an analysis could be done. Once we had entered all the data in excel, Dr Charu, our research supervisor ran some preliminary checks and calculated the overall score for students as well as section- and class-wise scores. She told everyone, 'I am surprised the schools in Bengal seem to be teaching very well and students have done very well. The NGOs (non-governmental organizations) are doing a commendable job by helping in education.'

'Hitler Chakra' (Sanjeev Chakrapani) was really happy and ordered coffee and samosas to celebrate a job well done and magnanimously told us,' Folks you may take the weekend off, and asked Charu, Why don't you show us the average scores across the classes? So, Charu showed us the figures on the OHP connected to her laptop. First we saw the Bangla score, then Maths and Science and then she came to English. The figures were really satisfying as there was no score less than 78.8 per cent. Then came the bombshell with English—5th grade had an average of 87.7 per cent, 6th, 79.9 per cent and then 8th had 103.4 per cent. We all sat upright and there was a pin-drop silence. How could the score in a 100-mark paper be 103.4 per cent?'

'Chakra yelled, Show us the column of the final grades of the students.' And, guess what, there were students with overall 150, 120, 135 and even 204. Emergency was declared. All samosas and coffee went to the dustbin, and all weekend plans flew out of the window.'

'But what had happened, how can someone make so many errors in a data entry?' asked Saraswati.

'Errors in one entry? No, when we opened the data files it was like a can of worms, there was not a single sheet without error. And, in most subjects a good many students were getting marks over 100 in a 100-mark paper.'

'Laila, the new intern, suddenly had a brainwave and said that we should look at the way scoring had been done in the answer scripts. Now, this suggestion was dangerous as all the coding for the answers had been done by Lord Chakra himself. Anyway, so we were told to examine a few scripts at random. And guess what happened?'

'There were 5- and 8-mark questions. If a person got most of the 5-mark question right, he was to be given a score of 4. The teacher had followed the instructions but had marked it as 8 and for an 8-mark question where she was supposed to give a 7, she had marked it 9'.

'Hey, do not confuse me Sana. Is this a riddle or a mystery? Please explain.'

'Look', said Sana, 'The teacher marked four and seven only but the numerals she wrote were in Bangla, where four is written as 8 and seven is written as 9. Now, at our end, when we entered the data we entered 8 and 9, which is more than the maximum score for the question. And obviously, the ultimate result was a 100+ score.'

'So, we as a team cross-checked all the scores on the excel sheets and wherever this discrepancy of 8 or 9 was found, we went back to the answer script and manually corrected each entry. The final scores, when we summed them across groups and classes, were dismal and, as expected, were mostly below 50 per cent across all the subjects.

So finally we have been let loose, to report on duty tomorrow morning and double check for the errors once more before the presentation for the client is made ready.'

'What a freak case, but just imagine if no one had seen the 100+ score, you would have been in deep trouble had the client discovered the mistake at a later date.'

Saraswati is right, because a freak error in entering the data could have had major repercussions in the outcome of the study and the subsequent conclusions. The critical job of the researcher begins after the data has been collected. He has to use this information to assess whether he had been correct or incorrect while making certain assumptions in the form of the hypotheses at the beginning of the study. The raw data that has been collected must be refined and structured in such a format that it can lend itself to statistical enquiry. This process of preparing the data for an analysis is a structured and sequential process (Figure 10.1).

The process starts by validating the measuring instrument, which could be questionnaire or any other qualitative technique as discussed in Chapter 6. This is followed by editing, coding, classifying and tabulating the obtained data. Sometimes, it might be essential to carry out some statistical modification of the data in order to be able to increase its generalizibility on the population under study. This is critical

FIGURE 10.1
The data-preparation process

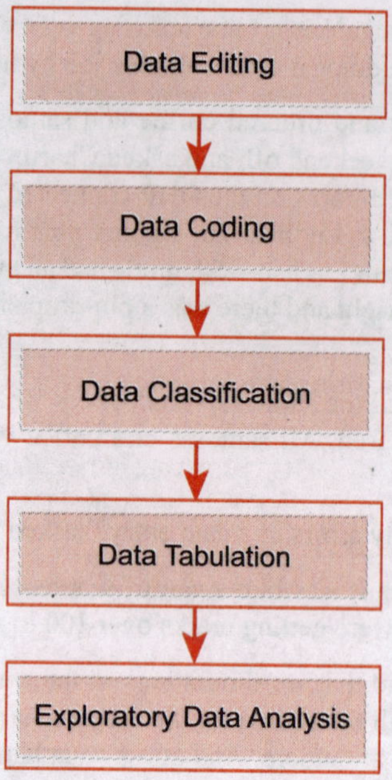

especially in applied research problems. The researcher should, then select an appropriate data analysis strategy.

The final data analysis strategy differs from the preliminary plan of data analysis due to the information and insights gained since the formulation of the preliminary plan. Data preparation should begin as soon as the first batch of questionnaires is received from the field, while the fieldwork is still going on. Thus, if any problems are detected, the fieldwork can be modified to incorporate the corrective action.

FIELDWORK VALIDATION

LEARNING OBJECTIVE 1
Understand the processing of the data collected before the data analysis.

The first step in the processing begins post the questionnaire/or primary data survey. The researcher needs to validate the fieldwork to check whether the execution of the study was handled properly. Thus, he must meticulously go over all the raw data forms and check them for errors and find out whether in the conducted interviews or schedules a standardized set of instructions and reporting was followed or not. As we stated earlier in Chapter 8, considerable validation is done at the pilot testing stage of the questionnaire formation. The significance of the validation becomes more important in the following cases:

- In case the form had been translated into another language, expert analysis to see whether the meaning of the questions in the two measures is the same or not. The second validation is done by measuring the reliability index of the original and the translated form.
- The second case could be that the questionnaire survey has to be done at multiple locations and one has outsourced to an outside research agency. In this case, it might be essential to carry out checks during the fieldwork as well to ensure that the process being followed is correct. As here there is both a time and a cost element involved, in case the investigators are erring it needs to be corrected immediately.

Post the survey there might be instances when the survey questionnaire cannot be used for analysis for multiple causes. It might be that:

- The answers that have been obtained and the question instructions that were given, such as qualifying instructions like, 'in case answer is __________ please answer the next set of questions, else go to question __________.' Were completely overlooked.
- The respondent seems to have used the same response category for all the questions; for example there is a tendency on a five point scale to give 3 as the answer for all questions.
- The form that is received back is incomplete, in the sense that either the person has not filled the answer to all questions, especially the open-ended ones, or in case of a multiple-page questionnaire, one or more pages are missing.
- The questionnaire is filled by someone who is not a representative of the population under study. For example, in a study on two-wheeler owners perception of Tata small car, Nano, people who have either no vehicle currently or have a small car might have filled in the questionnaire.
- The filled-in form is received after the deadline for receiving the questionnaires has elapsed and the researcher is on the data analysis and interpretation stage.
- The forms received are not in the proportion of the sampling plan. For example, instead of an equal representation from government and private sector employees, 65 per cent of the forms are from the government sector. In such a case the researcher either would need to discard the extra forms or get an equal number filled-in from private sector employees.

DATA EDITING

LEARNING OBJECTIVE 2

Understand and carry out the checking and editing of the primary data as well as be able to carry out the necessary fieldwork required.

Once the validation process has been completed, the next step is the editing of the raw data obtained. In this stage, all detectable errors and omissions have been examined and the necessary actions have been taken. While carrying out the editing the researcher needs to ensure that:

- The data obtained is complete in all respects.
- It is accurate in terms of information recorded and responses sought.
- Questionnaires are legible and are correctly deciphered, especially the open-ended questions.
- The response format is in the form that was instructed.
- The data is structured in a manner that entering the information will not be a problem.

To ensure that data screening and cleaning, which is essentially the requirement of the editing process, has been carried out, the researcher needs to carry out the process at two levels, the first of these is field editing and the second is central editing.

Field Editing

Raw data validation ensures that all detectable errors and omissions have been examined and the necessary steps have been taken.

Usually, the preliminary editing of the information obtained is done by the field investigators or supervisors. It is advisable that at the end of every field day the investigator(s) review the filled forms for any inconsistencies, non-response, illegible responses or incomplete questionnaires. This is to ensure that the fallacies found can be corrected immediately, as they are fresh in the investigator's mind and also because the recall would be better. Also, in case the investigator needs to contact the respondent who filled in the form, the clarifications required would be much easier.

The other advantage is that regular field editing ensures that one may also be able to check if the interviewer or the surveyor is able to handle the process of instructions and probing correctly or not. It might also happen that certain terms or abbreviations have been used in the instrument on which the investigator is not clear and could misinterpret the instructions. This most often happens with branching and skip questions. Thus, the process ensures that the researcher can advise and train the investigator on how to administer the questionnaire correctly. This, however, is only possible in case of a face-to-face interaction and not in the mailed surveys.

Some researchers, in order to ensure the authenticity of the data obtained, sometimes, carry out random interviews with the same respondents to cross-check whether the administration process was accurate.

Centralized In-house Editing

The second level of editing takes place at the researcher's end. The in-house editing can be handled by the researcher alone or by various members in the research team, as the case may be. It is recommended that even in a single-researcher study, the data should be screened by an outsider as well. At this stage there are two kinds of typical problems that the researcher might encounter.

First, one might detect an incorrect entry. For example, in case of a five-point scale one might find that someone has used a value more than 5. In another case, one might be asking a question like, 'how many days do you travel out of the city in a week?' and the person says '15 days'. Here one can carry out a quick frequency check of the responses; this will immediately detect an unexpected value. As for the above case, the frequency analysis would have shown an entry of 15, and then one can screen the column in which the data for the question has been entered for 15.

The second and the major problem that most researchers face is that of 'armchair interviewing' or a fudged interview. One way to handle this is to first scroll the answers to the open-ended questions, as generally if the investigator is filling in multiple forms faking these would be difficult. Thus, these could be highlighted with a different colour and cross-checked with the investigator or the respondent. In fact, it is advisable that wherever the researcher is making corrections he/she should use a different colour as that would indicate it being different from the original.

In fact, one should highlight what needs to be cross-checked (yellow colour) and also highlight what is corrected (red colour). It is also advisable, in case of a team of researchers, that the highlighting formats are shared as a uniform scheme by all.

The researcher has some standard processes available to him to carry out the editing process. These are discussed below. It is to be remembered that these are not absolute steps as sometimes it might be essential to troubleshoot specifically for some peculiar problems (as in the opening vignette) that the person encounters in his/her study.

Backtracking involves returning to the field and to the respondents, so as to follow up the unsatisfactory responses.

Backtracking: The best and the most efficient way of handling unsatisfactory responses is to return to the field, and go back to the respondents. This technique is best used for industrial surveys, where it is easier to track the respondent, who can be persuaded to give answers to the non-response or illegible answers. In individual surveys, this becomes a little difficult, as sometimes the person might have indicated only the locality he lives in and there is no contact detail. Another issue in this is that the antecedent states during the two administrations might be different and these could affect the answers the person would give at the second conduction.

Allocating missing values: This is a contingency plan that the researcher might need to adopt in case going back to the field is not possible. Then the option might be to assign a missing value to the blanks or the unsatisfactory responses. However, this works in case:

- The number of blank or wrong answers is small.
- The number of such responses per person is small.
- The important parameters being studied do not have too many blanks, otherwise the sample size for those variables becomes too small for generalizations.

Plug value: In cases such as the third condition above, when the variable being studied is the key variable, then sometimes the researcher might insert a *plug value*. Sometimes one can plug an average or a neutral value in such cases, for example a 3 for a five-point scale. Sometimes a decision rule based upon probability could be established and the researcher might decide on a thumb rule (for example, for a yes/no question, he might decide to put 'yes' the first time he encounters a missing value or no at the second and so on). Another way to handle this is to conduct an exploratory data analysis and see what the ratio of yes to no answers is and accordingly establish the decision rule.

Sometimes, the respondents' pattern of responses to other questions is used to extrapolate and calculate an appropriate response for the missing answer. Here, it may become a little subjective as the researcher needs to sift through the data and infer and predict the responses the person would have given had he/she answered the questions. There are statistical software and programmes available today to extrapolate and ascribe values for such missing responses.

Discarding unsatisfactory responses: If the response sheet has too many blanks/illegible or multiple responses for a single answer, the form is not worth correcting and editing. Hence, it is much better to completely discard the whole questionnaire. If too many forms are discarded then the sample for the study might become too small for an analysis or generalization, so, here it is advisable to carry out another round of field visits. However, the discarding of the forms might lead to elimination from the population of the group which had a contrary or a negative opinion than the ones who completed the forms. In a research study on orange juice, it happened that when the response to a product change proposition (more pulp in the drink) was studied and the completed forms were considered, they were all filled by people who liked the change, while those who did not answer all the questions had their forms rejected. Finally, when the new product was launched there were limited takers for it, as the proportion of people who did not like the drink in the studied sample was too small as compared to what existed in the actual market-place.

CONCEPT CHECK

1. Explain the steps involved in fieldwork validation.
2. How is data editing conducted?
3. Explain field editing and centralized in-house editing.

CODING

LEARNING OBJECTIVE 3
Code both the structured and unstructured questionnaires following certain guidelines.

The process of identifying and denoting a numeral to the responses given by a respondent is called coding. This is essentially done in order to facilitate the researcher's use for interpreting the answers and classifying and then subsequently recording the data from the questionnaire on a spreadsheet on the computer. It is advisable for the sake of computation to assign a numeric code even for the categorical data (e.g., gender). In fact, subsequently we will learn that even for open-ended questions, which are in a statement form, we will try to categorize them into numbers. The reason for doing this is that the quantification and graphic representation of data into charts and figures becomes easier.

Usually, the codes that have been formulated are organized into fields, records and files. For example, the gender of a person is one *field* and the codes used could be 0 for males and 1 for females. All related fields, for example, all the demographic variables like age, gender, income, marital status and education could be one *record*. Sometimes the researcher might not be interested in keeping multiple records and might decide to have all the answers a single respondent has given on the questionnaire as a single record. The records of the entire sample under study form a single *file*. The data that is entered in the spreadsheet, such as on EXCEL, is in the form of a data matrix, which is simply a rectangular arrangement of the data in rows and columns. Here, every row represents a single case or record. For example, consider the following representation from a study on two-wheeler buyers (Table 10.1):

The process of identifying and denoting a numeral to the responses given by a respondent is called **coding**.

TABLE 10.1
Sample record: Excel sheet for two-wheeler owners

Unit Column 1	Occupation Column 2	Vehicle Column 3	Km/day Column 4	Marital status Column 5	Family size Column 6
1	4	1	20	1	3
2	3	2	25	2	1
3	5	1	25	1	4
4	2	1	15	2	2
5	4	2	20	2	4
6	5	2	35	2	6
7	1	1	40	1	3
8	5	2	20	2	4

It is advisable to prepare a **schema** in advance to simplify and effectively manage the data entry process.

Here, the data matrix reveals that each field is denoted on the column head and each case record is to be read along the row. The data in the first column represents the unique identification given to a particular respondent (also marked on his/her questionnaire). The second column has data entered on the basis of a predetermined coding scheme where every occupation is given a numeral value (for example, 1 stands for government service and 5 stands for student and so on). Column 3 has 1 representing a motorcycle and 2 representing a scooter. The next value is of the average number of kilometres a person travels per day.
This is followed by the marital status, with 1 signifying unmarried and 2 married. The last column is again a ratio scale data with the number of family members. The researcher can enter the data on the spreadsheet of the software package he/she is using for the analysis. However, in case the data is being entered by the field investigator or someone not acquainted with the software package, one can also use a spreadsheet programme such as EXCEL to enter the data as most software have the provision of importing data from an EXCEL spreadsheet.

Codebook formulation: In order to simplify and effectively manage the data entry process, it is essential to prepare a schema in advance for entering the records in the spreadsheet. This formal standardization or the coding scheme for all the variables under study is called a *codebook*. Generally, while designing the rules, care must be taken to decide on some categories that are:

- *Appropriate to the research objective:* For example, in the two-wheeler study when the study was to be conducted on people in socio-economic classification (SEC)

A and B, then the occupation and education categories had to be comparable to the ones established in the classification. Secondly, if the comparison is to be done amongst people in different age groups then the age-class intervals (discussed later in the chapter) should be representative of the comparison to be carried out.

- *Comprehensive:* As far as possible, options should be given to the respondent in the closed-ended questions as probable response categories. This can be ensured by a thorough exploratory study and later on, after the conduction of the pilot study, which might result in discovering other responses in the 'any other ________.' These, then, can be written as independent response options in the final questionnaire.
- *Mutually exclusive:* The categories and codes devised must be exclusive or clearly different from each other. This will be further discussed in the classification rules that the person should employ.
- *Single variable entry:* The response that is being entered and the code for it should indicate only a single variable. For example, a 'working single mother' might seem an apparently simple category which one could code as 'occupation.' However, it needs three columns—occupation, marital status and family life cycle. So, one needs to have three different codes to enter this information.

Based on the above rules, one creates a code book that can be effectively used by the coders. This would generally contain information on the question number, variable name, response descriptors and coding instructions and the column descriptor. Table 10.2 gives an extract from a questionnaire designed to measure the consumer buying behaviour for the ready-to-eat food products. The coding instructions for the qualifying and the demographic variables are presented here.

Designating numeral codes to the designed responses before administration is called **pre-coding**.

As we have read in the earlier chapter, a questionnaire can have both closed-ended and open-ended questions. The process of coding the two kinds of questions is very different and requires a detailed discussion. When the questions are structured and the response categories are prescribed then one does what is called *pre-coding*, i.e., designating numeral codes to the designed responses before administration. However, if the questions are structured and the answers are open ended and not determined in advance, one needs to decide on the codes after the administration of the survey. This is called *post-coding* and requires skilled interpretation and categorization of the responses into homogenous grouped response categories and then these are assigned a numeric code.

Coding Closed-ended Structured Questions

The method of coding for structured questions is easier as the response categories are decided in advance. The researcher simply assigns a code for every answer for each question and specifies the appropriate field and columns in which the response codes are to be noted. The coding method to be followed for different kinds of questions is discussed below.

Dichotomous questions: For dichotomous questions, which are on a nominal scale, the responses can be binary, for example:

Do you eat ready-to-eat food? Yes = 1; No = 0.

This means if someone eats ready-to-eat food he/she will be given a score of 1 and if not, then 0.

TABLE 10.2 Codebook extract for ready-to-eat food study

Question No.	Variable Name	Coding Instruction	Symbol used for Variable Name
1.	Buy ready-to-eat food products	Yes = 1 No = 0	X1
2.	Use ready-to-eat food products	Yes = 1 No = 0	X2
22.	Age	Less than 20 years = 1, 21 to 26 years = 2, 27 to 35 years = 3, 36 to 45 years = 4, More than 45 years = 5	X22
23.	Gender	Male = 1 Female = 2	X23
24.	Marital status	Single = 1 Married = 2 Divorced/widow = 3	X24
25.	No. of children	Exact no. to be written	X25
26.	Family size	One to two = 1, Three to five = 2, Six and more = 3	X26
27.	Monthly household income	₹20,000 to ₹34,999 = 1, ₹35,000 to ₹50,000 = 2, ₹50,001 to ₹74,999 = 3 ₹75,000 and above = 4	X27
28.	Education	Less than graduation = 1 Graduation = 2 Postgraduation and above = 3	X28
29.	Occupation	Student = 1 Businessman = 2 Professional = 3 Service = 4 Housewife = 5 Others = 6	X29

Ranking questions: For ranking questions where there are multiple objects to be ranked, the person will have to make multiple columns, with column numbers equaling the number of objects to be ranked. For example, for the question on ranking TV serials in Chapter 8, the codebook would be as follows:

Q. No.	Variable Name	Coding Instructions	Variable Name
1.	*Balika Vadhu*	Number from 1-10	X10a
2.	*Sathiya*	Number from 1-10	X10b
3.	*Sasural Genda Phool*	Number from 1-10	X10c
4.	*Bidai*	Number from 1-10	X10d
5.	*Pathshala*	Number from 1-10	X10e
6.	*Bandini*	Number from 1-10	X10f
7.	*Lapataganj*	Number from 1-10	X10g
8.	*Sajan GharJaana Hai*	Number from 1-10	X10h
9.	*Tere liye*	Number from 1-10	X10i
10.	*Uttaran*	Number from 1-10	X10j

Checklists/multiple responses: In questions that permit a large number of responses, each possible response option should be assigned a separate column. For example, consider the following question:

Which of the following newspapers do you read? (Tick all that you read.)

The Times of India ________
The Hindustan Times ________
Mail Today ________
The Indian Express ________
Deccan Chronicle ________
The Asian Age ________
Mint ________

For this question, the number of columns required are seven, one for each newspaper. The coding instructions for each column would be as follows: in case the person ticks on a name, the paper = 1, and in case he does not tick, the paper = 0.

Scaled questions: For questions that are on a scale, usually an interval scale, the question/statement will have a single column and the coding instruction would indicate numerical assignment, i.e., what number needs to be allocated for the response options given in the scale. Consider the following question from Chapter 8.

Please indicate level of your agreement with the following statements.

	Compared to the Past (5–10 years)	SA	A	N	D	SD
1.	The individual customer today shops more					
2.	The consumer is well informed about market offerings					
3.	The consumer knows what he/she wants to buy before entering the store					
4.	The consumer today has more money to spend					
5.	There are more shopping options available to the consumer today					

SA – Strongly agree; A – Agree; N – Neutral; D – Disagree; SD – Strongly disagree.

The codebook for this will look as follows:

Col. no.	Variable Name	Coding Instructions	Variable Name
1.	Individual shops more	A number from 1 to 5 SA = 5, A = 4, N = 3, D = 2, SD = 1	X1a
2.	Well informed	- do -	X1b
3.	Knows what to buy	- do -	X1c
4.	More spending money	- do -	X1d
5.	More shopping options	- do -	X1e

The coding instructions for comparative scales would be slightly different. Consider the following comparative question:

Please rate Domino's and other pizza restaurants you frequent on the basis of your satisfaction level on an 11-point scale, based upon the following parameters: (1 = Extremely poor, 6 = Average, 11 = Extremely good). Circle your response.

a.	Variety of menu options	1	2	3	4	5	6	7	8	9	10	11
b.	Value for money	1	2	3	4	5	6	7	8	9	10	11
c.	Speed of service (delivery time)	1	2	3	4	5	6	7	8	9	10	11
d.	Promotional offers	1	2	3	4	5	6	7	8	9	10	11
e.	Food quality	1	2	3	4	5	6	7	8	9	10	11
f.	Brand name	1	2	3	4	5	6	7	8	9	10	11
g.	Quality of service	1	2	3	4	5	6	7	8	9	10	11
h.	Convenience in terms of takeaway location	1	2	3	4	5	6	7	8	9	10	11
i.	Friendliness of the salesperson on the phone	1	2	3	4	5	6	7	8	9	10	11
j.	Quality of packaging	1	2	3	4	5	6	7	8	9	10	11
k.	Adaptation to Indian taste	1	2	3	4	5	6	7	8	9	10	11
l.	Side orders/appetizers	1	2	3	4	5	6	7	8	9	10	11

Here, the number of columns required is not 12 but 2 (Domino's and others) X 12, that is 24 columns. The respondent is supposed to use the same parameters and the same scale but for each he is supposed to make one circle for Domino's and one for the other pizza restaurant. In case of multiple brands being rated on the same parameters it would be:

X_n (where X = number of parameters and n = number of objects being evaluated on each parameter).

Missing values: It is advisable to use a standard format for signifying a non-response or a missing value. For example, a code of 9 could be used for a single-column variable, 99 for a double-column variable, and 999 for a three character variable and so on. The researcher must take care as far as possible to use a value that is starkly different from the valid responses. This is one of the reasons why 9 is suggested. However, in case you have a scale that is like the one above, 9 cannot be used as a missing value.

Coding Open-ended Structured Questions

There are no **predefined response categories** for the coding of open-ended questions. This is due to the fact that they are unpredictable in terms of insufficient information.

The coding of open-ended questions is quite difficult as they are unpredictable in terms of insufficient information or a lack of hypotheses, which is why there are no predefined response categories. As discussed earlier, the respondents' exact answers are noted on the questionnaire. Then the researcher (either individually or as a team) looks for patterns and assigns a category code. Sometimes the researcher does what is termed as test tabulation, where he randomly looks at the answers from 20 per cent of the sample data and attempts to give codes to each of the responses identified. When deciding on the codes he/she must keep the criteria of appropriateness, exhaustive categorization, mutually exclusive categories and single distribution variable as the guiding principles.

The following example is a question that was used to study the reasons attributed to the lean management implementation in an organization.

If you think lean was a success so far, please specify three most significant reasons that have contributed to its success in your opinion.

As these were based upon the three most important reasons to be indicated, each case/record might have multiple answers. Thus, based upon the responses obtained, for the above question, the following post-code book was created:

Col. No.	Variable Name	Coding Instructions	Variable Name
63	Improvement at work place by eliminating waste.	Yes = 1 No = 0	X63a
64	To meet increasing demands of customers	Yes = 1 No = 0	X63b
65	To improve quality	Yes = 1 No = 0	X63c
66	To achieve corporate goal	Yes = 1 No = 0	X63d
67	It reduces cycle time of the manufacturing and production	Yes = 1 No = 0	X63e
68	Reduced response time	Yes = 1 No = 0	X63f
69	Enhanced innovation and creativity	Yes = 1 No = 0	X63g

When deciding on the codes, at times, it may be essential to use a code even when no one has mentioned them. Here, it may be critical as one of the hypothesized parameters has been negated. For example, for a question:

Why do you eat organic food products?

'Organic food is fashionable' was a reason why the researcher believes that people consume it. Thus, one of the predetermined/post-coded category coded as 1 was this. Along with these, the researcher might post-code the responses received. However, it may so happen that no one chose this option, thus while interpreting his findings one can state *that no one consumes the food simply because it is fashionable to do so.*

CONCEPT CHECK

1. Explain coding.
2. Discuss the various categories which constitute code book formulation.
3. How does one code the open-ended structured questions?

CLASSIFICATION AND TABULATION OF DATA

LEARNING OBJECTIVE 4

Carry out the tabulation and entry of data in the required format.

Sometimes, the data obtained from the primary instrument is bulky and voluminous and even structured response categories become tedious to interpret. In such cases, the researcher might decide to reduce the information into homogenous categories. This is essentially like post-coding of the open-ended questions, but here the grouping would be based upon structured questions. This method of arrangement is called classification of data. This can be done on the basis of common attributes or on the basis of class intervals.

Reducing the information into homogeneous categories on the basis of structured questions is called **classification of data.**

Classification on the basis of attributes: Here, what is done is that the person's score on a particular variable is computed by various combinations of the original data obtained. This process is called variable respecification. For example, in a study on schoolchildren mental growth was calculated on the basis of their answers given to the questions that were related to the conceptual knowledge plus the questions related to applications. In another study the person's age, marital status and presence and age of children could be used to compute their family life cycle stage. Similarly, as stated earlier, the socio-economic classification of a person could be identified upon the basis of his education and occupation.

Another respecification the researcher might carry out is collapsing the response categories. For example, suppose the original variable was plastic bag usage with 10 response categories. These might be collapsed into four categories: heavy, medium, light, and non-user. Other respecification of variables includes square root and log transformations, which are often applied to improve the fit of the model being estimated.

Another classification technique discussed in an earlier chapter on measurement and scaling and in the coding section here refers to the use of dummy variables for respecifying the categorical variables. Dummy variables are also called binary, dichotomous, instrumental, or qualitative variables. They are variables that may take on only two values, such as 0 or 1.

Classification by class intervals: Numerical data, like the ratio scale data, can be classified into *class intervals*. This is to assist the quantitative analysis of data. For example, the age data obtained from the sample could be reduced to homogenous grouped data, for example all those below 25 form one group, those 25–35 are another group and so on. Thus, each group will have class limits—an upper and a lower limit. The difference between the limits is termed as the class magnitude. One can have class intervals of both equal and unequal magnitude.

The decision on how many classes and whether equal or unequal depends upon the judgement of the researcher. Generally, multiples of 2 or 5 are preferred. Some researchers adopt the following formula for determining the number of class intervals:

$$i = R/(1 + 3.3 \log N)$$

where,

i = Size of class interval,

R = Range (i.e., difference between the values of the largest item and smallest item among the given items),

N = Number of items to be grouped.

The class intervals that are decided upon could be *exclusive*, for example:

10–15
15–20
20–25
25–30

In this case, the upper limit of each is excluded from the category. Thus we read the first interval above as 10 and under 15, the next one as 15 and under 20 and so on.

The other kind is *inclusive*, that is:

10–15
16–20
21–25
26–30

Here, both the lower and the upper limits are included in the interval. It says 10–15 but actually means 10–15.99. It is recommended that when one has continuous data it should be signified as 10–15.99, as then all possibilities of the responses are exhausted here. However, for discrete data one can use 10–15.

Tabulation involves an orderly arrangement of data into an array that is suitable for statistical analysis. This can be done both manually and with the assistance of a software.

Once the categories and codes have been decided upon, the researcher needs to arrange the same according to some logical pattern. This is referred to as *tabulation* of data. This involves an orderly arrangement of data into an array that is suitable for a statistical analysis. Usually, this is an orderly arrangement of the rows and columns. In case there is data to be entered for one variable, the process is a simple tabulation and, when it is two or more variables, then one carries out a cross-tabulation of data. This can be done manually or with the help of a computer.

Exploratory Data Analysis

Once the data has been cleaned and entered in a tabular form, the researcher is advised to do a preliminary data exploration, in order to assess the expected trends of the findings. Sometimes, these indicative trends may demonstrate that the data collection or instrument design is faulty and needs some corrections.

Preliminary data exploration is done to assess the expected trends of the findings. This is, basically, loosely structured.

Thus, before one goes about testing the formulated hypotheses, one carries out a loosely structured exploration. Most of the exploration is done on the basis of the graphical and visual display of the data patterns that seem to be emerging. In this section we will discuss some widely used and simplistic measures of displaying data.

Bar and pie charts: The data that is available as classification or demographic variable is most often on a categorical or nominal scale. Thus, the tabled data can be plotted to demonstrate the pattern of responses. For example, in a study on jewellery buying the age groups of the sample group and the occupations were as follows:

Occupation

	Frequency	Per cent
Business	14	14.0
Salaried	40	40.0
Professional	27	27.0
Housewife	19	19.0
Total	100	100.0

Age Group

	Frequency	Per cent
20–25	27	27.0
26–30	37	37.0
31–35	9	9.0
36–40	22	22.0
41–45	3	3.0
46 & Above	2	2.0
Total	100	100.0

Thus, a quick visual representation of the largest and the smallest group can be obtained by constructing a pie chart of the same (Figure 10.2).

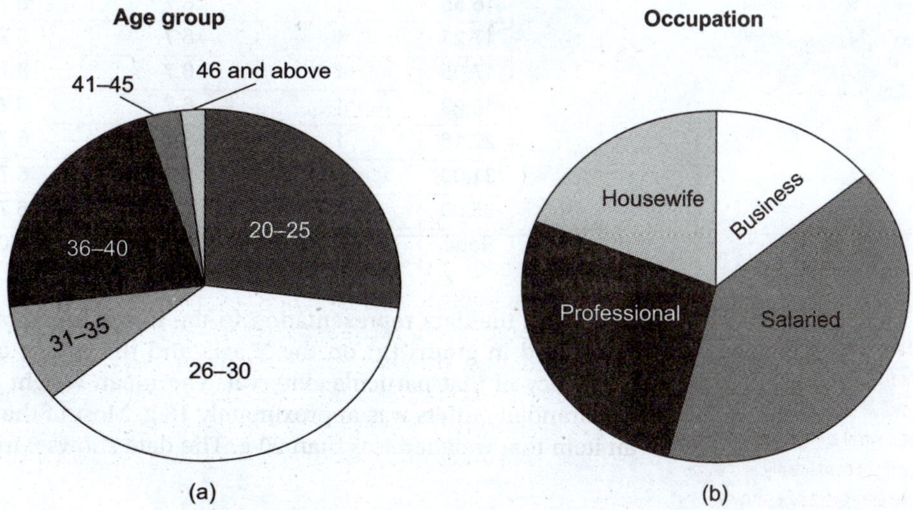

FIGURE 10.2 Pie chart showing the largest and smallest groups

In case one is interested in getting a comparative depiction of the same, the data in the above case is represented in a bar chart (Figure 10.3).

FIGURE 10.3

Comparative depiction of the groups through bar charts

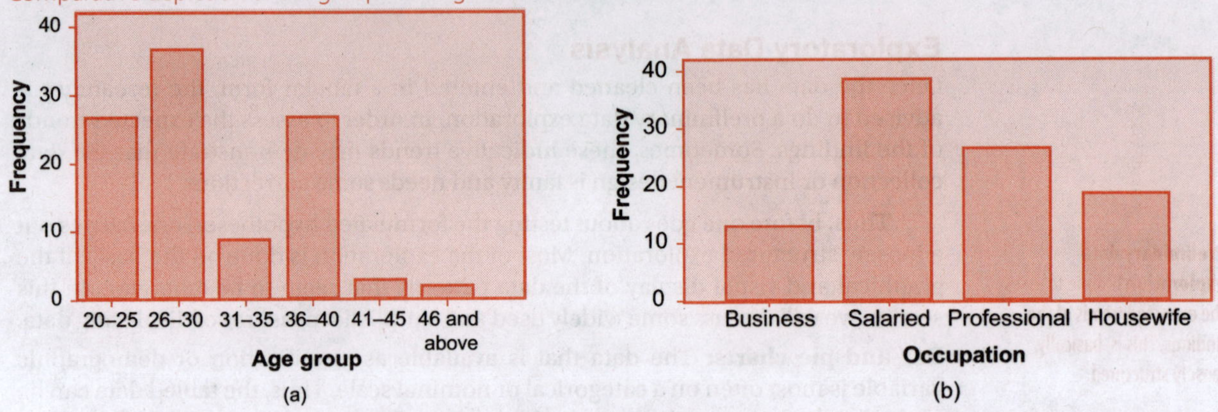

Histogram: For metric-interval and ratio scale data, the data is represented through a histogram (Figure 10.4). The representation would be able to demonstrate the distribution pattern in terms of whether it is normally distributed or demonstrates skewness. The following was the result of the distribution of 15 customers who purchased from branded jewellery outlets last year.

		Frequency	Per cent	Valid Per cent	Cumulative Per cent
Valid	13.10	1	6.7	6.7	6.7
	13.25	1	6.7	6.7	13.3
	13.26	1	6.7	6.7	20.0
	13.87	1	6.7	6.7	26.7
	15.64	1	6.7	6.7	33.3
	15.65	1	6.7	6.7	40.0
	15.84	1	6.7	6.7	46.7
	16.26	1	6.7	6.7	53.3
	16.55	1	6.7	6.7	60.0
	17.25	1	6.7	6.7	66.7
	17.65	1	6.7	6.7	73.3
	18.23	1	6.7	6.7	80.0
	22.18	1	6.7	6.7	86.7
	31.00	1	6.7	6.7	93.3
	35.60	1	6.7	6.7	100.0
	Total	15	100.0	100.0	

Thus, the data representation in the histogram shows the weight of the item purchased in grams (g) on the X-axis and the height of the bars represents the frequency of that particular interval. The mean weight of the items bought from the branded outlets was approximately 18 g. Most of the sample did a purchase of an item that weighed less than 20 g. The data shows 0 frequencies for the 23–30 g.

FIGURE 10.4
Histogram showing the distribution pattern of customers

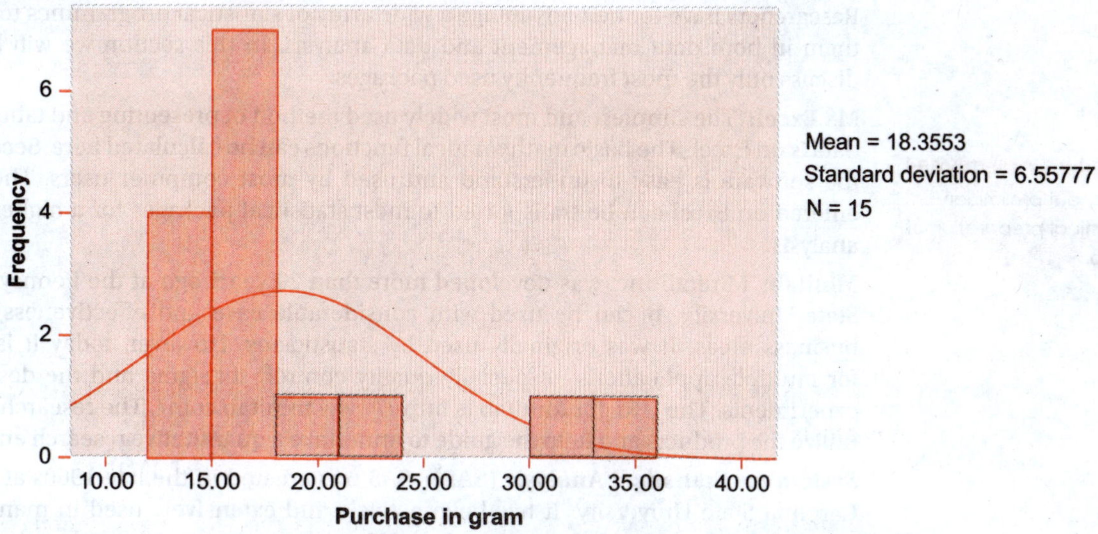

Thus, the display demonstrates that the sample selected is more skewed towards the purchasers of smaller items.

Stem and leaf display shows individual data values in each set as against the histogram which presents only group aggregates.

Stem and leaf displays: This is another way of displaying the metric data. It is very easy to compute and can be done manually or with the help of Minitab. It shows individual data values in each set as against the histogram which presents only group aggregates.

It shows the pattern of responses in each interval and yet can maintain the rank order for a quick approximation of the median or quartile. Each row or line is called a stem and each value on the line is a leaf. The same data that we represented on the histogram can also be depicted on a stem and leaf display as follows:

Stem	Leaf
13	1 3 3 9
15	6 6 8
16	3 6
17	3 7
18	2
22	2
31	0
35	6

If one looks at the tabled data for the jewellery purchase in the above stem and leaf display, the decimals have been rounded off the first place and in case of two similar entries the number 13.3 has been entered twice. In fact, if one rotates the above display by 90 degrees to the left one would get the histogram. The display is showing at a glance that the sample studied was concerned with the buying of mostly 13 g items.

There are other methods like box plots, which are a more detailed representation as compared to histograms. These are basically descriptive statistical values for the data obtained and these are based upon the measures of central tendency and dispersion. These statistical measures would be explained in detail in the next chapter.

CONCEPT CHECK

1. What is meant by tabulation of data?
2. Discuss exploratory data analysis.
3. Name the main statistical software packages available for data management.

STATISTICAL SOFTWARE PACKAGES

LEARNING OBJECTIVE 5
Carry out preliminary statistical preparation of data.

Researchers have to their advantage a wide array of statistical programmes to assist them in both data management and data analysis. In this section we will briefly discuss only the most frequently used packages.

MS Excel: The simplest and most widely used method of presenting and tabulating data is on Excel. The basic mathematical functions can be calculated here. Secondly, the software is easy to understand and used by most computer users. The data entered on Excel can be transported to most statistical packages for a higher level analysis.

Minitab: Minitab Inc. was developed more than 20 years ago at the Pennsylvania State University. It can be used with considerable ease and effectiveness in all business areas. It was originally used by statisticians. However, today it is used for multiple applications—especially quality control, six sigma and the design of experiments. The URL for Minitab is http://www.minitab.com/. The researcher can utilize the products and help the guide to undertake a quantitative research analysis.

System for Statistical Analysis (SAS): SAS was created in the late 1960s at North Carolina State University. It has been actively and extensively used in managing, storing and analysing information. It has the advantage of being able to manage really bulky data sets with considerable ease. Linear models (Regression, Analysis of variance, Analysis of covariance), Generalized linear models (including Logistic regression and Poisson regression), multivariate methods (MANOVA, Canonical correlation, Discriminant analysis, Factor analysis, Clustering), categorical data analysis (including log-linear models), and all the standard techniques for descriptive and confirmatory statistical analysis are possible with SAS. The statistical analyses may be interfaced with the graphical products to produce relevant plots such as q-q plots, residual plots, and other relevant graphical descriptions of the data. Forecasting and trend series can also be carried out using the package. It finds a higher usage amongst industry than students who are more comfortable with SPSS. The URL for package is http://www.sas.com/.

SPSS: Amongst the student community as well as with most research agencies, this is the most widely used package. It is adaptable to most business problems and is extremely user friendly. A reference URL for SPSS is http://www.spss.com/. The software is discussed in detail in Appendix 10.1 of the chapter.

There are a number of specific software programs like E Views for business forecasting and LISREL (Linear Structural Relations) for structural equation modelling. However, for most purposes, SPSS is the most widely used software.

SUMMARY

- After the data has been collected through different methods used by the researcher, the information needs to be refined and structured in a format that can lend itself to a statistical enquiry for testing the study hypotheses. The researcher first begins by validating the fieldwork that was conducted. The processing here refers to the primary data that has been collected specifically for the study.
- The researcher needs, to carry out a hawk-eyed scrutiny of the obtained data to ensure that no omissions or errors are there. This is the editing stage of the data processing step. Here, the researcher begins by conducting a field editing and is able to resolve some of the inconsistencies and issues of incomplete data. This process is conducted at the second stage at the central office level. At this stage, the research team conducts some data treatment such as allocating the missing values, if possible, backtracking and sometimes, plugging the incomplete data.

- Once this is completed, the researcher prepares a uniform code sheet for the questions and expected responses. This notepad of instructions is referred to as the code book. In case the question and answers are closed ended, the investigator is able to conduct a precoding of data, where he decides in advance what numeral value is to be assigned to each of the expected answer. The investigator then takes a decision on how to code the missing values, i.e. the questions whose answers have been left blank. This is critical to decide and record in the entered data as this might lead to an error in calculation.
- Classification into attributes or class intervals is carried out and the entered data is now ready for analysis in a tabular form. Before conducting formal and rigorous data analysis through a gamut of statistical technique, it is advisable to carry out a simple exploratory data analysis by portraying the data in figurative forms such as bar charts, pie charts, histograms and stem and leaf displays. This exploration can now be conducted in an extremely user-friendly and quick manner by using various software packages like MS Excel, SAS, Minitab and SPSS.

KEY TERMS

- Backtracking
- Bar chart
- Class intervals
- Classification of data
- Code book
- Coding
- Data editing
- Data processing
- Data tabulation
- Exclusive class intervals
- Field
- Field editing
- File
- Histogram
- Inclusive class intervals
- In-house editing
- Minitab
- Missing values
- MS Excel
- Pie chart
- Plug value
- Post-coding
- Pre-coding
- Record
- SAS
- Single variable entry
- SPSS
- Stem and leaf display
- Test tabulation

CHAPTER REVIEW QUESTIONS

Objective Type Questions

State whether the following statements are true (T) or false (F).

1. The first step in the data analysis process is data validation.
2. Field editing is possible for all types of primary data collected.
3. Armchair interviewing refers to face-to-face filling in of the questionnaire by the respondent.
4. Backtracking means going back to the respondent to check any errors during questionnaire administration.
5. Backtracking is best suited for industrial surveys.
6. Plug value refers to the fudged value that an investigator might put for a missing response.
7. The smallest code entry a researcher makes in a code book is a field.
8. Several fields together can be clubbed into a file.
9. In a data matrix every column represents a single case.
10. SEC refers to the sections in a typical data matrix.
11. All categories formulated for data entry must be mutually exclusive.
12. Post-coding is conducted on closed-ended questions.
13. In case the person is permitted more than one entry for a question that has six options the number of corresponding columns would be two.
14. In case the question is a Likert type question and it has agreement/disagreement on a five-point scale, the number of corresponding columns in the code book would be five.

15. Test tabulation is conducted on open-ended questions.
16. For classifying nominal data one can tabulate using class intervals.
17. For nominal data, pie charts are a good option for representation of data.
18. 10–15 years; 16–20 years; 21 years and beyond is an example of an exclusive class interval.
19. Histograms can be formulated for all levels of measurement.
20. Stem and leaf diagrams are a projective technique used for data collection.

Conceptual Questions

1. How do you edit a questionnaire? What are the precautions that a researcher must take while editing a questionnaire? Give suitable examples.
2. Processing of data involves editing, coding, classifying and tabulating. Explain each of these steps by taking an appropriate research example.
3. How has the use of SPSS become very handy for the modern researcher today?
4. How do you code data? What guidelines should be followed to carry out the task? Discuss by giving suitable examples.
5. What is tabulation of data? How does tabulation help in data analysis? Give two examples to illustrate your answer.
6. Distinguish between:

   (a) Inclusive and exclusive class intervals (b) Pre-coding and post-coding of data

   (c) Field and centralized editing
7. Write short notes on:

   (a) Stem and leaf displays (b) Histograms (c) Statistical software packages
8. For the questionnaire you developed with regard to safety of women in terms of Likert scale and semantic differential scale, prepare the codebook for the two versions that you have made. How do these differ from each other?

   What elements did you need to keep in mind while preparing the codebook?
9. Given below is a question related to parents' buying behaviour related to their children:

   Below are some product categories (used by children). Kindly advise who among you, your spouse and your child are the decision makers with regard to these products?

	I buy	My spouse buys	Either one of us buys	We buy together	Our kids accompany us and buy on their own
a. Clothes and Shoes					
b. Toys and Games					
c. Hobby Classes					
d. Soft Home Furnishing					
e. Eatables (Candies, etc.)					

   • Design the code sheet for the above question.
   • Conduct this question on 10 parents having children below 10 years of age and prepare a stem and leaf diagram of the data.

10. Given below is the data from 10 respondents with reference to their ice cream eating behaviour. The questions asked with their codes are as follows:

Question No.	Variable Name	Coding Instruction	Symbol used for variable name
1.	Customer ID	ACTUAL	X1
2.	Age (Actual rounded up)	ACTUAL	X2
3.	Gender	Male = 1 Female = 2	X3
4.	Frequency of consumption	ONCE A DAY = 1, ONCE A WEEK = 2, ONCE A MONTH = 3 ONLY ON OCCASIONS = 4	X4
5.	Average money spent on ice cream at one go(₹)	ACTUAL	X5

Ice cream eating behavior (n=10)

X1	X2	X3	X4	X5
1	20	1	1	20.00
2	32	1	2	150.00
3	41	1	2	100.00
4	18	2	1	45.00
5	28	2	3	100.00
6	21	1	3	110.00
7	17	1	4	500.00
8	30	2	1	30.00
9	16	1	2	50.00
10	18	1	2	100.00

(a) Can you convert any of the variables into class intervals? Which ones and how?

(b) Did you make exclusive or inclusive intervals? Why?

(c) What is the trend in terms of age and ice cream spend and frequency? How will you represent the data?

CASE 10.1

MAX NEW YORK LIFE INSURANCE

Max New York Life India decided to conduct an employee survey to find out the motivators for an effective performance. For this purpose, the following questionnaire was used:

1. Prepare a code book for the questionnaire designed.
2. Which questions require post-coding? Can you prepare your broad categories in advance? Give reasons for your answer.

Instructions

We solicit your co-operation and responses to the questions that follow. The responses and the consequent analysis will be used purely for academic purposes and the data shared will be kept strictly confidential.

Please tick the appropriate checkbox.

1. Are you an employee of Max New York Life Insurance?

   ☐ Yes ☐ No

2. For how long have you been working with the current organization?

   ☐ Less than 1 year ☐ 1–5 years
   ☐ 5–10 years ☐ 10–15 years
   ☐ More than 15 years

3. Your designation/job title:

4. Rate the factors listed in the table; on the following scale given below:

   1: Very unimportant 2: Unimportant 3: Indifferent 4: Important 5: Very important

	1	2	3	4	5
Participation in the decision-making process					
Clear communication, assistance and support provided by your supervisors					
Clarity in the objectives and performance expectations					
Encouragement provided to be creative, innovative and to search for better ways to get the job done					
Regard and value attached to its human resources by the organization					
Degree of responsibility, freedom and accountability					
Extent of rules, regulation, policies and supervision					

5. How much do the organizational culture factors listed above affect your work performance?

   ☐ Very low ☐ Low ☐ Moderate ☐ High ☐ Very high

6. Rate the following factors according to the scale given below:

   1: Very unimportant 2: Unimportant 3: Indifferent 4: Important 5: Very important

	1	2	3	4	5
Remuneration/take-home salary					
Job security					
Rewards and recognition					
Learning (training/self-development avenues)					
Work Ambience					
The degree of autonomy and decision-making in your job					
The creativity, meaningfulness and complexity of the work you perform					
Your interpersonal relationships with subordinates, superiors and peers					

7. How much do the motivational factors listed above affect your work performance?

   ☐ Very low ☐ Low ☐ Moderate ☐ High ☐ Very high

8. How do you define effective work performance?
   (Please tick what is relevant according to you.)

Being focused and working with the intention of creating results that benefit the stakeholders in any given situation	
Accomplishment of a given task measured against present standards of accuracy, completeness, cost, and speed	
Clearly and consistently performing all duties above expectations	
Attainment of specific results required by the job through specific actions while maintaining or being consistent with processes, procedures and conditions of the organizational environment	
Appropriate execution of processes and procedures	

9. Please indicate your age:
   - ☐ Below 25 years ☐ 25–35 years ☐ 35–45 years
   - ☐ 45–55 years ☐ Above 55 years
10. For how long have you been working in the insurance sector?
    - ☐ Less than 1 year ☐ 1–5 years ☐ 5–10 years
    - ☐ 10–15 years ☐ More than 15 years
11. Educational qualification (*you can tick more than one*).
    - ☐ BE ☐ B.Tech ☐ BSc ☐ BBA
    - ☐ BA ☐ MBA
    - ☐ MA ☐ MS ☐ M.Tech ☐ MSc

    Others (please specify): B.Com (P) ____________________
12. Please suggest other factors that you think affect your work performance. ____________

CASE 10.2

BRANDED JEWELLERY – IS THERE A DEMAND?

Sundri is a chain of branded jewellery outlets in Tamil Nadu. They intend to set up branded stores in North India as well. T Sivamani, the proprietor of the chain, wished to understand how consumers buy jewellery and the difference between those who buy jewellery from the traditional jewellers and those who visit branded outlets.

For the purpose, a small survey was conducted to study the consumers' buying behaviour. Given below is the questionnaire used for the study. The data has been collected and now needs to be entered.

1. Prepare a code book for the questionnaire.
2. How will you carry out an exploratory data analysis on the data obtained?

Consumer Questionnaire
Jewellery Buying Behaviour

Instructions

'Hi, we are students of _________ We are carrying out a survey to find out how people buy jewellery. Since you are a customer who buys jewellery, we would request your cooperation in filling up the following questionnaire. Your inputs are greatly valued.'

Name (optional) ________________

1. Why do you buy jewellery? (tick all that apply)
   - ☐ Fashion Statement
   - ☐ Status Symbol
   - ☐ Investment/Security
   - ☐ Gift
   - ☐ Any other
2. When do you buy jewellery? (tick all that apply)
   - ☐ At least once a month
   - ☐ At least once a quarter
   - ☐ At least once a year
   - ☐ Only on festivals
   - ☐ Only on special occasions
   - ☐ Any other

3. What kind of jewellery do you buy? (tick all that apply)
   - ☐ Gold
   - ☐ Diamond
   - ☐ Silver
   - ☐ Semi-precious
   - ☐ Precious gems
   - ☐ Pearls
   - ☐ Any other
4. Where do you buy the jewellery from? (tick all that apply)
   - ☐ Company showrooms
   - ☐ Jewellery shops
   - ☐ Branded jewellery showrooms
   - ☐ Multi brand outlets (e.g., Shoppers' Stop)
   - ☐ Any other

(Whoever ticked jewellery shops, take them to question 7)

5. What kind of designs do you buy? (tick all that apply)
   - ☐ Traditional Indian
   - ☐ Classic Western
   - ☐ Any other
6. Given below are some attributes that one considers while buying jewellery. Please evaluate them on their importance for you on the given five-point scale.

	VI	I	N	UI	VUI
Brand Name					
Variety of designs					
Location of the outlet					
Known jeweller					
Discount schemes					
Quality assurance					
Recommendation from friends/relatives					
Brand endorsement by a celebrity					
Cordial and helpful personnel at the shop					
Availability of desired grade of carat					

(VI – Very Important; I – Important; N – Neutral; UI – Unimportant; VUI – Very Unimportant)

7. What will encourage you to buy at branded jewellery outlets? Please evaluate them on their importance for you on the given five-point scale.

	VL	L	MB	UL	VUL
Discount schemes					
Variety of designs					
Brand endorsement by a celebrity					
Showroom at a convenient place					
Customization of designs					
Buy back of jewellery					
Quality certification					
Any other					

(VL – Very Likely; L – Likely; MB – May be; UL – Unlikely; VUL – Very Unlikely)

8. Please give the following personal details about yourself.
   (a) Gender
   ☐ Male ☐ Female
   (b) Age group
   ☐ 20 – 25 ☐ 26 – 30
   ☐ 31 – 35 ☐ 36 – 40
   ☐ 41 and above
   (c) Marital status
   ☐ Married ☐ Unmarried
   (d) Occupation
   ☐ Business ☐ Salaried
   ☐ Retired ☐ Housewife
   ☐ Student ☐ Any other
   (e) Family income (in INR/month)
   ☐ Less than 25,000 ☐ 25,000 – 50,000
   ☐ 50,000 – 1,00,000
   ☐ 1,00,000 and above
   (f) Address ______________________________
   ____
   ____

Appendix – 10.1: SPSS – AN INTRODUCTION

Statistical Package for Social Sciences (SPSS) is one of the most popular software packages to perform statistical analysis on survey data. Its first version was released in 1968 and since then, it has come a long way. It is used by researchers in educational institutes, research organizations, government, marketing firms, etc.

Launching SPSS

To start SPSS, go to *Start -> Programs-> SPSS* followed by its version. For example, SPSS 12, SPSS 14, SPSS 16, SPSS 17. A dialog box will open in front of SPSS grid listing several options to choose from. The following options will appear in the dialog box:

- Run the tutorial
- Type in data
- Run in existing query
- Create new query using Database Wizard
- Open an existing data source
- Open another type of file

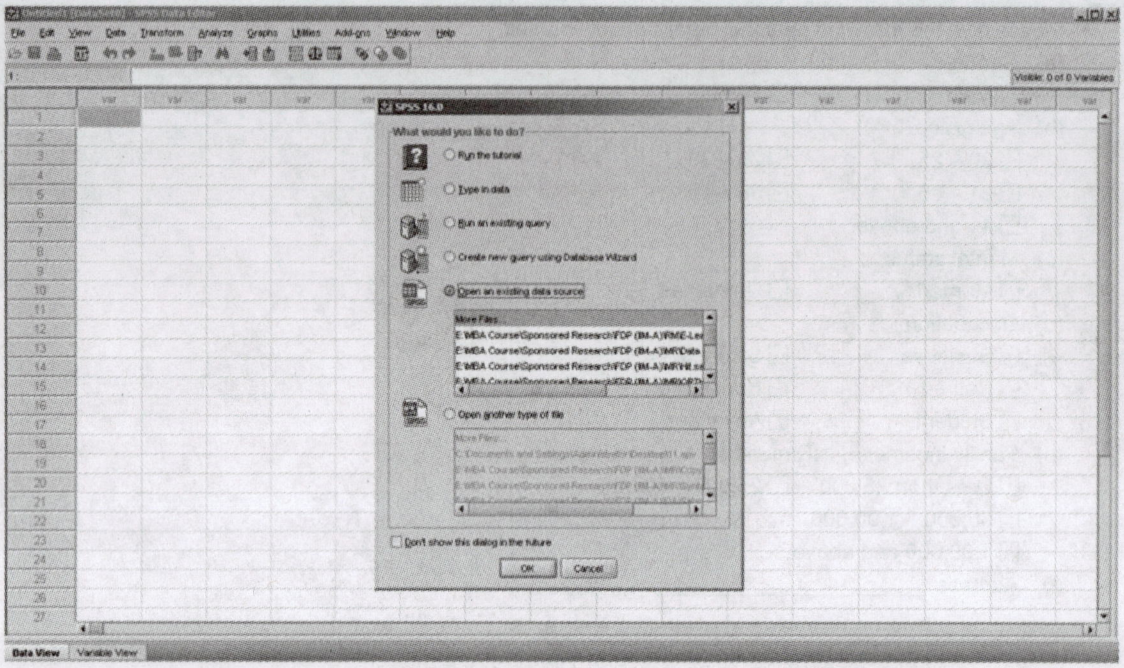

For the moment, we will concentrate on the second option, i.e., Type in data. Select this option and click Ok. By default, the Data Editor view is initially selected.

SPSS Data Editor

The SPSS Data Editor Window has two views: *Data View* and *Variable View*. Variable View is used to define variables that will store the data. Data View contains the actual data.

The first step is to open the 'Variable View' window of the Data Editor and define variables. Let us consider an example where Employee Data of an organization needs to be saved and analysed. The objective is to create a small data file for employees that consist of six variables as given in the following Table.

Variable name	Variable type
EmpID	Numeric
EmpName	String
Gender	Numeric (categories are Female = 1 and Male = 2)
Age	Numeric
Income	Numeric
MaritalStatus	Numeric (categories are Unmarried = 1 and Married = 2)

There are different types of variables in SPSS, the default one being **numeric**. To change variable type, in Variable View click on the variable in the column Type. A window similar to one below will open. Create all the variables and select appropriate Type as given in the table above.

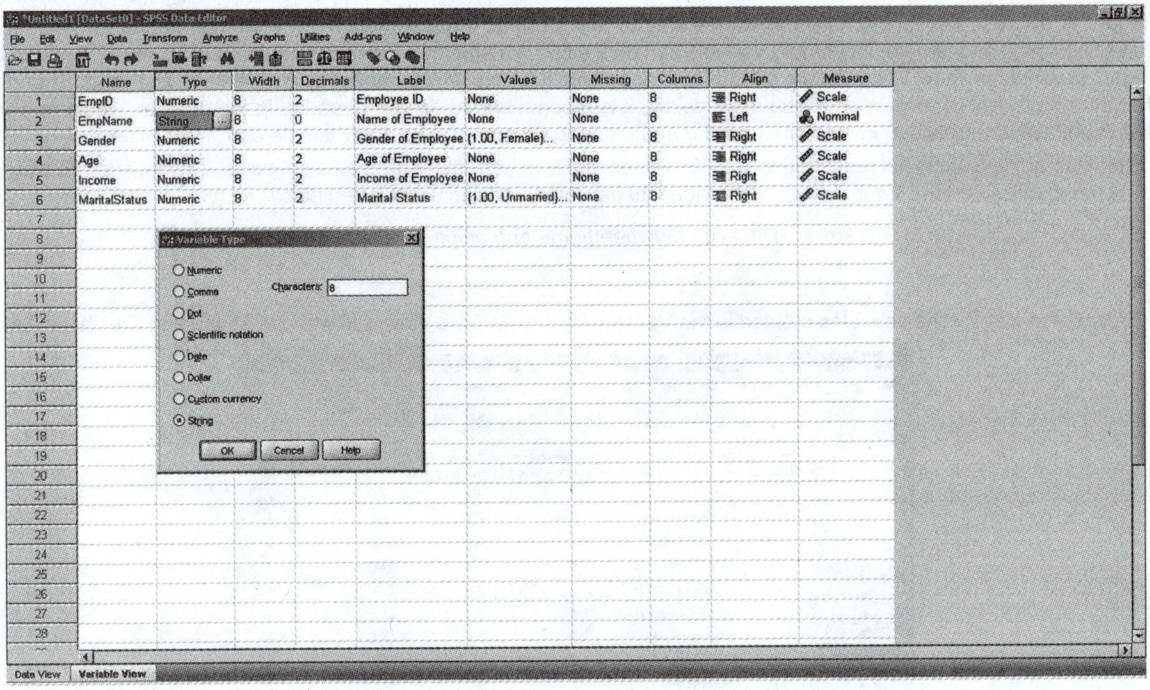

Note: While defining variable names empty spaces are not allowed.

E.g., Marital Status – Not allowed

MaritalStatus or Marital_Status – Correct

The third column in Variable view is *Width*, which specifies the number of characters allowed to be entered in the column. By default the width is 8 characters and can be modified depending upon the data being entered.

The fourth column is *Decimals*, which represents the number of decimal places. For numeric data type the default value is 0. Say, for example, EmpID does not require decimal places, therefore, it can be set to 0.

The fifth column is *Label*, which describes the variable.

The sixth column is *Values*. For example, Gender contains two categories (Female = 1 and Male = 2). In Data View, the gender will be entered as either 1 or 2. But what 1 or 2 represents is given in the Values as 1 represents Female and 2 Male.

The seventh column is *Missing*. Often while collecting data, you will have missing values within your data. This column is used in cases where no data is provided by a respondent. A missing value is chosen as an impossible value for that column. For example, the missing value for age can be entered as 1000 or -100 which are impossible entries for age. The objective of giving a missing value is to exclude that record while analysing the data.

The eighth column is *Columns*. It represents the width of the column. Default value is 8 and can be changed.

The ninth column is *Align*, which aligns the data at the left, centre or right of cell.

The last column is *Measure*. It can take values of Nominal, Ordinal or Scale.

The table below shows the different types of measurement, with examples:

Nominal	Category	Discrete	Eye colour
Ordinal	Ranking	Discrete	Ranking preference for various soft drinks
Interval	Scale	Continuous	Temperature
Ratio	Scale	Continuous	Age, years of education

Nominal Data: Discrete/category variable (limited number of values), e.g., Gender (Male or Female), Days of the week, Yes/No response in a questionnaire.

Ordinal Data: Discrete/category variable (limited number of ranks).

Interval Data: Continuous Data.

Ratio Data: Continuous Data.

Category or discrete measure consists of values that can be grouped into categories, for example, gender, which can be grouped into male and female. A category variable can be a string variable or a numeric variable but it is recommended that categorical variables should be numeric because strings contain letters which cannot be numerically analysed. Therefore, rather than representing female as 'f' and male as 'm', it is recommended as stated earlier in the chapter, where possible, use numeric values instead of letters when coding and entering data, e.g., use '1' for female and '1' for male.

Continuous measure is not restricted to specific values and is usually measured on a continuous scale, such as distance from home to office (in km). It will vary from individual to individual on a scale as given below.

0 km *Distance between home and office (in km)* 100 km

Enter some data for the variables created in the Variable View. The Data View grid will look something like shown below:

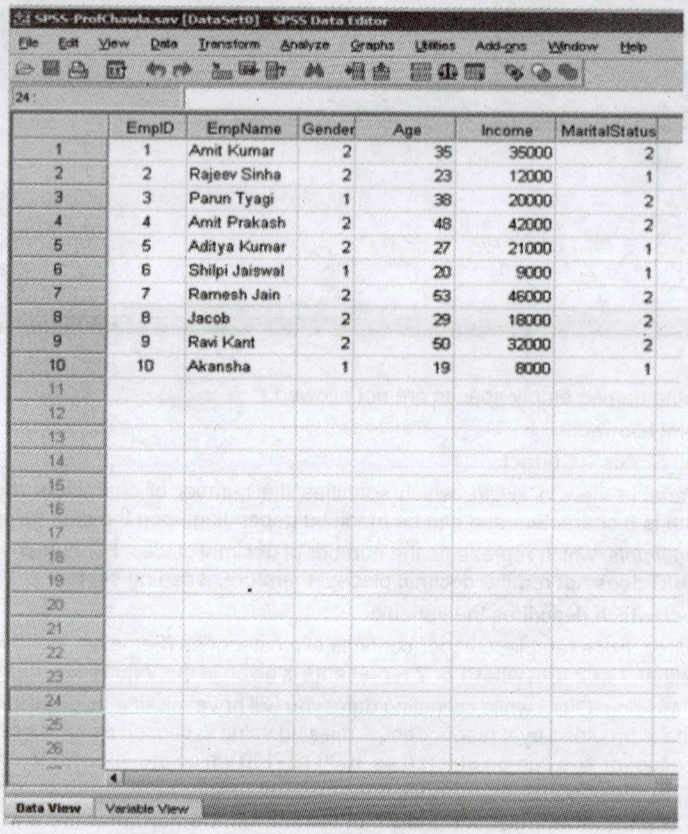

	EmpID	EmpName	Gender	Age	Income	MaritalStatus
1	1	Amit Kumar	2	35	35000	2
2	2	Rajeev Sinha	2	23	12000	1
3	3	Parun Tyagi	1	38	20000	2
4	4	Amit Prakash	2	48	42000	2
5	5	Aditya Kumar	2	27	21000	1
6	6	Shilpi Jaiswal	1	20	9000	1
7	7	Ramesh Jain	2	53	46000	2
8	8	Jacob	2	29	18000	2
9	9	Ravi Kant	2	50	32000	2
10	10	Akansha	1	19	8000	1

Recoding Variables

Recode is a very important feature in SPSS, which is used to convert continuous data into discrete or category data. One can recode values within the existing variable into a new variable.

Note: If you recode the values into the existing variable, the old values are lost. So it is recommended to recode a variable into a new variable wherever possible, so that your original values are retained.

Recode is available under *Transform* menu. There are three ways to recode the data.

1. Recode into same variables
2. Recode into new variables
3. Automatic recode

Now suppose, the variable income is to be categorized into three income categories based upon the below logic.

< =10000 – 1 *(Low income)*

>10000 - <=30000 - 2 *(Middle income)*

> 30000 as 3 *(High income)*

Go to Transform-> Recode into new variable. The variable income will be recoded into a new variable *(IncomeRe)* labeled as Income Redefined which is the Output Variable.

Click on the button Old and New Values. A window will open divided into two parts. Left side will be *Old Value* and right side shows *New Value*.

Since the first category is 10000, the Old Value option to be selected will be Range, Lowest through value: 10,000. New Value is 1.

The second category is a range >10000 and 30,000, the Old Value option to be selected is a Range, i.e., 10,000 through 30,000. New Value is 2.

The third category is > 3000, the Old value option to be selected is Range, value through Highest: 30,000. New Value is 3.

A snapshot of the recode screen is given below for reference. Click on Continue and Ok.

A new variable IncomeRe will be created based upon the income variable. Next, we need to label what are 1, 2 and 3 values. Go to Variable View and give the labels for the new variable *IncomeRe*.

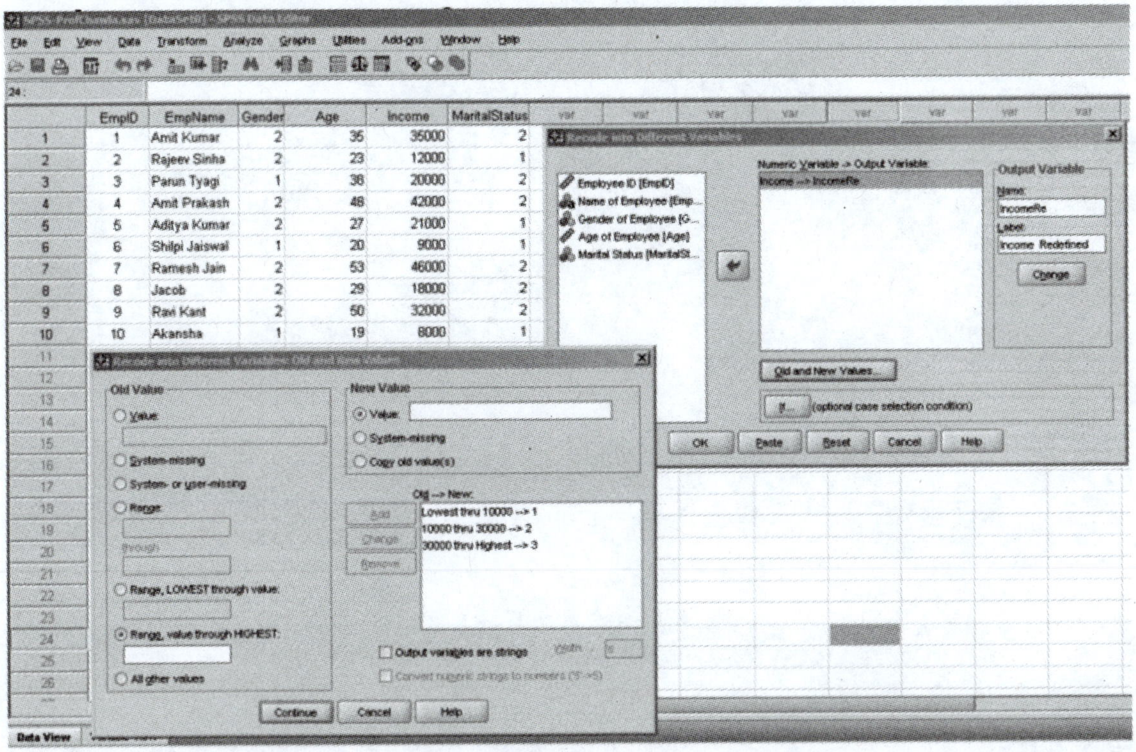

Answers to Objective Type Questions

1. True	2. False	3. False	4. True	5. True
6. False	7. True	8. False	9. False	10. False
9. True	12. False	13. False	14. False	15. True
16. False	17. True	18. False	19. False	20. False

BIBLIOGRAPHY

Boyd, Harper W Jr, Ralph Westfall and Stanley F Stasch. *Marketing Research: Text and Cases* Delhi: Richard D. Irwin, Inc., 2002.

Burns, Robert B. *Introduction to Research Methods.* London: Sage Publications, 2000.

Churchill, Gilbert A, Jr and Dawn Iacobucci, *Marketing Research Methodological Foundations:* 9th edition. New Delhi: Thompson South Western, 2007.

Green, Paul E and Donald S Tull, *Research for Marketing Decisions,* 4th edn. New Delhi: Prentice Hall of India Private Ltd, 1986.

Hair, Joseph F, Jr, Robert P Bush and David J Ortinau. *Marketing Research – A Practical Approach for the New Millennium.* New Delhi: McGraw-Hill Higher Education, 1999.

Kinnear, Thomas C and James R. Taylor. *Marketing Research: An Applied Approach*, 5th edn. New York: McGraw Hill, Inc., 1996.

Kothari, C R. *Research Methodology Methods and Techniques*, 2nd edn. New Delhi: Wiley Eastern Limited, 1990.

Malhotra, Naresh K. *Marketing Research – An Applied Orientation*, 3rd edn. New Delhi: Pearson Education, 2002.

Tull, Donald S and Del I Hawkins, *Marketing Research: Measurement and Method*, 6th edn. New Delhi: Prentice Hall of India Pvt. Ltd., 1993.

Zikmud, William G. *Business Research Methdos*. 5th edn. Thompson South–Western, 1997.

Section 4

PRELIMINARY DATA ANALYSIS AND INTERPRETATION

This section discusses the method of sample selection and the process of refining and collating the collected data.

Chapter 11 Univariate and Bivariate Analysis of Data

Chapter 11 is on univariate and bivariate analysis of data. It explains the type of descriptive analysis to be carried on nominal, ordinal, interval and ratio scale data. Preparation and interpretation of bivariate cross tables is discussed. The computation of Spearman's rank order correlation coefficient and its interpretation, along with the computation of summarized rank order of ranks of various attributes to find out the overall ranks obtained by various attributes of a product/service in question, is also discussed. The chapter also briefly outlines the transformation of original data into different formats for ease of analysis. The use of SPSS software for carrying out univariate and bivariate analysis of data is extensively illustrated.

Chapter 12 Testing of Hypotheses

Chapter 12 is on testing of hypothesis and it briefly discusses the various concepts used. The test of significance of mean of a single population and difference between the means of two populations are detailed using t and Z test. The concept of dependent sample (paired sample) and the testing procedure for examining the significance difference in the case of paired sample is also explained. The chapter outlines the procedure for testing the significance of a single population proportion and the difference between two population proportions using Z-test. The *p* value approach for testing of hypothesis is explained at length. Moreover, all the exercises are also worked out using SPSS software, the required instructions for which are given in the appendix at the end of the chapter.

Chapter 13 Analysis of Variance Techniques

Chapter 13 explains the meaning and assumptions of carrying out an analysis of variance exercise. The use of analysis of variance is made in completely randomized design, randomized block design, factorial design and Latin square design. The concept of interaction is introduced for a factorial design. The illustrations are also worked out using SPSS software.

Chapter 14 Non-Parametric Tests

Chapter 14 discusses the difference between parametric and non-parametric tests. It explains advantages and disadvantages of non-parametric tests and describes various non-parametric tests like chi-square, run test, one-sample and two-sample sign test, Man-Whitney U-test, Wilcoxon signed-rank test for paired sample and Kruskal-Wallis test. The SPSS procedure for conducting such tests is also explained in this chapter.

11

CHAPTER

Univariate and Bivariate Analysis of Data

Learning Objectives

By the end of the chapter, you should be able to:

1. Distinguish between univariate, bivariate and multivariate analysis.
2. Differentiate between descriptive and inferential analysis.
3. Discuss the type of descriptive univariate analysis to be carried on nominal, ordinal, interval and ratio scale data.
4. Explain the descriptive analysis of bivariate data.
5. Elaborate more on analysis of data by calculating rank order and using data transformation.

The average monthly household expenditure on food items in a town is ₹2,300. About 25 per cent of households spend more than ₹5,000 per month on food; 50 per cent of the households spend less than ₹2,800 per month on food. Three out of ten households send their children to government schools and 5 per cent of the households go abroad for holidays. Further, these households have earnings of more than ₹2 lakh per month. It is also known that the occupation of the head of the household in a town is 15 per cent in business, 30 per cent in the private sector, 45 per cent in government service and the remaining are occupied in odd jobs.

These findings illustrate the results of a typical descriptive analysis. This chapter discusses how to carry out a descriptive analysis. The focus is on univariate and bivariate analysis of data.

UNIVARIATE, BIVARIATE AND MULTIVARIATE ANALYSIS OF DATA

LEARNING OBJECTIVE 1
Distinguish between univariate, bivariate and multivariate analysis.

Once the raw data is collected from both primary and secondary sources, the next step is to analyse the same so as to draw logical inferences from them. The data collected in a survey could be voluminous in nature, depending upon the size of the sample. In a typical research study there may be a large number of variables that the researcher needs to analyse. The analysis could be univariate, bivariate and multivariate in nature. In the univariate analysis, one variable is analysed at a time. In the bivariate analysis two variables are analysed together and examined for any possible association between them. In the multivariate analysis, the concern is to analyse more than two variables at a time. The subject matter of multivariate analysis will be studied in detail in the chapters Correlation and Regression Analysis, Factor Analysis, Discriminant Analysis, Cluster Analysis and Multidimensional Scaling. These will be taken up in chapters 15 to 19. The subject matter of univariate and bivariate analysis will be taken up in chapters 11 to 14.

The type of statistical techniques used for analysing univariate and bivariate data depends upon the level of measurements of the questions pertaining to those variables. This has already been discussed in detail in the chapter, Attitude Measurement and Scaling, where it is explained what techniques are applicable for which type of measurement. Further, the data analysis could be of two types, namely, Descriptive and inferential. Below is mentioned a list of illustrative set of questions which are answered under both descriptive and inferential analysis.

DESCRIPTIVE VS INFERENTIAL ANALYSIS

LEARNING OBJECTIVE 2
Differentiate between descriptive and inferential analysis.

Descriptive Analysis

Descriptive analysis refers to transformation of raw data into a form that will facilitate easy understanding and interpretation. Descriptive analysis deals with summary measures relating to the sample data. The common ways of summarizing data are by calculating average, range, standard deviation, frequency and percentage distribution. The first thing to do when data analysis is taken up is to describe the sample. Below is a set of typical questions that are required to be answered under descriptive statistics:

The common ways of **summarizing data** are by calculating average, range, standard deviation, frequency and percentage distribution.

- What is the average income of the sample?
- What is the average age of the sample?
- What is the standard deviation of ages in the sample?
- What is the standard deviation of incomes in the sample?
- What percentage of sample respondents are married?
- What is the median age of the sample respondents?
- Which income group has the highest number of user of product in question in the sample?
- Is there any association between the frequency of purchase of product and income level of the consumers?
- Is the level of job satisfaction related with the age of the employees?
- Which TV channel is viewed by the majority of viewers in the age group 20–30 years?

Types of descriptive analysis

The type of descriptive analysis to be carried out depends on the measurement of variables into four forms—nominal, ordinal, interval and ratio. Table 11.1 presents the type of descriptive analysis which is applicable under each form of measurement.

TABLE 11.1
Descriptive analysis for various levels of measurement

Type of Measurement	Type of Descriptive Analysis
Nominal	Frequency table, Proportion percentages, Mode
Ordinal	Median, Quartiles, Percentiles, Rank order correlation
Interval	Arithmetic mean, Correlation coefficient
Ratio	Index numbers, Geometric mean, Harmonic mean

It is assumed that readers are acquainted with the methods of descriptive analysis as the material could be found in any elementary text on descriptive statistics. Here only a brief review of some of the methods is mentioned.

In an **inferential analysis,** inferences are drawn on population parameters based on sample results. A necessary condition is that the sample should be drawn at random.

Inferential Analysis

After descriptive analysis has been carried out, the tools of inferential statistics are applied. Under inferential statistics, inferences are drawn on population parameters based on sample results. The researcher tries to generalize the results to the population based on sample results. The analysis is based on probability theory and a necessary condition for carrying out inferential analysis is that the sample should be drawn at random. The following is an illustrative list of questions that are covered under inferential statistics.

- Is the average age of the population significantly different from 35?
- Is the average income of population significantly greater than ₹25,000 per month?
- Is the job satisfaction of unskilled workers significantly related with their pay packet?
- Do the users and non-users of a brand vary significantly with respect to age?
- Is the growth in the sales of the company statistically significant?
- Does the advertisement expenditure influences sale significantly?
- Are consumption expenditure and disposable income of households significantly correlated?
- Is the proportion of satisfied workers significantly more for skilled workers than for unskilled works?
- Do urban and rural households differ significantly in terms of average monthly expenditure on food?
- Is the variability in the starting salaries of fresh MBA different with respect to marketing and finance specialization?

As stated earlier, this chapter is focused on descriptive analysis for univariate and bivariate variables. For the purpose of illustration we have taken the data from a research study by Chawla and Behl, 2004. In this study, a sample of 500 users of cyber café was taken from five zones of Delhi, namely, Central, East, West, South and North. A sample of 414 usable questionnaires could be found for further analysis. Table 11.2 presents a data on some of the variables used in the study. The variables used in Table 11.2 are defined as:

- The variable X3 was framed as:

  When accessing the Internet at a cyber café, tick frequently used applications.

  1. E-mail (X3a)
  2. Chat (X3b)
  3. Browsing (X3c)
  4. Downloading (X3d)
  5. Shopping (X3e)
  6. Net telephone (X3f)
  7. Business and commerce (e-commerce) (X3g)
  8. Entertainment (X3h)
  9. Adult sites (X3i)
  10. Astrology and horoscope (X3j)
  11. Education (X3k)
  12. Any other, please specify (X3l)

- X3a was defined as

  e-mail = 1

  Otherwise = 0

TABLE 11.2
Data on select variables used in cyber café study

Resp No.	X3A	X3B	X3C	X3D	X3E	X3F	X3G	X3H	X3I	X3J	X3K	X3L	X6	X10	X11A	X12	X13	X15
1	1	1	1	1	0	0	0	1	1	1	1	0	4	72	3	1	1	5
2	1	0	0	0	0	0	0	0	0	0	1	0	4	60	4	2	1	2
3	1	1	0	0	0	0	0	0	0	0	0	0	4	12	3	1	1	2
4	1	1	1	0	0	0	0	0	0	0	1	0	4	24	5	1	1	3
5	1	0	1	0	1	0	0	0	0	0	0	0	4	72	4	1	2	2
6	1	0	0	1	0	0	0	0	1	0	1	0	4	60	4	1	2	2
7	1	1	1	0	0	0	0	0	0	1	0	0	3	12	5	2	1	3
8	1	1	1	0	0	0	0	0	0	0	0	0	5	12	5	2	1	3
9	1	0	0	0	0	0	0	0	0	0	0	0	3	60	5	2	1	2
10	0	0	0	0	0	1	1	1	0	0	0	0	1	120	4	1	1	1
11	1	0	1	1	1	0	0	0	0	1	0	0	5	24	5	1	1	2
12	1	1	1	1	0	0	0	0	1	0	1	0	4	36	4	2	2	2
13	1	1	0	0	0	1	0	1	0	0	0	0	5	48	4	1	1	4
14	1	0	1	0	0	0	0	1	1	0	0	0	5	60	5	1	2	4
15	1	1	1	0	0	0	0	1	0	0	0	0	4	24	4	1	1	3
16	1	0	1	1	0	0	0	0	0	0	1	0	5	36	2	1	1	3
17	1	1	0	0	0	0	0	0	0	0	0	0	2	12	4	2	2	5
18	1	1	0	0	0	0	0	0	1	0	1	0	2	36	1	1	1	4
19	1	1	1	0	0	0	0	0	0	0	0	0	4	36	3	2	1	4
20	1	1	1	1	0	0	0	1	0	0	1	0	5	60	3	1	1	4
21	1	0	0	0	0	0	0	0	0	1	0	0	3	42	4	2	1	3
22	0	0	0	1	0	0	0	0	0	0	0	0	4	36	3	2	1	1
23	1	0	1	0	0	0	0	0	0	0	0	0	4	12	4	2	2	6
24	1	0	0	0	0	0	0	0	0	0	0	0	4	36	4	2	2	2
25	1	0	1	0	1	0	0	0	0	0	1	0	4	12	4	2	2	3
26	1	1	0	1	0	0	0	0	0	0	1	0	1	12	4	2	1	3
27	1	1	1	1	0	0	0	0	0	0	0	0	1	60	3	2	1	2

28	1	0	1	1	0	0	0	0	0	0	1	0	4	24	2	2	1	3
29	1	0	1	1	0	0	0	0	0	0	0	1	3	36	3	1	1	3
30	1	1	1	0	0	0	0	0	0	0	0	0	4	42	4	1	1	3
31	1	1	1	1	0	1	0	1	0	0	0	0	5	48	4	1	2	4
32	1	0	0	1	0	0	0	0	0	0	1	0	4	24	4	1	1	2
33	1	1	1	1	0	0	0	0	0	0	0	0	4	24	4	1	2	4
34	1	0	1	0	0	0	0	0	0	0	1	1	4	18	4	1	1	4
35	1	1	0	0	0	0	1	0	0	0	0	0	5	36	4	1	1	3
36	1	1	0	1	0	0	0	1	0	0	0	0	3	24	4	1	1	4
37	0	1	1	0	0	0	0	1	1	0	0	0	5	36	3	1	1	4
38	1	1	0	0	0	0	0	0	0	0	1	0	4	36	3	1	1	1
39	1	0	1	0	0	0	0	0	0	1	0	0	4	36	5	1	1	4
40	1	0	1	1	0	0	0	0	0	0	1	0	5	48	3	1	1	1
41	1	0	0	1	0	0	1	1	0	0	0	0	3	48	4	1	2	4
42	1	1	1	1	0	1	1	0	0	0	1	0	5	48	4	1	2	5
43	1	1	1	1	0	0	0	0	0	0	1	0	5	48	4	1	2	4
44	1	1	1	1	0	0	0	1	0	1	0	0	4	24	4	2	1	2
45	1	1	1	1	0	0	0	1	0	0	1	0	4	36	3	1	2	4
46	1	1	1	1	0	1	0	0	0	0	1	0	1	24	4	1	1	9
47	1	0	1	0	0	0	0	0	0	1	1	0	4	24	3	1	1	3
48	1	1	1	1	0	0	0	1	0	0	1	0	5	48	4	1	1	4
49	1	1	1	1	0	0	0	0	0	0	0	0	3	36	4	1	1	4
50	1	1	1	0	0	0	0	0	0	0	0	1	5	60	4	1	1	3
51	1	1	1	1	0	0	0	0	0	0	1	0	2	24	4	2	2	5
52	1	0	1	1	0	0	0	0	1	0	0	0	5	48	5	1	1	6
53	1	0	0	0	1	0	0	1	1	0	0	0	5	24	5	2	1	1
54	1	1	0	1	0	0	1	1	1	0	0	0	4	36	4	1	1	3
55	1	1	1	1	0	1	0	1	0	0	0	0	5	36	4	1	2	5
56	1	0	0	0	0	0	1	0	0	0	0	0	4	48	1	1	1	1
57	1	1	0	1	0	0	0	0	0	0	1	0	3	12	4	1	1	2
58	1	1	0	1	0	0	0	0	1	0	0	0	2	36	4	1	1	1

Resp No.	X3A	X3B	X3C	X3D	X3E	X3F	X3G	X3H	X3I	X3J	X3K	X3L	X6	X10	X11A	X12	X13	X15
59	1	1	0	0	0	0	0	1	0	0	0	1	4	24	3	1	1	2
60	1	1	0	0	0	0	0	1	0	1	0	0	1	36	4	2	1	2
61	1	0	1	1	0	0	0	1	0	0	0	0	4	60	4	1	1	6
62	1	0	1	1	0	0	1	0	0	0	1	0	5	999	4	2	1	1
63	1	0	0	1	0	0	0	0	0	0	1	0	3	60	3	2	1	9
64	1	1	1	0	0	0	0	0	0	0	1	0	4	48	3	2	1	3
65	1	0	1	1	0	0	0	0	0	0	1	0	3	12	5	2	1	9
66	1	1	1	0	0	0	0	0	0	0	1	0	4	24	3	2	1	2
67	1	1	1	0	0	0	0	0	0	0	1	0	4	24	4	2	1	9
68	1	1	1	1	0	0	0	0	0	0	0	0	3	999	4	2	1	9
69	1	1	0	1	0	0	0	0	0	1	0	0	4	24	4	2	1	2
70	1	1	1	1	0	0	0	0	0	1	1	0	4	12	3	2	1	1
71	1	0	0	1	0	0	0	0	0	0	0	0	4	24	4	1	1	2
72	0	1	0	1	0	0	1	1	0	0	0	0	2	60	4	1	2	2
73	0	0	1	0	0	0	0	0	0	0	0	0	3	24	4	1	2	2
74	1	1	1	1	1	1	0	1	0	0	1	0	2	24	3	1	1	3
75	1	1	0	1	0	0	0	1	0	0	1	0	5	42	3	1	2	5
76	1	1	1	0	0	0	0	0	0	0	1	0	5	36	4	1	1	4
77	1	1	1	1	0	1	0	0	0	0	0	0	5	48	4	1	1	4
78	1	1	1	0	0	1	0	0	0	0	1	0	5	48	4	1	2	5
79	1	1	1	0	0	0	0	1	0	0	0	0	2	24	4	1	1	3
80	1	1	0	0	0	0	0	0	0	0	0	0	1	24	5	1	1	1
81	1	0	0	0	0	0	0	0	0	0	1	0	4	24	4	1	1	3
82	1	1	1	0	0	0	0	0	0	0	1	0	5	24	4	1	1	1
83	1	1	0	0	0	0	0	0	0	0	0	0	2	24	4	1	1	2
84	0	1	0	0	0	0	0	0	0	0	0	0	4	999	3	1	1	2
85	1	0	1	1	1	0	0	1	0	0	1	0	5	24	4	1	1	1
86	1	1	1	0	0	0	0	0	0	0	1	0	5	24	4	1	1	1
87	1	0	1	0	0	0	1	0	0	0	1	0	5	6	3	1	1	5

88	1	0	0	0	0	0	0	0	0	0	1	0	1	18	4	1	1	2
89	1	1	1	0	0	0	0	0	0	0	0	0	3	24	4	1	1	2
90	0	1	0	0	0	0	0	1	0	0	1	0	3	999	4	1	1	2
91	1	1	0	1	1	0	0	0	1	0	0	0	1	48	4	2	1	6
92	1	1	1	0	0	0	0	0	0	0	1	0	4	12	4	2	1	3
93	1	0	1	1	0	0	0	0	0	0	1	0	3	60	3	2	1	2
94	1	0	1	1	0	0	0	0	0	0	1	0	4	48	4	1	1	2
95	1	1	1	1	0	0	0	0	1	0	1	0	1	36	3	2	1	3
96	1	0	1	1	0	0	0	1	0	0	0	0	4	36	1	2	1	3
97	1	0	1	0	0	0	1	0	0	0	1	0	4	48	4	2	1	1
98	1	1	0	0	1	0	1	0	0	0	0	0	3	36	4	2	1	5
99	1	1	0	0	0	1	0	0	0	0	1	1	5	36	4	1	1	4
100	1	1	0	1	0	0	0	1	0	0	0	0	4	48	4	2	1	1
101	1	1	1	1	0	0	0	0	0	0	0	0	5	60	3	1	1	2
102	1	1	0	1	0	0	0	0	1	0	0	0	4	36	3	1	1	3
103	1	1	1	1	0	0	0	1	1	0	1	0	5	24	3	2	1	2
104	1	1	1	1	0	0	0	1	0	0	0	0	5	48	4	1	1	4
105	1	1	1	1	0	0	0	0	0	1	1	1	5	36	4	1	2	4
106	1	1	1	1	0	0	1	1	0	0	0	0	5	60	4	1	2	5
107	1	1	1	1	0	0	0	0	0	0	1	0	5	24	4	1	1	3
108	1	0	0	1	0	0	0	0	0	0	1	0	4	24	3	2	1	1
109	1	1	1	1	0	0	1	0	0	0	0	0	5	60	4	1	2	5
110	1	1	1	0	0	1	0	0	0	0	0	1	4	36	3	1	1	3
111	1	1	1	0	0	0	0	0	0	1	0	0	5	24	3	1	1	2
112	1	1	1	0	0	0	0	0	0	1	1	0	4	24	3	1	1	3
113	1	0	1	0	0	0	0	1	1	0	0	0	5	48	4	1	2	3
114	1	0	0	0	0	0	0	0	0	0	0	0	4	48	4	1	2	4
115	1	1	1	0	0	0	1	0	0	0	0	0	4	24	3	1	2	5
116	1	1	1	1	0	0	0	1	0	0	0	0	4	36	4	2	1	5
117	0	1	1	0	0	0	0	1	0	1	0	0	1	24	4	2	2	4
118	1	1	0	0	0	0	1	0	0	0	0	0	1	48	4	2	1	4

Resp No.	X3A	X3B	X3C	X3D	X3E	X3F	X3G	X3H	X3I	X3J	X3K	X3L	X6	X10	X11A	X12	X13	X15
119	1	0	0	0	0	0	1	1	0	0	0	0	1	60	4	1	2	5
120	0	0	1	0	0	0	0	0	0	0	1	0	5	30	4	1	2	4
121	1	1	0	0	0	0	0	0	0	0	1	0	4	36	3	2	1	2
122	1	1	0	0	0	0	0	0	0	0	1	0	4	12	4	2	2	6
123	1	1	1	0	0	0	1	1	1	0	0	0	4	60	4	1	2	3
124	0	1	1	0	0	0	0	1	1	1	0	0	5	60	4	1	2	4
125	1	1	1	1	0	0	0	0	0	1	0	0	4	36	4	2	1	2
126	1	1	0	0	0	0	0	1	1	0	0	0	5	36	3	1	1	1
127	1	1	1	0	0	0	0	0	0	0	1	0	4	24	4	1	2	4
128	1	0	0	0	0	0	1	0	0	0	0	0	4	12	3	1	1	3
129	1	1	1	0	0	0	0	0	1	0	0	0	5	42	3	1	1	2
130	1	1	0	1	0	0	0	1	0	0	1	0	4	48	4	1	1	2
131	1	0	1	0	1	0	0	0	0	1	0	0	3	30	3	2	2	4
132	1	1	0	0	0	0	0	0	0	0	0	0	3	42	4	2	1	3
133	1	0	1	1	0	0	0	0	0	0	1	0	3	42	4	2	1	4
134	1	1	1	1	0	0	1	0	1	1	0	0	5	60	4	1	2	4
135	1	1	1	0	0	0	0	0	0	0	1	0	4	60	4	2	2	3
136	1	0	1	1	0	0	0	0	0	0	0	0	4	66	4	1	2	2
137	1	1	1	1	0	0	1	0	1	0	0	0	4	84	4	1	1	3
138	1	1	0	0	0	0	0	0	0	0	1	0	3	48	4	2	1	2
139	1	1	0	0	0	0	0	0	0	0	0	0	3	24	4	2	2	3
140	1	1	1	0	0	0	0	1	0	0	0	0	5	24	3	1	1	2
141	1	1	1	1	0	0	0	1	1	0	1	0	5	60	3	1	1	1
142	1	0	0	1	0	0	0	1	0	0	0	0	5	36	4	1	1	1
143	1	0	0	0	0	0	0	0	0	0	0	0	5	72	4	1	1	2
144	1	0	0	0	0	0	0	0	0	0	0	0	5	72	4	1	2	1
145	1	0	1	1	0	0	0	0	0	0	1	0	5	24	3	1	1	2
146	1	0	1	1	0	1	0	0	0	0	0	0	5	60	3	1	1	2
147	1	1	0	0	0	0	0	0	0	1	0	0	4	60	3	1	1	1

148	1	1	1	0	0	0	0	1	1	0	0	0	5	42	4	1	1	2
149	1	0	1	0	1	0	0	0	0	0	0	0	3	36	4	2	2	3
150	1	0	1	1	0	0	0	0	0	0	0	0	4	78	4	1	2	4
151	1	1	1	0	1	0	0	0	0	1	0	0	2	60	4	2	2	3
152	1	1	0	1	0	0	0	0	0	0	1	0	4	36	4	1	1	2
153	1	1	1	1	0	0	0	0	0	0	1	0	1	24	4	2	1	3
154	1	1	1	1	0	0	0	0	0	0	1	0	4	36	4	1	1	4
155	1	1	1	1	0	0	0	1	1	0	1	0	5	36	4	1	1	2
156	1	1	1	1	0	0	0	1	0	1	1	0	4	30	4	1	1	4
157	1	1	1	0	0	0	0	1	0	0	0	0	4	36	4	1	1	6
158	1	1	1	0	0	0	0	0	1	0	0	0	4	24	4	1	1	6
159	1	1	1	1	0	0	0	0	0	0	0	0	1	24	4	1	1	6
160	1	0	1	1	0	0	1	0	0	0	0	0	4	48	3	1	1	6
161	1	1	1	1	0	0	0	0	0	0	0	0	5	24	4	1	2	6
162	1	1	1	0	0	0	1	0	0	0	0	0	3	24	3	1	2	6
163	1	1	1	0	0	0	0	0	1	0	0	0	4	36	3	2	1	6
164	1	1	0	0	0	0	1	0	0	0	1	0	5	36	4	2	2	6
165	1	1	1	0	0	0	0	1	0	0	0	0	4	24	3	1	1	6
166	1	1	1	0	0	0	1	0	0	0	0	0	4	12	3	1	1	6
167	1	1	1	1	0	0	0	0	0	0	0	0	4	48	4	2	1	2
168	1	1	1	1	0	1	0	0	0	0	0	0	5	36	4	1	1	4
169	1	1	1	1	0	1	0	1	0	0	0	0	5	48	4	1	1	2
170	1	1	1	1	0	0	0	0	0	0	0	0	5	72	4	1	2	5
171	1	1	0	0	0	1	0	0	0	0	1	0	5	30	4	1	1	2
172	1	1	1	1	0	0	0	0	0	0	1	0	4	72	4	1	1	4
173	1	1	1	1	0	1	0	0	0	0	0	0	5	24	4	1	1	5
174	1	1	1	1	0	1	0	0	0	0	0	0	5	36	4	1	1	2
175	1	1	1	1	0	0	0	0	0	0	0	0	2	60	4	1	1	3
176	0	1	1	0	0	0	0	0	1	0	0	0	4	36	3	1	2	3
177	1	1	1	1	0	0	0	1	0	0	1	0	5	24	4	1	1	5
178	1	1	0	1	0	0	1	0	0	1	1	0	5	42	4	1	2	5

Resp No.	X3A	X3B	X3C	X3D	X3E	X3F	X3G	X3H	X3I	X3J	X3K	X3L	X6	X10	X11A	X12	X13	X15
179	1	1	1	1	0	0	0	0	0	0	1	0	4	48	4	1	1	4
180	1	1	1	1	0	0	0	0	0	1	0	0	4	36	4	1	1	3
181	1	1	1	1	0	0	0	0	0	0	0	1	4	24	4	1	1	3
182	1	1	1	0	0	1	0	0	0	0	0	0	5	60	4	1	2	4
183	1	1	1	1	0	1	0	0	0	1	0	0	5	36	4	1	1	4
184	1	1	0	1	0	0	0	1	0	1	0	0	4	42	3	1	1	4
185	1	1	0	1	0	0	0	0	0	0	1	0	4	36	4	1	1	3
186	1	1	1	1	0	0	0	0	0	1	1	0	5	12	4	1	2	4
187	1	1	1	1	0	0	0	1	0	0	1	0	5	42	4	1	2	4
188	1	1	1	1	0	0	0	0	0	0	1	0	5	48	4	1	1	2
189	1	1	1	0	0	0	0	1	1	0	0	0	4	12	3	1	2	2
190	1	1	1	1	0	1	0	1	0	0	0	0	5	36	3	1	1	3
191	1	1	1	1	0	0	0	0	0	0	0	0	5	48	4	1	1	3
192	1	1	1	1	0	0	0	1	0	0	0	0	4	36	4	1	1	2
193	1	1	1	1	0	0	0	1	0	0	0	0	4	48	4	2	1	2
194	1	1	1	1	0	0	0	0	0	0	0	0	4	36	4	2	1	2
195	1	1	1	0	0	0	0	1	1	0	0	0	9	48	4	1	1	4
196	1	1	1	1	0	0	0	1	0	0	1	0	3	24	4	2	2	4
197	1	1	1	0	0	0	0	1	1	0	0	0	9	42	4	1	1	4
198	1	1	0	0	0	0	0	0	0	0	0	0	4	48	4	1	1	4
199	1	1	0	1	0	0	0	1	0	0	0	0	4	36	4	1	2	3
200	1	1	1	1	1	0	0	1	0	0	1	0	9	24	4	1	1	4
201	0	1	1	1	0	0	0	0	1	1	0	0	4	36	4	1	1	3
202	1	1	0	0	0	0	0	0	0	0	0	0	9	36	4	1	1	4
203	1	1	0	1	0	0	0	1	0	1	1	0	3	24	4	1	1	3
204	1	1	0	0	0	0	0	0	0	0	0	0	4	36	4	2	1	2
205	1	1	0	0	0	0	0	1	0	0	0	0	4	48	4	1	2	3
206	1	1	0	0	0	0	1	0	0	0	1	1	4	48	4	1	1	3
207	1	0	0	0	0	0	0	0	0	0	0	0	9	60	4	1	2	3

208	1	1	0	0	0	0	0	1	1	0	0	0	9	48	4	1	1	3
209	1	1	0	0	0	0	0	0	0	0	1	0	9	36	4	1	2	4
210	1	1	0	0	0	0	0	0	1	1	1	0	9	48	4	1	1	3
211	1	1	0	1	0	0	0	1	0	1	1	0	2	60	4	1	1	4
212	1	1	1	1	0	0	0	0	0	1	1	0	4	60	4	2	2	4
213	1	1	1	1	0	0	0	1	0	0	1	0	9	48	4	1	1	4
214	1	0	0	0	0	0	0	0	0	0	1	0	4	60	4	1	2	3
215	1	1	0	0	0	0	0	0	0	0	0	0	4	36	4	1	2	3
216	1	1	1	1	0	0	0	1	0	0	0	0	4	36	4	1	1	3
217	1	1	1	1	0	0	0	0	0	0	1	0	3	60	4	1	1	4
218	1	1	1	1	0	0	0	0	0	0	1	0	2	60	4	2	1	3
219	1	1	0	0	0	0	0	1	0	0	0	0	9	12	4	2	1	3
220	1	1	0	0	0	0	0	1	1	1	0	0	4	42	4	1	1	4
221	1	1	1	1	0	0	0	0	0	0	0	0	4	24	4	1	2	3
222	1	1	0	1	0	0	0	0	0	1	0	0	3	24	4	1	1	4
223	1	1	1	0	1	0	1	1	0	1	1	0	4	36	4	1	1	4
224	1	1	0	0	0	0	0	0	0	0	0	0	4	36	4	1	2	4
225	1	1	1	1	0	0	0	0	0	0	0	0	9	48	4	1	2	3
226	1	1	1	1	1	0	0	0	0	1	1	0	4	48	4	1	1	4
227	1	1	1	1	0	0	0	1	1	0	1	0	4	42	4	1	1	3
228	1	1	1	0	1	0	0	0	0	0	0	0	2	30	4	2	2	4
229	1	1	0	0	0	0	0	0	0	0	0	0	4	60	4	1	2	4
230	1	1	0	0	1	0	0	0	0	1	0	0	3	36	4	2	2	4
231	1	1	1	1	0	0	0	1	0	1	1	0	3	24	4	1	1	6
232	1	1	1	1	1	1	0	1	0	1	1	0	5	60	4	2	2	3
233	1	0	0	0	0	0	0	0	0	0	0	0	4	60	4	1	2	3
234	1	1	1	1	0	0	0	1	0	0	1	0	4	48	4	1	2	3
235	1	1	1	0	0	0	0	1	0	0	0	0	4	24	4	1	2	4
236	1	1	1	1	0	0	0	1	0	0	1	0	9	36	4	2	2	4
237	1	1	1	0	0	0	0	0	1	0	0	0	4	48	4	1	1	3
238	1	1	0	0	0	0	1	0	0	0	0	1	9	60	4	1	1	3

Resp No.	X3A	X3B	X3C	X3D	X3E	X3F	X3G	X3H	X3I	X3J	X3K	X3L	X6	X10	X11A	X12	X13	X15
239	1	1	1	1	1	1	0	1	1	1	0	0	9	60	4	1	2	3
240	1	1	1	1	0	0	1	0	1	0	1	0	3	36	4	1	1	1
241	1	1	1	0	0	0	0	1	0	0	0	0	2	36	4	2	2	3
242	1	1	1	1	0	0	0	1	1	0	1	0	4	48	4	1	1	2
243	1	0	0	0	0	0	0	0	0	0	0	0	4	24	4	1	1	3
244	0	1	1	1	0	0	0	0	0	0	1	0	4	60	4	1	1	5
245	1	1	0	0	0	0	0	0	0	0	0	0	3	24	4	2	2	4
246	1	1	1	1	0	0	0	0	1	0	1	0	5	48	4	1	2	4
247	1	1	0	1	0	0	1	0	0	0	0	0	9	24	4	1	1	3
248	1	1	1	1	0	0	0	1	1	0	1	0	4	30	4	1	2	3
249	1	1	0	1	0	0	0	0	0	0	1	0	4	48	4	2	1	1
250	1	1	1	1	0	0	0	0	0	0	0	0	1	12	2	2	1	3
251	1	1	0	1	0	0	0	0	0	0	1	0	3	24	3	1	1	3
252	1	1	1	1	0	0	0	0	0	0	0	0	5	24	4	2	1	2
253	1	0	1	1	0	0	0	0	0	0	1	0	4	36	3	2	1	6
254	1	0	1	1	0	0	0	0	0	0	1	0	5	48	3	1	1	2
255	1	0	1	1	0	0	0	0	0	0	1	0	5	24	3	2	1	4
256	1	1	1	1	0	0	0	0	0	0	1	0	4	48	4	2	1	9
257	1	1	0	1	0	0	0	0	0	0	1	0	3	42	4	1	1	3
258	1	1	1	0	0	0	0	0	0	0	1	0	4	24	4	2	1	3
259	1	1	0	1	0	0	0	0	0	0	1	0	5	36	4	2	1	2
260	1	1	1	0	0	0	0	1	0	0	0	0	4	36	4	1	2	4
261	1	1	1	1	0	0	0	1	1	1	1	0	4	60	4	1	2	4
262	1	1	0	0	0	0	0	1	1	0	0	0	4	60	4	1	1	4
263	1	0	0	1	0	0	0	1	0	0	1	0	4	36	3	2	1	2
264	1	1	1	1	0	0	0	0	0	0	1	0	1	42	3	2	2	5
265	1	1	0	0	0	0	0	0	0	0	0	0	4	48	4	1	1	3
266	1	1	0	0	0	0	0	0	0	0	0	1	9	48	4	1	1	4
267	1	1	0	0	0	0	0	0	0	0	0	0	9	12	4	2	2	3

268	1	1	0	0	0	0	0	1	0	1	0	0	4	999	4	1	1	4
269	1	1	1	1	1	1	0	1	0	0	0	0	9	60	4	1	1	4
270	1	1	0	0	0	0	0	1	0	0	0	1	4	36	4	1	1	3
271	1	1	1	0	0	1	0	0	1	1	0	0	9	36	4	1	2	3
272	1	1	0	1	0	0	1	1	0	0	0	0	4	36	4	1	1	4
273	1	0	1	0	0	0	0	0	1	1	0	0	4	24	4	1	2	3
274	1	1	0	0	0	0	0	0	0	0	0	0	4	36	4	2	1	1
275	1	1	0	0	0	1	1	0	0	0	0	0	4	30	4	1	2	4
276	1	1	1	1	0	1	1	0	1	1	0	0	3	48	4	1	1	4
277	1	1	1	1	0	0	1	1	0	0	0	0	4	48	4	1	2	4
278	1	0	1	1	0	0	0	1	0	0	0	0	9	36	4	1	2	4
279	1	1	1	1	0	0	0	0	0	0	0	0	9	48	4	1	1	3
280	1	1	1	1	0	0	0	0	0	0	1	0	9	60	4	1	1	3
281	1	1	1	1	0	0	0	1	1	0	1	0	9	48	4	1	1	3
282	1	0	1	1	0	0	0	0	0	0	0	0	2	24	4	1	1	2
283	1	1	0	0	0	0	0	0	0	0	0	0	4	36	4	1	1	1
284	0	1	0	0	0	0	0	0	0	0	0	0	4	60	4	1	1	4
285	1	1	1	0	0	0	0	1	0	0	1	0	3	36	4	2	1	4
286	1	1	1	0	0	0	0	1	0	0	0	0	4	24	3	1	2	3
287	1	0	1	0	0	0	0	0	0	0	1	1	1	12	4	1	1	2
288	1	1	1	0	0	0	0	0	0	0	1	0	9	48	4	1	1	4
289	1	1	1	0	0	1	0	0	0	0	0	0	3	24	4	1	2	3
290	1	0	1	1	0	0	0	1	1	1	1	0	3	60	4	2	1	2
291	1	0	0	0	0	0	0	0	0	0	0	0	4	100	1	2	1	4
292	1	1	1	1	0	0	0	0	0	0	0	0	5	24	3	1	1	4
293	1	1	1	0	0	0	0	0	0	0	1	0	4	60	4	2	1	5
294	1	1	0	1	0	0	0	0	0	0	1	0	4	12	2	1	1	2
295	1	1	1	1	1	0	0	1	1	1	0	0	9	36	4	2	2	4
296	1	0	0	0	0	0	0	0	0	0	0	0	9	60	4	1	2	3
297	1	1	0	0	0	0	0	1	0	0	0	0	9	30	4	1	1	3
298	1	1	1	0	0	0	0	1	0	1	1	0	9	30	4	1	1	4

Resp No.	X3A	X3B	X3C	X3D	X3E	X3F	X3G	X3H	X3I	X3J	X3K	X3L	X6	X10	X11A	X12	X13	X15
299	1	1	0	0	0	0	0	1	0	0	0	0	9	42	4	1	2	4
300	1	1	0	0	0	0	1	0	1	0	0	0	4	48	5	1	1	4
301	1	1	0	0	1	0	0	0	0	1	0	0	4	999	4	2	1	3
302	1	1	0	0	0	0	0	0	0	0	0	0	9	24	4	2	2	9
303	1	1	0	0	0	0	0	0	0	0	0	0	3	36	4	2	1	4
304	1	1	1	1	0	0	0	1	0	0	1	0	9	24	4	1	1	4
305	1	1	0	0	1	0	0	1	0	0	0	0	9	36	4	2	2	3
306	1	1	0	1	0	0	0	1	0	0	0	0	4	36	4	1	1	4
307	1	0	0	0	0	0	0	0	0	0	0	0	9	30	4	1	1	4
308	1	0	0	0	0	0	0	0	0	0	0	0	9	36	4	1	2	4
309	1	1	0	1	1	0	1	0	1	1	0	0	9	60	4	1	1	4
310	1	0	1	0	0	0	0	0	0	0	0	0	4	24	3	1	1	4
311	1	0	0	0	0	0	0	0	0	0	0	0	4	24	5	1	2	6
312	1	1	1	0	1	0	0	0	0	0	0	0	4	30	4	1	1	6
313	1	1	0	0	0	0	0	1	1	0	0	0	4	48	4	1	2	3
314	1	1	0	1	0	0	0	0	0	0	1	0	3	24	4	2	2	4
315	1	1	1	1	1	0	1	1	0	0	1	0	3	48	3	1	1	4
316	1	1	0	1	0	0	0	1	0	0	0	0	2	36	4	1	1	2
317	1	1	1	0	0	0	0	0	0	0	1	0	4	48	4	1	2	1
318	1	0	1	0	0	0	0	0	0	0	0	0	4	12	4	1	1	4
319	1	0	0	0	0	0	0	0	0	0	0	0	1	36	3	1	1	2
320	1	1	1	0	0	0	1	0	0	0	0	0	5	36	4	1	2	4
321	1	1	0	1	0	0	0	0	0	0	1	0	5	72	3	1	2	3
322	1	1	0	1	0	0	0	1	0	0	0	0	3	24	4	2	2	4
323	1	1	0	0	0	0	0	0	0	0	0	0	9	60	4	2	1	4
324	1	1	1	0	0	0	1	0	0	0	1	0	5	48	4	1	2	3
325	1	1	1	1	0	0	0	1	0	0	0	0	5	72	2	2	1	4
326	1	1	0	0	0	0	1	0	1	0	0	0	5	24	3	1	2	3
327	0	0	0	0	1	0	1	1	0	0	0	0	2	999	5	1	2	2

328	1	1	0	0	1	0	0	1	0	0	0	0	3	24	4	2	2	3
329	1	1	1	0	0	0	0	0	0	0	0	0	4	24	4	1	1	2
330	1	1	1	1	0	0	0	1	1	0	0	0	4	36	4	1	1	3
331	1	1	0	0	0	0	0	0	0	0	0	0	9	48	4	1	1	3
332	1	1	1	0	0	0	1	0	0	0	0	0	9	24	4	1	1	4
333	1	1	0	0	0	0	0	1	0	0	0	0	4	36	4	1	2	4
334	1	1	0	0	0	0	0	1	0	0	1	0	4	60	3	1	1	3
335	1	1	0	0	0	0	0	1	0	0	1	0	4	36	1	1	1	2
336	1	1	0	1	0	0	0	1	0	0	0	0	3	54	4	1	1	3
337	1	0	1	1	0	0	0	1	0	0	0	0	5	48	5	1	1	4
338	1	1	0	1	0	0	0	0	0	0	1	0	4	42	4	1	1	3
339	1	0	1	0	0	0	0	1	0	0	1	0	4	24	3	1	1	3
340	1	0	0	0	0	0	0	0	0	0	0	0	4	24	3	1	1	4
341	1	0	0	1	0	0	0	1	0	0	1	0	4	42	4	1	1	2
342	1	1	0	1	0	0	0	0	0	0	1	0	4	48	4	1	1	2
343	0	0	0	0	0	0	0	1	0	0	0	0	4	12	3	1	1	2
344	1	0	1	1	0	1	0	0	0	0	0	0	4	48	4	1	1	4
345	1	1	0	0	0	1	1	0	0	0	0	0	4	12	4	1	2	2
346	1	1	0	1	0	0	0	0	0	0	1	0	4	12	3	1	1	2
347	1	0	0	1	0	0	0	1	0	0	1	0	4	36	4	2	1	9
348	1	1	0	1	0	0	0	0	0	0	1	0	4	18	4	1	2	3
349	1	1	0	0	0	0	0	1	0	0	1	0	3	48	4	2	1	3
350	1	1	0	0	0	0	0	1	0	0	1	0	4	36	4	1	1	2
351	1	1	1	0	0	0	0	1	0	0	0	0	5	36	4	1	1	3
352	1	1	0	0	0	0	0	0	0	0	0	0	9	24	4	2	2	3
353	1	1	0	0	0	0	0	1	0	0	0	0	9	24	4	1	1	4
354	1	1	0	0	0	0	1	0	0	0	0	0	4	60	4	2	2	4
355	1	0	0	0	0	0	0	0	0	0	0	0	4	60	4	1	1	2
356	1	1	1	1	0	0	0	0	0	0	1	0	3	42	4	1	1	4
357	1	0	0	0	0	0	0	0	0	0	0	0	9	60	4	1	2	3
358	1	1	0	0	0	0	0	0	0	0	1	0	9	36	4	1	1	2

Resp No.	X3A	X3B	X3C	X3D	X3E	X3F	X3G	X3H	X3I	X3J	X3K	X3L	X6	X10	X11A	X12	X13	X15
359	1	1	0	1	0	0	0	0	0	1	1	0	3	48	4	2	1	4
360	1	1	0	0	0	0	0	1	1	0	1	0	9	60	4	1	1	3
361	0	0	0	0	0	0	0	1	0	0	0	0	9	36	4	1	1	3
362	1	1	0	0	0	0	1	1	0	0	0	0	4	24	4	2	1	3
363	1	0	0	0	0	0	1	0	0	0	0	0	4	60	4	1	2	4
364	1	1	1	1	0	0	0	0	0	0	0	0	3	60	4	2	1	3
365	1	1	0	1	0	0	0	0	0	0	1	0	2	36	4	1	1	4
366	1	1	0	0	0	0	0	0	0	0	1	0	3	36	4	2	1	3
367	1	1	0	0	0	0	0	0	0	0	0	0	4	48	4	1	1	3
368	1	1	0	0	0	0	0	1	0	0	1	0	3	60	4	1	1	3
369	1	1	1	0	1	0	0	0	0	0	0	0	9	24	3	2	2	4
370	1	1	1	0	0	0	0	1	1	0	1	0	3	42	4	1	1	3
371	1	1	0	0	0	0	0	1	0	1	0	0	4	48	4	1	2	4
372	1	1	0	0	0	0	0	1	1	0	0	0	4	36	5	1	1	3
373	1	1	0	1	0	0	0	0	0	0	1	0	3	60	4	2	1	3
374	1	1	0	0	0	0	1	0	0	1	1	0	4	30	4	1	2	4
375	1	1	1	1	0	0	0	0	0	0	0	0	9	60	4	1	1	3
376	1	0	0	0	1	0	0	1	0	0	0	0	3	36	4	1	2	4
377	1	0	0	0	0	0	0	0	0	0	0	0	3	12	4	1	2	3
378	1	1	0	0	0	0	0	0	0	0	0	0	4	60	4	2	1	3
379	1	0	0	0	0	0	0	0	0	0	0	0	4	24	4	1	2	4
380	1	1	1	0	0	0	0	0	0	0	0	0	3	42	4	1	1	3
381	0	0	0	0	0	0	0	0	0	0	0	0	4	60	4	1	2	4
382	1	1	0	0	0	0	1	0	1	0	1	0	3	36	4	1	1	3
383	1	0	1	1	0	0	0	0	0	0	0	0	4	48	4	1	1	3
384	1	1	0	0	0	0	1	1	0	0	1	0	4	36	4	2	2	4
385	1	1	1	1	0	0	0	1	0	0	1	0	4	42	4	1	1	5
386	1	1	0	0	0	0	0	1	0	0	1	0	3	48	4	1	1	2
387	1	0	1	1	0	0	0	0	0	0	1	0	4	999	4	1	1	3

388	1	1	0	0	0	0	0	1	0	0	1	0	3	48	4	1	2	4
389	1	1	0	0	0	0	0	0	0	0	0	0	3	24	4	2	9	9
390	1	1	0	0	0	0	0	0	0	0	0	0	3	48	4	1	2	3
391	1	1	0	0	0	0	0	1	1	0	0	0	9	48	4	1	1	3
392	1	0	0	0	0	0	0	0	0	0	0	0	4	36	4	1	2	3
393	1	0	1	1	0	0	0	0	0	0	0	0	4	60	4	1	2	4
394	1	1	0	0	0	0	0	0	0	0	1	0	9	24	4	2	2	4
395	1	1	0	0	0	0	0	1	0	0	0	1	3	36	4	2	1	5
396	1	1	0	0	0	0	0	0	0	0	0	0	4	48	4	1	1	3
397	1	1	1	1	0	0	0	0	0	0	0	0	3	36	4	1	1	5
398	0	1	0	0	0	0	0	0	0	0	0	0	4	48	4	2	1	3
399	1	1	1	1	0	0	0	0	0	0	0	0	5	60	4	1	2	4
400	1	1	1	1	0	0	0	0	0	0	0	0	5	36	4	1	1	2
401	0	0	0	0	0	0	0	0	0	0	0	0	4	24	4	1	1	2
402	1	1	1	1	0	0	0	0	0	0	0	0	5	42	4	1	1	2
403	1	1	1	0	0	0	0	0	0	0	0	0	4	36	4	1	1	2
404	1	1	1	1	0	0	0	0	0	0	1	0	5	24	4	2	1	2
405	1	1	1	1	0	0	0	0	0	0	0	0	4	24	4	1	2	2
406	1	1	1	1	0	0	1	0	0	0	0	0	4	60	4	1	1	3
407	0	1	1	0	1	0	0	1	0	0	0	0	5	24	4	1	2	4
408	1	1	1	1	0	0	0	0	0	0	0	0	5	24	4	1	1	2
409	1	1	1	1	0	0	0	0	0	0	1	0	4	42	4	1	1	9
410	1	1	1	1	0	0	0	0	0	0	0	0	5	36	4	2	1	3
411	1	0	0	0	0	1	1	0	0	0	0	0	5	60	4	1	2	4
412	1	1	1	1	0	0	0	0	0	0	0	0	5	30	4	1	1	2
413	1	1	1	1	0	0	0	0	0	0	1	0	5	36	4	1	1	3
414	1	1	1	1	0	0	0	0	0	0	0	0	4	36	4	1	1	3

'Missing Value' = 9 for all variables in the above table except for the variable X10, where it is denoted by 999.

- X3b was defined as

Chat	= 1
Otherwise	= 0

- X3c was defined as

Browsing	= 1
Otherwise	= 0

- X3d was defined as

Downloading	= 1
Otherwise	= 0

- X3e was defined as

Shopping	= 1
Otherwise	= 0

- X3f was defined as

Net-telephony	= 1
Otherwise	= 0

- X3g was defined as

e-commerce	= 1
Otherwise	= 0

- X3h was defined as

Entertainment	= 1
Otherwise	= 0

- X3i was defined as

Adult sites	= 1
Otherwise	= 0

- X3j was defined as

Astrology and horoscope	= 1
Otherwise	= 0

- X3k was defined as

Education	= 1
Otherwise	= 0

- X3l was defined as

Any other	= 1
Otherwise	= 0

- The variable X6 was framed as
  'At what time of the day do you prefer to use the cyber café?'

This was defined as	Morning	= 1
	Noon	= 2
	Afternoon	= 3
	Evening	= 4
	Night	= 5

- The variable X10 was framed as
  'How long have you been using the cyber café?'
  Actual number of months is reported.
- The variable X11A was framed as
  'The behaviour of the café owner is very cordial

Strongly disagree	= 1
Disagree	= 2
Neither agree nor disagree	= 3

Agree = 4
Strongly agree = 5

- X12 (Gender) - Defined as
  - Male = 1
  - Female = 2
- X13 (Marital status) - Defined as
  - Single = 1
  - Married = 2
- X15 (Income) - Defined as
  - < ₹10,000 = 1
  - 10,000 to 19,999 = 2
  - 20,000 to 29,999 = 3
  - 30,000 to 49,999 = 4
  - 50,000 to 64,999 = 5
  - 65,000 and above = 6

DESCRIPTIVE ANALYSIS OF UNIVARIATE DATA

LEARNING OBJECTIVE 3
Discuss the type of descriptive univariate analysis to be carried on nominal, ordinal, interval and ratio scale.

As indicated earlier, univariate procedures deal with analysis of one variable at a time. In this chapter only a brief review of various techniques is given. The first step under univariate analysis is the preparation of frequency distributions of each variable. The frequency distribution is the counting of responses or observations for each of the categories or codes assigned to a variable. The SPSS instructions for preparing a frequency distribution table are explained in Appendix 11.1. Consider a nominal scale variable—gender of respondents.

Table 11.3 shows both the raw frequency and the percentages of responses for each category in case of the variable gender, the data for which is presented in Table 11.2.

TABLE 11.3 Gender of the respondent

		Frequency	Per cent	Valid Per cent	Cumulative Per cent
Valid	Male	301	72.7	72.7	72.7
	Female	113	27.3	27.3	100.0
	Total	414	100.0	100.0	

This tabulation process can be done by hand using tally marks. However, in case of large sample, the frequency distribution table is prepared using computer software. In the present case, SPSS software is used. The results indicate that out of a sample of 414 respondents, 301 are male and 113 are female. The raw frequencies are often converted into percentages as they are more meaningful. In the present case, for example, there are 72.7 per cent male and 27.3 per cent female respondents.

Missing Data

There are situations when certain questions knowingly or unknowingly are not answered by the respondents. The responses corresponding to such respondents are treated as 'missing data'. The frequency distribution in case of the variable 'marital status' is presented in Table 11.4.

TABLE 11.4
Marital status of respondents

		Frequency	Per cent	Valid Per cent	Cumulative Per cent
Valid	Single	285	68.8	69.0	69.0
	Married	128	30.9	31.0	100.0
	Total	413	99.8	100.0	
Missing	9	1	0.2		
Total		414	100.0		

If the marital status variable is examined in Table 11.2, the respondent who did not answer the question on 'marital status' is coded as nine, which is being treated as the missing data. The missing value could as well be coded with another number. The only precaution to be kept in mind is that a missing observation should be assigned a number that should not be equal to the value of the variable obtained as part of the survey. If the value of the missing observation was available; it could perhaps lead to different research conclusions. The intensity of the deviation of the actual results from the observed depends upon the number of missing observations and the extent to which the missing data would be different from actual observation.

In case of Table 11.4, it may be noted that out of a sample of 414 respondents, 285 are single, 128 are married and one observation is missing. In the column on 'per cent' in this table, it is indicated that 68.8 per cent are single, 30.9 per cent are married and 0.2 per cent are missing observation. Here, the percentages are computed on a total sample of 414. As it is known that one observation is missing, the actual sample for this variable should be 413. Therefore, a column named 'valid per cent' has been included, where the percentages are computed based on a sample of 413. The result using the 'valid per cent' column indicates that 69.0 per cent of respondents are single, whereas 31 per cent are married. The results in both cases are almost similar. This is so because there was only one single missing value. Generally, if the volume of missing data is small, it is unlikely to affect the conclusion from the analysis. This may not always be the case. It is for this reason that the 'valid per cent' column should be used for interpreting the results.

Table 11.5 gives the frequency distribution of time of the day preferred to use café. It may be noted from this table that the number of missing observations in this case is 48, amounting to 11.6 per cent of the sample. As a consequence of this, the results of 'per cent' and 'valid per cent' vary, especially for 'afternoon', 'evening' and 'night' response categories.

It may be worth considering a variable where the cumulative frequencies in percentages may be very useful in interpretation of the results. Table 11.6 presents

TABLE 11.5
Preferred time of the day for using cyber café

		Frequency	Per cent	Valid Per cent	Cumulative Per cent
Valid	Morning	18	4.3	4.9	4.9
	Noon	18	4.3	4.9	9.8
	Afternoon	61	14.7	16.7	26.5
	Evening	178	43.0	48.6	75.1
	Night	91	22.0	24.9	100.0
	Total	366	88.4	100.0	
Missing	9	48	11.6		
Total		414	100.0		

TABLE 11.6
Monthly household income of cyber café users

		Frequency	Per cent	Valid Per cent	Cumulative Per cent
Valid	Less than ₹10,000	26	6.3	6.4	6.4
	₹10,000 to ₹19,999	83	20.0	20.5	27.0
	₹20,000 to ₹29,999	129	31.2	31.9	58.9
	₹30,000 to ₹49,999	123	29.7	30.4	89.4
	₹50,000 to ₹64,999	24	5.8	5.9	95.3
	₹65,000 and above	19	4.6	4.7	100.0
	Total	404	97.6	100.0	
Missing	9	10	2.4		
Total		414	100.0		

the frequency distribution of monthly household income of 414 respondents. It may be noted that there are 10 missing observations in this table. Therefore, the analysis should be applicable using a sample of 404 respondents. As discussed earlier the 'valid per cent' column should be used for interpretation of the results. For example, the results indicate that 20.5 per cent of the respondents have a monthly household income of ₹10,000 to ₹19,999, whereas 4.7 per cent of respondents have monthly income of ₹65,000 and more. The last column of Table 11.6 presents cumulative per cent. The results in Table 11.6 indicate that while 27 per cent of the respondents have a monthly household income less than or equal to ₹19,999, there are 95.3 per cent of them that have income less than or equal to ₹64,999.

Analysis of Multiple Responses

At times, the researcher comes across multiple category questions where respondents could choose more than one answer. In such a case, the preparation of frequency table and its interpretation is slightly different. If the question in the research study is multiple category question and the respondents are allowed to tick more than one choice, the percentage in such a case may not add up to 100. For example, one may consider the following question:

When accessing the internet at a cyber café, tick up to frequently used applications for which you use the cyber café.

1. E-mail
2. Chat
3. Browsing
4. Downloading
5. Shopping
6. Net telephony
7. Business and Commerce (e-commerce)
8. Entertainment
9. Adult sites
10. Astrology and Horoscope
11. Education
12. Any other, please specify.

It may be recalled that in Table 11.2, the coding for the variable X_3 has been in binary form where values one and zero are assigned. If the respondent uses a particular application, the value assigned is 1, otherwise 0. The resulting frequency table for the above-mentioned question is as presented in Table 11.7.

In Table 11.7 the percentages are computed on the total sample size of 414. If these percentages are added up, they would exceed more than 100 per cent. This is because of multiplicity of answers as respondents were given the chance to choose

TABLE 11.7 Frequently used applications at cyber café

Sl. No.	Application	Frequencies	Percentage (%)
1	Email	399	94.9
2	Chat	316	76.3
3	Browsing	232	56.0
4	Downloading	197	47.6
5	Shopping	30	7.2
6	Net telephony	30	7.2
7	E-commerce	51	12.3
8	Entertainment	135	32.6
9	Adult sites	59	14.3
10	Astrology and horoscopes	52	12.6
11	Education	159	38.4
12	Any Other	14	3.4
TOTAL RESPONDENTS		414	*

*Total exceeds 100% because of multiplicity of answers.

more than one answer. The interpretation of the table would be based on a sample of 414 and is given as:

- The most used application at a cyber café is e-mail. It is seen that 94.9 per cent of the users make use of this.
- The second popular application is chatting, and 76.3 per cent of the sample respondents make use of it.
- Similarly, other applications in order of preference are browsing (56 per cent), downloading (47.6 per cent), education 35.4 per cent), entertainment (32.6 per cent) and so on.

Analysis of Ordinal Scaled Questions

It is quite likely that there may be some respondents who might have used more than one brand of toothpaste in the last one year. These could be Colgate, Pepsodent, Close up, Neem, Sensodyne etc. The respondents could be asked to rank their preference for toothpaste. The question before the researcher is how to tabulate and interpret the responses to such questions. It could be done in two ways as would be shown in the following example. The questions asked of the respondents in such a case could be:

- Rank the following five attributes while choosing a restaurant for dinner. Assign a rank of 1 to the most important, 2 to the next important ... and 5 to the least important.
  - Ambience
  - Food quality
  - Menu variety
  - Service
  - Location

From a sample of 32, the responses obtained are given in Table 11.8. To construct univariate tables out of the given data, one can take up one column at a time from Table 11.8 and prepare the separate frequency tables. For example, distribution of rank assigned to attribute food quality may be considered in Table 11.9.

TABLE 11.8 Ranking of various attributes while selecting a restaurant for dinner

Respondent No.	Ambience	Food Quality	Menu Variety	Service	Location
1	3	1	4	2	5
2	5	2	1	4	3
3	1	2	5	3	4
4	3	1	5	2	4
5	2	1	5	3	4
6	1	3	2	4	5
7	3	2	4	1	5
8	1	2	5	3	4
9	4	2	3	5	1
10	4	3	1	2	5
11	2	1	5	3	4
12	5	1	4	3	2
13	3	1	5	4	2
14	4	1	2	5	3
15	3	2	5	1	4
16	1	2	5	4	3
17	3	1	4	2	5
18	5	2	1	3	4
19	2	1	4	3	5
20	3	2	4	5	1
21	4	1	5	2	3
22	3	2	1	4	5
23	5	1	4	3	2
24	3	2	5	1	4
25	5	1	4	3	2
26	2	1	3	5	4
27	3	1	4	2	5
28	3	2	1	4	5
29	3	1	5	2	4
30	4	2	1	3	5
31	2	1	5	3	4
32	3	4	1	2	5

TABLE 11.9 Distribution of ranks assigned to food quality

Rank	Frequency	Per cent
1	16	50.0
2	13	40.6
3	2	6.3
4	1	3.1
5	—	—
Total	32	100.0

It is seen from Table 11.9 that out of 32 respondents, 16 (50 per cent) have assigned rank one, 13 (40.6 per cent) have assigned rank two, 2 (6.3 per cent) have assigned rank three and 1 (3.1 per cent) has assigned rank four to food quality. This shows that food quality is given a lot of importance by the respondents. Similar analysis could be carried out for other attributes.

The other way of preparing a univariate table could be to find distribution of attribute which got various ranks. Table 11.10 indicates the distribution of attributes that received rank one.

Table 11.10 indicates that 50 per cent of the respondents gave food quality rank one, whereas 21.88 per cent gave menu variety as rank one, followed by ambience that was ranked one by 12.5 per cent of the respondents. Similar analysis could be carried out corresponding to the remaining attributes.

TABLE 11.10 Distribution of attributes that received rank one

Attribute	Number	Percentage
Ambience	4	12.50
Food Quality	16	50.00
Menu Variety	7	21.88
Service	3	9.38
Location	2	6.25
Total	32	100.00

Grouping Large Data Sets

Sometimes data collected is very large and needs to be collapsed for interpretation. For example, the variable X10 in Table 11.2 is worded as:

'How long you have been using cyber café?'

The respondents were to answer the question in actual number of months.' This is a ratio scale measurement. 'The frequency distribution for this variable is given in Table 11.11.'

TABLE 11.11 Distribution of respondents by duration of using cyber café in months

		Frequency	Per cent	Valid Per cent	Cumulative Per cent
Valid	6	1	0.2	0.2	0.2
	12	26	6.3	6.4	6.7
	18	3	0.7	0.7	7.4
	24	90	21.7	22.2	29.6
	30	13	3.1	3.2	32.8
	36	100	24.2	24.6	57.4
	42	24	5.8	5.9	63.3
	48	72	17.4	17.7	81.0
	54	1	0.2	0.2	81.3
	60	63	15.2	15.5	96.8
	66	1	0.2	0.2	97.0
	72	8	1.9	2.0	99.0
	78	1	0.2	0.2	99.3
	84	1	0.2	0.2	99.5
	100	1	0.2	0.2	99.8
	120	1	0.2	0.2	100.0
	Total	406	98.1	100.0	
Missing	999	8	1.9		
Total		414	100.0		

Table 11.11 indicates that there are too many categories to allow quick interpretation of the results. This could be facilitated by recoding the data into fewer broader categories. For example, X10 could be recoded as less than or equal to 30 months, 31 to 60 months, 61 to 90 months and 91 to 120 months. The frequency distribution for this is presented in Table 11.12.

Table 11.12 presents the grouped frequency distribution for 406 respondents as there are eight missing observations. The results show that while 32.8 per cent of the respondents are using cyber cafés for less than or equal to 30 months, 64 per cent are using it for 31 to 60 months (both values included).

Similar analysis could be carried out in the case of interval scale data. We have used variable X11A, which is an interval scale variable to prepare the frequency distribution for the behaviour of café owner. The results are presented in Table 11.13.

The results of Table 11.13 indicate that more than three-fourths of the respondents are of the view that the behaviour of the cyber café owner is cordial. It is only a very small proportion that does not agree with the statement. As this variable is an interval scale variable, mean, standard deviation and other statistics could be computed. The details on the computations are presented in the sebsequent sections.

The data such as presented in Table 11.2 could be further summarized by using measures of central tendency and dispersion.

TABLE 11.12 Grouped frequency distribution of respondents by the duration of using cyber café in months

		Frequency	Per cent	Valid Per cent	Cumulative Per cent
Valid	Less than or equal to 30 months	133	32.1	32.8	32.8
	31 to 60 months	260	62.8	64.0	96.8
	61 to 90 months	11	2.7	2.7	99.5
	91 to 120 months	2	0.5	0.5	100.0
	Total	406	98.1	100.0	
Missing	System	8	1.9		
Total		414	100.0		

TABLE 11.13 Behaviour of café owner

		Frequency	Percent	Valid Per cent	Cumulative Per cent
Valid	Strongly disagree	5	1.2	1.2	1.2
	Disagree	5	1.2	1.2	2.4
	Neither agree nor disagree	69	16.7	16.7	19.1
	Agree	319	77.1	77.1	96.1
	Strongly agree	16	3.9	3.9	100.0
	Total	414	100.0	100.0	

Measures of central tendency

There are three measures of central tendency that are used in research—mean, median and mode.

1. The mean represents the arithmetic average of a variable is appropriate for interval and ratio scale data. The mean is computed as:

$$\overline{X} = \frac{\sum_{i=1}^{n} X_i}{n}$$

where,

$\overline{X}$ = Mean of some variable X
X_i = Value of ith observation on that sample
n = Number of observations in the sample

It is also possible to compute the value of mean when interval or ratio scale data are grouped into categories or classes. The formula for mean in such a case is given by:

$$\overline{X} = \frac{\sum_{i=1}^{k} f_i X_i}{n}$$

where,

f_i = Frequency of ith class
X_i = Midpoint of ith class
k = Number of classes

Example 11.1

The percentage of dividend declared by a company over the last 12 years is 5, 8, 6, 10, 12, 20, 18, 15, 30, 25, 20, 16. Compute the average dividend.

Solution:

Let X_i denote the dividend declared in i^{th} year;

$$\sum X_i = 185 \quad \overline{X} = \frac{\sum X_i}{n} = 15.417$$

Therefore, the average dividend declared by the company in the last 12 years is 15.417 per cent.

Example 11.2

The sales data of 250 retail outlets in the garment industry gave the following distribution. Compute the arithmetic mean of the sales.

Sales (in ₹lakh)	No. of firms
0 – 20	6
20 – 40	16
40 – 60	34
60 – 80	46
80 – 100	75
100 – 120	42
120 – 140	20
140 – 160	11
Total	**250**

Solution:

Sales (in ₹lakh)	No. of firms (*f*)	Mid-point (*X*)	*X* × *f*
0 – 20	6	10	60
20 – 40	16	30	480
40 – 60	34	50	1700
60 – 80	46	70	3220
80 – 100	75	90	6750
100 – 120	42	110	4620
120 – 140	20	130	2600
140 – 160	11	150	1650
Total	**250**		**21080**

$$\Sigma X_i f_i = 21080 \quad \overline{X} = \frac{\Sigma X_i f_i}{\Sigma f_i} = \frac{21080}{250} = 84.32$$

Hence, the average sales of 250 retail outlets in the garments industry is ₹84.32 lakh. The main limitation of arithmetic mean as a measure of central tendency is that it is unduly affected by extreme values. Further, it cannot be computed with open-ended frequency distribution without making assumptions regarding the size of the class interval of the open-ended classes. In an extremely asymmetrical distribution, it is not a good measure of central tendency.

2. The median can be computed for ratio, interval or ordinal scale data. The median is that value in the distribution such that 50 per cent of the observations are below it and 50 per cent are above it. The median for the ungrouped data is defined as the middle value when the data is arranged in ascending or descending order of magnitude. In case the number of items in the sample is odd, the value of $(n + 1)/2$th item gives the median. However if there are even number of items in the sample, say of size $2n$, the arithmetic mean of nth and $(n + 1)$th items gives the median. It is again emphasized that data needs to be arranged in ascending or descending order of the magnitude before computing the median.

Example 11.3

The marks of 21 students in economics are given 62, 38, 42, 43, 57, 72, 68, 60, 72, 70, 65, 47, 49, 39, 66, 73, 81, 55, 57, 57, 59. Compute the median of the distribution.

Solution:
By arranging the data in ascending order of magnitude, we obtain: 38, 39, 42, 43, 47, 49, 55, 57, 57, 57, 59, 60, 62, 65, 66, 68, 70, 72, 72, 73, 81.

The median will be the value of the 11th observation arranged as above. Therefore, the value of median equals 59. This means 50 per cent of students score marks below 59 and 50 per cent score above 59.

Example 11.4

What would be the median score in the above example if there were 22 students in the class and the score of the 22nd student was 79.

Solution:
By arranging the data in ascending order of magnitude, we obtain: 38, 39, 42, 43, 47, 49, 55, 57, 57, 57, 59, 60, 62, 65, 66, 68, 70, 72, 72, 73, 79, 81.

The median is given by the average of 11th and 12th observation when arranged in ascending order of magnitude.

The value of 11th observation = 59.
The value of 12th observation = 60.
Mean of 11th and 12th observation = (59 + 60)/2 = 59.5.

Hence 50 per cent of the students score marks below 59.5 per cent and 50 per cent score above 59.5.

The median could also be computed for the grouped data. In that case first of all, median class is located and then median is computed using interpolation by using the assumption that all items are evenly spread over the entire class interval. The median for the grouped data is computed using the following formula

$$\text{Median} = l + \frac{\frac{N}{2} - CF}{f} \times h$$

where

l = Lower limit of the median class
f = Frequency of the median class
CF = Cumulating frequency for the class immediately below the class containing the median
h = Size of the interval of the median class.

Example 11.5 The distribution of dividend declared by 77 companies is given in the following table. Compute the median of the distribution.

Percentage of dividend declared	Number of Companies
0 – 10	6
10 – 20	8
20 – 30	23
30 – 40	18
40 – 50	14
50 – 60	6
60 – 70	2
Total	77

Solution:

Percentage of dividend declared	Number of Companies (f)	CF
0 – 10	6	6
10 – 20	8	14
20 – 30	23	37
30 – 40	18	55
40 – 50	14	69
50 – 60	6	75
60 – 70	2	77
Total	**77**	

$$\text{Median} = l + \frac{\frac{N}{2} - CF}{f} \times h$$

where

l = Lower limit of the median class = 30

f = Frequency of the median class = 1

CF = Cumulating frequency for the class immediately below the class containing the median = 37

h = Size of the interval of the median class = 10

Substituting these values in the formula for median, we get

Median = 30.83

The results show that half of the companies have declared less than 30.83 per cent dividend and the other half have declared more than 30.83 per cent dividend.

The limitations of median as a measure of central tendency is that it does not use each and every observation in its computation since it is a positional average.

3. The mode is that measure of central tendency which is appropriate for nominal or higher order scales. It is the point of maximum frequency in a distribution around which other items of the set cluster densely. Mode should not be computed for ordinal or interval data unless these data have been grouped first. The concept is widely used in business, e.g. a shoe store owner would be naturally interested in knowing the size of the shoe that the majority of the customers ask for. Similarly, a garment manufacturer is interested in determining the size of the shirt that fits most people so as to plan its production accordingly.

Example 11.6 The marks of 20 students of a class in statistics are given as under:

44, **52**, 40, 61, 58, **52**, 63, 75, 87, **52**, 63, 38, 44, 61, 68, 75, 72, **52**, 51, 50,

Solution: Compute the mode of the distribution

It is observed that the maximum number of students (four) have obtained 52 marks. Therefore, the mode of the distribution is 52.

In the case of grouped data, the following formula may be used:

$$\text{Mode} = l + \frac{f - f_1}{2f - f_1 - f_2} \times h$$

where,

l = Lower limit of the modal class

f_1, f_2 = The frequencies of the classes preceding and following the modal class respectively.

f = Frequency of modal class

h = Size of the class interval

Example 11.7 The data in the following frequency distribution is about monthly wages of semi-skilled worker in a town. Compute the modal wage.

Monthly wage (₹)	Number of workers
5000 – 6000	15
6000 – 7000	20
7000 – 8000	24
8000 – 9000	32
9000 – 10000	28
10000 – 11000	20
11000 – 12000	16
Total	155

Solution:

The mode is given by the formula

$$\text{Mode} = l + \frac{f - f_1}{2f - f_1 - f_2} \times h$$

where

l = Lower limit of the modal class = 8000

f_1, f_2 = The frequencies of the classes preceding and following the modal class respectively = 24, 28

f = Frequency of modal class = 32

h = Size of the class interval = 1000

$$\text{Mode} = 8000 + \frac{32 - 24}{64 - 24 - 28} \times 1000 = 8666.7$$

Hence, modal wages are ₹8666.7.

Another important concept is skewness, which measures lack of symmetry in the distribution. In case of symmetrical distribution, mean = median = mode. For a positively skewed distribution, mean > median > mode. In such a case, the longer tail of the distribution is towards the right, the mode falls under the peak and the mean changes its position as it is affected by extreme values. The same is the case with negatively skewed distribution where arithmetic mean < median < mode.

The skewness is measured by the difference between arithmetic mean and mode. If the value of arithmetic mean is greater than mode, skewness is positive and if the value of the expression is negative, skewness is negative.

Measures of dispersion

The measures of central tendency locate the centre of the distribution. However, they do not provide enough information to the researcher to fully understand the distribution being examined. For example, measures of central tendency do not indicate how items are spread out on either side of the centre. Therefore, there is a need to study the spread of a distribution of a variable and the methods which provide that are called measures of dispersion.

The study of dispersion could help in taking better decisions. This is because small dispersion indicates high uniformity of the items, whereas large variability denotes less uniformity. If returns on a particular investment show lot of variability (dispersion), it means a risky investment as compared to the one where variability is very small. A company may not only be interested in finding out the average sales of a product but also the variability in the sales over time. The various measures of dispersion are discussed below:

(i) **Range:** This is the simplest measure of dispersion and is defined as the distance between the highest (maximum) value and the lowest (minimum) value in an ordered set of values. In other words, range provides difference on the end points of a distribution when its values are arranged in an order. The range could be computed for interval scale and ratio scale data.

$$\text{Range} = X_{max} - X_{min}$$

where,

X_{max} = Maximum value of the variable

X_{min} = Minimum value of the variable

The limitation of range as a measure of dispersion is that it considers only the extreme value and ignores all other data points. The value of range could vary considerably from sample to sample. Even with this limitation, range as a measure of dispersion is widely used in industrial quality control for the preparation of control charts.

Example 11.8 The following are the prices of shares of a company from Monday to Friday: Calculate the range of the distribution.

Day	Price (₹)
Monday	125
Tuesday	180
Wednesday	100
Thursday	210
Friday	150

Solution:

L = Largest values = 210

S = Smallest value = 100

Therefore, range = $L - S = 210 - 100 = 110$.

In the case of a frequency distribution, range is calculated by taking the difference between the lower limit of the lowest class and upper limit of the highest class. The limitation of range is that it is not based on each and every observation of the distribution and, therefore, does not take into account the form of distribution within the range.

The **population standard deviation** is denoted by σ and can be computed by applying:

$$\sigma = \sqrt{\frac{\Sigma(X-\mu)^2}{N}}$$

(ii) **Variance and standard deviation:** Variance is defined as the mean squared deviation of a variable from its arithmetic mean. The positive square root of the variance is called standard deviation. The variance is a difficult measure to interpret and, therefore, standard deviation is used as a measure of dispersion. The population standard deviation is denoted by σ and computed using the following formula:

$$\sigma = \sqrt{\frac{\Sigma(X-\mu)^2}{N}}$$

where,

σ = Population standard deviation

X = Value of observations

μ = Population mean of observations

N = Total number of observations in the population.

However, in survey research, we generally take a sample from the population. If the standard deviation is computed from the sample data, the following formula may be used.

$$s = \sqrt{\frac{\Sigma(X-\bar{X})^2}{n-1}}$$

where,

s = Sample standard deviation

$\bar{X}$ = Sample mean

X = Value of observation

n = Total number of observations in the sample

Variance is defined as the mean squared deviation of a variable from its arithmetic mean.

In case of grouped data, the following formula for computing sample standard deviation may be used:

$$s = \sqrt{\frac{\Sigma f_i(X_i-\bar{X})^2}{n-1}}$$

where,

X_i = Value of ith observation
$\overline{X}$ = Sample mean
f_i = Frequency of ith class interval
n = Sample size

The standard deviation could be computed in case of interval and ratio scale data.

Example 11.9 Sample data of 10 days' sales from the two-month data collected on daily basis is given below. Compute the sample variance and standard deviation.

Sales in unit	15	28	32	16	19	26	38	40	25	13

Solution:

Sales in unit (X)	$x = X - \overline{X}$	$(X - \overline{X})^2$
15	–10.2	104.04
28	2.8	7.84
32	6.8	46.24
16	–9.2	84.64
19	–6.2	38.44
26	0.8	0.64
38	12.8	163.84
40	14.8	219.04
25	–0.2	0.04
13	–12.2	148.84
Total	**0**	**813.6**

$$\Sigma X = 252$$

$$\overline{X} = \frac{\Sigma X}{n} = \frac{252}{10} = 25.2$$

$$\Sigma(X - \overline{X})^2 = 813.6$$

$$\text{Variance} = s^2 = \frac{\Sigma(X - \overline{X})^2}{n-1} = \frac{813.6}{9} = 90.4$$

$$\text{Standard deviation} = s = \sqrt{90.4} = 9.508$$

Therefore, the standard deviation of sales of 10 days is 9.508 units.

Example 11.10 The data on dividend declared in percentage is presented in the following frequency distribution table for a sample of 107 companies. Compute the variance and standard deviation of the dividend declared.

Dividend declared (per cent)	Number of Companies
0 – 10	5
10 – 20	10
20 – 30	13
30 – 40	25
40 – 50	30
50 – 60	16
60 – 70	8
Total	**107**

Solution:

Dividend declared (per cent)	Number of Companies (f)	X	fX	$X-\bar{X}$	$(X-\bar{X})^2$	$f(X-\bar{X})^2$
0 – 10	5	5	25	–33.5514	1125.697	5628.483
10 – 20	10	15	150	–23.5514	554.6685	5546.685
20 – 30	13	25	325	–13.5514	183.6405	2387.326
30 – 40	25	35	875	–3.5514	12.61246	315.3114
40 – 50	30	45	1350	6.448598	41.58442	1247.533
50 – 60	16	55	880	16.4486	270.5564	4328.902
60 – 70	8	65	520	26.4486	699.5283	5596.227
Total			4125			25050.47

$$\Sigma fX = 4125$$

$$\bar{X} = \frac{\Sigma fX}{\Sigma f} = \frac{4125}{107} = 38.5514$$

$$\Sigma f(X-\bar{X})^2 = 25050.47$$

$$\text{Variance} = s^2 = \frac{\Sigma f(X-\bar{X})^2}{n-1} = \frac{25050.47}{106} = 236.3252$$

$$s = \text{standard deviation} = \sqrt{236.3252} = 15.373$$

Therefore, the standard deviation of the dividend declared of 107 companies is 15.373 per cent.

The standard deviation is a very useful measure as it has a relationship with mean in case of normal distribution. It is known that 68 per cent of the observations lie within one standard deviation of mean; 95.5 per cent of the observations lie within two standard deviations of mean; and 99.7 per cent of the observations lie within three standard deviations of mean in case of normal distribution. These properties are very useful in sampling, correlation, etc. Another common application of standard deviation is while testing the equality of two population means.

Coefficient of variation can be calculated by:

$$CV = \frac{s}{\bar{X}} \times 100$$

(iii) **Coefficient of variation:** This measure is computed for ratio scale measurement. The standard deviation measures the variability of a variable around the mean. The unit of measurement of standard deviation is the same as that of arithmetic mean of the variable itself. The measure of dispersion is considerably affected by the unit of measurement. In such a case, it is not possible to compare the variability of two distributions using standard deviation as a measure of variability. To compare the variability of two or more distributions, a measure of relative dispersion called the coefficient of variation can be used. This measure is independent of units of measurements. The formula of coefficient of variation is:

$$CV = \frac{s}{\bar{X}} \times 100$$

where,

CV = Coefficient of variation

s = Standard deviation of sample

$\bar{X}$ = Mean of the sample

Example 11.11

For the data given in Example 11.10, compute the coefficient of variation.

Solution:

$$CV = \frac{s}{\overline{X}} \times 100$$

where,

CV = Coefficient of variation

s = Standard deviation of sample = 15.373

$\overline{X}$ = Mean of the sample = 38.5514

$$\text{Therefore, } CV = \frac{15.373 \times 100}{38.5514} = 39.88 \text{ per cent}$$

Therefore, the coefficient of variation is 39.88 per cent. As already mentioned, coefficient of variation is useful for comparing the variability of two distributions. This is a more useful measure when two distributions are entirely different and the units of measurements are also different.

(iv) **Relative and absolute frequencies:** In the case of nominal scale data, the researcher could compute relative and absolute frequencies as measures of dispersions. Suppose a sample of 400 respondents is selected from different regions of the country as shown in Table 11.14. Absolute frequencies are the number of respondents in the sample that appear in each category of variable. For example, 130 respondents were selected from the south, 100 from the north, 90 from the west and 80 from the east. Relative frequencies denote the percentage of respondents that belong to each region and, therefore, it could be seen that 32.5 per cent of the respondents belong to the south, 25 per cent to the north, 22.5 per cent to west and 20 per cent to the east.

TABLE 11.14 Distribution of respondents from various regions of the country

Region of the Country	Absolute Frequency	Relative Frequency
East	80	20.0%
West	90	22.5%
North	100	25.0%
South	130	32.5%
Total	400	100%

CONCEPT CHECK

1. Differentiate between univariate, bivariate and multivariate analysis of data.
2. What is descriptive analysis?
3. Discuss inferential analysis.
4. How would you calculate variance and standard deviation of a variable?

DESCRIPTIVE ANALYSIS OF BIVARIATE DATA

LEARNING OBJECTIVE 4

Explain the descriptive analysis of bivariate data.

As already mentioned, bivariate analysis examines the relationship between two variables. There are three types of measures used for carrying out bivariate analysis. These are (a) Cross-tabulation, (b) Spearman's rank correlation coefficient, and (c) Pearson's linear correlation coefficient. The topic on linear correlation coefficient would be taken up later on in the chapter 'Correlation and Regression'. Here, the remaining two methods would be discussed.

Cross-tabulation

In simple tabulation, the frequency and the percentage for each question was calculated. In cross-tabulation, responses to two questions are combined and data is tabulated together. A cross-tabulation counts the number of observations in each cross-category of two variables. The descriptive result of a cross-tabulation is a frequency count for each cell in the analysis. For example, in cross-tabulating a two-category measure of income (low- and high-income households) with a two-category measure of purchase intention of a product (low and high purchase intentions) the basic result is a cross-classification as shown in Table 11.15.

TABLE 11.15 Cross-table of purchase intention and income

		Income	
		Low Income	High Income
Purchase Intention	Low purchase intention	120	60
	High purchase intention	80	190
		200	250

The results of cross-tabulation show the number of sample respondents with low income having low purchase intention, low income with high purchase intention, high income with low purchase intention and high income with high purchase intention. (At this juncture, it may be noted that the variable purchase intention was categorized as low purchase intention and high purchase intention; the SPSS instructions for the same are given in Appendix 11.2.)

As is the case with simple tabulations, the results of a cross-tabulation are more meaningful if cell frequencies are computed as percentages. The percentages can be computed in three-ways. As is the case of Table 11.15, the percentages can be computed (1) row-wise so that the percentages in each row add up to 100 per cent; (2) column-wise so that the percentages in each column add up to 100 per cent or (3) cell percentages, such that percentages added across all cells equal 100 per cent. The interpretation of percentages is different in each of the three cases. Therefore, the question arises which of these percentages is most useful to the researcher. What is the general rule for computing percentages?

The basis for calculating category percentage depends upon the nature of relationships between the variables.

The basis for calculating category percentage depends upon the nature of relationship between the variables. One of the variables could be viewed as dependent variable and the other one as independent variable. In the cross-tabulation presented in Table 11.15, the purchase intention could be treated as dependent variable, which depends upon income (independent variable). The rule is to cast percentages in the direction of independent (causal) variable across the dependent variable. For Table 11.15, there are 200 respondents with low income, out of which 120 have low purchase intention for the product. In terms of percentages, 60 per cent of the respondents with low income have low purchase intention for the product. Now there are 250 people with high income, out of which 60 have low purchase intention and 190 have high purchase intention for the product. By calculating percentages column wise, it is seen that 24 per cent have low purchase intention whereas 76 per cent have high purchase intention for the product. The results indicate that with increase in income, the purchase intention for the product increases. Table 11.16 presents the percentages column-wise as given below:

TABLE 11.16 Cross-table of purchase intention and income (column-wise percentages)

		Income	
		Low Income	High Income
Purchase Intention	Low purchase intention	60%	24%
	High purchase intention	40%	76%
		100%	100%

From the above example, it is clear that any two variables each having certain categories can be cross-tabulated. The interpretation of the cross-tabulation results may show a high association between two variables. That does not mean one of them, the independent variable, is the cause of the other variable—the dependent variable. Causality between the two variables is more of an assumptions made by the researcher based on his experience or expectations. Just because there is a high association between two variables, it does not imply a cause-and-effect relationship.

Cross-tabulation using survey data

Mahesh Enterprises (ME) has a chain of high class restaurants in Punjab and Haryana serving high quality multicuisine food at premium prices. The restaurants serve only lunch and dinner. The top management of the restaurants observes that the total sales revenues of the restaurants have been more or less stagnant, growing at a rate of 2 per cent only for the last three years. A meeting of the senior management personnel was called to discuss the issue. Some of them were of the opinion that young customers in the age group of 18 to 35 were switching to fast food. Further, they were of the view that the trend mainly is among people belonging to high income-group and to families where both partners' were economically employed.

In the series of meetings which the top management had, it was decided to launch a chain of fast food joints in states where they were already present. However, before starting the fast food joint, they got a survey conducted to understand the preference of people for fast food. A sample of 100 respondents was chosen. Table 11.17 gives the data on select variables.

Please note that in Table 11.17:

- First column indicates the respondent number.
- Second column indicates the preference for fast food. The respondents were asked to state their preference for fast food on a 5-point scale, where 1 = Not at all preferred, 2 = Not preferred, 3 = Neutral, 4 = Preferred, 5 = Very much preferred.
- Third column indicates the actual age of the respondent.
- Fourth column of the table states the household monthly income coded as:
  - 1 = Household income less than ₹25,000 per month (low income)
  - 2 = Household income of ₹25,000 per month but less than ₹50,000 per month (middle income)
  - 3 = Household income of ₹50,000 and above (high income)
- Fifth column of the table states the gender of the respondents coded as:
  Male = 1
  Female = 2

Questions

Divide the sample into two groups based on the preference scores. Those scoring from one to three could be regarded as respondents for whom fast food is 'not preferred' choice. Respondents having a score of four or five may be treated as having 'preferred' fast food.

(i) Cross-tabulate the above two groups against gender. Compute the percentages in the appropriate direction and interpret the results.

(ii) Prepare cross-tabulation table of the above-mentioned groups of preference for fast food with age, where respondents aged less than or equal to 40 may be treated as younger respondents, and those above 40 may be treated as older respondents. Again compute the percentages in the desired direction and interpret the result.

TABLE 11.17
Data on select variables on the survey for fast food

Resp. No.	Preference	Age	Income	Gender
1	1	46	2	2
2	2	24	1	1
3	4	22	3	1
4	4	18	3	1
5	2	46	1	1
6	2	38	1	1
7	1	47	1	2
8	2	54	2	2
9	5	50	3	2
10	4	46	3	1
11	3	29	1	1
12	2	32	2	2
13	4	26	2	1
14	5	19	2	1
15	4	41	3	1
16	2	20	1	1
17	3	36	2	2
18	4	31	3	1
19	5	28	1	2
20	2	54	1	1
21	4	30	1	2
22	2	46	2	1
23	3	37	3	1
24	4	22	3	2
25	3	26	1	2
26	4	47	3	2
27	3	45	1	2
28	2	50	1	1
29	2	54	2	2
30	5	26	3	2
31	3	41	1	1
32	5	42	2	1
33	1	61	3	1
34	2	31	1	1
35	1	19	3	1
36	3	20	1	1
37	4	29	3	2
38	3	26	2	1
39	4	31	3	1
40	4	28	3	2
41	3	41	2	2
42	2	51	1	1
43	1	49	1	1
44	5	31	3	1
45	3	46	2	1
46	4	26	1	1
47	5	31	3	1
48	4	35	2	1
49	5	32	3	2
50	4	39	3	2

(Contd.)

Resp. No.	Preference	Age	Income	Gender
51	1	52	2	1
52	3	46	1	2
53	2	21	2	1
54	4	21	3	2
55	5	18	3	1
56	5	29	2	2
57	4	51	3	1
58	1	52	2	2
59	2	46	2	2
60	2	31	1	2
61	3	34	3	2
62	3	46	3	1
63	4	60	3	2
64	4	18	3	2
65	5	27	2	1
66	5	25	3	2
67	2	31	1	2
68	1	32	3	1
69	3	47	3	1
70	5	42	2	1
71	1	59	3	1
72	2	50	3	2
73	3	26	1	2
74	4	28	3	1
75	5	31	2	2
76	5	52	2	1
77	4	41	3	2
78	3	38	1	1
79	2	46	2	2
80	1	41	3	1
81	3	46	2	1
82	5	24	3	2
83	3	44	1	2
84	4	27	2	1
85	2	58	2	1
86	1	56	1	1
87	4	29	3	2
88	3	52	3	2
89	4	26	3	2
90	3	24	2	2
91	5	42	3	1
92	5	34	3	1
93	4	22	3	2
94	2	22	3	2
95	3	26	2	1
96	2	38	2	2
97	4	33	3	1
98	4	33	3	2
99	5	28	1	2
100	1	19	3	2

(iii) Again cross-tabulate preference for fast food against the income level as defined earlier. Compute percentages in the right direction and interpret the results.

The above-mentioned three exercises on cross-tabulation can be carried out manually by using tally marks. Alternatively, SPSS software or other software such as SAS can be used for the purpose. It is required to convert the preference data into two categories for which required SPSS instructions and that of preparing cross-tables and percentages in the desired direction are provided in Appendix 11.2 and Appendix 11.3 respectively given at the end of this chapter.

For the purpose of preparation of cross-tabulation, the variable preference categorized into two groups would be taken row-wise and each of the other variables, namely, gender; age and income would be taken up column-wise. There is no hard and fast rule as to which variable should be presented row-wise and which one column-wise. Only precaution that needs to be taken is that percentages should be cast in the direction of independent (causal) variable. In each of three above-mentioned problems, the dependent variable is preference for fast food. The result of cross-tabulation of preference against gender is presented in Table11.18.

TABLE 11.18 Cross-table of preference for fast food with gender

			Gender		Total
			Male	Female	
Preference Redefined	Not preferred	Count	30	24	54
		% within Gender	56.6%	51.1%	54.0%
	Preferred	Count	23	23	46
		% within Gender	43.4%	48.9%	46.0%
Total		Count	53	47	100
		% within Gender	100.0%	100.0%	100.0%

It is observed from Table 11.18 that out of 53 male respondents, 30 have no preference for fast food, whereas 23 prefer fast food. This means 56.6 per cent of men do not prefer fast food. Similarly, it can be observed that out of 47 female respondents, 51.1 per cent do not prefer fast food, whereas 48.9 per cent prefer the same. It is seen that proportion of female preferring fast food is slightly higher. However, whether the difference is significant in statistical sense would be examined in the chapter on Non-Parametric Tests (Chapter 14).

The cross-tabulation of preference for fast food categorized as 'not preferred' and 'preferred' with the variable age categorized as younger and older respondent is presented in Table 11.19.

TABLE 11.19 Cross-tabulation of preference for fast food with age

			Age Redefined		Total
			Less than or equal to 40	Greater than 40	
Preference Redefined	Not preferred	Count	24	30	54
		% within Age Redefined	40.7%	73.2%	54.0%
	Preferred	Count	35	11	46
		% within Age Redefined	59.3%	26.8%	46.0%
Total		Count	59	41	100
		% within Age Redefined	100.0%	100.0%	100.0%

Table 11.19 indicates that there are 59 younger respondents and 41 older respondents. Out of the 41 older respondents, only 26.8 per cent prefer fast food, whereas 73.2 per cent have no preference for fast food. In case of younger respondents, 59.3 per cent have preference for fast-food, whereas 40.7 per cent of them do not prefer fast food. This shows that preference for fast food increases among younger population. This is quite understandable in the light of the growing popularity of fast food in the last decade among the younger population. The analysis of the results shows that preference for fast food is related to the age.

The cross-tabulation of preference for fast food (categorized as 'not preferred' and 'preferred') with the variable income classified as low income, middle income and high income is presented in Table 11.20.

TABLE 11.20 Cross-tabulation of preference for fast food with income

			Income			Total
			Low Income	Middle Income	High Income	
Preference Redefined	Not preferred	Count	22	19	13	54
		% within Income	84.6%	65.5%	28.9%	54.0%
	Preferred	Count	4	10	32	46
		% within Income	15.4%	34.5%	71.1%	46.0%
Total		Count	26	29	45	100
		% within Income	100.0%	100.0%	100.0%	100.0%

The analysis of Table 11.20 shows that there are 26 people belonging to low income, 29 belonging to middle income and 45 belonging to high-income group. Out of those belonging to low income, only 15.4 per cent prefer fast food. Of the 29 belonging to middle income, 34.5 per cent prefer fast food, whereas as of the 45 belonging to the high-income group, 71.1 per cent prefer fast food. It is, therefore, seen that with increase in income, the preference for fast food increases. A plausible reason for this could be that fast food is generally expensive and it is people with high income who can afford it.

Elaboration of Cross-tables

A **third variable** is introduced in the analysis to elaborate and refine the initial observed relationship between two variables.

Once the relationship between the two variables has been established, the researcher may introduce a third variable into the analysis to elaborate and refine the initial observed relationship between two variables. The main question being asked is whether the interpretation of the relationship is modified with the introduction of the third variable. There would be four possibilities on introducing the third variable. (i) It may refine the association that was observed originally between two variables. (ii) By introducing the third variable, it may be found that there was no association between initial variables or the original association was spurious. (iii) Introducing a third variable may indicate association between original two variables although no association was observed originally. (iv) Introduction of the third variable may not show any change in the initial association between two variables.

Refinining an initial relationship: The data reported in Table 11.21 represents the relationship between consumption of ice cream and income level. The respondents are divided into two categories—high consumption or low consumption based on the amount of ice cream consumed. Similarly, the variable income was divided into two categories—low income and high income.

TABLE 11.21
Cross-tabulation of consumption of ice cream by income

		Income	
		Low Income	High Income
Consumption of Ice Cream	High consumption	30%	55%
	Low Consumption	70%	45%
	Column Total	100%	100%
	No. of respondents	600	400

The above table indicates that 55 per cent of high income respondents fall into high consumption category as compared to 30 per cent of low income respondents. Before concluding that high income respondents consume more ice cream as compared to low income families, a third variable, namely, gender is introduced into the analysis. The results are reported in Table 11.22.

TABLE 11.22
Consumption of ice cream by income and gender

	Gender			
	Male		Female	
	Low Income	High Income	Low Income	High Income
High Consumption	40%	45%	10%	63.18%
Low Consumption	60%	55%	90%	36.82%
Column Total	100%	100%	100%	100%
No. of respondents	400	180	200	220

In Table 11.22, gender of the respondents was introduced as the third variable. The relationship between consumption of ice cream and income of respondents was reexamined in the light of the third variable. In case of female, 63.18 per cent with high income fall in the high consumption category as compared to 10 per cent of those with low income. In case of males, 45 per cent with high income fall in the high consumption category as compared to 40 per cent with low income. Therefore, it is seen that percentages are closer in case of males. Therefore, the relationship between ice cream consumption and income has been refined by introduction of a third variable, namely, gender. High income respondents are more likely to fall in the high consumption category and this is more so in case of females as compared to males.

Initial relationship was spurious: A study was conducted to examine the relation between the ownership of flat in high-rise buildings and education level. The ownership of flat was categorized as yes or no, whereas the variable education level was categorized as low education and high education. The results of the study are given in Table 11.23.

TABLE 11.23
Cross-tabulation of ownership of flats in high-rise buildings and education levels

		High education	Low education
Ownership of flats in high-rise buildings	Yes	35%	22%
	No	65%	78%
	Column Total	100%	100%
	No. of respondents	300	500

Table 11.23 indicates that 35 per cent of respondents with high education own a flat in a high-rise building as opposed to 22 per cent with low education. Now when a third variable 'income' categorized as low and high income is introduced, it results in Table 11.24.

TABLE 11.24 Ownership of flats in high-rise building by education and income

		Income			
		Low Income		High Income	
		High Education	Low Education	High Education	Low Education
Ownership of flats in high-rise buildings	Yes	15%	6.67%	45%	45%
	No	85%	93.33%	55%	55%
	Column Total	100%	100%	100%	100%
	No. of Respondents	100	300	200	200

In Table 11.24, it is found that irrespective of the education level, the ownership of flat in high-rise buildings depends upon the income level. It is more for the high-income respondents than that for the low-income respondents, indicating that the initial relationship was spurious.

Reveal suppressed association: A study was conducted to examine the relationship between the desire to visit temple and age. The respondents who desire to visit temple were categorized as low and high and the age categorized as younger respondents (age less than 35 years) and older respondents (at least 35 years of age). The cross-tabulation of data resulted in Table 11.25.

TABLE 11.25 Cross-tabulation of desire to visit temple and age

		Age	
		< 35	≥ 35 years
Desire to Visit Temple	High	50%	50%
	Low	50%	50%
	Column Total	100%	100%
	No. of respondents	400	400

Table 11.25 shows that desire to visit temple is independent of age. Now when gender is added as the third variable, the results obtained are summarized in Table 11.26.

It is seen from Table 11.26 that 56.67 per cent of males above 35 have a high desire to go to temple whereas 70 per cent of females below 35 have a high desire to go to temple. Therefore, the introduction of third variable has revealed the suppressed relationship between desire to visit temple and age.

No change in initial relationship: There are situations when the introduction of a third variable does not change the initial relationship. Consider the data in the cross Table 11.27, where one variable is the size of toothpaste bought by the families and the other variable is the size of the household. The size of toothpaste was categorized as small and large and size of household was categorized as small and large.

Table 11.27 indicates that 60 per cent of the large households buy large-sized toothpaste whereas 60 per cent of small households buy small-size toothpaste. Now if income categorized as low income and high income is introduced as third variable, the new table is presented in Table 11.28.

TABLE 11.26
Desire to visit temple by age and gender

	Gender			
	Male		Female	
	< 35	≥ 35	< 35	≥ 35
High	43.33%	56.67%	70%	30%
Low	56.67%	43.33%	30%	70%
Column Total	100%	100%	100%	100%
No. of respondents	300	300	100	100

TABLE 11.27
Cross-tabulation of size of household and size of toothpaste

		Household Size	
		Large	Small
Size of Toothpaste	Large	60%	40%
	Small	40%	60%
	Column Total	100%	100%
	No. of Respondents	200	300

TABLE 11.28
Cross-tabulation of size of household and size of toothpaste with income

		Income			
		Low Income		High Income	
		Large Household	Small Household	Large Household	Small Household
Size of Toothpaste	Large	60%	40%	60%	40%
	Small	40%	60%	40%	60%
	Column Total	100%	100%	100%	100%
	No. of respondents	100	150	100	150

It is found that even with the introduction of third variable, i.e., income, the initial relationship remains unchanged.

Spearman's Rank Order Correlation Coefficient

In the case of ordinal scale data, the measure of association between two variables is obtained through Spearman's rank order correlation coefficient. Suppose in a beauty contest two judges are asked to rank ten female participants. A rank correlation coefficient between the ranks awarded by two judges would give how consistent they are in awarding the rank. The Spearman's rank correlation coefficient is given by

Spearman's rank correlation coefficient is given by:

$$r_s = 1 - \frac{6\sum d_i^2}{n(n^2-1)}$$

$$r_s = 1 - \frac{6\sum d_i^2}{n(n^2-1)}$$

where, r_s = Spearman's rank correlation coefficient

n = Sample size

d_i = Difference in the ranking for the ith contestant

The rank correlation coefficient takes a value between -1 and +1. In case the value is +1, it indicates a complete agreement between the ranks assigned by two judges, whereas the value of -1 indicates a complete disagreement.

Example 11.12

Two judges in a beauty contest evaluate ten participants. A rank of one was assigned to the most beautiful candidate, two to the next and so on. Compute the rank order correlation and comment on the value.

The rankings are as follows:

Participant	Ranking by Judge 1	Ranking by Judge 2
I	10	9
II	1	3
III	5	4
IV	2	1
V	8	8
VI	3	2
VII	4	6
VIII	6	5
IX	7	7
X	9	10

Solution:

Participant	Ranking by Judge 1	Ranking by Judge 2	d_1	d_i^2
I	10	9	1	1
II	1	3	−2	4
III	5	4	1	1
IV	2	1	1	1
V	8	8	0	0
VI	3	2	1	1
VII	4	6	−2	4
VIII	6	5	1	1
IX	7	7	0	0
X	9	10	−1	1
			Total	14

$$r_s = 1 - \frac{6\sum d_i^2}{n(n^2 - 1)} = 1 - \frac{6 \times 14}{10(100 - 1)}$$

$$= 1 - \frac{84}{10 \times 99} = 1 - \frac{84}{990}$$

$$= 1 - 0.085 = 0.915$$

It is seen that there is a high degree of positive rank correlation coefficient which implies that there is a strong agreement between two judges on their opinion about the beauty of contestants.

As already mentioned, the detailed discussion on linear correlation is covered in the chapter on 'Correlation and regression'. Correlation measures the degree of linear association between two metric (interval or ratio scaled data) data.

CONCEPT CHECK

1. Define cross-tabulation.
2. Discuss the reasons for the elaboration of cross-tables.

MORE ON ANALYSIS OF DATA

LEARNING OBJECTIVE 5

Elaborate more on analysis of data by calculating rank order and using data transformation

Calculating Rank Order

In survey research, it is generally observed that respondents may be asked to indicate a rank ordering of various attributes of a product or rank ordering of brand preference or some other variable of interest. For example, data presented in Table 11.8 gives the ranking by 32 respondents on five attributes while choosing a restaurant for dinner. The data given in Table 11.8 can be used to prepare the summarized rank ordering of various attributes. The rankings of attributes given in Table 11.8 can be presented in the form of frequency distribution in Table 11.29.

TABLE 11.29 Frequency table of the rankings of the attributes while selecting a restaurant for dinner

Attribute	Rank				
	1	2	3	4	5
Ambience	4	5	13	5	5
Food Quality	16	13	2	1	0
Menu Variety	7	2	2	9	12
Service	3	8	11	6	4
Location	2	4	4	11	11
Total	**32**	**32**	**32**	**32**	**32**

To calculate a summary rank ordering, the attribute with the first rank was given the lowest number (1) and the least preferred attribute was given the highest number (5).

The summarized rank order is obtained with the following computations as:

Ambience	:	(4 × 1) + (5 × 2) + (13 × 3) + (5 × 4) + (5 × 5)	=	98
Food Quality	:	(16 × 1) + (13 × 2) + (2 × 3) + (1 × 4) + (0 × 5)	=	52
Menu Variety	:	(7 × 1) + (2 × 2) + (2 × 3) + (9 × 4) + (12 × 5)	=	113
Service	:	(3 × 1) + (8 × 2) + (11 × 3) + (6 × 4) + (4 × 5)	=	96
Location	:	(2 × 1) + (4 × 2) + (4 × 3) + (11 × 4) + (11 × 5)	=	121

The total lowest score indicates the first preference ranking. The results show the following rank ordering:

(1) Food quality
(2) Service
(3) Ambience
(4) Menu variety
(5) Location

Data Transformation

To achieve the **objectives of the study**, the researcher modifies the original data by creating new variables or changing the values of the scale data.

Under data transformation, the original data is changed to a new format for performing data analysis so as to achieve the objectives of the study. This is generally done by the researcher through creating new variables or by modifying the values of the scaled data. The following illustrations show how it is carried out.

(a) It is usually believed by researchers that the response bias will be less if instead of asking the question on the exact age, the question is asked on the date of birth. This does not create any problem in data analysis as having known the date of birth, it is always possible to compute the exact age of the respondent.

(b) At times it may become essential to collapse or combine adjacent categories of a variable so as to reduce the number of categories of original variables. In a 5-point Likert scale, having categories like strongly agree, agree, neither agree nor disagree, disagree and strongly disagree can be clubbed into three categories. One can combine strongly agree and agree category into one category. Similarly, disagree and strongly disagree responses could be clubbed into a separate category and neither agree nor disagree could be treated as a separate category. This is how a five-category scale can be collapsed into a three-category one.

(c) The researcher could create new variables by re-specifying the data with numeric or logical transformation. Suppose a multiple-item Likert scale designed to measure the perception of a customer towards the bank has 10 items. The total score of a respondent can be computed as:

Total score of ith respondent = Score of ith respondent on item 1 + Score of ith respondent on item 2 + ... + Score of ith respondent on item 10.

Once the total score for each of the respondent is computed, the average score can be obtained by dividing it by the number of items. It can be further categorized as favourable, neutral and unfavourable perception that could be related to various demographic variables depending upon the objectives of research.

CONCEPT CHECK

1. Explain the formula for calculating Spearman's rank order correlation coefficient.
2. What is data transformation?

SUMMARY

- This chapter introduces how the researcher should carry out data analysis once the data from primary and secondary sources have been collected. The data analysis could be univariate, bivariate or multivariate depending upon whether one variable, two variables or more than two variables are being analysed at a time. The analysis of data could be descriptive or inferential in nature. Descriptive analysis deals with describing the sample. It discusses summary measures relating to the sample data. They include summarizing data by calculating the average, frequency distribution, range, standard deviations and percentage distributions. In the inferential analysis, the concern is to draw inferences on population parameters based on sample results. The chapter focuses on the descriptive analysis of univariate and bivariate data.
- In the descriptive analysis of univariate data are discussed the frequency distributions and percentage distribution in case of nominal scale variable. The analysis is also explained for multiple category and multiple response category questions. The treatment of missing data is also covered here. The chapter explains how to analyse ordinal scale data.
- The various measures of central tendency like arithmetic mean, median and mode are discussed for interval and ratio scale data. The measures of dispersion discussed are range, variance and standard deviation. The concept of coefficient of variation is taken up using ratio scale measurement. All the measures of central tendency and dispersion are taken up with the help of various numerical examples.
- The descriptive analysis of bivariate data is taken upon using (i) cross-tabulation (ii) Spearman's rank correlation coefficient and (iii) Pearson's linear correlation coefficient. The third measure is discussed in the chapter 'Correlation and Regression' whereas the other two are duscussed in this chapter. The chapter explains the preparation and interpretation of cross-tables. For the interpretation of cross-tables, it is important to identify dependent and independent variables as the rules for calculating percentages depends upon that. The general rule is that percentages should be computed in the direction of independent variable across dependent variable. The chapter also discusses the impact of introduction of third variable on the initial relationship found with the two variables. There could be four different scenarios such as that the introduction of third variable (i) may refine the association that was observed originally between two variables, (ii) may indicate that the original association was spurious, (iii) may indicate association between original two variables although no observation was observed originally, and (iv) may not show any change in the initial association between two variables.

- ❖ The association between two ordinal scale data could be computed using Spearman's rank order correlation coefficient. The value of the rank correlation coefficient lies between –1 and +1. A ranking of +1 indicates a complete agreement on the ranks by the two respondents, whereas the value of (–1) indicates a complete disagreement on the ranks by the two respondents.
- ❖ There are situations where a researcher might have to transform the data from original format to a new one before carrying out the analysis. Three such situations are taken up in this context. Further the concept of calculating rank ordering of ranks of various attributes or of brand preference to indicate the overall rank obtained by various attributes is also discussed.

KEY TERMS

- Arithmetic mean
- Association
- Bivariate analysis
- Coefficient of variation
- Cross-tabulation
- Data transformation
- Dependent variable
- Descriptive analysis
- Elaboration of cross-tables
- Frequency distribution
- Grouped data
- Independent variable
- Inferential analysis
- Median
- Missing data
- Mode
- Multivariate analysis
- Pearson's linear correlation coefficient
- Percentage distribution
- Percentages across independent variable
- Range
- Rank order
- Relative and absolute frequencies
- Spearman's rank order correlation coefficient
- Standard deviation
- Univariate analysis
- Variance

CHAPTER REVIEW QUESTIONS

Objective Type Questions

State whether the following statements are true (T) or false (F).

1. The median could be computed for nominal scale data.
2. Mean, median and mode are the measures of central tendency.
3. Two variables are considered at a time in case of a frequency distribution.
4. The standard deviation of a variable can be negative.
5. Arithmetic mean can be computed for ordinal scale data.
6. The rank order correlation coefficient can take values between –1 and +1.
7. In a bivariate table, the percentages should be computed in the direction of dependent variable.
8. The introduction of a third variable in the case of a bivariate table may altogether change the interpretation.
9. Interval scale data could be used for computing coefficient of variation.
10. Median is that value in a distribution such that 50 per cent of the observations are below it and 50 per cent are above it.
11. Simultaneous tabulation of more than two variables is not called cross-tabulation.
12. The number of tabulations is a direct function of the number of variables.
13. Using an additional variable to refine the initial results is a basic technique of cross-tabulation.
14. The researcher does not need to specify the relationships to be investigated and the appropriate cross-tabulations before data collection.
15. A simple tabulation is also called a one-way frequency distribution.
16. The simplest way to look for association in a data set that requires only the ability to calculate percentages is cross-tabulation.
17. The arithmetic mean and standard deviation of a variable can only be calculated from interval and ratio scale data.

18. The median of a variable can also be computed from open-ended distribution.
19. In the case of normal distribution mean = median = mode.
20. For a positively skewed distribution arithmetic mean > median > mode.

Conceptual Questions

1. How does one go about preparing cross-table between two variables each having two categories? In what ways should percentages be calculated to interpret the results of a cross-tabulation? What is the role played by introducing a third variable in the cross-table?
2. What is elaboration? What could be found as a result of elaboration?

Application Questions

1. You are presented with the following table of frequency counts to show the nature of relationship between age and watching of movies in a cinema hall. What conclusion can be drawn?

Frequency of watching movies	Age	
	Under 35	35 & above
4 or more times in a month	200	80
Less than 4 times in a month	130	190
Total	330	270

2. The following bivariate table was prepared to understand the relationship between preference for continental food and monthly income of the respondents. What conclusion can be drawn?

		< ₹30,000	₹30,000 – ₹60,000	More than ₹60,000
Preference for continental food	Yes	20	32	17
	No	100	148	83
	Total	120	180	100

3. The table below presents the ranks which were assigned by three judges to the works of ten artists:

S. No.	1	2	3	4	5	6	7	8	9	10
Judge A	5	7	4	1	3	2	9	8	10	6
Judge B	4	8	3	2	7	1	10	6	9	5
Judge C	8	6	2	10	4	1	3	9	5	7

Compute the Spearman's rank order correlation coefficient for each pair of ranking and decide:

(a) Which two judges are most alike in their opinions about these artists?

(b) Which two judges are different in their opinions about their artists?

4. The raw data for the variable X10 (How long have you been using cyber café?) is given in Table 11.2. Using this data, compute mean, median, mode, standard deviation, coefficient of variation and skewness. Also interpret the results.

CASE 11.1

EATING-OUT HABITS OF INDIVIDUALS

The Indian economy has been growing at a tremendous pace for the last two years, with growth rates of 9.6 per cent in 2006 and 9.2 per cent in 2007. Despite the global slowdown that hit economies across the globe, India is considered to have survived it to a satisfactory extent. The economy did slow down to 6.7 per cent in 2008 but picked up beyond expectations to 7+ figures in the first half of 2009. What does this imply? Simply put, the Indian economy is growing at a steady pace with the direct impact being steadily rising income levels of the Indian population.

This rising income levels in the population is a very interesting phenomena because of two reasons. One being the fact that 55 per cent of the population is under the age of 25 years and secondly, the changed family structure of the population, especially in cities (nuclear families with more than one earning member).

What this leads to is an increase in spending, but an increase in spending with a changed consumer behaviour. This is also seen in the change in the eating-out habits of the population. It is seen that more and more people eat out these days and for a multitude of reasons, ranging from lack of option for a home- cooked meal to wanting to have a relaxing experience from a hard day at work to spending time with friends/family and so on. The avenues available to them have also increased over the last few years.

Rising disposable incomes and changing consumer behaviour brought about a complete change in the way people choose to eat out. The eating out frequency and habits have undergone a total change over the last decade. One reason for such a significant change has been along with the income and demographic profiles is the growing influence of the West. It is because of this that food habits of countries like India are changing and there is a rapid growth in the fast food industry.

It is seen that the trend of going to eat out has increased tremendously. And to cater to this demand a number of restaurants have come up. The eating out decision now no longer is based in the satisfaction of the *basic need* for food. There is a plethora of other factors on which this decision depends. Keeping this in mind, a study was conducted to understand the factors that influence the eating out decisions of the individuals.

A sample of 76 individuals was taken using convenience sampling. A questionnaire was designed for the purpose. The data needs of the study were identified using exploratory research. The questionnaire along with the coding scheme is presented below:

Questionnaire Along with Coding Scheme

1. How many times do you eat out in a week? (X1)

1 – 3	(1)
4 – 6	(2)
7 – 9	(3)
10 – 12	(4)
13 – 15	(5)
16 +	(6)

2. Which of the following categories of eateries do you visit the most? (X2)

Restaurant	(1)
Fast food	(2)
Food court	(3)
Dhaba	(4)
Home delivery	(5)

3. With whom do you eat out most frequently? (X3)

Alone	(1)
With partner	(2)
With family	(3)
With friends	(4)
With colleagues	(5)

4. Approximately how much do you spend per week on eating out? (X4)

0 – 300	(1)
301 – 600	(2)
601 – 900	(3)
901 – 1200	(4)
1201 – 1500	(5)
1500 +	(6)

5. For what reasons do you eat out? (X5a to X5e)

No option of home-cooked food (X5a)	0 = No 1 = Yes
Special occasion (X5b)	0 = No 1 = Yes
Leisure (X5c)	0 = No 1 = Yes
To spend time with friends and family (X5d)	0 = No 1 = Yes
Others, pls specify (X5e)	0 = No 1 = Yes

6. When do you prefer to eat out? (X6)

Weekdays	(1)
Weekends	(2)
Any day	(3)

7. Which meal of the day do you prefer to eat out? (X7a to X7d)

Breakfast (X7a)	0 = No 1 = Yes
Lunch (X7b)	0 = No 1 = Yes
Dinner (X7c)	0 = No 1 = Yes
Snacks (X7d)	0 = No 1 = Yes

Each question (X7a to X7d) is coded as 0 = No (Not ticked) 1 = Yes (Ticked).

8. Rank the following factors from 1 – 6, rank 1 being the most important and rank 6 being the least important (Ranked from 1 – 6, coded as 1 – 6.) (X8a to X8f)

Parameter	Rank
Food (X8a)	☐
Price (X8b)	☐
Service (X8c)	☐
Friends (X8d)	☐
Location (X8e)	☐
Brand (X8f)	☐

9. How do you rate the following when you decide to eat out. (X9a to X9o)

No.	Factors	Extremely important	Important	Neither important nor unimportant	Unimportant	Extremely unimportant
		(1)	(2)	(3)	(4)	(5)
1.	Taste of food (X9a)					
2.	Presentation of food (X9b)					
3.	External look and feel (X9c)					
4.	Ambience (X9d)					
5.	Price (X9e)					
6.	Menu-item variety (X9f)					
7.	Speed of service (X9g)					
8.	Friendliness of service personnel (X9h)					
9.	Cleanliness of the restaurant (X9i)					
10.	Promptness in handling of Complaints (X9j)					
11.	Transportation/accessibility to the place (X9k)					
12.	Brand perception (X9l)					
13.	Promotional offers (X9m)					
14.	Recommendation from friends and others (X9n)					
15.	Payment options offered (X9o)					

10. Age (X10)

< 20	(1)
20 – 30	(2)
31 – 40	(3)
41 – 50	(4)
51 – 60	(5)
60 +	(6)

11. Sex (X11)

    Male [(1)]

    Female [(2)]

12. Marital status (X12)

    Single [(1)]

    Married [(2)]

13. Profession (X13)

    Student [(1)]

    Professional [(2)]

    Self-employed [(3)]

    Retired [(4)]

    Housewife [(5)]

14. Do you own a vehicle? (X14)

    Yes [(1)]

    No [(2)]

15. What is your family's average monthly income? Question ignored.

    0 – 15,000 [(1)]

    15001 – 30000 [(2)]

    30001 – 45000 [(3)]

    45000 + [(4)]

16. Any other comments?

The data for the study is given in Table 11.30 in the data disk.

QUESTIONS

1. Carry out a univariate analysis for the data given in Table 11.30.
2. Prepare appropriate cross-tables for the data presented in Table 11.30. Compute the percentages in the appropriate direction. (You might have to redefine certain variables). What tables would you like to elaborate? Justify your answers.
3. Using the data of question no. 8 of the questionnaire, prepare a rank ordering of the six factors.
4. Interpret the results as obtained above. Write a management summary of your findings.

CASE 11.2

SECOND-HAND CLASSIFIED WEBSITES IN INDIA: USAGE AND TRUST AMONG CONSUMERS

There are a number of second-hand classified (SHC) websites that offer a forum for selling and buying second-hand items by posting ads. The leaders in this sector in India are OLX.com and Quikr.com. People can buy and sell anything—used car, bike, music system, mobile phone, laptop, furniture or household appliances. The information is publically available, but due to heavy information asymmetry in the marketplace, there is barely any trust, and the clearing rate stands as low as 28 per cent.

A survey was conducted in which the respondents were chosen using convenience sampling. A total of 1000 respondents were contacted for filling up the questionnaire, out of which only 600 successfully completed the survey. The questionnaire was prepared by identifying the variables by conducting unstructured interviews with 25 people. The objectives of the study were as follows:

- To gauge the level of awareness about the second-hand classified websites
- To identify the sources of information
- To understand the concerns of people while using the website for buying second-hand products
- To examine whether there is any relationship between the concerns of the respondents and the demographic variables
- To understand the steps needed to increase the clearing rate of this site

The results of the survey are given in the following tables:

Table 1 Age of the Respondents

Age group	Frequency
19 – 25	300
26 – 32	150
≥ 33	150
Total	600

Table 2 Gender of the Respondents

Gender	Frequency
Male	340
Female	260
Total	600

Table 3 Occupation of the Respondents

Occupation	Frequency
Student	340
Service	190
Business	50
Homemaker	20
Total	600

Table 4 Members in Social Circle of the Respondents

Social Circle Members	Frequency
≤ 100	90
101 – 200	150
201 – 400	150
401 +	210
Total	600

Table 5 Annual Household Income of the Respondents

Income Group (in ₹lakh)	Frequency
< 6	110
6 but less than 12	140
12 but less than 18	90
18 +	260
Total	600

Table 6 Awareness of SHC Websites

Awareness	Frequency
No	40
Yes	560
Total	600

Table 7 Sources of Information about SHC Websites

n = 560

Channels of Awareness	Frequency
TV ads	270
Online/Facebook ads	170
Word of Mouth	140

*There is multiplicity of answers.

Table 8 Usage of SHC Websites

Usage	Frequency
No	230
Yes	370
Total	600

Table 9 Trust on Sellers of Websites

Response	Frequency
No	520
Yes	80
Total	600

Table 10 Quality of Second-hand Goods

Response	Frequency
Low	360
High	240
Total	600

Table 11 Website Complicated and Difficulty to Use

Response	Frequency
No	380
Yes	220
Total	600

Table 12 Physical Evaluation of the Product

Response	Frequency
Not important	110
Important	490
Total	600

Table 13 Return Policy Associated with the Product

Response	Frequency
Not Important	180
Important	420
Total	600

Table 14 Usage of SHC Website by Age

Usage of SHC Website	Age		Total
	Below 26 years	26 years & above	
No	69.6%	30.4%	100.0%
Yes	69.6%	30.4%	100.0%

Table 15 Usage of SHC Website by Gender

Usage of SHC Website	Gender		Total
	Male	Female	
No	56.5%	43.5%	100.0%
Yes	56.8%	43.2%	100.0%

Table 16 Usage of SHC Website by Occupation

Usage of SHC Website	Occupation		Total
	Non-working	Working	
No	73.9%	26.1%	100.0%
Yes	51.4%	48.6%	100.0%

Table 17 Usage of SHC Website by Income

Usage of SHC Website	Income	
	Below ₹18 lakh	₹18 lakh and above
No	50.0%	23.1%
Yes	50.0%	76.9%
Total	100.0%	100.0%

Table 18 Trust on SHC Website by Age

Trust	Age	
	Below 26 years	26 years & above
No	83.3%	90.0%
Yes	16.7%	10.0%
Total	100.0%	100.0%

Table 19 Trust on SHC Website by Gender

Trust	Gender		Total
	Male	Female	
No	57.7%	42.3%	100.0%
Yes	50.0%	50.0%	100.0%

Table 20 Income by Trust

Income	Trust		Total
	No	Yes	
Below ₹18 lakh	82.4%	17.6%	100.0%
₹18 lakh and above	92.3%	7.7%	100.0%

Table 21 Trust by Occupation

Trust	Occupation		Total
	Non-working	Working	
No	57.7%	42.3%	100.0%
Yes	75.0%	25.0%	100.0%

Table 22 Quality by Age

Quality	Age		Total
	Below 26 years	26 years and above	
High quality	50%	50%	100.0%
Low quality	50%	50%	100.0%

Table 23 Quality by Gender

Quality	Gender		Total
	Male	Female	
High quality	58.3%	41.7%	100.0%
Low quality	55.6%	44.4%	100.0%

Table 24 Quality by Income

Quality	Income	
	Below ₹18 lakh	₹18 lakh and above
High quality	41.2%	38.5%
Low quality	58.8%	61.5%
Total	100.0%	100.0%

Table 25 Occupation by Quality

Occupation	Quality	
	High quality	Low quality
Non-working	50.0%	66.7%
Working	50.0%	33.3%
Total	100%	100%

Table 26 Age by Complicated Websites

Age	Complicated Websites		Total
	No	Yes	
Below 26 years	86.7%	13.3%	100.0%
26 years and above	40.0%	60.0%	100.0%

Table 27 Complicated Websites by Gender

Complicated Websites	Gender		Total
	Male	Female	
No	60.5%	39.5%	100.0%
Yes	50.0%	50.0%	100.0%

Table 28 Complicated Websites by Income

Complicated Websites	Income		Total
	Below ₹18 lakh	₹18 lakh and above	
No	68.4%	31.6%	100.0%
Yes	36.4%	63.6%	100.0%

Table 29 Occupation by Complicated Websites

Occupation	Complicated Websites	
	No	Yes
Non-working	76.3%	31.8%
Working	23.7%	68.2%
Total	100%	100%

Table 30 Evaluation by Age

Evaluation	Age		Total
	Below 26 years	26 years & above	
Not important	54.5%	45.5%	100.0%
Important	49.0%	51.0%	100.0%

Table 31 Evaluation by Gender

Evaluation	Gender	
	Male	Female
Not important	14.7%	23.1%
Important	85.3%	76.9%
Total	100.0%	100.0%

Table 32 Evaluation by Income

Evaluation	Income	
	Below ₹18 lakh	₹18 lakh and above
Not important	20.6%	15.4%
Important	79.4%	84.6%
Total	100.0%	100.0%

Table 33 Evaluation by Occupation

Evaluation	Occupation	
	Non Working	Working
Not important	8.3%	33.3%
Important	91.7%	66.7%
Total	100.0%	100.0%

Table 34 Return Policy by Age

Return Policy	Age	
	Below 26 years	26 years & above
Not important	43.3%	16.7%
Important	56.7%	83.3%
Total	100.0%	100.0%

Table 35 Return Policy by Gender

Return Policy	Gender		Total
	Male	Female	
Not important	61.1%	38.9%	100.0%
Important	54.8%	45.2%	100.0%

Table 36 Return Policy by Income

Income	Return Policy		Total
	Not important	Important	
Below ₹18 lakh	35.3%	64.7%	100.0%
₹18 lakh and above	23.1%	76.9%	100.0%

Table 37 Return Policy by Occupation

Return Policy	Occupation		Total
	Non-working	Working	
Not important	61.1%	38.9%	100.0%
Important	59.5%	40.5%	100.0%

QUESTIONS

1. What are your conclusions based on univariate analysis?
2. What conclusion can be drawn based on bivariate analysis? Are all the percentages cast in the correct direction for the interpretation of the table? In case the percentages are not cast in the right direction, correct them and interpret all the bivariate tables.
3. Suggest by identifying any bivariate table where a **'moderator variable'** could be used.
4. Write a note on the major findings of the study.

Appendix – 11.1: SPSS COMMANDS FOR PREPARING FREQUENCY DISTRIBUTION TABLES

In this chapter, frequency distribution Tables 11.3, 11.4, 11.5, 11.6 and many more have been prepared. Below are given the SPSS instructions to prepare any of the above tables. The raw data for Table 11.2 in the SPSS form is already given. The instructions for frequency distribution table for marital status as denoted by X13 are as below:

After the input data has been typed along with variable labels and value labels in the SPSS data files (see SPSS Table 11.2), to get the frequency table output for the variable X13 the following steps are used:

1. Click on ANALYSE on the SPSS menu bar.
2. Click on DESCRIPTIVE STATITICS, followed by FREQUENCIES.
3. On the dialogue box which appears, select the variable for which FREQUENCY TABLE are required, by clicking on the right arrow to transfer them from the variable list on the left to the VARIABLES box on the right.
4. Click OK to get the tables with counts and percentages, for each of the selected variables.

Similarly, frequency distribution table corresponding to the variable X3 can be prepared. Only thing which needs to be done is to prepare the table for each of the variables X3a, X3b, ..., till X3l and summarize the result in the form of Table 11.7 as given in the text.

Appendix – 11.2: SPSS COMMANDS FOR RECODING VALUE OF A VARIABLE INTO A NEW VARIABLE

After the input data has been typed along with variable labels and value labels in an SPSS data files, in order to transform a variable into a different variable proceed as follows: (the data of Table 11.16 will be used for the purpose.)

Example: One of the questions was on the preference for fast food. The respondents were asked to state their preference for fast food on a five-point scale where 1 = not at all preferred, 2 = not preferred, 3 = neutral, 4 = preferred, 5 = very much preferred. Our job is to divide the preference rating into two groups based on the preference scores. Those scoring from 1 to 3 could be regarded as such respondents for whom fast food is 'not preferred' choice. For those respondents having a score a 4 or 5 may be treated as respondents having 'preferred' fast food.

To do this exercise we choose the variable 'preference' given in the data sheet. The other steps are as follows:

1. We will come to TRANSFORM, and then choose RECODE and then INTO DIFFERENT VARIABLE.
2. Select the variable PREFERENCE and move it to the right hand side. Under output variable for name call it REPREFERENCE and LABEL it as PREFERENCE REDEFINED and then click on OLD AND NEW VALUES.
3. Under the box titled OLD VALUES, click the RANGE button on the left hand side and then type 1 through 3, and move to the right hand side box titled NEW VALUE and give it a value of 1 and then click on ADD button, you will

get **1 thru 3 → 1**. For the next, click the RANGE button on the left hand side and type 4 through 5 and move to the right hand side under NEW VALUES and give it a value of 2 and then click the ADD button. You will get **4 thru 5 → 2**.

4. Choose REPREFERENCE variable under variable view and select VALUES and define them as 1 = NOT PREFERRED, and 2 = PREFERRED. To do this you have to choose VALUE LABELS and give value of 1 under VALUE and label it as NOT PREFERRED under VALUE LABELS. Click on ADD and continue with the remaining labeling.

Appendix – 11.3: SPSS COMMANDS FOR CROSS-TABLES

After the input data has been typed along with variable labels and value labels in an SPSS data file, to get the CROSS-TABULATIONS and chi-squared test output for a problem, follow the following steps:

1. Click on ANALYSE at the SPSS menu bar.
2. Click on DESCRIPTIVE STATISTICS, followed by CROSS-TABS.
3. Select the row variable for a cross-tabulation by highlighting it in the variable list on the left side and clicking on the arrow leading to the row variable box. Similarly, select the variable you wish to be the column variable in the cross-tabulation.
4. Click on CELLS in the main dialogue box. Under 'Percentages', select either 'ROW' or 'COLUMN' depending on which is desired. Click CONTINUE to return to the main dialog box.
5. Click OK to get the output containing the required cross-tab, along with the percentages computed in the requested direction.

Answers to Objective Type Questions

1. False	2. True	3. False	4. False	5. False
6. True	7. False	8. True	9. False	10. True
11. False	12. True	13. True	14. False	15. True
16. True	17. True	18. True	19. True	20. True

REFERENCE

Chawla, Deepak and Ramesh Behl. *Management of Cyber Café*. Unpublished mimeograph, 2004.

BIBLIOGRAPHY

Churchill, Gilbert A Jr and Dawn Iacobucci. *Marketing Research Methodological Foundations*, 8th edn. New Delhi: Thompson South Western, 2002.

Cooper, Donald R. *Business Research Methods*. New Delhi: Tata McGraw Hill Publishing Company Ltd, 2006.

Emory, William C. *Business Research Methods*. Illinois: Richard D Irwin, 1976.

Gay, L R. *Research Methods for Business and Management*. New York: Macmillan Publishing Company, 1992.

Green, Paul E and Donald S Tull. *Research for Marketing Decisions*, 4th edn. New Delhi: Prentice Hall of India Private Ltd, 1986.

Kinnear, Thomas C and James R Taylor. *Marketing Research: An Applied Approach*, 5th edn. New York: McGraw Hill, Inc., 1996.

Kothari, C R. *Research Methodology: Methods and Techniques*, 2nd edn. New Delhi: Wiley Eastern Limited, 1990.

Malhotra, Naresh K. *Marketing Research – An Applied Orientation*, 3rd edn. New Delhi: Pearson Education, 2002.

Nargundkar, Rajendra. *Marketing Research (Text and Cases)*. New Delhi: Tata McGraw Hill Publishing Company Ltd, 2002.

Schwab, Donald P. *Research Methods for Organizational Studies*. Mahwah: Lawrence Erlaum Associates Publishers, 2005.

Sekaram, Uma. *Research Methods for Business: A Skill Building Approach*. Singapore: John Wiley & Sons (Asia) Pte Ltd, 2003.

Zikmund, William G. *Business Research Methods*. 5th edn. Fort Worth: Dryden Press, Harcourt Brace College Publishers, 1997.

Zikmund, William G. *Business Research Methods*. Fort Worth: Dryden Press, 2000.

12

CHAPTER

Testing of Hypotheses

Learning Objectives

By the end of the chapter, you should be able to:

1. Discuss the concepts used in the testing of hypothesis exercise.
2. Discuss the steps used in testing of hypothesis exercise.
3. Carry out the test of the significance of the mean of a single population using both t and Z-tests.
4. Illustrate the test of the significance of difference between two population means using t- and Z-tests.
5. Use SPSS software to conduct the testing of hypothesis.
6. Discuss the test of the significance of a single population proportion.
7. Carry out the test of the significance of the difference between two population proportions using a Z-test.

Mrs M makes home-made ice creams and desserts and sells them through her garage outlet at New Friends Colony, New Delhi. Now her son and daughter-in-law want to expand the business and sell cakes and confectionery as well. The daughter-in-law knows chocolate-making and believes that today the gift industry in India, especially the 'sweet nothings' industry, has a huge potential. So, she is planning to provide customized fancy chocolate boxes and assortments of candies that can be sold to individual customers.

However, this expansion would require investment in terms of capital, manpower and infrastructure. Thus, they would like to be able to test the acceptability and the probability of purchase for their products and customized service. Mrs M was very optimistic and said that she had spoken to some of her regular customers as well as their chef. Both of them felt that there was great potential and whatever they manufacture would sell—after all, they had been in the business for 25 years and knew the market pulse.

The daughter-in-law, a BSc in statistics, stated that certain scientific ways of testing whether their presumptions are true or not on a small sample of potential buyers are available. This would help cut the risk, as well as give some indication on what could be the numbers they can look at. Moreover, it will help in identifying the impact of the factors such as old customers of Mrs M, age of the customer, family size and lifestyle variables on the buying decision. Mrs M looked wonderingly at her daughter-in-law and asked whether the numerical testing learnt by her during academics could be put to use in the present scenario.

Well, the answer is yes. To recall, we hypothesized our assumptions formally in the form of a statement to be tested in the second chapter. In this chapter, we will be looking at how we can reduce the statements to mathematical forms and test them to ascertain their truth.

CONCEPTS IN TESTING OF HYPOTHESIS

LEARNING OBJECTIVE 1
Discuss the concepts used in the testing of hypothesis exercise.

A hypothesis is an assumption or a statement that may or may not be true. The hypothesis is tested on the basis of information obtained from a sample. Hypothesis tests are widely used in business and industry for making decisions. Instead of asking, for example, what the mean assessed value of an apartment in a multistoried building is, one may be interested in knowing whether or not the assessed value equals some particular value, say ₹80 lakh. Some other examples could be whether a new drug is more effective than the existing drug based on the sample data, and whether the proportion of smokers in a class is different from 0.30. The formulation of hypothesis has already been discussed in Chapter 2 of this book. The testing procedures are generally explained in any text on statistics. For the sake of revision, below are listed some concepts that are useful for carrying out a testing of hypothesis exercise.

Null hypotheses are proposed with the intent of receiving a rejection. These are denoted as H_0.

Null hypothesis: The hypotheses that are proposed with the intent of receiving a rejection for them are called null hypotheses. This requires that we hypothesize the opposite of what is desired to be proved. For example, if we want to show that sales and advertisement expenditure are related, we formulate the null hypothesis that they are not related. Similarly, if we want to conclude that the new sales training programme is effective, we formulate the null hypothesis that the new training programme is not effective, and if we want to prove that the average wages of skilled workers in town 1 is greater than that of town 2, we formulate the null hypotheses that there is no difference in the average wages of the skilled workers in both the towns. Since we hypothesize that sales and advertisement are not related, new training programme is not effective and the average wages of skilled workers in both the towns are equal, we call such hypotheses null hypotheses and denote them as H_0.

The **alternative hypotheses** can cover a whole range of value rather than a single point. These are denoted by H_1.

Alternative hypotheses: Rejection of null hypotheses leads to the acceptance of alternative hypotheses. The rejection of null hypothesis indicates that the relationship between variables (e.g., sales and advertisement expenditure) or the difference between means (e.g., wages of skilled workers in town 1 and town 2) or the difference between proportions have statistical significance and the acceptance of the null hypotheses indicates that these differences are due to chance. As already mentioned, the alternative hypotheses specify that values/relation which the researcher believes hold true. The alternative hypotheses can cover a whole range of values rather than a single point. The alternative hypotheses are denoted by H_1.

One-tailed and two-tailed tests: A test is called one-sided (or one-tailed) only if the null hypothesis gets rejected when a value of the test statistic falls in one specified tail of the distribution. Further, the test is called two-sided (or two-tailed) if null hypothesis gets rejected when a value of the test statistic falls in either one or the other of the two tails of its sampling distribution. For example, consider a soft drink bottling plant which dispenses soft drinks in bottles of 300 ml capacity. The bottling is done through an automatic plant. An overfilling of bottle (liquid content more than 300 ml) means a huge loss to the company given the large volume of sales. An underfilling means the customers are getting less than 300 ml of the drink when they are paying for 300 ml. This could bring bad reputation to the company. The company wants to avoid both overfilling and underfilling. Therefore, it would prefer to test the hypothesis whether the mean content of the bottles is different from 300 ml. This hypothesis could be written as:

$$H_0 \quad : \quad \mu \quad = \quad 300 \text{ ml.}$$
$$H_1 \quad : \quad \mu \quad \neq \quad 300 \text{ ml.}$$

The hypotheses stated above are called two-tailed or two-sided hypotheses. However, if the concern is the overfilling of bottles, it could be stated as:

$$H_0 \quad : \quad \mu \quad = \quad 300 \text{ ml.}$$
$$H_1 \quad : \quad \mu \quad > \quad 300 \text{ ml.}$$

Such hypotheses are called one-tailed or one-sided hypotheses and the researcher would be interested in the upper tail (right hand tail) of the distribution. If however, the concern is loss of reputation of the company (underfilling of the bottles), the hypothesis may be stated as:

$$H_0 \quad : \quad \mu \quad = \quad 300 \text{ ml.}$$
$$H_1 \quad : \quad \mu \quad < \quad 300 \text{ ml.}$$

The hypothesis stated above is also called one-tailed test and the researcher would be interested in the lower tail (left hand tail) of the distribution.

At this stage we advice the reader to turn to the descriptive and relational hypotheses narrated in statement form in Chapter 2 and reduce them to a statistical H_0 as well as the corresponding alternative hypotheses as H_1.

Type I and type II error: The acceptance or rejection of a hypothesis is based upon sample results and there is always a possibility of sample not being representative of the population. This could result in errors as a consequence of which inferences drawn could be wrong. The situation could be depicted as given in Figure 12.1.

FIGURE 12.1
Type I and Type II errors

	Accept H_0	Reject H_0
H_0 True	Correct decision	Type I error
H_0 False	Type II error	Correct decision

The level of significance denotes the probability of rejecting the null hypothesis when it is true. It is denoted by α.

If null hypothesis H_0 is true and is accepted or H_0 when false is rejected, the decision is correct in either case. However, if the hypothesis H_0 is rejected when it is actually true, the researcher is committing what is called a Type I error. The probability of committing a Type I error is denoted by alpha (α). This is termed as the level of significance. Similarly, if the null hypothesis H_0 when false is accepted, the researcher is committing an error called Type II error. The probability of committing a Type II error is denoted by beta (β). The expression $1 - \beta$ is called power of test.

STEPS IN TESTING OF HYPOTHESIS EXERCISE

LEARNING OBJECTIVE 2
Discuss the steps used in the testing of hypothesis exercise.

The following steps are followed in testing of a hypothesis:

Setting up of a hypothesis: First step is to establish the hypothesis to be tested. As it is known, these statistical hypotheses are generally assumptions about the value of the population parameter; the hypothesis specifies a single value or a range of values for two different hypotheses rather than constructing a single hypothesis. These two hypotheses are generally referred to as the (1) null hypotheses denoted by H_0 and (2) alternative hypothesis denoted by H_1.

The null hypothesis is the hypothesis of the population parameter taking a specified value. In case of two populations, the null hypothesis is of no difference or the difference taking a specified value. The hypothesis that is different from the null hypothesis is the alternative hypothesis. If the null hypothesis H_0 is rejected based upon the sample information, the alternative hypothesis H_1 is accepted. Therefore, the two hypotheses are constructed in such a way that if one is true, the other one is false and vice versa. There can also be situations where the researcher is interested in establishing the relationship between any two variables. In such a case, a null hypothesis is set as the hypothesis of no relationship between those two variables; whereas the alternative hypothesis is the hypothesis of the relationship between variables. The rejection of the null hypothesis indicates that the differences/relationship have a statistical significance and the acceptance of the null hypothesis means that any difference/relationship is due to chance.

The **level of significance** denotes the probability of rejecting the null hypothesis when it is true. It is denoted by α.

Setting up of a suitable significance level: The next step in the testing of hypothesis exercise is to choose a suitable level of significance. The level of significance denoted by α is chosen before drawing any sample. The level of significance denotes the probability of rejecting the null hypothesis when it is true. The value of α varies from problem to problem, but usually it is taken as either 5 per cent or 1 per cent. A 5 per cent level of significance means that there are 5 chances out of hundred that a null hypothesis will get rejected when it should be accepted. This means that the researcher is 95 per cent confident that a right decision has been taken. Therefore, it is seen that the confidence with which a researcher rejects or accepts a null hypothesis depends upon the level of significance. When the null hypothesis is rejected at any level of significance, the test result is said to be significant. Further, if a hypothesis is rejected at 1 per cent level, it must also be rejected at 5 per cent significance level.

Determination of a test statistic: The next step is to determine a suitable test statistic and its distribution. As would be seen later, the test statistic could be t, Z, χ^2 or F, depending upon various assumptions to be discussed later in the book.

Determination of critical region: Before a sample is drawn from the population, it is very important to specify the values of test statistic that will lead to rejection or acceptance of the null hypothesis. The one that leads to the rejection of null hypothesis is called the critical region. Given a level of significance, α, the optimal critical region for a two-tailed test consists of that α/2 per cent area in the right hand tail of the distribution plus that α/2 per cent in the left hand tail of the distribution where that null hypothesis is rejected. Therefore, establishing a critical region is similar to determining a 100 (1 – α) per cent confidence interval.

Computing the value of test-statistic: The next step is to compute the value of the test statistic based upon a random sample of size n. Once the value of test statistic is computed, one needs to examine whether the sample results fall in the critical region or in the acceptance region.

Making decision: The hypothesis may be rejected or accepted depending upon whether the value of the test statistic falls in the rejection or the acceptance region. Management decisions are based upon the statistical decision of either rejecting or accepting the null hypothesis.

If the hypothesis is being tested at 5 per cent level of significance, it would be rejected if the observed results have a probability less than 5 per cent. In such a case, the difference between the sample statistic and the hypothesized population parameter is considered to be significant. On the other hand, if the hypothesis is accepted, the difference between the sample statistic and the hypothesized population parameter is not regarded as significant and can be attributed to chance.

Test Statistic for Testing Hypothesis about Population Mean

If the **population standard deviation** σ is known, a Z statistic can be used. In case σ is unknown and is estimated using sample data, a t-test with appropriate degrees of freedom is used under the assumption that the sample is drawn from a normal population.

In this section, we will take up the test of hypothesis about population mean in a case of single population and the difference between the two means for two populations.

One of the important things that have to be kept in mind is the use of an appropriate test statistic. In case the sample size is large ($n > 30$), Z statistic would be used. For a small sample size ($n \leq 30$), a further question regarding the knowledge of population standard deviation (σ) is asked. If the population standard deviation σ is known, a Z statistic can be used. However, if σ is unknown and is estimated using sample data, a t-test with appropriate degrees of freedom is used under the assumption that the sample is drawn from a normal population. It is assumed that the readers have the knowledge of Z and t-distribution from the course on statistics. However, these would be briefly reviewed at the appropriate place. Table 12.1 summarizes the appropriateness of the test statistic for conducting a test of hypothesis regarding the population mean.

TABLE 12.1 Appropriateness of test statistic in testing hypotheses about means

Sample Size	Knowledge of Population Standard Deviation (σ)	
	Known	Not Known
Large (n > 30)	Z	Z
Small (n ≤ 30)	Z	t

TEST CONCERNING MEANS – CASE OF SINGLE POPULATION

LEARNING OBJECTIVE 3
Carry out the test of the significance of the mean of a single population using both t and Z-tests.

In this section, a number of illustrations will be taken up to explain the test of hypothesis concerning mean. Two cases of large sample and small samples will be taken up.

Case of Large Sample

As mentioned earlier, in case the sample size n is large or small but the value of the population standard deviation is known, a Z-test is appropriate. There can be alternate cases of two- tailed and one-tailed tests of hypotheses. Corresponding to the null hypothesis $H_0 : \mu = \mu_0$, the following criteria could be used as shown in Table 12.2.

The test statistic is given by,

$$Z = \frac{\overline{X} - \mu_{H_0}}{\frac{\sigma}{\sqrt{n}}}$$

where,

$\overline{X}$ = Sample mean

σ = Population standard deviation

μ_{H_0} = The value of μ under the assumption that the null hypothesis is true

n = Size of sample

TABLE 12.2 Criteria for accepting or rejecting null hypothesis under different cases of alternative hypotheses

S. No.	Alternative Hypothesis	Reject the Null Hypothesis if	Accept the Null Hypothesis if
1.	$\mu < \mu_0$	$Z < -Z_\alpha$	$Z \geq -Z_\alpha$
2.	$\mu > \mu_0$	$Z > Z_\alpha$	$Z \leq Z_\alpha$
3.	$\mu \neq \mu_0$	$Z < -Z_{\alpha/2}$ Or $Z > Z_{\alpha/2}$	$-Z_{\alpha/2} \leq Z \leq Z_{\alpha/2}$

If the population standard deviation σ is unknown, the sample standard deviation

$$s = \sqrt{\frac{1}{n-1}\Sigma(X-\overline{X})^2}$$

is used as an estimate of σ. It may be noted that Z_α and $Z_{\alpha/2}$ are Z values such that the area to the right under the standard normal distribution is α and α/2 respectively. Below are solved examples using the above concepts.

Example 12.1

A sample of 200 bulbs made by a company give a lifetime mean of 1540 hours with a standard deviation of 42 hours. Is it likely that the sample has been drawn from a population with a mean lifetime of 1500 hours? You may use 5 per cent level of significance.

Solution:

In the above example, the sample size is large (n = 200), sample mean ($\overline{X}$) equals 1540 hours and the sample standard deviation (s) is equal to 42 hours. The null and alternative hypotheses can be written as:

$$H_0 \quad : \quad \mu \quad = 1500 \text{ hrs}$$
$$H_1 \quad : \quad \mu \quad \neq 1500 \text{ hrs}$$

It is a two-tailed test with level of significance (α) to be equal to 0.05. Since n is large (n > 30), though population standard deviation σ is unknown, one can use Z-test. The test statistics are given by:

$$Z = \frac{\overline{X} - \mu_{H_0}}{\sigma_{\overline{X}}}$$

where, μ_{H_0} = Value of μ under the assumption that the null hypothesis is true

$\hat{\sigma}_{\overline{X}}$ = Estimated standard error of mean

Here, $\mu_{H_0} = 1500$, $\hat{\sigma}_{\overline{X}} = \frac{\hat{\sigma}}{\sqrt{n}} = \frac{s}{\sqrt{n}} = \frac{42}{\sqrt{200}} = 2.97$

(Note that $\hat{\sigma}$ is estimated value of σ.)

$$Z = \frac{\overline{X} - \mu_{H_0}}{\frac{s}{\sqrt{n}}} = \frac{1540 - 1500}{2.97} = \frac{40}{2.97} = 13.47$$

The value of α = 0.05 and since it is a two-tailed test, the critical value Z is given by $-Z_{\alpha/2}$ and $Z_{\alpha/2}$ which could be obtained from the standard normal table given in Annexure 1 at the end of the book.

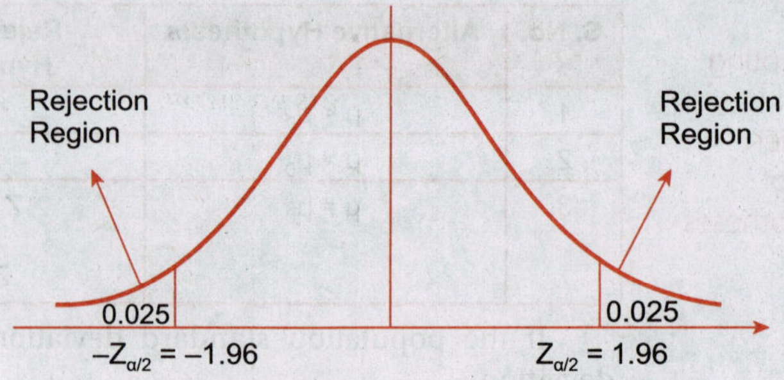

Rejection regions for Example 12.1

Since the computed value of Z = 13.47 lies in the rejection region, the null hypothesis is rejected. Therefore, it can be concluded that the average life of the bulb is significantly different from 1500 hours.

Alternative Approach to the Test of Hypothesis

There is an alternative approach called probability approach or simply p value approach to test the hypothesis. Under this approach, the researcher does not have to refer to Z table to determine the critical value. Referring to Example 12.1, the p value can be calculated as follows:

$$p = P(Z > 13.47) + P(Z < -13.47)$$

We know that the problem is that of a two-sided test and Z has a symmetric distribution, therefore,

$$p = 2P(Z > 13.47) = 2 \times 0 = 0$$

In a **probability approach** or a **p value approach**, the researcher does not have to refer to Z table to determine the critical value.

Now, the decision rule is:

Reject	H_0	if	$p \le \alpha$
Accept	H_0	if	$p > \alpha$

In this example, $\alpha = 0.05$ and p value is less than α, so the null hypothesis is rejected. Therefore, it may be noted that the same conclusion is arrived at and there is no need to look at the critical value of Z as given in the statistical table. These days, most computer software like SPSS, EXCEL, SAS, MINITAB provide both the computed value of test statistic and the corresponding p value. Please note that the p value provided there is for the two-sided test. In case the problem is of a one-sided test, the reported p value is divided by 2 to obtain the desired p value for the problem and then compared with alpha (α), the level of significance so as to either accept or reject the null hypothesis. This is possible since Z-distribution is a symmetrical distribution.

Example 12.2

On a typing test, a random sample of 36 graduates of a secretarial school averaged 73.6 words with a standard deviation of 8.10 words per minute. Test an employer's claim that the school's graduates average less than 75.0 words per minute using the 5 per cent level of significance.

Solution:

$$H_0 : \mu = 75$$
$$H_1 : \mu < 75$$

$\bar{X} = 73.6$, $s = 8.10$, $n = 36$ and $\alpha = 0.05$. As the sample size is large ($n > 30$), though population standard deviation σ is unknown, Z-test is appropriate.

The test statistic is given by:

$$Z = \frac{\bar{X} - \mu_{H_0}}{\hat{\sigma}_{\bar{X}}} = \frac{73.6 - 75}{1.35} = \frac{-1.4}{1.35} = -1.04$$

$$\left(\hat{\sigma}_{\bar{X}} = \frac{s}{\sqrt{n}} = \frac{8.10}{\sqrt{36}} = \frac{8.10}{6} = 1.35\right)$$

Since it is a one-tailed test and the interest is in the left hand tail of the distribution, the critical value of Z is given by $-Z_a = -1.645$. Now, the computed value of Z lies in the acceptance region, and the null hypothesis is accepted as shown below:

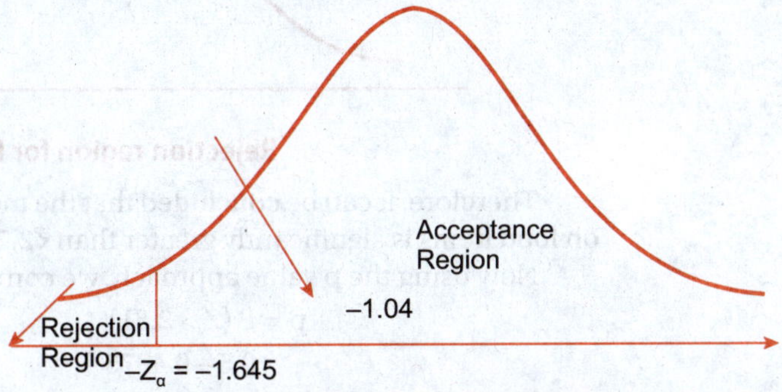

Rejection region for Example 12.2

Now, the same problem can be worked out using the p value approach.

$$p = P(Z < -1.04)$$
$$= 0.5 - 0.3508$$
$$= 0.1492 \text{ (From Annexure 1)}$$

Since the p value is greater than α, there is not enough evidence to reject the null hypothesis. Therefore, the average speed of the graduates of a secretarial school is not significantly different from 75.00 words per minute. Therefore, the claim of the employer is not valid.

Example 12.3 It is known from past studies that the monthly average household expenditure on the food items in a locality is ₹2,700 with a standard deviation of ₹160. An economist took a random sample of 25 households from the locality and found their monthly household expenditure on food items to be ₹2,790.0. At 0.01 level of significance, can we conclude that the average household expenditure on the food items is greater than ₹2,700?

Solution:

$$H_0 \quad : \quad \mu = 2700$$
$$H_1 \quad : \quad \mu > 2700$$

$\bar{X} = 2790$, $\sigma = 160$, $n = 25$, and $\alpha = 0.01$. It may be seen that although the sample size is small ($n < 30$), but since the population standard deviation is known, Z-test could be applied.

The test statistic is given by,

$$Z = \frac{\bar{X} - \mu_{H_0}}{\hat{\sigma}_{\bar{X}}} = \frac{2790 - 2700}{32} = \frac{90}{32} = 2.81$$

$$\left(\sigma_{\bar{X}} = \frac{\sigma}{\sqrt{n}} = \frac{160}{5} = 32\right)$$

Since it is a one-tailed test and the interest is in the right hand tail of the distribution, the critical value of Z is given by $Z_\alpha = Z_{.01} = 2.33$. Now, the computed value of Z lies in the rejection region, the null hypothesis is rejected as shown below:

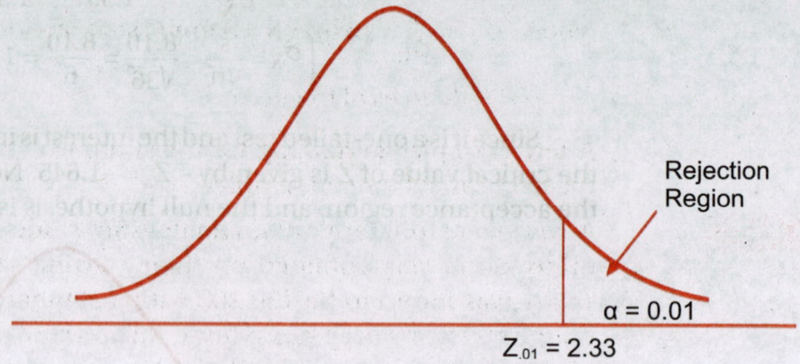

Rejection region for Example 12.3

Therefore, it can be concluded that the monthly average household expenditure on food items is significantly greater than ₹2,700.

Now using the p value approach, we compute it as:

$$p = P(Z > 2.81)$$
$$= 0.5 - 0.4975$$
$$= 0.0025 \text{ (From Annexure 1)}$$

Since the p value of 0.0025 is less than 0.01, there is enough evidence to reject H_0.

Case of Small Sample

In case the sample size is small ($n \leq 30$) and is drawn from a population having a normal population with unknown standard deviation σ, a t-test is used to conduct the hypothesis for the test of mean. The t-distribution is a symmetrical distribution just like the normal one. However, t-distribution is higher at the tail and lower at the peak. The t-distribution is flatter than the normal distribution. With an increase in the sample size (and hence degrees of freedom), t-distribution loses its flatness and approaches the normal distribution whenever $n > 30$. A comparative shape of t and normal distribution is given in Figure 12.2.

FIGURE 12.2
Shape of t and normal distribution

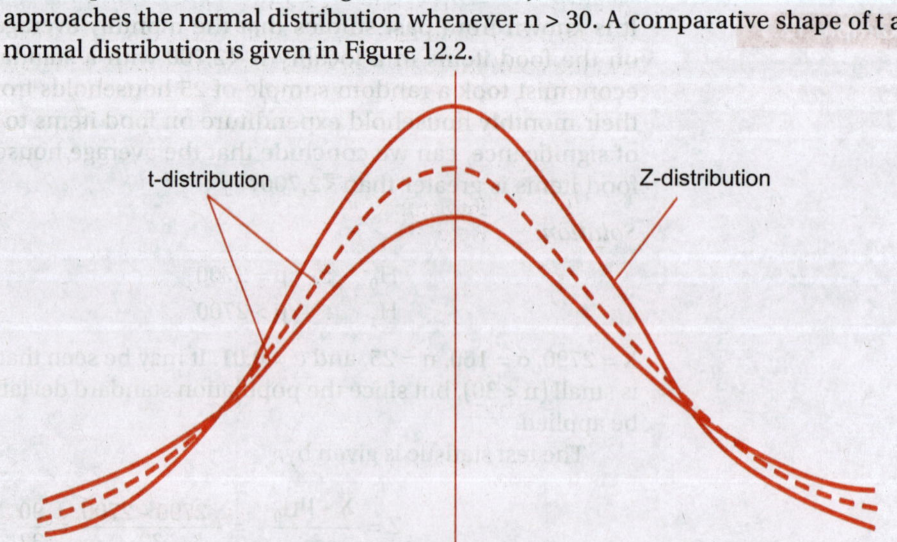

The procedure for testing the hypothesis of a mean is similar to what is explained in the case of large sample. The test statistic used in this case is:

$$t_{n-1} = \frac{\bar{X} - \mu_{H_0}}{\hat{\sigma}_{\bar{X}}}$$

where, $\hat{\sigma}_{\bar{X}} = \frac{s}{\sqrt{n}}$ (where s = Sample standard deviation)

n−1 = degrees of freedom

A few examples pertaining to 't' test are worked out for testing the hypothesis of mean in case of a small sample.

Example 12.4

A sample of 16 graduating engineering students of a college was taken and the information was obtained on their starting salary. The mean monthly starting salary was found to be ₹30,200 with a standard deviation of ₹960. The past data on the starting salary has given a mean value of ₹30,000. Using a 5 per cent level of significance, can we conclude that the average starting salary is different from ₹30,000?

Solution:

$$H_0 \quad : \quad \mu = 30{,}000$$
$$H_1 \quad : \quad \mu \neq 30{,}000$$

$\bar{X} = 30{,}200$, s = 960, n = 16 and $\alpha = 0.05$. As the sample size is small ($n < 30$), and population standard σ is unknown, one may use a t-test to examine the hypothesis in question.

The test statistic is given by:

$$t_{n-1} = \frac{\bar{X} - \mu_{H_0}}{\hat{\sigma}_{\bar{X}}} = \frac{\bar{X} - \mu_{H_0}}{\frac{s}{\sqrt{n}}} = \frac{30{,}200 - 30{,}000}{\frac{960}{\sqrt{16}}}$$

$$= \frac{200 \times 4}{960} = \frac{800}{960} = 0.83$$

Since it is a two-tailed test, the critical value of t with 15 degrees of freedom is given by $-t_{\alpha/2} = -2.131$ and $t_{\alpha/2} = 2.131$. These could be obtained from the t-distribution table given in Annexure 2 at the end of the book. It is seen from the curve given below that the computed value of t lies in the acceptance region.

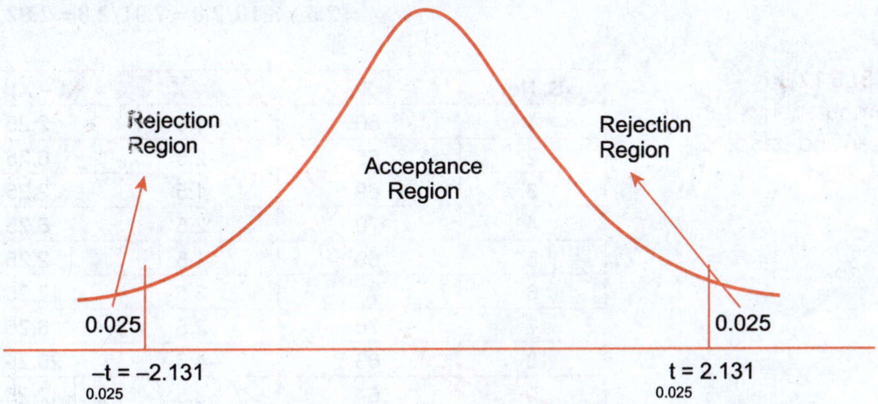

Rejection regions for Example 12.4

Therefore, there is not enough evidence to reject the null hypothesis. Hence, the average salary of graduating engineering students is not statistically different from ₹30,000 at 5 per cent level of significance.

For the p value approach, we examine the level of significance at which the computed value of t = 0.83 with 15 degrees of freedom falls. It is seen that the p value will be more than 10 per cent. This value of p is greater than the value of $\alpha = 0.05$. This means that the null hypothesis is accepted.

Example 12.5

Prices of share (in ₹) of a company on the different days in a month were found to be 66, 65, 69, 70, 69, 71, 70, 63, 64, and 68. Examine whether the mean price of shares in the month is different from 65. You may use 10 per cent level of significance.

Solution:

$$H_0 \quad : \quad \mu = 65$$
$$H_1 \quad : \quad \mu \neq 65$$

Since the sample size is n = 10, which is small, and the sample standard deviation is unknown, the appropriate test in this case would be t. First of all, we need to estimate the value of sample mean ($\bar{X}$) and the sample standard deviation (s). It is known that the sample mean and the standard deviation are given by the following formula.

$$\bar{X} = \frac{\Sigma X}{n} \qquad s = \sqrt{\frac{1}{n-1}\Sigma(X-\bar{X})^2}$$

The computation of $\bar{X}$ and s is shown in Table 12.3.

$$\Sigma X = 675, \qquad \bar{X} = \frac{\Sigma X}{n} = \frac{675}{10} = 67.5$$

$$\Sigma(X-\bar{X})^2 = 70.5$$

$$s^2 = \frac{1}{n-1}\Sigma(X-\bar{X})^2 = \frac{70.5}{9} = 7.83$$

$$s = \sqrt{7.83} = 2.80$$

The test statistic is given by:

$$t_{n-1} = \frac{\bar{X} - \mu_{H_0}}{\hat{\sigma}_{\bar{X}}} = \frac{\bar{X} - \mu_{H_0}}{\frac{s}{\sqrt{n}}} = \frac{67.5 - 65}{\frac{2.8}{\sqrt{10}}} = \frac{2.5 \times \sqrt{10}}{2.8}$$

$$= 2.5 \times 3.16/2.8 = 7.91/2.8 = 2.82$$

TABLE 12.3 Computation of sample mean and standard deviation

S. No.	X	$X-\bar{X}$	$(X-\bar{X})^2$
1	66	–1.5	2.25
2	65	–2.5	6.25
3	69	1.5	2.25
4	70	2.5	6.25
5	69	1.5	2.25
6	71	3.5	12.25
7	70	2.5	6.25
8	63	–4.5	20.25
9	64	–3.5	12.25
10	68	0.5	0.25
Total	675	0	70.5

The critical values of t with 9 degrees of freedom for a two-tailed test are given by –1.833 and 1.833. Since the computed value of t lies in the rejection region (see figure below), the null hypotheses is rejected.

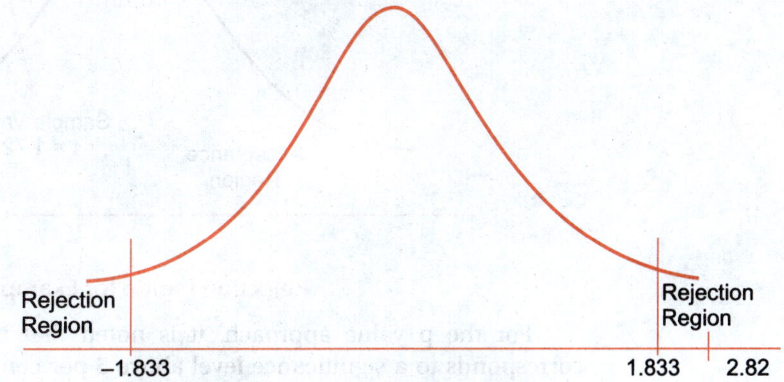

Rejection regions for Example 12.5

Therefore, the average price of the share of the company is different from 65. This problem could also be solved using the p value approach as explained in the previous example. It is left to the readers to verify the conclusion using these two approaches.

Example 12.6 The results of a household survey indicated that a sample of 20 households bought an average of 75 litres of milk per month with a standard deviation of 13.0 litres. Test the hypothesis that the value of the population mean is 70 litres against the alternative that it is more than 70 litres. Use 0.05 level of significance.

Solution:

$$H_0 \quad : \quad \mu = 70$$
$$H_1 \quad : \quad \mu > 70$$

$\bar{X} = 75, s = 13.0, n = 20, \alpha = 0.05$. This is the problem of a one-tailed test. The population standard deviation is unknown and the sample size is small (n < 30). Therefore, a t-test would be appropriate. The test statistic is given by:

$$t_{n-1} = \frac{\bar{X} - \mu_{H_0}}{\hat{\sigma}_{\bar{X}}} = \frac{\bar{X} - \mu_{H_0}}{s/\sqrt{n}} = \frac{75-70}{\frac{13}{\sqrt{20}}} = \frac{5}{2.91} = 1.72$$

$$\left(\hat{\sigma}_{\bar{X}} = \frac{s}{\sqrt{n}} = \frac{13}{\sqrt{20}} = 2.91\right)$$

The critical value of t with 19 degrees of freedom for a one-tailed test is given by 1.729 (see Annexure 2 on t-distribution given at the end of the book). As the computed value of t lies in the acceptance region, as shown in the figure below, the null hypothesis is accepted. Therefore, the average purchase of milk in a household per month is not significantly different from 70 litres.

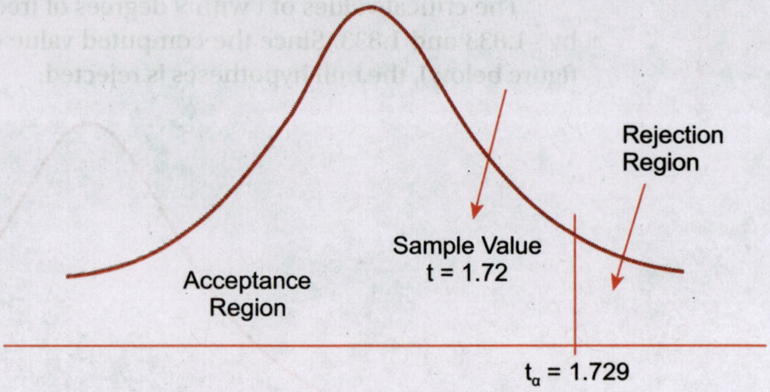

Rejection region for Example 12.6

For the p value approach, it is noted that the sample value of t statistic corresponds to a significance level above 5 per cent. The p value for this problem exceeds 0.05, thereofre the null hypothesis is accepted. Hence, the same conclusion as stated above would hold true.

Example 12.7 Past records indicate that a golfer has averaged 82 on a certain course. With a new set of clubs, he averages 7 over five rounds with a standard deviation of 2.65. Can we conclude that at 0.025 level of significance, the new club has an adverse effect on the performance?

Solution:

$H_0 \quad : \quad \mu = 82$

$H_1 \quad : \quad \mu < 82$

$\bar{X} = 7.9$, $n = 5$, $s = 2.65$, $\alpha = 0.025$. As the population standard deviation is unknown and the sample size is small ($n < 30$), a t-test would be appropriate. The test statistic is given by:

$$t_{n-1} = \frac{\bar{X} - \mu_{H_0}}{\hat{\sigma}_{\bar{X}}} = \frac{\bar{X} - \mu_{H_0}}{s/\sqrt{n}} = \frac{7.9 - 8.2}{1.185} = \frac{-0.3}{1.185} = -0.25$$

$$\left(\hat{\sigma}_{\bar{X}} = \frac{s}{\sqrt{n}} = \frac{2.65}{\sqrt{5}} = 1.185\right)$$

The critical value of t at 0.025 level of significance with four degrees of freedom is given by $-t_\alpha = -2.776$ (see Annexure 2). As the sample t value of -0.25 lies in the acceptance region, the null hypothesis is accepted (see figure below).

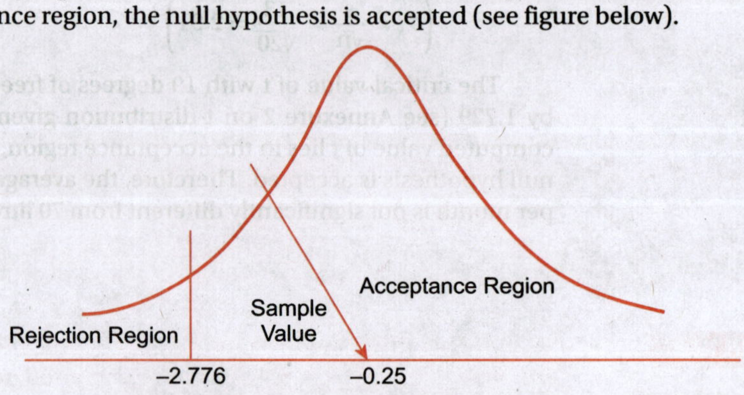

Rejection region for Example 12.7

CONCEPT CHECK	
	1. Define null hypothesis and alternative hypothesis.
	2. What are type I and type II errors?
	3. How would you test the hypothesis concerning mean in the case of single population?

Therefore, there is no adverse effect on the performance due to a change in the club and the performance can be attributed to chance.

TESTS FOR DIFFERENCE BETWEEN TWO POPULATION MEANS

LEARNING OBJECTIVE 4
Illustrate the test of the significance of difference between two population means using t- and Z-tests.

So far we have been concerned with the testing of means of a single population. We took up the cases of both large and small samples. It would be interesting to examine the difference between the two population means. Again, various cases would be examined as discussed below:

Case of Large Sample

In case both the sample sizes are greater than 30, a Z-test is used. The hypothesis to be tested may be written as:

$$H_0 \quad : \quad \mu_1 = \mu_2$$
$$H_1 \quad : \quad \mu_1 \neq \mu_2$$

where,

μ_1 = Mean of population 1

μ_2 = Mean of population 2

The above is a case of two-tailed test. The test statistic used is:

$$Z = \frac{(\bar{X}_1 - \bar{X}_2) - (\mu_1 - \mu_2)H_0}{\sqrt{\frac{\sigma_1^2}{n_1} + \frac{\sigma_2^2}{n_2}}}$$

$\bar{X}_1$ = Mean of sample drawn from population 1

$\bar{X}_2$ = Mean of sample drawn from population 2

n_1 = Size of sample drawn from population 1

n_2 = Size of sample drawn from population 2

If σ_1 and σ_2 are unknown, their estimates given by $\hat{\sigma}_1$ and $\hat{\sigma}_2$ are used.

$$\hat{\sigma}_1 = s_1 = \sqrt{\frac{1}{n_1 - 1}\sum_{i=1}^{n_1}(X_{1i} - \bar{X}_1)^2}$$

$$\hat{\sigma}_2 = s_2 = \sqrt{\frac{1}{n_2 - 1}\sum_{i=1}^{n_2}(X_{2i} - \bar{X}_2)^2}$$

The Z value for the problem can be computed using the above formula and compared with the table value to either accept or reject the hypothesis. Let us consider the following problem:

Example 12.8

A study is carried out to examine whether the mean hourly wages of the unskilled workers in the two cities—Ambala Cantt and Lucknow are the same. The random sample of hourly earnings in both the cities is taken and the results are presented in the Table 12.4.

TABLE 12.4 Survey data on hourly earnings in two cities

City	Sample Mean Hourly Earnings	Standard Deviation of Sample	Sample Size
Ambala Cantt	₹8.95 ($\overline{X}_1$)	0.40 (s_1)	200 (n_1)
Lucknow	₹9.10 ($\overline{X}_2$)	0.60 (s_2)	175 (n_2)

Using a 5 per cent level of significance, test the hypothesis of no difference in the average wages of unskilled workers in the two cities.

Solution:

We use subscripts 1 and 2 for Ambala Cantt and Lucknow respectively.

$$H_0 \quad : \quad \mu_1 = \mu_2 \quad \rightarrow \quad \mu_1 - \mu_2 = 0$$
$$H_1 \quad : \quad \mu_1 \neq \mu_2 \quad \rightarrow \quad \mu_1 - \mu_2 \neq 0$$

The following survey data is given:

$$\overline{X}_1 = 8.95,\ \overline{X}_2 = 9.10,\ s_1 = 0.40,\ s_2 = 0.60,\ n_1 = 200,\ n_2 = 175,\ \alpha = 0.05$$

Since both n_1, n_2 are greater than 30 and the sample standard deviations are given, a Z-test would be appropriate.

The test statistic is given by

$$Z = \frac{(\overline{X}_1 - \overline{X}_2) - (\mu_1 - \mu_2)H_0}{\sqrt{\frac{\sigma_1^2}{n_1} + \frac{\sigma_2^2}{n_2}}}$$

As σ_1, σ_2 are unknown, their estimates would be used.

$$s_1 = \hat{\sigma}_1, \qquad s_2 = \hat{\sigma}_2$$

$$\sqrt{\frac{\hat{\sigma}_1^2}{n_1} + \frac{\hat{\sigma}_2^2}{n_2}} = \sqrt{\frac{(0.4)^2}{200} + \frac{(0.6)^2}{175}} = \sqrt{0.0028} = 0.0053$$

$$Z = \frac{(8.95 - 9.10) - 0}{0.053} = -2.83$$

As the problem is of a two-tailed test, the critical values of Z at 5 per cent level of significance are given by $-Z_{\alpha/2} = -1.96$ and $Z_{\alpha/2} = 1.96$. The sample value of Z = −2.83 lies in the rejection region as shown in the figure below:

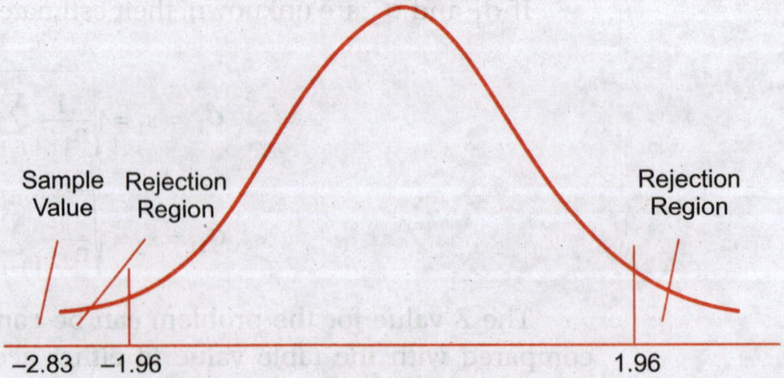

Rejection regions for Example 12.8

Therefore, the null hypothesis is rejected and it may be concluded that there is a difference in the average wages of unskilled workers in the two cities. Let us rework the same problem using the p value approach. As it is known that the problem is of a two-tailed test, the p value is given by:

$$\begin{aligned} p &= P(Z < -2.83) + P(Z > 2.83) \\ &= 2P(Z > 2.83) \\ &= 2 \times (0.5 - 0.4977) \\ &= 2 \times 0.0023 \\ &= 0.0046 \end{aligned}$$

As the value of p is less than α (0.05), the null hypothesis is rejected. Similarly, the problems on one-tailed tests can be solved.

Case of Small Sample

If the size of both the samples is less than 30 and the population standard deviation is unknown, the procedure described above to discuss the equality of two population means is not applicable in the sense that a t-test would be applicable under the assumptions:

(a) Two population variances are equal.
(b) Two population variances are not equal.

Population variances are equal

If the two population variances are equal, it implies that their respective unbiased estimates are also equal. In such a case, the expression becomes:

$$\sqrt{\frac{\hat{\sigma}_1^2}{n_1}+\frac{\hat{\sigma}_2^2}{n_2}} = \sqrt{\frac{\hat{\sigma}^2}{n_1}+\frac{\hat{\sigma}^2}{n_2}} = \hat{\sigma}\sqrt{\frac{1}{n_1}+\frac{1}{n_2}}$$

$$(\text{Assuming } \hat{\sigma}_1^2 = \hat{\sigma}_2^2 = \hat{\sigma}^2)$$

To get an estimate of $\hat{\sigma}^2$, a weighted average of s_1^2 and s_2^2 is used, where the weights are the number of degrees of freedom of each sample. The weighted average is called a 'pooled estimate' of σ^2. This pooled estimate is given by the expression:

$$\hat{\sigma}^2 = \frac{(n_1 - 1)s_1^2 + (n_2 - 1)s_2^2}{n_1 + n_2 - 2}$$

The testing procedure could be explained as under:

$$H_0 : \mu_1 = \mu_2 \quad \Rightarrow \quad \mu_1 - \mu_2 = 0$$
$$H_1 : \mu_1 \neq \mu_2 \quad \Rightarrow \quad \mu_1 - \mu_2 \neq 0$$

In this case, the test statistic t is given by the expression:

$$t_{n_1+n_2-2} = \frac{(\bar{X}_1 - \bar{X}_2) - (\mu_1 - \mu_2)H_0}{\hat{\sigma}\sqrt{\frac{1}{n_1}+\frac{1}{n_2}}}$$

where $\hat{\sigma} = \sqrt{\frac{(n_1 - 1)s_1^2 + (n_2 - 1)s_2^2}{n_1 + n_2 - 2}}$

The calculated value of t statistic is compared with the tabulated value at a level of significance α to arrive at a decision regarding the acceptance or rejection of hypothesis.

Once the value of t-statistic is computed from the sample data, it is compared with the tabulated value at a level of significance α to arrive at a decision regarding the acceptance or rejection of hypothesis. Let us work out a problem illustrating the concepts defined above.

Example 12.9

Two drugs meant to provide relief to arthritis sufferers were produced in two different laboratories. The first drug was administered to a group of 12 patients and produced an average of 8.5 hours of relief with a standard deviation of 1.8 hours. The second drug was tested on a sample of 8 patients and produced an average of 7.9 hours of relief with a standard deviation of 2.1 hours. Test the hypothesis that the first drug provides a significantly higher period of relief. You may use 5 per cent level of significance.

Solution:

Let the subscripts 1 and 2 refer to drug 1 and drug 2 respectively.

$$H_0 \quad : \quad \mu_1 = \mu_2 \quad \Rightarrow \quad \mu_1 - \mu_2 = 0$$

$$H_1 \quad : \quad \mu_1 > \mu_2 \quad \Rightarrow \quad \mu_1 - \mu_2 > 0$$

The following survey data is given:

$$\bar{X}_1 = 8.5, \bar{X}_2 = 7.9, s_1 = 1.8, s_2 = 2.1, n_1 = 12, n_2 = 8,$$

As both n_1, n_2 are small and the sample standard deviations are unknown, one may use a t-test with the degrees of freedom $= n_1 + n_2 - 2 = 12 + 8 - 2 = 18$ d.f.

The test statistics is given by:

$$t_{n_1+n_2-2} = \frac{(\bar{X}_1 - \bar{X}_2) - (\mu_1 - \mu_2)\,H_0}{\hat{\sigma}\sqrt{\frac{1}{n_1} + \frac{1}{n_2}}}$$

where,
$$\hat{\sigma} = \sqrt{\frac{(n_1 - 1)\,s_1^2 + (n_2 - 1)\,s_2^2}{n_1 + n_2 - 2}}$$

$$= \sqrt{\frac{(12-1)(1.8)^2 + (8-1)(2.1)^2}{12 + 8 - 2}} = \sqrt{\frac{11 \times 3.24 + 7 \times (4.41)}{18}}$$

$$= \sqrt{\frac{35.64 + 30.87}{18}} = \sqrt{\frac{66.61}{18}} = \sqrt{3.695} = 1.92$$

$$t_{18} = \frac{(8.5 - 7.9) - (0)}{1.92\sqrt{\frac{1}{12} + \frac{1}{8}}} = \frac{0.6}{1.92\sqrt{0.2083}}$$

$$= \frac{0.6}{1.92 \times 0.456} = \frac{0.6}{0.8755} = 0.685$$

The critical value of t with 18 degrees of freedom at 5 per cent level of significance is given by 1.734. The sample value of t = 0.685 lies in the acceptance region as shown in figure below:

Therefore, the null hypothesis is accepted as there is not enough evidence to reject it. Therefore, one may conclude that the first drug is not significantly more effective than the second drug. The same answer could be obtained using a p value approach. It is left to the readers to verify the same.

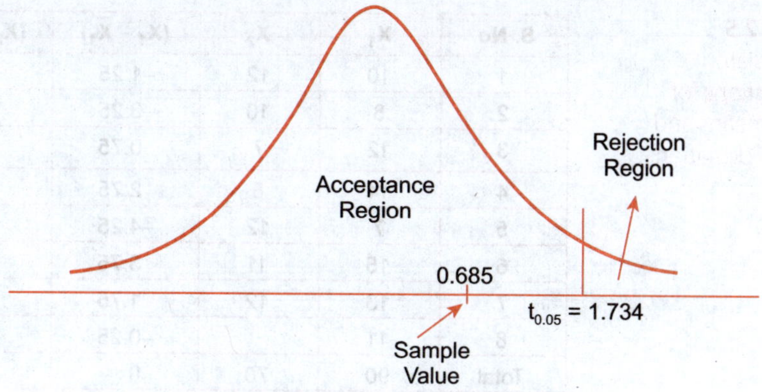

Rejection region for Example 12.9

When population variances are not equal

In case population variances are not equal, the test statistic for testing the equality of two population means when the size of samples are small is given by:

$$t = \frac{(\overline{X}_1 - \overline{X}_2) - (\mu_1 - \mu_2)H_0}{\sqrt{\frac{\hat{\sigma}_1^2}{n_1} + \frac{\hat{\sigma}_2^2}{n_2}}}$$

The degrees of freedom in such a case is given by the expression:

$$\text{d.f.} = \frac{\left(\frac{s_1^2}{n_1} + \frac{s_2^2}{n_2}\right)^2}{\frac{1}{n_1 - 1}\left(\frac{s_1^2}{n_1}\right)^2 + \frac{1}{n_2 - 1}\left(\frac{s_2^2}{n_2}\right)^2}$$

The procedure for testing of hypothesis remains the same as was discussed when the variances of two populations were assumed to be same. Let us consider an example to illustrate the same.

Example 12.10

There were two types of drugs (1 and 2) that were tried on some patients for reducing weight. There were 8 adults who were subjected to drug 1 and seven adults who were administered drug 2. The decrease in weight (in pounds) is given below:

Drug 1	10	8	12	14	7	15	13	11
Drug 2	12	10	7	6	12	11	12	

Do the drugs differ significantly in their effect on decreasing weight? You may use 5 per cent level of significance. Assume that the variances of two populations are not same.

Solution:

$$H_0 \quad : \quad \mu_1 = \mu_2$$
$$H_1 \quad : \quad \mu_1 \neq \mu_2$$

Let us compute the sample means and standard deviations of the two samples as shown in Table 12.5.

TABLE 12.5 Intermediate computations for sample means and standard deviations

S. No.	X_1	X_2	$(X_1-\bar{X}_1)$	$(X_2-\bar{X}_2)$	$(X_1-\bar{X}_1)^2$	$(X_2-\bar{X}_2)^2$
1	10	12	–1.25	2	1.5625	4
2	8	10	–3.25	0	10.5625	0
3	12	7	0.75	–3	0.5625	9
4	14	6	2.75	–4	7.5625	16
5	7	12	–4.25	2	18.0625	4
6	15	11	3.75	1	14.0625	1
7	13	12	1.75	2	3.0625	4
8	11		–0.25		0.0625	
Total	90	70	0	0	55.5	38
Mean	11.25	10				

$$n_1 = 8, \qquad n_2 = 7,$$

$$\bar{X}_1 = \frac{\Sigma X_1}{n_1} = \frac{90}{8} = 11.25 \qquad \bar{X}_2 = \frac{\Sigma X_2}{n_2} = \frac{70}{7} = 10$$

$$s_1^2 = \frac{\Sigma(X_1-\bar{X}_1)^2}{n_1-1} = \frac{55.5}{7} = 7.93$$

$$s_2^2 = \frac{\Sigma(X_2-\bar{X}_2)^2}{n_2-1} = \frac{38}{6} = 6.33$$

$$\hat{\sigma}_{\bar{X}_1-\bar{X}_2} = \sqrt{\frac{s_1^2}{n_1}+\frac{s_2^2}{n_2}} = \sqrt{\frac{7.93}{8}+\frac{6.33}{7}} = \sqrt{0.99+0.90} = \sqrt{1.89} = 1.37$$

$$\text{d.f.} = \frac{\left(\dfrac{s_1^2}{n_1}+\dfrac{s_2^2}{n_2}\right)^2}{\dfrac{1}{n_1-1}\left(\dfrac{s_1^2}{n_1}\right)^2+\dfrac{1}{n_2-1}\left(\dfrac{s_2^2}{n_2}\right)^2} = \frac{\left(\dfrac{7.33}{8}+\dfrac{6.33}{7}\right)^2}{\dfrac{1}{7}\left(\dfrac{7.33}{8}\right)^2+\dfrac{1}{6}\left(\dfrac{6.33}{7}\right)^2}$$

$$= \frac{3.314}{0.12+0.136} = \frac{3.314}{0.12+0.136} = 12.996 = 13 \text{ (approx.)}$$

The test statistic t is computed as:

$$t = \frac{(\bar{X}_1-\bar{X}_2)-(\mu_1-\mu_2)H_0}{\sqrt{\dfrac{\hat{\sigma}_1^2}{n_1}+\dfrac{\hat{\sigma}_2^2}{n_2}}}$$

$$t = \frac{11.25-10}{1.37} = \frac{1.25}{1.37} = 0.912$$

The table value (critical value) of t with 13 degrees of freedom at 5 per cent level of significance is given by 2.16. As computed t is less than tabulated t, there is not enough evidence to reject H_o.

Case of Paired Sample (Dependent Sample)

Our discussion so far was concentrated upon two independent samples. At times, however, it makes sense to choose samples that are not independent of each other.

In a **paired** or **dependent sample** two observations are taken from the same respondent, one prior to the treatment and the other post-treatment.

In case of dependent samples (paired sample), two observations are taken from each respondent one prior to administering a treatment and the other after the treatment has been administered. For example, some customers may be questioned on their perception about a product and later on, a television commercial may be shown to them about the same product. After seeing the advertisement, they may again be questioned on their perception about the product. Such a sample is called dependent or paired sample because on the same respondent, two observations are taken—one prior to treatment and the other after being subjected to treatment. The objective of doing this could be to examine whether that perception has undergone a change after the subjects viewed the advertisement, and if so, in what direction?

The use of dependent sample enables us to perform a more precise analysis as it allows the controlling of extraneous variables. The difference is that we convert the problem from two samples to a one-sample problem. Suppose we are interested in comparing two teaching methods on the basis of average scores obtained by the management trainees divided randomly into two equal sizes, one taught by each method. After obtaining the scores by two methods, the null hypothesis of average scores being equal by two methods is written as:

$$H_0 \quad : \quad \mu_1 = \mu_2$$
$$H_1 \quad : \quad \mu_1 \neq \mu_2$$
$$\text{Let } \mu_d = \mu_1 - \mu_2$$

Since the pair sample observations are taken, the hypothesis is converted to:

$$H_0 \quad : \quad \mu_d = 0$$
$$H_1 \quad : \quad \mu_d \neq 0$$

This means that we want to test that the average difference in score is zero against the alternative hypothesis that it is not so. Here, d denotes the difference in scores by two methods:

The test statistic in such a case,

$$t = \frac{\bar{d}}{\frac{s}{\sqrt{n}}}$$

which follows a t-distribution with n - 1 degrees of freedom,

where, $\bar{d}$ = Mean of difference $= \frac{\sum di}{n}$

s = standard deviation of differences $= \sqrt{\frac{\sum(d-\bar{d})^2}{n-1}}$

n = number of paired observations in the sample

For a given level of significance α, the computed t statistic is compared with the tabulated (critical) t with n - 1 degrees of freedom to accept or reject the null hypothesis. Let us consider the following example.

Example 12.11 A company selects eight salesmen at random and their sales figures for the previous month are recorded. They then undergo a training course devised by a business consultant, and their sales figures for the following month are compared as shown in the table. Has the training course caused an improvement in the salesmen's ability? You may use a 0.05 level of significance.

Previous Month	75	90	94	95	100	90	70	64
Following Month	77	101	93	92	105	88	76	68

Solution:

Let P and F stand for the previous and the following months:

$$H_0 \quad : \quad \mu_d = 0$$
$$H_1 \quad : \quad \mu_d > 0$$
$$d = F - P,$$

The required computations are given in Table 12.6.

TABLE 12.6 Intermediate computations for mean and standard deviation

S. No.	P	F	d	$(d - \bar{d})$	$(d - \bar{d})^2$
1	75	77	2	–0.75	0.5625
2	90	101	11	8.25	68.0625
3	94	93	–1	–3.75	14.0625
4	95	92	–3	–5.75	33.0625
5	100	105	5	2.25	5.0625
6	90	88	–2	–4.75	22.5625
7	70	76	6	3.25	10.5625
8	64	68	4	1.25	1.5625
Total			22	0	155.5
Mean			2.75		

$$\sum d = 22, \qquad \bar{d} = \frac{\sum d}{8} = \frac{22}{8} = 2.75,$$

$$s^2 = \frac{\sum (d - \bar{d})^2}{n - 1} = \frac{155.5}{7} = 22.214, \quad s = 4.713$$

$$t_{n-1} = \frac{\bar{d} - \mu d}{\frac{s}{\sqrt{n}}} = \frac{(2.75 - 0)\sqrt{8}}{4.713} = \frac{2.75 \times 2.828}{4.713} = \frac{7.777}{4.713} = 1.650$$

$$\text{tab t (5 per cent)} = 1.895$$

As computed t is less than tabulated t, there is not enough evidence to reject H_0. Therefore, the training has not caused any improvement in the salesmen's ability.

CONCEPT CHECK

1. What is the difference between an independent and a dependent sample?
2. What is the degree of freedom when testing the difference between two population means assuming equal variances?

USE OF SPSS IN TESTING HYPOTHESIS CONCERNING MEANS

LEARNING OBJECTIVE 5
Use SPSS software to conduct the testing of hypothesis.

The SPSS software can be used for testing the hypothesis concerning means. The researcher would have to make use of the raw data instead of the summarized data. Examples 12.5, 12.10 and 12.11 make use of raw data. The illustrations correspond to one sample, two-independent samples and paired sample test. They can be worked out by using SPSS software. Example 12.11 has been reworked using SPSS in Example 12.14. The reader can work out the Examples 12.5 and 12.10 using SPSS.

In Chapter 11 (Univariate and Bivariate Analysis of Data), we mentioned a study on 'Management of Cyber Café' (Chawla and Behl, 2004). A sample of 500 users of cyber café was taken from five zones of Delhi, namely, central, east, west, south and north. A sample of 414 usable questionnaires was used for further analysis. In Table 11.2, data on select variables from the study is reported. One of the variables used in the study was. 'How long have you been using a cyber café?' The response was to be in number of months. The variable in the table was symbolized as 'X10'. The missing value was denoted by '999'. This data is also available in SPSS data file for this table. We will show the use of t-test using this variable.

Example 12.12 Using the data on the variable 'How long have you been using cyber café?', which is represented by 'X10', test the hypothesis that the mean number of months for which the cyber café is used is 36 against the alternative hypothesis that it is more than 36. You may use 5 per cent level of significance.

Solution:

$$H_0 \quad : \quad \mu = 36$$
$$H_1 \quad : \quad \mu > 36$$

This is a one-tailed test. You will find that there are eight missing observations and, therefore, the analysis is carried out on 406 observations. The SPSS instructions for carrying out the test are given in Appendix 12.1. You would find that a t-test is being used. This would be the case in most of the software that is available for carrying out the statistical analysis. Since with a large sample it will not make a difference whether a Z or a t-test is used due to the fact that with an increase in sample size, the t-distribution approaches the Z-distribution. The computed value of t would be the same as that of the Z value. The only minor difference may be found in the critical value of t, which for a large sample could be ignored. The computer results corresponding to this problem are presented in Tables 12.7(a) and 12.7(b).

We find that the p value for the test is given by 0.000. As shown in the computer printout above, this is denoted by 'significance' (two-tailed). The software gives the p value for a two-tailed test. Our problem is that of a one-tailed test. As we know that the t-distribution is a symmetrical distribution and, therefore, the relevant value of p for a one-tailed test would be the given figure in the computer printout divided by 2. Therefore, the relevant p remains 0.00. Now, since this p value is less than $\alpha = 0.05$, there is enough evidence to reject the null hypothesis. Therefore, it can be concluded that the users of cyber café use it for more than 36 months.

The same conclusion can be arrived at by comparing the sample value of t, which from the computer printout is 3.861 with the critical value of t with 405 degrees of freedom at 1 per cent level of significance. You will find that the table value of t would approximately equal 1.645, which would imply that the null hypothesis is rejected in the favour of the alternative hypothesis.

We will now take the case of two independent sample tests and use SPSS software for testing the equality of the two means.

TABLE 12.7(a)
One-sample statistics

	N	Mean	Std. Deviation	Std. Error Mean
How long have you been using cyber café	406	39.02	15.784	0.783

TABLE 12.7(b)
One-sample test

	Test Value = 36					
	t	d.f.	Sig. (2-tailed)	Mean Difference	95% Confidence Interval of the Difference	
					Lower	Upper
How long have you been using cyber café	3.861	405	0.000	3.025	1.48	4.56

Example 12.13 In the study on 'Management of Cyber Cafe' the data for which was reported in Table 11.2, there were two variables—'How long have you been using the cyber café?' denoted by 'X10' and another variable 'Gender' denoted by 'X12'. The male respondents were coded as 1, whereas female respondents were coded as 2. We want to test the hypothesis that the average number of months of cyber café use by male and female respondents is same or different. We want to conduct the test at 5 per cent level of significance.

Solution:

$$H_0 \quad : \quad \mu_1 = \mu_2$$
$$H_1 \quad : \quad \mu_1 \neq \mu_2$$

Please note that the subscript 1 is for the male respondent and subscript 2 is for the female respondent. The way data is to be presented for using SPSS to carry out the test for these two independent samples is explained in Appendix 12.1. Here we would only report the results and carry out the interpretation of the results. The computer results are reported in Tables 12.8(a) and 12.8(b).

As discussed earlier, the t-test for testing the equality of two population means is carried out using these two assumptions:

TABLE 12.8(a) Group statistics

	Sex	N	Mean	Std. Deviation	Std. Error Mean
How long has the subject been using cyber café?	Male	296	40.01	15.535	.903
	Female	110	36.36	16.208	1.545

TABLE 12.8(b) Independent samples test

		Levene's Test for Equality of Variances		t-test for Equality of Means						
									95% Confidence Interval of the Difference	
		F	Sig.	t	df	Sig. (2-tailed)	Mean Difference	Std. Error Difference	Lower	Upper
How long has the subject been using cyber café?	Equal variances assumed	0.065	0.800	2.079	404	0.038	3.650	1.755	0.199	7.101
	Equal variances not assumed			2.039	188.032	0.043	3.650	1.790	0.119	7.181

1. Population variances are equal.
2. Population variances are not equal.

In the computer printout mentioned above, both t and p values under the two assumptions listed above are reported. The p values given by significance (two-tailed) in the SPSS output show that in both the cases, they are less than the level of significance, which is 0.05. Therefore, the null hypothesis is rejected and we can conclude that there is a significant difference in the usage of cyber café by the males and females. Even using the computed t-values and comparing it with the critical value one would arrive at the same conclusions. It is left to the readers to verify the same.

We have talked about dependent sample (paired sample) t-test in the text. We would now use SPSS software to illustrate the same.

Example 12.14 Use the data presented in Example 12.11 to carry out the test as required in this example using SPSS software. You may use 5 per cent level of significance.

Solution:

$H_0 \quad : \quad \mu_f = \mu_p$

$H_1 \quad : \quad \mu_f > \mu_p$

The subscript f stands for the following month and subscript p stands for the previous month. This is a one-tailed test. The above hypothesis may be rewritten as:

$H_0 \quad : \quad \mu_d = 0$

$H_1 \quad : \quad \mu_d > 0$

(where $d = f - p$)

The SPSS instructions for carrying out the test are also given in Appendix 12.1. The SPSS output is given in Tables 12.9(a), 12.9(b) and 12.9(c).

TABLE 12.9(a) Paired sample statistics

		Mean	N	Std. Deviation	Std. Error Mean
Pair 1	Sales in following month	87.5000	8	12.88410	4.55522
	Sales in previous month	84.7500	8	13.20984	4.67039

TABLE 12.9(b) Paired sample correlations

		N	Correlation	Sig.
Pair 1	Sales in the following month and Sales in the previous month	8	0.935	0.001

TABLE 12.9(c) Paired samples test

		Paired Differences					t	df	Sig. (2-tailed)
		Mean	Std. Deviation	Std. Error Mean	95% Confidence Interval of the Difference				
					Lower	Upper			
Pair 1	Sales in the following month - sales in the previous month	2.75000	4.71320	1.66637	-1.19034	6.69034	1.650	7	0.143

The results presented above indicate the p value to be .143. Since it is a one-tailed test, the applicable p value would be $.143/2 = .0715$. This is greater than $\alpha = .05$. Therefore, the null hypothesis is accepted as there is not enough evidence to reject it. Therefore, the sales training programme has not caused any improvement in the salesman's ability.

TESTS CONCERNING POPULATION PROPORTION

LEARNING OBJECTIVE 6

Discuss the test of the significance of a single population proportion.

We have already discussed the tests concerning population means. In the tests about proportion, one is interested in examining whether the respondents possess a particular attribute or not. For example, the interest could be in the proportion of students who are smokers or the proportion of consumers who use a particular brand of product or the percentage of skilled employees in a company who are not satisfied with their present job.

As the sample size increases, **binomial distribution** approaches the normal distribution in characteristics.

We note that in the examples cited above, the random variable in a question is a binary one in the sense it takes only two values—yes or no. As we know that either a student is a smoker or not, a consumer either uses a particular brand of product or not and lastly, a skilled worker may be either satisfied or not with the present job. At this stage it may be recalled that the binomial distribution is a theoretically correct distribution to use while dealing with proportions. Further as the sample size increases, the binomial distribution approaches the normal distribution in characteristic. To be specific, whenever both np and nq (where n = number of trials, p = probability of success and q = probability of failure) are at least 5, one can use the normal distribution as a substitute for the binomial distribution. The test of hypotheses would be discussed in the case of single and two population proportions. We will take these cases one by one.

The Case of Single Population Proportion

Suppose we want to test the hypotheses,

$$H_0 \quad : \quad p = p_0$$
$$H_1 \quad : \quad p \neq p_0$$

For large sample, the appropriate test statistic would be:

$$Z = \frac{\bar{p} - p_{H_0}}{\sigma_{\bar{p}}}$$

where, $\bar{p}$ = sample proportion

p_{H_0} = the value of p under the assumption that null hypothesis is true

$\sigma_{\bar{p}}$ = Standard error of sample proportion

The value of $\sigma_{\bar{p}}$ is computed by using the following formula:

$$\sigma_{\bar{p}} = \sqrt{\frac{p_{H_0} q_{H_0}}{n}}$$

where, $q_{H_0} = 1 - p_{H_0}$

n = Sample size

For a given level of significance α, the computed value of Z is compared with the corresponding critical values, i.e. $Z_{\alpha/2}$ or $-Z_{\alpha/2}$ to accept or reject the null hypothesis. We will consider a few examples to explain the testing procedure for a single population proportion.

Example 12.15

An officer of the health department claims that 60 per cent of the male population of a village comprises smokers. A random sample of 50 males showed that 35 of them were smokers. Are these sample results consistent with the claim of the health officer? Use a level of significance of 0.05.

Solution:

Sample size (n) = 50

Sample proportion $= \bar{p} = \frac{x}{n} = \frac{35}{50} = 0.70$

$$H_0 \quad : \quad p = 0.60$$
$$H_1 \quad : \quad p > 0.60$$

The test statistic is given by:

$$Z = \frac{\bar{p} - p_{H_0}}{\sigma_{\bar{p}}} = \frac{0.70 - 0.60}{0.069} = \frac{0.10}{0.069} = 1.44$$

$$\left(\sigma_{\bar{p}} = \sqrt{\frac{p_{H_0} q_{H_0}}{n}} = \sqrt{\frac{0.6 \times 0.4}{50}} = \sqrt{\frac{0.24}{50}} = 0.069\right)$$

It is a one-tailed test. For a given level of significance $\alpha = 0.05$, the critical value of Z is given by $Z_\alpha = Z_{0.05} = 1.645$. It is seen that the sample value of Z = 1.44 lies in the acceptance region as shown below (see figure).

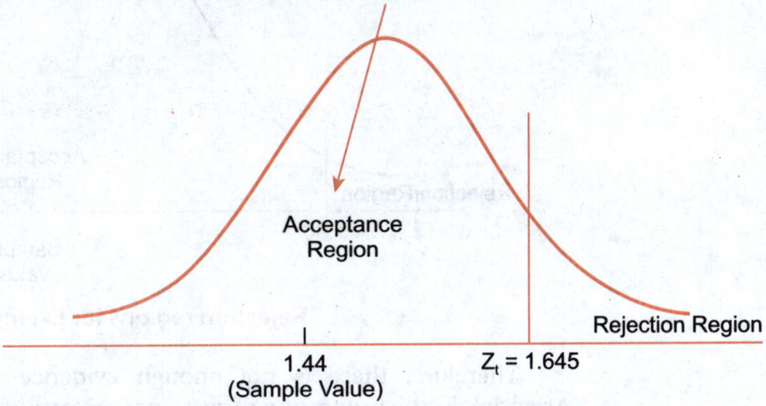

Rejection region for Example 12.15

Therefore, there is not enough evidence to reject the null hypothesis. So it can be concluded that the proportion of male smokers is not statistically different from 0.60.

Using the p value approach, the p value for this problem is given by:

$$\begin{aligned} p &= P(Z > 1.44) \\ &= 0.5 - P(0 < Z < 1.44) \\ &= 0.5 - 0.4251 \\ &= 0.0749 \end{aligned}$$

Since the p value is greater than $\alpha = 0.05$, the null hypothesis is accepted. Therefore, it is seen that same conclusion is arrived at by using the p value approach.

Example 12.16 A food processing company wants to know whether the proportion of customers who prefer the new packaging to the old one is 0.65. What can be concluded at the level of significance $\alpha = 0.05$ if 74 of the 100 randomly selected customers prefer the new kind of packaging and alternative hypothesis is $p \neq 0.65$.

Solution:

$$H_0 : p = 0.65$$
$$H_1 : p \neq 0.65$$

$$x = 74, \quad n = 100, \quad \bar{p} = \frac{x}{n} = \frac{74}{100} = 0.74, \quad \alpha = 0.05$$

The problem is of a two-tailed test. The test statistic is given as:

$$Z = \frac{\bar{p} - p_{H_0}}{\sigma_{\bar{p}}} = \frac{0.74 - 0.65}{0.0477} = 1.89$$

$$\left(\sigma_{\bar{p}} = \sqrt{\frac{p_{H_0} q_{H_0}}{n}} = \sqrt{\frac{0.65 \times 0.35}{100}} = \sqrt{.002275} = 0.0477\right)$$

For 5 per cent level of significance, the critical values are given by $-Z_{\alpha/2} = -Z_{.025} = -1.96$ and $Z_{\alpha/2} = Z_{0.025} = 1.96$. The computed value of Z lies in the acceptance region as shown in the figure below:

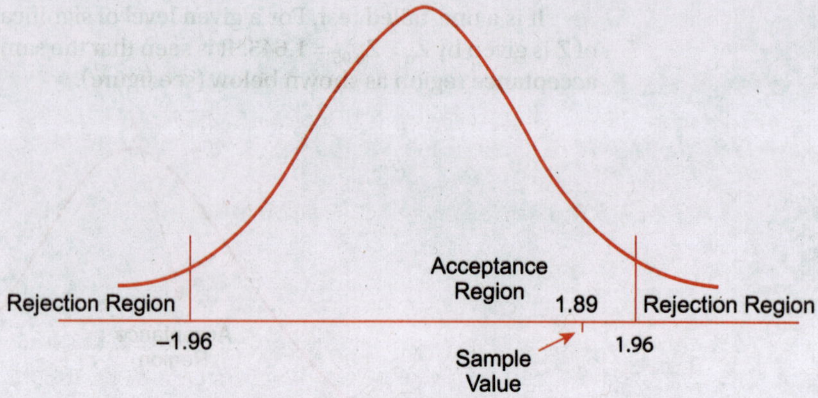

Rejection regions for Example 12.16

Therefore, there is not enough evidence to reject the null hypothesis. Accordingly, the proportion of customer preferring new kind of packaging to the old one is not significantly different from 0.65.

The same problem could be worked out using the p value approach. The p value for this problem could be computed as:

$$\begin{aligned} p &= P(Z > 1.89) + P(Z < -1.89) \quad \text{(it is a two-tailed test.)} \\ &= 2 \times P(Z > 1.89) \\ &= 2 \times (0.5 - P(0 < Z < 1.89)) \\ &= 2 \times (0.5 - 0.4706) \\ &= 0.0588 \end{aligned}$$

As p value is greater than 0.05, the level of significance, the null hypothesis is accepted. Therefore, we arrive at the same conclusion.

TWO POPULATION PROPORTIONS

LEARNING OBJECTIVE 7
Carry out the test of the significance of the difference between two population proportions using a Z-test.

Here, the interest is to test whether the two population proportions are equal or not. The hypothesis under investigation is:

$$H_0 : p_1 = p_2 \Rightarrow p_1 - p_2 = 0$$
$$H_1 : p_1 \neq p_2 \Rightarrow p_1 - p_2 \neq 0$$

The alternative hypothesis assumed is two sided. It could as well have been one sided. The test statistic is given by:

$$Z = \frac{\bar{p}_1 - \bar{p}_2 - (p_1 - p_2)\,H_0}{\sigma_{\bar{p}_1 - \bar{p}_2}}$$

where, $\bar{p}_1$ = Sample proportion possessing a particular attribute from population 1

$\bar{p}_2$ = Sample proportion possessing a particular attribute from population 2

$\sigma_{\bar{p}_1 - \bar{p}_2}$ = Standard error of difference between proportions.

$(p_1 - p_2)_{H_0}$ = Value of difference between population proportion under the assumption that the null hypothesis is true.

The formula for $\sigma_{\bar{p}_1 - \bar{p}_2}$ is given by:

$$\sigma_{\bar{p}_1-\bar{p}_2} = \sqrt{\frac{p_1q_1}{n_1} + \frac{p_2q_2}{n_2}}$$

We do not know the value of p_1, p_2, etc., but under the null hypothesis $p_1 = p_2 = p$.

$$\sigma_{\bar{p}_1-\bar{p}_2} = \sqrt{\frac{pq}{n_1} + \frac{pq}{n_2}} = \sqrt{pq\left(\frac{1}{n_1} + \frac{1}{n_2}\right)}$$

The best estimate of p is given by:

$$\hat{p} = \frac{x_1 + x_2}{n_1 + n_2}$$

where,
x_1 = Number of successes in sample 1
x_2 = Number of successes in sample 2
n_1 = Size of sample taken from population 1
n_2 = Size of sample taken from population 2

It is known that $\bar{p}_1 = \frac{x_1}{n_1}$ and $\bar{p}_2 = \frac{x_2}{n_2}$. Therefore $x_1 = n_1\bar{p}_1$, and $x_2 = n_2\bar{p}_2$.

Therefore,

$$\hat{p} = \frac{n_1\bar{p}_1 + n_2\bar{p}_2}{n_1 + n_2}$$

Therefore, the estimate of standard error of difference between the two proportions is given by:

$$\hat{\sigma}_{\bar{p}_1-\bar{p}_2} = \sqrt{\hat{p}\hat{q}\left(\frac{1}{n_1} + \frac{1}{n_2}\right)}$$

where $\hat{p}$ is as defined above and $\hat{q} = 1 - \hat{p}$. Now, the test statistic may be rewritten as:

$$Z = \frac{\bar{p}_1 - \bar{p}_2 - (p_1 - p_2)H_0}{\sqrt{\hat{p}\hat{q}\left(\frac{1}{n_1} + \frac{1}{n_2}\right)}}$$

$$Z = \frac{\bar{p}_1 - \bar{p}_2 - (p_1 - p_2)H_0}{\sqrt{\hat{p}\hat{q}\left(\frac{1}{n_1} + \frac{1}{n_2}\right)}}$$

Now, for a given level of significance α, the sample Z value is compared with the critical Z value to accept or reject the null hypothesis. We consider below a few examples to illustrate the testing procedure described above.

Example 12.17

A company is interested in considering two different television advertisements for the promotion of a new product. The management believes that advertisement A is more effective than advertisement B. Two test market areas with virtually identical consumer characteristics are selected. Advertisement A is used in one area and advertisement B in the other area. In a random sample of 60 consumers who saw advertisement A, 18 tried the product. In a random sample of 100 customers who saw advertisement B, 22 tried the product. Does this indicate that advertisement A is more effective than advertisement B, if a 5 per cent level of significance is used?

Solution:

$H_0 \quad : \quad p_a = p_b$

$H_1 \quad : \quad p_a > p_b$

$n_A = 60, \quad x_A = 18, \quad n_B = 100, \quad x_B = 22$

$$\left(\bar{p}_A = \frac{x_A}{n_A} = \frac{18}{60} = 0.3\right) \quad \left(\bar{p}_B = \frac{x_B}{n_B} = \frac{22}{100} = 0.22\right)$$

$$Z = \frac{\bar{P}_A - \bar{P}_B - (p_A - P_B)H_0}{\sigma_{\bar{P}_A - \bar{P}_B}} = \frac{0.3 - 0.22 - 0}{\sqrt{\hat{p}\hat{q}\left(\frac{1}{n_A} + \frac{1}{n_B}\right)}}$$

$$= \frac{0.08}{\sqrt{0.25 \times 0.75\left(\frac{1}{60} + \frac{1}{100}\right)}} = \frac{0.08}{\sqrt{0.25 \times 0.75(0.0267)}} = \frac{0.08}{0.071} = 1.3$$

$$\left(\hat{p} = \frac{x_A + x_B}{n_A + n_B} = \frac{18 + 22}{60 + 100} = \frac{40}{160} = 0.25\right)$$

The critical value of Z at 5 per cent level of significance is 1.645. The sample value of Z = 1.13 lies in the acceptance region as shown in the figure below:

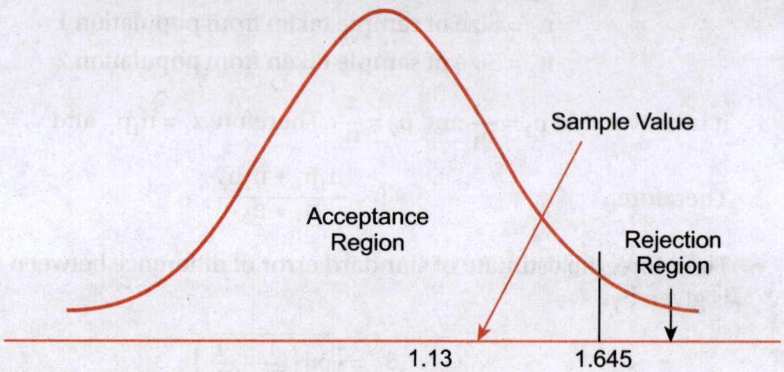

Rejection region for Example 12.17

Therefore, we accept the null hypothesis. It can be concluded that there is no difference in the effectiveness of two advertisements. We could work out the same problem using the p value approach. The p value may be calculated as:

$$p = P(Z > 1.13)$$
$$= 0.5 - P(0 < Z < 1.13)$$
$$= 0.5 - 0.3708$$
$$= 0.1292$$

The p value of 0.1292 is greater than 0.05, therefore, we accept the null hypothesis as was done with the other approach.

Example 12.18 In a random sample of 100 persons taken from village A, 60 were found to be consuming tea. In another sample of 200 persons taken from village B, 100 persons were found to be consuming tea. Does the data reveal a significant difference between the two villages so far as the habit of taking tea is concerned? You may use a 5 per cent level of significance.

Solution:

$$H_0 \quad : \quad p_A = p_B$$
$$H_1 \quad : \quad p_A \neq p_B$$

$n_A = 100$, $x_A = 60$, $\bar{p}_A = \frac{x_A}{n_A} = \frac{60}{100} = 0.6$

$n_B = 200$, $x_B = 100$, $\bar{p}_B = \frac{x_B}{n_B} = \frac{100}{200} = 0.5$

The test statistic to be used here is:

$$Z = \frac{\bar{p}_A - \bar{p}_B - (p_A - p_B)H_0}{\sigma_{\bar{p}_A - \bar{p}_B}} = \frac{\bar{p}_A - \bar{p}_B - 0}{\sqrt{\hat{p}\hat{q}\left(\frac{1}{n_A} + \frac{1}{n_B}\right)}}$$

$$= \frac{0.6 - 0.5 - 0}{\sqrt{.533 \times .467\left(\frac{1}{100} + \frac{1}{200}\right)}} = \frac{0.10}{\sqrt{.533 \times .467 \times 0.015}}$$

$$= \frac{0.10}{\sqrt{0.00373}} = \frac{0.10}{0.061} = 1.64$$

$$\left(\hat{p} = \frac{x_A + x_B}{n_A + n_B} = \frac{60 + 100}{100 + 200} = \frac{160}{300} = \frac{8}{15} = 0.533\right)$$

$$(\hat{q} = 1 - \hat{p} = 1 - 0.533 = 0.467)$$

Tab Z = 1.96 Accept H_0

$$p = P(Z > 1.64) + P(Z < -1.64)$$
$$= 2P(Z > 1.64)$$
$$= 2\,(0.5 - 0.4495)$$
$$= 2 \times 0.0505$$
$$= 0.101$$

Since $p > \alpha = 0.05$, H_0 is accepted. Therefore, there is no difference in the proportions of persons consuming tea in the two villages.

In this chapter, we have discussed the test of significance for the mean and proportions of the single and two populations. In the next chapter, the discussion will be on testing the equality of more than two population means. The test of equality of more than two population proportions will be taken up in Chapter 14, besides other non-parametric tests.

CONCEPT CHECK	1. Outline the procedure for testing the significance of single population proportion. 2. List the steps required for testing the equality of two population proportions.

SUMMARY

- A hypothesis is a statement or an assumption regarding a population, which may or may not be true. This chapter briefly explains the various concepts that are used while testing for a hypothesis. These concepts are null hypothesis, alternative hypothesis, one-tailed and two-tailed tests, type I and type II errors. The sequences of steps that need to be followed for the testing of hypothesis are also explained.
- The test procedure concerning the mean of a single population is explained. The cases of both large and small samples are discussed. For a large sample (sample size greater than 30), a Z-test is used. For a small sample, if the population standard deviation is known, a Z-test is used. If population standard deviation σ is unknown, a t-test is appropriate under the assumption that the sample is drawn from a normal population.
- The test procedure for examining the equality of two population means is discussed for both large and small independent samples. For the large samples, a Z-test is appropriate whereas for the small samples, a t-test is used under the two cases where: (i) population variances are equal and (ii) population variances are not equal. The case of the two related samples is also discussed in the chapter.

- The testing procedures concerning the proportion of a single population and the difference between two population proportions are also explained. The hypotheses concerning them are carried out using a Z-test under the assumption that the normal distribution could be used as an approximation to the binomial distribution for a large sample.
- All the testing procedures are explained with the help of solved examples. A p-value approach for the testing of hypothesis also finds a place here. The use of SPSS software for conducting the test of hypothesis exercise is explained with the help of raw data. The necessary instructions for carrying out these tests using SPSS are explained in Appendix 12.1 given at the end of chapter.

KEY TERMS

- Acceptance region
- Alternative hypothesis
- Binomial distribution
- Confidence level
- Critical region
- Critical value
- Dependent sample (paired sample t-test)
- Independent sample
- Large sample
- Level of significance (α)
- Null hypothesis
- One-tailed tests
- p value
- Population standard deviation
- Power of test
- Rejection region
- Sample standard deviation
- Small sample
- t-test
- Test of difference between means of two population
- Test of mean of one population
- Test of proportion of one population
- Test statistic
- Two-tailed tests
- Type I error
- Type II error
- Z-test

CHAPTER REVIEW QUESTIONS

Objective Type Questions

State whether the following statements are true (T) or false (F).

1. The null hypothesis could be specified as $H_0 : p > 0.22$.
2. Accepting a null hypothesis when it is false is called Type II error.
3. The hypothesis which is specified with the hope of rejecting it is called null hypothesis.
4. Alternative hypotheses specify the value that the researcher believes to hold true.
5. For testing the value of the population mean, a Z-test should be used when the sample size is small and the population standard deviations are unknown.
6. If a hypothesis is rejected at 5 per cent level, it must also be rejected at 1 per cent level.
7. The alternative hypothesis $H_1 : \mu \neq 35$ is an example of a two-tailed test.
8. A Z-test could be used to test population mean when population standard deviation is known, though sample size is small.
9. Whenever the degrees of freedom exceed 30, the t-distribution can be approximated by Z-distribution.
10. If p value is less than α, the level of significance, the null hypothesis should be accepted.
11. The standard error of mean increases with the increase in sample size.

12. The degrees of freedom in the two sample t-test for testing the equality of means is given by $n_1 + n_2 - 2$.
13. The paired sample t-test could be used when on the same respondent two observations are taken, one before the experiment and the other after the experiment.
14. The sample test statistic is based on the assumption that the alternative hypothesis is true.
15. Quantity demanded and the price of the product are related is an example of null hypothesis.
16. An estimate of the combined proportion while testing for the equality of two population proportion is given by the total number of successes in the two samples divided by the sum of sizes of two samples.
17. Normal distribution may be used as an approximation to a binomial distribution whenever both np and nq are at least 5, where the notations have their usual meanings.
18. For testing hypothesis for equality of the two means using t statistics, the p value as obtained in the SPSS printout is for a one-tail test.
19. The sample standard deviation could be used as an unbiased estimate of the population standard deviation.
20. An alternative hypothesis while testing the equality of two population means could be written as $H_1 : \mu_1 = \mu_2$.

Conceptual Questions

1. Explain the following concepts.
   (a) Null and alternative hypothesis
   (b) One and two-tailed test
   (c) Type I and type II error
   (d) Level of significance
   (e) Power of test
2. Explain the various steps involved in the tests of hypothesis exercise.
3. In a before–after experiment if two sets of observations are related, what type of statistical test should be employed? What would be the null hypothesis? How would the test statistic be calculated?
4. Indicate whether a Z or t-distribution is applicable in each of the following cases while conducting test for population mean.

(i)	n = 31	s = 12
(ii)	n = 15	s = 9
(iii)	n = 64	s = 8
(iv)	n = 28	σ = 10
(v)	n = 56	σ = 6

Application Questions

1. The company XYZ manufacturing bulbs hypothesizes that the life of its bulbs is 145 hours with a known standard deviation of 210 hours. A random sample of 25 bulbs gave a mean life of 130 hours. Using a 0.05 level of significance, can the company conclude that the mean life of bulbs is less than the 145 hours?
2. The manager of a hotel is trying to decide which of the two supposedly equally good cigarette–vending machines to install, tests each machine 500 times, and finds that machine I fails to work (neither delivers the cigarettes nor returns the money) 26 times and machine II fails to work 12 times. Using a 0.05 level of significance, can he conclude that two machines are not equally good?
3. If 54 out of a random sample of 150 boys smoke, while 31 out of random sample of 100 girls smoke, can we conclude at the 0.05 level of significance that the proportion of male smokers is higher than that of female smokers?
4. Advertisements claim the average nicotine content of a certain kind of cigarette is 0.30 mg. Suspecting that this figure is too low, a consumer protection service takes a random sample of 15 of these cigarettes from different production lots and finds that their nicotine content has a mean of 0.33 mg with a standard deviation of 0.018 mg. Use the 0.05 level of significance to test the null hypothesis $\mu = 0.30$ against the alternative hypothesis $\mu > 30$.

5. In a study of the effectiveness of physical exercise in weight reduction, a group of 11 persons engaged in a prescribed programme of physical exercise for 45 days showed the following results:

S. No.	Weight before (pounds)	Weight after (pounds)	S. No.	Weight before (Pounds)	Weight after (Pounds)
1	209	196	7	158	159
2	178	171	8	180	180
3	169	170	9	170	164
4	212	207	10	153	152
5	180	177	11	183	179
6	192	190			

Use the 0.05 level of significance to test the null hypothesis that the prescribed programme of exercise is not effective in reducing weight.

6. In a departmental store's study designed to test whether the mean balance outstanding on 30-day charge account is same in its two suburban branch stores, random samples yielded the following results:

$n_1 = 60$ $\quad \overline{X}_1 = ₹6420$ $\quad s_1 = ₹1600$

$n_2 = 100$ $\quad \overline{X}_2 = ₹7141$ $\quad s_2 = ₹2213$

where the subscripts denote branch store 1 and branch store 2. Use the 0.05 level of significance to test the hypothesis against a suitable alternative.

7. A product is produced in two ways. A pilot test on 6th times from each method indicates that product of method 1 has sample mean tensile strength 106 lbs and a standard deviation 12 lbs, whereas in method 2 the corresponding values of mean and standard deviation are 100 lbs and 10 lbs respectively. Greater tensile strength in the product is preferable. Use an appropriate large sample test of 5 per cent level of significance to test whether or not method 1 is better for processing the product. State clearly the null hypothesis. *[MBA, DU, 2003]*

8. 500 units from a factory are inspected and 12 are found to be defective; 800 units from another factory are inspected and 12 are found to be defective. Can it be concluded at 5 per cent level of significance that the production at the second factory is better than at the first factory? *[MBA, DU, 2002, 2007]*

9. Two types of new cars produced in India are tested for petrol mileage. One group consisting of 36 cars averaged 14 km per litre while the other group consisting of 72 cars averaged 12.5 km per litre.
   (a) What test statistic is appropriate if $\sigma_1^2 = 1.5$ & $\sigma_2^2 = 2.0$?
   (b) Test, whether there exists a significant difference in the petrol consumption of two types of cars (use $\alpha = 0.01$). *[MBA, IIT Roorkee, 2000]*

10. Intelligence tests on two groups of boys and girls gave the following results:

Gender	Mean	Standard Deviation	Sample Size
Girls	75	15	150
Boys	70	20	250

Is there a difference in the mean scores obtained by the boys and girls? Let the level of significance be 5 per cent. *[MBA, Kumaun Univ., 2002]*

11. In two large populations, there are 30 per cent and 25 per cent fair coloured people respectively. Is this difference likely to be hidden in the samples of 1200 and 900 respectively from two populations? (Given the tabulated value of the test statistics at 5 per cent level of significance is 1.96) *[MBA, IGNOU, 2004]*

12. A filling machine at a soft drink factory is defined to fill bottles of 200 ml with a standard deviation of 10 ml. A random sample of 50 filled bottles was taken and the average volume of soft drink was computed to be 198 ml per bottle. Test the hypothesis that the mean volume of soft drink per bottle is not less than 200 ml at 5 per cent level of significance. *[MBA, IGNOU, 2007]*

13. Two brands of bulbs are quoted at the same price. A buyer tested a random sample of 100 bulbs of each brand and found the following:

Brand	Mean Life (hrs.)	Standard Deviation
Brand I	1300	82
Brand II	1248	83

Is there a significant difference in the quality of two brands of bulbs at 5 per cent level of significance?
[MBA, DU, 1999, 2006]

14. A company is considering two different television advertisements for the promotion of a new product. Management believes that the advertisement A is more effective than advertisement B. Two test market areas with virtually identical consumer characteristics are selected: advertisement A is used in one area and advertisement B in another area. In a random sample of 60 customers who saw advertisement A, 18 tried the product. In a random sample of 100 customers who saw advertisement B, 22 tried the product. Does this indicate that advertisement A is more effective than advertisement B, if a 5 per cent level of significance is used?
[MBA, DU, 2000, 2005]

15. Two salesmen A and B are employed by a company. The comparative data pertaining to sales made by the two salesmen are as follows:

	Salesman A	Salesman B
No. of Sales	30	35
Average Sales (₹)	600	700
Standard Deviation	50	40

Do the average sales of the two salesmen differ significantly? Assume alpha-risk of 0.05.

16. Average annual income of the employees of a company has been reported to be ₹18,750. A random sample of 100 employees was taken. Then average annual income was found to be ₹19,240 with a standard deviation of ₹2,610. Test at 5 per cent level of significance whether the sample results are representative of population results.

17. Intelligence test on students of MBA and MCA gave the following results:

MBA	MCA
$n_1 = 35$	$n_2 = 80$
Average marks $\overline{X} = 75$	$\overline{X} = 79$
$\sigma_1 = 12$	$\sigma_2 = 13$

Examine whether the difference is significant.

CASE 12.1

COMPARATIVE PERCEPTION OF MESS FOOD VIS-À-VIS DHABAS – A CASE OF IIFT

The Indian Institute of Foreign Trade (IIFT) was set up by the Government of India in 1963. This is an autonomous organization engaged in teaching, training, research and consultancy in the area of foreign trade management. Besides students, it has provided training to executives of both the corporate sector and the Government in the field of international business. The institute runs a two-year MBA programme in International Business at New Delhi, Kolkatta and Dar-e-Salaam. It also conducts a three-year part-time MBA course in New Delhi and Kolkatta. The Institute also holds executive Masters Programme and a certificate programme in export management at Delhi.

The institute has conducted a number of research studies for WTO, World Bank, UNCTAD and Ministry of Commerce & Industry. The Institute has also trained more than 40,000 business executives across 30 countries through its Management Development Programmes.

IIFT MBA(IB) programme has 260 students under it, both first and second year. There is one mess serving all of these students. There are a few eating options outside in the local roadside dhabas. It has been observed that many students do not like the mess food. As a result, students frequently eat at the dhabas outside IIFT.

Recently, a scheme of taking four meals under the plan of ₹1,800 or two meals under the plan of ₹1,200 was launched by the IIFT mess and some students have availed of the latter plan and some are planning to avail it. This has led to the identification, the various reasons because of which students are not taking mess food.

The students of IIFT conducted a comparative study of both IIFT mess and the dhabas to find out the factors that could improve mess for the benefit of the student community at IIFT. It was felt that the results of the study could help the mess committee in coming up with some innovative plans to make it better.

A qualitative research was undertaken that helped in outlining the various attributes which could be incorporated in the design of the questionnaire. The questionnaire was emailed to 260 students but only 45 responses were obtained. The response rate was 17.3 per cent. Among the various questions asked to differentiate the perception of mess with dhabas around IIFT, the following attributes were considered:

1. Taste of food
2. Quality of ingredients
3. Hygiene
4. Cost
5. Ambience
6. Nutrition
7. Menu variety
8. Quality of service
9. Timing at which they are open
10. Total time taken for the meal

The following questions were asked incorporating the above attributes:

- How do you rate IIFT mess/*dhabas* on a scale of 1 – 5 on the following parameters? (1 = Extremely Unsatisfied, 2 = Unsatisfied, 3 = Neutral, 4 = Satisfied, 5 = Extremely Satisfied)

S. No.	Parameters	IIFT Mess (X)	Dhabas (Y)
1.	Taste		
2.	Menu variety		
3.	Cost		
4.	Quality of ingredients		
5.	Hygiene		
6.	Service quality		
7.	Ambience		
8.	Nutrition		
9.	Timings at which they are open		
10.	Total time taken for the meal		

The survey data on a sample of 45 respondents is given in Table 12.10.

It may be noted that the data on variables X_1, X_2, - - - -, X_{10} correspond to the ratings of ten attributes for IIFT mess, whereas Y_1, Y_2, - - - -, Y_{10} are the corresponding rating for *dhabas*.

Table 12.10 Data on rating of various attributes of IIFT mess and outside *dhabas*

Resp. No.	X_1	X_2	X_3	X_4	X_5	X_6	X_7	X_8	X_9	X_{10}	Y_1	Y_2	Y_3	Y_4	Y_5	Y_6	Y_7	Y_8	Y_9	Y_{10}
1	2	2	4	3	4	4	4	3	4	4	4	4	4	3	2	3	4	3	4	4
2	2	1	1	2	4	4	3	3	3	4	4	4	4	3	2	2	2	2	4	2
3	3	1	3	2	4	5	1	4	4	4	5	5	3	3	2	2	1	3	5	5
4	3	3	5	4	4	4	4	4	3	4	5	4	2	3	2	3	4	3	4	3
5	4	4	3	3	3	4	4	3	5	4	2	2	3	3	3	3	3	3	2	3
6	4	3	3	3	2	4	4	4	3	3	4	4	4	3	3	4	2	2	5	3
7	5	4	3	4	4	4	4	3	3	3	5	4	4	3	3	4	4	4	4	3
8	2	1	4	3	3	2	3	3	4	5	4	4	2	1	1	1	1	1	4	3
9	1	1	4	2	2	2	4	3	1	4	5	4	3	2	3	2	3	4	2	1
10	3	4	3	3	1	2	2	4	2	4	4	4	2	2	1	3	4	3	4	4
11	1	2	3	3	1	2	3	2	5	4	4	4	2	2	1	4	3	2	5	4
12	1	1	3	4	3	4	4	4	2	5	5	5	3	3	2	2	4	3	4	2
13	2	1	3	2	1	2	3	3	3	3	4	5	4	4	2	2	2	2	5	3
14	1	3	5	3	4	1	1	3	1	5	3	5	2	2	1	3	1	3	5	4
15	3	2	3	2	3	3	3	2	4	4	4	4	4	3	3	4	3	3	4	4
16	2	4	4	3	3	3	4	4	4	4	4	4	4	3	2	4	2	2	2	2
17	3	3	2	3	4	2	3	2	3	3	4	4	4	2	2	2	2	2	4	3
18	2	1	3	3	3	3	2	3	1	4	4	3	4	2	3	4	3	1	5	4
19	4	4	4	4	3	3	3	3	4	3	2	2	2	3	4	3	4	4	2	2
20	2	2	3	3	3	3	3	4	3	4	4	4	4	4	2	2	2	2	4	2

Resp. No.	X_1	X_2	X_3	X_4	X_5	X_6	X_7	X_8	X_9	X_{10}	Y_1	Y_2	Y_3	Y_4	Y_5	Y_6	Y_7	Y_8	Y_9	Y_{10}
21	1	1	1	1	3	4	4	2	5	5	4	4	2	3	2	3	2	3	4	4
22	2	2	3	3	3	3	3	3	4	4	2	2	2	3	3	3	3	3	2	3
23	3	4	4	3	4	3	3	4	5	4	4	3	4	3	1	3	2	3	5	4
24	1	3	3	2	2	3	2	1	1	3	4	3	4	2	1	3	2	2	4	4
25	1	1	3	1	1	1	5	5	5	5	4	4	4	2	1	4	4	2	4	4
26	5	4	5	2	2	3	3	3	4	5	4	3	3	1	1	2	2	2	5	3
27	2	1	1	2	3	4	4	3	4	3	4	3	3	2	3	3	2	1	3	3
28	1	1	4	3	2	2	1	4	4	5	4	4	2	3	1	3	1	2	5	2
29	3	3	3	4	4	4	4	3	3	4	4	4	4	4	2	3	3	3	3	3
30	1	1	3	2	2	3	3	1	4	4	4	4	2	2	2	3	4	3	4	2
31	1	1	3	2	2	3	3	1	4	4	4	4	2	2	2	3	4	3	4	2
32	3	4	4	3	4	4	4	4	4	4	1	1	1	1	1	1	1	1	1	1
33	3	2	4	3	3	2	3	4	5	4	4	4	2	2	2	3	2	1	2	3
34	1	2	4	4	3	4	5	3	5	5	5	4	2	3	2	4	2	3	2	2
35	1	1	1	2	2	2	2	2	1	1	4	4	5	3	3	4	2	3	5	4
36	1	1	2	1	2	2	3	1	2	4	4	4	4	3	1	4	4	3	4	4
37	3	4	5	3	2	5	3	4	2	4	4	5	3	2	2	4	3	3	5	4
38	1	2	2	2	2	3	3	2	4	4	4	2	3	3	2	4	2	2	4	3
39	3	3	3	3	3	3	3	3	3	3	4	4	4	3	3	3	3	3	3	3
40	2	3	3	2	3	4	3	2	3	3	5	5	2	3	2	2	2	2	3	2
41	3	2	3	2	4	3	2	2	3	2	4	3	4	4	3	2	3	2	3	4
42	3	4	4	4	4	4	4	3	4	4	2	2	3	3	3	3	3	3	2	2
43	3	3	2	3	4	3	3	2	4	3	5	5	4	3	2	3	3	1	5	5
44	2	2	4	3	3	4	4	3	3	3	5	4	4	3	3	3	3	3	4	4
45	2	2	4	2	4	3	3	4	4	3	4	4	4	4	2	4	2	3	4	4

QUESTIONS

1. By using a paired sample t-test, identify the parameters on which the *dhaba* food has an edge over the mess food. You may use a 5 per cent level of significance.
2. Based on the results obtained, what are your recommendations?
(Use the SPSS data provided in Table 12.10 to answer the above questions.)

Note: *The case is based on a project done by IIFT students Manvi Bajpai, Manoj Chakravarthy, Mayur Toshniwal, Mohit Jyotishkaran and Mohit Bhatia as a part of Business Research Methods course.*

CASE 12.2

PERCEPTION OF PEOPLE ABOUT BAN ON PLASTIC BAGS IN DELHI

Plastic bags play an integral role in our daily life. Be it carrying groceries from the local kirana store or the storing of household articles in a poly-bag, we never actually run out of plastic bags. The omnipresence of this utility object brought to the fore an impending problem that needed to be resolved. The problem associated with using plastic bags is that they are not biodegradable and in fact take close to 60 years to decompose. Apart from that, they are also the cause of various other problems such as clogging of drain pipes and death of cattles that accidentally chew on plastic bags.

This prompted the Delhi government to finally take notice and introduce a blanket ban on plastic bags in 2009. The storage and sale of plastic bag in all places, including shops, is banned. The penalty for violating the ban, could be a fine of ₹1,00,000 or five years', imprisonment or both.

The officials empowered to enforce the ban are the staff of the health and environment department. Food and supply officers and subdivisional magistrates are also empowered to enforce the ban.

The Delhi Pollution Control Committee (DPCC) has been assigned the task of implementation. It has formed a special inspection team for the purpose. The team would visit manufacturing units and retail shops, and would initiate punishment for the violators. The scope of this ban has been widened by including four-star hotels under its purview.

The imposition of this widespread ban has prompted researchers to analyse the impact and effectiveness of the ban from the perspective of both the consumer and the vendor. They first checked whether the consumers and vendors are aware of the ban or not. Along with that they analysed the preference, choices and willingness of the consumers and vendors from diverse backgrounds to switch to eco-friendly alternatives so as to ascertain the effectiveness of the ban on plastic bags.

A survey was conducted in Delhi to understand the perception of consumers about the plastic bag ban. The statements related to the respondents perceptions are listed below:

What are your views about plastic bags since the ban? (Tick one for each answer)

Parameters	Strongly Agree (1)	Moderately Agree (2)	Neither Agree Nor Disagree (3)	Moderately Disagree (4)	Strongly Disagree (5)
Plastic bag is a must when buying groceries/vegetables. (X12a)					
Plastic bag is harmful for the environment. (X12b)					
I do not wish to quit using plastic bags. (X12c)					
I try to avoid plastic bags as much as I can. (X12d)					
Plastic bag ban is not enforced properly. (X12e)					
Paper bag is not a useful substitute for plastic bag. (X12f)					

A sample of 44 respondents was chosen randomly. The data is presented in Table 12.11 and is also available in SPSS/EXCEL file in the data disk.

Table 12.11
Select data on perception and demographic profile of consumers regarding ban on plastic bags

Resp No.	X12a	X12b	X12c	X12d	X12e	X12f	Age	Gender
1	1	2	3	4	2	2	2	1
2	2	1	3	4	1	5	2	1
3	4	1	4	3	2	4	2	1
4	1	1	3	3	2	4	2	2
5	3	1	5	4	1	5	2	2
6	2	1	3	3	1	2	2	1
7	3	1	4	2	2	4	2	1
8	1	5	5	5	3	1	3	1
9	3	2	3	3	2	2	2	2
10	2	1	5	2	2	4	2	1
11	5	1	1	1	1	2	1	1
12	5	1	2	2	1	2	2	1
13	2	1	3	2	1	2	2	2
14	3	1	2	2	1	2	2	1
15	2	1	5	2	2	4	2	2
16	2	1	4	4	1	5	2	1
17	2	3	3	3	4	1	2	2
18	2	2	4	2	2	3	3	1
19	2	1	4	4	1	5	2	1
20	1	2	2	3	3	2	3	1
21	5	1	3	2	2	2	3	1
22	5	1	4	1	1	5	2	1
23	2	2	4	2	2	2	2	2
24	3	1	3	2	2	2	2	1
25	4	1	5	1	1	2	1	2
26	2	1	3	2	1	2	2	1
27	2	4	5	2	4	5	2	1
28	2	1	2	5	2	5	2	1
29	2	1	4	2	1	2	2	2
30	1	1	4	3	2	4	2	1
31	1	1	2	5	2	4	2	1
32	5	1	5	3	1	5	2	2
33	5	3	2	4	4	2	2	1
34	5	1	5	2	2	2	2	1
35	4	1	2	1	3	1	2	1
36	3	1	5	3	1	2	2	2
37	2	1	4	2	1	5	2	1
38	4	1	3	2	1	4	2	1
39	5	1	5	2	2	4	2	1
40	5	1	5	3	4	4	2	1
41	2	2	2	5	1	4	2	1
42	2	1	3	2	1	3	2	2
43	2	1	4	4	1	4	2	1
44	2	2	2	4	2	3	2	2

- The variable age is coded as:
  1 = Below 18 years
  2 = 18 to 30 years
  3 = 31 to 50 years
- The variable gender is coded as:
  1 = Male 2 = Female

QUESTIONS

1. By using a one-sample t-test, identify the parameters of the plastic bags ban on which the consumers have a favourable opinion. (**Hint:** Test the null hypothesis: $\mu = 3$ against an appropriate alternative hypothesis.)
2. Using a two-sample independent t-test, examine whether the views of the male and the female respondents are the same.
3. Divide all the respondents into two groups by taking respondents aged 30 and below as the younger respondents and those who are 31 and above as older respondents. Now statistically examine whether the views on the ban on plastic bags are different for the younger and older respondents.
4. Write a summary of your findings.

Note: *The case is based on a project done by IIFT students Manu Pathak, Madhuri Ghosh, Navin Agarwal and Nitesh Luthra as a part of Business Research Methods course.*

CASE 12.3

CHANGE IN THE LIFESTYLE OF YOUTH AFTER THE GANGRAPE INCIDENT OF DECEMBER 16, 2012

A 23-year-old girl and her male friend were returning home on the night of 16 December 2012 after watching the film *Life of Pi* in a multiplex in Saket, Delhi. Both of them got into a chartered bus at Munirka for Dwarka at 9.30 p.m. The bus was being driven by joyriders, and besides the driver, there were five others. One of them, a minor had called out to them, saying that the bus was going to their desired destination. After they boarded the bus, the doors of bus were shut, and it started deviating from the route. When the girl's friend objected, the six of them taunted them, asking what they were up to at such a late hour. The boy was beaten up with an iron rod and knocked unconscious. The girl, after being beaten with the iron rod, was dragged to the rear of the bus and raped as the bus continued to move. As per the medical reports, the girl suffered serious injuries to her abdomen, intestines and genitals due to the assault. According to the doctors, the iron rod could have been used for penetration. The victim tried to fight off the rapists by biting three of them.

After being raped, the girl and her male friend, both unconscious and partially clothed, were thrown out of the moving bus near Mahipalpur. Both of them were found on the road at around 11.00 pm by a passerby who reported the matter to the Delhi Police. They were then taken to the Safdarjung Hospital.

The incident led to a huge outrage, not only from women groups but from the general public as well. It generated widespread coverage in both the national and international media. Delhi and other cities around India saw a series of protests against the incident, as well as the government for not providing adequate security to women. The major participants in these protests were the youth in the age group of 16 to 35 years. This incident made the public (especially the youth) more introspective, and more conscious about such incidents. It also showed how frequent such incidents had become in our society.

Some questions were being commonly discussed keeping in mind the following two perspectives:

1. Has the rape incident followed by the protest and prominence of similar cases brought about any change in the lifestyle of the youth? If yes, in what respect? Are they taking any precautionary measures? Has there been any attitude change? Has the trust towards police or authorities reduced? The essence was to find out whether this incident had brought about any change in youths. If yes, whether this change was temporary or permanent.
2. Have some businesses such as restaurants and nightclubs been impacted? Is any business feeling threatened as a consequence of the incident? Have new business opportunities such as cabs driven by lady drivers and self-defence training programs been created? What more can be done?

Some of these issues were addressed in a survey conducted among 70 respondents in the age group of 15–35 who are the residents of Delhi (staying in Delhi at least for the last 6–8 months). The respondents were chosen using convenience sampling.

The objective of the study was to determine the lifestyle change among the youth after the rape incident. A focus group discussion was conducted to identify the variables which need to be studied. Focus group consisted of 8 individuals—5 females and 3 males. Out of these, 1 female and 1 male were professional and the rest were students of B-school. Among the students, some had work experience, while others were freshers. The participants were aged 21–35 years. The identified variables were used in designing the questionnaire. A selected part of the questionnaire is given below:

1. Are you familiar with the Damini Rape Case?
   - i Yes [1]
   - ii No [0]

2(a). What kind of public places do you prefer to go out to?
   - i Malls [Yes = 1, No = 0]
   - ii Theatres/ Cinemas [Yes = 1, No = 0]
   - iii Restaurants [Yes = 1, No = 0]
   - iv Historical Monuments [Yes = 1, No = 0]
   - v Pubs/ Night-clubs [Yes = 1, No = 0]
   - vi Other: ____________________ (Actual place to be mentioned.)

2(b). Out of the above places, which ones have been affected with regard to frequency and time of visit after the incident?
   - i Malls [Yes = 1, No = 0]
   - ii Theatres/ Cinemas [Yes = 1, No = 0]
   - iii Restaurants [Yes = 1, No = 0]
   - iv Historical Monuments [Yes = 1, No = 0]
   - v Pubs/ Nightclubs [Yes = 1, No = 0]
   - vi Other: ____________________ (Actual place to be mentioned.)

3. What security measures have you undertaken after the rape incident?
   - A. Carrying a Knife [Yes = 1, No = 0]
   - B. Chilli/ Pepper spray [Yes = 1, No = 0]
   - C. Mobile app (such as BeSafe) [Yes = 1, No = 0]
   - D. Self-defence training [Yes = 1, No = 0]
   - E. No measure [Yes = 1, No = 0]
   - F. Other: ____________________ (Actual measure to be mentioned.)

4. Given below are some statements regarding behaviour changes after the rape incident. You are requested to state your degree of agreement/ disagreement with each of the statements as mentioned below on a 5-point scale.

Statement	Completely Disagree	Disagree	No opinion	Agree	Completely Agree
	[1]	[2]	[3]	[4]	[5]
a) Your parents intervene regarding late-hour outings					
b) Your parents are more concerned about the company you hang out with					
c) You have reduced frequency of late night outings					
d) You have reduced outings with your friends of opposite gender					
e) You mind travelling alone at night					

Statement	Completely Disagree	Disagree	No opinion	Agree	Completely Agree
	[1]	[2]	[3]	[4]	[5]
f) You prefer public transport at night					
g) You have started using lady-driven cab instead of a normal cab					
h) You are comfortable in taking lifts (R)					
i) You have reduced drinking outside due to increased police patrolling					

(R) stands for reverse coding.

5. Gender
   - i Male [1]
   - ii Female [0]
6. You belong to age group
   - i 15–20 years [1]
   - ii 21–25 years [2]
   - iii 26–30 years [3]
   - iv 31 and above [4]
7. Marital status
   - i Single [1]
   - ii Married [2]
   - iii Widow/ divorced [3]
8. You belong to a
   - i Nuclear family [1]
   - ii Joint family [0]
9. What is your occupation?
   - i Student [1]
   - ii Home-Maker [2]
   - iii Businessman [3]
   - iv Professional/ Service [4]
   - v Unemployed [5]
10. Your monthly household income
    - i Up to ₹25,000 [1]
    - ii 25,001–50,000 [2]
    - iii 50,001–1,00,000 [3]
    - iv 1,00,001 and above [4]

The data collected is presented in the Table 12.12 given at the end of the case.

QUESTIONS

1. Carry out a descriptive univariate analysis of data.
2. Conduct an appropriate statistical test to examine whether there is an (a) increase in parents' intervention, (b) reduction in late night outings, (c) change in trust, (d) change in travelling behaviour and (e) reduction in drinking habits after the gangrape incident. *[Hint: Parents' intervention may be identified by questions numbering 4(a) and 4(b), reduction in late night outings by 4(c), trust issues by 4(d) and 4(h), change in travelling behaviour by 4(e), 4(f) and 4(g) and reduction in drinking habits by 4(i).]*
3. Carry out an independent sample t-test to examine the differences in (a) increase in parents' intervention, (b) reduction in late night outings, (c) changes in trust, (d) changes in travelling behaviour and (e) reduction in drinking habits with respect to (i) gender and (ii) occupation such as students and professionals.

Table 12.12 Select data on variables used in survey of gangrape incident of 16 December 2012

Resp No	X1	X2A1	X2A2	X2A3	X2A4	X2A5	X2A6	X2B1	X2B2	X2B3	X2B4	X2B5	X2B6	X3A	X3B	X3C	X3D	X3E	X3F	X4A	X4B	X4C	X4D	X4E	X4F	X4G	X4H	X4I	X5	X6	X7	X8	X9	X10
1	1	1	1	1	1	0		0	0	0	0	0		0	0	0	0	1		4	4	4	5	4	3	1	2	5	1	2	1	1	1	1
2	1	1	1	1	1	1		0	1	0	0	1		0	1	0	0	0		4	5	5	2	5	5	3	5	5	0	2	1	1	1	4
3	1	1	0	0	0	0		0	0	0	1	1		0	0	0	0	1		4	4	4	2	5	5	2	5	4	0	2	1	1	4	2
4	1	1	1	1	0	0		0	0	0	0	1		0	0	0	0	1		4	4	4	1	4	4	2	5	4	0	2	1	1	1	3
5	1	1	0	0	0	0		0	0	0	0	1		0	0	0	1	0		1	4	4	2	2	4	3	4	3	1	1	1	1	1	2
6	1	1	1	1	1	0		1	1	0	1	0		0	0	1	0	0		5	4	4	2	5	5	2	5	3	0	2	1	1	1	4
7	1	0	1	1	0	0		0	0	0	0	0		0	0	0	0	1		3	3	2	2	5	1	2	4	3	1	2	1	1	4	2
8	1	1	1	1	1	0		0	0	0	0	0		0	0	0	0	1		2	2	3	1	3	4	2	2	3	0	2	1	1	1	3
9	1	1	1	1	0	0		0	0	0	0	0		0	0	0	0	1		2	4	1	1	1	1	3	4	4	1	2	1	1	4	4
10	1	0	0	0	0	1		0	0	0	0	1		0	0	0	1	0		4	4	2	2	4	3	1	4	5	1	2	1	1	4	4
11	1	0	0	0	0	1		0	0	0	0	1		0	0	0	1	0		3	5	5	4	1	1	5	5	5	1	2	1	1	3	4
12	1	1	1	1	1	0		0	0	0	1	0		0	0	0	1	0		5	4	5	3	5	5	4	5	3	0	2	1	0	1	2
13	1	0	0	1	0	0		0	0	0	0	1		0	0	0	1	0		2	2	4	1	4	3	2	5	4	1	1	1	1	1	2
14	1	1	1	0	0	0		0	0	0	0	1		0	0	0	1	0		3	4	4	3	5	5	3	5	3	0	1	1	1	1	2
15	1	1	1	1	0	0		0	0	0	0	1		0	0	0	1	0		5	2	4	1	5	4	3	5	3	0	2	1	1	1	4
16	1	1	1	1	0	1		0	0	0	0	0		0	0	0	1	0	More careful with respect to surroundings	4	3	2	2	2	3	2	5	4	1	2	1	1	1	3
17	1	0	0	1	0	0	Religious Place	0	0	0	0	1		0	0	0	0	1		4	4	4	2	5	1	3	5	3	0	3	1	1	1	2
18	1	1	1	1	0	0		0	0	0	0	0		0	0	0	0	1		4	4	4	2	5	5	3	5	3	0	2	1	1	1	2
19	1	1	1	1	1	1		0	0	0	0	0		0	0	0	0	1		4	4	3	3	3	2	1	2	4	1	2	1	0	4	4
20	1	1	1	1	1	0		0	1	0	1	0		1	1	1	0	0		2	2	4	2	4	3	3	5	3	0	3	2	1	4	3
21	1	1	1	1	1	0		0	1	0	0	0		0	0	0	0	1		2	4	4	2	1	5	3	2	3	0	3	2	1	4	2
22	1	0	1	0	0	0		0	0	0	0	1		0	0	0	0	1		4	3	4	2	2	3	1	5	4	1	2	1	0	1	2
23	1	1	1	1	1	1		1	1	0	0	1	Railway Metro Stations	0	1	0	0	0		5	3	2	5	5	1	5	1	5	1	2	1	1	1	3
24	1	1	1	1	1	0		0	0	0	1	0		0	0	0	1	0		5	4	5	2	5	5	3	4	3	0	2	1	0	1	4
25	1	1	1	1	1	1		0	0	0	0	1		0	0	1	99	0		2	4	4	2	5	4	3	5	2	0	2	1	1	1	4
26	1	1	1	1	0	0	Markets	1	0	0	0	0	Markets	0	1	0	1	0		5	5	5	4	5	1	3	5	3	0	2	1	1	1	4
27	1	1	1	1	0	0		0	0	0	0	0		0	0	0	0	0	Avoid Night outings	4	3	5	1	4	2	3	5	3	0	2	1	1	4	2
28	1	1	1	1	1	0		0	1	0	0	0		0	0	0	0	1		2	4	4	4	4	4	2	5	3	1	2	1	0	4	3
29	1	0	0	0	1	0		0	0	0	0	1		0	0	0	0	1		4	4	4	5	1	5	2	5	3	0	2	1	1	1	3
30	1	0	1	0	0	0		0	0	0	0	1		0	0	0	1	0		4	5	2	4	2	2	1	4	2	1	2	1	1	5	2
31	1	1	1	1	1	0		0	0	0	0	0		0	0	0	0	1		4	4	3	2	4	4	3	4	1	1	2	1	1	4	4
32	1	1	1	0	0	1		0	1	0	0	1		0	1	0	1	0		5	4	4	4	4	2	4	2	4	1	2	1	1	4	2
33	1	1	1	1	0	1		1	0	0	0	1		0	0	0	0	1		4	3	4	4	3	3	3	3	4	1	2	1	0	4	2
34	1	1	1	1	1	0		0	1	0	0	0		0	0	0	0	1		4	3	4	2	3	5	4	3	4	1	2	1	0	1	4

Resp No	X1	X2A1	X2A2	X2A3	X2A4	X2A5	X2A6	X2B1	X2B2	X2B3	X2B4	X2B5	X2B6	X3A	X3B	X3C	X3D	X3E	X3F	X4A	X4B	X4C	X4D	X4E	X4F	X4G	X4H	X4I	X5	X6	X7	X8	X9	X10
35	1	1	0	0	0	0		0	0	0	0	0		0	0	0	0	0	Avoid odd time to travel	2	2	2	2	1	5	2	5	2	1	3	1	1	4	3
36	1	1	1	1	1	1		0	0	0	0	0		0	0	0	0	1		1	1	1	1	1	5	1	5	1	1	3	1	1	4	2
37	1	1	1	0	1	0		0	0	0	0	1		1	1	0	1	0		4	4	4	2	2	2	4	4	5	0	2	1	1	1	2
38	1	1	1	1	1	1		0	0	0	0	1		0	0	0	0	1		4	4	4	2	4	4	2	4	2	0	2	1	1	1	1
39	1	1	1	1	1	0		0	0	0	0	0		0	0	0	0	1		1	1	1	1	5	1	1	1	3	1	2	1	1	1	1
40	1	1	1	1	1	0		0	0	0	0	0		0	0	0	0	1		4	4	3	3	4	4	3	4	3	0	2	1	1	1	2
41	1	1	1	1	0	0		0	0	0	1	1		1	1	0	0	0		4	1	5	1	5	5	3	5	3	0	2	1	0	4	2
42	1	1	1	1	0	0		1	0	0	0	1		0	1	0	0	0		5	5	4	2	4	2	3	2	3	0	2	1	1	1	2
43	1	1	1	1	0	0		1	0	0	0	0		0	0	0	0	1		4	3	4	5	1	3	2	2	3	1	3	1	1	1	3
44	1	1	1	1	0	0		0	0	0	0	1		1	1	0	0	1		4	5	5	2	3	5	3	5	5	0	2	1	1	4	2
45	1	1	1	1	0	1		0	1	0	0	1		0	0	0	0	1		1	1	1	2	1	5	1	5	2	1	2	1	1	4	2
46	1	0	1	1	0	0		0	0	0	1	0		0	0	0	0	1		4	4	4	4	3	4	3	5	3	1	2	1	1	4	3
47	1	1	0	0	0	0		0	0	0	0	1		0	0	0	0	1		5	5	5	5	5	1	3	3	3	0	3	1	0	4	1
48	1	1	1	1	0	0		0	0	0	0	0		0	0	0	0	1		5	3	3	3	3	2	3	2	3	1	2	1	0	4	2
49	1	1	1	1	0	0		0	1	0	1	0		0	0	0	0	1		4	2	2	2	4	4	2	4	2	0	2	1	1	1	4
50	1	1	1	1	0	1		0	0	0	0	0		0	0	0	0	1		4	4	2	1	2	3	3	3	5	1	2	1	1	1	4
51	1	1	1	1	0	0		0	0	0	0	0		0	0	0	0	1		4	4	2	2	2	4	1	5	5	1	2	1	1	1	3
52	0	1	1	1	1	1		1	1	0	0	1		0	0	0	0	1		4	4	2	2	2	4	3	4	2	1	2	1	1	1	1
53	1	1	1	1	0	0		0	0	0	0	1		0	0	0	0	1		4	4	5	5	3	3	2	5	3	0	2	1	0	4	2
54	1	1	1	0	0	0		1	0	0	0	1		0	1	1	0	0		4	4	4	2	4	4	3	5	2	0	2	1	0	1	1
55	1	1	1	0	0	0		1	1	0	0	0		0	1	0	1	0		5	5	5	2	4	5	3	1	5	0	2	1	1	4	2
56	1	1	1	0	0	0		0	0	0	0	0		0	0	0	0	1		2	2	3	1	1	3	3	3	4	1	2	1	0	3	1
57	1	1	1	0	0	0		0	1	0	0	1		0	1	1	0	0		2	4	4	4	4	2	2	4	3	0	2	1	1	4	4
58	1	1	1	0	0	0		1	1	0	0	0		0	0	0	0	1		4	4	5	5	5	4	3	5	1	0	3	1	1	1	2
59	1	1	1	0	0	0		0	0	0	0	1		0	0	0	0	1		4	4	4	2	2	4	2	5	5	1	2	1	1	1	2
60	1	1	0	0	0	0		0	0	0	0	1		0	0	0	0	1		2	4	4	5	2	5	5	2	4	1	2	1	0	4	2
61	1	1	1	1	0	1		1	0	1	0	1		0	0	0	0	1		5	5	5	4	5	2	4	3	3	0	2	1	1	4	2
62	1	1	1	1	1	1		1	1	1	1	1		0	1	0	0	0		5	5	4	4	5	4	3	5	3	0	2	1	1	1	4
63	1	1	1	1	1	0		0	1	1	0	0		0	0	1	0	0		4	4	4	2	3	1	3	4	3	0	2	1	0	1	3
64	1	1	0	1	0	0		1	0	1	0	0		0	0	0	0	1		1	5	4	4	5	1	3	5	3	0	2	1	1	4	3
65	1	1	1	1	1	0		1	1	1	1	0		1	0	0	0	0		4	3	5	3	5	5	3	5	3	0	2	1	1	4	2
66	1	0	0	1	0	0		0	0	1	0	0		0	0	0	0	1		4	1	3	1	3	4	2	5	3	0	2	1	1	1	3
67	1	1	1	1	0	0		1	1	1	0	0		0	1	1	1	0		5	5	4	3	2	2	3	2	4	1	2	1	1	1	3
68	1	1	1	1	1	0		0	1	1	0	0		0	0	0	0	1		3	2	2	2	3	3	3	3	3	1	2	1	1	1	3
69	1	1	1	1	1	0		1	1	1	0	0		1	1	1	0	0		4	5	5	4	5	1	4	5	2	0	3	1	1	1	4
70	1	1	1	0	0	0		0	0	1	0	1		0	0	1	0	0		2	5	3	2	2	3	3	5	4	0	2	1	1	4	1

CASE 12.4

PERCEIVED ORGANIZATIONAL SUPPORT, ROLE OVERLOAD AND WORK-FAMILY CONFLICT IN IT INDUSTRY[1]

Organizations are always looking for higher productivity from their employees. There are various factors that affect employee performance and productivity. While many of these stem from the organizational context, a number of factors are related to a person's individual context stemming from his/ her family and personal life.

Perceived organizational support (POS) is defined as employees' global beliefs about the extent to which the organization values their contributions and cares about their well-being. This construct has been examined in several work-family studies. POS should increase performance of standard job activities and actions favorable to the organization that go beyond assigned responsibilities. Employees who experience a strong level of POS theoretically feel the need to reciprocate favorable organizational treatment with attitudes and behaviors that in turn benefit the organization.

Role overload can be defined as the additional and excessive responsibilities given to an employee due to which the set goals and targets are either not met or not completed up to a particular satisfaction level. Role overload occurs when people are assigned positions with excessive demands. Role overload causes personal wear and tear and performance deterioration. A clear understanding of obligations, a sense of priorities, open communication channels, and perceived organizational support are expected to reduce or prevent role overload. Role stressors such as role conflict, role overload, and role ambiguity have been found to increase levels of work-family conflict.

Work-family conflict (WFC) is a form of inter-role conflict in which participation in the work role is made more difficult by virtue of participation in the family role. Conflict between work and family can originate in either domain such that work can interfere with family needs or family can interfere with work responsibilities. WFC, the main concept, has been associated with an array of negative outcomes such as poor job attitudes, ineffective work performance, dissatisfaction within the family domain, diminished psychological well-being, and physical and behavioural symptoms of distress. Work-family conflict exists when pressures arising in work role are incompatible with pressures arising in family role and when participation in one role is made more difficult by virtue of participation in another role. The situational variables of role conflict, role ambiguity and role overload have been found to directly and positively relate to work-family conflict. An important organizational outcome that might result from POS is reduced work-family conflict.

In sum, perceived organizational support makes the employees less prone to role overload state. Moreover, the employees who perceive high levels of organizational support are likely to report less work-family conflict, since their supportive organization may offer family-friendly policies or flexible work arrangements to better balance work and family.

A study was undertaken to examine the relationship between the three discussed concepts and to examine the variations in these concepts due to demographic variables.

A sample of 31 respondents from the IT industry was chosen using convenience sampling. All the respondents were married and belonged to the age group 25–40 years. The perceived organizational support, role overload and work–family conflict were measured using a Likert scale with the code1 = strongly disagree, 2 = disagree, 3 = undecided, 4 = agree, 5 = strongly agree. In the case of negative statements, reverse code was used with 5 = strongly disagree .... and 1 = strongly agree. The survey instrument is given below:

1. Sex (**X_1**) : Male [1]
   Female [2]
2. Experience (**X_2**) : ____________________
   (No. of Years)
3. Is your partner working (**X_3**): Yes [1]
   No [2]
4. Do you have any children (**X_4**): Yes [1]
   No [2]
5. Given below are some statements. You are requested to indicate the extent to which you agree with each statement to describe your job and the experience or feelings about it. (**X_5**)

[1] *This case is based on a project done by Aayush Singhal, Geetika Khosla, Nishtha Sharma and Saurabh Pushpraj, participants of PGDM-HR (2012–14), IMI New Delhi.*

S. No.	Statement	Strongly disagree	Disagree	Undecided	Agree	Strongly agree
a	The organization values my contribution to its well-being.					
b	The organization fails to appreciate any extra effort from me. (R)					
c	The organization would ignore any complaint from me. (R)					
d	The organization really cares about my well-being.					
e	Even if I did the best job possible, the organization would fail to notice. (R)					
f	The organization cares about my general satisfaction at work.					
g	The organization shows very little concern for me. (R)					
h	The organization takes pride in my accomplishments at work.					
i	I have to do a lot of work in this job					
j	Owing to excessive workload I have to manage with insufficient number of employees and resources.					
k	I have to complete my work hurriedly owing to excessive workload.					
l	I have to do such work as ought to be done by others.					
m	I am unable to carry out my assignments to my satisfaction on account of excessive workload and lack of time.					
n	My working hours prevent me from having more quality time with my family					
o	My work responsibility time, demands more of me than my responsibility with my family					
p	My family is able to adapt to my working hours and work demands. (R)					
q	I still spend productive time with my family even when I spend overtime at work or working over the weekend (R)					
r	Taking care of my dependents affect my working time					
s	My family is stressed because of my working-hour and work responsibilities					
t	I am confident that my family understands my working situation/demands (R)					
u	I spend the weekends with my family (partner and children) (R)					

Note: R stands for reverse coding.

The statements (a) to (h) are for perceived organizational support (POS), (i) to (m) are for role overload and (n) to (u) for work–family conflict. The data for the 31 respondents for the above questionnaire is presented in Table 12.13 at the end of the case.

QUESTIONS

1. Conduct an independent sample t-test to determine the difference in the (i) perceived organizational support, (ii) role overload, and (iii) work–family conflict because of
   a. Gender b. Working of the spouse c. Possessing children
2. How does work–family conflict influence perceived organizational support?*
3. What is the impact of role overload on perceived organizational support?*
4. How is the role overload related to work–family conflict?

Note: Please note that questions numbering 2, 3 and 4 may be taken up after Chapter 15 on Correlation and Regression.

Table 12.13 Data on perceived organizational support, role overload, work–family conflict and demographic variables

S. No.	x_1	x_2	x_3	x_4	x_{5a}	x_{5b} (R)	x_{5c} (R)	x_{5d}	x_{5e} (R)	x_{5f}	x_{5g} (R)	x_{5h}	x_{5i}	x_{5j}	x_{5k}	x_{5l}	x_{5m}	x_{5n}	x_{5o}	x_{5p} (R)	x_{5q} (R)	x_{5r}	x_{5s}	x_{5t} (R)	x_{5u} (R)
1	1	6	1	2	3	4	3	2	2	2	1	3	2	2	3	5	2	5	4	2	2	3	4	3	2
2	2	7	1	2	4	3	4	4	3	2	4	3	3	2	4	4	4	4	4	2	2	3	4	4	1
3	2	4	1	2	2	4	4	3	4	2	2	2	3	1	2	3	2	3	3	1	2	1	1	5	1
4	2	5	1	2	4	4	4	4	4	4	2	4	3	2	4	2	3	2	2	2	4	4	1	1	1
5	1	5	2	2	3	2	4	3	3	2	3	3	4	2	3	4	4	3	4	2	3	1	2	1	2
6	2	3.5	1	2	4	4	5	4	4	4	4	4	5	4	2	4	2	4	3	2	2	2	3	2	2
7	1	4	2	2	4	2	2	1	1	1	1	1	2	2	5	5	4	1	2	3	5	3	3	3	3
8	1	2.5	2	2	4	4	4	4	4	3	4	4	4	4	2	4	3	2	4	2	4	2	1	2	3
9	1	5	1	1	5	3	4	3	1	2	3	4	2	4	1	1	5	2	3	2	4	3	2	2	1
10	2	7	1	2	3	2	4	1	3	2	3	4	5	4	2	3	5	5	5	1	5	5	4	2	1
11	1	5	1	2	1	3	2	2	2	2	1	3	2	3	2	2	4	2	2	4	2	4	4	5	5
12	1	7	1	2	3	3	4	3	2	3	3	2	1	1	1	2	1	1	2	2	1	4	3	4	5
13	2	2	1	2	4	5	2	3	4	3	4	4	4	4	4	4	4	4	4	3	2	3	4	3	1
14	1	4	1	2	4	4	4	3	3	3	4	2	4	2	2	2	3	4	4	2	4	4	3	2	2
15	2	3.5	1	2	3	5	4	2	5	2	4	4	3	2	2	3	3	4	3	3	2	3	2	2	5
16	1	10	1	1	4	3	4	4	3	2	4	3	2	3	4	3	1	2	2	4	2	3	2	4	4
17	1	15	2	1	3	4	4	4	4	3	4	3	4	3	3	4	4	4	4	4	2	2	4	3	3
18	1	2	2	2	4	5	4	4	5	4	4	3	3	2	2	2	2	4	3	3	3	3	3	2	1
19	1	17	1	1	4	4	4	4	4	4	4	4	4	4	2	4	2	4	4	2	3	2	4	2	3
20	1	4	2	1	3	4	3	3	3	2	4	2	3	2	3	3	3	4	2	3	3	2	3	3	4
21	1	17	2	1	4	4	4	4	4	4	4	4	3	4	3	3	3	5	4	2	3	2	4	2	1
22	1	16	2	1	4	4	4	4	4	4	4	4	4	1	2	2	2	2	1	1	5	1	1	1	2
23	1	10	1	2	4	4	5	2	5	2	5	4	5	3	2	2	1	3	1	3	3	1	1	1	2
24	1	4	1	2	5	3	3	4	2	4	4	5	4	4	4	5	3	4	4	3	5	4	4	3	1
25	1	3	1	2	5	4	4	4	3	4	2	5	4	1	4	2	3	2	4	4	3	1	1	3	4
26	2	4	1	2	4	3	3	4	2	3	3	3	5	2	3	3	4	5	5	1	1	3	4	4	4
27	1	5	1	2	3	3	4	5	1	5	2	4	4	4	4	3	2	4	3	3	4	4	3	2	3
28	2	3	1	2	5	4	2	3	3	2	3	1	5	5	2	4	5	3	2	1	5	3	3	2	1
29	1	5	1	2	4	4	1	2	4	3	1	5	5	3	4	3	4	1	4	4	2	4	1	1	5
30	2	4	1	2	3	4	4	4	5	4	4	3	2	4	5	5	3	5	5	2	3	4	2	4	3
31	1	2	1	2	4	3	4	4	4	3	4	4	4	2	2	4	2	2	2	2	2	4	2	2	1

Appendix – 12.1: SPSS COMMANDS FOR DATA INPUTS AND t-TEST

Data in SPSS

When you start the SPSS program, you will get a blank screen like a blank EXCEL spreadsheet.

1. Type in your data for the problem (or from a survey which has to be processed) in this file. Data should be numerical (coded if nominal scale).
2. To define the data format, variable labels, and value labels for each variable, double-click on the headings of the respective column. Fill the details in the relevant boxes/cells.
3. Save this file with a FILE SAVE command.

t-test (for one sample)

1. Click on ANALYSE at the SPSS menu bar.
2. Click on COMPARE MEANS, followed by 'One sample t-test'.
3. Select the test variable for which this test is to be done, by clicking on the arrow after highlighting the appropriate variable to transfer it from left to right. In our case, the test variable is X10.
4. Specify the test value which is the hypothesized value and say OK. In our case the test value is 36, which could vary from problem to problem.

t-tests (independent sample)

After the input data has been typed along with the variable labels and value labels in an SPSS file, to get the t-test output for an independent sample t-test for comparing the means of two metric variables, proceed as follows:

1. Click on ANALYSE at the SPSS menu bar.
2. Click on COMPARE MEANS, followed by 'Independent sample t-test'.
3. Select the test variable for which this test is to be done, by clicking on the arrow after highlighting the appropriate variable to transfer it from left to right. In our case, it is variable X10.
4. Select the GROUPING VARIABLE in the same way, and transfer it to the right side box. This variable defines the codes for segregating the test variable into two groups. In our case grouping variable is X12.
5. Then define the codes for the two groups by clicking on DEFINE GROUPS just below the GROUPING VARIABLE and typing in the codes (1, 2 for example, or as are used in our case).
6. Click OK to get the output for an independent sample t-test.

For the paired sample t-test

1. Repeat step 1 above, after your data is typed and the labels are defined.
2. Click on COMPARE MEANS, followed by 'paired sample t-test'.
3. Select two variables from the variable list appearing on the left side. These should be transferred to the box on the right by clicking on the arrow.
4. Click OK to get the desired output.

Note: In all these tests, you can set a confidence level by clicking on OPTIONS in the dialog box and choosing the desired confidence level for the t-test. The default value would generally be 95 per cent if you do not choose any.

Answers to Objective Type Questions

1. False	2. True	3. True	4. True	5. False
6. False	7. True	8. True	9. True	10. False
11. False	12. True	13. True	14. False	15. False
16. True	17. True	18. False	19. True	20. False

BIBLIOGRAPHY

Bhattacharyya, Dipak Kumar. *Research Methodology*. New Delhi: Excel Books, 2006.

Cooper, Donald R. *Business Research Methods*. New Delhi: Tata Mcgraw-Hill Publishing Company Ltd, 2006.

Emory, William C. *Business Research Methods*. Illinois: Richard D. Irwin, 1976.

Gay, L R. *Research Methods for Business and Management*. New York: Macmillan Publishing Company, 1992.

Graziano, Anthony M. *Research Methods: A Process of Inquiry*. Boston: Allyn and Bacon, 2000.

Green, Paul E. and Donald S Tull. *Research for Marketing Decisions*. 4th edn. New Delhi: Prentice Hall of India Private Ltd., 1986.

Kinnear, Thomas C and James R Taylor. *Marketing Research: An Applied Approach*. 5th edn. New York: McGraw Hill, Inc., 1996.

Kothari, C R. *Research Methodology: Methods and Techniques*. New Delhi: Wiley Eastern, 1990.

Malhotra, Naresh K. *Marketing Research – An Applied Orientation*. 3rd edn. New Delhi: Pearson Education, 2002.

Nargundkar, Rajendra. *Marketing Research (Text and Cases)*. New Delhi: Tata McGraw Hill Publishing Company Ltd., 2002.

Nation, Jack R. *Research Methods*. New Jersey: Prentice Hall, 1997.

Sekaram, Uma. *Research Methods for Business: A Skill Building Approach*. Singapore: John Wiley & Sons (Asia) Pte Ltd., 2003.

Sethna, Beherug N. *Research Methods in Marketing Management*. New Delhi: Tata McGraw-Hill Publishing Company Ltd, 1984.

Tripathi, P.C. *A Textbook of Research Methodology in Social Sciences*. New Delhi: Sultan Chand & Sons, 2007.

Zikmund, William G. *Business Research Methods*. Fort Worth: Dryden Press, 2000

13

CHAPTER

Analysis of Variance Techniques

Learning Objectives

By the end of the chapter, you should be able to:

1. Explain the meaning and assumptions of conducting analysis of variance.
2. Describe completely randomized design.
3. Apply SPSS in conducting a one-way analysis of variance.
4. Describe the randomized block design in two-way analysis of variance.
5. Illustrate the use of SPSS in two-way analysis of variance.
6. Explain a factorial design and the use of SPSS in the same.
7. Describe a Latin square design.

Rakesh Mehta, a student of MBA (HR programme) of a top business school took up his summer internship with NC Consultants—an HR consulting firm. He was assigned the task of comparing the average wages of unskilled workers in five cities of UP—Lucknow, Kanpur, Allahabad, Noida and Varanasi. Rakesh collected data on the wages of 100 unskilled workers from each of the five cities mentioned above. He took the mean of the wages of these workers, compared them and reported it to his supervisor. The supervisor, however, wanted to know whether there was any statistically significant difference in the wages in the five cities. Rakesh decided to compare the wages of two cities at a time using a Z-test and approached the supervisor for his approval. The supervisor told him that this method would involve 10 comparisons in order to accept or reject the hypothesis of equal mean wages of unskilled workers in five cities. The supervisor wanted a shorter method where this could be done in one go. Rakesh decided to consult his statistics professor, who advised him that he needed to learn a technique called analysis of variance which can help him carry out the job.

This chapter is devoted to the analysis of variance techniques as applied in different settings. It talks about the necessary assumptions that need to be satisfied before applying this technique.

WHAT IS ANOVA?

In the last chapter, we discussed the test of hypothesis concerning the equality of two population means using both the Z and t-tests. However, if there are more than two populations, the test for the equality of means could be carried out by considering

LEARNING OBJECTIVE 1
Explain the meaning and assumptions of conducting analysis of variance.

The **analysis of variance** technique helps to draw inferences whether the samples have been drawn from populations having the same mean.

two populations at a time. This would be a very cumbersome procedure. One easy way out could be to use the analysis of variance (ANOVA) technique. The technique helps in performing this test in one go and, therefore, is considered to be important technique of analysis for the researcher. Through this technique it is possible to draw inferences whether the samples have been drawn from populations having the same mean.

The technique has found applications in the fields of economics, psychology, sociology, business and industry. It becomes handy in situations where we want to compare the means of more than two populations. Some examples could be to compare:

- The mean cholesterol content of various diet foods.
- The average mileage of, say, five automobiles.
- The average telephone bill of households belonging to four different income groups and so on.

As mentioned earlier, considering all combinations of two populations at a time would require not only a large number of tests but could also be very time consuming. Further, it may not be possible to identify certain relationships, called the interaction effect, among the independent variables (factors). For details on the interaction effect, see Chapter 4. The technique of ANOVA becomes handy as it helps to compare the differences among the means of all the populations simultaneously.

R A Fisher developed the theory concerning ANOVA. The basic principle underlying the technique is that the total variation in the dependent variable is broken into two parts—one which can be attributed to some specific causes and the other that may be attributed to chance. The one which is attributed to the specific causes is called the variation between samples and the one which is attributed to chance is termed as the variation within samples. Therefore, in ANOVA, the total variance may be decomposed into various components corresponding to the sources of the variation. For example, the sales of chairs could differ because of the various styles and the sizes of the stores selling them. Similarly, one could study the differences among the various types of drugs for curing a specific disease or the differences in the cholesterol content of various diet foods or differences in the yield of crops due to varieties of seeds, fertilizers or soils.

In **ANOVA**, the total variance may be decomposed into various components corresponding to the sources of the variation.

In general, the ANOVA techniques investigate any number of factors which are supposed to influence the dependent variable of interest. It is also possible to investigate the differences in various categories within each of these factors. In ANOVA, the dependent variable in question is metric (interval or ratio scale), whereas the independent variables are categorical (nominal scale). If there is one independent variable (one factor) divided into various categories, we have one-way or one-factor analysis of variance. In the two-way or two-factor analysis of variance, two factors each divided into the various categories are involved. However, if the set of an independent variable consists of both the metric and the categorical variables, the technique is called analysis of covariance (ANOCOVA). The discussion of ANOCOVA is beyond the scope of this text.

In **analysis of variance**, the dependent variable in question is metric (interval or ratio scale) whereas the independent variables are categorical (normal scale).

In ANOVA, it is assumed that each of the samples is drawn from a normal population and each of these populations has an equal variance. Another assumption that is made is that all the factors except the one being tested are controlled (kept constant). Basically, two estimates of the population variances are made. One estimate is based upon between the samples and the other one is based upon within the samples. The two estimates of variances can be compared for their equality using F statistic (for details on comparing the equality of variances of the two populations, refer to any textbook on statistics). Below, we discuss the concept of ANOVA in various experimental designs. (You may like to refresh the discussion done on these designs in Chapter 4.)

COMPLETELY RANDOMIZED DESIGN IN A ONE-WAY ANOVA

LEARNING OBJECTIVE 2
Describe completely a randomized design.

Completely randomized design involves the testing of the equality of means of two or more groups. In this design, there is one dependent variable and one independent variable. The dependent variable is metric (interval/ratio scale) whereas the independent variable is categorical (nominal scale). A sample is drawn at random from each category of the independent variable. The size of the sample from each category could be equal or different. Let us consider a few examples to illustrate a one-way analysis of variance.

Numericals

Example 13.1

Suppose we want to compare the cholesterol contents of the four competing diet foods on the basis of the following data (in milligrams per package) which were obtained for three randomly taken 6-ounce packages of each of the diet foods:

Diet Food A	3.6	4.1	4.0
Diet Food B	3.1	3.2	3.9
Diet Food C	3.2	3.5	3.5
Diet Food D	3.5	3.8	3.8

We want to test whether the difference among the sample means can be attributed to chance at the 5 per cent level of significance.

Solution:

As explained earlier, the total variation in the data set can be expressed as a sum of the variations that can be attributed to specific sources (in this example, the various diet foods) plus the one which is attributed due to chance. The total variation in the data set is called the total sum of squares (TSS) and is computed as:

$$TSS = \sum_{i=1}^{k}\sum_{j=1}^{n} x_{ij}^2 - \frac{1}{kn}\bullet T_{\bullet\bullet}^2$$

where, (i=1, ... k and j=1, 2,....n)

x_{ij} = The jth observation of the ith sample (diet food)

$T_{\bullet\bullet}$ = Grand total of all the data

k = 4 (Number of diet foods)

n = 3 (Number of observations in each sample)

The term $\frac{1}{kn}\bullet T_{\bullet\bullet}^2$ is referred to as the correction factor. The variation between the sample means which is attributed to specific sources or causes is referred to as the treatment sum of squares (TrSS). This is computed using the following formula:

$$TrSS = \frac{1}{n}\sum_{i=1}^{k} T_{i\bullet}^2 - \frac{1}{kn}\bullet T_{\bullet\bullet}^2$$

where, $T_{i\bullet}$ = Total of observations for the ith treatment.

The variation within the sample, which is attributed to chance, is referred to as the error sum of squares (SSE). This could be computed by subtracting the treatment sum of squares from the total sum of squares. This is shown as:

$$SSE = TSS - TrSS = \left[\sum_{i=1}^{k}\sum_{j=1}^{n} x_{ij}^2 - \frac{1}{kn}\bullet T_{\bullet\bullet}^2\right] - \left[\frac{1}{n}\sum_{i=1}^{k} T_{i\bullet}^2 - \frac{1}{kn}\bullet T_{\bullet\bullet}^2\right]$$

In order to test the null hypothesis,

$$H_0 : \mu_A = \mu_B = \mu_C = \mu_D$$

against the alternative hypothesis

H_1 : At least two means are not equal
(Treatment means are not equal)

If there are **k treatments** then the corresponding degrees of freedom will become k – 1.

We test the equality of TrSS with SSE. The necessary workings required for this are presented in Table 13.1, which is called one-way analysis of the variance table. The first column of the table indicates the sources of variation. The second column lists the degrees of freedom. There are k treatments; therefore the corresponding degrees of freedom are k – 1. Similarly, the total number of observations in the data set is kn and therefore, the corresponding degrees of freedom are kn – 1. The degrees of freedom for errors are obtained by subtracting from the total degrees of freedom, the degrees of freedom corresponding to the treatment, i.e., (kn – 1) – (k – 1) = k (n – 1). The third column lists the sum of squares due to the various sources of variation. The fourth column lists the mean square due to treatment $\left(MSTr = \frac{TrSS}{k-1}\right)$ and the mean square due to error $\left(MSE = \frac{SSE}{k(n-1)}\right)$ obtained by dividing the corresponding sum of squares by their degrees of freedom. The last column indicates the F statistic given as the ratio of the two mean squares with k – 1 degrees of freedom for the numerator and k (n – 1) degrees of freedom for the denominator. For a given level of significance, α, the computed F statistic is compared with the table value of F with k – 1 degrees of freedom in the numerator and k (n – 1) degrees of the freedom for the denominator. If the computed F value is greater than the tabulated F value, the null hypothesis is rejected.

The required computations in case of Example 13.1 are given below:

$$k = 4, \quad n = 3$$

TABLE 13.1
One-way ANOVA

Source of Variation	Degrees of Freedom	Sum of Squares	Mean Square	$F_{k(n-1)}^{k-1}$
Treatments (Diet food)	k – 1	TrSS	$MSTr = \frac{TrSS}{k-1}$	$\frac{MSTr}{MSE}$
Error	k (n – 1)	SSE	$MSE = \frac{SSE}{k(n-1)}$	
Total	kn – 1	TSS		

$T_{\bullet\bullet}$	=	3.6 + 4.1 + 4.0 + 3.1 + 3.2 + 3.9 + 3.2 + 3.5 + 3.5 + 3.5 + 3.8 + 3.8	=	43.2
$T_{1\bullet}$	=	3.6 + 4.1 + 4.0	=	11.7
$T_{2\bullet}$	=	3.1 + 3.2 + 3.9	=	10.2
$T_{3\bullet}$	=	3.2 + 3.5 + 3.5	=	10.2
$T_{4\bullet}$	=	3.5 + 3.8 + 3.8	=	11.1
$\sum_{i=j}^{4}\sum_{j=1}^{3} x_{ij}^2$	=	$(3.6)^2 + (4.1)^2 + (4.0)^2 + (3.1)^2 + (3.2)^2 + (3.9)^2 + (3.2)^2 + (3.5)^2 + (3.5)^2 + (3.5)^2 + (3.8)^2 + (3.8)^2$	=	156.70

$$TSS = \sum_{i=j}^{4}\sum_{j=1}^{3} x_{ij}^2 - \frac{1}{kn} \bullet T_{..}^2$$

$$= 156.70 - \frac{1}{12}(43.2)^2 = 1.18$$

$$TrSS = \frac{1}{n}\sum_{i=1}^{4} T_{1\bullet}^2 - \frac{1}{kn} \bullet T_{..}^2$$

$$= \frac{1}{3}[11.7^2 + 10.2^2 + 10.2^2 + 11.1^2] - \frac{1}{12}(43.2)^2 = 0.54$$

$$SSE = TSS - TrSS = 1.18 - 0.54 = 0.64$$

The above results corresponding to Example 13.1 could be set up in the ANOVA Table 13.2.

TABLE 13.2 ANOVA table for Example 13.1

Source of Variation	Degrees of Freedom	Sum of Squares	Mean Square	F_8^3
Treatments (Diet Food)	3	0.54	0.18	2.25
Error	8	0.64	0.08	
Total	11	1.18		

Assuming the level of significance to be 5 per cent, the table value of F with 3 degrees of freedom in the numerator and 8 degrees of freedom in the denominator equals 4.07 (See Annexure 4 at the end of the book). Since the computed F is less than the tabulated F, there is not enough evidence to reject the null hypothesis. Therefore, the difference in the cholesterol contents in the four diet foods could be attributed to chance.

Strength of Association

There is a statistic which is used for measuring the strength of association, called ρ (rho). Rho is computed as the ratio of the sum of squares for the treatment (TrSS) to the total sum of squares (TSS). In Example 13.1, the value of ρ is given by 0.54/1.18 = 0.458. This means 45.8 per cent of the variation in the cholesterol content is explained by the treatment (diet foods).

It is known that the sample value (ρ) tends to be upward biased; it is useful to have an estimate of the population strength of association (ω^2, omega squared) between the treatment (diet foods) and the dependent variable (cholesterol content). A sample estimate of this population value can be computed as:

$$\hat{\omega}^2 = \frac{TrSS - (k-1)MSE}{TSS + MSE}$$

$$= \frac{0.54 - 3(0.08)}{1.18 + 0.08}$$

$$= \frac{0.54 - 0.24}{1.26}$$

$$= \frac{0.30}{1.26} = 0.238$$

This means that 23.8 per cent of total variation in the data (cholesterol content) is explained for by the treatment (diet food).

As mentioned earlier, the size of the sample from each category (treatment) need not be same. If there are n_i observations corresponding to i^{th} treatment, the computing formula for the sum of squares would look like:

$$TSS = \sum_{i=1}^{k} \sum_{j=1}^{n_i} x_{ij}^2 - \frac{1}{N} \bullet T_{..}^2$$

$$TrSS = \sum_{i=1}^{k} \frac{T_{i.}^2}{n_i} - \frac{1}{N} T_{..}^2$$

$$SSE = TSS - TrSS$$

where, $N = n_1 + n_2 + \ldots. + n_k$

The total number of degrees of freedom in the case is N – 1, and the degrees of freedom are k – 1 for the treatments and N – k for the error. Let us consider a few more examples.

Example 13.2

The following are the number of words per minute which a secretary typed on several occasions on three different typewriters.

Typewriter 1	71	78	70	69	77	72	65	69
Typewriter 2	74	76	72	70	69	68	72	73
Typewriter 3	70	72	66	64	63	67	69	70

Test whether the differences among the mean of the three samples (typewriters) can be attributed to chance. You may use a 5 per cent level of significance.

Solution:

$H_0 : \mu_1 = \mu_2 = \mu_3$ (the mean difference in the typing speed between the three typewriters can be attributed to chance.)

H_1 : At least two means are not equal

$K = 3, \quad n = 8$

$T_{..}$	=	71 + 78 + 70 + 69 + 77 + 72 + 65 + 69 + 74 + 76 + 72 + 70 + 69 + 68 + 72 + 73 + 70 + 72 + 66 + 64 + 63 + 67 + 69 + 70	=	1686
$T_{1.}$	=	71 + 78 + 70 + 69 + 77 + 72 + 65 + 69	=	571
$T_{2.}$	=	74 + 76 + 72 + 70 + 69 + 68 + 72 + 73	=	574
$T_{3.}$	=	70 + 72 + 66 + 64 + 63 + 67 + 69 + 70	=	541
$\sum_{i=j}^{3} \sum_{j=1}^{8} x_{ij}^2$	=	$(71)^2 + (78)^2 + (70)^2 + (69)^2 + (77)^2 + (72)^2 + (65)^2 + (69)^2 + (74)^2 + (76)^2 + (72)^2 + (70)^2 + (69)^2 + (68)^2 + (72)^2 + (73)^2 + (70)^2 + (72)^2 + (66)^2 + (64)^2 + (63)^2 + (67)^2 + (69)^2 + (70)^2$	=	118774

$$TSS = \sum_{i=1}^{3} \sum_{j=1}^{8} x_{ij}^2 - \frac{1}{kn} \bullet T_{..}^2$$

$$= [71^2 + 78^2 + \ldots\ldots 69^2 + 70^2] - \frac{1}{3 \times 8}(1686)^2$$

$$= 118774 - 118441.5 = 332.5$$

$$TrSS = \frac{1}{n} \sum_{i=1}^{3} T_{i.}^2 - \frac{1}{kn} \bullet T_{..}^2$$

$$= \frac{1}{8}[571^2 + 574^2 + 541^2] - \frac{1}{3 \times 8}(1686)^2$$

$$= 118524.8 - 118441.5 = 83.25$$

$$SSE = TSS - TrSS = 332.5 - 83.25 = 249.25$$

The one-way ANOVA table in the case of Example 13.2 can be set up as shown in Table 13.3.

TABLE 13.3
One-way ANOVA for Example 13.2

Source of Variation	Degrees of Freedom	Sum of Squares	Mean Square	F^2_{21}
Typewriter (Between groups)	2	83.25	41.625	3.507
Error (with groups)	21	249.25	11.869	
Total	23	332.50		

The computed value of $F^2_{21} = 3.507$. The table value of F^2_{21} with 5 per cent level of significance equals 3.47. As the computed F statistic is greater than the corresponding tabulated value, we reject the null hypothesis. Therefore, the difference in the average number of the words typed on the three typewriters cannot be attributed to chance.

Once the null hypothesis is rejected, it will be interesting to examine in which typewriter the number of words typed per minute is significantly higher compared to the other typewriter(s). This issue would be taken up later. Let us now, consider another example where the size of the sample from each treatment is different.

Example 13.3

The following are the number of kilometres/litre which a test driver with three different types of cars has obtained randomly on different occasions.

Car 1	15	14.5	14.8	14.9		
Car 2	13	12.5	13.6	13.8	14	
Car 3	12.8	13.2	12.7	12.6	12.9	13

Using a 5 per cent level of significance, perform a one-way ANOVA to examine the hypothesis that the difference in the average mileage in the three types of cars can be attributed to chance.

Solution:

$H_0: \mu_1 = \mu_2 = \mu_3$ (Average mileage in the three types of cars is the same)

H_1 : At least two types of cars do not have the same mileage.

$$K = 3, \quad n_1 = 4, \quad n_2 = 5, \quad n_3 = 6$$

$$N = n_1 + n_2 + n_3 = 4 + 5 + 6 = 15$$

$T_{..}$	=	15 + 14.5 + 14.8 + 14.9 + 13 + 12.5 + 13.6 + 13.8 + 14 + 12.8 + 13.2 + 12.7 + 12.6 + 12.9 + 13	=	203.3
$T_{1.}$	=	15 + 14.5 + 14.8 + 14.9	=	59.2
$T_{2.}$	=	13 + 12.5 + 13.6 + 13.8 + 14	=	66.9
$T_{3.}$	=	12.8 + 13.2 + 12.7 + 12.6 + 12.9 + 13	=	77.2
$\sum_{i=1}^{3}\sum_{j=1}^{ni} x_{ij}^2$	=	$(15)^2 + (14.5)^2 + (14.8)^2 + (14.9)^2 + (13)^2 + (12.5)^2 + (13.6)^2 + (13.8)^2 + (14)^2 + (12.8)^2 + (13.2)^2 + (12.7)^2 + (12.6)^2 + (12.9)^2 + (13)^2$	=	2766.49

$$TSS = \sum_{i=1}^{3}\sum_{j=1}^{ni} x_{ij}^2 - \frac{1}{N} \bullet T_{..}^2$$

$$= 2766.49 - \frac{1}{15}(203.3)^2$$

$$= 2766.49 - 2755.393 = 11.097$$

$$TrSS = \sum_{i=1}^{3} \frac{T_{i\bullet}^2}{n_i} - \frac{1}{N} T_{\bullet\bullet}^2$$

$$= \left[\frac{59.2^2}{4} + \frac{66.9^2}{5} + \frac{77.2^2}{6} \right] - \frac{1}{15}(203.3)^2$$

$$= 2764.5886 - 2755.3926 = 9.196$$

$$SSE = TSS - TrSS = 11.097 - 9.196 = 1.901$$

The ANOVA table in the case of Example 13.3 can be set up as shown in Table 13.4.

TABLE 13.4 One-way ANOVA for Example 13.3

Source of Variation	Degrees of Freedom	Sum of Squares	Mean Square	F_{12}^2
Treatments (Between groups)	2	9.196	4.598	29.02
Error (within groups)	12	1.901	0.158	
Total	14	11.097		

The computed F statistics equals 29.02. The table value of F with 2 degrees of freedom in the numerator and 12 degrees of freedom in the denominator at a 5 per cent level of significance is given by 3.89. As the computed F statistic is greater than the table F value, the null hypothesis is rejected. Therefore, the average mileage in these types of cars is statistically different. It would, therefore, be interesting to examine which car significantly gives a higher mileage than the other. This will be taken up in the next section.

CONCEPT CHECK

1. Define ANOVA.
2. State an example to illustrate the completely randomized design in a one-way ANOVA.

USE OF SPSS IN CONDUCTING ONE-WAY ANOVA

LEARNING OBJECTIVE 3
Apply SPSS in conducting a one-way ANOVA.

The SPSS software can be used to conduct a one-way ANOVA. For the purpose of illustration, Examples 13.1 to 13.3 would be reworked. The SPSS instructions for conducting a one-way ANOVA are given in Appendix 13.1. In case of Example 13.1, the data in SPSS format would be as given in Table 13.5.

The variable CC denotes the cholesterol content which is the dependent variable. The DF denotes diet foods which is an independent variable (factor) and is coded as 1 = Diet Food A, 2 = Diet Food B, 3 = Diet Food C, and 4 = Diet Food D.

TABLE 13.5 Data for Example 13.1 in SPSS format

S. No.	CC	Diet Food
1	3.6	1
2	4.1	1
3	4	1
4	3.1	2
5	3.2	2
6	3.9	2
7	3.2	3
8	3.5	3
9	3.5	3
10	3.5	4
11	3.8	4
12	3.8	4

TABLE 13.6
ANOVA table for Example 13.1

Cholesterol Content

	Sum of Squares	Degrees of Freedom	Mean Square	F	Sig.
Between Groups (Diet Food)	0.540	3	0.180	2.250	0.160
Within Groups (Error)	0.640	8	0.080		
Total	1.180	11			

The hypothesis to be tested is:

H_0 : $\mu_A = \mu_B = \mu_C = \mu_D$

H_1 : At least two means are not equal.

The SPSS output for the Example 13.1 is given in Table 13.6.

It could be noted that the results in the above table are identical to when the problem was worked out manually. The p value (sig.) for this problem is 0.160, which is greater than α = 0.05, the level of significance. Therefore, there is not enough evidence to reject the null hypothesis. This means that the difference in the cholesterol content of various diet foods could be attributed to chance.

Let us now attempt Example 13.2 using the SPSS software. As mentioned before, the instructions for conducting a one-way ANOVA are given in Appendix 13.1. The data for Example 13.2 in the SPSS spreadsheet would appear as given in Table 13.7.

X = Number of words typed per minute.

Type = The type of the typewriter which takes value 1, 2 or 3 depending upon the typewriter which the secretary used for typewriting.

The hypothesis to be tested in Example 13.2 is reproduced below:

H_0 : $\mu_1 = \mu_2 = \mu_3$

H_1 : At least two means are not equal.

TABLE 13.7
Data for Example 13.2 in SPSS format

S. No.	X	Type
1	71	1
2	78	1
3	70	1
4	69	1
5	77	1
6	72	1
7	65	1
8	69	1
9	74	2
10	76	2
11	72	2
12	70	2
13	69	2
14	68	2
15	72	2
16	73	2
17	70	3
18	72	3
19	66	3
20	64	3
21	63	3
22	67	3
23	69	3
24	70	3

The SPSS output for Example 13.2 is given in Tables 13.8 and 13.9.

TABLE 13.8 Descriptive statistics for Example 13.2

Typing Speed

Typewriter	N	Mean	Std. Deviation	Std. Error	95% Confidence Interval for Mean		Minimum	Maximum
					Lower Bound	Upper Bound		
Typewriter 1	8	71.3750	4.30739	1.52289	67.7739	74.9761	65.00	78.00
Typewriter 2	8	71.7500	2.65922	0.94017	69.5268	73.9732	68.00	76.00
Typewriter 3	8	67.6250	3.15945	1.11704	64.9836	70.2664	63.00	72.00
Total	24	70.2500	3.80217	0.77612	68.6445	71.8555	63.00	78.00

TABLE 13.9 ANOVA table for Example 13.2

Typing Speed

	Sum of Squares	Degrees of Freedom	Mean Square	F	Sig.
Between Groups	83.250	2	41.625	3.507	0.049
Within Groups	249.250	21	11.869		
Total	332.500	23			

It may be noted that the results in Table 13.9 are identical to when this problem was worked out manually. The p value for the problem works out to be 0.049, which is less than 0.05, the assumed level of significance. Therefore, the null hypothesis is rejected. As the null hypothesis is rejected, the interest would be in examining which of the typewriters have speeds that are significantly different. To carry out this, post hoc analysis is carried out. Example 13.4 illustrates this.

Example 13.4

The following set of data is obtained for the sales of a product corresponding to three price levels—₹39, ₹44, and ₹49. The data pertains to five randomly selected retail stores where the product was sold.

Price Level	Sales (in ₹ lakhs)				
₹39	8	12	10	9	11
₹44	7	10	6	8	9
₹49	4	8	7	9	7

Test whether the difference in sales corresponding to various price levels can be attributed to chance at 5 per cent level of significance. In case of significant difference, carry out further analysis.

Solution:

In this example, dependent variable is sales and the independent variable is price level. A one-way analysis of variance was carried out using SPSS software. The results are presented in the ANOVA Table 13.10.

TABLE 13.10 ANOVA Table for Example 13.4

Sales

	Sum of Squares	df	Mean Square	F	Sig.
Between Groups	23.333	2	11.667	4.118	0.043
Within Groups	34.000	12	2.833		
Total	57.333	14			

The hypothesis to be tested for this example is

$$H_0 : \mu_1 = \mu_2 = \mu_3$$
$$H_1 : \text{At least two } \mu\text{s are different.}$$

(μ_1, μ_2, μ_3 are the average sales corresponding to price levels of ₹39, ₹44, and ₹49 respectively.)

In the above ANOVA table, it is seen that p value equals 0.043, which is less than 0.05, the assumed level of significance. Therefore, we reject the null hypothesis. This means the difference in the sales due to various price levels cannot be attributed to chance.

Now that the null hypothesis is rejected, we would be interested in examining which pair of prices are significantly different. For this, post hoc analysis is carried out. To carry out the post hoc analysis, we follow the instructions as given in Appendix – 13.1. The results would be obtained as presented in Table 13.11.

TABLE 13.11 Multiple comparisons for Example 13.4

(I) Price	(J) Price	Mean Difference (I–J)	Std. Error	Sig.	95% Confidence Interval	
					Lower Bound	Upper Bound
₹39	₹44	2.00000	1.06458	0.187	–0.8402	4.8402
	₹49	3.00000(*)	1.06458	0.038	0.1598	5.8402
₹44	₹39	–2.00000	1.06458	0.187	–4.8402	0.8402
	₹49	1.00000	1.06458	0.627	–1.8402	3.8402
₹49	₹39	–3.00000(*)	1.06458	0.038	–5.8402	–0.1598
	₹44	–1.00000	1.06458	0.627	–3.8402	1.8402

* The mean difference is significant at the 0.05 level.

The above table compares the sales corresponding to price of ₹39 with ₹44. No statistically significant difference is found as the p value works out to be 0.187 although in absolute terms, the sales for price ₹39 is more than for ₹44. The difference is 2.00 as indicated in the column 'mean difference'. Similarly, the sales for price of ₹39 is compared with corresponding sales for price of ₹49 and p value is found as 0.038, which is less than the level of significance of 0.05. This indicates that there is a significant difference in the sales corresponding to price of ₹39 and ₹49. Further, the difference in sales is positive.

Similarly, sales corresponding to price of ₹44 is compared with ₹39 and ₹49 and we find no significant difference in the sales. The same exercise is carried for comparing the sales corresponding to the price of ₹49 with price of ₹39 and ₹44. It is seen that there is a significant difference in the sales for price of ₹49 with that of ₹39 as the p value is 0.038, which is less than the assumed level of significance of 0.05. The difference is –3.00, as indicated in the column 'mean difference'. However, no difference is found in the sales corresponding to ₹49 and ₹44.

From the above discussion, it is seen that the sales corresponding to price of ₹39 is the highest, followed by the sales for price of ₹44 and ₹49 respectively. Further, there is a significant difference in sales corresponding to the prices of ₹39 and ₹49.

Table 13.12 presents the homogeneous subsets.

TABLE 13.12 Homogeneous subsets for Example 13.4

Tukey's HSD Test[a]

Price	N	Subset for alpha = 0.05	
		1	2
₹49	5	7.0000	
₹44	5	8.0000	8.0000
₹39	5		10.0000
Sig.		0.627	0.187

Means for groups in homogeneous subsets are displayed.
[a]Uses Harmonic Mean Sample Size = 5.000.

In subset 1, it is seen that the sales corresponding to price of ₹49 and ₹44 are put in one group and this group is homogeneous in the sense that the p value for this is equal to 0.627. This means that there is no difference in the sales corresponding to these prices.

The sales corresponding to ₹44 and ₹39 are kept in the second homogeneous group. The group is homogeneous because there is no statistical difference in their sales as the p value for this is given as 0.187.

To conclude, we reject the hypothesis of no difference in sales due to various price levels. As per the post hoc analysis, the statistical difference in sales is found corresponding to price levels of ₹39 and ₹49. There are two homogenous subsets—one for the sales corresponding to price levels of ₹49 and ₹44 and the remaining one corresponding to price of ₹44 and ₹39.

Example 13.3 could also be worked out using the SPSS software as was done for Examples 13.1 and 13.2. It is left to the reader to work out this exercise.

RANDOMIZED BLOCK DESIGN IN TWO-WAY ANOVA

LEARNING OBJECTIVE 4
Describe the randomized block design in two-way analysis of variance.

In Example 13.1, it could not be shown that there really is a significant difference in the average cholesterol content of the four diet foods. The results were not statistically different because there was a considerable difference in the values within each of the samples resulting in a large experimental error. However, if we have additional information that each of the value was randomly measured in the three different laboratories in such a way that the first value of each sample came from laboratory 1, the second value from laboratory 2, and the third value from laboratory 3. (the random assignment of test units to labs) In such a case, a two way Analysis of variance is suggested. We had earlier partitioned the total sum of squares into two components—one which is due to the differences between the sample (treatment sum of squares) and the other one due to the differences within the samples (error sum of squares). Now, this error sum of square includes the sum of squares due to laboratories (called blocks) as an extraneous factor. In two-way analysis of variance, we remove the effect of the extraneous factors (laboratories or blocks) from the error sum of squares. Therefore, the total sum of square is partitioned into three components—one due to treatment, second due to block, and the third one due to chance (called the error sum of squares). It may be noted that the total sum of squares (TSS) and the treatment sum of squares (TrSS) would remain the same as computed earlier in Example 13.1. In addition, we will have another component called Block sum of squares (SSB), which is due to different laboratories and is computed as:

Block sum of squares is computed as:

$$SSB = \frac{1}{k} \cdot \sum_{j=1}^{n} T_{\cdot j}^2 - \frac{1}{kn} \cdot T_{\cdot\cdot}^2$$

$$SSB = \frac{1}{k} \cdot \sum_{j=1}^{n} T_{\cdot j}^2 - \frac{1}{kn} \cdot T_{\cdot\cdot}^2$$

where, $T_{\bullet j}$ = Total of the values in the jth block.
The error sum of squares would be computed as:

$$SSE = TSS - TrSS - SSB$$

There will be two hypotheses to be tested:

I. *Diet Food*

$H_0 : \mu_A = \mu_B = \mu_C = \mu_D$
H_1 : At least the two means are not same.

II. *Blocks or Labs*

$H_0 : \nu_1 = \nu_2 = \nu_3$
(Average cholesterol content in the three labs is same.)
H_1 : At least two means are not same.

Now, we would need to test the equality of TrSS with SSE and SSB with SSE. The necessary working required for this are presented in Table 13.13 called Two-way Analysis of variance table.

TABLE 13.13
Two-way ANOVA

Source of Variation	Degrees of Freedom	Sum of Squares	Mean Square	F
Treatments	k – 1	TrSS	$MSTr = \frac{TrSS}{k-1}$	$F^{k-1}_{(k-1)(n-1)} = \frac{MSTr}{MSE}$
Blocks	n – 1	SSB	$MSB = \frac{SSB}{n-1}$	$F^{n-1}_{(k-1)(n-1)} = \frac{MSB}{MSE}$
Error	(k – 1) (n – 1)	SSE	$MSE = \frac{SSE}{(k-1)(n-1)}$	
Total	kn – 1	TSS		

The various columns of the above table are filled up in the same fashion as was done for Table 13.1. Example 13.1 can be rewritten as Example 13.5.

Example 13.5

Suppose in Example 13.1, the measurement of the cholesterol content was performed in three different laboratories. The first value of each sample came from one laboratory, the second value came from another laboratory, and the third value came from a third laboratory. The data is presented below:

Diet Food	Laboratory		
	One	Two	Three
Diet Food A	3.6	4.1	4.0
Diet Food B	3.1	3.2	3.9
Diet Food C	3.2	3.5	3.5
Diet Food D	3.5	3.8	3.8

Perform a two-way ANOVA using a 0.05 level of significance.

Solution:

There will be two hypotheses to be tested in this case; one corresponding to the treatment (diet food) and the other corresponding to laboratories (blocks). These are listed below:

I. *Diet Food*

$H_0 : \mu_A = \mu_B = \mu_C = \mu_D$ (Average cholesterol content of the four diet foods is same.)

H_1 : At least two means are not same.

II. *Blocks or labs*

$H_0 : v_1 = v_2 = v_3$ (Average cholesterol content in the three labs is same.)

H_1 : At least two means are not same.

The TSS and TrSS here would be the same as computed in Example 13.1. As mentioned earlier, the block sum of square would be required in this problem using the formula:

$$SSB = \frac{1}{k} \bullet \sum_{j=1}^{n} T_{\bullet j}^2 - \frac{1}{kn} \bullet T_{\bullet\bullet}^2$$

where, $T_{\bullet j}$ = Total of the values in the jth block.

The error sum of squares would be obtained as:

$$SSE = TSS - TrSS - SSB$$

The required computations for the two-way ANOVA are as under:

$$T_{\bullet 1} = 3.6 + 3.1 + 3.2 + 3.5 = 13.4$$
$$T_{\bullet 2} = 4.1 + 3.2 + 3.5 + 3.8 = 14.6$$
$$T_{\bullet 3} = 4.0 + 3.9 + 3.5 + 3.8 = 15.2$$

$$SSB = \frac{1}{k} \bullet \sum_{j=1}^{n} T_{\bullet j}^2 - \frac{1}{kn} \bullet T_{\bullet\bullet}^2$$
$$= \frac{1}{4}[13.4^2 + 14.6^2 + + 15.2^2] - \frac{1}{12}(43.2)^2$$
$$= 155.94 - 155.52$$
$$= 0.42$$

We have already computed in Example 13.1, the values of TSS & TrSS as under:

$$TSS = 1.18, \quad TrSS = 0.54$$

Therefore,

$$SSE = TSS - TrSS - SSB$$
$$= 1.18 - 0.54 - 0.42$$
$$= 0.22$$

We note that the SSE in Example 13.1 was 0.64, whereas here it is 0.22. This is because the earlier SSE has been partitioned into two components, namely, the block sum of squares (SSB) having a value of 0.42 resulting in 0.22 as the new error sum of squares (SSE). The required results for the testing of the two hypotheses are presented in the ANOVA Table 13.14.

TABLE 13.14
Two-way ANOVA table for Example 13.5

Source of Variation	Degrees of Freedom	Sum of Squares	Mean Square	F
Treatments (Diet Food)	3	0.54	0.18	$F_6^3 = \frac{0.18}{0.0367} = 4.90$
Block (Laborataries)	2	0.42	0.21	$F_6^2 = \frac{0.21}{0.0367} = 5.72$
Error (Chance)	6	0.22	0.0367	
Total	11	1.18		

The table value of F_6^3 and F_6^2 at a 5 per cent level of significance is given by 4.76 and 5.14 respectively. The corresponding sample F values for both are 4.90 and 5.72. Since the computed F values are greater than the corresponding table values, the null hypothesis is rejected in both the cases. Therefore, it can be concluded that there is a difference in the average cholesterol content due to various diet foods and because of the laboratories where the measurements were taken. Let us consider one more example.

Example 13.6

The following table presents the number of the defective pieces produced by three workmen operating in turn on three different machines:

	Machine 1	Machine 2	Machine 3
Workman 1	27	34	23
Workman 2	29	32	25
Workman 3	22	30	22

Conduct a two-way ANOVA to test at 5 per cent level of significance, whether:

(i) The difference among the means obtained for the three workmen can be attributed to chance.

(ii) The differences among the means obtained for the three machines can be attributed to chance.

Solution:

The following two hypotheses are to be tested:

I. *Workman*

$H_0 : \mu_1 = \mu_2 = \mu_3$ (Average numbers of the defectives produced by the three workmen are the same.)

H_1 : At least two means are different.

II. *Machines*

$H_0 : \nu_1 = \nu_2 = \nu_3$ (Average numbers of the defectives produced by the three machines are the same.)

H_1 : At least two means are different.

Using the notations explained in this chapter, we may compute:

$$T_{\bullet\bullet} = 27 + 34 + 23 + 29 + 32 + 25 + 22 + 30 + 22 = 244$$
$$T_{1\bullet} = 27 + 34 + 23 = 84$$
$$T_{2\bullet} = 29 + 32 + 25 = 86$$
$$T_{3\bullet} = 22 + 30 + 22 = 74$$
$$T_{\bullet 1} = 27 + 29 + 22 = 78$$
$$T_{\bullet 2} = 34 + 32 + 30 = 96$$
$$T_{\bullet 3} = 23 + 25 + 22 = 70$$

$$\sum_{i=1}^{k}\sum_{j=1}^{n} x_{ij}^2 = (27)^2 + (34)^2 + (23)^2 + (29)^2 + (32)^2 + (25)^2 + (22)^2 + (30)^2 + (22)^2 = 6772$$

$$TSS = \sum_{i=1}^{k}\sum_{j=1}^{n} x_{ij}^2 - \frac{1}{kn} \bullet T_{\bullet\bullet}^2$$

$$= 6772 - \frac{1}{9}(244)^2$$

$$= 6772 - 6615.111$$
$$= 156.889$$

$$\text{TrSS} = \frac{1}{n}\sum_{i=1}^{k} T_{i\bullet}^2 - \frac{1}{kn} \bullet T_{\bullet\bullet}^2$$

$$= \frac{1}{3}[84^2 + 86^2 + 74^2] - \frac{1}{9}(244)^2$$

$$= \frac{19928}{3} - 6615.111$$

$$= 27.556$$

$$\text{SSB} = \frac{1}{k}\sum_{j=1}^{n} T_{\bullet j}^2 - \frac{1}{kn} \bullet T_{\bullet\bullet}^2$$

$$= \frac{1}{3}[78^2 + 96^2 + 70^2] - \frac{1}{9}(244)^2$$

$$= 6733.333 - 6615.111$$
$$= 118.222$$

$$\text{SSE} = \text{TSS} - \text{TrSS} - \text{SSB}$$
$$= 156.889 - 27.556 - 118.22$$
$$= 11.111$$

To test the two hypotheses, the results can be summarized in the form of a two-way ANOVA as shown in Table 13.15.

TABLE 13.15 Results of two-way ANOVA

Source of Variation	Degrees of Freedom	Sum of Squares	Mean Square	F
Treatments (Workmen)	2	27.556	13.778	$F_4^2 = 4.96$
Block (Machines)	2	118.222	59.111	$F_4^2 = 21.28$
Error	4	11.111	2.778	
Total	8	156.889		

The table value of F with 2 degrees of freedom at the numerator and 4 in the denominator equals 6.94. The computed values of F_4^2 are 4.96 and 21.28 for the 1st and the 2nd hypothesis respectively. Therefore, there is not enough evidence to reject the null hypothesis in the first case whereas it is rejected for the 2nd case. This means that there is no difference in the average number of the defectives produced by three workmen, whereas there is a significant difference in the average number of the defectives produced by the three machines. Thus, it can be concluded that the efficiency of the three machines to produce good items is different.

USE OF SPSS IN CONDUCTING TWO-WAY ANOVA

LEARNING OBJECTIVE 5
Illustrate the use of SPSS in two-way analysis of variance.

The SPSS software can be used to conduct a two-way ANOVA. The necessary instructions for this are given in Appendix 13.2. For the purpose of illustration, let us consider Examples 13.5 and 13.6.

In Example 13.5, there were two hypotheses to be tested, which are reproduced below:

I. *Diet Food*

H_0 : $\mu_A = \mu_B = \mu_C = \mu_D$ (Average cholesterol content of the four diet foods is the same.)

H_1 : At least two means are not the same.

II. *Blocks or Labs*

H_0 : $\nu_1 = \nu_2 = \nu_3$ (Average cholesterol content measured in the three labs is the same.)

H_1 : At least two means are not the same.

The data in SPSS format would be as given in Table 13.16.

TABLE 13.16
Data for Example 13.5 in SPSS format

CC	DF	LAB
3.6	1	1
4.1	1	2
4	1	3
3.1	2	1
3.2	2	2
3.9	2	3
3.2	3	1
3.5	3	2
3.5	3	3
3.5	4	1
3.8	4	2
3.8	4	3

where, CC = Cholesterol content

DF = Diet Food *which takes values*

1 = Diet Food A

2 = Diet Food B

3 = Diet Food C

4 = Diet Food D

LAB = Laboratory *which takes values*

1 = Laboratory 1

2 = Laboratory 2

3 = Laboratory 3

The SPSS results are given in Table 13.17.

TABLE 13.17
Results of two-way ANOVA for Example 13.5

Dependent Variable: Cholesterol Content

Source	Type III Sum of Squares	Degrees of Freedom	Mean Square	F	Sig.
Corrected Model	0.960[a]	5	0.192	5.236	0.034
Intercept	155.520	1	155.520	4241.455	0.000
DF	0.540	3	0.180	4.909	0.047
Lab	0.420	2	0.210	5.727	0.041
Error	0.220	6	0.037		
Total	156.700	12			
Corrected Total	1.180	11			

[a] R-squared = 0.814 (Adjusted R-squared = 0.658).

The results in the above table are exactly the same as when this exercise was carried out manually. The p value corresponding to both hypotheses is less than 0.05, the level of significance. This means that there is enough evidence to reject both of them. This helps us conclude that the average content in the four diet foods is different and the difference is also due to the three laboratories where the measurements were taken.

Now let us consider Example 13.6. The two hypotheses to be tested are:

I. *Workmen*

$H_0 : \mu_1 = \mu_2 = \mu_3$ (Average numbers of defectives produced by three workmen are the same.)

H_1: At least two means are different.

II. *Machine*

$H_0: \nu_1 = \nu_2 = \nu_3$ (Average numbers of defectives produced by three machines are the same.)

H_1: At least two means are different.

The data in the SPSS format would be as given in Table 13.18.

TABLE 13.18 Data for Example 13.6 in SPSS format

Y	M	W
27	1	1
29	1	2
22	1	3
34	2	1
32	2	2
30	2	3
23	3	1
25	3	2
22	3	3

where, Y = Number of defective pieces

M = Machine *which takes values*

1 = Machine 1

2 = Machine 2

3 = Machine 3

W = Workman *which takes values*

1 = Workman 1

2 = Workman 2

3 = Workman 3

The SPSS results are given in Table 13.19.

The results in Table 13.19 are exactly similar to when the problem was worked out manually. The p values corresponding to the hypothesis for the machines and workmen are 0.007 and 0.083 respectively. The assumed level of significance is 0.05 As the p value corresponding to the hypothesis for the machines is less than the

TABLE 13.19 Results of two-way ANOVA for Example 13.6

Dependent Variable: No. of Defectives

Source	Type III Sum of Squares	Degrees of Freedom	Mean Square	F	Sig.
Corrected Model	145.778[a]	4	36.444	13.120	0.014
Intercept	6615.111	1	6615.111	2381.440	0.000
M	118.222	2	59.111	21.280	0.007
W	27.556	2	13.778	4.960	0.083
Error	11.111	4	2.778		
Total	6772.000	9			
Corrected Total	156.889	8			

[a] R-Squared = 0.929 (Adjusted R-Squared = 0.858).

level of significance, the null hypothesis in such a case is rejected. This means that the average number of defects for various machines is different. For the hypothesis, corresponding to the workmen, the null hypothesis is accepted. Therefore, it can be concluded that the average number of the defectives items produced by the three workmen does not vary significantly.

FACTORIAL DESIGN

LEARNING OBJECTIVE 6
Explain a factorial design and the use of SPSS in the same.

In the factorial design, the dependent variable is the interval or the ratio scale and there are two or more independent variables which are nominal scale. In the factorial design, it is possible to examine the interaction between the variables. If there are two independent variables each having three categories, there would be a total of nine interactions. The details on this are already explained in Chapter 4 (Experimental Research Designs). Let us consider an illustration to explain factorial design.

It is generally observed that there are differences in the pay packages offered to fresh MBA graduates. The variations could be either due to the type of business school where they have studied or it could be due to their area of specialization. The variation can also be due to an interaction between the business school and the area of specialization. For example, the specialization in finance at one business school might fetch a better package. All these presumptions could be tested with the help of the factorial design explained with the help of the following example.

Example 13.7

The following data refers to the salary package (in ₹ lakhs) offered to MBA graduates with different specializations and having studied at four different business schools. For the sake of simplification, only two students are taken for each interaction between the institute and field of specialization.

Specialization	Business School			
	I	II	III	IV
Marketing	6	4	8	6
	5	5	6	4
Finance	7	6	6	9
	6	7	7	8
Operations	8	5	10	9
	7	5	9	10

Test the hypothesis: (i) whether the difference between the pay packages offered by different business schools can be attributed to chance, (ii) average pay packages by all specializations are equal, (iii) the average pay package for 12 interactions are equal.

You may use a 5 per cent level of significance.

Solution:
The following set of hypotheses is required to be tested.

Business schools:

H_0 : Average pay package for all the institutions are equal.

H_1 : Average pay package for all the institutions are not equal.

Specialization:

H_0 : Average pay package for all the specializations are equal.

H_1 : Average pay package for all the socializations are not equal.

Interaction:

H_0 : Average pay package for all 12 interactions are equal.

H_1 : Average pay package for all 12 interactions are not equal.

Let us compute the following:

$$\text{Correction factor (CF)} = \frac{(\text{Sum of all observations})^2}{\text{Total number of observations}}$$

$$= \frac{(163)^2}{24} = \frac{26569}{24} = 1107.04$$

Total sum of squares= (Sum of squares of observations) – CF

$$= 6^2 + 4^2 + 8^2 + 6^2 + - - - + 7^2 + 5^2 + 9^2 + 10^2 - 1107.04$$

$$= 1179 - 1107.04$$

$$= 71.96$$

Sum of squares due to specialization (row)/SSR

$$= \frac{44^2}{8} + \frac{56^2}{8} + \frac{63^2}{8} - CF$$

$$= 1130.13 - 1107.04$$

$$= 23.08$$

where,

Sum total for Marketing = 44

Sum total for Finance = 56

Sum total for Operations = 63

Sum of squares due to school (column)/SSC

$$= \frac{39^2}{6} + \frac{32^2}{6} + \frac{46^2}{6} + \frac{46^2}{6} - CF$$

$$= 1129.5 - 1107.04$$

$$= 22.46$$

where,

Sum total for Business School 1 = 39

Sum total for Business School 2 = 32

Sum total for Business School 3 = 46

Sum total for Business School 4 = 46

Sum of squares due to interactions (SSI) = $n\sum(\bar{x}_{ij} - \bar{x}_{i\bullet} - \bar{x}_{\bullet j} + \bar{x}_{\bullet\bullet})^2$

where,

n = Number of observations for each interaction

$\bar{x}_{i\bullet}$ = Mean of observations of ith row

$\bar{x}_{\bullet j}$ = Mean of observation of jth column

$\bar{x}_{\bullet\bullet}$ = Grand mean of all the observations

$\bar{x}_{ij}$ = Mean of observation of ith row and j^{th} column

The above terms can be calculated by first calculating the means of all the interactions and also the means of the corresponding rows and columns. These are presented in the table below:

Specialization	Business School				
	I	II	III	IV	$\bar{x}_{i\bullet}$
Marketing	5.5	4.5	7	5	5.5
Finance	6.5	6.5	6.5	8.5	7
Operations	7.5	5	9.5	9.5	7.88
$\bar{x}_{\bullet j}$	6.5	5.33	7.67	7.67	$\bar{x}_{\bullet\bullet} = 6.793$

Therefore,

$$\text{SSI} = 2\sum\sum(\bar{x}_{ij} - \bar{x}_{i\bullet} - \bar{x}_{\bullet j} + \bar{x}_{\bullet\bullet})^2$$

$$= 2[(5.5 - 5.5 - 6.5 + 6.79)^2 + (4.5 - 5.5 - 5.33 + 6.79)^2 + \text{---} + (9.5 - 7.88 - 7.67 + 6.79)^2]$$

$$= 2 \times 8.96 = 17.92$$

Sum of Squares due to error (SSE):

$$\text{SSE} = \text{TSS} - \text{SSR} - \text{SSC} - \text{SSI}$$

$$= 71.96 - 23.08 - 22.46 - 17.92$$

$$= 8.5$$

Therefore, the ANOVA table for factorial design could be prepared as given in Table 13.20.

TABLE 13.20 Results of ANOVA table for factorial design

Source of Variation	Sum of Squares	Degrees of Freedom	Mean Sum of Squares	F
Row (Specialization)	23.08	2	11.54	16.26
Column (Business School)	22.46	3	7.49	10.55
Interaction	17.92	6	2.96	4.17
Error	8.50	12	0.71	
Total	71.96	23		

The table values of F^2_{12}, F^3_{12} and F^6_{12} (at 5 per cent level of significance) are given as 3.885, 3.490 and 2.996 respectively. As the computed value for the hypothesis concerning specialization, business school and interaction are greater than the corresponding tabulated values; the three null hypotheses are rejected. This means that it can be concluded that the packages offered to the graduates vary due to their specialization, the type of business school in which they have studied and their interactions.

It may be noted that in the above example, we have used all the 12 interactions. However, a fractional factorial design could be used if the interest is in studying only a few of the interactions.

Use of SPSS in a Factorial Design

The above problem can also be worked out using the SPSS software, the instructions for which are provided in Appendix 13.3. The hypotheses to be tested are:

Business schools:

H_0 : Average pay package for all the institutions are equal.

H_1 : Average pay package for all the institutions are not equal.

Specialization:

H_0 : Average pay package for all the specializations are equal.

H_1 : Average pay package for all the specializations are not equal.

Interaction:

H_0 : Average pay package for all 12 interaction are equal.

H_1 : Average pay package for all 12 interaction are not equal.

The data in SPSS format for Example 13.7 would be as given in Table 13.21.

where, S_PACKAGE = Salary package

SP_ZATION = Specialization *which takes values*
1 = Marketing
2 = Finance
3 = Operations

B_SCHOOL = Business school *which takes values*
1 = Business School I
2 = Business School II
3 = Business School III
4 = Business School IV

The SPSS results are given in Table 13.22.

If we compare these results with the one presented in Table 13.20, where the problem was solved manually, we find almost identical results. The p values given in the last column of Table 13.22 are all less than 0.05, the assumed level of significance. Therefore, we reject the entire three hypotheses (concerning business school, specialization and interaction). Therefore, it can be concluded that there is a difference in the average pay package depending on where the students have studied, their area of specialization and the interaction between the two.

Table 13.21
Data for Example 13.7 in SPSS format

S_PACKAGE	SP_ZATION	B_SCHOOL
6	1	1
5	1	1
7	2	1
6	2	1
8	3	1
7	3	1
4	1	2
5	1	2
6	2	2
7	2	2
5	3	2
5	3	2
8	1	3
6	1	3
6	2	3
7	2	3
10	3	3
9	3	3
6	1	4
4	1	4
9	2	4
8	2	4
9	3	4
10	3	4

TABLE 13.22
Results of ANOVA table for Example 13.7 using SPSS

Dependent Variable: Salary Package (in ₹ lakh)

Source	Type III Sum of Squares	Degrees of Freedom	Mean Square	F	Sig.
Corrected Model	63.458[a]	11	5.769	8.144	0.001
Intercept	1107.042	1	1107.042	1562.882	0.000
sp_zation	23.083	2	11.542	16.294	0.000
b_school	22.458	3	7.486	10.569	0.001
sp_zation * b_school	17.917	6	2.986	4.216	0.016
Error	8.500	12	0.708		
Total	1179.000	24			
Corrected Total	71.958	23			

[a] R-Squared = 0.882 (Adjusted R-Squared = 0.774).

LATIN SQUARE DESIGN

LEARNING OBJECTIVE 7
Describe a Latin square design.

Latin square design was introduced in Chapter 4. In this design, it is possible to remove the influence of two extraneous variables. This design is an improvement over the randomized block design, which involved a type of stratification of the experimental units into homogeneous groups. This was done by incorporating a control variable which helped in eliminating the unwanted sources of variation from the analysis.

In a **Latin square design**, a control variable is incorporated which helps in eliminating the unwanted sources of variation from the analysis.

The Latin square design has three important characteristics:

1. The number of categories must be equal for the two extraneous (control) variables.
2. The number of experimental (treatment) groups should equal to the numbers of categories in the control variables.
3. Each experimental (treatment) group must appear only once in every row and column.

Let us try to recapitulate the example of the Latin square design as explained in Chapter 4. Assuming that we are interested in studying the impact of the price categorized as low (A), medium (B), and high (C) on sales. Two extraneous variables, namely, the store size and the type of packaging could also influence sales. As already stated, the number of categories of the two extraneous variables should equal the number of categories of treatment. In the present case, the store size could be small (1), medium (2), and large (3), whereas the type of packaging could be labelled as I, II, and III. Therefore, if there are three treatments as well as the replication for each treatment, the total number of experimental units for this design would be 3 × 3. The 3 treatments are assigned to 3 × 3 units at random in such a way that each treatment occurs once and only once in each row (store) and each column (packaging). The layout of the Latin square design for this problem could be as shown in Table 13.23.

TABLE 13.23
Latin square for various levels of price

Store Size	Packaging		
	I	II	III
Small (1)	A	B	C
Medium (2)	C	A	B
Large (3)	B	C	A

To carry out the analysis and for preparing the ANOVA table to test the null hypothesis that all the treatments (price levels) have an equal effect on the dependent variable (sales), we would compute the following as:

$T_{\bullet\bullet}$ = Sum total of all observations

n = Total number of observations

$$CF = \text{Correction factor} = \frac{(\text{Sum of all observations})^2}{n}$$

R_i = Sum of observations of ith row ($i = 1$ to m)

C_j = Sum of observations of jth column ($j = 1$ to m)

T_k = Sum of observations of kth treatment ($k = 1$ to m)

x_{ij} = Observation corresponding to i^{th} row and j^{th} column.

$$\text{Total sum of squares (TSS)} = \sum_{i=1}^{m}\sum_{j=1}^{m} x_{ij}^2 - CF$$

$$\text{Treatment sum of squares (TrSS)} = \frac{1}{m}\sum_{k=1}^{m} T_k^2 - CF$$

$$\text{Row sum of squares (RSS)} = \frac{1}{m}\sum_{i=1}^{m} R_i^2 - CF$$

$$\text{Column sum of squares (CSS)} = \frac{1}{m}\sum_{j=1}^{m} C_j^2 - CF$$

$$\text{Error sum of squares (ESS)} = TSS - TrSS - RSS - CSS$$

The ANOVA table can be set up as shown in Table 13.24.

TABLE 13.24
Analysis of variance table for an m × m Latin square design

Source of Variation	d.f.	Sum of Squares	Mean Square	F
Rows	m – 1	RSS	$MSR = \frac{RSS}{m-1}$	
Columns	m – 1	CSS	$MSC = \frac{CSS}{m-1}$	
Treatment	m – 1	TrSS	$MST = \frac{TrSS}{m-1}$	$F_{(m-1),(m-1)(m-2)} = \frac{MST}{MSE}$
Error	(m – 1) (m – 2)	ESS	$MSE = \frac{ESS}{(m-1)(m-2)}$	
Total	$m^2 - 1$			

Let us consider an example to illustrate the design.

Example 13.8

A company tried to study the effect of three price levels (₹12 = A, ₹15 = B, ₹18 = C) on the sales of its product in a Latin square design by controlling the influence of three types of stores (small, medium, large) and three types of packaging labelled as Packaging I, II, and III. The data is presented in the table below:

Store Size	Packaging		
	I	II	III
Small (1)	65 A	50 C	59 B
Medium (2)	55 B	68 A	46 C
Large (3)	52 C	58 B	72 A

Set up an ANOVA table for a 3 × 3 Latin square design to examine whether the three price levels have an equal effect on sales. (Sales figures are in lacs of rupees per month). You may use a 5 per cent level of significance.

Solution:

The hypothesis to be tested is:

H_0 : Three price levels have the same effect on sales.

H_1 : Three price levels do not have the same effect on sales.

Sum of all observations $T_{..}$ $= 65 + 55 + 52 + 50 + 68 + 58 + 59 + 46 + 72$

$= 525$

Correction factor (CF) $= \dfrac{T_{..}^2}{m \times m} = \dfrac{525^2}{9} = \dfrac{275625}{9} = 30625$

Total sum of squares (TSS) $= \sum_{i=1}^{3}\sum_{j=1}^{3} x_{ij}^2 - CF$

$= [65^2 + 55^2 + 52^2 + 50^2 + 68^2 + 58^2 + 59^2 + 46^2 + 72^2] - 30625$

$= 31223 - 30625$

$= 598$

$R_1 = 174, \quad R_2 = 169, \quad R_3 = 182$

Row sum of square (RSS) $= \dfrac{1}{m}\sum_{j=1}^{m} R_i^2 - CF$

$= \dfrac{1}{3}[174^2 + 169^2 + 182^2] - 30625$

$= 30653.667 - 30625$

$= 28.667$

$C_1 = 172, \quad C_2 = 176, \quad C_3 = 177$

Column sum of squares (CSS) $= \dfrac{1}{m}\sum_{j=1}^{m} C_i^2 - CF$

$= \dfrac{1}{3}[172^2 + 176^2 + 177^2] - 30625$

$= \dfrac{91889}{3} - 30625$

$= 30629.667 - 30625$

$= 4.667$

$T_1 = 205, \quad T_2 = 172, \quad T_3 = 148$

Treatment sum of square (TrSS) $= \dfrac{1}{m}\sum_{k=1}^{3} T_k^2 - CF$

$= \dfrac{1}{3}[205^2 + 172^2 + 148^2] - 30625$

$= \dfrac{93513}{3} - 30625$

$= 31171 - 30625$

$= 546$

Error Sum of Squares (ESS) $= TSS - TrSS - RSS - CSS$

$= 598 - 546 - 28.667 - 4.667$

$= 18.667$

The ANOVA table could be prepared as shown in Table 13.25.

TABLE 13.25
ANOVA table for 3 × 3 Latin square design

Source of Variation	d.f.	S.S	MS	F
Rows	2	28.667	14.3335	
Columns	2	4.667	2.3335	
Treatments	2	546	273	$F_2^2 = \frac{273}{9.3335} = 29.25$
Error	2	18.667	9.3335	
Total	8			

The table value of F with 2 degrees of freedom in the numerator and 2 degrees of freedom in the denominator at a 5 per cent level of significance is given by 19.00. As computed value of F = 29.25 is greater than the tabulated value, we reject the null hypothesis. Therefore, it can be concluded that the effect of the three price levels is significantly different on the sales of the product.

It may be noted that the concept of analysis of variance is also applicable in the case of non-metric data. The discussion on this will find a place in Chapter 14 (Non-parametric Tests).

CONCEPT CHECK

1. What is a factorial design?
2. Define Latin square design.
3. What are the two hypotheses to be tested in randomized block design?

SUMMARY

- R A Fisher developed the theory of analysis of variance. This technique could be used to test the equality of more than two population means in one go. The basic principle underlying the technique is that the total variations in the dependent variable can be broken into two components—one which can be attributed to specific causes and the other one may be attributed to chance. In analysis of variance, the dependent variable is metric, where as, the independent variable is categorical (nominal scale). The assumption in analysis of variance is that each sample is drawn from a NORMAL population and each of these populations has an equal variance. Another assumption made under analysis of variance is that all the factors except the one being tested are kept constant.
- The analysis of variance techniques in this chapter are illustrated through the completely randomized design, randomized block design, Latin square design and factorial design. In a completely randomized design, there is one dependent and one independent variable. The dependent variable is metric whereas the independent variable is categorical. Random samples are drawn from each category of the independent variable. The sample size from each category could be same or different. In the randomized block design, there is one independent variable and one extraneous factor (block). Both independent variable and extraneous factor (block) are nominal scale variables. The effect of the extraneous factor is removed from the analysis. In the factorial design, the dependent variable is metric and there are two or more independent variables which are non-metric. In this design, it is possible to examine the interaction between the variables. If there are two independent variables each having three cells, there would be a total of nine interactions. A fractional factorial design would also be used if we are interested in studying only a few of the interactions. All these designs except the Latin square design are also illustrated through the use of the SPSS software.
- In the Latin square design, there is one treatment and there are two extraneous variables. The number of categories of treatment and the extraneous variables are equal. In this design, it is possible to remove the effect of two extraneous variables from the analysis. In this design, each treatment appears once and only once in each row and column of the Latin square table.
- The Post Hoc analysis is carried out if results of one-way ANOVA are significant.

KEY TERMS

- Between sample variance
- Block sum of squares
- Completely randomized design
- Degrees of freedom
- Error sum of squares
- F statistic
- Factorial design
- Interaction
- Latin square design
- Mean square
- One-way ANOVA
- Randomized block design
- Sum of squares
- Sum of squares due to interaction
- Total sum of squares
- Treatment sum of squares
- Two-way ANOVA
- Within sample variance

CHAPTER REVIEW QUESTIONS

Objective Type Questions

State whether the following statements are true (T) or false (F).

1. The theory of ANOVA was developed by R A Fisher.
2. Using analysis of variance, it is possible to compare the means of more than two populations simultaneously.
3. In one-way ANOVA, both the dependent and the independent variables have metric measurements.
4. In analysis of variance, the sample need not be drawn from the normal populations.
5. The equality of variances between the sample and within the samples is compared using an F statistic in one-way ANOVA.
6. In completely randomized design, the dependent variable is metric, whereas the independent variable is categorical.
7. The degree of freedom corresponding to the total sum of squares equals the total number of observations less one.
8. In a two-way analysis of variance, the effect of the extraneous factors is removed from the value of the error sum of squares as obtained in a one-way analysis of variance.
9. In analysis of variance, the null hypothesis is that the means of all the categories are not equal.
10. In the analysis of co-variance, the independent variables are both metric and categorical.
11. In a factorial design with two independent variables, one having two categories and second having three categories, the total number of interactions is six.
12. In two-way analysis of variance, the equality of the treatment sum of squares with the error sum of squares and the block sum of squares with the error sum of squares is tested.
13. In the Latin square design it is possible to remove the influence of two extraneous variables.
14. In the Latin square design each treatment must appear once and only once in every row and column.
15. The number of categories of the two extraneous variables and that of the treatment must be equal in Latin square design.
16. In a Latin square design, the treatments can be assigned to the experimental units arbitrarily.
17. In a randomized block design, the effect of one extraneous variable is removed.
18. In the Latin square design, the degrees of freedoms corresponding to rows, columns and treatments need not be equal.
19. A randomized block design is an improvement over the Latin square design.
20. If the sample means between the groups are almost equal, it will imply a very small value of variance.

Conceptual Questions

1. What is the analysis of variance? What are the assumptions of the technique? Give a few examples where the technique could be used.
2. Differentiate using suitable examples between the one-way and two-way analysis of variance.

3. Discuss the procedure involved in analysis of variance. Tabulate the ANOVA table in both the one-way and the two-way classification.
4. What are the characteristics of the Latin square design?
5. Compare a randomized block design with Latin square design.
6. What is a factorial design? Explain the terms, main effects and interaction effects in relation to factorial design.
7. Give the layout and analysis of (i) randomized block design and, (ii) Latin square design.
8. How is the analysis of variance related to the randomized block design, the Latin square design and the factorial design?
9. Explain the meaning of interaction between the variables with the help of a suitable example.

Application Questions

1. An oil company is interested in testing four different blends of gasoline for fuel efficiency by controlling the variability of four different drivers and four different models of cars. The fuel efficiency was measured as kilometre per litre after driving the cars over a standard clause. Data is presented in a 4 × 4 Latin square design.

Fuel efficiencies (km litre) for four blends of gasoline

Driver	Car Model			
	I	II	III	IV
1	A 13	D 9.4	C 10.6	B 12
2	B 12.4	C 10.2	A 13.6	D 8.7
3	C 9.9	B 12.6	D 9.3	A 13.4
4	D 9.8	A 14.0	B 12.7	C 10.5

Use 5 per cent level of significance to test the appropriate hypothesis.

2. As the head of a department of a consumer research organization, you have the responsibility for testing and comparing the lifetime of four brands of electric bulbs. Suppose you test the lifetime of three electric bulbs of each of the four brands. The data is shown below, each entry representing the lifetime of an electric bulb, measured in hundreds of hours.

Brand			
A	B	C	D
20	25	24	23
19	23	20	20
21	21	22	20

Can we infer that the mean lifetimes of the four brands of electric bulbs are equal?

(MBA, University of Roorkee)

3. Amit Merchandising Company wishes to test whether its three salesmen A, B, and C make sales of the same size or whether they differ in their selling ability as measured by the average size of their sales. During the last week, out of the 14 sales, A made 5, B made 4, and C made 5 calls. The following is the weekly sales (in ₹ '000) record of three salesmen.

A	B	C
300	600	700
400	300	300
300	300	400
500	400	600
0	–	50

Test whether the three salesmen's average sales differ in size. *(MBA, Bharathidasan Univ., 2001)*

4. As part of the investigation of the collapse of the roof of a building, a testing laboratory is given the entire available stock of bolts that connect the steel structure at three different positions on the roof. The forces required to share each of these bolts (coded values) are as follows:

Position 1	90	82	79	98	83	91	
Position 2	105	89	93	104	89	95	86
Position 3	83	89	80	94			

Perform an analysis of variance test at the 0.05 level of significance to find out whether the differences among the sample means at the three positions are significant. *(BE/B.Tech., Madras Univ., 2003)*

5. The following data represents the numbers of units produced by four operators during three different shifts:

Shifts	**Operator**			
	A	**B**	**C**	**D**
I	10	8	12	13
II	10	12	14	15
III	12	10	11	14

Perform a two-way analysis of variance and interpret the result. *(MBA, Madras Univ., 2005)*

6. The following data pertain to the numbers of units of a product manufactured per day by five workmen from four different brands of machines.

Workmen	**Machine Brands**			
	A	**B**	**C**	**D**
1	46	40	49	38
2	48	42	54	45
3	36	38	46	34
4	35	40	48	35
5	40	44	51	41

(i) Test, whether the mean productivity is the same for four brands of machines.

(ii) Test whether the five different workmen differ with respect to productivity. *(M.Com., DU, 1999)*

7. The following are the number of mistakes made in five excessive days by four technicians working for a photographic laboratory. Test at a level of significance $\alpha = 0.01$, whether the differences among the four sample means can be attributed to chance.

Mistakes	**Technician**			
	I	**II**	**III**	**IV**
Day 1	6	14	10	9
Day 2	14	9	12	12
Day 3	10	12	7	8
Day 4	8	10	15	10
Day 5	11	14	11	11

(MBA, Anna Univ., 2007)

CASE 13.1

PAID KIDS' CARE UNIT IN A MALL

In the past few years, a large number of malls have sprouted in the Indian metros. Malls are not only meant for shopping but are also combined with multiplexes and provide other indoor modes of recreation. In this context, it has become a place to hang out for most of the younger population.

Many young parents go to malls, usually with their children in tow. While it can be a terrific family outing, sometimes a break from the children while shopping can also be a pleasant experience. A kid's care centre in a mall can give parents a fantastic place to drop off their children while shopping or while exploring the mall for other modes of entertainment or recreation.

Such facilities are already available in European markets. A study was conducted to examine whether Indians need such a facility.

The unit of analysis for the study was young parents having kids in the age group 1 to 6 years. The visit to a mall was considered to be the most appropriate method to find the target population. A sample of 30 respondents was selected while they were visiting malls. A questionnaire was administered to the respondents. A few questions that were asked of the respondents were:

- If you are provided with a paid kids' care facility in a mall, for the kids aged 1–6 years, would you be interested in availing of the facility? (Y)
  (a) Very Interested - (5)
  (b) Interested - (4)
  (c) Indifferent - (3)
  (d) Not interested - (2)
  (e) Not at all interested - (1)
- According to you what should be the charge on an hourly basis, for a kids' care centre in a mall? (X_1)
  (a) ₹100 – ₹150 - (1)
  (b) ₹151 – ₹200 - (2)
  (c) ₹201 – ₹250 - (3)
  (d) ₹251 and above - (4)
- Your sex (X_2)
  (a) Male - (1)
  (b) Female - (2)
- Your education (X_3)
  (a) Undergraduate - (1)
  (b) Graduate - (2)
  (c) Postgraduate and above - (3)
- Your monthly household income (X_4)
  (a) Less than or equal to ₹15,000 - (1)
  (b) ₹15,001 – ₹30,000 - (2)
  (c) ₹30,001 – ₹45,000 - (3)
  (d) ₹45,001 and above - (4)
- Are both you and your spouse working (X_5)
  (a) Both - (1)
  (b) One - (2)
- You belong to (X_6)
  (a) Nuclear family - (1)
  (b) Joint family - (2)

The data on the variable Y is in the interval scale, whereas the data on the remaining variables—X_1, X_2 up to X_6—is nominal scale. The coding for X variables is shown within parenthesis. The values taken by the interval scale variable Y are shown within the brackets. The entire data is reproduced below in Table 13.26 and is also available in the SPSS format in the data disk.

Table 13.26 Data for select variables

S. No.	Y	X_1	X_2	X_3	X_4	X_5	X_6
1	4.00	1.00	2.00	2.00	3.00	1.00	1.00
2	3.00	1.00	1.00	3.00	3.00	1.00	1.00
3	2.00	1.00	2.00	3.00	3.00	2.00	1.00
4	4.00	1.00	2.00	3.00	3.00	1.00	1.00
5	5.00	1.00	2.00	2.00	4.00	2.00	1.00
6	3.00	1.00	2.00	2.00	3.00	2.00	1.00
7	5.00	1.00	1.00	2.00	4.00	2.00	2.00
8	2.00	1.00	2.00	3.00	4.00	2.00	2.00
9	2.00	1.00	1.00	3.00	4.00	2.00	2.00
10	3.00	1.00	1.00	3.00	3.00	2.00	1.00
11	5.00	1.00	2.00	2.00	4.00	2.00	1.00
12	4.00	1.00	1.00	3.00	4.00	1.00	1.00
13	5.00	1.00	1.00	2.00	4.00	2.00	2.00
14	5.00	1.00	1.00	2.00	3.00	2.00	2.00
15	4.00	2.00	1.00	2.00	3.00	2.00	2.00
16	5.00	2.00	2.00	3.00	4.00	2.00	2.00
17	2.00	3.00	2.00	3.00	4.00	1.00	2.00
18	2.00	1.00	1.00	2.00	3.00	1.00	2.00
19	3.00	1.00	1.00	3.00	4.00	2.00	1.00
20	4.00	1.00	2.00	3.00	3.00	1.00	1.00
21	5.00	1.00	1.00	3.00	4.00	1.00	2.00
22	5.00	1.00	1.00	1.00	3.00	1.00	1.00
23	4.00	2.00	2.00	1.00	3.00	1.00	1.00
24	4.00	3.00	2.00	3.00	4.00	1.00	1.00
25	5.00	1.00	1.00	2.00	4.00	2.00	2.00
26	5.00	2.00	2.00	2.00	4.00	2.00	2.00
27	5.00	2.00	2.00	2.00	4.00	1.00	2.00
28	3.00	1.00	1.00	2.00	4.00	2.00	2.00
29	4.00	1.00	1.00	2.00	4.00	2.00	2.00
30	5.00	2.00	2.00	2.00	4.00	2.00	2.00

QUESTIONS

1. Treat X_1, X_2 and X_6 as independent variables. Run a one-way analysis of variance using the independent variables X_1, X_3 and X_4 with interest in the Kids' Care Centre (Y) as a dependent variable. If the results are significant, carry out POST HOC analysis and interpret the results.
2. Conduct an appropriate test to examine whether there is a difference in the interest in the Kids' Care Centre because of gender (X_2), spouse working (X_5) and type of family (X_6). Interpret the result.
3. Divide the interest in the Kids' Care Centre into two groups—low interest with a score of 1 to 3 and high interest with a score to 4 or 5. Cross-tabulate it with the gender (X_2), spouse working (X_5) and type of family (X_6). Interpret the results.
4. Write a management summary of the findings.

CASE 13.2

MALHOTRA SPICES COMPANY PVT. LTD.

Malhotra Spices Company came into operation in 1960 and has its operations in all parts of the country. It was in the business of manufacturing and selling spices suitable for the Indian kitchen. They ventured into the export markets in the 1980s as there was a huge demand for the spices in North America, Europe, Australia and in the Middle East. This is because the number of the Indians residing in these countries had been increasing at an exponential rate. The spices were packed into tetrapacks containing spices in different quantities like 100, 150, 200, 250 and 500 gm. The 500 gm packages were mostly used by restaurants and hoteliers. Mr K P Malhotra, Chairman of Malhotra Spices, was wondering whether they should change the packaging from tetrapack to plastic or glass bottle packaging. Before taking a final decision, as an experiment, the company introduced plastic and glass bottle packaging in addition to the existing tetrapacks packaging in the national capital region (NCR) of Delhi. Mr Malhotra was thinking that switching over to a new packaging would involve a huge investment and if the results were not different for the other two types of packaging, they would drop the idea of change in packaging.

The company on an experimental basis came up with three types of packaging—plastic, glass bottles and tetrapacks—for the NCR market. They wanted to observe the sales of spices for the three types of packaging. Mr Malhotra's younger brother told him that it is not only the type of packaging that influenced the sales but also some external factors like the size of the store selling the spices. The relevant results taken for 30 months are reported in Table 13.27.

Table 13.27 Data for select variables

S. No.	Sales (₹ in lakh)	Type of Packaging	Stores
1	120	1	1
2	90	2	1
3	110	3	1
4	150	1	2
5	100	2	2
6	120	3	2
7	140	1	3
8	110	2	3
9	130	3	3
10	138	1	1
11	100	2	1
12	126	3	1
13	145	1	2
14	125	2	2
15	130	3	2
16	130	1	3
17	110	2	3
18	120	3	3
19	140	1	1
20	111	2	1
21	125	3	1
22	110	1	2
23	100	2	2
24	105	3	2
25	120	1	3
26	100	2	3
27	110	3	3
28	127	1	1
29	98	2	1
30	107	3	1

Type of packaging

1 = Plastic

2 = Glass

3 = Tetrapacks

Type of store

1 = Large store

2 = Medium store

3 = Small store

QUESTIONS

1. Use a one-way analysis of variance to examine whether the type of packaging has any effect on the sales volume. If a significant difference exists, carry out an appropriate further analysis. Write a summary of your findings.
2. If the size of the store is to be treated as a block, carry out the two-way analysis of variance to examine whether the size of the store has any impact upon the sales of the spices.

CASE 13.3

KUMAR SOFT DRINK BOTTLING COMPANY

Kumar Soft Drink Bottling Company came into operation in 1984 and was operating in the NCR of Delhi and in the states of Punjab and Haryana. The turnover of the company was ₹1.5 crore in 2010 and it was growing at the rate of 10 per cent per annum. The chairman of the company, Mr. Kumar, wanted to examine whether the flavour of the soft drink and the price level had any impact upon the sales. He wanted this because the results could have implications for changing the product mix if required. Three types of flavours were considered, namely, pineapple, mango and orange. Further, three level of prices were taken into consideration—₹10, ₹12, and ₹14. An experiment was conducted by randomly choosing a sample of 18 stores where the flavour of the soft drink and the price level were varied. The experiment period was one month. The result of the experiment is shown in Table 13.28

Table 13.28 Data for select variables

Store No.	Sales (in ₹ lakh)	Flavour	Price
1	5.5	1	1
2	4.2	2	1
3	3.7	3	1
4	3.6	1	2
5	2.9	2	2
6	2.5	3	2
7	2.0	1	3
8	1.9	2	3
9	2.8	3	3
10	5.6	1	1
11	4.3	2	1
12	5.4	3	1
13	4.0	1	2
14	3.8	2	2
15	3.2	3	2
16	2.6	1	3
17	2.8	2	3
18	2.0	3	3

Coding for flavour:	Pineapple	=	1
	Mango	=	2
	Orange	=	3
Coding for price:	₹10/-	=	1
	₹12/-	=	2
	₹14/-	=	3

QUESTIONS

1. Is there any impact of the flavour or the price level independently upon the sales? Conduct the test using a 5 per cent level of significance.
2. Examine if there is any combined effect of the flavour and the price level (interaction effect) on sales.

CASE 13.4

PERCEPTION OF DELHIITES ABOUT DELHI METRO

The construction of Delhi Metro commenced on 3 May 1995, with the aim of providing relief to people of Delhi and NCR from the increasing traffic snarls and to reduce air pollution in the city.

With the completion of Phase-I and Phase-II, the Delhi Metro now covers a total distance of 190 km. There are six lines, with 142 metro stations. The trains run at a maximum speed of 80 km/h and stop for about 20 second at each station. The frequency of trains is from 2.5 to 10 minutes from 6.00 am to 11.00 pm. Many of the metro stations have facilities like ATMs, food outlets, convenience stores and mobile recharge. There are a total of 200 train sets, of which 69 have six coach formations. The total distance covered by the Delhi Metro is over 69,000 km per day.

The Delhi Metro Rail Corporation (DMRC) has become one of the main modes of transport for the people residing in Delhi and NCR. This has proved to be an effective solution for the traffic problem that Delhi was facing. Other notable benefits include reduction in pollution, as more people now prefer to use the Metro rather than their private vehicles, easing of pressure on the bus transport system, reduction in fuel consumption, less congested roads and increase in comfort levels of public transport.

A study was conducted to examine how effective the Delhi Metro has been in achieving its set objectives. To capture the perceptions of people on various parameters, an exploratory research was conducted using unstructured interviews with 15 commuters. By using the identified parameters, a questionnaire was designed and perception was measured on a 5-point Likert scale. The main objective was to examine whether the perception on various parameters vary across certain demographic variables and the frequency of use of Delhi Metro. A select portion of the questionnaire is reproduced below:

1. How frequently do you use the Delhi Metro? ***(X1)***
   - Daily [1]
   - 2-4 times a week [2]
   - Once a week [3]
   - Once or twice a month [4]
   - Once or twice a year [5]

2. Indicate to what extent you agree or disagree with the following statements. (***X2***)

Statements	Strongly Disagree	Disagree	Neither Agree nor Disagree	Agree	Strongly Agree
(a) The fare of commuting by the Metro is high (R)					
(b) Travelling by Metro is safer for women as compared to other means of public transport					
(c) The connectivity provided by the Metro across Delhi is good					
(d) The waiting time for the Metro at the platform is high (R)					
(e) I normally get a seat in the Metro					
(f) Swapping of Metro card takes less time as compared to buying ticket for other means					
(g) The maps and signage of the Delhi Metro are confusing (R)					
(h) Metro train is comfortable in terms of temperature levels maintained inside the coaches					
(i) Metro trains take more time to reach the destination (R)					
(j) The Metro is helping reduce environmental pollution in Delhi					
(k) Feeder bus service has made Metro stations more accessible					

- *R – Stands for reverse statement.*
- *For a favourable statement, the coding was 1 = strongly disagree, 2 = disagree, 3 = neither agree nor disagree, 4 = agree, and 5 = strongly agree.*
- *For unfavourable statements, the coding was reversed.*

3. Please specify your age (***X3***)
   - 18-30 [1]
   - 31-50 [2]
   - > 50 [3]
4. Gender (***X4***)
   - Male [1]
   - Female [2]
5. What is your profession? (***X5***)
   - Student [1]
   - Business [2]
   - Service [3]
   - Homemaker [4]

The questionnaire was administered on 127 respondents using convenience sampling. The data collected is presented in Table 13.29.

Table 13.29 Perception Data about Delhi Metro

Resp No.	X1	X2a_R	X2b	X2c	X2d_R	X2e	X2f	X2g_R	X2h	X2i_R	X2j	X2k	X3	X4	X5
1	5	4	4	3	3	2	4	4	4	4	5	3	2	2	3
2	5	4	4	4	3	2	4	2	4	4	5	3	3	1	3
3	1	4	5	4	4	1	4	4	4	4	4	4	1	2	1
4	4	4	4	4	4	1	5	5	4	4	4	3	1	1	1
5	4	4	4	4	4	2	4	4	4	4	4	2	1	2	1
6	4	4	5	4	4	4	5	4	4	4	5	4	1	2	1
7	5	3	5	4	4	2	4	2	4	5	5	4	1	1	3
8	3	5	5	4	5	2	5	5	5	4	4	4	1	1	3
9	4	4	5	5	4	3	5	2	4	4	5	4	1	2	1
10	2	3	4	4	3	4	4	4	4	2	4	4	1	2	1
11	3	4	4	4	4	4	1	2	1	3	1	3	1	1	3
12	4	4	5	4	3	4	4	2	4	4	4	4	1	2	1
13	3	3	4	4	4	3	5	2	5	4	5	4	1	1	1
14	5	4	3	4	4	2	5	2	4	3	3	3	1	2	1
15	3	4	5	4	4	4	5	4	5	5	4	4	1	2	1
16	2	4	4	3	4	2	5	4	3	3	4	3	1	2	1
17	3	3	5	5	4	3	5	4	4	3	5	3	1	1	3
18	4	4	4	4	4	1	4	4	5	4	3	2	1	1	1
19	1	3	5	4	4	1	5	3	4	4	5	4	1	1	3
20	3	4	5	4	3	3	5	4	5	4	5	5	1	1	1
21	3	5	4	5	5	3	5	5	4	3	3	4	1	2	1
22	3	4	4	4	4	1	4	5	4	5	4	3	1	1	1
23	2	4	5	4	4	2	5	4	3	4	5	3	1	1	1
24	3	4	4	4	4	2	4	4	5	4	5	5	1	1	3
25	3	3	5	3	4	2	5	4	4	4	1	3	1	1	3
26	3	3	4	4	2	2	5	4	4	4	4	4	1	2	3
27	3	2	4	4	4	1	5	4	4	4	3	3	1	2	3
28	3	3	4	3	3	2	4	3	4	3	4	3	1	1	3
29	4	3	4	4	3	3	3	4	5	5	5	5	1	2	3
30	5	3	5	4	3	1	5	2	4	2	4	3	1	2	3
31	4	4	4	4	3	1	4	5	4	4	4	2	1	1	1
32	4	4	5	4	3	2	5	4	2	2	2	3	1	2	1
33	5	4	4	4	4	1	5	2	1	2	5	5	1	1	2
34	5	3	5	5	4	4	3	5	5	3	5	2	1	1	2
35	5	3	4	3	4	2	5	4	3	3	5	4	1	1	3
36	5	4	4	4	3	1	3	4	4	5	4	4	1	1	3
37	2	3	5	5	4	4	5	2	4	4	4	1	1	2	3
38	1	1	5	4	4	4	3	4	5	5	1	4	1	1	1
39	4	4	5	3	4	2	5	5	4	3	5	4	1	1	1
40	1	5	5	5	4	3	4	3	4	4	4	4	1	1	3
41	2	3	5	4	4	4	4	4	4	4	4	4	1	1	1
42	1	4	4	4	4	2	5	4	5	1	4	4	1	2	1
43	2	4	5	5	4	2	4	4	4	5	5	3	1	2	3
44	2	2	4	4	4	1	5	4	2	4	4	3	1	1	1
45	4	5	3	4	5	1	4	5	5	3	5	4	1	1	1
46	2	5	5	4	4	3	5	5	4	4	1	4	3	1	3
47	3	3	4	4	4	3	4	3	4	4	5	2	1	2	3
48	4	4	4	4	2	2	4	4	4	4	2	4	1	1	2
49	4	4	4	3	4	1	4	4	4	5	4	5	1	1	1
50	4	5	5	4	4	3	5	5	5	4	5	5	1	1	1

Resp No.	X1	X2a_R	X2b	X2c	X2d_R	X2e	X2f	X2g_R	X2h	X2i_R	X2j	X2k	X3	X4	X5
51	4	4	5	3	5	2	4	4	5	4	4	3	1	2	1
52	2	5	5	5	4	4	5	2	4	4	1	5	1	2	1
53	4	2	4	4	3	1	3	5	5	5	4	3	1	1	3
54	4	4	4	4	4	2	4	3	4	4	4	3	1	1	1
55	2	3	4	5	2	2	5	3	4	4	5	3	1	1	3
56	3	4	5	5	4	3	4	4	4	4	4	4	1	2	1
57	1	3	4	4	3	2	4	3	4	4	5	4	1	2	3
58	1	4	5	4	5	2	5	5	4	4	5	4	1	2	1
59	4	4	4	4	3	2	3	3	3	3	3	3	1	1	1
60	4	3	4	5	3	2	5	5	4	4	4	4	1	1	1
61	4	4	4	4	4	2	4	4	4	4	5	3	1	1	1
62	3	4	5	4	3	2	4	4	4	4	5	4	1	2	1
63	4	5	5	4	4	3	5	5	5	5	5	4	1	1	1
64	4	5	4	4	5	3	4	4	4	4	5	4	1	1	1
65	5	3	4	4	4	3	4	2	4	3	5	5	1	1	3
66	4	4	4	4	5	2	4	4	5	5	5	3	1	1	1
67	2	4	4	4	3	2	4	4	4	4	3	3	1	1	1
68	5	4	4	4	3	1	5	4	4	3	4	4	1	1	1
69	3	4	5	5	2	3	5	4	4	4	5	2	1	2	1
70	3	4	2	5	3	3	3	4	4	2	5	4	1	1	1
71	4	2	5	4	3	4	5	4	4	5	4	4	1	2	1
72	2	4	2	2	4	2	2	4	2	4	2	2	1	1	1
73	2	4	4	4	2	1	5	5	4	5	5	4	1	2	1
74	4	5	5	3	5	1	5	5	4	3	5	3	1	1	1
75	5	3	4	4	3	2	1	3	2	5	3	4	1	1	1
76	4	4	5	4	5	4	4	3	5	4	4	3	2	2	3
77	1	3	4	3	2	2	5	2	4	4	5	4	2	1	4
78	4	5	5	4	5	2	5	2	4	5	5	3	2	1	3
79	3	4	5	3	4	2	4	4	4	4	5	3	2	2	3
80	5	3	4	4	3	4	4	4	4	4	4	2	1	2	3
81	1	3	5	4	4	1	5	4	5	4	4	4	1	2	1
82	5	2	2	4	4	2	4	3	4	3	4	4	1	1	1
83	4	4	4	4	2	2	4	2	5	3	4	4	2	1	3
84	2	4	4	4	3	1	3	5	3	4	3	3	1	1	1
85	4	4	4	3	4	2	5	4	5	2	3	3	2	2	3
86	1	2	4	4	4	3	4	4	4	3	4	3	2	2	3
87	4	4	4	3	3	5	3	2	4	3	4	4	1	1	1
88	2	1	5	4	1	2	5	2	5	4	5	3	2	1	3
89	4	3	4	4	4	1	5	4	5	4	4	4	2	1	2
90	4	5	5	4	5	4	4	5	4	5	4	4	2	2	1
91	1	5	5	3	4	1	4	4	4	2	5	1	2	1	3
92	2	2	4	5	4	2	4	4	4	4	5	4	2	1	2
93	3	4	4	4	3	1	5	4	4	3	5	3	1	1	1
94	2	4	3	4	4	4	5	5	4	4	3	4	1	1	1
95	4	4	4	4	2	2	5	3	5	4	5	4	1	2	1
96	3	4	3	5	3	2	5	5	5	5	5	3	2	2	1
97	3	2	4	3	2	4	3	2	4	3	4	4	1	1	1
98	1	4	5	5	4	4	4	4	4	3	5	4	1	2	3
99	5	5	4	4	4	3	5	4	3	4	4	4	1	1	3
100	4	4	4	4	4	3	5	4	4	4	5	5	1	1	3
101	3	2	4	3	4	2	5	4	4	1	4	3	1	1	1

Resp No.	X1	X2a_R	X2b	X2c	X2d_R	X2e	X2f	X2g_R	X2h	X2i_R	X2j	X2k	X3	X4	X5
102	3	4	4	4	4	3	2	4	4	4	3	4	1	1	3
103	4	4	5	4	3	2	5	5	2	3	4	4	1	2	3
104	1	3	5	4	2	1	4	3	2	4	5	3	2	1	3
105	3	3	4	4	4	3	5	4	4	3	4	3	1	2	3
106	1	3	5	3	4	1	5	4	4	2	4	1	1	2	3
107	4	2	5	4	3	4	4	4	4	4	4	4	1	1	1
108	2	5	4	3	4	2	5	5	5	3	4	3	1	1	3
109	1	4	5	4	4	3	5	4	3	5	5	5	1	2	1
110	1	4	4	4	2	2	5	5	4	5	2	4	1	1	1
111	1	4	5	5	2	1	5	4	5	4	4	5	1	2	1
112	1	4	4	4	4	1	5	4	4	4	4	4	1	2	1
113	4	4	3	4	2	4	3	3	4	2	3	3	2	1	1
114	1	2	5	5	3	3	5	4	4	3	5	4	1	2	1
115	1	2	4	3	3	4	4	3	4	3	4	3	3	2	3
116	4	4	4	3	5	2	4	4	4	5	5	1	3	1	3
117	5	1	4	3	3	2	4	3	4	4	4	4	3	1	3
118	3	4	5	4	4	2	4	3	4	4	4	4	3	1	3
119	5	4	4	4	2	4	4	3	3	4	4	4	2	2	3
120	4	2	4	4	3	3	4	4	5	4	4	4	2	2	3
121	2	2	4	4	1	4	5	2	4	1	4	5	3	1	3
122	5	4	4	4	4	2	4	4	4	3	4	4	2	1	3
123	1	3	5	4	4	3	4	4	4	3	4	3	2	1	3
124	5	4	4	4	4	3	4	4	4	4	4	3	2	1	3
125	4	3	4	4	4	2	5	4	3	4	4	4	1	1	1
126	4	5	4	4	4	2	4	3	4	5	5	4	3	1	3
127	5	4	5	4	4	3	4	3	4	4	4	3	3	2	4

QUESTIONS

1. Conduct a one-way analysis of variance to examine whether there is any difference in the mean perception of the commuters because of
   (a) Frequency of using Delhi Metro
   (b) Age
   (c) Gender
   (d) Profession
2. What further analysis would you carry out in case the difference is significant due to the factors mentioned in Question 1?
3. Write a management summary based on your results.

Appendix – 13.1: SPSS COMMANDS FOR ONE-WAY ANOVA

After the input data has been typed along with the variable labels and the value labels in an SPSS file, to get the output for a ONE-WAY ANOVA problem, follow the following steps:

1. Click on ANALYSE at the SPSS menu bar.
2. Click on COMPARE MEANS.
3. Click on ONE-WAY ANOVA.
4. Select the appropriate variable as the dependent variable (interval or ratio scale) and take it to the right hand side box called DEPENDENT LIST, then select another appropriate variable as a factor (independent variable) that

appears from the list of the variables on the left hand side of the box and click it towards the arrow directing to the FACTOR box.

5. Then click OPTION followed by DESCRIPTIVES.
6. Click CONTINUE to return to the main dialog box.
7. Click on option Post HOC followed by Tukey under equal variance assumed.
8. Click OK to get the output for one-way ANOVA.

Appendix – 13.2: SPSS COMMANDS FOR TWO-WAY ANOVA

After the input data has been typed along with the variable labels and the value labels in an SPSS file, to get the output for a TWO-WAY ANOVA problem, follow the following steps:

1. Click on ANALYSE at the SPSS menu bar.
2. Click on GENERAL LINEAR MODEL followed by UNIVARIATE.
3. Take the appropriate variable as the dependent variable box (interval or ratio scale), then select another appropriate two variables as FIXED FACTORS. The independent variable is the first factor and the block variable is the second factor.
4. Then click MODEL followed by CUSTOM.
5. Take both the factors one by one to the right hand side box called MODEL.
6. Click CONTINUE to return to the main dialog box.
7. Click OK to get the output for two-way ANOVA.

Appendix – 13.3: SPSS COMMANDS FOR FACTORIAL DESIGN

After the input data has been typed along with variable labels and value labels in an SPSS file, to get the output for a FACTORIAL DESIGN problem, follow the following steps:

1. Click on ANALYSE at the SPSS menu bar.
2. Click on GENERAL LINEAR MODEL followed by UNIVARIATE.
3. Take the appropriate variable as the Dependent variable box (interval or ratio scale), then select other appropriate two or more variables as the case may be as FIXED FACTORS.
4. Then click MODEL followed by FULL FACTORIAL.
5. Click CONTINUE to return to the main dialog box.
6. Click OK to get the output for FACTORIAL DESIGN.

Answers to Objective Type Questions

1. True	2. True	3. False	4. False	5. True
6. True	7. True	8. True	9. False	10 True
11. True	12. True	13. True	14. True	15. True
16. False	17. True	18. False	19. False	20. True

BIBLIOGRAPHY

Beri, G.C. *Marketing Research*. 3rd edn. New Delhi: Tata McGraw Hill Publishing Company Ltd, 2000.

Bhatnagar, O P. *Research Methods and Measurements in Behavioural and Social Sciences*. New Delhi: Agricole Publishing Academy, 1981.

Bhattacharyya, Dipak Kumar. *Human Resource Research Methods*. New Delhi: Oxford University Press, 2007.

Bhattacharyya, Dipak Kumar. *Research Methodology*. New Delhi: Excel Books, 2006.

Cooper, Donald R and Pamela S Schindler. *Business Research Method*. 6th edn. New Delhi: Tata McGraw Hill Publishing Company Ltd, 1998.

Kazmier, Leonard J. *Schaum's Outline of Theory and Problems of Business Statistics*. 4th edn. New York: McGraw Hill Professional, 2004.

Keller, Gerald. *Statistics for Management and Economics*. 7th edn. Ohio: South-Western Cengage Learning, 2005.

Kinnear, Thomas C and James R Taylor. *Marketing Research: An Applied Approach*. 5th edn. New York: McGraw Hill, Inc., 1996.

Kothari, C R. *Research Methodology: Methods and Techniques*. New Delhi: Wiley Eastern, 1990.

Luck, David J and Ronald S Rubin. *Marketing Research*. 7th edn. New Delhi: Prentice Hall of India Ltd, 1992.

Nargundkar, Rajendra. *Marketing Research (Text and Cases)*. New Delhi: Tata McGraw Hill Publishing Company Ltd, 2002.

Spiegel, Murray R. *Schaum's Outline Series of Theory and Problems of Probability and Statistics*, SI (metric) edition. New York: McGraw Hill Book Company, 1975.

Tull, Donald S and Del I Hawkins. *Marketing Research: Measurement & Method*. 6th edn. New Delhi: Prentice Hall of India Pvt. Ltd., 1993.

Zikmund, William G. *Business Research Methods*. 7th edn. Ohio: South Western Cengage Learning, 2003.

14

CHAPTER

Non-Parametric Tests

Learning Objectives

By the end of the chapter, you should be able to:

1. Learn about the advantages and disadvantages of non-parametric tests.
2. Discuss various applications of chi-square tests.
3. Explain the run test of randomness for metric and non-metric data.
4. Describe one-sample and two-sample sign tests.
5. Explain the procedure for conducting the Mann-Whitney U test.
6. Discuss Wilcoxon signed-rank test for a paired sample.
7. Describe the Kruskal-Wallis test.

Jagdish Kapur and Jaya Mehta were working in a research firm as management trainees after completing their MBA from a top business school in Western India. Their first assignment was a perception study of a high-class restaurant. As part of the study, a questionnaire was designed. Some of the questions in the questionnaire were on nominal scale like gender, marital status, profession, age group and income groups. There was an ordinal scale question where the respondents were asked to rank various attributes like food quality, food variety, ambience, price and location of the restaurants. Jagdish and Jaya found out that the data on these variables did not follow a normal distribution. They also realized that such could also be the case with the data obtained from any qualitative research study. They had learnt in their course on statistics that it was either necessary for the population to follow a normal distribution or the sample size had to be large before any standard tests of significant could be used. In fact, in the case of nominal or ordinal scale data, the normality assumption does not hold true. They were wondering how they could then relate the perception about the various attributes of the restaurants with the demographic variables.

This chapter introduces the readers to a set of statistical tests where the sample size may be relatively small or the normality assumptions used in the tests described in Chapter 12 do not hold true. The name given to such tests is 'distribution-free tests' as they do not require any distribution to be satisfied before their application.

The population mean (μ), standard deviation (σ), and proportion (p) are called the parameters of a distribution. In Chapter 12, tests of hypotheses concerning the mean and proportion were discussed. These tests were based on the assumption that the population(s) from where the sample is drawn is normally distributed.

In Chapter 13, the ANOVA technique to test the equality of more than two population means is based upon the assumption that the populations from where the samples are drawn is, approximately, normally distributed. The test on the parameters like mean, standard deviation and proportion are called parametric tests.

However, there are situations where the populations under study are not normally distributed. The data collected from these populations is extremely skewed. In such a situation, an option could be used to increase the sample size. This is because the central limit theorem assumes that the distribution of sample estimates approximately has a normal distribution for large samples; whatever the shape of the population distribution. The other option is to use a Non-parametric test. These tests are called the distribution-free tests as they do not require any assumption regarding the shape of the population distribution from where the sample is drawn. However, some non-parametric tests do depend on a parameter such as median but they do not require a particular distribution for their application. These tests could also be used for the small sample sizes where the normality assumption does not hold true.

Non-parametric tests are called distribution-free tests as they do not require any assumption regarding the shape of the population distribution from where the sample is drawn.

ADVANTAGES AND DISADVANTAGES OF NON-PARAMETRIC TESTS

LEARNING OBJECTIVE 1
Learn about the advantages and disadvantages of non-parametric tests.

There are many advantages of a non-parametric test. These are:

- They can be applied to many situations as they do not have the rigid requirements of their parametric counterparts, like the sample having been drawn from the population following a normal distribution. A researcher can encounter an application where a numeric observation is difficult to obtain but a rank value is not. For example, it is easy to obtain the rank data on the preference of consumer for the various brands of toothpaste rather than assigning a numerical value to them. By using ranks, it is possible to relax the assumptions regarding the underlying populations.
- Non-parametric tests can often be applied to the nominal and ordinal data that lack exact or comparable numerical values. For example, the respondents may be asked a question on their religion—Hindu, Sikh, Christian, or Muslim. This is a nominal scale data and can only be analysed by non-parametric methods.
- Non-parametric tests involve very simple computations compared to the corresponding parametric tests.

Non-parametric tests involve very simple computations compared to the corresponding parametric tests.

However, the methods are not without their own drawbacks and there are certain disadvantages of non-parametric tests. These are:

- A lot of information is wasted because the exact numerical data is reduced to a qualitative form. For example, in one of the non-parametric tests like the sign test, the increase or the gain is denoted by a plus sign whereas a decrease or loss is denoted by a negative sign. No consideration is given to the quantity of the gain or loss. A gain of ₹1 or ₹1 lakh would both receive a plus sign.
- Non-parametric methods are less powerful than parametric tests when the basic assumptions of parametric tests are valid. Therefore, there is more risk of accepting a false hypothesis and thus committing a type II error.
- Null hypothesis in a non-parametric test is loosely defined as compared to the parametric tests. Therefore, whenever the null hypothesis is rejected, a non-parametric test yields a less precise conclusion as compared to the parametric test. For example, corresponding to the null hypothesis that the means of the two populations are equal in the parametric test, the null hypothesis in a non-parametric test is that the two populations have same probability distributions.

In such a situation, rejecting a null hypothesis under the parametric test would imply that the means of the two populations are different whereas under a non-parametric test, it means that the two population distributions are different but the specific form of the difference between the two populations is not clearly defined.

In the following sections, we will discuss non-parametric tests such as chi-square, run test, sign test, the Mann-Whitney U test, the Wilcoxon matched-pair rank test and the Kruskal–Wallis test. The differences between parametric and non-parametric tests are summarized below.

	Parametric Tests	Non-Parametric Tests
Assumptions:	Normality assumption is required.	Normality assumption is not required.
	Uses the metric data.	Ordinal or interval scale data is used.
	Can be applied for both small and large samples.	Can be applied for small samples.
Applications:	One sample using Z or t statistics.	One sample using the sign test.
	Two independent samples using a t or z test.	Two independent samples using the Mann-Whitney U statistics.
	Two paired samples using a t or z test.	Two paired samples using the sign test and Wilcoxon matched pair rank test.
	Randomness – no test in parametric is available.	Randomness – using runs test.
	Several independent samples using F test in ANOVA.	Several independent samples using Kruskal–Wallis test.

CHI-SQUARE TESTS

LEARNING OBJECTIVE 2
Discuss various applications of chi-square tests.

For the use of a chi-square test, the data is required in the form of frequencies. The data expressed in percentages or proportion can also be used, provided it could be converted into frequencies. The majority of the applications of chi-square (χ^2) are with the discrete data. The test could also be applied to continuous data, provided it is reduced to certain categories and tabulated in such a way that the chi-square may be applied.

Some of the important properties of the chi-square distribution are:

- Unlike the normal and t distribution, the chi-square distribution is not symmetric (Figure 14.1).

FIGURE 14.1
Shape of chi-square (χ^2) distribution

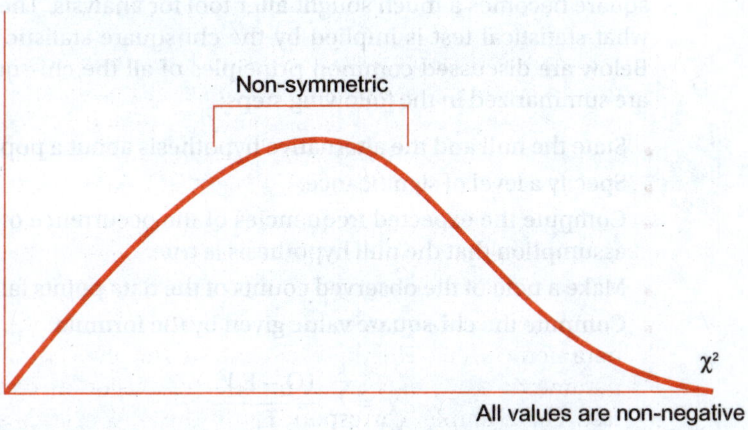

FIGURE 14.2
Shape of chi-square distribution with varying degrees of freedom

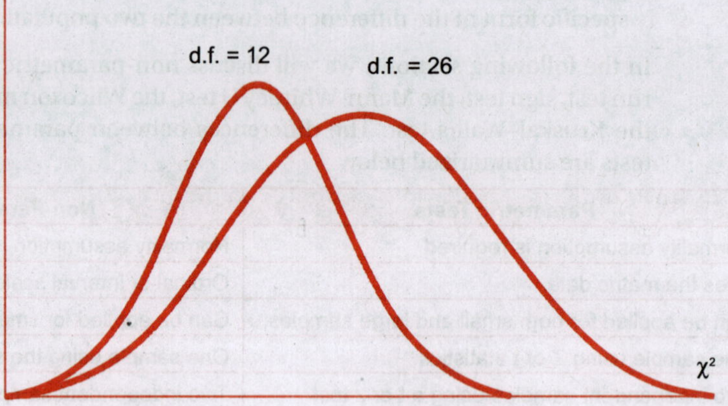

A chi-square is symbolically represented as χ^2 and for the use of a chi-square test the data is required in the form of frequencies.

- The values of a chi-square are greater than or equal to zero.
- The shape of a chi-square distribution depends upon the degrees of freedom. With the increase in degrees of freedom, the distribution tends to normal (Figure 14.2).

Application of Chi-square

There are many applications of a chi-square test. Some of them are explained below:

- A chi-square test for the goodness of fit.
- A chi-square test for the independence of variables.
- A chi-square test for the equality of more than two population proportions.

A chi-square test for the goodness of fit

As discussed before, the data in chi-square tests is often in terms of counts or frequencies. The actual survey data may be on a nominal or higher scale of measurement. If it is on a higher scale of measurement, it can always be converted into categories. The real world situations in business allow for the collection of count data, e.g., gender, marital status, job classification, age and income. Therefore, a chi-square becomes a much sought after tool for analysis. The researcher has to decide what statistical test is implied by the chi-square statistic in a particular situation. Below are discussed common principles of all the chi-square tests. The principles are summarized in the following steps:

- State the null and the alternative hypothesis about a population.
- Specify a level of significance.
- Compute the expected frequencies of the occurrence of certain events under the assumption that the null hypothesis is true.
- Make a note of the observed counts of the data points falling in different cells
- Compute the chi-square value given by the formula.

$$\chi^2_{k-1} = \sum_{i=1}^{K} \frac{(O_i - E_i)^2}{E_i}$$

where,

O_i = Observed frequency of ith cell

E_i = Expected frequency of ith cell
k = Total number of cells
k-1 = Degrees of freedom

- Compare the sample value of the statistic as obtained in previous step with the critical value at a given level of significance and make the decision.

A goodness of fit test is a statistical test that determines the validity of the observed data regarding the assumption about the distribution of a population.

A goodness of fit test is a statistical test of how well the observed data supports the assumption about the distribution of a population. The test also examines that how well an assumed distribution fits the data. Many a times, the researcher assumes that the sample is drawn from a normal or any other distribution of interest. A test of how normal or any other distribution fits a given data may be of some interest.

Consider for example the case of the multinomial experiment which is the extension of a binomial experiment. In the multinomial experiment, the number of the categories k is greater than 2. Further, a data point can fall into one of the k categories and the probability of the data point falling in the ith category is a constant and is denoted by p_i where i = 1, 2, 3, 4, ..., k. In summary, a multinomial experiment has the following features:

- There are fixed number of trials.
- The trials are statistically independent.
- All the possible outcomes of a trial get classified into one of the several categories.
- The probabilities for the different categories remain constant for each trial.

Consider as an example that a respondent can fall into any one of the four non-overlapping income categories. Let the probabilities that the respondent will fall into any of the four groups may be denoted by the four parameters p_1, p_2, p_3, and p_4. Given these, the multinomial distribution with these parameters, and n the number of people in a random sample, specifies the probabilities of any combination of the cell counts.

Given such a situation, we may use a multinomial distribution to test how well the data fits the assumption of k probability $p_1, p_2, ..., p_k$ of falling into the k cells. The hypothesis to be tested is:

H_0: Probabilities of the occurrence of events $E_1, E_2, ..., E_k$ are given by the specified probabilities $p_1, p_2, ..., p_k$

H_1: Probabilities of the k events are not the p_i stated in the null hypothesis.

Such hypothesis could be tested using the chi-square statistics. Below are given a set of illustrated examples.

Example 14.1

The manager of ABC icecream parlour has to take a decision regarding how much of each flavour of icecream he should stock so that the demands of the customers are satisfied. The icecream supplier claims that among the four most popular flavors, 62 per cent customers prefer vanilla, 18 per cent chocolate, 12 per cent strawberry and 8 per cent mango. A random sample of 200 customers produces the results below. At the $\alpha = 0.05$ significance level, test the claim that the percentages given by the supplies are correct.

Flavour	Vanilla	Chocolate	Strawberry	Mango
Number preferring	120	40	18	22

Solution:

Let

p_v : Proportion of customers preferring vanilla flavour.
p_c : Proportion of customers preferring chocolate flavour.
p_s : proportion of customers preferring strawberry flavour.
p_m : proportion of customers preferring mango flavour.

$H_0: \; p_v = 0.62, p_c = 0.18, p_s = 0.12, p_m = 0.08$
$H_1:$ Proportions are not that specified in the null hypothesis

The expected frequencies corresponding to the various flavors under the assumption that the null hypothesis is true are:

Vanilla = 200 × 0.62 = 124
Chocolate = 200 × 0.18 = 36
Strawberry = 200 × 0.12 = 24
Mango = 200 × 0.08 = 16

The computations for χ_3^2 are as under: $\sum_{i=1}^{K} \frac{(O_i - E_i)^2}{E_i}$

Flavour	O (Observed Frequencies)	E (Expected Frequencies)	O – E	$(O - E)^2$	$\frac{(O-E)^2}{E}$
Vanilla	120	124	–4	16	0.129
Chocolate	40	36	4	16	0.444
Strawberry	18	24	–6	36	1.500
Mango	22	16	6	36	2.250
Total					4.323

The computed value of chi-square is 4.323.
Table χ_3^2 (5 per cent) = 9.488 (see Annexure 3 at the end of the book.)

Rejection region for Example 14.1.

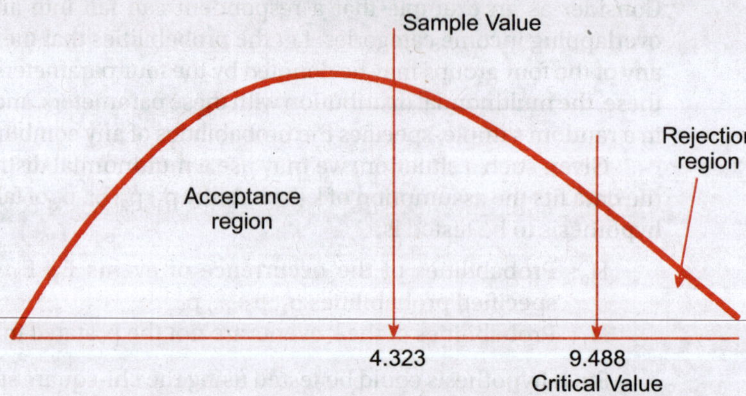

As sample χ^2 lies in the acceptance region, accept H_0. Therefore, the customer preference rates are as stated. Using the p value approach, we find that the sample χ^2 value lies as shown below:

χ^2 with 3 d.f.	11.345	7.815	6.251	↓
Level of significance	1 per cent	5 per cent	10 per cent	4.323 (sample χ^2)

It is seen that the sample χ^2 corresponds to a p value greater than 10 per cent. Therefore, there is not enough evidence to reject the null hypothesis. This means that the customer preference rates are as stated in the null hypothesis.

For the application of a **chi-square test**, the expected frequency in each cell should be at least 5.0.

It may be worth pointing out that for the application of a chi-square test, the expected frequency in each cell should be at least 5.0. In case it is found that one or more cells have the expected frequency less than 5, one could still carry out the chi-square analysis by combining them into meaningful cells so that the expected number has a total of at least 5. Another point worth mentioning is that the degree of freedom, usually denoted by *df* in such cases, is given by k – 1, where k denotes the number of cells (categories).

It may be noted that in Example 14.1, the hypothesized probabilities were not equal. There are situations where the hypothesized probabilities in each category are equal or in other words, the interest is in investigating the uniformity of the distribution. The following example would illustrate it.

Example 14.2

An insurance company provides auto insurance and is analysing the data obtained from fatal crashes. A sample of the motor vehicle deaths is randomly selected for a two-year period. The number of fatalities is listed below for the different days of the week. At the 0.05 significance level, test the claim that accidents occur on different days with equal frequency.

Day	Monday	Tuesday	Wednesday	Thursday	Friday	Saturday	Sunday
Number of Fatalities	31	20	20	22	22	29	36

Solution:

Let

p_1 = Proportion of fatalities on Monday
p_2 = Proportion of fatalities on Tuesday
p_3 = Proportion of fatalities on Wednesday
p_4 = Proportion of fatalities on Thursday
p_5 = Proportion of fatalities on Friday
p_6 = Proportion of fatalities on Saturday
p_7 = Proportion of fatalities on Sunday

$H_0 : p_1 = p_2 = p_3 = p_4 = p_5 = p_6 = p_7 = \frac{1}{7}$

H_1 : At least one of these proportions is incorrect.

n = Total frequency = 31 + 20 + 20 + 22 + 22 + 29 + 36 = 180

The expected number of fatalities on each day of the week under the assumption that the null hypothesis is true is given as under:

$$\text{Monday} = 180 \times \frac{1}{7} = 25.714$$

$$\text{Tuesday} = 180 \times \frac{1}{7} = 25.714$$

$$\text{Wednesday} = 180 \times \frac{1}{7} = 25.714$$

$$\text{Thursday} = 180 \times \frac{1}{7} = 25.714$$

$$\text{Friday} = 180 \times \frac{1}{7} = 25.714$$

$$\text{Saturday} = 180 \times \frac{1}{7} = 25.714$$

$$\text{Sunday} = 180 \times \frac{1}{7} = 25.714$$

The computation of sample chi-square value is given in the following table:

Day	Observed Frequencies (O)	Expected Frequencies (E)	O – E	$(O – E)^2$	$\frac{(O-E)^2}{E}$
Monday	31	25.714	5.286	27.942	1.087
Tuesday	20	25.714	–5.714	32.650	1.270

Day	Observed Frequencies (O)	Expected Frequencies (E)	O – E	$(O - E)^2$	$\frac{(O-E)^2}{E}$
Wednesday	20	25.714	–5.714	32.650	1.270
Thursday	22	25.714	–3.714	13.794	0.536
Friday	22	25.714	–3.714	13.794	0.536
Saturday	29	25.714	3.286	10.798	0.420
Sunday	36	25.714	10.286	105.802	4.114
		Total			9.233

The value of sample $\chi^2 = \Sigma \frac{(O-E)^2}{E} = 9.233$

Degrees of freedom $= 7 - 1 = 6$

Critical (Table) $\chi_6^2 = 12.592$

Since the sample chi-square value is less than the tabulated χ^2, there is not enough evidence to reject the null hypothesis as shown in the figure below.

Rejection region for Example 14.2.

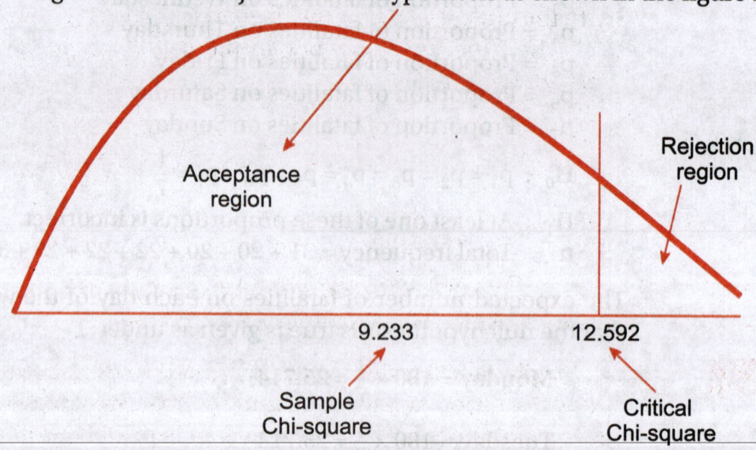

The problem can also be worked out using the p-value approach. The sample value of $\chi^2 = 9.233$ with 6 df is less than the critical value 10.645, which corresponds to an area of 10 per cent. Therefore, the p value in this problem is greater than 10 per cent, which is higher than the level of significance $\alpha = 0.05$. Therefore, the null hypothesis is accepted. This means that the accidents occur on different days with equal frequencies.

A chi-square test for independence of variables

Contingency tables are also referred to as cross-tabs with the cells corresponding to a cross classification of attributes or events.

The chi-square test can be used to test the independence of two variables each having at least two categories. The test makes a use of contingency tables also referred to as cross-tabs with the cells corresponding to a cross classification of attributes or events. A contingency table with 3 rows and 4 columns (as an example) is shown in Table 14.1.

Assuming that there are r rows and c columns, the count in the cell corresponding to the ith row and the jth column is denoted by O_{ij}, where i = 1, 2, ..., r and j = 1, 2, ..., c. The total for row i is denoted by R_i whereas that corresponding to column j is denoted by C_j. The total sample size is given by n, which is also the sum of all the r row totals or the sum of all the c column totals.

TABLE 14.1 Layout of a contingency table

Second Classification Category	First Classification Category				
	1	2	3	4	Total
1	O_{11}	O_{12}	O_{13}	O_{14}	R_1
2	O_{21}	O_{22}	O_{23}	O_{24}	R_2
3	O_{31}	O_{32}	O_{33}	O_{34}	R_3
Total	C_1	C_2	C_3	C_4	n

The hypothesis test for independence is:

H_0 : Row and column variables are independent of each other.

H_1 : Row and column variables are not independent.

The hypothesis is tested using a chi-square test statistic for independence given by:

$$\chi^2 = \sum_{i=1}^{r} \sum_{j=1}^{c} \frac{(O_{ij} - E_{ij})^2}{E_{ij}}$$

The degrees of freedom for the chi-square statistic are given by (r – 1) (c – 1).

For a given level of significance α, the sample value of the chi-square is compared with the critical value for the degree of freedom (r – 1) (c – 1) to make a decision.

The expected frequency in the cell corresponding to the ith row and the jth column is given by:

$$E_{ij} = \frac{R_i \times C_j}{n}$$

where, R_i = Total for the ith row,

C_j = Total for the jth column,

n = Total sample size.

Let us consider a few examples:

Example 14.3

A sample of 870 trainees was subjected to different types of training classified as intensive, good and average and their performance was noted as above average, average and poor. The resulting data is presented in the table below. Use a 5 per cent level of significance to examine whether there is any relationship between the type of training and performance.

Performance	Training			
	Intensive	Good	Average	Total
Above average	100	150	40	290
Average	100	100	100	300
Poor	50	80	150	280
Total	250	330	290	870

Solution:

H_0 : Attribute performance and the training are independent.

H_1 : Attribute performance and the training are not independent.

The expected frequencies corresponding the ith row and the jth column in the contingency table are denoted by E_{ij}, where i = 1, 2, 3 and j = 1, 2, 3.

$$E_{1,1} = \frac{290 \times 250}{870} = 83.33$$

$$E_{1,2} = \frac{290 \times 330}{870} = 110.00$$

$$E_{1,3} = \frac{290 \times 290}{870} = 96.67$$

$$E_{2,1} = \frac{300 \times 250}{870} = 86.21$$

$$E_{2,2} = \frac{300 \times 330}{870} = 113.79$$

$$E_{2,3} = \frac{300 \times 290}{870} = 100.00$$

$$E_{3,1} = \frac{280 \times 250}{870} = 80.46$$

$$E_{3,2} = \frac{280 \times 330}{870} = 106.21$$

$$E_{3,3} = \frac{280 \times 290}{870} = 93.33$$

The table of the observed and expected frequencies corresponding to the ith row and the jth column and the computation of the chi-square is given in the table.

Row, Column	O_{ij}	E_{ij}	$(O_{ij} - E_{ij})^2$	$\frac{(O_{ij} - E_{ij})^2}{E_{ij}}$
1,1	100	83.33	277.89	3.335
1,2	150	110.00	1600.00	14.545
1,3	40	96.67	3211.49	33.221
2,1	100	86.21	190.16	2.21
2,2	100	113.79	190.16	1.671
2,3	100	100.00	0	0.000
3,1	50	80.46	927.81	11.53
3,2	80	106.21	686.96	6.468
3,3	150	93.33	3211.49	34.41
		Total		107.39

$$\text{Sample } \chi^2 = \sum_{i=1}^{r} \sum_{j=1}^{c} \frac{(O_{ij} - E_{ij})^2}{E_{ij}} = 107.39$$

The critical value of the chi-square at 5 per cent level of significance with 4 degrees of freedom is given by 9.49. The sample value of the chi-square falls in the rejection region as shown in the figure on next page.

Therefore, the null hypothesis is rejected and one can conclude that there is an association between the type of training and performance.

Using a p value approach, it can be seen that the computed value of chi-square (107.39) with 4 df is higher than the critical value (13.28) at 1 per cent level of significance. Therefore, the p value of this problem is less than 0.01 which is far below the level of significance. Therefore, the null hypothesis is rejected. This means that there is a relationship between the type of training and the performance.

Rejection region for Example 14.3.

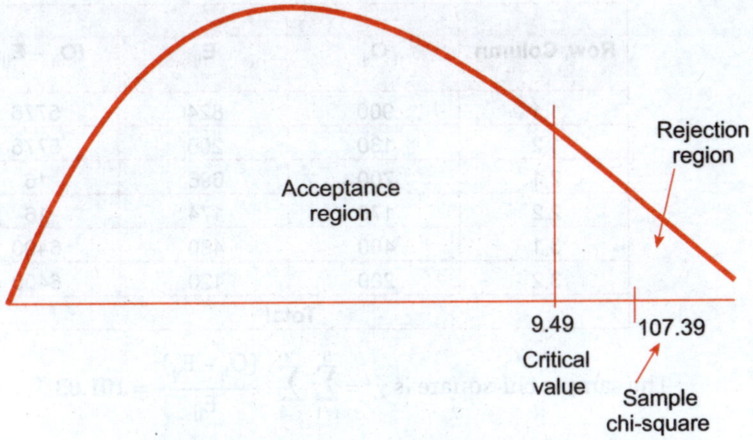

Example 14.4 The following table gives the number of good and defective parts produced by each of the three shifts in a factory:

Shift	Good	Defective	Total
Day	900	130	1030
Evening	700	170	870
Night	400	200	600
Total	2000	500	2500

Is there any association between the shift and the equality of the parts produced? Use a 0.05 level of significance. *[MBA, Kumoun Univ, 2000; MBA, DU, 2003, 2005]*

Solution:

H_0 : There is no association between the shift and the quality of parts produced.

H_1 : There is an association between the shift and quality of parts.

The computations of the expected frequencies corresponding to the ith row and the jth column of the contingency table are shown below: (i = 1, 2, 3) and (j = 1, 2).

$$E_{1,1} = \frac{1030 \times 2000}{2500} = 824$$

$$E_{1,2} = \frac{1030 \times 500}{2500} = 206$$

$$E_{2,1} = \frac{870 \times 2000}{2500} = 696$$

$$E_{2,2} = \frac{870 \times 500}{2500} = 174$$

$$E_{3,1} = \frac{600 \times 2000}{2500} = 480$$

$$E_{3,2} = \frac{600 \times 500}{2500} = 120$$

The table of the observed and expected frequencies corresponding to the ith row and the jth column and the computation of the chi-square is given below:

Row, Column	O_{ij}	E_{ij}	$(O_{ij} - E_{ij})^2$	$\frac{(O_{ij} - E_{ij})^2}{E_{ij}}$
1,1	900	824	5776	7.010
1,2	130	206	5776	28.039
2,1	700	696	16	0.023
2,2	170	174	16	0.092
3,1	400	480	6400	13.333
3,2	200	120	6400	53.333
		Total		**101.83**

The sample chi-square is $\chi^2 = \sum_{i=1}^{3} \sum_{j=1}^{2} \frac{(O_{ij} - E_{ij})^2}{E_{ij}} = 101.83$

The critical value of the chi-square with 2 degrees of freedom at 5 per cent level of significance is given by 5.991. The null hypothesis is rejected as the sample chi-square lies in the rejection region as shown in the figure below. Therefore, the quality of parts produced is related to the shifts in which they were produced.

Rejection region for Example 14.4.

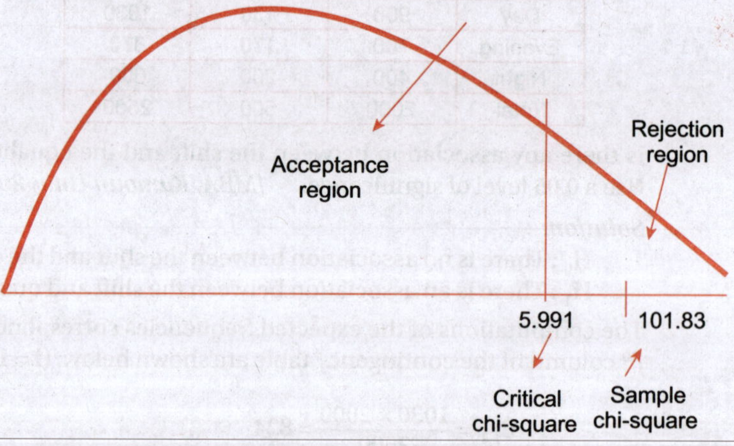

Using a p value approach, the same decision would be arrived at. It is left for the readers to show it.

It may be worth mentioning again that for the application of a chi-square test of independence, the sample should be selected at random and the expected frequency in each cell should be at least 5.

A chi-square test for the equality of more than two population proportions

In certain situations, the researchers may be interested to test whether the proportion of a particular characteristic is the same in several populations. The interest may lie in finding out whether the proportion of people liking a movie is the same for the three age groups, 25 and under, over 25 and under 50, and 50 and over. To take another example, the interest may be in determining whether in an organization, the proportion of the satisfied employees in four categories—class I, class II, class III, and class IV employees—is the same. In a sense, the question of whether the proportions are equal is a question of whether the three age populations of different categories are homogeneous with respect to the characteristics being studied. Therefore, the

The tests for the equality of proportions across several populations are also called tests of homogeneity.

tests for equality of proportions across several populations are also called tests of homogeneity.

The analysis is carried out exactly in the same way as was done for the other two cases. The formula for a chi-square analysis remains the same. However, two important assumptions here are different.

(i) We identify our population (e.g., age groups or various class employees) and the sample directly from these populations.

(ii) As we identify the populations of interest and the sample from them directly, the sizes of the sample from different populations of interest are fixed. This is also called a chi-square analysis with fixed marginal totals. The hypothesis to be tested is as under:

H_0 : The proportion of people satisfying a particular characteristic is the same in population.

H_1 : The proportion of people satisfying a particular characteristic is not the same in all populations.

The expected frequency for each cell could also be obtained by using the formula as explained earlier. There is an alternative way of computing the same, which would give identical results. This is shown in the following example:

Example 14.5

An accountant wants to test the hypothesis that the proportion of incorrect transactions at four client accounts is about the same. A random sample of 80 transactions of one client reveals that 21 are incorrect; for the second client, the number is 25 out of 100; for the third client, the number is 30 out of 90 sampled and for the fourth, 40 are incorrect out of a sample of 110. Conduct the test at $\alpha = 0.05$.

Solution:

Let p_1 = Proportion of incorrect transaction for 1st client
p_2 = Proportion of incorrect transaction for 2nd client
p_3 = Proportion of incorrect transaction for 3rd client
p_4 = Proportion of incorrect transaction for 4th client

Let $H_0 : p_1 = p_2 = p_3 = p_4$
H_1 : All proportions are not the same.

The observed data in the problem can be rewritten as:

Transactions	Client 1	Client 2	Client 3	Client 4	Total
Incorrect transactions	21	25	30	40	116
Correct transactions	59	75	60	70	264
Total	80	100	90	110	380

An estimate of the combined proportion of the incorrect transactions under the assumption that the null hypothesis is true:

$$p = \frac{21 + 25 + 30 + 40}{80 + 100 + 90 + 110} = \frac{116}{380} = 0.305$$

q = Combined proportion of the correct transaction

$$= 1 - p = 1 - 0.305 = 0.695$$

Using the above, the expected frequencies corresponding to the various cells are computed as shown below:

Transactions	Client 1	Client 2	Client 3	Client 4	Total
Incorrect transactions	80 × 0.305 = 24.4	100 × 0.305 = 30.5	90 × 0.305 = 27.45	110 × 0.305 = 33.55	115.9
Correct transactions	80 × 0.695 = 55.6	100 × 0.695 = 69.5	90 × 0.695 = 62.55	110 × 0.695 = 76.45	264.1
Total	80	100	90	110	380

In fact, the sum of each row/column in both the observed and expected frequency tables should be the same. Here, a bit of discrepancy is found because of the rounding of the error. It can be easily verified that the expected frequencies in each cell would be the same using the formula $E_{ij} = \frac{R_i \times C_j}{n}$ as already explained. Now the value of the chi-square statistic can be calculated as:

$$\chi^2 = \sum_{i=1}^{2}\sum_{j=1}^{4}\frac{(O_{ij}-E_{ij})^2}{E_{ij}} = \frac{(21-24.4)^2}{24.4} + \frac{(25-30.5)^2}{30.5} + \frac{(30-27.45)^2}{27.45} + \frac{(40-33.55)^2}{33.55} + \frac{(59-55.6)^2}{55.6} + \frac{(75-69.5)^2}{69.5}$$

$$+ \frac{(60-62.55)^2}{62.55} + \frac{(70-76.45)^2}{76.45}$$

$$= 0.474 + 0.992 + 0.237 + 1.240 + 0.208 + 0.435 + 0.104 + 0.544$$

$$= 4.234$$

Degrees of freedom (df) = (2 – 1) × (4 – 1) = 3

The critical value of the chi-square with 3 degrees of freedom at 5 per cent level of significance equals 7.815. Since the sample value of χ^2 is less than the critical value, there is not enough evidence to reject the null hypothesis. Therefore, the null hypothesis is accepted. Therefore, there is no significant difference in the proportion of incorrect transaction for the four clients.

Use of SPSS in the Chi-square Analysis

In Chapter 11, Table 11.17 presented the data on 100 respondents regarding their preference for fast food. The other variables contained in that table were gender, age and income. The preference data was on a 5-point interval scale where 1 = Not at all preferred, 2 = Not preferred, 3 = Neutral, 4 = Preferred, and 5 = Very much preferred. Gender was a nominal scale variable, coded as Male = 1 and Female = 2. Income was divided into three categories, coded as 1 = household income less than ₹25,000 per month (low-income group), 2 = household income of ₹25,000 per month and above but less than ₹50,000 per month (middle income group), 3 = household income of ₹50,000 and above (high-income group). Age of the respondents was the actual age presented in Table 11.17 and is of the ratio scale measurement. We had earlier asked three questions on the cross-tabulation and used percentages in the direction of causal variables for the analysis. We will carry out the same analysis using a chi-square test. For the sake of ease, we reproduce below the same three questions with a bit of modification.

Questions:

Divide the sample into two groups based upon the preference scores. Those scoring from 1 to 3 could be regarded as respondents for whom fast food is 'not a preferred' choice. The respondents having a score of 4 or 5 may be treated as those who 'prefer' fast food.

(i) Prepare a cross-tabulation table of the above mentioned groups on their preference for fast food with age groups, where respondents aged less than or equal to 40 may be treated as younger respondents, and above 40 may be treated as older respondents. Find the association between age and preference for fast food.

(ii) Again, cross-tabulate the preference for fast food against the income level as defined earlier. Examine whether preference is related to income.

(iii) Cross-tabulate the above two groups against gender. Find out the association between gender and preference for fast food.

The coded data for the above problem is already available in SPSS (refer to SPSS Table 11.17). The chi-square results (which would follow soon) are used to test the following hypothesis for the first question.

H_0 : Age and preference for fast food are independent.
H_1 : Age and preference for fast food are related.

One could follow the SPSS instructions as given in Appendix 14.1. Table 14.2 gives observed and expected frequencies for the above problem. Using the formula for the expected frequencies discussed in this chapter, one can check to see that the expected frequencies reported are correct.

The chi-square value can be computed using the formula explained earlier in the chapter and which using the SPSS is shown in Table 14.3. The value of the computed chi-square is 10.282, which is highly significant if we use the level of significance to be 5 per cent. This is so because the p-value for this problem is 0.001 as shown in the significance (2-sided) in the computer printout, (Table 14.3) which is below 0.05, the assumed level of significance.

TABLE 14.2
Preference redefined vs age redefined cross-tabulation

Preference Redefined	Count/ Expected Count	Age Redefined		Total
		Younger Respondent	Older Respondent	
Not preferred	Count	24	30	54
	Expected Count	31.9	22.1	54.0
Preferred	Count	35	11	46
	Expected Count	27.1	18.9	46.0
Total	Count	59	41	100
	Expected Count	59.0	41.0	100.0

TABLE 14.3
Chi-square tests

	Value	df	Asymp. Sig. (2-sided)	Exact Sig. (2-sided)	Exact Sig. (1-sided)
Pearson Chi-Square	**10.282[b]**	**1**	**0.001**		
Continuity Correction[a]	9.015	1	0.003		
Likelihood Ratio	10.573	1	0.001		
Fisher's Exact Test				0.002	0.001
Linear-by-Linear Association	10.179	1	0.001		
N of Valid Cases	100				

[a] Computed only for a 2 × 2 table
[b] 0 cells (.0 per cent) have expected count less than 5. The minimum expected count is 18.86.

Since the chi-square value is significant it means that we can reject the null hypothesis. This means that there is enough evidence to conclude that age and the preference for fast food are related. The next question that comes to our mind is, how strong is this relationship? The answer to this is given by a statistic called contingency coefficient, which is used only when the null hypothesis is rejected.

Contingency coefficient: The contingency coefficient is computed when the number of rows and the number of columns in a contingency table are equal. The value of the contingency coefficient is given by:

The contingency coefficient is computed when the number of rows and the number of columns in a contingency table are equal. It is given by:

$$C=\sqrt{\frac{\chi^2}{n+\chi^2}}$$

$$C=\sqrt{\frac{\chi^2}{n+\chi^2}}$$

In the present case n = 100, sample $\chi^2 = 10.282$

Therefore, $$C=\sqrt{\frac{10.282}{100+10.282}}=\sqrt{\frac{10.282}{110.282}}=0.305$$

We need to know the lower and upper limit of the contingency coefficient (C) to determine how strong is the relationship between age and preference. The lower limit of C equals zero when χ^2 is zero. The χ^2 will take a value of zero when the variables are independent. The upper limit of C when the number of rows is equal to the number of columns is given by the expression:

$$\sqrt{\frac{r-1}{r}}$$

where, r = number of rows

Therefore, the upper limit of $C=\sqrt{1/2}=0.707$. Now, the computed value of the contingency coefficient is 0.305 (Table 14.4) which is approximately midway between 0 and 0.707. This means that there is a moderate relationship between the variables.

Phi coefficient (φ): There is another statistic called the phi-coefficient which can be used to determine the strength of a relationship only in a 2 × 2 contingency table. The phi-coefficient like the correlation coefficient can assume any value between –1 and 1. Let us rewrite Table 14.2 as Table 14.5:

TABLE 14.4
Symmetric measures

		Value	Approx. Sig.
Nominal by Nominal	Phi	–0.321	0.001
	Cramer's V	0.321	0.001
	Contingency Coefficient	0.305	0.001
N of Valid Cases		100	

Phi-coefficient (φ) may be computed by using the following formula:

Phi coefficient can be used only in a case of 2 × 2 contingency table. It can assume any value between –1 and 1.

$$\varphi=\frac{ad-bc}{\sqrt{(a+b)(c+d)(a+c)(b+d)}}$$

$$\varphi=\frac{ad-bc}{\sqrt{(a+b)(c+d)(a+c)(b+d)}}$$

$$=\frac{24\times 11-30\times 35}{\sqrt{(54)(46)(59)(41)}}$$

$$=\frac{-786}{2451.286}=-0.321$$

TABLE 14.5
Preference redefined vs age redefined cross-tabulation

Preference Redefined	Age Redefined		Total
	Younger Respondent	Older Respondent	
Not preferred	24 (a)	30 (b)	54 (a + b)
Preferred	35 (c)	11 (d)	46 (c + d)
Total	59 (a + c)	41 (b + d)	100 (a + b + c + d)

This computed value of φ is shown in Table 14.4 also. The phi-coefficient can assume a positive or negative value. However, the sign of the phi-coefficient does not have any particular meaning. If the responses were concentrated in the cells a and d instead of b and c, the sign of phi-coefficient would have been positive.

The value of φ^2 (the square of φ coefficient) measures the proportion of one variable that is explained by the other variable. In the present case $\varphi^2 = 0.1034$, which indicates that 10.34 per cent of variations in the preference are explained by age.

Table 14.6 gives a description of the strength of a relationship for a given particular phi value.

TABLE 14.6
Value of φ and implied strength of relationship

Value of ± φ	Strength of Relationship
Greater than 0.80	Strong
0.40 to 0.80	Moderate
0.20 to 0.40	Weak
0.00 to 0.20	Negligible

Source: Luck and Rubin (1992).

$V = \sqrt{\frac{\chi^2}{n(f-1)}}$

Cramer's V statistic: When the number of rows is not equal to the number of columns, we may use the statistic called Cramer's V statistic given by:

$$V = \sqrt{\frac{\chi^2}{n(f-1)}}$$

where, f = Min (rows, columns)

In Question (ii), we prepared a 2 × 3 cross-table between the preference for fast food and income. The hypothesis to be tested in this case is:

H_0 : Preference is not related to income.
H_1 : Preference is related to income.

The table of observed and expected frequencies is given in Table 14.7.

TABLE 14.7
Preference redefined vs income cross-tabulation

Preference Redefined	Count/ Expected Count	Income			Total
		Low Income	Middle Income	High Income	
Not preferred	Count	22	19	13	54
	Expected Count	14.0	15.7	24.3	54.0
Preferred	Count	4	10	32	46
	Expected Count	12.0	13.3	20.7	46.0
Total	Count	26	29	45	100
	Expected Count	26.0	29.0	45.0	100.0

TABLE 14.8
Chi-square tests

	Value	df	Asymp. Sig. (2-sided)
Pearson Chi-Square	22.783[a]	2	0.000
Likelihood Ratio	24.197	2	0.000
Linear-by-Linear Association	21.938	1	0.000
N of Valid Cases	100		

[a] 0 cells (.0 per cent) have expected count less than 5. The minimum expected count is 11.96.

The sample chi-square can be obtained by making use of the formula already discussed and its value is given as 22.783 as shown in Table 14.8. The χ^2 value is significant as the p value (0.000) is less than $\alpha = 0.05$.

Therefore, the null hypothesis of no relationship between the income and preference is rejected. To determine the strength of relationship between the two variables, Cramer V statistic is used as mentioned earlier since the number of rows is not equal to the number of columns. The value of Cramer V statistics is obtained as:

$$V = \sqrt{\frac{\chi^2}{n(f-1)}} = \sqrt{\frac{22.783}{100}} = 0.477$$

The value of Cramer's V statistic using SPSS is given in Table 14.9.

TABLE 14.9
Symmetric measures

		Value	Approx. Sig.
Nominal by Nominal	Phi	0.477	0.000
	Cramer's V	**0.477**	**0.000**
	Contingency Coefficient	0.431	0.000
N of Valid Cases		100	

The **chi-square** takes a zero value when the variables are independent. The **maximum value of a chi-square** equals n (f–1).

To determine the strength of a relationship, we need to find the lower and upper limit of Cramer's V statistic. The lower limit of V is zero, when the value of the chi-square is zero. The chi-square takes a zero value when the variables are independent. The maximum value of a chi-square equals n (f–1). Therefore, the upper limit of the V statistic equals one when χ^2 is maximum. In the present case, the value of V is 0.477 which implies that there is a moderate relationship between the variables.

Similarly, a chi-square analysis could be performed by using the SPSS software to examine the relationship between preference and gender. It is left for the readers to carry out the exercise and interpret the results.

Another use of the SPSS for a χ^2 analysis is to test whether the observed data in a frequency distribution is uniform over all the classes. In Table 11.6, the income variable was categorized as less than ₹25,000, between ₹25,000 and ₹50,000 and ₹50,000 and above. Suppose we want to test whether 100 respondents are uniformly distributed over the three income classes. The hypothesis could be written as:

H_0 : Respondents are uniformly distributed over all the three income classes.
H_1 : Respondents are not uniformly distributed over all the three income classes.

The observed frequency distribution for each of the income classes can be obtained by using the income variable data. The expected frequencies for each class under the assumption that the null hypothesis is true is 100/3 = 33.33. Now using the observed and expected frequencies of each class, the sample chi-square can be computed using SPSS, the instructions for which are given in Appendix 14.2.

TABLE 14.10
Observed and expected frequencies of respondent categorized into income groups

Income Groups	Observed N	Expected N	Residual
Low Income	26	33.3	–7.3
Middle Income	29	33.3	–4.3
High Income	45	33.3	11.7
Total	100		

TABLE 14.11
Test statistics

	Income
Chi-square[a]	6.260
Df	2
Asymp. Sig.	0.044

[a] 0 cells (.0 per cent) have expected frequencies less than 5. The minimum expected cell frequency is 33.3.

The observed and expected frequencies using SPSS software are given in Table 14.10.

Table 14.11 gives the computed chi-square value of 6.260 with 2 degrees of freedom. The p value corres-ponding to the chi-square is 0.044, which is less than 0.05, the level of significance. Therefore, the null hypothesis that the respondents are uniformly distributed over the three income categories is rejected.

CONCEPT CHECK

1. Discuss the advantages and disadvantages of non-parametric tests.
2. What is a chi-square test?
3. Illustrate a chi-square test for independence of variables.

RUN TEST FOR RANDOMNESS

LEARNING OBJECTIVE 3
Explain the run test of randomness for the metric and non-metric data.

One of the assumptions that are usually made by researchers is that a random sample is drawn from the population. Most of the tests of significance based upon the Z, t or F distribution make use of this assumption. Here, we will discuss a test called the run test to examine the randomness of the sample. As the test on randomness is based upon the concept of run, it is appropriate at this stage to define a run.

Run: A run is defined as a sequence of like elements that are preceded and followed by different elements or no elements at all. The concept of run to examine the randomness of a sample is discussed in the following examples.

Example 14.6

Run test is used to examine the randomness of the sample. A run is a sequence of like elements that are preceded and followed by different elements or no elements at all.

To explain the concept of run, consider an example where the sex of a customer entering a restaurant is noted. Suppose the following sequence is obtained:

M M F M F F F M M M M F F F M M F F F M M M M M F F M M M F F F M F F F F F M M F F F F F

where, M and F denote the male and female entrant respectively. The number of runs (r) in the above sample of the 45 entrants of a restaurant is shown below:

<u>M M</u> <u>F</u> <u>M</u> <u>F F F</u> <u>M M M M</u> <u>F F F</u> <u>M M</u> <u>F F F</u> <u>M M M M M</u> <u>F F</u> <u>M M M</u> <u>F F F</u> <u>M</u> <u>F F F F F</u> <u>M M</u> <u>F F F F F</u>

The total number of runs is 16 as shown by the lines below the identical symbols. In the above example:

n (Total size of the sample) = 45
n_1 (Number of males in the sample) = 20

n_2 (Number of females in the samples) = 25
r (Number of runs) = 16

Too many or too few runs in a sequence indicates a lack of randomness. For large samples, either $n_1 > 20$ or $n_2 > 20$, the distribution of runs (r) is normally distributed with mean:

$$\mu_r = 1 + \frac{2n_1n_2}{n_1 + n_2}$$

and standard deviation:

$$\sigma_r = \sqrt{\frac{2n_1n_2(2n_1n_2 - n_1 - n_2)}{(n_1 + n_2)^2(n_1 + n_2 - 1)}}$$

The hypothesis is to be tested is:

H_0 : The pattern of sequence is random.
H_1 : The pattern of sequence is not random.

For a large sample, the test statistic is given by $Z = \frac{r - \mu_r}{\sigma_r}$

$$\mu_r = 1 + \frac{2n_1n_2}{n_1 + n_2} = 1 + \frac{2(20)(25)}{20 + 25}$$

$$= 1 + \frac{1000}{45} = 1 + 22.22$$

$$= 23.22$$

$$\sigma_r = \sqrt{\frac{2n_1n_2(2n_1n_2 - n_1 - n_2)}{(n_1 + n_2)^2(n_1 + n_2 - 1)}} = \sqrt{\frac{2 \times 20 \times 25\,(2 \times 20 \times 25 - 20 - 25)}{(20 + 25)^2(20 + 25 - 1)}}$$

$$\sigma_r = \sqrt{\frac{1000\,(1000 - 45)}{(45)^2(44)}} = \sqrt{\frac{1000 \times 955}{2025 \times 44}} = \sqrt{\frac{955{,}000}{89{,}100}} = \sqrt{10.72} = 3.27$$

The sample Z statistic could be computed as:

$$Z = \frac{r - \mu_r}{\sigma_r} = \frac{16 - 23.22}{3.27} = \frac{-7.22}{3.27} = -2.21$$

Assuming a 5 per cent level of significance, the critical value of Z is given by ± 1.96. As the absolute Z value is greater than the absolute critical value of Z, the null hypothesis is rejected. Therefore, the sequence of this observation is not randomly generated.

The example discussed above clearly fits into two categories (nominal measurement). The test for randomness can also be applied to the interval or ratio scale data. What is required is that the interval/ratio scale data should be converted into a nominal scale measurement. To partition the data into two categories, one could use the value of mean or median and randomness can be tested for the numerical data above or below the median. For illustration purposes, consider the following example.

Example 14.7

The data listed below is the lifetime of batteries in hours produced by ZIDA company in a particular order.

270,	280,	248,	260,	220,	285,	270,	266,	269,	266,	272,
225,	228,	290,	284,	282,	276,	269,	250,	249,	262,	273,
277,	258,	264,	269,	276,	278,	249,	286,	282,	264,	201,
215,	222,	238,	212,	242,	236,	247,	249,	248,	256,	271,
282,	305,	217,	303,	305,	309,	320,	262,	244,	262,	267.

Assuming a significance level of 5 per cent, determine whether the sample lifetime of the batteries produced by ZIDA is random.

Solution:

H_0 : Lifetime of batteries is random.

H_1 : Lifetime of batteries is not random.

There are 55 observations. We will first compute the median of the distribution by arranging the data in an ascending order of magnitude shown below:

201, 212, 215, 217, 220, 222, 225, 228, 236, 238, 242,
244, 247, 248, 248, 249, 249, 249, 250, 256, 258, 260,
262, 262, 262, 264, 264, **266, 266,** 267, 269, 269, 269,
270, 270, 271, 272, 273, 276, 276, 277, 278, 280, 282,
282, 282, 284, 285, 286, 290, 303, 305, 305, 309, 320,

As there are 55 observations, the value of the middle (28th) observation when data is arranged in an ascending order of magnitude gives the median of distribution. Please note that the 28th observation when the data is arranged in an ascending order of magnitude is 266. There are two observations having a value of 266. Therefore, these two are discarded and for further analysis we will have 53 observations. Now the original data will be divided into two categories—above the median denoted by (A) and below the median denoted by (B). The number of runs could be obtained as shown below:

A A B B B A A A B B A A A A A B B B A A B B A A A B A A

B B B B B B B B B B B   A A A B A A A A B B B A

The total number of runs (r) = 17

Number of observations above median (n_1) = 26

Number of observations below median (n_2) = 27

Total number of observations (n) = 53

As both n_1 and n_2 are greater than 20, the distribution of runs (r) could be approximated by normal distribution with mean:

$$\mu_r = 1 + \frac{2n_1n_2}{n_1 + n_2} = 1 + \frac{2(26)(27)}{26+27}$$

$$= 1 + \frac{1404}{53} = 1 + 26.49 = 27.49$$

and standard deviation:

$$\sigma_r = \sqrt{\frac{2n_1n_2(2n_1n_2 - n_1 - n_2)}{(n_1+n_2)^2(n_1+n_2-1)}} = \sqrt{\frac{2\times 26\times 27\,(2\times 26\times 27 - 26 - 27)}{(26+27)^2(26+27-1)}}$$

$$\sigma_r = \sqrt{\frac{1404\,(1404-53)}{(53)^2(52)}} = \sqrt{\frac{1404\times 1351}{2809\times 52}} = \sqrt{\frac{1896804}{146068}} = \sqrt{12.99}$$

$$= 3.60$$

The sample Z statistic can be computed as:

$$Z = \frac{r - \mu_r}{\sigma_r} = \frac{17 - 27.49}{3.60} = \frac{-10.49}{3.60} = -2.91$$

Assuming a 5 per cent level of significance, the critical value of Z is given by ± 1.96. As the absolute computed value of Z is greater than the absolute critical value of Z, the null hypothesis is rejected. Therefore, the sequence of the observations indicating the lifetime of batteries is not random.

Example 14.8 A researcher conducts a survey to find out whether the inhabitants of a metro town are in favour of capital punishment (F) or against it (A). The sequence of responses to the question asked is given below. Use the run test at $\alpha = 0.05$ to test whether the responses are random.

F	F	A	F	F	F	A	A	A	A	A	F	F	A
A	A	F	F	A	A	A	A	A	A	F	F	A	A
A	A	A	A	F	F	F	A	A	A	F	A	F	F
F	F	A	A	A	A	F	F	F	A	A	A	F	F

Solution:

H_0: The sequence of the responses is random.
H_1: The sequence of the responses is not random.

Total number of runs (r) = 19
Number of observations in favour of capital punishment (n_1) = 24
Number of observations against capital punishment (n_2) = 32
Total number of observations (n) = 56

$$\mu_r = 1 + \frac{2n_1n_2}{n_1 + n_2} = 1 + \frac{2(24)(32)}{24 + 32}$$

$$= 1 + \frac{1536}{56} = 1 + 27.43 = 28.43$$

$$\sigma_r = \sqrt{\frac{2n_1n_2(2n_1n_2 - n_1 - n_2)}{(n_1 + n_2)^2 (n_1 + n_2 - 1)}} = \sqrt{\frac{2 \times 24 \times 32(2 \times 24 \times 32 - 24 - 32)}{(24 + 32)^2 (24 + 32 - 1)}}$$

$$\sigma_r = \sqrt{\frac{1536(1536 - 56)}{(56)^2 (55)}} = \sqrt{\frac{1536 \times 1480}{3136 \times 55}} = \sqrt{\frac{2273280}{172480}} = \sqrt{13.18}$$

$$= 3.63$$

The sample Z statistic could be computed as:

$$Z = \frac{r - \mu_r}{\sigma_r} = \frac{19 - 28.43}{3.36} = \frac{-9.43}{3.63} = -2.60$$

The absolute computed value of Z is greater than the absolute critical value of Z = 1.96. Therefore the hypothesis that the responses are random is rejected.

Use of SPSS in Conducting a Run Test

We can conduct a run test using both metric data as given in Example 14.7 and non-metric data as given in Example 14.8. The SPSS instructions for the conduct of the test are given in Appendix 14.3. The computer output corresponding to Example 14.7 is given in Table 14.12. The data for Example 14.7 is given in the SPSS file in the data disk.

In the Table 14.12, the median value is 266, and the number of observation below the median and greater than or equal to the median are 27 and 28 respectively. Please note that the same example was solved manually and we had taken values strictly above the median and that is the reason n_2 equals 26 there. For this reason,

TABLE 14.12
Runs test for data given in Example 14.7

	Life of Batteries (in hours)
Test Value[a]	266.00
Cases < Test Value	27
Cases >= Test Value	28
Total Cases	55
Number of Runs	17
Z	–3.129
Asymp. Sig. (2-tailed)	0.002

[a] Median.

the value of Z is slightly different in the SPSS printout. The p value here is 0.002, which is less than $\alpha = 0.05$, the assumed level of significance. This shows that the null hypothesis of randomness is rejected. The same results were obtained when the above example was worked out manually.

Example 14.8 is also solved using SPSS. It may be noted that the scale of data is nominal—F or A. For the SPSS we gave a value of 1 for F and –1 for A. The test value was taken as 0. The detailed instructions are in Appendix 14.4. The data for Example 14.18 is given in the SPSS file in the data disk. The computer output is given in Table 14.13.

In Table 14.13, one can verify the results with Example 14.8 that was worked out

TABLE 14.13
Runs test for data given in Example 14.8

	Opinion about Capital Punishment
Test Value[a]	0.0000
Total Cases	56
Number of Runs	19
Z	–2.597
Asymp. Sig. (2-tailed)	.009

[a] User-specified.

manually. It could be seen that the results are identical. The p value is 0.009, which is less than 0.05, the level of significance. Therefore, the null hypothesis of randomness is rejected. Therefore, the sequence of response for or against capital punishment is not random.

ONE-SAMPLE SIGN TEST

LEARNING OBJECTIVE 4
Describe the one-sample and two-sample sign tests.

The test discussed in Chapter 12 is based upon the assumption that the samples are drawn from a population having roughly the shape of a normal distribution. This assumption gets violated, especially while using the non-metric data (ordinal or nominal). In such situations, the standard tests can be replaced by a non-parametric test. In this section, one such test, namely, the one-sample sign test would be explained.

Suppose the interest is in testing the null hypothesis $H_0 : \mu = \mu_0$ against a suitable alternative hypothesis. Let n denote the size of sample for any problem. To conduct a sign test, each sample observation greater than μ_0 is replaced by a plus sign, whereas each value less than μ_0 is replaced by a minus sign. In case a sample observation equals μ_0, it is omitted and the size of the sample gets reduced accordingly.

Testing the given null hypothesis is equivalent to testing that these plus and minus signs are the values of a random variable having a binomial distribution with p = ½.

For a small sample, the test is performed by computing the binomial probabilities. For a large sample when both np and nq are at least 5, the normal approximation to the binomial distribution is used. In such a situation, the Z score corresponding to the value of the binomial variable X is given by:

$Z = \frac{X - \mu}{\sigma} = \frac{X - np}{\sqrt{npq}}$

$$Z = \frac{X - \mu}{\sigma} = \frac{X - np}{\sqrt{npq}}$$

where, μ = Mean of binomial distribution = np

σ = Standard deviation of binomial distribution = $\sqrt{npq}$

As the binomial distribution is a discrete one whereas the normal distribution is a continuous distribution, a correction for continuity is to be made. For this, X is decreased by 0.5 if X > np and increased by 0.5 if X < np. As under the null hypothesis, $p = ½$, therefore $\mu = np = \frac{n}{2} = 0.5\,n$ and $\sigma = \sqrt{npq} = \sqrt{n \times \frac{1}{2} \times \frac{1}{2}} = \frac{\sqrt{n}}{2} = 0.5\sqrt{n}$. Let us consider a few examples to illustrate the sign test.

Example 14.9

The interest is to test the hypothesis that the median value of a distribution is 19 against the alternative hypothesis that it is greater than 19. A sample of 24 observations is taken with the following results:

18, 24, 20, 26, 23, 17, 24, 21,
22, 20, 16, 27, 25, 25, 14, 20,
15, 18, 22, 21, 24, 26, 27, 29,

You may use a 5 per cent level of significance.

Solution:

$H_0 : p = ½$

$H_1 : p > ½$

Replacing each value greater than 19 by a plus sign and those with less than 19 by a minus sign, we get:

− + + + + − + +
\+ + − + + + − +
− − + + + + + +

There are 18 plus and 6 minus signs. Since both np = 24 × ½ = 12 and nq = 24 × ½ = 12 are greater than 5, a normal approximation to the binomial distribution can be used.

Therefore, the test statistic is given by:

$$Z = \frac{X - np_o}{\sqrt{np_o(1 - p_o)}}$$

$$= \frac{(18 - .05) - 0.5 \times 24}{0.5\sqrt{n}} = \frac{17.5 - 12}{0.5 \times \sqrt{24}} = \frac{5.5}{0.5 \times 4.9} = \frac{5.5}{2.45} = 2.24$$

The critical value of Z at 5 per cent level of significance equals 1.645. As the sample value of Z is greater than the critical value, the null hypothesis is rejected and the median of the distribution is greater than 19.

Example 14.10 A survey was conducted to understand the preference for fast food by the inhabitants of a small town. A sample of 100 respondents indicated that 54 do not prefer fast food whereas 46 have a preference for the fast food. By using a sign test, examine the hypothesis that half of the inhabitants of the town prefer fast food. Let the level of significance be 5 per cent.

Solution:

$H_0 : p = ½$

$H_1 : p \neq ½$

where, p = Proportion not preferring fast food.

Denote those not preferring fast food by a plus sign and those preferring fast food by a minus sign. Therefore, there are 54 plus signs and 46 minus signs. The test statistic in this case is:

$$Z = \frac{(X - 0.5) - 0.5n}{0.5\sqrt{n}} = \frac{54 - 0.5 - 0.5 \times 100}{0.5\sqrt{100}} = \frac{53.5 - 50}{5} = \frac{3.5}{5} = 0.7$$

The critical value of Z at 5 per cent level of significance is ± 1.96. As the absolute sample value of Z is less than the critical value of Z, the null hypothesis is accepted. Therefore, the proportion of inhabitants not preferring fast food is not significantly different from the ones preferring fast food.

Example 14.11 A random sample of 80 batteries of TYZ company indicates that exactly 35 of them last 40 hours or more. Use the sign test to test the claim that the median life of a TYZ company battery is at least 40 hours. You may use a 5 per cent level of significance.

Solution:

H_0 : Median is at least 40 hrs (Median ≥ 40).

H_1 : Median is less than 100 (Median < 40).

We use a plus sign for the batteries having a life of at least 40 hours and a minus sign for those having a life of less than 40 hours. Therefore, we have 35 plus signs and 45 minus signs. We would use the Z statistic to test the hypothesis:

$$Z = \frac{(X + 0.5) - 0.5n}{0.5\sqrt{n}} = \frac{35 + 0.5 - 0.5 \times 80}{0.5\sqrt{80}} = \frac{35.5 - 40}{0.5 \times 8.94} = \frac{-4.5}{4.47} = -0.96$$

The critical value of Z = −1.645. As the absolute computed value of Z is less than the absolute critical value, there is not enough evidence to reject H_0. Thus, the median life of the batteries is at least 40 hours.

TWO-SAMPLE SIGN TEST

The **two-sample sign** test is a non-parametric test based upon the sign of a pair of observations.

The two-sample sign test is a very simple non-parametric test to use. In Chapter 12, we discussed the dependent sample (paired sample) test based upon a t distribution. The two-sample sign test is a non-parametric version of it. It is based upon the sign of a pair of observations. Suppose a sample of respondents is selected and their views on the image of a company are sought. After some time, these respondents are shown an advertisement, and thereafter, the data is again collected on the image of the company. For those respondents, where the image has improved, there is a positive and for those where the image has declined there is a negative sign assigned and for the one where there is no change, the corresponding observation is dropped from the analysis and the sample size reduced accordingly. The key concept underlying the test is that if the advertisement is not effective in improving the image of the company, the number of positive signs should be approximately equal to the number of negative signs. For small samples, a binomial distribution could be used, whereas for a large sample, the normal approximation to the binomial distribution could be used, as already explained in the one-sample sign test. Let us consider a few examples.

Example 14.12

Two psychology professors have developed their own version of an IQ test. A psychologist administered them on 17 individuals. The results are presented below. Using a 5 per cent level of significance, test the claim that there is no significant difference between two versions.

Individuals	Version 1	Version 2
1	96	102
2	110	106
3	105	105
4	109	97
5	98	102
6	104	103
7	96	97
8	111	112
9	88	85
10	109	107
11	110	112
12	96	94
13	89	91
14	88	95
15	100	103
16	106	104
17	99	102

Solution:

H_0: There is no significant difference between the two versions.

H_1: There is a significant difference between the two versions.

We note that there are 7 plus signs (score of Version 1 is more than that of Version 2), 9 minus signs (score of Version 1 is less than that of Version 2). There is one case with an identical score and therefore, this observation is dropped from the analysis and accordingly the sample size is reduced to 16.

Now, the Z statistic may be applied to test the hypothesis. This is because both np and nq are greater than 5 (16 × ½ = 8);

$$Z = \frac{(X - 0.5) - 0.5n}{0.5\sqrt{n}} = \frac{(9 - 0.5) - 0.5 \times 16}{0.5\sqrt{16}} = \frac{8.5 - 8}{0.5 \times 4} = \frac{0.5}{2} = 0.25$$

The critical value of Z at a 5 per cent level of significance is ± 1.96 (two-tailed test). As the absolute sample value of Z is less than the absolute critical value, there is not enough evidence to reject H_0. Therefore, there is no statistical difference between the IQ scores of the two versions. Therefore, it is safe to use any of the versions for measuring IQ.

Example 14.13

The following data represents the amount of money spent by 20 households when they eat at a Chinese and an Indian restaurant.

S. No.	Amount (in ₹) Spent at		S. No.	Amount (in ₹) Spent at	
	Chinese Restaurant	Indian Restaurant		Chinese Restaurant	Indian Restaurant
1	2780	2600	11	2700	2720
2	3200	3400	12	2600	2500
3	1800	1600	13	1200	1100
4	2000	1900	14	1000	1200
5	1800	1875	15	1400	1350
6	1600	1700	16	2500	2300
7	3000	3100	17	2100	2000
8	1600	1300	18	1800	1900
9	1400	1450	19	1600	1700
10	1500	1350	20	1500	1300

Use the sign test to examine the hypothesis that households on an average spend more money at a Chinese restaurant. You may use a 5 per cent level of significance.

Solution:

We will assign a positive sign to a household if the amount spent at a Chinese restaurant is more than at the Indian restaurant. A negative sign will be assigned if the amount spent at an Indian restaurant is higher than at the Chinese restaurant. In case of ties, the observation will be dropped from the analysis and the sample size would be reduced accordingly. We note that there are 12 plus and 8 minus signs. As both np and nq are greater than 5 (np = nq = 20 × ½ = 10), the normal approximation to binomial will be used for the purpose of testing the following hypothesis:

H_0 : The average amount spent by the households at a Chinese and an Indian restaurant is the same.

H_1 : The average amount spent at a Chinese restaurant is more than at an Indian restaurant.

$$Z = \frac{(X - 0.5) - 0.5n}{0.5\sqrt{n}} = \frac{(12 - 0.5) - 0.5 \times 20}{0.5\sqrt{20}} = \frac{11.5 - 10}{0.5 \times 4.47} = \frac{1.5}{2.24} = 0.67$$

The critical value of Z at a 5 per cent level of significance is 1.645. Since, the sample value of Z is less than the critical value of Z, the null hypothesis is accepted. Therefore, there is no difference in the average amount spent by the households while eating at a Chinese or an Indian restaurant.

MANN-WHITNEY U TEST FOR INDEPENDENT SAMPLES

LEARNING OBJECTIVE 5
Explain the procedure for conducting the Mann-Whitney U test.

This test was developed by H B Mann and R Whitney in the 1940s. The test is used to examine whether two samples have been drawn from populations with same locations (mean). This test is an alternative to a t test for testing the equality of means of two independent samples discussed in Chapter 12. The application of a t test involves the assumption that the samples are drawn from the normal population. If the normality assumption is violated, this test can be used as an alternative to a t test. This is a very powerful non-parametric test as this can be used both for qualitative and quantitative data. A two tailed hypothesis for a Mann-Whitney test could be written as:

H_0: Two samples come from identical populations

or

Two populations have identical probability distribution.

H_1: Two samples come from different populations

or

Two populations differ in locations.

The procedure involved in the use of Mann-Whitney U test is very simple and is described in the following steps:

(i) The two samples are combined (pooled) into one large sample and then we determine the rank of each observation in the pooled sample. If two or more sample values in the pooled samples are identical, i.e., if there are ties, the sample values are each assigned a rank equal to the mean of the ranks that would otherwise be assigned.

(ii) We determine the sum of the ranks of each sample. Let R_1 and R_2 represent the sum of the ranks of the first and the second sample whereas n_1 and n_2 are the respective sample sizes of the first and the second sample. For convenience, choose n_1 as a small size if they are unequal so that $n_1 \leq n_2$. A significant difference between R_1 and R_2 implies a significant difference between the samples.

(iii) Define $$U_1 = n_1 n_2 + \frac{n_1(n_1+1)}{2} - R_1$$

and $$U_2 = n_1 n_2 + \frac{n_2(n_2+1)}{2} - R_2$$

Please note that the following expression will hold true:

$$U_1 + U_2 = n_1 n_2$$

Mann-Whitney test for a large sample: If n_1 or n_2 is greater than 10, a large sample approximation can be used for the distribution of the Mann-Whitney U statistic. For this purpose, either of U_1 or U_2 could be used for testing a one-tailed or a two-tailed test. In this test, U_2 will be used for the purpose.

Under the assumption that the null hypothesis is true, the U_2 statistic follows an approximately normal distribution with mean:

$$\mu_{u_2} = \frac{n_1 n_2}{2}$$

and standard deviation:

$$\sigma_{u_2} = \sqrt{\frac{n_1 n_2 (n_1 + n_2 + 1)}{12}}$$

The test statistic is:

$$Z = \frac{U_2 - \mu_{u_2}}{\sigma_{u_2}}$$

The test statistic is: $Z = \frac{U_2 - \mu_{u_2}}{\sigma_{u_2}}$

Assuming the level of significance as equal to α, if the absolute sample value of Z is greater than the absolute critical value of Z, i.e., $Z_{\alpha/2}$, the null hypothesis is rejected. A similar procedure is used for a one tailed test. For a one sided upper tail test if the sample value of Z is greater than the critical Z_α, the null hypothesis is rejected. For a one-sided lower tail test, the null hypothesis is rejected if the sample Z is less than $-Z_\alpha$. Let us consider a few examples to illustrate the Mann-Whitney U test.

Example 14.14 The table below represents the number of bounced cheques in two banks—Bank A and Bank B—on randomly chosen 12 days for Bank A and 15 days for Bank B. Use a Mann-Whitney U test to examine at a 5 per cent level of significance whether Bank A has more bounced cheques as compared to Bank B.

Bank A	42	65	38	55	71	60	47	59	68	57	76	42			
Bank B	22	17	35	19	8	24	42	14	28	17	10	15	20	45	50

Solution:

H_0 : Two populations have identical probability distributions.
H_1 : Population A is shifted to the right of population B.

We pool both the samples and rank them. This is shown below:

Number of Bounced Cheques	Bank	Rank
8	B	1
10	B	2
14	B	3
15	B	4
17	B	5.5
17	B	5.5
19	B	7
20	B	8
22	B	9
24	B	10
28	B	11
35	B	12
38	A	13
42	A	15
42	A	15
42	B	15
45	B	17
47	A	18
50	B	19
55	A	20
57	A	21
59	A	22
60	A	23
65	A	24
68	A	25
71	A	26
76	A	27

We consider the sample of Bank B as coming from the population B whereas that of Bank A belonging to the population A.

$$R_1 = \text{Sum of ranks of Bank A} = 249$$
$$R_2 = \text{Sum of ranks of Bank B} = 129$$

$$\therefore \quad U_2 = n_1 n_2 + \frac{n_2(n_2+1)}{2} - R_2$$

$$= 12 \times 15 + \frac{15(15+1)}{2} - 129 = 180 + \frac{240}{2} - 129$$

$$= 180 + 120 - 129 = 300 - 129$$
$$= 171$$

The mean (μ_{u_2}) and standard deviation (σ_{u_2}) of the U_2 statistic are given as:

$$\mu_{u_2} = \frac{n_1 n_2}{2} = \frac{12 \times 15}{2} = 90$$

$$\sigma_{u_2} = \sqrt{\frac{n_1 n_2 (n_1 + n_2 + 1)}{12}} = \sqrt{\frac{(12)(15)(28)}{12}} = \sqrt{420} = 20.49$$

$$Z = \frac{U_2 - \mu_{u_2}}{\sigma_{u_2}} = \frac{171 - 90}{20.49} = \frac{81}{20.49} = 3.95$$

The critical value of Z at a 5 per cent level of significance is given by 1.645. The sample value of Z exceeds the critical value of Z and the null hypothesis is rejected. Therefore, Bank A has a larger number of bounced cheques as compared to Bank B.

Example 14.15

The data on the weekly expenditure (in ₹) on entertainment by 14 MBA students of college A and 16 students of college B is reported below. Test using a 1 per cent level of significance that there is no difference in the average expenditure of the students of the two colleges.

College A	250	300	350	180	280	260	400	190	320	340	370	160	500	550		
College B	380	130	400	450	360	270	500	480	450	470	500	550	575	470	480	220

Solution:

H_0 : Two populations have same location parameter.
H_1 : Two populations differ in location.

Consider the data on college A and college B as belonging to population 1 and 2 respectively. The two samples in the question are independent and therefore hypothesis could be tested using the Mann-Whitney U statistic. For this, we pool both the samples and rank them. This is shown below.

Weekly Expenditure (in ₹) on Entertainment	College	Rank
130	B	1
160	A	2
180	A	3
190	A	4
220	B	5
250	A	6
260	A	7
270	B	8
280	A	9
300	A	10
320	A	11
340	A	12
350	A	13
360	B	14
370	A	15
380	B	16

(Contd.)

Weekly Expenditure (in ₹) on Entertainment	College	Rank
400	A	17.5
400	B	17.5
450	B	19.5
450	B	19.5
470	B	21.5
470	B	21.5
480	B	23.5
480	B	23.5
500	A	26
500	B	26
500	B	26
550	A	28.5
550	B	28.5
575	B	30

R_1 = Sum of ranks of College A = 164
R_2 = Sum of ranks of College B = 301
$n_1 = 14$
$n_2 = 16$

$$\therefore \quad U_2 = n_1 n_2 + \frac{n_2(n_2+1)}{2} - R_2$$
$$= 14 \times 16 + \frac{16 \times 17}{2} - 301$$
$$= 224 + 136 - 301$$
$$= 59$$

The mean (μ_{u_2}) and the standard deviation (σ_{u_2}) of the U_2 statistic are given as:

$$\mu_{u_2} = \frac{n_1 n_2}{2} = \frac{14 \times 16}{2} = 112$$

$$\sigma_{u_2} = \sqrt{\frac{n_1 n_2 (n_1 + n_2 + 1)}{12}} = \sqrt{\frac{(14)(16)(31)}{12}} = \sqrt{\frac{6944}{12}} = \sqrt{578.67} = 24.055$$

The sample statistic Z is given by:

$$Z = \frac{U_2 - \mu u_2}{\sigma_{u_2}} = \frac{59 - 112}{24.055} = \frac{-53}{24.055} = -2.203$$

The critical value of Z at the 1 per cent level of significance is given by ±2.575. As the absolute value of the computed Z is less than the absolute value of the critical Z, there is not enough evidence to reject the null hypothesis. Therefore, we can conclude that there is no difference in the average expenditure on entertainment by the students of two colleges.

Use of SPSS in Conducting a Mann-Whitney U test

Examples 14.14 and 14.15 on the Mann-Whitney U test can be reworked by using the SPSS software. The instructions for the Mann-Whitney U test are given in Appendix 14.5. In Example 14.14 we were to test the following hypothesis:

H_0 : The number of bounced cheques in bank A and B are equal.
H_1 : The number of bounced cheques in Bank A is greater than bank B.

For this, the Mann-Whitney U test for a large sample was used. The data on a SPSS spreadsheet would as shown in Table 14.14.

Note: 1 = Bank A
2 = Bank B

The SPSS results for the Mann-Whitney U test are given in Tables 14.15 and 14.16.

TABLE 14.14
Data for Example 14.14 in SPSS format

S. No.	No. of Bounced Cheques	Label
1	42	1
2	65	1
3	38	1
4	55	1
5	71	1
6	60	1
7	47	1
8	59	1
9	68	1
10	57	1
11	76	1
12	42	1
13	22	2
14	17	2
15	35	2
16	19	2
17	8	2
18	24	2
19	42	2
20	14	2
21	28	2
22	17	2
23	10	2
24	15	2
25	20	2
26	45	2
27	50	2

TABLE 14.15
Ranks for Example 14.14

	Bank	N	Mean Rank	Sum of Ranks
Number of Bounced Cheques	Bank A	12	20.75	249.00
	Bank B	15	8.60	129.00
	Total	27		

TABLE 14.16
Test statistics for Example 14.14

	Number of Bounced Cheques
Mann-Whitney U	9.000
Wilcoxon W	129.000
Z	−3.955
Asymp. Sig. (2-tailed)	0.000
Exact Sig. [2*(1-tailed Sig.)]	0.000[a]

[a] Not corrected for ties.

We note from Table 14.15 that the sum of the ranks for Bank A equals 249 and for Bank B it is 129. The same results were obtained when we worked out the problem manually. The value of Z statistic in Table 14.16 is –3.95, whereas manually it is worked out to be +3.95. This has happened because the alternative hypothesis is taken in an opposite way in the software. (Bank A has more number of bounced cheques than Bank B is equivalent to writing that Bank B has a less number of bounced cheques as compared to Bank A.) However, our inferences remain the same. The p value for the problem is 0.000, which is less than 0.05, the assumed level of significance. This means that the null hypothesis is rejected in favour of the alternative hypothesis. Therefore, we can conclude that Bank A has more number of bounced cheques as compared to Bank B.

Similarly, Example 14.15 was reworked using the SPSS. The hypothesis to be tested in this case is:

H_0 : The weekly expenditure on entertainment by the students of college A and college B is the same.

H_1 : The weekly expenditure on entertainment by the students of college A and college B is different.

The data on Example 14.15 in SPSS format is presented in Table 14.17.

Note: 1 = College A
2 = College B

TABLE 14.17
Data for Example 14.15 in SPSS format

S. No.	Weekly Expenditure on Entertainment by Students	Label
1	250	1
2	300	1
3	350	1
4	180	1
5	280	1
6	260	1
7	400	1
8	190	1
9	320	1
10	340	1
11	370	1
12	160	1
13	500	1
14	550	1
15	380	2
16	130	2
17	400	2
18	450	2

S. No.	Weekly Expenditure on Entertainment by Students	Label
19	360	2
20	270	2
21	500	2
22	480	2
23	450	2
24	470	2
25	500	2
26	550	2
27	575	2
28	470	2
29	480	2
30	220	2

TABLE 14.18
Ranks for Example 14.15

	College	N	Mean Rank	Sum of Ranks
Weekly Expenditure on Entertainment by Students	College A	14	11.71	164.00
	College B	16	18.81	301.00
	Total	30		

TABLE 14.19
Test statistics for Example 14.15

	Weekly Expenditure on Entertainment by Students
Mann-Whitney U	59.000
Wilcoxon W	164.000
Z	–2.205
Asymp. Sig. (2-tailed)	0.027
Exact Sig. [2*(1-tailed Sig.)]	0.028[a]

[a] Not corrected for ties.

The SPSS results are presented in Tables 14.18 and 14.19. We note that the sum of ranks for college A equals 164 and for college B it is 301. The same results were obtained when the problem was worked out manually.

The sample Z value in the SPSS printout as given in Table 14.19 is –2.205. When the problem was worked out manually, approximately the same results were obtained. As the p value in this case is 0.027, which is higher than 0.01, the assumed level of significance, there is not enough evidence to reject the null hypothesis. Therefore, we can conclude that there is no difference in the weekly expenditure on entertainment by the students of college A and B.

CONCEPT CHECK

1. Discuss the run test for randomness.
2. What is a one-sample sign test?
3. Discuss the Mann-Whitney U test for independent samples.

WILCOXON SIGNED-RANK TEST FOR PAIRED SAMPLES

LEARNING OBJECTIVE 6
Discuss Wilcoxon signed-rank test for a paired sample.

The Mann-Whitney U test just discussed assumes that the two samples are independent. However, there are instances when the sample data consists of paired observations. Examples of paired samples include a study where husband and wife are matched or where subjects are studied before and after experimentation or observations are taken on a variable for brother and sister. The case of paired sample (dependent sample) was discussed in Chapter 12 using a t distribution. The use of t distribution is based on the normality assumption. However, there are instances when the normality assumption is not satisfied and one has to resort to a non-parametric test. One such test earlier discussed was the two-sample sign test. In this test, only the sign of the difference (positive or negative) was taken into account and no weightage was assigned to the magnitude of the difference. The Wilcoxon matched-pair signed rank test takes care of this limitation and attaches a greater weightage to the matched pair with a larger difference. The test, therefore, incorporates and makes use of more information than the sign test. This is, therefore, a more powerful test than the sign test.

The test procedure is outlined in the following steps:

(i) Let d_i denote the difference in the score for the ith matched pair. Retain signs, but discard any pair for which d = 0.
(ii) Ignoring the signs of difference, rank all the d_i's from the lowest to highest. In case the differences have the same numerical values, assign to them the mean of the ranks involved in the tie.
(iii) To each rank, prefix the sign of the difference.
(iv) Compute the sum of the absolute value of the negative and the positive ranks to be denoted as T_- and T_+ respectively.
(v) Let T be the smaller of the two sums found in step iv.

When the number of the pairs of observation (n) for which the difference is not zero is greater than 15, the T statistic follows an approximate normal distribution under the null hypothesis, that the population differences are centered at 0. The mean μ_T and standard deviation σ_T of T are given by:

$$\mu_T = \frac{n(n+1)}{4} \quad \text{and} \quad \sigma_T = \sqrt{\frac{n(n+1)(2n+1)}{24}}$$

The test statistic is given by:

The **test statistic** is given by:
$$Z = \frac{T - \frac{n(n+1)}{4}}{\sqrt{\frac{n(n+1)(2n+1)}{24}}}$$

$$Z = \frac{T - \frac{n(n+1)}{4}}{\sqrt{\frac{n(n+1)(2n+1)}{24}}}$$

For a given level of significance α, the absolute sample Z should be greater than the absolute $Z_{\alpha/2}$ to reject the null hypothesis. For a one-sided upper tail test, the null hypothesis is rejected if the sample Z is greater than Z_α and for a one-sided lower tail test, the null hypothesis is rejected if sample Z is less than $-Z_\alpha$. Let us consider an example to illustrate the Wilcoxon-Rank test for a paired sample.

Example 14.16

A sample of 16 salesmen was selected in an organization and their score on performance appraisal was noted. The salesmen were sent for a three-week training programme and in the next appraisal, their scores were noted again. The appraisal scores before and after the training are given below:

Salesman	1	2	3	4	5	6	7	8	9	10	11	12	13	14	15	16
Scores Before Training	85	76	64	59	72	68	43	54	57	61	71	82	39	51	54	57
Scores After Training	82	79	68	52	75	69	40	53	50	67	74	83	54	59	51	58

Use a 5 per cent level of significance to test the hypothesis that the training has not caused any change in the performance appraisal score.

Solution:

H_0 : There is no difference in the appraisal score because of training.

H_1 : There is a difference in the appraisal score because of training.

The value of the T statistic can be worked out as follows:

S. No.	Score Before Training	Score After Training	Difference	Absolute Difference	Rank of Absolute Difference	Negative Rank	Positive Rank
1	85	82	–3	3	7.5	7.5	
2	76	79	3	3	7.5		7.5
3	64	68	4	4	11		11
4	59	52	–7	7	13.5	13.5	
5	72	75	3	3	7.5		7.5
6	68	69	1	1	2.5		2.5
7	43	40	–3	3	7.5	7.5	
8	54	53	–1	1	2.5	2.5	
9	57	50	–7	7	13.5	13.5	
10	61	67	6	6	12		12
11	71	74	3	3	7.5		7.5
12	82	83	1	1	2.5		2.5
13	39	54	15	15	16		16
14	51	59	8	8	15		15
15	54	51	–3	3	7.5	7.5	
16	57	58	1	1	2.5		2.5
			Total			52	84

$$T_+ = \text{Sum of positive ranks} = 84$$
$$T_- = \text{Sum of negative ranks} = 52$$
$$T = \text{Min}\,(T_-, T_+) = 52$$

$$\mu_T = \frac{n(n+1)}{4} = \frac{16 \times 17}{4} = 68$$

$$\sigma_T = \sqrt{\frac{n(n+1)(2n+1)}{24}} = \sqrt{\frac{16 \times 17 \times 33}{24}} = \sqrt{374} = 19.34$$

The test statistic Z is written as:

$$Z = \frac{T - \mu_T}{\sigma_T} = \frac{52 - 68}{19.34} = \frac{-16}{19.34} = -0.83$$

The critical value of Z at 5 per cent level of significance is ± 1.96. As the absolute computed value of Z is less than the absolute critical value, the null hypothesis is accepted. Therefore, there is no change in the performance appraisal score because of training.

Use of SPSS in Conducting a Wilcoxon Signed-rank Test for Paired Samples

Example 14.16 was also solved using the SPSS software, the instructions of which are given in Appendix 14.6. The hypothesis to be tested in this problem is reproduced below:

H_0 : There is no difference in the appraisal score because of training.

H_1 : There is a difference in the appraisal score because of training.

The data required in the SPSS format is given in Table 14.20.

The SPSS results for the problem are given in Tables 14.21 and 14.22. It is seen that the sum of positive ranks works out to be 84, whereas the sum of negative ranks works out to be 52. The same results are obtained when the problem is worked out manually.

In Table 14.22, the Z value is –0.834 and has a p-value of 0.404, which is greater than 0.05, the assumed level of significance. Therefore, there is not enough evidence to reject the null hypothesis, thereby indicating that the score on the performance appraisal has not undergone a change after the training programme.

TABLE 14.20 Data for Example 14.16 in SPSS format

Salesman	Score Before Training	Score After Training
1	85	82
2	76	79
3	64	68
4	59	52
5	72	75
6	68	69
7	43	40
8	54	53
9	57	50
10	61	67
11	71	74
12	82	83
13	39	54
14	51	59
15	54	51
16	57	58

TABLE 14.21 Ranks for Example 14.16

		N	Mean Rank	Sum of Ranks
Score After Training – Score Before Training	Negative Ranks	6[a]	8.67	52.00
	Positive Ranks	10[b]	8.40	84.00
	Ties	0[c]		
	Total	16		

[a] Score After Training < Score Before Training
[b] Score After Training > Score Before Training
[c] Score After Training = Score Before Training

TABLE 14.22 Test statistics for Example 14.16

	Score After Training—Score Before Training
Z	–0.834[a]
Asymp. Sig. (2-tailed)	0.404

[a] Based on the negative ranks

THE KRUSKAL-WALLIS TEST

LEARNING OBJECTIVE 7
Describe the Kruskal-Wallis test.

When testing the equality of more than two population means, one-way ANOVA technique was used in Chapter 13. One of the assumptions used in ANOVA is that all the involved populations from where the samples are taken are normally distributed. If this assumption does not hold true, the F-statistic used in ANOVA becomes invalid. The normality assumptions may not hold true when we are dealing with ordinal data or when the size of the sample is very small.

The Kruskal-Wallis test comes to our rescue during such situations. This is, in fact, a non-parametric counterpart to the one-way ANOVA. The test is an extension of the Mann-Whitney U test discussed in this chapter. Both methods require that the scale of the measurement of a sample value should be at least ordinal.

The hypothesis to be tested in-Kruskal-Wallis test is:

H_0 : The k populations have identical probability distribution.
H_1 : At least two of the populations differ in locations.

The procedure for the test is listed below:

(i) Obtain random samples of size $n_1, ..., n_k$ from each of the k populations. Therefore, the total sample size is $n = n_1 + n_2 + ... + n_k$
(ii) Pool all the samples and rank them, with the lowest score receiving a rank of 1. Ties are to be treated in the usual fashion by assigning an average rank to the tied positions.
(iii) Let r_i = the total of the ranks from the ith sample.

The Kruskal-Wallis test uses the χ^2 to test the null hypothesis. The test statistic is given by:

$H = \frac{12}{n(n+1)} \sum_{i=1}^{k} \frac{r_i^2}{n_i} - 3(n+1)$

$$H = \frac{12}{n\,(n+1)} \sum_{i=1}^{k} \frac{r_i^2}{n_i} - 3(n+1),$$

which follows a χ^2 distribution with the k–1 degrees of freedom.

where, k = Number of samples
n = Total number of elements in k samples.

The null hypothesis is rejected, if the computed χ^2 is greater than the critical value of χ^2 at the level of significance α. Let us take up a problem to illustrate the test.

Example 14.17

Three machines are used in the packaging of 16 kg of wheat flour. Each machine is designed so as to pack on an average 16 kg of flour per bag. Samples of six bags were selected from each machine and the amount of wheat packaged in each bag is shown below:

Machine 1	15.8	15.9	16.2	15.7	16.3	15.8
Machine 2	16.5	16	15.4	15.9	16.2	16.1
Machine 3	15.7	16.4	16.2	15.9	15.7	16.3

Use a 5 per cent level of significance to test the hypothesis that the amount of wheat packaged by the three machines is the same.

Solution:

H_0 : Amount of wheat packaged by the three machines is same.
H_1 : Amount of wheat packaged by at least two machines is different.

Pool the elements of the different samples and rank them. These rankings are shown below:

Weight	Rank	Machine	Weight	Rank	Machine
15.4	1	2	16	10	2
15.7	3	1	16.1	11	2
15.7	3	3	16.2	13	1
15.7	3	3	16.2	13	2
15.8	5.5	1	16.2	13	3
15.8	5.5	1	16.3	15.5	1
15.9	8	1	16.3	15.5	3
15.9	8	3	16.4	17	3
15.9	8	2	16.5	18	2

r_1 (Total of ranks from machine 1) = 50.5
r_2 (Total of ranks from machine 2) = 61
r_3 (Total of ranks from machine 3) = 59.5

Therefore, $$H = \frac{12}{n(n+1)} \sum_{i=1}^{k} \frac{r_i^2}{n_i} - 3(n+1)$$

$$= \frac{12}{18(19)} \left[\frac{50.5^2}{6} + \frac{61^2}{6} + \frac{59.5^2}{6} \right] -3\,(18+1)$$

$$= \frac{12}{342} [425.04 + 621.17 + 590.04] -57$$

$$= \frac{12}{342} [1636.25] -57 = \frac{19635}{342} - 57$$

$$= 57.41 - 57 = 0.41$$

We know that H follows a χ^2 distribution with 2 degrees of freedom. The sample value of χ^2 of 0.41 is to be compared with the critical value of χ^2, which in the present case is 5.99. As sample χ^2 is less than the critical χ^2, the null hypothesis is accepted. Therefore, there is no significant difference in the amount of wheat packaged by the three machines.

Use of SPSS in Conducting the Kruskal-Wallis Test

The Kruskal-Wallis test can also be conducted using the SPSS software, the instructions for which are given in Appendix 14.7. This is done for Example 14.17. The required data for this example in the SPSS format is given in Table 14.23.

Note: 1 = Machine 1
2 = Machine 2
3 = Machine 3

The hypothesis to be tested in this problem is stated as follows:

H_0 : Amount of wheat packaged by three machines is same.
H_1 : Amount of wheat packaged by at least two machines is different.

The SPSS results for the problem are given in Tables 14.24 and 14.25. It is seen that the sum of the ranks for machine 1, machine 2 and machine 3 work out to be 50.5, 61 and 59.5 respectively, which is the same as when computed manually.

TABLE 14.23
Data for Example 14.17 in SPSS format

S. No.	Weight	Label
1	15.8	1
2	15.9	1
3	16.2	1
4	15.7	1
5	16.3	1
6	15.8	1
7	16.5	2
8	16.0	2
9	15.4	2
10	15.9	2
11	16.2	2
12	16.1	2
13	15.7	3
14	16.4	3
15	16.2	3
16	15.9	3
17	15.7	3
18	16.3	3

TABLE 14.24
Ranks for Example 14.17

	Machine	N	Mean Rank
Weight (in kg)	Machine 1	6	8.42
	Machine 2	6	10.17
	Machine 3	6	9.92
	Total	18	

TABLE 14.25
Test statistics for Example 14.17

	Weight (in Kg)
Chi-square	0.383
df	2
Asymp. Sig.	0.826

Note: 1. Kruskal-Wallis Test
2. Grouping Variable: Machine

The computed chi-square value as reported in Table 14.25 is 0.383, which is approximately the same as obtained when the problem was solved manually. The p value for this problem works out to be 0.826, which is greater than 0.05, the assumed level of significance. Therefore, we accept the null hypothesis and conclude that there is no difference in the weight of bags as measured by the three packaging machines.

CONCEPT CHECK

1. Illustrate the use of Wilcoxon signed-rank test for paired samples.
2. Discuss the Kruskal-Wallis test.

SUMMARY

- The tests of significance discussed in Chapter 12 are based on t, Z and F distribution and use the assumption of normality for them to be valid. These tests are called parametric test. A researcher may come across many situations where the normality assumptions do not hold. There can be an instance where our sample size is small or the collected data is ordinal or nominal in measurement. In such situations, a non-parametric test comes to the rescue of the researchers. These tests are called distribution-free tests and do not require any normality assumption for their use. They can be used in case of a small sample and are more suitable for analysing the nominal and ordinal scale data. Further, these tests require very few arithmetic computations. Corresponding to almost every parametric test, there are parallel non-parametric tests.
- In this chapter, we discussed the applications of various non-parametric tests such as chi-square, run test, one-sample sign test, two-sample sign test, the Mann-Whitney U test, Wilcoxon matched-pairs signed rank test and Kruskal-Wallis Test. Three applications of the chi-square test are discussed: (i) test for the goodness of fit, (ii) test for the independence of variables (iii) test for the equality of more than two population proportions. The application of chi-square involves a minimum expected frequency in each cell to be 5. The run test is used to test the randomness of the sample. It is explained for both metric (interval or ratio) and non-metric (ordinal or nominal) data. The test is explained for large samples.
- Corresponding to the test of significance of mean in a parametric test based upon the t and Z statistic, a corresponding non-parametric sign test is used, which is again illustrated for a large sample. In Chapter 12, a paired sample (dependent sample) t-test was discussed. A corresponding non-parametric test is the two-sample sign test, which is based on the signs of the differences of the paired sample observations. The test is explained for a large sample. A parametric test for testing the equality of means of two populations was based on the t statistic. The corresponding non-parametric test is the Mann-Whitney U test, which is illustrated for a large sample.
- One of the main limitations of the two-sample sign test is that it considers only the sign of the differences of the paired observations and does not give any importance to the magnitude of the differences. The Wilcoxon signed rank test for paired samples takes care of this limitation of the two-samples sign test. The hypothesis to be tested here is the same as that in a two-sample sign test. Further, this test is also explained for a large sample.
- To test the equality of more than two population means under a parametric test, the one-way ANOVA is based on the assumptions that each population from where the sample is drawn follows a normal distribution. If this assumption is violated, the non-parametric version of this is given by the Kruskal-Wallis test, which is based on the chi-square distribution. The test is explained with the help of an example.
- All the tests explained in this chapter barring the sign tests are also explained using the SPSS software. The SPSS instructions for using these tests are given in Appendix at the end of this chapter.

KEY TERMS

- Binomial distribution
- Chi-square test
- Kruskal-Wallis test
- Mann-Whitney U test
- Metric measurement
- Non-metric measurement
- Non-parametric test
- Non-symmetric distribution
- Normal approximation to binomial distribution
- One-sample sign test
- One-way ANOVA
- Parametric tests
- Run test
- Symmetric distribution
- Test for equality of proportions
- Test for goodness of fit
- Test for the independence of variables
- Ties
- Two-sample sign test
- Wilcoxon signed-rank test for paired samples

CHAPTER REVIEW QUESTIONS

Objective Type Questions

State whether the following statements are true (T) or false (F).

1. Run test is not available for the interval or ratio scale data.
2. Too many runs indicate that a sample is drawn randomly from a population.
3. Non-parametric tests are also called distribution-free tests.
4. Wilcoxon matched-pair rank test is more powerful than a two-sample sign test.
5. For the application of a chi-square test, the expected frequency in each cell should be at least five.
6. The sample value of the chi-square can be negative.
7. The shape of the chi-square distribution is asymmetrical.
8. Parametric tests involve the population distribution to be normal.
9. To apply a continuity correction in a sign test, 0.5 should be added to X, if X > np, where the notations have their usual meaning.
10. The sample mean ($\overline{X}$) and the sample standard deviation (s) are called the parameters of distribution.
11. The normality assumption is not satisfied for ordinal scale data.
12. Non-parametric tests do not involve simple arithmetic computations.
13. If 2nd, 3rd and 4th observations, when arranged in an ascending order of the magnitude are equal, the rank assigned to each observation is 3.
14. Non-parametric test could be used with the interval or the ratio data when no assumption can be made regarding the probability distribution of the population.
15. An alternative to a two-independent sample t-test is provided by the Mann-Whitney U test.
16. In a contingency table with 3 rows and 4 columns, the degree of freedom equals 6.
17. Kruskal-Wallis test is an extension of the Mann-Whitney U test.
18. In one-way ANOVA, the various populations from where the samples are drawn need not follow a normal distribution.
19. Kruskal-Wallis test is a non-parametric alternative to a one-way ANOVA.
20. One-tailed test cannot be performed with a one-sample sign test.

Conceptual Questions

1. Under what condition is the Kruskal-Wallis test used as an alternative to analysis of variance? Explain.
2. How would you conduct a run test of randomness for metric data?
3. When do we use contingency coefficient? What are its limitations? How does Cramer's V statistic overcome its limitations?
4. What are non-parametric tests? How are they different from parametric tests? Explain the advantages and disadvantages of the non-parametric tests.
5. Both the two-sample sign test and the Wilcoxon signed-rank test for paired samples can be used to test the same hypothesis. However, the latter is preferred. Explain the reasons.
6. What is a χ^2 test? Point out its applications. Under what conditions is this test applicable?
7. What is χ^2 test of the goodness of fit? What cautions are necessary while applying this test? Point out its role in business decision-making.

Application Questions

1. A sample analysis of the examination results of 200 MBA students was done. It was found that 46 students had failed, 68 had secured a third division, 62 had secured a second division and the rest obtained first division. Are these figures commensurate with the general examination result, which is in the ratio of 2 : 3 : 3 : 2 for various categories respectively? *[MBA, DU, 2002]*

2. Of the 1000 workers in a factory exposed to an epidemic, 700 in all were attacked, 400 had been inoculated and of these, 200 were attacked. On the basis of this information can it be said that the inoculation and attack are independent? [MBA, HPU, 1998]
3. The following figures show the distribution of the digits in numbers chosen at random from a telephone directory:

Digit	0	1	2	3	4	5	6	7	8	9	Total
Frequency	1026	1107	997	966	1075	933	1107	972	964	853	10,000

Test whether the digits may be taken to occur equally in the directory. [MBA, IIT, Roorkee, 2000]
4. The number of automobile accidents per week in a certain city was as follows:

12, 8, 20, 2, 14, 10, 15, 6, 9, 4

Are these frequencies in agreement with the belief that the accident conditions were the same during the 10-week period? [MBA, DU, 1999]
5. The divisional manager of a retail chain believes that the average number of customers entering each of the five stores in his division weekly is the same. In a given week, a manager reports the following number of customers in the stores:

3000, 2960, 3100, 2780, 3160

Test the divisional manager's belief at a 10 per cent level of significance.
6. A cigarette company interested in the relation between sex of a person and the type of cigarettes smoked has collected the following data from a random sample of 150 persons:

Cigarette	Male	Female	Total
A	25	30	55
B	40	15	55
C	30	10	40
Total	95	55	150

Test whether the type of cigarette smoked and the sex are independent. [MBA, Osmania Univ., 2006]
7. Two sample polls of the votes for two candidates A and B for a public office are taken, one from among the residents of a rural area and one from urban areas. The results are given below. Examine whether the nature of the area is related to the voting preference in this election.

Area	Votes for		Total
	A	B	
Rural	620	380	1000
Urban	550	450	1000
Total	1170	830	2000

[MBA, IGNOU, 2001]
8. A sample of parts provided the following data on the quality of parts delivered by the production shift:

Shift	Number good	Number Defective	Total
First	368	32	400
Second	285	15	300
Third	176	24	200
Total	829	71	900

Use a five per cent level of significance to test the hypothesis that the quality of parts is independent of the production shift. [MBA, DU, Oct 2003]
9. The following table gives the number of aircraft accidents that occurred during various days of the week. Test whether the accidents are uniformly distributed over the week.

Days	Monday	Tuesday	Wednesday	Thursday	Friday	Saturday
No. of Accidents	14	18	12	11	15	14

[MBA, IGNOU, 2006]
10. A survey was carried out in a state among the doctors belonging to the rural health service cadre (500 doctors) and among the medical education directorate cadre (300 teaching doctors). They were asked a question, 'Would it

be acceptable to you, if the government proposes to hire all the doctors on a fixed period contractual basis?' The doctors were to answer either as 'Acceptable' or 'Not Acceptable'. There was no third category 'Undecided'. The following was the data compiled in a cross-tabulated format:

Doctors	Acceptable	Not Acceptable	Total
Rural Cadre	195	305	500
Teaching Cadre	140	160	300
Total	335	465	800

Test an appropriate hypothesis using a 5 per cent level of significance. *[MBA, DU, 2002]*

11. A machine produces acceptable and the defective items in the following sequence:

A A A A D D D D D A D D D A A A A A D D D D A A A A D A D A A A A A D D A A D D D D A A A A D D D D

where, A = Acceptable item

D = Defective item

Test the claim that the sequence is random. Let the level of significance be 5 per cent.

12. A man had to wait 7, 5, 4, 6, 3, 8, 7, 6, 10, 8, 11, 9, 2, 10, 9, 8, 7, 9, 6 minutes on randomly chosen 19 occasions to meet his boss. Use the sign test at a 5 per cent level of significance to test the hypothesis that he has to wait on an average 8 minutes to meet the boss.

13. A sample of 20 persons engaged in a prescribed programme of physical exercise for 50 days to reduce weight gave the following results:

S. No.	Weight Before (Pounds)	Weight After (Pounds)	S. No.	Weight Before (Pounds)	Weight After (Pounds)
1	169	175	11	206	180
2	180	172	12	186	174
3	176	170	13	180	184
4	175	178	14	240	210
5	169	170	15	180	184
6	182	182	16	170	176
7	170	173	17	190	195
8	176	169	18	186	174
9	189	175	19	210	190
10	184	182	20	180	174

Use a two-sample sign test to test that the prescribed programme of exercise is effective. Use a 5 per cent level of significance. Will the answer to the problem change if Wilcoxon matched-pair rank test is used?

14. The time spent (in minutes) by 20 students in the age group 18 – 22 years in a mall is given as:

100, 80, 160, 70, 90, 100, 115, 130, 96, 102, 104, 105, 145, 136, 108, 97, 85, 99, 103, 109

Use a one-sample sign test to test the hypothesis that the median time spent is at least 101 minutes. Let the level of significance be 5 per cent.

15. A sample is selected from each of these makes of ropes and their breaking strengths (in pounds) are found as reported below:

I	II	III
72	73	84
80	83	75
76	77	69
75	76	70
71	71	73
	70	76
		80

Using the Kruskal-Wallis test, examine at a 5 per cent level of significance whether there is any difference in their breaking strengths.

16. The number of typing errors per page made by 17 students who joined a typing institute before and after the training is given below. Use a 5 per cent level of significance to test the hypothesis that the average number of typing errors decreased after the training.

Students No.	1	2	3	4	5	6	7	8	9	10	11	12	13	14	15	16	17
Errors before Training	10	6	9	13	7	8	6	3	7	9	4	3	2	7	8	6	5
Errors after Training	7	5	11	10	9	10	4	3	5	6	7	4	0	3	4	3	6

17. Two drugs 'A' and 'B' were tried on certain patients for reducing weight—10 persons were subjected to drug A and 15 were given drug B. The decease in weight (in pounds) is given below:

Drug A	7	5	8	9	6	8	10	11	2	4					
Drug B	6	4	5	10	9	8	7	5	6	11	12	7	6	5	8

Do the two drugs differ significantly with regard to their effect in reducing the weight (Hint: use the Mann-Whitney U test)

18. Twenty housewives were selected and their perceptions on a detergent were recorded. They were later shown a commercial on the benefits of the detergent and their perception score was again noted. For respondents whose perception has improved, a positive sign and where it has declined, a negative sign is used, as shown below:

$$- + + + - + - - + + + - + + - - - + -$$

Use an appropriate non-parametric test to examine the effect of the advertisement upon the perception.

19. Eight of light bulbs A and 14 of light bulb B were selected and their lifetime (in hours) on a continuous use is given below:

Bulb A	380	420	450	416	375	395	401	412						
Bulb B	404	410	370	390	382	410	415	472	480	430	360	370	390	426

Use the Mann-Whitney test at a 1 per cent level of significance to determine whether there is no difference in the average lifetime of the two types of bulbs.

20. The following are the mileage (km/litre) that a driver got from five tank fuels each full of three kinds of petrol:

Petrol I	9.8	10.2	11	10.6	10.8
Petrol II	8.9	9.6	10	10.2	10.5
Petrol III	10.5	10.8	10.7	11.2	9.9

Use an approximate test at the level of significance of 1 per cent to test whether there is no difference in the average mileage of three kinds of petrol.

21. A random sample of 12 first year and 14 second year students of a management programme of a business school spent the following amount (in ₹) when they went to Agra for an excursion:

First Year	2800	3200	4200	3600	2500	4300	
	4100	4900	2900	3300	3900	4500	
Second Year	3600	3500	5200	4700	4600	3800	4300
	4700	4900	5100	5300	5200	4700	4800

Use an appropriate non-parametric test to examine that the second year students spend on average more money than first year students when they go for an excursion. Use a 5 per cent level of significance.

CASE 14.1

COMPARATIVE CONSUMER PERCEPTION OF JET AIRWAYS *VIS-À-VIS* INDIAN AIRLINES[1]

The Indian aviation sector till recently was highly regulated by the government. During the 1980s, it saw the introduction of some new initiatives like the air taxi scheme, whose main objective was to boost tourism.

Till recently, Indian Airlines had a monopoly in the sector. However, in 1993 the skies were opened for private participation and eight airlines got the nod to commence operations. High costs of operating, low passenger traffic and a fiercely growing competition forced many players to ground their aircraft.

Domestic passenger traffic in India is projected to grow annually at 12.5 per cent year on year over the next decade.

Thus, currently the domestic aviation industry has only two private players—Jet Airways and Sahara Airlines, who have managed to survive.

Over the last five years, Jet Airways is being seen as a major threat to Indian Airlines and has been able to retain its premium image in the Industry.

In spite of all the odds, Sahara Airlines has somehow managed to stay in the fray with a very small market share.

The market share of Indian Airlines *vis-à-vis* private players is given below:

Airlines	Market Share	Aircrafts Owned
Indian Airlines	47 per cent	55
Private Airlines*	53 per cent	35

Source: India Infoline Site – Industry Reports

Therefore, it is seen that the private airlines are taking a major share in the domestic market. Out of the two private airlines Sahara and Jet, Jet is emerging as a major player. Sahara is lagging behind in comparison to both the Jet and the Indian Airlines. The present study investigates the perceptions that the air travellers have in their mind about Jet airways and Indian Airlines. Therefore, the objectives of the study are:

Research Objective

- To compare the consumer perception of the Jet Airways vis-à-vis Indian Airlines.
- To find out if the perception is related to demographic and psychographic variables.

Statement of Hypothesis

The above stated objectives can be achieved by testing a set of hypotheses listed in exhibits 1 to 3.

Exhibit 1: Statement of hypotheses regarding the perception of Indian Airlines and Jet Airways

Hypothesis 1 : There is no difference in the overall average perception of Indian Airlines and Jet Airways.
Hypothesis 2 : There is no difference in average perception regarding ticketing/reservation.
Hypothesis 3 : There is no difference in the average perception regarding the airport services.
Hypothesis 4 : There is no difference in the average perception regarding in-flight services.
Hypothesis 5 : There is no difference in the average perception regarding food.
Hypothesis 6 : There is no difference in the average perception regarding safety..
Hypothesis 7 : There is no difference in the average perception regarding miscellaneous variables.

Alternative hypothesis corresponding to each of the above-mentioned null hypotheses is that the average perception of Jet Airways is better than that of Indian Airlines on all the attributes mentioned above.

[1]Prepared by Dr Deepak Chawla for classroom discussion only. The material for the case study is based on a project carried out by Gagan Kapoor, Gautam Sareen, Raman Chawla, Sandeep Bansal and Sonya V Kapoor, participants of PGPM (2001-04) at the International Management Institute (IMI), New Delhi. The facts presented in the case pertain to the year 2002.

Exhibit 2: Statement of hypotheses regarding the relationships between demographic/psychographic variables and the perception about Indian Airlines

Hypothesis 8	: The frequency of travel and perception about Indian Airlines are statistically independent variables.
Hypothesis 9	: Age and perception about Indian Airlines are statistically independent variables.
Hypothesis 10	: Education and perception about Indian Airlines are statistically independent variables.
Hypothesis 11	: Profession and perception about Indian Airlines are statistically independent variables.
Hypothesis 12	: Income and perception about Indian Airlines are statistically independent variables.
Hypothesis 13	: Club membership and perception about Indian Airlines are statistically independent variables.
Hypothesis 14	: Type of vehicle owned and perception about Indian Airlines are statistically independent variables.
Hypothesis 15	: Ownership of house and perception about Indian Airlines are statistically independent variables.
Hypothesis 16	: Frequency of holidays taken and perception about Indian Airlines are statistically independent variables.
Alternative hypotheses in all the above cases would be that the two variables are statistically related.	

Exhibit 3: Statement of hypotheses regarding the relationships between the demographic/psychographic variables and the perception about Jet Airways

Hypothesis 17	: The frequency of travel and perception about Jet Airways are statistically independent variables.
Hypothesis 18	: Age and perception about Jet Airways are statistically independent variables.
Hypothesis 19	: Education and perception about Jet Airways are statistically independent variables.
Hypothesis 20	: Profession and perception about Jet Airways are statistically independent variables.
Hypothesis 21	: Income and perception about Jet Airways are statistically independent variables.
Hypothesis 22	: Club membership and perception about Jet Airways are statistically independent variables.
Hypothesis 23	: Type of vehicle owned and perception about Jet Airways are statistically independent variables.
Hypothesis 24	: Ownership of the house and perception about Jet Airways are statistically independent variables.
Hypothesis 25	: Frequency of the holidays taken and perception about Jet Airways are statistically independent variables.
Alternative hypotheses in all the above cases would be that the two variables are statistically related.	

Research Design

In the present study, a descriptive research examined the consumer perception towards Jet Airways *vis-à-vis* Indian Airlines, and how it varies with the demographic variables like age, income level, etc.

Unit of Analysis

A customer who has travelled either by Jet Airways and/or Indian Airlines or both.

Methodology

1. **Information needs:** An exploratory research was carried out on a set of travellers of Jet Airways and Indian Airlines to identify the information needs which have been grouped under the following heads:

   Ticketing/reservations

   - Accessibility of telephone numbers for ticketing/reservations
   - Staff efficiency/effectiveness in dealing with customers

Airport services

- Baggage handling
- Check-in procedures/tele-check-in facilities
- Ground staff hospitality
- Airport announcements

In-flight hospitality

- Behaviour of the crew
- Overall personality of the crew
- Food and beverages
- Adequate leg room in seating
- Clarity of the in-flight announcements
- In-flight decor

Food/beverages

- Quality/quantity of meal
- Presentation of the meal
- Variety of meals

Safety

- Passenger safety
- Smoothness of take-off/landing operations
- Demonstration of the safety instructions
- Age of aircrafts

Other Variables

- Adherence to the flight schedule/ cancellation information
- Care for kids, old and handicapped people
- Frequent flyer programmes
- Connectivity of flights
- Holiday/discount offers

2. **Data collection:** Using the above information needs, a questionnaire was designed (Please refer to Annexure 1 for the questionnaire.) The questionnaire was administered to the respondents and the data was collected.
3. **Sampling**

   Selection of sample – For the purpose of data collection, we selected our sample by using a convenience sampling technique and thus our sample population consisted of our co-students from IMI, as well as colleagues at our work places.

   Sample size – The sample size for the purpose of the study was to be 30 to 35 respondents who would have travelled by Jet Airways and/or Indian Airlines. Data was collected from 36 respondents, out of which six respondents gave response for one airline only. For convenience in the research analysis, and the comparison of perception of the two airlines, these six responses were excluded.
4. **Coding scheme:** The questionnaire presented in Annexure 1 was coded using the coding scheme presented in Annexure 2.
5. **Statistical methods used to test hypothesis:** The research study tried to compare the consumer perception with respect to Jet Airways *vis-à-vis* Indian Airlines and keeping the same in view, the following statistical tests were carried out to analyse the data collected through the questionnaire:

   Step 1: The mean scores were calculated for an Overall perception and various subgroups namely, Ticketing and reservations, airport services, in-flight services, food, safety and other variables. These mean scores were calculated for both Indian Airlines and Jet Airways.

   Step 2: Using the mean scores as calculated above, the group used a paired t test for comparing the perception on all the subgroups and for the overall perception of Indian Airlines *vis-à-vis* Jet Airlines.

Step 3: A chi-square test was applied to check the existence of the relationship between key elements like frequency of travel, age, education, profession and the perception of each airline.

Analysis

- The primary data in respect of 30 respondents was entered in the SPSS package and frequency distribution tables (refer Annexure 3 for Tables 1 to 14) worked out.
- The mean scores for the overall perception and various subgroups for both Indian Airlines and Jet Airways are tabulated at the end of this case.
- The results of the paired t-test are tabulated in Table 16 (Annexure 5).
- The results of the chi-square tests for Indian Airlines and Jet Airways are presented in Tables 17 and 18 respectively (Annexure 6).

Case Questions

1. Comment on the methodology used in the study.
2. Describe the sample by analysing univariate Tables 1 to 14 (Annexure 3).
3. Compare the perception of Jet Airways *vis-à-vis* Indian Airlines by analysing the results presented in Tables 15 and 16 (Annexure 4 and 5).
4. Analyse the results of the chi-square tests for Indian Airlines and Jet Airways as given in Tables 17 and 18 (Annexure 6).
5. Write a management report of the findings of the study.

Annexure 1: Questionnaire

1. How often do you travel out of station? (Tick one of the options).
   (Once a week/month/year)
   Frequency of travel __________ (Specify number of times for the option as ticked)
2. What mode of travel do you use? (Respondent may tick more than one option)
   (a) Air
   (b) Rail
   (c) Road transport
   (d) Own transport
   If Answer to Question 2 is Air, then proceed to Question 3, else terminate the questionnaire.
3. What is the purpose of your travel?
   (a) Business
   (b) Personal
   (c) Both
4. Which airlines do you choose for travel?
   (a) Indian Airlines
   (b) Jet Airways
5. If you are a business traveller, do you have any restrictions in choice of airlines?
   Yes/No
6. If yes, please indicate your preference (had there been no restrictions).
   (a) Indian Airlines
   (b) Jet Airways

7. On a scale of 1 to 7, rate the following attributes for the airlines on which you have travelled (where 1: Extremely Poor, 2: Very Poor, 3: Poor, 4: Neither Poor or Good, 5: Good, 6: Very Good, 7: Extremely Good)

Attribute	Indian Airlines	Jet Airways
Ticketing/Reservations		
• Accessibility of telephone numbers for		
(a) Reservations		
(b) Inquiry		
(c) Airport		
(d) Tele check-in		
• During reservations, please relate your experiences w.r.t.		
(a) Staff efficiency		
(b) Staff courtesy		
Airport Services		
(a) Check-in procedures		
(b) Ease in finding check-in counter for the flight		
(c) Adequacy of number of check-in counters		
(d) Personality of ground staff		
(e) Staff efficiency		
(f) Baggage handling		
(g) Boarding announcements		
(h) If flight delayed, how well is the situation handled?		
In-flight		
(a) Friendly welcome/greeting at the time of boarding		
(b) Help during the embarkation phase (guidance, hand luggage and stowage)		
(c) Adequacy of leg space		
(d) Behaviour of the crew		
(e) Cabin crew announcements		
(f) Reading material/newspapers		
(g) Temperature in the cabin		
(h) Cleanliness of the cabin		
(i) Cleanliness of the washroom		
Food		
(a) Quality of the meal		
(b) Presentation of the meal		
(c) Appropriateness of the menu for the time of day		
(d) Quantity of the meal		
(e) Variety of Meal		

Attribute	Indian Airlines	Jet Airways
Safety		
(a) Smoothness of take-off/landing operations		
(b) Demonstration of the safety instructions		
(c) Age of the Fleet		
Other Variables		
(a) Adherence to the flight schedule/cancellation information		
(b) Frequent flyer programmes		
(c) Holiday/discount offers		
(d) Care for kids, old and handicapped people		
(e) Connectivity of flights		

8. Demographic profile of the respondent:

Age • Between 22 and 30 • 31 and above	
Education	
Profession • Government Service • Private Company • Businessman • Professional • Student • Any other (Pls specify)	
Income Group • Less than 3 lakh per annum • 3 to 6 lakh • More than 6 lakh	
Club Membership	
Type and make of the vehicle owned by respondent	
House • Owned • Rented (personal lease) • Company lease	
How often do you go for a holiday?	

Annexure 2

1. The data was converted into the number of travels per quarter and then the following coding scheme was used.

1 to 8 time	coded as	1
9 to 16	coded as	2
17 to 24	coded as	3
Above 24	coded as	4

2. Mode of travel

Air	coded as	1
Others	coded as	0

3. Purpose of travel

Business	coded as	1
Personal	coded as	2
Both	coded as	3

4. Choice of airline

Indian Airlines	coded as	1
Jet Airways	coded as	2

5. Restriction in choice of airlines

Yes	coded as	1
No	coded as	0

6. Preference if there was no restriction

Indian Airlines	coded as	1
Jet Airways	coded as	2

7. Rating of the attributes for the airlines

   There were 36 attributes divided into six categories. The actual score varied from 1 to 7 and that was mentioned in the spreadsheet.

   - Ticketing category variables were labelled as T-1 to T-6.
   - Airport services variables were labelled as A-1 to A-8.
   - In-flight variables were labelled as I-1 to I-9.
   - Food variables were labelled as F-1 to F-5.
   - Safety variables were labelled as S-1 to S-3.
   - Other variables (miscellaneous) were labelled as M-1 to M-5.

8. Demographic and psychographic profile of respondent

Age

22 to 30 years	coded as	1
31 year and above	coded as	2

Education

Graduation	coded as	1
Above graduation	coded as	2

Profession

Private company	coded as	1
Others	coded as	2

Income Group

Less than 3 lakh	coded as	1
3 to 6 lakh	coded as	2
Above 6 lakh	coded as	3

Club Membership

Yes	coded as	1
No	coded as	0

Type of Vehicle

Less than 1000 cc	coded as	1
1000 cc and above	coded as	2

House

Owned	coded as	1
Rented (Personal lease)	coded as	2
Company Lease	coded as	3

Frequency of taking holiday

Once a year	coded as	1
More than once a year	coded as	2

For testing the hypothesis given in Exhibits 2 and 3, the overall average perception score for both the airlines was categorized as follows:

1 to 3.5 as poor perception	coded as	1
3.501 to 4.5 as neutral perception	coded as	2
4.501 to 7 as high perception	coded as	3

Annexure 3

Table 1 Frequency Distribution of Travelling Out of Station Per Quarter

		Frequency	Per cent	Valid Per cent	Cumulative Per cent
Valid	1 to 8	23	76.7	76.7	76.7
	9 to 16	6	20.0	20.0	96.7
	25 & above	1	3.3	3.3	100.0
	Total	30	100.0	100.0	

Table 2 Frequency Distribution of Mode of Travel

		Frequency	Per cent	Valid Per cent	Cumulative Per cent
Valid	Air	30	100.0	100.0	100.0

Table 3 Frequency Distribution of the Purpose of Travel

		Frequency	Per cent	Valid Per cent	Cumulative Per cent
Valid	Business	16	53.3	53.3	53.3
	Personal	4	13.3	13.3	66.7
	Both	10	33.3	33.3	100.0
	Total	30	100.0	100.0	

Table 4 Frequency Distribution of the Choice of Airline

		Frequency	Per cent	Valid Per cent	Cumulative Per cent
Valid	Indian Airlines	9	30.0	30.0	30.0
	Jet Airways	21	70.0	70.0	100.0
	Total	30	100.0	100.0	100.0

Table 5 Frequency Distribution of Restriction in Choice of Airline

		Frequency	Per cent	Valid Per cent	Cumulative Per cent
Valid	No Restriction	22	73.3	73.3	73.3
	Restriction	8	26.7	26.7	100.0
	Total	30	100.0	100.0	

Table 6 Frequency Distribution of Preference of Airline if no Restriction

		Frequency	Per cent	Valid Per cent	Cumulative Per cent
Valid	Indian Airlines	6	20.0	20.0	20.0
	Jet Airways	24	80.0	80.0	100.0
	Total	30	100.0	100.0	

Table 7 Frequency Distribution of Age

		Frequency	Per cent	Valid Per cent	Cumulative Per cent
Valid	22 to 30 yrs	19	63.3	63.3	63.3
	Above 30 yrs	11	36.7	36.7	100.0
	Total	30	100.0	100.0	

Table 8 Frequency Distribution of Education

		Frequency	Per cent	Valid Per cent	Cumulative Per cent
Valid	Graduate	14	46.7	46.7	46.7
	Above Graduation	16	53.3	53.3	100.0
	Total	30	100.0	100.0	

Table 9 Frequency Distribution of Profession

		Frequency	Per cent	Valid Per cent	Cumulative Per cent
Valid	Private Company	24	80.0	80.0	80.0
	Others	6	20.0	20.0	100.0
	Total	30	100.0	100.0	

Table 10 Frequency Distribution of Income

		Frequency	Per cent	Valid Per cent	Cumulative Per cent
Valid	Less than 3 lakh	7	23.3	23.3	23.3
	3 to 6 lakhs	10	33.3	33.3	56.7
	More than 6 lakh	13	43.3	43.3	100.0
	Total	30	100.0	100.0	

Table 11 Frequency Distribution of Club Membership

		Frequency	Per cent	Valid Per cent	Cumulative Per cent
Valid	No	17	56.7	56.7	56.7
	Yes	13	43.3	43.3	100.0
	Total	30	100.0	100.0	

Table 12 Frequency Distribution of the Type of Vehicle

		Frequency	Per cent	Valid Per cent	Cumulative Per cent
Valid	Less than 1000 cc	23	76.7	76.7	76.7
	1000 cc and above	7	23.3	23.3	100.0
	Total	30	100.0	100.0	

Table 13 Frequency Distribution of House

		Frequency	Per cent	Valid Per cent	Cumulative Per cent
Valid	Owned	19	63.3	63.3	63.3
	Rented	8	26.7	26.7	90.0
	Company Lease	3	10.0	10.0	100.0
	Total	30	100.0	100.0	

Table 14 Frequency Distribution of going for a Holiday

		Frequency	Per cent	Valid Per cent	Cumulative Per cent
Valid	Once in a year	15	50.0	50.0	50.0
	More than once in a year	15	50.0	50.0	100.0
	Total	30	100.0	100.0	

Annexure 4

Table 15 Paired Sample Statistics of Indian Airlines vs Jet Airways

	Attributes	Mean	N	Std. Deviation	Std. Error Mean
Pair 1	Overall perception of Indian Airlines	4.081667	30	0.79283	0.14475
	Overall perception of Jet Airways	5.082	30	0.74017	0.135136
Pair 2	Perceptions for ticketing about Indian Airlines	3.844667	30	0.88291	0.161196
	Perceptions for ticketing about Jet Airways	5.304333	30	0.910107	0.166162
Pair 3	Perceptions for airport services about Indian Airlines	4.177333	30	0.835488	0.152539
	Perceptions for airport service about Jet Airways	5.268	30	0.762832	0.139273
Pair 4	Perceptions for in-flight service about Indian Airlines	4.089333	30	0.922765	0.168473
	Perceptions for in-flight service about Jet Airways	5.096333	30	0.8135	0.148524
Pair 5	Perceptions for food about Indian Airlines	3.82	30	1.194643	0.218111
	Perceptions for food about Jet Airways	4.486667	30	1.201933	0.219442
Pair 6	Perceptions for safety about Indian Airlines	4.377333	30	0.949246	0.173308
	Perceptions for safety about Jet Airways	5.156	30	0.791213	0.144455
Pair 7	Perceptions for miscellaneous variables about Indian Airlines	4.286667	30	0.903149	0.164892
	Perceptions for miscellaneous variables about Jet Airways	5.04	30	0.772635	0.141063

Annexure 5

Table 16 Paired Samples t-Test to Compare Perception – Indian Airlines vs Jet Airways

Indian Airlines (Minus) Jet Airways		Paired Differences			t
		Mean	Std. Deviation	Std. Error Mean	
Pair 1	Overall Perception	−1.0003	1.20966	0.22085	−4.529
Pair 2	Ticketing/Reservation	−1.4596	1.45893	0.26636	−5.479
Pair 3	Airport Services	−1.0906	1.27152	0.23214	−4.698
Pair 4	In-flight Service	−1.007	1.3036	0.23800	−4.231
Pair 5	Food	−0.6666	1.55659	0.28419	−2.345
Pair 6	Safety	−0.7786	1.20015	0.21911	−3.553
Pair 7	Miscellaneous	−0.7533	1.25140	0.228475	−3.29723

Annexure 6

Table 17 Tests of Hypothesis Investigating the Relationship between the Demographic/Psychographic Variables and Perception about Indian Airlines

Hyp. No.	Variables	DF	Computed χ^2
8	Frequency of Travel vs Perception	4	12.695
9	Age vs Perception	2	0.839
10	Education vs Perception	2	3.857
11	Profession vs Perception	2	4.342
12	Income vs Perception	4	2.82
13	Club membership vs Perception	2	1.136
14	Type of vehicle owned vs Perception	2	1.866
15	Ownership of house vs Perception	4	3.616
16	Frequency of holiday vs Perception	2	3.474

Table 18 Tests of Hypothesis Investigating the Relationship between the Demographic/Psychographic Variables and Perception about Jet Airways

Hyp. No.	Variables	DF	Computed χ^2
17	Frequency of Travel vs Perception	4	0.739
18	Age vs Perception	2	2.672
19	Education vs Perception	2	3.884
20	Profession vs Perception	2	4.760
21	Income vs Perception	4	9.874
22	Club membership vs Perception	2	0.971
23	Type of vehicle owned vs Perception	2	1.405
24	Ownership of house vs Perception	4	1.010
25	Frequency of holiday vs Perception	2	4.615

CASE 14.2

CHOICE OF SPECIALIZATION IN A MANAGEMENT PROGRAMME

The number of students completing MBA has increased exponentially from under 5000 in 1960 to over 100,000 in 2000. MBA programmes have witnessed a 40 per cent increase in applications since 2000. An MBA degree is considered to be a ticket to the corporate world, and therefore, more and more students are opting for it. Eighty per cent of the working executives feel that a graduate degree in business is important to reach senior ranks within most companies.

Due to the complexity and size of today's organizations, a typical organization is divided into various departments. Each department takes care of a specific work in the organization like finance, marketing, HR, etc., and hence requires a special knowledge and training on the part of the employees to be able to handle the respective departments. This is where specialization courses in MBA come to the fore.

Choice of specialization of an MBA student is influenced by various factors—both internal as well as external. It depends upon his field of study during graduation, his field of previous work experience, the experience of his friends and family, his interactions with his seniors and the alumni of his institute and also with the corporate and other formal and informal interactions he is exposed to during the course of his study. In the present study, an attempt is made to study such variables that influence one's choice of specialization during MBA and try to draw conclusions.

Reasons for the Study

Choosing a field of specialization is a daunting task faced by MBA students. The fact that most students have a vague idea about the specializations adds to the complexity and hence they try to get some references from external factors. The growing demand for MBA graduates by companies for managing their businesses and the stiff competition at every step makes this a very crucial decision, and hence the need for complete knowledge before deciding.

Objective of the Study

The objective of the study is to analyse the factors that lead to the choice of patterns of the students while deciding about their specializations. A correlation between the environmental factors and their effect on the decision of the students in choosing their MBA specializations is attempted. Choosing the right specialization is the first and the most important decision taken by MBA students, for this decision decides the course of their careers. The study aims at analysing the factors that influence this decision.

Scope of the Study

The study has been conducted on the first and second year students of an MBA programme.

Methodology of the Study

An exploratory research was conducted to identify the information needed for the study. This was used for designing the questionnaire which was administered to the first and second year students. The responses were obtained through an online survey. A total of 69 students participated in the study. Table 14.26 presents the survey data on select variables. The select variables are explained as:

State your views on the following on a 5-point scale (where 1 = completely disagree, 2 = disagree, 3 = no opinion, 4 = agree and 5 = strongly agree) while choosing the specialization in the second year of the programme.

- Previous work experience affects the choice. (X_1)
- Placement of a senior affects the choice. (X_2)
- Experience with the courses and the professors in the first three trimesters affects the choice. (X_3)
- Future job prospects affect the choice. (X_4)

Table 14.26
Data on select variables used in the study

Resp No.	X_1	X_2	X_3	X_4	Resp No.	X_1	X_2	X_3	X_4
1	4	4	4	3	36	4	4	4	1
2	4	4	3	2	37	4	3	4	2
3	4	4	4	1	38	4	4	4	2
4	4	4	4	4	39	5	2	5	2
5	4	5	5	2	40	3	5	4	2
6	4	2	5	4	41	4	2	2	4
7	3	5	4	5	42	3	2	4	2
8	1	1	5	1	43	4	4	5	3
9	4	4	5	2	44	4	1	5	3
10	4	4	4	4	45	2	4	4	4
11	3	3	4	2	46	2	4	5	3
12	5	4	3	4	47	3	3	4	5
13	4	5	5	4	48	2	5	5	2
14	4	4	5	3	49	3	5	4	2
15	3	2	4	4	50	3	2	5	1
16	4	2	2	2	51	4	4	5	4
17	4	4	5	2	52	4	2	4	3
18	4	4	4	2	53	3	4	5	4
19	2	4	4	2	54	4	1	4	3
20	2	4	4	2	55	4	1	4	3
21	4	5	5	3	56	2	4	4	1
22	5	4	5	4	57	5	2	4	3
23	2	4	5	4	58	2	2	4	2
24	2	4	4	1	59	5	2	3	3
25	4	2	4	4	60	5	4	5	2
26	3	3	3	3	61	5	2	5	3
27	3	4	4	2	62	2	2	4	2
28	5	3	2	2	63	3	2	4	1
29	5	4	4	3	64	2	4	4	2
30	2	2	2	2	65	4	5	5	2
31	2	2	4	3	66	4	4	5	2
32	4	2	2	2	67	4	2	2	3
33	4	4	4	4	68	4	4	3	4
34	2	2	2	2	69	5	4	5	3
35	4	4	4	1					

QUESTIONS

1. Conduct an appropriate non-parametric test to examine the hypothesis that there is no difference in the four variables considered in the study in choosing the electives. Use a 5 per cent level of significance.
2. In case the null hypothesis of no difference in the above question is rejected, use two non-parametric tests to test which variable influences most the choice of electives and which the least. Compare your answers for both the tests used. You may use a 5 per cent level of significance.
3. Write a management summary of your findings.

Appendix – 14.1: SPSS COMMANDS FOR CROSS-TABS AND CHI-SQUARED TEST

After the input data has been typed along with the variable labels and the value labels in an SPSS data file, to get the CROSS-TABULATIONS and chi-squared test output for a problem, follow the following steps:

1. Click on ANALYSE at the SPSS menu bar.
2. Click on DESCRIPTIVE STATISTICS, followed by CROSS-TABS.
3. Select the row variable for a cross-tabulation by highlighting it in the variable list on the left side and clicking on the arrow leading to the row variable box. Similarly, select the variable you wish to be the column variable in the cross-tabulation.
4. Click on STATISTICS in the main dialogs box. Then click on 'Chi-square'. In the box titled 'Nominal', click on 'Contingency Coefficient', 'Phi and Cramer's V', and 'Lambda' to give you these statistics associated which measure the strength of the association in a cross-tab. Click CONTINUE to return to the main dialog box.
5. Click OK to get the output containing the required cross-tab, along with the chi-squared test and the measures of association like Lambda and Contingency Coefficients.

Note: The chi-squared test requires counts to be in the cross-tables, and not percentages. Original data should have counts when using this test.

Appendix – 14.2: SPSS COMMANDS FOR TESTING THE EQUALITY OF VARIOUS POPULATION PROPORTIONS

After the input data has been typed along with the variable labels and value labels in an SPSS data file to test the hypothesis of uniformity of distribution among the various categories, follow the following steps:

1. Click on ANALYSE at the SPSS menu bar.
2. Click on NON-PARAMETRIC STATISTICS followed by CHI-SQUARE.
3. Take the concerned variable to the right hand box.
4. Under EXPECTED VALUE click ALL CATEGORIES EQUAL.
5. Click OK.

Appendix – 14.3: SPSS COMMANDS FOR RUN TEST THE CASE OF INTERVAL OR RATIO SCALE MEASUREMENT

After the input data has been typed along with the variable labels and value labels in an SPSS data file to test the hypothesis of randomness using interval or ratio scale data, follow the following steps:

1. Click on ANALYSE at the SPSS menu bar.
2. Click on NON-PARAMETRIC STATISTICS followed by RUNS.
3. Take the concerned variable to the right hand box.
4. Tick on MEDIAN or MEAN depending upon which one you want it as your cut-off value.
5. Click OK.

Appendix – 14.4: SPSS COMMANDS FOR A RUN TEST THE CASE OF NOMINAL SCALE MEASUREMENT

After the input data has been typed along with the variable labels and the value labels in an SPSS data file to test the hypothesis of randomness using nominal scale data, follow the following steps:

1. Click on ANALYSE at the SPSS menu bar.
2. Click on NON-PARAMETRIC STATISTICS followed by RUNS.
3. Take the concerned variable to the right hand box.

4. Since the nominal scale data needs to be coded, the appropriate coding could be 1 for male and –1 for female or 1 for married and –1 for single or 1 for user of a brand of a product and –1 for non-user of the brand of a product, click CUSTOM and give it a 0 value.
5. Click OK.

Appendix – 14.5: SPSS COMMANDS FOR THE MANN-WHITNEY U TEST

After the input data has been typed along with the variable labels and the value labels in an SPSS data file to test the hypothesis of the equality of two location parameters, follow the following steps:

1. The variable 1 has to be typed in a column and the values of the second variable should follow below it. In the next column use code 1 or 2 to indicate whether the observation belongs to group 1 or group 2.
2. Click on ANALYSE at the SPSS menu bar.
3. Click on NON-PARAMETRIC STATISTICS followed by TWO INDEPENDENT SAMPLES.
4. Take the test variable on the right hand box and the coded grouping variable in the box labelled GROUPING VARIABLES followed by define groups, which should be the coded values as explained in step 1.
5. Click MANN-WHITNEY U TEST.
6. Click OK.

Appendix – 14.6: SPSS COMMANDS FOR THE WILCOXON MATCHED PAIR RANK SUM TEST

Type the two variables of interest in the two columns and label them accordingly in the SPSS data file. Now to test the hypothesis of equality of two location parameters in paired sample follow the following steps:

1. Click on ANALYSE at the SPSS menu bar.
2. Click on NON-PARAMETRIC STATISTICS followed by TWO RELATED SAMPLES.
3. Take these two variables simultaneously in the right hand side box.
4. Click WILCOXON TEST.
5. Click OK.

Appendix – 14.7: SPSS COMMANDS FOR THE KRUSKAL-WALLIS TEST

Type the variable of interest in a column, once you finish typing this variable, type the data on other variables below it. In the next column type 1 or 2 or 3 depending upon the group from where data has come. The Kruskal-Wallis Test is used to test the equality of various location parameters and for this follow the following steps:

1. Click on ANALYSE at the SPSS menu bar.
2. Click on NON-PARAMETRIC STATISTICS followed by K INDEPENDENT SAMPLE.
3. Take the test variable to the right hand side box and below that click the box of DEFINE GROUPS and give the coded value from minimum to maximum.
4. Click KRUSKAL-WALLIS TEST.
5. Click OK.

Answers to Objective Type Questions

1. False	2. False	3. True	4. True	5. True
6. False	7. True	8. True	9. False	10. False
11. True	12. False	13. True	14. True	15. True
16. True	17. True	18. False	19. True	20. False

REFERENCE

Luck, David J and Ronald S Rubin. *Marketing Research*. 7th edn. New Delhi: Prentice Hall of India Ltd, 1992.

BIBLIOGRAPHY

Aczel, Amir D and Jayavel Sounderpandian. *Complete Business Statistics*. 5th edn. USA: McGraw Hill Irwin.

Aczel, Amir D and Jayavel Sounderpandian. *Complete Business Statistics*. 6th edn. New Delhi: Tata McGraw Hill Publishing Company Ltd, 2006.

Bhatnagar, OP. *Research Methods and Measurements in Behavioural and Social Sciences*. New Delhi: Agricole Publishing Academic, 1981.

Bhattacharyya, Dipak Kumar. *Human Resource Research Methods*. New Delhi: Oxford University Press, 2007.

Bhattacharyya, Dipak Kumar. *Research Methodology*. New Delhi: Excel Books, 2006.

Black, Ken. *Business Statistics for Contemporary Decision Making*. 4th edn. Singapore: John Wiley & Sons (Asia) Pte. Ltd., 2004.

Downie, N M and W Robert. *Heath, Basic Statistical Methods*. New York: Harper & Row Publishers, 1983.

Kothari, C R. *Research Methodology: Methods and Techniques*. New Delhi: Wiley Eastern, 1990.

Kvanli, Alan H, C Stephen Guynes and Robert J Pavur. *Introduction to Business Statistics—A computer Integrated, Data Analysis Approach*. 4th edn. West Publishers Company, 1996.

Newbold, Paul, William L Carlson and Betty Thorne. *Statistics for Business and Economics*. 6th edn. New Delhi: Pearson Education.

Spiegerl, Murray R and Larry J Stephens. *Theory and Problems of Statistics*. 3rd edn. New Delhi: Tata McGraw Hill Publishing Company Ltd, 2000.

Triola, Mario F and Leroy A Franklin. *Business Statistics—Understand Populations & Processes*. Addison-Wesley Publishing Company, 1994.

Tripathi, P.C. *A Textbook of Research Methodology in Social Sciences*. New Delhi: Sultan Chand & Sons, 2007.

Zikmund, William G. *Business Research Methods*. Fort Worth: Dryden Press, 2000.

Section 5

ADVANCED DATA ANALYSIS TECHNIQUES

This section deals with the advanced data analysis techniques. There are five chapters in this section.

Chapter 15 Correlation and Regression Analysis

Chapter 15 distinguishes between correlation and regression. It talks about the limitation of correlation analysis, so that the use of the concept of regression analysis is justified. Both simple and multiple regressions are explained. The test of significance of the individual regression coefficients and goodness of fit is also discussed. The chapter also introduces the concept of dummy variables that make use of qualitative variables as regressors in the regression model. The emphasis is on the interpretation of results. The use of SPSS software is also illustrated.

Chapter 16 Factor Analysis

Chapter 16 on factor analysis is a data reduction technique. The chapter begins by stating the conditions under which factor analysis exercise could be carried out. The chapter explains both principal component and varimax rotation methods with the help of examples. The empirical work in this chapter is supported by the use of SPSS software.

Chapter 17 Discriminant Analysis

Chapter 17 on discriminant analysis is about predicting group membership. The distinction between two- and multiple-group discriminant analysis is made. This chapter is devoted to two-group discriminant analysis. It discusses the estimation and interpretation of the discriminant function and explains the procedure for determining the statistical significance of the discriminant function and relative contribution of independent variables in discriminating between groups. The procedure for assigning a new object to a particular group and the interpretation of the confusion matrix is also outlined in this chapter. The chapter makes use of SPSS software in model estimation.

Chapter 18 Cluster Analysis

Chapter 18 deals with the multivariate grouping technique of classification, namely, cluster analysis. The technique is essentially based on squared Euclidean distance. It groups objects/cases on the basis of similarity/inter-respondent distance on multiple variables. The technique can be successfully executed on both metric and non-metric data. The chapter discusses at length both computations and derivations for the two assumptions. Validation of the cluster solution and profiling of the obtained cluster solution is discussed at length. Step-wise computation of data, along with SPSS instructions for all conditions, is provided at the end of the chapter.

Chapter 19 Multidimensional Scaling and Perceptual Mapping

Chapter 19 discusses the most commonly used method of perceptual mapping—multidimensional scaling. The technique can be applied to similarity and distance data, as well as ranking and preference of objects/brands/cases. The basic statistical function is Kruskal's stress formula on the basis of which a uni-to-multidimensional map representing the studied objects can be presented in geometrical space. Mathematical assumptions and statistical explanation with SPSS conduction of analysis are presented for both similarity and preference data.

Chapter 20 Conjoint Analysis

Chapter 20 discusses the various concepts that are involved in a conjoint exercise, which attempts to identify the most desirable attributes that could be offered in a new product or service.

This section deals with the [illegible] of data [illegible]. [illegible] chapters in this section [illegible]

Chapter 15 [illegible] correlation and regression [illegible] correlation analysis, so that the use of the concept of regression analysis [illegible], both simple and multiple regression [illegible]. The test of significance of the individual regression coefficients [illegible] are discussed. The chapter also introduces the concept of dummy variables [illegible] of qualitative variables [illegible] in the regression model [illegible] the interpretation of results [illegible] are also illustrated.

Chapter 16 on factor analysis [illegible] data reduction technique [illegible] by stating the conditions under which factor analysis [illegible] the chapter [illegible] both principal component and common factor methods with the help of examples. The [illegible] chapter is supported by the use of SPSS [illegible]

Chapter 17 [illegible] analysis about predicting group membership and the distinction between two and multiple group discriminant analysis [illegible]. This chapter [illegible] two group discriminant analysis [illegible] discusses the estimation and [illegible] of the discriminant function [illegible] the procedure [illegible] the statistical significance of the discriminant function and relative contribution of independent variables in discriminating between groups. The procedure for assigning a new object to a particular group and the interpretation of the [illegible] issues outlined in this chapter. The chapter makes use of SPSS [illegible]

Chapter 18 deals with the multivariate grouping technique of cluster analysis. The technique is essentially based on [illegible] Euclidean distance [illegible] distance or [illegible] The chapter discusses [illegible] computations [illegible] validation of the cluster solution and profiling of the obtained cluster solution [illegible] step by step computation [illegible] along with SPSS instructions [illegible] at the end of the chapter.

Chapter 19 discusses the most commonly used method of [illegible] multidimensional scaling. The technique can be applied to similarity and dissimilarity data as well as ranking/preference of objects/brands [illegible]. The basic [illegible] representing the [illegible] explanation with SPSS [illegible]

Chapter 20 discusses the [illegible] conjoint analysis, which [illegible] most desirable attributes that could be offered in a new product or service.

15

CHAPTER

Correlation and Regression Analysis

Learning Objectives

By the end of the chapter, you should be able to:

1. Understand the concept of correlation and distinguish between various types of correlation.
2. Find a numerical estimate of the correlation coefficient and test for its statistical significance.
3. Understand the concept of regression analysis and estimate a simple linear regression model.
4. Conduct tests of the significance of regression parameters and the overall goodness of fit.
5. Use the regression analysis in prediction.
6. Learn alternative method of testing the significance of r^2.
7. Use SPSS software to estimate the regression equation.
8. Introduce the concept of multiple regression.
9. Use qualitative variables (dummy variables) as regressors in the regression model.
10. Apply regression analysis in research.

Mr V K Malhotra, the Marketing Manager of S P Pickles Pvt. Ltd. was wondering about the reasons for the decline in the sale of the company's pickles for the last two years. He called a meeting of his team to discuss the possible reasons for the decline. The members suggested that it may be worthwhile to list the variables that influence the sale of the pickles. They listed the average price of the pickles sold by them, the competitor's average price, consumer's income, taste and preference and the amount spent on advertising. Having done so, they were wondering what to do next. How can they determine the important variables influencing the sale of their pickles? What is the relative contribution of these variables in explaining the sales and how can they manipulate these variables to achieve the desired level of sales?

This chapter will attempt to estimate the relationship between sales and the variables affecting it. It will also try to point out the relative importance of the variables that influence sales and provide guidelines for manipulating of sales.

INTRODUCTION

LEARNING OBJECTIVE 1
Understand the concept of correlation and distinguish between various types of correlation.

Correlation and regression analysis are generally performed together. Correlation measures the degree of the association between two or more set of variables. Regression, on the other hand, is used to explain the variations in one variable—usually called the dependent variable—by a set of independent variables. It identifies the nature of the relationship. The number of independent variables in regression analysis could be one or more. In case of one independent variable, we classify it as a simple regression, whereas in case of more than one independent variable, it is called a multiple regression analysis.

Correlation

Correlation measures the degree of association between two or more variables. When we are dealing with two variables, we are talking in terms of simple correlation and when more than two variables are involved, the subject matter of interest is called multiple correlation. In this chapter, we will start the discussion of simple correlation and extend the analysis to multiple correlation. There are three types of correlation:

When two variables X and Y **move in the same direction,** the correlation between the two variables is positive.

1. **Positive correlation:** When two variables X and Y move in the same direction, the correlation between the two is positive. If one variable increases, the other variable also increases and if one variable decreases, the other variable also decreases. The examples of positive correlation are a particular quantity supplied of a commodity and the price of the commodity, the sales revenue and the advertising expenditure, consumption expenditure and the disposable income. The scatter of the points of the variables X and Y is clustered around a positively sloped line/curve in such a case as shown in Figure 15.1. In the figure, we note that the two variables X and Y move in the same direction.

When the two variables X and Y **move in the opposite direction**, the correlation is negative.

2. **Negative correlation:** When two variables X and Y move in the opposite direction, the correlation is negative. If one variable increases, the other decreases and vice versa. The examples of negative correlation are usually the quantity demanded and the price of the commodity. The scatter of the points on the variables X and Y is clustered around a negatively sloped straight line/curve in such a situation as shown in Figure 15.2. In the figure, we find that the variables X and Y are moving in the opposite direction.

FIGURE 15.1
Positive correlation

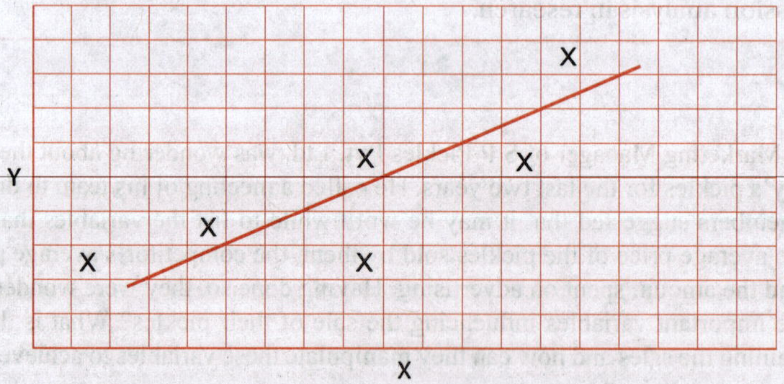

FIGURE 15.2
Negative correlation

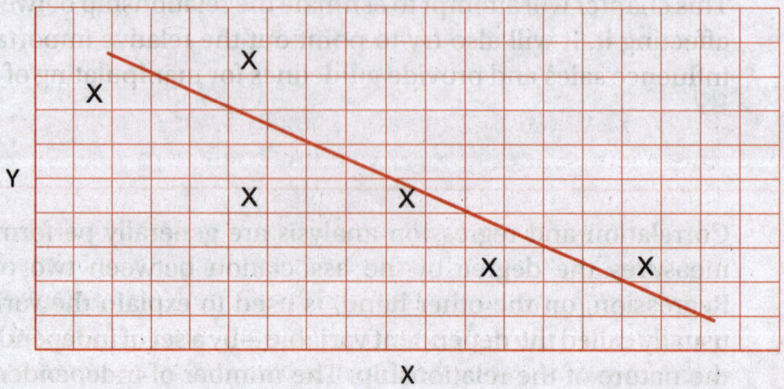

FIGURE 15.3
Zero correlation

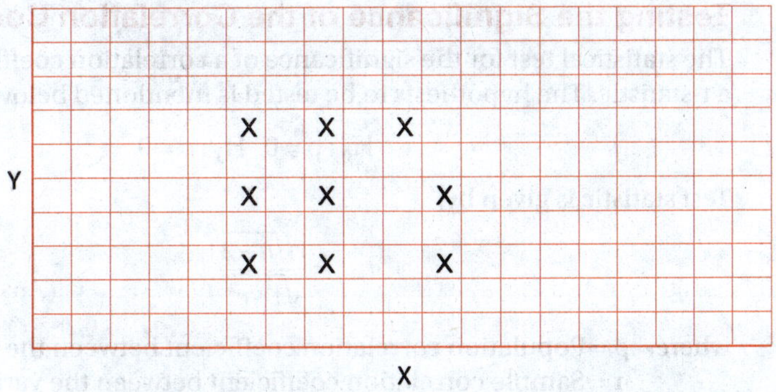

3. **Zero correlation:** The correlation between two variables X and Y is zero when the variables move in no connection with each other. If the variable X increases, Y may increase or decrease in some situation. The scatter of the points of the variables X and Y in case of zero correlation is given in Figure 15.3. Zero correlation does not mean that the variables are not related. We are, here, dealing with a linear correlation and there could be a non-linear relation between them.

QUANTITATIVE ESTIMATE OF A LINEAR CORRELATION

LEARNING OBJECTIVE 2
Find a numerical estimate of the correlation coefficient and test for the statistical significance of the correlation coefficient.

A quantitative estimate of a linear correlation between two variables X and Y is given by Karl Pearson as:

$$r_{xy} = \frac{\sum_{i=1}^{n} (X_i - \overline{X})(Y_i - \overline{Y})}{\sqrt{\sum_{i=1}^{n} (X_i - \overline{X})^2} \sqrt{\sum_{i=1}^{n} (Y_i - \overline{Y})^2}} \qquad (15.1)$$

which may be rewritten as:

$$r_{xy} = \frac{\sum_{i=1}^{n} X_i Y_i - n\overline{X}\,\overline{Y}}{\sqrt{\sum_{i=1}^{n} X_i^2 - n\overline{X}^2} \sqrt{\sum_{i=1}^{n} Y_i^2 - n\overline{Y}^2}} \qquad (15.2)$$

where, r_{xy} = Correlation coefficient between X and Y

$\overline{X}$ = Mean of the variable X

$\overline{Y}$ = Mean of the variable Y

n = Size of the sample

The **linear correlation coefficient** can take a value between −1 and +1.

It may be noted that the above-mentioned formulae are for the linear correlation coefficient. The linear correlation coefficient takes a value between -1 and +1 (both values inclusive). If the value of the correlation coefficient is equal to 1, the two variables are perfectly positively correlated and the scatter of the points of the variables X and Y will lie on a positively sloped straight line. Similarly, if the correlation coefficient between the two variables X and Y is -1, the scatter of the points of these variables will lie on a negatively sloped straight line and such a correlation will be called a perfectly negative correlation. It may be noted that the closer the scatter of points to the line, higher is the degree of correlation between the variables.

Testing the Significance of the Correlation Coefficient

The statistical test for the significance of a correlation coefficient is conducted using a t-statistic. The hypothesis to be tested is mentioned below:

$$H_0: \rho = 0 \quad H_1: \rho \neq 0$$

Test statistic is given by,

$$t_{n-2} = \frac{r\sqrt{n-2}}{\sqrt{1-r^2}}$$

Test statistic is given by,

$$t_{n-2} = \frac{r\sqrt{n-2}}{\sqrt{1-r^2}} \tag{15.3}$$

where, ρ = Population correlation coefficient between the variables X and Y
r = Sample correlation coefficient between the variables X and Y
n - 2 = The degrees of freedom

Given the value of r and n, the value of the test statistic t could be computed. Now for a given level of significance, if computed |t| is greater than tabulated |t| with n - 2 degrees of freedom, the null hypothesis of no correlation between X and Y is rejected.

REGRESSION ANALYSIS

LEARNING OBJECTIVE 3
Understand the concept of regression analysis and estimate a simple linear regression model.

Zero correlation does not mean that the variables are not related. They may be non-linearly related.

One of the problems with Karl Pearson's formula of correlation coefficient is that it is applicable only when the relationship between the two variables is linear. There can, however, be situations when the variables are connected by a non-linear relationship. It may be noted that zero correlation and the independence of the two variables are not the same thing. Zero correlation does not mean that the variables are not related. They may be non-linearly related. However, the statistical independence implies that there is a zero correlation between the variables. Another problem with the simple correlation coefficient is that it does not indicate which variable is influencing which one. If, for example, the correlation coefficient between the variables X and Y is 0.96, it can only be said that the variables X and Y are positively and highly correlated. We cannot say that whether the variable X influences Y or Y influences X or there may be a third variable Z which may be influencing both these variables, thus resulting in a high correlation between X and Y. To overcome this limitation of the correlation analysis, we have another concept called the regression analysis.

Regression analysis could be used for a variety of purposes in research. It could be used to test whether an overall relationship exists between the dependent variable and a set of independent variables (concepts to be explained later). It can also be used to measure the relative importance of various independent variables in explaining the dependent variable. The other use of regression analysis is for a prediction of the values of dependent variable, that is, knowing the values of the independent variables one can predict the values of the dependent variable. For example, food expenditure by households could be predicted by using family income and family size as independent variables in regression. As another example, the amount spent by a consumer at a retail store in the last three months can be explained by the store's location, prices, credit policy, merchandise quality and speed of service by using the regression analysis. Likewise, another example could be to predict the sales volume of a photocopier by using a set of independent variables like the size of sales force, amount of the advertising budget and the consumer attitudes towards the company's product. Similarly, the willingness to export the product by the small entrepreneurs could be explained by the employee size, firm revenue and the years of operation in the domestic market.

In regression analysis, it is assumed that there is a variable that is influencing another variable. For example, we may write,

$$Y = f(X)$$

This indicates that the values of Y depend upon the values of X. Further, there is a one-way causation between X and Y in the sense that it is X which influences the values of Y and not the other way round. The variable Y is called a dependent variable or an effect variable, whereas the variable X is called an independent variable, explanatory variable, causal variable or a regressor. The relationship between Y and X may be assumed to be linear and we may write the following expression as:

$$Y = \alpha + \beta X$$

The above expression shows that if we have a pair of data on the variables X and Y, the scatter of all the points between these two variables will lie on a positively or negatively sloped straight line depending upon whether the sign of beta (β) is positive or negative. This means that the correlation coefficient between X and Y will either be +1 or –1. In fact, in reality such a thing rarely happens. If we plot the data on the variables X and Y on a two-dimensional plane, all the scatter of points would not lie on either positively or negatively sloped straight line. This is because the variable Y is not only influenced by the variable X but by many other variables which we have ignored for various reasons. The possible reasons for ignoring those variables could be the non-availability of data or poor knowledge about the existence of such variables influencing the dependent variable Y or the errors of measurements in the variables X and Y or the researcher's inability to quantify such variables. Therefore, to account for those variables which have been omitted for one reason or the others, a stochastic error term is added to the above equation which appears as:

$$Y = \alpha + \beta X + U \tag{15.4}$$

where, U = Stochastic error term

α, β = Parameters to be estimated

Simple linear regression equation can be presented as $Y = \alpha + \beta X + U$

The above equation is called a simple linear regression equation. This is so because there is one dependent variable and one independent variable. In case of multiple regression, there are at least two independent variables. The equation is estimated using the ordinary least squares (OLS) method of estimation. The OLS method of estimation states that the regression line should be drawn in such a way so as to minimize the error sum of squares. The method of least square is explained as follows:

If we plot the scatter of points on the variable X and Y, the scatter may look as shown in Figure 15.4.

Let us assume that $\hat{\alpha}$ and $\hat{\beta}$ are the OLS estimates of α and β respectively. Then, the estimated regression line ($\hat{Y} = \hat{\alpha} + \hat{\beta}X$) would look as given in the Figure 15.4. Now corresponding to X_1, there is an observed Y_1 and an estimated value as $\hat{Y}_1$. Therefore, the error is given by $\hat{U}_1 = Y_1 - \hat{Y}_1$ which is positive. Similarly, corresponding to X_2 we have observed Y_2 and estimated $\hat{Y}_2$ and the error is given by $\hat{U}_2 = Y_2 - \hat{Y}_2$ which is negative. Now, for the given value of X_3, the values of Y_3 and $\hat{Y}_3$ are equal as these points lie on the estimated regression line. Therefore, the error is zero. Now the error sum of squares would be given by:

$$\sum_{i=1}^{n} \hat{U}_i^2 = \sum (Y - \hat{Y})^2 = \sum (Y - \hat{\alpha} - \hat{\beta}X)^2 \tag{15.5}$$

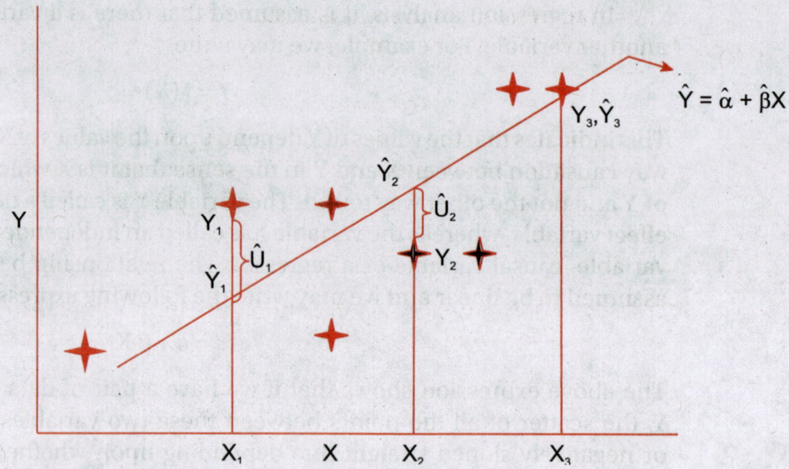

FIGURE 15.4 Scatter of points and the estimated regression line

As mentioned earlier, OLS method aims at minimizing the error sum of square. Therefore, by taking the partial derivative of the above expression with respect to $\hat{\alpha}$ and $\hat{\beta}$ and setting the resulting expression to zero, we get the following:

$$\sum Y = n\hat{\alpha} + \hat{\beta}\sum X \qquad (15.6)$$

$$\sum XY = \hat{\alpha}\sum X + \hat{\beta}\sum X^2 \qquad (15.7)$$

(We have purposely ignored the derivations and have assumed that the second order conditions for minimization are satisfied.)

The above two equations (15.6 and 15.7) are called normal equations and using algebraic manipulations it can be shown that the OLS estimates of α and β are given as:

$$\hat{\beta} = \frac{\sum_{i=1}^{n} (X_i - \overline{X})(Y_i - \overline{Y})}{\sum_{i=1}^{n} (X_i - \overline{X})^2} \qquad (15.8)$$

$$= \frac{\sum_{i=1}^{n} X_i Y_i - n\overline{X}\overline{Y}}{\sum_{i=1}^{n} X_i^2 - n\overline{X}^2} \qquad (15.9)$$

Once $\hat{\beta}$ is estimated, the value of α may be computed as:

$$\hat{\alpha} = \overline{Y} - \hat{\beta}\overline{X} \qquad (15.10)$$

Standard error of estimate

$$= \hat{\sigma}_u = \sqrt{\frac{\sum_{i=1}^{n} \hat{U}_i^2}{n-k}}$$

After having estimated the regression equation, the estimate of the error (residual) term is obtained as $\hat{U} = Y - \hat{Y}$ where $\hat{U}$ is equal to the estimated value of the error term, Y is the observed value of the dependent variable and $\hat{Y}$ is the estimated value of the dependent variable Y. The estimate of the variance of the error term is given by:

$$V(\hat{U}) = \hat{\sigma}_U^2 = \frac{\sum_{i=1}^{n} \hat{U}_i^2}{n-k} \qquad (15.11)$$

Its square root gives the standard error of estimate of the regression equation which is given below:

$$\text{Standard error of estimate} = \hat{\sigma}_U = \sqrt{\frac{\sum_{i=1}^{n}\hat{U}_i^2}{n-k}} \tag{15.12}$$

The **standard error of estimates** indicates how close the scatter of the points is to the regression line.

In the above expression, n and k denote the sample size and the number of parameters to be estimated in a given regression. The standard error of estimates indicates how close the scatter of the points is to the regression line. However, this measure suffers from the defect that it depends upon the units of measurement and, therefore, the fit of the two regression equations with different standard errors of estimates cannot be compared. To overcome this problem, we will introduce the concept of R^2, the coefficient of determination, later in the text.

TEST OF SIGNIFICANCE OF REGRESSION PARAMETERS

LEARNING OBJECTIVE 4

Conduct tests of the significance of regression parameters and the overall goodness of fit.

We need to test the significance of the regression coefficients α and β, which is carried out with the help of the t statistic. The hypothesis to be tested for the slope coefficient is mentioned below as:

$$H_0 : \beta = 0 \quad H_1 : \beta \neq 0$$

The acceptance of the null hypothesis (H_0) would indicate that the variable X does not influence Y. In the above case we have used a two-tailed test. The decision whether a researcher should use a two-tailed or a one-tailed alternative depends upon whether the direction of the relationship between the dependent and the causal variable is known or not. If we know the direction of the relationship between the causal variable and the dependent variable, we should go for a one-tailed test and if there is no clue about the direction of relationship between the two variables, it is suggested that a two-tailed alternative should be adopted.

The test statistic to be used to test the significance of the slope coefficient is given by:

$$t_{n-k} = \frac{\hat{\beta} - \beta}{SE(\hat{\beta})} \tag{15.13}$$

where, $\hat{\beta}$ = Estimated value of beta (β)

$SE(\hat{\beta})$ = Standard error of estimate of β

We know that: $$V(\hat{\beta}) = \frac{\hat{\sigma}_U^2}{\Sigma(X-\bar{X})^2} \tag{15.14}$$

Therefore, $$SE(\hat{\beta}) = \frac{\hat{\sigma}_u}{\sqrt{\Sigma(X-\bar{X})^2}} \tag{15.15}$$

Once we compute the t statistic, it is compared with table value of t with n – k degrees of freedom where n is the number of the observations in the sample and k represents the number of parameters to be estimated in a regression equation (in the present case k = 2). In case the computed value of |t| is greater than the tabulated valued of |t| at a given level of significance, the null hypotheses is rejected.

Goodness of Fit of Regression Equation

The coefficient of determination of a regression equation takes values between 0 and 1 (both values inclusive).

A researcher would be interested in knowing how good the estimated regression equation is. To answer this question, there is a measure r^2 which, in the case of simple linear regression model, is simply the square of the correlation coefficient. This measure is also called the coefficient of determination of a regression equation and it takes values between 0 and 1 (both values inclusive). It indicates the explanatory power of the regression model. If for a particular regression model, r^2 is equal to 0.86, it means that 86 per cent of the variations in the dependent variable Y are explained by the variations in the independent variable X. The r^2 may be computed as:

$$r^2 = 1 - \frac{\sum \hat{U}^2}{\Sigma(Y-\bar{Y})^2} \quad (15.16)$$

$$= r_{xy}^2 \quad (15.17)$$

$$= r_{y\hat{y}}^2 \quad (15.18)$$

$$= \frac{\Sigma(\hat{Y}-\bar{Y})^2}{\Sigma(Y-\bar{Y})^2} \quad (15.19)$$

The measure r^2 is free from the units of measurements and, therefore, can be used to compare the goodness of fit of two or more regressions. The test for the goodness of fit is carried out by using the F statistic. The hypothesis to be tested is:

$$H_0 : r^2 = 0 \quad H_1 : r^2 > 0$$

The test statistic F is given by the expression:

$$F_{n-k}^{k-1} = \frac{r^2/(k-1)}{(1-r^2)/(n-k)} \quad (15.20)$$

For a given level of significance α, the computed value of the F statistic is compared with the tabulated value of F with k - 1 degrees of freedom in the numerator and n - k degrees of freedom in the denominator. If the computed F exceeds the tabulated F, the null hypothesis is rejected in favour of the alternative hypothesis.

CONCEPT CHECK

1. If correlation coefficient between two variables is zero, does it mean that the variables are independent? Explain.
2. What test is used to examine the statistical significance of correlation coefficient?
3. Why is error term included in the regression model?
4. What is the test statistics used to test the significance of r^2?

USES OF REGRESSION ANALYSIS IN PREDICTION

LEARNING OBJECTIVE 5
Use the regression analysis in prediction.

The regression analysis can be employed for prediction. The prediction estimates could be both point and interval. Further, the interval prediction can be approximate as well as exact.

To get the point prediction estimate corresponding to $X = X_0$, we substitute the value of X_0 in the estimated regression $\hat{Y} = \hat{\alpha} + \hat{\beta}X$ to obtain the predicted value of the dependent variable as:

$$\hat{Y}_0 = \hat{\alpha} + \hat{\beta}X_0$$

The $(1 - \alpha)$ per cent approximate prediction interval for $X = X_0$ is given as:

Lower limit of approximate prediction interval $= \hat{Y}_0 - t_{\alpha/2}\hat{\sigma}_u$ (15.21)

Upper limit of approximate prediction interval $= \hat{Y}_0 + t_{\alpha/2}\hat{\sigma}_u$ (15.22)

where $\hat{\sigma}_u$ is the standard error of estimate and the table value of $t_{\alpha/2}$ corresponds to $n - 2$ degrees of freedom.

To get the exact prediction interval, the standard error of estimate $\hat{\sigma}_u$ is replaced by the standard error of prediction given by:

$$Sp = \hat{\sigma}_u \sqrt{1 + \frac{1}{n} + \frac{(\bar{X} - X_0)^2}{\Sigma X^2 - n\bar{X}^2}} \quad (15.23)$$

Therefore, $(1 - \alpha)$ per cent exact prediction interval is given as:

Lower limit $= \hat{Y}_0 - t_{\alpha/2}Sp$ (15.24)

Upper Limit $= \hat{Y}_0 + t_{\alpha/2}Sp$ (15.25)

We will now explain all the concepts discussed so far with the help of a numerical example.

Example 15.1

Consider the data on the quantity demanded and the price of a commodity over a ten-year period as given in the following table:

Year	Demand	Price
1996	100	5
1997	75	7
1998	80	6
1999	70	6
2000	50	8
2001	65	7
2002	90	5
2003	100	4
2004	110	3
2005	60	9

Questions

1. Estimate the correlation coefficient between the quantity demanded and price and interpret the same.
2. Test the statistical significance of the correlation coefficient at a 5 per cent level.
3. Estimate the linear regression equation of demand on price and interpret the same. Use the estimated equation to compute the average point price elasticity of demand.
4. Test the statistical significance of the slope coefficient of the estimated regression equation.
5. Compute r^2 and interpret the same.
6. Test the significance of r^2 at a 5 per cent level.
7. Find a 95 per cent approximate prediction interval for demand when price (X) equals 8.

Solution:

This problem will be attempted first by showing all the detailed computations and later on the same will be worked out using the SPSS software.

$$r_{xy} = \frac{\sum_{i=1}^{n} X_i Y_i - n\,\overline{X}\overline{Y}}{\sqrt{\sum_{i=1}^{n} X_i^2 - n\overline{X}^2}\sqrt{\sum_{i=1}^{n} Y_i^2 - n\overline{Y}^2}}$$

The required computations are shown in the following table:

Year	Demand (Y)	Price (X)	XY	X²	Y²
1996	100	5	500	25	10000
1997	75	7	525	49	5625
1998	80	6	480	36	6400
1999	70	6	420	36	4900
2000	50	8	400	64	2500
2001	65	7	455	49	4225
2002	90	5	450	25	8100
2003	100	4	400	16	10000
2004	110	3	330	9	12100
2005	60	9	540	81	3600
Total	800	60	4500	390	67450

$\Sigma XY = 4500 \qquad \Sigma X^2 = 390$

$\Sigma Y^2 = 67{,}450 \qquad \Sigma Y = 800$

$\Sigma X = 60 \qquad n = 10$

$$\overline{Y} = \frac{\Sigma Y}{n} = \frac{800}{10} = 80 \qquad \overline{X} = \frac{\Sigma X}{n} = \frac{60}{10} = 6$$

Substituting these values in the formula for the correlation coefficient, we get:

$$r_{xy} = \frac{4500 - 10 \times 6 \times 80}{\sqrt{390 - 10 \times 6 \times 6}\ \sqrt{67450 - 10 \times 80 \times 80}}$$

$$= \frac{4500 - 4800}{\sqrt{390 - 360}\ \sqrt{67450 - 64000}}$$

$$= \frac{-300}{\sqrt{30}\ \sqrt{3450}} = \frac{-300}{5.477 \times 58.737}$$

$$= \frac{-300}{321.701} = -0.9325$$

The value of the correlation coefficient between the quantity demanded and price is −0.9325, which is negative and very high. This shows that the quantity demanded and price move in the opposite directions. Now, in order to test the statistical significance of the correlation coefficient, we use the following test.

$$H_0 : \rho = 0 \quad H_1 : \rho \neq 0$$

Test statistic is given by $t_{n-2} = \dfrac{r\sqrt{n-2}}{\sqrt{1 - r^2}}$

where, $r = -0.9325$

$n = 10$

$r^2 = 0.8696$

By substituting these values in the t-statistic formula given above, we obtain:

$$t_8 = \frac{-0.9325\sqrt{10-2}}{\sqrt{1-0.8696}} = \frac{-0.9325\sqrt{8}}{\sqrt{0.1304}}$$

$$= \frac{-0.9325 \times 2.8284}{0.3611} = -7.30402$$

Let us choose the level of significance (α) to be 5 per cent. Therefore, table value of |t| with 8 degrees of freedom at 5 per cent is equal to 2.306, whereas the computed |t| is equal to 7.304. As the computed |t| is greater than the tabulated |t|, we reject H_0 which shows that the correlation coefficient is significant.

In order to estimate the linear regression model, we need to get the values of β and α as given below:

$$\hat{\beta} = \frac{\sum_{i=1}^{n}(X_i - \bar{X})(Y_i - \bar{Y})}{\sum_{i=1}^{n}(X_i - \bar{X})^2} = \frac{\sum_{i=1}^{n} X_i Y_i - n\bar{X}\bar{Y}}{\sum_{i=1}^{n} X_i^2 - n\bar{X}^2}$$

$$\hat{\alpha} = \bar{Y} - \hat{\beta}\bar{X}$$

By substituting the values of,

$$\Sigma XY = 4500 \qquad \Sigma X^2 = 390$$
$$\Sigma Y = 800 \qquad \bar{Y} = 80$$
$$\Sigma X = 60 \qquad n = 10$$
$$\bar{X} = 6$$

in the formula for $\hat{\beta}$, we obtain:

$$\hat{\beta} = \frac{4500 - 10 \times 6 \times 80}{390 - 10 \times 6 \times 6} = \frac{4500 - 4800}{390 - 360}$$

$$= \frac{-300}{30} = -10$$

Therefore, $\hat{\alpha} = \bar{Y} - \hat{\beta}\bar{X}$ may be obtained as:

$$\hat{\alpha} = 80 - (-10) \times 6$$
$$= 80 + 60 = 140$$

Therefore, the estimated regression equation is $\hat{Y} = 140 - 10X$. This regression equation shows that as the price goes up by 1 unit, the quantity demanded goes down by 10 units. The price elasticity of demand at the mean value of price ($\bar{X}$) and demand ($\bar{Y}$) is given by:

$$\text{Price elasticity of demand} = \frac{dY}{dX} \cdot \frac{\bar{X}}{\bar{Y}} = \frac{-10 \times 6}{80}$$

$$= \frac{-60}{80} = -0.75$$

This shows that as price goes up by 1 per cent, the quantity demanded goes down by 0.75 per cent.

To test the statistical significance of the slope coefficient, it is required to find an estimate of the standard error of estimate $\hat{\sigma}_u = \sqrt{\frac{\Sigma \hat{u}_i^2}{n-2}}$ for which the following computations are required:

Year	D(Y)	P (X)	$\hat{Y}$ = 140–10X	$\hat{U}$	$\hat{U}^2$
1996	100	5	90	10	100
1997	75	7	70	5	25
1998	80	6	80	0	0
1999	70	6	80	–10	100
2000	50	8	60	–10	100
2001	65	7	70	–5	25
2002	90	5	90	0	0
2003	100	4	100	0	0
2004	110	3	110	0	0
2005	60	9	50	10	100
Total	800	60	800	0	450

Therefore, the standard error of estimate is obtained as:

$$\hat{\sigma}_u = \sqrt{\frac{\Sigma \hat{u}_i^2}{n-2}} = \sqrt{\frac{450}{8}} = 7.5$$

To test the significance of the slope coefficient, the following hypothesis is to be tested:

$$H_0 : \beta = 0 \quad H_1 : \beta \neq 0$$

The test statistic to be used for testing the hypothesis is as given below:

$$t_{n-2} = \frac{\hat{\beta} - \beta}{SE(\hat{\beta})}$$

where, $\hat{\beta}$ = Estimated value of β

$SE(\hat{\beta})$ = Standard error of estimate of slope term

The estimate of the standard error of slope term is given by the following formula:

$$SE(\hat{\beta}) = \frac{\hat{\sigma}_u}{\sqrt{\Sigma X^2 - n\bar{X}^2}}$$

where, $\hat{\sigma}_u$ = Standard error of estimate.

We have already computed the values of the expression in the numerator and denominator as 7.5 & $\sqrt{30}$ respectively. Substituting these values in the expression for $SE(\hat{\beta})$ we obtain:

$$SE(\hat{\beta}) = \frac{7.5}{\sqrt{30}} = 1.37$$

Therefore, the value of t-statistic could be computed as:

$$t_{n-2} = \frac{\hat{\beta} - \beta}{SE(\hat{\beta})} = \frac{-10 - 0}{1.37} = -7.3$$

If we choose the level of significance to be 5 per cent, we obtain the table value of t as 2.306, since the absolute computed value of t is greater than the tabulated value of t we reject the null hypothesis and conclude that the price affects the quantity demanded significantly.

The value of r^2, the coefficient of determination is computed as:

$$r^2 = 1 - \frac{\Sigma \hat{U}^2}{\Sigma (Y - \bar{Y})^2} = 1 - \frac{\Sigma \hat{U}^2}{\Sigma Y^2 - n\bar{Y}^2}$$

$$= 1 - \frac{450}{3450} = 1 - 0.13 = 0.87$$

This means that 87 per cent of the variations in the quantity demanded are explained by price. In order to test the statistical significance of r^2, we proceed as follows.

The hypothesis to be tested is:

$$H_0 : r^2 = 0 \quad H_1 : r^2 > 0$$

The alternative hypothesis is taken as one sided as r^2 can't be negative:

$$\underset{n-k}{\overset{k-1}{F}} = \frac{\dfrac{r^2}{(k-1)}}{\dfrac{(1-r^2)}{(n-k)}} = \frac{\dfrac{0.87}{1}}{\dfrac{0.13}{8}} = \frac{0.87 \times 8}{0.13} = 53.538$$

The computed value of F is to be compared with the tabulated value of $\underset{8}{\overset{1}{F}}$ at a 5 per cent level of significance. The tabulated value of $\underset{8}{\overset{1}{F}}$at a 5 per cent level of significance equals 5.32. Since the computed F is greater than the tabulated F, null hypothesis is rejected. This means that r^2 is significant at a 5 per cent level of significance. The estimated regression equation is:

$$\hat{Y} = 140 - 10X$$

Point prediction of demand when X = 8 is obtained by substituting the value of X in the above equation:

$$\hat{Y} = 140 - 10 \times 8$$
$$= 140 - 80$$
$$= 60$$

The 95 per cent approximate prediction interval when X = 8 is obtained as:

Lower limit of approximate prediction interval $= \hat{Y} - t_{0.025}\, \hat{\sigma}_u$

$$= 60 - 2.306 \times 7.5$$
$$= 42.705$$

Upper limit of approximate prediction interval $= \hat{Y} + t_{0.025}\, \hat{\sigma}_u$

$$= 60 + 2.306 \times 7.5$$
$$= 77.295$$

Therefore, the 95 per cent prediction interval for demand when price X = 8 is given by (42.705, 77.295). This means that the true demand is likely to lie between the two limits.

ALTERNATIVE WAY OF TESTING THE SIGNIFICANCE OF r^2

LEARNING OBJECTIVE 6
Learn alternative method of testing the significance of r^2.

Another way of testing the significance of r^2 is by using the analysis of variance approach. Here, the total variance in Y is decomposed into two components, viz., one explained by the regression line and the other one being unexplained. We know:

Total Variance = Explained variance + Unexplained variance

$$\Sigma(Y-\bar{Y})^2 = \Sigma(\hat{Y}-\bar{Y})^2 + \Sigma(Y-\hat{Y})^2$$
$$= \Sigma(\hat{Y}-\bar{Y})^2 + \Sigma\hat{U}^2 \qquad (15.26)$$

Since r^2 measures explanatory power of the model, it may be written as:

$$r^2 = \frac{\Sigma(\hat{Y}-\bar{Y})^2}{\Sigma(Y-\bar{Y})^2} \qquad (15.27)$$

where,

$\Sigma(Y-\bar{Y})^2$ = Total sum of squares or total variation (TSS)

$\sum(\hat{Y}-\bar{Y})^2$ = Explained sum of squares or variations explained by regression (ESS)
$\sum(Y-\hat{Y})^2 = \sum\hat{U}^2$ = Error sum of squares or residual sum of squares

The analysis of variance (ANOVA) table can be set up as:

Source of Variation	Sum of Squares	d.f.	Mean Square	F^{k-1}_{n-k}
Regression	$r^2\sum(Y-\bar{Y})^2$	k – 1	$\frac{r^2\sum(Y-\bar{Y})^2}{k-1}$	$\frac{r^2/(k-1)}{(1-r^2)/(n-k)}$
Error	$(1-r^2)\sum(Y-\bar{Y})^2$	n – k	$\frac{(1-r^2)\sum(Y-\bar{Y})^2}{n-k}$	
Total	$\sum(Y-\bar{Y})^2$	n – 1		

The computed value of F can be obtained from the above table and compared with the table value for accepting or rejecting the null hypothesis that r^2 equals zero.

USE OF SPSS IN THE SIMPLE LINEAR REGRESSION MODEL

LEARNING OBJECTIVE 7
Use SPSS software to estimate the regression equation.

Example 15.1 can be worked out using the SPSS software. The instructions for obtaining the simple correlation coefficient and simple regression are given in Appendices 15.1 and 15.2 respectively. The results of the correlation between demand and price are presented in Table 15.1.

The results indicate that the correlation between demand and price is –0.933, which is the same as was obtained when the problem was worked out manually. The p value for the correlation coefficient is 0.000, which is less than 0.01, the assumed level of significance. This implies that the correlation coefficient between the quantity demanded and the price is negative, high and statistically significant.

The simple regression results are presented in Tables 15.2 to 15.4.

TABLE 15.1
Correlation matrix

		Demand	Price
Demand	Pearson Correlation	1	–0.933**
	Sig. (2-tailed)		0.000
	N	10	10
Price	Pearson Correlation	–0.933**	1
	Sig. (2-tailed)	0.000	
	N	10	10

**Correlation is significant at the 0.01 level (2-tailed).

TABLE 15.2
Model summary

Model	R	R Square	Adjusted R Square	Std. Error of the Estimate
1	0.933[a]	0.870	0.853	7.50000

[a] Predictors: (Constant), Price

TABLE 15.3
ANOVA[b]

Model		Sum of Squares	d.f.	Mean Square	F	Sig.
1	Regression	3000.000	1	3000.000	53.333	0.000[a]
	Residual	450.000	8	56.250		
	Total	3450.000	9			

[a] Predictors: (Constant), Price [b] Dependent Variable: Demand

TABLE 15.4
Coefficients[a]

Model	Unstandardized Coefficients		Standardized Coefficients	t	Sig.
	B	Std. error	Beta		
1 (Constant)	140.000	8.551		16.372	0.000
Price	–10.000	1.369	–0.933	–7.303	0.000

[a] Dependent Variable: Demand

By using the results presented in Table 15.4, we can write the estimated regression equation as:

Demand = 140.00 – 10.00 Price
t = (16.372) (–7.303)

We note that the intercept and the slope terms are 140 and –10.00, respectively, which is exactly the same as when the problem was worked out manually. The value of the t statistic corresponding to the coefficient of price is –7.303, which is the same when the example was worked out manually. The value of $r^2 = 0.87$ as presented in Table 15.2 also matches exactly. The F statistic used to test the significance of r^2 as given in Table 15.3 equals 53.333, which is significant as indicated by the p value (sig.) as given in the last column. Therefore, all the results are identical when the example was worked out manually. The interpretation of the results has already been discussed in Example 15.1. Now onwards, all the results would be from the SPSS output.

MULTIPLE REGRESSION MODEL

LEARNING OBJECTIVE 8
Introduce the concept of multiple regression.

In the multiple regression model, there are at least two independent variables. The linear multiple regression model with two independent variables would look like:

$$Y = b_0 + b_1 X_1 + b_2 X_2 + U$$

The **linear multiple regression model** with the two independent variables would look like:
$Y = b_0 + b_1 X_1 + b_2 X_2 + U$

In the above model, there are three parameters b_0, b_1, and b_2 that are to be estimated. One of the very crucial assumptions for the estimation of the multiple regression is that there should not be any perfect positive or a negative correlation between X_1 and X_2. If the correlation coefficient between X_1 and X_2 is either +1 or –1, the model cannot be estimated and this is called the problem of perfect multicollinearity. The estimation is carried out using the OLS estimates, where the sum of the squared residuals is minimized. This results into following three normal equations:

$$\Sigma Y = n\hat{b}_0 + \hat{b}_1 \Sigma X_1 + \hat{b}_2 \Sigma X_2 \quad (15.28)$$

$$\Sigma X_1 Y = \hat{b}_0 \Sigma X_1 + \hat{b}_1 \Sigma X_1^2 + \hat{b}_2 \Sigma X_1 X_2 \quad (15.29)$$

$$\Sigma X_2 Y = \hat{b}_0 \Sigma X_2 + \hat{b}_1 \Sigma X_1 X_2 + \hat{b}_2 \Sigma X_2^2 \quad (15.30)$$

Now, there are three equations with three unknowns ($\hat{b}_0$, $\hat{b}_1$, and $\hat{b}_2$). These equations can be solved simultaneously to obtain the estimated values of b_0, b_1, and b_2. It can be shown that by certain algebraic manipulations, the above equations would result in the following:

$$\hat{b}_0 = \bar{Y} - \hat{b}_1 \bar{X}_1 - \hat{b}_2 \bar{X}_2 \quad (15.31)$$

$$\hat{b}_1 = \frac{(\Sigma x_1 y)(\Sigma x_2^2) - (\Sigma x_2 y)(\Sigma x_1 x_2)}{(\Sigma x_1^2)(\Sigma x_2^2) - (\Sigma x_1 x_2)^2} \quad (15.32)$$

$$\hat{b}_2 = \frac{(\Sigma x_2 y)(\Sigma x_1^2) - (\Sigma x_1 y)(\Sigma x_1 x_2)}{(\Sigma x_1^2)(\Sigma x_2^2) - \Sigma (x_1 x_2)^2} \tag{15.33}$$

where,

$$x_1 = X_1 - \overline{X}_1$$
$$x_2 = X_2 - \overline{X}_2$$

Please note that b_1 and b_2 are called partial regression coefficients and b_0 the constant term.

In case of multiple regression model, we have the concept of the multiple correlation squared given by $R^2_{Y.X_1X_2}$ which indicates the explanatory power of the model. This shows the percentage of the variations in the dependent variable Y that is explained together by the two independent variables X_1 and X_2. It may be noted that after Y, a dot is put, followed by X_1, X_2 indicating that Y is the dependent variable and X_1 and X_2 are independent variables. The various formulae for R^2 are given as under:

$$R^2_{Y.X_1X_2} = \frac{\Sigma \hat{y}^2}{\Sigma y^2} = \frac{\Sigma(\hat{Y} - \overline{Y})^2}{\Sigma(Y - \overline{Y})^2} = 1 - \frac{\Sigma \hat{u}^2}{\Sigma y^2} = \frac{\Sigma y^2 - \Sigma \hat{u}^2}{\Sigma y^2}$$

$$= \frac{\hat{b}_1 \Sigma y x_1 + \hat{b}_2 \Sigma y x_2}{\Sigma y^2} = (r_{Y\hat{Y}})^2 \tag{15.34}$$

where, $y = Y - \bar{Y}$

The test of significance of the individual parameters is conducted using the t statistic. To be able to use the t statistic we need the estimates of the variance of the estimated coefficients of the regression equation. These are presented below:

$$\text{var}(\hat{b}_0) = \hat{\sigma}^2 \left[\frac{1}{n} + \frac{\overline{X}_1^2 \Sigma x_2^2 + \overline{X}_2^2 \Sigma x_1^2 - 2\overline{X}_1 \overline{X}_2 \Sigma x_1 x_2}{\Sigma x_1^2 \Sigma x_2^2 - (\Sigma x_1 x_2)^2}\right] \tag{15.35}$$

$$\text{var}(\hat{b}_1) = \hat{\sigma}^2 \frac{\Sigma x_2^2}{\Sigma x_1^2 \Sigma x_2^2 - (\Sigma x_1 x_2)^2} \tag{15.36}$$

$$\text{var}(\hat{b}_2) = \hat{\sigma}^2 \frac{\Sigma x_1^2}{\Sigma x_1^2 \Sigma x_2^2 - (\Sigma x_1 x_2)^2} \tag{15.37}$$

where,

$$\hat{\sigma}^2 = \frac{\Sigma \hat{u}^2}{n - k} \tag{15.38}$$

$$\hat{u} = Y - \hat{Y}$$

Let us assume that we want to test the significance of the slope coefficient of the variable X_1. We can write the null and alternative hypothesis as:

$$H_0 : b_1 = 0$$
$$H_1 : b_1 \neq 0$$

The test statistic may be written as:

$$t_{n-k} = \frac{\hat{b}_1 - b_{1H_0}}{\sqrt{V(\hat{b}_1)}} \tag{15.39}$$

The value of the test statistic t is computed and compared with the table value of t for a given level of significance. If the computed value of |t| is greater than table value of |t|, we reject H_0 in favour of the alternative hypothesis H_1. That would show that X_1 has a significant impact upon the dependent variable Y.

The test for the significance of R^2 is carried out using the F statistic, which is already explained in the case of the two variable linear regression model. The hypothesis to be tested is listed as under:

$$H_0 : b_0 = b_1 = b_2 = 0 \Rightarrow R^2 = 0$$
$$H_1 : \text{All b's are not zero} \Rightarrow R^2 > 0$$

If R^2 is equal to 0 that means all the coefficients are equal to zero since none of the independent variables would explain any variations in Y.

TABLE 15.5
ANOVA table for multiple regression

Source	Sum of Squares	d.f.	Mean Square	F
Due to Regression	$R^2\Sigma y^2$	K – 1	$\frac{R^2\Sigma y^2}{K-1}$	$\frac{R^2(n-K)}{(1-R^2)(K-1)}$
Due to Residual	$(1-R^2)\Sigma y^2$	n – K	$\frac{(1-R^2)\Sigma y^2}{n-K}$	
Total	Σy^2	n – 1		

The test for the significance of R^2 is shown through the analysis of variance (ANOVA) in Table 15.5 already discussed under the two variable linear models.

We will take up an example to illustrate the estimation of the multiple regression model and the inferences thereupon.

In the last example, we had taken the data on the quantity demanded and the price and had estimated the simple linear regression model. We would add another variable i.e. income, and estimate the linear regression of demand on the price and income. The question may be written as follows:

Example 15.2

The following table gives the data on the quantity demanded, price and income of a commodity for the period 1996 to 2005.

Year	Demand (Y)	Price (X)	Income (I)
1996	100	5	1000
1997	75	7	600
1998	80	6	1200
1999	70	6	500
2000	50	8	300
2001	65	7	400
2002	90	5	1300
2003	100	4	1100
2004	110	3	1300
2005	60	9	300

Questions

1. Estimate the linear regression of the demand on the price and income.
2. Conduct a test of significance for the slope coefficients of the price and income.

3. Estimate R^2, interpret it and test for its statistical significance. Set up an analysis of the variance table for the purpose.
4. Compute the price and income elasticity of demand at the mean value of price and income.
5. Examine what happens to the value of R^2 when we move from a simple linear regression model to the multiple regression models as in this case.

Solution:

We will estimate the regression model using the SPSS software as the algebraic estimation is quite cumbersome. The results are presented in the Tables 15.6 to 15.8.

The value of R^2 equals 0.894, indicating that 89.4 per cent of the variations in the demand are explained by the price and income (Table 15.6). It may be seen that the value of R^2 in the simple linear regression model was 0.870, which has increased to 0.894 with the inclusion of an additional variable (income) in the regression model. This is always the case as the value of R^2 increases when an additional explanatory variable is added to the model. The value of R^2 is significant as indicated by the p value (0.000) of F statistic as given in ANOVA Table 15.7. The estimated regression equation as obtained in Table 15.8 may be written as:

$$Y = 111.692 - 7.188\,X + 0.014\,I$$

$$\text{P value} = (0.002)\;(0.026)\qquad(0.240)$$

where, Y = Demand

X = Price

I = Income

The above estimated regression equation indicates that the price is negatively related with demand as is evident from the negative value of its coefficient (–7.188).

TABLE 15.6
Model summary

Model	R	R Square	Adjusted R Square	Std. Error of the Estimate
1	0.946[a]	0.894	0.864	7.21326

[a] Predictors: (Constant), Income, Price

TABLE 15.7
ANOVA[b]

Model	Sum of Squares	d.f.	Mean Square	F	Sig.
1 Regression	3085.782	2	1542.891	29.653	0.000[a]
Residual	364.218	7	52.031		
Total	3450.000	9			

[a] Predictors: (Constant), Income, Price
[b] Dependent Variable: Demand

TABLE 15.8
Coefficients[a]

Model	Unstandardized Coefficients		Standardized Coefficients	t	Sig.
	B	Std. error	Beta		
1 (Constant)	111.692	23.531		4.747	0.002
Price	–7.188	2.555	–670	–2.813	0.026
Income	0.014	0.011	0.306	1.284	0.240

[a] Dependent Variable: Demand

Similarly, the income is positively related to the demand as the coefficient for the income variable is positive (0.014). The results indicate that if the price goes up by one unit, the quantity demanded will go down by 7.188 units while keeping the income constant. If the income goes up by one unit, the quantity demanded would go up by 0.014 units while keeping price constant. The results indicate that the price significantly influences demand, whereas the impact of income upon demand is insignificant. This is evident for the p value of price (0.026) and the income variable, which is 0.240. The significance of the coefficient is indicated if the p value is less than or equal to the level of significance (alpha), which is assumed to be 0.05 in the present case.

The relative importance of the independent variables is obtained by the absolute value of the standardized regression coefficients given in Table 15.8. In the present case, it shows that the price is relatively more important than the income in explaining the demand. This is because the absolute value of the standardized coefficient for price and income is 0.670 and 0.306 respectively.

The regression coefficients can be used to compute the price and income elasticity of the demand at the mean values of the variables. We know the mean values of the variables as $\overline{Y} = 80$, $\overline{X} = 6$, and $\overline{I} = 800$. Using these values, the price elasticity of demand is computed as:

$$\text{Price elasticity of demand} = \frac{\partial Y}{\partial X} \times \frac{\overline{X}}{\overline{Y}} = -7.188 \times \frac{6}{80} = -0.5391$$

The interpretation of the price elasticity of demand is that if the price goes up by 1 per cent, the quantity demanded goes down by 0.54 per cent while keeping the income constant. This could be useful for decision-making and future planning. If our objective is to increase the demand by 5 per cent, what one needs to do is to reduce the price by (5/.54 = 9.26) 9.26 per cent. Similarly, the income elasticity of demand could be computed as:

$$\text{Income elasticity of demand} = \frac{\partial Y}{\partial I} \times \frac{\overline{I}}{\overline{Y}} = 0.014 \times \frac{800}{80} = 0.14$$

This shows that if the income goes up by 1 per cent, the quantity demanded goes up by 0.14 per cent while keeping price constant.

DUMMY VARIABLES IN REGRESSION ANALYSIS

LEARNING OBJECTIVE 9
Use qualitative variables (dummy variables) as regressors in the regression model.

In regression analysis, the **dependent variable** is generally metric in nature and it is most often influenced by other metric variables.

In regression analysis, the dependent variable is generally metric in nature and it is most often influenced by other metric variables. For example, income, output, prices, etc., However, there could be situations where the dependent variable may be influenced by the qualitative variables like gender, marital status, profession, geographical region, colour, or religion. For instance, the demand for cosmetics is not only influenced by the price of cosmetics and consumer's income but also by the gender of the respondents. This is important because we have reasons to believe that females use more cosmetics than males. Therefore, its inclusion in the regression model as the regressor (independent variable) is required. The important question which comes to our mind is how to quantify the qualitative variable mentioned as above. In situations like this, the dummy variables come to our rescue. They are used to quantify the qualitative variables. The number of dummy variables required in the regression model is equal to the number of categories of data less one. For example, in the case of gender (male and female) we will use one dummy variable. In case we are considering four religions (Hindu, Sikh, Christian and Muslim) there would be three dummy variables required in the model. Dummy variable usually assumes, two values 0 and 1. There is no hard and fast rule for assigning a dummy variable a value of 0 and 1. It can be –1 and +1 or any other value. These assignments of the numbers do not change the results. The advantage of assigning a value of 0 and 1 helps us in better interpreting the results and make the comparisons between various categories easy.

Let us consider an example to illustrate the concept of dummy variables. Suppose the starting salary of a college lecturer is influenced not only by years of teaching experience but also by gender. Therefore, the model could be specified as:

$$Y = f(X, D) \tag{15.40}$$

where, Y = Starting salary of a college lecturer in thousands ₹ per month
X = No. of years of work experience
D is a dummy variable which takes values
D = 1 (if the respondent is a male)
= 0 (if the respondent is a female)

The model could be written as:

$$Y = \alpha + \beta X + \gamma D + U \tag{15.41}$$

This can be estimated by using ordinary least squares (OLS) techniques. Suppose the estimated regression equation looks like:

$$\hat{Y} = \hat{\alpha} + \hat{\beta} X + \hat{\gamma} D \tag{15.42}$$

Now, for the male respondents, the salary equation would look like:

$$\hat{Y} = \hat{\alpha} + \hat{\beta} X + \hat{\gamma} \tag{15.43}$$

$$\hat{Y} = (\hat{\alpha} + \hat{\gamma}) + \hat{\beta} X \tag{15.44}$$

For the female respondents, the salary equation would look like:

$$\hat{Y} = \hat{\alpha} + \hat{\beta} X \tag{15.45}$$

The above two equations (15.44 and 15.45) differ by the amount $\hat{\gamma}$. It is known that $\hat{\gamma}$ can be positive or negative. If $\hat{\gamma}$ is positive it would imply that the average salary of a male lecturer is more than that of a female lecturer by the amount $\hat{\gamma}$ while keeping the number of years of experience constant. Further, if γ is statistically significant then it would imply that the difference in the salary of males and the females is statistically different. This can be shown empirically. We have taken the data on 14 respondents which is presented in the Table 15.9.

The regression model was estimated using the SPSS software and the results are presented in Tables 15.10 to 15.12.

From Table 15.12, the following estimated equation can be written.

$$\hat{Y} = 17.321 + 1.545\,X + 3.286\,D \tag{15.46}$$
$$p\text{ value} = (0.000)\ \ (0.000)\ \ (0.000)$$

The above estimated equation states that by keeping the other things constant as the experience increases by one year, the average starting salary increases by 1.545 thousands of rupees. Further, other things being constant, the starting salary of a male lecturer is more than the starting salary of a female lecturer by ₹3.286 thousands. Further, both the numbers of years of experience as well as the gender are found to

TABLE 15.9
Data on salaries (in ₹ '000 per month) of college lecturers in relation to years of teaching experience and gender

S. No.	Y	X	D
1	22.0	1	1
2	18.5	1	0
3	24.0	2	1
4	21.0	2	0
5	25.5	3	1
6	21.0	3	0
7	27.0	4	1
8	24.0	4	0
9	25.0	5	0
10	28.0	5	1
11	29.5	6	1
12	27.0	6	0
13	28.0	7	0
14	31.5	7	1

TABLE 15.10
Model summary

Model	R	R Square	Adjusted R Square	Std. Error of the Estimate
1	0.993[a]	0.987	0.984	0.45895

[a] Predictors: (Constant), Gender, No. of Years of Experience

TABLE 15.11
ANOVA[b]

Model		Sum of Squares	d.f.	Mean Square	F	Sig.
1	Regression	171.397	2	85.699	406.862	0.000[a]
	Residual	2.317	11	0.211		
	Total	173.714	13			

[a] Predictors: (Constant), Gender, No. of Years of Experience
[b] Dependent Variable: Starting Salary of a Lecturer (in ₹ '000 per month)

TABLE 15.12
Coefficients[a]

Model		Unstandardized Coefficients		Standardized Coefficients	t	Sig.
		B	Std. Error	Beta		
1	(Constant)	17.321	0.300		57.651	0.000
	No. of Years of Experience	1.545	0.061	0.877	25.186	0.000
	Gender	3.286	0.245	0.466	13.394	0.000

[a] Dependent Variable: Starting Salary of a Lecturer (in ₹ '000 per month)

be significant variables as the p values for their coefficients is 0.000. Here, through an example, we have shown that the constant term varies for the male and the female salary functions.

The R^2 for the model is 0.987 (Table 15.10) which is high and significant as seen from the p value of the F statistic (Table 15.11).

It would be interesting to examine the impact of the years of experience of a male and female lecturer on the starting salary. Therefore, for this we need a dummy variable for the slope term and we would be examining whether the slope term is different for the male and female lecturers corresponding to the variable number of years of experience. The function in its unspecified form would look like:

$$Y = f(X, D X) \qquad (15.47)$$

where the notations are as defined above. The model in its specified form would look like:

$$Y = \alpha + \beta X + \delta (DX) + U \qquad (15.48)$$

The OLS estimated version of the above model would look like:

$$\hat{Y} = \hat{\alpha} + \hat{\beta} X + \hat{\delta} (DX) \qquad (15.49)$$

For the male respondents, the estimated salary function would look like:

$$\hat{Y} = \hat{\alpha} + (\hat{\beta} + \hat{\delta})X \qquad (15.50)$$

For the female respondents, the estimated salary function would look like:

$$\hat{Y} = \hat{\alpha} + \hat{\beta} X \qquad (15.51)$$

The difference in the slope term of the two functions is $\hat{\delta}$, which may be positive or negative. If it is positive, it would imply that the impact of experience on the starting salary is more for the male lecturers than for the female lecturers. If $\hat{\delta}$ is negative, it would imply that the impact of experience on the starting salary is higher for the female lecturers than for the male lecturers. Further δ could be significant or insignificant. The data matrix in the SPSS format for this problem would look as presented in Table 15.13.

The regression model (15.48) was estimated using OLS technique and the results are presented in Table 15.14 to 15.16.

TABLE 15.13
Data on salaries of college lecturers in relation to years of teaching experience and gender

S. No.	Y	X	Dx
1	22.0	1	1
2	18.5	1	0
3	24.0	2	2
4	21.0	2	0
5	25.5	3	3
6	21.0	3	0
7	27.0	4	4
8	24.0	4	0
9	25.0	5	0
10	28.0	5	5
11	29.5	6	6
12	27.0	6	0
13	28.0	7	0
14	31.5	7	7

TABLE 15.14
Model summary

Model	R	R Square	Adjusted R Square	Std. Error of the Estimate
1	0.966[a]	0.934	0.922	1.02224

a. Predictors: (Constant), Gender X No. of Years of Experience, No. of Years of Experience

TABLE 15.15
ANOVA[b]

Model		Sum of Squares	df	Mean Square	F	Sig.
1	Regression	162.220	2	81.110	77.619	0.000[a]
	Residual	11.495	11	1.045		
	Total	173.715	13			

a Predictors: (Constant), Gender X No. of Years of Experience, No. of Years of Experience
b Dependent Variable: Starting Salary of a Lecturer (in ₹ '000 per month)

TABLE 15.16
Coefficients[a]

Model		Unstandardized Coefficients		Standardized Coefficients	t	Sig.
		B	Std. Error	Beta		
1	(Constant)	18.964	0.611		31.043	0.000
	No. of Years of Experience (X)	1.225	0.150	0.696	8.186	0.000
	Gender X No. of Years of Experience (DX)	0.639	0.122	0.445	5.232	0.000

a. Dependent Variable: Starting Salary of a Lecturer (in ₹ '000 per month)

The estimated regression model would look like as obtained from Table 15.16.

$$\hat{Y} = 18.964 + 1.225\,X + 0.639\,DX \tag{15.52}$$
$$\text{p value} = (0.000)\quad(0.000)\quad(0.000)$$

All the coefficients are highly significant as indicated by the p values of the model. The salary function for the male lecturers would look like:

$$\hat{Y} = 18.964 + 1.225\,X + 0.639\,X \tag{15.53}$$
$$= 18.964 + 1.864\,X \tag{15.54}$$

The salary function for the female lecturers would be:

$$\hat{Y} = 18.964 + 1.225\,X \tag{15.55}$$

It is seen that the impact of the years of experience on the starting salary is more for the male than for the females. In fact a male lecturer would get ₹639 more per month than the female lecturer for every year of experience. Moreover, this difference is significant as indicated by the p value of the coefficient of DX.

The value of R^2 for the model is 0.934 (Table 15.14). which is highly significant as given by the p value corresponding to the F statistic (Table 15.15).

CONCEPT CHECK

1. What is the difference between approximate prediction interval and exact prediction interval?
2. What happens to the value of R^2 when the number of independent variables in a regression model are increased?
3. How do we incorporate dummy variable to measure the shift in slope term in a regression model?

APPLICATIONS OF REGRESSION ANALYSIS IN RESEARCH IN VARIOUS FUNCTIONAL AREAS OF MANAGEMENT

LEARNING OBJECTIVE 10
Apply regression analysis in research.

A study attempting at finding out the variables affecting the work exhaustion and hence turnover intention was carried out in the NCR between May and October 2007.[1] The study was confined to women BPO employees working at the executive level and women school teachers teaching class 6 and above. A sample of 75 respondents each from school teachers and BPO employees was taken. The following hypotheses were tested for the school teachers, as well as for the BPO executives.

H_1: Perceived workload will positively influence work exhaustion (WE) among the working women. If perceived work load is high then the WE will be more.

H_2: Job autonomy will negatively influence WE among the working women. If job autonomy is low then the WE will be high.

H_3: Work-family conflict (WFC) will positively influence work exhaustion among the working women. If WFC is high then work exhaustion will also be high.

H_4: Fairness of reward will negatively influence work exhaustion among the working women. If the fairness of reward is high then the work exhaustion will be low.

H_5: Work Exhaustion will positively influence the turnover intention among the working women. If the work exhaustion is high, the turnover intention will also be high.

To test the above hypothesis, a questionnaire was prepared having subscales measuring each of the constructs listed in the Moore's model. The subscales were assessed by using an 8-point Likert scale. The subscales were on: job autonomy, work-family conflict, work exhaustion, perceived workload, fairness of reward and turnover intentions.

Before analysing the data obtained from the filled-in questionnaire, the reliability and validity of the scales used in the study for both the BPO executives and school teachers was tested. To check the reliability of the scale, cronbach alpha was used and the value was found to be quite high, indicating that a further analysis could be carried on the data. The confirmatory factor analysis was conducted to assess the validity of the scale, both among the BPO teachers, as well as among school teachers. The results were in accordance with the scale formulated.

The five hypotheses could be mathematically written as:

$$WE = f(PWL, FoR, JA, WFC) \tag{1}$$

$$TI = g(WE) \tag{2}$$

where, PWL = Perceived Workload
FoR = Fairness of Rewards
JA = Job Autonomy
WFC = Work-Family Conflict
WE = Work Exhaustion
TI = Turnover Intention

[1] Neena Sondhi, Deepak Chawla, Prachi Jain and Monika Kashyap. "Applications in HR (Work-exhaustion – A Consequential Framework: Validating the model in the Indian Context", *The Indian Journal of Industrial Relations* 43(4): 2008.

Equation (1) states that work exhaustion depends upon the perceived workload, fairness of reward, job autonomy and work-family conflict. Equation (2) states that the turnover intention depends upon work exhaustion.

The regression model as given in equation (1) was estimated using the OLS method for the BPO executives, school teachers and for the combined sample of the BPO executives and School teachers. The results are reported below for each one of the categories.

Regression equation of work exhaustion for BPO executives:

$$\text{WE} = 3.464 + 0.061\ \text{PWL} - 0.021\ \text{JA} + 0.395\ \text{WFC} - 0.308\ \text{FOR}$$
$$\text{t value} = (5.04)^{*}\quad (0.564)\quad (0.237)\quad (3.924)^{*}\quad (3.533)^{*}$$

* = Significant at 1 per cent

$R^2 = 0.449$

F value = 14.268

The regression results indicate that both the perceived workload and the work-family conflict positively influence the work exhaustion. This is evident from the positive signs of the estimated coefficients of the corresponding variables. This means if the perceived workload and work-family conflict increase, there is increased work exhaustion. Further, job autonomy and fairness of reward negatively influence work exhaustion. This is evident from the negative signs of the estimated coefficients of the corresponding variables. This means that if these two are increased in an organization, it will result in a reduction of the work exhaustion. It is found that work-family conflict and fairness of reward are significant variables in influencing work exhaustion as indicated by the one-tailed t test at a 1 per cent level. Work-family conflict is found to be the most important variable in influencing work exhaustion followed by the fairness of reward, perceived workload and job autonomy. The significance of R^2 as tested by the F statistic indicates that the regression equation is significant. The results indicate that the hypotheses numbering 1 to 4 hold true.

Regression Equation of Work Exhaustion for School Teachers

The regression results for school teachers are given below:

$$\text{WE} = 5.401 - 0.282\ \text{PWL} - 0.21\ \text{JA} + 0.423\ \text{WFC} - 0.254\ \text{FOR}$$
$$\text{t value} = (5.241)^{*}\quad (2.615)^{**}\quad (1.848)^{**}\quad (3.183)^{*}\quad (2.708)^{*}$$

* = Significant at 1 per cent

$R^2 = 0.371$

** = Significant at 5 per cent

F value = 10.325

The above regression equation indicates that the perceived workload, job autonomy and fairness of reward negatively influence work exhaustion. This means an increase in their value would result in the reduction of work exhaustion. Further, the fairness of reward is significant at a 1 per cent level, whereas the remaining two are significant at a 5 per cent level. The results indicate the negation of the first hypothesis, which states that with the increased perceived workload, the work exhaustion should increase. The variable work-family conflict significantly and positively influences the work exhaustion at 1 per cent level. The R^2 for the regression equation is 0.371 resulting in an F value of 10.325, which is significant. The results indicate that except for the first hypothesis, all other (H_2, H_3, and H_4) hold true.

Regression Equation of the Turnover Intention for School Teachers

The results of the regression equation using work exhaustion as a predictor variable to explain turnover intention is given below:

$$TI = 2.277 + 0.293\ WE$$

$$t\ value = (3.85)^{*}(2.039)^{**}$$

* = Significant at 1 per cent level

** = Significant at 5 per cent level

$$R^2 = 0.054$$

$$F\ value = 4.158$$

The regression results indicate that work exhaustion is positively related to the turnover intention of a school teacher as indicated by the positive slope coefficient of the work exhaustion variable. Further, it is significant at a 5 per cent level of significance as indicated by the t statistic. The R^2 value is 0.054, which is quite low but is significant at a 5 per cent level. The regression indicates that with an increase in work exhaustion among school teachers, their intention to leave the job increases, thereby showing that hypothesis number 5 holds true.

Regression Equation of the Turnover Intention for the Combined Sample of BPO Executives and School Teachers

The estimated regression equation to explain the turnover intention for the combined sample is given below:

$$TI = 2.131 + 0.391\ WE$$

$$t\ value = (5.539)^{*}\ (4.036)^{*}$$

* = Significant at 1 per cent level

$$R^2 = 0.099$$

$$F\ value = 16.29$$

It is seen from the regression equation that the work exhaustion positively influences the turnover intentions of the workers. Further, it is a significant variable at a 1 per cent level of significance. The regression results in an R^2 value of 0.099, which is poor but significant as indicated by the F value. The positive relationship between the work exhaustion and the turnover intention indicates the validity of hypothesis numbering 5.

Therefore, it can be concluded that among the BPO respondents, the work-family conflict emerged as the most significant independent variable that impacts work exhaustion, that is, H3 of the study was proven and the results were found to be significant. Similar results have been reported by Salaff (2002) and Ahuja et al. (2007). The next significant variable found for the group was the fairness of rewards, that is, H4 of the study and was found to be true and significant. Thus, it might be that the fairness of rewards received by the BPO workers might mitigate the effect of the work exhaustion. Perceived work overload was the next variable to impact the work exhaustion, the H1 of the study was found to be true but statistically insignificant. This could probably be because of the moderating effect of the individual differences amongst the respondents in terms of their personality, where the work responsibilities might be perceived as very stressful by some individuals and, at the same time, not at all exhausting from another perspective. The last variable impacting the work exhaustion was job autonomy, thus H2 was found to be true but statistically insignificant.

Amongst the school teacher sample also the work-family conflict was found to be the most important variable, followed by the fairness of rewards, and both these results were found to be statistically significant. The next variable was the perceived workload but the impact was the opposite and, thus, the H1 of the study was negated for the school teachers, and this result was statistically significant. The last variable was the job autonomy, thus H2 was found to be true at the 5 per cent level of significance.

The results clearly indicate that the dissonance that arises from managing a professional career and personal roles by the women workers is what is most stressful for them. These results were true both for the BPO and the school teacher populations.

The findings have significant implications for any employer who can retain and maintain a more loyal and consistent workforce if the organization looks at refurbishing its work schedules and policies to accommodate the personal roles and responsibilities of its women employees.

The above-mentioned results take on an added significance when we analyse the impact of this work-related exhaustion with the turnover intentions. Consistently across the school teachers (significant at a 5 per cent level), and the BPO workers (significant at a 1 per cent level) there was a statistically significant impact of the work exhaustion upon the turnover intentions, i.e., the higher the exhaustion higher are the turnover intentions—H5 of the study was found to be true.

Another study attempted to test the validity of the capital asset pricing model (CAPM) for the Indian stock market.[2] The study has been carried out based upon the S and P CNX Nifty companies that were part of the index from 1 January 2003 to 1 February 2008. Nifty stocks represented about 54 per cent of the total market capitalization as on 31 December 2007 and accounted for 21 sectors of the economy. These companies are well traded and belong to diverse industry groups. While the aforementioned index consists of 50 stocks, other scrips that were replaced on or after 1 January 2003 were also included in the study. The list included 69 companies. The final list was reduced to 50 companies owing to the unavailability of data for 19 companies for the entire period under consideration.

The S and P CNX 500 has been taken as the market proxy, being India's first broad-based benchmark. It represents more than 90 per cent of the total market capitalization and accounts for 72 industry indices. The required data on the stocks and indices was collected from the Centre for Monitoring Indian Economy (CMIE) database, PROWESS, the National Stock Exchange (NSE) website and the Yahoo! Finance website. For the risk-free rate, the 91-day Treasury bill rates have been taken as a proxy. The required data was collected from the CMIE Database of Economic Intelligence.

For the purpose of the study, weekly data was used for all the variables. This is because, daily data, though better for estimating the risk-return relationships, is very noisy and, monthly data, owing to the longer duration, distorts the risk-return relationships. Thus, the weekly data has been considered as it suits best the purpose of the study.

The steps followed in carrying out the research are as under:

- For the market index (S and P CNX 500) and each of the 50 stocks, daily returns through a natural logarithm of the price relatives were calculated, followed by the

[2] Debarati Basu and Deepak Chawla. "Applications in Finance "An Empirical Test of CAPM – the Case of the Indian Stock Market". Paper presented at the International Conference on Finance, Accounts and Global Investment at the International Management Institute, New Delhi, 22–24 August 2008.

calculation of the weekly returns, from one Wednesday to next to ensure that there is no impact of day-of-the-week and weekend.

- This was followed by estimating beta for each of the 50 stocks by regressing the weekly stock returns on the weekly market returns.
- The stocks were then arranged in the descending order of beta and grouped into 10 portfolios of 5 stocks each such that portfolio 1 contains the first 5 stocks representing the 5 highest beta values and portfolio 10 contains the last 5 stocks representing the 5 lowest beta values. This was done to achieve a diversification and thus reduce any errors that might occur due to the presence of any unsystematic risk.
- Finally, using the daily returns, portfolio returns, and portfolio beta, the residual variance was calculated for each portfolio at the weekly intervals resulting in 256 observations for each of the variables for each of the weeks.

Returns can be explained through the following regression:

$$R_{it} = R_{ft} + \beta_i R_{mt} + u_t$$

where, R_{it} is the return on portfolio i at time t
R_{ft} is the return on the risk-free asset at time t
R_{mt} is the market return at time t
u_t is the stochastic error term at time t

The above regression, interpreted according to CAPM's theory, implies that returns are a linear function of the risk-free rate and a risk premium for the systematic risk undertaken, as measured by the coefficient of the market return. Thus, beta is supposed to be the only factor influencing the excess portfolio returns, i.e., portfolio returns as reduced by the risk-free rate. This suggests that the validity of this theory depends on: a) a positive linear relationship between beta and excess returns and b) sole dependence of the excess returns on the systematic risk as measured by the beta.

This model was thus, tested using the following regression:

$$R_{it} - R_{ft} = \gamma_0 + \gamma_1 \beta_{it} + \gamma_2 \beta_{it}^2 + \gamma_3 RV_{it} + \varepsilon_t$$

where, R_{it} is the return on portfolio i at time t
R_{ft} is the return on the risk-free asset at time t
β_{it} is the beta of portfolio i at time t, representing systematic risk
β_{it}^2 is the beta of portfolio i at time t squared, representing non-linearity of returns
RV_{it} is the residual variance of portfolio i at time t, representing unsystematic risk
ε_t is the stochastic error term at time t

For this purpose, the excess weekly portfolio returns were regressed on beta, beta-squared and residual variance, as obtained from the data preprocessing stage, to test the statistical significance of the coefficients using the standard t test. For the CAPM to hold true, the following hypotheses should be satisfied.

- $\gamma_0 = 0$, as any excess return earned should be zero for a zero-beta portfolio
- $\gamma_1 > 0$, as there should be a positive price for the risk taken
- $\gamma_2 = 0$, as the security market line should represent a linear relationship
- $\gamma_3 = 0$, as residual risk which can be diversified away should not affect the return

The regression model was estimated using the OLS method and the tests of significance were carried out at a 5 per cent level using the following framework:

- The intercept term, the coefficient of beta-squared and the residual variance have been hypothesized as not being statistically different from zero and, therefore, a two-tailed test is appropriate.
- The coefficient of beta should be positive and thus, significant, as explained above, and, therefore, a one-tailed test is used.

The results indicate that for all the ten portfolios, the intercept term is significantly different from zero, the coefficient of beta-squared is significant in five cases and the coefficient of the residual variance is significant in four cases. These are against the validity of CAPM.

Further, the coefficient of beta falters in nine out of the ten portfolios where the coefficient of beta is found to be negative but it is insignificant in six of these cases. Overall, the beta coefficients are found insignificant in seven of the ten cases. These results again question the validity of CAPM and its risk-return theory in the context of the Indian stock market. Also, the R^2 values in the ten regressions varies from 1.55 per cent to 7.78 per cent, which is very low, although significant in six cases as indicated by the p value corresponding to its F statistic. There is also a problem of the first degree autocorrelation in the case of two regressions as evident from the Durbin-Watson (DW) statistic.

Thus, the results reveal that, in the Indian context, CAPM fails to explain the excess portfolio returns earned in an adequate manner. For each of the regressions, the CAPM performs below expectations with respect to the signs and significance of the coefficients while displaying very low R-squared values across all ten portfolios. As demonstrated by the empirical evidence, the application of this model has yielded varied results under different market conditions over varying sample periods. Accordingly, this analysis helps in finding further evidence for CAPM's downfall in explaining the excess returns in the emerging market.

SUMMARY

- Simple correlation measures the association between the two variables. It can be positive, negative or zero. A quantitative measure of the linear association between the two variables X and Y is given by Karl Pearson's correlation coefficient, denoted by r_{XY}. The correlation coefficient can take any value between –1 and +1 (both values inclusive). In case it takes a value of +1, it is called a perfect positive correlation, and if takes a value of –1, it is called a perfect negative correlation. The main limitation of the correlation analysis is that if there is a zero correlation between the two variables does not mean that the variables are not related. The variables could be non-linearly related as the Karl Pearson correlation coefficient measures the linear association between the two variables. The other limitation of the correlation analysis is that it does not talk about the cause-and-effect relationship.
- To overcome the limitations of the correlation analysis, a regression analysis is proposed, which assumes a cause-and-effect relationship between the variables. In a simple regression, there is one dependent and one independent variable whereas in multiple regressions there is one dependent and at least two independent variables. A linear relationship between the dependent and independent variables is assumed. An error term U is added in the regression model for capturing the effect of the omitted variables. The estimation of the regression model is carried out by the ordinary least squares (OLS) method. The OLS method aims at minimizing the error sum of the squares while estimating the regression model. A t test is conducted for testing the significance of the individual regression coefficients. The overall fit of the regression is given by R^2 that is called the coefficient of determination and is a measure of the explanatory power of the model. The value of R^2 lies between 0 and 1 (both values inclusive). The closer the value of R^2 to one, the better is the goodness of fit. The significance of R^2 is carried out by using the F statistic. The use of regression in estimating the point and interval prediction is shown. Also is demonstrated the computation of elasticity and its use in decision making.

- Many a times, the qualitative variables may have to be introduced as the independent variables in the regression model. Dummy variables are used to quantify the qualitative variables in an approximate manner. Dummy variables usually take values of 0 and 1. In this chapter, the use of dummy variables to measure the shift in the intercept and slope term is shown. The use of the SPSS software is also demonstrated for estimating the simple and multiple regression models in this chapter.

KEY TERMS

- ANOVA
- Coefficient of determination
- Dummy variables
- Error sum of squares
- Error term
- Estimate of error variance
- Explained sum of squares
- Explanatory power of the model
- F statistic
- Goodness of fit of the regression equation
- Multiple regression
- p value
- Perfect multicollinearity
- Perfect negative correlation
- Perfect positive correlation
- Qualitative variables
- Significance of the individual coefficients
- Significance of the simple correlation coefficient
- Simple correlation coefficient
- Simple regression
- Standard error of estimate
- Standardized coefficients
- t statistic
- Total sum of squares
- Zero correlation

CHAPTER REVIEW QUESTIONS

Objective Type Questions

State whether the following statements are true (T) or false (F).

1. Simple correlation measures the degree of association between two variables.
2. In multiple regression, there are at least two independent variables.
3. The significance of R^2 is tested by the t statistic.
4. If the simple correlation coefficient between two variables is zero, the variables must be independent.
5. The independent variables in a regression model are also called effect variables.
6. R^2 cannot be negative.
7. The simple correlation coefficient r takes values between –1 and +1.
8. If all the scatter of points on the variables X ad Y lie on a positively sloped straight line, then the correlation coefficient would be +1.
9. The standard error of the estimate is independent of the units of measurements.
10. The significance of the individual regression coefficients is tested by a t statistic.
11. There is no relationship between the standard error of estimate and the standard error of prediction.
12. The value of R^2 may go down with an increase in the independent variables in the regression model.
13. The significance of the simple correlation coefficient is tested by a t statistic.
14. One of the reasons for including the error term U in the regression model is because of the omitted variables from the regression model.
15. The degrees of freedom corresponding to the residual sum of squares is n – 1, where n = size of sample.
16. The value of R^2 always equals $r^2_{Y\hat{Y}}$ when $r_{Y\hat{Y}}$ is the simple correlation coefficient between the dependent variable Y and its estimated value.
17. The numbers of the dummy variables to be used in the regression model are equal to the number of categories less one.

18. The residual is the difference between the observed value of the dependent variable (Y) and its predicted value ($\hat{Y}$) by the regression equation.
19. If all the slope coefficients of a multiple regression equations are not significantly different from zero, it will imply that R^2 is close to zero.
20. If the correlation coefficients between any two independent variables are ±1, then the multiple regression equation cannot be estimated.

Conceptual Questions

1. Define the following:
(a) Correlation coefficient
(b) Ordinary least square method
(c) Dummy variables
(d) R^2
2. Distinguish between correlation and regression with the help of an example. How are the two concepts used together?
3. Define the standard error of estimate. Point out its limitation in comparing the goodness of fit of two regressions. How is R^2 a better measure than the standard error of estimate?
4. Discuss how you will use the dummy variables to capture the seasonal effect on the profits of a firm when you have a quarterly data on profits and sales.
5. Explain the difference between the point and interval prediction. Discuss the role of the standard error of estimate in computing the approximate and exact interval prediction.
6. Outline briefly the procedure for testing the significance of the slope coefficient in a regression analysis.

Application Questions

1. The manufacturers of a particular brand of chocolate were interested in examining the relationship between the sales of chocolates and the shelf space allocated to that brand of chocolate by various stores. Data was collected from 10 stores as indicated below:

Store No.	Sales (₹ '000)	Shelf Space (Sq. Ft)
1	25	5
2	15	3.2
3	28	5.4
4	30	6.1
5	17	4.3
6	16	3.1
7	12	2.6
8	21	6.4
9	19	4.9
10	27	5.7

(a) Is there any association between the sales and the shelf space? Test it at a 5 per cent level of significance.
(b) Can we predict the sales using the shelf space?
(c) Name other variables that would influence the sales.

2. Conduct a survey of property dealers in your city. Collect the data on the price of a flat, area in square feet covered by the flat, the number of rooms, the number of bathrooms/toilets, distance from the nearest community centre, distance from the nearest shopping centres and hospitals. Take a minimum of 50 observations from various parts of your city. Run a suitable regression model and identify the most important variable influencing the price of a flat. Can you list some other variables that have not been considered in the mentioned study?

3. The following model is estimated for the demand function of domestically produced automobiles:

$$\hat{D}_x = 1584 - 12P_x + 18P_f + 0.6Y \qquad R^2 = 0.88$$
$$SE = (320) \quad (3) \quad (2) \quad (0.1) \qquad n = 30$$

where, $\hat{D}_x$ = Demand for domestically produced cars
P_x = Price of domestically produced cars
P_f = Price of imported cars
Y = Disposable income
SE = Standard error of the regression coefficient

(i) Evaluate the above estimated demand function on the basis of the economic theory and the statistical inference (R^2, significance of coefficients, etc.).
(ii) Estimate the demand for domestically produced cars if P_x = 3,000, P_f = 2,500, Y = 250,000.
(iii) Estimate the average price elasticity, cross elasticity, and income elasticity, given $\overline{D}_x$ = 60,000 $\overline{P}_x$ = 4,000, $\overline{P}_f$ = 3,500 and $\overline{Y}$ = 1,50,000.

4. (a) The standard error of estimate for a regression (Y = a+bX+U) was calculated to be 18.69. When treated separately, the sum of squared deviations around the mean was 20.25 for X value and 59.12 for Y values based upon a sample of n = 10 observation. Find the standard error of the slope coefficient.
(b) A linear regression line was calculated using eight points. The sum of the Xs was 77 and the sum of X^2s was 782. Also the standard error of the estimate was 8.71. To gain an exact prediction interval for Y when X = 13, find the standard error of the prediction.

5. A sample of ten-yearly observations on a firm corresponding to the regression model:

$$C = a + b X + U$$

where, C = Total cost (in '000 dollars)
X = Quantity produced ('000 of units)

gave the following data:

$$\sum X = 777 \quad \sum C = 1657 \quad \sum CX = 132{,}938 \quad \sum X^2 = 70{,}903 \quad \sum C^2 = 277{,}119$$

(i) Estimate the parameters of the model by the OLS method.
(ii) Find the standard error of estimate.
(iii) Find the correlation coefficient between the total cost and the total output and test for its statistical significance at a 5 per cent level.

6. A company collects data about its advertising expenditure and the corresponding sales figure over a period of consecutive months as shown in the table below:

Month	Expenditure (£,00)	Sales (£,000)
1	3.00	7.00
2	3.20	8.30
3	3.50	9.00
4	4.00	10.00
5	4.40	10.50
6	4.70	10.80
7	5.20	11.00
8	5.50	11.10

(i) Estimate the linear regression of sales on the advertising expenditure and interpret the results.
(ii) Compute the standard error of estimate.
(iii) Test for the statistical significance of the slope coefficient of the estimated regression equation using a 5 per cent level of significance.
(iv) Interpret the above results.

7. A simple linear regression equation was estimated using the data on living area (measured in square feet) and the selling price (thousands of dollars). The results of the regression equation and the other summary statistics are as follows:

$$\hat{Y} = 71.0 + 4.64\,X$$

where, Y = Selling price (thousands of dollars)
X = Living area (measured in square feet)
n = 8

$\sum X = 165$; $\sum Y = 1334$; $\sum XY = 29611$; $\sum X^2 = 3855$; $\sum Y^2 = 241394$

(i) Interpret the above estimated regression equation.
(ii) Find the standard error of estimates.
(iii) Find a 95 per cent approximate and the exact prediction interval when the living area = 19 square feet.
(iv) Find the r^2 and interpret it.

8. The firm of Smithson Financial Consultants has been hired by Blackburn Industries to determine whether a relationship exists between the age of the unmarried male Blackburn employees (including, never married, divorced, or widowed male employees) and the amount of the individual liquid assets. The main question of interest is whether a linear relationship exists between these two variables, where X is defined as the age of the employee and Y is the percentage of annual income allocated to the liquid assets (such as cash, savings accounts, and tradable stocks and bonds). A random sample of 12 observations gave the following results:

$$Y = -0.814 + 0.353\,X$$

where, Y = Percentage of annual income allocated to the liquid assets
X = Age of the employee

$r = 0.672$
$\sum X = 524$
$\sum Y = 175$
$\sum X^2 = 24150$

(i) Interpret the estimated regression model.
(ii) Find a 95 per cent exact prediction interval for a person whose age is 53 years.
(iii) Conduct a test of significance for the slope coefficient of the regression using an appropriate alternative hypothesis and assuming the level of significance (α) to be equal to 10 per cent.
(iv) Compute the total sum of squares, explained sum of squares and the error sum of squares.

9. A research project was undertaken to determine if there is a relationship between the years of experience on the job (E) and the efficiency rating of employees (R). The objective of the study is to predict the efficiency rating of an employee based upon the years on the job. The sample results are given below:

S. No.	Employee	Years of Job (E)	Efficiency Rating (R)
1	Arun	1	6
2	Ravinder	20	5
3	Anoop	6	3
4	Rakesh	8	5
5	Mohan	2	2
6	Jatin	1	2
7	Rajesh	14	4
8	Puneet	8	3
9	Balvinder	4	3
10	Gurinder	6	4

$$\sum E = 70;\ \sum R = 37$$
$$\sum E^2 = 818;\ \sum R^2 = 153$$

(i) What is the dependent variable?
(ii) Estimate the linear regression equation.
(iii) Test the significance of the slope coefficient of regression at a 5 per cent level of significance.
(iv) For 8 years on the job, what is the exact 99 per cent prediction interval for the efficiency rating?
(v) Find the r^2 for the regression line and interpret it.
(vi) Write a brief note on the findings of the study based on the above computations.

10. A sample of 10 observations based upon the data for the period 1991 to 2000 corresponding to the following regression model:

$$Y = a + bX + U;$$

where, Y = Quantity supplied (millions tons)
X = Export price ($ per ton)

gave the following results:

$$\sum X = 51;\ \sum X^2 = 309;\ \sum XY = 355;\ \sum Y = 59;\ \sum Y^2 = 419$$

(i) Estimate the parameters of the model using the OLS method.
(ii) Find the value of r^2.
(iii) Estimate the standard error of the estimate of regression.
(iv) Examine whether the export price affects the quantity supplied by testing a suitable hypothesis. You may use a 1 per cent level of significance.
(v) Estimate a 95 per cent approximate prediction interval when the export price equals $6.5 per ton.
(vi) Estimate the price elasticity of supply at the mean values of the variable.
(vii) Interpret and evaluate the results computed in the above six parts.

11. A study was taken to estimate a linear demand function. The data on the quantity demanded and the price of a commodity was collected for 8 periods. The data is given below:

S. No.	Demand (Y) (in kg)	Price (X) (in 00 ₹)
1	16	10
2	20	8
3	18	12
4	21	6
5	13	13
6	15	9
7	17	11
8	22	7

(i) Estimate the linear demand function Y = a + bX + u. Also interpret the estimated regression.
(ii) Find an exact 95 per cent prediction interval for demand when price is equal to ₹800.
(iii) Compute r^2 and interpret it.

12. A sample of eight observations corresponding to the regression model Y= a + bX + U gave the following results:

$$\sum X = 33.5;\ \sum Y = 77.7;\ \sum XY = 334.27;\ \sum X^2 = 146.23;\ \sum Y^2 = 769.99$$

where, Y = Sales (in £,000)
X = Advertising Expenditure (in £,00)
a, b = Parameters to be estimated
U = Random error term

(i) Estimate the linear regression of the sales on the advertising expenditure.
(ii) Estimate the promotional elasticity of sale at the mean values of the variables.
(iii) Compute the standard error of estimate.
(iv) Test the hypothesis that the advertisement expenditure influences sales. You may use $\alpha = 0.01$.
(v) Interpret the above results.

13. A property dealer wants to predict the selling price of a house using a simple linear regression equation with the living area as a predictor variable. A sample of eight houses corresponding to the following linear regression model Y = a + bX + U gave the following results:

$$\sum X = 165;\ \sum Y = 1{,}334;\ r = 0.7167;\ \sum X2 = 3{,}855;\ \sum Y2 = 241{,}394$$

where, Y = Selling price of a house (in thousand dollars)
X = Living area (in hundred square ft.)
a, b = Parameters to be estimated
U = Error term

(i) Estimate the parameters of the linear regression equation.
(ii) Test for the significance of the slope coefficient using a 5 per cent level of significance. State clearly your null and alternative hypothesis.
(iii) Compute the explained and error sum of squares.
(iv) Interpret your results.

14. To estimate the sales of a company in various districts, the following regression of the sales of the company in ten districts based upon the total disposable income of the inhabitants of these districts was estimated.

$$Y = b_0 + b_1 X + U$$

where, Y = Sales of the company in a district ($ million)
X = Total disposable income of inhabitants of the district ($ million)
U = Random error

The following results were obtained:

$$\sum Y = 200;\ \sum X = 160;\ \sum Y^2 = 4{,}108;\ \sum XY = 3{,}306;\ r = 0.955$$

(i) Estimate the parameters b_0 and b_1. Also interpret the estimated regression.
(ii) Can the company use the disposable income as a basis for predicting the sales in a district? You may use a 5 per cent level of significance.
(iii) Predict the sales of a district whose total disposable income is $18 million. Also find a 98 per cent exact confidence interval for the forecast.

CASE 15.1

MRP BISCUIT COMPANY PVT. LTD.

The Indian biscuit industry has a turnover of around ₹3,000 crore. India is the second largest manufacturer of biscuits, after USA. The industry employs almost 3.5 lakh people directly and 30 lakh people indirectly. The biscuit industry can be segmented into the organized and unorganized sectors. There are about 150 small and medium sector units besides a few large units. The proportion of the production in the organized to unorganized sector is in the ratio of 55 to 45 per cent. Exports of biscuits have been generally to the tune of 10 per cent of annual production. The industry is showing an annual growth rate of about 14 to 16 per cent since 2003. The per capita consumption of biscuits in India is only 1.8 kg per annum as compared to 2.5 kg to 5.5 kg in the South East Asian countries, European countries and USA. The biscuits could be broadly classified into various categories such as Glucose, Marie, Sweet, Salty, Cream and Milk.

MRP Biscuit Company started its operations in Ambala city, Haryana, in 2001. The company was growing at an annual rate of 20 per cent, which was above the industry average. However, for the last three years, the growth has been only to the tune of 5 to 6 per cent. This very factor has been of a main concern to the top management of the company. Mr P K Malhotra, the Senior Vice President, Marketing, had a meeting of the senior marketing team and was wondering why their company, which has been doing so well, has slowed down in the last few years. During the discussion it was suggested by one of the senior managers to identify the factors which influence the preference for biscuits. It was argued that once these are known, it will help the company to concentrate on those factors accordingly. Therefore, the company decided to get a study done from a research agency to identify the various factors that influence the preference for biscuits. A sample of 40 individuals was chosen randomly from Ambala. The data was collected on variables like preservation, quality, taste, nutrition value and preference on a 7-point scale with the higher number indicating a more positive rating. The data is presented in Table 15.17.

Table 15.17 Data on preference for biscuits

S. No.	Preference	Nutrition Value	Taste	Preservation Quality
1	7	5	6	5
2	6	4	6	6
3	5	5	7	4
4	6	6	7	5
5	4	3	2	4
6	2	2	1	2
7	3	3	2	3
8	6	5	6	5
9	7	7	7	6
10	5	6	5	4
11	4	4	3	2
12	3	6	2	3
13	1	1	2	1
14	2	2	3	1
15	4	5	4	3
16	4	4	5	4

S. No.	Preference	Nutrition Value	Taste	Preservation Quality
17	3	2	1	3
18	6	7	5	4
19	6	5	5	6
20	7	6	4	5
21	7	5	6	6
22	3	2	3	4
23	2	2	1	1
24	5	5	4	4
25	6	5	6	4
26	7	6	5	7
27	2	1	1	2
28	4	2	1	2
29	6	4	5	5
30	7	6	5	5
31	6	3	6	5
32	5	4	4	4
33	2	1	1	2
34	3	2	1	1
35	4	3	2	2
36	6	5	7	6
37	7	6	7	6
38	7	5	6	7
39	4	3	2	3
40	5	3	4	3

QUESTIONS

1. Run a multiple regression explaining the preference for the brand of biscuits in terms of the nutrition value, taste and preservation quality.
2. Interpret the partial regression coefficients.
3. Test the overall significance of the regression using the ANOVA table.
4. Examine the significance of the partial regression coefficient using a 5 per cent level of significance.
5. As a marketing manager of the biscuit company, on what attributes will you concentrate more so as to improve the marketability of the brand?

CASE 15.2

SHYAM FOODS PVT. LTD.

Mr Shyam Banerjee, the Chairman and Managing Director of Shyam Foods Pvt. Ltd, was contemplating introducing a breakfast cereal to his existing list of ready-to-eat food products. Currently, in the list of ready-to-eat products were *aloo mutter*, *pav bhaji*, *tadka dal*, *vegetable pulav*, *methi malai mutter*, *chana masala*, *kadhi pakora*, *dal makhani*, *palak paneer*, *Kashmiri dum aloo*, *shahi mutter paneer*, *gajar halwa*, *chhole chawal*, chowmein, canned *sarson ka saag*, *dahi kachori* and chicken korma curry.

The breakfast cereal in question was a high-protein and low-carbohydrate product. Shyam was of the opinion that there was a ready market for such a product because of increasing health consciousness among the people especially the women. Before launching the product, Shyam called a meeting of the senior management to discuss the matter. As the product was going to be high in protein and low in carbohydrates, it was agreed that the female population would prefer the product. Women these days were playing an important role in the service sectors and were deviating more from the household work. The share of women in the Indian workforce was increasing. It was estimated that women constituted 31.2 per cent of all economically active individuals. Further, educated women these days were well informed, and their decision making ranged not only from day-to-day purchase of food requirement but also to the impact it was going to have on health. They further discussed that this was typical of women, irrespective of which state do they belonged to. The fact was that women preferred to look slim, and as such the product would be a great success. One member said that it was not only women, but men also preferred to look slim, as was evident from the increasing rush in gyms all over the country. Thus, the present lifestyle would encourage people to go for such a product. As this product was going to be expensive, income would play an important role in the acceptance of the product.

The company conducted a survey where the respondents were briefed about the product and asked questions on their willingness to buy the new breakfast cereal on an 11-point scale, where 1 = not at all willing, to 11 = very much willing. There were many other questions in the survey. The other variables on which data was collected were age, income level and gender. The question on age (how old are you?) was measured using ratio-scale measurement.

The respondents were divided into three income groups coded as:

Low income	1
Middle income	2
High income	3

The gender was coded as:

Female	1
Male	0

The data for 100 respondents is given in Table 15.18

Table 15.18 Data on Willingness to Buy Breakfast Cereal

Resp. No.	Willingness	Age	Income Group	Gender
1	3	32	2	0
2	10	48	3	1
3	8	36	2	1
4	4	26	1	0
5	5	29	1	1
6	10	52	3	1

Resp. No.	Willingness	Age	Income Group	Gender
7	9	49	3	1
8	8	49	3	1
9	6	30	2	1
10	4	26	1	0
11	3	22	1	0
12	2	25	1	0
13	9	43	2	0
14	10	36	3	1
15	8	34	1	1
16	9	42	2	0
17	5	33	2	0
18	7	38	3	0
19	9	51	3	1
20	2	39	1	0
21	7	36	2	1
22	10	46	3	1
23	11	57	3	1
24	4	27	1	0
25	9	41	2	1
26	11	51	3	1
27	4	37	2	0
28	8	49	3	1
29	6	32	2	0
30	4	27	2	0
31	10	46	3	1
32	11	51	3	0
33	3	31	1	1
34	4	40	1	0
35	5	32	2	0
36	8	36	2	1
37	11	48	3	1
38	3	22	1	0
39	10	41	3	1
40	7	50	2	0
41	9	42	2	1
42	10	51	3	1
43	2	22	1	0
44	2	20	1	0
45	3	25	2	0
46	7	39	2	1

Resp. No.	Willingness	Age	Income Group	Gender
47	8	42	2	1
48	9	45	3	1
49	10	41	3	1
50	10	45	3	1
51	2	29	1	0
52	8	34	2	0
53	6	27	2	1
54	7	34	1	1
55	5	23	1	0
56	4	28	1	0
57	6	22	1	0
58	3	29	1	0
59	5	33	2	0
60	10	47	3	1
61	11	54	3	1
62	9	53	3	1
63	7	47	2	0
64	4	31	2	1
65	2	27	1	0
66	1	26	1	0
67	3	20	1	1
68	6	31	2	1
69	8	32	2	1
70	7	39	3	0
71	3	42	1	0
72	2	26	1	0
73	5	29	2	0
74	6	32	2	1
75	8	40	3	1
76	1	23	1	0
77	10	57	3	1
78	10	58	3	1
79	3	30	1	0
80	6	32	2	0
81	8	37	2	1
82	9	40	2	1
83	7	39	2	1
84	5	36	2	0
85	3	27	1	0
86	1	29	1	0

Resp. No.	Willingness	Age	Income Group	Gender
87	2	22	1	0
88	4	20	1	0
89	6	22	2	1
90	8	29	2	1
91	11	31	3	1
92	9	26	3	1
93	5	40	3	0
94	4	36	2	0
95	1	22	1	0
96	7	23	2	1
97	9	28	3	0
98	6	37	3	1
99	10	45	3	1
100	5	35	2	0

QUESTIONS

1. If our objective is to examine the impact of age, income and gender on willingness to buy the breakfast cereal, identify the variables for which dummy variables should be used.
2. Write down the data matrix for the above exercise.
3. Estimate the regression model and interpret the results
4. Discuss how the management of Shyam Foods Pvt. Ltd can use the result to their advantage.

Appendix – 15.1: SPSS COMMANDS FOR CORRELATION

After the input data has been typed along with the variable labels and the value labels in an SPSS file, to get the output for a correlation problem, carry out the following steps:

1. Click on ANALYSE at the SPSS menu bar.
2. Click on CORRELATE, followed by BIVARIATE.
3. On the dialogue box which appears, select all the variables for which the correlations are required by clicking on the right arrow to transfer them from the variable list on the left. Then select Pearson under the heading Correlation coefficients, and select *2-tailed* under the heading Tests of Significance.
4. Click OK to get the matrix of the pair-wise Pearson correlations among all the variables selected, along with the two-tailed significance of each pair-wise correlation.

Appendix – 15.2: SPSS COMMANDS FOR REGRESSION

Type the data along with the variable labels and the value labels in an SPSS file, and to get the output for a regression problem, follow the directions:

1. Click on ANALYSE at the SPSS menu bar.
2. Click on REGRESSION, followed by LINEAR.

3. In the dialogue box which appears, select a dependent variable by clicking on the arrow leading to the dependent box after highlighting the appropriate variable from the list of the variables on the left side.
4. Select the independent variables to be included in the regression model in the same way, transferring them from left side to the right side box by clicking on the arrow leading to the box called independent variables or independents.
5. In the same dialogue box, select the METHOD. Choose:
   - ENTER as the method if you want all independent variables to be included in the model.
   - STEPWISE if you want to use forward stepwise regression.
   - BACKWARD if you want to use a backward stepwise regression.
6. Select OPTIONS if you want additional output options, select the ones you want, and click CONTINUE.
7. Select PLOTS if you want to see some plots such as residual plots, select those you want, and click CONTINUE.
8. Click OK from the main dialogue box to get the REGRESSION output.

Answers to Objective Type Questions

1. True	2. True	3. False	4. False	5. False
6. True	7. True	8. True	9. False	10. True
11. False	12. False	13. False	14. True	15. False
16. True	17. True	18. True	19. True	20. True

REFERENCES

Ahuja, M, Katherine M Chudoba, and C J Kacmar. "IT Road Warriors: Balancing Work-Family Conflict, Job Autonomy and Work Overload to Mitigate Turnover Intentions", *MIS Quarterly*, 31 (2007): 1–17.

Salaff, J F. "Where Home is the Office: The New Form of Flexible Work", Working paper. Department of Sociology, Centre for Urban and Community Studies, Univerisity of Toronto, 2002.

BIBLIOGRAPHY

Basu Debarati and Deepak Chawla. "An Empirical Test of CAPM – The Case of Indian Stock Market". Paper presented at the International Conference on Finance, Accounts & Global Investment, International Management Institute, New Delhi, 22–24 August 2008.

Boyd, Harper W, Ralph Westfall, Jr and Stanley F Stasch. *Marketing Research: Text and Cases.* 7th edn. Richard D. Irwin, Inc., 2002.

Churchill, Gilbert A, Jr and Dawn Iacobucci. *Marketing Research Methodological Foundations.* 8th edn. Thompson South Western, 2002.

Schwab, Donald P. *Research Methods of Organizational Studies.* Mahwah: Lawrence Erlaum Associates Publishers, 2005.

Cooper, Donald R. *Business Research Methods.* New Delhi: Tata McGraw-Hill Publishing Company Ltd, 2006.

Gay, L R. *Research Methods for Business and Management.* New York: Macmillan Publishing Company, 1992.

Gujarati, Damodar N and Sangeetha. *Basic Econometrics*, 4th edn. New Delhi: Tata McGraw Hill Publishing Co., 2007.

Johnston, J. *Econometric Methods*, 3rd edn. McGraw Hill International Company, 1984.

Kothari, C.R. *Research Methodology: Methods and Techniques.* New Delhi: Wiley Eastern, 1990.

Koutsoyiannis, A. *Theory of Econometrics*, 2nd edn. Macmillan Press Ltd, 1979.

Malhotra Naresh K. *Marketing Research – An Applied Orientation.* 3rd edn. New Delhi: Pearson Education, 2002.

Michael, V.P. *Research Methodology in Management.* Mumbai: Himalaya Publishing House, 2000.

Sethna, Beherug N. *Research Methods in Marketing Management.* New Delhi: Tata McGraw-Hill Publishing Company Ltd, 1984.

Sondhi, Neena, Deepak Chawla, Prachi Jain and Monika Kashyap. "Work-exhaustion – A Consequential Framework: Validating the Model in the Indian Context". *The Indian Journal of Industrial Relations*, 43 (2008).

Tull, Donald S and Hawkins, Del I. *Marketing Research: Measurement & Method*, 6th edn. New Delhi: Prentice Hall of India Pvt. Ltd, 1993.

Emory, William C. *Business Research Methods.* Illinois: Richard D. Irwin Inc., 1976.

Zikmund, William G. *Business Research Methods*, 5th edn. The Dryden Press, Harcourt Brace College Publishers, 1997.

16

CHAPTER

Factor Analysis

Learning Objectives

By the end of the chapter, you should be able to:

1. Describe the uses of factor analysis.
2. State conditions under which a factor analysis could be carried out.
3. Understand the steps involved in a factor analysis exercise.
4. Explain the concepts and statistics associated with factor analysis with the help of an example.
5. Carry out the applications of factor analysis in other multivariate techniques.

Mr K P Singh, Director of BPS Business School, was worried about the sharp decline in the number of applicants for admission to full-time Postgraduate Diploma in Management (PGDM) programme. BPS Business School was 12 years old and was situated in Jaipur. It had an intake of 120 students and had been receiving on an average 5000–6000 applications for the programme. However, for the current year, much to the surprise of Mr Singh, the number of applications dipped to 1500. The admission to PGDM was through CAT and there was a 20 per cent decline in the CAT registration for the current year. However, the decline for BPS was much more, which was the cause of worry for Mr Singh.

Mr Singh called a faculty meeting to discuss the possible cause of sharp decline in applications. After a brainstorming session, it was decided to conduct a survey of prospective students to find out what makes them choose a business school for pursuing a PGDM programme. A random sample of 200 respondents was chosen to fill up a specially designed questionnaire for the purpose. There were about 70 variables on which information was sought. Having obtained such information Mr Singh was wondering how to draw inferences from the same as many of the variables seemed to be interrelated. Dr Gupta, the faculty for research methods, was approached for the purpose. Dr Gupta suggested that a factor analysis of 70 variables should be carried out to detect the factors that could be extracted from these variables. The present chapter is an attempt in this direction.

Factor analysis is a multivariate statistical technique in which there is no distinction between dependent and independent variables. In factor analysis, all variables under investigation are analysed together to extract the underlined factors. Factor analysis is a data reduction method. It is a very useful method to reduce a large number of variables resulting in data complexity to a few manageable factors. These factors explain most part of the variations of the original set of data. A market researcher might have collected data on say, more than 50 attributes (or items) of a product which may become very difficult to analyse. Factor analysis could help to reduce the data on 50 odd attributes to a few manageable factors. It helps in identifying the underlying structure of the data.

A factor is a linear combination of variables. It is a construct that is not directly observable but that needs to be inferred from the input variables.

A *factor* is a linear combination of variables. It is a construct that is not directly observable but that needs to be inferred from the input variables. The factors are statistically independent. We will show you their application in a regression analysis as the factor scores, when used as independent variables in regression analysis, help to solve the problem of multicollinearity. (The problem of multicollinearity in a regression model arises when the independent variables are so highly correlated that it becomes difficult to separate out the influence of each of the independent variables on the dependent variable.) The factor scores could also be used in other multivariate techniques.

USES OF FACTOR ANALYSIS

LEARNING OBJECTIVE 1
Describe the uses of factor analysis.

The technique of factor analysis has multiple uses as discussed in the following situations:

Scale construction: Factor analysis could be used to develop concise multiple item scales for measuring various constructs. We have already discussed in the chapter Attitude Measurement and Scaling the process of developing a multiple item scale that typically starts generating a large set of items (statements) relating to the attitude being measured. This is done as part of exploratory research. Factor analysis can reduce the set of statements to a concise instrument and at the same time, ensure that the retained statements adequately represent the critical aspects of the constructs being measured. Suppose we want to prepare a multiple item scale for measuring the job satisfaction of skilled workers in an organization. As the first step, we would generate a large number of statements, numbering say 100 or so as part of exploratory research. These statements could be subjected to factor analysis and let us assume that we get three factors out of it. Now, if we want to construct a 15-item scale to measure job satisfaction, what could be done is to separate five items in each of the factors having the highest factor loading. The concept of factor loading will be discussed later in the book. This way, a 15-item scale to measure job satisfaction could be developed.

Establish antecedents: This method reduces multiple input variables into grouped factors. Thus, the independent variables can be grouped into broad factors. For example, all the variables that measure the safety clauses in a mutual fund could be reduced to a factor called safety clause. Thus, the company could know about the broad benefit that an investor seeks in a fund.

Different independent variables can be grouped to measure independent factors. These are later used for identifying personality types. This is called **psychographic profiling**.

Psychographic profiling: Different independent variables are grouped to measure independent factors. These are then used for identifying personality types. One of the most well known inventories based on this technique is called the 16 PF inventory.

Segmentation analysis: Factor analysis could also be used for segmentation. For example, there could be different sets of two-wheelers-customers owning two wheelers because of different importance they give to factors like prestige, economy consideration and functional features.

Marketing studies: The technique has extensive use in the field of marketing and can be successfully used for new product development; product acceptance research, developing of advertising copy, pricing studies and for branding studies. For example we can use it to:

- identify the attributes of brands that influence consumers' choice;
- get an insight into the media habits of various consumers;
- identify the characteristics of price-sensitive customers.

CONDITIONS FOR A FACTOR ANALYSIS EXERCISE

LEARNING OBJECTIVE 2
State conditions under which a factor analysis could be carried out.

Factor analysis requires some specific conditions that must be ensured before executing the technique. These are mentioned in detail in this section.

- Factor analysis exercise requires metric data. This means the data should be either interval or ratio scale in nature. The variables for factor analysis are identified through exploratory research which may be conducted by reviewing the literature on the subject, researches carried out already in this area, by informal interviews of knowledgeable persons, qualitative analysis like focus group discussions held with a small sample of the respondent population, analysis of case studies and judgement of the researcher. Generally in a survey research, a five or seven-point Likert scale or any other interval scales may be used.

The **factor analysis exercise** requires metric data, which should be either interval or ratio scale in nature.

- As the responses to different statements are obtained through different scales, all the responses need to be standardized. The standardization helps in comparison of different responses from such scales. The standardization is carried out using the following formulae:

$$\text{Standardized score of i}^{\text{th}}\text{ respondent on a statement} = \frac{\text{Actual score of i}^{\text{th}}\text{ respondent on statement} - \text{Mean of all respondents on the statement}}{\text{Standard deviation of all respondents on the statement}}$$

- The size of the sample respondents should be at least four to five times more than the number of variables (number of statements).
- The basic principle behind the application of factor analysis is that the initial set of variables should be highly correlated. If the correlation coefficients between all the variables are small, factor analysis may not be an appropriate technique. A correlation matrix of the variables could be computed and tested for its statistical significance. The hypothesis to be tested may be written as:

  H_0 : Correlation matrix is insignificant, i.e., correlation matrix is an identity matrix where diagonal elements are one and off diagonal elements are zero.

  H_1 : Correlation matrix is significant.

  The test is carried out by using a Barttlet test of sphericity, which takes the determinant of the correlation matrix into consideration. The test converts it into a chi-square statistics with degrees of freedom equal to $[(k(k-1))/2]$, where k is the number of variables on which factor analysis is applied. The significance of the correlation matrix ensures that a factor analysis exercise could be carried out.

- Another condition which needs to be fulfilled before a factor analysis could be carried out is the value of Kaiser-Meyer-Olkin (KMO) statistics which takes a value between 0 and 1. For the application of factor analysis, the value of KMO statistics should be greater than 0.5. The KMO statistics compares the magnitude of observed correlation coefficients with the magnitudes of partial correlation coefficients. A small value of KMO shows that correlation between variables cannot be explained by other variables.

STEPS IN A FACTOR ANALYSIS EXERCISE

LEARNING OBJECTIVE 3
Understand the steps involved in a factor analysis exercise.

There are basically two steps that are required in a factor analysis exercise.

1. **Extraction of factors:** The first and the foremost step is to decide on how many factors are to be extracted from the given set of data. This could be accomplished by

$F_i = W_{i1}X_1^* + W_{i2}X_2^* + W_{i3}X_3^* + ... + W_{ik}X_k^*$

various methods like the centroid method, the principal component method and the maximum likelihood method. Here, only the principal component method will be discussed very briefly. As we know that factors are linear combinations of the variables which are supposed to be highly correlated, the mathematical form of the same could be written as:

$$F_i = W_{i1}X_1^* + W_{i2}X_2^* + W_{i3}X_3^* + ... + W_{ik}X_k^*$$

where,

X_i^* = i^{th} standardized variable
F_i = Estimate of ith factor
W_i = Weight or factor score coefficient for i^{th} standardized variable.
k = Number of variables

The principal component methodology involves searching for those values of W_i so that the first factor explains the largest portion of total variance. This is called the first principal factor. This explained variance is then subtracted from the original input matrix so as to yield a residual matrix. A second principal factor is extracted from the residual matrix in a way such that the second factor takes care of most of the residual variance. One point that has to be kept in mind is that the second principal factor has to be statistically independent of the first principal factor. The same principle is then repeated until there is little variance to be explained. Theory may be used to specify how many factors should be extracted or it may be based on the criterion of the Kaiser Guttman method. This method states that the number of factors to be extracted should be equal to the number of factors having an eigenvalue of atleast 1. Since each of the variables in the original data set has a variance of 1 (eigenvalue of 1), therefore, if there are 50 variables then the total variation in the data set will be 50.

We know that a factor is a linear combination of the various variables. Now eigenvalue for each of the factor is computed and only those factors that have an eigenvalue at least 1 are accepted as per Kaiser Guttman method. All those factors having eigenvalues less than 1 are rejected. This is because each of the variables has a variance of 1 and, therefore, a linear combination of these variables called factor should not have an eigenvalue less than 1.

Another output of the factor analysis exercise is a *factor score*, which is computed for each of the factors corresponding to each respondent. Most software, including SPSS, provide factor score for each respondent and each factor. As the factor scores are statistically independent, they can be used in regression and discriminant analysis as independent variables. This will be explained briefly in the text later on.

Factor loading is the correlation coefficient of the extracted factor score with a variable.

The correlation coefficient of the extracted factor score with a variable is called the *factor loading*. In most computer printouts, a matrix of factor loadings called factor matrix or component matrix is presented. Factor loadings play a very important role in the computations of eigenvalues of each factor and also in computing the communalities of each variable. These concepts would be discussed in depth with the help of a numerical exercise.

2. **Rotation of factors:** The second step in the factor analysis exercise is the rotation of initial factor solutions. This is because the initial factors are very difficult to interpret. Therefore, the initial solution is rotated so as to yield a solution that can be interpreted easily. Most of the computer software would give options for *orthogonal rotation, varimax rotation* and *oblique rotation*. Generally, the varimax rotation is used as this results in independent factors. The varimax rotation

The basic idea of **rotation** is to get some factors that have a few variables that correlate high with that factor and some that correlate poorly with that factor.

method maximizes the variance of the loadings within each factor. The variance of the factor is largest when its smallest loading tends towards zero and its largest loading tends towards unity. The basic idea of rotation is to get some factors that have a few variables that correlate high with that factor and some that correlate poorly with that factor. Similarly, there are other factors that correlate high with those variables with which the other factors do not have significant correlation. Therefore, the rotation is carried out in such way so that the factor loadings as in the first step are close to unity or zero. This procedure avoids problems of having factors with all variables having midrange correlations. This is done for a better interpretation of the results and for the ease obtained in naming the factors. Once this is done, a cut off point on the factor loading is selected. There is no hard and fast rule to decide on the cut-off point. However, generally it is taken to be greater than 0.5. All those variables attached to a factor, once the cut-off point is decided, are used for naming the factors. This is a very subjective procedure and different researchers may name same factors differently. Another point to be noted is that a variable which appears in one factor should not appear in any other factor. This means that a variable should have a high loading only on one factor and a low loading on other factors. If that is not the case, it implies that the question has not been understood properly by the respondent or it may not have been phrased clearly. Another possible cause could be that the respondent may have more than one opinion about a given item (statement).

The total variance explained by all the factors taken together remains the same after rotation. However, the amount of variations for each individual factor may undergo a change. The communalities for each variable under the two procedures remain unchanged. This would be shown in the example to follow.

CONCEPT CHECK

1. Explain the use of factor analysis.
2. What are the main conditions for a factor analysis exercise?
3. Discuss the various steps involved in a factor analysis.

ILLUSTRATION OF FACTOR ANALYSIS EXERCISE

LEARNING OBJECTIVE 4
Explain the concepts and statistics associated with factor analysis with the help of an example.

We will explain all that is discussed above with the help of a numerical example.

A study was carried out in 2007 to understand and analyse the investment behaviour of the employees of public sector units (PSUs) and government. A sample of 80 respondents was drawn from the PSU and government employees in the vicinity of Delhi. The respondents were asked to state their level of agreement or disagreement on the following parameters on a 5-point scale, where 1 = strongly disagree, 2 = disagree, 3 = neutral, 4 = agree, and 5 = strongly agree. The parameters in question were the importance given to risk averseness, returns, insurance cover, tax rebate, maturity time, credibility of the financial institution, and easy accessibility while making an investment. The data is presented in the Table 16.1.

where, X_1 = Score on risk averseness
X_2 = Score on returns
X_3 = Score on insurance cover
X_4 = Score on tax rebate
X_5 = Score on maturity time
X_6 = Score on credibility of the financial institution
X_7 = Score on easy accessibility
999 = Represents missing value in the data

TABLE 16.1 Data used for the study on investment behaviour

Resp No.	X_1	X_2	X_3	X_4	X_5	X_6	X_7	Resp No.	X_1	X_2	X_3	X_4	X_5	X_6	X_7
1	4	4	4	4	4	4	4	41	4	5	5	5	5	5	4
2	4	4	3	4	3	4	4	42	4	4	4	4	4	4	4
3	4	5	3	4	2	3	3	43	4	4	5	5	3	4	3
4	5	4	1	5	4	5	3	44	3	3	3	3	3	3	3
5	3	5	3	5	5	3	3	45	3	5	3	3	4	4	4
6	4	4	4	4	4	4	4	46	5	4	2	4	3	5	4
7	4	5	3	5	5	5	5	47	4	4	3	4	4	5	4
8	4	4	5	4	4	4	3	48	5	4	3	4	3	5	4
9	5	5	5	5	5	5	4	49	5	5	3	5	3	4	3
10	4	5	2	4	4	4	4	50	5	4	2	4	2	5	4
11	5	4	4	4	3	4	5	51	5	4	1	5	3	4	2
12	5	4	1	4	4	5	3	52	5	4	3	4	2	5	4
13	4	3	5	4	3	4	3	53	5	4	2	5	4	4	3
14	5	5	3	3	5	5	5	54	5	5	4	5	3	5	5
15	5	5	4	3	4	5	4	55	5	4	2	4	3	4	4
16	4	5	2	3	4	4	3	56	5	5	1	5	4	5	3
17	4	2	3	5	4	4	4	57	5	4	3	5	3	5	5
18	999	3	4	4	3	5	5	58	5	4	1	5	2	5	2
19	5	5	5	5	5	5	5	59	5	5	2	4	3	4	3
20	5	5	4	5	3	4	3	60	5	3	1	3	3	5	4
21	5	5	5	5	5	5	5	61	5	4	3	4	4	4	2
22	4	3	4	3	3	3	3	62	5	4	1	5	3	5	4
23	3	5	5	4	4	4	4	63	4	5	2	1	5	5	2
24	4	5	4	5	4	5	5	64	4	4	4	4	2	4	2
25	5	5	3	4	4	5	5	65	4	4	4	4	4	4	4
26	4	4	4	5	4	5	4	66	3	3	4	4	4	4	4
27	4	4	4	4	4	4	4	67	5	5	5	4	5	5	5
28	4	4	5	4	2	2	2	68	5	4	4	4	4	5	4
29	2	5	5	5	5	5	5	69	4	5	3	4	4	4	4
30	4	4	4	5	4	4	4	70	5	4	2	3	3	5	4
31	2	5	4	5	4	5	4	71	4	4	4	4	4	5	5
32	4	4	3	4	4	4	4	72	3	5	3	5	4	4	4
33	3	3	4	4	4	5	4	73	4	4	4	4	4	4	4
34	5	4	3	5	4	5	3	74	3	4	3	5	5	5	5
35	5	5	3	4	4	5	4	75	5	4	4	4	3	5	3
36	5	4	4	4	4	3	4	76	4	5	5	3	3	4	3
37	4	4	5	5	3	3	3	77	5	5	2	5	4	5	4
38	4	3	4	4	4	4	3	78	4	5	2	5	3	5	3
39	1	5	4	4	5	5	5	79	4	4	3	4	5	4	4
40	4	4	4	5	5	4	4	80	2	4	3	4	3	4	2

Establishing the Strength of the Factor Analysis Solution

In order to establish the strength of the factor analysis solution it is essential to establish the reliability and validity of the obtained reduction. As discussed earlier, this is done with the KMO and the Bartlett's test of sphericity.

Using SPSS 14.0 a factor analysis was carried out. The results on KMO and Bartlett's test are given in Table 16.2.

TABLE 16.2 KMO and Bartlett's test

Kaiser-Meyer-Olkin Measure of Sampling Adequacy		0.591
Bartlett's Test of Sphericity	Approx. Chi-Square	80.004
	d.f.	21
	Sig.	0.000

It may be noted that the value of KMO statistics is greater than 0.5, indicating that factor analysis could be used for the given set of data. Further, Bartlett's test of sphericity testing for the significance of the correlation matrix of the variables indicates that the correlation coefficient matrix is significant as indicated by the p value corresponding to the chi-square statistic. The p value is 0.000, which is less than 0.05, the assumed level of significance, indicating the rejection of the hypothesis that the correlation matrix of the variables is insignificant. It may be noted that the sample size of 80 is more than 5 times the number of variables (seven). All these justify the use of factor analysis for this problem.

The Factor Score Coefficient Matrix

As stated earlier, based on the correlation between the original variables, one attempts to explain the variance between these based on some common factor. Based on the component score coefficients we are able to obtain the factor scores for the extracted factors.

The component score coefficient matrix for the above data is given as shown in Table 16.3.

There are two factors that can be extracted from the data. This will be shown later on. The factor scores for the two factors can be computed as:

$$\text{Factor score for } 1^{st} \text{ factor} = -0.086\, X_1^* + 0.257\, X_2^* + 0.163\, X_3^* + 0.150\, X_4^* + 0.372\, X_5^* + 0.277\, X_6^* + 0.386\, X_7^*$$

$$\text{Factor score for } 2^{nd} \text{ factor} = 0.486\, X_1^* + 0.103\, X_2^* - 0.456\, X_3^* + 0.080\, X_4^* - 0.128\, X_5^* + 0.408\, X_6^* + 0.030\, X_7^*$$

TABLE 16.3 Component score coefficient matrix

	Component	
	1	2
Risk averseness	–0.086	0.486
Returns	0.257	0.103
Insurance cover	0.163	–0.456
Tax rebate	0.150	0.080
Maturity time	0.372	–0.128
Credibility of the financial institution	0.277	0.408
Easy accessibility	0.386	0.030

Extraction Method: Principal Component Analysis.
Component Scores.

where $$X_i^* = \frac{X_i - \overline{X}_i}{SD\,(X_i)} \qquad i = 1, 2, 3, \ldots\ldots\ldots\ldots, 7$$

$\overline{X}_i$ = Mean of ith variable

$SD\,(X_i)$ = Standard deviation of X_i

The factor scores for the two factors corresponding to each of the 80 respondents are given in Table 16.4.

TABLE 16.4 Factor scores for two factors corresponding to each respondent

S. No.	Factor Score 1	Factor Score 2	S. No.	Factor Score 1	Factor Score 2
1	0.04651	−0.70451	41	1.61059	−0.38924
2	−0.53408	−0.1644	42	0.04651	−0.70451
3	−1.45202	−0.49099	43	−0.50594	−0.86923
4	−0.31279	1.68553	44	−1.86938	−1.61166
5	0.17155	−1.39535	45	0.18383	−0.82756
6	0.04651	−0.70451	46	−0.36616	1.37648
7	1.78276	0.42285	47	0.31246	0.27959
8	−0.2645	−1.12811	48	−0.22733	0.98799
9	1.51256	0.16754	49	−0.50323	0.61705
10	0.14726	0.22498	50	−0.80791	1.5281
11	−0.04343	0.03898	51	−1.60916	1.20643
12	−0.51309	1.57826	52	−0.66907	1.1396
13	−1.08466	−1.129	53	−0.57874	0.70142
14	1.28413	0.76509	54	0.94007	0.89436
15	0.53138	0.49311	55	−0.77095	0.78087
16	−0.50288	0.08262	56	0.06563	1.83803
17	−0.64887	−0.51376	57	0.42281	1.13035
18	.	.	58	−1.64612	1.95366
19	1.9624	0.20264	59	−0.84237	0.89828
20	−0.36439	0.22855	60	−1.08372	1.50521
21	1.9624	0.20264	61	−1.09004	0.17056
22	−1.82858	−1.44338	62	−0.3047	1.87225
23	0.6618	−1.49728	63	−0.50679	0.27698
24	1.47985	0.18597	64	−1.73666	−0.47148
25	1.04268	1.02398	65	0.04651	−0.70451
26	0.65159	−0.00164	66	−0.23388	−1.4138
27	0.04651	−0.70451	67	1.7621	0.09537
28	−2.4074	−2.0512	68	0.35326	0.44788
29	2.2565	−1.4677	69	0.28609	−0.16351
30	0.24681	−0.59725	70	−0.56646	1.26922
31	1.22608	−0.96269	71	0.90113	−0.0738
32	−0.09233	−0.31602	72	0.58443	−0.61303
33	0.17091	−0.81819	73	0.04651	−0.70451
34	−0.03512	0.90854	74	1.50237	−0.28644
35	0.59284	0.98888	75	−0.53833	0.56439
36	−0.45631	−0.74334	76	−0.52812	−0.93126
37	−0.91073	−1.46484	77	0.6543	1.48464
38	−0.78175	−0.89212	78	−0.13925	1.04437
39	2.0154	−1.74325	79	0.34942	−0.46763
40	0.68855	−0.74886	80	−1.23768	−1.34816

Factor Loadings and Computation of Eigenvalues

The correlation coefficient between the factor score and the variables included in the study is called factor loading and is presented in Table 16.5, called factor matrix (component matrix). The result presented below could always be verified by computing the correlation coefficient between the relevant factor score with the original standardized variables.

TABLE 16.5
Component matrix[a]

	Component	
	1	2
Risk averseness	–0.176	0.753
Returns	0.527	0.160
Insurance cover	0.335	–0.707
Tax rebate	0.309	0.125
Maturity time	0.765	–.198
Credibility of the financial institution	0.570	0.633
Easy accessibility	0.793	0.047

Extraction Method: Principal Component Analysis.
[a] 2 components extracted.

In the above component matrix, the elements of the matrix are called factor loadings. The correlation coefficient between first variable, namely, risk averseness and factor 1 is –0.176. Similarly, the correlation coefficient between factor 2 and the variable 3, namely, insurance cover is –0.707. The factor loadings could be used to compute eigenvalues for each factor. For example, the eigenvalue for factor 1 is computed as:

$$\text{Eigenvalue of factor 1} = (-0.176)^2 + (0.527)^2 + (0.335)^2 + (0.309)^2 + (0.765)^2 + (0.570)^2 + (0.793)^2 = 2.054$$

$$\text{Eigenvalue of factor 2} = (0.753)^2 + (0.160)^2 + (-0.707)^2 + (0.125)^2 + (-0.198)^2 + (0.633)^2 + (0.047)^2 = 1.551$$

Total Variance Accounted by the Extracted Factors

We note that there are two factors with eigenvalues greater than one. The percentage of variance explained by each of the factor can be computed using the eigenvalues. As there are seven variables, the total variance equals seven. Therefore, the variance explained by each of the factors can be computed as:

$$\text{Percentage of variance explained by factor 1} = \frac{\text{Eigenvalue of factor 1}}{\text{Sum total of the eigenvalues}} \times 100$$

$$= \frac{2.054}{7} \times 100 = 29.346 \text{ per cent}$$

Similarly,

$$\text{Percentage of Variance explained by factor 2} = \frac{\text{Eigenvalue of factor 2}}{\text{Sum total of the eigenvalues}} \times 100$$

$$= \frac{1.551}{7} \times 100 = 22.16 \text{ per cent}$$

The total variance explained by both factors = 29.346 + 22.16 = 51.506 per cent

The above computations as obtained from SPSS output are presented in Table 16.6.

TABLE 16.6
Total variance explained

Component	Initial Eigenvalues			Extraction Sums of Squared Loadings		
	Total	% of Variance	Cumulative %	Total	% of Variance	Cumulative %
1	2.054	29.346	29.346	2.054	29.346	29.346
2	1.551	22.160	51.506	1.551	22.160	51.506
3	0.970	13.857	65.363			
4	0.848	12.109	77.472			
5	0.711	10.151	87.622			
6	0.490	7.003	94.626			
7	0.376	5.374	100.000			

Extraction Method: Principal Component Analysis.

Communality: Explanation of the Original Variable's Variance

Communality is denoted by h^2. It indicates how much of each variable is accounted for by the underlying factors taken together.

It may be appropriate to introduce another concept known as *communality* denoted by h^2 at this stage. It indicates how much of each variable is accounted for by the underlying factors taken together. In other words, it is a measure of the percentage of variable's variation that is explained by the factors. A relatively high communality shows that not much of the variable is left over after whatever the factors represent is taken into consideration. The communality for each variable is computed as given in Table 16.7. The factor matrix (component matrix) as presented in Table 16.5 could be used to compute communalities for each variable.

TABLE 16.7
Communalities for variables

Communality for risk averseness (X_1)	=	$(-0.176)^2 + (0.753)^2$	=	0.598
Communality for returns (X_2)	=	$(0.527)^2 + (0.160)^2$	=	0.304
Communality for insurance cover (X_3)	=	$(0.335)^2 + (-0.707)^2$	=	0.612
Communality for tax rebate (X_4)	=	$(0.309)^2 + (0.125)^2$	=	0.111
Communality for maturity time (X_5)	=	$(0.765)^2 + (-0.198)^2$	=	0.624
Communality for credibility of the financial institution (X_6)	=	$(0.570)^2 + (0.633)^2$	=	0.725
Communality for easy accessibility (X_7)	=	$(0.793)^2 + (0.047)^2$	=	0.631

The communality for the first variable is 0.598, which means 59.8 per cent of the variance or information content of the first variable, namely, risk averseness (X_1) is explained by the two factors. Similarly, the communalities for the other variables could be computed.

Establishing the Statistical Independence of Extracted Factors

As mentioned earlier, the two factors should be statistically independent. This means the correlation coefficient between the two factors scores should be zero. To verify this, correlation between the two factor scores was computed using SPSS software and the results are presented in Table 16.8.

The correlation matrix given in Table 16.8 indicates that the correlation between the two factor scores is zero.

TABLE 16.8 Correlations between factor scores

		REGR Factor Score 1 for Analysis 1	REGR Factor Score 2 for Analysis 1
REGR factor score 1 for analysis 1	Pearson Correlation	1	0.000
	Sig. (2-tailed)		1.000
	N	79	79
REGR factor score 2 for analysis 1	Pearson Correlation	0.000	1
	Sig. (2-tailed)	1.000	
	N	79	79

Rotation of Factors

The next task is to interpret the factor loading matrix called the component matrix. In order to do so and to be able to interpret the results in a better way a factor rotation is desired. Many of the software have a provision for Varimax rotation which results in independent factors. The purpose of rotation is to have the factor loading in such a way that they are either close to zero or to –1 or +1. This means that the factor loadings are high on some variable and low on some other variables. In the present case, the results obtained after Varimax rotations are given in Table 16.9.

The **purpose of rotation** is to have the factor loading in such a way that they are either close to zero or to –1 or +1.

TABLE 16.9 Rotated component matrix[a]

	Component	
	1	2
Risk averseness	.057	.771
Returns	.551	.004
Insurance cover	.109	.775
Tax rebate	.332	–.027
Maturity time	.671	.417
Credibility of the financial institution	.732	–.435
Easy accessibility	.771	.192

Extraction Method: Principal Component Analysis.
Rotation Method: Varimax with Kaiser Normalization.
[a] Rotation converged in 3 iterations.

In order to interpret the results of Table 16.9, a cut-off point is decided. As mentioned earlier, there is no hard and fast rule to decide the cut-off point, but generally it is taken above 0.5. Now using 0.7 as the cut-off point, the two variables corresponding to factor 1 having a factor loading above 0.7 are credibility of the financial institutions and ease of accessibility. The variables corresponding to factor 2 for which the factor loadings are greater than 0.7 are risk averseness and insurance cover. A variable which appears in one factor does not appear in other.

Labelling or Naming the Factors

Our next job is to name these factors. The factor 1 comprising of the credibility of financial institution and ease of accessibility could be named as *Perceived value of service* and the factor 2 comprising of the variables risk averseness and insurance cover could be named as *Security factor*. This shows that the most important factor explaining the investment behaviour of PSU and government employees is the perceived value of service followed by the security factor.

As stated earlier, total variance explained by the two methods remains the same although the variance explained by each factor may undergo a change. Further, the communalities of each variable under the two procedures do not change. This can be shown below as:

Using the factor loadings as given in rotated component matrix, the eigenvalue of factor 1 can be computed as:

$$\text{Eigenvalue for factor 1} = (0.057)^2 + (0.551)^2 + (0.109)^2 + (0.332)^2 + (0.671)^2 + (0.732)^2 + (0.771)^2 = 2.01$$

$$\text{Eigenvalue for factor 2} = (-0.771)^2 + (0.004)^2 + (0.775)^2 + (-0.027)^2 + (0.417)^2 + (-0.435)^2 + (0.192)^2 = 1.60$$

$$\text{Variance explained by factor 1} = \frac{2.01}{7} \times 100 = 28.71 \text{ per cent}$$

$$\text{Variance explained by factor 2} = \frac{1.60}{7} \times 100 = 22.86 \text{ per cent}$$

$$\text{Total variance explained by two factors} = 28.71 + 22.86 = 51.57 \text{ per cent}$$

Therefore, we note that although variance explained by the two factors individually has changed slightly after rotation, the total variance explained by the two factors together has remained same.

Now using the rotated factor component matrix, the communalities for each variable could be computed as:

Communality for risk averseness (X_1)	=	$(0.057)^2 + (-.771)^2$	=	0.598
Communality for returns (X_2)	=	$(0.551)^2 + (0.004)^2$	=	0.304
Communality for insurance cover (X_3)	=	$(0.109)^2 + (0.775)^2$	=	0.612
Communality for tax rebate (X_4)	=	$(0.332)^2 + (-0.027)^2$	=	0.111
Communality for maturity time(X_5)	=	$(0.671)^2 + (0.417)^2$	=	0.624
Communality for credibility of the financial institution (X_6)	=	$(0.732)^2 + (-0.435)^2$	=	0.725
Communality for easy accessibility (X_7)	=	$(0.771)^2 + (0.192)^2$	=	0.631

From the above we may note that the communalities for each of the variables remain unchanged under varimax rotation. The total picture could be summarized in Table 16.10 as obtained from the SPSS printout.

CONCEPT CHECK

1. Discuss the factor score coefficient-matrix.
2. Define communality.

TABLE 16.10
Total variance explained

Component	Initial Eigenvalues			Extraction Sums of Squared Loadings			Rotation Sums of Squared Loadings		
	Total	Percentage of Variance	Cumulative Percentage	Total	Percentage of Variance	Cumulative Percentage	Total	Percentage of Variance	Cumulative Percentage
1	2.054	29.346	29.346	2.054	29.346	29.346	2.010	28.708	28.708
2	1.551	22.160	51.506	1.551	22.160	51.506	1.596	22.798	51.506
3	0.970	13.857	65.363						
4	0.848	12.109	77.472						
5	0.711	10.151	87.622						
6	0.490	7.003	94.626						
7	0.376	5.374	100.000						

Extraction Method: Principal Component Analysis.

APPLICATIONS OF FACTOR ANALYSIS IN OTHER MULTIVARIATE TECHNIQUES

LEARNING OBJECTIVE 5
Carry out the applications of factor analysis in other multivariate techniques

One of the ouputs of factor analysis, namely, factor scores, could be used as an input in various multivariate techniques like multiple regression, discriminant analysis, cluster analysis and multidimensional scaling. The uses are briefly described below:

Multiple regression: One use of factor analysis is to overcome the problem of multicollinearity in a multiple regression model. One of the assumptions of the multiple regression models is that all the independent variables should be statistically independent. However, in reality this is hardly the case. We would show with the help of an example how factor analysis would come to our rescue and help overcome the problem of multicollinearity.

A study was conducted to determine the factors responsible for measuring the satisfaction levels among consumers of aerated drinks. A survey was conducted with a sample size of 100 consumers of soft drinks from different age and income groups. The respondents were a mix of male and female. Some of the questions asked in the survey were the following:

		Strongly Disagree	Disagree	Neither Disagree nor Agree	Agree	Strongly Agree
1	Aerated soft drinks are refreshing (X_1)					
2	are bad for health (X_2)					
3	are very convenient to serve (X_3)					
4	should be avoided with age (X_4)					
5	are very tasty (X_5)					
6	are not good for children (X_6)					
7	should be consumed occasionally (X_7)					
8	should not be taken in large quantity (X_8)					
9	are not as good as energy drinks (X_9)					
10	are better than fruit juices (X_{10})					

The question on satisfaction towards the aerated drinks was measured using the following questions.

	Strongly Disagree	Disagree	Neither Disagree nor Agree	Agree	Strongly Agree
You would recommend aerated drinks to others. (S)	1	2	3	4	5

The data for the 100 respondents is given in Table 16.11.

The satisfaction level was used as a dependent variable and regressed on the remaining 10 independent variables labelled as X_1, X_2, ... X_{10}. The regression results are given in Tables 16.12 and 16.13.

TABLE 16.11 Data for study on aerated drinks

Resp	X_1	X_2	X_3	X_4	X_5	X_6	X_7	X_8	X_9	X_{10}	S
1	4	4	4	5	4	4	4	4	4	2	4
2	3	5	4	5	3	5	5	5	3	1	5
3	3	3	3	3	4	3	4	5	4	4	2
4	1	4	4	4	5	1	5	3	3	4	3
5	2	5	3	4	4	4	2	4	5	4	2
6	3	4	4	3	3	4	4	4	4	2	5
7	3	4	4	4	5	3	3	4	4	3	3
8	2	5	4	4	3	5	4	4	4	1	4
9	3	5	4	3	4	5	4	5	4	1	5
10	5	5	4	3	4	4	4	2	4	4	2
11	3	5	4	4	5	5	4	5	4	2	4
12	4	4	4	3	5	3	4	3	2	3	4
13	4	3	4	4	4	4	4	4	4	2	5
14	4	2	4	2	4	2	5	3	3	3	3
15	4	4	5	5	4	5	4	4	4	1	5
16	4	4	4	5	3	4	4	4	4	4	1
17	4	1	4	2	3	3	2	4	5	1	5
18	4	3	4	4	4	3	3	4	3	2	4
19	4	4	5	4	3	4	4	4	2	2	5
20	3	5	4	5	3	5	4	3	3	1	4
21	4	4	5	3	4	5	5	5	3	1	5
22	4	4	3	4	4	4	3	4	5	2	4
23	3	4	4	4	4	5	3	5	4	2	3
24	4	4	4	4	4	4	4	4	2	1	4
25	3	2	4	3	4	2	4	4	4	2	4
26	4	2	4	4	5	3	4	4	4	4	1
27	4	3	4	2	4	2	3	3	2	4	2
28	3	5	4	3	3	5	5	5	5	1	5
29	4	4	4	3	3	2	4	4	5	1	4
30	4	4	4	3	4	4	5	5	4	3	3
31	4	2	5	3	5	4	3	4	5	5	1
32	3	4	4	4	3	4	4	4	4	2	4
33	4	4	4	3	4	3	3	3	3	2	5
34	2	4	4	4	2	4	4	4	4	1	5

Resp	X_1	X_2	X_3	X_4	X_5	X_6	X_7	X_8	X_9	X_{10}	S
35	2	4	4	4	3	4	4	4	4	2	4
36	4	4	4	4	4	4	4	4	4	2	4
37	2	4	4	4	3	4	4	4	4	2	5
38	4	4	4	4	4	4	4	4	4	2	4
39	4	3	4	4	4	3	3	3	3	3	3
40	2	3	4	4	2	4	4	4	5	1	4
41	3	5	5	5	4	4	5	5	5	2	4
42	5	3	4	3	4	4	3	4	4	1	5
43	4	4	4	4	5	5	5	5	3	3	4
44	4	4	5	3	4	5	5	5	3	1	3
45	2	5	4	4	4	5	5	5	5	2	4
46	3	4	4	4	4	4	4	4	4	2	3
47	3	5	4	5	3	5	5	3	3	1	4
48	4	4	4	4	5	3	3	4	3	5	2
49	4	5	4	5	4	5	5	5	5	1	5
50	3	5	4	5	4	5	5	5	5	1	4
51	5	4	4	4	5	4	4	4	4	2	3
52	4	5	4	5	3	5	5	5	4	1	4
53	4	5	5	3	5	3	4	4	4	3	3
54	3	5	4	5	3	4	5	4	3	1	4
55	4	4	4	4	5	4	4	4	3	3	4
56	3	5	4	4	4	4	4	4	4	2	5
57	4	5	4	4	4	5	4	4	4	2	5
58	3	5	4	5	3	5	5	4	4	2	4
59	3	5	4	5	3	5	5	5	3	1	4
60	5	4	5	4	5	4	4	4	5	3	4
61	4	4	4	3	5	4	4	4	4	1	5
62	4	4	4	5	3	4	4	4	4	2	4
63	3	5	5	4	4	5	4	4	4	1	5
64	4	5	4	3	4	5	5	4	2	2	4
65	4	5	4	4	4	5	4	4	4	1	5
66	4	4	4	3	4	4	4	4	4	1	5
67	4	4	5	4	4	4	4	3	4	1	4
68	3	4	5	3	4	3	3	3	3	2	3
69	3	4	4	3	3	4	4	5	5	1	4
70	2	5	4	3	3	4	4	1	5	1	3
71	2	4	5	4	4	4	4	4	4	1	3
72	4	5	4	5	4	5	5	5	5	1	4
73	2	4	2	4	2	4	4	5	1	1	5
74	4	4	4	4	4	4	4	3	3	3	3
75	5	5	5	5	5	5	2	3	4	1	5
76	2	4	4	4	4	4	4	5	4	1	4
77	1	5	5	5	5	5	5	5	1	1	4
78	1	4	2	3	2	3	3	3	3	3	4
79	5	5	5	5	5	5	5	3	1	4	2
80	4	4	4	4	3	4	3	4	3	3	1

(Contd.)

Resp	X_1	X_2	X_3	X_4	X_5	X_6	X_7	X_8	X_9	X_{10}	S
81	4	2	4	3	4	3	3	4	4	3	2
82	5	5	5	5	5	5	5	5	1	1	4
83	4	4	4	4	5	5	5	4	4	1	4
84	4	4	2	4	4	4	4	4	4	2	5
85	4	4	4	4	4	4	4	4	4	2	3
86	4	4	4	4	4	4	4	1	2	4	2
87	4	4	5	3	3	4	4	4	4	4	1
88	4	3	5	2	3	1	2	4	2	4	1
89	4	4	4	4	4	4	3	3	3	2	4
90	5	5	5	5	5	5	5	5	1	5	1
91	4	4	3	3	2	3	3	4	5	1	4
92	4	4	4	4	4	4	4	4	1	1	5
93	4	4	4	4	4	4	4	4	4	4	2
94	1	5	5	5	5	5	5	5	5	5	1
95	5	5	5	1	5	3	3	3	5	5	1
96	4	4	4	3	3	3	3	5	5	4	2
97	5	5	5	5	5	5	5	5	2	2	4
98	1	5	5	5	5	5	5	5	1	5	1
99	2	5	5	5	2	5	5	5	5	1	4
100	4	4	4	2	4	3	1	5	1	1	5

TABLE 16.12 Model summary

Model	R	R Square	Adjusted R Square	Std. Error of the Estimate
1	0.845[a]	0.713	0.681	0.704

[a] Predictors: (Constant), x_{10}, x_3, x_9, x_1, x_8, x_2, x_7, x_5, x_4, x_6

TABLE 16.13 Coefficients[a] of satisfaction function for aerated drinks

Model		Unstandardized Coefficients		Standardized Coefficients	t	Sig.
		B	Std. Error	Beta		
1	(Constant)	6.185	0.797		7.758	0.000
	x_1	0.026	0.080	0.021	0.329	0.743
	x_2	0.069	0.113	0.046	0.610	0.543
	x_3	–0.384	0.127	–0.191	–3.029	0.003
	x_4	–0.048	0.107	–0.034	–0.453	0.652
	x_5	0.211	0.104	0.141	2.028	0.046
	x_6	–0.021	0.125	–0.016	–0.172	0.864
	x_7	0.003	0.104	0.002	0.024	0.981
	x_8	0.017	0.095	0.012	0.183	0.855
	x_9	–0.035	0.065	–0.031	–0.535	0.594
	x_{10}	–0.859	0.067	–0.861	–12.818	0.000

[a] Dependent Variable: S

The results indicate that 71.3 per cent of the variations in the dependent variable, i.e. satisfaction, is explained by the set of 10 independent variables. The variables X_3, X_5 and X_{10} are significant variables. The coefficient of the variable X_{10} indicates that the consumers do not perceive aerated drinks to be better than fruit juices and that has resulted in a negative and significant coefficient of the variable.

This shows that the aerated Drink Company can perceive fruit juices as a potential threat. Further, the variable X_3 that aerated drinks are very convenient to serve appears as a negative sign, which is surprising. Moreover, the coefficient of this variable is significant. Similarly, the fifth variable, that aerated drinks are very tasty, is significant and positive. This shows that this variable is very important and contributing to the satisfaction of the consumers. Therefore, the aerated drinks company should try to cash on this and this should be reflected in their advertisements. All other variables have the correct signs. The sign of the coefficient of X_3 could be due to the problem of multicollinearity. One way to overcome the problem of multicollinearity is to run a factor analysis of the ten independent variables (X_1, X_2, ..., X_{10}) and use the factor score output as independent variables in the regression.

The results of the factor analysis carried out on ten independent variables are presented in Tables 16.14 to 16.18.

TABLE 16.14 KMO and Bartlett's test

Kaiser-Meyer-Olkin Measure of Sampling Adequacy.		0.722
Bartlett's Test of Sphericity	Approx. Chi-Square	224.769
	d.f.	45
	Sig.	0.000

TABLE 16.15 Communalities

	Initial	Extraction
x_1	1.000	0.597
x_2	1.000	0.587
x_3	1.000	0.523
x_4	1.000	0.632
x_5	1.000	0.686
x_6.	1.000	0.771
x_7	1.000	0.564
x_8	1.000	0.364
x_9	1.000	0.526
x_{10}	1.000	0.547

Extraction Method: Principal Component Analysis.

TABLE 16.16 Total variance explained

Component	Initial Eigenvalues			Extraction Sums of Squared Loadings			Rotation Sums of Squared Loadings		
	Total	Percentage of Variance	Cumulative Percentage	Total	Percentage of Variance	Cumulative %	Total	Percentage of Variance	Cumulative %
1	2.935	29.349	29.349	2.935	29.349	29.349	2.857	28.572	28.572
2	1.842	18.424	47.773	1.842	18.424	47.773	1.623	16.231	44.803
3	1.020	10.202	57.975	1.020	10.202	57.975	1.317	13.172	57.975
4	0.922	9.223	67.198						
5	0.833	8.335	75.532						
6	0.699	6.994	82.526						
7	0.554	5.540	88.066						
8	0.487	4.870	92.936						
9	0.442	4.423	97.359						
10	0.264	2.641	100.000						

Extraction Method: Principal Component Analysis.

TABLE 16.17
Component matrix[a]

	Component		
	1	2	3
X_1	−0.245	0.535	0.500
X_2	0.745	0.067	−0.167
X_3	0.241	0.632	0.255
X_4	0.767	0.059	−0.200
X_5	0.012	0.825	0.079
X_6	0.861	0.040	0.166
X_7	0.734	0.103	−0.120
X_8	0.486	−0.103	0.343
X_9	−0.039	−0.422	0.588
X_{10}	−0.395	0.517	−0.353

Extraction Method: Principal Component Analysis.
[a] 3 components extracted.

TABLE 16.18
Rotated component matrix[a]

	Component		
	1	2	3
X_1	−0.277	0.715	0.095
X_2	0.766	−0.023	−0.015
X_3	0.253	0.675	−0.056
X_4	0.793	−0.047	−0.035
X_5	0.082	0.747	−0.349
X_6	0.815	0.127	0.301
X_7	0.750	0.032	0.004
X_8	0.400	0.093	0.442
X_9	−0.191	−0.058	0.697
X_{10}	−0.267	0.257	−0.640

Extraction Method: Principal Component Analysis.
Rotation Method: Varimax with Kaiser Normalization.
[a] Rotation converged in 5 iterations.

The results indicate that a factor analysis can be applied to the set of given data as the value of KMO statistics is greater than 0.5 and the Bartlett's test of Sphericity is significant (Table 16.14). There are three factors resulting from the analysis explaining a total of 57.975 per cent of the variations in the entire data set (Table 16.16). The percentage of variation explained by the first, second and third factors are 28.572, 16.231 and 13.172 per cent respectively after varimax rotation is performed. We will use the rotated component matrix using 0.63 as a cut-off point for factor loading for naming the factors (See Table 16.18). In this way we will get three factors. Factor 1 will comprise variables X_2 (aerated drinks are bad for health), X_4 (aerated drinks should be avoided with age), X_6 (aerated drinks are not good for children) and X7 (aerated drinks should be consumed occasionally). This factor can be named as HEALTH RELATED CONCERNS. Factor 2 comprises X_1 (aerated drinks are refreshing), X_3 (aerated drinks are convenient to serve), X_5 (aerated drinks are very tasty). Therefore, factor 2 can be named as PRODUCT BENEFITS. The third factor comprises X_9 (aerated drinks are not as good as energy drinks) and X10 (aerated drinks are better than fruit juices). This factor can be labelled as COMPARATIVE FACTOR. It would be interesting to know that the factor loading for factor 3 with variable X_{10} is negative. Since the variable X_{10} means that aerated drinks are better than fruit juices, a negative of this statement would be that fruit juices are better than aerated drinks and this is the reason why the factor loading came out to be negative.

The three factors would result in three factor scores, which one can obtain using SPSS software. The factor scores for the three factors corresponding to 100 respondents are given in Table 16.19.

TABLE 16.19 Factor scores for three factors

Resp No.	Factor Score 1	Factor Score 2	Factor Score 3
1	0.2025	0.15719	0.1914
2	1.51105	−0.79256	0.39788
3	−1.00077	−0.66562	−0.2532
4	−0.23284	−1.26276	−2.96895
5	−0.45369	−1.29626	−0.40107
6	−0.36795	−0.68686	0.4222
7	−0.58014	0.19074	−0.58813
8	0.75699	−1.26523	0.48518
9	0.43582	−0.02072	1.10006
10	−0.56425	0.54785	−0.97364
11	0.78306	0.45198	0.39853
12	−0.59783	0.4272	−1.754
13	−0.46812	0.29976	0.45389
14	−1.73298	0.08667	−0.94528
15	0.62587	0.90645	0.84731
16	0.09846	−0.25195	−0.35152
17	−2.87113	0.03163	2.03164
18	−0.94379	0.10934	−0.18649
19	0.18923	0.23788	−0.43658
20	0.96208	−1.08996	−0.35469
21	0.51703	1.12285	0.94085
22	−0.69195	−0.34228	0.85841
23	0.0838	0.01981	0.79749
24	0.15092	0.01193	−0.34626
25	−1.55816	−0.28752	0.06447
26	−1.10319	0.84932	−0.55592
27	−1.94396	0.01105	−1.78376
28	0.58774	−0.45048	1.72915
29	−1.16845	−0.37279	1.15197
30	−0.06348	0.51132	0.44107
31	−1.5239	1.87952	0.1172
32	−0.03277	−0.76861	0.28016
33	−1.05747	−0.02494	−0.58442
34	0.09781	−1.82459	0.59433
35	0.10986	−1.27013	0.03485

(Contd.)

Resp No.	Factor Score 1	Factor Score 2	Factor Score 3
36	–0.13268	0.23894	0.33345
37	0.10986	–1.27013	0.03485
38	–0.13268	0.23894	0.33345
39	–1.08838	0.00256	–0.9735
40	–0.3641	–1.67448	1.23835
41	1.10082	0.50986	0.76742
42	–1.23638	0.84763	1.29522
43	0.72192	0.96046	–0.21328
44	0.51703	1.12285	0.94085
45	1.07761	–0.4793	0.78232
46	0.00995	–0.26259	0.08814
47	1.28319	–1.10298	–0.4412
48	–0.65762	0.69985	–1.60134
49	1.15819	0.39357	1.49835
50	1.30082	–0.10796	1.25305
51	–0.2326	1.24649	0.38675
52	1.24195	–0.20174	1.16678
53	–0.28972	1.38371	–0.32258
54	1.11609	–1.06193	–0.22496
55	0.00584	0.70411	–0.74962
56	0.34538	–0.32341	–0.03229
57	0.48378	0.29228	0.41631
58	1.23999	–0.81004	0.13446
59	1.51105	–0.79256	0.39788
60	–0.27805	2.06775	0.62801
61	–0.39449	0.77827	0.65096
62	0.15978	–0.34883	0.38342
63	0.76876	0.42585	0.62361
64	0.72266	0.18243	–0.57532
65	0.51444	0.24384	0.78378
66	–0.4372	0.27225	0.84297
67	–0.10427	0.71883	0.36652
68	–0.80315	0.15706	–0.74459
69	–0.34983	–0.49079	1.7328
70	–0.3275	–1.674	–0.3111
71	0.29492	–0.12902	0.29544
72	1.15819	0.39357	1.49835
73	0.36779	–3.30432	–0.72718
74	–0.15081	0.04288	–0.97714
75	0.10523	1.72402	0.53364

Resp No.	Factor Score 1	Factor Score 2	Factor Score 3
76	0.29717	−0.65734	0.62984
77	2.24638	−0.27862	−1.4388
78	−0.96904	−3.86021	−1.47407
79	1.35601	1.56239	−2.39904
80	−0.4007	−0.2949	−0.27909
81	−1.77153	0.38964	0.23212
82	1.67586	1.7275	−0.45757
83	0.54283	0.79765	0.6257
84	−0.35606	−1.12813	0.16317
85	−0.13268	0.23894	0.33345
86	−0.28286	−0.3084	−2.70727
87	−0.46022	0.59509	0.01772
88	−2.3632	0.24265	−1.20387
89	−0.44126	0.00747	−0.52317
90	1.55321	1.92125	−1.92743
91	−1.36294	−1.43516	1.54864
92	0.2774	−0.07736	−0.86985
93	−0.19401	0.33582	−0.40148
94	1.61784	0.27229	−0.81431
95	−1.72556	2.09271	−0.33755
96	−1.18659	0.05492	0.75891
97	1.51872	1.86523	−0.30144
98	2.12373	−0.08486	−2.90867
99	1.46971	−0.93799	1.4769
100	−1.5234	0.16627	−0.11

Now, these factor scores could be used as independent variables (instead of using $X_1, X_2, ..., X_{10}$) and satisfaction level (S) as a dependent variable and the following regression could be obtained as given in Tables 16.20 and 16.21.

The regression results indicate that 33.4 per cent of the variations in the satisfaction level are explained by three factors. Further, the coefficients of all the factors are significant. The third factor works out to be the most important factor in explaining the satisfaction, followed by the second and the first factor. This is because the absolute standardized coefficient is highest for the third factor followed by the second and first factors.

TABLE 16.20
Model summary

Model	R	R Square	Adjusted R Square	Std. Error of the Estimate
1	0.578[a]	0.334	0.313	1.034

[a] Predictors: (Constant), REGR factor score 3 for analysis 1, REGR factor score 2 for analysis 1, REGR factor score 1 for analysis 1

TABLE 16.21
Coefficients[a]

Model		Unstandardized Coefficients		Standardized Coefficients	t	Sig.
		B	Std. Error	Beta		
1	(Constant)	3.600	0.103		34.817	0.000
	REGR factor score 1 for analysis 1	0.243	0.104	0.195	2.339	0.021
	REGR factor score 2 for analysis 1	-0.284	0.104	-0.228	-2.737	0.007
	REGR factor score 3 for analysis 1	0.616	0.104	0.494	5.923	0.000

[a] Dependent Variable: S

Simplifying the discrimination solution: In the next chapter, Discriminant Analysis, a number of independent variables are used as antecedent variables to measure causation for a non-metric variable. In this exercise the independent variables can be reduced to a manageable number of factors which are formulated by the grouping of variables using factor analysis.

Simplifying the cluster analysis solution: Factor analysis is also able to simplify the data used in a cluster analysis. This technique will be discussed in detail in Chapter 18. The technique involves grouping objects, cases or entities on the basis of multiple variables. Here, again, to make the data manageable, the variables selected for grouping can be reduced to a more manageable number using a factor analysis and the obtained factor scores can then be used to cluster the objects/cases under study.

Perceptual mapping in multidimensional scaling: In Chapter 19 (Multidimensional Scaling) we would be discussing the techniques of deriving the spatial map of objects or brands multidimensional scaling. The technique forms a part of a larger group called perceptual mapping. Factor analysis that results in factors can be used as dimensions with the factor scores as the coordinates to develop attribute-based perceptual maps where one is able to comprehend the placement of brands or products according to the identified factors under study.

Therefore, it is noted that factor analysis is a very powerful technique of data reduction and the factor scores have applications in various other multivariate techniques.

SUMMARY

- Factor analysis is a multivariate data reduction technique. All the variables under investigation are analysed together to extract the underlying factors. Factor analysis helps in identifying underlying structure of the data. Factor analysis makes use of metric data. A factor is a linear combination of variables.
- The variables for factor analysis are gathered through exploratory research, which is carried out by conducting focus group discussions, unstructured interviews with knowledgeable people, literature survey, and analysis of case studies, etc. The variables used in factor analysis are standardized. The basic condition for applying factor analysis is that the variables should be highly correlated. The significance of correlation matrix is conduced using Bartlett's test of sphericity. Further, the number of observations in the sample should be at least four to five times the number of variables. Finally, the value of KMO statistics should be greater than 0.5. The KMO statistic compares the magnitude of the observed correlation coefficients with the magnitude of partial correlation coefficients.
- The most important step in factor analysis is to decide about how many factors are to be extracted from the given set of data. For this, the principal component method is used. Here the first factor is extracted in such a way that it explains the largest portion of total variance. This explained variance is subtracted from the original input matrix so as to yield

a residual matrix. A second principal factor is extracted from the residual matrix in such a way that the second takes care of most of the residual variance and so on, and this procedure is repeated until there is a very little variance to be explained. How many factors are to be extracted is based on the criterion of the Kaiser Guttman method.

- The concept of factor score is discussed in this chapter. The correlation coefficient between the factor score and variable is called factor loading. In most computer printouts, the matrix of factor loadings or a factor matrix or a component matrix is presented. Factor loadings are used to compute eigenvalues for each factor and the communalities of each variable.
- For the interpretation of factors, the factor loading matrix is rotated. There are various methods of rotations and here varimax method is used. The purpose of rotation is to bring the smallest loadings close to zero and its largest loadings towards unity. The idea is to get some factors that have a few variables that are correlated high with that factor and some that are correlated poorly with that factor. Once this is done, a cut-off point for factor loadings is selected. There is no hard and fast rule for deciding the cut-off point but generally it is chosen above 0.5. Therefore the variables attached to a factor with a loading of 0.5 and above are used for naming a factor. This is very subjective exercise and different researchers may name same factors differently. It may be noted that if a variable belongs to one factor, then it should not belong to another factor. If this happens it means that the question has either not been understood properly by the respondent or it might not have been phrased properly.
- It may be emphasized here that the total variances explained by all the factors taken together remain the same after rotation. The variance for individual factor may undergo a change. However, the communalities for each variable remain unchanged. Factor analysis could be used to design a multiple item scale. Further, it could be used in regression analysis to overcome the problem of multicollinearity.
- Factor analysis also has applications in other multivariate techniques like discriminant analysis, cluster analysis and multidimensional scaling.

KEY TERMS

- Bartlett's test of sphericity
- Chi-square statistic
- Cluster analysis
- Communalities
- Component matrix
- Correlation matrix
- Eigenvalue
- Factor loading
- Factor score
- Factor score coefficient
- Kaiser's method
- KMO statistic
- Multicollinearity
- Principal component method
- Regression analysis
- Rotated component matrix
- Standardized coefficients
- Standardized score
- Total variance explained
- Varimax rotation

CHAPTER REVIEW QUESTIONS

Objective Type Questions

State whether the following statements are true (T) or false (F).

1. Factor analysis is a data reduction technique.
2. There is no distinction between a dependent and independent variable while conducting factor analysis.
3. Factors are statistically independent.
4. The significance of the correlation matrix in factor analysis is carried out using KMO statistics.
5. If there are 20 variables on which factor analysis is performed, the degrees of freedom corresponding to chi-square statistics for Barttlet test of sphericity is 30.
6. The communality of each variable remains unchanged whether we use principal component method or varimax rotation.
7. The total variance explained under both the principal component and varimax rotation is the same while the variance for individual factor may vary for the two methods.
8. Factor loading gives the correlation coefficient between a factor score and a variable.
9. A factor is a linear combination of variables.
10. The variables to be used for factor analysis need not be standardized before carrying out factor analysis.

11. One of the important conditions for carrying out factor analysis is that the variables are statistically independent.
12. Factor scores could be used as independent variables in the regression model to overcome the problem of multicollinearity.
13. The purpose of carrying out varimax rotation is to get some factors that have a few variables that correlate high with that factor and some that correlate poorly with that factor.
14. Any factor could have an eigenvalue of less than one.
15. Factor analysis examines whether the set of variables are independent or not.
16. For the application of factor analysis, the size of the sample should be at least four times the number of variables.
17. It is difficult to interpret the factors arising from unrotated factor loading matrix.
18. The criterion of Kaiser method states that only those factors having an eigenvalue of greater than or equal to 1 should be selected.
19. A variable could appear in more than one factor.
20. Factor analysis could be used for segmentation exercise.

Conceptual Questions

1. What is a factor loading matrix? How is it obtained? How can the entries in the table can be used to compute eigenvalues for each factor and communality for each variable?
2. What is the basic purpose of factor analysis? Explain the conditions that are required to be satisfied before carrying out a factor analysis exercise.
3. Explain briefly the concept of Kaiser method in deciding the number of factors to be extracted.
4. Describe the following:
   (i) Eigenvalue
   (ii) Communality
   (iii) Factor loading
   (iv) Bartlett's test of sphericity
   (v) Component matrix
   (vi) Varimax rotation
5. Why is varimax rotation method used instead of the principal component method?
6. What is the role of communalities in measuring the total variance explained by the extracted factors?

Application Questions

1. Interpret the results of a factor analysis done on the following questions to determine why people work in an organization. The interpretation would involve the following:
   (a) Interpret the rotated solutions and name the factors.
   (b) Calculate the eigenvalues of each factor.
   (c) Calculate the communalities for each variable.
   (d) What is the contribution of the identified factors towards the total variance?

Table 1 KMO and Bartlett's Test

Kaiser-Meyer-Olkin Measure of Sampling Adequacy.		0.698
Bartlett's Test of Sphericity	Approx. Chi-Square	1267.330
	d.f.	15
	Sig.	0.000

Table 2 Rotated Component Matrix

Attributes	Component 1	Component 2
Add to image of company	–0.028	0.221
I enjoy working in the company	0.928	0.194
My company is well respected	0.976	0.142
The fellow workers are helpful	0.376	0.902
Team working is recognized by the company	0.375	0.903
We have a very relaxed working atmosphere in the company	0.953	0.145

2. Interpret the results of a factor analysis done on the following questions to interpret the underlying dimensions related to attitudes towards job anxiety. The interpretation would involve:
   (a) Interpret the rotated solutions and name the factors.
   (b) Calculate the eigenvalues of each factor.
   (c) Calculate the communalities for each variable.
   (d) What is the contribution of the identified factors towards the total variance?

Table 1 KMO and Bartlett's Test

Kaiser-Meyer-Olkin Measure of Sampling Adequacy		0.760
Bartlett's Test of Sphericity	Approx. Chi-Square	1552.631
	d.f.	15
	Sig.	0.000

Table 2 Rotated Component Matrix

Attributes	Component 1	Component 2
I get heart palpitations when my boss calls me	0.971	0.088
Work life also spills over to personal life	0.050	0.974
I do not feel like meeting people after I go home from office	0.085	0.920
A sitting job leads to digestive problems	0.975	0.095
I always like to stay back after working hours in the office	–0.083	–0.971
When I retire I might not be physically fit to enjoy my retired life	0.977	0.040

CASE 16.1

PURCHASE OF B-SEGMENT CARS IN INDIA

The Indian automobile market is expected to grow at a compound annual growth rate (CAGR) of 9.5 per cent amounting to ₹13,008 million by 2010. The contribution of the commercial vehicle segment has been tremendous to the growth of the automobile industry.

The contribution of foreign companies to the automobile industry in India is in terms of technology transfers, joint ventures, strategic alliance and financial collaborations.

The purchase of motorcycles and cars in rural as well as urban areas is increasing. In India, the sales figure of major car manufacturers was 67.4 lakh units for the year ending March 2007, whereas that of export of cars was 39,295 units.

It is known that the B segment forms the largest part of the consumer vehicle market in India. With the boom in the Indian economy post 1990s, a large number of consumers have graduated from two-wheelers to cars, thus leading to a boom in the B-segment market. The B-segment car market constitutes the likes of Maruti 800, Alto, Wagon R, Hyundai Santro, Tata Indica and Fiat Palio. Now with the increasing income levels, consumers are opting for more than one car per family, with the second car generally belonging to the B-segment.

A study was carried out to understand what influences the purchase of B-segment cars in India. An exploratory research was conducted in the form of personal unstructured interviews with B-segment car users. A lot of literature was also reviewed on the subject. Based on the insight obtained from the exploratory research, a number of variables were identified that influence consumers' buying behaviour in B-segment cars. Using the information identified, a questionnaire was prepared. A part of the questionnaire seeking information on the importance the consumers attach to various attributes is reproduced below. A sample of 100 current car owners of B-segment cars in the NCR region was contacted for filling up the questionnaires. Only 75 responded to the survey. The question seeking information on the criterion for the purchase of B-segment car was phrased as:

How important according to you are the following criteriea in the purchase of B-segment cars? Please rate them on a 7-point scale (where 1 = extremely important, 2 = very important, 3 = important, 4 = neither important nor unimportant, 5 = unimportant, 6 = very unimportant, 7 = extremely unimportant) by putting a tick (✓) at the appropriate place.

Criteria	Extremely Important	Very Important	Important	Neither Important nor Unimportant	Unimportant	Very Unimportant	Extremely Unimportant
(a) Price on road (X_1)							
(b) Brand name (X_2)							
(c) Engine capacity (X_3)							
(d) Looks and design (exterior and interior) (X_4)							
(e) Fuel efficiency (X_5)							
(f) Discount schemes (X_6)							
(g) Resale value (X_7)							
(h) After sale services (X_8)							
(i) Running and maintaining cost (X_9)							
(j) Convenience features (power steering, power windows, etc.) (X_{10})							
(k) Purpose of purchase (X_{11})							
(l) Performance information available (X_{12})							
(m) Driving pleasure (X_{13})							
(n) Car image and positioning (X_{14})							
(o) Economical (X_{15})							
(p) Colors available (X_{16})							
(q) Advertising and marketing (X_{17})							
(r) Safety (X_{18})							

The data pertaining to the 75 respondents is given in Table 16.22.

Table 16.22 Data of select variables for the purchase of B-segment cars in India

Resp. No.	X_1	X_2	X_3	X_4	X_5	X_6	X_7	X_8	X_9	X_{10}	X_{11}	X_{12}	X_{13}	X_{14}	X_{15}	X_{16}	X_{17}	X_{18}
1	1	1	2	4	2	4	4	4	2	2	3	2	1	4	2	1	6	1
2	1	1	2	2	1	2	4	3	2	2	3	4	3	3	2	4	3	3
3	1	1	1	1	1	3	2	3	2	1	3	3	1	2	3	3	4	2
4	1	1	1	1	1	4	2	2	2	2	2	3	2	3	1	3	3	2
5	2	1	4	3	2	3	3	2	2	3	3	4	1	3	2	3	2	2
6	2	2	2	3	2	3	5	2	2	2	2	3	1	3	1	1	3	1
7	1	1	1	1	1	2	2	2	1	1	4	4	1	4	1	5	4	1
8	1	1	3	3	3	4	5	2	2	1	3	4	1	4	2	1	4	1
9	3	1	2	1	3	4	4	3	3	1	1	3	1	3	3	1	2	1
10	1	1	1	1	3	4	4	3	3	1	4	4	1	5	2	1	3	3
11	4	1	4	1	1	3	3	2	2	1	2	3	1	3	2	1	4	1
12	1	1	2	1	2	3	3	3	3	1	2	2	1	1	3	5	3	2
13	3	2	3	1	3	4	4	3	3	1	4	4	1	3	3	1	4	2
14	1	2	1	1	1	4	2	2	2	2	1	2	3	4	1	4	5	3
15	2	1	1	1	2	2	2	1	2	1	3	2	1	1	3	1	5	1
16	2	2	4	2	1	2	2	1	1	2	5	4	2	3	1	3	5	1
17	2	3	1	2	1	5	3	3	2	1	4	2	2	5	2	3	4	1
18	3	2	3	2	2	3	3	2	2	2	3	999	2	3	4	3	4	4
19	3	2	1	4	1	3	4	2	1	3	2	4	3	4	2	5	5	1
20	1	1	2	999	2	3	4	999	2	2	1	3	2	2	3	2	2	1
21	1	1	3	1	1	3	3	2	1	3	1	3	1	4	3	4	4	3
22	1	1	2	1	1	2	2	2	1	3	1	1	1	5	3	1	4	3
23	1	2	3	3	1	3	3	2	2	3	3	3	3	3	2	3	2	2
24	1	1	1	3	2	3	3	2	1	2	1	4	3	5	1	4	4	1
25	2	1	1	2	1	3	2	3	1	3	3	1	2	3	3	2	5	1
26	3	2	4	1	3	4	4	2	2	1	4	1	1	1	2	1	5	1
27	1	2	3	3	3	2	1	1	2	2	3	3	3	2	3	4	3	3
28	1	3	2	4	2	3	4	3	2	3	2	3	3	4	1	4	4	3
29	1	1	1	1	1	2	1	1	1	1	1	1	1	1	1	1	1	1
30	1	2	1	3	1	4	3	3	2	2	4	3	4	5	2	6	7	1
31	2	2	3	2	4	3	2	3	3	3	3	5	3	2	3	5	3	3
32	2	1	3	2	3	3	2	1	3	1	1	2	1	3	3	5	4	1
33	2	1	1	1	2	5	4	2	2	3	1	2	2	2	4	4	1	1
34	2	2	4	3	2	3	3	3	2	3	3	3	3	3	2	7	3	2
35	2	1	2	1	1	1	5	1	3	1	4	2	2	4	2	1	1	1
36	1	2	1	3	1	1	2	2	1	2	2	1	2	2	1	2	4	2
37	3	2	4	3	1	4	3	2	1	1	3	2	1	1	1	4	3	1
38	1	1	1	1	1	3	2	2	1	3	2	3	2	2	1	4	4	2

Resp. No.	X_1	X_2	X_3	X_4	X_5	X_6	X_7	X_8	X_9	X_{10}	X_{11}	X_{12}	X_{13}	X_{14}	X_{15}	X_{16}	X_{17}	X_{18}
39	3	2	1	1	1	4	4	1	1	1	2	2	1	2	2	1	4	1
40	1	2	3	1	2	3	2	3	2	1	3	4	3	3	3	1	3	2
41	2	2	4	2	3	3	3	3	5	2	1	4	2	3	3	4	5	4
42	3	2	2	2	1	4	2	2	3	3	3	2	2	3	3	4	7	3
43	3	2	2	2	2	3	2	1	2	2	2	3	2	2	2	3	3	1
44	3	1	2	3	2	4	4	3	3	4	3	5	1	2	3	3	3	1
45	3	2	3	2	2	4	3	1	1	1	4	2	2	2	1	2	4	1
46	2	2	2	3	1	2	2	2	3	1	3	2	2	3	2	3	2	2
47	3	3	2	2	3	2	2	1	1	2	3	2	1	5	3	3	5	2
48	3	2	2	2	2	3	3	2	2	2	4	3	3	3	2	6	3	3
49	1	2	2	3	2	4	1	2	2	3	4	3	2	2	2	1	3	2
50	2	2	3	2	2	4	3	1	2	2	4	3	2	3	2	3	4	2
51	2	2	3	1	2	3	4	1	2	2	4	3	1	2	3	3	3	2
52	1	2	3	3	2	1	2	3	3	2	4	3	1	3	1	4	5	1
53	2	3	4	3	2	2	3	1	1	1	2	1	1	2	1	3	4	1
54	1	2	3	2	4	5	4	1	3	2	7	1	3	4	6	1	3	1
55	1	3	4	3	2	3	3	2	3	3	4	3	3	3	2	5	5	4
56	3	1	2	1	1	4	3	2	2	1	2	4	1	4	2	4	2	1
57	1	2	2	3	1	4	2	2	1	3	1	2	2	2	1	4	4	2
58	2	1	3	1	2	2	2	5	3	2	3	2	3	2	2	1	4	1
59	3	3	3	3	3	3	4	3	3	3	999	4	3	3	3	4	4	3
60	2	2	3	1	2	2	4	3	1	2	2	3	1	2	2	1	3	1
61	3	2	4	1	3	5	6	4	5	4	3	5	6	7	5	7	7	5
62	3	2	1	2	1	4	4	2	2	1	999	2	1	4	2	5	6	1
63	3	2	2	2	2	3	4	2	3	2	1	2	1	1	2	2	4	2
64	1	2	2	2	1	2	2	1	1	1	1	1	1	1	1	1	1	1
65	2	1	2	3	1	4	3	3	1	2	2	3	3	4	1	4	4	1
66	2	2	2	3	3	1	2	2	2	2	3	3	2	2	2	2	3	2
67	2	1	1	1	3	3	2	2	3	1	3	2	1	3	2	3	4	1
68	2	2	3	3	2	2	3	1	2	1	4	3	2	3	2	3	3	2
69	1	1	1	1	1	1	1	1	1	3	3	2	2	3	2	4	3	2
70	1	1	3	3	3	4	4	3	3	3	3	3	2	3	2	3	4	1
71	1	1	4	2	2	2	2	2	2	3	1	4	2	2	1	2	2	1
72	2	2	3	3	2	2	3	1	2	1	1	3	2	4	2	3	3	2
73	3	3	2	2	1	4	4	2	2	2	3	3	2	3	1	3	2	2
74	1	1	2	1	1	4	3	2	1	1	3	3	3	3	3	5	3	2
75	2	3	2	2	1	3	4	2	2	3	2	1	1	3	1	3	4	2

Notes: X_1, X_2, X_3 ..., X_{18} are already explained in the questionnaire.
999 = Missing value

QUESTION

1. Conduct a factor analysis to identify the underlying factors that are important to the buyers of B-segment cars. Give appropriate names to the factors.

CASE 16.2

DIRECT SELLING OF COSMETICS

In direct selling, the product or service is sold from person to person. There are no intermediaries involved. The products are sold to the consumers by independent salespeople who are called consultant representatives or distributors. The products are sold in parties or in home product demonstrations and one-on-one selling.

Worldwide, the direct selling industry is huge and accounts for sales of US$ 109 billion through the activities of more than 58 million direct salespersons in 165 countries.

Direct selling is one of the fastest growing Industries in India with an estimated current turnover of over ₹3,110 crore. The industry is experiencing dynamic growth that is expected to continue for many years to come.

Direct selling offers consumers a convenient and more informed way to buy along with money back guarantee and refund policies.

There is a growing middle class in the country and, therefore, companies are targeting consumers in smaller towns in addition to bigger towns and metros.

There can be a number of innovations in the direct selling industry to meet today's customers' ever-changing demands and improve their standards of living. Recession does not worry direct selling companies. As people like to pamper themselves, the sales of cosmetics also grow.

At present, direct selling companies like Amway, Modicare, Avon and Oriflame dominate the market in the country. However, there are several other players operating in the segment, which are acting as impediments to the sector's growth.

Customers value the advantages of direct selling in the form of:

- Personalized attention
- A good selection of products
- Convenience of a one-to-one basis

Agents play an important role in direct selling business as they are the intermediaries between the direct selling company and the ultimate consumer.

- They influence the buying decision of consumers.
- They are the representatives of the company and carry the image of the company they are working for.
- As they directly interact with clients, they are the ones who build the feeling of trust among consumers.
- The consumers' perception about the company and its products is through the agents' ability to deal with them.
- After-sales service is also an important consideration for the consumer while judging a business.

In today's world of rapid change, direct selling offers the companies a direct distribution channel that can be accessed immediately, bypassing rigid and costly traditional distribution channels.

The Indian Direct Selling Association (DSA) is an association of companies engaged in the business of direct selling in India. Its members are of high national and international repute having set standards in delivering quality goods and in following ethical business practices.

The Indian Direct Selling Association was formed in 1996. It is a self-regulatory body for direct selling member companies in India. It is affiliated to the World Federation of Direct Selling Association, USA (an umbrella body for 58 DSAs across the world).

The association conducts various research products for the benefit of the industry and is a valuable source of information on the direct selling industry. The Indian DSA handles all India operations of the industry from New Delhi.

The objectives of the Indian Direct Selling Association (IDSA) is to provide an ambience of growth for everyone involved in the experience of direct selling in any form. The mission is accomplished through the following objectives:

- To promote and protect the interests of the direct selling industry and of consumers.
- To support and protect the character and status of the direct selling industry and to assist and guide in maintaining qualitative standards in direct selling.

The IDSA will work towards the enhancement of direct selling as a profession so that all those engaged in it can work in a congenial ambience of growth and achieve their objectives to earn, learn, and become independent and well respected. The concept of direct selling creates the need for a code of conduct which would protect the rights of the customer and ensure that the companies and their sales people practise ethical behaviour.

Leading Players in the Market

(a) **Mary Kay Cosmetics Pvt. Ltd** plans to invest about ₹1,000 crore in the next three years in India. It is one of the largest direct selling chains of cosmetic products. The brand Mary Kay was launched in India in September 2007. It has a sales force of over 3000 women. The company plans to train its workforce and consolidate its distribution network and sales force.

(b) **Amway India Enterprises Pvt. Ltd** plans to expand fast. Its sales in 2007 was ₹8 billion which increased to ₹11.28 billion in 2008 thereby registering a growth of 40 per cent. They are looking for a growth of 25 per cent next year. They feel that recession in not going to have any adverse impact on their business as their industry is not affected by recession. They plan to enhance the production capacities in 2009 so as to reach a sales target of ₹25 crore by 2012.

(c) **Oriflame** is growing very fast trying to gain the market share. It has more than one lakh consultants and plans to increase the sales at least three times over the next five years.

A survey was carried out using a sample of 129 female respondents to understand the underlying factors important to the consumers while buying cosmetics. The sample was selected using convenience sampling design in the NCR region. The following question was asked of the respondents:

Please rate the importance of the following variables on a 7-point scale (where 1 = Highly important, ..., 7 = Least important) while buying cosmetics.

1. Price	**Highly Important**	1	2	3	4	5	6	7	**Least Important**
2. Availability	**Highly Important**	1	2	3	4	5	6	7	**Least Important**
3. Durability	**Highly Important**	1	2	3	4	5	6	7	**Least Important**
4. Brand name	**Highly Important**	1	2	3	4	5	6	7	**Least Important**
5. Previous Experience	**Highly Important**	1	2	3	4	5	6	7	**Least Important**
6. Dealer's knowledge	**Highly Important**	1	2	3	4	5	6	7	**Least Important**
7. Variety	**Highly Important**	1	2	3	4	5	6	7	**Least Important**
8. Refund Policy	**Highly Important**	1	2	3	4	5	6	7	**Least Important**
9. Word of mouth	**Highly Important**	1	2	3	4	5	6	7	**Least Important**
10. Demonstration	**Highly Important**	1	2	3	4	5	6	7	**Least Important**
11. Packaging	**Highly Important**	1	2	3	4	5	6	7	**Least Important**
12. Advertising	**Highly Important**	1	2	3	4	5	6	7	**Least Important**
13. Herbal contents	**Highly Important**	1	2	3	4	5	6	7	**Least Important**
14. Offers	**Highly Important**	1	2	3	4	5	6	7	**Least Important**

A factor analysis was conducted using the data on 129 respondents. Some of the results of factor analysis are given below (Tables 1 and 2).

Table 1 KMO and Bartlett's test

Kaiser-Meyer-Olkin Measure of Sampling Adequacy		0.526
Bartlett's Test of Sphericity	Approx. Chi-Square	392.049
	d.f.	91
	Sig.	0.000

Table 2 Rotated component matrix[a]

	Component				
	1	2	3	4	5
Price	0.666	0.209	−0.180	-0.310	0.028
Availability	0.097	0.759	0.163	0.056	0.041
Durability	−0.049	0.809	0.000	0.143	0.097
Brand name	−0.251	0.453	0.410	0.143	−0.123
Previous experience	−0.006	0.014	−0.009	−0.026	0.869
Dealer's knowledge	0.040	0.154	0.182	0.560	0.528
Variety	0.113	0.213	−0.072	0.810	0.085
Refund Policy	0.856	−0.101	−0.035	0.311	−0.045
Word of mouth	0.415	−0.436	0.341	−0.053	0.259
Demonstration	0.676	0.047	0.105	0.036	0.052
Packaging	0.210	0.276	0.704	−0.138	0.063
Advertising	−0.003	−0.046	0.793	0.230	0.000
Herbal contents	−0.091	0.021	0.280	0.564	−0.358
Offers	0.684	−0.140	0.105	−0.013	−0.009

Extraction Method: Principal Component Analysis.
Rotation Method: Varimax with Kaiser Normalization.
[a] Rotation converged in 6 iterations.

QUESTIONS

1. Prepare the labels for the factors given in the rotated component matrix and explain your rationale. Also interpret these factors.
2. Compute the amount of variations explained by each factor. Interpret your findings.
3. Determine the variance summarized by these factors combined. Explain the meaning of the total variance summarized.
4. Compute the communalities for each of the 14 variables and interpret the same.
5. If a cut-off point of 0.5 for the factor loading is selected for labelling of the factor, what problems would you face? Explain the possible reason for such a problem.
6. Comment on the factor analysis exercise carried above.

CASE 16.3

B-SEGMENT CAR RATING STUDY

The following three tables present the output of a factor analysis conducted on the ratings of 75 respondents who were asked to evaluate a particular B-segment car using 18 attributes on a 7-point scale. The same respondents were used for all the three B-segment cars, namely, Santro, Indica and Wagon R. The results are given in Tables 1 to 2:

Table 1 Factor loadings for Santro (varimax rotation) rotated component matrix[a]

	Component				Communality
	1	2	3	4	
San-Price	0.018	0.159	–0.003	0.740	0.573
San-Brand	0.197	0.089	0.323	0.614	0.527
San-Eng	0.369	–0.163	0.642	0.158	0.601
San-Looks	0.725	0.042	0.226	0.316	0.678
San-Fueleff	–0.021	0.364	0.678	0.193	.629
San-Disc	0.479	0.402	0.110	0.477	0.631
San-Resale	0.157	0.383	0.453	0.440	0.570
San-AftrSaleSer	0.307	0.697	0.086	0.308	0.683
San-R&M	0.734	0.094	0.069	0.435	0.742
San-Conven	0.635	–0.059	0.443	0.371	0.740
San-Purpose	0.814	0.249	0.157	-0.020	.749
San-PerfInf	0.487	0.225	0.587	0.033	0.633
San-DrivPleas	0.202	0.772	0.101	0.244	0.707
San-Image	0.679	0.267	0.194	0.157	0.595
San-Econ	0.616	0.435	0.243	–0.029	0.629
San-Colours	0.585	0.342	0.466	–0.127	.693
San-AdvMark	0.651	0.367	0.046	0.124	0.576
San-Safety	0.487	0.495	0.325	–0.218	0.635

Extraction Method: Principal Component Analysis.

Rotation Method: Varimax with Kaiser Normalization.

[a] Rotation converged in 46 iterations.

Table 2 Factor loadings for Indica (varimax rotation) rotated component matrix[a]

	Component			Communality
	1	2	3	
Ind-Price	0.154	0.762	–0.071	0.609
Ind-Brand	0.112	.709	0.354	0.640
Ind-Eng	0.474	0.480	0.265	0.525
Ind-Looks	0.717	0.247	0.145	0.596
Ind-Fueleff	0.015	0.169	0.735	0.569
Ind-Disc	0.481	0.567	0.331	0.662
Ind-Resale	0.480	0.382	0.385	0.525
Ind-AftrSaleSer	0.161	0.637	0.351	0.555

	Component			Communality
	1	2	3	
Ind-R&M	0.636	0.531	0.163	0.713
Ind-Conven	0.415	0.604	0.219	0.585
Ind-Purpose	0.825	0.239	0.203	0.778
Ind-PerfInf	0.742	0.221	0.399	0.759
Ind-DrivPleas	0.341	0.178	0.615	0.527
Ind-Image	0.454	0.437	–0.019	0.398
Ind-Econ	0.652	0.264	0.096	0.503
Ind-Colours	0.807	0.188	–0.215	0.734
Ind-AdvMark	0.737	0.274	0.280	0.697
Ind-Safety	0.744	0.009	0.413	0.723

Extraction Method: Principal Component Analysis.
Rotation Method: Varimax with Kaiser Normalization.
[a] Rotation converged in 5 iterations.

Table 3 Factor loadings for Wagon-R (varimax rotation rotated component matrix[a])

	Component					Communality
	1	2	3	4	5	
Wag-Price	0.031	0.080	0.852	0.034	0.025	0.735
Wag-Brand	0.280	0.513	0.596	–0.050	–0.150	0.722
Wag-Eng	0.035	0.728	0.437	0.019	–0.088	0.730
Wag-Looks	0.500	0.638	0.035	0.327	–0.009	0.765
Wag-Fueleff	0.212	0.198	0.693	–0.002	0.132	0.582
Wag-Disc	0.601	0.212	0.469	0.170	–0.212	0.700
Wag-Resale	0.601	0.294	0.288	0.032	–0.190	0.568
Wag-AftrSaleSer	0.677	–0.376	0.377	0.209	0.070	0.790
Wag-R&M	0.641	0.250	–0.150	0.552	0.122	0.816
Wag-Conven	0.094	0.110	0.012	0.798	–0.106	0.669
Wag-Purpose	0.798	0.193	–0.086	0.293	0.260	0.835
Wag-PerfInf	0.782	0.205	0.164	–0.014	–0.003	0.680
Wag-DrivPleas	–.0071	–0.062	0.020	0.044	0.798	0.647
Wag-Econ	–0.040	–0.168	0.482	0.493	0.350	0.627
Wag-Colours	0.225	0.767	0.090	0.229	0.126	0.715
Wag-AdvMark	0.447	0.110	0.116	0.424	0.410	0.572
Wag-Safety	0.485	0.327	0.077	–0.063	0.543	0.647

Extraction Method: Principal Component Analysis.
Rotation Method: Varimax with Kaiser Normalization.
[a] Rotation converged in 29 iterations.

QUESTIONS

1. Label the factors as obtained from the three tables. Compare these factors. What are the reasons for them to be different?
2. Compute the total variance explained and the variance explained for each of the factors in three tables.
3. Analyse and contrast the communalities for each of the variables in three tables.

Appendix – 16.1: SPSS COMMANDS FOR FACTOR ANALYSIS

After the input data has been typed along with variable labels and value labels in an SPSS file, to get the output for a **factor analysis** problem proceed as mentioned below:

1. Click on ANALYSE on the SPSS menu bar.
2. Click on DATA REDUCTION, followed by FACTOR.
3. On the dialog box which appears, select all the variables required for the factor analysis by clicking on the right arrow to transfer them from the variable list on the left to the variables box on the right.
4. Click on EXTRACTION in the lower part of the dialog box.
   (i) Select 'Principal Components' as the Method.
   (ii) Under DISPLAY, select 'Unrotated Factor Solution'.
   (iii) Under EXTRACT, select 'Eigenvalues over 1'.
   (iv) Under ANALYSE, choose 'Correlation Matrix'.
   (v) Click CONTINUE.
5. Click on ROTATION in the lower part of the main dialog box. Select VARIMAX from the options under METHOD. Click CONTINUE.
6. Click on DESCRIPTIVE in the lower part of the dialog box. Click KMO and BARTLETT'S TEST OF SPHERICITY and CONTINUE.
7. Click on SCORES, click on SAVE AS VARIABLE and select method as REGRESSION, then click on DISPLAY FACTOR SCORE COEFFICIENTS.
8. Click OK to get the FACTOR ANALYSIS output, including the unrotated factor matrix, the rotated factor matrix using varimax rotation and the extracted factors along with eigenvalues and cumulative variance. Communality figures would also be a part of the output.

Answers to Objective Type Questions

1. True	2. True	3. True	4. False	5. False
6. True	7. True	8. True	9. True	10. False
11. False	13. True	13. True	14. False	15. False
16. True	17. True	18. True	19. False	20. True

BIBLIOGRAPHY

Aaker, David A V Kumar and George S Day. *Marketing Research*. 7th edn. Singapore: John Wiley & Sons, Inc., 2001.

Bhattacharyya, Dipak Kumar. *Human Resource Research Methods*. New Delhi, Oxford University Press, 2007.

Boyd, Harper W Jr, Ralph Westfall and Stanley F Stasch. '*Marketing Research—Text and Cases*'. 7th edn. Richard D. Irwin, Inc., 2002.

Churchill, Gilbert A Jr and Iacobucci, Dawn. *Marketing Research Methodological Foundations*. 8th edn. Thompson South Western, 2002.

Cooper, Donald R. *Business Research Methods*, New Delhi: Tata McGraw Hill Publishing Company Ltd, 2006.

Green, Paul E, Donald S Tull and Gerald Albaum. *Research for Marketing Decisions*. 5th edn. New Delhi: Prentice-Hall of India Pvt. Ltd., 1992.

Kinnear, Thomas C and James R Taylor. *Marketing Research—An Applied Approach*. 3rd edn. New York: McGraw-Hill Book Company 1987.

Kothari, CR. *Research Methodology: Methods and Techniques*. 2nd edn. New Delhi: Wiley Eastern, 1990.

Luck, David J and Ronald S Rubin. *Marketing Research*. 7th edn. New Delhi: Prentice Hall of India Ltd., 1992.

Malhotra, Naresh K. *Marketing Research—An Applied Orientation*. 3rd edn. New Delhi: Pearson Education, 2002.

Nargundkar, Rajendra. *Marketing Research—Text and Cases*. 2nd edn. New Delhi: Tata McGraw Hill Publishing Co. Ltd., 2004.

Parasuraman, A, Dhruv Grewal and R Krishnan. *Marketing Research*. Biztantra, First Indian adaptation, 2004.

Sethna, Beherug N. *Research Methods in Marketing Management*. New Delhi: Tata Mcgraw-Hill Publishing Company Ltd., 1984.

Zikmund, William G. *Business Research Methods*. Fort Worth: Dryden Press, 2000.

17

CHAPTER

Discriminant Analysis

Learning Objectives

By the end of the chapter, you should be able to:

1. Explain the purpose of discriminant analysis.
2. Discuss the concepts and statistics associated with discriminant analysis using an illustration.
3. Explain the methods of assessing the classification accuracy of the model.
4. Judge the out-of-sample performance of the discriminant model.

Mr S P Ghosh owns a restaurant named *Rasoi*, which serves Indian and Chinese cuisine. The restaurant is more than 20 years old, located in a posh locality of Delhi and caters to upscale consumers. About three years back, another restaurant came up in the vicinity of *Rasoi*. In the beginning Mr Ghosh did not observe any significant impact of the competition. However, with the passage of time, the clientage of *Rasoi* declined sharply. Mr Ghosh wondered about the possible reasons for this. He wanted to know the variables that differentiate between the choice of *Rasoi* to that of the competition. He also wanted to know the relative importance of variables in discriminating between the choice of *Rasoi* to that of the competition. He was wondering if it was possible to predict whether a prospective customer would choose *Rasoi* or not. The present chapter is an attempt in this direction. It attempts to answer the above questions and many more.

Discriminant analysis is used to predict group membership. This technique is used to classify individuals/objects into one of the alternative groups on the basis of a set of predictor variables. The dependent variable in discriminant analysis is categorical and on a nominal scale, whereas the independent or predictor variables are either interval or ratio scale in nature. When there are two groups (categories) of dependent variable, we have two-group discriminant analysis and when there are more than two groups, it is a case of multiple discriminant analysis. In case of two-group discriminant analysis, there is one discriminant function, whereas in case of multiple discriminant analysis, the number of functions is one less than the number of groups.

OBJECTIVES AND USES OF DISCRIMINANT ANALYSIS

LEARNING OBJECTIVE 1
Explain the purpose of discriminant analysis.

The objectives of discriminant analysis are the following:

- To find a linear combination of variables that discriminate between categories of dependent variable in the best possible manner.
- To find out which independent variables are relatively better in discriminating between groups.
- To determine the statistical significance of the discriminant function and whether any statistical difference exists among groups in terms of predictor variables.
- To develop the procedure for assigning new objects, firms or individuals whose profile but not the group identity are known to one of the two groups.
- To evaluate the accuracy of classification, i.e., the percentage of customers that it is able to classify correctly.

Discriminant analysis can be a very powerful technique of analysis in multiple situations. Some areas in which it is extensively used are as follows:

Discriminant analysis is used to identify the variables or statements that are discriminating and on which people with diverse views will respond differently.

Scale construction: Discriminant analysis is used to identify the variables/ statements that are discriminating and on which people with diverse views will respond differently. For example, in case one wants to assess people who believe that corporate governance is the responsibility of policy-makers against those who think it needs to be self driven or individual centric, one may generate a number of statements and then conduct a pilot study and select only those statements on which the two groups differ significantly.

Segment discrimination: Most business managers recognize that the population under consideration can never be totally homogeneous in composition. Therefore, to understand what are the key variables on which two or more groups differ from each other, this technique is extremely useful. Questions to which one may seek answers are as follows:

- What are the demographic variables on which potentially successful salesmen and potentially unsuccessful salesmen differ?
- What are the variables on which users/non-users of a product can be differentiated?
- What are the economic and psychographic variables on which price-sensitive and non-price sensitive customers be differentiated?
- What are the variables on which the buyers of local/national brand of a product be differentiated?

Perceptual mapping: The technique is also used extensively to create attribute-based spatial maps of the respondent's mental positioning of brands. The advantage of the technique is that it can present brands or objects and the attributes on the same map. Therefore, the business manager can determine what attribute is the unique selling proposition (USP) of which brand and which are the attributes that are valued by the respondent but there is no brand that currently satisfies that need.

Discriminant Analysis Model

The mathematical form of the discriminant analysis model is:

$$Y = b_0 + b_1 X_1 + b_2 X_2 + b_3 X_3 + \ldots + b_K X_K$$

where, Y = Dependent variable

b_s = Coefficients of independent variables

X_s = Predictor or independent variables

It may be kept in mind that the dependent variable Y should be a categorized variable, whereas the independent variables X_s should be continuous. As the dependent variable is a categorized variable, it should be coded as 0, 1 or 1, 2 and 3, similar to the dummy variable coding.

The method of estimating b_s is based on the principle that the ratio of between group sum of squares to within group sum of squares be maximized. This will make the groups differ as much as possible on the values of the discriminant function.

The **method of estimating** b_s is based on the principle that the ratio of between group sum of squares to within group sum of squares be maximized.

After having estimated the model, the b_s coefficients (also called discriminant coefficient) are used to calculate Y, the discriminant score by substituting the values of X_s in the estimated discriminant model. For any new data point that we want to classify into one of the groups, a decision rule is formulated for this purpose to determine the cut-off score, which is usually the midpoint of the mean discriminant scores of the two groups in case of two-group discriminant analysis, provided the size of the samples in the two groups are same. The accuracy of classification is determined by using a classification matrix (also called confusion matrix).

The relative importance of the independent variables could be determined from the standardized discriminant function coefficient and the structure matrix. The difference between the standardized and unstandardized discriminant function is that in the un-standardized discriminant function we have a constant term, whereas in the standardized discriminant function, there is no constant term.

ILLUSTRATION OF DISCRIMINANT ANALYSIS

LEARNING OBJECTIVE 2
Discuss the concepts and statistics associated with discriminant analysis using an illustration.

We will illustrate the estimation and the use of the discriminant model in the case of two groups with the help of an example.

A wool manufacturer is interested in getting information on the possible commercial acceptance of a new yarn. He wants to know the characteristics of the fibers that differentiate between prospective buyers/non-buyers of the product. He is interested primarily in ascertaining the relative importance of the following yarn characteristics.

- Durability
- Lightness in weight
- Low investment in conversion facilities
- Rot resistance

The above stated points affect a potential buyer's overall evaluation of the yarn's desirability. The ratings in Table 17.1 pertain to the product being considered and represent the judgements of 18 potential buyers regarding the individual characteristic ratings and 'buy' versus 'not buy' response. Thus, each respondent rates the product according to each of the four characteristics and then indicates whether he would be a prospective buyer of the product or not. The rating is done on an 11-point scale (where 0 represents very poor and 10 excellent). The data for the exercise is reported in Table 17.1.

It may be important to mention that the actual size of the sample was 26, but the above 18 observations reported in Table 17.1 were used for a model estimation, and the remaining 8 observations presented in Table 17.13 were used as a hold-out sample for validation of the discriminant model.

We would conduct a discriminant analysis to find out:

- The percentage of sample that it is able to classify correctly.
- Statistical significance of the discriminant function.

TABLE 17.1 Ratings of four characteristics of yarn

S. No.	Buyer/ Non-buyer	Durability	Light Weight	Low Investment	Rot Resistance	Discriminant Score (Y)
1	Buyer	9	8	7	6	1.06
2	Buyer	7	6	6	5	0.28
3	Buyer	10	7	8	2	2.18
4	Buyer	8	4	5	4	1.35
5	Buyer	9	9	3	3	2.23
6	Buyer	8	6	7	2	1.18
7	Buyer	7	5	6	2	0.81
8	Buyer	5	4	2	3	0.22
9	Buyer	4	3	3	4	−0.69
10	Non-buyer	4	4	4	6	−1.24
11	Non-buyer	3	6	6	3	−1.88
12	Non-buyer	6	3	3	4	0.55
13	Non-buyer	2	4	5	2	−2.04
14	Non-buyer	1	2	2	1	−1.83
15	Non-buyer	4	6	5	6	−1.54
16	Non-buyer	6	7	5	6	−0.36
17	Non-buyer	7	5	6	2	0.81
18	Non-buyer	3	2	3	3	−1.09

- Which variables (durability, light weight, low investment and rot resistance) are relatively better in discriminating between the two groups.
- How to classify a person as a potential buyer or non-buyer.

The discriminant analysis exercise is carried out using the SPSS software. The instruction for carrying out the same is given in Appendix 17.1.

Descriptive Statistics

As the two groups (buyer/non-buyer) are to be compared on the basis of four characteristics of the yarn, namely, durability, light weight, low investment and rot resistance, it will be useful to compute their mean values to get an idea of the differences in their mean score. The mean scores, along with the standard deviations of the four characteristics of the yarn are presented in Table 17.2.

We observe from Table 17.2 that the mean score for durability for the buyer group is 7.444, whereas for the non-buyer group, it is 4.0. The difference in the score for light weight for the buyer group is 5.778, whereas it is 4.33 for the non-buyer group. Similar results are obtained for low investment. However, for the characteristics rot resistance the score for the non-buyer (3.667) is slightly higher than that of the buyer (3.444). Therefore, at the outset one may expect that all these predictor variables except for rot resistance could be useful in discriminating between prospective buyers and non-buyers. However, in terms of variability, the standard deviations of variables like low investment and rot resistance seem to vary a lot.

TABLE 17.2
Group statistics

Buyer/Non-buyer	Characteristics	Mean	Std. Deviation	Valid N (listwise)	
				Unweighted	Weighted
Non-buyer	Durability	4.0000	2.00000	9	9.000
	Light Weight	4.3333	1.80278	9	9.000
	Low Investment	4.3333	1.41421	9	9.000
	Rot Resistance	3.6667	1.93649	9	9.000
Buyer	Durability	7.4444	1.94365	9	9.000
	Light Weight	5.7778	1.98606	9	9.000
	Low Investment	5.2222	2.10819	9	9.000
	Rot Resistance	3.4444	1.42400	9	9.000
Total	Durability	5.7222	2.60781	18	18.000
	Light Weight	5.0556	1.98442	18	18.000
	Low Investment	4.7778	1.80051	18	18.000
	Rot Resistance	3.5556	1.65288	18	18.000

Note: In the SPSS data sheet, buyer is coded as 1, whereas non-buyer is coded as 0.

TABLE 17.3
Tests of equality of group means

Characteristics	Wilks' Lambda	F	d.f.1	d.f.2	Sig.
Durability	0.538	13.729	1	16	0.002
Light Weight	0.860	2.610	1	16	0.126
Low Investment	0.935	1.103	1	16	0.309
Rot Resistance	0.995	0.077	1	16	0.785

Tests for Differences in Group Means

However, to know for which of the characteristics a significant difference exists between the means of two groups, a one-way ANOVA is carried out for each of the characteristics, where each of the predictor variable (durability, light weight, low investment, and rot resistance) is treated as a dependent variable and the non-buyer/buyer group as an independent variable. The results are presented in Table 17.3.

It is observed from the Table 17.3 that the significant difference in the mean exists for the durability, for which the p value is 0.002, which is less than 0.05, the assumed level of significance. There does not seem to be any significant difference in the means of the remaining three characteristics as the p value in each of these cases is greater than 0.05.

Correlation Matrix

The pooled within-group matrices in Table 17.4 present the correlation matrix for the entire predictor variables. It is very important to examine this for detecting the problem of multicollinearity (a high correlation between pairs of predictor variables). If it is noticed that the correlation coefficient between any pair of predictor variables is greater than 0.75, it indicates that both the variables in that particular pair share a large amount of common shared variance and might reflect the same attribute. Under such a circumstance, one of the two variables could be eliminated for further analysis. In our case, the correlation matrix is presented in Table 17.4.

Table 17.4 indicates that the correlation between any pair of predictor variables does not exceed 0.75. Therefore, there does not seem to be any serious problem of

TABLE 17.4
Pooled within-groups matrices[a]

		Durability	Light Weight	Low Investment	Rot Resistance
Correlation	Durability	1.000	0.633	0.549	0.209
	Light Weight	0.633	1.000	0.541	0.327
	Low Investment	0.549	0.541	1.000	0.064
	Rot Resistance	0.209	0.327	0.064	1.000

[a] The covariance matrix has 16 degrees of freedom.

multicollinearity. In case of a serious multicollinearity, the reliability of the model would be less and, therefore, the researcher should be cautious about it.

Unstandardized Discriminant Function

As was mentioned earlier, the basic principle in the estimation of a discriminant function is that the variance between the groups relative to the variance within the group should be maximized. The ratio of between group variance to within group variance is given by eigenvalue. A higher eigenvalue is always desirable. The estimated unstandardized discriminant function is given in Table 17.5.

TABLE 17.5
Canonical discriminant function coefficients

Variable	Function 1
Durability	0.618
Light Weight	–0.055
Low Investment	–0.188
Rot Resistance	–0.157
(Constant)	–1.800

Unstandardized coefficients.

The results in Table 17.5 can be written in the form of discriminant function as:

$$Y = -1.80 + 0.618\,X_1 - 0.055\,X_2 - 0.188\,X_3 - 0.157\,X_4$$

where, Y = Discriminant score
X_1 = Durability
X_2 = Light weight
X_3 = Low investment
X_4 = Rot resistance

Given the values of X_1, X_2, X_3 & X_4, the discriminant score for each respondent could be calculated. In case of respondent number 1, the values of X_1 to X_4 are given in Table 17.1. Substituting these values in the discriminant function, the score for the first respondent could be obtained as:

$$Y = -1.80 + 0.618 \times 9 - 0.055 \times 8 - 0.188 \times 7 - 0.157 \times 6 = 1.064$$

Similarly, the discriminant scores for the remaining respondents could be obtained. To save space, the scores are presented in the last column of Table 17.1. In fact, the SPSS software has a provision to provide the discriminant scores for each respondent and saving it in the data sheet.

The eigenvalue for the above estimated discriminant function is 1.033, as shown in Table 17.6 with 100 per cent variance explained.

TABLE 17.6 Eigenvalues

Function	Eigenvalue	Percentage of Variance	Cumulative Percentage	Canonical Correlation
1	1.033[a]	100.0	100.0	0.713

[a] First canonical discriminant functions were used in the analysis.

The last column of Table 17.6 indicates canonical correlation, which is the simple correlation coefficient between the discriminant score and their corresponding group membership (buyer/non-buyer). The value of this is 0.713, which the readers may verify. The square of the canonical correlation is $(0.713)^2 = 0.508$, which means 50.8 per cent of the variance in the discriminating model between a prospective buyer/non-buyer is due to the changes in the four predictor variables, namely, durability, light weight, low investment, and rot resistance.

Classification of Cases Using the Discriminant Function

One can also compute the mean discriminant scores of the buyer and non-buyer groups separately. This is known as group centroids. This works out to be –0.958 for a non-buyer and 0.958 for a buyer. This is presented in Table 17.7.

TABLE 17.7 Functions at group centroids

Buyer/Non-buyer	Function 1
Non-buyer	–0.958
Buyer	0.958

Unstandardized canonical discriminant functions evaluated at group means.

The value of the function at group centroids (means) given in Table 17.7 can be used for designing a decision rule to classify a customer into the buyer/non-buyer category. If the size of the sample for the two groups is the same while estimating the model, the cut-off score used for classification into the buyer/non-buyer category can be obtained by taking the average of the two-group centroid. In the present case, the average works out to be (–0.958 + 0.958)/2 = 0. It is shown below as:

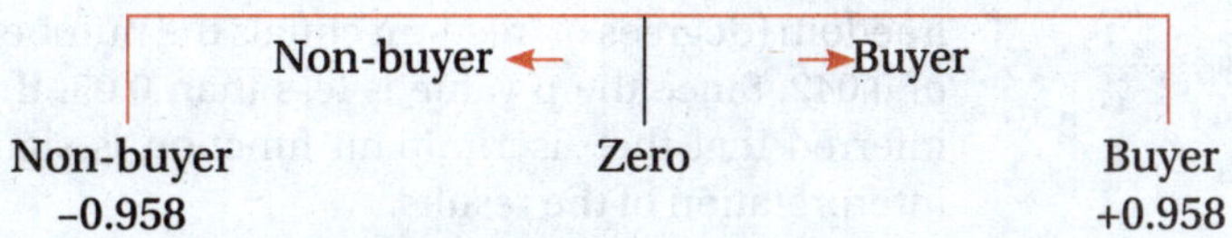

Now, any respondent whose discriminant score is greater than zero would be classified as a prospective buyer, whereas the one with score less than zero would be classified as a non-buyer. Therefore, it may be inferred that a high score on durability is likely to classify a respondent into the buyer group, whereas a high score on light weight, low investment and rot resistance would classify the respondent into the non-buyer category.

In case the size of sample in the two groups is not equal, the cut-off score for classification is computed as given below:

$$C = \frac{(n_2 \bar{Y}_1 + n_1 \bar{Y}_2)}{(n_1 + n_2)}$$

where, $\bar{Y}_1$ and $\bar{Y}_2$ = Mean discriminant score for group 1 (non-buyer) and group 2 (buyer).

n_1 and n_2 = Sizes of groups 1 and 2 respectively.

Significance of Discriminant Function Model

It is very important that the discriminant function is statistically significant as this will enhance the reliability that the differentiation between the groups exists. In case the discriminant function is not significant, it should not be used for interpretation as the discrimination can only be attributed to a sampling error. There is a statistic called Wilks' lambda which is computed by finding the ratio of within-group sum of squares to total sum of squares in a one way ANOVA where the dependent variable is the discriminant score for each respondent and the predictor variable is the category (one or zero) to which the respondent belongs. The results of a one-way analysis of variance are presented in Table 17.8.

TABLE 17.8 ANOVA with the dependent variable as discriminant scores

	Sum of Squares	d.f.	Mean Square	F	Sig.
Between Groups	16.536	1	16.536	16.536	0.001
Within Groups	16.000	16	1.000		
Total	32.536	17			

As we have defined Wilks' lambda as the ratio of within-group sum of squares to total sum of squares, its values should equal (16.0/32.536) = 0.492. The same is reported in Table 17.9 obtained from SPSS computer printout.

TABLE 17.9 Wilks' Lambda

Test of Function(s)	Wilks' Lambda	Chi-square	d.f.	Sig.
1	0.492	9.936	4	0.042

We find that the value of Wilks' lambda is 0.492, which is the same as obtained using the results of the one-way ANOVA. The Wilks' lambda takes a value between 0 and 1 and lower the value of Wilks' lambda, the higher is the significance of the discriminant function. Therefore, a 0 (zero) value would be the most preferred one. The statistical test of significance for Wilks' lambda is carried out with the chi-squared transformed statistic, which in our case is 9.936 (refer Table 17.9) with 4 degrees of freedom (degrees of freedom equals the number of predictor variables) and a p value of 0.042. Since the p value is less than 0.05, the assumed level of significance, it is inferred that the discriminant function is significant and can be used for further interpretation of the results.

We had already discussed the concept of eigenvalue, which is given by the ratio of between-sum of squares to within-sum of squares in the one-way ANOVA (see Table 17.8). This ratio is obtained as (16.536/16) = 1.033, which is the same as reported in Table 17.6.

Standardized Discriminant Function Coefficient

A small value of the discriminant coefficient means that the impact of a unit change in a predictor variable is small in the **discriminant function score.**

We can interpret the standardized discriminant function coefficient exactly in the same way as a standardized regression coefficient. This means that each coefficient reflects the relative contribution of each of the predictor variable on the discriminant function. A small value of the discriminant coefficient means that the impact of a unit change in a predictor variable is small in the discriminant function score.

As mentioned earlier, the standardized discriminant function does not have a constant term in it, whereas the unstandardized discriminant function has a constant term. The coefficients of unstandardized discriminant function depend upon the units of measurement, whereas the coefficients of standardized discriminant function are

TABLE 17.10 Standardized canonical discriminant function coefficients

Characteristics	Function 1
Durability	1.219
Light Weight	–0.104
Low Investment	–0.338
Rot Resistance	–0.268

TABLE 17.11 Structure matrix

Characteristics	Function 1
Durability	0.911
Light Weight	0.397
Low Investment	0.258
Rot Resistance	–0.068

Pooled within-group correlations between discriminating variables and standardized canonical discriminant functions.
Variables ordered by absolute size of the correlation within function.

independent of the units of measurements. The absolute values of the coefficients in standardized discriminant function indicate the relative contribution of the variables in discriminating between the two groups. Table 17.10 gives the standardized canonical discriminant function coefficients. It indicates that durability is the most important characteristic, which discriminates between the buyer and non-buyer group, followed by low investment, rot resistance, and light weight.

Structural Coefficients

Structural coefficients are obtained by computing the correlation between the discriminant score and each of the independent variables.

Another way of finding the relative contributions of the predictor variables in discriminating between the buyer and non-buyer groups is through comparing the structural coefficients of the predictor variables. The structural coefficients are obtained by computing the correlation between the discriminant score and each of the independent variables. These are also called discriminant loadings. The structure matrix is presented in Table 17.11.

The correlation coefficient between the discriminant score and the variable durability is 0.911, whereas the correlation with light weight, low investment and rot resistance is 0.397, 0.258 and –0.068 respectively. It is observed from Table 17.11 that durability is the most important characteristic in discriminating between a buyer and a non-buyer followed by light weight, low investment and rot resistance. One can observe that the relative importance of the variables have undergone a change from what we obtained through the standardized discriminant coefficient. Durability remains the most important characteristic using both the methods. Light weight, low investment and rot resistance are the next important characteristics in order of relative importance in discriminating between the buyers and non-buyers. The change in the relative importance of variables using structure matrix in comparison to what is obtained through standardized coefficients is due to an inter-correlation between predictor variables.

CONCEPT CHECK

1. State the objectives and uses of discriminant analysis.
2. Illustrate the discriminant analysis model.
3. Define the correlation matrix.
4. What is the significance of discriminant function model?
5. Define standardized discriminant coefficient.

ASSESSING CLASSIFICATION ACCURACY

LEARNING OBJECTIVE 3
Explain the methods of assessing the classification accuracy of the model.

The classification accuracy can be assessed in the following ways:

Hit ratio: In our case, the discriminant score for each of the respondents was computed (refer Table 17.1) and, as already mentioned, if the discriminant score is greater than zero, the individual is classified into the buyer group; otherwise into the non-buyer group. Using this, results of classification for all the cases are presented in Table 17.12, which classifies each respondent into the buyer/non-buyer category. This table is also called confusion matrix or classificatory table. It may be seen from Table 17.12 that out of the 9 respondents who were actually prospective buyers, 8 were predicted by the model as buyers. Similarly, out of the 9 respondents that were actually non-buyers, 7 of them were predicted as non-buyers. The overall classificatory ability of the model measured by the hit ratio is given as:

$$\text{Hit ratio} = \frac{\text{No. of correct predictions}}{\text{Total number of cases}}$$

In this case, there were 15 correct predictions out of 18; therefore, the hit ratio works out to be 83.3 per cent.

Maximum vs proportional chance criterion: We may ask the question about how reliable is a hit ratio. If the sample sizes were equal in both the groups, the chance would be 50 per cent. In our case, getting 83.33 per cent accuracy appears to be very good. The question is what happens if the sizes of the sample are not the same in the two cases. Suppose our sample comprises 70 per cent buyers and 30 per cent non-buyers. As per the maximum chance criteria, the best thing to do would be to classify each respondent belonging to the buyer group so that we can get 70 per cent accuracy. This way we could maximize the percentage of cases correctly classified. This type of rule is not useful as we cannot classify any case belonging to the non-buyer category correctly. Our purpose is however, to make correct predictions about both the groups. In such a case, proportional chance criterion is used as the standard for evaluation. It is given by:

$$C_{prop} = \alpha^2 + (1 - \alpha)^2$$

TABLE 17.12 Classification results [b,c]

		Buyer/Non-Buyer	Predicted Group Membership		Total
			Non-Buyer	Buyer	
Original	Count	Non-Buyer	7	2	9
		Buyer	1	8	9
	%	Non-Buyer	77.8	22.2	100.0
		Buyer	11.1	88.9	100.0
Cross-validated[a]	Count	Non-Buyer	6	3	9
		Buyer	2	7	9
	%	Non-Buyer	66.7	33.3	100.0
		Buyer	22.2	77.8	100.0

[a] In cross-validation, each case is classified by the functions derived from all cases other than that case.
[b] 83.3% of original grouped cases correctly classified.
[c] 72.2% of cross-validated grouped cases correctly classified.

where, α = proportion of individuals belonging to group 1.
$1 - \alpha$ = proportional of individuals belonging to group 2.
For 70 per cent buyers and 30 per cent non-buyers, the index equals:

$$C_{prop} = (0.70)^2 + (0.30)^2$$
$$= 0.49 + 0.09$$
$$= 0.58$$

If by using a discriminant function, a classification accuracy of 65 per cent (say) is obtained, the hit ratio would look good compared to chance alone (0.58). However, this would not be as attractive as the maximum chance criteria.

Cross-validation: This method is known as leave-one-out classification method in SPSS. In our example, we had 18 observations. Here, the first observation is deleted and the discriminant model is estimated on the remaining 17 observations. Based on this discriminant model, the excluded case is predicted to belong to a specific category. In the same way, the second observation is eliminated and the discriminant model is estimated using the remaining 17 observations. Again based on this model, the excluded case is predicted to belong to a specific category. This process is repeated 18 times. That is why this method is called the leave-one-out-classification.

The second part of Table 17.12 gives the results, wherein we see that 72.2 per cent of the cases are classified correctly. This is slightly less than the original hit ratio. Based on cross-validation results, it is expected that 72.2 per cent of the cases would be classified correctly.

CONCEPT CHECK

1. What is maximum chance criteria?
2. Define hit ratio.
3. Explain the one leave-out classification method.

OUT-OF-SAMPLE PERFORMANCE

LEARNING OBJECTIVE 4
Judge the out-of-sample performance of the discriminant model.

This method is used to test the validity of the discriminant model. Table 17.1 presents data on four predictor variables on which the model was built. The total number of observations used to build the model was 18. As a matter of fact, the survey contained 26 observations, of which 18 were used to build the model. The remaining 8 observations were kept as 'hold-out' samples to test the out-of-sample performance of the model. The data on the hold-out sample is presented in Table 17.13.

TABLE 17.13 Data on hold-out sample

S. No.	Buyer/ Non-Buyer	Durability	Light Weight	Low Investment	Rot Resistance
1	Buyer	3	5	4	3
2	Buyer	9	5	6	5
3	Buyer	8	7	4	4
4	Buyer	8	6	5	5
5	Non-buyer	3	6	6	3
6	Non-buyer	4	6	5	2
7	Non-buyer	7	2	3	2
8	Non-buyer	5	5	6	4

Using the estimated discriminant function:

$$Y = -1.8 + 0.618\,X_1 - 0.055\,X_2 - 0.188\,X_3 - 0.157\,X_4$$

The discriminant score corresponding to the 8 hold-out observations can be computed as:

1	Y =	−1.80 +0.618 × 3 – 0.055 × 5 – 0.188 × 4 – 0.157 × 3	=	−1.444
2	Y =	−1.80 +0.618 × 9 – 0.055 × 5 – 0.188 × 6 – 0.157 × 5	=	1.574
3	Y =	−1.80 +0.618 × 8 – 0.055 × 7 – 0.188 × 4 – 0.157 × 4	=	1.379
4	Y =	−1.80 +0.618 × 8 – 0.055 × 6 – 0.188 × 5 – 0.157 × 5	=	1.089
5	Y =	−1.80 +0.618 × 3 – 0.055 × 6 – 0.188 × 6 – 0.157 × 3	=	−1.875
6	Y =	−1.80 +0.618 × 4 – 0.055 × 6 – 0.188 × 5 – 0.157 × 2	=	−0.912
7	Y =	−1.80 +0.618 × 7 – 0.055 × 2 – 0.188 × 3 – 0.157 × 2	=	1.538
8	Y =	−1.80 +0.618 × 5 – 0.055 × 5 – 0.188 × 6 – 0.157 × 4	=	−0.741

It is noted that out of 4 buyers, 3 are classified correctly as their discriminant score is greater than zero. Further, out of the 4 non-buyers in the hold-out samples, 3 are classified correctly, as their discriminant score is less than zero. Therefore, out of 8 cases, 6 cases are correctly classified resulting in an out-of-sample accuracy of 75 per cent.

We have illustrated the case of the two-group discriminant analysis by estimating a discriminant function. There are instances where a dependent variable can be classified into one of three or more groups. In such a situation, the number of discriminant functions required is one less than the number of groups. The discussion of multiple discriminant analysis is beyond the scope of this book.

If the number of predictor variables in discriminant analysis is large, they can first be subjected to factor analysis and the factor scores can be used as predictor variables in estimating discriminant function.

SUMMARY

- Discriminant analysis is used to predict group membership. The basic principle underlying a discriminant model is to choose linear combinations of the predictor variables that will maximize between-group variance to within-group variance. The dependent variable in a discriminant analysis is categorical, whereas the independent variables are continuous. The numbers of discriminant functions to be estimated are one less than the number of categories of the dependent variable. The main objectives of discriminant analysis are:
  - To estimate the percentage of respondents that the discriminant model is able to classify correctly.
  - To determine the statistical significance of the discriminant function.
  - To find out which of the predictor variables are relatively better in discriminating between the two groups.
  - To classify a new respondent into one of the two groups by building a decision rule and a cut-off score.
- The discussion of discriminant analysis is illustrated through an example. Various concepts like eigenvalue, canonical correlation, Wilks' lambda, standardized discriminant function coefficients, structure matrix are explained. Eigenvalue indicates the ratio between group variance to within-group variance. Canonical correlation is the simple correlation between the discriminant score and the coded values of groups. The discriminant scores are obtained by substituting the values of the predictor variables in unstandardized discriminant function. The square of canonical correlation indicates the percentage of variation in the discriminant model that is explained by the predictor variables. Wilks' lambda is used to test the significance of a discriminating function. If the discriminant function is not significant, it should not be interpreted. It is obtained by computing the ratio of within-group sum of squares to total sum of squares. Wilks' lambda takes a value ranging from 0 to 1. The lower the value the better is the function in discriminating between the groups. Wilks' lambda follows a chi-squared statistic, which is used for examining the statistical significance of a discriminant function.

- The relative contribution of each predictor variable in discriminating between the groups is obtained through the absolute value of the standardized coefficients of a discriminant function. The higher the absolute value of the coefficient, more is the importance attached to the corresponding variable. Another way of obtaining relative importance is through the coefficient of structure matrix, which is obtained by computing a simple correlation between the discriminant score and the predictor variables. Again, the absolute values are used for finding the relative importance of variables. The two methods may give varying results if there is a very high correlation among the predictor variables.
- The decision rule to classify a new object into a group is discussed. The classificatory ability of the discriminat model is presented in the classification table, which is also called confusion matrix. Three ways of assessing classification accuracy are discussed—(i) hit ratio (ii) maximum vs proportional chance criteria and (iii) cross-validation.
- The out-of-sample performance of the discriminant model is assessed using a hold-out sample, which should be done if our original sample is large enough to be divided into two groups, one on which the model is built and the other to be used for testing the accuracy of the model.

KEY TERMS

- Between-group variance
- Canonical correlation
- Chi-square
- Classificatory ability
- Confusion matrix
- Correlation matrix
- Dependent variable
- Discriminant coefficients
- Eigenvalue
- Hit ratio
- Multiple discriminant analysis
- One-way ANOVA
- Predictor variable
- Standardized coefficient
- Standardized discriminant function
- Structure matrix
- Total variance
- Two group discriminant analysis
- Un-standardized discriminant function
- Wilks' lambda
- Within group variance

CHAPTER REVIEW QUESTIONS

Objective Type Questions

State whether the following statements are true (T) or false (F).

1. In discriminant analysis, the dependent variable is interval or ratio scale in nature.
2. Discriminant analysis is used to predict group membership.
3. Eigenvalue is given by the ratio of between-group variance to within-group variance.
4. The number of discriminant functions should be one more than the number of groups.
5. Hit ratio is obtained as the ratio of the number of correct predictions to the total number of cases.
6. The value of Wilks' lambda is greater than 0.5.
7. The higher the value of Wilks' lambda, better is the discriminant model.
8. Wilks' lambda is obtained as the ratio of within-group sum of squares to total sum of squares.
9. The predictor variables in the discriminant model should be continuous.
10. The standardized discriminant function does not contain a constant term.
11. The discriminant scores are obtained from standardized discriminant function.
12. Canonical correlation is the simple correlation between the discriminant score and the various groups.
13. The significance of a discriminant function is tested by significance of Wilks' lambda.
14. The classification results table is also called confusion matrix.
15. The square of canonical correlation gives the percentage of variations in the discriminant model that are explained by the predictor variables.

16. The results of standardized discriminant coefficients and structure matrix are always the same.
17. There is no limitation of maximum criteria in checking the accuracy of a discriminant model.
18. The unstandardized discriminant function depends on the units of measurements.
19. The 'cut-off' score is obtained by computing the average of scores at a two-group centroid if the size of the samples in two groups is same.
20. The degree of freedom for a chi-square corresponding to the Wilks' lambda is one less than the number of predictor variables.

Conceptual Questions

1. Briefly explain different methods of assessing the classificatory ability of the model.
2. Distinguish between a standardized discriminant coefficient and a structure matrix. Under what conditions can the interpretation in the two cases be different?
3. How can discriminant analysis be used for prediction and structural interpretation? Explain with the help of an example.
4. What is discriminant analysis? Explain the various steps in carrying out a discriminant analysis exercise.
5. What is Wilks' lambda? How it is computed? What is its role in a discriminant analysis?
6. What is canonical correlation? How is it computed? How is it used in discriminant analysis?
7. List a few studies where discriminant analysis could be applied and explain how.
8. Find out the similarities and difference between a regression and discriminant analysis.

Application Questions

1. The following discriminant function was developed to classify salespersons into the categories of successful and unsuccessful salespersons:

$$Z = 0.53\ X_1 + 2.1\ X_2 + 1.5\ X_3$$

Where, X_1 = No. of sales call made by salesperson

X_2 = No. of customers developed by salesperson

X_3 = No. of units sold by salesperson

The following decision rule was developed.

If $Z \geq 10$, classify the salesperson as successful.

If $Z < 10$, classify the salesperson as unsuccessful.

Salespersons A and B were considered for promotion on the basis of being classified as successful or unsuccessful. Only the successful salesperson would be promoted. The relevant data on A and B is given below. Whom will you promote?

	A	B
X_1	10	11
X_2	2	1.5
X_3	1	0.5

CASE 17.1

PREDICTING HIGH/LOW USER OF SOCIAL NETWORKING SITES AMONG STUDENTS

Social networking is the grouping of individuals into specific groups like small rural communities or a neighbourhood subdivision. Although social networking is possible in person, especially in the workplace, universities, and schools, it is most popular online. This is because the Internet is filled with millions of individuals who are looking to meet other people, to gather and share first-hand information and experiences about any number of topics—from golfing, gardening, developing friendships to professional alliances.

When it comes to online social networking, websites are commonly used. These websites are known as social networking sites. They function like online communities of internet users. Depending on the website in question, many of these online community members share common interests in hobbies, religion, or politics. Once you are granted access to a social networking website you can begin to socialize. This socialization may include reading the profile pages of other members and possibly even contacting them.

Contrary to the widely held assumption that people fake themselves on social networking sites, a new study has claimed that netizens use their profiles to communicate real personalities, instead of an idealized virtual identity.

According to scientists at the University of Texas, Austin, online social networking profiles like on Facebook convey rather accurate images of the profile owners, either because people aren't trying to look good or because they are trying and failing to pull it off.

'I was surprised by the findings because the widely held assumption is that people are using their profiles to promote an enhanced impression of themselves,' said lead author Sam Gosling of the research of over 700 million people worldwide who have online profiles.

He said, 'These findings suggest that online social networks are not so much about providing positive spin for the profile owners but are instead just another medium for engaging in genuine social interactions, much like the telephone'.

A brief survey of literature on social networking sites reveals that there has been an upsurge of interest in the study of this relatively new domain in the past few years. Academic researchers have started studying the use of social networking sites, with questions ranging from their role in identity construction and expression (Boyd and Heer, 2006) to the building and maintenance of social capital (Ellison, Steinfeld, and Lampe, 2007) and concerns about privacy. Majority of these studies generally use Facebook as the subject of study, reflecting the popularity and huge user base of Facebook.

Williams and Gulati (2007) showed that Facebook had a significant role in the campaigns of the 2006 mid-term elections of the US Congress, both in terms of being embraced by a significant percentage of major-party candidates and in terms of the final vote. They found that 32 per cent of candidates for the US Senate and 13 per cent of candidates for the House updated their Facebook profiles. In addition, incumbents added 1.1 per cent to their vote share by doubling the number of supporters on Facebook, while open-seat candidates added 3 per cent by achieving the same increase. 'Taken together, the evidence from the analyses provides a compelling case that Facebook played an important role in the 2006 Congressional races and that social networking sites have the capability of affecting the electoral process.'

Hargittai (2007), conducted a study to look at the predictors of social networking sites usage among a diverse group of mainly 18- and 19-year-old college students studying in the University of Illinois, Chicago. He found that a person's gender, race and ethnicity, and parental educational background are all associated with use, but in most cases only when the aggregate concept of social networking sites is disaggregated by service. Additionally, people with more experience and autonomy of use are more likely to be users of such sites.

Ellison, Steinfield and Lampe (2007) stated that 'our findings demonstrate a robust connection between Facebook usage and indicators of social capital, especially of the bridging type. Internet use alone did not predict social capital accumulation, but intensive use of Facebook did.' Stressing the role of social networking sites in the formation of social capital, the study shows a strong linkage between Facebook use and high school connections, and that social networking sites help maintain relations as people move from one offline community to another. Social networking sites may also facilitate connections when students graduate from college, with alumni keeping their school e-mail address and using Facebook to stay in touch with the college community. Such connections could have strong payoffs in terms of jobs, internships, and other opportunities.

A study was conducted to identify the variables which distinguish between heavy/light users of social networking sites among students. A questionnaire was designed for the purpose. The social networking sites considered for the study were Facebook, Orkut, Linked-In, Twitter, etc. The online survey was conducted on a sample of 61 students in the age group of 20–30. The following questions were asked of the respondent:

1. How much time do you spend daily on networking sites during weekdays (Monday to Friday)? (X_1)
   (a) Less than 1 hour [1]
   (b) 1 to less than 3 hours [2]
   (c) 3 to less than 5 hours [3]
   (d) More than 5 hours [4]
2. How much time do you spend daily on networking sites during weekends (Saturday and Sunday)? (X_2)
   (a) Less than 2 hours [1]
   (b) 2 to less than 4 hours [2]
   (c) 4-6 hours [3]
   (d) More than 6 hours [4]
3. Rate the uses of social networking on a scale of 1 to 5 (1 being least useful and 5 being extremely useful) with respect to the following parameters:
   (a) To link with professionals (X_3A)
   (b) Messaging/chatting (X_3B)
   (c) Networking with friends/relatives (X_3C)
   (d) To make new friends (X_3D)
   (e) To promote events/information (X_3E)
   (f) Blogging (X_3F)
   (g) News updates (X_3G)
   (h) Games (X_3H)
   (i) Educational (X_3I)
   (j) Photo-sharing (X_3J)
   (k) Job seeking (X_3K)
   (l) Online dating (X_3L)

The data for the study is reported in Table 17.14.

Table 17.14 Select data for social networking study

S. No.	X_1	X_2	X_3A	X_3B	X_3C	X_3D	X_3E	X_3F	X_3G	X_3H	X_3I	X_3J	X_3K	X_3L
1	2	3	1	2	3	5	2	3	2	5	4	2	2	1
2	4	3	4	4	5	2	2	3	4	2	2	4	4	1
3	2	3	1	5	3	2	2	5	3	1	1	4	1	1
4	2	3	5	4	5	3	4	5	5	4	5	5	3	3
5	2	2	4	4	5	4	3	3	3	2	3	4	3	2
6	2	2	2	4	5	1	1	2	2	1	2	3	2	1
7	1	2	2	2	3	1	1	1	2	1	1	3	2	1
8	4	1	5	3	3	2	2	2	2	2	2	5	5	1
9	2	2	3	5	4	4	4	3	2	4	5	5	3	2

S. No.	X_1	X_2	X_3A	X_3B	X_3C	X_3D	X_3E	X_3F	X_3G	X_3H	X_3I	X_3J	X_3K	X_3L
10	1	1	3	5	5	1	3	2	1	1	2	4	2	1
11	1	1	5	1	2	5	3	3	3	4	4	2	5	5
12	4	1	3	4	4	3	3	3	3	3	3	4	4	2
13	2	2	5	4	4	2	5	3	3	2	2	4	3	1
14	1	1	5	1	1	5	5	5	3	5	3	3	5	5
15	1	1	3	4	5	1	3	4	4	3	3	4	1	1
16	1	1	5	1	1	2	5	5	5	5	3	5	5	5
17	1	1	1	4	4	4	4	2	2	1	1	4	1	2
18	2	2	3	2	4	1	4	2	4	5	3	5	3	1
19	4	1	2	3	2	2	2	2	3	4	4	3	2	2
20	1	1	5	4	4	2	1	1	1	1	5	4	1	5
21	3	1	3	4	5	4	4	4	3	3	2	2	3	4
22	1	1	2	4	5	1	2	2	2	3	3	5	3	1
23	3	1	4	5	5	5	4	4	3	3	3	5	4	3
24	1	1	3	5	5	4	4	4	5	5	5	5	3	3
25	1	1	2	3	3	3	3	3	3	3	3	4	2	1
26	1	1	4	4	4	3	3	3	3	1	3	4	2	2
27	1	1	4	4	5	3	4	4	4	4	5	5	5	3
28	3	2	4	4	4	4	4	4	4	4	4	4	4	1
29	2	2	2	3	4	2	3	4	4	4	3	2	2	1
30	1	3	4	4	4	4	4	5	4	4	5	5	2	4
31	1	1	4	4	5	2	5	3	5	2	5	5	3	1
32	2	2	3	4	4	4	2	2	2	2	2	2	2	2
33	1	2	3	1	2	4	4	3	2	2	4	2	1	1
34	1	1	4	4	5	4	3	3	3	4	4	4	3	4
35	1	4	1	4	4	5	4	4	3	4	3	4	4	5
36	2	4	2	3	3	4	4	3	4	3	4	4	3	5
37	2	3	3	2	3	3	4	4	4	5	4	5	2	4
38	2	3	1	3	3	4	3	3	3	4	3	4	3	4
39	1	3	1	4	4	5	2	3	2	2	3	5	3	5
40	2	3	1	2	3	3	3	4	4	4	4	5	4	4
41	2	3	2	3	4	3	5	5	4	4	5	4	3	3
42	1	3	4	1	1	1	3	2	1	1	4	2	4	3
43	2	3	2	2	3	4	4	4	3	3	3	4	2	4
44	1	2	2	2	4	3	2	2	3	4	1	4	2	4
45	4	4	4	1	1	2	3	2	1	2	5	3	4	4
46	1	3	1	3	4	3	4	3	4	4	3	4	3	3
47	1	1	1	5	5	5	1	1	1	1	1	5	1	1
48	1	2	1	2	3	3	2	2	3	3	2	3	2	3
49	1	2	1	2	3	3	2	2	3	3	2	4	3	4
50	1	2	1	2	3	4	3	2	3	4	2	4	2	4
51	1	1	5	3	3	4	2	2	3	3	2	4	4	2
52	2	2	4	5	4	4	4	4	2	3	3	4	4	5
53	2	1	4	3	4	4	3	2	3	3	3	4	3	3
54	4	4	4	4	4	4	3	3	3	3	3	3	3	3
55	4	4	1	5	5	5	5	5	1	5	1	5	1	5

S. No.	X_1	X_2	X_3A	X_3B	X_3C	X_3D	X_3E	X_3F	X_3G	X_3H	X_3I	X_3J	X_3K	X_3L
56	4	4	2	4	4	3	3	2	2	5	2	4	2	5
57	1	2	2	3	4	4	2	2	2	3	2	4	4	4
58	1	3	2	4	4	4	2	2	2	4	3	5	4	4
59	1	2	2	4	4	5	2	2	3	4	3	5	3	4
60	1	4	2	4	4	4	1	2	3	4	3	5	3	4
61	1	2	1	5	5	5	2	2	3	4	3	4	2	3

QUESTIONS

1. Divide the sample into two groups—one that is using the social networking site for less than one hour on weekdays (low users) and the second which is using the social networking site for one or more hours (high users). Run a two-group discriminant analysis with high/low user as a dependent variable and the variables X_3A to X_3L as independent variables to:
   (a) Compute the percentage of respondents that it is able to classify correctly.
   (b) Determine the statistical significance of the discriminant function.
   (c) Identify which of the predictor variables are relatively better in discriminating between the two groups.
   (d) Classify a new respondent into one of the two groups by building a decision rule and a cut-off score.
2. Divide the sample into two groups—one that is using the social networking site for less than four hours on weekends (low users) and the second which is using the social networking site for four or more hours (high users) and repeat the analysis as carried out in the first question.

CASE 17.2

BUYING BEHAVIOUR OF READY-TO-EAT FOOD CONSUMERS

Ready-to-eat food products are prepared in advance and can be eaten as sold. This is a relatively new concept and a growing industry in India. The size of the ready-to-eat market is approximately ₹600 – ₹700 million. The main producers of ready-to-eat food are MTR, Kohinoor, Tasty Bites, Indo-Nissin, Currie Classic and ITC. The major brands available in markets are Maggie, Sunfeast, MTR meals and Nissin's cup noodles. Because of the change in lifestyle – nuclear families, working couples, more disposable income and less time to cook—more and more people are opting for ready-to-eat food in a big way.

A survey was conducted to understand the buying behaviour of ready-to-eat food consumers. A questionnaire was prepared for the purpose and was administered to 58 respondents in the age group 18 to 55 with 40 male members and 18 female members. The sample had 53 single and 5 married respondents. One of the objectives of the study was to discriminate between heavy users and light users of ready-to-eat food. The following questions were asked:

1. How often do you eat 'ready-to-eat' foods? (X_1)
   (a) Rarely (once a month) – *Coded as 1*
   (b) Weekly (1-2 times/week) – *Coded as 2*
   (c) Regularly (3-5 times/week) – *Coded as 3*
2. Kindly tick any one as your opinion on the parameters given below:
   Strongly agree (5)
   Agree (4)
   Neither agree/nor disagree (3)
   Disagree (2)
   Strongly disagree (1)

(a) 'Ready-to-eat' packs are very convenient to use (X_2A)
(b) 'Ready-to-eat' makes my work very easy (X_2B)
(c) 'Ready-to-eat' packs are very time saving (X_2C)
(d) 'Ready-to-eat' food is easily available whenever I need it (X_2D)
(e) 'Ready-to-eat' packs are reasonably priced (X_2E)
(f) 'Ready-to-eat' packs have reasonable amount of nutrition and calories (X_2F)
(g) 'Ready-to-eat' meal is not as tasty as freshly cooked food (X_2G)
(h) 'Ready-to-eat' packs are manufactured at accepted quality standards (X_2H)
(i) 'Ready-to-eat' packs are a good option while travelling (X_2I)
(j) Even if I buy a 'ready-to-eat' curry, making chapattis separately takes up my time. (X_2J)

The required data is given in Table 17.15.

Table 17.15 Select data for ready-to-eat study

S. No.	X_1	X_2A	X_2B	X_2C	X_2D	X_2E	X_2F	X_2G	X_2H	X_2I	X_2J
1	1	4	4	4	4	2	2	2	4	2	2
2	3	4	4	4	4	4	3	3	3	3	3
3	1	4	4	4	5	4	3	2	3	4	3
4	2	5	4	3	2	3	4	5	1	3	2
5	3	2	2	2	2	4	4	4	2	2	4
6	1	3	4	4	3	2	1	1	4	5	3
7	1	4	4	4	4	4	4	4	4	4	2
8	2	4	5	5	3	2	2	4	4	4	2
9	1	5	4	5	5	2	1	3	3	5	5
10	1	4	4	4	4	4	2	3	4	5	4
11	1	4	4	4	4	4	2	2	3	4	3
12	1	4	4	4	4	4	4	1	5	3	3
13	1	4	4	4	4	4	1	2	2	4	2
14	1	5	5	5	4	3	2	1	3	4	5
15	1	4	4	4	4	3	2	2	3	4	2
16	2	5	5	5	4	4	3	3	3	4	3
17	3	5	5	4	4	4	1	1	3	4	3
18	1	4	4	3	2	1	1	2	3	4	3
19	2	4	4	4	4	4	2	1	2	2	4
20	1	4	4	3	2	3	2	3	4	5	3
21	1	5	5	5	4	3	3	3	3	3	3
22	1	3	3	3	3	2	3	1	3	4	5
23	2	5	5	5	4	4	2	5	2	3	3
24	2	4	4	4	4	3	2	2	3	2	2
25	1	4	4	4	3	3	3	3	3	4	2
26	2	5	3	4	4	4	2	2	4	4	3
27	2	5	4	4	3	2	2	3	3	4	2
28	2	4	4	5	5	5	3	3	3	4	3
29	1	5	5	5	2	3	3	4	3	5	2
30	2	4	5	5	3	4	3	3	4	4	2

S. No.	X_1	X_2A	X_2B	X_2C	X_2D	X_2E	X_2F	X_2G	X_2H	X_2I	X_2J
31	3	3	4	5	5	3	3	2	3	5	2
32	1	4	4	4	4	2	2	1	3	4	3
33	1	5	4	3	2	1	2	3	4	5	2
34	1	5	5	5	5	4	4	1	4	4	2
35	1	4	4	4	3	2	3	2	4	4	3
36	2	5	5	5	3	3	3	4	4	4	4
37	2	5	5	3	4	4	3	2	4	3	3
38	2	5	3	5	2	3	3	4	3	5	3
39	1	3	3	4	4	2	2	3	3	4	4
40	1	4	4	3	2	2	1	2	4	4	2
41	1	5	5	5	5	5	5	1	5	5	1
42	2	4	4	4	3	3	3	3	3	4	2
43	2	5	4	4	4	4	2	3	3	5	3
44	1	5	5	4	4	3	3	2	3	3	3
45	1	4	3	4	2	3	3	1	4	4	3
46	1	4	4	5	5	3	2	1	3	4	3
47	1	4	3	3	2	1	1	1	2	4	4
48	2	1	3	4	4	4	3	2	5	4	1
49	1	4	4	4	4	3	3	3	3	4	3
50	1	5	4	5	5	4	3	2	3	4	3
51	1	4	3	4	5	4	3	2	4	5	2
52	1	4	3	5	1	1	3	3	3	4	3
53	1	3	4	4	4	3	3	1	3	4	3
54	1	4	4	4	3	2	2	1	4	4	2
55	3	5	5	5	4	3	2	3	4	2	4
56	3	4	5	5	5	4	4	3	4	5	2
57	1	5	5	4	1	2	3	2	4	4	1
58	1	5	4	5	3	4	3	2	3	5	3

QUESTION

1. Divide the sample into two groups—those who rarely consume 'ready-to-eat' food are to be labelled as 'light consumers' and those eating 1–2 times or more weekly as 'high consumers' of 'ready-to-eat' food. Using the variables listed in Question 2 as predictor variables, estimate a discriminant function to differentiate between high and low consumers of ready-to-eat food and answer the following questions:
   (a) Compute the percentage of respondents that it is able to classify correctly.
   (b) Determine the statistical significance of the discriminant function.
   (c) Identify which of the predictor variables are relatively better in discriminating between the two groups.
   (d) Classify a new respondent into one of the two groups by building a decision rule and a cut-off score.

Appendix – 17.1: SPSS COMMANDS FOR DISCRIMINANT ANALYSIS

After the input data has been typed along with the variable labels and value labels in an SPSS file, to get the output for a **Discriminant Analysis** problem proceed as mentioned below:

1. Click on ANALYSE at the SPSS menu bar.
2. Click on CLASSIFY, followed by **DISCRIMINANT**.
3. On the dialogue box which appears, select the GROUPING VARIABLE (dependent categorical variable in discriminant analysis) by clicking on the right arrow to transfer it from the variable list on the left to the grouping variable box on the right.
4. Define the range of values of the grouping variable by clicking on DEFINE RANGE just below the grouping variable box. Fill in the minimum and maximum values (the codes used in our problem is 0 and 1) of the variable in the box which appears. Then click CONTINUE.
5. Select all the independent variables for discriminant analysis from the variable list by clicking on the arrow which transfers them to the INDEPENDENTS box on the right.
6. Just below the INDEPENDENTS box select 'Enter independents together' if you want all the selected independent variables (that are in the box) in the discriminant model. (Here you have an option to use a STEPWISE discriminant analysis by selecting 'Use Stepwise Method' instead of 'Enter independents together').
7. Click on STATISTICS on the lower part of the main dialog box. This opens up a smaller dialog box. Under STATISTICS, click on MEANS and UNIVARIATE ANOVAS. Under the title FUNCTION COEFFICIENTS, choose UNSTANDARDIZED to obtain the unstandardized coefficients of the discriminant function. These are used to classify a new object in a discriminant analysis. Under MATRICES click on WITHIN GROUP CORRELATION. Click on CONTINUE to return to the main dialog box.
8. Click on CLASSIFY on the lower part of the main dialog box. Select SUMMARY TABLE and LEAVE-ONE-OUT CLASSIFICATION under the heading DISPLAY in the smaller dialog box that appears. This gives you the classification table (also called the confusion matrix) that judges the accuracy of the discriminant model when applied to the input data points. Click on CONTINUE to return to the main dialog box.
9. Click on SAVE and then select PREDICTED GROUP MEMBERSHIP and DISCRIMINANT SCORES.
10. Click OK to get the discriminant analysis output.

Answers to Objective Type Questions

1. False	2. True	3. True	4. False	5. True
6. False	7. False	8. True	9. True	10. True
11. False	12. True	13. True	14. True	15. True
16. False	17. False	18. True	19. True	20. False

REFERENCES

Boyd, D and J. Heer. *Profiles as conversation: Networked identity performance on Friendster*. Proceedings of the Thirty-Ninth Hawai'i International Conference on System Sciences. Los Alamitos, CA: IEEE Press, 2006.

Ellison, N B, C Steinfeld and C Lampe. '*The benefits of Facebook Friends:* Social capital and college students' use of online social network sites. *Journal of Computer-Mediated Communication,* 12 (4): 2007.

Hargittai, E. 'Whose space? Differences among users and non-users of social network sites.' *Journal of Computer-Mediated Communication*, 13(1): 2007.

Williams, Christine B and G J Gulati. 'Social Networking in Political Campaigns: Facebook and the 2006 Midterm Elections'. Paper presented at the American Political Association annual meeting, Chicago, Illinois, 2007.

BIBLIOGRAPHY

Aaker, David A, V Kumar and George S Day. *Marketing Research*. 7th edn. Singapore: John Wiley & Sons, Inc., 2001.

Boyd, Harper W Jr, Ralph Westfall and Stanley F Stasch. *Marketing Research – Text & Cases*. 7th edn. New Delhi: Richard D. Irwin, Inc., 2002.

Churchill, Gilbert A, Jr., Dawn Iacobucci and D Israel. *Marketing Research – A South Asian Perspective*. New Delhi: Cengage Learning India Pvt. Ltd., India Edition, 2009.

Cooper, Donald R. *Business Research Methods*. New Delhi: Tata Mcgraw-Hill Publishing Company Ltd., 2006.

Green, Paul E, Donald S Tull and Gerald Albaum. *Research for Marketing Decisions*. 5th edn. Prentice-Hall of India Pvt. Ltd., 1992.

Luck, David J and Ronald S Rubin. *Marketing Research*. 7th edn. New Delhi: Prentice Hall of India Ltd., 1992.

Malhotra, Naresh K. *Marketing Research – An Applied Orientation*. 3rd edn. New Delhi: Pearson Education, 2002.

Nargundkar, Rajendra. *Marketing Research – Text and Cases*. 2nd edn. New Delhi: Tata McGraw Hill Publishing Co. Ltd., 2004.

Sethna, Beherug N. *Research Methods in Marketing Management*. New Delhi: Tata Mcgraw Hill Publishing Company Ltd., 1984.

Zikmund, William G. *Business Research Methods*. Fort Worth: Dryden Press, 2000.

18 CHAPTER

Cluster Analysis

Learning Objectives

By the end of the chapter, you should be able to:

1. Understand the technique of cluster analysis.
2. Understand the usage of cluster analysis.
3. Understand the underlying statistics used in obtaining a cluster solution.
4. Identify the key concepts used in cluster analysis.
5. Comprehend the process of clustering.
6. Discuss the hierarchical, non-hierarchical and combination methods for obtaining a cluster analysis.

11 August 2010, Caravan Travel desk: M Gad sat at his travel desk at People's Organization Travel Corporation (POTC), Janpath, and wondered what would happen to his commission for the months of July and August 2010. Gad handled the customized tour packages to exotic locations, especially Egypt. Today was the first day of *Ramadan*, the one-month period of abstinence for Muslims.

Thus, tourist outflow from India to Egypt might get curtailed. His commissions in May and June had also not been so great. People did not want to travel in the heat and there were other more exciting and cooler options available. He was eyeing a new car for himself and wanted his commissions to fund the purchase. He racked his brains on what to do, how to get people interested in the exotic Egypt package and how he should identify his potential customers.

His boss Mallvika had advised him to sift through the database of POTC to get a pool of a probable group of people who could be given exciting offers and deals to get them to opt for the package. Interesting idea, he thought to himself and went to Sukrit, who was managing the database. When he saw the database, he was stupefied. Good heavens! The list just went on and on. How was he going to make sense of the data and sort out a smaller pool to which he could send a mail and expect some conversions to happen?

'Any ideas Sukrit?' asked Gad. 'What's the problem sir?' queried Sukrit. 'Well, you see I would like to identify a group of probables who have earlier had a pleasant experience with POTC and send them an informative mail on special incentives for an exotic Egypt trip during the period of *Ramadan*, when the traffic generally is low? Can there be multiple groups to whom I can sell the package differently by pointing out different positives of the package?'

'Not a problem,' said Sukrit, who was a statistics graduate, 'We have the age group, occupation, group members/family details, time of travel, place of travel and mode of payment of the customers, also in some cases where customization was done for them, we have peculiar requests. Based on these multiple variables, I can group the customers into groups using a technique we had learned in college called cluster analysis. The clustering is done on some underlying commonality, on the basis of which any data can be reduced to smaller and more homogenous groups.' 'Are you serious, can I really get a scientifically robust solution to my problem?' asked Gad. 'Definitely, I have a cousin of mine studying at Indian Statistical Institute (ISI), where she has access to software packages. I will carry the data and conduct the analysis for you. I also feel rusted and would love to have an opportunity to use my learning. In fact, if it works and you get your conversions by identifying the 'could be interested' clusters, we can suggest this as a sorting tool to be used by the custom relationship management (CRM) department for any off-season promotions that we want to offer our past customers.'

LEARNING OBJECTIVE 1
Understand the technique of cluster analysis.

Sukrit is right, we constantly try to make sense of all the objects, individuals or even topics of study by identifying one or more similarity or similarities by grouping them. This is scientifically done in physical science (e.g., legumes and *homo sapiens*) as well as in social sciences (e.g., classifying people as personality types). In management sciences, it takes on an added advantage as grouping can help design focused strategies targeted at specific segments.

CLUSTER ANALYSIS—A CLASSIFICATION TECHNIQUE

Cluster analysis is also referred to as a classification technique, numerical taxonomy and Q analysis. The grouping can be done for objects, individuals and entities.

One such grouping technique is cluster analysis. The basic assumption underlying the technique is the fact that similarity is based on multiple variables, and the technique attempts to measure the proximity in terms of the study variables. The emerging groups are homogenous in their composition and heterogeneous as compared to the other groups. The grouping can be done for objects, individuals, entities and products. The researcher identifies a set of clustering variables which have been assumed as significant for the purpose of classifying the objects into groups. Thus, it is also referred to as a classification technique, numerical taxonomy and Q analysis. This is basically because the technique is used in various branches of social science, like psychology, sociology, engineering and management. If one were to plot the groups geometrically, a robust cluster analysis is one where individual objects in one cluster are concentrated together and where the individual clusters are far apart from each other. Figure 18.1(a) shows a simple cluster solution of breakfast food based on people who seek nutrition and convenience (ease of preparation).

However, the actual situation might be different as the person might be using different criteria for a weekday and for a weekend breakfast. Thus, as the criteria for decision-making become multiple, the grouping does not happen on a simple two-dimensional space but becomes multidimensional [Figure 18.1(b)]. Thus, the researcher is able to group people on these three dimensions and the point

FIGURE 18.1(a)
Ideal cluster solution

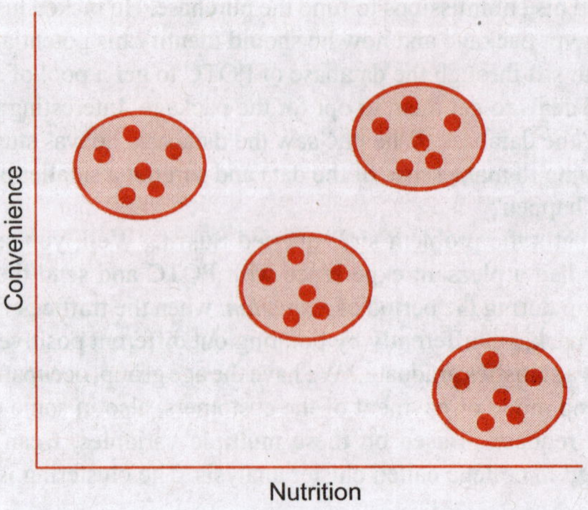

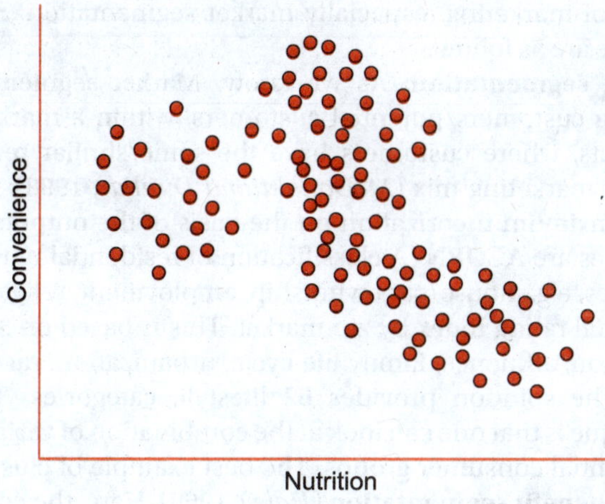

FIGURE 18.1(b)
Actual cluster solution

regarding the interpretation of benefits sought becomes clear as one understands the multidimensionality of needs. Thus, a bakery/confectionery shop selling sandwiches, patties, bread rolls as well as freshly ground idli batter, using the solution would know: (1) the lucrative segment, (2) the segment which might be motivated to buy if one takes care of their weekday/weekend needs, and (3) A segment which is currently not interested in getting a 'ready-to-eat' breakfast solution and might not look at the bakery as an outlet to visit in the morning. Once the homogenous clusters emerge, the next step is to determine the profile of the group in terms of who they are? What is their gender, age group, family size, etc.? What deals motivate them to buy from a particular store when they are buying eatables in general?

Differentiating Cluster Analysis

In cluster analysis, the whole population sample is undifferentiated and the attempts to assess similarity in response to variables and the grouping happens post the clustering.

In terms of the nature of the technique vis-á-vis the other multivariate techniques, cluster analysis is similar in terms of analysing the function of multiple independent variables. However, there are essential differences between the other data reduction techniques and cluster analysis.

In factor analysis, the objective was to reduce the original correlated variables to a more manageable number of orthogonal or oblique factors. However, the data reduction was carried out on the columns of the data matrix. On the other hand, in cluster analysis the focus is on the rows, or the individuals or entities and the objective is to group the individuals on the variables.

The other data classification technique we read about in the previous chapter was two group discriminant analyses. Here also, one might wish to group individuals or objects into groups, but the classification or identification of groups is *a priori*. Thus, in the technique one has an established classification rule and the objective of the technique is to validate the information to attest whether the groups obtained by the identified function are correctly classified or not. In cluster analysis, the whole population/sample is undifferentiated and the attempts to assess similarity in response to variables and the grouping happens *post* the clustering.

USAGE OF CLUSTER ANALYSIS

LEARNING OBJECTIVE 2
Understand the usage of cluster analysis.

Cluster analysis has widespread applicability in all the branches of social sciences and management. In management science, its most valuable contribution is in the area of marketing, especially market segmentation. Some applications of the technique are as follows:

ACORN and PRIZM are prime examples of the **market segmentation technique.** Here, one can look at the combination of variables to predict consumer or potential consumer groups.

- **Market segmentation:** As we know, Market segmentation is the process of splitting customers/potential customers, within a market into different groups/ segments, where customers have the same/similar requirement satisfied by a distinct marketing mix (*McDonald and Dunbar*, 1998). This is one area that has seen maximum theorization on the basis of the outputs of the technique. Some examples are **ACORN** (A classification of residential neighbourhood based on 40 variables, e.g., house/car ownership, employment, religion, lifestyle, etc.), ***PRIZM*** (Potential rating index by zip market. This is based on 39 variables (for example, education, affluence, family life cycle, urbanization, race and ethnicity, mobility, etc.). The solution provides 62 lifestyle categories. The advantage with the technique is that one can look at the combination of variables to predict consumer or potential consumer groups. The best example of clustered solutions are in the area of **benefit segmentation** (*Haley*, 1968). Here, the consumers are divided into groups based on the benefits they seek from the product category. These, then, could be across age groups, gender and other variables. Thus, a marketer could design his product on the basis of this segmentation approach. Yankelovich (1964) segmented consumers in terms of 'what they look for in a watch' and classified people into those who are *price driven, durability* and *quality driven*, and those driven by *occasion-bound symbolism*. Sinha (2003) classified food shoppers into *fun* and *work shoppers* based on the benefits they seek from grocery/food purchase. Sondhi and Singhvi (2005) classified grocery shoppers *into transition shoppers, traditional shoppers, thrifty shoppers* and *indifferent shoppers*.

A cluster analysis is the **best classification technique** when multiple factors are involved in data collection.

- **Segmenting industries/sectors:** The researcher could also go about grouping products or sectors (e.g., health or education) into blocks that have some common trait(s). This makes it easier for both the organizations and policy-makers while planning or evaluating the performance of the group.
- **Segmenting markets:** Cities or regions with some common traits like population mix, infrastructure development, climatic or socio-economic conditions could be clustered together. If one city in Kerala and another in Andhra Pradesh are in one cluster, then the organization is able to plan and execute a similar business approach in the two areas.
- **Career planning and training analysis:** In the area of human resources (HR) the technique can be used to group people into clusters on the basis of their educational qualification, experience, aptitude and aspirations. This grouping can assist the HR division to effectively manage training and manpower development for the members of different clusters effectively.
- **Segmenting financial sectors/instruments:** This is an emerging area where different factors like raw material cost, financial allocations, seasonality and other factors are being used to group sectors together to understand the growth and performance of a group of industries. This also assists the policy-makers and the financial analysts in assessing the monetary implications. A number of researchers are making use of clustering principles to group consumers and their investment behaviour on the basis of the combination of different variables and benefits sought (behavioural finance).

The basic premise of the above technique is, as we said earlier, wherever a researcher wants to manage the data (especially individual or organizational) and he/she perceives that there could be multiple factors involved, cluster analysis is the best classification technique at his/her disposal.

CONCEPT CHECK	
	1. Define cluster analysis.
	2. What are the uses of the cluster analysis technique?

STATISTICS ASSOCIATED WITH CLUSTER ANALYSIS

LEARNING OBJECTIVE 3
Understand the underlying statistics used in obtaining a cluster solution.

Before we review the statistics involved with the technique, it is essential once again to examine the simplicity of the technique. Unlike the other multivariate techniques that we have discussed till now, cluster analysis is the simplest in terms of mathematical derivations. The simplest way to explain the technique is to understand that it simply measures the distance between objects on the basis of multiple variables and looks for similarity as a function of distance, i.e., the shorter the distance between two objects, the more similar they are.

Metric data analysis: For obtaining a cluster solution to data that is collected on an interval or ratio scale the statistical assessment of the distance between two objects can be done by calculating the Euclidean distance between them. In case the study has two variables (as stated in the earlier example of nutrition and ease of preparation) then the distance between person A and B can be calculated:

For data that is interval or ratio **Euclidean distance** is used to measure the distance between the two objets.

$$d_{A,B} = \sqrt{(X_{B1} - X_{A1})^2 + (X_{B2} - X_{A2})^2}$$

where X_{B1} represents the coordinate of person B on nutrition (interval scale data).

A note of caution here: The Euclidean distance is not 'scale invariant'. It may happen that the relative ordering of the objects in terms of their similarity can be affected by a simple change in the scale by which one or more of the variables are measured. Thus, it is advisable that the data is standardized before being subjected to any analysis. However, it may sometimes happen that standardization can reduce the differences between the groups on the variables that may well be the best discriminators of group differences. Thus, care needs to be taken initially in questionnaire designing to keep the variables measurement scales as roughly of more or less than the same range and avoid standardizing them. Only if the variables are measured on widely different units, standardization is needed to prevent the variables measured in larger units from dominating the cluster solution.

In the example, the two variables were placed on a 10-point scale of importance (with 1 = very important and10 = very unimportant). The values selected by person A and B were as follows:

Person	Nutrition	Ease of preparation
A	1	2
B	5	2

Then the distance between the two is,

$$d_{A,B} = \sqrt{(5-1)^2 + (2-2)^2} = 4.0$$

Suppose there was a third person C who had selected

Person	Nutrition	Ease of preparation
C	6	2

Then the distance between A and C would be 5.0 and between B and C would be 1.0.

Thus, B and C are the most similar pair as the inter-person distance is the least and, as stated earlier, the shorter the distance, the greater the similarity.

If, in addition to having nutrition and ease of preparation for breakfast, we also had a variable that measured cost, we would effectively have a 3-dimensional solution. Then the formula would have been:

$$d_{A,B} = \sqrt{(X_{B1} - X_{A1})^2 + (X_{B2} - X_{A2})^2 + (X_{B3} - {}_{A3})^2}$$

And generally, for any two objects, i and j:

$$d_{ij} = \sqrt{\sum_{k=1} (X_{ik} - X_{jk})^2}$$

where,

d_{ij} = Distance between person i and j
k = Variable (interval/ratio)
i = Object/person
j = Object/person

Manhattan distance between two objects is the sum of the absolute differences in the values for each variable.

Also, there are other distance measures available like the city-block or *Manhattan distance* between two objects, which is the sum of the absolute differences in the values for each variable. Another distance measure is the *Chebychev distance* between two objects, which is the maximum absolute difference in values for any variable. However, the most commonly used measure is the squared Euclidean distance. A point to be noted here is that clustering with squared Euclidean distance is faster than the regular Euclidean distance. Thus, for the purpose of clustering, we make use of squared Euclidean distance. The equation for this is the same as the Euclidean distance; only the square root is not calculated.

Then, based on the distance calculated, a distance matrix is created and clusters are created by moving from the most to the least similar pair based on a clustering method. To illustrate how the grouping of cases is done and then its conversion into a pictorial representation of clusters we take a small example here.

Cluster Analysis: A Simplified Illustration of the Technique

Enchante is a jewellery designer who wishes to know if the population of young teenage girls aged 13–19 can be divided into smaller groups who might be looking at jewellery very differently.

- The following six statements were given to a group of 10 girls to understand what jewellery meant to them. The questionnaire was on a five-point Likert scale ranging from 1 = strongly agree to 5 = strongly disagree.

TABLE 18.1 Data table jewellery preferences of ten teenage girls

Respondent Number	X_1	X_2	X_3	X_4	X_5
1	1.00	3.00	5.00	4.00	3.00
2	2.00	3.00	4.00	5.00	2.00
3	3.00	2.00	3.00	3.00	3.00
4	5.00	5.00	1.00	2.00	4.00
5	4.00	4.00	2.00	2.00	3.00
6	2.00	2.00	4.00	3.00	2.00
7	3.00	3.00	4.00	4.00	3.00
8	2.00	1.00	3.00	3.00	2.00
9	4.00	4.00	2.00	2.00	3.00
10	5.00	4.00	1.00	1.00	3.00

X_1 = I like to wear jewellery that glitters.
X_2 = My jewellery should match my dress.
X_3 = I want everyone to admire my jewellery.
X_4 = I take my friends with me when I go jewellery shopping.
X_5 = Beautiful jewellery adds to a girl's beauty.

Now, using the squared Euclidean distance formula, we get a 10 × 10 data matrix of the distances computed. The matrix obtained would be as follows:

TABLE 18.2 Data matrix of distances

	Squared Euclidean Distance									
	1	2	3	4	5	6	7	8	9	10
1	0.000	4.000	10.000	41.000	23.000	5.000	5.000	11.000	23.000	42.000
2		0.000	8.000	35.000	19.000	5.000	3.000	9.000	19.000	36.000
3			0.000	19.000	7.000	3.000	3.000	3.000	7.000	16.000
4				0.000	4.000	32.000	22.000	34.000	4.000	3.000
5					0.000	14.000	10.000	16.000	.000	3.000
6						0.000	4.000	2.000	14.000	27.000
7							0.000	8.000	10.000	23.000
8								0.000	16.000	27.000
9									0.000	3.000
10										0.000

Now following the 'shortest distance = closest pair' logic, examine the shortest distance, which in this case is 0 between person 5 and 9. Thus:

At a distance of 0 there is one cluster of persons 5, 9.

The next distance is 2 so at a distance of 2 there are two clusters,

Cluster 1 = 5, 9
Cluster 2 = 6, 8

The next distance is 3 and here we have,

Cluster 1 = 5, 9, 4, 10
Cluster 2 = 6, 8, 3, 2, 7

The reason for the grouping that we have above is based on a deductive logic, i.e., if a = b and b = c then a = c. Taking this in the above case if 4 = 10; 5 = 10 and then 4 = 5.

FIGURE 18.2 Dendrogram of jewellery group

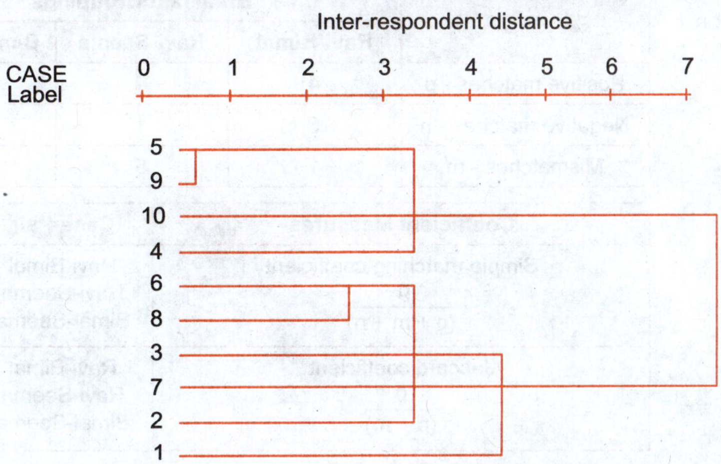

At a distance of 4 we have,

Cluster 1 = 5, 9, 4, 10

Cluster 2 = 6, 8, 3, 2, 7, 1

Next, based on the data obtained, we plot the inter-respondent distance against the cases based on proximities and we get a grouping of the 10 teenage girls into two distinct clusters. This plot is called a *dendrogram* (to be discussed in detail later).

Next, if we look at the original values or statements that they agreed with, we find that the first cluster (5, 9, 10, 4) seems to be the *socially concerned* group as they show a higher degree of agreement with X_3 and X_4. The other girls (6, 8, 3, 7, 2, 1) are more *self-driven* as they show a higher degree of agreement with X_1, X_2 and X_5.

Non-metric data analysis: The task of handling data on the non-metric scales, i.e., those placed on the nominal or ordinal scale (e.g., marital status, ethnic background, religious preference, stage in the life cycle) is different. Either it needs to be binary (0 = absence, 1 = presence of an attribute), or matching coefficients (e.g., two customers are more similar if they both consume bread and butter), or are the coefficients to reflect categories (e.g., someone who eats bread, butter, patties, bagels, doughnuts and so on).

A matching coefficient represents the number of qualities that the two objects share.

A number of formulas and computations have been made and rather than using distance or correlations to measure similarity, a matching coefficient is used. A matching coefficient represents the number of qualities that the two objects share. That is, if both give the same answer, say, a 'yes,' then it is a match, else no match. A number of computations have been made with positive matches, negative matches or both kinds.

To illustrate this, let us consider the example of three people who consume various options for their respective breakfast. If two people eat the product (a positive match) then the score is 1-1, a 0-0 indicates that neither person eats the product – (that's a negative match), a 1-0 means that the first person eats it but the second does not, whereas a 0-1 indicates the opposite, implying a mismatch in the eating habits.

TABLE 18.3(a) Breakfast consumption

	Breakfast Options									
Person	Toast Butter	Parantha	Idli	Poha	Dhokla	Patties	Bagels	Sprouts	Juice	Milk
Ravi	0	0	1	0	1	0	0	1	1	1
Bimal	0	0	1	0	1	0	0	1	1	0
Seema	1	1	1	0	0	1	1	1	1	1

TABLE 18.3(b) Breakfast consumption match

	Breakfast Groupings		
	Ravi-Bimal	Ravi-Seema	Bimal-Seema
Positive matches - p	4	4	3
Negative matches - n	5	1	1
Mismatches - m	1	5	6

TABLE 18.3(c) Similarity measures

Coefficient Measures	Case-Pair	Value
Simple matching coefficient $\frac{p}{(p + m + n)}$	Ravi-Bimal Ravi-Seema Bimal-Seema	0.4 0.4 0.3
Jaccard coefficient $\frac{p}{(p + m)}$	Ravi-Bimal Ravi-Seema Bimal-Seema	0.8 0.4 0.3

There are several formulas available for the purpose of clustering; however, we are mentioning the most popular ones here, namely the *simple matching coefficient* and the Jaccards' coefficient. Both are predominantly based on positive matches. The formulae and the calculated values for the three consumers is given in Table 18.3(c).

Let us see how the similarity between Ravi and Bimal was calculated using the simple matching coefficient formula. The positive matches between Ravi and Bimal [Table 18.3(b)] were 4, negative matches were 5 and mismatches were 1. Thus, we used the formula given in Table 18.3(c) 4/(4 + 1 + 5) = 0.4. Similarly, we calculated the similarity between Ravi and Seema, and Bimal and Seema. The values are given in Table 18.3(c).

The Jaccard coefficient does not make use of negative matches. Thus, the similarity between Ravi and Bimal using the Jaccard coefficient works out to be 4/(4 + 1) = 0.8. Similarly, we calculate the values for the other two pairs. Thus, we find that the most similar pair for breakfast options is Ravi and Bimal, which means, they like similar options for breakfast, say, *pakodas* and tea and perhaps, *parantha* and curd. The next similar pair is Ravi and Seema, which means that Ravi and Seema also have some common preferances for breakfast, say, milk and toast, and also perhaps, eggs, toast and coffee. The most dissimilar pair was Bimal and Seema, which means that they both like some food options that are not alike. This means that a breakfast place that sells Indian options like *parantha* and curd and *pakodas* should look at Ravi and Bimal. However, for one selling milk and toast or eggs and coffee should look at a pair like Ravi and Seema.

Most computer programs like SPSS and SAS have provisions for conducting the association analysis. One can simply select the measurement scale as binary and then select either one of these as the clustering measure.

Mixed (Metric and Non-metric) Data Analysis

There have also been extensions that are able to accommodate different measurement scales in the same equation. The most efficient of these is *Gower's coefficient* of similarity. It can manage binary (e.g., marital status), multicategory (e.g., newspaper preference), and quantitative (e.g., income) characteristics. The formula is as follows:

Gower's coefficient of similarity can be used when questions used for clustering are on varying levels of measurement.

$$S_{ij} = \frac{\sum_{k=1}^{m} W_k S_{ijk}}{\sum_{k=1}^{m} W_k}$$

where, S_{ij} = The similarity of objects i and j,

S_{ijk} is the similarity of objects i and j on the kth characteristic, with m characteristics in all. (The value S_{ijk} must be > = 0 and < = 1).

With qualitative characters, it is 1 when there is a match and 0 when there is a mismatch.

With quantitative characters $S_{ijk} = (|X_{ik} - X_{jk}|)/R_k$, where X_{ik} and X_{jk} are the values of attribute k for the ith and j^{th} objects,

R_k = The range of character k in the sample,

W_k = The weight attached to the kth attribute.

Another method is the log-likelihood method. The measure basically places a probability distribution on the variables. Continuous variables are assumed to be normally distributed, while categorical variables are assumed to be multinomial. All variables are assumed to be independent.

KEY CONCEPTS IN CLUSTER ANALYSIS

LEARNING OBJECTIVE 4
Identify the key concepts used in cluster analysis.

The following statistics and concepts are associated with cluster analysis.

Agglomeration schedule: A hierarchical method that provides information on the objects, starting with the most similar pair and then at each stage, provides information on the object joining the pair at a later stage.

ANOVA table: The univariate or one-way ANOVA statistics for each clustering variable. The higher is the F value, the greater is the difference between the clusters on that variable.

Cluster variate: The variables or parameters used to cluster and calculate the similarity between objects.

Cluster centroid: The average values of the objects on all variables in the cluster variate.

Cluster seeds: Initial cluster centres in the non-hierarchical clustering that are the initial points from which one starts. Then the clusters are created around these seeds.

Cluster membership: The address or the cluster to which a particular person/object belongs.

Dendrogram: This is a tree-like diagram that graphically presents the cluster results. The vertical axis represents the objects and the horizontal represents the inter-respondent distance. The figures are to be read from left to right.

Distances between final cluster centres: These are the distances between the individual pairs of clusters. A robust solution that is able to demarcate the groups distinctly is the one where the inter-cluster distance is large; the larger the distance the more distinct are the clusters.

Entropy group: Individuals or small groups that do not seem to fit into any cluster.

Entropy group: Individuals or small groups that do not seem to fit into any cluster.

Final cluster centres: The mean value of the cluster on each of the variables that is part of the cluster variate.

Hierarchical methods: A step-wise process that starts with the most similar pair and formulates a tree-like structure composed of separate clusters.

Non-hierarchical methods: Cluster seeds or centres are the starting points and one builds individual clusters around it based on some pre-specified distance of the seeds.

Proximity matrix: A data matrix that consists of pair-wise distances/similarities between the objects. It is an N × N matrix, where N is the number of objects being clustered.

Summary: Number of cases in each cluster is indicated in the non-hierarchical clustering method.

Vertical icicle diagram: Quite similar to the dendrogram, it is a graphical method to demonstrate the composition of clusters. The objects are individually displayed at the top. At any given stage, the columns correspond to the objects being clustered, and the rows correspond to the number of clusters. An icicle diagram is read from bottom to top.

CONCEPT CHECK

1. How would you conduct a metric data analysis?
2. How is the data on a non-metric scale tackled?
3. Discuss some of the key concepts in cluster analysis.

PROCESS OF CLUSTERING

LEARNING OBJECTIVE 5
Comprehend the process of clustering.

Even though it is a simple technique, cluster analysis requires a step-wise execution. The first step is to establish the research objectives of the study, which essentially indicates a clustering problem. The next step is to design a mechanism for obtaining information on the cluster variate. After the researcher has designed his measuring instrument, the next step is to decide on the clustering method. As we saw in the statistics section, a number of measures are available to the researcher depending on the scale used. The clustering algorithm to be used (in terms of hierarchical or non-hierarchical or a combination) needs to be specified next. Taking a decision on the number of clusters is a matter of quantitative analysis as well as the subjective judgment on the part of the researcher. The cluster solution obtained then needs to be interpreted with reference to the original variate and a cluster profile has to be formulated in terms of the classification variables. Lastly, the researcher must assess the validity of the clustering process. This sequential model is presented as a flow diagram in Figure 18.3.

The selected variables should be included in a study on the basis of their **relevance** to the research objective and **ability** to discriminate between clusters.

Establishing the research objectives: The first stage in cluster analysis is linked to the initial stage of defining the research problem. This could be of an exploratory or a descriptive nature. For example, in the study on organic food products, one might wish to understand the nature of food purchase and to examine whether customers differ in terms of their criteria for selection or outlet decision or the mode of purchase. Thus, here, one would do an exploratory study and look at identification of the variate (specific variables) for clustering the population. The other kind of research, either based on an exploratory study or the researcher's judgment, might involve having a predetermined set of criteria which are used as the defining variables. This step becomes extremely critical in the cluster analysis method as in this method, unlike the others stated earlier, all the specified variables which are a part of the clustering variate are used to segment or group the population under study. A single or two irrelevant variables may distort an otherwise useful clustering solution. Thus, it may happen that an entropy group is created because of an irrelevant variable. Thus, the selected variables should be included in the study on the basis of their (a) relevance to the research objective and (b) ability to discriminate between clusters.

Establishing the cluster assumptions: The next step in the technique is to take a decision on how the clustering variables would be portrayed in the measuring instrument. The first step here is to identify the scale on which the response categories would be based. That is, the level of measurement to be used. This could be either based on metric or non-metric data.

Since the objective of the method is to classify the objects that are similar in composition, the next step is to select the statistical technique applicable for the selected level of measurement. As we learned in the earlier section on statistics, the distance measure for the nominal level of measurement and where the output was binary in nature, the technique to be used is simple matching coefficient. Most statistical packages, e.g. SPSS, have the provision for carrying out the cluster analysis for nominal data.

Alternatively the response categories could be formulated on an interval scale of measurement, and then the distance measure used would be squared Euclidean distance. This analysis is also possible on most statistical packages like SPSS. To understand the step-wise process of cluster analysis, we are going to discuss an example, where the clustering variable were on a 5-point Likert scale, that is, metric data.

For conducting this analysis, please refer to instructions in Appendix 18.1 in the section on hierarchical cluster analysis. This is interval-scale data, so ignore instruction points 8 and 9. Further to this, please note the section on K-means

FIGURE 18.3
Cluster analysis process

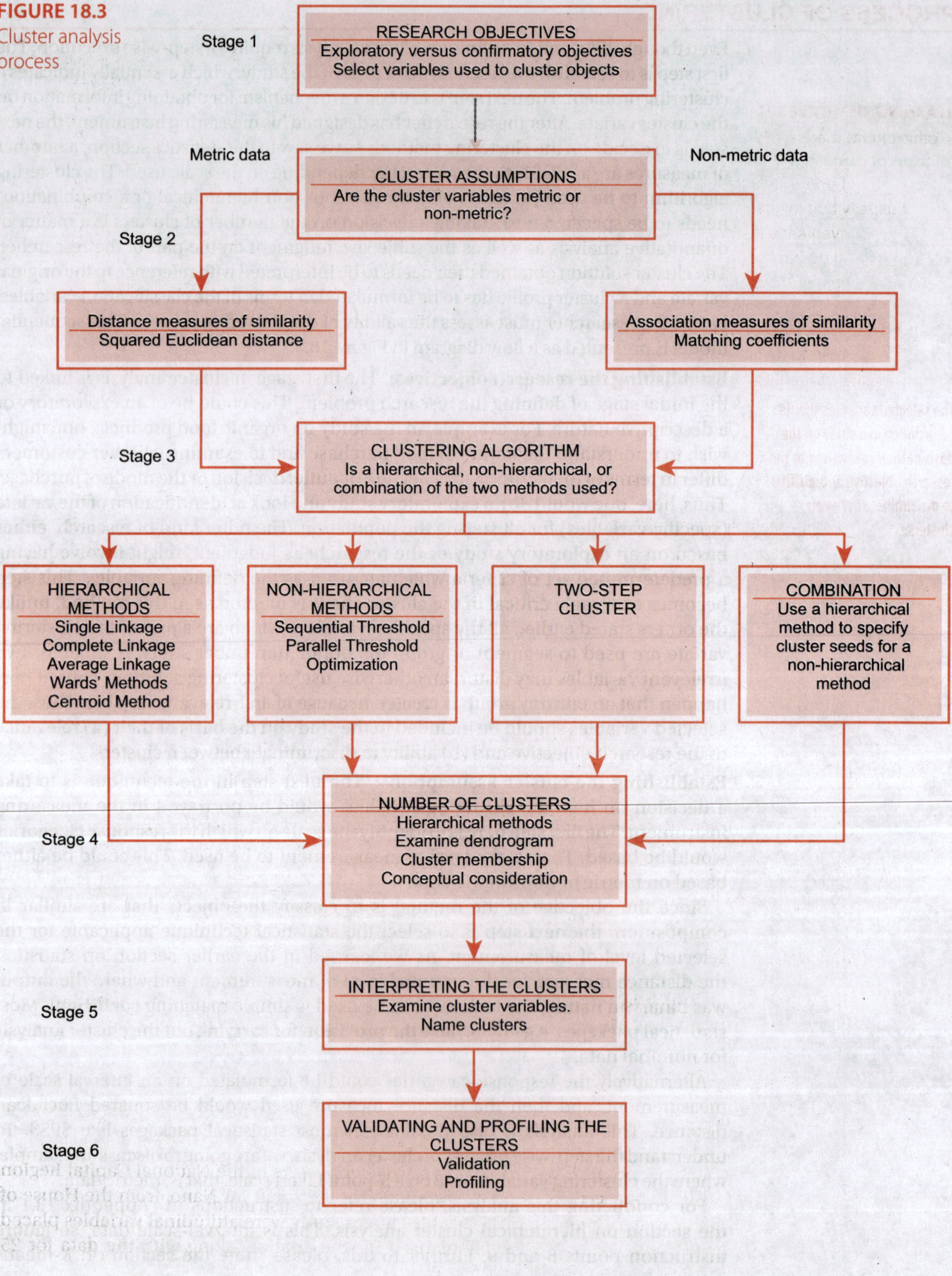

Codebook for the Nano study

Variable Name	Coding Instruction	Symbol used for Variable Name
Respondent ID.	Serially numbered	ID
I think in India we have been able to achieve technological standard of high order	A number from 1 to 5 SA = 5, A = 4, N = 3, D = 2, SD = 1	1a
I prefer to buy things made in India	- do -	1b
I usually buy things which provide value for money	- do -	1c
Convenience is more important than style	- do -	1d
I do not like wasteful expenditure	- do -	1e
When it comes to safety I believe there should be no compromises.	- do -	1f
I'm a 'saver' rather than a 'spender.'	- do -	1g
I like to try new and different things.	- do -	1h
I always want to be a part of changing world	- do -	1i
In the near future I would like to purchase a Nano car.	Yes = 1 No = 0	2
Occupation	1 = Government 2 = private 3 = self-employed	3
Family monthly household income	< 1 lakh = 1, 1–1.5 lakh = 2, 1.6-2.0 lakh = 3 > 2 lakh = 4	4
Family size	One to two = 1, Three to five = 2, Six and more = 3	5
Marital Status	Married = 1 Single = 2	6
Education	10th grade = 1 12th grade = 2 Graduation = 3 Post-graduation and above = 4	7
Age group	21–30 yrs = 1 31–40 yrs = 2 41–50 yrs = 3 >50 yrs = 4	8
Nature of job	Desk job = 1 Travelling = 2 Both = 3	9

clustering is to be followed completely as that is meant for interval and ration scale data only and is not applicable to non-metric data.

CLUSTER ANALYSIS: METRIC DATA

Illustration 18.1: Nano Sample Survey (metric data)

A study was conducted on 200 two-wheeler owners in the National Capital Region (NCR) to assess their purchase intention for the small car Nano, from the House of Tata Motors. The clustering variables under study were attitudinal variables placed on a Likert scale. The questions used for the analysis along with the data for 25 customers are presented below:

TABLE 18.4
Two-wheeler Study: Nano Sample Survey

ID	1a	1b	1c	1d	1e	1f	1g	1h	1i	2	3	4	5	6	7	8	9	10
1	5	5	3	2	3	3	4	1	1	1	2	4	2	1	3	3	1	3
2	3	3	5	4	4	5	4	1	1	0	2	2	1	2	3	2	1	1
3	1	1	1	2	1	2	1	4	4	0	2	1	3	1	3	1	1	2
4	5	5	4	2	3	4	3	2	2	1	2	4	2	1	3	3	1	3
5	2	2	4	5	4	5	4	2	2	0	2	4	3	2	3	2	1	1
6	2	2	1	2	1	1	1	5	5	1	2	4	2	1	3	1	1	2
7	3	3	2	1	1	1	1	5	4	0	3	2	1	2	4	1	3	2
8	1	1	1	2	1	2	1	4	4	0	2	1	3	2	3	2	1	2
9	4	5	3	3	3	3	4	1	1	1	2	4	2	1	3	3	1	3
10	1	1	4	4	3	4	4	2	2	0	2	1	2	2	3	3	1	1
11	2	2	1	2	1	1	1	5	5	1	2	4	2	1	3	1	1	2
12	5	4	3	2	3	2	2	2	2	0	1	2	3	2	3	3	3	3
13	3	3	2	1	1	1	1	5	4	0	3	2	1	2	4	1	3	2
14	5	5	2	2	2	3	1	1	1	1	2	3	2	1	3	2	1	3
15	3	2	5	5	5	5	4	2	1	0	2	1	3	2	3	3	2	1
16	4	5	2	2	3	1	1	1	1	1	2	3	2	1	3	3	1	3
17	2	1	5	5	5	4	5	1	1	0	3	2	2	2	3	2	1	1
18	2	3	2	2	1	1	1	5	4	1	2	3	2	1	3	2	1	2
19	4	5	3	3	3	2	2	1	1	1	2	3	2	1	3	3	1	3
20	4	4	2	1	3	2	1	1	2	0	2	3	3	2	3	3	1	3
21	2	2	1	2	1	1	1	5	5	1	2	4	1	1	3	1	1	2
22	2	1	5	5	5	5	4	1	1	0	2	2	3	2	3	2	3	1
23	4	4	2	2	2	3	4	1	2	1	2	4	3	2	3	3	1	3
24	4	5	3	2	3	3	4	1	1	0	1	4	3	1	3	2	1	3
25	2	3	2	2	1	1	1	5	4	1	2	4	2	1	3	1	1	2

ESTABLISHING THE CLUSTERING ALGORITHM

LEARNING OBJECTIVE 6
Discuss the hierarchical, non-hierarchical and combination methods for obtaining a cluster analysis.

The next stage involves determining how many clusters are statistically robust-homogenous within themselves and heterogeneous when compared to others. For this, one needs to specify the clustering algorithm to be used. The commonly used algorithms are hierarchical methods, non-hierarchical methods and two-step methods of clustering. These are briefly discussed below:

Hierarchical Methods

As stated in the previous section, this group of methods involves constructing a hierarchy of objects based on similarity and starting with the most similar pair and going to the most dissimilar one. There are two kinds of hierarchical procedures. The first is agglomerative, where each person/object starts off as a cluster, at the next it combines with a similar object to form a new aggregate. Thus, at each stage, the

FIGURE 18.4
Dendrogram showing hierarchical clustering

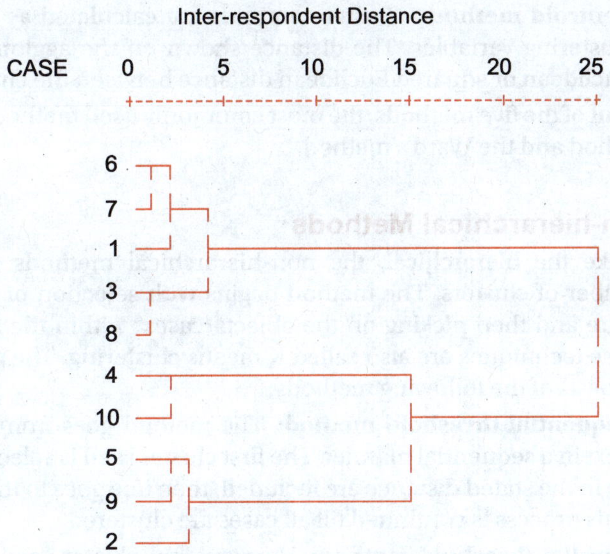

number of clusters keeps on reducing as more and more objects cluster together. Thus, in a sample of n objects, n-1 clustering stages occur. Thus, the cluster of an initial stage gets nested with the aggregation of a later stage. This can be observed when we plot the inter-object distance on the horizontal axis and the objects on the vertical axis (Figure 18.4). For example, in case 6, 7 who clustered at stage 1 are joined by case 1, 3 and 8 to form a two-cluster solution. This tree like structure is referred to as a dendrogram.

The other hierarchical method is the divisive method. This is the exact opposite of the agglomerative methods, as here, one begins with one large mass which is the entire sample being clustered as one group and then at each stage, the dissimilar objects break away and form smaller clusters until everyone is an individual cluster. Typically, in the above diagram, if one reads from left to right it is an agglomerative representation and if one moves from right to left, it is divisive. Most software packages present the divisive method as icicles.

Agglomerative methods have been further modified by different researchers. The individual formulation is as follows:

1. **Single linkage method or nearest neighbour approach:** This is based on minimum distance. The first two most similar pair(s) are put in the first cluster and then the next closest person(s) join and this moves on at every stage. At every stage, the agglomeration schedule shows the shortest distance between the two clusters as the shortest distance between their two closest points.
2. **Complete linkage method:** This is the exact opposite of the single linkage. Rather than minimum distance, the clustering is based on the maximum distance between the two elements.
3. **Average linkage method:** The cluster criterion here is the average distance from all the elements in one cluster with the other entire cluster. Thus, here, one is not looking at paired data at each stage, but it is based on all the elements of the cluster. Thus, the cluster created would also ensure grouping objects with a small variance and thus homogeneity would be higher.
4. **Ward's method:** Here, the distance between two clusters is the sum of squares between the two clusters across all the clustering variables. Thus, in this case the with-in cluster variance is reduced to a minimum.

In **Ward's method**, the distance between two clusters is the sum of squares between the two clusters across all the clustering variables.

5. **Centroid method:** Cluster centroids are calculated as the mean values for the clustering variables. The distance shown on the agglomeration schedule is the Euclidean or squared Euclidean distance between the cluster centroids.

Out of the five methods, the most commonly used methods are the average linkage method and the Ward's method.

Non-hierarchical Methods

Non-hierarchical methods start with a predefined number of clusters and are also called **K-means clustering.**

Unlike the hierarchical, the non-hierarchical methods start with a predefined number of clusters. The method begins with selection of a cluster seed or cluster centre and then picking on the objects/cases within the predetermined distance. These techniques are also called K-means clustering. The grouping can be done on the basis of the following methods:

1. **Sequential threshold method:** The method goes from one cluster seed to the next in a sequential manner. The first cluster seed is selected and all the cases that lie in the stated distance are included, then one goes to the next seed and the next. This process is continued till all cases are clustered.
2. **Parallel threshold method:** Here, several cluster seeds are selected at one go and different cases are categorized into clusters where the object-seed distance is minimal. Here, sometimes the threshold distance is adjusted by the presence of more or less cases near the cluster seed. It may also happen that some cases remain unclustered if they are not close to any cluster seed.
3. **Optimizing procedures:** This method allows for a re-alignment of cases. It begins like the other two and begins by allotting cases to the clusters based on the threshold distance. In case, after clustering, some cases seem to be deviant with their original classification and seem to belong more to another group, to optimize the homogeneity of the solution the divergent element is moved to the other more similar cluster.

Two-step Clustering

There are other cluster methods available as well; one frequently used as an alternative is the two- step cluster analysis. It has the advantage of being compatible with both continuous and categorical data. As the name rightly indicates, the analysis is done at two stages. At the first stage, it uses an agglomeration schedule to start with the closest and then goes on to make homogenous groups of all the objects considered for analysis. Like the K-means clustering and hierarchical cluster, here also the researcher can ask for a specified number of clusters, else the technique first determines the optimal number of clusters automatically by comparing the values across different clustering solutions.

At the second stage, the technique calculates measures–of-fit to assess how many ideal clusters should be used for analysis. Two options exist for calculating the goodness of fit-Bayes information criteria (BIC) and Akaike's information criteria (AIC). They compare multiple combinations with varying number of clusters predictive capabilities of the model. Both are based on the likelihood model. When calculating AIC, what is obtained is a constant plus the distance between the actual but unknown likelihood function of the number of clusters that actually exist in the population with the fitted function of the model. BIC is on the other hand based on the posterior probability of the model being true under certain Bayesian conditions. In both cases, a lower value indicates a better fit between the fitted and the true model. However, while AIC tends to overestimate the best solution in terms of number of clusters, the BIC model takes a more conservative approach and underestimates. Thus, you can see the results by both the methods by using statistical software like SPSS. In most cases, the solution would be more or less comparable, with may be a difference in predicting the goodness of fit (this is illustrated later in the chapter). This method can be used to validate the results obtained by the other two methods.

Combination Method

There are different schools of thought about the question which is better-hierarchical or non-hierarchical? In practice, most researchers use them in combination. That is, one uses hierarchical to establish how many clusters would be ideal and then carries out a non-hierarchical with the pre-specified number of clusters. This output is then used to interpret the cluster solution. This will be demonstrated in a subsequent section.

Determining the number of clusters: An important step in the cluster analysis is determining the number of clusters that need to be considered. There are numerous guidelines for this purpose:

(a) Sometimes, one may make an *a priori* decision about a viable and manageable number of clusters. For example, if the purpose of clustering is to identify market segments, one needs to divide the consumers into groups large enough to be commercially viable.

(b) The *hierarchical cluster methods* can also be used for this purpose. Here, there are three measures available to the researcher. The methods are demonstrated by conducting a cluster analysis on the Nano sample survey (for conducting the hierarchical cluster analysis go to Appendix 18.1 and follow steps from 1-12; however do not conduct steps 8 and 9).

(c) One can take a decision by observing the agglomeration schedule, obtained by using the average linkages method, given in Table 18.5(a) when we examine the distance coefficient values in the 'coefficients' column.

Before we go on to the interpretation of how we arrive at the ideal number of clusters, let us first examine how we arrive at an agglomeration schedule. To illustrate this, we take the example of five consumers (case numbers-1, 24, 4, 7, 18) and the distance matrix computed between them using the Euclidean distance formula. This distance has been calculated using their answers to the nine questions in the Nano study (refer data given in Table 18.4). We will call this matrix $D^{(1)}$.

Matrix $D^{(1)}$

	A (case 1)	B (case 24)	C (case 4)	D (case 7)	E (case18)
A (case 1)	0.0	1.0	5.00	52.00	56.00
B (case 24)	1.0	0.0	6.00	49.00	51.00
C (case 4)	5.00	6.00	0.0	43.00	47.00
D (case 7)	52.00	49.00	43.00	0.0	2.00
E (case 18)	56.00	51.00	47.00	2.00	0.0

Now, the coefficients at various stages using the average distance rule formula is

$$\frac{1}{n_1 n_j}\sum_i \sum_j d_{ij} \text{ where}$$

d_{ij} = The distance between object i in cluster 1 and object j in cluster 2. The summation is done across all possible pairings of the variables between the two clusters.

n_i and n_j = Number of objects in the respective clusters.

Thus, the coefficients obtained are as follows:

Stage 1: The shortest distance as we can see above is 1.0 between person 1 and person 24.

Stage 2: Now if we take this distance as 0 and calculate the average of d_{AB} with all the other objects as follows:

$$d_{(AB),C} = \frac{dAC + dBC}{2 \times 1} = \frac{5+6}{2} = 5.5$$

$$d_{(AB),D} = \frac{dAD + dBD}{2} = \frac{52+49}{2} = 50.5$$

$$d_{(AB),E} = \frac{dAE + dBE}{2} = \frac{56+51}{2} = 53.5$$

$d_{(CD)} = 43$
$d_{(CE)} = 47$
$d_{(DE)} = \mathbf{2}$

The $D^{(2)}$ Matrix looks as follows:

Matrix $D^{(2)}$

	AB	C	D	E
AB	0.0	5.5	50.5	53.5
C	5.5	0.0	43.0	47.00
D	50.5	43.00	0.0	2.00
E	53.5	47.00	2.00	0.0

Thus, at stage 2 the shortest distance is 2 (between D and E)

Now we take d_{DE} as the Shortest distance and therefore take it as equal to 0; again we follow the same calculations as we did for $D^{(2)}$:

$$d_{(AB),C} = \frac{dAC + dBC}{2 \times 1} = \frac{5+6}{2} = 5.5$$

$$d_{(AB),(DE)} = \frac{dAD + +dAE + dBD + BE}{2 \times 2} = \frac{52+56+49+51}{2 \times 2} = \frac{208}{4} = 52$$

$$d_{(DE),C} = \frac{dDC + +dEC}{2 \times 1} = \frac{43+47}{2} = 45$$

and we get $D^{(3)}$ matrix as follows:

Matrix $D^{(3)}$

	AB	C	DE
AB	0.0	5.5	52.0
C	5.5	0.0	45.0
DE	52.0	45.0	0.0

And thus, we can see the shortest distance at stage 3 is 5.5. Thus the agglomeration schedule would look like this:

Stage	Cluster Combined		Coefficients	Stage Cluster First Appears		Next Stage
	Cluster 1	Cluster 2		Cluster 1	Cluster 2	
1	A	B	1.0	0	0	3
2	D	E	2.0	0	0	4
3	C	A	5.5	0	1	0
4	D	A	45.0	2	1	0

Next Object joins at Stage 3

Object A appears at Stage 1

At stage 1, A and B would join as their distance is minimum (1). At stage 0, A and B were single objects (did not belong to any cluster). The next pair is D and E, which meet at the next distance of 2.0 and in the previous stage (0) they were standalone. At stage 3, which is shown in the first cell of the last column, C enters the cluster of A and B and now the shortest distance between AB and C is 5.5. The cluster containing D and E are (see last column, stage 2) are joined by more objects like A, B, C at stage 4 and the coefficient is 45.0

This example illustrated the method of agglomerating the cases. Now, let us see the agglomeration schedule for the whole sample of 25. This can now be used to determine how many distinctly different clusters exist. Using Table 18.5(a) of the

TABLE 18.5(a) Agglomeration schedule: Nano survey data

Stage	Cluster Combined		Coefficients	Stage Cluster First Appears		Next Stage
	Cluster 1	Cluster 2		Cluster 1	Cluster 2	
1	18	25	0.000	0	0	9
2	11	21	0.000	0	0	4
3	7	13	0.000	0	0	9
4	6	11	0.000	0	2	12
5	3	8	0.000	0	0	20
6	9	24	1.000	0	0	7
7	1	9	1.500	0	6	13
8	17	22	2.000	0	0	11
9	7	18	2.000	3	1	12
10	16	20	4.000	0	0	16
11	15	17	4.000	0	8	18
12	6	7	4.000	4	9	20
13	1	23	4.667	7	0	19
14	12	19	5.000	0	0	16
15	5	10	5.000	0	0	21
16	12	16	6.000	14	10	17
17	12	14	6.250	16	0	22
18	2	15	6.667	0	11	21
19	1	4	7.000	13	0	22
20	3	6	7.857	5	12	24
21	2	5	8.500	18	15	23
22	1	12	11.800	19	17	23
23	1	2	40.667	22	21	24
24	1	3	59.222	23	20	0

Nano survey, we start with the last coefficient when all objects group into a single cluster value (stage 24). Next, we subtract the coefficient from the 2 cluster (stage 23) as follows:

$$59.222 - 40.667 = 18.55$$

Then, we look at the difference between 2 clusters (stage 23) and 3 cluster (stage 22):

$$40.667 - 11.800 = 28.867.$$

The next difference is

$$11.800 - 8.50 = 3.5$$

Thus, we can see from the data above that the maximum variation happens when we move from a two-cluster to a three-cluster solution. Thus, we assume that a three-cluster solution is adequate and distinct enough for analysis. Or simply put, the 25 respondents selected for the Nano survey can be grouped into three distinct clusters.

(d) **Cluster membership:** In the hierarchical cluster solution one can also examine the cluster membership of cases for an a apriori selected number of clusters. For example, in the Nano example let us examine the cluster membership of the 25 cases for a 2, 3, 4, 5 cluster solutions [Table 18.5(b)].

TABLE 18.5(b)
Cluster membership: Nano sample survey

Case	6 Clusters	5 Clusters	4 Clusters	3 Clusters	2 Clusters
1	1	1	1	1	1
2	2	2	2	2	1
3	3	3	3	3	2
4	1	1	1	1	1
5	4	4	2	2	1
6	5	3	3	3	2
7	5	3	3	3	2
8	3	3	3	3	2
9	1	1	1	1	1
10	4	4	2	2	1
11	5	3	3	3	2
12	6	5	4	1	1
13	5	3	3	3	2
14	6	5	4	1	1
15	2	2	2	2	1
16	6	5	4	1	1
17	2	2	2	2	1
18	5	3	3	3	2
19	6	5	4	1	1
20	6	5	4	1	1
21	5	3	3	3	2
22	2	2	2	2	1
23	1	1	1	1	1
24	1	1	1	1	1
25	5	3	3	3	2

For a 2 Cluster solution(examine the last column): The customer IDs of the people in each cluster:

Cluster 1: 1, 2, 4, 5, 9, 10, 12, 14, 15, 16, 17, 19, 20, 22, 23, and 24.

Cluster 2: 3, 6, 7, 8, 11, 13, 18, 21, 25.

As one can see, when we move from a two- to a three-cluster solution, 9 cases move to the third cluster, and when the movement is from a three- to a four-cluster solution, only 5 cases moved. As the movement after a three-cluster solution was less, again a three-cluster solution is recommended.

(e) **Dendrogram:** The third way of assessing the number of clusters is to physically observe the dendrogam of the distance matrix. Figure 18.5 shows the tree graph. As we examine here as well there are clearly three clusters that are distinctly different from each other.

Interpreting and profiling the clusters: This step is carried out by conducting the K-means clustering. (Refer to the SPSS instruction in Appendix 18.1 for K-means clustering: step 1-6). The interpretation is conducted by following the steps as listed below.

Step I: Examine the F values from the ANOVA tables to establish the discriminating power of each clustering variable. This is important as the interpretation would then

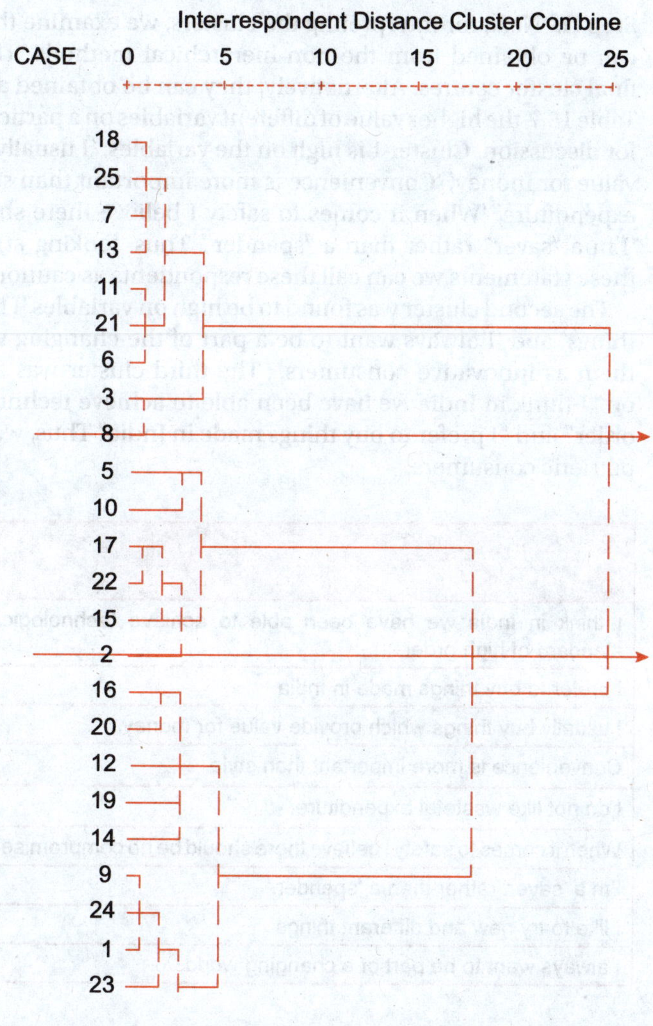

FIGURE 18.5 Dendrogram of Nano sample survey

ignore the variables on which all clusters have more or less the same views. For the Nano sample survey, an ANOVA table for the attitudinal statements under study was constructed (Table 18.6). Please note that for the nominal data this will not be done.

TABLE 18.6 ANOVA table for Nano sample survey

	F	Sig.
I think in India we have been able to achieve technological standard of high order.	39.036	0.000
I prefer to buy things made in India.	44.896	0.000
I usually buy things which provide value for money.	53.716	0.000
Convenience is more important than style.	65.008	0.000
I do not like wasteful expenditure.	92.103	0.000
When it comes to safety I believe there should be no compromises.	50.579	0.000
I'm a 'saver' rather than a 'spender.'	23.468	0.000
I like to try new and different things.	164.223	0.000
I always want to be part of a changing world.	96.749	0.000

As can be observed from the above results, all the variables were significant at the 5 per cent level of significance and may be used for the interpretation.

Step II: Next, for interpreting the clusters, we examine the cluster centroids. These can be obtained from the non-hierarchical methods. They are referred to as the final cluster centres. Alternatively, they can be obtained as descriptive(s) as well. In Table 18.7 the higher value of different variables on a particular cluster is emboldened for discussion. Cluster 1 is high on the variables, 'I usually buy things which provide value for money', 'Convenience is more important than style', 'I do not like wasteful expenditure', 'When it comes to safety I believe there should be no compromises', 'I'm a "saver" rather than a "spender"'. Thus, looking at the common elements in these statements we can call these respondents as cautious consumers.

The second cluster was found to be high on variables 'I like to try new and different things' and 'I always want to be a part of the changing world'. Thus, we can name them as innovative consumers. The third cluster was found to have high values on "I think in India we have been able to achieve technological standard of a high order" and "I prefer to buy things made in India". Thus, we decided to call this group patriotic consumers.

TABLE 18.7 Cluster centroids for Nano sample survey

	Cluster		
	1	2	3
I think in India we have been able to achieve technological standard of high order.	2.17	2.00	**4.40**
I prefer to buy things made in India.	1.67	2.22	**4.70**
I usually buy things which provide value for money.	**4.67**	1.44	2.70
Convenience is more important than style.	**4.67**	1.78	2.10
I do not like wasteful expenditure.	**4.33**	1.00	2.80
When it comes to safety I believe there should be no compromises.	**4.67**	1.22	2.60
I'm a 'saver' rather than a 'spender.'	**4.17**	1.00	2.60
I like to try new and different things.	1.50	**4.78**	1.20
I always want to be part of a changing world.	1.33	**4.33**	1.40

When we conduct the K-means clustering (refer Appendix 18.1) we also SAVE the cluster membership so that the data table now has a new variable, which is 'cluster membership'. This data can be seen in the last column of Table 18.4, which represents cluster membership. Please note that to save space this data has been saved in the original table for illustration.

Based on the cluster membership of the saved solution, the non-hierarchical solution also gives a summary table of the number of cases in each cluster, as shown in Table 18.8.

TABLE 18.8 Cluster summary: Nano sample survey

	Cluster 1 (cautious consumer)	6.000
	Cluster 2 (innovative consumer)	9.000
	Cluster 3 (patriotic consumer)	10.000
Valid		25.000
Missing		0.000

Profiling the clusters and validating the cluster solution: Once, the clusters have been duly categorized and given a name, it is useful to profile the clusters in terms of variables that were not used for clustering. Thus, based on the demographic, psychographic or any other classification data one is able to create a cluster profile. In fact, it is also possible to go to their typical shopping behavior/decision making behavior/economic spend/media habits/leisure activities and create a profile. This profiling is useful as the developed strategies can be disseminated to the cluster on the basis of the information for each cluster. To illustrate this, presented below is the cluster profile of the Nano sample survey. If we go back to the data set, we can see that there are some demographic variables listed that can be used for the profiling.

Cluster profile: Nano Sample survey: The clusters obtained by cross-tabulating the cluster membership with the demographic variables for age, marital status, occupation, education, family size and nature of job. To illustrate how this is done, the cross-tabulated data for cluster membership and occupation is presented below (Table 18.9).

TABLE 18.9 Cross-tabulation of cluster membership with occupation

		Occupation			Total
		Government	Private	Self-employed	
Cluster membership	Cautious consumer	0	5	1	6
	Innovative consumer	0	7	2	9
	Patriotic consumer	2	8	0	10
Total		2	20	3	25

Thus, if we see the above charts we formulate the following conclusions about the three clusters:

Cautious consumer: This group was composed of people in the age bracket of 31 and above with a large majority in the age group of 31–40 years. They were all single, graduate males living mostly in large families. Most of them were working in the private sector and had a desk job. Their family income was less than 1.5 lakh per month.

FIGURE 18.6(a)
Cluster profile (Nano) – occupation

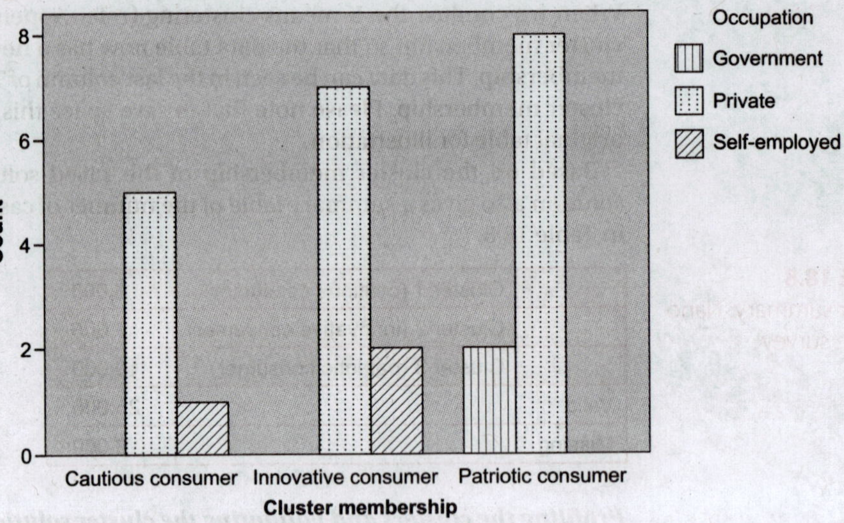

FIGURE 18.6(b)
Cluster profile (Nano) – education

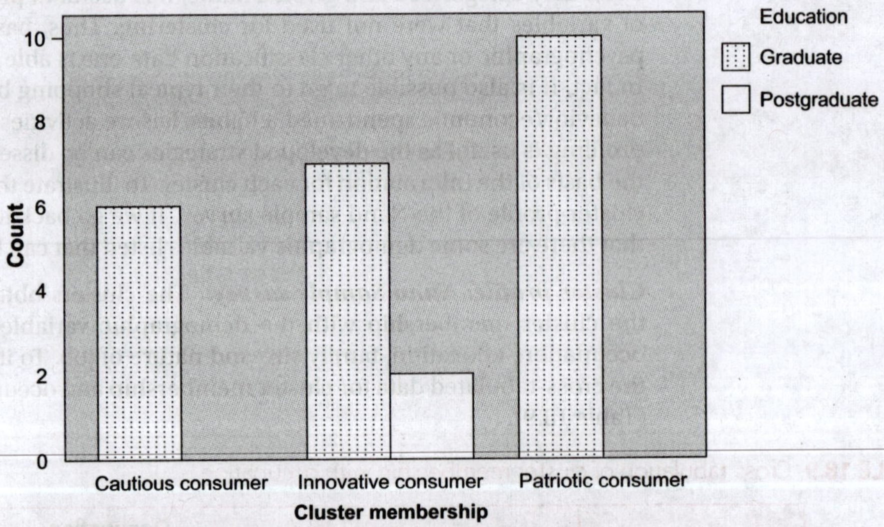

FIGURE 18.6(c)
Cluster profile (Nano) – nature of job

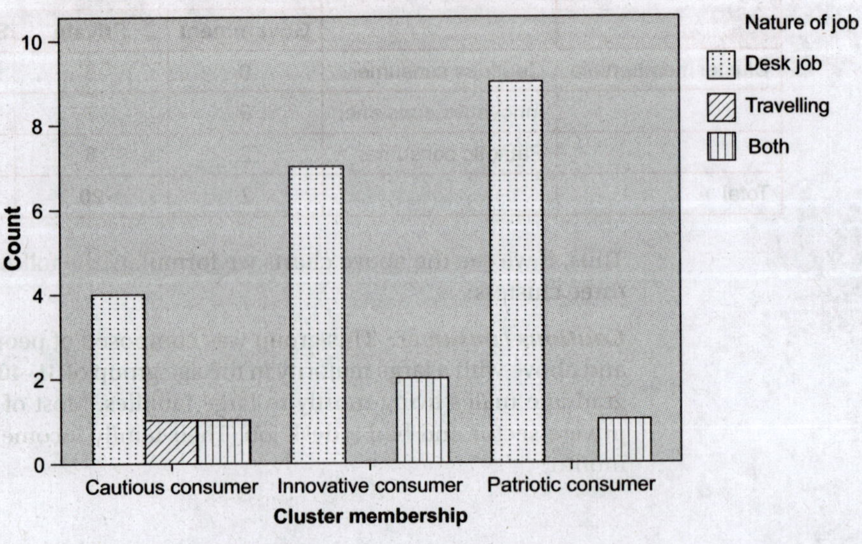

FIGURE 18.6(d)
Cluster profile (Nano) – age

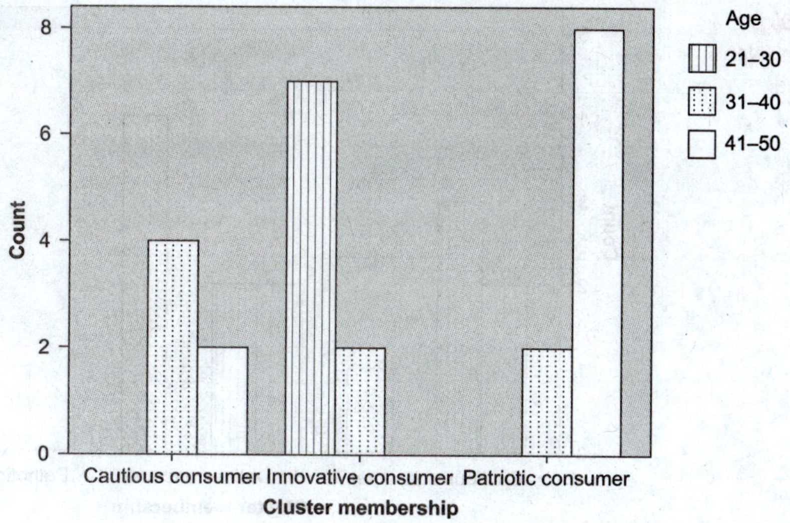

FIGURE 18.6(e)
Cluster profile (Nano) – marital status

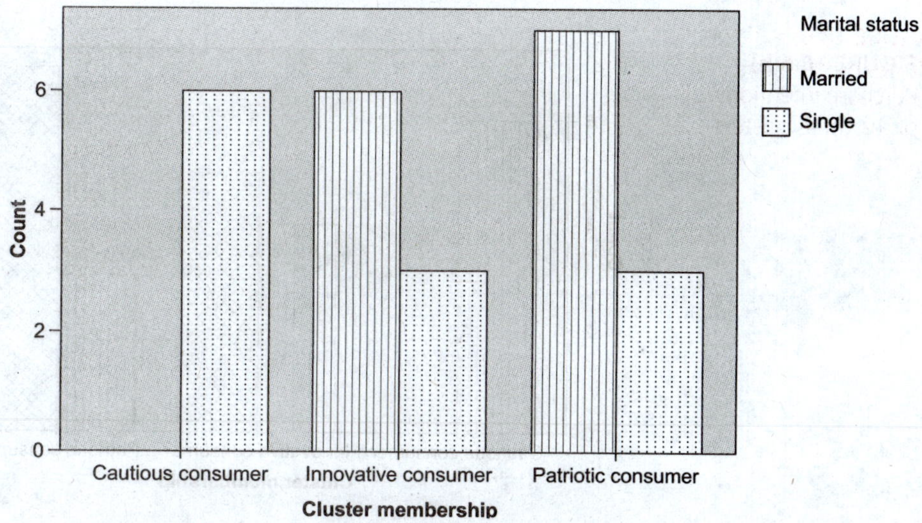

FIGURE 18.6(f)
Cluster profile (Nano) – family size

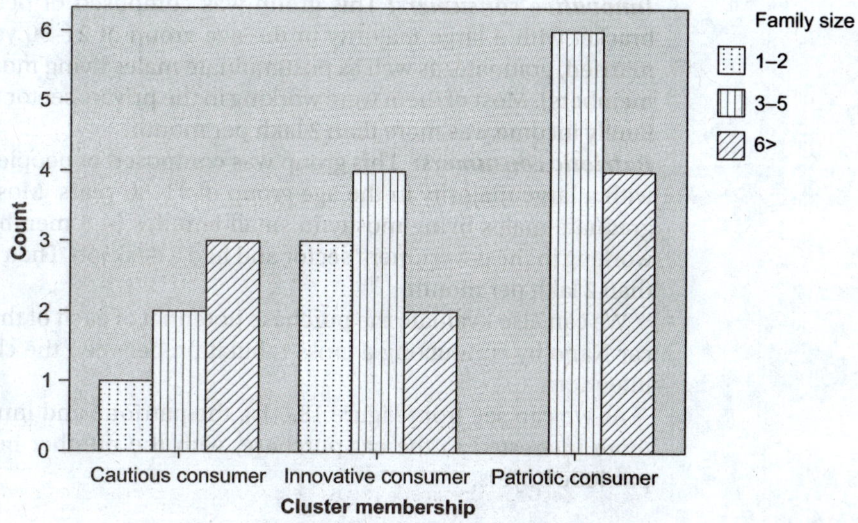

FIGURE 18.6(g)
Cluster profile (Nano) – family income

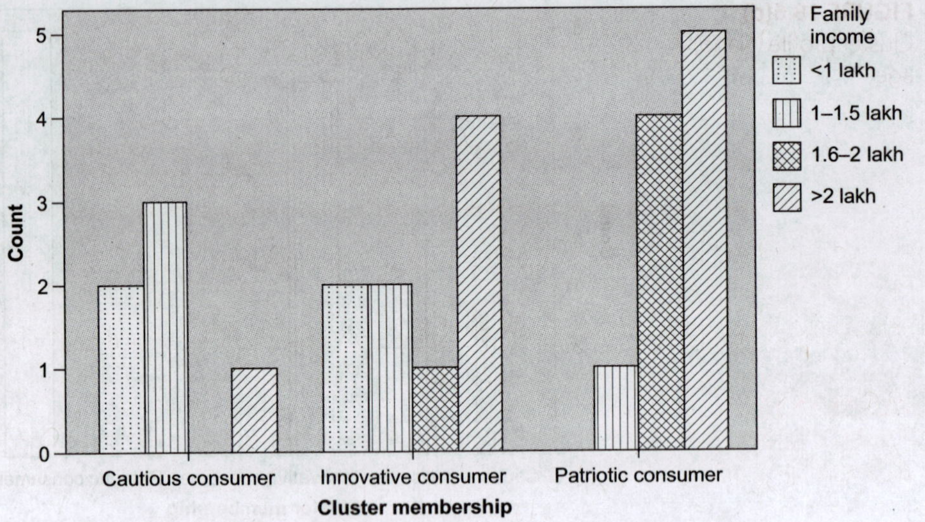

FIGURE 18.6(h)
Purchase intentions of the three clusters

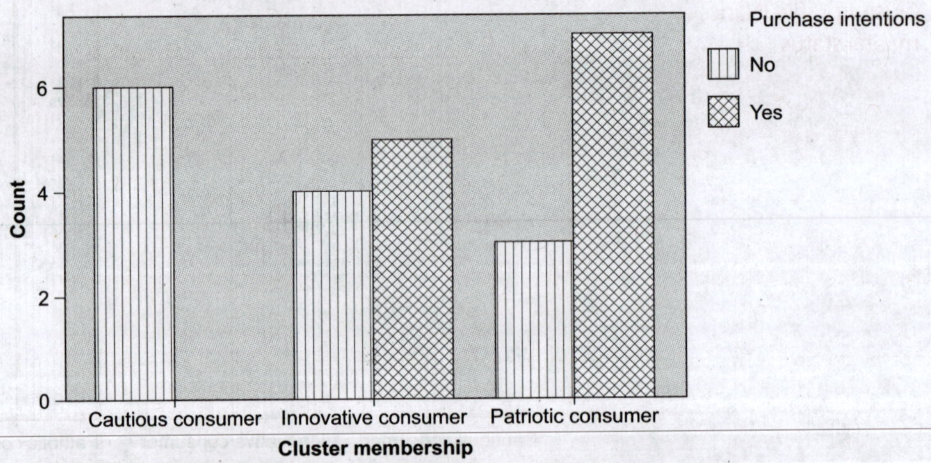

Innovative consumers: This group was composed of people in the younger age bracket with a large majority in the age group of 21–30 years. Most of them were married, graduate, as well as postgraduate males living mostly in small families (< 5 members). Most of them were working in the private sector and had a desk job. Their family income was more than 2 lakh per month.

Patriotic consumers: This group was composed of people in the older age bracket with a large majority in the age group of 41–50 years. Most of them were married, graduate males living mostly in small families (< 5 members). Most of them were working in the government sector and had a desk job. Their family income was more than 2 lakh per month.

We can also evaluate the purchase potential of each of the clusters for Tata's small car Nano by conducting a cross-tabulation between the clusters and the purchase intentions.

As we can see from Figure 18.6(h), the patriotic and innovative consumers were more interested in the car purchase, with the number being higher amongst the patriotic buyers.

Validating the cluster solution: The last stage in the cluster analysis is establishing the validity of the obtained solution. Formal procedures are available for establishing the validity; however, here we would just point out some simple procedures for establishing the same.

- One can use different clustering algorithms and check for the stability of solution. For example, using different hierarchical and non-hierarchical methods and further validating it using a two-step clustering solution (Appendix 18.1- two-step clustering–steps 1-8 and ensure in step 3 you chose Euclidean distance). As discussed earlier in the chapter, this technique first establishes clusters or groups and then assesses the viability of results by the AIC or BIC technique. In this case, we are giving the goodness of fit obtained with both. The result is as presented in Figures 18.7(a) and (b).

FIGURE 18.7(a) Two-step clustering–BIC method

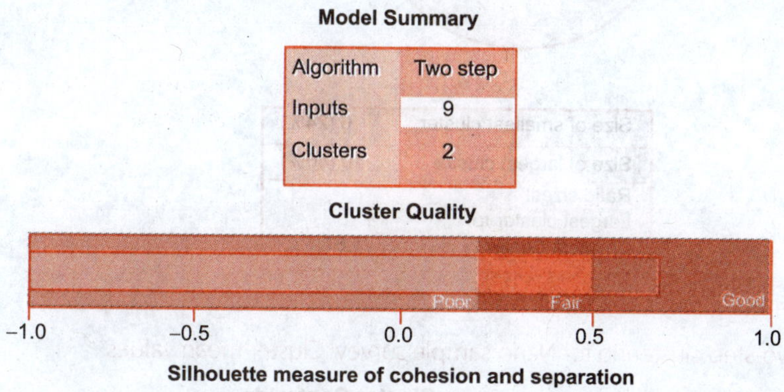

FIGURE 18.7(b) Two-step clustering–AIC method

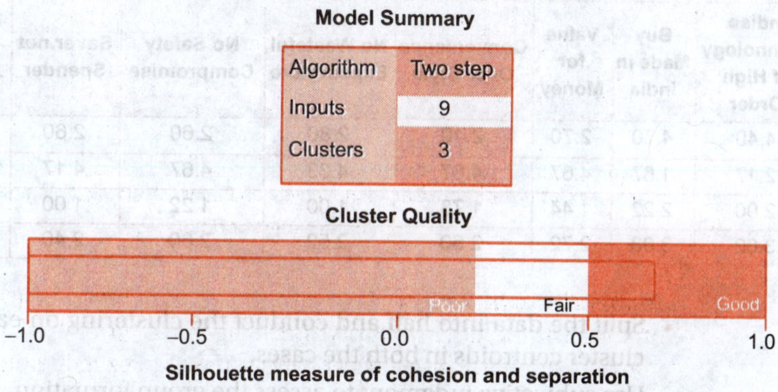

As we can see, the above reveal the likelihood of first, whether there are distinct clusters and secondly, the statistical significance of the results obtained. Both BIC and AIC methods result in coefficient that ranges from –1.0 to +1.0. However, for all practical purposes, a coefficient value ranging from -0.5 to +1.0 is considered to be acceptable and good solution. As we can see from the illustration of AIC and BIC in Figure 18.7(a) and 18.7(b), respectively, the software also plots the obtained value on a scale of –0.1 to 0.1 and indicates whether the solution is good or not.

Thus, as we can see for the Nano survey data, the two-clustering solution the BIC method gives a two-cluster solution, while the AIC method establishes that there are three distinct clusters. Since the other two methods also revealed the existence of three distinct clusters, we decide to go for a three-cluster solution. There is also 'good' cohesion within the obtained clusters and 'good' difference between them. Thus, the obtained model has sound predictive capability.

Next, we look at the cluster size and centroids-on the nine parameters/variables in the study [Figure 18.7 (c) and Table 18.10]. As we can see, the clustering result for the Nano sample survey is the same for K-means and the two-step clustering.

FIGURE 18.7(c) Two-step clustering for Nano sample survey

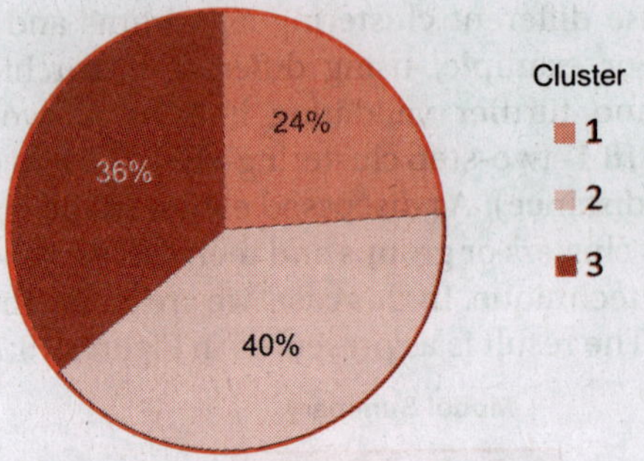

Size of smallest cluster	6 (24%)
Size of largest cluster	10 (40%)
Ratio sizes: Largest cluster to Smallest cluster	1.67

TABLE 18.10 Two-step clustering for Nano sample survey: Cluster mean values

Cluster Centroids

		Indian Technology of High Order	Buy Made in India	Value for Money	Convenience Over Style	No Wasteful Expenditure	No Safety Compromise	Saver not Spender	Try New Things	Part of Changing world	Std. Deviation
Cluster	1	4.40	4.70	2.70	2.10	2.80	2.60	2.60	1.20	1.40	0.516
	2	2.17	1.67	4.67	4.67	4.33	4.67	4.17	1.50	1.33	0.516
	3	2.00	2.22	1.44	1.78	1.00	1.22	1.00	4.78	4.33	0.500
Combined		3.00	3.08	2.72	2.60	2.52	2.60	2.40	2.56	2.44	1.530

- Split the data into half and conduct the clustering on each half and compare the cluster centroids in both the cases.
- Use subjective judgment to assess the group formation. For example, in the Nano study the innovative buyers are younger and more educated as compared to the other two and, thus, are more open to change.

CONCEPT CHECK

1. What is clustering?
2. What are the hierarchical and non-hierarchical methods?
3. Illustrate the use of a combination method.

CLUSTER ANALYSIS: NON-METRIC DATA

The same process of conduction is required for non-metric data as was the case for metric data. However, there are certain steps and assumptions that need to be handled differently. Given below is a step-wise illustration of a nominal data set.

Illustration 18.2: Milk supplement study

A study was conducted to assess the purchase behaviour of 40 housewives with reference to the milk supplement that they bought for their family. Data was also collected about their family size and children above (ch>18) and children below 18(ch<18). The purchase was related to different available brands [Bo = Bournvita, Mi = Milo, Co = Complan, Ho = Horlicks, Pr = Protinex, Zc = Zandu chyawanprash, Dr = Dabur Red Chywanprash, Db = Dabur Blue Chyawanprash, Bc = Baidyanath Chyawanprash] as shown in the following table. If the brand was purchased, the respondent was to put a 'yes' against the brand name. Every 'yes' was assigned a value of 1 and 'no' of 0, while entering the data.

TABLE 18.11 Milk supplement [presence =1; absence = 0]

Id	size	ch<18	ch>18	Bo	Mi	Zc	Dr	Db	Pr	Ho	Bc	Co
1	3	1	0	1	1	0	0	0	0	1	0	0
2	6	0	2	0	0	1	0	1	0	0	1	0
3	4	1	1	0	0	0	0	0	1	1	0	1
4	4	0	2	1	1	0	0	0	0	1	0	0
5	3	1	0	1	1	0	0	0	0	1	0	1
6	4	0	2	0	0	0	0	0	1	1	0	1
7	8	0	3	0	0	1	1	1	0	0	1	0
8	6	0	1	0	0	1	0	1	0	0	1	0
9	7	0	2	0	0	0	1	1	0	0	1	0
10	4	2	0	1	1	0	0	0	0	1	0	0
11	3	1	0	1	1	0	0	0	0	1	0	0
12	4	2	0	1	1	0	0	0	1	1	0	1
13	4	1	1	0	0	0	0	0	1	1	0	1
14	4	0	2	0	0	0	0	0	1	1	0	1
15	3	1	0	1	1	0	0	0	0	1	0	0
16	4	1	1	0	0	0	0	0	1	1	0	1
17	4	0	2	1	1	0	0	0	0	1	0	0
18	8	0	3	0	0	1	1	1	0	0	1	0
19	3	1	0	1	1	0	0	0	0	1	0	1
20	4	2	0	1	1	0	0	0	0	1	0	0

Establishing the Cluster Assumptions

Here, the variables under study were on the nominal scale and the response to be given were in terms of categorical data.

Please note that, here, only a sample of 20 has been used to illustrate the technique. In practice, the sample size is considerably larger. To arrive at the cluster solution, please go to Appendix 18.1 and follow the hierarchical cluster analysis instructions. The steps to be followed are 1-12, except step 7 and 9.

Establishing the clustering algorithm: As was the case for metric data, similarly we establish this through the agglomeration schedule; cluster membership and dendrogram analysis.

TABLE 18.12(a) Agglomeration schedule: Milk supplement data

Stage	Cluster Combined		Coefficients	Stage Cluster First Appears		Next Stage
	Cluster 1	Cluster 2		Cluster 1	Cluster 2	
1	17	20	1.000	0	0	4
2	5	19	1.000	0	0	14
3	7	18	1.000	0	0	15
4	1	17	1.000	0	1	9
5	14	16	1.000	0	0	7
6	11	15	1.000	0	0	9
7	3	14	1.000	0	5	12
8	6	13	1.000	0	0	12
9	1	11	1.000	4	6	13
10	4	10	1.000	0	0	13
11	2	8	1.000	0	0	16
12	3	6	1.000	7	8	18
13	1	4	1.000	9	10	17
14	5	12	.889	2	0	17
15	7	9	.889	3	0	16
16	2	7	.778	11	15	19
17	1	5	.778	13	14	18
18	1	3	.556	17	12	19
19	1	2	.000	18	16	0

Agglomeration schedule: To determine the optimum clusters for nominal data we use the complete linkage/furthest neighbor method to obtain the agglomeration schedule:

Here, the most similar pair will reveal a perfect match which would mean a score of 1. Please remember as explained earlier in the chapter when discussing the non-metric data example, the similarity between two objects is directly proportional to the coefficient obtained. In the schedule, again when we examine the difference between coefficients; we see that this occurs between stage 17(three cluster) and 18(2 cluster) and here a three cluster solution is advocated.

Cluster membership: here again we established the grouping by using an a priori selected number of clusters. In the case of the milk supplement data the following clustering solutions were obtained.

TABLE 18.12(b) Cluster membership: Milk supplement data

Case	5 Clusters	4 Clusters	3 Clusters	2 Clusters
1	1	1	1	1
2	2	2	2	2
3	3	3	3	1
4	1	1	1	1
5	4	4	1	1
6	3	3	3	1
7	5	2	2	2
8	2	2	2	2
9	5	2	2	2

(Contd.)

Case	5 Clusters	4 Clusters	3 Clusters	2 Clusters
10	1	1	1	1
11	1	1	1	1
12	4	4	1	1
13	3	3	3	1
14	3	3	3	1
15	1	1	1	1
16	3	3	3	1
17	1	1	1	1
18	5	2	2	2
19	4	4	1	1
20	1	1	1	1

FIGURE 18.8
Dendrogram of milk supplement data

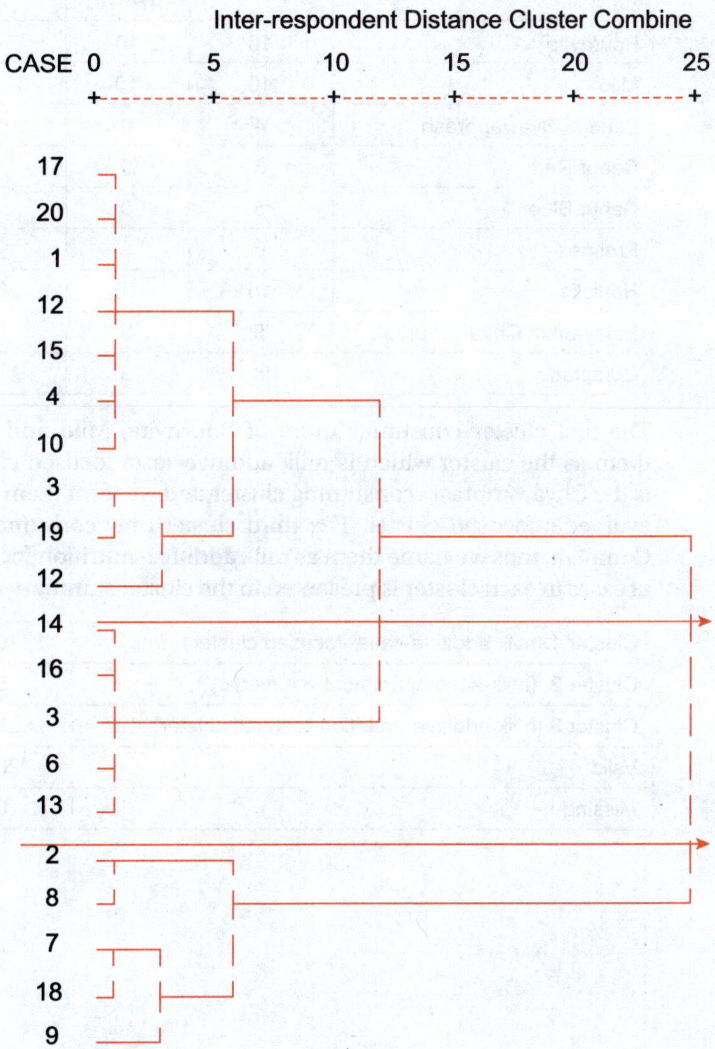

As can be observed when one moves from a two- to a three-cluster solution, five members of cluster 1 move to 3 and when we go to a four cluster solution only two elements move, thus a three cluster solution is recommended here.

Dendrogram: The dendrogram for the milk supplements study is given below in Figure 18.8. As can be seen here, three clusters can be physically identified.

Interpreting and profiling the clusters: For the milk supplement study, there are different computation principles to be adapted, as we recall this data was on a nominal scale, thus, distances could not be calculated. Instead, we had used matching coefficient to assess similarity between the cases/objects. Thus, to profile the clusters, there is an option of saving a three-cluster membership using the hierarchical method as stated earlier and then looking at the presence/absence of the brand in that cluster. Based on this, we prepare a frequency of the consumption table, which shows overall consumption of the brand in the sample, as well as the individual consumption pattern in different clusters (Table 18.13). For example, the total number of people consuming Bournvita is 10 and all the 10 respondents belong to cluster 1.

TABLE 18.13 Frequency of consumption for milk supplement survey

		1(N=10)	2(N=5)	3(N=5)
Bournvita	10	10	0	0
Milo	10	10	0	0
Zandu Chyawanprash	4	0	4	0
Dabur Red	3	0	3	0
Dabur Blue	5	0	5	0
Protinex	6	1	0	5
Horlicks	15	10	0	5
Baidyanath Chyawanprash	5	0	5	0
Complan	8	3	0	5

The first cluster consumes more of Bournvita, Milo and Horlicks, thus we name them as the cluster which is milk additive-taste focused cluster. The second cluster is the Chyawanprash-consuming cluster and we term them as milk-accompaniment-ayurvedic focused cluster. The third cluster only consumes Protinex, Horlicks and Complan, thus we name them as milk additive-nutrition focused cluster. The number of cases in each cluster is presented in the cluster summary below (Table 18.14)

TABLE 18.14 Cluster summary: milk supplement survey

Cluster 1 (milk additive–taste-focused cluster)	10.000
Cluster 2 (milk-accompaniment-ayurvedic)	5.000
Cluster 3 (milk additive–nutrition-focused cluster)	5.000
Valid	20.000
Missing	0.000

FIGURE 18.9(a)
Cluster profile (milk supplement): family size

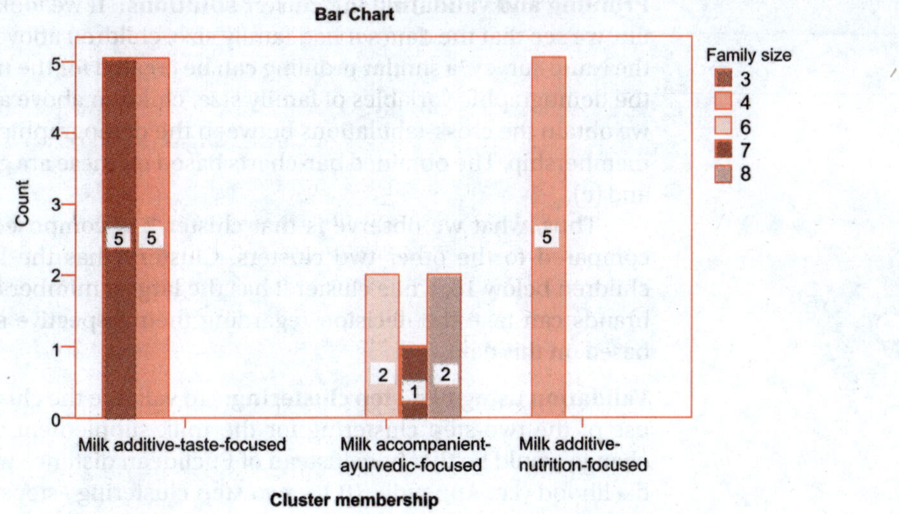

FIGURE 18.9(b)
Cluster profile (milk supplement): children below 18

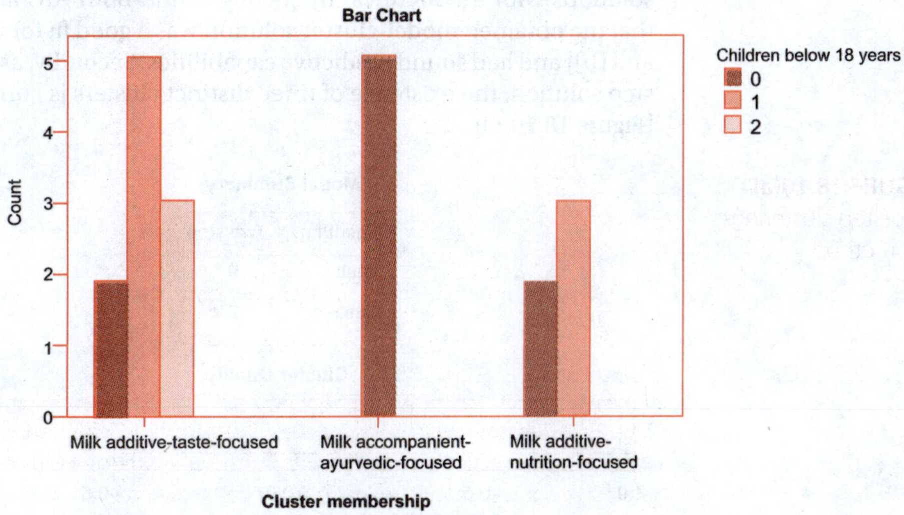

FIGURE 18.9(c)
Cluster profile (milk supplement): children above 18

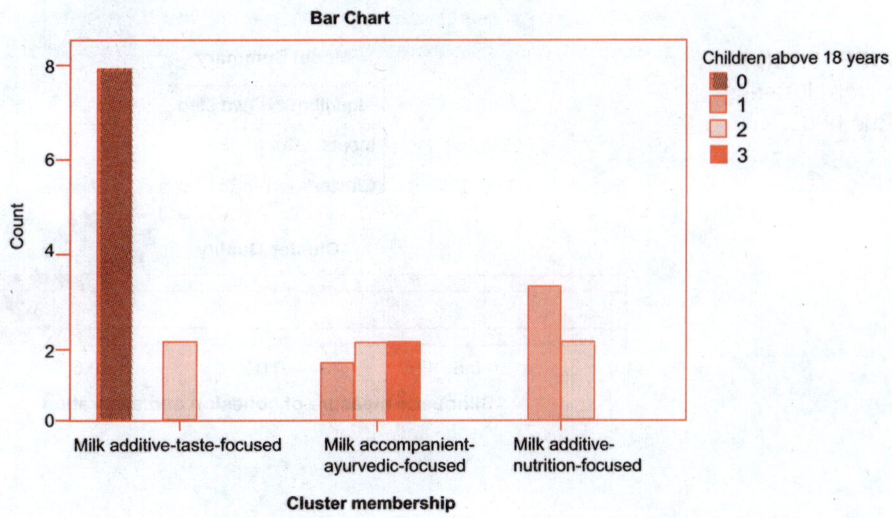

Profiling and validating the cluster solutions: If we look back at the original data file, we see that the data set had family size, children above and below 18. Thus, like the Nano survey; a similar profiling can be created for the milk supplement study for the demographic variables of family size, children above and below 18. Here again, we obtain the cross-tabulations between the demographic variables and the cluster membership. The obtained bar-charts based on these are given in Figure 18.9(a), (b) and (c).

Thus, what we observe is that cluster 2 is composed of larger family size as compared to the other two clusters. Cluster 1 has the largest number of young children below 18, while cluster 2 has the largest number of children above 18. The brands can take the decision regarding their respective strategies for the clusters based on this data.

Validation using two-step clustering: To validate the cluster solution we can make use of the two-step clustering for the milk supplement study. However, the only change would be that here instead of Euclidean distance we would make use of log-likelihood (i.e. Appendix 18.1 – two step clustering –steps 1-8 and ensure in step 3 you chose LOG-LIKELIHOOD) and one would perceive again the same three-cluster solutions with the identical frequency count. Both AIC and BIC analysis revealed that the obtained model-cluster solution was a good fit for the data [Figures 18.10(a) and (b)] and had sound predictive capabilities. Secondly, as we can see from the two-step solution, the existence of three distinct clusters is corroborated by the analysis [Figure 18.10(c)].

FIGURE 18.10(a) Two-step clustering–BIC method

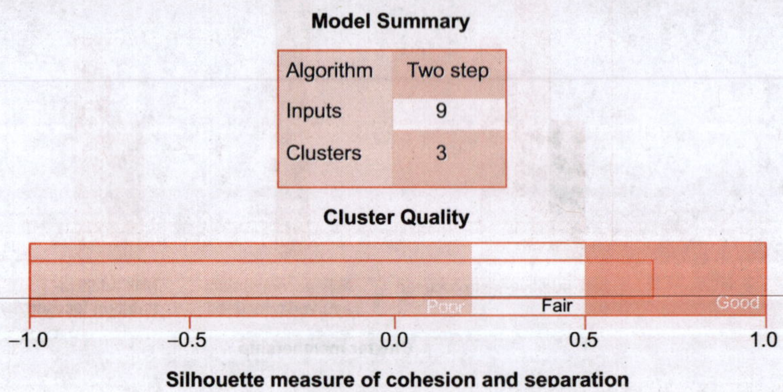

FIGURE 18.10(b) Two-step clustering–AIC method

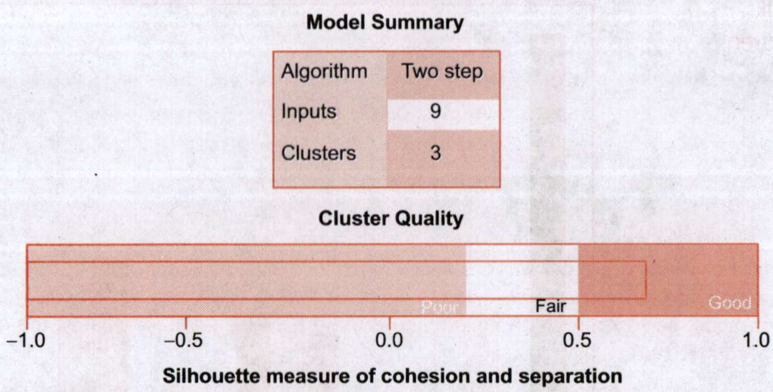

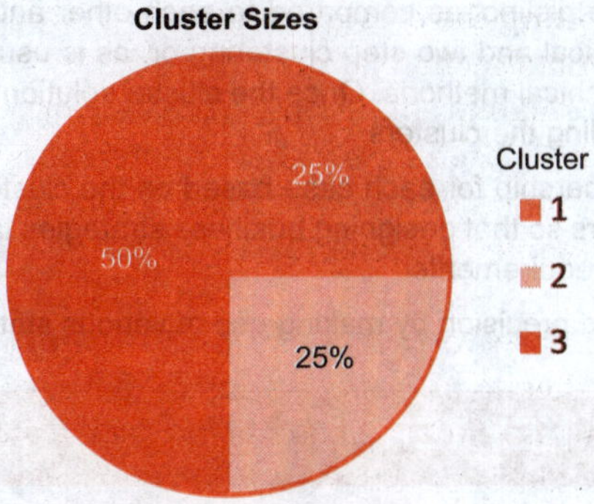

FIGURE 18.10(c) Two-step clustering solution (milk supplement data): cluster composition

Size of smallest cluster	5 (25%)
Size of largest cluster	10 (50%)
Ratio sizes: Largest cluster to Smallest cluster	2.00

Statistical Software

SPSS: On the SPSS, cluster analysis comes under the classification techniques. Based on the measurement scale on which the clustering variable has been designed, one selects a distance measure and starts by conducting the hierarchical clustering of objects using the hierarchical cluster analysis. To be able to interpret and profile the non-hierarchical clustering, the K-means cluster program is to be used. On the basis of this one is able to determine the cluster membership for each case and using the membership data one is able to profile the groups. (refer to SPSS command to carry out cluster analysis in Appendix 18.1).

Both SAS and MINITAB are able to generate both the hierarchical and non-hierarchical solutions. To draw the dendrogram in SAS one needs to use the Tree diagram. Excel, however, is not able to generate a cluster solution.

SUMMARY

- Most of the times, the data and the information obtained from surveys are voluminous and the researcher is required to reduce the data in order to make some semblance of order to the data obtained. Cluster analysis is one such grouping technique. The basic premise behind the method is to group variables or respondents based on the commonality found in the primary data. It needs to be understood, however, that the technique is unique as it measures similarity as a function of multiple variables. This is also the reason it comes under multivariate analysis of data.
- Cluster analysis is typically used in management in the field of marketing. Here it is used to segment and group the customers into distinctly homogenous groups, which requires specific strategies in order to target them. The segmentation can be extended to industries, sectors, as well as markets. In the area of human resources the method can be effectively used to group people into clusters and then devise an overall career growth plan.
- The other significant advantage of clustering method is that it can be successfully carried out on non-metric and metric data. For metric data the basic statistics involved is squared Euclidean distance, the assumption being the shorter the distance between the objects the higher is the similarity and homogeneity amongst like- minded people. For nominal data, perfect match and mismatch is used to measure the similarity; the higher the match higher is the similarity amongst individuals.
- The conduction of a typical cluster analysis requires a step-wise procedure. Based on the research objectives, one designs the research instrument. Depending on the scale of measurement, one selects the appropriate statistical formula. Next, one decides on the clustering algorithm, which would enable the researcher to reduce the data to

a manageable number of clusters that are distinct as compared to each other and homogenous in composition. These could be Hierarchical, Non-hierarchical and two step clustering or, as is usually done, one makes use of a combination of hierarchical and non-heirarchical methods. Once the cluster solution has been obtained, one needs to interpret the results by naming and profiling the clusters.

- The researcher can save the cluster membership for each case based on the cluster solution and then arrive at a complete demographic profile of the clusters so that designing business strategies targeted at the groups are more synchronized and focused on the group's requirements.
- Cluster analysis can be done with ease and precision by making use of various statistical software like SPSS.

KEY TERMS

- A priori decision
- Agglomeration schedule
- Average linkage method
- Benefit segmentation
- Centroid method
- Chebychev distance
- Classification technique
- Cluster analysis
- Cluster centroid
- Cluster seeds
- Cluster variate
- Complete linkage method
- Dendrogram
- Entropy group
- Euclidean distance
- Final cluster centre
- Gower's coefficient of similarity
- Hierarchical methods
- Jaccards' coefficient
- K-means clustering
- Manhattan distance
- Market segmentation
- Metric data analysis
- Non-hierarchical methods
- Non-metric data analysis
- Proximity matrix
- Simple matching coefficient
- Single linkage method
- Two-step clustering
- Vertical icicle diagram
- Ward's method

CHAPTER REVIEW QUESTIONS

Objective Type Questions

State whether the following statements are true (T) or false (F).

1. Cluster analysis is a classification technique.
2. Cluster analysis is possible only on interval and ratio level of measurement.
3. Numerical taxonomy is another name for cluster analysis.
4. In benefit segmentation the members of a cluster may not be of the same demographic group.
5. Euclidean distance is the underlying statistics for cluster analysis.
6. Euclidean distance is a statistics that is not scale variant.
7. Chebychev distance is the absolute difference in values for any variable.
8. Matching coefficient represent the number of presence or absence of qualities that two objects share.
9. Matching coefficient is the statistics used for clustering objects based on nominal data.
10. For mixed variable clustering we make use of the Jaccard coefficient .
11. The variables used to cluster objects are called the cluster variates.
12. Cluster seeds are the respondents that are clustered by the cluster variates.
13. The group that does not fit into any group is called the entropy group.
14. In the vertical icicle the columns correspond to the objects being clustered.
15. The cluster solution can be represented graphically in the form of a dendrite.
16. The within cluster variance is reduced to a minimum in Ward's method.
17. Optimizing procedure is a non-hierarchical method of clustering.

18. To validate the cluster solution one can make use of the non-hierarchical methods.
19. Another method of validating the cluster solution is the *a priori* decision.
20. The ANOVA table is a method of selecting the significant cluster variates.

Conceptual Questions

1. 'Selecting the cluster variables is a more difficult task than the variables included in any other multivariate technique.' Examine the validity of the above statement by giving suitable examples.
2. What is cluster analysis? Explain in brief the underlying assumptions of the technique.
3. What are hierarchical and non-hierarchical methods? When is it advisable to choose one over the other? Explain.
4. Explain in detail the steps involved in carrying out a cluster analysis. Use suitable examples to do so.
5. What is an agglomeration schedule? How does the technique help in taking a clusering decision?
6. What is the significance of profiling clusters? How would these be of value for the decision-maker?
7. What is the difference between the following:
   (a) Dendrogram and icicle diagram.
   (b) K-means clustering and two-step clustering.
   (c) Complete linkage and Ward's method.

Application Questions

1. Cos Mode conducted a scaled survey on the residents of Delhi to find out their opinion on expansion plans for the city. Responses of five members of this sample to questions on 'pubs and bars' and 'specialty coffee shops' on a five-point scale (1-very favourable and 5-very unfavourable) are presented below:

Sample	Pubs and Bars	Speciality Coffee Shops
1	1	4
2	2	5
3	5	2
4	1	5
5	4	3

   (i) Determine the similarity of each pair of respondent by computing the Euclidean distance between them.
   (ii) Using the single-linkage method, prepare a dendrogram.
   Cos Mode does not want to consider clusters above an inter-respondent distance of 5. How many clusters exist at a maximum Euclidean distance of 5 and, based on what they want, what do you recommend—pubs or coffee shops?

2. A fast food chain survey examined the relative importance of eight attributes of a fast food restaurant. The interval scaled question had nine response categories ranging from 9 = very important to 1 = very unimportant. A K-means cluster output is as follows:

Variable	Cluster I (n = 62)	Cluster II (n = 55)	Cluster III (n = 83)
Ambience	8.6	4.5	7.8
Taste	8.6	8.1	8.5
Hygiene	8.2	5.6	6.8
Preparation time	3.8	7.7	8.8
Other diners	8.5	4.5	7.8
Variety in menu	4.4	6.7	8.8
Location	5.5	8.7	8.7
Bill amount	3.2	8.1	5.5

(i) How would you validate the cluster results?
(ii) How would you interpret the cluster results?
(iii) What elements should a fast food restaurant be careful about when designing an offering for each of the clusters?
(iv) In case these clusters had to be profiled what questions would you have asked?

CASE 18.1

MILK FOR HEALTH

ABC India Ltd. is India's largest milk cooperative and wants to map the profile of its target customers in terms of lifestyle, attitude, and perceptions. ABC's marketing managers prepare a set of 15 psychographic statements, which emerged out of a focus group discussion that was conducted with housewives and mothers. These were assumed to reflect health concerns. The respondents had to agree or disagree with each statement on a scale of 1 to 5.

1 = Completely agree
2 = Agree
3 = Neither agree nor disagree
4 = Disagree
5 = Completely disagree

The following 15 statements were prepared by the ABC marketing team:

1. I prefer to skip breakfast as I do not have time in the morning.
2. I always keep ready-to-eat packets in my kitchen cupboard.
3. I like watching family-based TV serials.
4. A healthy and sumptuous breakfast is the best meal to have in a day.
5. Skill based education is the need of the hour in India.
6. Its better to buy packaged milk products.
7. I keep in touch with my friends on Facebook.
8. In today's times a wife has got to work to support her husband.
9. Women's empowerment is an essential step for any nation to grow.
10. Sunday evenings are for enjoying oneself.
11. Today the consumer is very conscious about the quality of a product.
12. I do not like making meals at home during weekends.
13. Mobile phones have become a very important part of an Indian's life.
14. India in the next decade is going to be a force to reckon with.
15. The quality of Indian milk products has improved greatly in the last decade.

Input Data

ABC India Ltd. has done this market research with 40 respondents who answered the above questionnaire. The input data matrix is shown in Table 18.15.

Table 18.15 Input data

Case	Q1	Q2	Q3	Q4	Q5	Q6	Q7	Q8	Q9	Q10	Q11	Q12	Q13	Q14	Q15
1	1.00	2.00	3.00	2.00	4.00	1.00	1.00	3.00	2.00	1.00	1.00	1.00	1.00	2.00	3.00
2	2.00	3.00	3.00	2.00	4.00	3.00	2.00	2.00	2.00	4.00	3.00	3.00	3.00	1.00	4.00

Case	Q1	Q2	Q3	Q4	Q5	Q6	Q7	Q8	Q9	Q10	Q11	Q12	Q13	Q14	Q15
3	4.00	4.00	3.00	3.00	3.00	3.00	3.00	5.00	2.00	5.00	4.00	2.00	3.00	1.00	3.00
4	3.00	2.00	2.00	4.00	2.00	3.00	1.00	2.00	3.00	4.00	3.00	2.00	2.00	4.00	2.00
5	1.00	2.00	2.00	3.00	1.00	2.00	2.00	5.00	2.00	3.00	2.00	1.00	2.00	3.00	2.00
6	3.00	2.00	3.00	3.00	1.00	1.00	3.00	2.00	2.00	1.00	1.00	2.00	2.00	3.00	2.00
7	4.00	4.00	3.00	2.00	4.00	5.00	1.00	2.00	5.00	3.00	5.00	3.00	2.00	3.00	4.00
8	2.00	4.00	3.00	2.00	3.00	4.00	2.00	2.00	2.00	2.00	5.00	3.00	1.00	3.00	5.00
9	2.00	4.00	5.00	2.00	4.00	3.00	3.00	2.00	3.00	2.00	4.00	1.00	2.00	3.00	4.00
10	1.00	2.00	3.00	1.00	2.00	2.00	4.00	1.00	2.00	1.00	1.00	2.00	3.00	1.00	2.00
11	2.00	3.00	4.00	4.00	3.00	3.00	3.00	3.00	3.00	2.00	4.00	4.00	1.00	1.00	1.00
12	3.00	5.00	1.00	3.00	2.00	4.00	2.00	3.00	3.00	2.00	4.00	4.00	3.00	3.00	5.00
13	1.00	2.00	2.00	2.00	3.00	2.00	1.00	3.00	2.00	1.00	3.00	3.00	1.00	2.00	3.00
14	3.00	2.00	2.00	1.00	3.00	2.00	2.00	2.00	2.00	3.00	2.00	1.00	1.00	2.00	2.00
15	1.00	2.00	3.00	2.00	4.00	1.00	1.00	3.00	2.00	1.00	1.00	1.00	1.00	2.00	3.00
16	1.00	1.00	5.00	4.00	4.00	3.00	2.00	4.00	3.00	3.00	4.00	3.00	2.00	2.00	4.00
17	4.00	4.00	3.00	2.00	4.00	5.00	1.00	2.00	5.00	3.00	5.00	3.00	2.00	3.00	4.00
18	2.00	4.00	3.00	2.00	3.00	4.00	2.00	2.00	2.00	2.00	5.00	3.00	1.00	3.00	5.00
19	2.00	4.00	5.00	2.00	4.00	3.00	3.00	2.00	3.00	2.00	4.00	1.00	2.00	3.00	4.00
20	1.00	2.00	3.00	1.00	2.00	2.00	4.00	1.00	2.00	1.00	1.00	2.00	3.00	1.00	2.00
21	3.00	3.00	2.00	1.00	2.00	1.00	3.00	1.00	1.00	3.00	4.00	3.00	1.00	2.00	1.00
22	3.00	2.00	3.00	5.00	4.00	2.00	1.00	3.00	4.00	2.00	1.00	1.00	2.00	2.00	1.00
23	2.00	2.00	2.00	1.00	1.00	3.00	2.00	3.00	4.00	2.00	1.00	3.00	2.00	3.00	3.00
24	3.00	3.00	2.00	1.00	2.00	1.00	3.00	1.00	1.00	3.00	4.00	3.00	1.00	2.00	1.00
25	3.00	2.00	3.00	5.00	4.00	2.00	1.00	3.00	4.00	2.00	1.00	1.00	2.00	2.00	1.00
26	2.00	2.00	2.00	1.00	1.00	3.00	2.00	3.00	4.00	2.00	1.00	3.00	2.00	3.00	3.00
27	2.00	4.00	1.00	2.00	1.00	4.00	2.00	4.00	4.00	2.00	5.00	3.00	2.00	2.00	2.00
28	4.00	4.00	1.00	3.00	5.00	5.00	1.00	5.00	4.00	2.00	5.00	2.00	2.00	2.00	5.00
29	2.00	4.00	1.00	2.00	1.00	4.00	2.00	4.00	4.00	2.00	5.00	3.00	2.00	2.00	2.00
30	4.00	4.00	1.00	3.00	5.00	5.00	1.00	5.00	4.00	2.00	5.00	2.00	2.00	2.00	5.00
31	1.00	1.00	5.00	4.00	4.00	3.00	2.00	4.00	3.00	3.00	4.00	3.00	2.00	2.00	4.00
32	2.00	3.00	4.00	4.00	3.00	3.00	3.00	3.00	3.00	2.00	4.00	4.00	1.00	1.00	1.00
33	3.00	5.00	1.00	3.00	2.00	4.00	2.00	3.00	3.00	2.00	4.00	4.00	3.00	3.00	5.00
34	1.00	2.00	2.00	2.00	3.00	2.00	1.00	3.00	2.00	1.00	3.00	3.00	1.00	2.00	3.00

Case	Q1	Q2	Q3	Q4	Q5	Q6	Q7	Q8	Q9	Q10	Q11	Q12	Q13	Q14	Q15
35	3.00	2.00	2.00	1.00	3.00	2.00	2.00	2.00	2.00	3.00	2.00	1.00	1.00	2.00	2.00
36	2.00	3.00	3.00	2.00	4.00	3.00	2.00	2.00	2.00	4.00	3.00	3.00	3.00	1.00	4.00
37	4.00	4.00	3.00	3.00	3.00	3.00	3.00	5.00	2.00	5.00	4.00	2.00	3.00	1.00	3.00
38	3.00	2.00	2.00	4.00	2.00	3.00	1.00	2.00	3.00	4.00	3.00	2.00	2.00	4.00	2.00
39	1.00	2.00	2.00	3.00	1.00	2.00	2.00	5.00	2.00	3.00	2.00	1.00	2.00	3.00	2.00
40	3.00	2.00	3.00	3.00	1.00	1.00	3.00	2.00	2.00	1.00	1.00	2.00	2.00	3.00	2.00

QUESTIONS

1. Conduct a quick clustering on the data and arrive at a three-cluster solution.
2. Interpret and name the clusters.
3. What are the implications for the decision-maker in this case?

CASE 18.2

'SUNDARTA MANE….'

A national cosmetics company wants to know what kind of women would be interested in their range of products. The purpose is to determine what does personal grooming mean to most women.

Ten statements are made in order to assess the lifestyle and attitude of urban women. The statements were designed on a Likert scale and require the person to indicate her level of agreement/disagreement with these (1 = Strongly agree, 2 = Agree, 3 = Neither agree nor disagree, 4 = Disagree, 5 = Strongly disagree).

1. I do not buy products that are not from an established brand.
2. I buy new products only when they have been tried and tested as safe.
3. I know the names of most cosmetic brands in the market.
4. I do not think one company can provide a complete personal care solution.
5. I plan my shopping trips very carefully.
6. Personal care product companies need to do lot of research before coming up with a product.
7. It is very important to look good and presentable in today's times.
8. I like experimenting with new trends and styles.
9. I always go by what the film stars endorse.
10. I believe that what I wear reflects who I am.

Table 18.16 Input data matrix

Case	Q1	Q2	Q3	Q4	Q5	Q6	Q7	Q8	Q9	Q10
1	2.00	3.00	2.00	1.00	3.00	5.00	1.00	3.00	5.00	3.00
2	2.00	2.00	2.00	2.00	3.00	2.00	3.00	4.00	4.00	3.00
3	3.00	4.00	2.00	3.00	2.00	3.00	4.00	3.00	5.00	3.00
4	4.00	5.00	4.00	3.00	4.00	4.00	2.00	2.00	4.00	3.00
5	3.00	4.00	4.00	2.00	2.00	4.00	2.00	2.00	5.00	3.00
6	2.00	3.00	4.00	2.00	4.00	3.00	3.00	5.00	4.00	4.00

Case	Q1	Q2	Q3	Q4	Q5	Q6	Q7	Q8	Q9	Q10
7	4.00	2.00	5.00	1.00	3.00	2.00	4.00	4.00	1.00	2.00
8	1.00	1.00	5.00	4.00	5.00	1.00	1.00	5.00	4.00	5.00
9	1.00	2.00	1.00	2.00	1.00	5.00	3.00	4.00	4.00	2.00
10	5.00	3.00	2.00	5.00	2.00	4.00	3.00	2.00	5.00	1.00
11	5.00	2.00	2.00	4.00	3.00	3.00	2.00	1.00	2.00	1.00
12	1.00	5.00	3.00	3.00	4.00	4.00	4.00	3.00	2.00	5.00
13	2.00	2.00	3.00	4.00	3.00	2.00	2.00	3.00	3.00	4.00
14	5.00	2.00	2.00	4.00	3.00	3.00	2.00	1.00	2.00	1.00
15	1.00	5.00	3.00	3.00	4.00	4.00	4.00	3.00	2.00	5.00
16	2.00	2.00	3.00	4.00	3.00	2.00	2.00	3.00	3.00	4.00
17	3.00	5.00	4.00	1.00	3.00	2.00	4.00	2.00	5.00	1.00
18	4.00	4.00	5.00	2.00	2.00	4.00	1.00	5.00	4.00	2.00
19	3.00	2.00	5.00	3.00	3.00	1.00	3.00	4.00	3.00	2.00
20	2.00	2.00	4.00	5.00	2.00	1.00	5.00	1.00	2.00	4.00
21	1.00	2.00	3.00	3.00	1.00	5.00	3.00	5.00	5.00	5.00
22	4.00	1.00	3.00	3.00	5.00	4.00	2.00	4.00	4.00	1.00
23	5.00	1.00	3.00	1.00	2.00	3.00	2.00	2.00	5.00	2.00
24	2.00	3.00	2.00	1.00	3.00	5.00	1.00	3.00	5.00	3.00
25	2.00	2.00	2.00	2.00	3.00	2.00	3.00	4.00	4.00	3.00
26	3.00	4.00	2.00	3.00	2.00	3.00	4.00	3.00	5.00	3.00
27	4.00	2.00	5.00	1.00	3.00	2.00	4.00	4.00	1.00	2.00
28	1.00	1.00	5.00	4.00	5.00	1.00	1.00	5.00	4.00	5.00
29	1.00	2.00	1.00	2.00	1.00	5.00	3.00	4.00	4.00	2.00
30	5.00	3.00	2.00	5.00	2.00	4.00	3.00	2.00	5.00	1.00
31	4.00	5.00	4.00	3.00	4.00	4.00	2.00	2.00	4.00	3.00
32	3.00	4.00	4.00	2.00	2.00	4.00	2.00	2.00	5.00	3.00
33	2.00	3.00	4.00	2.00	4.00	3.00	3.00	5.00	4.00	4.00
34	3.00	5.00	4.00	1.00	3.00	2.00	4.00	2.00	5.00	1.00
35	4.00	4.00	5.00	2.00	2.00	4.00	1.00	5.00	4.00	2.00
36	3.00	2.00	5.00	3.00	3.00	1.00	3.00	4.00	3.00	2.00
37	2.00	2.00	4.00	5.00	2.00	1.00	5.00	1.00	2.00	4.00
38	1.00	2.00	3.00	3.00	1.00	5.00	3.00	5.00	5.00	5.00
39	4.00	1.00	3.00	3.00	5.00	4.00	2.00	4.00	4.00	1.00
40	5.00	1.00	3.00	1.00	2.00	3.00	2.00	2.00	5.00	2.00

QUESTIONS

1. Conduct a quick clustering on the data and arrive at a two-cluster solution.
2. Interpret and name the clusters.
3. What are the implications for the decision-maker in this case?

CASE 18.3

DANISH INTERNATIONAL (D)

Raghu Narang had hired Shameem Naqib as a company counselor at Danish International. Naqib was asked to identify the reason for lack of motivation amongst the company employees. He evaluated the merit of conducting a survey amongst old and new employees. However, after an exploratory survey, he found that apathy was more amongst the new employees.

Thus, Shameem Naqib decided to do a short survey of the new employees at Danish. He decided that he would do this study on all those who had been handpicked by Raghu Narang from various organizations and constituted what he termed as his dream team. The total number given to him by the HR for this group was 143. Thus he prepared a short questionnaire having nine statements on a Likert scale. The scale was a 5-point scale ranging from strongly disagree=1 to strongly agree=5. The total completed questionnaire on which he could complete the analysis stood at 120. He also obtained their agreement/ disagreement on a similar 5-point scale about their satisfaction with their current job role.

Next, by conducting a hierarchical analysis on the 9 statements, he obtained a three-cluster solution and further on conducting the K-means cluster analysis he obtained the output as given below.

Table 18.17 Final cluster centres of the obtained clusters

Final Cluster Centers

S. No.	Statements	Cluster 1	Cluster 2	Cluster 3
1.	I like to finish my assignments on time	4.66	4.67	3.85
2.	My supervisor seek my inputs on important decisions	4.08	3.90	2.70
3.	I like taking the responsibility and accountability of the work as it comes up	4.58	4.35	3.55
4.	I like taking work home as and when required	3.55	2.49	2.36
5.	I get time to attend all the social events at home.	2.89	3.65	2.73
6.	I am not irritable at home, because my job is not stressful	3.29	3.47	3.06
7.	I am expected to work late nights and also on weekends.	3.92	1.98	2.91
8.	I often get support from my manager/ supervisor or colleagues	4.24	3.84	3.12
9.	My superior inquires about my training needs and helps me sharpen my skills	4.12	3.71	2.21

Table 18.18 ANOVA table for the cluster solution

ANOVA

S. No.	Statements	F	Sig.
1	I like to finish my assignments on time	13.472	0.000
2	My supervisor seek my inputs on important decisions	27.716	0.000
3	I like taking the responsibility and accountability of the work as it comes up	19.317	0.000
4	I like taking work home as and when required	14.490	0.000
5	I get time to attend all the social events at home.	9.858	0.000
6	I am not irritable at home, because my job is not stressful	1.342	0.265
7	I am expected to work late nights and also on weekends.	51.136	0.000
8	I often get support from my manager/ supervisor or colleagues	18.427	0.000
9	My superior inquires about my training needs and helps me sharpen my skills	54.634	0.000

Table 18.19 Number of cases in each cluster

Number of Cases in each Cluster		
Cluster	1	33.000
	2	38.000
	3	49.000
Valid		120.000
Missing		0.000

He saved the three-cluster solution. Next, he recoded the job satisfaction from the 5-point scale. Response category 1, 2 and 3 were recoded into "low job satisfaction" and 4 and 5 were recoded into "high Job-satisfaction". On running the cross-tabulation with the obtained cluster solution, he obtained the following data.

Table 18.20 Job Satisfaction of the cluster segments

Cluster	LOW	HIGH
Cluster 1	12	21
Cluster 2	20	18
Cluster 3	32	17

QUESTIONS

1. Interpret the cluster solution for Shameem Naqib.
2. For the cross tabulated result conduct the appropriate inferential analysis to arrive at a suitable conclusion about the level of job satisfaction of the three clusters.
3. What hypotheses would you test for the data presented in Table 4? Are the results statistically significant? Interpret the results.
4. In the light of the above answers do you have any clear cut suggestions about how to work on the clusters to obtain a suitable dream team as envisaged by Raghu Narang. What suggestions do you think Shameem should make?

Appendix – 18.1: CLUSTER ANALYSIS COMMANDS FOR SPSS

The following steps are suggested to be carried out in a step-wise manner for conducting a cluster analysis using SPSS for Windows:

Hierarchical Cluster Analysis

1. On the top of the screen go to Analyse……Classify…….. Hierarchical Cluster.
2. A dialog box will open for the technique. Now select all the variables to be used for the analysis by dragging them to the right, into the VARIABLES box.
3. Then select CASES (default option), as we are going to cluster the sample.
4. In the DISPLAY box, check STATISTICS and PLOTS (default options).
5. Now go to METHOD. For CLUSTER METHOD select 'between groups linkages'. In the MEASURE box check the scale as 'Interval' or 'count' or 'binary' as the case may be for the clustering variables.
6. Once you select the measure, the options for calculating distance for the measure would get activated.
7. For interval data select SQUARED EUCLIDEAN DISTANCE. Click CONTINUE.
8. For binary data select SIMPLE MATCHING COEFFICIENT. Click CONTINUE.
9. For count data select CHI-SQUARE. Click CONTINUE.
10. Now go to STATISTICS. In the pop-up window, check AGGLOMERATION SCHEDULE. Click CONTINUE.
11. Click on PLOTS and click on DENDROGRAM. Next for the ICICLE box check 'all clusters' (default) and in the ORIENTATION box, check 'vertical'. Click CONTINUE.

12. Go to the main menu box and click on OK.

The method is the same if you would like to cluster the variables. In that case, in Step 3, click on VARIABLES.

K-Means Cluster Analysis

1. On the top of the screen go to Analyse……Classify……..K-MEANS CLUSTER.
2. A dialog box will open for the technique. Now select all the variables to be used for the analysis by dragging them to the right, into the VARIABLES box.
3. Under this there is an option for NUMBER OF CLUSTER; enter a number here (as identified by the hierarchical cluster analysis).
4. Click on OPTIONS. In the pop-up window, in the STATISTICS box, check INITIAL CLUSTER CENTERS, ANOVA and CLUSTER INFORMATION FOR EACH CASE. Click CONTINUE.
5. Go to SAVE and click on SAVE CLUSTER MEMBERSHIP.
6. Go to the main menu box and click on OK.

Two-Step Cluster Analysis

1. On the top of the screen go to Analyse……Classify…….. TWO-STEP CLUSTER.
2. A dialog box will open for the technique. Now select all the variables to be used for the analysis by dragging them to the right, into the CONTINUOUS and CATEGORICAL (as the case may be) VARIABLES box.
3. For the DISTANCE MEASURE (in case the variables are continuous) select EUCLIDEAN, for categorical or mixed select LOG-LIKELIHOOD.
4. For CLUSTERING CRITERION select AKAIKE'S INFORMATION CRITERION (AIC).
5. For NUMBER OF CLUSTER select DETERMINE AUTOMATICALLY (DEFAULT 15).
6. At the bottom, go to PLOTS and select CLUSTER PIE CHART.
7. Next go to OUTPUT and select DESCRIPTIVES BY CLUSTER and CLUSTER FREQUENCIES.
8. Go to the main dialog box and click on OK.

Answers to Objective Type Questions

1. True	2. False	3. True	4. True	5. True
6. True	7. False	8. True	9. True	10. False
11. True	12. False	13. True	14. True	15. False
16 True	17. True	18. False	19. False	20. True

REFERENCES

Haley, R I. "Benefit Segmentation", *Journal of Marketing* 32 (1968): 30–35.

McDonald, Malcolm and Ian K Dunbar. *Market Segmentation: How to Do it, How to Profit from it.* London: Macmillan Business, 1998.

Sinha, P. "Shopping Orientation in the Evolving Indian Shoppers", *Vikalpa* 27 (2003): 13–28.

Sondhi N and Singhvi S R. "A Typology of Consumer Buying Behaviour: Packaged Grocery Products", *JIMS* 10 (2), 2005.

Yankelovich. "New Criteria for Market Segmentation", *Harvard Business Review* 42 (2): 83–90, 1964.

BIBLIOGRAPHY

Bhattacharyya, Dipak Kumar. *Research Methodology.* New Delhi: Excel Books, 2006.

Boyd, Harper W Jr, Ralph Westfall and Stanley F Stasch. *Marketing Research: Text and Cases,* 7th edn. Delhi: Richard D. Irwin, Inc, 2002.

Churchill, Gilbert A Jr and Dawn Iacobucci. *Marketing Research Methodological Foundations*, 8th edn. New Delhi: Thompson South Western, 2002.

Dwivedi, R S. *Research Methods in Behavioural Sciences.* New Delhi: Macmillan India Ltd, 1997.

Graziano, Anthony M. *Research Methods: A Process of Inquiry.* Boston: Allyn and Bacon, 2000.

Green, Paul E and Donald S Tull. *Research for Marketing Decisions*, 4th edn. New Delhi: Prentice Hall of India Pvt. Ltd, 1986.

Haley, R I. "Benefit segmentation", *Journal of Marketing*, 32 (1968): 30-35.

Kothari, C R. *Research Methodology: Methods and Techniques,* 2nd edn. New Delhi: Wiley Eastern Limited, 1990.

Malhotra, Naresh K. *Marketing Research – An Applied Orientation*, 3rd edn. New Delhi: Pearson Education, 2002.

Nargundkar, Rajendra. *Marketing Research (Text and Cases).* New Delhi: Tata McGraw Hill Publishing Company Ltd, 2002.

Pannerselvam, R. *Research Methodology*. New Delhi: Prentice Hall of India Pvt. Ltd, 2004.

Tull, Donald S and Del I Hawkins. *Marketing Research: Measurement and Method*, 6th edn. New Delhi: Prentice Hall of India Pvt. Ltd, 1993.

19

CHAPTER

Multidimensional Scaling and Perceptual Mapping

Learning Objectives

By the end of the chapter, you should be able to:

1. Understand the nature and scope of multidimensional scaling (MDS) in business research and appreciate its application in all areas of business.
2. Understand the significance and usage of MDS.
3. Carry out the step-wise process for conducting an MDS.
4. Conduct a similarity-based MDS.
5. Identify the optimal number of dimensions required to configure the respondent data.
6. Conduct a preference-based MDS.
7. Establish the strength of the MDS solution.
8. Conduct attribute-based perceptual maps.
9. Formulate perceptual maps using factor analysis.

'Isn't it intriguing to marvel at the capacity and capability of the human brain? At a single moment in time, one is bombarded with so many sensations that act on us and, yet, the information is attended to, absorbed and selectively addressed in its own peculiar and effortless way. No matter how much the mechanical brain's clone–the computer–advances in terms of the way it assimilates, stores and responds to information, it can never come close to matching the original', said Prof. Krishna Raju to his class, as he explained the phenomena of selective sensory attention and response.

'Sir, how does the individual handle man-made stimuli when he is bombarded with artificial exposure to brands and needs to make sense of it? Secondly sir, what if the person gets positive or negative information about the brand? How does the brain account for it?' asked Karthik S.

'Very interesting Karthik, you see what the brain does is to make sense of the data that it captures based on the unique codes of similarity or dissimilarity. On the basis of these features, it tries to group the data so that in his mind a schema of the objects is created, which is essentially like a spatial map. The brands or objects are then plotted at different locations which represent the standing of the objects on the features or attributes or some logic that the individual is using to evaluate and sift the information. And as the consumer gets positive or negative feedback about the plotted brands, the position of the brands automatically changes. Does it make sense? Do you understand?'

'Umm…mm…Sir … Can you please give an example of this?' asked Karthik, hesitatingly.

'Sure, imagine a consumer who is looking at investing in a health insurance scheme. He gathers a lot of information about different service providers and finally shortlists one government and three private mediclaim options. Now he is concerned about certain things like the premium amount to be paid and the network of hospitals the scheme covers.

So, he evaluates the four options before him on these dimensions of value. Thus, what you would get is an imaginary two-dimensional map that the person creates in his mind and the brands would be like four plotted points on this. Now, suppose he hears that one of the private players has a lot of constraints in his plan, then the map would be based on three dimensions instead of two. Hence the positions of the brands would change again. If the hospital network of the private player is reduced because of some reason, this will lower the value of the company on the 'network of hospital' dimension and thus impact the positioning of the service provider on the map. And all this is carried out in a fraction of a second and effortlessly by the brain', explained Prof. K.

'Amazing sir! And, moreover, if these maps can be plotted on an actual physical diagram it could have a huge potential for any strategist who wants to create a space for himself in the individual's mind', marvelled Karthik.

'Very true, Karthik, these mental maps or perceptual maps are the essential tools of any brand manager managing the sensory imaging of his brand in isolation and in comparison with other competing brands…'

One of the ways in which Prof. Krishna advocated the creation of spatial maps is by the use of a multivariate technique called multidimensional scaling (MDS). The usage of the technique has increased enormously after the advent of computer software that has made the creation of representations from simple two-dimensional to multidimensional seem like child's play.

MULTIDIMENSIONAL SCALING—A MAPPING TECHNIQUE

LEARNING OBJECTIVE 1
Understand the nature and scope of multidimensional scaling in business research and appreciate its application in all areas of business.

The underlying presumptions that one makes while creating an MDS are:

- The individual tries to group objects together.
- The grouped objects are usually evaluated and compared with each other so that they can coexist on a spatial map.
- The basis of evaluation is not unidimensional and the user is at all times (consciously or unconsciously) using an underlying multidimensional space to evaluate the objects.

MDS essentially visually plots the perceptions and preferences of individuals singly and as a group, regarding a group of objects, individuals or both; even when the information about the dimensions or bases of evaluations is minimal.

Multidimensional scaling usually plots the perceptions and preferences of individuals singly and as a group even when the information about the dimensions or bases of evaluations is minimal.

Thus, the technique uses powerful mathematical tools in order to condense the data by creating visual representations based on the similarities or dissimilarities of data on a spatial map (Schiffman, *et al.* 1981). The map dimensions are hypothesized to be the attributes or features that the person uses to form certain impressions about the object. One of the most widely used mathematical methods to create the maps is based on Kruskal's (1964) stress calculations (to be discussed further in the chapter).

MDS, as stated earlier, usually involves a comparison of sorts to create a relative position of the considered objects. The comparison could be made on *defined dimensions*, or the apparent basis of comparison, as was the case with the premium charged by the insurance service providers in the illustration used by Prof. Krishna (refer case vignette). However, more often than not, people make use of their own peculiar and sometimes subjective or *perceived dimensions* to make the comparison. For example, it could be the trust or faith in the service provider in handling the insured person's problems effectively. Thus, two objects or brands with the same defined dimensions might be perceived very differently by the person because:

- The evaluations might not be solely based on defined or observed parameters.
- The subjective and the objective dimensions might be absolutely unrelated.

To simplify the process further, the technique presents the dependent variable (which might be a similarity or dissimilarity between the object or preferences) and then tries to figure out what were the underlying independents or antecedents that led to the obtained map. The advantage of this method is that the researcher's influence where he/she attempts to provide the dimensions of comparison gets minimized. The disadvantage, however, would be to clearly figure out the dimension the respondents might have used for the comparison.

Thus, the researcher needs to be fairly well versed with the probable parameters that a person might use for comparison. These perceived parameters might emerge from a qualitative analysis of the respondents' decision process or through the researcher's review of the secondary literature about the product. The inputs obtained would have to be objectively—without any element of personal bias—assessed to comprehend the defined or apparent and the hidden or subjective dimensions being used.

A simple explanation of the concept: To understand the concept of mapping the respondent's choices, let us look at a very simple example of a consumer who buys bread every day for his family breakfast. Now, we ask him which bread he buys. He tells us, 'Harvest Gold, Britannia and Perfect.' Next, we ask him the similarity between two bread brands, say, Harvest Gold and Britannia, on a 7-point scale, where 1 is very similar and 7 is very dissimilar. He says, the similarity is 1 . What this means is that:

- If we were to take a mental model of his brain when he said this, the two brands would be very close to each other.
- Suppose we say that the consumer was thinking of price and availability when he was telling us this. Thus, the unconscious evaluation that he did was on the two dimensions of 'price' and 'brand.' So, these two brand are two points close to each other in this two-dimensional map.
- The two manufacturers have to understand that there is no brand loyalty from the customer, as he could very easily buy the competing brand as they are almost identical to each other in his 'mind.'

Now, suppose, we ask him if he has consumed Harvest Gold multi-grain bread, and he says, 'yes.' So we now ask him to tell us the similarity between Harvest Gold regular and Harvest Gold multi-grain bread on the same 7-point scale. His answer is 6. Now, what will happen if we use the same dimensions as in the above case? The brand is the same for both, thus using a two-dimensional map would not be wise as the consumer may be now looking at the health benefit or nutritional content in the breads also as a dimension. Thus this means:

- The bread brands now need a three-dimensional representation to represent their relative positioning in the consumers mind.
- Harvest Gold multi-grain need not worry about competition with the other two as the consumer who buys the multi-grain will not buy them as a substitute as they are very different from the bread they eat regularly.

MDS is only one of the wide array of statistical techniques available for obtaining the object map. The whole range of these methods grouped together is termed as perceptual mapping techniques.

Before discussing the process of conducting the MDS, let us briefly attempt to understand the underlying algorithms of MDS.

- The inputs obtained by the respondents could be in terms of objects, individuals, brands, corporations or countries.

- The comparison could be in terms of similarities/dissimilarities, e.g. how similar is Delhi to Mumbai on a 7-point scale ranging from the most dissimilar to the most similar; or preferences, e.g. out of the five listed brands, indicate the one you prefer the most to the one that is least preferred.
- As you can observe, the respondent is NOT given any dimension to measure similarity or dissimilarity.
- The preferences could be based on ranked data.
- The respondent might be asked to conduct a paired comparison of the data.

Multidimensional Map: An Illustration

Assume Delhi (D) Mumbai (M) and Bengaluru (B) are the cities compared for similarity and the scale is 7 = most similar and 1 = least similar. And the scores obtained were as follows:

Delhi-Mumbai 3
Delhi-Bengaluru 1
Mumbai-Bengaluru 6

Now, we convert the similarity into distance, assuming that there is an inverse relationship between the two. Remember, we had three cities, so we did three comparisons, so the city pair that is most similar would be at the least distance. Let us call it 1. The second similar pair would be at a distance of 2 and the third would be at a distance of 3. Thus, when we got the answers, we saw that the respondent reported that the most similar cities were Mumbai and Bangalore (6). Thus, if we inverse this and say, the more similar a pair, the smaller the distance between them, we convert this into the smallest distance, that is, 1. Similarly, the most dissimilar pair was Delhi and Bangalore (1). Now, going by the same logic, we convert this into the most distant pair, so the equivalent distant would be 3. And the second pair, that is, Delhi-Mumbai, has the second highest similarity, so accordingly, we put the cities at a distance of 2. Thus, the data would look something like this:

Pair	*Similarity*	*Distance*
Delhi – Mumbai	3	2
Delhi – Bengaluru	1	3
Mumbai – Bengaluru	6	1

Now, using the scale of dissimilarities and making the basic assumption that when the respondents conveyed the similarity between the cities, physical distance was not the only measure used by the individual to compare the stated pair. The researcher now needs to try and assess the probable number of dimensions. The approaches that are usually practised involve:

1. The review of earlier work done on the topic
2. Based on the primary inputs that the researcher has obtained through in-depth interviews or focus group studies.
3. Derived from random points generated from an approximately normally distributed configuration.

Going by the third logic, let us look at an emerging map representing the three cities on a two dimensional map (Figure 19.1). As we can see in the conversion of similarity to distance, we found that the cities which were closer to each other were Bangalore and Mumbai. Thus, what we do is, we draw two points on a spatial two-dimensional map. These two points represent Mumbai and Bangalore. Now, since Delhi is

FIGURE 19.1
Spatial map of three Indian metros based on similarity data

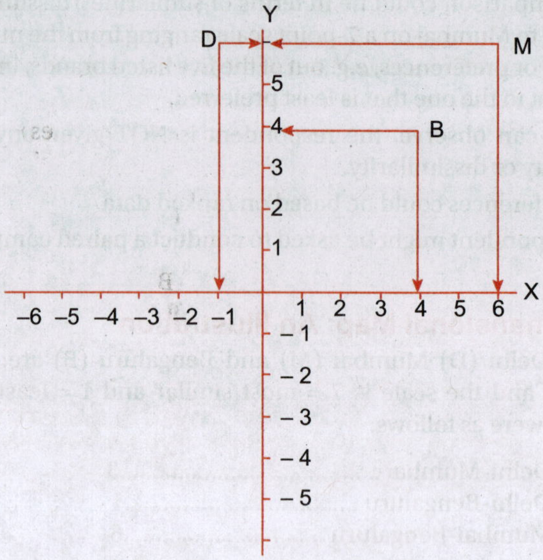

considered to be most dissimilar as compared to Bangalore, we draw the third point representing Delhi as the furthest apart. As you can see now, the D represents Delhi, B is for Bangalore and M is for Mumbai. For simplicity of explanation and understanding, we are taking an assumption of a two-dimensional map. Broadly speaking, this means that the respondent who evaluated the similarity and difference between the three cities was, in his conscious or unconscious evaluation, making use of two parameters or characteristics or features for making the comparison. This assumption might or might not be correct. The method of assessing, whether we were correct or not, will be discussed subsequently.

Next, we drop a perpendicular to these hypothetical dimensions from each of the points. So, we drop a perpendicular from point B to the X-axis, the arrow drops at 4. Similarly, from B we drop another perpendicular on the Y-axis. This point is also 4; we follow the same process for Delhi (D) and Mumbai (M). Now, from all the three cities, we measure the coordinates on the X and Y axis for each—Delhi is *(-1; 6), Mumbai is (6; 6), Bengaluru is (4; 4)*. Now, these values are used to arrive at the squared Euclidean distance between the cities. Please note, when we had converted the similarity ratings of the respondent into distance, that was the actual distance as per the respondent.

Now, we are looking at how the researcher interprets the distance. Thus this is called the 'derived distance' based on the researcher's 'derivation' of the data. Let us see how we calculate the distance between Delhi and Mumbai using the squared Euclidean distance formula. For example, the distance between Delhi and Mumbai is calculated as follows:

$$d_{DM} = (-1 - 6)^2 + (6 - 6)^2 = \mathbf{49.0}$$

Similarly, we can obtain the data for different pairs of cities as shown below:

Pair	*Similarity*	*'Distance'*	*'Derived distance'*
Delhi – Mumbai	3	2	49 (3)
Delhi – Bengaluru	1	3	29 (2)
Mumbai – Bengaluru	6	1	8 (1)

Thus, we can see that the Mumbai-Bengaluru derived distance (8) is the smallest and so was the case when the respondents' similarity (6) was converted into distance (1), so the error between the respondent's judgment and the researcher's interpretation about the assessment is 0. Now let us look at the case of Delhi-Bangalore. Here the similarity between the cities was 1, thus the distance between them was 3. Now look at the derived distance between the two cities which is 29 and this is the second highest distance and not the highest as it should have been had the researcher and respondent assessment matched. Thus we say that there has been an "error" on the part of the researcher when he was trying to map the cities based on the respondent's judgment. The most popular measure for measuring this "error difference" is with the Kruskal's Stress. Here, Stress score is defined as the measure of the goodness of fit and assesses the discrepancy between the actual distance (d_{ij}) and the derived distance ($\hat{d}_{ij}$).

Now let us move the point representing Bengaluru a little to the top right (B′), as shown in the following configuration (Figure 19.2).

FIGURE 19.2 Spatial map of three Indian metros based on similarity data (new coordinates)

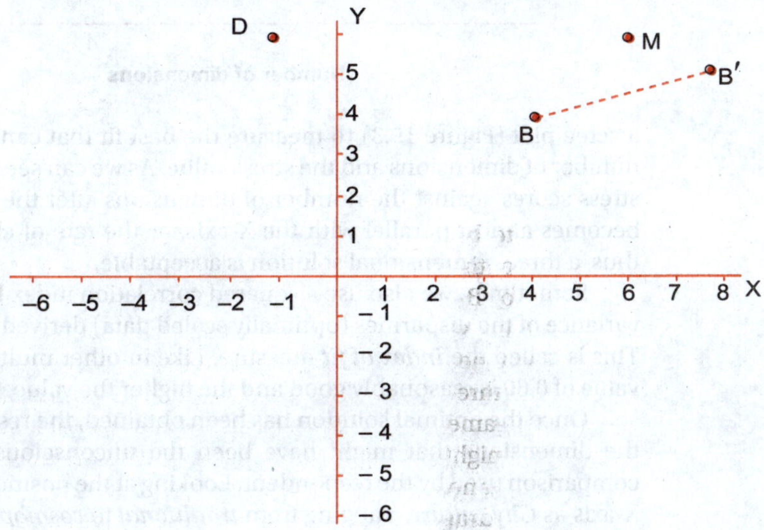

Now, you might ask why we moved the point representing Bengaluru a little further from its original place. The reason is that since the distance between the city pairs should be highest for Delhi-Bengaluru, we try to physically take the point further, i.e. more distant from Delhi. So, the new point is far from Delhi and yet not too far from Mumbai, which should be the shortest distance. Now, we again follow the same process as we did earlier. From the B′ let us drop a perpendicular to the X-axis and one to the Y-axis. The new coordinates for B′ now are B (8, 5). Now the distance between Delhi and Bangalore, according to the squared Euclidean distance, is as follows:

$$\mathbf{D_{DB'} = (-1-8)^2 + (6-5)^2 = 82}$$

Thus, the picture that emerges is as follows:

Pair	*Similarity*	*'Distance'*	*'Derived distance'*
Delhi – Mumbai	3	2	49 (2)
Delhi – Bengaluru	1	3	82 (3)
Mumbai – Bengaluru	6	1	5 (1)

Kruskal's stress measures the discrepancy between actual and derived distance. Lower the stress value, better the 'fit'.

As can be observed, the discrepancy between the respondents assessment of the cites and the researcher's interpretation of how the respondent assessed the similarity/distance between them is zero. Thus 'stress' value between derived and actual distance would be zero. The lower the stress value, the better the 'fit.' Stress can be understood by equating it with R^2 in multiple regression, where we know that the R^2 value can increase with additional causal variables. Similarly, stress will keep on reducing as one increases the number of dimensions. Thus, one can carry out

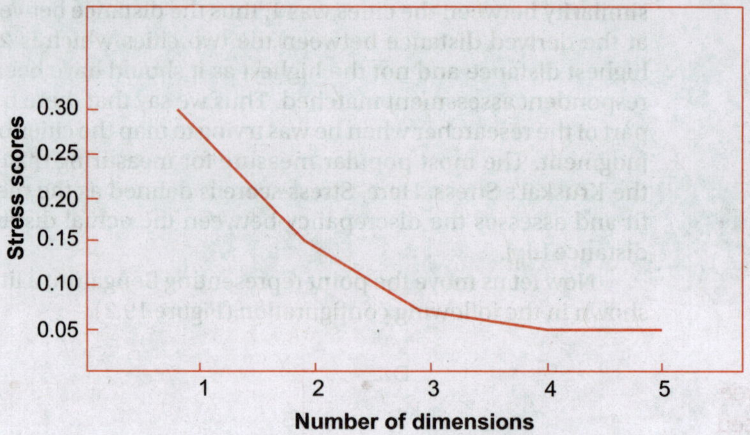

FIGURE 19.3 Scree plot for assessing optimal MDS solution

a scree plot (Figure 19.3) to measure the best fit that can be obtained between the number of dimensions and the stress value. As we can see in Figure 19.3, plotting the stress scores against the number of dimensions after the third dimension, the plot becomes almost parallel with the X-axis, or the rate of change becomes zero and, thus, a three- dimensional solution is acceptable.

Sometimes, we also use a squared correlation index R^2, which is essentially the variance of the disparities (optimally scaled data) derived from the MDS procedure. This is called the *index of fit* measure. Like in other multivariate techniques, an R^2 value of 0.60 is reasonably good and the higher the value, the better the solution.

Once the optimal solution has been obtained, the researcher attempts to name the dimensions that might have been the unconscious underlying basis of the comparison used by the respondent. Looking at the position of the cities, let us name X-axis as *City culture,* ranging from *traditional* to *cosmopolitan.* Let us name Y-axis as *job opportunities,* ranging from *low* to *high.*

It is interesting to understand that the MDS solution would have been more accurate if the researcher had used:

- Past data or qualitative research to comprehend the basis of comparison.
- More cities with varied composition and then observed the derived optimal solution.

Today, there are multiple computer programs like ALSCAL, PROXCAL, INDSCAL, MDSCAL, PREFMAP and MULTISCAL available to the researcher to effectively arrive at an MDS solution.

USAGE OF MULTIDIMENSIONAL SCALING

LEARNING OBJECTIVE 2
Understand the significance and usage of MDS.

The MDS technique has multiple uses for the decision-maker in the business world. However, the prime use of the technique is in the discipline of marketing.

Scale construction: As we can see, the multidimensional scaling gives a composite picture about how the respondent views the object/brand/city, etc., when compared to others in the category. This can be done using similarity or preference data. Next, the researcher tries to name the dimensions that could have been the basis of the comparison. For example, in the illustration about the cities, the researcher felt that the two dimensions used by the respondent were *city culture* and *job opportunities.* Next, what the researcher can do is use these as attributes variables on which he may ask the respondent to evaluate the same or more cities. And if the two - MDS spatial map and the attribute-based map - match, then we can confidently use them to develop a scale to measure city attractiveness. Thus, MDS is a simplistic, yet powerful tool that can help in scale construction.

Brand image analysis: Many marketers use the technique to measure the possible gaps between a company's or a brand's positioning with the consumer's brand image perception.

New product development: MDS is one of the most powerful tools to be used at the idea generation or concept testing stage. It helps us identify quadrants that are less crowded and where a clear product launch opportunity exists. Also if the product team has come up with more than one probable concept, the preference of the consumers regarding these could be tested by placing the preference on a spatial map to see which concept finds higher acceptability on multiple dimensions.

Pricing studies: The marketer can use subjective maps to assess whether price is making a difference to the preference or demand of the brand by measuring a spatial map of the competing brand with and without the criteria of price to assess whether the positioning of the brand is affected by price or not.

Assessing communication effectiveness: The brand manager could design a 'before' and 'after' study to assess the placement of the brand before and after a specific repositioning or a new advertising campaign to see the impact of the same on the brand perception.

In fact, the MDS finds wide usage in the discipline of marketing, as the input data required is easy to comprehend by the respondent and not too tedious in terms of assessing the same with multiple variables. Secondly, with the availability of numerous computer programs, perceptual maps can be easily drawn. And lastly, in a cluttered marketplace, a brand uses subjective and psychological perceptions to create a brand image that stands out and is also difficult to clone and copy by the competitor. The consumer respondent tries to make some semblance of order in a world bombarded with brands and particularly associates one image with one brand only.

CREATING SPATIAL MAPS USING MULTIDIMENSIONAL SCALING

LEARNING OBJECTIVE 3
Carry out the step-wise process for formulating an MDS.

This section is devoted to understanding how the process of a research study using MDS as an assessment tool is carried out. The entire process has been demonstrated as a flow diagram in Figure 19.4.

Formulating the Research Objectives

The method of MDS is used under two conditions:

1. In case the researcher is carrying out an exploratory study in order to decipher the probable underlying attributes or the causes of certain observed patterns of behaviour.
2. It can also be used in descriptive research studies. The objective is simply to present the comparative evaluations of objects, individuals or brands in the consumer's mind space.

Thus, in both cases, the diffused approach to addressing the research topic is a common factor. The strength of the technique is the ability of being able to present a probable spatial map of respondent choices even without any stated attributes

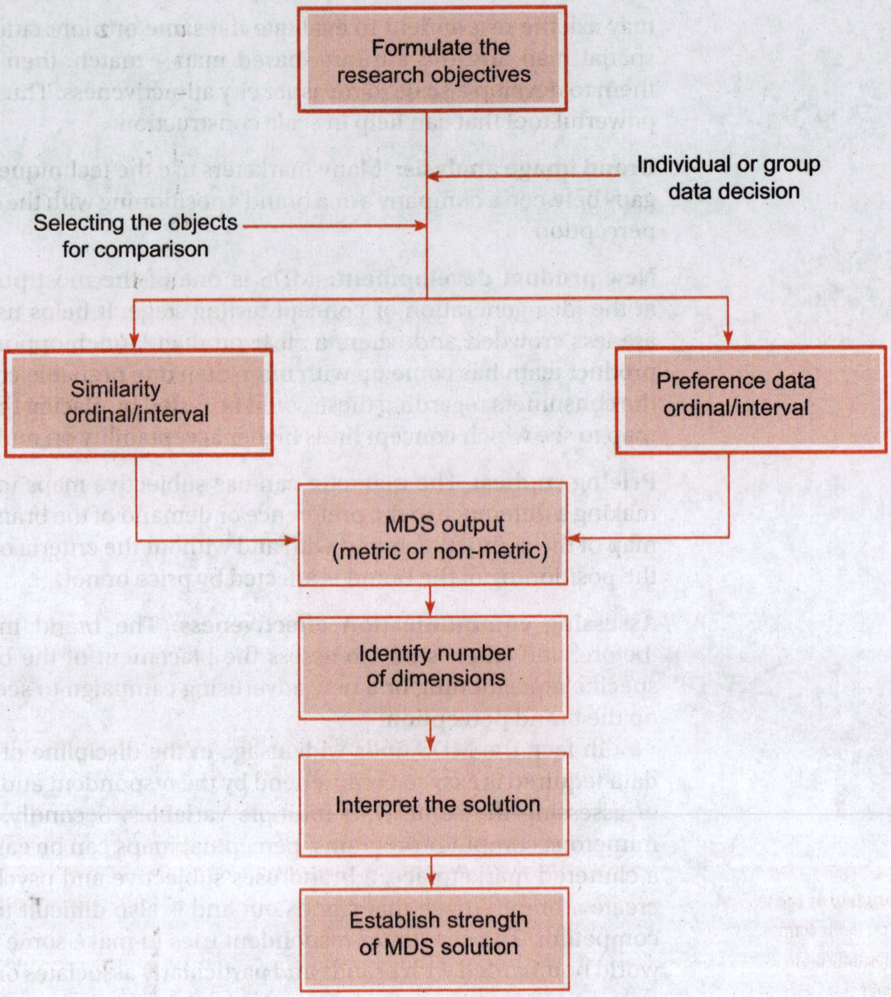

FIGURE 19.4 The process of multidimensional scaling

of comparison. Thus, the onus to improve the solution obtained by the technique depends on the researcher's skill and knowledge of the topic under study as he/she should be able to identify the possible dimensions used accurately. In order to correctly arrive at the decisions the researcher needs to decide on the following:

- The unit of analysis, i.e. would the comparison be for individuals, the subgroups, clusters or for the entire sample under study?
- Secondly, the objects, brands or elements to be compared have to be carefully selected.
- Lastly, the decision on whether the study requires the respondent to identify:
  - the placement of the selected objects in the individual's mental map. Thus, the distance, or similarities, between the objects needs to be ascertained.
  - whether the objective is to measure the order of preference amongst the objects/brands.

The advantage of MDS is that it can present the placement of objects in a unique configuration for each individual as well as for the entire group.

Establishing Individual or Grouped Data Decision

The advantage of MDS is also that it can present the placement of objects in a unique configuration for each individual as well as for the entire group. In case of multiple individual maps, however, the researcher will constantly need to figure out the commonality of placement to make any targeted decision.

However, in case the objective is to customize offerings—like holiday packages or event planning—then individual maps would be the ones to be considered. Also, when the sample under study is very small—for example, a panel of judges measuring advertising effectiveness or measuring the impact of different repositioning alternatives, these are situations that might warrant the use of individual maps.

There are also situations when the placement of objects at the macro or group level needs to be assessed as the objective is to design strategies focused on a targeted population. In case the population is not homogenous in composition and exists as small, more distinctly homogenous clusters, then the researcher might look at the subgroup or clustered plots to assess which is the segment in which the object/brand is valued more or less as compared to the category leader. Also, the subgroup plots might identify new product opportunities in some clusters because when we look at the existing map of the objects in that cluster, the options being considered are too few and there is ample opportunity to enter the zone.

Selecting the Objects for Comparison

Once the research objective has been established and the decision on the unit of analysis has been made, the next decision is to identify the objects that need to be compared for the analysis. For example, in the study on cities the difficulty encountered was that the number of cities was not sufficient to cover the spectrum on the probable dimensions. Thus, the selection of cities that have a more rigid city culture or are more cosmopolitan and also which vary in the kind of occupational opportunities available there was too small. Thus, we cannot state with certainty whether the dimensions identified were the ones that were at the back of the respondent's mind when the comparative evaluations were made.

Secondly, the objects to be considered must have some underlying dimension of an observable or a subjective characteristic because sometimes, including an object or two which are oddities in the group might not do justice to the spatial representation. For example, if we give the consumer a list of small cars like Alto, Santro, i10, Zen, Beat, Spark and include in the comparison Reva, which is an electric car, or Beetle, which is a collector's item, we are creating a dilemma in the consumer's mind and here, the perception will be very different for a person who is unconsciously using environment-friendly as the basis and another who is using mileage and engine power as the dimensions for evaluation.

The researcher should not use **very few or too many objects.** In the former case, it becomes difficult to ascertain the dimensions used and in the latter it becomes bothersome for the respondent.

Lastly, the researcher also needs to take care not to use very few or too many objects. If the number is less, it becomes difficult to ascertain the dimensions used and too many would be bothersome for the respondent, who would need to compare or rank too many objects or the combination of objects. Even though there are no hard and fast rules, it is advisable to have a minimum of eight objects and going beyond 25 objects is usually to be avoided. Another way to select the number of objects is based on the number of desired or perceived dimensions of comparison. Generally, as a thumb rule, we select objects in a 4 : 1 ratio of the dimensions desired. Thus, for a one-dimensional solution, we pick up at least four objects and at least eight for a two- and 12 for a three-dimensional solution.

To illustrate the technique we are taking eight business and general interest magazines namely – *India Today*, *Outlook*, *Open*, *Frontline*, *Business India*, *Business world*, *Investor* and *Society*. The objective of the business development manager of a popular publication house was to see whether a new magazine could be launched, and if so, how should he compose and position the magazine. A study of 100 readers in North India, where the magazine would be launched, was carried out to see what their perception about these magazines was and which ones were the preferred magazines.

Thus, as we can see that the unit of analysis is the reader residing in North India who is aware of all the eight magazines. This takes us to the question of scale construction to obtain the respondents input. On the basis of the listed objectives, here, the data obtained should be on the basis of similarity and secondly, on the basis of preference.

To illustrate the technique we will take the same eight magazines and demonstrate how to obtain the inputs and analyse the results.

CONCEPT CHECK

1. Discuss MDS as a mapping technique.
2. In what areas can MDS be applied?
3. What are the various steps involved in the creation of spatial maps?

CONDUCTING MDS WITH SIMILARITY DATA

LEARNING OBJECTIVE 4
Conduct a similarity-based MDS.

When the objective is to determine the grouping of objects then the intention is to see the plotting of the objects in an imaginary space on the basis of whether they seem close to or far apart as compared to each other. To measure similarity, we make use of a paired comparison scale and give the respondent different pairs (as was the case in the earlier chapter illustration of the three Indian cities—Delhi, Mumbai and Bengaluru). This comparison can take two different orientations. The first is based on the rank-order scale and the second is based on interval scale. In this section, we will discuss both by using suitable examples.

Similarity Measured on Interval Scale Data

Here, to measure similarity we use an Interval scaled question as follows:

> *Given below are sets of magazines that you know of/have read. You are requested to evaluate them on whether you think they are similar or different when compared to each other.*

Thus, all the possible pairs [(n (n – 1)/2, where n is the number of stimuli)] are given to the respondent to evaluate. The idea being that the individual will use his own judgment to evaluate the similarities between the magazine. The matrix of comparison would be as follows:

	VS								VDS
India Today-Outlook	1	2	3	4	5	6	7	8	9	10
India Today-Frontline	1	2	3	4	5	6	7	8	9	10
Business India-Business World	1	2	3	4	5	6	7	8	9	10
Open-Investor	1	2	3	4	5	6	7	8	9	10

where VS (very similar) = 1, to VDS (very dissimilar) = 10

Here, the data obtained is metric or on an interval scale. It is also possible to get non-metric or ordinal scale data, where paired magazines are given to the respondent and he/she is asked to rank them from the most similar pair to the most dissimilar pair. However, there is no problem of analysis as most software programs are able to conduct the analysis on both the metric as well as the non-metric data.

Obtaining the Data Output for Conducting MDS

Once the data from all respondents has been gathered, it is collated to represent the aggregate (group plots were to be computed) dissimilarities between the brands and we get a matrix that looks as given in Table 19.1. Let us see how we get this:

TABLE 19.1 MDS input data for magazines (n = 100)

	Frontline	Society	India Today	Outlook	Business World	Open	Investor	Business India
Frontline	0.00	3.00	4.00	7.00	1.00	5.00	1.00	8.00
Society	3.00	0.00	2.00	4.00	7.00	7.00	8.00	6.00
India Today	4.00	2.00	0.00	1.00	3.00	6.00	7.00	3.00
Outlook	7.00	4.00	1.00	0.00	2.00	4.00	7.00	7.00
Business world	1.00	7.00	3.00	2.00	0.00	2.00	4.00	5.00
Open	5.00	7.00	6.00	4.00	2.00	0.00	3.00	6.00
Investor	1.00	8.00	7.00	7.00	4.00	3.00	0.00	2.00
Business India	8.00	6.00	3.00	7.00	5.00	6.00	2.00	0.00

For example, we show the responses of the first 10 respondents who gave the following data regarding the similarity between *Frontline* and *Society*:

3, 4, 3, 4, 5, 3, 3, 3, 3, 3

The mean of the above responses equals 3.1, which could be rounded off to 3.0 (for simplicity of understanding here). Similarly, we could obtain the average similarity rating based on the comparison made by all 100 respondents. The actual values might go into two or three decimal places. However, for simplicity of illustration, we have rounded the obtained average of 3.1 to the nearest whole number ,that is, 3. Thus, as we can see, we get an 8 × 8 data matrix, where the rows and columns are mirror images and reflect the magazines we were evaluating.

Obtaining the MDS Solution

The MDS solution to get the spatial map of the consumer's perception can be obtained by using any of the software as listed earlier. The nature of the input data in this case was interval or metric. Thus, the data can be treated as distance. The nature of the input data—that is, metric or non-metric—will determine the next step. For non-metric data, the software will produce or create distances in a given dimensionality. The rank order of the estimated distances (*distances would be based on derived distances as explained earlier*) would try to match the 'actual (respondent's)' ranked data as far as possible.

On the other hand, in case the data is metric and intervally placed, as in our example, the match between the output (*which is metric Euclidean distances*) and the input (*that is interval data*) is stronger. However, in most instances, the results from metric and non-metric inputs are comparable and both can be used with equal ease and reliability.

Thus, from the composite input data of Table 19.1 different spatial maps were obtained for the data. These maps were obtained from a unidimensional to a three-dimensional solution. For getting the MDS solution, go to Appendix 19.1 of this chapter. and follow the step-wise instructions. Omit Step 4 from the instructions, as this was an interval scale and, therefore, metric data. However, you must also remember that this was a paired comparison of the magazines that you did, and paired comparison places the obtained data on an ordinal scale (refer Chapter 7). Thus, when you go to Step 5 and click on MODEL, you must not forget to specify the level of measurement as Ordinal.

IDENTIFYING THE NUMBER OF DIMENSIONS

LEARNING OBJECTIVE 5
Identify the optimal number of dimensions required to configure the respondent data.

As stated in the earlier sections, usually, as the number of probable dimensions increases the interpretation of the respondent's mental map of the objects improves. However, too many dimensions can make a map tedious to interpret. Thus, one needs to balance the number of dimensions with the magnitude of stress measure that is acceptable to the researcher. In practice, there are some rules that are used to assist in this decision.

- **Subject knowledge** or familiarity with the product category might be used by the researcher very often to figure out the underlying dimensions. However, this method needs to be used with caution, as it requires a complete objective approach and minimization of the researcher's own evaluative criteria and bias.
- **Reader's comprehension:** Even though multiple dimensions might be more accurate, for the reader comprehending configurations' beyond a two-dimensional map is often not easy. Thus, if the stress score is manageable and R-square value is 0.6 or above the researcher might go along with a two-dimensional map only.
- **Scree plots:** As stated earlier, another way of ascertaining the optimal balance between accuracy and dimensions is to use the scree plot. The stress scores obtained are plotted against the number of dimensions and wherever the rate of change is negligible and the plotted line becomes almost parallel to the X-axis is the point at which one decides to stop and accept the solution.

Subject knowledge requires a **complete objective approach** and minimization of the researcher's own evaluative criteria and bias.

For the above example, we made use of the ALSCAL process in SPSS and obtained three spatial maps for three-, two-, and one-dimensional solutions. The obtained stress scores were plotted against the corresponding dimensions and we obtained the plot shown in Figure 19.5. This scree plot is not generated through

FIGURE 19.5
Scree plot for magazines: similarity data

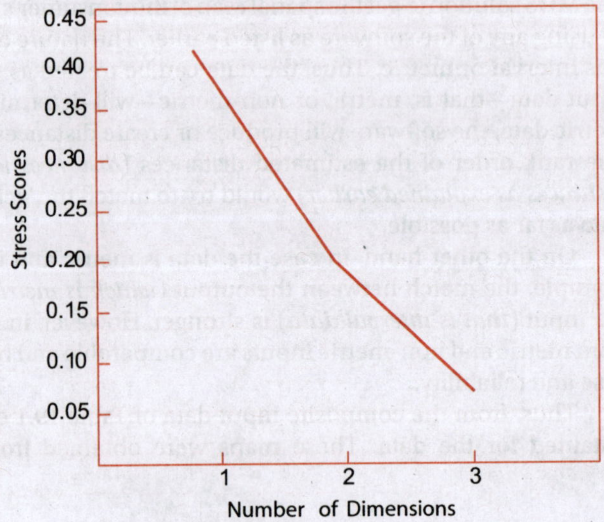

the ALSCAL process. One can make this plot in EXCEL as well. You enter the Dimension number in the First column and the stress scores in the second column and get the line graph. As we can see, the elbow is lying somewhere between a two- and a three-dimensional solution.

- **R-square value:** Another criterion that the researcher might like to use is the R-square value. In case the R-square value is 0.6 or above, the solution is acceptable. As we can see from Table 19.2, the two-dimensional solution is an acceptable one.

TABLE 19.2
Stress scores and R-square values of the similarity data

Number of Dimensions	Stress Value	R-square Values
3	0.09042	0.87006
2	0.20997	**0.62649**
1	0.42502	0.40979

Interpreting the MDS Solution

After determining the ideal or optimal dimensions, the next step is to identify the possible dimensions used. One way of doing this is to go back to the respondents and ask them about what basis they used for comparison. Based on the research work done on the topic, the researcher might attempt to identify the dimensions. One may check the objective measures of difference. For example, in the above illustration, the magazine content or the price of the magazine can be used to evaluate the difference and to figure out what could have been the dimensions. The MDS output always gives the coordinates on the identified dimensions. Along with these and the proximity of values one might try to figure out what could have been the basis.

In the stated example, let us first examine the coordinates for a three-dimensional solution. The obtained coordinates are presented in Table 19.3.

To name these dimensions, let us look at the extreme values and the grouping of brands. As we can see on dimension 1, *Investor* is the highest (1.69) and *Society, India Today* and *Outlook* are close to each other. Now, if we go by the reported content in these magazines, *Investor* mostly has information related to financial matters, while the other three magazines are more of general interest in nature. Thus, we can name this dimension as 'magazine content', ranging from specialized to general interest.

To name the second dimension, let us examine the highest and lowest and the clustered values. Here we see *Frontline* and *Society* scoring high and *Open* scoring low. For this we examined the reporting nature of the article and found that the depth and attention paid to detailed information was high in both *Frontline* and *Society*, while in *Open* and *Outlook* the articles were superficial and did not provide

TABLE 19.3
Coordinates for a three-dimensional solution

Magazines	Dimension 1	Dimension 2	Dimension 3
Frontline	0.6532	1.3542	0.9130
Society	–1.4403	1.2012	–0.3738
India Today	–1.3882	0.2484	–0.3070
Outlook	–1.2960	–1.0636	0.5045
Business World	0.4481	–0.5772	1.1583
Open	0.7140	–1.5063	0.4570
Investor	1.6944	0.4127	–0.4527
Business India	0.6148	–0.0692	–1.8993

a comprehensive perspective on the issue reported. The reading in the end seemed inconclusive at best. Thus, we named the dimension as 'Attention to detailing' ranging from comprehensive to brief.

The last dimension puzzled us as *Business World* and *Business India* were diametrically opposite to each other. Then we identified the volume, size or number of pages and found that the *Business World* volume was the smallest and *Business India* was the bulkiest and had the most number of pages. Thus we named the dimension as 'Magazine volume' ranging from small to large.

As a two-dimensional solution also had an acceptable stress score and a significant R-square, we are presenting below the two-dimensional solution as a spatial map (Figure 19.6).

The computer program also gives us the coordinates of the eight magazines on two dimensions (Table 19.4). Thus, we consider the placement of the magazines and the corresponding coordinates to name the dimensions.

If we examine the first dimension, we find that *Society* is the highest here, with *India Today* and *Outlook* close together and the last on this dimension is *Investor*. This seems to be the 'Magazine content' ranging from general interest to specific interest.

The second dimension has *Business India* at the top and *Open* at the bottom and looking at the placement of the other six magazines, this seems to be '*Subscription base*', ranging from corporate readership to general reader ship.

In the spatial map, the magazines that are closer to each other have a similar benefit or image in the consumer's mind. Thus the competition between them is higher as compared to the names that are further apart. The brand that appears

TABLE 19.4
Coordinates for a two-dimensional solution

Magazines	Dimension 1	Dimension 2
Frontline	−0.1735	−1.4487
Society	1.6737	−0.4389
India Today	0.9264	0.6538
Outlook	1.1472	0.0258
Business World	−0.6590	0.3820
Open	−0.8459	−1.0233
Investor	−1.6313	0.0970
Business India	−0.4375	1.7522

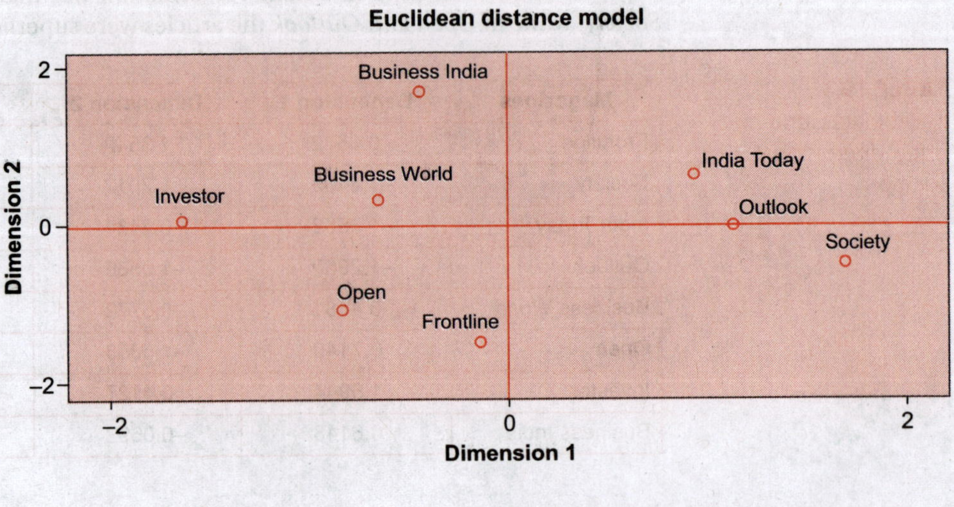

FIGURE 19.6
Spatial map of magazines based on similarity data

isolated has a unique image and stands out clearly and, generally, can be assured of no real competition.

Manager's decision: Thus, based on the similarity analysis, the management concluded that *Society* was a magazine that was of general interest and seemed to be enjoying an uncluttered space. Thus, rather than looking at a specialized and a corporate base, the new magazine would be a general interest magazine that will cover on everyday issues. It would not be high on political content like *India Today* or *Outlook* but would focus on lifestyle issues. The name of the monthly magazine would be *Life & Times.*

Similarity Measured on Ranked Scale

As stated earlier in the section, similarity-based MDS can also be obtained from ranked data. The researcher gave the following five magazines as pairs (n (n-1)/2) to the respondents and asked the following question:

Given below are different pairs of magazines that you know of/have read. You are requested to rank the pairs in terms of which according to you is the most similar pair to the most dissimilar. Remember to give a rank of 1 to the most similar pair and so on till you reach the last pair and give it a rank of 10.

Pair no.	Magazine Pair	Rank
X1	India Today-Outlook	
X2	India Today-Open	
X3	India Today-Frontline	
X4	India Today-Society	
X5	Outlook-Open	
X6	Outlook-Frontline	
X7	Outlook-Society	
X8	Open-Frontline	
X9	Open-Society	
X10	Frontline-Society	

Obtaining the Data Output for Conducting MDS

This question will generate ranks from 1 to 10 for each respondent. Then this data can be entered in an EXCEL or an SPSS spreadsheet. This data can be used to prepare summarized ranks. To illustrate how to enter the data and arrive at the data matrix, a small part of the above research question is given below. This is an illustration for five respondents for the 10 magazine pairs as above.

SAMPLE TABLE A
Data sheet of responses for the above-mentioned 10 magazine pairs (n = 5)

Res.id	X1	X2	X3	X4	X5	X6	X7	X8	X9	X10
1	1	7	6	10	3	8	9	5	4	2
2	1	7	7	9	3	8	10	5	4	2
3	2	7	7	10	3	8	9	4	5	1
4	1	7	7	9	3	10	8	4	5	2
5	2	6	6	9	3	10	8	5	4	1

The next step is to calculate the summarized ranks based on the above data. Once the summarized ranks are available the lowest value is given a rank of 1 - in this case 7 = rank 1 and so on:

Summation of ranks	Rank
X1 = (1x3) + (2x2) + (3x0) + (4x0) + (5x0) + (6x0) + (7x0) + (8x0) + (9x0) + (10x0) = 7	1
X2 = (1x0) + (2x0) + (3x0) + (4x0) + (5x0) + (6x1) + (7x4) + (8x0) + (9x0) + (10x0) = 34	7
X3 = (1x0) + (2x0) + (3x0) + (4x0) + (5x0) + (6x2) + (7x3) + (8x0) + (9x0) + (10x0) = 33	6
X4 = (1x0) + (2x0) + (3x0) + (4x0) + (5x0) + (6x0) + (7x0) + (8x0) + (9x3) + (10x2) = 47	9
X5 = (1x0) + (2x0) + (3x5) + (4x0) + (5x0) + (6x0) + (7x0) + (8x0) + (9x0) + (10x0) = 15	3
X6 = (1x0) + (2x0) + (3x0) + (4x0) + (5x0) + (6x0) + (7x0) + (8x3) + (9x0) + (10x2) = 44	8
X7 = (1x0) + (2x0) + (3x0) + (4x0) + (5x0) + (6x0) + (7x0) + (8x2) + (9x2) + (10x1) = 54	10
X8 = (1x0) + (2x0) + (3x0) + (4x2) + (5x3) + (6x0) + (7x0) + (8x0) + (9x0) + (10x0) = 23	5
X9 = (1x3) + (2x2) + (3x0) + (4x3) + (5x2) + (6x0) + (7x0) + (8x0) + (9x0) + (10x0) = 22	4
X10 = (1x2) + (2x3) + (3x0) + (4x0) + (5x0) + (6x0) + (7x0) + (8x0) + (9x0) + (10x0) = 8	2

* *Please note the lowest aggregated value means more preferred and thus 7 becomes rank 1.*

Next we prepare a 10 by 10 matrix on the basis of this data as follows:

SAMPLE TABLE B
MDS input data for ranked pairs of magazines (n = 5)

Magazines	India Today	Outlook	Open	Frontline	Society
India Today	0.00	1.00	7.00	6.00	9.00
Outlook	1.00	0.00	3.00	8.00	10.00
Open	7.00	3.00	0.00	5.00	4.00
Frontline	6.00	8.00	5.00	0.00	2.00
Society	9.00	10.00	4.00	2.00	0.00

The same process was employed for the sample size of 100. Then the final table of the composite ranks for all the respondents (n = 100) would look like this:

TABLE 19.5
MDS input data for ranked pairs of magazines (n = 100)

Magazines	India Today	Outlook	Open	Frontline	Society
India Today	0.00	1.00	4.00	6.00	10.00
Outlook	1.00	0.00	3.00	5.00	9.00
Open	4.00	3.00	0.00	2.00	7.00
Frontline	6.00	5.00	2.00	0.00	8.00
Society	10.00	9.00	7.00	8.00	0.00

Obtaining the MDS Solution

Since the data that was generated for this paired comparison matrix was based on ordinal (ranked) scale, the first step to be taken is to *create distances from the data.*

For getting the MDS solution, go to Appendix 19.1 of this chapter and follow the step-wise instructions. Omit Step 3 from the instructions, as the scale was ordinal and, thus, non-metric data. However, you must also remember that this was a paired comparison of the magazines that you did and, thus, the obtained data is on an ordinal scale (refer Chapter 7). Thus, when you go to Step 5 and click on MODEL, you must not forget to specify the level of measurement as Ordinal.

Please note that since the number of paired objects for comparison were 10, we are going for a two-dimensional solution, as at least 12 objects are required for a three-dimensional solution (Refer to earlier section on selecting the objects for comparison). The two-dimensional solution resulted in the following Kruskal stress value and R-squared values.

TABLE 19.6
Stress value and R square value for rank data

Number of Dimensions	Stress Value	R-square Value
2	0.000	1.00

Interpreting the MDS Solution

For the two-dimensional solution we obtained the following coordinates on the two dimensions:

TABLE 19.7
Coordinates for a two-dimensional solution

Magazines	Dimension 1	Dimension 2
India Today	1.0228	–0.7168
Outlook	0.9830	–0.4423
Open	0.3665	0.5877
Frontline	0.0195	0.9618
Society	–2.3918	–0.3904

To name the dimensions, we will look at the extreme values on the two dimensions and how the magazines are grouping together. On dimension 1, *India Today* is the highest; *Outlook* is very close, and the magazine on the other extreme is *Society*. Now, if go by the content of these magazines, *India Today* and *Outlook* are general interest magazines, with covering everything from politics to sports. On the other hand, *Society* mostly has articles and coverage about celebrities and their lifestyle. Thus, this dimension is one of *magazine content,* ranging from general interest to social gossip.

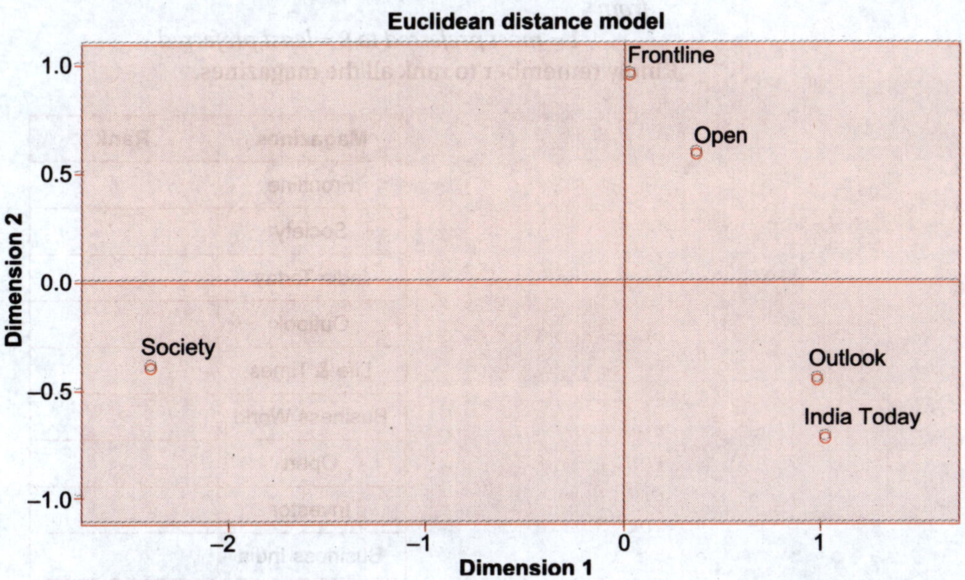

FIGURE 19.7
MDS map for ranking data (n = 100)

Let us look at Dimension 2. Here *Frontline* is the highest and *India Today* is the lowest. This could be related to type of articles. In *Frontline*, the nature of articles is more reporting of information, while in *India Today*, the articles are more opinion based and clearly reflect the analysis of the writer. Thus, there is more depth in the article as compared to *Frontline*. Thus, we name the dimension as *reporting style*—ranging from general to opinion based.

Thus it can be clearly seen that there are two magazine pairs- India Today and Outlook and Frontline and Open which exist together in the readers mind. Society seems to be by itself and has no competition for this group of readers.

Manager's decision: Thus looking at existing general interest magazines, it seems that there lies a clear opportunity for the manager to come out with a magazine that can focus on celebrity reporting but could either be similar to Society by being more opinion based (it is also low on dimension 2) or have a mix of opinion based articles and also carries reports of celebrity events . This would ensure that it can create a space for itself that is above Society.

CONDUCTING MDS WITH PREFERENCE DATA

LEARNING OBJECTIVE 6
Conduct a preference-based MDS.

As the name suggests, the object is not to measure similarity or dissimilarity but to measure selection or rejection of objects or brands. Usually, the data is based on ordinal level—either based on a simple ranking or on the basis of paired-comparison scale. However, it is also possible to ask interval-scaled questions and then conduct an MDS. In this section we will illustrate all the three conditions with examples.,

Preference Illustration (Simple Ranking Scale)

One year after the launch of the Life and Times magazine, a survey of 250 subscribers (those who had read at least three issues of the magazine) was conducted. Out of these, the usable sample was of 130 respondents.

In our study of nine magazines, we have used the ranking scale.

Given below are the names of common magazines that you know of/have read. You are requested to kindly rank them in your order of preferred reading, ranging from

1 = most preferred to 9 = least preferred.

Kindly remember to rank all the magazines.

Magazines	Rank
Frontline	
Society	
India Today	
Outlook	
Life & Times	
Business World	
Open	
Investor	
Business India	

Another way of getting the data is through paired comparison, where the respondent is given a pair of magazines every time and has to choose the preferred magazine from the pair. Both of these are non-metric inputs of data and, as stated earlier, these would be converted into distances to arrive at the spatial map.

In some instances the preference can be obtained through rating scales ranging from 'like a lot' to 'dislike a lot'.

It needs to be remembered that the difference in the similarity map could be very different from the preference map, as it might happen that two objects that are very different from each other are both preferred by the respondent or two brands that appear to be very similar might end up at the two ends of the preference continuum.

Obtaining the Data Output for Conducting the MDS

Once the ranked data is gathered from entire respondents, one takes a decision of individual or group plots. In this case, we look at the aggregate maps as it is the subscribers'/readers' perception that we are interested in. The data sheet looks like the data from 10 respondents displayed in Table 19.8 (for the complete data set refer to Table 19.8 in the data disc).

TABLE 19.8
Sample data for 10 respondents–magazine rankings

S. No.	India Today	Outlook	Business World	Open	Investor	Business India	Society	Frontline	Life & Times
1	4	3	2	9	5	1	7	6	8
2	9	6	7	4	5	8	2	3	1
3	9	1	2	8	6	3	4	5	7
4	7	3	2	9	4	1	5	6	8
5	8	3	2	9	4	1	5	6	7
6	9	4	2	8	6	5	1	3	7
7	9	7	6	5	4	8	1	2	3
8	1	5	4	9	3	2	7	6	8
9	1	7	6	9	2	3	5	4	8
10	1	5	4	9	3	2	7	6	8

Obtaining the MDS Solution

Based on the data from 130 respondents, an MDS solution was constructed using ALSCAL. In order to get the MDS solution, go to Appendix 19.1 of this chapter. You are required to follow the step-wise instructions for getting the MDS solution. Omit Step 3 from the instructions, as the scale was ordinal and thus non-metric data. However, you must also remember that this was ranking data. Thus, when you go to Step 5 and click on MODEL, you must not forget to specify the level of measurement as Ordinal. As the data was in ranks, the distances were created from the input. Based on the aggregate grouped plots, four solutions were arrived at for a one-dimensional, a two-dimensional, three-dimension and a four-dimensional spatial map.

Identifying the Number of Dimensions

Next, based on the scree plot (Figure 19.8) and the R-square values (Table 19.9) it was decided to accept a two-dimensional solution as the stress value was good (10 per cent) and the R-square value was significantly high (0.95).

FIGURE 19.8
Scree plot for magazines: ranked data

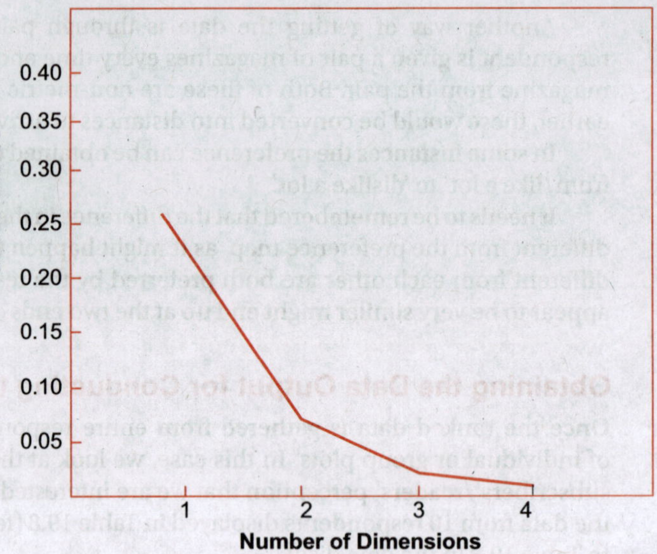

TABLE 19.9
Stress scores and R-square values of the ranked data

Number of Dimensions	Stress Value	R-square Values
4	0.00058	1.0
3	0.00256	0.99993
2	0.07677	**0.95947**
1	0.26536	0.78040

Interpreting the MDS Solution

Once the decision has been made about a two-dimensional map, we need to get the output as a spatial map and the coordinates of the identified dimensions. The map and the coordinates are presented below.

FIGURE 19.9
MDS map of ranking data obtained for nine magazines (N = 130)

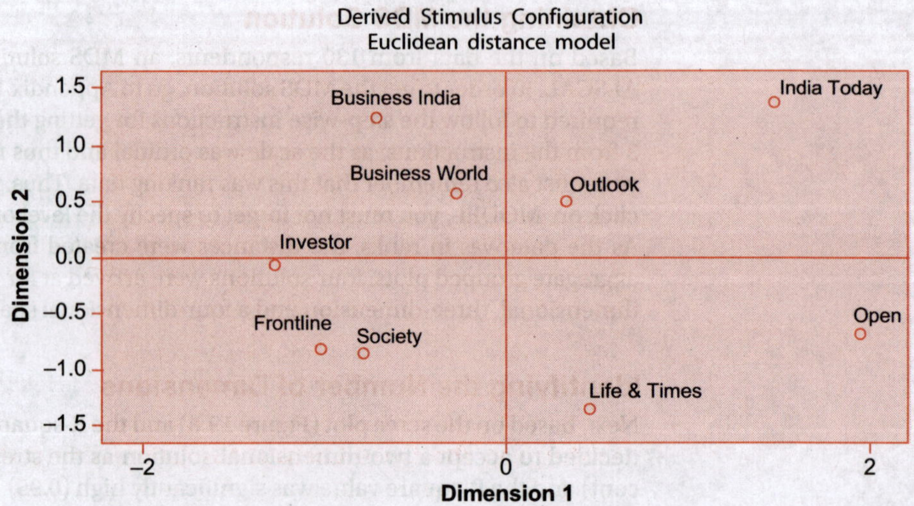

Looking at the placement of the magazines we can see that *India Today* is gaining on both the dimensions. The first dimension or Dimension 1 seems to be based on *coverage.* One end of the dimension might be wider in scope, as in the case of *Open* and *India Today* to the other end would, however, be narrow in scope, for example, Investment behaviour and advice in *Investor* and lifestyle and trends in *Society*. Dimension 2 seems to be the *credibility*, or trust factor. The respondent has more faith in the reporting of *India Today* and *Business India*, followed by *Business World* and *Outlook*. *Frontline*, *Society*, as well as *Life & Times* need to do substantial work in this direction.

TABLE 19.10
Coordinates for a two-dimensional solution

Magazines	Dimension 1	Dimension 2
Frontline	–1.0337	–0.8097
Society	–0.8504	–0.8599
India Today	1.4473	1.3989
Outlook	0.3202	0.4932
Business World	–0.2705	0.5955
Open	1.9368	–0.6654
Investor	–1.2852	–0.525
Business India	–0.7182	1.2562
Life & Times	0.4536	–1.3564

Thus, if we look at the magazine launch, we have been able to create a space for ourselves as a general interest magazine. However, some credible sources need to publish with us or else we need to ensure a more comprehensive research for the articles that are published with us. This also depends on what is our benchmark—in this case, we are assuming it to be *India Today*.

Preference Illustration (Paired Comparison Scale)

In this format, the respondent is given one pair to evaluate at a time and he/she indicates which brand he prefers. The brands considered for the study were: Pizza Hut, Dominoes, Slice of Italy, Spaghetti, Pizza Corner, Flavors and local pizzeria. This scale has been explained in depth in Chapter 7). Thus, here we are giving the question that was asked:

Given below are pairs of pizza brands that you have heard of/have consumed pizza from. Please indicate in the box which one of the pizza brands you prefer. Put a tick in the box representing the pizza you prefer. Remember to tick only one brand in each pair.

Pair Number	Brand	Brand
1	Pizza Hut	Dominoes
2	Pizza Hut	Slice of Italy
3		
21	Spaghetti	Local pizzeria

This question consisting of 21 possible pairs was given to 20 respondents.

Obtaining the Data Output for Conducting the MDS

To illustrate how to obtain the data matrix from the paired comparison that is carried out, a small illustration from the same example is given below. The data is for 10 respondents and for simplicity we have taken 4 brands – thus 6 paired comparisons were made.

SAMPLE TABLE C

Data entry for 6 paired comparisons for 4 pizza brands (n=10) [Pizza Hut = PH; Dominoes = DO; Slice of Italy = SOI; Local pizzeria = LP]

Res. ID	Pizza Hut-Dominoes	Pizza Hut-Slice of Italy	Pizza Hut-local pizzeria	Dominoes-Slice of Italy	Dominoes-Local pizzeria	Slice of Italy-Local pizzeria
1	Pizza Hut	Pizza Hut	Pizza Hut	Slice of Italy	Dominoes	Slice of Italy
2	Pizza Hut	Pizza Hut	Pizza Hut	Slice of Italy	Dominoes	Slice of Italy
3	Pizza Hut	Pizza Hut	Pizza Hut	Dominoes	Local pizzeria	Slice of Italy
4	Dominoes	Slice of Italy	Pizza Hut	Dominoes	Dominoes	Slice of Italy
5	Pizza Hut	Slice of Italy	Pizza Hut	Dominoes	Dominoes	Slice of Italy
6	Pizza Hut	Slice of Italy	Pizza Hut	Dominoes	Dominoes	Slice of Italy
7	Dominoes	Pizza Hut	Local pizzeria	Slice of Italy	Dominoes	Slice of Italy
8	Dominoes	Pizza Hut	Local pizzeria	Slice of Italy	Local pizzeria	Local pizzeria
9	Pizza Hut	Pizza Hut	Pizza Hut	Dominoes	Dominoes	Slice of Italy
10	Pizza Hut	Pizza Hut	Pizza Hut	Dominoes	Dominoes	Slice of Italy
%	PH=70	PH=70	PH=80	SOI=40	DO=80	SOI=90
%	DO=30	SOI=30	LP=20	DO=60	LP=20	LP=10

Based on the frequency of preference available in each paired comparison, we prepare a 6 by 6 data matrix of the sample data. The data matrix obtained would be as follows:

SAMPLE TABLE D

Data entry for 6 paired comparisons for 4 pizza brands (n=10)

BRANDS	Pizza Hut	Dominoes	Slice of Italy	Local pizzeria
Pizza Hut	0.00	0.30	0.30	0.20
Dominoes	0.70	0.00	0.40	0.20
Slice of Italy	0.70	0.60	0.00	0.10
Local pizzeria	0.80	0.80	0.90	0.00

Similarly, for the actual study once the preferences were obtained from all the respondents, the data matrix of preference that emerged was as follows:

TABLE 19.11

MDS data on paired comparisons (n = 20)

BRANDS	Pizza Hut	Dominoes	Slice of Italy	Pizza Corner	Flavors	Spaghetti	Local pizzeria
Pizza Hut	0.00	0.40	0.30	0.10	0.60	0.70	0.10
Dominoes	0.60	0.00	0.50	0.40	0.80	0.80	0.20
Slice of Italy	0.70	.50	0.00	0.50	0.60	0.80	0.20
Pizza Corner	0.90	0.60	0.50	0.00	0.70	0.70	0.50
Flavors	0.40	0.20	0.40	0.30	0.00	0.60	0.20
Spaghetti	0.30	0.20	0.20	0.30	0.40	0.00	0.20
Local pizzeria	0.90	0.80	0.80	0.50	0.80	0.80	0.00

Thus we can see 60 percent of respondents prefer Pizza Hut over Dominoes and 40 per cent prefer Dominoes over Pizza Hut. Similarly, 90 per cent of the consumers prefer Pizza Hut over the local pizzeria and 10 per cent prefer local pizzeria over Pizza Hut.

Obtaining the MDS Solution

Once the data matrix was prepared, the MDS solution was obtained using ALSCAL. In order to get the MDS solution, go to Appendix 19.1 of this chapter. You are required to follow the step-wise instructions for getting the MDS solution. Omit Step 3 from the instructions as this was an Ordinal and, therefore, non-metric data. However, as stated earlier, this was a paired comparison of the pizzas that you did and paired comparison places data on an ordinal scale (refer Chapter 7). Thus, when you go to Step 5 and click on MODEL, you must not forget to specify the level of measurement as Ordinal.

Identifying the Number of Dimensions

For the conduction we obtained a three-dimensional to a one-dimensional solution. The obtained stress scores and R-square values are given below:

TABLE 19.12 Stress scores and R-square values of the paired comparison data

Number of Dimensions	Stress Value	R-square Value
3	0.00485	0.99986
2	**0.00560**	**0.99985**
1	0.03271	0.99593

As we can see from the solution above, a two-dimensional solution is an excellent solution. Even though the three-dimensional solution has a better stress value, it is easier for the reader to comprehend a two-dimensional map. Thus, we decide to go for a two-dimensional map. The coordinates for a two-dimensional map are as follows:

TABLE 19.13 Coordinates for a two-dimensional solution

Brands	Dimension 1	Dimension 2
Pizza Hut	0.9637	0.5623
Dominoes	-0.2502	0.4662
Slice of Italy	-0.3321	0.1099
Pizza Corner	-1.2369	-0.5130
Flavors	1.1917	-0.1908
Spaghetti	1.9344	-0.4533
Local pizzeria	-2.2706	0.0188

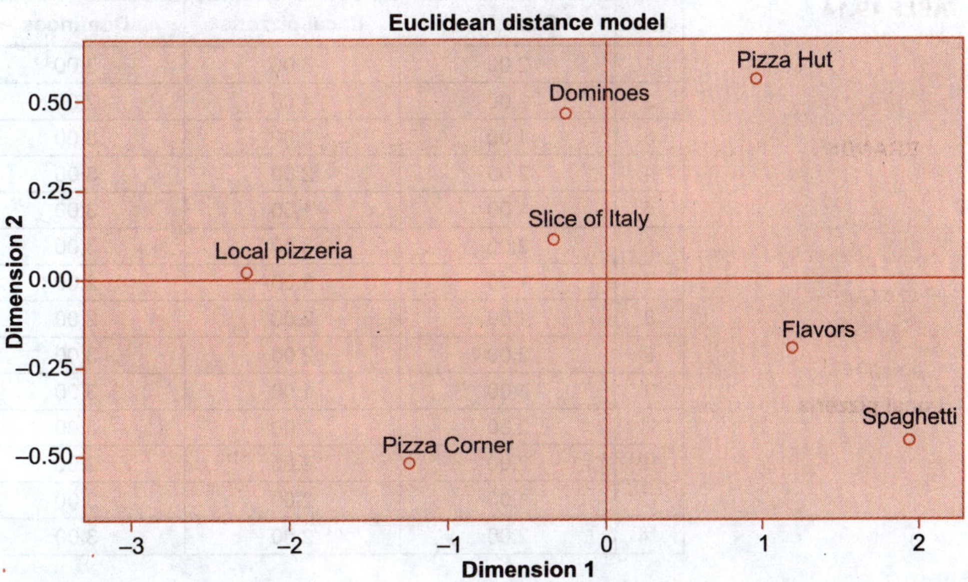

FIGURE 19.10 MDS two-dimensional map of paired comparison data (n = 20)

Interpreting the MDS Solution

Let us look at the placement of the pizza brands where Spaghetti is the highest and the local pizzeria is on the other end. The dimension is clearly that of *restaurant experience*, ranging from fine dining to utilitarian space. The second dimension has Pizza Hut and Dominoes very high and Spaghetti and Pizza Corner are very low. Here, the researcher might call this as *delivery time* or service speed, where Pizza Hut delivers fast and Spaghetti has a leisurely pace of delivery. One may also call it *pizza popularity*, where Pizza Hut is very popular and Spaghetti has a select clientele. Thus the solution gives an interesting illustration on how two researchers could interpret the same result differently. Thus, what can be done is that the dimensions identified by the researcher can be converted into attributes and the respondent can evaluate these brands on the said attributes. This will be discussed later in the chapter in attribute-based perceptual mapping.

Preference Illustration (Interval Scale)

Consumer preference scan also be tested on an interval-scaled data. For example, in the same pizza study, the respondent was asked to rate the pizza brand. The question asked was as follows:

Given below are four pizza brands available in the market that you may have consumed. Please indicate your liking for the brand on the following scale, where 1 = like a lot; 2 = somewhat like it; 3 = not sure; 4 = somewhat dislike it; 5 = dislike it a lot.

Brand	1	2	3	4	5
Pizza Hut					
Dominoes					
Pizza Corner					
Local pizzeria					

Obtaining the Data Output for Conducting the MDS

Once the liking for the pizza brands was obtained from 20 respondents, the data matrix of liking looked like this:

TABLE 19.14 Liking data (interval scale) for Pizza brands (n = 20)

No.	Pizza Hut	Local pizzeria	Dominoes	Pizza Corner
1	2.00	3.00	3.00	3.00
2	2.00	4.00	2.00	4.00
3	1.00	2.00	3.00	3.00
4	2.00	2.00	3.00	2.00
5	1.00	1.00	3.00	2.00
6	2.00	3.00	3.00	3.00
7	1.00	3.00	2.00	3.00
8	1.00	2.00	2.00	4.00
9	2.00	2.00	3.00	4.00
10	1.00	1.00	3.00	2.00
11	2.00	2.00	3.00	3.00
12	2.00	2.00	2.00	3.00
13	1.00	2.00	3.00	3.00
14	2.00	2.00	3.00	2.00

No.	Pizza Hut	Local pizzeria	Dominoes	Pizza Corner
15	1.00	1.00	3.00	2.00
16	2.00	2.00	3.00	2.00
17	1.00	1.00	3.00	2.00
18	2.00	3.00	4.00	3.00
19	1.00	3.00	3.00	3.00
20	1.00	2.00	4.00	5.00

Obtaining the MDS Solution

Once the data has been entered in the SPSS spread sheet, the data is subjected to ALSCAL. Since this is interval scale data go to Appendix 19.1 of this chapter. Omit step 4 from the instructions as this is interval scaled data and thus data is already into distances. However, when you go to step 5 and click on MODEL, you must not forget to specify the level of measurement as Interval.

For this question we asked for a one-dimensional to a two-dimensional map. The stress scores and the R-square values obtained are as follows:

TABLE 19.15 Stress scores and R-square values of the liking data (n = 20)

Number of Dimensions	Stress Value	R-square Value
2	**0.17901**	**0.52423**
1	0.36968	0.27894

As we can see from the table the stress value is less than 20 per cent and the R-squared value is also more than 0.5, we consider the solution to be an acceptable solution. For the two-dimensional solution the coordinates were as follows:

TABLE 19.16 Coordinates for a two-dimensional solution

Brands	Dimension 1	Dimension 2
Pizza Hut	0.3465	0.9475
Local Pizzeria	–0.3766	–1.14172
Dominoes	1.5193	–0.0777
Pizza Corner	–1.4892	0.5475

Interpreting the MDS Solution

As we can see from the placement of the brands on the two dimensions, Dominoes is the highest on dimension 1 and Pizza Corner is the lowest. Moreover, since we are aware of Dominoes' 3-minute promise, this dimension is definitely *speed of delivery* or delivery time. On the second dimension, the brand that is at the top is Pizza Hut and on the other end, there is the local pizzeria. Thus this dimension is probably *authentic Italian taste*.

Pizza corner decision: If we were to look at Pizza Corner and based on the perceptual map we need to advise the brand manager on how to improve its business model; it would simply be to tell the organization to work on their delivery process as it is not doing so badly on taste so if it works on the delivery speed it can have a sizeable number of consumers. Even the Dominoes consumers might shift, as we can see Dominoes is very good on delivery but is not so good on taste.

FIGURE 19.11 Spatial map of Pizza brands – interval scale data (n = 20)

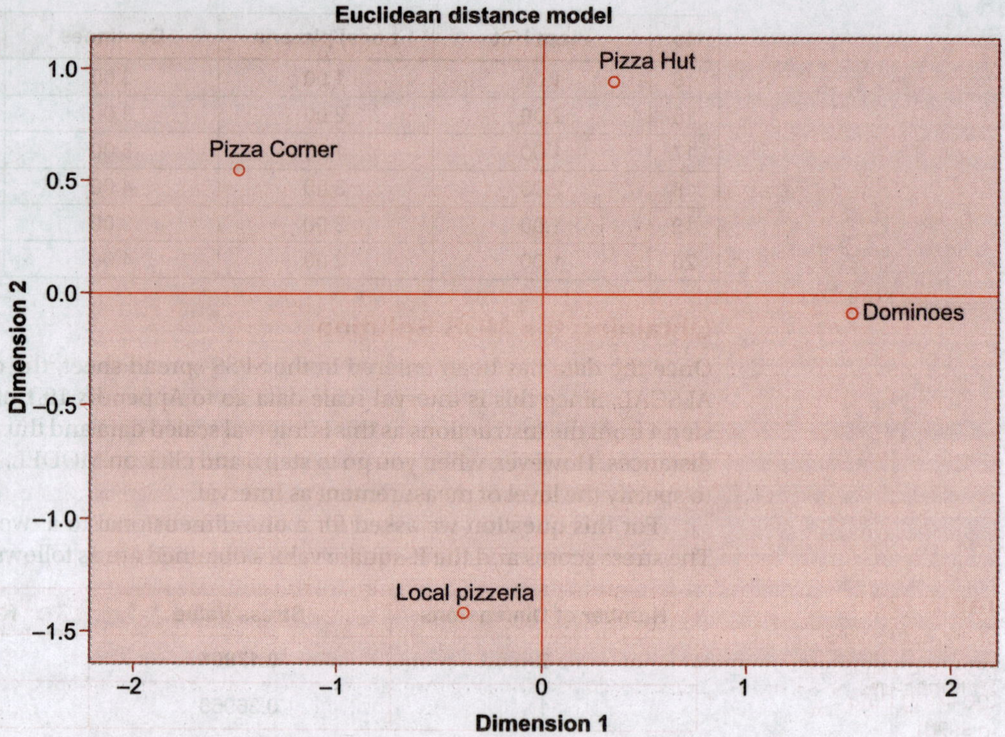

Establishing the Strength of the MDS Solution

LEARNING OBJECTIVE 7
Establish the strength of the MDS solution.

As mentioned earlier, the flexibility of approach in MDS is both an advantage and a disadvantage of the technique. Since the labelling of the dimension is at the discretion of the researcher and he/she is trying to work backwards from the apparent output to what might have been the inputs, it becomes extremely important to establish the reliability and validity of the obtained solution. The methods of evaluating the robustness of the solution have been suggested earlier as well, we repeat them here again.

- The Kruskal stress scores are the discrepancy scores obtained between the derived distances on a configured map and the actual distance as indicated by the respondents' choice. The ideal representation would be a stress value of 0. However, it is acceptable to consider a solution till a 20 per cent stress between the actual and the derived configuration.
- The R-square value measures the proportion of the variance of the final scaled solution that can be accounted for by the MDS procedure. The ideal would be 1. However, an R-square value of 0.6 or above is acceptable.
- Another measure of establishing the reliability of the answers obtained is to conduct a split-half technique, where the entire sets of obtained responses can be split into two groups and the MDS obtained by the two groups should more or less match with each other. However, some cases might reveal a totally different placement of brands as the underlying basis used by the groups could be different. In such cases it is wiser to:
  - (a) Go back to the diverging groups
  - (b) Consider the two groups as independent clusters and check with their demographic or psychographic variables to understand the reason for the difference.

- The same group could be checked at a different interval in time (test-retest) to see if the placement (similarity and selection-preference of the brand) stays constant.
- The leave-one-out technique or eliminating one brand to measure the resulting spatial map is another way of observing the consistency of results.

As there is subjectivity involved both at the respondent's end, as well as the researcher's end, wherever possible, the obtained solution must be validated with different samples and at different intervals in time.

MULTIDIMENSIONAL SCALING AND PERCEPTUAL MAPPING

As mentioned earlier in the chapter, some scholars and researchers use multidimensional scaling interchangeably with perceptual mapping. Perceptual mapping is a very powerful attempt to recreate the mental map of a human mind as he/she evaluates different objects and products and brands to make some semblance of order in his world. Multidimensional scaling is an attribute-free test that looks at the pattern of comparison and tries to decipher the antecedents or criteria that were used by the person. There are other approaches which are attribute based and, thus, yield a more accurate placement of the objects on the respondent's spatial map. The attribute-based data can be subjected to a factor analysis or a discriminant analysis.

Multidimensional scaling is an attribute-free test that looks at the pattern of comparison and tries to decipher the antecedents or criteria that were used by the person.

Then, by making use of the factor scores, one can configure an attribute-based representation. This can also be done by using the discriminant scores, in fact discriminant analysis has an added advantage of providing the metric attributes with the categories or brands on the same map. Thus, one can even measure the distance between a particular attribute and a brand.

Another technique that can also result in similar perceptual maps is correspondence analysis, where in a joint space one can show attributes and brands on the same representation.

In this section, we will discuss the factor analysis derivation of arriving at a perceptual map.

CONCEPT CHECK	
	1. How would you conduct MDS with similarity data?
	2. Discuss the use of MDS with preference data.

Attribute-based Perceptual Mapping: Factor Analysis

As discussed earlier the more accurate placement of brands in a spatial map is when it is based on evaluation of the brand on concrete attributes or benefits that the consumer is looking for. The process is different from the MDS process thus we will discuss this in detail here.

Formulating the attribute-based comparisons

The researcher may identify certain attributes that are relevant in the product/ service decision. This can be obtained from:

- Secondary data and past studies
- Exploratory or qualitative research done at the beginning of the study
- The MDS solution might serve to identify some possible dimensions

The researcher can then ask the respondent to evaluate the brands/objects/ companies/ideas on these attributes. We are taking the example of ice creams. The question asked to the respondent was as follows:

TABLE 19.17 Data for five ice cream brands on five attributes(n = 60)

id	X1	X2	X3	X4	X5	X6	X7	X8	X9	X10	X11	X12	X13	X14	X15	X16	X17	X18	X19	X20	X21	X22	X23	X24	X25
1	4	3	5	4	3	2	5	3	4	5	4	5	3	4	5	4	3	5	4	5	4	5	3	5	4
2	4	4	3	4	3	4	4	3	3	3	3	3	3	3	3	3	3	3	4	3	2	4	4	4	1
3	3	3	3	3	3	4	3	4	3	3	5	5	5	5	5	4	2	4	2	1	2	4	4	4	3
4	1	3	3	3	1	4	2	1	2	4	5	1	4	4	5	3	4	2	5	3	2	5	5	1	2
5	4	4	4	4	4	5	4	2	4	4	4	4	5	4	4	2	2	2	4	4	2	4	4	4	5
6	3	3	3	3	3	3	3	3	3	3	4	5	5	3	3	5	5	5	5	5	3	3	3	3	3
7	5	3	3	3	3	5	4	5	3	3	4	5	5	5	4	4	4	4	4	3	5	5	5	4	5
8	4	5	4	4	3	5	5	4	4	4	4	5	4	4	4	4	4	3	4	3	4	3	4	4	4
9	1	4	4	1	1	3	5	5	2	2	2	2	1	3	3	5	1	2	4	4	4	3	3	5	5
10	3	2	3	3	1	3	3	3	3	3	4	5	4	4	4	5	5	5	5	5	4	5	3	4	5
11	5	3	2	3	3	4	3	3	4	3	5	4	3	4	5	4	4	3	3	3	5	5	5	4	5
12	1	2	3	4	5	5	4	3	2	1	1	2	4	3	5	1	3	2	5	4	5	4	3	2	1
13	5	2	2	3	3	3	5	5	4	3	3	4	4	4	4	3	3	3	3	3	1	5	5	3	3
14	3	3	3	3	3	3	3	3	3	3	4	4	3	4	2	3	3	3	4	4	2	5	5	5	4
15	3	3	3	3	4	3	3	3	3	4	5	5	5	5	5	4	5	5	4	4	4	5	5	5	4
16	3	3	3	4	2	3	3	3	4	2	4	3	3	4	2	4	4	4	4	3	3	4	3	4	4
17	4	4	3	3	3	4	4	3	3	3	3	5	5	4	5	4	5	4	4	4	3	2	4	3	3
18	3	3	3	3	3	3	4	3	4	4	4	4	4	4	4	4	3	4	3	4	4	5	4	5	5
19	3	3	3	4	3	4	3	4	4	2	3	4	4	4	4	2	4	5	4	1	2	4	4	4	3
20	3	3	3	3	3	3	5	3	4	3	3	5	5	4	5	5	3	3	2	5	3	2	2	2	1
21	5	1	1	3	1	5	3	3	3	3	4	5	4	4	5	4	4	5	4	1	3	5	5	4	2
22	3	4	3	4	3	4	4	4	4	4	3	4	3	4	3	5	5	5	5	4	3	3	3	3	3
23	3	3	3	4	3	4	4	3	4	3	4	4	4	4	4	3	3	3	4	3	4	4	4	5	4
24	4	5	3	3	3	3	3	3	3	3	4	5	5	4	3	4	4	4	4	4	5	4	5	4	5
25	4	4	4	5	5	3	3	3	4	4	1	1	1	3	1	2	2	2	2	3	3	3	3	1	2
26	4	4	3	3	3	3	3	3	3	3	3	3	3	3	3	3	3	3	3	3	3	3	3	3	3
27	5	2	3	3	3	5	3	3	3	4	5	4	3	3	4	5	5	3	3	5	3	5	4	3	3
28	1	2	3	4	5	1	2	3	4	5	1	3	5	2	4	3	5	4	1	2	3	4	5	2	1
29	4	3	5	3	3	4	4	4	4	4	4	4	4	4	4	5	5	5	5	5	3	3	3	3	3
30	4	3	3	3	3	4	4	3	4	3	3	2	2	3	3	3	2	2	3	3	2	3	4	3	3
31	5	2	3	3	3	3	3	3	3	3	4	5	5	5	5	4	4	4	5	5	4	4	4	4	4
32	4	3	4	4	2	99	4	4	3	4	5	5	4	5	5	2	4	4	3	3	4	5	2	3	4
33	4	4	4	4	4	4	3	4	3	3	4	4	5	4	5	4	4	5	4	4	3	4	4	4	3
34	4	4	4	3	3	5	4	3	3	4	3	5	4	4	2	4	5	4	4	4	3	4	4	4	4
35	5	3	4	5	4	4	5	4	4	3	4	5	4	3	3	3	3	3	3	3	3	3	3	3	3
36	3	3	3	3	2	3	1	3	3	3	3	2	2	1	2	3	2	3	3	3	3	3	3	3	3
37	4	3	3	4	3	4	3	4	4	3	2	4	4	3	5	3	3	3	3	3	2	5	5	4	3
38	3	3	3	3	3	3	3	3	3	3	4	4	4	4	4	4	4	4	3	2	5	5	5	5	5
39	3	2	3	4	4	3	2	2	3	2	4	4	5	4	4	3	2	2	3	2	4	4	4	4	4
40	5	3	3	4	4	4	3	3	4	4	4	5	5	5	4	5	5	4	5	4	3	5	5	5	4
41	3	2	4	3	3	3	3	2	3	3	5	5	5	5	5	4	4	4	4	4	3	3	4	3	3
42	4	4	4	4	4	4	4	4	3	3	4	5	5	5	5	5	5	5	5	5	4	4	4	4	4
43	4	2	2	2	2	4	4	3	3	3	4	4	3	4	3	4	4	4	4	4	2	4	4	4	2
44	3	4	5	4	3	3	4	2	3	2	3	3	3	3	3	2	3	3	3	3	3	4	5	2	2
45	4	2	2	4	2	4	2	4	4	2	2	5	4	4	4	3	1	2	2	1	1	4	3	4	4
46	3	3	4	3	3	3	3	3	4	4	2	3	5	4	5	4	5	4	4	5	4	5	5	4	5
47	3	2	3	3	2	3	3	3	3	3	4	5	5	3	5	4	5	4	4	5	3	4	4	4	4
48	4	3	3	4	4	4	5	5	5	4	4	5	5	5	4	4	4	5	4	4	4	4	4	4	3
49	3	3	3	3	3	5	5	5	5	5	4	4	4	4	4	3	3	3	3	3	5	5	5	5	5
50	3	3	3	3	3	4	4	4	4	3	4	5	5	5	5	5	5	5	5	5	5	4	4	4	4
51	3	3	3	3	3	3	4	3	3	4	4	4	4	4	4	3	3	3	4	3	4	4	4	5	4
52	3	3	3	4	3	3	99	3	3	3	3	3	3	3	3	3	2	2	3	2	4	2	2	2	2
53	2	2	2	2	2	3	3	3	3	3	5	4	4	4	4	4	5	5	4	4	3	3	3	3	3
54	5	3	4	5	5	4	4	4	4	4	3	5	5	5	5	5	4	4	4	5	3	4	5	5	5
55	3	3	4	3	3	3	3	3	4	3	3	2	3	5	2	3	5	2	2	4	2	4	5	3	3
56	4	4	4	4	4	3	3	4	4	3	2	5	5	5	5	5	5	5	5	5	2	3	2	2	2
57	4	3	2	3	3	4	3	2	3	3	4	5	4	4	4	4	4	3	4	3	2	4	5	4	3
58	5	3	3	3	4	3	5	3	4	5	5	5	4	5	5	2	5	5	5	4	2	5	5	5	3
59	3	3	4	4	3	3	3	4	3	3	4	3	3	3	3	5	3	5	3	4	5	5	5	5	4
60	4	3	2	4	3	5	4	3	3	2	2	3	5	4	3	4	5	3	4	3	5	2	4	3	2

Given below are some popular ice cream brands. Please evaluate the brands that you have consumed on the criteria given below. Please remember 1 = Very good; 2 = Good; 3 = Average; 4 = bad; 5 = very bad.

Brands	Price	Taste	Brand Value	Availability	Assortment
Vadilal					
Amul					
Mother Dairy					
Kwality Walls					
Local ice cream					

The total number of columns that were needed to enter the data were 5(ice-cream brands) × 5(attributes) = 25. The data on these brands were obtained on 150 respondents. However, for illustration, we are looking at the 60 who by and large had consumed/tasted all these brands.

Obtaining Data from the Interval Question

Once the data has been obtained from all the 60 respondents the data sheet looks like the way it is presented in Table 19.17.

The code book for the question was as follows: *The first five column codes are given to you for your reference; the others are the same for the remaining brands. So, for each ice-cream brand you would have 5 similar columns.*

Question	Question Code	Response Categories
X1	Vadilal (price)	1= Very good; 2=Good; 3= Average; 4= bad; 5= very bad.
X2	Vadilal (taste)	1= Very good; 2=Good; 3= Average; 4= bad; 5= very bad.
X3	Vadilal (brand value)	1= Very good; 2=Good; 3= Average; 4= bad; 5= very bad.
X4	Vadilal (availability)	1= Very good; 2=Good; 3= Average; 4= bad; 5= very bad.
X5	Vadilal (assortment)	1= Very good; 2=Good; 3= Average; 4= bad; 5= very bad.

- X6, X7.......to X10: represent price, taste brand value, availability and assortment for Amul.
- X11......to X15 : represent the various attributes for Mother Dairy
- X16.......to X20: represent the attributes for Kwality Walls
- X21........to X 25: represent the attributes for local ice cream brand.

TABLE 19.18 Mean values for the 25 evaluations (n = 60)

	X1	X2	X3	X4	X5	X6	X7	X8	X9	X10	X11	X12	X13
n	60	60	60	60	60	59	59	60	60	60	60	60	60
Mean	3.53	3.03	3.20	3.42	3.05	3.61	3.53	3.30	3.43	3.25	3.57	4.02	3.98
	X14	X15	X16	X17	X18	X19	X20	X21	X22	X23	X24	X25	
n	60	60	60	60	60	60	60	60	60	60	60	60	
Mean	3.92	3.92	3.68	3.73	3.65	3.72	3.55	3.27	3.97	3.97	3.67	3.38	

Next, from the data we obtain the mean values for each of the 25 combinations i.e. the 5 brand × 5 attribute combination that the respondent had evaluated in the questionnaire. The table of mean values is presented in Table 19.19.

Now from these values we obtain a 5 x 5 matrix as follows:

TABLE 19.19
Mean scores of the five brands on the five attributes (n=60)

Brands	Taste	Price	Brand Value	Availability	Assortment
Vadilal	3.53	3.03	3.20	3.42	3.05
Amul	3.61	3.53	3.30	3.43	3.25
Mother Dairy	3.57	4.02	3.98	3.92	3.92
Kwality Walls	3.68	3.73	3.65	3.72	3.55
Local	3.27	3.97	3.97	3.67	3.38

This table can now be transposed to an SPSS spreadsheet for factor analysis.

Obtaining a Factor Analysis of Brands and Attributes

Now, using the data from the above table, the data reduction technique of factor analysis is applied on the data. Please note that the factor solution is not for respondents but for the five brands that we had considered. The factor analysis can be obtained using the factor analysis commands as given in Chapter 16 (Appendix 16.1). The factor analysis tables that we get are as follows:

TABLE 19.20
Total Variance explained

Component	Initial Eigenvalues			Extraction Sums of Squared Loadings			Rotation Sums of Squared Loadings		
	Total	Percentage Variance	Cumulative Percentage	Total	Percentage Variance	Cumulative Percentage	Total	Percentage Variance	Cumulative Percentage
1	3.638	72.760	72.760	3.638	72.760	72.760	3.577	71.548	71.548
2	1.202	24.041	96.801	1.202	24.041	96.801	1.263	25.253	96.801
3	0.138	2.760	99.561						
4	0.022	0.439	100.000						
5	4.282E-016	8.565E-015	100.000						

TABLE 19.21
Rotated component matrix

	Component	
	1	2
Price	–0.037	**0.995**
Taste	**0.920**	–0.255
Brand	**0.915**	–0.397
Availability	**0.979**	0.041
Assortment	**0.967**	0.223

Thus, we note that we have got a two-factor solution. Now, you can consider these two factors as similar to two dimensions that we had got in the MDS map. However, the difference is that this is more authentic as this is based on actual attributes that were later grouped into two factors. Thus, with these two factors we can make a two-dimensional map. In case you get three factors you would get a three-dimensional map and so on.

In this case, based on the factor loadings, we name the first factor as *product mix* as it has all components from brand value, taste, availability and assortment high on this factor. The second factor has a single variable, that is, taste, so we keep the name of the factor also as *price.*

Since we had saved the factor scores as variables we will also get the factor scores for each brand on the two factors. The data matrix for variables would be as follows:

TABLE 19.22 Factor coordinates for the ice cream brands

Brands	Product Mix	Price
Vadilal	−1.27746	0.04708
Amul	−0.67763	0.40069
Mother Dairy	1.30088	0.39498
Kwality Walls	0.36336	0.86822
Local	0.29085	−1.71097

Obtaining the Factor Generated Perceptual Map

Next, using these coordinates one can generate a two-dimensional map. This can be obtained both with SPSS (Refer to 19.2) or one may obtain the same results with EXCEL. The obtained map would look as given in Figure 19.12.

Interpretation of the Perceptual Map

As we can see from the above perceptual map, on the dimension of *price*, Kwality Walls is perceived to be more expensive and can be considered as premium as compared to other brands and has very little competition. However, Mother Dairy has a much better product strategy as it is doing extremely well on the dimension of *product mix*. The local ice-cream may not be doing so good on the product mix but has a considerable advantage in terms of being perceived as low priced and therefore affordable. Amul and Vadilal are considered as more high priced but the real issue is that the two brands are not considered as having a good product mix. Thus they need to do a thorough consumer research to understand the elements of the product mix on which they lose out.

Thus as we can see Perceptual Mapping makes the visual representation of brands/objects with reference to each other very simple and effective. One of the

FIGURE 19.12 Spatial map using Factor scores (n = 60)

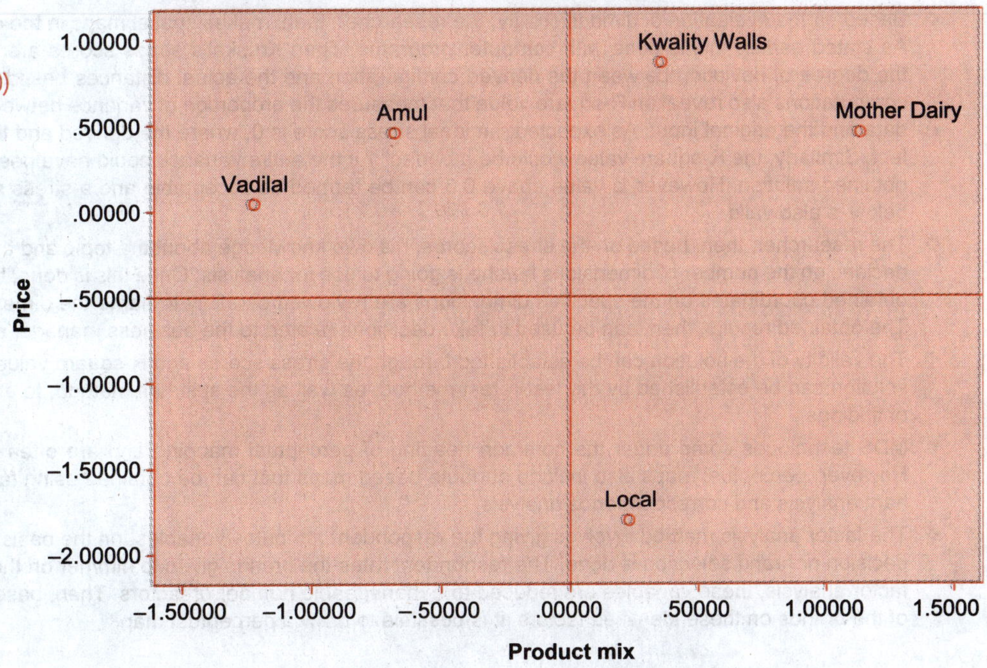

most critical starting points for assessing and designing marketing strategies is based on their brand positioning. This is powerful as it is easy to comprehend and work on.

SUMMARY

- Multidimensional scaling (MDS) is a unique multivariate technique that does not identify the variables and then attempts to measure the impact of these variables. It starts with the end result and tries to figure out the unique variable(s) that led to the composition.
- Its underlying assumption is that human beings compare objects, individuals and brands all the time. For this comparison, rather than the objective observable parameters, the underlying dimensions might be subjective in nature and a complex interplay between these dimensions will result in a mental map of the objects in the individual's mind.
- The technique has wide applicability in the area of marketing, where it can be used to study subjective brand perceptions, impact of repositioning and advertising strategies on brand image, the congruence of brand image and brand identity. It has been actively used for identifying new product opportunities. It can also be used to assess the relative role of price in determining object selection or purchase.
- The basic underlying logic of MDS is to first collect data from respondents. These could be based on identifying the similarities or dissimilarities between selected objects. Another way the information is obtained is by asking for respondent preferences.
- The data obtained could be non-metric in the form of paired comparisons or ranking scales or the same could be metric in nature and obtained through rating scales and through Likert-scale type questions. The choice of the scale would depend on the researcher's discretion and also the respondent's ease in answering questions which might be more for non-metric data.
- Once the data is collected, the next step is to decide whether the plots are to be constructed for every individual or aggregated across groups or are to be made separately for each subgroup or cluster. These decisions are based on the size of the sample and the nature of decision to be made.
- The data that is collected, then, is subjected to a computer software program. There are multiple methods available for this, including INDSCAL, ALSCAL, MDSCAL, PROXSCAL and PREFMAP. The programs convert the similarity or preference data into distances from the closest to the furthest. Then the researcher works backward from this point and tries to figure what might have been the dimensions that the respondent had used for his comparison. This could be based on either past researches, expert opinion and qualitative analysis of the sample group or simply the researcher's judgment. Since the involvement of the human element in this instance is large, extreme care has to be taken to be as objective as possible and not to introduce personal biases into the analysis.
- Based on the evaluation of dimensionality, the researcher, then, makes spatial maps in the desired dimensionality. As stated earlier, this is done with computer programs. Then Kruskal's stress scores are calculated to measure the degree of deviation between the derived configuration and the actual distances based on the input data. The computations also reveal an R-square value that measures the proportion of variance between the optimally scaled data and the original input. As expected, an ideal stress score is 0, where the derived and the actual map are perfect. Similarly, the R-square value would be a perfect 1 if the entire variance could have been accounted for by the obtained solution. However, a value above 0.6 can be termed as acceptable and a stress score of 20 per cent or below is also valid.
- The researcher, then, based on the stress scores, his own knowledge about the topic and the objects under study, decides on the number of dimensions he/she is going to use for analysis. Once this is done, the spatial map and the obtained coordinates on the specified dimensions are reviewed carefully to name the dimensions and label them. The obtained results, then, can be used to take decisions related to the business manager's problem.
- The validity of the solution can be established through the stress scores and R-square values. The reliability of the solution can be established by the test-retest method, as well as the split half method, to analyse the consistency of findings.
- MDS techniques come under the common heading of perceptual mapping and are often used interchangeably. However, perceptual maps also include attribute-based maps that can be obtained using factor analysis, discriminant analysis and correspondence analysis.
- The factor analysis method involves giving the respondent attributes/variables, on the basis of which the purchase decision or brand selection is done. The respondent rates the brands given to him/her on these dimensions. Using factor analysis, these variables are reduced to a manageable number of factors. Then, based on the factor scores of the brands on these identified factors, it is possible to draw a perceptual map.

KEY TERMS

- Actual distance
- ALSCAL
- Attribute-based mapping
- Brand image analysis
- Derived distance
- Group plots
- Index of fit
- Individual plots
- Kruskal's stress formula
- Leave-one-out method
- Multidimensional scaling
- Non-attribute based mapping
- Perceptual dimensions
- Perceptual mapping
- Preference data
- PROXSCAL
- R-square value
- Scale construction
- Scree plot
- Similarity data
- Split half method

CHAPTER REVIEW QUESTIONS

Objective Type Questions

State whether the following statements are true (T) or false (F).

1. There are perceptual mapping techniques other than multidimensional scaling.
2. Respondent fatigue in questionnaire completion is very high in multidimensional scaling.
3. The underlying statistics behind a multidimensional map is Euclidean distance.
4. The underlying statistics behind a multidimensional map is Kruskal's stress.
5. The spatial map prepared is called the scree plot.
6. The maximum usage of MDS is in finance and insurance.
7. MDS can be conducted on attribute-based questions.
8. MDS is usually conducted on brands.
9. R-square is an index of fit measure used in MDS.
10. An R-square value of 0 means an excellent fit in an MDS solution.
11. A stress value of 0 means an excellent fit in an MDS solution.
12. As the number of dimensions in an MDS increases the stress value decreases.
13. ALSCAL is a software program to generate an MDS solution.
14. Preference data used to obtain an MDS solution is based on ranking data.
15. Similarity scores used to create an MDS are always interval data.
16. To conduct an MDS it is advisable not to have less than eight objects to evaluate.
17. To conduct an MDS it is advisable not to have more than 15 objects to evaluate.
18. A perceptual map is possible with all multi-variate techniques.
19. Factor analysis cannot be used to generate perceptual maps.
20. Discriminant analysis can be used to generate perceptual maps.

Conceptual Questions

1. 'Conducting the multidimensional scaling exercise is very peculiar. It is extremely easy to administer but extremely difficult to interpret.' Examine the validity of this statement by giving suitable examples.
2. What is Multidimensional scaling? Explain in brief the underlying assumptions of the technique.
3. What are the essential requirements for conducting and creating an MDS?
4. Explain in detail the steps involved in carrying out a similarity-based MDS. Use suitable examples to do so.
5. Explain in detail the steps involved in carrying out a preference-based MDS. Use suitable examples to do so.
6. Explain the concept of stress in MDS. How does one account for this and attempt to reduce it? Illustrate by giving suitable examples.
7. 'Perceptual mapping and multidimensional Scaling are termed as interchangeable.' Examine the truth of this statement.

8. How will you establish the reliability and validity of the MDS solution? Explain in detail what could be the possible errors that you need to take care of.
9. Is it possible to create perceptual maps with data that is attribute-based? How?
10. How does one take decision on dimensionality in terms of:
    (a) The number of dimensions to be included in the study.
    (b) The labelling of dimensions.
11. What is the difference between the following?
    (a) Actual and derived distance.
    (b) Similarity and preference data.
    (c) Stress scores and R-square values.
    (d) Individual and group plots.
    (e) Metric and non-metric data inputs for MDS.

Application Questions

1. A food chain survey in Delhi was conducted. The survey required the respondents to compare the similarity between nine restaurants ranging from 1 = most similar pair to 9 = most dissimilar pair. The following were the stress and R-square vales that were obtained.

   Stress = 0.01087, RSQ = 0.99953

   The spatial map obtained is as follows:

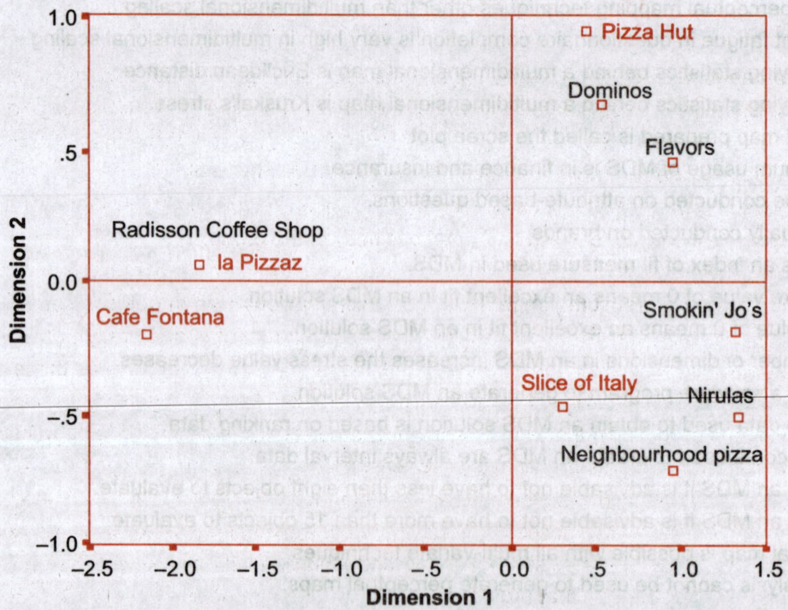

   (a) Comment on the robustness of the solution.
   (b) Name the dimensions.
   (c) What advice do you have for Cafe Fontana?
   (d) What advice do you have for Slice of Italy?
   (e) What advice do you have for Pizza Hut?
2. Go to Chapter 7 of the book and go to the brand data in Table 7.2. Obtain an MDS for this data. If you were to imagine these to be sports goods manufacture, where A = Nike, B = Reebok, D = Adidas, C = Puma and E = Lotto.
   (a) Name the dimensions.
   (b) Where do you foresee a new product opportunity? Why?
   (c) Is this a robust solution? Why? Why not?

3. In Chapter 7, go to the Question 5 and obtain an MDS for the five tyre brands.
   (a) Is this a good solution? Why?
   (b) Name the dimensions.
   (c) Which brand do you think has a unique brand image? Why?
   (d) Which brand needs to do extensive work to improve its preference?
4. Identify 10 popular sports personalities of the today. Collect data from 30 of your colleagues—15 males and 15 females—in terms of their liking for one or the other celebrity on a 7-point scale. Based on the data collected, create a composite and two independent gender-specific MDS solutions—for males and females. Be prepared to discuss your findings with your colleagues in terms of:
   (a) The decision on personality selection.
   (b) The number of dimensions used for the map.
   (c) Key findings.
   (d) Dimensions that could have been used.
   (e) Strength of the solution.
   (f) Discrepancy, if any, between the three maps.

CASE 19.1

MALLS, MALLS, EVERYWHERE...

Shivani Malhotra had joined JB Real Estates six months ago. She had worked for a world renowned Spa company based in Bangkok, Thailand. A graduate from the JJ school of Arts, she also held a degree in Management from Nottingham Trent University. Mr Shailesh Singh (SS), CEO of JB, had handpicked her and granted her almost total autonomy in JB' Group's latest venture—entering the fast growing retail sector.

The group had to its credit residential spaces with the company going into complete townships. The company had grown as an offshoot of the larger cement and hotel business of the group.

Even though it was the third largest business house operating from Delhi, somehow the group had not been recognized as one having a premium image. Now, with this ambitious plan of golf courses and premium townships, SS felt that getting into high-end mall construction and letting the retail space to high-end premium brands would increase brand awareness as well as enhance the brand image of JB. However, SS was of the opinion that the Indian customer was unique and had his own set of values which were both traditional and, yet, with a global influence, more experimental. Thus, the proposition that worked with this paradoxical customer had to be truly unique.

This was the two-pronged agenda he had assigned Shivani and told her to report directly to him the marketing strategy that she would devise on for the business development plan.

Shivani attributed her runaway success at her previous assignment not to her business acumen alone. She had done a comprehensive study of the existing offerings and identified with careful analysis and inference the unique selling proposition (USP) of the spa that they set up. She was a great believer in the Blue Ocean strategy and was always concerned about identifying the gaps amongst customer needs and available products.

Thus, she had outsourced a comprehensive survey of 200 residents of Delhi to understand what their preferred choice was when they wanted to visit a mall. For this purpose, the first step was to identify the malls that were visited most frequently. This resulted in a list of 12 malls. These were then assessed by amongst the group of 200 for their most to the least preferred mall. The data obtained was subjected to an MDS and the resulting two-dimensional map of the malls is on next page.

Shivani examined the map closely in order to identify what was going on in the customers' mind when this image was portrayed in his/her mind. She wondered where the actual ideal mall should be positioned? Did she go along with what was the customers' popular choice? Was SS right when he had spoken about the unique Indian offering? Her experience of the spa's strategic rollout and her global exposure had taught her differently.

As she gathered her papers and walked towards SS' office she tried to crystallize her strategic proposal for the new JB mall.....

Figure 19.13

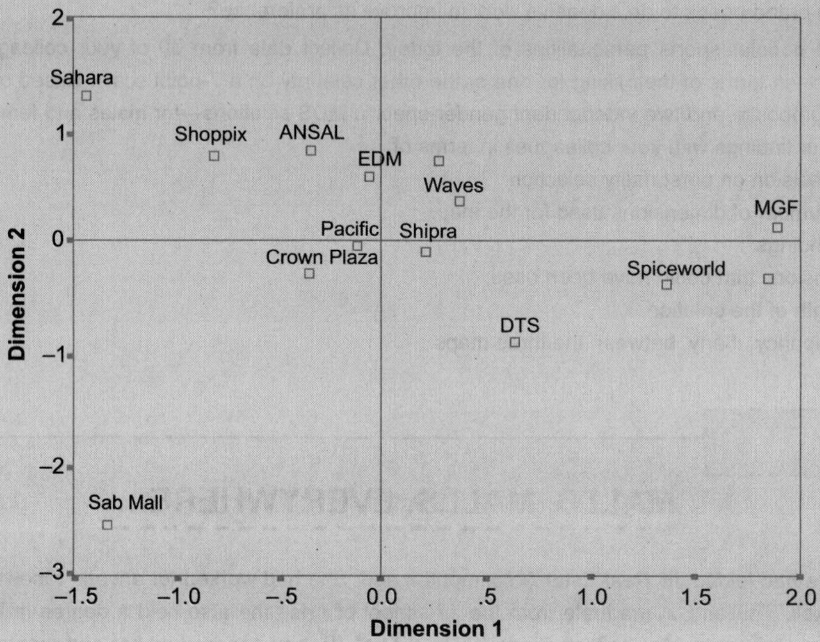

QUESTIONS

1. What in your opinion is the reliability of the obtained solution?
2. What do you think was the basic dimension being used by a typical Delhite in selecting a mall?
3. Interpret the solution.
4. Based on the solution and the mandate, what do you think will be Shivani's stratetgic recommendation to SS?

CASE 19.2

CANDY HO! (B)

Sagar Ahuja realized that for launching the new Moondrops bubblegum he needed to decide on the unique positioning of the brand. Thus, the market analysis and the qualitative analysis should be supported by a brand perception study of the consumer's bubblegum choices. Thus, a dipstick survey was carried out among 200 children and teenagers to assess the similarity/dissimilarity among 11 brands of bubblegums, namely Boomer (BMR), Big Babool (BBL), Centrefresh (CF), Orbit (ORB), Dubble Bubble (DB), Happydent (HD), Centershock (CNS), Chiclets (CHK), Wrigley's Fruity Juice (WJF), Wrigley's Spearmint (WSP), and Wrigley's Double Mint (WDM). The respondent was asked to measure the similarity between brands on a 10-point scale ranging from 1 = most similar to 10 = most dissimilar.

The data from the 200 respondents was collated to arrive at an input data matrix as follows:

Table 19.23

	BMR	WSP	WJF	DB	CNS	BBL	WDM	CF	HD	CHK	ORB
BMR	0.00	3.00	6.00	8.00	1.00	2.00	7.00	8.00	8.00	3.00	8.00
WSP	3.00	0.00	4.00	6.00	4.00	5.00	2.00	5.00	3.00	6.00	3.00

	BMR	WSP	WJF	DB	CNS	BBL	WDM	CF	HD	CHK	ORB
WJF	6.00	4.00	.00	3.00	2.00	4.00	6.00	1.00	7.00	7.00	7.00
DB	8.00	6.00	3.00	0.00	3.00	5.00	4.00	7.00	6.00	6.00	8.00
CNS	1.00	4.00	2.00	3.00	0.00	2.00	8.00	5.00	5.00	8.00	4.00
BBL	2.00	5.00	4.00	5.00	2.00	.00	3.00	6.00	7.00	2.00	7.00
WDM	7.00	2.00	6.00	4.00	8.00	3.00	.00	5.00	1.00	7.00	3.00
CF	8.00	5.00	1.00	7.00	5.00	6.00	5.00	0.00	6.00	5.00	4.00
HD	8.00	3.00	7.00	6.00	5.00	7.00	1.00	6.00	.00	7.00	3.00
CHK	3.00	6.00	7.00	6.00	8.00	2.00	7.00	5.00	7.00	0.00	5.00
ORB	8.00	3.00	7.00	8.00	4.00	7.00	3.00	4.00	3.00	5.00	0.00

QUESTIONS

1. Conduct an MDS on the above data.
2. Evaluate the strength of the solution.
3. Construct and interpret a two-dimensional solution for Mr Ahuja.
4. What advice will you give to Mr Ahuja?

CASE 19.3

A SHIRT ON MY BACK

The textile industry in the vicinity of Mumbai had taken a turn for the worse in the last two decade. Depending on their individual circumstances and aspirations of the manufacturers, most had gone into alternative businesses, opened a retail outlet or moved to Coimbatore. Shiva Savarkar was a third generation Maharastrian and for him the smell and feel of textile looms was his life blood and due to family constraints he had to give his natural instincts a back seat and for the past fifteen years he had been playing safe and running a conservative retail shop at Bangud Road in Gore Gaon Mumbai. However, for the last five years he had been following an exciting trend which he believed was here to stay and could spell new beginnings for a long term business opportunity.

The urban male shopper was increasing becoming style and fashion conscious. This shopper was experimental and wanted to look good even when he was in a formal office setting. The time for tailored shirts was going to be a thing of the past, when, depending on his pocket, the male shopper would only look at branded tailored shirts.

Shiva discussed this emerging trend with Anjan , his son. Anjan had just completed his masters in management form a premier B-school and was a true chip of the old block for whom cloth and entrepreneurial spirit was in line with that of his father. Anjan felt the idea of getting into branded formal wear for Men had a lot of merit.

He collected extensive branded apparel industry reports and also explored various options of setting up a manufacturing unit or alternately outsourcing from the local units and then selling under his own brand, with setting up a self-owned manufacturing unit staggered to a later period. Anjan after an extensive market study told Shiva that the first stage of their business plan should be to start with Men's shirts and then get into trousers, casuals and also accessories and then personal care .

Shiva looked at Anjan with pride and told him that he had full faith in his son's business sense and was there to provide support in whichever way he could. Anjan remembered his marketing fundamentals and the significance of positioning his brand correct. Thus he felt that before going ahead with developing their business strategy they must take a firm decision on how they want to position themselves.

And being an enthusiastic Management graduate his next step was to contact his friend Ayesha who was working with Quintum research inc. to conduct a quick dipstick across the western region and provide leads on the current positioning of popular brands in the regional market. Ayesha conducted a survey with 546 young (22-29yrs) male professionals in and around Mumbai and presented the following data to Anjan. The survey was based on a similarity based perceptual map of selected brands by the respondents. The scale was an interval scale where 1= most similar and 7=most dissimilar.

Table 19.24 Iteration with stress and R squares values

Iteration	S-stress	Improvement
1	0.14624	
2	0.12966	0.01658
3	0.12857	0.00109
4	0.12834	0.00022

For Matrix:
Stress = 0.09282 RSQ = 0.94028

Figure 19.14 Spatial map of existing brands

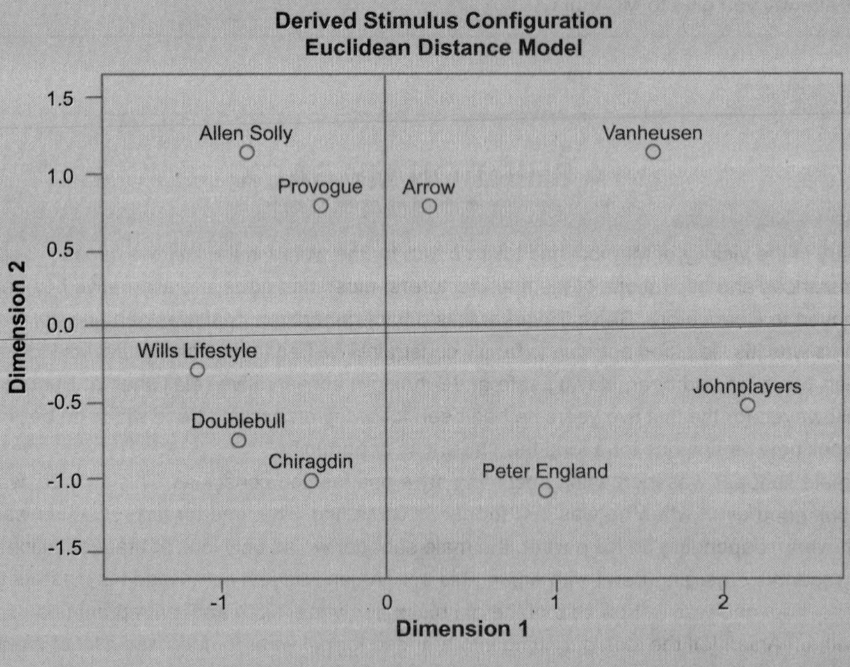

Anjan looked quizzically at Ayesha and said –"this is more confusing, all the choices seem to be all over the place. How do I decide what to do?"

"Well, you have to remember your short term and long term, at the Marketing research end we can only present a portrayal of what exists. What needs to be decided on the basis of the existing patterns depends on what you as a business manager read into the results. I am sure you will be able to arrive at an answer."

Anjan went back and shared the data with his father Shiva, his younger brother Niranjan who was studying at a fashion technology institute in Delhi; and told them that this was the data he had got from the survey that had been conducted. Based on this and their business plans he asked them to independently pin the point at which their brand needs to be positioned and have a strong argument for the suggested stance. "In the meanwhile I will work on this independently. Let us meet tomorrow evening at the club and then see where we are going. Remember we want to possess every Mumbaikar's wardrobe in the long run..................................

QUESTIONS

1. What is the reliability of the solution given by Ayesha?
2. What in your opinion are the two benefits (dimensions) that a young male looks for in the shirt that he buys?
3. In the light of the business objectives of the company where would you recommend they position their brand? Be prepared to defend your stance.

Appendix – 19.1: MULTIDIMENSIONAL SCALING COMMANDS FOR SPSS

The following steps are suggested to be carried out in a step-wise manner for conducting an MDS using SPSS for Windows:

Multidimensional Scaling

1. On top of the screen go to Analyse......Scale........Multidimensional scaling (ALSCAL).
2. A dialog box will open for the technique. Now select all the objects/brands to be used for the analysis by dragging them to the right, into the VARIABLES box.
3. Now the command would be different for metric and non-metric data. In case the data is metric, go along with 'Data are distances'.
4. In case the data is non-metric, click on 'Create distances from data'.
5. Next, go to the box that says Model. For all paired comparison and ranked data, enter the level of measurement as ORDINAL. In case of Interval data, enter level of measurement as INTERVAL.
6. The scaling model is, as we stated, EUCLIDEAN DISTANCE and the CONDITIONALITY is matrix.
7. In the DIMENSIONS box by default it would be minimum-2 and maximum-2. You may change this to whatever is the desired dimensionality. Click OK.
8. Next, go to the OPTIONS box. Here you may click on GROUP PLOTS or INDIVIDUAL PLOTS depending on what is the objective. Next ask for DATA MATRIX, MODEL AND OPTIONS SUMMARY. Press CONTINUE.
9. Go to the main menu box and click on OK.

Appendix 19.2: FACTOR ANALYSIS PERCEPTUAL MAP FROM SPSS

1. On top of the screen go to ANALYZE.——————DESCRIPTIVE STATISTICS—Go to Descriptives.
2. A dialogue box will open. Now take all the variables to the VARIABLES box.
3. On the side, there is OPTION———CLICK only for Mean.
4. Now, open a new SPSS spreadsheet and enter the data , by putting brands in the first variable and every attribute is entered as a separate variable after this
5. The mean values obtained for each brand on each attribute should be entered in the corresponding cell.
6. Now, run a Factor Analysis [Appendix 16.1 (Step 1-8)].
7. Now, go back to the data sheet, you will see new variables corresponding to the number of factors obtained.
8. You may name the factors and enter the factor names in the LABEL for the respective factor.
9. Now click on the icon next to ANALYZE. This is called GRAPHS.
10. When you click on this, there will be an option called LEGACY DIALOGUES.
11. Click on LEGACY DIALOGUES——————SCATTER——————SIMPLE SCATTER.

12. Then click on DEFINE.
13. Now, take the first factor in X-AXIS and second factor in Y-AXIS.
14. Enter the BRANDS in LABEL CASES BY.
15. Now, go to OPTIONS and click on DISPLAY CHART WITH LABELS————Press CONTINUE————OK.
16. Now, you will get the two-dimensional plot but no axis line.
17. You need to right click the graph————and then EDIT CONTENT.....IN SEPARATE WINDOW
18. Now, in this editing window————go to OPTIONS and click on X-AXIS line. And then Y-AXIS line.

Answers to Objective Type Questions

1. True	2. False	3. True	4. True	5. False
6. False	7. True	8. True	9. True	10. False
11. False	12. True	13. True	15. True	15. False
16. True	17. False	18. False	19. False	20. True

REFERENCES

Kruskal, J B. "Multidimensional Scaling by Optimizing Goodness of fit to a Nonmetric Hypothesis", *Psychometrika* 29 (1964): 1-27.

Schiffman, Susan S, M Lance Reynolds and Forrest W Young. *Introduction to Multidimensional Scaling*. New York: Academic Press, 1981.

BIBLIOGRAPHY

Boyd, Harper W Jr, Ralph Westfall and Stanley F Stasch. *Marketing Research: Text and Cases*, 7th edn. Richard D. Irwin, Inc, 2002.

Burns, Robert B. *Introduction to Research Methods*. London: Sage Publications, 2000.

Churchill, Gilbert A Jr and Dawn Iacobucci. *Marketing Research Methodological Foundations*, 8th edn. New Delhi: Thompson South Western, 2002.

Dwivedi, R S. *Research Methods in Behavioural Sciences*. New Delhi: Macmillan India Ltd, 1997.

Easwaran, Sunanda and Sharmila J Singh. *Marketing Research—Concepts, Practices and Cases*. New Delhi: Oxford University Press, 2006.

Green, Paul E. "On the Robustness of Multidimensional Scaling Techniques", *Journal of Marketing Research* 12 (1975): 73–81.

Green, Paul E and Vithala Rao. *Applied Multidimensional Scaling*. New York: Holt, Rinehart and Winston, 1972.

Hair, Joseph F Jr, Robert P Bush and David J Ortinau. *Marketing Research—A Practical Approach for the New Millennium*. Delhi: McGraw-Hill Higher Education, 1999

Kinnear, Thomas C and James R Taylor. *Marketing Research: An Applied Approach*, 5th edn. New York. McGraw Hill, Inc., 1996.

Kruskal, Joseph B and Myron Wish. "Multidimensional Scaling" In *Sage University Paper Series on Quantitative Applications in the Social Sciences*, 07–011. Beverely Hills, California: Sage, 1978.

Malhotra, Naresh K. *Marketing Research—An Applied Orientation*, 3rd edn. Pearson Education, 2002.

Maholtra, Naresh. "Validity and Structural Reliability of Multidimensional Scaling", *Journal of Marketing Research* 24 (1987): 164–73.

Pannerselvam R. *Research Methodology*. New Delhi: Prentice Hall of India Pvt Ltd, 2004.

Nargundkar, Rajendra. *Marketing Research (Text and Cases)*. New Delhi: Tata McGraw Hill Publishing Company Ltd, 2002.

Shajahan, S. *Marketing Research–Concepts and Practices in India*. New Delhi: McMillan India Ltd, 2005.

Tull, Donald S and Del I Hawkins. *Marketing Research: Measurement and Method*, 6th edn. New Delhi: Prentice Hall of India Pvt. Ltd, 1993.

Zikmund, William G. *Business Research Methods*, 5th edn. Dryden Press, Harcourt Brace College Publishers, 1997.

20

CHAPTER

Conjoint Analysis

Learning Objectives

By the end of the chapter, you should be able to:

1. Discuss the concept of conjoint analysis.
2. Explain the various steps involved in a conjoint exercise.
3. Conduct conjoint analysis with the help of actual data using SPSS software and interpret results.
4. Explain the uses of conjoint analysis.
5. Discuss the issues involved in carrying out conjoint analysis.

Malhotra Spices Company had taken a decision to diversify into the manufacturing of pickles which they wanted to sell in packs of 400 gm. They were considering three packaging options—glass bottle, plastic bottle and tetrapack. Four varieties—Mango, Lemon, Garlic and Mixed Vegetables were under consideration. The three levels of prices—₹50, ₹65 and ₹75—were being debated. Management was considering the combination that would be most preferred by the consumers. This chapter deals with this kind of analysis and facilitates in answering the questions posed.

CONCEPT OF CONJOINT ANALYSIS

Conjoint analysis makes use of subjective evaluation of the combinations presented to the consumer.

Conjoint analysis uses nominal-scale data. It attempts to identify the most desirable attributes that could be offered in a product or service. An attempt is made to determine the relative importance that consumers attach to the attributes and the utilities that they attach to the levels of attributes. The values assumed by the attributes are called levels. The utilities describe the importance that consumer attach to the levels of each attribute. Here, the respondents are told about the various combinations of the attribute levels and are asked to evaluate the combinations in terms of their desirability. The evaluation can be done either using ordinal or interval-scale data. This will be explained later in the chapter. It may be worth noting that conjoint analysis makes use of subjective evaluation of the combinations presented to the consumer. It makes use of such data to identify the most desirable combinations of the levels of attributes to be included in the new product. In fact, the major business domain where the technique is used is marketing, though it is also applied in the area of HR, Finance and Operations. The various uses of conjoint analysis are to:

- Determine the relative importance of the attributes in the choice process of the consumers
- Determine the market share of brands that differ in attribute levels
- Segment the market based on similarly of preference for attribute levels

For conducting the **conjoint analysis,** the researcher is required to identify the attributes and the levels of the attributes that could be used in constructing the stimuli for presentation to the respondents.

For conducting the conjoint analysis, the researcher is required to identify the attributes and the levels of the attributes that could be used in constructing the stimuli for presentation to the respondents. The attributes and its various levels could be identified using exploratory research which could be conducted by discussion with management and industry experts; informal interviews with prospective customers, analysis of secondary data and case studies. Once the attributes and its various levels are identified, the respondents are presented with combinations of attributes with levels to show their preference for various combinations. This is illustrated in the following example.

Suppose we ask a set of respondents to express their preference among movies that varied on three attributes, each with two levels as shown below:

- Hero of the movie : Shahrukh Khan or Akshay Kumar
- Type of movie : Action or comedy
- Price of ticket : ₹150 or ₹200

There are in total 2 × 2 × 2 = 8 combinations of these features. Each of these features is presented to, say, respondent number 1. The various features would look like:

Feature 1 – Shahrukh Khan, Action, ₹150
Feature 2 – Shahrukh Khan, Action, ₹200
Feature 3 – Akshay Kumar, Action, ₹150
Feature 4 – Akshay Kumar, Action, ₹200
Feature 5 – Shahrukh Khan, Comedy, ₹150
Feature 6 – Shahrukh Khan, Comedy, ₹200
Feature 7 – Akshay Kumar, Comedy, ₹150
Feature 8 – Akshay Kumar, Comedy, ₹200

The respondent could be presented with the above eight combinations and asked to give their preferences in terms of desirability of the feature, either on an interval scale or ordinal scale.

STEPS IN CONJOINT ANALYSIS

The following steps are involved in carrying out a conjoint analysis exercise.

1. Identification of Attributes

One has to be careful in selecting the attributes since only a limited number could be used in a **conjoint study.**

As a first step, the researcher needs to identify the various attributes that may be used in constructing stimuli. It is important from the point of view of both the consumer and the company. From the consumer point of view, only those attributes that influence the consumers' choice will be selected. This is determined through exploratory research, for example, through managerial judgments. From the point of view of the company, it gains importance because the company has to see whether it has the technological or other resources which could be used to incorporate consumer preferences. One has to be careful in selecting the attributes since only a limited number could be used in a conjoint study.

2. Determination of Attribute Levels

This involves specifying the actual levels for each attribute. In a study on the sale of juices, if the attribute of interest is flavour, then the possible corresponding levels could be mango, orange, and pineapple. The number of levels of each attribute has a direct bearing on the number of stimuli which the respondents could be assumed to evaluate. To ensure the quality of data, it is advisable to have as small number of levels for each attribute as possible. The goal is to end up with good estimates of the utility of each attribute level.

Empirical evidence suggests that the more the levels used for an attribute, the more important that attribute is going to be inferred in the analysis.

While creating stimuli for conjoint judgment task, the researcher has to keep in mind that there is a relationship between the number of levels used to measure an attribute and the inferred importance of the attribute. Empirical evidence suggests that the more the levels used for an attribute, the more important that attribute is going to be inferred in the analysis.

The choice of attribute levels depends upon their effect on consumer choice. If the chosen attribute levels lie outside the range that is usually encountered, it decreases the believability by respondents but could increase the accuracy by which parameters can be estimated. A combination such as very low price and high quality is unbelievable, but it could result in increase in accuracy by which parameters can be estimated.

3. Determination of Attribute Combinations

In the third stage, the specific combination of various attributes is decided upon. If there are three attributes each with three levels, the total number of stimuli to be presented to the respondents would be 3 × 3 × 3 = 27. Suppose each of the attributes has 5 levels—this would result in 5 × 5 × 5 = 125 stimuli. It will certainly be very difficult for respondents to provide meaningful judgments on their preference of such a large number of stimuli. The analyst, instead of using the full factorial design where the respondent is to indicate preference for all stimuli, uses a fractional factorial design where only select stimuli are selected.

4. Nature of Judgment on Stimuli

The next step is to ascertain the nature of judgment on stimuli. This can be done in two ways. One is to ask the respondents to rank order the various stimuli according to their preference or intention to buy. The advantages of ranking are their ease of use by consumers, ease of administration, etc. The second way is to use a rating scale. The respondent may be asked to rate their preference on a 5-point or 7-point rating scale. The advantages of using rating scale are that it is less time consuming, more convenient to use and easier to analyse. In the rank-order approach, relative judgments are sought, whereas in rating scale, respondents are asked to indicate their degree of preference for each stimuli.

The **advantages of using rating scale** are that it is less time consuming, more convenient to use and easier to analyse.

5. Aggregation of Judgments

The fifth step is to decide how the responses from various individual consumers are aggregated. One option is to estimate the utility function for each individual. The problem with such an analysis is that individual-level functions cannot be used for formulating marketing strategies. On the other extreme, one could pool the results across all respondents and estimate one overall utility function. This approach ignores the heterogeneity that may exist among respondents. The best option would be to group respondents in the form of segments. This will have clear marketing

The best option would be to group respondents in the form of **segments**.

strategy implications for managers. The main question, however, is how to form segments. The segments formed are homogenous with respect to the benefits that respondents want from product or service.

6. Choice of Technique of Analysis

The last step would be to choose the technique so that the input data can be analysed. As our purpose is to estimate the utilities for each level of each attribute, a dummy variable regression would be quite appropriate. The dummy variable regression is explained in Chapter 15 of the book. This will be illustrated through the following illustration.

Illustration of Conjoint Analysis with an Example

As another example, consider the case of a soft drink bottling company that wants to enter the fruit juice market, as the demand for aerated drinks is showing a stagnant trend because of increasing health consciousness among the consumers. Before the launch of fruit juices, the company wants to undertake a study to determine what combination of attributes with various levels would be the most desired one. The three attributes considered in the study are flavour, packaging and price each of them having three levels (Table 20.1).

TABLE 20.1
Fruit juice attributes and levels

Attribute	Number	Level Description
Flavour	3	Mixed Fruit
	2	Orange
	1	Mango
Packaging	3	Tetra pack
	2	Plastic Bottle
	1	Glass Bottle
Price	3	₹90/-
	2	₹75/-
	1	₹65/-

Two approaches are used for constructing conjoint analysis stimuli: the pair-wise approach and full profile approach. The full profile approach lists all the stimuli in terms of all attributes by using the attribute levels specified by the design. This chapter does not make use of the pair-wise approach. The full profile approach is a multiple factor evaluation and is being used in the present example. In this approach, complete profiles are considered for all the attributes. Each profile is described on a card and respondent is asked to evaluate the same in terms of its preference on a 9 - point interval scale where 1 = least preferred to 9 = most preferred. Given three attributes, defined at three levels each, a total of 3 × 3 × 3 = 27 profiles can be constructed.

The purpose of fractional factorial design is to reduce the number of stimuli profile to be evaluated out of the full profile.

In order to reduce the task of respondent evaluation, a fractional factorial design is employed and the set of nine profiles is constructed. The purpose of fractional factorial design is to reduce the number of stimuli profile to be evaluated out of the full profile. In the present example, the set of nine profiles is constructed, which constitutes the estimation stimuli (Table 20.2).

TABLE 20.2
Fruit juice profiles and their ratings

Profile No.	Flavour	Packaging	Price	Preference Rating
1	1	1	1	5
2	1	2	2	6
3	1	3	3	5
4	2	1	2	7
5	2	2	3	7
6	2	3	1	9
7	3	1	3	4
8	3	2	1	8
9	3	3	2	7

Conjoint analysis makes use of dummy variable regression, where dependent variable preference is treated as utility or the Part-worth of the level of attributes. The utility model is written as:

$$U = b_0 + b_1X_1 + b_2X_2 + b_3X_3 + b_4X_4 + b_5X_5 + b_6X_6 + U$$

where, X_1, X_2 = dummy variables representing flavour
X_3, X_4 = dummy variables representing packaging
X_5, X_6 = dummy variables representing price

where, X_1 = 1, if choice is for mango
= 0, Otherwise
X_2 = 1, if choice is for orange
= 0, Otherwise
X_3 = 1, if choice is for glass bottle
= 0, Otherwise
X_4 = 1, if choice is for plastic bottle
= 0, Otherwise
X_5 = 1, if choice is for ₹65/-
= 0, Otherwise
X_6 = 1, if choice is for ₹75/-
= 0, Otherwise
U = Preference rating or utility

We have used level 3 as the base level. The data for respondent number 1 is presented in Table 20.3.

TABLE 20.3
Fruit juice data for dummy variable regression

S. No.	X_1	X_2	X_3	X_4	X_5	X_6	Y
1	1	0	1	0	1	0	5
2	1	0	0	1	0	1	6
3	1	0	0	0	0	0	5
4	0	1	1	0	0	1	7
5	0	1	0	1	0	0	7
6	0	1	0	0	1	0	9
7	0	0	1	0	0	0	4
8	0	0	0	1	1	0	8
9	0	0	0	0	0	1	7

The estimated regression equation is given below:

$$U = 5.778 - 1.00X_1 + 1.333X_2 - 1.667X_3 + 0.000X_4 + 2.000X_5 + 1.333X_6$$

Here,

$b_0 = 5.778$
$b_1 = -1.00$

$$b_2 = 1.333$$
$$b_3 = -1.667$$
$$b_4 = 0.000$$
$$b_5 = 2.000$$
$$b_6 = 1.333$$

U stands for utility.

As discussed in the chapter 'Correlation and Regression' each dummy variable coefficient represents the difference in the part-worth for that level minus the part-worth for the base level. For flavour, we have the following:

$$\alpha_{11} - \alpha_{13} = b_1$$
$$\alpha_{12} - \alpha_{13} = b_2$$

An additional constraint is required since the part-worths are estimated on an interval scale, which has an arbitrary origin. The additional constraint looks like:

$$\alpha_{11} + \alpha_{12} + \alpha_{13} = 0$$

The equations for fruit juice are:

$$\alpha_{11} - \alpha_{13} = -1.00$$
$$\alpha_{12} - \alpha_{13} = 1.333$$
$$\alpha_{11} + \alpha_{12} + \alpha_{13} = 0$$

Solving these equations, we get

$$\alpha_{13} = -0.111$$
$$\alpha_{12} = 1.333 - 0.111$$
$$= 1.222$$
$$\alpha_{11} = -1.111$$

The equations for second attribute (packaging) are:

$$\alpha_{21} - \alpha_{23} = b_3$$
$$\alpha_{22} - \alpha_{23} = b_4$$
$$\alpha_{21} + \alpha_{22} + \alpha_{23} = 0$$
$$\alpha_{21} - \alpha_{23} = -1.667$$
$$\alpha_{22} - \alpha_{23} = 0$$
$$\alpha_{21} + \alpha_{22} + \alpha_{23} = 0$$
$$\therefore \quad \alpha_{23} = 0.556$$
$$\alpha_{21} = -1.111$$
$$\alpha_{22} = 0.556$$

Similarly, for the third attribute (price), we have

$$\alpha_{31} - \alpha_{33} = b_5$$
$$\alpha_{32} - \alpha_{33} = b_6$$
$$\alpha_{31} + \alpha_{32} + \alpha_{33} = 0$$
$$\alpha_{31} - \alpha_{33} = 2.000$$
$$\alpha_{32} - \alpha_{33} = 1.333$$
$$\alpha_{31} + \alpha_{32} + \alpha_{33} = 0$$
$$\alpha_{33} = -1.111$$
$$\alpha_{31} = 0.889$$
$$\alpha_{32} = 0.222$$

The relative importance of attributes indicates which attributes are important in influencing the choice of the consumers. The relative importance weights are calculated based on ranges of part-worths as follows:

$$\text{Sum of ranges of part-worths} = [1.222 - (-1.111)] + [0.556 - (-1.111)] + (0.889 - (-1.111))$$
$$= 2.333 + 1.667 + 2.0$$
$$= 6.000$$

$$\text{Relative importance of flavour} = \frac{[1.222 - (-1.111)]}{6.0} = \frac{2.333}{6.0} = 0.39$$

$$\text{Relative importance of packaging} = \frac{[0.556 - (-1.111)]}{6.0} = \frac{1.667}{6.0} = 0.28$$

$$\text{Relative importance of price} = \frac{[0.889 - (-1.111)]}{6.0} = \frac{2.0}{6.0} = 0.33$$

The results for part-worths and relative contribution of attributes are given in Table 20.4:

The estimation of part-worths and the relative importance of weights provide the basis for interpreting the results. In the case of our respondent, the weight assigned by him to flavour, price and packaging are 39, 33 and 28 per cent respectively. It is seen that the respondent prefers orange flavour, followed by mixed fruit and mango. The respondent is indifferent between plastic and tetra packaging. As expected, the price of ₹65/- has the highest utility and the price of ₹90/- has the lowest utility.

TABLE 20.4
Results of conjoint analysis

Attribute	Number	Description	Utility	Importance
Flavour	3	Mixed fruit	–0.111	0.39
	2	Orange	1.222	
	1	Mango	–1.111	
Packaging	3	Tetra pack	0.556	0.28
	2	Plastic bottle	0.556	
	1	Glass bottle	–1.111	
Price	3	₹90/-	–1.111	0.33
	2	₹75/-	0.222	
	1	₹65/-	0.889	

The results can be interpreted better by plotting the part-worth function in Figure 20.1, which is self-explanatory.

Uses of Conjoint Analysis

The main uses of Conjoint Analysis are as follows:

- **Segmentation:** Cluster analysis, discussed in Chapter 18 of this book, is a technique that could be used to segment the respondents of conjoint analysis exercise. The

FIGURE 20.1
Part-worth functions

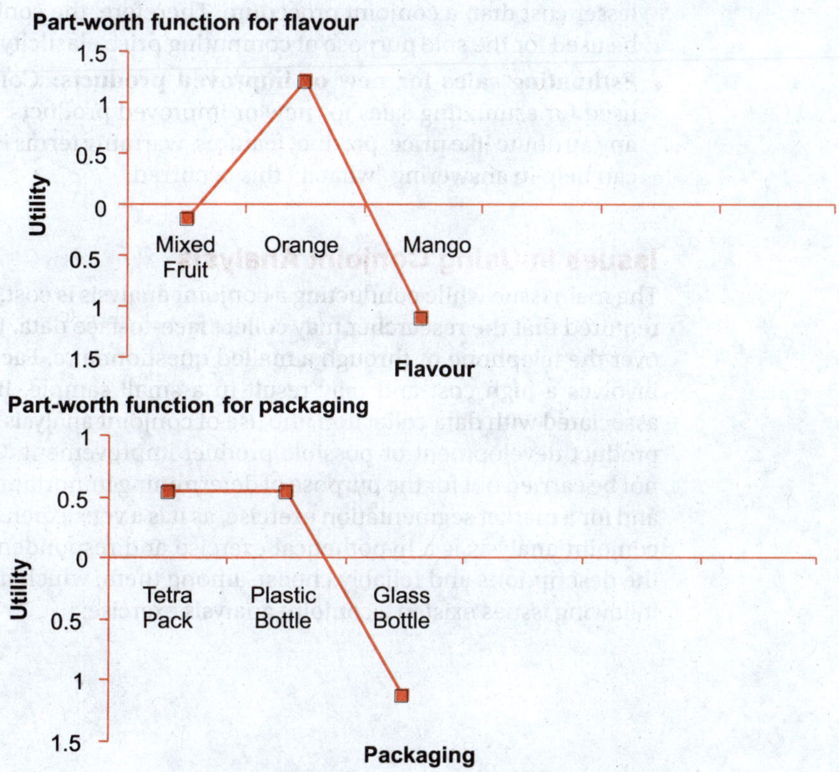

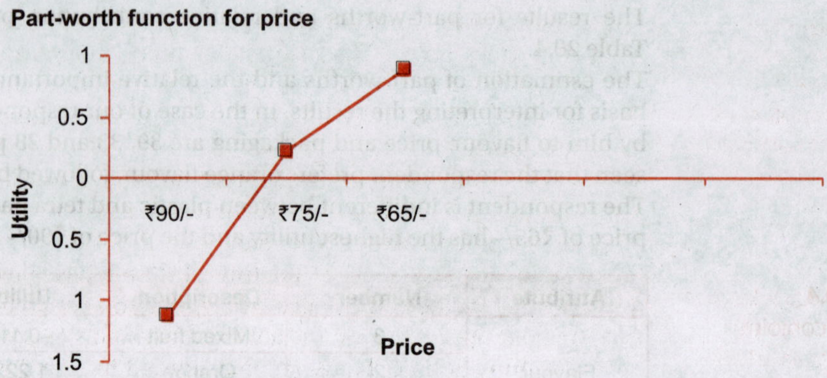

segmentation exercise could be based on the similarities/dissimilarities in the utilities that are attached to the levels of various attributes. The analysis could group customers of two-wheelers that care about different attributes—there could be respondents to whom product features are important, some for whom economic considerations are important, while others may attach importance to pride of ownership.

The **segmentation exercise** could be based on the similarities/dissimilarities in the utilities that are attached to the levels of various attributes.

- **Computation of price elasticity:** In case price is included in the conjoint analysis, one of the outputs obtained could be a utility function for price, which could be used for computation of elasticity. Elasticity information can be obtained at a lower cost from such data rather than from conjoint analysis.

  To get elasticity information for a mixer grinder, describe the product to the respondents and ask whether they would be willing to pay ₹X for it. Divide the respondents into several groups, say, five to six, and give a different value of X. Develop a rough demand curve by plotting the percentage of respondents who would buy at each price. This would provide information about price elasticity at lesser cost than a conjoint procedure. Therefore, the conjoint analysis should not be used for the sole purpose of computing price elasticity.
- **Estimating sales for new or improved products:** Conjoint analysis could be used for estimating sales for new or improved products. The effect of changes in any attribute like price, product features, warranty terms in the conjoint procedure can help in answering "what if" this occurred.

Issues in Using Conjoint Analysis

The main issue while conducting a conjoint analysis is cost. In conjoint analysis, it is required that the researcher may collect face-to-face data. Data cannot be collected over the telephone or through a mailed questionnaire. Face-to-face data collection involves a high cost and may result in a small sample. Because of the high cost associated with data collection, the use of conjoint analysis may be restricted to new product development or possible product improvement. Conjoint analysis should not be carried out for the purpose of determining important attributes of the product and for a market segmentation exercise, as it is a very expensive proposition. Further, conjoint analysis is a hypothetical exercise and respondents are asked to visualize the descriptions and reliably choose among them, which may not be that easy. The following issues exist in a conjoint analysis exercise:

Conjoint analysis is a hypothetical exercise and respondents are asked to visualize the descriptions and reliably choose among them, which may not be that easy.

The second point to be kept in mind is that the analyst has chosen the appropriate levels of the attributes. **Exclusion of some levels** may lead to management taking a poor decision.

(i) The conjoint procedure assumes that the attributes being considered are the important ones. This means that there should be some evidence that the considered attributes are the most important ones. Perhaps a previous factor analysis study might have identified the most important features or attributes.

(ii) The second point to be kept in mind is that the analyst has chosen the appropriate levels of the attributes. Exclusion of some levels may lead to management taking a poor decision.

(iii) As already discussed, evaluating all stimuli based on full factorial design may not be feasible. This is because respondents would find it extremely difficult to rank or rate all the profile. It is because of this reason that a fractional factorial design is desired. However, it is advised to take the help of an expert before dropping some combinations.

(iv) It is very important that all respondents must be properly motivated as the form of ranking or rating various combinations may be taken very seriously. It is advised that generally not more than 30 profiles be offered to the respondents.

SUMMARY

- Conjoint analysis uses nominal-scale data. It attempts to identify the most desirable attributes that can be offered in a product or service. Respondents are presented in various combinations of attribute levels and asked to evaluate combinations in terms of their desirability. The evaluation of the combinations can be done using either ordinal- or interval-scale data.
- There are six steps involved in carrying out the conjoint analysis exercise. These are identification of attributes, determination of attribute level, determination of attribute combination, nature of judgment on stimuli, aggregation of judgment, and choice of techniques of analysis.
- In conjoint analysis, the relative importance of various attributes is calculated and utilities attached to the various levels are computed. The relative importance of the attributes depends upon the number of levels of the attributes. Higher the number of levels of the attributes, more important will be that attribute.
- Conjoint analysis could be used for market segmentation, computation of price elasticity, market share of a product and estimating sales for new or improved products. The various issues in using conjoint analysis are also discussed.

KEY TERMS

- Attributes
- Consumer preference
- Dummy variables
- Expert
- Face to face
- Factorial design
- Fractional factorial design
- Improved products
- Judgment
- Levels
- Mailed questionnaire
- New products
- Price elasticity
- Rank order
- Segmentation
- Stimuli
- Utility
- Utility function

CHAPTER REVIEW QUESTIONS

Objective Type Questions

State whether the following statements are true (T) or false (F).

1. Conjoint analysis makes use of continuous data.
2. Conjoint analysis is typically used to identify the most desirable features to be offered in a product or service.
3. Conjoint analysis computes utility for each level.
4. If for an attribute, there are four levels, the number of dummies to be used would be five.
5. If there are three attributes with three levels each, the total number of profiles for evaluation of respondents would be 27.
6. Less the number of levels for an attribute, more is its relative importance among the attributes.
7. The various stimuli could be rated on ordinal or interval scale.
8. Conjoint analysis could be used to compute price elasticity.
9. Administering rating scale is very time consuming.
10. The rank-order approach of evaluating stimuli seeks relative judgment of the respondents.
11. Estimating individual level utility function for each respondent is useful for formulating marketing strategies.
12. Segmentation exercise in conjoint analysis is based on similarities/dissimilarities in utilities that are attached to the levels of various attributes.
13. Conjoint results in data which is less expensive as compared to the survey data in the determination of price elasticity.
14. Conjoint analysis exercise makes use of small sample because of cost consideration.
15. Conjoint analysis is a 'hypothetical' exercise.
16. If some levels of an attribute are not chosen due to mistake, it may result in poor management decision.
17. It is advised that some levels of an attribute could be dropped at the advice of the expert.
18. A factor analysis exercise could help in identifying important attributes.
19. For computing price elasticity, a conjoint analysis is recommended.
20. Because of cost considerations, the conjoint analysis may be restricted to new product development or improvement in the existing products.

Conceptual Questions

1. How conjoint analysis can be used for segmentation exercise?
2. What are the important issues involved in carrying out a conjoint analysis?
3. What is the role of dummy variables in calculating utilities for each level of the attribute?
4. Why some of the data collecting procedures cannot be used in conducting conjoint analysis exercise?
5. Briefly explain the following:

   (a) Level

   (b) Utility function

   (c) Fractional factorial design

   (d) Full profile

   (e) Relative importance of attributes

CASE 20.1

BURMAN TEA COMPANY PVT. LTD.

India ranks second in the production of tea in the world, after China, and accounts for 26 per cent of the world production. There are 1680 tea manufacturers, 9 auction centres and 280 registered tea associations. The market for tea is growing at a rate of 12.27 per cent per annum. About 79 per cent of the produced tea is exported to the global market.

The domestic market for tea is saturated and served by only two market leaders, namely, Tata Tea Ltd and Hindustan Unilever Ltd (HUL). The combined market share of these two companies is 33 per cent. The major tea brands in India are Tata, Society, Brook Bond Red Label, Duncan's Double Diamond, Taj Mahal, Lipton, Tetley and Pataka. All the brews available are to be prepared in traditional method. The ready-to-make supplement is only available in the coffee segment. Market leaders Tata and HUL do not cater to this segment.

The Burman Tea Company, incorporated in 1995 in Kolkata, is engaged in growing and cultivating tea plantations. It also manufactures tea. The company owns a tea estate and a factory in the state of Assam. The main business of the company is growing, manufacturing and sale of tea. After a survey conducted by the company indicated a favourable response towards 'ready-to-make tea', the company decided to go for this kind of tea. This was to be available in the form of sachets. The company considered the options for the sachet size, and the possible alternatives were one, two and three cups. They considered four price levels i.e. ₹12, ₹14, ₹18 and ₹21. The options of offering with and without sugar and with and without milk were also considered. If they considered all the combinations, it would work out to be $3 \times 4 \times 2 \times 2 = 48$ combinations. It was practically impossible to get a survey conducted and ask every respondent to give their preference for all the 48 combinations. Therefore, they decided to go for a fractional factorial design and considered only 11 combinations. The details of various attributes, their levels and dummy variable coding are given in Table 20.5.

Table 20.5 Attributes of Ready-to-make Tea, Levels and Coding

Attribute	Level	Lever description	Coding		
Sachet Size	3	3 cups	0	0	
	2	2 cups	0	1	
	1	1 cup	1	0	
Price	4	₹21	0	0	0
	3	₹18	0	0	1
	2	₹14	0	1	0
	1	₹12	1	0	0
Sugar	2	Without sugar	0		
	1	With sugar	1		
Milk	2	Without milk	0		
	1	With milk	1		

Table 20.6 details the profiles that were offered to the 110 respondents, along with their average preference rating. The respondents were asked to rate the profiles on a 9-point scale where 1 = least preferred and 9 = most preferred.

Table 20.6 Ready-to-Make Tea Profile and Their Ratings

Profile No.	Sachet Size	Price	Sugar	Milk	Preference Rating
1	1 cup	₹12	With sugar	With milk	7
2	2 cups	₹18	Without sugar	With milk	8
3	3 cups	₹21	With sugar	With milk	7
4	2 cups	₹21	Without sugar	Without milk	6
5	1 cup	₹14	With sugar	Without milk	6

Profile No.	Sachet Size	Price	Sugar	Milk	Preference Rating
6	3 cups	₹18	With sugar	With milk	9
7	1 cup	₹14	Without sugar	With milk	7
8	2 cups	₹18	With sugar	With milk	8
9	3 cups	₹21	Without sugar	With milk	8
10	2 cups	₹12	Without sugar	Without milk	9
11	1 cup	₹14	With sugar	With milk	7

The data matrix for the conjoint analysis is presented in Table 20.7.

Table 20.7 Ready-to-make Tea Data for Dummy Variable Regression (n = 110)

S. No.	X_1	X_2	X_3	X_4	X_5	X_6	X_7	Preference rating (Y)
1	1	0	1	0	0	1	1	7
2	0	1	0	0	1	0	1	8
3	0	0	0	0	0	1	1	7
4	0	1	0	0	0	0	0	6
5	1	0	0	1	0	1	0	6
6	0	0	0	0	1	1	1	9
7	1	0	0	1	0	0	1	7
8	0	1	0	0	1	1	1	8
9	0	0	0	0	0	0	1	8
10	0	1	1	0	0	0	0	9
11	1	0	0	1	0	1	1	7

where X_1, X_2 = dummy variables representing sachet size
X_3, X_4, X_5 = dummy variables representing price
X_6 = dummy variable representing sugar
X_7 = dummy variable representing milk

where X_1 = 1, if the choice is for one cup
= 0, Otherwise
X_2 = 1, if the choice is for two cups
= 0, Otherwise
X_3 = 1, if the price is ₹12
= 0, Otherwise
X_4 = 1, if the price is ₹14
= 0, Otherwise
X_5 = 1, if the price is ₹18
= 0, Otherwise
X_6 = 1, if tea is with sugar
= 0, Otherwise
X_7 = 1, if tea is with milk
= 0, Otherwise

QUESTIONS

1. Carry out a conjoint analysis to determine:
   a. Relative contribution of various attributes.
   b. The importance assigned to various levels within the attribute.
   c. The combination which consumers prefer the most.
2. What are the limitations of such an analysis? Explain.

Answers to Objective Type Questions

1. False	2. True	3. True	4. False	5. True
6. False	7. True	8. True	9. False	10. True
11. False	12. True	13. False	14. True	15. True
16. True	17. True	18. True	19. False	20. True

REFERENCES

David A Aaker, V Kumar and George S Day, *Marketing Research*, 7th edn (John Wiley & Sons, Inc., 2001).

Harper W Boyd, Jr, Ralph Westfall and Stanley F Stasch, *Marketing Research – Text and Cases*, 7th edn (Richard D. Irwin, Inc., 2002).

Naresh K Malhotra, *Marketing Research – An Applied Orientation*, 3rd edn (Pearson Education, 2002).

Seymour Sudman and Edward Blair, *Marketing Research: A Problem Solving Approach*, (McGraw Hill, 1998).

Section 6
REPORTING RESEARCH RESULTS

Introduction

Chapter 21 Report Writing and Presentation of Results

Chapter 21 begins by introducing the kind of reports that are usually formulated to record the results of a research study. These might be brief or detailed reports. They may be technical or business reports. A typical report has a preliminary section, followed by background, methodology, findings and conclusions. The definite format and method of reporting of a typical research are provided with illustrations. Guidelines are provided for report writing, data reporting, as well as referencing. The chapter concludes by discussing simple to advanced options of presenting the study results.

21

CHAPTER

Report Writing and Presentation of Results

Learning Objectives

By the end of the chapter, you should be able to:

1. Understand the basic objectives behind writing a research report.
2. Classify the various types of research reports.
3. Understand the process of report writing and presentation in business research.
4. Understand the key features to be kept in mind in terms of the report format.
5. Identify the needs of the reader and formulate a report to match the requirements.
6. Design effective and focused presentation of findings.
7. Understand the relevance of oral presentations of research.

The scene was dismal and morose at the Jigyasa Educational Research Centre, Thiruvelli office. It was November 2010, and it had been eleven months since 6 January that the team had undertaken an in-depth study of the rural customers of Tamil Nadu to measure the impact of different media vehicles like the radio, television, mobile advertising and OOH (out-of-home) on the consumer groups at the bottom of the pyramid. 'We followed the research process to the book. We structured it the way Ankita (IIM-A graduate 2009) had suggested. Now after formulating the hypotheses, doing extensive background secondary study of the past work done in the area, and formulating and standardizing a questionnaire, what do we find? The hypothesis does not hold good and the impact of the medium is negligible. So, the entire effort has gone waste and we have nothing to show as output for the past so many months. This is so disheartening. Ah ha, here comes Ankita.'

'Hey folks. So, what's on the agenda today? And why is everyone looking so miserable?' B Nagesh, the project leader, updates her on the results and the despondency. 'It's still great work folks, all we have done now needs to be compiled in the form of a report. So let's get going.' 'Ankita, are you all right, have you not understood, we have nothing to show.' 'Who says we have nothing to show? We need to document all that we have done in a sequential and logical manner. The results that show that the impact is negligible are not difficult to explain. The point I am making is that the report will serve a dual purpose:

- It will show our potential clients the work we are capable of; and
- The results will indicate findings that have to be interpreted and can be taken further in a subsequent research.

The nascent nature of the exposure and the influence of other variables like cultural and group factors that might have acted as outside moderators could have been responsible for the findings. You need to understand that the scientific nature of our study now needs to be showcased in a professional report. The task is only half done at this stage, because now we need to compile the research report and be ready to professionally, as well as academically, present the results of the research.' 'Good heavens, why didn't I think of this?' Nagesh wondered aloud.

One cannot overemphasize the significance of a well-documented and structured research report. This step is often taken as extremely rudimentary and is, thus, ignored. However, just like all the other steps in the research process, this requires careful and sequential progression. In this chapter, we would be discussing in detail the formation and presentation of the research study. The format and the steps might be moderately adjusted and altered based on the reader's requirement. Thus, it might be for an academic and theoretical purpose or might need to be clearly spelt and linked with the business manager's decision dilemma.

NEED FOR EFFECTIVE DOCUMENTATION: IMPORTANCE OF REPORT WRITING

LEARNING OBJECTIVE 1
Understand the basic objectives behind writing a research report.

On completion of the research study and after obtaining the research results, the real skill of the researcher lies in terms of analysing and interpreting the findings and linking them with the propositions formulated in the form of research hypotheses at the beginning of the study. The statistical or qualitative summary of results would be little more than numbers or conclusions unless one is able to present the documented version of the research endeavour.

Depending on the business researcher's orientation, the intention might be different and would be reflected in the form of the presentation but the significance is critical to both. Essentially, this is so because of the following reasons:

The **research report** fulfills the historical task of serving as a concrete proof of the study that was undertaken.

- The research report fulfills the historical task of serving as a concrete proof of the study that was undertaken. This serves the purpose of providing a framework for any work that can be conducted in the same or related areas.
- It is the complete detailed report of the research study undertaken by the researcher, thus it needs to be presented in a comprehensive and objective manner. This is a one-way communication of the researcher's study and analysis to the reader/manager, and thus needs to be all-inclusive and yet neutral in its reporting.
- For academic purpose, the recorded document presents a knowledge base on the topic under study and for the business manager seeking help in taking more informed decisions, the report provides the necessary guidance for taking appropriate action.
- As the report documents all the steps followed and the analysis carried out, it also serves to authenticate the quality of the work carried out and establishes the strength of the findings obtained.

Thus, effective recording and communicating of the results of the study becomes an extremely critical step of the research process. Based on the nature of the research study and the researcher's orientation, the report can take different forms.

TYPES OF RESEARCH REPORTS

LEARNING OBJECTIVE 2
Classify the various types of research reports.

The form and structure of the research report might change according to the purpose for which it has been designed. Based on the size of the report, it is possible to divide the report into the following types:

Brief Reports

These kinds of reports are not formally structured and are generally short, sometimes not running more than four to five pages. The information provided is of a limited scope and is prepared either for immediate consumption or as a prelude to the formal structured report that would subsequently follow. These reports could be designed in several ways.

- ***Working papers*** or ***basic reports*** are written for the purpose of collating the process carried out in terms of scope and framework of the study, the methodology followed and instrument designed. The results and findings would also be recorded here. However, the interpretation of the findings and study background might be missing, as the focus is more on the present study rather than past literature. These reports are significant as they serve as a reference point when writing the final report or when the researcher wants to revisit the detailed steps followed in collecting the study-related information.
- ***Survey reports*** might or might not have an academic orientation. The focus here is to present findings in easy-to-comprehend format that includes figures and tables. The reader can then study the patterns in findings to arrive at appropriate conclusions, essential for resolving the business dilemma. The advantage of these reports is that they are simple and easy to understand and present the findings in a clear and usable format.

The aim of a **survey report** is to present the findings in a comprehensive format that includes figures, charts and tables.

Detailed Reports

These are more formal and pedantic in their structure and are essentially either academic, technical or business reports. Sometimes, the researcher may prepare both kinds—for an academic as well as for a business purpose. The language, presentation and format of the two kinds of reports would be vastly different as they would need to be prepared for the understanding of the reader's capabilities and intentions.

Detailed reports are more formal and pedantic in their structure and constitute academic, technical or business reports.

Technical Reports

These are major documents and would include all elements of the basic report, as well as the interpretations and conclusions, as related to the obtained results. This would have a complete problem background and any additional past data/records that are essential for comprehending and interpreting the present study output. All sources of data, sampling plan, data collection instrument(s), data analysis outputs would be formally and sequentially documented.

Business Reports

These reports would not have the technical rigour and details of the technical report and would be in the language and include conclusions as understood and required by the business manager. The tables, figures and numbers of the first report would now be pictorially shown as bars and graphs and the reporting tone would be more in business terms rather than in conceptual or theoretical terms. If needed, the tabular data might be attached in the appendix.

CONCEPT CHECK

1. Is effective report writing crucial to the fundamental framework of a study?
2. What is the difference between a technical report and a business report?
3. Define a brief report.

REPORT PREPARATION AND PRESENTATION

LEARNING OBJECTIVE 3
Understand the report writing and presentation process in business research.

Whatever the type of report, the reporting and dissemination of the study and its findings require a structured format and by and large, the process is standardized. As stated above, the major difference amongst the types of reports is that all the elements that essentially constitute a research report would be present only in a detailed technical report. In the management report, the information on the sampling techniques follows the research intention, and the questionnaire design details need not be reported. The review of past literature would be perfunctory in the management report; however, they would be detailed and accompanied with the bibliography in the technical report. Usage of theoretical and technical jargon would be higher in the technical report and visual presentation of data would be higher in the management report.

In the **management report,** the information on the sampling techniques follows the research intention, and the questionnaire design details need not be reported.

The process of report formulation and presentation is presented in Figure 21.1. As can be observed, the preliminary section includes the rudimentary parts, for example the title page, followed by the letter of authorization, acknowledgements, executive summary and the table of contents. Then come the background section, which includes the problem statement, introduction, study background, scope and objectives of the study and the review of literature (depends on the purpose). This

FIGURE 21.1
The process of report formulation and writing

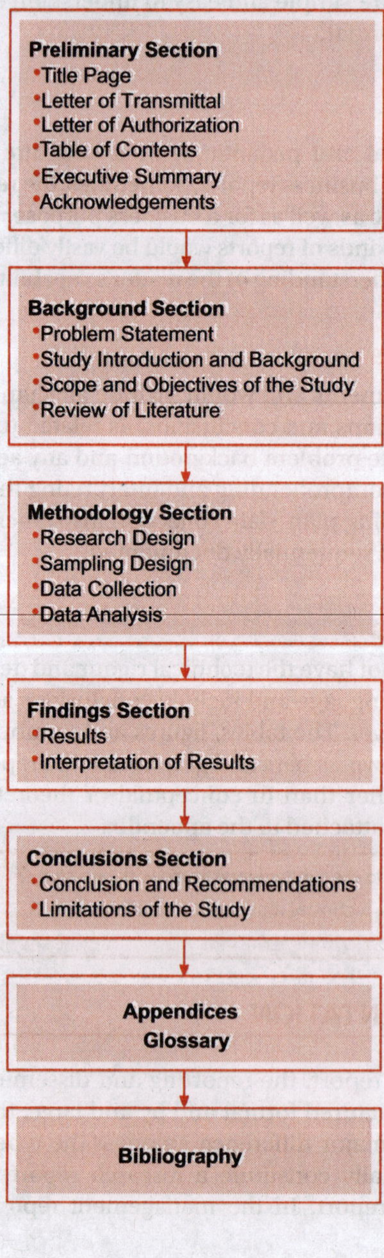

is followed by the methodology section, which, as stated earlier, is again specific to the technical report. This is followed by the findings section and then come the conclusions. The technical report would have a detailed bibliography at the end.

In the management report, the sequencing of the report might be reversed to suit the needs of the decision-maker, as here the reader needs to review and absorb the findings. Thus, instead of simply summarizing the statistical results, the findings need to be presented in such a way that they can be used directly as inputs for decision-making. Thus, the last section would be presented immediately after the study objectives and a short reporting on methodology could be presented in the appendix.

Thus, the entire research project needs to be recorded either as a single written report or into several reports, depending on the need of the readers. The researcher would need to assist the business manager in deciphering the report, executing the findings, and in case of need, to revise the report to suit the specific actionable requirements of the manager.

REPORT STRUCTURE

LEARNING OBJECTIVE 4
Understand the key features to be kept in mind in terms of the report format.

As presented in Figure 21.1, most research reports include the following sections:

Preliminary Section

This section mainly consists of identification information for the study conducted. It has the following individual elements:

Title page: This includes classification data about:

- The target audience, or the intended reader of the report.
- The report author(s), including their name, affiliation and address.
- The title of the study presented in a manner to clearly indicate the study variables; the relationship or status of the variables studied and the population to which the results apply. The title should be crisp and indicative of the nature of the project, as illustrated in the following examples.
  - Comparative analysis of BPO workers and schoolteachers with reference to their work–life balance
  - Segmentation analysis of luxury apartment buyers in the National Capital Region (NCR).
  - An assessment of behavioural factors impacting consumer financial investment decisions.

Letter of transmittal goes alongside the formalized copy of the final report and it refers to the purpose behind the study.

Letter of transmittal: This is the letter that goes alongside the formalized copy of the final report. It broadly refers to the purpose behind the study. The tone in this note can be slightly informal and indicative of the rapport between the client-reader and the researcher. A sample letter of transmittal is presented in Exhibit 21.1. The letter broadly refers to three issues. It indicates the term of the study or objectives; next it goes on to broadly give an indication of the process carried out to conduct the study and the implications of the findings. The conclusions generally are indicative of the researcher's interest/learning from the study and in some cases may be laying the foundation for future research opportunities.

Letter of authorization: Sometimes the letter of authorization may be redundant as indications of the formal approval for conducting the study might be included in the letter of transmittal. The author of this letter is the business manager or corporate

EXHIBIT 21.1
Sample letter of transmittal

To:	Mr Prem Parashar	**From:**	Nayan Navre
Company:	Just Bondas Corporation (JBC)	**Company:**	Jigyasa Associates
Location:	Mumbai 116879	**Location:**	Sabarmati Dham, Mumbai
Telephone:	48786767; 4876768	**Telephone:**	41765888
Fax:	48786799	**Fax:**	41765899

Addendums: Highlight of findings (pages: 20)

15 January 2011

Dear Prem,

Please find the enclosed document which covers a summary of the findings of the November-December 2010 study of the new product offering and its acceptibility. I would be sending three hard copies of the same tomorrow.

Once the core group has discussed the direction of the expected results I would request you to kindly get back with your comments/queries/suggestions, so that they can be incorporated in the preparation of the final report document.

The major findings of the study were that the response of the non-vegetarians consuming the new *keema bonda pav* at Just Bondas was positive. As you can observe, however, the introduction of the non-vegetarian *bonda* has not been well received by the regular customers who visit the outlets for their regular *alloo bonda*. These findings, though on a small respondent base, are significant as they could be an indication of a deflecting loyal customer base.

Best regards,
Nayan

representative who formally gives the permission for executing the project. The tone of this letter, unlike the above document, is very precise and formal, leaving no room for speculation or interpretation.

As explained, this letter is not critical to submission, in case reference to the same has been made in the transmittal letter. However, in case it is to be included in the report, it is advisable to reproduce the exact prototype of the original letter.

Table of contents: All reports should have a section that clearly indicates the division of the report based on the formal areas of the study as indicated in the research structure. The major divisions and subdivisions of the study, along with their starting page numbers, should be presented. The subheadings and the smaller sections of a topic need not be indicated here as then the presentation of the content seems cluttered.

Once the major sections of the report are listed, the list of tables come next, followed by the list of figures and graphs, exhibits (if any) and finally the list of appendices.

In most instances, business managers read only the **executive summary** in its complete detail and just glance through the rest of the report.

Executive summary: This is the last and the most critical element of the preliminary section. The summary of the entire report, starting from the scope and objectives of the study to the methodology employed and the results obtained, have to be presented in a brief and concise manner. In case the research requirement was to provide recommended changes based on the findings, it is advisable to provide short pointers here. Interestingly, it has been observed that in most instances the business managers read only the executive summary in its complete detail and most often just glance through the rest of the report. Thus, it becomes extremely critical to present a Gestaltan view of the entire report in a suitable condensed form.

The **executive summary** is a standalone document which is often circulated independently to the interested managers who might be directly or indirectly related to the study.

The executive summary essentially can be divided into four or five sections. It begins with the study background, scope and objectives of the study, followed by the execution, including the sample details and methodology of the study. Next comes the findings and results obtained. The fourth section covers the conclusions which are more or less based on the opinion of the researcher. Finally, as stated earlier, in case the study objectives necessitates implications, the last section would include recommendations and suggestions.

Acknowledgements: A small note acknowledging the contribution of the respondents, the corporates and the experts who provided inputs for accomplishing the study is to be included here.

Though the executive summary comes before the main body of the report, it is always prepared after the entire report has been finalized and is ready in its final form. The length of this section is one or two pages only and the researcher needs to effectively present the most significant parts of the study in a succinct form. It has been observed that the executive summary is a standalone document that is often circulated independently to the interested managers who might be directly or indirectly related to the study.

Main Report

This is the most significant and academically robust part of the report. The sections of this division follow the essential pattern of a typical research study.

Problem definition includes the elaboration of the research problem and intention.

Problem definition: This section begins with the formal definition of the research problem. The problem statement is the research intention and is more or less similar to what was stated earlier as the title of the research study.

Study background: Study background presents details of the preliminary conceptualization of the management decision problem and all the groundwork done in terms of secondary data analysis, industry experts' perspectives and any other earlier reporting of similar approaches undertaken. Thus, essentially, the section begins by presenting the decision-makers' problem and then moves on to a description of the theoretical and contemporary market data that laid the foundation that guided the research.

In case the study is an academic research, there is a separate section devoted to the review of related literature, which presents a detailed reporting of work done on the same or related topic of interest.

Study scope and objectives: The logical arguments then conclude in the form of definite statements related to the purpose of the study. A clear definition of the scope and objective of the study is presented usually after the study background; in case the study is causal in nature, the formulated hypotheses are presented here as well.

Methodology of research: This section would not be sequentially placed here, for short reports or for a business report. In such reports, a short description of the methodology followed would be documented in the appendix. However, for a technical and academic report, this is a significant and primary contribution of the research study. The section would essentially have five to six sections specifying the details of how the research was conducted. These would essentially be:

- *Research framework or design:* The variables and concepts being investigated are clearly defined, with a clear reference to the relationship being studied. The justification for using a particular design has to be presented in a sequential and step-wise manner enlisting the experimental and control conditions, in case of a causal study. The researcher must take care to keep the technical details of the execution in the appendix and present the execution details in simple language, in the main body.

- *Sampling design:* The entire sampling plan in terms of the population being studied, along with the reasons for collecting the study-related information from the given group is given here. The execution details, in terms of sample size calculations, sampling frame considered and field work details can be recorded in the appendix rather than in the main body of the report. However, the sample profile and identification details are included in the main section. As stated earlier, the report needs to be reader-friendly, and too much technical information might not be required by the decision-maker.
- *Data collection methods:* In this section, the researcher should clearly list the information needed for the study as drawn from the study objectives stated earlier. The secondary data sources considered and the primary instrument designed for the specific study are discussed here. However, the final draft of the measuring instrument can be included in the appendix, which includes the execution details in terms of how the information was collected; how the open ended or opinion-based questions were handled; and how irregularities were handled and accounted for in the study. These and similar information enable a clear insight into the standardization of procedures maintained.
- *Data analysis:* Here, the researcher again needs to revisit the research objectives and the study design in order to justify the analytical tools and techniques used in the study. The assumptions and constraints of the analysis need to be explained here in simple, non-technical terms. There is no need to give a detailed description of the statistical calculations here.
- *Study results and findings:* This is the most critical chapter of the report and requires special care; it is probably also one of the longest chapters in the document. The researcher could, thus, consider either breaking this into subchapters or at least clear subheadings.

The result should be organized according to the information areas on which the data was collected or on the basis of the research objectives.

Researchers commonly divide the chapter on the basis of the data collection plan, i.e., there is a section on interview analysis, another one on focus group discussion and the third referring to the questionnaire analysis. This, however, does not serve any purpose as the results would then seem repetitive and disjointed. Instead, the result should be organized according to the information areas on which the data was collected or on the basis of the research objectives. There are also times when the data would be presented for the whole sample and then will be split and presented for the sub-population studied. For example, in the study on work-life balance, the findings were presented for the whole sample and then at the micro level for the BPO sector and separately for the school teacher segment. For each group, first the sample profile in terms of the demographic details of age, education, income (individual and family), years of experience, marital status, family size and other details was presented. Next, the descriptive data was made available on the seven sub-scales studied—and lastly—the predictive data-based on a multiple regression analysis with work-life balance as the dependent variable and the seven variables as independent, was presented. There was only one open-ended question related to the individual's suggestion as to what support was required from one's place of work to achieve work-life balance. This was presented last in the form of a bar chart showing variability in the responses given. Again as advised earlier, it is essential to present the findings in the form of simplified tables, graphs and figures, with the same being explained in simple text subsequently.

Interpretations of Results and Suggested Recommendations

The section study results and findings, i.e., the main report, presents a bird's eye view of the information as it exists in a summarized and numerical form. This kind of information might become difficult to understand and convert into actionable steps, thus the real skill of the researcher lies in simplifying the data in a reader-friendly language. Here, it is recommended that this section should be more analytical and opinion based. The results could be supported by the data that was presented earlier, for example, industry forecasts or the expert opinion. In case the report had an earlier section on literature review, the researcher could demonstrate the similarity of findings with past studies done on the topic. For example, in a study conducted on analysing the antecedents of turnover intention, the results obtained were explained as follows:

The results of the logit regression indicate that organizational commitment, age and martial status are significant at 5 per cent and 10 per cent levels respectively. The results indicate that as organizational commitment increases, the log of odd ratios in the favour of high turnover intention reduces, which is very logical. This is in accordance with the results obtained by Mobley, et al. (1978), Cotton and Tuttle (1986), Igbaria and Greenhaus (1992), Ahuja, et al. (2007). Thus, when employees feel committed to an organization, they are more likely to stay with the organization.

Sometimes, the research results obtained may not be in the direction as found by earlier researchers. Here, the skill of the researcher in justifying the obtained direction is based on his/her individual opinion and expertise in the area of study. For example, in the same study on turnover intentions, contrary findings were explained as follows:

...the results indicate that the log of odd ratios in favour of high turnover intention is more in the case of older respondents; this is contrary to the findings of Zeffane and Gul (1995) and Finegold, et al. (2002). However, this has to be understood in the light of the profession, as in India, most people take the BPO sector as a stop-gap career and use the time at the BPO employment as an opportunity to enhance their academic qualification and then move on, which is also one of the reasons why this sector is a young sector.

Subsequent to the subsection on the interpretation of results, sometimes, the study requirement might be to formulate indicative recommendations to the decision-makers as well. Thus, in case the report includes recommendations, they should be realistic, workable and topically related to the industry studied. For example, to the business manager of organic food products, the following recommendation was made to build awareness amongst potential customers about the benefits of organic products:

Organic food study: An illustration: *The power of the print media in promoting a high-involvement product is unsurpassed. Thus, articles by leading nutritionists and doctors (88 per cent of consumers are influenced by others in consuming health alternatives) on any aspect of organic food would work well. The organic players need to take care that they do not advertise only their product offerings and price alone but they also need to educate the consumer on the health benefits of the products in their advertisements.*

The article/advertisement could be placed in the Sunday supplements of newspapers so that people would read them at leisure. The major decision-makers for groceries are women thus magazines like Femina, Health and Savvy would be likely choices (the magazines suggested are English fortnightlies and have a reader profile similar to our sample profile). This is also because the product is a premium and niche product and thus requires selective exposure.

Limitations of the Study

The last in this section is a brief discussion of the problems encountered during the study and the constraints in terms of time, financial or human resources. There could also have been constraints in obtaining the required information, either because the data about the topic of interest has not been collected or because it is not readily available to all. These clear revelations about the drawbacks are thus kept in mind by the reader when analysing the results and the implications of the study.

End Notes

The final section of the report provides all the supportive material in the study. Some of the common details presented in this section are as follows:

Appendices: The appendix section follows the main body of the report and essentially consists of two kinds of information:

1. Secondary information like long articles or in case the study uses/is based on/ refers to some technical information that needs to be understood by the reader. Or long tables or articles or legal or policy documents.
2. Primary data that can be compressed and presented in the main body of the report. This includes: Original questionnaire, discussion guides, formula used for the study, sample details, original data, long tables and graphs which can be described in statement form in the text.

MS Word 2007 can generate a bibliography automatically based on the information and sources provided.

Bibliography: This is an important part of the final section as it provides the complete details of the information sources and papers cited in a standardized format. It is recommended to follow the publication manuals from the American Psychological Association (APA) or the Harvard method of citation for preparing this section. In fact, with the advancement in computer technology the Microsoft office Word 2007 can automatically generate a bibliography based on any of these formats, based on the source information provided in the document.

The reporting content of the bibliography could also be in terms of:

- **Selected bibliography:** Selective references are cited in terms of relevance and reader requirement. Thus, the books or journals, that are technical and not really needed to understand the study outcomes are not reported.
- **Complete bibliography:** All the items that have been referred to, even when not cited in the text, are given here.
- **Annotated bibliography:** Along with the complete details of the cited work, some brief information about the nature of information sought from the article is given. This could run into three or four lines or a brief paragraph.

At this juncture we would like to refer to another method of citation that an author might wish to use during report writing. This could be in the form of a footnote. To explain the difference we would first like to explain what a typical footnote is:

A footnote refers to a source that the author has referred to or it may be an explanation of a specific concept.

Footnote: A typical footnote, as the name indicates, is part of the main report and comes at the bottom of a page or at the end of the main text. This could refer to a source that the author has referred to or it may be an explanation of a particular concept referred to in the text.

The referencing protocol of a footnote and bibliography is different. In a footnote, one gives the first name of the person first and the surname next. However, this order is reversed in the bibliography. Here we start first with the surname and then the first name. In a bibliography, we generally mention the page numbers of the article or the total pages in the book. However, in a footnote, the specific page from which the information is cited is mentioned. A bibliography is generally arranged alphabetically depending on the author's name, but in the footnote the reporting is based on the sequence in which they occur in the text.

Glossary of terms: In case there are specific terms and technical jargon used in the report, the researcher should consider putting a glossary in the form of a word list of terms used in the study. This section is usually the last section of the report.

CONCEPT CHECK	
	1. Discuss the process of report presentation.
	2. Elaborate upon the structure of a report and its main constituents.
	3. What constitutes an ideal executive summary?

REPORT WRITING: REPORT FORMULATION

LEARNING OBJECTIVE 5
Identify the needs of the reader and formulate a report to match the requirements.

An important point to remember in report writing is that the document compiled is meant for specific readers. Thus, one needs to design the same according to the needs of the reader. Listed below are some features of a good research study that should be kept in mind while documenting and preparing the report.

Clear report mandate: While writing the research problem statement and study background, the writer needs to be focused, precise and very explicit in terms of the problem under study, the background that provided the impetus to conduct the research and the study domain. This is prepared on the assumption that the writer at no point in time needs to be physically present in order to clarify the research mandate. One cannot make an assumption that the reader has earlier insights into the problem situation. The writer needs to be absolutely clear on the need for lucidity of thought and dissemination of this knowledge to the reader.

Clearly designed methodology: Any research study has its unique orientation and scope and thus has a specific and customized research design, sampling and data collection plan. The writer, thus, needs to be explicit in terms of the logical justification for having used the study methods and techniques. However, as stated earlier, the language should be non-technical and reader friendly and any technical explanations or details must be provided in the appendix. In researches, that are not completely transparent on the set of procedures, one cannot be absolutely confident of the findings and resulting conclusions.

The **sample base** is very important in justifying a trend or taking a strategic decision.

Clear representation of findings: The sample size for each analysis, any special conditions or data treatment must be clearly mentioned either as a footnote or as an endnote, so that the reader takes this into account while interpreting and understanding the study results. The sample base is very important in justifying a trend or taking a strategic decision; for example, if amongst a sample of bachelors we say that 100 per cent young bachelors want to buy grocery online or on the telephone and the recommended strategy is to suggest this as the delivery channel, one might be making an error if the size of the bachelors was four out of a total sample of 100 grocery buyers considered. Thus, complete honesty and transparency in stating the treatment and editing of missing or contrary data is extremely critical.

A good **research report** is also explicit in terms of extent and scope of the results obtained, and in terms of the applicability of findings.

Representativeness of study finding: A good research report is also explicit in terms of extent and scope of the results obtained, and in terms of the applicability of findings. This is also dependent on whether the assumptions and preconditions made for formulating the conclusions and recommendations of the study have been explicitly stated.

In order to ensure that one has been able to achieve the above stated objective, the reader must ensure a standardization of procedures in writing the document as well as follow standard protocols for preparing graphs and tables. In the following section we will briefly discuss some simple rules that the researcher can use as guidelines for this.

GUIDELINES FOR EFFECTIVE DOCUMENTATION

LEARNING OBJECTIVE 6
Design effective and focused presentation of findings.

To illustrate the formulation style a sample report (brief version) is presented in Appendix 21.1.

Command over the medium: Even though one may have done an extremely rigorous and significant research study, the fundamental test still remains as to how the learning has been disseminated. Regardless of how effective the graphs and figures are in showcasing the findings, the verbal description and explanation—in terms of why it was done, how it was done, and what was the outcome, still remain the acid test.

Thus, a correct and effective language of communication is critical in putting ideas and objectives in the vernacular of the reader/decision-maker. The writer may, thus, be advised to read professionally written reports and, if necessary, seek assistance from those proficient in preparing business reports.

Phrasing protocol: There is a debate about whether or not one makes use of personal pronoun while reporting. To understand this, one needs to revisit the responsibility of the researcher, which is to present the findings of his/her study, with complete objectivity and precision. The use of personal pronoun such as 'I think.....' or 'in my opinion.....' lends a subjectivity and personalization of judgement. Thus, the tone of the reporting should be neutral. For example:

'Given the nature of the forecasted growth and the opinion of the respondents, it is likely that the......'

Whenever the writer is reproducing the verbatim information from another document or comment of an expert or published source, it must be in inverted commas or italics and the author or source should be duly acknowledged. For example:

Sarah Churchman, Head of Diversity, PricewaterhouseCoopers, states *'At PricewaterhouseCoopers we firmly believe that promoting work-life balance is a 'business-critical' issue and not simply the 'right thing to do.' Profitable growth and sustainable business depends on attracting and retaining top talent and we know, from our own research and experience that work-life policies are an essential ingredient of successful recruitment and retention strategies.'*

The writer should avoid long sentences and break up the information in clear chunks, so that the reader can process it with ease.

The writer should avoid long sentences and break up the information in clear chunks, so that the reader can process it with ease. Similar is the case in structuring of the chapters or sections of the report that can be logically broken down into smaller sections that are comprehensive and complete and yet maintain a strong but logical link with the flow of reporting.

With the onset of the use of abbreviated communications in SMS and emails, most people tend to use shortened form as 'cd.' for could and 'u' for you, etc. Also the use of colloquial language and slangs must be avoided, as this is a formal document and one must maintain the sanctity of the formal documentation required in a research report.

Simplicity of approach: Along with grammatically and structurally correct language, care must be taken to avoid technical jargon as far as possible. The business

Along with grammatically and structurally correct language, care must be taken to avoid **technical jargon** as far as possible.

manager, might have been a business student who had prepared a research report in his academic pursuits but now understands simple common terms and does not have the time or inclination to juggle the dictionary and the report together. In case it is imperative to use certain terminology, then, as stated earlier, the definition of these terms can be provided in the glossary of terms at the end of the report.

Sometimes the writer may prepare different research reports for the same study to suit the need of diverse readers, for example, the business report needs to be crisp and simple with definable and workable recommendations. On the other hand, an academic report could discuss extensively the literature review section, as well as the statistical analysis and interpretation.

Report formatting and presentation: In terms of paper quality, page margins and font style and size, a professional standard should be maintained. The font style must be uniform throughout the report. The topics, subtopics, headings and subheadings must be construed in the same manner throughout the report. Sometimes certain academic reports have a mandated format for presentation which the writers need to follow, in which case there is no choice in presentation.

The **researcher** can provide data relief and variation by adequately supplementing the text with graphs and figures.

However, when this is not clear, it is advisable that the writer creates his/her own formatting rules and saves it on a notepad so that they can be implemented in a standardized and professional manner.

The researcher can provide data relief and variation by adequately supplementing the text with graphs and figures. Pictorial representations are simple to comprehend and also break the monotony and fatigue of reading. They should be used effectively whenever possible in the report.

Guidelines for Presenting Tabular Data

Most research studies involve some form of numerical data, and even though one can discuss this in text, it is best represented in tabular form. The advantage of doing this is that statistical tables present the data in a concise and numeral form, which makes quantitative analysis and comparisons easier. Tables formulated could be general tables following a statistical format for a particular kind of analysis. These are best put in the appendix, as they are complex and detailed in nature. The other kind is simple summary tables, which only contain limited information and yet, are, essentially critical to the report text.

The mechanics of creating a summary table are very simple and are illustrated below with an example (Table 21.1). The illustration has been labelled with numbers which relate to the relevant section.

Table identification details: The table must have a title (1a) and an identification number (1b). The table title should be short and usually would not include any verbs or articles. It only refers to the population or parameter being studied. The title should be briefly yet clearly descriptive of the information provided. The numbering of tables is usually in a series and generally one makes use of Arabic numbers to identify them.

The **title of a table** should be short and concise referring to the population or parameter being studied.

Data arrays: The arrangement of data in a table is usually done in an ascending manner. This could either be in terms of time, as shown in Table 21.1 (column-wise) or according to sectors or categories (row-wise) or locations, e.g., north, south, east, west and central. Sometimes, when the data is voluminous, it is recommended that one goes alphabetically, e.g., country or state data. Sometimes there may be subcategories to the main categories, for example, under the total sales data—a column-wise component of the revenue statement—there could be subcategories

TABLE 21.1
Automobile domestic sales trends

Marker		1b		2a			3
1a			Year-wise data (number of cars)				
2b	Category		2002-2003	2003-2004	2004-2005	2006-2007	2007-2008
4b, 4a, 4c	Passenger vehicles......		707,198	902,096	1,061,572	1,143,076	1,379,979
	Commercial Vehicles......		190,682	260,114	318,430	351,041	467,765
	Three-wheelers......		231,529	284,078	307,862	359,920	403,910
7a	Two-wheelers......		4,812,126	5,364,249	6,209,765	7,052,391	7,872,334
	Grand Total*		5,941,535	6,810,537	7,897,629	8,906,428	10,123,988

5b — *Does not include second hand car sales.

6a — *Source:* SIAM

of department store, chemists and druggists, mass merchandisers and others. Then these have to be displayed under the sales data head, after giving a tab command as follows:

Total sales
Mass market
Department store
Drug stores
Others (including *paan beedi* outlets)

Measurement unit: The unit in which the parameter or information is presented should be clearly mentioned.

Spaces, Leaders and Rulings (SLR): For limited data, the table need not be divided using grid lines or rulings. Simple white spaces add to the clarity of information presented and processed. In case the number of parameters are too many and the data seems to be bulky to be simply separated by space, it is advisable to use vertical ruling. Horizontal lines are drawn to separate the headings from the main data, as can be seen in Table 21.1. When there are a number of subheadings as in the sales data example, one may consider using leaders (.......) to assist the eye movement in absorbing and processing the information.

Total sales
Mass market.........
Department store.........
Drug stores.........
Others (including *paan beedi* outlets).........

Assumptions, details and comments: Any clarification or assumption made, or a special definition required to understand the data, or formula used to arrive at a particular figure, e.g., total market sale or total market size can be given after the main tabled data in the form of footnotes.

Data sources: In case the information documented and tabled is secondary in nature, complete reference of the source must be cited after the footnote, if any.

Special mention: In case some figure or information is significant and the reader should pay special attention to it, the number or figure can be bold or can be highlighted to increase focus.

Guidelines for Visual Representations: Graphs

Similar to the summarized and succinct data in the form of tables, the data can also be presented through visual representations in the form of graphs. The visual representation of the findings in the form of lines or boxes and bars relative to a number line is easy to comprehend and interpret. There are some standard rules and procedures available to the researcher for this; also there are computer programs like MS Excel and SPSS, where the numbered data can be converted with ease into graphical form.

The **line graph** is able to clearly portray any change in pattern that needs to be shown as occurring during a particular time period.

Line and curve graphs: Usually, when the objective is to demonstrate trends and some sort of pattern in the data, a line chart is the best option available to the researcher as the line is able to clearly portray any change in pattern during a particular time period. On the same chart, it is also possible to show patterns of growth of different sectors or industries in the same time period or to compare the change in the studied variable across different organizations or brands in the same industry. Certain points to be kept in mind while formulating line charts include:

- The time units or the causal variable being studied are to be put on the X-axis, or the horizontal axis.
- If the intention is to compare different series on the same chart, the lines should be of different colours or forms (Figure 21.2).

FIGURE 21.2
Comparative analysis of vehicles (including Nano) on features desired by consumers

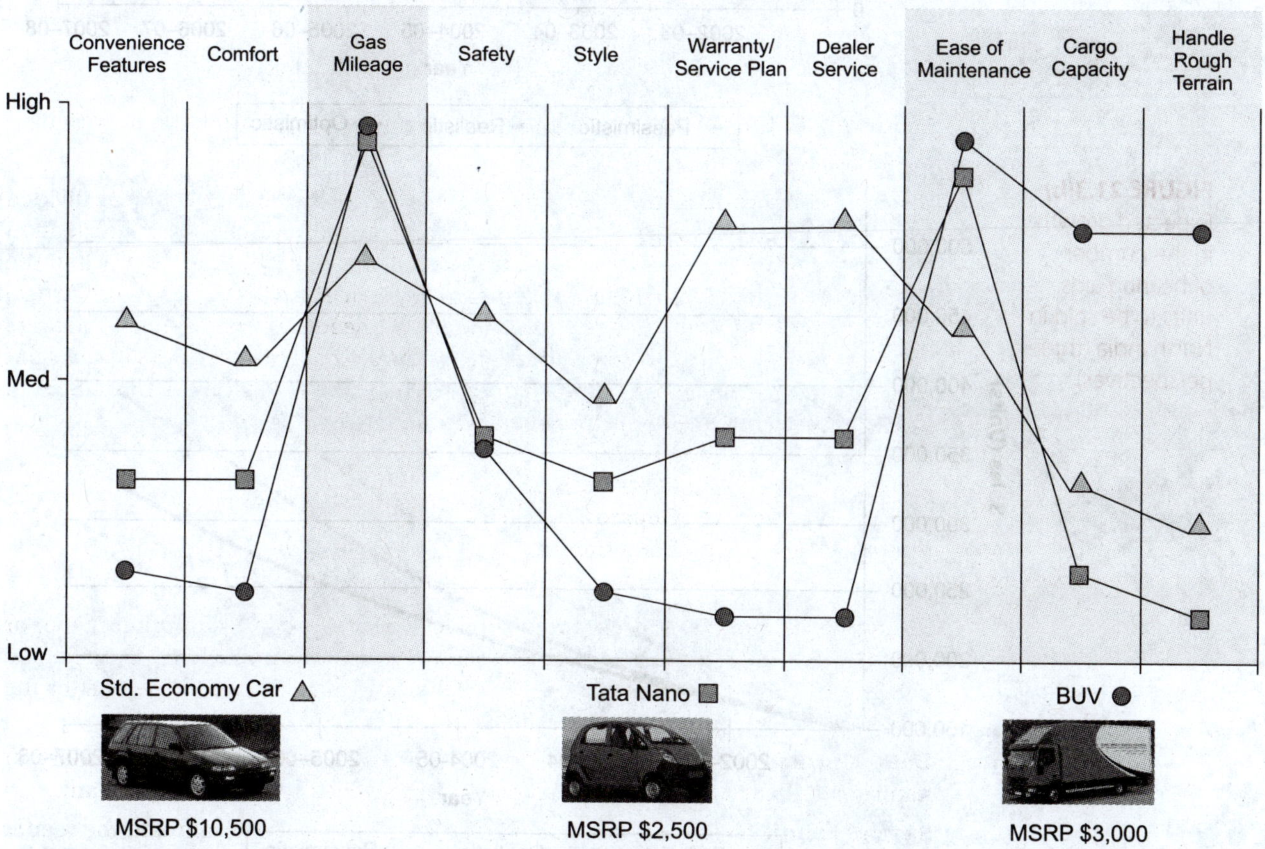

Source: vytrak.com

Too many lines are not advisable on the same chart as the data becomes too cluttered.

- Too many lines are not advisable on the same chart as then the data becomes too cluttered; an ideal number would be five or less than five lines on the chart.
- The researcher also must take care to formulate the zero baseline in the chart as otherwise, the data would seem to be misleading. For example, in Figure 21.3(a), in case the zero baseline is (as shown in the chart) the expected change in the number of hearing aids units to be sold over the time period 2002–03 to 2007–08, it can be accurately perceived. However, in Figure 21.3(b), where the zero is at 1,50,000 units, the rate of growth can be misjudged to be more swift.

FIGURE 21.3(a) Expected growth in the number of hearing aids units to be sold in North India (three perspectives)

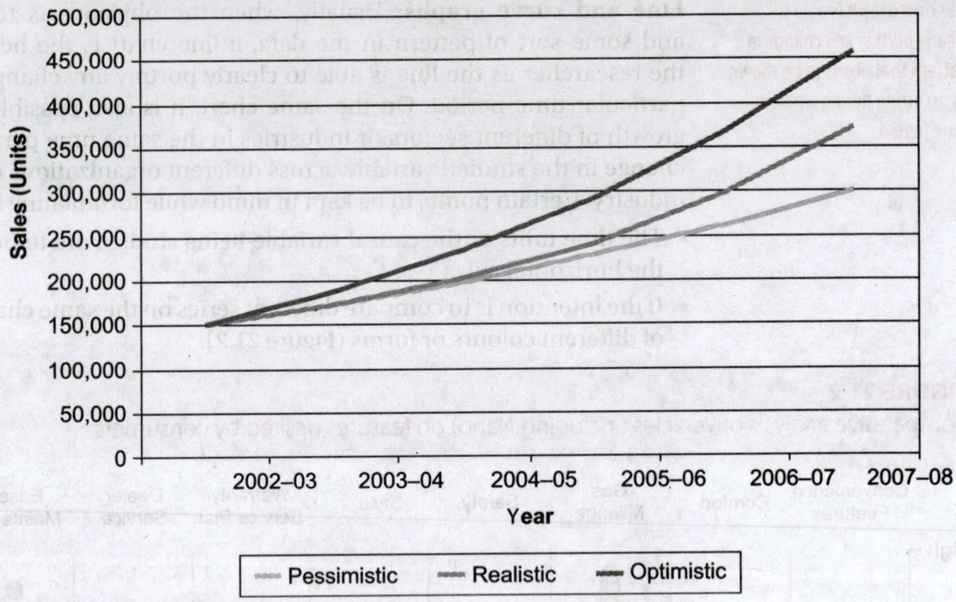

FIGURE 21.3(b) Expected growth in the number of hearing aids units to be sold in North India (three perspectives)

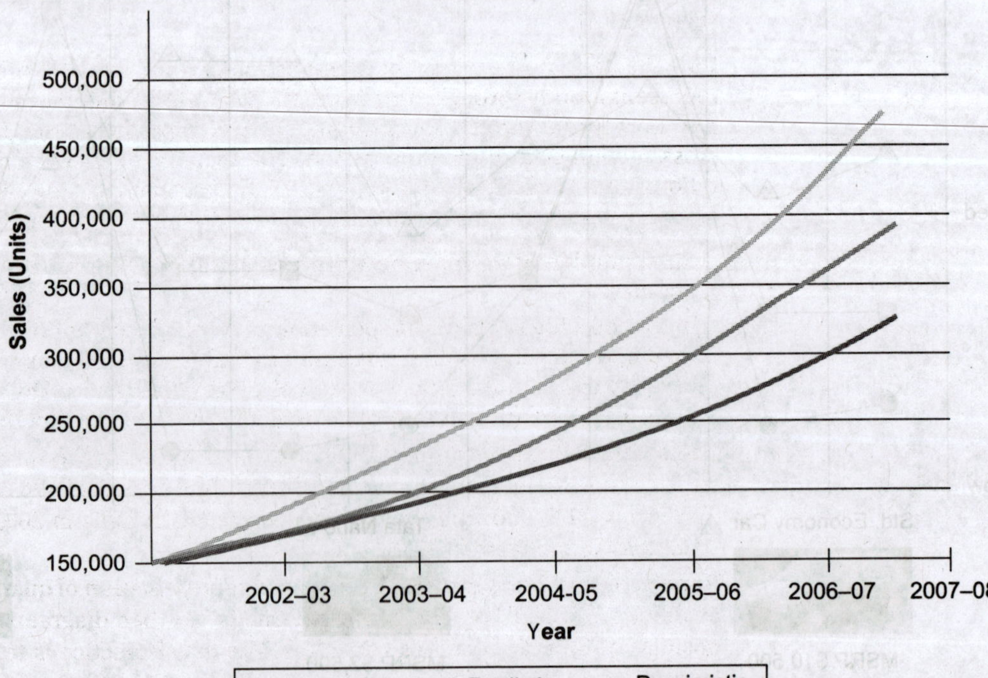

FIGURE 21.4
Perception of Nano by three psychographic segments of two-wheeler owners

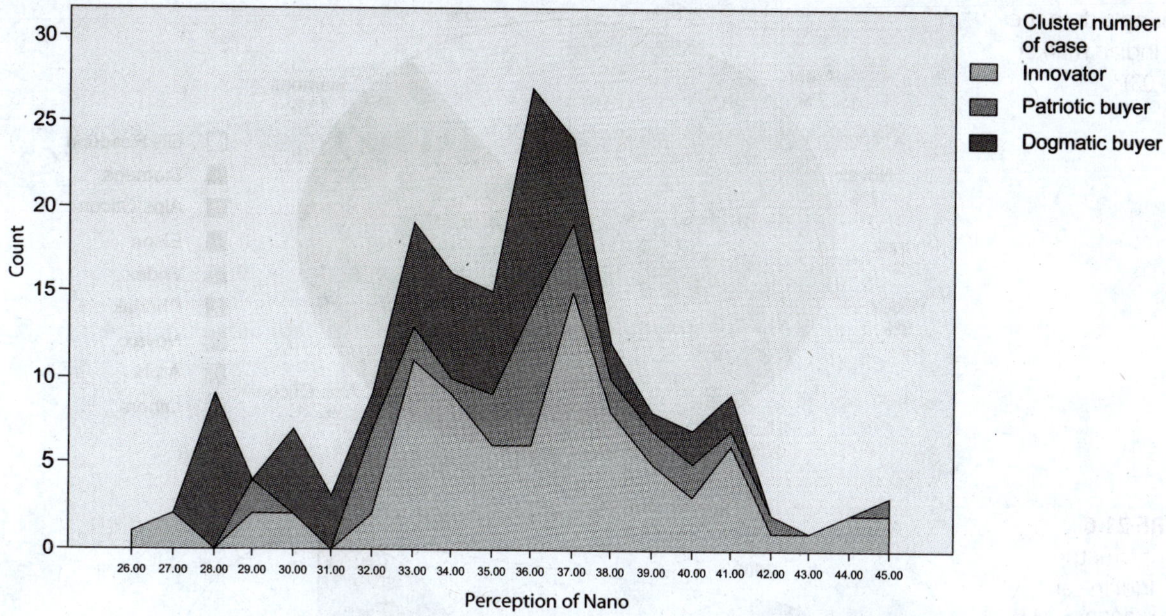

Area or stratum charts: Area charts are like the line charts, usually used to demonstrate changes in a pattern over a period of time. However, here there are multiple lines that are essentially components of the original composite data. What is done is that the change in each of the components is individually shown on the same chart and each of them is stacked one on top of the other. The areas between the various lines indicate the scale or volume of the relevant factors/categories (Figure 21.4).

Pie charts: Another way of demonstrating the area or stratum or sectional representation is through the pie charts. The critical difference between a line and pie chart is that the pie chart cannot show changes over time. It simply shows the cross-section of a single time period. The sections or slices of the pie indicate the ratio of that section to the total area of the parameter being displayed. There are certain rules that the researcher should keep in mind while creating pie charts.

- The complete data must be shown as a 100 per cent area of the subject being graphed.
- It is a good idea to have the percentages displayed within or above the pie rather than in the legend as then it is easier to understand the magnitude of the section in comparison to the total. For example, Figure 21.5 shows the brand-wise sales in units for the existing brands of hearing aids in the North Indian market.
- Showing changes over time is difficult through a pie chart, as stated earlier. However, the change in the components at different time periods could be demonstrated as in Figure 21.6, showing share of the car market in India in 2009 and the expected market composition of 2015.

Bar charts and histograms: A very useful representation of quantum or magnitude of different objects on the same parameter are bar diagrams. The comparative position of objects becomes very clear. The usual practice is to formulate vertical bars; however, it is possible to use horizontal bars as well if none of the variable is time related [Figure 21.7(a)]. Horizontal bars are especially useful when one is showing

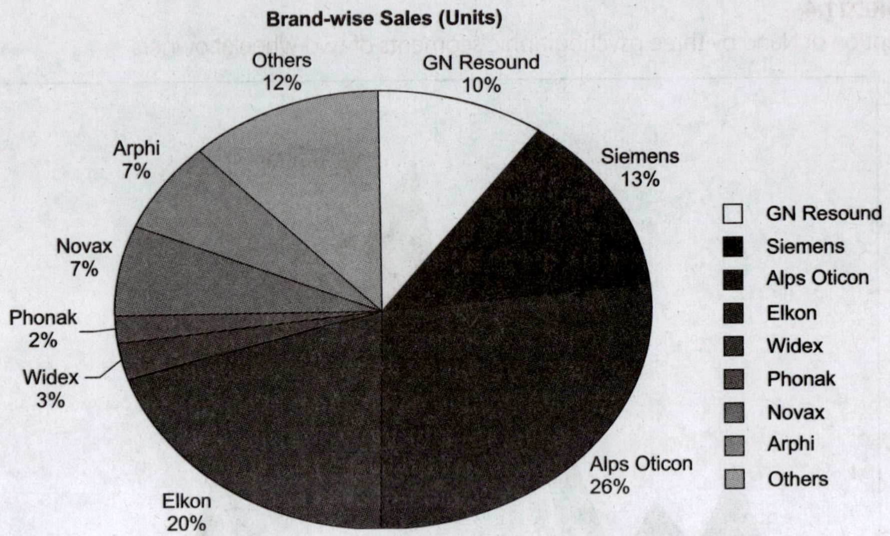

FIGURE 21.5 Brand-wise sales (units) of hearing aids in the North Indian market (2002–03)

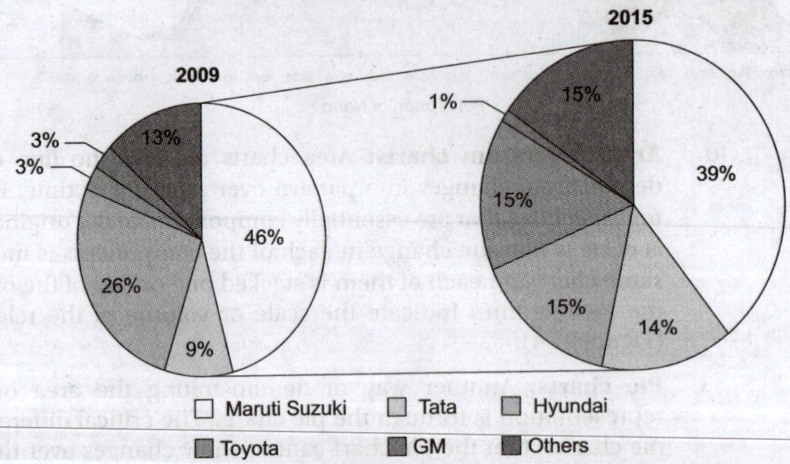

FIGURE 21.6 Current structure of the Indian car market (2009) and the forecasted structure for 2015

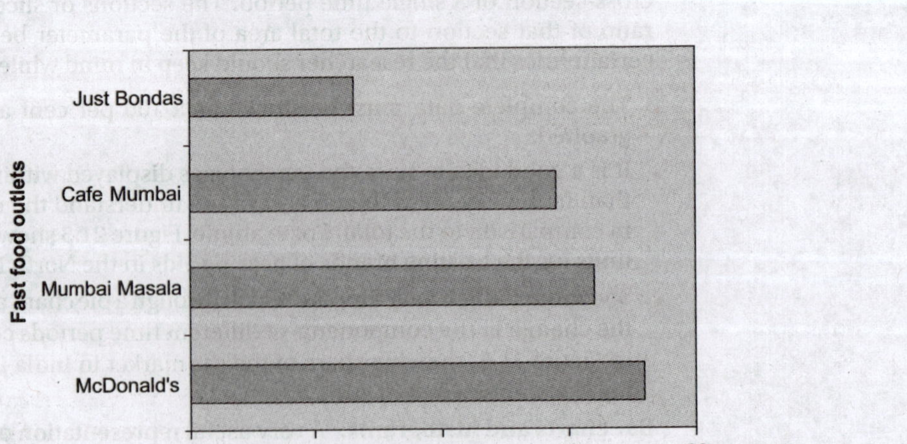

FIGURE 21.7(a) Bar chart per day, unit sales (thousands) at fast food outlets in Mumbai

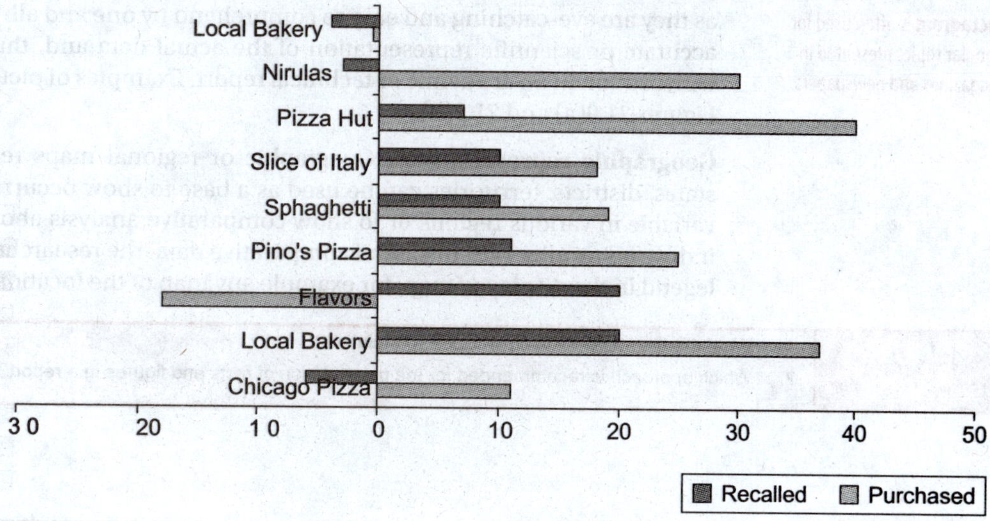

FIGURE 21.7(b) Bilateral bar chart—the brand recall and brand purchase response for pizza joints in the NCR

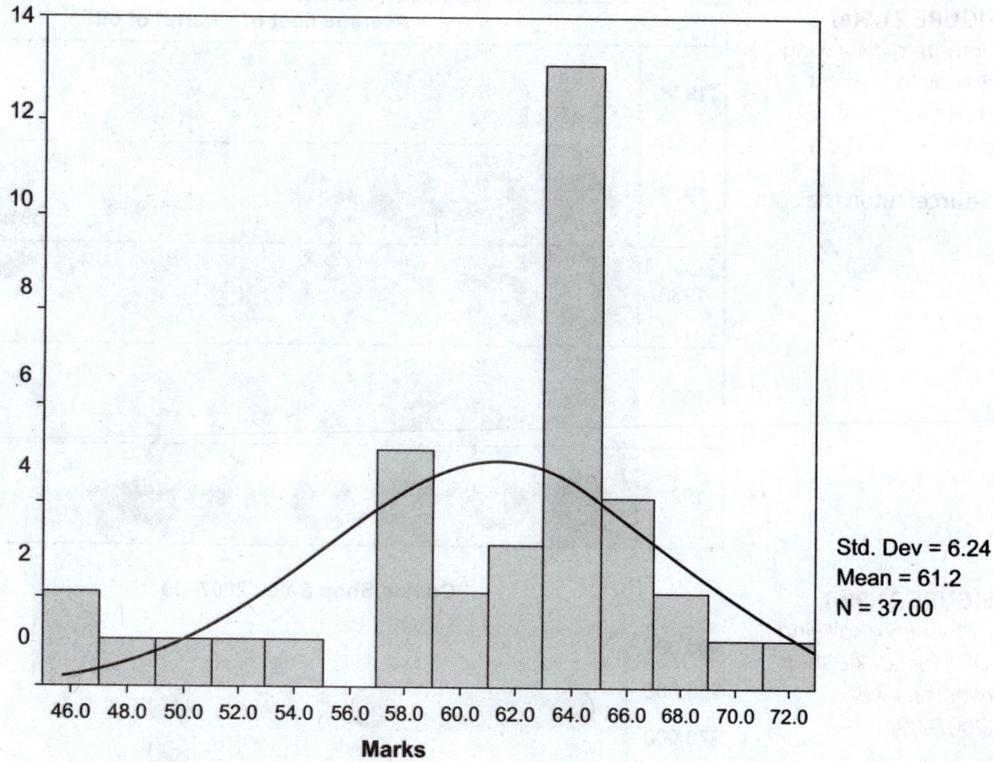

FIGURE 21.8 Histogram (with normal curve) displaying marks in a course on research methods for management

both positive and negative patterns on the same graph [Figure 21.7(b)]. These are called bilateral bar charts and are especially useful to highlight the objects or sectors showing a varied pattern on the studied parameter. It is possible to generate bar graphs with relative ease with computer programs today and the distance between the bars can be extremely precise as compared to those created by hand.

Another variation of the bar chart is the histogram (Figure 21.8) here the bars are vertical and the height of each bar reflects the relative or cumulative frequency of that particular variable.

Pictogram: A pictogram shows graphical representation of data. Pictograms are most often used in popular and general read such as in magazines and newspapers,

Pictogram is often used for popular topics presented in magazines and newspapers.

as they are eye-catching and easy to comprehend by one and all. They are not a very accurate or scientific representation of the actual data and, thus, should be used with caution in an academic or technical report. Examples of pictograph are given in Figures 21.9(a) and 21.9(b).

Geographic representation: Geographic or regional maps related to countries, states, districts, territories can be used as a base to show occurrence of the studied variable in various regions or to show comparative analysis about major brands or industries or minerals. In case of comparative data, the researcher must provide the legend in the displayed map, for example any map of the location may be given.

CONCEPT CHECK

1. What are the steps involved in report formulation?
2. Which approach is recommended for the presentation of facts and figures in a report?

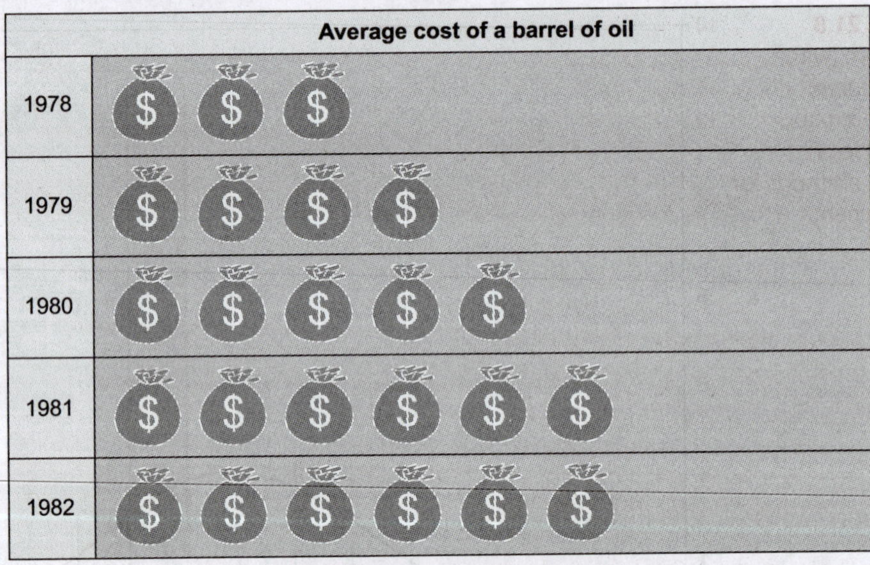

FIGURE 21.9(a) Pictogram displaying change in the cost of oil over a five-year block (1978–1982)

Source: tutorvista.com

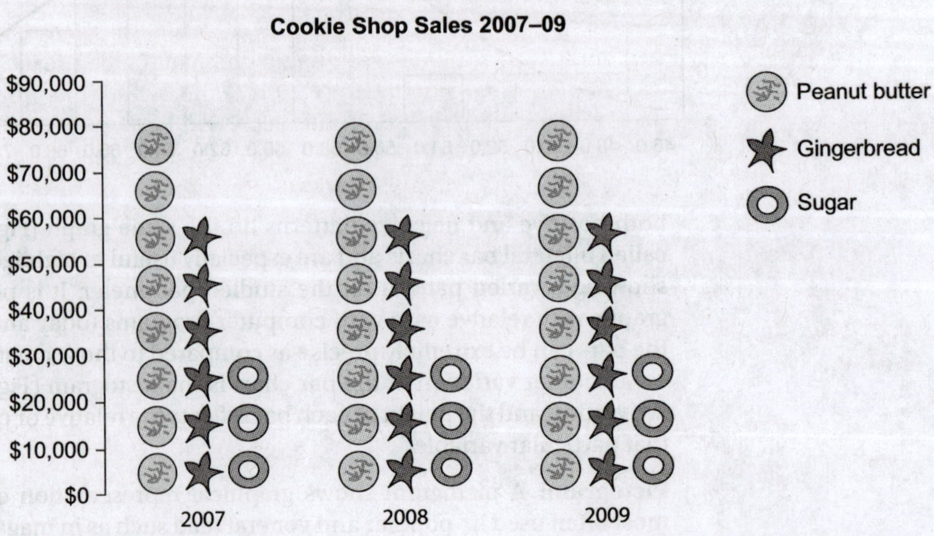

FIGURE 21.9(b) Pictogram displaying sales for cookie shop over three years (2007–09)

Source: 4spreadsheets.pbworks.com

RESEARCH BRIEFINGS: ORAL PRESENTATION

LEARNING OBJECTIVE 7
Understand the relevance of oral presentations of research.

Once the final draft of the research report is prepared and documented, the last stage is sharing the findings and research implications with the client or interested audience. This is usually done orally and with the support of visual aids. The presentation that the researcher might be making could be detailed for his team members or for an academic audience. However, in case the presentation is for the client or for a business audience, brevity and focus of the presentation is critical. A thumb rule for this is not to go beyond 20 minutes with more time for question and answers and interactive discussion on the findings.

A thumb rule for an **oral presentation** is that the speaker should not go beyond 20 minutes and should reserve some time for a healthy interactive discussion.

Regardless of the audience for the presentation, the most critical aspect of the presentation is two-fold:

(a) Who is the listener? What does he/she seek from the presentation?
(b) What is the core of the briefing—is it background, or methodology, key findings or decision directions that the findings are indicating?

Once the researcher is clear on this, he needs to need to focus on three key aspects:

The **researcher** must be able to demonstrate clearly the link between the study objectives and the findings.

Study background: This should be essentially 10–15 per cent of the entire presentation. It should explain the impetus behind the study as briefly and with suitable emphasis as possible.

Study findings: The major conclusions of the study need to be shared in simple words and with appropriate supportive visuals or material. The researcher must be able to demonstrate clearly the link between the study objectives and the findings.

Study implications: In case this was agreed upon between the researcher and the client or was specified as a study objective by the researcher, this section would be the last section of the presentation. The link between what was found and what is suggested must be clear to the audience. The researcher may vary the discussion time between the earlier section and this as 45 per cent each or 30–70 or 70–30, depending on the study objective, i.e., more findings or more implication oriented.

As supportive material the researcher can make use of:

Handouts: These could be in the form of the primary questionnaire designed for the study or company brochures and other related secondary material. They should be distributed to the audience when the presenter is referring to them.

Slides: These are created today with the help of computer programmes. There are endless possibilities enhancing the material be presented and for engaging the listener. The designing and creation of the material requires considerable skill and care to ensure that the presentation style should be the supportive aid for an effective delivery and not a showcase of the computer graphics that the researcher is well versed with. Too much clutter and a random mix of text and graphics should be avoided. Animation of the data in synchronization with the vocal delivery makes the presentation more forceful.

Chalkboards and flipcharts: These are additional visual aids that could be kept as standby for the question-and-answer session when an idea might have to be highlighted or demonstrated in the response of some query raised by the listeners. However, use of these means during an active presentation should be avoided as they necessitate the presenter to be engaged with the medium at the cost of losing contact with the listener.

Video and audio tapes: Again, these are supportive materials that can be used to emphasize a point.

The world has become smaller as a consequence of technological innovations that make dissemination of knowledge seem like child's play. Thus, the significance of communication and presentation of this learning cannot be overemphasized.

CONCEPT CHECK	1. How can an oral presentation be made effective? 2. Apart from oral presentations, what other means can be employed by the researcher to enhance the presentation process?

SUMMARY

- Once a research project has reached its conclusions, the most important task ahead of the researcher is to document the entire work done in the form of a well structured research report. This step is significant not only for the client or business manager for whom the task was undertaken, but also for documenting the work formally as research done in the topic of interest. This would be useful as historical or secondary data available for anyone who wishes to study the topic in future.
- The orientation and structure of the report will depend on what kind of report is being constructed. There are brief reports which, as the name suggests, are of a shorter length and could be in the form of working papers or short survey reports. These might be expanded while preparing the detailed report. The detailed report may vary in scope and style depending on the requirement of the reader for whom it is to be created. These could be in the form of highly structured and comprehensive technical reports or simpler action-oriented business reports.
- However, no matter what is the orientation, reports generally follow a standardized structure. The entire report can be divided into three main sections—the preliminary section, the main body and endnotes. The preliminary section typically includes the title page, the table of contents and the letter of authorization and the letter of transmittal. The most significant section of this part is a short but succinct executive summary, which summarizes the main report.
- The main report includes the background of the study, scope and framework and the methodology of the study, including the data collection and sampling plan. The section culminates into the most important part of the report, the study findings and interpretation of these results. The last section includes the bibliography and all the supportive documents like measuring instrument (questionnaire), the sample details and any relevant document that needs to be referred to comprehend the report.
- Any well documented report must be clear and explicit in its reporting. There must be no ambiguity in either presenting the findings or representativeness of the findings. The designed report must be formulated, keeping the reader and the researcher's capabilities in mind. The author must follow a widely mandated and followed protocol for reporting and referencing in the report. The reporting needs to be objective and simple rather than complex and opinionated.
- Visual relief for the written can be provided through figures, tables and graphs. These simple and yet effective means of representing the data are made simpler and more variegated today with the help of computer and graphic technology.
- The researcher at times might need to verbally present the research study. These presentation sessions need to be brief and crisp, with the thrust being more on the methodology and findings. Communicating and presenting the research results is both a skill and an art and the richness of the research findings needs to be appropriately shared with the interested listeners in a manner best suited to their individual needs.

KEY TERMS

- Appendices
- Bibliography
- Brief report
- Business report
- Data arrays
- Detailed report
- Endnotes
- Executive summary
- Flipcharts
- Footnote
- Geographic representation
- Glossary of terms
- Handouts
- Letter of authorization
- Letter of transmittal
- Line and curve graph
- Phrasing protocol
- Preliminary section
- Research framework
- Research report
- Slides
- SLR
- Stratum charts
- Study background
- Survey report
- Technical report
- Working paper

CHAPTER REVIEW QUESTIONS

Objective Type Questions

State whether the following statements are true (T) or false (F).

1. In case the study hypotheses are disproved one need not write the research report.
2. The letter of transmittal is written at the commencement of the study.
3. The tone of the letter of transmittal is informal.
4. Executive summary of the report gives a short description of the impetus behind the study.
5. Survey reports do not make use of secondary data.
6. Technical reports are meant for technical heads in an organization.
7. The major emphasis in a working paper is on the methodology of the study.
8. Endnotes include all the supportive documents used to prepare the report.
9. Annotated bibliography has small snippets about the citations made in the report.
10. Selected bibliography refers to the referred articles which are from selective and prestigious journals and sources.
11. In a bibliography one gives the name of the person first, followed by the surname.
12. In the footnote one gives the name of the person first, followed by the surname.
13. The arrangement of data in a table is usually done in descending order.
14. SLR refers to the lens of the device used to make graphs and charts.
15. While making a graph, care must be taken to put the causal variable on the X-axis.
16. The ideal number of lines in a chart is 10.
17. The area between the lines in a stratum chart represents the volume of the factors represented there.
18. Histograms show both positive and negative patterns on the same graph in the shape of bars.
19. Histograms assume normality of the distribution.
20. The thumb rule for oral presentation of findings is ideally not to go beyond 20 minutes.

Conceptual Questions

1. Discuss in detail the steps that a researcher needs to follow to formulate a good research report. Do the criteria become different for different kinds of reports? Explain with examples.
2. What should be the ideal structure of a research report? What are the elements of the structure defined by you?
3. What are the guidelines for effective report writing? Illustrate with suitable examples.
4. 'Visual representations of results are best understood by a reader, thus special care must be taken for this formulation.' Examine the truth of this statement by giving suitable examples.
5. What are the guidelines a researcher must follow for graphical and tabular representation of the research results?

6. What are the guidelines for effectively presenting the research results through oral presentation? How can a researcher make his presentation more effective? What are the audio-visual aids available for the purpose?
7. What is the difference between the following:
   (a) Brief report and long report
   (b) Line charts and pie charts
   (c) Technical and business report
   (d) Geographic representation and pictograms

Application Questions

1. Find a technical and business report from your library or on the internet and examine the contents of the report against what has been discussed in the chapter. What deviations did you find from the stated structure? What do you think could have been the reason for this?
2. Examine online research reports available and evaluate the process of reporting by them. Do you think that the structure followed by them is effective and efficient? Comment.
3. There are a number of sites available for educating a researcher on making presentations. Study the methodology suggested by these and prepare a presentation of not more than 20 minutes to share with your class colleagues.

Appendix – 21.1: SAMPLE REPORT (BRIEF VERSION)

Marketing of organic food products in the Delhi market

Prepared for Dr Ms V Krishna
Nirmal Corporation
January 2005

by
Jigyasa Associates
Research Services
Sabarmati Dham
Mumbai - 119988

CONFIDENTIAL
Only for limited circulation

Executive Summary

Organic pulses, cereals and spices are more in demand as compared to the other products. X brand has maximum sale and close to it is Y. Retailing is not done professionally. Organic food products (OFP) consumption is confined to rich people only as it is quite expensive. Retailers think that OFP demand will grow by 10 to 50 per cent. Organic sale has been picking up in the last two years but the proportion of organic demand is still low. However, wheat atta, wheat dalia and Rajma (brown and white) have maximum demand. Consumers demand quality assurance and thus branded products are preferred. Organic consumers are more concerned about the safety of food.

Potential retail market will grow if the retailers are educated about OFP and if OFP will be made available easily. If media is used more extensively for creating awareness about OFP with health benefits in focus, potential consumer markets will grow much faster than they are doing today. Quality assurance and easy availability are the key issues for potential consumers. Doctors, dieticians and chefs can be used as ambassadors for increasing awareness and promoting OFP as they believe that the nutrition value of OFP is better.

Introduction

The present study focuses on marketing of organically grown agricultural produce and products. With growing awareness and concern for the environment and health, it is only a matter of time before the number of the consumers who prefer organic produce grows by leaps and bounds with not enough supply for the same. Thus, it is a highly lucrative and a potential market, and there is an urgent need to explore the current organic market and assess its growth potential. The second aim of the research is to focus on the marketing strategies required to meet the organic demand. The organic awareness and market are predominantly in the urban metros, Delhi being one of them, thus the research is confined to the Delhi NCR region.

Objectives and Scope of the Study

To study the existing organic market: This would involve categorizing the organic products available in Delhi into grain, snacks, herbs, pickles, squashes, and fruits and vegetables; estimating the demand pattern of various products for each of the categories and to understand the marketing strategies adopted by different players for promoting and propagating organic products.

Consumer diagnostic research: This would entail studying the existing consumer profile, i.e., perception and attitudes towards organic products and purchase and consumption patterns.

Methodology

Information areas as relevant for the study are discussed as follows:

***Organic food products (OFP*):** What are formally defined as OFP, what are the; certification procedures; what are the production estimates and what is the nature of government and private support (if any).

Organic market: An analysis of the major players in the NCR in terms of background information, products available, sales figures or indications, marketing strategy, channels of distribution, and market composition.

Organic Consumers: With reference to their demographic profile, lifestyle patterns, attitudes towards health and importance of nutrition, awareness and perception about OFP products, Grocery purchase, OFP purchase/purchase intentions, OFP benefits/attributes sought, OFP purchase decision-making, and OFP consumption as well as availability of OFP.

Sample

The organic consumers (OCs) were also divided into three strata. The consumers were from the NCR, i.e., Delhi, Noida and Gurgaon. The sample was more biased towards Delhi as the researchers felt that the availability of the OFP was more in Delhi than in the suburbs. Focus group discussions were conducted for OCs. One was conducted in Nirmal's office and another in Noida to collect qualitative information. Number of the participants was according to the availability. A total of 100 OCs were interviewed through questionnaire for a quantitative data collection.

The Questionnaire

The questionnaire begins with identification details of the respondent. It is divided into four parts. Part A consists of 23 statements about the respondent's lifestyle and attitude. All statements are on a 5 point Likert scale.

Part B has Question 1-6 related to grocery purchase behaviour. Question 7 ascertains respondent's attitude towards grocery. Question 8 is a product vs type, brand, frequency, and quantity of purchase. Questions 1–6 are multiple-choice questions while 7 is on a semantic differential scale. Question 8 is ratio scaled. (Presented in Appendix 1).

Part C measures awareness of OFP. Questions 1, 2 and 4 are related to duration, proportion and grocery budget implications of OFP. Question 3 requires the respondent to name and evaluate his/her OFP retailer. Question 5 is related to satisfaction with OFP. Question 6 is related to problems with purchase and usage of OFP. Questions 4 and 5 are multiple-choice questions. Question 3 is on a Likert scale. Questions 1, 2 and 6 are open-ended.

Part D consists of 29 statements about the respondent's post-consumption perception about OFP.

All statements are on a 5-point Likert scale. Sample questions from questionnaire are available in the annexure.

Study findings

Though awareness about organic food in Delhi is increasing, supply is often sporadic and there is no systematic data bank of organic outlets from where the consumers can buy their monthly ration or where they can treat a friend to an environment-friendly menu. The market comprises both the organized sector, which is largely composed of the certified branded players, and the unorganized sector, a mixed bag. That is, it has the certified players who do not have regular distribution channels and rely mostly on fairs and meets, and secondly, the non-certified unbranded players who operate more on faith.

Available to the consumer is a gamut of products that cover almost the entire food grocery basket. The various product categories selling in the Delhi market are:

Cereals: Atta-wheat, maize and ragi, Amaranth-plain, popped and breakfast cereal, wheat dalia and wheat puffed, jhangar, ragi and maize.

Rice: Kasturi, red, kelas, sela, ramjaran, hansraj, unpolished, basmati (different varieties).

Pulses: Arhar, bhatt, moong dhuli, moong saboot, masoor saboot, malka masoor, naurangi, kulath, urad dhuli, urad whole, kabli chana, chana daal, rajma (all varieties) and lobiya.

Snacks: Bread, cookies, biscuits and namkeens.

Preserves and pickles: Squashes, pickles, jams and chutneys

Herbs: Oregano, lemongrass, thyme, etc.

Tea: Herbal, normal and flavoured.

Fruits and vegetables: These are only seasonal fruits and vegetables as the shelf life for the products is low and the demand for the product is not sufficient to warrant cold stocking.

The consumer responses to organic product revealed the following:

Product benefits

1. 64 per cent think that OFPs are important for family diet, whereas 21 per cent do not think so and 15 per cent did not have any opinion.
2. 96 per cent agreed that organic farming is necessary to manage soil.
3. 49 per cent of the OCs relates OFPs with health.
4. Majority of OCs think that OFP are less contaminated and so good for health and for growing children.
5. Comparing taste of OFPs with non OFPs, only 23 per cent think that OFPs are tastier whereas rest of them are not able to differentiate taste.
6. However, 81 per cent think that the nutrition value of OFP is higher.
7. It is a general notion that cooking organic ingredients takes more time.
   According to our finding, 85 per cent do not think so only 11 per cent think it tastes differently. Most of the respondents find it easy to cook OFPs and are happy with the look of OFPs.
8. 27 per cent of the OC families have developed a taste for OFPs in a short period of time.
9. 66 per cent OCs consume OFPs to maintain their good looks and physique and 48 per cent of the families were positive about the extra expenses on OFPs.
10. Most of OCs consume OFPs for health, not because of fashion.
11. 62 per cent recommend OFPs to others but only 20 per cent of them support any organization promoting the organic cause.

Product negatives

1. 85 per cent think OFPs are expensive.
2. Only 33 per cent think they can differentiate OFPs and non OFPs.

Marketing insights

1. 81 per cent preferred frequent home delivery, while 93 per cent prefer to buy according to their needs.
2. 94 per cent agree that OFPs should be branded, and 47 per cent indicate brand loyalty.
3. Only 14 per cent think that OFPs are easily available while the rest of them have difficulty in acquiring OFPs.

Conclusions

The current research conducted in the NCR conveyed some significant findings:

- Majority of the market players are either social activists, or have passion for OFP due to their benefits. None of the organic brands are managed or marketed commercially.
- Findings of the study also indicate that the size of organic market is very small. Even though the products have been there for more than a decade in the domestic retail market, they have only picked up largely in the last one or two years. With growing popularity of OFP and bigger profits, every year, new entrants are joining the organic bandwagon. For example, FabIndia, an apparel retailer in Delhi, has started selling OFP from their shops. Thus, organic market has been growing both vertically and laterally. A lot of lifestyle stores like Life Springs, Good Things and Food Plus, recognizing future trends, have created shelf space for OFPs. This has resulted in competition among the few leading players and, thus, managing of the organic market has become important for everyone. Present marketing strategies used by the marketeers are based upon market demand and customer relations. Stocking and selling of the item depends upon demand. Customer relationship is built up by making them members of the organization or registration for required services. However, things are changing very fast and it is only a matter of time before a large organization enters the organic market and works on building a competitive edge. Thus, in order to retain the leading position in the market, one would need to develop strategic competitiveness by providing value to the customer.

Appendix – 21.2: SAMPLE FROM THE QUESTIONNAIRE

Part–B*

Grocery Purchase

1. Where do you purchase grocery? **(Could be ≥ 1)**
   - ☐ Doorstep vendor
   - ☐ Neighbourhood *kirana* store
   - ☐ Semi-whole sellers
   - ☐ Departmental stores
   - ☐ Specialty stores
   - ☐ Any other ___________
2. How is it purchased? **(Could be ≥ 1)**
   - ☐ Personal visit
   - ☐ Telephone (home delivery)
   - ☐ Domestic help
   - ☐ Internet
   - ☐ Any other ___________
3. What are the preferred days for shopping?
   - ☐ Weekdays
   - ☐ Weekends
   - ☐ Any day
4. What is the preferred time for shopping?
   - ☐ Before 11.00 hrs
   - ☐ 11.00–17.00 hrs.
   - ☐ 17.00–21.00 hrs
   - ☐ Any time
5. How much time is spent on grocery shopping?
   - ☐ <1 hr
   - ☐ 1–1½ hrs
   - ☐ 1 ½–2 hrs.
   - ☐ >2 hrs.
6. What is the preferred mode of payment?
   - ☐ Cash
   - ☐ Credit card
   - ☐ Both
7. Grocery shopping is:

   Please rate your overall shopping experience on a 5-point scale

	1	2	3	4	5	
Expensive	☐	☐	☐	☐	☐	Cheap
Useful	☐	☐	☐	☐	☐	Useless
Uninteresting	☐	☐	☐	☐	☐	Interesting
Enjoyable	☐	☐	☐	☐	☐	Unenjoyable

*As stated in the report text, there were four parts of the final questionnaire. This annexure consists of a few questions from Part-B of the questionnaire.

Answers to Objective Type Questions

1. False	2. False	3. True	4. False	5. True
6. False	7. True	8. True	9. True	10. False
11. False	12. True	13. False	14. False	15. True
16. False	17. True	18. False	19. True	20. True

REFERENCES

Ahuja, M, Katherine M Chudoba and C J Kacmar. 'IT Road Warriors: Balancing Work-Facilty Conflict, Job Autonomy and Work Overload to Mitigate Turnover Intentions', *MIS Quarterly* 31 (2007): 1–17.

Cotton, J and J Tuttle. 'Employee turnover: a meta analysis and review with implications for research', *Academy of Management Review* (11) 1986: 55–70.

Finegold, D, S Mohrman and G M Spreitzer. 'Age effects on the predictors of technical workers' commitment and willingness to turnover', *Journal of Organisational Behavior* 23 (5) 2002: 655–674

Igbaria M, and J H Greenhaus. 'Determinants of MIS employees turnover intentions: A structural equation model', *Communications of the ACM,* (35:2) 1992: 35–49.

Mobley, W H, S O Horner and A T Hollingsworth. 'An evaluation of precursors of hospital employee turnover,' *Journal of Applied Psychology,* 63 (4) 1978: 408–414.

Zeffane, R A and F A Gul. 'Determinants of employee turnover intentions: An exploration of a contingency (P-O) model', *International Journal of Employment Studies* 3 (2) 1985: 91–116.

BIBLIOGRAPHY

Boyd, Harper W Jr, Ralph Westfall and Stanley F Stasch. *Marketing Research: Text and Cases,* 7th edn. Richard D. Irwin, Inc, 2002.

Department of Agriculture and Rural Development (2000), 'Organic production, a viable alternative for Northern Ireland'. Available at http://www.organic-research.com/news/2000/2000112.htm.

Dryer, Jerry. 'The Organic Option', *Dairy Foods*. 105 (9) 2004: 24.

Dwivedi, R S. *Research Methods in Behavioural Sciences.* New Delhi: Macmillan India Ltd, 1997.

GoI (Government of India). *Report of the Working Group on Organic and Bio Dynamic Farming* for the 10th Five-Year Plan. New Delhi: Planning Commission, 2001.

Kothari, C R. *Research Methodology: Methods and Techniques,* 2nd edn. New Delhi: Wiley Eastern Limited, 1990.

Malhotra, Naresh K. *Marketing Research – An Applied Orientation*, 3rd edn. New Delhi: Pearson Education, 2002.

Pannerselvam R. *Research Methodology*. New Delhi: Prentice Hall of India Pvt Ltd, 2004.

Tull, Donald S and Del I Hawkins. *Marketing Research: Measurement and Method,* 6th edn. New Delhi: Prentice Hall of India Pvt. Ltd, 1993.

Zikmund, William G. *Business Research Methods,* 5th edn. Dryden Press, Harcourt Brace College Publishers, 1997.

Comprehensive Cases

CASE 1: MANAGING BALANCE IN WORK AND LIFE

Work-life balance is an important matter of consideration in the professional world, both for men and women. However, it is felt that the concept has a special significance from the perspective of women professionals. A number of research studies have examined the role of women in management by evaluating the work done on equality, differences and stereotyping. Most studies point towards gender discrimination and role stress. It has been suggested that in examining the relationship between work and personal life, gender is a significant moderating variable. It is found that even though women's participation in the workforce is widely accepted, majority of the caring responsibilities of the family lie with the fairer sex. Though this phenomenon has global relevance, the application of this is more significant for a developing country like India.

As a country surges towards development and enlightenment, the social structure becomes more open and progressive in providing equal opportunities to all members of the society. In India, this development has resulted in better opportunities for Indian women in terms of education and employment opportunities. With exposure to the Western world and a desire for better quality of life, educated women are entering the industrial, professional and academic sectors. Thus, statistics show a large number of dual-career families. However, the similarity with the Western world stops here as the work-family dilemmas faced by the Indian woman are starkly different from that of her Western counterpart. More often than not, this results in lowered career aspirations for women professionals as compared to men. Else, the woman relies on extended familial support or hired domestic help to manage and balance the work-personal pressures. There are also indications of individual concessions that the women sometimes get at an informal level from empathetic supervisors, but this is exceptional and not a norm. Organizations are becoming more sensitive to the needs of women professionals and make systematic policy changes to assist them in maintaining the balance between their professional and personal goals. However, a lot more needs to be done to cognize Indian corporate houses of the need for gender empathetic policies required for half the professional workforce of the country.

The Research Study

Thus, it was decided to undertake a study to try and comprehend not only the pressures faced by professional women in contemporary India, but also the pressure on organizations to attract and retain women in the workforce. The changing socio-cultural balances in India and the increase in the number of working women make the issue more relevant for the study.

Work-life balance needs to be studied from two perspectives. One would need to focus on work-related factors and their impact on family life, while the second perspective could focus on family-focused factors and their effect on the work life. It was perceived that this study would provide insights for the integration of these two perspectives in investigating both the work and family pressures and their influence on the performance of working women.

Two distinct segments of working women were considered for the study—school teachers and BPO employees. The reason for choosing these were that working women in these two sectors have altogether different demands, which require different approaches to maintain a healthy work and personal life.

In India, just like in other countries around the world, teachers are required to have specialized education and professional certification. They are supposed to cope with the changing curriculum and growth in knowledge. The situation with respect to the demand for teachers is not uniform across different states in India. With population growing apace and the performance in terms of children's participation in schooling far from satisfactory, the demand is expected to grow even further.

At present there are 2515 primary schools, 635 middle schools and 1712 secondary and senior secondary schools in Delhi (Economic Survey of Delhi 2005–06).

The number of school teachers in primary and pre-primary is as follows (Economic Survey of Delhi 2005–06): total (93,100), primary/pre-primary (24,744), middle (9,210), sec./sr sec (59,146).

Business process outsourcing, or BPO, is the contracting of specific business tasks to a third party service provider. It is usually a cost-saving measure. The rapid expansion in the scope of BPO has been accompanied by an equally rapid adoption across a range of vertical industries. The Indian ITES-BPO segment has witnessed a steady growth and is expected to grow exponentially.

Nearly fifty per cent of BPO workers are women. The participation of women in the BPO workforce is seen as a critical enabling factor for the continuing growth of the industry. A BPO worker's job is characterized by shift duties which can extend to up to twelve hours a day, and the shift can change at short notice. The problem is more for women working in night shifts and the long, irregular hours take a toll on the mental and physical health of the employees.

School teachers have an early start and early end to the workday whereas it is diametrically opposite for BPO workers. The teachers' job is a day job like that of a banker or chartered accountant, whereas the BPO worker's job is similar to that of nurses, airline staff and hotel employees. Thus, by selecting two different respondent populations we hoped to cover the entire stretch of professions that Indian women are likely to pursue.

Case Questions

Chapter 1

1. Business research can be typically classified into various categories. What kind of research is being advocated in the above case? Give reasons for your classification.
2. In case you were to expand the scope of research, how would you do so? Explain in detail.
3. While pursuing this further, what criteria do you advocate for the researcher to keep in mind?
4. Formulate a research proposal for the above situation and include all the relevant sections with clearly defined justifications/arguments for the same.

Chapter 2

1. What is the decision maker's problem in this case?
2. Based on the steps defined in the chapter, convert the decision problem into a research problem.
3. Identify all the elements of the problem identified by you in terms of unit of analysis, variables and the coordinates of the study.
4. Can you formulate a theoretical model or framework to assist in developing a perspective on the research problem?
5. Formulate three research questions for the problem and develop the working hypotheses for the same.

Chapter 3

1. Can an exploratory research design be advocated in the above situation? How?
2. Would it be possible to conduct a descriptive research study here? Which one would you recommend—cross-sectional or longitudinal? Why?

Chapter 4

1. Work-life balance is assumed to be influenced by the following factors: job autonomy, work-family conflict, organizational commitment, work exhaustion, perceived workload and fairness of reward. Is

it possible to carry out a causal research here? Which design would you recommend here? Identify the variables, the test units and the hypothesized framework for the study.

2. What are the factors that could impact the internal and external validity of the experiment? How can we go about controlling them?
3. Suppose a BPO introduces three different service conditions for its women professionals, ranging from regular shifts (A) to work-from-home (B) and flexi-time (C). Women are to be classified in the age group of 18–22, 23–26 and 27–35 years. To measure the work–life balance score under these conditions, which research design would you recommend here? Why? Identify hypotheses, variables, test units and provide the framework for investigation.

Chapter 5

1. Can syndicate data sources be useful here? Why/why not?
2. What government publications would be of use here? Can the information obtained be authenticated from alternative methods/sources? How?
3. What academic data can be accessed for the study? What could be the possible source of this data?
4. For all the above questions, how would you establish the credibility of the information obtained?

Chapter 6

1. To understand the concept of work–life balance, it is essential to conduct a qualitative research on the identified population. Which qualitative techniques would you suggest?
2. Can we use sociometry for studying any of the identified variables? Which one and why?
3. Design an interview guide to be used for discussion with a Psychotherapist to get her view on the current status on work-life balance? Give reasons for the questions designed by you. Conduct a one-to-one interview base on this and summarize your findings indicating some possible recommended solutions.
4. Can any of the projective techniques be used for the study? Design some questions based on the technique identified by you.
5. Can you use observations for your study? What would be the limitations/shortcomings of this method?

Chapter 7

1. For measuring the constructs under study, design 10 questions using:
   (a) Itemized rating scales
   (b) Graphic rating scales
   (c) Rank order scales
   (d) Comparative rating scales
2. Out of Likert scale, semantic differential scale and constant sum scale, which scale would you advocate for the study? Why?
3. How will you measure the reliability of the scale identified by you?
4. How will you measure the validity of the scale identified by you?

Chapter 8

1. Examine the following questions in terms of the study variables. Can the questions be better structured? How?

(a)	Do you have job autonomy in your organization?	Yes/no
(b)	I am overloaded and stressed in my job.	Sometimes/often/never
(c)	Don't you think the organization is overtaxing you?	Yes/no
(d)	I belong to	Upper class/middle class/lower class
(e)	You have a mother-in-law and a help who take care of the family when you are working.	Yes/no
(f)	There is gender bias in most organizations in India.	Definitely/maybe/not sure

2. Design a questionnaire to be used for the study. Would you devise different questions for the two identified groups? Why/why not?

Chapter 9

1. Who would be the identified population to be studied here?
2. What sampling frame(s) can you use for this?
3. What sampling technique would you recommend and why?
4. What sampling and non-sampling errors will you attempt to minimize in the study? How?
5. It is estimated that nearly 50 per cent of BPO workers are women. Determine how large a sample size should be taken for a study of BPO workers with an error margin of 6 per cent with 90 per cent confidence.

Chapter 10

1. Prepare a code book for the questionnaire attached in Appendix A–1.
2. Conduct a preliminary analysis of the data (SPSS data file: Comp Case A – (BPO Data); Comp Case B – (School Teacher Data) and use the suggested techniques in the chapter to represent the results.
3. Compute the subscale scores for each of the seven parameters tested in the study (SPSS data file: Comp Case A – (BPO Data); Comp Case B – (School Teacher Data), namely, Job Autonomy (Question 3A), Work-family Conflict (Question 3B), Organizational Commitment (Question 3C), Work Exhaustion (Question 3D), Perceived Work Overload (Question 3E), Fairness of Rewards (Question 3F) and Turnover Intentions (Question 3G).

Chapter 11

1. Prepare the frequency distribution tables for components of questions on Job Autonomy (Question 3A), Work-family Conflict (Question 3B), Organizational Commitment (Question 3C), Work Exhaustion (Question 3D), Perceived Work Overload (Question 3E), Fairness of Rewards (Question 3F) and Turnover Intentions (Question 3G) and interpret the results of the frequency table. Conduct the exercise separately for the two segments (SPSS data file: Comp Case A – (BPO Data); Comp Case B – (School Teacher Data).
2. Divide the score of Question 3K into two groups—one which is able to maintain a perfect work–life balance and the other that is not able to maintain a perfect work–life balance and cross-tabulate it with the demographic variables like Age (Question 4), marital status (Question 5), Number of children (Question 6A), Age group of children (Question 6B), Family Type (Question 7A), Family Income Question (8B), Job Travelling Frequency (Question 9B) and Domestic help (Question 10). Compute the percentages in each of the cross-tables in the appropriate direction, interpret the results and write a summary of your findings. Conduct the exercise separately for the two segments (SPSS data file: Comp Case A – (BPO Data); Comp Case B – (School Teacher Data).

Chapter 12

1. Use the score of Question 3K of the questionnaire (SPSS data file: Comp Case A – (BPO Data); Comp Case B – (School Teacher Data) for BPO and school teacher and divide them into two groups of married and unmarried employees (see Question 5) and conduct an appropriate statistical test to examine whether the work–life balance differs in the two cases.
2. Repeat the above exercise by using Family Type (Question 7A) as the two groups (SPSS data file: Comp Case A – (BPO Data); Comp Case B – (School Teacher Data).

Chapter 13

In case of significant result, what further analysis would be carry out?

1. By using the score on work-life balance as dependent variable and each of the following variables as separate independent variables, conduct a one-way ANOVA for each of the cases below:
   - Age (Question 4)
   - Age group of children (Question 6B)
   - Family income (Question 8B)

State the null and alternative hypotheses and any assumption which may be appropriate for carrying out ANOVA. Conduct the exercise separately for the two segments (SPSS data file: Comp Case A – (BPO Data); Comp Case B – (School Teacher Data).

Chapter 14

1. Rework Question 2 of Chapter 11 by computing chi-square statistics in various cross-tables. State the appropriate hypotheses and test the same. In case the chi-square works out to be significant, go for further analysis by computing contingency coefficient or Cramer's V statistics (whichever is applicable, and interpret the tables. Conduct the exercise separately for the two segments. (SPSS data file: Comp Case A – (BPO Data); Comp Case B – (School Teacher Data).

Chapter 15

1. Treat the score on Question 3K (work–life balance as dependent variables and regress it on the aggregate values of the following variables: Job Autonomy (Question 3A), Work-family Conflict (Question 3B), Organizational Commitment (Question 3C), Work Exhaustion (Question 3D), Perceived Work Overload (Question 3E) and Fairness of Rewards (Question 3F).
2. Conduct the exercise separately for the entire sample and then for the two segments—BPO and school teachers—separately. (SPSS data file: Comp Case A – (BPO Data); Comp Case B – (School Teacher Data). What difference (if any) did you find in the three analyses? Interpret the results.

Chapter 16

1. You may note that Question 3A has four components; similarly 3B to 3G have various components. Conduct a factor analysis for the components of each question separately and examine whether you get only one factor (this is called confirmatory factor analysis). Conduct the exercise separately for the two segments (SPSS data file: Comp Case A – (BPO Data); Comp Case B – (School Teacher Data) and examine in how many cases it holds true.

Chapter 17

1. The variable turnover intention was divided into two groups (high turnover intentions and low turnover intentions). Treat this categorical variable as the dependent variable and use the aggregate score of the seven subscales (SPSS data file: Comp Case A – (BPO Data); Comp Case B – (School Teacher Data) as independent variable and build a discriminant model. Test statistically whether the discriminant model is significant and which of the independent variable are relatively more important in discriminating between the two groups. Examine the classificatory model and comment and interpret the results of the model.

Chapter 18

1. Conduct a cluster analysis using all the aggregate scores of the subscales (SPSS data file: Comp Case A – (BPOData); Comp Case B – (School Teacher Data). Using the hierarchical cluster analysis and, interpret the solution. Please note that the analysis is to be done separately for the two groups.
2. Conduct a three-cluster solution using Question 11 by the K-means cluster analysis technique. Interpret the solution. Name the clusters.
3. Using the demographic questions, formulate the cluster profiles and interpret the solution.
4. Question 3K has been recoded as high, medium and low work–life balance. Conduct a cross-tabulation between the cluster membership and work–life balance. Which group showed more balance? What do you think is the reason for this difference? Explain.

Chapter 19

1. Make a list of 10 private schools in your city. Now make a 10 × 10 matrix for carrying out a paired comparison test. Take a sample size of 15 private school teachers and 15 government school teachers and ask them to select from each pair:

- The school that any teacher would like to work in
- The school any parent would like to send their child to

Using the data prepare an MDS for each solution and interpret the solution. What was the similarity/dissimilarity between the two maps that you obtained? What do you think was the reason for this?

2. Make a list of 10 BPOs in your city. Take a sample size of 30 BPO employees and ask them to select from each pair. Now ask them to rank the BPOs in terms of the best one to work for. Using the data, prepare an MDS for the solution and interpret the solution.

Chapter 21

1. Write a report based on the entire process of research and analysis carried out for the 19 chapters.
2. What recommendations do you have for:
   (a) A school in your city in terms of facilitating/enhancing their employees' work-life balance
   (b) A BPO in your city in terms of facilitating/enhancing their employees work-life balance.

Appendix A-1: WORK–LIFE BALANCE QUESTIONNAIRE

1. Working as:

   BPO employee ☐ Teacher ☐

2. Name of the organization: ______________

3A. **JOB AUTONOMY**

Indicate the extent to which these statements reflect your feelings about your current job.

(1 = Strongly Disagree, 2 = Disagree, 3 = Somewhat Disagree, 4 = No Opinion, 5 = Somewhat Agree, 6 = Agree, 7 = Strongly Agree)

1. I control the content of my job. ☐
2. I have a lot of freedom to decide how I perform assigned tasks. ☐
3. I set my own schedule for completing assigned tasks. ☐
4. I have the authority to initiate projects at my job. ☐

3B. **WORK–FAMILY CONFLICT**

If you are not married and/or do not have children, you can choose to respond to these questions in terms of your life outside of work in general (for example, replace 'family' with 'friends' and think of your other commitments, such as gymnasiums, book clubs, or any other hobbies). Reverse.

(1 = Strongly Disagree, 2 = Disagree, 3 = Somewhat Disagree, 4 = No Opinion, 5 = Somewhat Agree, 6 = Agree, 7 = Strongly Agree)

1. The demands of my work interfere with my home and family life. ☐
2. The amount of time my job takes up makes it difficult to fulfil family responsibilities. ☐
3. Things I want to do at home do not get done because of the demands my job puts on me. ☐
4. My job causes strain that makes it difficult to fulfil family duties. ☐
5. Due to work-related duties, I have to make changes to my plans for family activities. ☐
6. I can't remember the last time I read—and finished—a book that I was reading purely for pleasure. ☐
7. I wish I had more time for some outside interests and hobbies. ☐
8. I am forced to do certain things to save my job because many people (children/partners/parents) depend on me for support. ☐

3C. ORGANIZATIONAL COMMITMENT

(1 = Strongly Disagree, 2 = Disagree, 3 = Somewhat Disagree, 4 = No Opinion, 5 = Somewhat Agree, 6 = Agree, 7 = Strongly Agree)

Think about your organization. Indicate the extent to which you agree or disagree with these statements.

1. I am willing to put in effort beyond the norm for the success of the organization.
2. For me, this is the best of all possible organizations for which to work.
3. I am extremely glad to have chosen this organization to work for over other organizations.
4. This organization inspires the very best in the way of job performance.
5. I show by my actions that I really care about the fate of this organization.

3D. WORK EXHAUSTION

(1 = Strongly Disagree, 2 = Disagree, 3 = Somewhat Disagree, 4 = No Opinion, 5 = Somewhat Agree, 6 = Agree, 7 = Strongly Agree)

1. I feel emotionally drained from my work.
2. I feel used up at the end of the workday.
3. I feel fatigued when I get up in the morning and have to face another day on the job.
4. I feel burned out from my work.
5. I feel physically weak due to the pressure of my job.
6. My immunity to illness has reduced since I started working.
7. I can't remember the last time I was able to find the time to take a day off to do something fun— something just for me.
8. Since I started working I feel emotionally drained.

3E. PERCEIVED WORK OVERLOAD

(1 = Strongly Disagree, 2 = Disagree, 3 = somewhat Disagree, 4 = No Opinion, 5 = Somewhat Agree, 6 = Agree, 7= Strongly Agree)

1. I feel that the number of requests I deal with is more than expected.
2. I feel that the amount of work I do interferes with how well it is done.
3. I feel rushed to complete the job
4. I feel pressured by my job responsibilities.
5. It sometimes feels as though I never even have a chance to catch my breath before I have to move on to the next project/crisis.
6. I usually bring work home with me.
7. I've missed many of my family's important events because of work-related time pressures and responsibilities.

3F. FAIRNESS OF REWARDS

(1 = Strongly Disagree, 2 = Disagree, 3 = somewhat Disagree, 4 = No Opinion, 5 = Somewhat Agree, 6 = Agree, 7 = Strongly Agree)

1. My organization has processes that ensure that all team members are treated fairly and equitably.
2. I work in an environment in which good procedures make things fair and impartial.
3. In my workplace, sound practices exist that help ensure fair and unbiased treatment of all team members.
4. Fairness to employees is built into how issues are handled in my work environment.
5. In my organization sex discrimination is non-existent.
6. All members of the team are given equal opportunities for growth in terms transfers/ promotions.

3G. TURNOVER INTENTIONS

(1 = Strongly Disagree, 2 = Disagree, 3 = Somewhat Disagree, 4 = No Opinion, 5 = Somewhat Agree, 6 = Agree, 7 = Strongly Agree)

1. There is no way I would be working at the same company this time next year. ☐
2. I would take positive steps during the next year to secure a job at a different company. ☐
3. There is no chance that I will be with this company five years from now. ☐
4. I will probably look for a job at a different company in the coming year. ☐
5. Sometimes I feel as though I've lost sight of what I am and why I chose this job/career. ☐

3H. According to you, what practices are being followed by you CURRENTLY to maintain work-life balance?

1. ______________________________
2. ______________________________
3. ______________________________
4. ______________________________
5. ______________________________

3I. According to you, what are the initiatives you would take in FUTURE to improve your work-life balance?

1. ______________________________
2. ______________________________
3. ______________________________
4. ______________________________
5. ______________________________

3J. According to you, what are the initiatives YOUR COMPANY should take to help you maintain your work-life balance?

1. ______________________________
2. ______________________________
3. ______________________________
4. ______________________________
5. ______________________________

3K. I am able to maintain a perfect work-life balance.

Strongly agree	☐	Agree	☐
Somewhat agree	☐	Somewhat disagree	☐
Disagree	☐	Strongly disagree	☐

Personal Details:

4. Age:

20–25	☐	26–35	☐
31–35	☐	36–40	☐
41–45	☐	Above 45	☐

5. Marital Status:

Married ☐
Unmarried ☐
Other ☐

6A. Children

None	☐	One	☐
Two	☐	More than two	☐

6B. Please indicate how many children are there in each age group.

Age group	No. of children
0–5	
6–15	
16–25	
Above 25	

7A. Family type:

Joint ☐ Nuclear ☐

7B. Number of family members ______

8A. Income per month in ₹ (self)

Below 10,000 ☐ 10,001–25,000 ☐
25,001–50,000 ☐ Above 50,000 ☐

8B. Income per month in ₹ (Family)

Below 10,000 ☐ 10,001–25,000 ☐
25,001–50,000 ☐ Above 50,000 ☐

9A. Spouse profession: (answer if applicable)

Service ☐
Self-employed ☐
Others ☐

9B. Job travelling: (Frequency)

1–2 times a week ☐ Not at all ☐
1–2 times a fortnight ☐ Stationed in a different city ☐
1–2 times a month ☐

10. Domestic help

Full time ☐
Part time ☐
None ☐

11. Work Experience:

(A) In present job ☐
(B) Total work experience ☐

Instructions for Filling up the Questionnaire

1. To be filled up by women working in BPO/teaching in schools.
2. Name and phone number are not mandatory.
3. Please answer Question 3B to 3G by indicating a number from 1–7 (1 = strongly disagree to 7 = strongly agree) or 8 if not applicable.
4. Question 6 (Parts A and B) to be filled up by married women only.
5. Question 9 (Parts A and B) to be filled up by married women only.

CASE 2: TUPPERWARE: SERVICING THE INDIAN HOUSEWIFE

Tupperware is the world's largest plastic food container company. Marketing its products in over 100 countries across the globe, it is today a household name in every corner of the world. The company's products have been listed in the *Guinness Book of World Records* as one of the best inventions of the 20th century.

Tupperware India: Tupperware India Pvt. Ltd is a wholly owned subsidiary of US-based Tupperware Corporation, the world's leading manufacturer of high quality plastic food storage and serving containers. The company started its operations in India in 1996 and has been recognized as the fastest growing market by Tupperware Worldwide. Its products were launched in Delhi in November 1996, followed by Mumbai in April 1997 and Bangalore and Chennai in October the same year. Pune, Chandigarh and Hyderabad followed in 1998.

Tupperware Marketing Strategy: The sales promotions are one of the key focus areas for the company to push the sales. The company has regular sales promotion programmes for the sales force and consumers. These promotions are mainly new products sold at special price and various discounts attached to the minimum order. Also, there are various promotion schemes to push recruiting activity of housewives who serve as direct selling agents. These incentives are over and above the normal commissions of the channel partners. With the objective of accelerating Tupperware's rapid growth and which meant reaching out to a wider consumer base and increasing brand awareness, the company worked on a strategy that essentially involved going 'retail'.

New Business Tactics: Some of the marketing initiatives by the company with the objective of widening the consultant base/increasing consumer awareness, in addition to the party plan system, are as under:

The Caravan Programme: Under the Integrated Direct Access strategy, the Caravan Programme, the first of its kind by any direct selling company, is an endeavour to increase the brand awareness, generate leads for recruiting and reaching new customers. The caravan, a display of Tupperware products manned by its consultants, has been travelling across various cities and states recruiting new people. Each distributor gets three days to man the caravan, which is then rotated through the other consultants.

The Showcase Programme: In addition, a 'Showcase Programme' was initiated in June 2002 and temporary kiosks were placed at Ansal Plaza mall in Delhi, and Ebony stores in Delhi, Noida and Mumbai. The company has plans to open similar showcases in other parts of the country as well.

Products

The company classified its products under various categories depending upon the purpose they serve. The main product lines of the company are grouped as follows:

- Dry Storage – Modular Mates, Canisters, etc.
- Tableware – Bread Server, Butter Dish, Curry Server, etc.
- Food Preparation – Masala Keeper, Magic Flow, Quick Shakes
- Microwave – Soup Mugs, Crystalwave Medium
- Refrigerator – Cool n Fresh Series, Wondlier Bowls, Ice Trays
- Lunch & Outdoors – Tumblers, Lunch Boxes
- Canister – Store-all-Canisters, Oasis Jug
- Classics – Classic Slim Launch, Tropical Cups.

Tupperware India has specially designed selected products tailormade for the Indian homemaker to fulfil the unique needs of the Indian kitchen. 'Cinnamon microwave dish' in dark blue colour keeps in mind the haldi stains, 'masala storage box', which can store up to seven dry spices, and a range of *thalis, katoris, roti-keeper*, pickle container and oil containers have already been introduced in the market. The products combine aesthetics and functionality. They are ingeniously designed offering versatility and convenience. Tupperware products have won several design awards worldwide. The products are manufactured with 100 per cent food grade virgin plastic and offer a lifetime guarantee against chipping, cracking or breaking under normal non-commercial use. They are light, unbreakable, non-toxic and odourless. They also have special airtight and liquidtight seals, which lock in freshness and flavour. The products are not only designed elegantly and add functionality but also add vibrancy and colour to any kitchen and dining table. The products are available in soothing colours such as red, blue, pastels, and green to match kitchen décor and consumer preference.

Distribution Strategy: Tupperware products are sold to consumers through a direct marketing channel, the Home Party Plan. Tupperware items are not sold through retail distribution channels. In the Home Party Plan, consultants predominantly recruit housewives and working women to hold Tupperware parties in their homes or workplaces. The consultants have a business relationship with the independent distributors and are recruited by the managers. Tupperware India has 75 distributors, 1500 managers and approximately 35,000 consultants spread across India.

The Home Party Plan is a method of selling products to the consumer using direct selling techniques. Tupperware pioneered the Home Party Plan. However, other companies also engage in direct selling, such as Amway, Avon Products Inc., Oriflame and Modicare among others. Tupperware has cultivated the Home Party Plan into a highly successful method for the selling its products.

Consumers are solicited by hostesses to attend a 'Tupper Party.' The consumers normally tend to be friends, neighbours, or co-workers of the hostess. The hostess is given gifts, commonly referred to as 'thank you gifts', for hosting the party. These gifts vary depending upon the volume of Tupperware products sold during the party; if more products are sold during the party, a larger gift is rewarded to the hostess.

At the party a consultant or manager or, occasionally, a distributor will show products and their uses to the consumers. The consumer places order for Tupperware products at the party with the consultant. The consultant collects the order and passes it on to the managers. Distributors collect the orders from their managers, consolidate it on a weekly basis and place the order to Tupperware India.

Tupperware distributors are not stockholding distributors and, thus, do not maintain significant inventory. At most, they keep a few pieces of only the fast moving items. Every Monday, each distributor holds an 'assembly'. Consultants come to the assembly and put in their orders. The distributor consolidates and places an order to Tupperware India. After receiving the orders, consultants then deliver the products to the hostess, who further hands them over to the customers.

The distribution manager is responsible for controlling the inventory levels and in that role works closely with the marketing team. Tupperware India has 13 warehouses spread across India. The distribution manager is responsible for maintaining adequate stock in these warehouses keeping in mind the historical demand in the region and the plan given by the marketing team. He is also responsible for efficient planning of logistics and arranges for the transportation of goods to various warehouses. The transportation of goods from the warehouse to the various distributors is arranged by the respective warehouse.

Reason for the Success of Party Plan

- All in all, the Party Plan creates an informal platform for interested housewives to get together and experience the joy of Tupperware.
- Further, the Party Plan clicks excellently in India because it fits in with the urban and semi-urban culture of 'kitty parties'.

Advantages of the Party System are Two-fold

- It does not put pressure on the hostess — she isn't forced to become a consultant if she does not want to.
- It allows the company to physically demonstrate the utility of its premium-priced products apart from creating consumer awareness.

Tupperware Distributor – Manager – Consultant Winning Combination

Tupperware follows a single-level marketing channel concept to distribute its products. The various channel partners in the order are as under

Company → Distributor → Manager → Consultant

Tupperware follows the single-level compensation structure where everything earned is performance-based, right from the consultant to the manager to the distributor.

Channel Partner	Remuneration
Distributor	Basic commission, plus variable sales margin that increases in direct proportion to the volume of sales.
Manager typically operating with a team of six consultants	Standard consultant's 25 per cent plus a 3 per cent commission on her unit's sales.
Consultant	Standard commission structure of 25 per cent based on sales.

The consultants are at the lowest level in the distribution chain, approximately 35,000 in number and spread across 35 cities. Anyone can become a Tupperware consultant because it is an investment-free opportunity. They are 'the Tupperware ladies.'

The next level is that of the Tupperware manager, who is one rung above the consultant and typically operates a team of six members. She has to hold a minimum of three parties a week, build her team and recruit one consultant per week (i.e., 52 consultants a year). A consultant can be a part-timer, but a manager needs to be reasonably career-oriented because she needs to put in at least four or five hours every day towards training the team, recruiting new consultants and, of course, increasing sales and brand awareness.

The next step up is the distributor, who holds a full-time job. Distributors need to be registered with the company. Here, in addition to the basic commission, the earnings increase in direct proportion to the volume of sales. Distributors play an important role in the value chain. They have conduct a weekly meeting with their entire unit called the ASSEMBLY, wherein the weekly sales and other results are declared. They also motivate and recognize the sales force based on performance.

The fourth level is Tupperware corporate hierarchy, comprising a strong and well-motivated sales team headed by the national sales director. The country is divided into four regions and is supported by a regional sales development manager, sales trainers and sale assistants. The whole team works very closely with the distributors.

Servicing of the Channel: The managers take orders from consultants and pass it on to the distributors every Monday/Tuesday and the same is passed on to the company for servicing. The company based on the credit terms of the distributors supplies the stock to them latest by Thursday. These credit terms are predecided at the time the distributor gets inducted in the channel and are evaluated in case there is a need to give extra credit quarterly or annually, whichever is earlier.

There are weekly promotions announced by the company and the same is then communicated to the distributors. The distributors' accounts in terms of commission/credit notes for promotions are settled on a monthly basis.

Need for the Study: The company is growing rapidly and uses the direct selling method to reach its end customers. The company has never conducted a perception study. This is necessary because Tupperware is facing competition from Modicare, Pearlpet and Reallife and the results of the study will help it in consolidating its market position by identifying its strength and weaknesses. Further, it would indicate why and on what parameters the perception of consumers versus non-consumers is different. This could enable the company to formulate appropriate strategies to attract the non-consumers.

Case Questions

Chapter 1

1. Tupperware has certain issues that require your expert advice. What kind of research would you suggest be carried out by Tupperware? Give reasons for your classification.
2. In case you were to expand the scope of research, how would you do so? Explain, in detail.
3. While pursuing this further, what criteria do you advocate the researcher to keep in mind?
4. Formulate a research proposal for Tupperware and include all the relevant sections with clearly defined justifications/arguments for the same.

Chapter 2

1. Based on the case, narrate the problems facing the management of Tupperware.
2. Based on the steps defined in the chapter, convert the decision problem into a research problem.
3. Identify all the elements of the problem identified by you in terms of unit of analysis, variables and the coordinates of the study.
4. Is it possible to formulate a theoretical model or framework to assist in developing a perspective on the research problem? Why/why not?
5. Formulate three research questions for the problem and develop the working hypotheses for the same.

Chapter 3

1. Can an exploratory research design be advocated in the above situation? How?
2. Would it be possible to conduct a descriptive research study here? Which one would you recommend—cross-sectional or longitudinal? Why?

Chapter 4

1. Take a random sample of 30 housewives who use Tupperware products and have almost similar socio-economic background. Divide the 30 housewives randomly into two groups. Members of these two groups should be invited to a party at home by consultants. Both the groups have demonstration of Tupperware products. In the first group an incentive scheme for ordering Tupperware products is introduced, whereas in the second one, no such scheme is introduced. After 15 days of the party, keep a record of the orders placed by housewives in the two groups.
   (a) Define the dependent and independent variables. What could be the extraneous variables in such an experiment?
   (b) Diagram the experiments.
   (c) Comment on the internal and external validity of the experiment.
   (d) How would you be able to conclude the results of the study?

Chapter 5

1. Can syndicate data sources be useful here? Why/why not?
2. What government publications would be of use here? Can the information obtained be authenticated from alternative methods/source? How?
3. What internal data sources would you recommend be collected from Tupperware? Can you identify the problems one might face in this?
4. For all the above questions, how would you establish the credibility of the information obtained?

Chapter 6

1. To understand the perceptions of the products of Tupperware it was felt that a qualitative research be carried out with the following groups:
   (a) Consultants, that is, the direct selling channel partners.
   (b) Users of Tupperware products.
   (c) Non-users of Tupperware products.

   Which qualitative techniques would you suggest? Would there be certain issues that one must be careful about in each group? Explain.
2. Design an interview guide to be used for discussion with a consultant to get her view on the perception of the user/general public about Tupperware. What should the company do to work on this?
3. Can any of the projective techniques be used for the study? Design some questions based on the technique identified by you.

Chapter 7

1. For measuring the constructs under study, design 10 questions using:
   (a) Itemized rating scales
   (b) Graphic rating scales
   (c) Rank order scales
   (d) Comparative rating scales
2. Out of Likert scale, semantic differential scale and constant sum rating scale, which scale would you advocate be used for the study? Why?
3. How will you measure the reliability of the scale identified by you?
4. How will you measure the validity of the scale identified by you?
5. Can you use observations for your study? What would be the limitations/shortcomings of this method?

Chapter 8

1. Based on the inputs of the activities carried out in chapter 7 design three questionnaires for the three identified groups. Would you devise different questions for the groups under study? Why/why not?

Chapter 9

1. If you were to carry out a perception study of Tupperware users/non-users, how would you define the sampling universe?
2. If, in a survey it is found that 70 per cent of the residents of DLF phase I and II use Tupperware products, how large a sample should be taken if we want a confidence level of 90 per cent with an error margin not exceeding 7 per cent.
3. What would be the appropriate sampling design? Justify your answer.

Chapter 10

1. Prepare a code book for the questionnaire attached in Case 7.1 at the end of Chapter 7.
2. Conduct a preliminary analysis of the data (SPSS data file: Tupperware data) and use the suggested techniques in the chapter to represent the results.

Chapter 11

1. Carry out a frequency distribution analysis for the users and non-users of Tupperware products. (The required data are given in the data disk).
2. The questionnaire for the study is given in Chapter 7. Now use the items of Question 11 and compute the average perception score for each individual. Divide this perception score into two groups—those having a score from 1 to 3 are to be treated as having poor perception and those having a score above 3 are to be treated as having a favourable perception. Now cross-tabulate this with the demographic variables as given in the case. Analyse and interpret your results.

Chapter 12

1. You know there are 128 users and 55 non-users of Tupperware products. You can compute the average perception scores corresponding to each of the user and non-user of the products. Attempt to test the following hypothesis:
   - Is there any difference in the average perception of the users and non-users of Tupperware products?
2. Question 18 of the questionnaire in Case 7.1 at the end of Chapter 7 tries to find out whether the users/non-users possesses credit card, four wheeler, and house or club membership. Test the hypothesis whether the proportion of users possessing each of these four items is different from that of the non-users.

Chapter 13

1. You have computed the average perception scores for the users/non-users of Tupperware. Treat this score as a dependent variable and use each of the demographic variables like type of family, marital status, employment category, age group, education group and household income as independent variables. Carry out one-way analysis of variance and interpret the results.
   In case of significant result, what further analysis would be carry out?

Chapter 14

1. In Question 2 corresponding to Chapter 11 of this case, you were asked to prepare a cross-table. Carry out a chi-square analysis to know whether there is any relationship between perception and any of the demographic variables. In case a significant relationship exists, carry out a further analysis to determine the strength of the relationship between variables.

Chapter 15

1. Using the questionnaire given to you in Chapter 7, add the following question to it:
   How satisfied are you with your Tupperware products?
   Very satisfied/satisfied/neutral/dissatisfied/very dissatisfied.
2. Now conduct a survey of 35-40 Tupperware customers and using the data conduct the following analysis: Take Question 11 as the independent variable and the above stated question as the dependent variable and conduct a multiple regression analysis.
3. What are your findings? Why do you think you got such a result?
4. What more could have been done to increase the strength of the regression equation?

Chapter 16

1. To extract the underlying factors of the perceptions of the users/non-users of Tupperware products, carry out a factor analysis by using the statements in Question 11. Name the identified factors and interpret the results of factor analysis for each of these cases.

Chapter 17

1. There are two groups, namely, users and non-users of Tupperware products. Use them as a categorical dependent variable and the statements in Question 11 of the questionnaire as independent variables and carry out a discriminant analysis to answer the following questions:
   (a) Is the discriminant function statistically significant?
   (b) What is the relative importance of the variables in discriminating between the users and non-user groups?
   (c) How would we build a decision rule to classify a perspective respondent into the user/non-user category?
   (d) What is the classificatory ability of the model?

Chapter 18

1. Conduct a cluster analysis using all the sub questions of Question 11 using the hierarchical cluster analysis. Interpret the solution.
2. Conduct a three-cluster solution using Question 11 by the K-means cluster analysis technique. Interpret the solution. Name the clusters.
3. Using the demographic questions, formulate the cluster profiles and interpret the solution.
4. Could a better profiling have been done by adding some additional questions? Explain.

Chapter 19

1. Make a list of 10 brands manufacturing products similar to Tupperware. Classify them as to why you consider them competition.

2. Now make a 10 × 10 matrix for carrying out a paired comparison test. Take a sample size of 15 users of Tupperware products and 15 non-users of the products and ask them to select from each pair:
   - The brands that they consider most similar to ones they consider most dissimilar.
   - The brand they prefer more over the other one.

   Using the data prepare an MDS for each of the solution and interpret the solution.
3. Now make a list of 10 brands and go to 10 users and 10 non-users of the product and ask them to rank the brands in terms of the best to the worst. What was the similarity/dissimilarity between the two maps that you obtained? What do you think was the reason for this?

Chapter 21

1. Write a report based on the entire process of research and analysis carried out for the 19 chapters.
2. What recommendations do you have for Tupperware to improve its India operations?

CASE 3: EXPLORING NEW OPPORTUNITIES: DAAG ACHHE HAIN!

The last decade has shown new trends among the Indian consumers due to the onset of liberalization and increased urbanization. Categories like health foods, personal care and fitness have seen stupendous growth and categories like soap, cooking oil, and detergents have taken a beating. With little difference between the brands and constant sales promotion activities, the consumer is spoilt for choice and does not look on these products as a category requiring any loyalty. Thus, because of brand switching, brands show stagnating and sometimes unpredictable sales figures. This has led the big FMCG giants to look elsewhere. One of the business opportunities that companies are exploring are smaller tier-II cities (cities with resident population of around 1 million, for example, Pune, Dehradun, Mangalore).

A predominant FMCG giant was conducting a research in tier-II cities in Uttarakhand . The company had successfully launched its washing machine variants that they had come out with in tier-II cities in neighbouring states. The state composition was by and large replicable to Uttarakhand, thus the intention was to do a simple survey of the households.

Study Objectives

- Find out the demographic profile of the potential consumer segment.
- Identify their washing rituals and pattern.
- Find out the most commonly used detergents in the market.
- Measure the ratio of the likelihood of a front load vs a top load retail potential.
- Make suitable recommendations to the organization in the light of the above findings.

The study methodology: The researcher first looked at all the 17 districts in Uttarakhand. Then he selected two districts at random. From each of the districts, he took one tier-II city. Then from each city, he decided to take a sample of 300 households each. The study was done by a door-to-door survey. The final sample of usable questionnaire was for 520 households in the identified cities. The researcher went at random to households in posh localities of the city, where they felt that there would be households owning a washing machine.

The study instrument: The study instrument was designed to understand the consumer washing habits, specifically in terms of washing role, such as the place of washing, whether at home or laundry. Also, the respondent was questioned in terms of his buying behaviour for detergents in terms of frequency of buying, quantity purchased, brands purchased, preferred packaging and major influences in detergent decision. The respondent was also asked to rate the product benefits considered on a 5- point scale (1 = very unimportant, 2 = unimportant, 3 = neither important nor unimportant, 4 = important and 5 = very important). The respondent was also questioned whether they would shift preference from their existing brands in case a popular detergent brand came up with a washing machine variant. This was on a 5-point interval scale (Will definitely buy=5, Will probably buy=4, Not sure=3, Will probably not buy=2 and Will definitely not buy=1). The instrument ended with obtaining demographic details, including washing machine ownership.

The major findings of the survey are given below:

TABLE 1 Washing location (n = 520)

Washing conducted	Frequency
At launderette(dhobhi)	120
At home	400

TABLE 2 Washing role (n = 400)

Washing role	Frequency
Yourself	142
Maid servant	258

TABLE 3 Detergent purchase (n = 400)

Detergent purchase	Frequency
Yes	400
No	0

TABLE 4 Frequency of purchase (n = 400)

Detergent Purchase	Frequency
15 days	110
Monthly	230
1–2 months	60

TABLE 5 Quantity of purchase (n = 400)

Quantity of detergent purchased	Frequency
< 1Kg	100
1–2 kg	190
2–3 kg	60
3–4 kg	40
> 4 kg	10

TABLE 6 Packaging preference (n = 400)

Packaging preference	Frequency
Sachets	30
Packets	210
Jars	90
Bigger containers	50
Others	20

TABLE 7 Brands purchased* (n = 400)

Brands purchased	Frequency
Surf	350
Wheel	240
Nirma	210
Tide	130
Rin	90
Ariel	70
Others/loose powder	210

**Note: Response to multiple response category question*

TABLE 8 Evaluation of Product benefits (n = 400)

Product benefits	Mean	Standard deviation
Removes stains	3.06	1.140
Lather	3.56	1.044
Easy on hands	2.85	1.026
Easy on fabric	3.77	0.886
Whiteness	3.88	0.918

TABLE 9 Influencers in purchase decision* (n = 400)

Major influences in detergent decision	Frequency
Friends	30
Neighbours	40
Self-experience	190
Maid servant	56
Advertisements	130
Promotional scheme /offers	230
Others	12

**Note: Response to multiple response category question.*

TABLE 10 Gender distribution (n = 400)

Male	52
Female	348

TABLE 11 Age-wise distribution (n = 400)

<25	70
25–34	140
35–44	120
>44	70

TABLE 12 Marital status (n = 400)

Single	100
Married	283
Widowed	17

TABLE 13 Family size distribution (n = 400)

1–2	72
3–5	243
6–7	69
>7	16

TABLE 14 Occupation wise distribution (n = 400)

Student	100
Self-employed	27
Service	43
Housewife	230

TABLE 15 Monthly income ('000) distribution (n = 400)

<25	60
25–30	140
31–40	100
>40	100

TABLE 16 Washing habits by income class (n = 400)

Washing role	Income group (000/mths)				TOTAL
	<25	25–30	31–40	>40	
Yourself	40	50	42	10	142
Maid servant	20	90	58	90	258
Total	60	140	100	100	400

x^2 value = 55.6982; p value = 0.000

TABLE 17 Ownership of washing machine (n = 400)

Washing machine	Frequency
Yes	240
No	160

TABLE 18 Purchase intention for washing machine variant (n = 240)

Purchase intention	washing machine	n	Mean	Std. deviation	Std. error of mean
Will you switch to an exclusive washing machine powder?	Top loaded	170	3.5882	1.63753	0.12559
	Front-loaded	70	2.5714	1.68171	0.20100

TABLE 19 Test statistics (n = 240)

		Levene's test for equality of variance		t-test for equality of means		
Will you switch to an exclusive washing machine powder?	assumption	F	Sig.	T	df	Sig.
	Equal variances assumed	1.196	0.275	4.338	238	0.000
	Equal variances not assumed			4.290	125.579	0.000

TABLE 20 Regression analysis: model summary (n = 240)

Model Summary

Model	R	R Square	Adjusted R Square	Std. Error of the Estimate
1	0.693a	0.480	0.458	0.575

TABLE 21 Regression analysis: ANOVA (n = 240)

ANOVA[a]

Model		Sum of Squares	df	Mean Square	F	Sig.
1	Regression	34.868	5	6.974	43.451	0.000[b]
	Residual	37.723	235	0.1605		
	Total	72.592	239			

a. Dependent Variable: Purchase intention

TABLE 22 Regression analysis: coefficient table (n=240)

Coefficients[a]

Model		Unstandardized Coefficients		Standardized Coefficients	t	Sig.
		B	Std. Error	Beta		
1	(Constant)	-0.230	0.356		-0.645	0.520
	Removes stains	0.108	0.051	0.157	2.125	0.036
	Whiteness	0.244	0.065	0.326	3.787	0.000
	Easy on fabric	0.178	0.082	0.209	2.169	0.032
	Lather	0.219	0.069	0.249	3.195	0.002
	Easy on hand	0.044	0.055	0.057	0.794	0.429

a. Dependent Variable: purchase intention

QUESTIONS

1. Based on the data given in the above tables, interpret the following:
   (a) What is the typical profile of a consumer in Uttarakhand's tier-II cities?
   (b) What is his/her typical washing behaviour?
   (c) Using Table 16, compute the percentage in the appropriate direction to interpret the results.
   (d) Is there any significant relation between how a person washes his/her clothes and the income class that the person belongs to? Carry out further analysis if you think it is appropriate to do so.
   (e) Which types of consumers are more likely to buy a washing machine variant (powder)?
   (f) Which factors influence the purchase intention for the washing machine variant? Interpret the results based on the relative importance.
2. Based on the answers of the above questions, prepare a management summary of the results. What recommendations would you give the FMCG company that wants to sell its washing machine detergent powder in the tier II cities?
3. Prepare a business report (hint: refer to Types of reports in Chapter 21) of the study. If you were to present the results to the management, how would you do so? Explain with suitable presentation material.

ADDENDUM 1

Online Research: New Age Techniques

If the 1960s was the era of rationality and the search for universal paradigms and absolute truths which could stand the test of time and boundaries; the 1990s saw turmoil and uncertainty. As the aftermath of nuclear warfare and environmental calamities like pollution, global warming and genetic malformations led to post-modernism and a questioning mindset characterized by hostility and despair with the state of things. This resulted in hyper realities, where more and more people across the world sought a world that was surreal and thus free from the chaos and disappointments as well as threats of the real world. The need was ably supported by the extremely fast digital growth that was happening across the world. Today, almost two decades later, more than one million people across physical boundaries stand connected through online communities, networks, groups, forums and podcasts. The huge success of virtual social worlds such as Second life is a definite proof of the fact that more and more consumers are taking on an alternative identity (or avatar), which has no constraints or rules. This is only one part of it—the success of social communities (Facebook), virtual product sales (on forums such as Flipkart and Snapdeal) gaming (World of Warfare) and knowledge/opinion sharing (Twitter and Wikipedia) all point towards the relevance of seeking time and information from data sources that are available (secondary) and can be sought (primary) in a virtual environment.

THE RELEVANCE AND DOMAIN OF ONLINE RESEARCH

In the last decade, what we saw was the recognition of the Internet as a useful source of secondary information, such as databases and online resources. However, today it is being recognized as a separate method as it involves unique challenges and processes related to sampling, data collection and measurement metrics which are not prevalent in traditional research as we know it. Thus, it is critical to understand these issues from the perspective of using the medium effectively for conducting a research study.

A typical phenomenon of virtual space is that companies now have to face the true aspects of designing consumer centric strategies. Thus, for the new era of co-creation by consumers and business managers, the business researcher needs to be "listening" to what the brand communities are saying; "talking" with them for co creation; "energizing" and "supporting" to complete the engagement with the consumer. The medium is exciting and has huge potential, yet it is in an evolving stage as it faces constant challenges of changes in terms of business-customer interface as well as ethical constraints. Thus, both perspectives on recognizing the value of the process as well as serious concerns exist about it. Thus, before we go on to the specifics of the online research process, let us briefly examines the pros and cons of using the method.

Advantages and Disadvantages of Online Research

Just like the traditional research process we have gone through in the textbook this also has strengths and weaknesses associated with it. Some of these are listed below:

Advantages

- **Low cost:** The most supportive argument is the cost of conducting the online research. Researchers have found it to be almost 30% cheaper to conduct a study online. The only significant cost the investigator may incur is in the use of the software to generate the study questionnaire. This has also been resolved to a certain extent as a number of free sites are available that can be used for designing and uploading the instrument. The second is the saving in the negligible to zero cost of reaching the sample respondents.

- **Quick response time:** This is both in terms of secondary data as well as collecting data that is primary in nature from the sample group.
- **Better respondent engagement:** With the innovation in design and tools available on the net the questionnaire and the information seeking can be made very engaging and interesting for the respondent.
- **Extensive reach:** The advantage of the virtual medium is that there are no distances in terms of approaching the sample group. Also, with advanced software available it is possible to enable an almost instant translation of the questions into the language of the respondent.
- **Anonymity and answering:** Since the researcher/investigator is in most instances not there, the respondent feels freer to answer and the relative anonymity gives them the assurance to answer, sensitive and open ended questions
- **Accuracy in data entry:** Since the response categories for the closed ended questions is done in the beginning there is no likelihood of human error in filling the answers in the spread sheet. The other records in terms of time off access and time taken to complete the questionnaire, etc., are precisely recorded and again this ensures zero error.
- **Authentic data sources:** With more and more companies and research agencies realizing the merit of the medium, reputed companies like Nielsen, Forrester and Euromonitor are establishing online divisions to cater to the needs of the business and academic researcher.

Disadvantages

- **Skewed sample:** The constraint of the method is that the data collected, especially primary, can only be conducted on people who are Internet-savvy. Thus, there is the issue of generalizability.
- **Representativeness and authenticity:** The anonymity of the respondent is also a problem as one does not know who is on the other side as the person might not reveal his/her true identity, age or gender. Thus, one may conduct and formulate conclusion based on a sample group that was not matching the population under study.
- **Significant cues:** A lot of physical cues that come from body language and voice modulations is lost in an online survey. Though this issue is being resolved to a certain extent by audio and video interviews and also analysis of emoticons (smiley face and punctuation and word forms) in the text is being researched to try and overcome this weakness.
- **Malicious responses:** Once the questionnaire is posted for response one has no control over who responds. It might happen that a disgruntled employee or customer might be extremely negative and fill the questionnaire not once but multiple times and thus deform the output.
- **Design problems:** The online surveys are more engaging provided one knows how to make effective use of the software features. Thus, they are also difficult to design and the average online researcher might not be proficient in doing so.

The online research process is by and large the same in terms of steps involved. However, special mention needs to be made of three important issues-sampling; data collection and data metrics.

SAMPLING FOR ONLINE RESEARCH STUDIES

One of the major challenges in online studies is designing an effective sampling plan and obtaining a representative sample. Since no concrete sampling frame exists of internet users, obtaining a probability sample is a difficult task. As a result of non-representativeness in sampling the sampling error becomes considerable and thus raising doubts with reference to the results of the study. In case the research study is being conducted on a finite group as amongst employees in a company or even students in universities, the population is finite and thus chances of error are minimized. Hence in the absence of sampling frame one should disperse the questionnaire on all relevant platforms, mailing lists, chat room, news group etc. However, there is still no way of knowing whether the sample who responded is representative of the population one wanted to study.

Added to the challenge is the fact that the same user may have multiple accounts. And updating and comprehending the accounts on which he is active/inactive is difficult to obtain. To a certain extent there are various companies across the Globe that have recognized the web-opportunity in the gap and provide the service of sampling users directly from various websites. Netzero is one such free Internet service provider. The company has a barter strategy and in exchange of complete profiling and tracking rights of user's site behavior, it offers the use of free internet access. Despite the invasion of privacy, the company has more than 8 million users. Thus the firm has a data base of consumers and can to a certain extent assist in improving the representative nature of the sample and also based on the profile of consumers manage an experimental design of experimental and control group, better.

Another company utilizing this barter strategy is Knowledge Networks. This company uses RDD (random digit dialing) methods to recruit individuals for a household panel survey. This would need to be longitudinal in nature. The recruited and screened panelist is provided free Web TV receiver and internet access in exchange for agreeing to participate in the online panels/surveys.

There are some typical ways of sampling on the net.

Open-Internet samples: This sample includes people who, for whatever reason volunteered to complete the online questionnaire survey. Some also opt for being part of online panels. This method suffers from the problem of self selection. The second problem is that if the survey is too long they might get bore or lose interest and quit without completing the survey. Also, these are sometimes mailed and sometimes they might be rolled out as pop-up surveys. The challenge with executing pop-up surveys, being that most Internet users these days have a pop-up blocker. Sometimes, the researcher also does Internet-intercept survey, which involves interjecting into an Internet user's activity on a typical homepage of any site.

Screened-Internet samples: This screened sample could be from the open-sample group or they might be part of a particular data base or service provider like Net zero. They are first administered a screening questionnaire and then requested based on the study requirement to complete the survey. Sometimes using the screener it is also possible to classify them into separate segments. In this case it is possible to direct them towards separate questions based on their characteristics. For example in a study on compensation and rewards, there might be groups of Public sector workers as well as private, so they are directed towards different sections.

Recruited sample: These are members who are generally accessed like the traditional method that is once they are representative of the population under study they are contacted through mail, email, telephone or in person. And after they agree to answer the survey they are sent the questionnaire or the link to the questionnaire, with a password to complete it.

DATA COLLECTION METHODS FOR ONLINE RESEARCH

As is the case with traditional research process, online research also has the same basic two broad categories of data collection—primary and secondary.

Secondary Methods

Secondary data collection methods have been discussed at length in Chapter 5, where secondary methods—both internal and published sources, especially online sources—have been discussed. However, there are three secondary sources which require special discussion and are detailed below:

Search engines

Today, one of the most powerful and most frequently used sources of secondary data is the Internet. A number of companies like Google, Wikipedia, MSN search, and Yahoo search have recognized the merit of having a full-fledged division dedicated to this. The search engines have their own programmed web crawlers, web spiders (these are like web robots and they systematically "crawl" the Internet to search and index sites/information) of taking the "searcher" to various sites. Some popular methods are based on keywords and their density, after which they look at the link popularity—in terms of how many times it has been accessed—and today with monetization of sites, how much does one need to pay per click. There are again general search engines like Google and Yahoo and more specific in terms of, say, when you are looking for specifics in terms of let's say statistical data related to Indian demographics, one goes to *www.censusindia.gov.in*. Because of the huge number of websites available with a single key term one may get 1000 or 10000 options and it is near impossible to tackle all of them, the other challenge is that a lot of sites , especially scholarly search sites like *www.hbsp.harvard.edu* (Harvard Business School publishing) require a password and cannot be accessed normally . Thus, the researchers may like to move to focused and reliable sites like Pathfinders. Pathfinders are basically sites that take the user to a limited portfolio of sites that are provided by credible sources. *www.pathfinderhealth.in* is a pathfinder that is focused on informational sites related to health and relevant to the Indian user/practitioner. These sites have what are known as intelligent crawlers that index specific topic-related results.

Newsgroups

These are quite similar to other social media platforms. They are called newsgroups because they are a primary method of communication in a virtual world with like minded professionals (e.g. marketing academicians—*www.marketingpower.com*) or special interest groups (e.g. management aspirants— *www.pagalguy.com*). The "Internet reader" can view threads (conversation histories); pose questions to other group members or rebuke or disagree with points of views more or less as in a face-to-face argument. A typical newsgroup message looks very similar to an email. There is a sender, a subject title and the actual message. These threads are powerful sources of information as you as a researcher can browse through an entire thread and get a first hand qualitative insight into what the respondent population is thinking and doing.

Blogs

Blogs originated in the late 1990s when they were usually managed by an enthusiast who gave a chronological index of sites of interest and also provided a personal commentary on the links or sites. However, later people created their own private blogs, which were like public sharing of private, personal views and thoughts. The fact that they are in the public domain means they are accessible and sometimes ones expression of discontent or despair that reflects a personal misery creates a reaction and sometimes can lead to an uprising, as can be seen in a number of cases of rebellion in the years 2011-12. Marketing researchers find blogs as very interesting as they are able to understand the lifestyle and beliefs about any consumer segment rather than merely the product or the brand, thus making targeting and positioning strategies more focused and meaningful. In fact there are search engines like *www.blogsearch.com* that can help a researcher conduct a blog search on any topic of interest.

Primary Methods

The premise of using the primary methods and the basic nuances of the techniques remain the same. In this section, we will highlight the aspects that are different and thus need to be taken care of while making use of any of these. There are also some primary methods-netnography—that are unique to this medium and will be dealt with in the end in some detail.

Before we proceed further, let us examine some categorization of online primary methods. One is between a web-based method in which the researcher could make use of a web designed questionnaire and collect the data from the respondent. The other is a communication method, which is more personalized and targeted towards collecting specific information from identified sample group. This involves using the email as a personalized platform for collecting information.

The other method is synchronized vs non-synchronized. In the first the researcher/interviewer asks questions and the respondent answers in real time while in the second case the questionnaire is sent to the respondent and he/she answers as per her convenience at a later time slot.

Online focus groups

The focus group is as rich in its conduct and usefulness as it is the real world. Here the focus croup could be both in the form of chat or discussion forums—where the group members are already familiar with each other or else they are selected through the internet. The method could also be synchronized where all members and the moderator are discussing at a single moment in time. However, there could also be non-synchronized focus groups where the members might post their comments and then move out of the group to conduct other activities and someone else may respond much later and the user when he returns then responds to the comment. These are typically called bulletin boards.

As the method involves usually typing ones response it is recommended that since there could be simultaneous response from the group members rather than 8-10 as is the practice in a regular focus group one should limit oneself to 6-8 members. Secondly, the moderator must be fast in typing on the keyboard and be very familiar with handling diversions and interjections on the software platform. A typical online focus group last for about two hours. While some group members might be keying in their response others might react with emoticons like smileys, etc., to express their feelings for the statement or comment. Since there could be multiple people who respond at the same time, it might be prudent to use two moderators so that multiple reactions can be handled at the same time. Just like the traditional method the online methods have their own challenges and advantages. The advantage primarily being in terms of cost, geographic reach and to a certain extent they do not involve facing a group. The disadvantages are that the richness of non-verbal cues are lost here.

Social network analysis

This method has its origin in Sociometry (discussed in Chapter 6). Here, essentially one tries to study social or virtual social ties. This involves studying the structure—hierarchy and patterns of networks that emerge between social or virtual actors. There are essentially two aspects one is analyzing—nodes (the net users) and the ties (their relationship with each other). The ties could be a sharing of ideas, information a business transaction or an emotional transaction. One can do things in a social network—either observe the way the information is flowing—in terms of who is the centre of the network(opinion leader), who is the loner, are their two people who communicate more with each other (dyads). The second method is to ask questions and find out with whom the group members would interact for emotional problems or information/knowledge seeking. Basically, the idea being to assess how decisions are taken in group settings and how group dynamics influence individual or group behavior in a particular network.

Online surveys

The online survey may be conducted in both real time and non-synchronized. The survey could involve either of the following two methods:

- **E-mail-based surveys:** These are generally conducted after the sampling has been done and the email address of the respondent has been made available. Post which the study instrument may be attached with the mail or be embedded in the mail. in this case there would be a short introduction to the study and the respondent answers the questions and then carry out the simple action of reply , the filled questionnaire returns back to the researcher. The other method is that there is an attachment which needs to be downloaded and then filled in. This can be either sent back as an attachment or the physical copy can be mailed back to the researcher.
- **Web-based surveys:** These involve using software or a program to generate a questionnaire. This method has a huge advantage in terms of design capabilities. One can make the questionnaire engaging and interesting by making use of computer programs. Secondly, the option of filter and branching question that are tedious when done in the traditional manner are handled very efficiently here. In most instances the instrument requires the respondent to punch/key in the button indicating their response. There are multiple web survey packages available today that can help the researcher to efficiently design a web survey, e.g. Web surveyor; Perseus Survey Monkey; Zoomerang, etc. The software further segregate and categorize

data by tabulating the responses. Thus the task of making a data entry and coding the data is saved as the human error in data entry is eliminated here. The basic challenge lies not in designing but in getting the respondent to the instrument and motivating them to complete the survey.

Netnography

Robert Z. Kozinets (2010) came up with an online method that has its roots in ethnographic analysis. Ethnography is basically an anthropological technique used quite actively today in the field of marketing and consumer research today. The method is distinguished from other primary methods as it uses multiple methods in conjunction with each other to arrive at a rich and holistic picture about a culture or a community. The methods popularly used are the observation method, semiotics, films, documentaries, conversational and discourse analysis, videography. The idea being to use every possible piece of communication/information that has been spouted/created by the user of that community to understand the apparent and latent aspects about the community.

Kozinet took the participant-observation method to understand discourse and conversations on the computer as the source of data. Thus the premise is that along with its other methods, ethnographic analysis must take into account the data obtained from a netnographic analysis.

Ethnography to netnographic analysis can be viewed as a continuum. At the one end is a face to face interaction-observation, dialogue, data collection, which is an ethnographic analysis. Let us say we want to study the world or challenges face by single mothers of autistic children. Now, let us say that these single mothers spend considerable time online, thus at the next stage we study these communities online and both the face to face and online methods provide us a rich understanding of their group in its entirety. The last stage is when we study only online communities—second life—and our observation are limited to only their online interaction. This method is called netnography. The method has its own set of peculiarities that need to be understood before we discuss the method of netnographic analysis. The first is alteration—the technology-based medium in which the interaction is happening is different from the traditional interaction as people move in and out of the platform, come back sometimes instantly and sometimes after days to respond to a message or communication. The second is the anonymous nature of the medium that lets the community member give vent to behavior, feelings and expression, that may never be possible in the actual world, however this can also be a challenge as it becomes extremely difficult to identify the community or even gender this person belongs to. The third aspect is accessibility, once part of an online community, one is privy to everything and anything that the person is doing in their virtual world and the last is that because of its very nature of storage, historical archiving of activity and communication is extremely easy.

A typical netnographic analysis involves adopting a structured approach.

- **Step 1- Identifying the research question and objectives:** Once done and you have identified what kind of information or knowledge that you seek about the community. You first need to visit sites frequented by the communities (secondary data) to understand their typical lingos, their concerns and patterns of communicating with each other.

- **Step 2- Identifying and approaching the communities:** Once you have understood them to a certain degree, the next thing is to identify the forums or groups on which they interact- these could be chat forums, bulletin board, and social networking sites. Next one needs to shortlist the communities that one wants to enter. It is suggested that one enters the groups that are interactive, active, heterogeneous and also the communication content is rich.

- **Step 3- Ethical immersion and participation in the communities:** At every stage in the study the researcher must follow an ethical path to the introduction and participation in a community. Thus the time when the researcher enters the community, explains the academic purpose of the desire to enter the community. The data collection here is also multi fold. It involves posting comments, posing questions, getting feedback, taking online initiative and taking leadership roles. The researcher has to decide about how the communication and online behavior is to be recorded. It is advised however, that the researcher maintains observational field notes on these communication pieces.

- **Step 4- Data analysis and interpretation:** Like any other qualitative method, researcher needs to make sense of the huge amount of conversation pieces that he has gathered and tries and discerns the underlying or common patterns of ideas or behavior. This can be done manually, where the researcher attempts to draw categories and tries to establish possible relationships or links between observed attitude or behavior. Please understand this is not interpretation but analysis that is very similar to content analysis. There are also software programs such as CAQDAS (computer assisted qualitative data analysis) that do the same analysis in terms of looking at identifying and coding recurrent themes.
- **Step 5- Evaluating and interpreting netnographic data:** Kozinets has identified 10 criteria that a netnographic analysis must meet in order to consider the findings of the analysis as an accurate ground for establishing accurately any characterization about the community or culture under study. The premise essentially being that the developed ideas and constructs must be distinct from each other. They should be grounded in some theoretical framework, allow for flexibility of interpretation by other researchers and be able to inspire some kind of applied social action with reference to the community.

Today, netnography is a technique that is being applied to blogs, tweets, and social networking sites like face book, podcasts and videocasts. The technique becomes increasingly important as it is able to provide insights into how people think and react. The companies are able to connect with their customers/stakeholders better if they understand the person's inner world. The third use is that the research can provide valuable means of communicating with these communities in a manner and language that they understand and believe in.

Online data metrics

The research process involved in an online research study is very similar to that conducted otherwise. However there are certain variable measurements that are unique to online research. It is not possible to discuss each one of them at length; however, an attempt is made to give the reader a substantive idea about what to look for and how to measure it.

1. **Cookie:** Is the historical record on your computer of your visiting any website. Every cookie has an ID number, a domain name and an expiry date , thus becomes useful in tracking user behavior.
2. **Webserver log files:** Most web hosts who create the website have an inbuilt mechanism of storing any request made there. Thus details about the user who accessed your site are available to you. One can program the web analytic software to record the visitor information in the manner you wish to.
3. **Page tagging:** Besides the web site one can tag individual pages on the website and record details of those who visited the page. As this is related to what we referred to as intelligent crawling where the user might be looking for specific information. there are free analytic services like Google analytics that can sssist in this form of tracking.

Key performance indicator

Key performance indicators (KPIs) are essentially measures of outcome or the dependent variable and the researcher can decide what he/she wants to assess depending on the objective of the research study. Some Popular KPIs are:

1. **Ad impression:** This is a measure of the number of times an ad banner is displayed on the Internet.
2. **Cost per thousand impressions (CPM):** This model based on impressions or essentially awareness was the model used till 1997. Post that the web marketer was more concerned about the viewer and the company paid for being seen by the user.
3. **CTR:** Click through rate is a percentage figure which is the ratio between the numbers of impressions an ad gets upon the number of times the ad was shown.
4. **Bounce rate:** Bounce rate indicates the number of people who visit a website's landing page and bounce back without browsing further.

5. **Open rate:** In case some information or link was sent by e-mail. then the open rate is the number of people who opened the e-mail. this requires the HTML or image to open and in case this has been disabled by the recipient it cannot be used as a metrics
6. **CTOR (click to open rate):** In case a link was sent on an email then the CTOR measures the number of people who opened the link vs those who opened the e-mail.
7. **Conversion rate:** This is the proportion of people who visit your site vs those who carry out a specific action, say, purchase.
8. **Abandonment rate:** Those who start an action but quit before completing the required activity. say making a payment at the payment gateway.
9. **Page views:** the number of pages on your site viewed by a site visitor.
10. **Absolute unique visitor:** The details of the visitor who visited your website at a unique time period- say an online promotion.
11. **New vs returning visitors:** Those who arrive at the page for the first time vs those who have visited the site earlier.
12. **Cost per click (CPC):** The ratio of the advertising spend vs the number of clicks the sponsored search or banner advertisement got. This was more important than CPM as a click would mean a higher probability that the user would convert into a purchase at the site.
13. **Transaction conversion rate (TCR):** This is the ratio of the fixed cost of advertising vs the numbers of conversions post the advertisement.
14. **Take rate = CTR X TCR:** Is the number of times a visitor clicks and then converts into a transaction.
15. **Return on ad dollars (ROA):** Is a measure of total revenue made (TCR)/ cost of internet marketing.
16. **Word of mouth (WOM):** this is an important metrics for evaluating social media effectiveness =

$$\frac{\text{Number of direct clicks + Number of clicks based on recommendation}}{\text{Number of direct clicks}}$$

These are examples of the output in terms of what is the objective of an online strategy. The business researcher might study either the pattern of these matrices across segments or communities or alternatively try to establish the antecedents of these as these insights are what are necessary for the business manager who wants to better manage his/her e-commerce activities.

REFERENCES

Bickerton, P, M Bickerton and U Pardesi, *Cyber Marketing: How to Use the Internet to Market Your Goods and Services*, 2nd edn, New Delhi: Butterworth Heinemann, 2002.

Gay. R, A Charlesworth and R Esen, *Online Marketing: A Customer-led Approach.* 2007. Oxford university press. New Delhi

McDaniel. C (jr.) and R Gates, *Marketing Research*, 8th edn, New Delhi: Wiley, 2010.

Bryman, A and E Bell, *Business Research Methods*, 3rd edition, New Delhi: Oxford University Press, 2011.

Ryan, D and C Jones, *Understanding Digital Marketing: Marketing Strategies for Engaging the Digital Generation,* New Delhi: Kogan Page India, 2009.

Jeffery M, *Data-driven Marketing: The 15-metrics Everyone in Marketing Should Know*. New Delhi: Wiley India. 2010

Kozinets. R V, *Netnography: Doing Ethnographic Research Online*, New Delhi: Sage Publications, 2010.

Kaplan,.A M and Haenlein, M, "The fairyland of second life: virtual social worlds and how to use them." *Business Horizons*, 52, 563-572, 2009.

ADDENDUM 2

Ethical Issues in Business Research

In the preceding chapters, we have understood the process of research as it exists in the different business domains. However, one needs to be cognizant of the fact that like every other aspect of the working environment, the investigative research process also has to be guided and monitored by a regulatory code of ethics. Rowley (2004) has put it very succinctly as '*conducting research ethically is concerned with respecting privacy and confidentiality, and being transparent in the use of research data. Ethical practices hinge on respect and trust and approaches that seek to build rather than demolish relationships.*'

Since research involves investigation, collection, interpretation and documentation, it becomes important that the researcher adheres to the defined protocol. Russ-Eft *et al.* (1999) advocated that while conducting business research, the approach must be professional and responsible, the data collection must be attempted with the respondent's consent under appropriate and ethically correct control, and, last but not the least, the interpretation has to be done in a careful manner. A number of corporations have developed their own code of ethics, regarding the conduct of research. While this practice of defining business ethics, which includes research ethics, is prevalent in most organizations in the West, in India this is spelt out and documented in the pharmaceutical sector and some banks like HSBC. Besides this, there are also well established and detailed tenets available from international bodies, for example, the Social Research Association's (SRA's) ethical guidelines, the American Psychological Association (APA) code of ethics, code of standards and ethics for survey research designed by the Council of American Survey Research Organizations (CASRO), American Marketing Association (AMA) and Business Marketing Association (BMA) code of conduct and ethics.

To understand the principles and code of ethics involved in research, one needs to understand the three significant stakeholders involved in any research, namely:

1. The **sponsoring clients** or decision-makers.
2. The **respondents** from whom one seeks the information.
3. The **researcher** himself/herself while administering and compiling the study.

Each one of these entities has their own specific interests and needs and, thus, the ethical concerns regarding each one would be unique and require different regulations. Thus, the following sections present brief guidelines on the ethical issues and their management.

The Client/Decision-Maker

Similar to any other business transaction, research is also an exchange process between various entities. The first of these is the one between the sponsoring client and the investigator. Thus both parties have an ethical obligation towards the other.

Client's ethical code: In case the study is being conducted for a business client, then in order to ensure real time research the objectivity of acquiring and interpreting information is a must. It has been observed that the client might be a business manager who because of his own personal interests might coerce or steer the results in a specific direction in order to fulfil a hidden agenda. For example, in case a warehousing organization is looking at business expansion and hires a research supplier to provide directions, it might so happen that the manager who is interfacing between the organization and the supplier has a family business of a transport fleet and thus wants the researcher to recommend courier and transit warehousing services as business opportunities that the company can go into.

It has been commonly found amongst small and relatively younger firms to solicit proposals from research agencies for the conduct of a study. However, once they obtain the details of the intended methodology, they usually get the study conducted by their own team or by trainees at a low to minimal cost to the company. And since the proposals are the first stage of a research bid, the company is under no obligation to pay for the research methodology collected by them in an underhand manner.

Another instance could be that even though the initial exploratory research and literature review indicate the nature of the respondent population, the client might, based on his own notions, force the researcher to undertake the study on a specific population. For example, if a new technology is being introduced in the company and the usage requires computer literacy, the client might ask the researcher to measure the acceptability of the product amongst only the computer-savvy population. Thus the results would automatically be skewed towards acceptance.

Sometimes the interpretation and recommendations might be beyond the scope of a study. For example, in the organic food study, which was conducted amongst retailers and consumers, the client might ask the researcher to suggest strategies for educating and building usage and recommendations amongst dieticians and doctors.

It is recommended in this instance that the researcher must conduct a comprehensive exploratory research and develop clearly stated objectives that do not leave any scope for unethical intervention. Secondly, he must educate with conviction and objectivity the significance of unbiased results; also the researcher, in case of an unethical manager client, should try to avoid making recommendations and formulating strategies and leave the use or non-use of the data to the manager. Of course, failing all possible paths, it is best to terminate the research study as unethical reporting and compilation is bound to backfire on the researcher's integrity.

The researcher is the key action agent in the study and hence owes it to both the client as well as the respondent group, to ensure that the entire study follows the quality checks and standards that should be maintained at a professional level. At the same time it is his/her moral responsibility that the study does not hurt/harm the sentiments or privacy rights of any person associated with the study. There are well constructed standards that have been devised in order to ensure these. The ethical and desired norms are discussed briefly in the section below:

Researcher's ethical code:

Quality control: A very important consideration, both short-term and long-term, is to maintain the standards of precision and quality in the conduct of the study. The researcher must be absolutely objective and correct in adapting the research design that would be appropriate for the study. For example, for studying the impact of a mathematics study programme on an experimental group of children, the researcher must have a matched control group of children with a similar understanding of mathematics but with no special treatment in order to isolate the effect of the designed intercession .

Sometimes the client might be unaware of the analytical rules and conditions for the result to be valid, thus it is the responsibility of the researcher to be absolutely transparent about the significance of the results obtained and refrain from emphasizing findings that might be of very little strength or value.

Privacy control: The most significant and important ethical concern of a research study is the issue of trust and confidentiality. At no cost must the researcher reveal any aspect of the study without the consent of the client. This could be in terms of not revealing the ***name*** of the company. For example, if the client is interested in finding out the comparative standing of their product with the competitor's product, it becomes critical to conduct the study amongst users of the product category rather than only the company brand in order to get an unbiased evaluation.

The researcher might also need to guard the reason or ***purpose*** of the study. For example if the client wants to measure a new product potential, then revealing the reason for the study might lead to the concept or idea being adopted and converted into a product prototype by someone else before the client is out with the offering. The third level of confidentiality that the researcher must ensure is the complete confidentiality of the findings till the research outcome has been converted into a business decision. For example, based on the organizational health index of its workers and the attrition rate, the correlation between the two variables might be alarming enough to require a major restructuring of the existing employee benefits and work policy. Or the research study might involve a comprehensive and detailed study of potential candidates being considered for the role of the CEO, as the existing leader is due for retirement. Thus, revelation of the findings of such research might lead to turbulence and divided opinion in the organization. Thus the results should not be made available to all till they have been brought into action.

Research Respondents

The most important and vulnerable person in the research study is the respondent from whom the data is to be collected. Every association and organization that is directly or indirectly involved with research has laid down clear and detailed guidelines for ensuring that unethical treatment of the respondent does not happen. The American Association for Public Opinion Research has formulated the following code of ethics for survey researchers, with reference to the respondent:

- *We shall strive to avoid the use of practices or methods that may harm, humiliate or seriously mislead survey respondents.*
- *Unless the respondent waives confidentiality for specific uses, we shall hold as privileged and confidential all information that might identify a respondent with his or her responses. We shall also not disclose or use the names of respondents for non-research purposes unless the respondent grants us permission to do so.*

Study disclosure: Complete and transparent information regarding the purpose of collecting data and what sort of information would be required from the respondent. The person must know what kind of questioning would be done, so that he is able to perceive what the researcher is looking for and whether he has the information, whether he wants to share all or part of it and also how much time and effort would the exercise entail. For example, for a new concept test or a segmentation analysis or an organizational climate survey the administration would require considerable time and commitment from the respondent. Secondly, if it is a before-and-after product acceptability or usage study, again the person would be contacted twice to assess the experience.

Thus the researcher needs to be absolutely truthful about the nature and objectives of the study.

Coercion and influence: The researcher should not at any stage, either before or during the data collection stage, try to pressurize the respondent through persuasive influence or by forcing him to share information. For example, if the respondent has been through some traumatic experience, he/she might not want to share all with a stranger, even if it is for an objective study. Schinke and Gilchrist (1993) state that *Under standards set by the National Commission for the protection of human subjects, all informed-consent procedures must meet three criteria: participants must be competent to give consent, sufficient information must be provided to allow for a reasonable decision and consent must be voluntary and uncoerced.*

Sometimes, it may so happen that the respondent is too young or too old or not literate and thus, unable to understand when the researcher might be either leading him/her to give certain preset answers or trying to force the person to share information that he does not want to reveal or which once shared might be misconstructed.

Sensitivity and respect: There are certain issues like shoplifting or sexual orientation, which are not topics that can be managed in a structured, impersonal manner. The researcher should devote more time here and also keep the questions more open-ended, and usually such situations need a considerable rapport formation and formulatuion of non-threatening question. The researcher, at all times, would need to treat the respondent with due respect and be transparent about the nature and objective of the questioning.

Experimentation and implication: In case the respondent is going to be part of the experimental group subjected to any sort of treatment, for example, a new shampoo trial or an intervention programme that may involve some behavioural change, complete information must be given regarding the course of the experiment and any risk, even minimal, which might be involved. The researcher, thus, must ensure minimal risk to the respondent and should in no way cause any harm to the person, even if it is for the quest of knowledge.

Bailey (1978) describes this 'harm' as *not only hazardous or medical experiments but also any social research that might involve such things as discomfort, anxiety, harassment, invasion of privacy or demeaning or dehumanizing procedures.*

Agreement or consent: Once the researcher has clearly communicated the purpose, the nature and likely outcome of the study, it is advisable for both concerned to formulate a mutual written or unwritten contract. This ensures that there are no non-pleasantries or legal confrontation on either side. Another advantage of this is that in case a point was not very clear the issue gets clarified. For example, for a personal care usage study the consumer might be under the impression that a questionnaire on usage would be filled in when actually the researcher wants to observe/record the usage ritual. This might entail some invasion of privacy by the researcher, thus taking the consent beforehand would make things clear for both the parties.

Sometimes, the nature of the study might require that the name of the company be disguised. For example, one cannot start a study by saying, 'We are conducting a survey for Mother Dairy milk; which do you think is the best milk in the city?' Thus, here the debriefing about the company sponsoring the research can be revealed after the data has been collected, and the purpose of the disguise can be revealed. This ensures respondent goodwill and cooperation.

Researcher's Professional Code

Besides ensuring that specific protocols and codes be followed for the two benefactors (client) and contributors (respondents) there are some basic tenets that the researcher must not forego. These are significant not only for the body of knowledge that the researcher is contributing to but also for the society in which we exist.

Professional creed: We have already discussed this in detail in both the sections above. However, here we refer to the overall demeanor of the researcher, who has to stand tall and be truthful during all phases of the study, whether in the conceptualization, conduction or presentation of the research study.

- At no stage should the researcher exaggerate or underplay the expense or effort incurred in the conduct of the study. Thus, sometimes the investigator might overclaim the expense incurred in travel or field visit. On the other hand, he might underpay the field investigators that he has kept for data collection by hiring undergraduate students rather than professional investigators.
- The respondent group being studied should be a true representative of the identified respondent population studied and not a skewed and biased sample. Another unethical practice observed is that the researcher might conduct the study with a professional group of respondents who are well versed in the response technique and thus give 'good' or predictable answers.
- The data and the questionnaire completed should be on authentic, real-time conduction, with actual respondents representative of the population under study and not fake completion done by the field investigators themselves.
- The findings and results should be presented as they were found based on actual conduction and under no circumstances must the researcher attempt to fudge or manipulate the results of the study.

Professional confidentiality: The researcher must bear the responsibility to maintain the confidentiality of the research findings and not making public any aspects of the study, in an apparent or camouflaged manner. This code of ethics applies both to the sponsoring client, as well as the respondent. The anonymity and privacy of the respondent is to be respected and not violated. Also, recording private or personal behaviour with hidden devices is considered a monumental violation of an individual's right to privacy (e.g., observing people in a fitting room with a hidden camera).

The right to privacy and confidentiality takes on a new meaning in cyberspace, where the respondent's personal and demographic details are made available to the researching company and this could be compiled and collated and sold as databases to various service providers as authentic locational details for tapping potential customers. Thus, maintaining anonymity and confidentiality of information shared is a professional norm that any ethical researcher should follow. In case the data is to be shared, it must be done with the consent of the respondent.

Professional objectivity: As a true researcher and contributor to the existing body of knowledge, the researcher must maintain the objectivity of an absolutely neutral reporter of facts. He must maintain objectivity in all phases of the study while:

- Designing the research objectives which must be based on facts and sound analysis rather than simple opinion.
- Collecting information by using a standard and not differential set of instructions. For example, in the intervention study quoted earlier, the researcher must give the instructions in the same way to both the experimental and control group and in no way try to exaggerate the actual impact of the treatment.
- Interpreting and presenting the findings as they are and not in a particular direction based on the researcher's own gut feel or liking. For example, a researcher who is a consumer of organic food will attempt to exaggerate the health benefits of the products not because that is what was found but because as a consumer of the category, that is what he believes.

Thus, as stated earlier, just like any other business function a code of ethics for conducting research is well structured and laid out by almost every business association. At all times, the researcher must remember that besides aiding in business decision-making, research also contributes to the huge domain of management knowledge. Thus, an authentic, transparent and objective reporting and compilation of the research becomes that much more critical.

REFERENCES

Bailey, K D. *Methods of Social Research*. 3rd edn. New York: the Free Press, 1978.

Russ-Eft, D, et al. 'Standards on ethics and integrity'. *Performance Improvement Quarterly* 12(3) 1999: 5–30.

Rowley, J. 'Researching people and organizations'. *Library Management* 15(4/5) 2004: 208-215.

Annexures 1–4

ANNEXURE 1

Area under standard normal distribution between the mean and successive value of Z

Z	0.00	0.01	0.02	0.03	0.04	0.05	0.06	0.07	0.08	0.09
0.0	0.0000	0.0040	0.0080	0.0120	0.0160	0.0199	0.0239	0.0279	0.0319	0.0359
0.1	0.0398	0.0438	0.0478	0.0517	0.0557	0.0596	0.0636	0.0675	0.0714	0.0753
0.2	0.0793	0.0832	0.0871	0.0910	0.0948	0.0987	0.1026	0.1064	0.1103	0.1141
0.3	0.1179	0.1217	0.1255	0.1293	0.1331	0.1368	0.1406	0.1443	0.1480	0.1517
0.4	0.1554	0.1591	0.1628	0.1664	0.1700	0.1736	0.1772	0.1808	0.1844	0.1879
0.5	0.1915	0.1950	0.1985	0.2019	0.2054	0.2088	0.2123	0.2157	0.2190	0.2224
0.6	0.2257	0.2291	0.2324	0.2357	0.2389	0.2422	0.2454	0.2486	0.2517	0.2549
0.7	0.2580	0.2611	0.2642	0.2673	0.2704	0.2734	0.2764	0.2794	0.2823	0.2852
0.8	0.2881	0.2910	0.2939	0.2967	0.2995	0.3023	0.3051	0.3078	0.3106	0.3133
0.9	0.3159	0.3186	0.3212	0.3238	0.3264	0.3289	0.3315	0.3340	0.3365	0.3389
1.0	0.3413	0.3438	0.3461	0.3485	0.3508	0.3531	0.3554	0.3577	0.3599	0.3621
1.1	0.3643	0.3665	0.3686	0.3708	0.3729	0.3749	0.3770	0.3790	0.3810	0.3830
1.2	0.3849	0.3869	0.3888	0.3907	0.3925	0.3944	0.3962	0.3980	0.3997	0.4015
1.3	0.4032	0.4049	0.4066	0.4082	0.4099	0.4115	0.4131	0.4147	0.4162	0.4177
1.4	0.4192	0.4207	0.4222	0.4236	0.4251	0.4265	0.4279	0.4292	0.4306	0.4319
1.5	0.4332	0.4345	0.4357	0.4370	0.4382	0.4394	0.4406	0.4418	0.4429	0.4441
1.6	0.4452	0.4463	0.4474	0.4484	0.4495	0.4505	0.4515	0.4525	0.4535	0.4545
1.7	0.4554	0.4564	0.4573	0.4582	0.4591	0.4599	0.4608	0.4616	0.4625	0.4633
1.8	0.4641	0.4649	0.4656	0.4664	0.4671	0.4678	0.4686	0.4693	0.4699	0.4706
1.9	0.4713	0.4719	0.4726	0.4732	0.4738	0.4744	0.4750	0.4756	0.4761	0.4767
2.0	0.4772	0.4778	0.4783	0.4788	0.4793	0.4798	0.4803	0.4808	0.4812	0.4817
2.1	0.4821	0.4826	0.4830	0.4834	0.4838	0.4842	0.4846	0.4850	0.4854	0.4857
2.2	0.4861	0.4864	0.4868	0.4871	0.4875	0.4878	0.4881	0.4884	0.4887	0.4890
2.3	0.4893	0.4896	0.4898	0.4901	0.4804	0.4906	0.4909	0.4911	0.4913	0.4916
2.4	0.4918	0.4920	0.4922	0.4925	0.4927	0.4929	0.4931	0.4932	0.4934	0.4936
2.6	0.4953	0.4955	0.4956	0.4957	0.4959	0.4960	0.4961	0.4962	0.4963	0.4964
2.8	0.4974	0.4975	0.4976	0.4977	0.4977	0.4978	0.4979	0.4979	0.4980	0.4981
2.9	0.4981	0.4982	0.4982	0.4983	0.4984	0.4984	0.4985	0.4985	0.4986	0.4986
3.0	0.4987	0.4987	0.4987	0.4988	0.4988	0.4989	0.4989	0.4989	0.4990	0.4990

ANNEXURE 2

Some critical values of 't'

	Level of Significance		
Degrees of Freedom	1%	5%	10%
1	63.657	12.706	6.314
2	9.925	4.303	2.920
3	5.841	3.182	2.353
4	4.604	2.776	2.132
5	4.032	2.571	2.015
6	3.707	2.447	1.943
7	3.499	2.365	1.895
8	3.355	2.306	1.860
9	3.250	2.262	1.833
10	3.169	2.228	1.812
11	3.106	2.201	1.796
12	3.055	2.179	1.782
13	3.012	2.160	1.771
14	2.977	2.145	1.761
15	2.947	2.131	1.753
16	2.921	2.120	1.746
17	2.898	2.110	1.740
18	2.878	2.101	1.734
19	2.861	2.093	1.729
20	2.845	2.086	1.725
21	2.831	2.080	1.721
22	2.819	2.074	1.717
23	2.807	2.069	1.714
24	2.797	2.064	1.711
25	2.787	2.060	1.708
26	2.779	2.056	1.706
27	2.771	2.052	1.703
28	2.763	2.048	1.701
29	2.756	2.045	1.699
α	2.576	1.960	1.645

Note: **These table values of '*t*' are in respect of two-tailed tests. If we use the *t*-distribution for one-tailed test then we are interested in determining the area located in one tail. So to find the appropriate *t*-value for a one-tailed test say at a 5% level with 12 degrees of freedom, then we should look in the above table under the 10% column opposite the 12 degrees of freedom row. (This value will be 1.782). This is true because the 10% column represents 10% of the area under the curve contained in both tails combined, and so it also represents 5% of the area under the curve contained in each of the tails separately.**

ANNEXURE 3

Some critical values of χ^2 for specified degrees of freedom

Degrees of Freedom	Level of Significance		
	10%	5%	1%
1	2.706	3.841	6.635
2	4.605	5.991	9.210
3	6.251	7.815	11.345
4	7.779	9.488	13.277
5	9.236	11.071	15.086
6	10.645	12.592	16.812
7	12.017	14.067	18.475
8	13.362	15.507	20.090
9	14.684	16.919	21.666
10	15.987	18.307	23.209
11	17.275	19.675	24.725
12	18.549	21.026	26.217
13	19.812	22.362	27.688
14	21.064	23.685	29.141
15	22.307	24.996	30.578
16	23.542	26.296	32.000
17	24.769	27.587	33.409
18	25.989	28.869	34.805
19	27.204	30.144	36.191
20	28.412	31.410	37.566
21	29.615	32.671	38.932
22	30.813	33.924	40.289
23	33.007	35.172	41.638
24	33.196	36.415	42.980
25	34.382	37.652	44.314
26	35.363	38.885	45.642
27	36.741	40.113	46.963
28	37.916	41.337	48.278
29	38.087	42.567	49.588
30	40.256	43.773	50.892

Note: For degrees of freedom greater than 30, the quantity $\sqrt{2x^2} - \sqrt{2v-1}$ may be used as a normal variate with unit variance.

ANNEXURE 4a

Significance points of the variance-ratio 'F' 5 per cent points of F

$v_1 \rightarrow$ / $v_2 \downarrow$	1	2	3	4	5	6	8	12	24	∞
1	161.4	199.5	215.7	224.6	230.2	234.0	238.9	243.9	249.0	254.3
2	18.51	19.00	19.16	19.25	19.30	19.33	19.37	19.41	19.45	19.50
3	10.13	9.55	9.28	9.12	9.01	8.94	8.84	8.74	8.64	8.53
4	7.71	6.94	6.59	6.39	6.26	6.16	6.04	5.91	5.77	5.63
5	6.61	5.79	5.41	5.19	5.05	4.95	4.82	4.68	4.53	4.36
6	5.99	5.14	4.76	4.53	4.39	4.28	4.15	4.00	3.84	3.67
7	5.59	4.74	4.35	4.12	3.97	3.87	3.73	3.57	3.41	3.23
8	5.32	4.46	4.07	3.84	3.69	3.58	3.44	3.28	3.12	3.93
9	5.12	4.26	3.86	3.63	3.48	3.37	3.23	3.07	2.90	2.71
10	4.96	4.10	3.71	3.48	3.33	3.22	3.07	2.91	2.74	2.54
11	4.84	3.98	3.59	3.36	3.20	3.09	2.95	2.79	2.61	2.40
12	4.75	3.88	3.49	3.26	3.11	3.00	2.85	2.69	2.50	2.30
13	4.67	3.80	3.41	3.18	3.02	3.92	2.77	2.60	2.42	2.21
14	4.60	3.74	3.34	3.11	2.96	2.85	2.70	2.53	2.35	2.13
15	4.54	3.68	3.29	3.06	2.90	2.79	2.64	2.48	2.29	2.07
16	4.49	3.63	3.24	3.01	2.85	2.74	2.59	2.42	2.24	2.01
17	4.45	3.59	3.20	2.96	2.81	3.70	2.55	2.38	2.19	1.96
18	4.41	3.55	3.16	2.93	2.77	2.66	2.51	2.34	2.15	1.92
19	4.38	3.52	3.13	2.90	2.74	2.63	2.48	2.31	2.11	1.88
20	4.35	3.49	3.10	2.87	2.71	2.60	2.45	2.28	2.08	1.84
21	4.32	3.47	3.07	2.84	2.68	2.57	2.42	2.25	2.05	1.81
22	4.30	3.44	3.05	2.82	2.66	2.55	2.40	2.23	2.03	1.78
23	4.28	3.42	3.03	2.80	2.64	2.53	2.38	2.20	2.00	1.76
24	4.26	3.40	3.01	2.78	2.62	2.51	2.36	2.18	1.98	1.73
25	4.24	3.38	2.99	2.76	2.60	2.49	2.34	2.16	1.96	1.71
26	4.22	3.37	2.98	2.74	2.59	2.47	2.32	2.15	1.95	1.69
27	4.21	3.35	2.96	2.73	2.57	2.46	2.30	2.13	1.93	1.67
28	4.20	3.34	2.95	2.71	2.56	2.44	2.29	2.12	1.91	1.65
29	4.18	3.33	2.93	2.70	2.54	2.43	2.28	2.10	1.90	1.64
30	4.17	3.32	2.92	2.69	2.53	2.42	2 .27	2.09	1.89	1.62
40	4.08	3.23	2.84	2.61	2.45	2.34	2.18	2.00	1.79	1.51
60	4.00	3.15	2.76	2.52	2.37	2.25	2.10	1.92	1.70	1.89
120	2.92	3.07	2.68	2.45	2.29	2.17	2.02	1.83	1.61	1.25
∞	3.84	2.99	2.60	2.37	2.21	2.09	1.94	1.75	1.52	1.00

v1 = Degrees of freedom for greater variance.
v2 = Degrees of freedom for smaller variance.

ANNEXURE 4b

Significance points of the variance-ratio 'F'1 per cent points of F

$v_1 \rightarrow$ / $v_2 \downarrow$	1	2	3	4	5	6	8	12	24	∞
1	4052	5000	5403	5625	5764	5859	5982	6106	6235	6366
2	98.50	99.00	99.17	99.25	99.30	99.33	99.37	99.42	99.46	99.50
3	34.12	30.82	29.46	28.71	28.24	27.91	27.49	27.05	26.60	26.13
4	21.20	18.20	16.69	15.88	15.52	15.21	14.80	14.37	13.93	13.45
5	16.26	13.27	12.06	11.39	10.97	10.67	10.29	9.89	9.47	9.02
6	13.75	10.92	9.78	9.15	8.75	8.47	8.10	7.72	7.31	6.88
7	12.25	9.55	8.45	7.85	7.46	7.19	6.84	6.47	6.07	5.65
8	11.26	8.65	7.59	7.01	6.63	6.37	6.03	5.67	5.28	4.86
9	10.56	8.02	6.99	6.42	6.06	5.80	5.47	5.12	4.73	4.31
10	10.04	7.56	6.55	5.99	5.64	5.39	5.06	4.71	4.33	3.91
11	9.65	7.21	6.22	5.87	5.32	5.07	4.74	4.40	4.02	3.60
12	9.33	6.93	5.95	5.41	5.06	4.82	4.50	4.16	3.78	3.36
13	9.07	6.70	5.74	5.21	4.86	4.62	4.30	3.96	3.59	3.17
14	8.86	6.51	5.56	5.04	4.69	4.46	4.14	3.80	3.43	3.00
15	8.68	6.36	4.42	4.89	4.56	4.32	4.00	3.67	3.29	2.87
16	8.53	6.23	5.29	4.77	4.44	4.20	3.89	3.55	3.18	2.75
17	8.40	6.11	5.18	4.67	4.34	4.10	3.79	3.46	3.08	2.65
18	8.29	6.01	5.09	4.58	4.25	4.01	3.71	3.37	3.00	2.59
19	8.18	5.93	5.01	4.50	4.17	3.94	3.63	3.30	3.92	2.49
20	8.10	5.85	4.94	4.43	4.10	3.87	3.56	3.23	2.86	2.42
21	8.02	5.78	4.87	4.37	4.04	3.81	3.51	3.17	2.80	2.36
22	7.95	5.72	4.82	4.31	3.99	3.76	3.45	3.12	2.75	2.31
23	7.88	5.66	4.76	4.26	3.94	3.71	3.41	3.07	2.70	2.26
24	7.82	5.61	4.72	4.22	3.90	3.67	3.36	3.03	2.66	2.21
25	7.77	5.57	4.68	4.18	3.85	3.63	3.32	2.99	2.62	2.17
26	7.72	5.53	4.64	4.14	3.82	3.59	3.20	2.96	2.58	2.10
27	7.68	5.49	4.60	4.11	3.78	3.56	3.26	2.93	2.45	2.13
28	7.64	5.45	4.57	4.07	3.75	3.53	3.23	2.90	2.52	2.06
29	7.60	5.42	4.54	4.04	3.73	3.50	3.20	2.87	2.49	2.03
30	7.56	5.39	4.51	4.02	3.70	3.47	3.17	2.84	2.47	2.01
40	7.31	5.18	4.31	3.83	3.51	3.29	2.99	2.66	2.29	1.80
60	7.08	4.98	4.13	3.65	3.34	3.12	2.82	2.50	2.12	1.60
120	6.85	4.79	3.95	3.48	3.17	2.96	2.66	2.34	1.95	1.38
∞	6.64	4.60	3.78	3.32	3.02	2.80	2.51	2.18	1.79	1.00

v_1 = Degrees of freedom for greater variance.
v_2 = Degrees of freedom for smaller variance.

Subject Index

Author Index